3 FREE Minutes

of weather information and save up to 60% on long distance calls!

Let The Weather Channel® help you pack! Get all the information you need before you leave.

- Current conditions & forecasts for over 900 cities worldwide
- Severe weather information including winter and tropical storm updates
- Wake-up call complete with your local forecast
- Special interest forecasts featuring ski resort, boating and other outdoor conditions

Remove card and see instructions on back.

Plus:

After selecting any additional payment option, you will receive 5 FREE MINUTES of long distance service!

Easy. Convenient. Fast.

It's The Only Phone Card You Will Ever Need!

During your free call, an automated operator will offer you an option to add $10, $20 or $30 to your phone card using any major credit card.

Use your card to:

- Save 20% on comprehensive weather information!

- Save up to 60% on long distance calls to **anywhere** in the U.S., **anytime**!

- Save 20% on other helpful information including lottery, sports, and more!

Domestic long distance service costs $0.25 per minute and all other options cost $0.75 per minute when using your TWC phone card.

Take the worry out of wondering! Carry the power to access all of these essential services with you in your wallet, wherever **Frommer's** may take you!

THE WEATHER CHANNEL ®

No place on Earth has better weather.™

Travel Discount Coupon

This coupon entitles you to special discounts
when you book your trip through the

☁ *TRAVEL NETWORK*®
RESERVATION SERVICE

Hotels ♦ Airlines ♦ Car Rentals ♦ Cruises
All Your Travel Needs

Here's what you get: *

♦ A discount of $50 USD on a booking of $1,000** or
  more for two or more people!

♦ A discount of $25 USD on a booking of $500** or more
  for one person!

♦ Free membership for three years, and 1,000 free miles
  on enrollment in the unique Miles-to-Go™ frequent-
  traveler program. Earn one mile for every dollar spent
  through the program. Earn free hotel stays starting at
  5,000 miles. Earn free roundtrip airline tickets starting
  at 25,000 miles.

♦ Personal help in planning your own, customized trip.

♦ Fast, confirmed reservations at any property
  recommended in this guide, subject to availability.***

♦ Special discounts on bookings in the U.S. and around
  the world.

♦ Low-cost visa and passport service.

♦ Reduced-rate cruise packages.

Visit our website at http://www.travnet.com/Frommer or
call us globally at 201-567-8500, ext. 55. In the U.S., call
toll-free at 1-888-940-5000, or fax 201-567-1838. In
Canada, call toll-free at 1-800-883-9959, or fax 416-922-
6053. In Asia, call 60-3-7191044, or fax 60-3-7185415.

---

* To qualify for these travel discounts, at least a portion of your trip must
  include destinations covered in this guide. No more than one coupon discount
  may be used in any 12-month period, for destinations covered in this guide.
  Cannot be combined with any other discount or program.
**These are U.S. dollars spent on commissionable bookings.
***A $10 USD fee, plus fax and/or phone charges, will be added to the cost of
  bookings at each hotel not linked to the reservation service. Customers
  must approve these fees in advance.

Valid until December 31, 1998. Terms and conditions of the Miles-to-
Go™ program are available on request by calling 201-567-8500, ext 55.

NEN123

Frommer's® 97

New England

by Wayne Curtis,
Herbert Bailey Livesey,
and Marie Morris

with Stephen Jermanok
and Sandy MacDonald

Macmillan • USA

MACMILLAN TRAVEL

A Simon & Schuster Macmillan Company
1633 Broadway
New York, NY 10019

Find us online at **http://www.mgr.com/travel**
or on America Online Keyword: **Frommer's.**

ISBN 0-02-861149-7
ISSN 1044-2286

Editors: Philippe Wamba and Ian Wilker
Thanks to Lisa Renaud
Production Editor: Lynn Northrup
Map Editor: Douglas Stallings
Design by Michele Laseau
Digital Cartography by Ortelius Design, Peter Bogaty, and Roberta Stockwell

SPECIAL SALES

Bulk purchases (10+ copies) of Frommer's and selected Macmillan travel guides are
available to corporations, organizations, mail-order catalogs, institutions, and charities at
special discounts, and can be customized to suit individual needs. For more information
write to: Special Sales, Macmillan General Reference, 1633 Broadway, New York, NY
10019.

Manufactured in the United States of America

ABOUT THE AUTHORS

Wayne Curtis (Chapters 1, 2, and 11–13) is the author of *Maine: Off the Beaten Path* (Globe Pequot) and numerous travel articles in newspapers and magazines, including the *New York Times, National Geographic Traveler,* and *Outside.* He lives in Portland, Maine, where he endeavors to support local microbreweries and minor-league baseball.

Herbert Bailey Livesey (Chapters 1 and 8–10) is a native New Yorker and a former New York University administrator. After leaving his career in higher education, he worked briefly as an artist before devoting himself to writing full time. He is the author of several travel guides, nine books on education and sociology, and a novel.

Marie Morris (Chapters 1, 4, and 5) is a native New Yorker and a graduate of Harvard College, where she studied history. She has worked for the *New York Times, Boston* magazine, and the *Boston Herald,* and is also the author of *Frommer's Boston '97.* She lives in Boston, not far from Paul Revere.

Stephen Jermanok (Chapters 1 and 2) has explored more than fifty countries in the past decade and has written for the *Washington Post, Travel & Leisure, Town & Country, New York,* the *Miami Herald,* and *Art & Antiques,* and is also the author of *Outside Magazine's Adventure Guide to New England.*

Sandy MacDonald (Chapters 1, 6, and 7) is a freelance writer who lives in Cambridge, MA. She has written a number of travel books, including *Frommer's Cape Cod,* as well as articles for *Boston,* the *Boston Globe, New England Monthly, Travel & Leisure, Yankee Traveler,* and others.

Contents

List of Maps

AN INVITATION TO THE READER

In researching this book, we discovered many wonderful places—hotels, restaurants, shops, and more. We're sure you'll find others. Please tell us about them, so we can share the information with your fellow travelers in upcoming editions. If you were disappointed with a recommendation, we'd love to know that, too. Please write to:

Frommer's New England '97
Macmillan Travel
1633 Broadway
New York, NY 10019

AN ADDITIONAL NOTE

Please be advised that travel information is subject to change at any time—and this is especially true of prices. We therefore suggest that you write or call ahead for confirmation when making your travel plans. The authors, editors, and publisher cannot be held responsible for the experiences of readers while traveling. Your safety is important to us, however, so we encourage you to stay alert and be aware of your surroundings. Keep a close eye on cameras, purses, and wallets, all favorite targets of thieves and pickpockets.

WHAT THE SYMBOLS MEAN

✪ Frommer's Favorites

Hotels, restaurants, attractions, and entertainment you should not miss.

Ⓢ Super-Special Values

Hotels and restaurants that offer great value for your money.

The following abbreviations are used for credit cards:

AE	American Express	EU	Eurocard
CB	Carte Blanche	JCB	Japan Credit Bank
DC	Diners Club	MC	MasterCard
DISC	Discover	V	Visa
ER	enRoute		

The Best of New England

One of the greatest challenges of traveling in New England is choosing from an abundance of superb restaurants, accommodations, and attractions. Where to start? Here's an entirely biased list of our favorite destinations, the places we always return to time and time again. Over years of traveling through the region, we've discovered that these are places worth more than just a quick stop when we're in the area. They're all worth a major detour.

1 The Best of Small-Town New England

- **Marblehead** (MA): Marblehead has major picture-postcard potential, especially in the summer, when the harbor fills with sailboats and yachts. From downtown, a short distance inland, make your way toward the water down the narrow, flower-dotted streets. The first glimpse of blue sea and blue sky is breathtaking. See Chapter 5.

- **Chatham** (MA): Only Provincetown offers better strolling-and-shopping options, and this version is G-rated. In summer, Friday-night band concerts draw multigenerational crowds in the thousands. For a glimpse of nature's awesome forces at work (it's busy rearranging the shoreline, with little eye to local real estate values), take an aerial tour with the Cape Cod Flying Circus: loop-de-loops are optional. Look for the hordes of seals on uninhabited Monomoy Island. See Chapter 6.

- **Washington** (CT): A classic, with a Congregational church facing a green surrounded by clapboard Colonial houses, all of them with black shutters. See Chapter 9.

- **Grafton** (VT): Just a few decades ago Grafton was a down-at-the-heels mountain town slowly being reclaimed by termites and the elements. A wealthy family took it on as a pet project, and has lovingly restored the village to its former self—even burying the electric lines to reclaim the landscape. It doesn't feel like a living-history museum; it just feels right. See Chapter 11.

- **Woodstock** (VT): Woodstock has a stunning village green, a whole range of 19th-century homes, woodland walks leading just out of town, and a settled, old-money air. This is a good place to explore by foot or bike, or to just sit on a porch and watch summer unfold. See Chapter 11.

- **Montpelier** (VT): This is the way all state capitals should be: slow-paced, small enough so you can walk everywhere, and full of shops that still sell nails and strapping tape to real people. Montpelier also shows a more sophisticated edge, with its Culinary Institute, a theater showing art-house films, and several fine bookshops. But at heart it's a small town, where you just might run into the governor buying a wrench at the corner store. See Chapter 11.
- **Exeter** (NH): Exeter boasts a small history museum covering life in revolutionary times, but the whole town is a living monument to a bygone era. The brick commercial downtown is trim and bustling; the prestigious Exeter Academy prep school recalls the era of Holden Caulfield of *Catcher in the Rye.* See Chapter 12.
- **Fitzwilliam** (NH): With its sleepy, lost-in-time feel, Fitzwilliam seems caught in a time warp from the 1830s. You half expect to see a horse-drawn carriage circling around the idyllic green, which is ringed with some of the most charming architecture in the region. This is a great destination for explorers—few urban refugees have yet discovered the place, and it still has a beguiling, raw-around-the-edges feel. See Chapter 12.
- **Castine** (ME): Soaring elm trees, a peaceful harborside setting, plenty of grand historic homes, and a selection of good inns make this a great spot to soak up some of Maine's coastal ambience off the beaten path. See Chapter 13.

2 The Best Places to See Fall Foliage

- **Walden Pond** (Concord, MA): Walden Pond is hidden from the road by the woods where Henry David Thoreau built a small cabin and lived from 1845 to 1847. When the leaves are turning, it's hard to imagine why he left. Take Route 2 from Cambridge and follow signs to Route 126, park and stroll down to see the trees reflected in the water. See Chapter 5.
- **Litchfield Hills** (CT): Route 7, running south to north through the rugged northwest corner of Connecticut roughly along the course of the Housatonic River, explodes with color in the week fore and aft of Columbus Day. It's something to see the fallen leaves whirling down the foaming river. See Chapter 9.
- **I-91** (VT): An interstate? Don't scoff (the traffic can be terrible on state roads). If you like your foliage viewing wholesale, cruise I-91 from White River Junction to Newport. You'll be overwhelmed with gorgeous terrain, from the gentle Connecticut River Valley to the sloping hills of the Northeast Kingdom. See Chapter 11.
- **Route 100** (VT): Route 100 winds the length of the Vermont from Reads-boro to Newport. It's the major north-south route through the center of the Green Mountains, and it's surprisingly undeveloped along most of its length. You won't exactly have it to yourself along the southern stretches on autumn weekends, but as you head farther north you'll leave the crowds behind. One of the most spectacular stretches runs between Rochester on up to the Mad River Valley, through which the road traverses the wild, narrow Granville Gulf. See Chapter 11.
- **Aboard the M/S *Mount Washington*** (NH): One of the more majestic views of the White Mountains is from Lake Winnipesaukee to the south. The vista is especially appealing as seen from the deck of the *Mount Washington,* an uncommonly handsome 230-foot-long vessel that offers a variety of tours through mid-October, when the lake is trimmed with a fringe of fall color along the shoreline. See Chapter 12.

- **Crawford Notch** (NH): Route 302 passes through this scenic valley, where you can see the brilliant red maples and yellow birches high on the hillsides. Mount Washington stands guard in the background, and in fall is likely to be dusted with an early snow. See Chapter 12.
- **The Blueberry Barrens of Downeast Maine:** Maine's wild blueberry barrens are ablaze with a brilliant cranberry-red hue in the fall. Wander the dirt roads northeast of Cherryfield through the upland barrens, or just drive on Route 1 between Harrington and Machias past the experimental farm atop aptly named Blueberry Hill. See Chapter 13.

3 The Best Ways to View Coastal Scenery

- **Strolling Around Bearskin Neck** (Rockport, MA): Rockport centers around a small harbor and spreads out along the rugged, rocky coastline of Cape Ann. From the end of Bearskin Neck, the view is spectacular—fishing and pleasure boats in one direction, roaring surf in the other. See Chapter 5.
- **Biking or Driving the Outer Cape** (MA): Cape Cod's "forearm," from Chatham all the way to Provincetown, offers an endless array of dazzling ocean vistas. The entire coast is under the protective auspices of the Cape Cod National Seashore, a federal park initiated in 1961. A series of visitor centers offer interpretive services and parking, and the lookouts from each are uniquely rewarding. Old County Road between Wellfleet and Truro traverses some truly unique landscape, and the bike paths through the Province Lands, just outside Provincetown, have no peer—the shifting sands of the swooping dunes regularly swallow whole trees. See Chapter 6.
- **Biking or Driving "Up-Island"** (Martha's Vineyard, MA): Many visitors to Martha's Vineyard never venture beyond the port towns of Vineyard Haven, Oak Bluffs, and Edgartown. Though each has its charms, the scenery actually gets a lot more spectacular "up-island," where towering trees give way to moorlike meadows marked off by stone walls. At the westernmost tip await the dazzling colored cliffs of Wampanoag-owned Gay Head, and beyond, the quaint fishing port of Menemsha. See Chapter 7.
- **Biking Route 1A from Hampton Beach to Portsmouth** (NH): You'll get a taste of all sorts of coastal scenery pedaling along New Hampshire's miniscule coastline. You'll begin with sandy beaches, then pass rocky headlands and handsome mansions before coasting into the region's most scenic seaside city. See Chapter 12.
- **Kayaking Merchant's Row** (ME): The islands between Stonington and Isle au Haut, rimmed with pink granite and capped with the stark spires of spruce trees, are simply spectacular. Exploring by sea kayak will get you to islands inaccessible by motorboat. Outfitters offer overnight camping trips on the islands. See "Sea Kayaking & Camping Along 'Merchant's Row'" in Chapter 13.
- **Hiking Monhegan Island** (ME): The village of Monhegan is clustered around the harbor, but the rest of this 700-acre island is all picturesque wildlands, with miles of trails crossing open meadows and winding along rocky bluffs. See Chapter 13.
- **Driving the Park Loop Road at Acadia National Park** (ME): This is the region's premier ocean drive. You'll start high along a ridge with views of Frenchman Bay and the Porcupine Islands, then dip down along the rocky shores to watch the surf crash against the dark rocks. Plan to do this 20-mile loop at least twice to get the most out of it. See Chapter 13.

4 The Best Places to Rediscover America's Past

- **The Old State House** (Boston): It towered over its surroundings when it was built in 1713, and today, dwarfed by office towers, the Old State House stands as a reminder of British rule (the exterior features a lion and a unicorn) and its overthrow. The Declaration of Independence was read from the balcony, which overlooks a traffic island where a circle of bricks represents the site of the Boston Massacre. See Chapter 4.

- **Faneuil Hall** (Boston): Faneuil Hall is known nowadays as a shopping destination, but if you head upstairs instead of out into the marketplace, you'll find yourself transported back in time. A recent restoration has left the second-floor auditorium in tip-top shape, and park rangers are on hand to talk about the building's role in the Revolution. Tune out the sound of sneakers squeaking across the floor, and you can almost hear Samuel Adams (his statue is out front) exhorting the Sons of Liberty. See Chapter 4.

- **The Old North Bridge** (Concord, MA): British troops headed here after putting down the uprising in Lexington, and the bridge stands (well, it's a replica) as a testament to the Minutemen who fought there. The Concord River and its peaceful green banks give no hint of what took place. On the path in from Monument Street, placards and audio stations provide a fascinating narrative. See Chapter 5.

- **Plymouth Rock** (MA): Okay, so it's a fraction of its original size and looks like something you might find in your garden (especially if your garden is in rocky New England soil), but it makes a perfect starting point for exploration. Close by is the *Mayflower II,* a replica of the alarmingly small original vessel. The juxtaposition reminds you of what a dangerous undertaking the Pilgrims' voyage was, something to keep in mind as you explore the town. See Chapter 5.

- **Portsmouth** (NH): Portsmouth is a salty coastal city that just happens to boast some of the most impressive historic homes in New England. Start at Strawbery Banke, a historic 10-acre compound of 42 historic buildings. Then visit the many other grand homes in nearby neighborhoods, like the house John Paul Jones occupied while building his warship during the Revolution. See Chapter 12.

- ***Old Ironsides*** (Boston): Formally known as the USS *Constitution, Old Ironsides* was launched in 1797 and made a name for itself fighting Barbary pirates and during the War of 1812. Last used in battle in 1815, it was periodically threatened with destruction until a complete renovation in the late 1920s started its career as a floating monument. The staff consists of sailors on active duty who wear 1812 dress uniforms, conduct tours, and can answer just about any question you throw at them. See Chapter 4.

- **Nantucket:** It looks like the whalers just left, leaving behind their grand houses and cobbled streets. Throughout the 18th century and the first half of the 19th, whaling was king here; the industry and its trappings are on display at the excellent Whaling Museum. See Chapter 7.

- **Deerfield** (MA): Arguably the best preserved colonial village in New England, Deerfield has stubbornly persisted through three centuries; there are scores of houses in town dating back to the 17th and 18th centuries, and none of the clutter of modernity has intruded here. Fourteen of them on the main avenue ("The Street"), can be visited through tours conducted by the organization known as Historic Deerfield. See Chapter 8.

- **Plymouth** (VT): Pres. Calvin Coolidge was born in this high upland valley, and the state has done a superb job preserving his hometown village. You'll get a good sense of the president's roots, but also gain a greater understanding of how a New England village works. Don't miss the cheese shop still owned by the president's son. See Chapter 11.
- **Manchester** (NH): New England's history isn't all farming and shipbuilding. A driving tour of downtown Manchester, with its hulking and impressive 19th-century factories of brick lining the Merrimack River, will show another side of New England's storied past. See Chapter 11.
- **Sabbathday Lake Shaker Community** (New Gloucester, ME): This is the last of the active Shaker communities in the nation—the only Shaker community that voted to accept new converts rather than to die out. The 1,900-acre farm, about 45 minutes outside of Portland, has a number of exceptional buildings, including some dating back to the 18th century. Visitors come to view examples of historic Shaker craftsmanship, and buy locally grown Shaker herbs to bring home. See Chapter 13.

5 The Best Literary Landmarks

- **Concord** (MA): Literary ghosts crowd round this village. Homes of Ralph Waldo Emerson, Nathaniel Hawthorne, Henry David Thoreau, and Louisa May Alcott are popular destinations, and look much as they did during the "flowering of New England" in the mid-19th century. See Chapter 5.
- **Salem** (MA): Native son Nathaniel Hawthorne might still feel right at home here. A hotel and a boulevard bear his name, the Custom House where he found an embroidered scarlet "A" still stands, and his birthplace is open for tours. It has been moved into the same complex as the House of the Seven Gables, a cousin's home that inspired the classic novel. See Chapter 5.
- **The Outer Cape** (MA): In the last century the communities at the far end of the Cape—Wellfleet, Truro, and particularly Provincetown—have been a veritable HQ of bohemia—more writers and artists have holed up here than you could shake a stick at. Distinguished literati such as Edna St. Vincent Millay and Edmund Wilson, Eugene O'Neill, Jack Kerouac, Tennessee Williams, and many others have taken refuge among the dunes here—make sure to take one of Art's Dune Tours for a very candid account of these various luminaries' time here. See Chapter 6.
- **Mark Twain & Harriet Beecher Stowe Houses** (Hartford, CT): Samuel Clemens's home is a fascinating example of the late 19th-century style sometimes known as Picturesque Gothic, and the interior shows his enthusiasm for new-fangled gadgets—there is a primitive telephone in the entrance hall. About 60 yards across the lawn from the porte-cochere of the Twain residence is the smaller home of Harriet Beecher Stowe, author of *Uncle Tom's Cabin*. Come to see them during "Mark Twain Days" in mid-August, packed with such events as frog jumping and fence painting, sack races and riverboat rides, and performances of plays based on Twain's life or works. See Chapter 9.
- **Naulakha** (Brattleboro, VT): During his sojourn in Vermont, British writer Rudyard Kipling gained a reputation as being something of a strange bird. But his neighbors' whispers didn't stop him from writing *The Jungle Book* or *Captains Courageous* while living in Naulakha, a house he built outside of Brattleboro.

Today, you can rent the home by the week and follow Kipling's footsteps through the countryside during your stay. See Chapter 11.

- **Robert Frost Farm** (Sugar Hill, NH): Two of the most famous New England poems—"The Road Not Taken" and "Stopping by Woods on a Snowy Evening"—were composed by Robert Frost at this farm just outside of Franconia. Explore the woods and read the verses posted along the pathways, and tour the farmhouse where Frost lived with his family earlier this century. See Chapter 11.
- **West Branch of the Penobscot River** (ME): Henry David Thoreau ventured down this river by canoe in the mid-19th century, and found the woods all "moosey and mossy." They're still that way along the river today. A four-day canoe trip along part of his route includes a stop at tiny Chesuncook Village, where you can find the grave of Thoreau's host in a quiet, wooded cemetery. See Chapter 13.

6 The Best Activities for Families

- **Visiting the Boston Museum of Science:** Built around demonstrations, experiments, and interactive displays that never feel like homework, this museum is guaranteed to be a place your kids will go nuts over. Explore the exhibits (this can fill a couple of hours or a whole day), then take in a show at the planetarium or the Omni Theater. Before you know it, everyone will have learned something, painlessly. See Chapter 4.
- **Free Friday Flicks at the Hatch Shell** (Boston): The Hatch, on Boston's Esplanade shows family films (*The Wizard of Oz* or *E.T.: The Extraterrestrial,* for example)—yes, free—on Friday nights in the summer. The lawn in front of the Hatch Shell, an amphitheater usually used for concerts, turns into a giant, car-less drive-in movie as hundreds of people picnic and wait for the sky to grow dark. Bring sweaters in case the breeze off the river grows chilly. See Chapter 4.
- **Visiting the New England Aquarium** (Boston): Holds the interest of the most easily distracted child—or adult. The marine mammal show alone is reason enough to visit, and it's just a small part of the experience. The centerpiece, a mammoth saltwater tank, is hypnotically peaceful, an oasis in the midst of equally interesting but noisier hands-on exhibits and shows. See Chapter 4.
- **A Trip to Woods Hole** (MA): For junior oceanologists, the place to be. You can try the hands-on exhibits at the Woods Hole Oceanographic Institute, observe experiments at the Marine Biological Laboratory, explore the touch tanks at the country's oldest aquarium, and even collect crucial data with the "Ocean Quest" crew. See Chapter 6.
- **A Stay in Chatham** (MA): Still a stellar example of Main Street, U.S.A., Chatham draws thousands Friday evenings in summer for its spirited band concerts. Also appealing are its Railroad Museum, overlooking the vast and imaginative Play-a-Round Park (free and open to the public). Well-heeled scions favor the Chatham Bars Inn, whose attractions include a private beach, full resort facilities, and supervised children's programs day and night. And most children will enjoy a nature cruise around Monomoy Island, where thousands of birds and a large seal colony make their homes. See Chapter 6.
- **A Learn-to-Ski Vacation at Jiminy Peak** (MA): More than 70% of Jiminy Peak's trails are catered toward beginners and intermediates, making it one of the premier places to learn to ski in the East. The mountain is located in the heart of the Berkshires, near Mt. Greylock. See Chapter 8.

- **An Afternoon of Deep-Sea Fishing:** Charter fishing boats these days usually have high-tech fish-finding gear—imagine how your kids will react to reeling in one big bluefish after another. The top spots to mount such an expedition are Hyannis, on Cape Cod; Point Judith, at the southern tip of Rhode Island; and the Maine Coast.
- **Visiting Mystic Seaport & Mystic Marinelife Aquarium** (CT): The double-down winner in the family-fun sweeps has to be this combination—performing dolphins and whales, full-rigged tall ships, penguins and sharks, and river rides on a perky little 1906 motor launch are the kinds of G-rated attractions that have no age barriers. See Chapter 9.
- **Visiting the Montshire Museum** (Norwich, VT): This new children's museum, in a soaring, modern space on the Vermont–New Hampshire border, has wonderful interactive exhibits inside and nature trails winding along the Connecticut River. See Chapter 12.
- **A Stay in Weirs Beach** (NH): This is the trip your kids would plan if you didn't get in the way. Weirs Beach on Lake Winnipesaukee offers passive amusements like train and boat rides that appeal to younger kids, and plenty of active adventures for young teens—like go-kart racing, waterslides, and video arcades. Their parents can recuperate while lounging on the lakeside beach. See Chapter 12.
- **A Ride on Cog Railroad** (Crawford Notch, NH): It's fun! It's terrifying! It's a great glimpse into history. Kids love this ratchety climb to the top of New England's highest peak aboard trains that were specially designed to scale the mountain in 1869. As a technological marvel, the railroad attracted tourists by the thousands a century ago. They still come to marvel at its sheer audacity. See Chapter 12.
- **A Trip to Monhegan Island** (ME): Kids from 8 to 12 years old especially enjoy overnight excursions to Monhegan Island. The mail boat from Port Clyde is rustic and intriguing, the hotels are an adventure, and the woods are filled with magical fairy houses. See Chapter 13.

7 The Best Downhill Skiing

- **Stowe** (VT; ☎ 802/253-3000): One of the oldest ski resorts in New England, Stowe deserves its reputation as one of the finest. Its berth on Mount Mansfield, the largest and most rugged of Vermont's peaks, yields some of the toughest old-school skiing in the East, typified by the fearsome challenge of the Front Four. Across from the main mountain is Spruce Peak, with plenty of beginner and intermediate terrain. See Chapter 11.
- **Killington** (VT; ☎ 802/422-3333): Run! Hide! Killington is the Godzilla of eastern skiing. With 165 trails on six interconnected mountains, you can be sure that somewhere on this hill you'll find the trails of your dreams. The problem is finding them; sometimes negotiating Killington can be reminiscent of driving the New Jersey Turnpike outside of New York—and during rush hour. But the raging nightlife scene and the occasional gift, days after a storm, of fresh powder makes a ski trip here worthwhile. See Chapter 11.
- **Sugarbush** (VT; ☎ 802/583-2381): My favorite Vermont ski resort: Its two big, lovely mountains (3,975-foot Lincoln Peak and 4,135-foot Mt. Ellen) have more of the classic narrow, cascading trails that are the epitome of New England skiing than any other in the state. And the Mad River Valley retains a bucolic feel while offering all the amenities you'd expect at a major resort town. On powder days

watch for "woodchucks" on the expert runs (you know—bearded native Vermonters in hunter's clothing, skiing on ancient planks, who nonetheless can ski the pants
off anyone else on the hill. After all, they were born and raised on the sport). See
Chapter 11.

- **Mad River Glen** (VT; ☎ 802/496-3551): This notably feisty ski area, just up
  the road from Sugarbush, hasn't given in to passing whims—like high-speed
  chairlifts and snowmaking—and maintains a stubborn pride in its challenging
  slopes and no-frills skiing. Longtime owner Betsy Pratt sold the mountain in 1995,
  and the cooperative of skiers who bought it seems determined to maintain its
  cranky charm. See Chapter 11.
- **Loon Mountain** (NH; ☎ 603/745-8111): New Hampshire's most popular skiing destination has a good assortment of intermediate runs. It only sells a limited
  amount of tickets to keep lift lines down. Within easy reach of Boston, Loon has
  loads of wide, groomed cruising runs built for speed. See Chapter 12.
- **Wildcat Mountain** (NH; ☎ 603/466-3326): Set amid New Hampshire's White
  Mountain National Forest, Wildcat is a wonderful, remote ski area with a good
  range of slopes and the best mountain views of any ski area in New England. See
  Chapter 12.
- **Sugarloaf/USA** (ME; ☎ 207/237-2000): At first sight, Sugarloaf/USA is an
  impressive sight. This big, brooding mountain has a friendly, bustling resort at its
  base and some superb skiing on its upper flanks. This is the place to be after a
  heavy snowstorm, when the snowfields offer the only lift-served above-treeline skiing in the East. It's popular with families. See Chapter 13.

8 The Best Warm-Weather Sports

- **Nature Walks:** In every corner of New England you'll find wildlife refuges, parks,
  even flat-out wilderness cut by trail systems that make the areas accessible to
  everyone. The pay-off for your exertions can be immense: thousands of nesting
  terns and plovers at Cape Cod's Wellfleet Bay Wildlife Sanctuary; wildflowers,
  rugged bluffs, and innumerable songbirds along Block Island's Greenway Trail;
  Newport's Cliff Walk, which both hangs above the ocean and provides views of
  the "cottages" of the Gilded-Age industrialists who summered here; views from
  atop 150-foot-high cliffs at Maine's Quoddy Head State Park, at the easternmost
  point of the United States; a short walk through lush, mossy woods to 125-foot-
  high Hamilton Falls, in Vermont. You'll find suggestions throughout this book.
- **Fly-Fishing on the Housatonic River** (CT): Vermont's Batten Kill River gets
  more attention—but perhaps that's why rumors circulate that the river is being
  fished out a bit. The stretch of the Housatonic River near Housatonic Meadows
  State Park is a nine-mile trout management area, with three miles reserved for fly-
  fishing. Browns and rainbows are plentiful. See Chapter 9.
- **Road Biking in Central & Northern Vermont:** The only negative thing you
  could say about the cycling in many parts of New England is that it's just too
  popular—on Block Island, for example, the cycling is lovely but in peak season
  you're likely to experience the closest thing to two-wheel gridlock most of us will
  ever see. The northern reaches of Vermont, however, are remote and thus fairly
  uncrowded. Arguably the best regions for cycling are the Champlain Islands, the
  Northeast Kingdom, and Central Vermont east of the Green Mountains. Each of
  these places feature plenty of elbow room on serpentine two-lane blacktop; on the
  islands you'll travel through a flat, austerely beautiful landscape where a new lake

vista appears at every turn; the latter two offer you verdant hills and tumbling streams—and much more challenging cycling. See Chapter 11.

- **Hiking the Presidential Mountains** (NH): These rugged peaks in the White Mountains draw hikers from all over the globe, attracted by the history, the beautiful vistas, and the exceptional landscapes along the craggy ridgelines. You can make day-hike forays and retreat to the comfort of an inn at night, or stay in the hills at the Appalachian Mountain Club's historic high huts. See Chapter 12.

- **Backpacking the Appalachian Trail's "Hundred-Mile Wilderness"** (ME): It's not really wilderness—there's abundant evidence of the vast logging operations at work in the North Woods—but there is nonetheless a uniquely raw, wild feel to this 100-mile, 10-day trek on the very northern tip of the Appalachian Trail. For one thing, there's more wildlife than can be seen on any other long-distance hike in the East—black bears, moose, and loons on the many lakes. See Chapter 13.

- **Mountain Biking at Acadia National Park** (ME): Devotees of hellbent downhills on single-track will probably want to head straight for places like Randolph, Stowe, and Craftsbury in Vermont, where there are serious mountain-biking communities, but Acadia's carriage roads are the perfect introduction to this sport—anyone who's reasonably fit can enjoy rides here. John D. Rockefeller Jr. built the carriage roads of Mount Desert Island so the gentry could enjoy rambles in the woods with their horses, away from pesky cars. Today, this extensive network makes for some of the most enjoyable, aesthetically pleasing mountain biking anywhere. See Chapter 13.

- **Canoeing and Kayaking Maine's Waters:** Maine has thousands of miles of flowing rivers and streams, hundreds of glass-smooth lakes, and hundreds of miles of shoreline along remote ponds and lakes. Bring your tent, sleeping bag, and cooking gear, and come prepared to spend a night under the stars listening to the sounds of the loons. See Chapter 13.

- **Sailing Penobscot Bay** (ME): Newport and Narragansett Bay in Rhode Island, the Connecticut coast, Vermont's Lake Champlain—these are but a few of the waters that make New England one of the world's best places to sail. But perhaps the most intriguing of all is Penobscot Bay, where the many pine-studded islands entice sailors. They come for the chance to test their skills—to fight the fog, currents, wide tidal range, and cold waters, only to see the sun seep through and the waters calm upon their next tack. That you can also weigh anchor for a night on your own little island is the kicker. Bay Island Yacht Charters in Rockland (☎ 800/421-2492) offer 15 bareboats and American Sailing Association accredited instruction. See Chapter 13.

9 The Best Country Inns

- **Hawthorne Inn** (Concord, MA; ☎ 508/369-5610): The Hawthorne Inn rings all the bells: Everything—the 1870 building, the garden setting a stone's throw from the historic attractions, the antique furnishings, the eclectic decorations, the accommodating innkeepers—is top of the line. See Chapter 5.

- **Inn on Cove Hill** (Rockport, MA; ☎ 508/546-2701): The Inn on Cove Hill isn't in the country, but you might be fooled when you're having breakfast on the lawn at this relaxing spot near the center of the coastal town. Built in 1791 and beautifully decorated, it's a delightful place. See Chapter 5.

- **The Inn at West Falmouth** (West Falmouth, MA; ☎ 508/540-6503): If you're looking for a perfect country inn worthy of *Architectural Digest,* this shingle-style

1900 manse overlooking Buzzards Bay should do the trick. The decor is sumptuous, though never overdone, and each room—lavished with piquant antiques and fine linens—comes with a marble Jacuzzi. There's a tiny pool set in the deck, a tennis court, lovely gardens, and a placid beach a country walk away. The only aspect lacking is a restaurant, but the innkeeper is willing to prepare a private nuovo Italian feast on request. See Chapter 6.

- **The Wequassett Inn** (Chatham, MA; ☎ 508/432-5400): This Chatham institution occupies its own little peninsula on Pleasant Bay and offers excellent sailing and tennis clinics. You'll be mightily tempted just to goof off, though—especially if you score one of the clapboard cottages, done up in an upscale country mode, right on the water. The restaurant, housed in the 18th-century Eben Ryder House, holds its own with the top Cape contenders. See Chapter 6.
- **The Inn at Blueberry Hill** (Chilmark, MA; ☎ 800/336-3322 or 508/645-3799): Rural sophistication is the rule at this country estate in Chilmark, Martha's Vineyard. The Shaker-like simplicity of the decor is supremely refreshing, especially when combined with such sensual treats as down duvets and a festive restaurant, Theo's, which revels in fresh regional fare. There's a tennis court, lap pool, and health club on the premises, and 56 acres of adjoining conservation land to roam. See Chapter 7.
- **Mayflower Inn** (Washington, CT; ☎ 860/868-9466): Not a tough call at all for this part of the region: Immaculate in taste and execution, the Mayflower is as close to perfection as any such enterprise is likely to be. A genuine Joshua Reynolds hangs in the hall. See Chapter 9.
- **The Old Tavern at Grafton** (Grafton, VT; ☎ 800/843-1801 or 802/843-2231): This elegant village inn sits amid one of the most charming historic villages of northern New England. Modernized and thoroughly made over, the Old Tavern offers contemporary elegance with plenty of historic flair. See Chapter 11.
- **Windham Hill Inn** (West Townshend, VT; ☎ 800/944-4080 or 802/874-4080): New innkeepers made over this historic inn in 1995, adding welcome amenities like air-conditioning while still preserving the antique charm of this 1823 farmhouse. It's at the end of a remote dirt road in a high upland valley, and guests are welcome to explore 160 private acres on a network of walking trails. See Chapter 11.
- **Kedron Valley Inn** (South Woodstock, VT; ☎ 800/836-1193 or 802/457-1473): Set at a quiet country crossroads just south of Woodstock, the Kedron Valley Inn offers genuine comfort—this is no stuffy museum-quality setting. Guests enjoy exquisite bedrooms, a private pond with two sand beaches, and a creative dining room that wins raves from discriminating diners. See Chapter 11.
- **Twin Farms** (Woodstock, VT; ☎ 800/894-6327 or 802/234-9999): Just north of Woodstock is the most elegant inn in New England. The price will appall many of you (rooms start at $700 for two, including all meals and liquor), but you'll certainly be pampered here. Novelist Sinclair Lewis once lived on this 300-acre farm, and today it's an aesthetic retreat that offers serenity and exceptional food. See Chapter 11.
- **The Inn at Thorn Hill** (Jackson, NH; ☎ 603/383-4242): Designed by famed architect Stanford White in 1895, this handsome inn is maintained in a style that would make the master proud. It's decorated in a Victorian motif, with comfortable guest rooms, lovely common areas, and a well-regarded dining room—all within easy walking (or skiing) distance of the town of Jackson. See Chapter 12.
- **The White Barn Inn** (Kennebunkport, ME; ☎ 207/967-2321): Much of the White Barn staff hails from Europe, and guests are treated with a continental

graciousness. The rooms are a delight, and the meals (served in the barn) are among the best in Maine. See Chapter 13.

10   The Best Luxury Hotels & Resorts

- **The Four Seasons Hotel or the Ritz-Carlton** (Boston; ☎ **617/338-4400** for the former, ☎ **617/536-5700** for the latter): The undisputed winner in this debate is . . . the guest. At both hotels, the service is legendary, the atmosphere elegant, the accommodations plush. The more contemporary Four Seasons opened in 1985; the Ritz-Carlton has been a Boston institution since 1927. See Chapter 4.
- **The Wauwinet** (Nantucket, MA; ☎ **800/426-8718** or 508/228-0145): Far from the bustle of Nantucket town, and nestled between a bay beach and an ocean beach, this opulently restored landmark offers the ultimate retreat. Everything a summering sybarite could want is close at hand, including tennis courts, a launch to drop you off on your own secluded beach (part of a 1,100-acre wildlife refuge), and an outstanding New American restaurant, Topper's. See Chapter 7.
- **Summer House** (Nantucket, MA; ☎ **508/257-4577**): Rather more homespun than the Wauwinet, and therefore more faithful to true Nantucket style, this cluster of rose-covered cottages commands a crow's-nest view of dunes and ocean. A short stroll from the center of quaint Siasconset, a fishing village turned summer colony at the turn of the century, the Summer House has a celebrated restaurant that's nostalgic in atmosphere, cutting-edge in cuisine. See Chapter 7.
- **Wheatleigh** (Lenox, MA; ☎ **413/637-0610**): A gracious replica of a Florentine palazzo with an ambitious dining room—and it stays open all year, unlike certain other heavily-touted Berkshire retreats. In paradoxical summation, the cheapest rooms are too small to merit their exorbitant cost, whereas the most expensive are so lavish as to almost seem reasonably priced. See Chapter 8.
- **Inn at National Hall** (Westport, CT; ☎ **203/221-1351**): Relatively new, the Inn at National Hall is an event stopover with decor to which the overused word unique can accurately be applied. A playful elegance is on display throughout, and Zanghi, the inn's restaurant, is without peer in the area. See Chapter 9.
- **Cliffside Inn** (Newport, RI; ☎ **401/847-1811**): Newport's champ is the Cliffside Inn, with whirlpools, fireplaces, terry robes, and generously deployed antiques. And so you don't have to wait until you get downstairs for breakfast, they bring an anticipatory pot of coffee and juice to your room. See Chapter 10.
- **Woodstock Inn & Resort** (Woodstock, VT; ☎ **800/448-7900** or 802/457-1100): The 140-room inn was built in the 1960s with a strong Colonial Revival accent. Located right on the green in picturesque Woodstock, the inn offers easy access to the village, along with plenty of other activities, including golf on a course designed by Robert Trent Jones, indoor and outdoor pools, hiking, and skiing (both downhill and cross-country) in winter. See Chapter 11.
- **White Mountain Hotel & Resort** (North Conway, NH; ☎ **800/448-7900** or 802/457-1100): This tasteful, upscale resort opened just a few years ago, but it's imbued with old-fashioned comfort and charm. Located a few miles from the tacky bustle of North Conway, the White Mountain Resort offers golf, swimming, and hiking right at its front door. See Chapter 12.
- **Mount Washington Hotel** (Bretton Woods, NH; ☎ **800/258-0330** or 603/278-1000): The last of the grand Edwardian resorts, the Mount Washington has come back from the brink of bankruptcy with its famed flair intact. This is the place to play golf, climb Mount Washington, or just sit on the broad porch and feel important. See Chapter 12.

- **Balsams Grand Resort Hotel** (Dixville Notch, NH; ☎ 800/255-0600 or 603/255-3400; 800/255-0800 in NH): It's like having your own castle on your own private estate. Set on 15,000 acres in far northern New Hampshire, the Balsams has been offering superb hospitality and gracious comfort since 1866. It has two golf courses, miles of hiking trails, and, in winter, its own downhill and cross-country ski areas. See Chapter 12.
- **The Colony** (Kennebunkport, ME; ☎ 800/552-2363 or 207/967-3331): This rambling, gleaming white resort dates back to 1914, and has been nicely upgraded over the years without losing any of the charm. You can play shuffleboard, putt on the green, or lounge in the ocean-view pool. More vigorous souls cross the street to brave the cold Atlantic waters. See Chapter 13.

11 The Best Moderately Priced Accommodations

- **Harvard Square Hotel** (Cambridge, MA; ☎ 617/864-5200): Smack in the middle of Cambridge's heart, the Harvard Square Hotel recently underwent an overhaul (and name change—it used to be the Harvard Manor House). It remains a comfortable place to stay in a great location. See Chapter 5.
- **John Carver Inn** (Plymouth, MA; ☎ 508/746-7100): The John Carver is centrally located whether you're immersing yourself in Pilgrim lore or passing through on the way from Boston to Cape Cod. Ask about the "Passport to History" packages for a good deal. See Chapter 5.
- **Summer House** (Sandwich, MA; ☎ 508/888-4991): A century ago, you'd have had to be a prosperous whaling captain to bed down in one of these handsome four-square rooms, flooded with light and accoutered with hand-stitched quilts. Sandwich has a number of charming B&Bs, but this one takes the cake—gourmet breakfast and tea, too—with prices negligibly higher than those of an ordinary motel. See Chapter 6.
- **Isaiah Hall B&B Inn** (Dennis, MA; ☎ 508/385-9928): Fancy enough for the Broadway luminaries who star in summer stock at the nearby Cape Cod Playhouse, this former farmhouse in Dennis is the antithesis of glitz. The "great room" doubles as a green room—that is, actors' hangout—and breakfast is celebrated communally in the country kitchen. The plainer rooms will set you back less than a pair of orchestra tix. See Chapter 6.
- **Nauset House Inn** (East Orleans, MA; ☎ 508/255-2195): One half-expects to spot Heathcliff roaming the surrounding moors, so romantic is this 1810 inn. The turn-of-the-century conservatory is the perfect place in which to peruse a novel languidly while waiting for the sky to clear; Nauset Beach is a 10-minute, hand-in-hand walk. See Chapter 6.
- **Even'Tide Motel** (South Wellfleet, MA; ☎ 508/349-3410): That rarity, a motel with style, this popular establishment embodies the best aspects of the '60s: handsome blond oak furniture, a rather hedonistic 60-foot heated indoor pool, and a ³/₄-mile nature trail leading to the sea. It's a low-key, low-cost family haven. See Chapter 6.
- **Wesley Hotel** (Oak Bluffs, MA; ☎ 508/693-6611): The few surviving grand hotels recently treated to makeovers tend to be priced right out of a reasonable range, but this 1879 Vineyard landmark, overlooking the harbor, re-creates the middle-class comforts of the Victorian age, including a long line of porch rockers. See Chapter 7.
- **Tollgate Hill Inn** (Litchfield, CT; ☎ 860/567-4545): No sacrifices in comfort will be made when you stay here, and you'll enjoy the marvelously atmospheric 1745 tavern that serves thoroughly up-to-date eclectic-fusion cuisine. On

weekends, they have live jazz, and Sunday brunch beside the fireplace in winter couldn't be more New England. See Chapter 9.

- **Beech Tree** (Newport, RI; ☎ **401/847-9794**): Arrive on Friday afternoon at the Beech Tree in Newport and they sit you down to a complimentary bowl of chowder, fresh bread, and a glass of wine. Breakfast the next morning, huge and cooked to order, makes lunch irrelevant. All rooms have air-conditioning, TVs, and phones, unlike most B&Bs. See Chapter 10.
- **Mad River Barn** (Waitsfield, VT; ☎ **802/496-3310**): It takes a few minutes to adapt to the Spartan rooms and no-frills accommodations here. But you'll soon discover that the real action takes place in the living room and dining room, where skiers relax and chat after a day on the slopes, and share heaping helpings at mealtime. Rooms with breakfast are $65 for two in summer, and $95 in winter. See Chapter 11.
- **Inn of Exeter** (Exeter, NH; ☎ **603/772-5901**): The dark, richly appointed lobby feels like a private gentleman's club. The location, adjacent to one of the most exclusive prep schools in the nation, only enhances the clubby mood. Rooms are a good value at $75 to $100 for two. See Chapter 12.
- **Red Hill Inn** (Center Harbor, NH; ☎ **603/279-7001**): Situated in the lush hills between Lake Winnipesaukee and the White Mountains, the Red Hill Inn has a faded Victorian grandeur that's been nicely updated without destroying the mood. It's hard to pry yourself away from the fireplace in the common room, but try to stir yourself, if only to explore the forest and fields around the inn. See Chapter 12.
- **Philbrook Farm Inn** (Shelburne, NH; ☎ **603/466-3831**): Go here if you're looking for a complete getaway. The inn has been taking in travelers since the 1850s, and they know how to do it right. The farmhouse sits on 1,000 acres between the Mahoosuc Mountains and the Androscoggin River, and guests can hike with vigor or relax in leisure with equal aplomb. Rooms for two are $130 or under, and that includes both breakfast and dinner. Ask about discounts for longer stays. See Chapter 12.
- **Maine Stay** (Camden, ME; ☎ **800/950-2117**) or 207/236-9636: It's by no means a budget inn (rooms run $80 to $130 for two), but you get a lot of hospitality for the money, and the accommodations are as nice as others I've seen for twice the price. The inn is within walking distance of both downtown Camden and the Camden Hills. See Chapter 13.

12 The Best Destinations for Serious Shoppers

- **Filene's Basement** (Boston): The one, the only. It's impossible to exaggerate enthusiasts' feelings about this world-famous shrine of discounting. From socks and underwear to the swankiest designer duds, it's all here. Wade into the crowds around the automatic-markdown racks (or arrive early and have them practically to yourself), and join the club. See Chapter 4.
- **Newbury Street** (Boston): From the genteel Arlington Street end to the cutting-edge Massachusetts Avenue end, Newbury Street is eight blocks of pure temptation in the form of galleries, boutiques, jewelry and gift shops, bookstores, and more. Set aside your idea of what you "need" (actual necessities are in short supply), and wear the numbers right off your credit cards. See Chapter 4.
- **Chatham** (MA): Old-fashioned, tree-shaded Main Street is packed with inviting storefronts, including the Spyglass for nautical antiques, Pentimento for casual clothing and curious gifts, and gourmet treats-to-go at Chatham Cookware. See Chapter 6.

- **Provincetown** (MA): Overlooking the import junk that's awash in the center of town, the 3-mile gamut of Commercial Street is a shopoholic's dream. It's all here, seemingly direct from Soho: art, jewelry, antiques, antique jewelry . . . and more sensual, cutting-edge clothing (for every sex and permutation thereof) than we could even begin to address in this book. See Chapter 6.
- **Nantucket** (MA): Imagine Martha Stewart cloned a hundredfold, and you'll have some idea of the tenor of shops in this well-preserved nineteenth-century town. Centre Street—known as "Petticoat Row" in whaling days—still caters to feminine tastes, and the town's many esteemed antique stores would never deign to present anything less than the genuine article. See Chapter 7.
- **Woodbury** (CT): Even in this antique-choked part of the country, few towns can match the more than 30 shops along Woodbury's Main Street. See Chapter 9.
- **Newport** (RI): Spring Street's shops mix crafts and folk art with pricey American and imported antiques along its nearly mile-long run. See Chapter 10.
- **Manchester** (VT): The dozens of outlet stores clustered in this handsome village include the usual high-fashion suspects, along with some notable individual shops. Head to Orvis, the maker of noted fly-fishing equipment, for a selection of outdoor gear and clothing. See Chapter 11.
- **Portsmouth** (NH): Downtown Portsmouth offers a grab-bag of small, manageable, eclectic shops, ranging from funky shoe stores to high-quality art galleries. The downtown district may be small enough to browse leisurely on foot, but it packs in a broad assortment of stuff for sale that will appeal to most any taste. See Chapter 12.
- **North Conway** (NH): Combine a trip bent on outdoor adventure with some serious shopping along the 3-mile stretch of discount outlet stores that makes up most of North Conway. Look for Anne Klein, American Tourister, Izod, Dansk, Donna Karan, Levi's, Polo/Ralph Lauren, Reebok/Rockport, J. Crew, and Eddie Bauer in town, along with dozens of others. See Chapter 12.
- **Route 1** (Kittery to Kennebunk, ME): Antique hounds delight in this stretch of less-than-scenic Route 1. Antique mini-malls and high-class junk shops alike are scattered along the route, though there's no central antique zone. Among the best shops is Jorgensen's Antiques on Route 1 in Wells, which has a good selection of American and European furniture in two large buildings. See Chapter 13.
- **Freeport** (ME): L.L. Bean is the big name in this thriving town of outlets, but you'll also find Nike, Patagonia, J. Crew, Dansk, Brooks Brothers, and about 100 others. This is the most aesthetically pleasing of the several outlet centers in northern New England. See Chapter 13.

Planning a Trip to New England

2

by *Wayne Curtis and Stephen Jermanok*

This chapter is designed to provide most of the nuts-and-bolts travel information you'll need before setting off for New England. Browse through this section before you hit the road to ensure you've touched all the bases.

1 Visitor Information

It often seems that New England's leading cash crop is the brochure. Shops, hotels, and restaurants frequently feature racks of colorful pamphlets touting local sights and accommodations. These mini-centers can be helpful in turning up unexpected attractions, but for a more comprehensive overview you should head for the state information centers or the local chambers of commerce. Chamber addresses and phone numbers are provided for each region in the chapters that follow. If you're a highly organized traveler, you'll call in advance and ask for information to be mailed to you. If you're like the rest of us, you'll swing by when you reach town and hope the office is still open.

All six states are pleased to send out general visitor information packets and maps to travelers who call or write ahead. Here's the contact information: **Connecticut Department of Economic Development, Tourist Division,** 865 Brook St., Rocky Hill, CT 06067-3405 (☎ **800/282-6863** or 203/258-4355); **Maine Publicity Bureau,** P.O. Box 2300, Hallowell, ME 04347 (☎ **800/533-9595** or 207/623-0360); **Massachusetts Office of Travel and Tourism,** 100 Cambridge St., 13th Floor, Boston, MA 02202 (☎ **800/447-6277** or 617/727-3201); **New Hampshire Office of Travel and Tourism,** P.O. Box 1856, Concord, NH 03302 (☎ **800/258-3608** or 603/271-2343); **Rhode Island Department of Economic Development,** 7 Jackson Walkway, Providence, R.I. 02903 (☎ **800/556-2484** or 401/277-2601); **Vermont Travel and Tourism,** 134 State St., Montpelier, VT 05602 (☎ **800/837-6668** or 802/828-3237 for general information, or 800/833-9756 for information by fax).

If you're connected to the Internet, there's a rapidly growing horde of information available on the World Wide Web. Many inns and restaurants are putting up their own sites, and entrepreneurs offer packaged tourism information. Many of these sites are simply electronic brochures, offering the same information you'd find at tourist racks. Be sure to distinguish which are paid advertising, and which are the opinions of travelers or residents. (Some cagey advertisers try to make it sound as if they're offering independent advice.)

My favorite sites are those run by cranky folks offering honest and sometimes jaundiced views of various destinations. Find these by using a search engine like Alta Vista (http://www.altavista.digital.com/). Type in a string of terms outlining your interest (for example, "new hampshire white mountains hiking"). You'll get a huge haul of sites, most of which you'll throw back but some of which will be helpful.

Other good places to begin an Internet search are the official information pages maintained by each state. The Web addresses are: **Connecticut:** http://www.state.ct.us/. **Maine:** http://www.state.me.us/. **Massachusetts:** http://ww.ma.us/. **New Hampshire:** http://www.cit.state.vt.us/.**Vermont:** http://www.cit.state.vt.us/. At press time, Rhode Island's site was not yet up and running on the Web.

2　When to Go

THE SEASONS

The well-worn joke about the climate in New England is that it has just two seasons: winter and August. There's a kernel of truth to that, but it's mostly a canard to keep outsiders from moving here. In fact, the ever-shifting seasons are one of those elements that make New England so distinctive.

SUMMER　The peak summer season runs from July 4th to Labor Day. Vast crowds surge into New England during these two holiday weekends, and activity remains high throughout July and August. This should be no surprise: Summers are exquisite here. Forests are verdant and lush, and in the mountains, warm (rarely hot) days are the rule, followed by cool nights. Along the coast, ocean breezes keep temperatures down, and often produce fogs that linger for days. Cape Cod and the Islands, for example, are generally 10 degrees cooler than the mainland in summer.

The weather in summer is determined by the winds. Southwest winds bring haze, heat, and humidity. The northwest winds bring cool weather and knife-sharp vistas. These systems tend to alternate, and the change from hot to cool will sometimes occur in a matter of minutes. Rain is never far away—some days it's an afternoon thunderstorm, other days a steady drizzle that brings a four-day soaking. Regardless, travelers should come prepared for it.

For most of the region, especially the coastal areas, mid-summer is the prime season. Expect to pay premium prices at hotels and restaurants except for around the empty ski resorts of northern New England, where you can often find bargains. Also be aware that early summer brings out black flies and mosquitoes who have spoiled many north country camping trips. Outdoorspeople are best off waiting until after July 4.

AUTUMN　Don't be surprised to smell the tang of fall approaching as early as mid-August, a time when you'll also notice a few leaves turned blaze-orange in otherwise verdant maples at the edges of wetlands. Fall comes early to New England, puts its feet up on the couch, and stays for some time. The foliage season begins in earnest in the northern part of the region by the third week in September; in the south, it reaches its peak by the middle of October.

Fall in New England is one of the great natural spectacles of the United States as rolling hills are blanketed by brilliant reds and stunning oranges. Keep in mind that this is the most popular time of year to travel—bus tours flock here in early October. Also, city dwellers are fond of loading their bikes into the car and heading for the country on weekends, stopping off at local farm stands on their way home for rations of fresh apple cider, pumpkins, squash, and cranberries. As a result, hotels are invariably booked solid. Reservations are essential, and you can also expect to pay a foliage surcharge of $10 or $20 per room at many inns.

WINTER   New England winters are like wine—some years are good, some are lousy. During a good season (like the winter of 1995–96), plenty of light, fluffy snow covers the deep woods and ski slopes. A good New England winter offers profound peace as the muffling qualities of fresh snow bring a thunderous silence to the region. During these winters, exploring the forest on snowshoes or cross-country skis is an experience that borders on the magical.

During the *other* winters, the lousy ones, the weather brings a nasty mélange of rain and sleet. It's bone-numbing cold, and bleak, bleak, bleak. Look into the eyes of the residents on the street during this time. They are all thinking of the Caribbean.

The higher you go in the mountains, and the farther north you head, the better your odds of finding snow and avoiding rain. Winter coastal vacations can be spectacular (nothing beats cross-country skiing at the edge of the pounding surf), but it's a high-risk venture that could definitely yield rain rather than snow.

Ski areas naturally are crowded during the winter months. They're especially so during school vacations, when most resorts tend to jack up their rates.

SPRING   Spring lasts only a weekend or so, often around mid-May, but sometimes it arrives as late as June. One day the ground is muddy, the trees are barren, and gritty snow is still piled in shady hollows. The next day, temperatures are reaching into the 80s, trees are blooming, and kids are swimming in the lakes. Travelers must be very crafty and alert if they want to experience spring in New England. It's also known as the mud season, and a time when many innkeepers and restaurateurs close up for a few weeks for either vacation or renovation. Be aware that New England plays host to a slew of colleges and universities and as a result the periods around graduation (mid- to late May and early June) produce unusually high hotel occupancy rates, particularly around major cities like Boston. As always, it's best to book rooms in advance.

Average Temperatures in Burlington, Vermont

	Jan	Feb	Mar	Apr	May	Jun	July	Aug	Sep	Oct	Nov	Dec
Avg. High (°F)	25	27	38	53	66	76	80	78	69	57	44	30
Avg. Low (°F)	8	9	21	33	44	54	59	57	49	39	30	15

NEW ENGLAND CALENDAR OF EVENTS

January

○ **New Year's & First Night Celebrations,** regionwide. Boston, Mass.; Portland, Me.; Providence, R.I.; Stamford, Conn.; Portsmouth, N.H.; Burlington, Vt.; and many other cities and towns, including Cape Cod and Martha's Vineyard, celebrate the coming of the New Year with plenty of festivities. Check with local chambers of commerce for details. New Year's Eve.

February

• **Dartmouth Winter Carnival,** Hanover, N.H. Huge and elaborate ice sculptures grace the Green during this festive celebration of winter, which includes numerous sporting events and other winter-related activities. Call **603/646-1110.** Mid-month.

• **Mt. Washington Valley Chocolate Festival,** North Conway, N.H. Earn your chocolate by cross-country skiing from inn to inn, picking up sweets at each stop. Look for other events sure to please the chocoholic in and around town. Call **800/367-3364.** Late February.

- **Stowe Derby,** Stowe, Vt. The oldest downhill/cross-country ski race in the nation features racers who scramble from the wintry summit of Mt. Mansfield into the village on the Stowe Rec path. Call **802/253-3423** for details. Late February.

March

- **St. Patrick's Day/Evacuation Day.** Parade, South Boston; celebration, Faneuil Hall Marketplace. The 5-mile parade salutes the city's Irish heritage and the day British troops left Boston in 1776. Head to Faneuil Hall Marketplace for music, dancing, and food and plenty of Irish spirit. Call **800/888-5515.** March 17.
- **New England Spring Flower Show,** Dorchester, Mass. This annual harbinger of spring presented by the Massachusetts Horticultural Society (☎ **617/536-9280**) draws huge crowds starved for a glimpse of green. Second or third week of the month.
- **Super Winterfest,** Ludlow, Vt. A weeklong festival throughout the town featuring skiing, ice fishing, snow hockey, fireworks, and a parade. Call **802/228-1229.** Early March.

April

- ❂ **Patriots Day,** Boston (Paul Revere House, Old North Church, Lexington Green, Concord's North Bridge). The events of April 18–19, 1775, which signified the start of the Revolutionary War, are commemorated and reenacted. Participants dressed as Paul Revere and William Dawes ride to Lexington and Concord to warn the Minutemen that "the regulars are out" (not that "the British are coming"— most colonists considered themselves British). Mock battles are fought at Lexington and Concord. Third Monday of the month, a state holiday. Call the Lexington Visitor's Center (☎ **617/862-1450**), or the Concord Chamber of Commerce (☎ **508/369-3120**).
- **Boston Marathon,** from Hopkinton, Mass., to Boston. International stars and local amateurs run in the world's oldest and most famous marathon. The noon start means elite runners hit Boston about two hours later; weekend runners stagger across the Boylston Street finish line as many as six hours after that. Call the Boston Athletic Association (☎ **617/236-1652**). Third Monday of the month.
- **Sugarbush Spring Fling,** Waitsfield, Vt. Ski-related events herald the coming of spring and the best season for skiing. Special events for kids. Call **802/583-2381.**
- ❂ **Daffodil Festival,** Nantucket. Spring's arrival is heralded with masses of yellow blooms adorning everything in sight, including a cavalcade of antique cars (☎ **508/228-1700**). Late April.

May

- **Annual Basketry Festival,** Stowe, Vt. A weeklong event with displays and workshops by talented weavers. Mid-May. Call the Stowe Area Association at **800/24-STOWE.**
- **Lilac Sunday,** Shelburne, Vt. See the famed lilacs (more than 400 bushes) at the renowned Shelburne Museum when they're at their most beautiful. Call **802/985-3346** for details. Mid- to late May.
- **Mayfest,** Bennington, Vt. Main Street is blocked off to cars and filled with food vendors and craftsman at this late spring/early summer community event. Call **802/442-5758.** Late May.
- **Lobsterfest,** Mystic, Conn. An old-fashioned lobster bake and live music on the banks of the Mystic River. Call **860/572-5315.** Late May.
- **Brimfield Antiques Fair,** Brimfield, Mass. Up to 2,000 dealers fill several fields near this central Massachusetts town, with similar fairs in early or mid-July and mid-September. Call **508/347-2761.** Mid-May.

- **Open Studio Weekend,** throughout Vermont. Artists throughout the state open their doors to the public, offering a first-hand glimpse at how it's all done. Call **802/223-3380.** Late May.
- **Cape Maritime Week,** Capewide. A multitude of cultural organizations mount special events—such as lighthouse tours—highlighting the region's nautical history. Call **508/362-3225.** Mid-May.
- **Figawi Sailboat Race,** Hyannis to Nantucket. The largest race on the East Coast. Call **508/778-1691.** Late May.

June

- **Old Port Festival,** Portland, Me. A day-long block party in the heart of Portland's historic district with live music, food vendors, and activities for kids. Call **207/ 772-2249.** Early June.
- **Yale-Harvard Regatta,** on the Thames River in New London, Conn. One of the oldest collegiate rivalries in the country. Call **203/432-4747.** Early June.
- **Market Square Weekend,** Portsmouth, N.H. This lively street fair attracts hordes from throughout southern New Hampshire and Maine into downtown Portsmouth to dance, listen to music, sample food, and enjoy summer's arrival. Call **603/436-2848.** Early June.
- **Lake Champlain Balloon and Craft Festival,** Essex Junction, Vt. New England's largest balloon festival draws thousands of spectators to see these graceful craft float above the quiet landscape. Call **802/899-2993.** Early June.
- **Taste of Hartford,** Hartford, Conn. One of New England's largest outdoor festivals. Many area restaurants serve up their specialties. You'll also get a "taste" of local music, dance, magic, and comedy. Call **860/728-3089.** Mid-month.
- **Motorcycle Week,** Loudon & Weirs Beach, N.H. Tens of thousands of bikers descend on the Lake Winnipesaukee region early each summer to compare their machines and cruise the strip at Weirs Beach. The Gunstock Hill Climb and the Loudon Classic race are the centerpieces of the week's activities. Call **603/ 783-4931.** Mid-June.
- **Taste of Block Island Seafood Festival,** Block Island, R.I. Chowder cookoff, games, crafts, and live entertainment. Call **800/383-2474.** Mid-June.
- **ESPN X (Extreme) Games,** in and around Newport and Providence, R.I. Hundreds of top athletes from around the world compete in this seven-day alternative-sport extravaganza featuring in-line skating, rock climbing, bungee jumping, sky surfing, and more. Call **401/846-1133.** Late June.
- *Boston Globe* **Jazz Festival,** Boston. Big names and rising stars of the jazz world appear at lunchtime, after-work, evening, and weekend events, some of which are free. Contact the *Globe* (☎ **617/929-2000**) or pick up a copy of the paper for a schedule when you arrive in town. Some events require tickets purchased in advance. Third week of June.
- **Great Kennebec Whatever Week,** Augusta, Me. A community celebration to mark the cleaning up of the Kennebec River, culminating in a wacky race involving all manner of watercraft, some more seaworthy than others. Call **207/623-4559** for details. Late June.
- ✪ **Jacob's Pillow Dance Festival,** Becket, Mass. The oldest dance festival in America features everything from ballet to modern dance and jazz. For a season brochure, call **413/243-0745.** Late June to August.
- **Williamstown Theater Festival,** Williamstown, Mass. This nationally distinguished theater festival presents everything from the classics to uproarious comedies and contemporary works. Scattered among the drama are literary readings and cabarets. Call **413/597-3399.** Late June through August.

July

- **Boston Harborfest,** Downtown (along Boston Harbor and the Harbor Islands). The city puts on its Sunday best for the Fourth of July, which has become a gigantic weeklong celebration of Boston's maritime history and an excuse to just get out and have fun. Events include concerts, guided tours, cruises, fireworks, the Boston Chowderfest, and the annual turnaround of the USS *Constitution*. In 1997, in celebration of its 200th birthday, the *Constitution* will be under sail for the first time in more than a century. Call **617/227-1528.** First week in July.

- **Boston Pops Concert and Fireworks Display,** Hatch Memorial Shell on the Esplanade. Independence Week culminates in the famous Boston Pops Fourth of July concert. People wait from dawn till dark for the music to start. The program includes the *1812 Overture* with actual cannon fire that coincides with the fireworks. July 4.

- **Independence Day,** regionwide. Communities throughout all three states celebrate July 4th with parades, cookouts, road races, and fireworks. The bigger the town, the bigger the fireworks. Contact local chambers of commerce for details.

- **Newport Music Festival,** Newport, R.I. Outdoor chamber music concerts are held among the opulent mansions. For information call **401/846-1133.** Second and third weeks in July.

- **Historic Homes Tour,** Litchfield, Conn. One day is your only opportunity to tour this beautiful town's historic houses and gardens. Call **860/567-9423.** Mid-month.

- **Barnstable County Fair,** East Falmouth, Mass. (on Cape Cod). An old-time county fair complete with rides, food, and livestock contests. Call **508/563-3200.** Late July.

- **Friendship Sloop Days,** Rockland, Me. This three-day event is a series of boat races that culminates in a parade of sloops. Call **207/596-0376.** Mid-month.

- **Wickford Art Festival,** Wickford, R.I. Over 200 artists gather in this quaint village for one of the East Coast's oldest art festivals. Wickford is the ancestral home of author John Updike and is allegedly the setting for his book *The Witches of Eastwick*. Call **401/295-5566.** Mid-month.

- **Vermont Quilt Festival,** Northfield, Vt. Displays are only part of the allure of New England's largest quilt festival. You can also attend classes, and have your heirlooms appraised. Call **802/485-7092.** Mid-July.

- **Revolutionary War Days,** Exeter, N.H. Learn all you need to know about the War of Independence during this historic community festival, which features a Revolutionary War encampment and dozens of reenactors. Call **603/772-2622.** Mid-July.

- **Marlboro Music Festival,** Marlboro, Vt. This is a popular six-week series of classical concerts featuring talented student musicians performing in the peaceful hills outside of Brattleboro. Call **802/254-2394** for information. Weekends from July through mid-August.

- ✪ **Tanglewood,** near Lenox, Mass. The Boston Symphony Orchestra makes its summer home at this fine estate bringing symphony, chamber concerts, and solo recitals to the Berkshire Hills. Call the Tanglewood Concert Line at **413/637-1666** (July and August only) or Symphony Hall **617/266-1492.** July to August.

August

- **SoNo Arts Festival,** South Norwalk, Conn. For three days artists, craftspeople, dancers, and other performers from around the country celebrate throughout South Norwalk's historic waterfront area. Call **203/866-7916.** Early August.

- **Maine Lobster Festival,** Rockland, Me. Fill up on the local harvest at this event marking the importance and delectability of Maine's favorite crustacean. Enjoy a boiled lobster or two, and take in the ample entertainment during this informal waterfront gala. Call **207/596-0376** or 800/562-2529. Early August.
- **Southern Vermont Crafts Fair,** Manchester. More than 200 artisans show off their fine work at this popular festival, which also features creative food and good music. Early August.
- **Newport Folk Festival & JVC Jazz Festival,** Newport, R.I. Thousands of music lovers congregate at Fort Adams State Park for concerts on alternate weekends in July and August. It's one of the premier jazz concerts in the country. Performers have included big names like B.B. King, Suzanne Vega, Ray Charles, and Tony Bennett. For information on schedules and tickets call **401/847-3700** or call TicketMaster (☎ **401/331-2211**). Second week.
- **Annual Star Party,** St. Johnsbury, Vt. The historic Fairbanks Museum and Planetarium hosts special events and shows, including night viewing sessions, during the lovely Perseid Meteor Shower. Call **802/748-2372.** Mid-August.
- **Martha's Vineyard Agricultural Fair,** West Tisbury, Mass. An old-fashioned country fair featuring horse pulls, livestock shows, musician and woodsman contests, and plenty of carnival action. Call **508/693-4343.** Mid-month.
- **Blueberry Festival,** Machias, Me. A festival marking the harvest of the region's wild blueberries. Eat to your heart's content. Call **207/794-3543.** Mid-month.
- **Blue Hill Fair,** Blue Hill, Me. A classic country fair just outside one of Maine's most elegant villages. Call **207/374-9976.** Late August to Labor Day.

September
- **Vermont State Fair,** Rutland, Vt. All of Vermont seems to show up for this grand event, with a midway, live music, and plenty of agricultural exhibits. Call **802/775-5200** for details. Early September.
- **Providence Waterfront Festival,** Providence, R.I. Performances, art exhibits, games, rides, and entertainment. Don't miss the Pasta Challenge, a local restaurant competition in which the public samples and votes for the best pasta sauces. Call **401/785-9450.** Labor Day weekend.
- **Cambridge River Festival,** Cambridge, Mass. A salute to the arts, with music, dancing, children's activities, and international food in an outdoor setting. Call **617/349-4380.** Early September.
- **Norwalk Oyster Festival,** Norwalk, Conn. This waterfront festival celebrates Long Island Sound's seafaring past. Highlights include oyster shucking and slurping contests, harbor cruises, concerts, and fireworks. Call **203/838-9444.** Early September.
- **Windjammer Weekend,** Camden, Me. Come visit Maine's impressive fleet of oldtime sailing ships, which host open houses throughout the weekend at this scenic harbor. Call **207/236-4404.** Early September.
- **Eastern States Exhibition,** West Springfield, Mass. "The Big E" is New England's largest agricultural fair with a midway, games, rides, rodeo and lumberjack shows, country music stars, and lots of eats. Call **413/737-2443** or 413/787-1548. Mid-September.
- **Provincetown Arts Festival,** Provincetown, Mass. (Cape Cod). One of the country's oldest art colonies celebrates its past and present with local artists giving open studios. It's an extraordinary opportunity for collecting 20th-century works. Call the Provincetown Chamber of Commerce (☎ **508/487-3424**). Late September.

- **Common Ground Fair,** Windsor, Me. An old-time state fair with a twist: The emphasis is on organic foods, recycling, and wholesome living. Call **207/ 623-5515.** Late September.

October

❂ **Northeast Kingdom Fall Foliage Festival,** Northeast Vermont. A cornucopia of events staged in towns and villages throughout Vermont's northeast corner heralds the arrival of the fall foliage season. Be the first to see colors at their peak. Call **802/748-3678** for information. Early October.

- **Bourne Farm Pumpkin Festival,** West Falmouth, Mass. (Cape Cod). A fun-for-the-whole-family day of pumpkin picking, hayrides, and pony rides at a 1775 farmstead. Call **508/548-0711.** Early October.

- **Fryeburg Fair,** Fryeburg, Me. Cotton candy, tractor pulls, live music, and huge vegetables and barnyard animals at Maine's largest agricultural fair. There's also harness racing in the evening. Call **207/985-3278.** A week in early October.

- **Mystic Chowderfest,** Mystic, Conn. A festival of soup served from bubbling cauldrons set on wood fires. Call **860/572-5315.** Mid-month.

- **Harvest Day,** Canterbury, N.H. A celebration of the harvest season, Shaker-style. Lots of autumnal exhibits and children's games. Call **603/783-9511.** Mid-month.

- **Cranberry Harvest Festival,** Nantucket. Bog tours, inn tours, and a cranberry cookoff, just when the foliage is at its burnished prime. Call **508/228-1700.** Mid-October.

- **Salem Haunted Happenings,** Salem, Mass. Parades, parties, fortune-telling, cruises, and candlelight tours of historic homes. It all leads up to a ceremony on the big day. Call **508/744-0004.** Last two weeks of the month.

❂ **Head of the Charles Regatta,** Boston and Cambridge. High school, college, and postcollegiate rowing teams and individuals—some 4,000 in all—race in front of hordes of fans along the banks of the Charles River. This event always seems to fall on the crispest, most picturesque Sunday of the season. Call the **Metropolitan District Commission Harbor Master** (☎ 617/727-0537) for information. Late October.

November

- **Victorian Holiday,** Portland, Me. From late November until Christmas Portland decorates its Old Port in a Victorian Christmas theme. Enjoy the window displays, take a free hayride, listen to costumed carolers sing. Call **207/772-6828** for details.

- **Thanksgiving Celebration,** Plymouth, Mass. The holiday that put Plymouth on the map is observed with a "stroll through the ages," showcasing 17th- and 19th-century Thanksgiving preparations in historic homes. Nearby Plimoth Plantation, where the colony's first years are re-created, wisely offers a Victorian Thanksgiving feast (reservations required). Call the Plymouth Visitors Center (☎ 800/ USA-1620) or the Plimoth Plantation (☎ 508/746-1622). Thanksgiving Day.

- **Brookfield Holiday Craft Exhibition & Sale,** Brookfield, Conn. Thousands of unique, elegant, and artful gifts are displayed in gallery settings on three floors of a restored grist mill. Call **203/775-4526.** Late November to Christmas.

December

- **Christmas Prelude,** Kennebunkport, Me. This scenic coastal village greets Santa's arrival in a lobster boat, and marks the coming of Christmas with street shows, pancake breakfasts, and tours of the towns' inns. Call **207/967-3286.** Early December.

- **Christmas Tree Lighting,** Boston, Prudential Center. Carol singing precedes the lighting of a magnificent tree from Nova Scotia—an annual expression of thanks from the people of Halifax for Bostonians' help in fighting a devastating fire more than 70 years ago. First Saturday of December. Call the Greater Boston Convention and Visitors Bureau (☎ 617/536-4100).
- **Boston Tea Party Reenactment,** Boston, Congress Street Bridge. Chafing under British rule, the colonists rose up on December 16, 1773, to strike a blow where it would cause real pain—in the pocketbook. Call **617/338-1773.** Mid-December.
- ✪ **Candlelight Stroll,** Portsmouth, N.H. Historic Strawberry Banke gets in a Christmas way with old-time decorations and more than 1,000 candles lighting the 10-acre grounds. Call **603/433-1100** for information. First two weekends of December.
- **Woodstock Wassail Celebration,** Woodstock, Vt. Enjoy classic English grog, along with parades and dances, at this annual event. Call **802/457-3555.** Early December.
- **Christmas Eve and Christmas Day.** Special festivities throughout New England. In Newport, R.I., several of the great mansions have special tours; Mystic, Conn., has a special program of Christmas festivities; Nantucket, Mass., features carolers in Victorian garb, art exhibits, and tours of historic homes. December 24–25.

3 The Active Vacation Planner

New England is a superb destination for those who don't consider it a vacation unless they find some outdoor adventure. One terrific resource is another Frommer's publication, *Outside Magazine's Adventure Guide to New England.* It covers all kinds of outings for travelers of every ability level.

For pointers on where to head, see the "Enjoying the Great Outdoors" section at the beginning of each state chapter in this book. More detailed information on local services is included in each regional section.

Guidebooks to the region's backcountry are plentiful and diverse. L.L. Bean in Freeport, Maine, and the Green Mountain Club headquarters in Waterbury, Vermont, both have an excellent selection of guidebooks, as do many local bookshops throughout the region. For a catalog of local guidebooks contact the **Appalachian Mountain Club,** 5 Joy St., Boston, MA 02108 (☎ 617/523-0636) or **Backcountry Publications,** P.O. Box 175, Woodstock, VT 05091 (☎ 800/245-4151).

Local outdoor clubs are also a good source of information, and some offer trips open to nonmembers. The most established of the bunch is the Appalachian Mountain Club (see address above), whose chapters run group trips almost every weekend throughout the region, but especially in northern New Hampshire. Other groups include the **Green Mountain Club,** R.R. #1, Box 650, Route 100, Waterbury Center, VT 05677 (☎ 802/244-7037) and the **Maine Outdoor Adventure Club (MOAC),** P.O. Box 11251, Portland, ME 04104 (☎ 207/828-0918 for a recorded hotline in Portland).

Another obvious but often overlooked source of information are shops that cater to active travelers. Cross-country ski shops, bike dealers, fishing suppliers, and camping shops are all potentially rich resources about the best local destinations. Clerks, managers, and other customers might be able to point you to the best trails and rivers.

Outdoor enthusiasts with Web access will want to check out **GORP**'s resource listings for on-line information on New England area parks and recreational activities. Head for **http://www.gorp.com/gorp/location/us/us.htm**, then choose one or more of the six New England states.

BIKING   New England's diversity of terrain, rich history, and compact size have all helped to make it one of the top road biking destinations in the country. Go East, young man and woman, and you'll find thousands of miles of road that form hundreds of loops ranging from 10 to 110 miles long. And, contrary to popular belief, car traffic is not a problem. Most of the congested roads are found around urban centers, not in the rural countryside.

The hardest decision is whether you should go with an outfitter or on your own. The biggest advantage of hiring a guide is the complete and utter lack of responsibility on your part. Most outfitters will find a way to relieve all your vacation worries, from accommodations to food to equipment. You also have a chance to make new friends. The downside is the additional cost and the lack of privacy. There's no place better than a lonely backcountry road to collect your thoughts and gain a sense of serenity. This is especially true if you live in a city like I do. If you do decide to go with an outfitter, ask the following questions before you put your money down:

- **What's the cost and what's included in the price?** Be sure to discuss accommodations and whether or not all meals are included. Some companies skip lunch or an occasional dinner. Also ask about shuttles to and from airports and the cost of bike rentals.
- **What level of fitness is required?** By far, the most important question. Get a feel for the tour. Is this an obstacle course better suited for Marines, or a walk in the park, or somewhere in between? Will I bike 20, 40, or 60 miles a day? Do I have options for each day? Can I go shopping or sightseeing one day while my wife bikes to her legs' delight?
- **How long have you been in business?** Credentials are important, but not nearly as important as the next question.
- **What are the age and experience of the guides?** Many outfitters are desperate enough to hire young guides who, until very recently, had no experience in that sport or are from an entirely different part of the country.
- **How many people are in the group?** What is the guide to client ratio? Do I have to compete with 30 or 5 other people for the guide's attention?
- **Is it mostly singles or couples?** Guided tours are a great place to befriend other singles or couples. Find out which trip best suits your needs.
- **What equipment is required? What type of equipment can I rent?** If you have your own bike, make sure its adequate for the trip. Ask what bikes they offer. Do they rent 3-speed Raleighs or 21-speed Cannondales and Treks?
- **What happens if it rains?** Do you have alternative plans for foul weather or do you expect me to bike around the Vineyard in a downpour?

The following is a list of outfitters that offer overnight bike trips. In my opinion, you really can't go wrong with any trip to Vermont or the Atlantic islands:

Backroads, 1516 Fifth St., Berkeley, CA 94710-1740, (☎ **800/GO-ACTIVE**) features five-day biking tours of Penobscot Bay, Me.; Southern Vermont; Northern Vermont; and Cape Cod and The Islands. **Bike Vermont,** P.O. Box 207, Woodstock, VT 05091 (☎ **800/257-2226**), offers weekend, three-day, five-day, and six-day tours to all regions of the state. **L.L. Bean Outdoor Discovery Program,** Freeport, ME 04033 (☎ **800/341-4341, ext. 6666**), offers instructional trips, so expect to leave with better pedaling power. They also have weekend bike trips to Bethel, Me., home of Sunday River Ski Resort. **Vermont Bicycle Touring,** P.O. Box 711, Bristol, VT 05433 (☎ 800/245-3868), organizes six five-day biking tours and eight weekend tours to every region of Vermont; a five-day trip to Cape Cod and the Islands; and three- to five-day tours of Penobscot Bay, Boothbay Harbor, and Acadia National Park.

Discover a unique mountain biking experience with **Back Country Excursions,** RFD 2, P.O. Box 365, Limerick, ME 04048 (☎ 207/625-8189). The owner has created a mountain biking playground called the "Palace." The 4,000-square-foot garden has over 100 tons of stones, log-packed trailways, bridges, and stairs, all situated in a natural half-pipe. Once you tire of this, you can take one of many guided tours through 60 miles of connected trails in the Sebago Lake area, near the New Hampshire border.

CANOEING   Whether you're a flatwater or white-water canoeist, the long sinuous rivers, lakes, and hidden ponds that blanket the Northeast offer some of the finest canoeing in the country. Hundreds of camping sites occupy the shores and islands, tucked between tall firs and spruces.

Not surprisingly, many of the best waterways are in Northern Maine, where wildlife outnumbers people. The 92-mile Allagash Wilderness Waterway, a series of pristine rivers, lakes, and ponds, takes between 7 and 10 days to complete. Development is prohibited within 500 feet of the corridor and there are 65 authorized campsites within the zone. The put-in is Allagash or Chamberlain Lake. Takeout is usually around the village of Allagash near the St. John River junction. Most of the water is flat, except for two Class II and III stretches known as Chase Rapids and Twin Brook Rapids. Chase Rapids is located at the beginning of the Allagash River. A ranger at Churchill Dam will truck you, your equipment, and your canoe around the rapids if you prefer not to paddle down the white water.

St. John River is mostly Class II and III white water. Early May to mid-June is the only time to cruise down the rapids. By the end of June, the river might be too shallow. Remember to bring your bug repellent since this is the heart of black fly season. The put-in for the 7- to 10-day St. John trip is Baker Lake. Like the Allagash trip, most canoeists end at Allagash Village. However, it's possible to paddle into New Brunswick, Canada.

Folsom's Air Service, Greenville, Me. (☎ 207/695-2821), will transport you, your gear, and your canoe on seaplane to most destinations in the North Woods. They will also pick you up once you're finished.

There's a long list of rentals, shuttles, and guide services. **Allagash Guide Service** in Allagash (☎ 207/398-3418), rents canoes, paddles, and offers transport and car pick-up from the Allagash Waterway or St. John River.

Gil Gilpatrick, author of *Allagash, The Canoe Guide's Handbook* and *Building a Strip Canoe,* is a highly recommended Registered Maine Guide. Contact him at **Gilpatrick's Guide Service,** P.O. Box 461, Skowhegan, ME 04976 (☎ 207/453-6959).

Alexandra and Garrett Conover are also Registered Maine Guides who run **North Woods Ways,** R.R. #2 Box 159A, Willimantic, ME 04443 (☎ 207/997-3723). They visit Allagash, St. John, the West Branch of the Penobscot, and other waterways (ask them about their 16-day trip to Grand River, Labrador).

L.L. Bean Paddling Schools, Freeport, ME 04033 (☎ 800/341-4341, ext. 6666), offer several canoe trips led by Registered Maine Guides. Two five-day trips head to the Allagash River, two four-day trips go to Moose River in Jackman. They also offer instruction on the shores of Moose Pond, Bridgton.

Outside of Maine, the best overnight canoeing is in Vermont, and the longest journeys are in the northern part of that state. The Winooski, Lamoille, and Missisquoi rivers are all tributaries of Lake Champlain. One recommendable outfit in this area is **Vermont Waterways,** R.R. #1, P.O. Box 322, East Hardwick, VT 05836-9707 (☎ 800/492-8271), which visits the White, Winooski, Connecticut, and Lamoille rivers on their weekend or five-day tours. Prices start at $350 per person, including accommodations and all meals.

FISHING   From the trout and landlocked salmon caught in the Battenkill, Penobscot, and Kennebec rivers to the stripers, blues, cod, and tuna found in the Atlantic, you have to try hard not to hook anything in the waters of New England.

Before you break out your pole, make sure you have a permit. Contact the Departments of Fish and Wildlife listed under each region in this book. Many of these offices also publish useful guides. If you don't know the area, hire a guide who can show you around and explain which flys, hooks, and lines to use.

There are so many places to fish and so many different techniques, from fly-fishing to surf casting, that it would be impossible to list them all. Here's a small sampling of my favorite destinations and trips in New England:

The Maine Woods, with rivers and lakes stocked with trout and salmon, is the premier spot for freshwater fishing in New England. If you're looking for a respected guide in the Carrabassett Valley region, contact Steve Warren (☎ 207/246-4042). In Rangeley, contact Ned Stearns at **Grey Ghost Guide Service** (☎ 207/864-5314). In Moosehead Lake, contact Bob Lawrence (☎ 800/346-4666 or 207/534-7709). On the Kennebec, contact Caroll Ware (☎ 207/474-5430).

Fishing camps are as prolific as the fish in the Maine Woods. Only serious fly-fishermen need apply at **Grant's Kennebago Camps,** P.O. Box 786, Oquossoc, ME 04964 (☎ 800/633-4815 or 207/864-3608). The 18 camps, replete with dock and boat, were built on Kennebago Lake in 1905. The cost is $92 per day, including all meals. **Tim Pond Wilderness Camps,** Eustis, ME 04936 (☎ 207/243-2947) has been in business since the 1860s and is billed as "the oldest continuously operating sporting camp in America." Fly-fishermen don't have to venture far from their log cabins to find the secluded pond. The price for one of $98 per day includes all meals.

The **L.L. Bean Fly-Fishing School,** Freeport, ME 04033 (☎ 800/341-4341, ext. 6666), offers a five-day intermediate fly-fishing school at Weatherby's in Grand Lake Stream for $1,295.

The 27-mile-long Battenkill River is famous for its brown and brook trout fishing and runs south from Manchester Village, Vermont to Arlington and then west to New York. **Orvis,** Manchester, VT 05254 (☎ 800/235-9763), runs one of the top fly-fishing schools in the country here. The two- to two-and-a-half-day classes are offered twice a week from early April to mid-July, then weekends only through August. They also offer parent/child and women-only weekends.

All along the Atlantic coast, party and private boats offer deep-sea fishing excursions. You can also surf cast from the shores. Cape Cod and the Islands are to blues and stripers what Montana is to trout—a fishing frenzy. Between late July and October, the bluefish are abundant. Striped bass are a bit more elusive, but still very catchable. Locals start hooking "keepers" in late May and continue throughout the summer.

There's elephant tuna, blue tuna, and bonita to be had when you venture offshore, but most likely you'll catch scup, tautog, fluke, sea bass, and other bottom fish. *On the Cape Hy-line* and the 65-foot *Navigator* operate out of Hyannis's **Ocean Street Docks** (☎ 508/790-0696). In Martha's Vineyard, **Coop's Bait and Tackle,** 147 West Tisbury Rd., near Edgartown (☎ 508/627-3909), comes highly recommended. In Nantucket, try the **Albacore** (☎ 508/228-5074) located on Slip #17, Straight Wharf, and **Just Do It Too** (☎ 508/228-7448) Slip #13, Straight Wharf.

In Rhode Island, Point Judith is the best place to find party boats and charters. Captain Frank Blount (☎ 401/783-4988) has three boats taking anglers out on half-day, full-day, and night trips for cod, blues, porgies, blackfish, and fluke. He also has overnight trips where you can reel in pollack, tuna, bonita, and shark. For more information call the **Rhode Island Party & Charterboat Association** (☎ 401/737-5812).

HORSEBACK RIDING   You don't have to venture to the Wild West for an over-night riding trip. **Kedron Valley Stables,** Route 106, South Woodstock (☎ 802/457-1480), offers four- to six-day inn-to-inn trips in the Green Mountain National Forest. Paul Kendall, the owner, will guide you through secluded woods and historic villages like South Woodstock, Grafton, and Proctorsville. Get used to your saddle because you'll be on it for five to six hours at a stretch over the four-day jaunt.

In a state known for their Morgans, the small pony-size horses at **Vermont Icelandic Farms,** P.O. Box 577, Waitsfield, VT 05673 (☎ 802/496-7141), are a special treat. Icelandics move at a very steady pace without much rocking, much like driving with good shocks. Owner Christina Calabrese offers half-day to three-day rides for experienced riders only.

For day riders, hundreds of stables offer lessons and guided trail rides throughout New England. The various sites include the shores of Block Island, the steep trails of the White Mountains, and the 200-year-old villages of northeastern Connecticut. Consult local chambers of commerce for further information.

SAILING   New England's portion of the Atlantic deserves its reputation as one of the world's leading cruising grounds. Almost every day in summer you'll see numerous sails tacking in and out of legendary bays like Narragansett in Rhode Island and Penobscot off the mid-Maine coast. With hundreds of picturesque anchorages like Potter's Cove at the north end of Prudence Island in Narragansett Bay, Isle au Haut in Maine's Penobscot Bay, and Tarpaulin Cove on the south side of Naushon Island (off Cape Cod), there's more than enough harbors to spend a day or evening. And let's not forget about the large lakes that lie inland. Champlain, Winnipesaukee, Moosehead, Squam, and many smaller bodies of water are just as popular with sailors.

There are numerous places to bareboat charter (renting a large sailboat without its crew for day or overnight trips). Schooling and prior sailing experience are necessary to bareboat charter, especially on the Maine coast where fog, currents, wide tidal range, and a merciless shoreline can wreak havoc. Less experienced sailors should consider renting lasers, rhodes, or sunfishes.

Hinckley Yacht Charters, Bass Harbor Marine, Bass Harbor, ME 04653 (☎ 800/HYC-SAIL), is based in a small fishing village on the southwestern shores of Mt. Desert Island. They have 25 boats, ranging from a 34-foot Sabre ($1,775–$1,975 a week) to a 49-foot Hinckley ($3,775–$4,200 a week). **Bay Island Yacht Charters,** 120 Tillson Ave., Rockland, ME (☎ 800/421-2492), offers 15 bare boats, from a 26-foot Nonsuch ($1,100 a week) to a 43-foot Taswell ($2,950 a week). **Winds of Ireland,** P.O. Box 2286, S. Burlington, VT 05407 (☎ 802/863-5090), charters five Hunters, from 30 to 40 feet, on a day or weekly rate. Prices start at $145 per day and a captain costs extra. Winds of Ireland also offers two-hour daysails and sunset sails. **McKibben Sailing Vacations,** 176 Battery St., Burlington, VT 05407 (☎ 800/522-0028 or 802/864-7733), offers bareboat and crewed charters on Lake Champlain.

If you don't have the experience to charter a sailboat, try the next best thing—a Windjammer cruise off the mid-Maine coast. Unlike most of the wooden ships offering trips along the Atlantic coast, the majority of schooners docked in Rockland, Rockport, and Camden were working vessels in the early 1900s.

One good example is the *Wendameen,* P.O. Box 506, Camden, ME 04843 (☎ **207/236-3472**), a 67-foot yacht built in 1912. Its passengers once included Eugene O'Neil and Katherine Porter, and the boat now accommodates 14 guests. An overnight stay, including breakfast and dinner costs $143. Rates for private charters start at $1,250 per day. For further information contact the **Maine Windjammer Association,** P.O. Box 317, Rockport, ME (☎ **800/614-6380**).

SKIING   See Chapter 1, "The Best of New England," for information on downhill ski resorts. We've detailed every downhill area and cross-country touring center in the regional chapters that follow.

SPORTS CAMPS   Camps are not just for children any more. The list of sporting camps catering to adults is growing. Here's a small sampling of the camps available in New England.

Call the **Appalachian Mountain Club,** P.O. Box 298, Gorham, NH 03581 (☎ **603/466-2727**), for a catalog of their extensive overnight courses. You'll find everything from mushroom foraging to canoeing to backpacking. **Bigelow Bike Tours,** P.O. Box 75, Stratton, ME 04982 (☎ **207/246-7352**) runs six-day mountain bike camps in Carrabassett Valley, Me. Also, **Mt. Snow,** 305 Mountain Rd., Westover, VT 05356 (☎ **800/245-SNOW**), runs one of the top mountain biking camps in the Northeast. **Maine Sport Outdoor School,** P.O. Box 956, Route One, Rockport, ME 04856 (☎ **800/722-0826**), provides instructional camps in sea kayaking, canoeing, and fishing on an island in Muscongus Bay, Me.

If you're looking to work on your golf swing for a few days, you might consider **The Golf School** (☎ **800/240-2555**) with locations in in Carrabassett Valley, Me., and Mt. Snow, Vt. Tennis anyone? The **Killington School for Tennis,** c/o Killington Resort Village, R.R. 1 Box 2460, Killington, VT 05751 (☎ **800/ 343-0762**), offers two-, three-, and five-day camps on their eight outdoor courts in a relaxing mountain setting.

Having problems with your ball handling in the open court? Don't sweat it. **Never Too Late Basketball Camps,** P.O. Box 235, West Medford, MA 02155 (☎ **888/ NTL-HOOP** or **617/488-3333**), could be just what the doctor ordered. Steve Bzomowski, a former Harvard University coach, offers weekend retreats in the Berkshires and Durham, N.H.

WHITE-WATER RAFTING   It's been more than 20 years since crazed adventurer Wayne Hockemeyer and a group of his buddies braved the tumultuous Kennebec River in a 20-foot raft. Today, white-water rafting is one of the most popular sports in Maine. Drive north on Route 201 from Bingham to West Forks and you'll soon realize that there are as many white-water outfitters in Maine as there are doughnut shops in New England. More than 60,000 people every summer participate in the sport, ranging in age from 8 to 80, and they all walk away exhilarated from an adventurous day. People are thrown off the rafts, but rarely does anyone get hurt (just wet).

No longer is the Kennebec the only river to raft down in Maine. Operations have moved to the raging Penobscot and Dead rivers. Daily water releases from dams ensure high water from May to October. However, there are only six big water releases on the Dead, in May, June, September, and October. No matter which river you choose, after the ride, your adrenaline will be flowing just as fast as the rapids.

Northern Outdoors, P.O. Box 100, Route 201, The Forks, ME 04895 (☎ 207/
663-4466), hosts trips to the Penobscot, Kennebec and Dead rivers. Cost is $75
weekdays, $95 weekends. They also offer accommodations at the Penobscot Outdoor
Center and The Forks Resort Center.

Eastern River Expeditions, P.O. Box 1173, Moosehead Lake, Greenville, ME
04441 (☎ 800/634-RAFT); **Maine Whitewater,** P.O. Box 633, Bingham, ME
04920-0633 (☎ 800/345-6246); and **New England Whitewater Center,** P.O. Box
21, Caratunk, ME 04925 (☎ 800/766-7238), are regarded highly. For more information, contact **Raft Maine** (☎ 800/RAFT-MEE) for a listing of nine white-
water rafting outfitters and their accommodations.

4 Special-Interest Vacations

FALL FOLIAGE ITINERARIES   The beginning of autumn in the Northeast is
a time to savor the final moments of summer against the countryside's mosaic backdrop of reds, yellows, oranges, and purples before the chill of winter.

This is not news to most of us. Indeed, fall in New England has become cliché.
There are 24-hour toll-free numbers to keep you abreast of nature's progress and even
a Connecticut-based touring company offering fall foliage tours in a chauffeured Rolls
Royce. And then there's the traffic. It often seems like the entire populations of
New York City and Boston have fled to New England's roadways during this
season. But, there are ways to avoid the masses and it only takes a little effort and
ingenuity.

Let's start with Vermont since most of us leaf peepers (what New Englanders call
fall foliage seekers) consider it the heart of nature's annual light show. Fall foliage in
southern Vermont usually occurs during the last week in September and the first two
weeks in October. In the northern areas leaves start to change color in early to mid-
September. Columbus Day weekend is absolute madness. Avoid Route 7 from
Bennington to Rutland, concentrating rather on eastern and northern Vermont.

From White River Junction, take **Route 14 north** along Vermont's White River.
At South Royalton, follow **Route 107 west** to Stockbridge and continue north on
Route 100 to Rochester before turning around. Another fine drive starts farther north
at Montgomery Center and follows **Route 58 east** through Hazen's Notch to Lowell.
Continue on Route 58 east to **Routes 5 and 14 south** until you reach one of my
favorite villages in Vermont, Craftsbury Common. From here, start back on the
same roads.

If time restrictions keep you from the far corners of the state, stick to the smaller
routes where the traffic is lighter, the farmland fertile, and the villages, replete with
white steeples, ooze with New England charm. I've found the most picturesque drives
traveling east to west through the gaps and notches of the Green Mountains. The
most spectacular is the **Lincoln Gap** between Lincoln and Warren on Lincoln Gap
Road. Then there's dramatic **Smuggler's Notch,** which can be reached from Stowe
or Jeffersonville on Route 108.

The one problem with a fall foliage trip is that one person has to drive. Prime leaf-
watching soon becomes tiresome road-watching. Your copilot revels in the bright
colors for miles, while you barely catch a glimpse of the scenery, often causing severe
neck strain. So, I recommend activities where you can both slow down and stop to
appreciate Mother Nature in her most flamboyant dress. Consider leaving your car
behind for part of the trip to hike, bike, or canoe.

Fall foliage is certainly not restricted to Vermont. Just across the Connecticut
River, New Hampshire has just as many types of trees and brilliant peak colors. In

fact, 80 percent of the state is covered with forest, so finding good foliage is rarely a problem. The 34-mile **Kancamagus Highway** (Route 112), or "Kanc" as the locals call it, is the state's centerpiece for foliage. At 3,000 feet, the Kanc snakes through the verdant forests and granite cliffs of the White Mountains. The pass can be heavily traveled, so stop and take one of the hikes at road's edge. **The Boulder Loop Trail** begins at the Covered Bridge Campground, 6 miles west of Conway. The 2.8-mile circuit takes about three hours to complete and provides vistas of Mount Chocorua.

Route 2 from Gorham, N.H., to Saint Johnsbury, Vt., is another worthwhile ride. If you drive in the early morning or twilight hours, you have a very good chance of spotting a moose slurping one of the rivers at roadside. **Route 108,** near Durham, is resplendent with color, especially the ride around the University of New Hampshire campus. Farther west, the **White Dot and White Cross trails** lead to the summit at Mount Monadnock where, on a clear day, you can see the highest peak in New England, Mt. Washington. In Connecticut, ride or bike along the southernmost part of the Connecticut River.

Leaf lovers instinctively take to the hills to find their favorite foliage spot, but it would be a mistake to overlook the Atlantic coast, especially **Acadia National Park** in Maine, where both mountains and ocean loom. The drive around the **Park Loop** to Cadillac Mountain is on everyone's itinerary, but a good second choice is a canoe ride on **Long Pond.** Only the rhythm of your stroke breaks the mirror-like waters in this serene setting. Then there's Acadia's noted network of Carriage Path trails. Financed by John D. Rockefeller Jr. between 1917 and 1933, this 43-mile network of trails crisscrosses the entire eastern half of Mt. Desert Island. They are off-limits to motorized vehicles.

An added bonus to the splendor of fall foliage in New England are the cranberry bogs of Nantucket. In early October, the cranberries turn beet red and are ready for harvesting. A 23-mile bike loop takes you past the cranberry bogs and moors to the charming town of 'Sconset. Contact the **Nantucket Island Chamber of Commerce**, 48 Main St., Nantucket, MA 02554 (☎ **508/228-1700**).

The United States Forest Service operates a foliage hotline, (☎ **800/354-4595**), with reports updated several times a week by diligent field employees. Besides the Forest Service's foliage line, you can call the following numbers for conditions in particular states; **Vermont** (☎ 800/VERMONT); **New Hampshire** (☎ 800/258-3608); **Connecticut** (☎ 800/282-6863); **Maine** (☎ 800/533-9595); **Massachusetts** (☎ 800/632-8038); **Rhode Island** (☎ 800/556-2484).

COASTAL DRIVES   With miles of jagged coastline stretching from Lubec, Me., to Greenwich, Conn., you might think that there are numerous scenic coastal drives. On the contrary, the chances of finding the ocean on the side of the road are pretty slim. New England has no equivalent of California's Pacific Coast Highway. So, if you want to catch a glimpse of the Atlantic, you'll have to turn to much smaller routes.

I-95 connects New York to Brunswick, Me., running close to the Atlantic, but very rarely producing decent views. In Brunswick, the highway veers inland toward Bangor, while Route 1 continues northeast along the rugged Maine coast all the way to Calais, Me. You can take Route 1 from Boston all the way to Brunswick, but don't expect much sand and sea—tawdry shops line most of the strip. Unfortunately, Route 1 north of Brunswick is just as commercial with the exception of the 27-mile stretch from Rockland to Belfast. Look off to your right near Camden and Rockport and you can see the Penobscot Bay Islands of Islesboro, North Haven, and Vinalhaven.

Nevertheless, there are several stunning drives in New England. You just have to know where they are. The most famous is the 27-mile **Park Loop Road** around

Acadia National Park. This one-way road circles Cadillac Mountain, the highest point on the eastern seaboard. Other sights include Thunder Hole, where waters spew in and out of a small cave, and shell-covered Sand Beach. In the distance, schooners slice through the islands of Frenchman Bay. This route is best taken during spring or fall to avoid the summer crowds.

Northeast of Acadia, two of my favorite drives are on **Route 187 south** to the small fishing village of Jonesport and Beals Island, and **Route 191 east** from Cutler to Quoddy Head State Park. Carved by the battering surf below, cliffs rise from 90 to 150 feet at Quoddy, the easternmost point in the United States.

South of Portland, Me., congested beaches and citified waterfronts line most of the coast. The next scenic drive is around Cape Ann, Mass., on **Route 128.** Highlights include Gloucester's lively fishing port, the boulders at Halibut Point, and the shops at Bearskin Neck in Rockport, Me. Bizarre as it might sound, Massachusetts' more famous Cape offers little in the way of scenic drives. The main thoroughfare to Provincetown is Route 6, which travels directly through the center of Cape Cod, offering no coastal views whatsoever.

Obviously, the ocean has a certain allure, but consider driving around New England's largest lakes. Vermont's **Route 2** heads north from Burlington to the Lake Champlain Islands, rewarding you with vistas of this vast lake on either side of the road. New Hampshire's **Route 109** goes north from Wolfeboro to Moultonborough along the eastern shores of Lake Winnipesaukee, with the White Mountains hovering in the distance.

SPAS   Services in New England's spas are no longer confined within the walls of a resort. More and more spas are taking advantage of their bucolic surroundings, whisking guests outside to breathe in the clean, crisp air, before returning them to the rejuvenating massage and aromatherapy rooms indoors. Considering that many of the region's spas are located in the mountains, on lakes, or near the ocean, it's a shrewd move. Obviously, aerobics classes, weight rooms, and other indoor services are still in place, but northeastern spas are finally realizing that you don't have to be in warm-weather climate year-round to savor the spectacular surroundings. Here's a list of some reputable spas in New England:

In the Berkshires there's **Canyon Ranch,** 165 Kemble St., Lenox, MA 01240 (☎ 800/742-9000), which boasts 40 aerobics classes, wholesome food, and seven types of massage and hydrotherapy. The resort's Outdoor Sports Department takes their clientele on the best hikes, bike rides, canoe jaunts, and cross-country skiing trails the Berkshires has to offer. Director Jude McCarthy has implemented a program that caters to all levels of experience from an early morning Tai Chi walk on the 120-acre grounds to a strenuous mountain bike ride on fire roads up Lenox Mountain. It's arguably the finest spa in New England. Week-long packages range from $1,900 to $2,280 per person, including meals, facilities, and outdoor recreation.

The Equinox, Route 7A, Manchester Village, VT 05254 (☎ 800/362-4747), a prestigious 225-year-old resort, will pamper you with body scrubs, therapeutic herbal wraps, and massages. Rates per person, including all meals, facilities, one herbal wrap, one loofah salt glow scrub, and a daily short massage costs $794 for four days.

Set in a grove of old evergreens, the **Spa at Grand Lake,** Route 207, Lebanon, CT 06249 (☎ 203/642-4306), is known for its no-frills casual atmosphere. Rates per person, including all meals, facilities, and six half-hour massages range from $949 to $1,075 per week. You'll discover a spiritual path to health at **Kripalu Center for Yoga and Health,** P.O. Box 793, Lenox, MA 01240 (☎ 800/967-3577), which features yoga and meditation courses. Rates per person, including all meals, facilities, and basic services range from $471 to $535 for a seven-night stay.

Like the name implies, **New Life: The Inn of the Six Mountains,** Killington Road, Killington, VT 05751 (☎ 800/545-9407), specializes in changing poor health habits through yoga, smart eating, and hiking. Rates per person, including all meals, facilities, and two one-hour massages range from $899 to $999 for a five-night package. **Topnotch at Stowe,** Mountain Road, Stowe, VT 05672 (☎ 800/451-8686), caters to sports enthusiasts and gives every client a "Fitness Profile" for planning a customized exercise regimen. Rates per person, including all meals, facilities, and one daily personal service of your choice range from $1,200 to $1,800 for a seven-night package.

Northern Pines Health Resort, 559 State Route 85, Raymond, ME 04071 (☎ 207/655-7624), is located 40 minutes west of Portland and emphasizes a holistic approach to stress control and weight loss. Rates per person, including all vegetarian meals, spa facilities, and basic services range from $780 to $1,170 for a seven-night stay. **Norwich Inn & Spa,** 607 W. Thames St., Route 32, Norwich, CT 06369 (☎ 800/ASK-4-SPA), is an intimate retreat offering a long list of services like invigorating loofah scrubs, clay wraps, and thalassotherapy, a sea water–based treatment. They sponsor an "Outdoor Adventure Week" where guides bring visitors on ocean walks and boating trips. Rates per person, including all meals, spa facilities, and two daily personal services range from $2,275 to $2,975 for seven nights.

FOR WILDLIFE ENTHUSIASTS With the Atlantic coast to the east and a slew of national forests and state parks, **bird watching** opportunities are virtually unlimited. More than 300 species have been observed in the region over the past decade, including herons, ospreys, warblers, puffins, and snowy egrets.

There are so many special places to view birds in New England that it's impossible to name them all. Some spots where you'll never go wrong include Machias Sea Island, Me.; Wellfleet Bay Wildlife Sanctuary, Wellfleet, Mass.; Monomoy Island, Mass.; Umbagog Lake, Errol, N.H.; and Acadia National Park, Bar Harbor, Me.

Also, the **National Audubon Ecology Camp,** 613 Riversville Rd., Greenwich, CT 06831 (☎ 203/869-2017) runs stellar birding programs for budding and experienced naturalists in New England.

Another popular activity among visitors to New England's coastal areas is **whale watching.** Almost every day from mid-April to November, boats leave the mainland in search of the biggest mammal on the planet. Experts on board discuss the various species you might see, migratory patterns, and the dangers of water pollution and other threats to the species' survival. The waters off Cape Cod are arguably some of the best for whale watching in the Northeast. One of the most reputable outfits is Provincetown's **Dolphin Fleet Whale Watching** (☎ 800/826-9300), which sends boats out daily from Provincetown Harbor. The cost is $17.50 per person and the trips last about four hours.

5 Tips for Travelers with Special Needs

FOR TRAVELERS WITH DISABILITIES Prodded by the Americans with Disabilities Act, a growing number of inns and hotels are retrofitting some of their rooms for people with special needs. Outdoor recreation areas, especially on state and federal lands, are also providing trails and facilities for those who've been effectively barred in the past.

Accessibility is improving regionwide, but improvements are far from universal. When in doubt, call ahead to ensure that you'll be accommodated.

Wilderness Inquiry, Fifth Street SE, Box 84, Minneapolis, MN 55414 (☎ 800/728-0719 or 612/379-3858), offers adventure travel packages for disabled travelers nationwide, including a canoe trip on the Moose River in Maine.

FOR SENIORS   New England is well-suited for older travelers, with a wide array of activities for seniors and discounts often available. It's wise to request a discount at hotels or motels when booking the room, not when you arrive. An identification card from the **American Association of Retired Persons (AARP),** 601 E St. NW, Washington, DC 20049 (☎ 202/434-2277), can be invaluable in obtaining discounts.

Excellent programs for seniors are offered by **Elderhostel,** which is based in Boston. These educational programs for people over 55 years old are reasonably priced, and include lodging and meals. Participants can study everything from the art of downhill skiing to the art of autobiography. The locations where these classes are held are often intriguing and dramatic. For more information, contact Elderhostel, 75 Federal St., Boston, MA 02110 (☎ 617/426-7788).

FOR FAMILIES   Few families don't find a raft of things to do with kids in New England. The natural world seems to hold tremendous wonder for the younger set— an afternoon exploring the mossy banks and rocky streambeds is an adventure. Older kids like the challenge of climbing a high mountain peak or learning to paddle a canoe in a straight line. And there's always the beach.

Be sure to ask about family discounts when visiting attractions. Many places offer a flat family rate that is less expensive than paying for each ticket individually. Some parks and beaches charge by the car rather than the head.

Be aware that many inns cater to couples, and kids aren't exactly welcomed with open arms. Many inns don't allow kids, or strongly prefer only children over a certain age. Innkeepers will let you know when you make your reservation, but you should mention that you're traveling with kids. Anyway, it's often wise to mention that you're a family when booking a room; often you'll get accommodations nearer the game room or the pool, making everyone's life a bit easier.

Recommended destinations for families include Cape Cod and the Islands in Massachusetts, Weirs Beach and Hampton Beach in New Hampshire, and York Beach and Acadia National Park in Maine. North Conway, N.H., also makes a good base for exploring with kids. The town has lots of motels with pools, and there are nearby train rides, aquaboggans, streams suitable for splashing around, easy hikes, and the distraction known as Story Land. Also don't forget about all of the exciting and family-friendly activities offered by New England's major cities like Boston, Portland, Providence, and Hartford.

Several specialized guides offer more detailed information for families on the go. Try *Best Hikes with Children in Vermont,* or *New Hampshire & Maine* by Cynthia and Thomas Lewis.

FOR GAY & LESBIAN TRAVELERS   New England isn't exactly a hotbed of gay culture, with some exceptions like Provincetown (Cape Cod), a world-renowned gay vacation capital, and the region's larger cities. But many gay men and lesbians live and travel here and have found the region accepting if not always welcoming.

In Boston, the **Gay and Lesbian Helpline** offers information (☎ 617/267-9001) Monday through Friday from 4 to 11pm, Saturday 6 to 8:30pm, and Sunday 6 to 10pm. You can also contact the **Boston Alliance of Gay and Lesbian Youth,** or BAGLY (☎ 800/422-2459). *In Publications* (258 Shawmut Ave., Boston, MA 02118; ☎ 617/426-8246) and *Bay Windows* (1523 Washington St., Boston, MA

02118; ☎ **617/266-6670**) are weekly newspapers that concentrate on upcoming gay-related events, news, and features.

Portland, Me., has a substantial gay population, attracting many refugees who've fled the crime and congestion of Boston and New York. Portland hosts a sizable gay pride festival early each summer that includes a riotous parade and a dance on the city pier. Check with the local gay newspaper, *Community Pride Reporter,* for dates and details (☎ **207/879-1342**).

As for resort areas, Provincetown, as we mentioned earlier, hosts a large gay community on vacation in the summer. Also, Ogunquit on the southern Maine coast is a hugely popular destination among gay travelers and features a lively beach and bar scene in the summer. In the winter, it's decidedly more mellow.

For a more detailed directory of gay-oriented enterprises in New England, track down a copy of *The Pink Pages*, published by KP Media (66 Charles St., #283, Boston, MA 02114; e-mail kpmedia@aol.com).

More adventurous souls should consider linking up with the **Chiltern Mountain Club,** P.O. Box 407, Boston, MA 02117 (☎ **617/859-2843**), an outdoor adventure club for gay men and lesbians that organizes trips in northern New England.

6 Getting There

BY CAR   Getting to New England by car doesn't require much in the way of special knowledge. Coming from the south, I-95 is the major interstate highway serving Connecticut, Rhode Island, and Massachusetts. The quickest route from New York to Boston is via Hartford, Conn., using I-84 and the Massachusetts Turnpike. If you want to approach northern New England from the south there are two main interstate highway corridors. I-91 heads more or less due north from Hartford, Conn., along the Vermont–New Hampshire border, then through northern Vermont. The other major interstate corridor skirts Boston. Follow I-93 north from Boston if your destination is the White Mountains; for Maine, take I-95, which parallels the southern Maine coast before veering inland.

If scenery is your priority, the most picturesque way to enter northern New England is from the west. Drive through New York's Adirondack Mountains to Port Kent, N.Y., on Lake Champlain, then catch the car ferry across the lake to Burlington.

BY PLANE   The central gateways to New England are Boston, New York City, and Montréal. Major commercial carriers also serve Hartford, Conn.; Burlington, Vt.; Manchester, N.H.; and Portland, Me. Several smaller airports in the region are served by feeder airlines and charter companies (see regional chapters for more information). Many of the scheduled flights from Boston to northern New England and Cape Cod and the Islands are aboard smaller prop planes; ask the airline or your travel agent if this is an issue for you.

Many people who travel to New England find they pay less and have a wider choice of flight times by flying into Boston's Logan Airport, then renting a car. Boston is about two hours by car from Portland, less than three hours from the White Mountains. If you're heading to the Bennington or Manchester area of Vermont, Albany, N.Y., is the closest major airport.

Airlines serving New England include **American** (☎ **800/433-7300**), **Colgan** (☎ **800/272-5488**), **Continental** (☎ **800/525-0280**), **Delta** (☎ **800/221-1212**), **Northwest** (☎ **800/225-2525**), **TWA** (☎ **800/221-2000**), **United** (☎ **800/ 241-6522**), and **USAir** (☎ **800/247-8786**).

Carriers to Cape Cod and the Islands include all of the above except TWA plus, **Cape Air** (☎ **800/352-0714** or 508/771-6944), **Island Airlines** (☎ **800/248-7779** or 508/775-6066), and **Nantucket Airlines** (☎ **800/635-8787** or 508/790-0300). Charter flights are offered by Cape Air and Nantucket Airlines, as well as by **Air New England** (☎ **508/693-8899**), **Hyannis Air Service** (☎ **508/775-8171**), **Island Air Charter** (☎ **508/778-8360**), **King Air Charters** (☎ **800/247-2427**), and **Westchester Air** (☎ **800/759-2929**).

BY BUS Bus service is well run en route to New England. You'll be able to reach the major cities and tourist destinations, but few of the remote villages in northern New England are accessible by bus.

The major bus lines serving New England are **Bonanza** (☎ **800/ 556-3815** or 617/720-4110), **Concord Trailways** (☎ **800/639-3317** or 617/426-8080), **Greyhound** (☎ **800/231-2222** or 617/526-1810), **Peter Pan** (☎ **800/343-9999** or 617/426-7838), and **Vermont Transit** (☎ **800/451-3292**).

Vermont Transit is affiliated with Greyhound and serves Vermont, New Hampshire, and Maine with frequent departures from Boston. **Concord Trailways** serves New Hampshire and Maine, including some smaller towns in the Lake Winnipesaukee and White Mountains area. Concord buses are a bit more luxurious (and a few dollars more) than Vermont Transit.

BY TRAIN Most passengers who come to New England by train take the *Northeast Corridor* line offered by **Amtrak** (☎ **800/872-7245**). It runs from Washington, D.C., to Boston via Philadelphia and New York City. Amtrak also runs *The Capecodder* on summer weekends from New York and Boston to Hyannis. Train service to Northern New England is more limited; however, Amtrak's *Vermonter* departs Washington, D.C., with stops in Baltimore, Philadelphia, and New York before following the Connecticut River northward. Stops in Vermont include Brattleboro, Bellows Falls, Claremont (N.H.), White River Junction, Montpelier, Waterbury, Burlington/Essex Junction, and St. Albans.

Rail service from Boston to Portland, Me., also serving seacoast New Hampshire, was slated to begin in 1994, but the process has been delayed. At press time, it looked reasonably hopeful for service to resume in early or mid-1997. Contact Amtrak for more information.

For rail service between New York and Connecticut, try cheaper **Metro North** (☎ **800/223-6052** or 212/532-4900), which runs commuter trains connecting many towns from New Haven to New York City.

FAST FACTS: New England

AAA Members can get help with trip planning, road service in the event of a breakdown, and discount tickets to events and attractions. Call **800/222-4357** for more information on membership and branch locations throughout New England.

American Express American Express offers travel services, including check cashing and trip planning, through several affiliated agencies in the region. Call **800/ 221-7282.**

Business Hours Most offices are open from 8 or 9am to 5 or 6pm. Shops usually open around 9:30 or 10am. Banks typically close at 3 or 4pm, but many have cash card machines available 24 hours. Post offices in larger cities may be open past 5pm, but it's best to call ahead before going out of your way. A few supermarkets are open 24 hours a day, but they're not terribly common in this part of the world.

If you need quick provisions, look for one of the brightly lit convenience stores (Christy's and Cumberland Farms are among the chains here), which are usually open until at least 10 or 11pm.

Federal Express   For the location of the nearest drop-off box, or to arrange a pickup, call **800/238-5355.**

Liquor Laws   The legal age to consume alcohol is 21. In Maine, New Hampshire, and Vermont, liquor is sold at government-operated stores only; in Connecticut, Massachusetts, and Rhode Island, liquor is sold privately. Liquor is not sold on Sunday, though most restaurants and bars with liquor licenses may serve by the drink on Sundays. Restaurants that don't have liquor licenses sometimes allow patrons to bring their own adult beverages. Always ask first.

Maps   Maps of the region and individual states are commonly available at convenience stores and supermarkets for $2 or $3. All three states also offer free road maps at their official tourist information centers (you usually have to ask at the desk). If you're a connoisseur of back roads and off-the-beaten-track exploring, check out DeLorme's atlases. They offer an extraordinary level of detail, right down to logging roads and public boat launches on small ponds. **DeLorme's (☎ 207/ 865-4171)** headquarters and map store is in Freeport, Me., but their products are available widely at book and convenience stores throughout the region.

Members of **AAA (☎ 800/222-4357)** should contact their local offices for road maps of New England. If you know exactly where you want to go in advance, AAA's maps and customized Triptiks are a useful tool for getting around this region.

Newspapers/Magazines   The *Boston Globe* and the *New York Times* are distributed throughout New England. Almost every small town seems to have a daily or weekly newspaper covering the events and happenings of the area. These are good sources of information for small-town events and specials at local restaurants—the day-to-day things that slip through the cracks at the tourist bureaus.

Speed Limits   The speed limit on interstate highways in the region is generally 65 miles per hour, although this is reduced to 55 miles per hour near cities. State highways are a less formal network, and the speed limits (and the conditions of the roads) vary widely. Watch for speed limits to drop in one or two stages as you approach a destination.

Taxes   The current state sales taxes are: Connecticut, 8%; Maine, 6% (7% on lodging); Massachusetts, 5% (9.7% on lodging); New Hampshire, 8%; Rhode Island, 7% (12% on lodging); and Vermont, 6%.

For Foreign Visitors 3

Most of the general information to ensure a pleasant trip will be found in the preceding introductory chapters. Some aspects of U.S. laws, customs, and culture that might be perplexing to visitors from Canada and overseas are covered in this chapter.

1 Preparing for Your Trip

ENTRY REQUIREMENTS

DOCUMENTS   Canadian citizens have it easiest when visiting the United States. Canadians need only present some form of identification at the border; a passport isn't necessary unless you plan to stay more than 90 days, although it may be helpful as identification for certain transactions, especially financial.

A number of countries are currently participating in the visa waiver pilot program, which allows travelers from these countries to enter the United States with just a valid passport and a visa waiver form. Check with your travel agency for the current rules and participating airlines and cruise lines. (At press time, the countries in this program were Andorra, Austria, Belgium, Brunei, Denmark, Finland, France, Germany, Iceland, Ireland, Italy, Japan, Liechtenstein, Luxembourg, Monaco, Netherlands, New Zealand, Norway, San Marino, Spain, Sweden, Switzerland, and the United Kingdom.)

Other foreign visitors should apply for a U.S. visa at the embassy or consulate with jurisdiction over their permanent residence. You can apply for a visa in any country, but it's generally easier to get a visa in your own. Applicants must have a passport that's valid for at least six months beyond the dates they propose to visit, a passport-size photo (1.5 inches square), and some indication that they have a residence outside the United States to which they plan to return. Applicants must also fill out a Form OF-156 (available free at all U.S. embassies and consulates). If you have a letter of invitation from a U.S. resident, that's sometimes helpful. Drug addicts and anarchists need not apply.

Bear in mind that the U.S. government assumes that everyone visiting the United States plans to immigrate here illegally. Some regard this as a little presumptuous and cynical, but that's how the system works under U.S. law. Therefore, it's up to the traveler to convince U.S. authorities otherwise. The more evidence you assemble to that effect, the easier it will be to get a visa. Especially helpful is an indication of how your trip will be financed.

Once in the country, foreign visitors come under the jurisdiction of the Immigration and Naturalization Service (INS). If you'd like to change the length or the status of your visa (for instance, from nonimmigrant to immigrant) contact the nearest INS office. Look in the local phone book under "U.S. Government."

Be sure to carefully check the valid dates on your visa. If you overstay one or two days, it's probably no big deal. If it's more than that, you may be on the receiving end of an interrogation by customs officials on your way out of the country, and it may hinder efforts to get another visa the next time you apply for one.

MEDICAL REQUIREMENTS   Unless you've recently been in an area suffering from an epidemic (such as yellow fever or cholera), no inoculations are needed to enter the United States.

Not all prescription drugs that are sold overseas are necessarily available in the United States. If you bring your own supplies of prescription drugs (and especially syringes), it's wise to carry a physician's prescription in case you need to convince customs officials that you're not a smuggler or drug addict.

CUSTOMS REQUIREMENTS   Jet and ship passengers will be asked to fill out a customs form declaring what goods they are bringing into the country. Visitors planning to spend at least 72 hours in the United States may bring 200 cigarettes, 3 pounds of smoking tobacco, or 100 cigars (but no Cuban cigars), and $100 worth of gifts without paying any duties. Anything over these amounts will be taxed. No food may be brought into the country (this includes canned goods); live plants are also prohibited. Up to US$10,000 in cash may be brought in or out of the country without any formal notification. If you are carrying more than that amount, you must notify customs officials when either entering or departing the country.

MONEY

The basic unit of U.S. currency is the dollar, which is about enough to buy a large cup of coffee. The dollar consists of 100 cents. Common coins include penny (1¢), nickel (5¢), dime (10¢), and quarter (25¢). You may come across a 50¢ or $1 coin, but these are relatively rare. Dollar bills and coins are accepted everywhere, but some smaller shops won't accept larger bills ($50 or $100) because they lack sufficient change or are fearful of counterfeit bills. It's best to travel with a plentiful supply of $10 and $20 bills.

CURRENCY EXCHANGE   Foreign exchange bureaus, so common in many countries, are rare in the United States, and are virtually nonexistent in northern New England. Many banks will exchange foreign currency for dollars, but it's often a time-consuming and expensive process. It's best to plan ahead and obtain dollars or dollar-based traveler's checks in your own country before departure.

Canadian dollars are commonly accepted in Maine, New Hampshire, and Vermont (all of which border Canada), although it's generally easier to use Canadian currency the closer to the border you are. Most hotels and many restaurants will accept Canadian currency at a discount close to its current trading value. Some places will periodically accept Canadian currency at face value as a part of a promotion to attract Canadian tourists; look for signs and advertisements to this effect in your travels.

If you're arriving in Boston a great place to exchange foreign money is at Logan International Airport at **Bay Bank,** in Terminal C (☎ **617/569-1172**) and Terminal E (☎ **617/556-6050**).

TRAVELER'S CHECKS   Traveler's checks are considered as good as cash in most U.S. shops and banks. Widely recognized brands include American Express, Barclay's, and Thomas Cook. With other types of checks, you might meet with some resistance, particularly in smaller towns. Some small shops may not cash checks of $100 or more if they have insufficient change; it's best to cash these at hotels or banks. Most banks will cash traveler's checks without charge.

CREDIT CARDS   Credit cards are becoming an increasingly common form of payment throughout the United States for everything from expensive hotel rooms to inexpensive gifts. It's not impractical to travel the country with no cash, just a credit card in your back pocket. Among the most commonly accepted credit cards are American Express, Discover, MasterCard, and Visa. Because American Express charges a higher rate for processing its transactions, a number of hotels and restaurants will claim not to accept the card, but will if it's the only card you have. It's highly recommended to have at least one credit card (fully paid up) when you travel in the United States. Credit cards are commonly accepted in lieu of deposits when renting a car or a hotel room and are often allowed as a form of identification.

Many ATM (automatic teller machines) will debit your credit card and provide cash on the spot. Don't ever give your card to anyone as a deposit; they should record the information on it and return it to you. Also be careful with your credit card receipts, as the information on them may be used by the unscrupulous to make purchases.

INSURANCE

Foreign visitors who are not insured are strongly urged to take out a traveler's insurance policy to cover any emergencies that may arise during their stay here. The United States does not offer national medical coverage for its residents; medical services are paid for either in cash or, more commonly, by an individual's insurance company. Be aware that hospital and doctors' costs are extremely high in the United States, and even a minor medical emergency could result in a huge extra expense for those traveling without insurance.

Comprehensive policies available in your country may also cover other disasters, including bail (in the event you are arrested), automobile accidents, theft or loss of baggage, and emergency evacuation to your country in the event of a dire medical situation. Check with your local automobile association (if there is one) or insurance company for detailed information on travelers' insurance.

Packages such as "Europe Assistance Worldwide Services" in Europe are sold by automobile clubs and travel agencies at attractive rates. **Travel Assistance International (TAI)** (☎ **800/821-2828** or 202/347-2025) is the agent for Europe Assistance Worldwide Services, Inc., so holders of this company's policies can contact TAI for assistance while in the United States.

Canadians should check with their provincial health scheme offices or call **HealthCanada** (☎ **613/957-3025**) to find out the extent of their coverage and what documentation and receipts they must take home in case they are treated in the United States.

SAFETY

New England, especially Maine, Vermont, and New Hampshire, boasts some of the lowest crime rates in the country. However, crime is on the increase everywhere in the United States, particularly in urban areas, and all travelers are advised to take the usual precautions against theft, robbery, and assault.

Avoid any unnecessary displays of wealth when in public. Don't bring out big wads of cash from your pocket, and save your best jewelry for private occasions. If you are approached by someone who demands money, jewelry, or anything else from you, do what most Americans do: Hand over what the mugger requests. Don't argue. Don't negotiate. Just do what they say. Then immediately contact the police (see "Emergencies," below).

The crime you're statistically most likely to encounter is theft from your automobile. Break-ins can occur any time of the day or night. Don't leave any items of value in plain view; that offers a target that's tempting for even the casual miscreant. At the least, store your valuables locked securely in your trunk. Better still, keep them with you at all times.

Late at night you should look for a well-lighted area to get gas or if you need to step out of your car for any reason. Also, don't sleep in your car at night at highway rest areas, which can leave you vulnerable to robbers passing through the area.

Take the usual precautions against leaving cash or valuables in your hotel room when you're not present. Larger hotels have safe-deposit boxes. Smaller inns and hotels will not, although it can't hurt to ask to leave small items in the house safe. A good number of small inns don't even have locks on guest room doors. Don't be alarmed; if anything, this is a good sign, indicating that there have been no problems here in the past. If you're feeling at all nervous about this, lock your valuables in your car trunk.

2 Getting to New England

Chances are you will reach your final destination by car. Bus and train service reaches parts of Maine, New Hampshire, and Vermont, but it tends to be quite spotty and relatively expensive in northern New England, especially if two or more are traveling together (it's often much cheaper to rent a car at the airport than to pay for two tickets). The New England states are best seen by exploring the countryside, which is virtually inaccessible by mass transportation.

Most international travelers come to New England via Boston's Logan Airport or the three New York City area airports. Boston offers the easiest access to New England. If you're coming from one of the three New York area airports, figure on at least five hours of driving time to most attractions. European visitors heading to Maine should inquire about flights to Bangor; while the city isn't a major European destination, a number of flights en route to the West Coast stop here to refuel and it's sometimes possible to disembark.

Dozens of airlines serve New York and Boston airports from overseas, although New York gets far more overseas traffic. Some helpful numbers to call in London include: **American Airlines** (☎ 0181/572-5555), **British Airways** (☎ 0345/222-111), **Continental** (☎ 4412/9377-6464), **Delta** (☎ 0800/414-767), **United** (☎ 0181/990-9900), and **Virgin Atlantic** (☎ 0293/747-747).

Canadian readers may want to check flight availability and fares on **Air Canada** (☎ 800/268-7240 in Canada) and **Canadian Airlines International** (☎ 800/426-7000 in Canada).

Those coming from Latin American, Asia, Australia, or New Zealand will probably arrive in New England through gateway cities like Miami, Los Angeles, or San Francisco, clearing customs there before connecting onward.

Bus service is available from Boston's Logan Airport to several cities in New England and some train service is also offered. See "Getting Around" in the previous chapter.

FAST FACTS: For The Foreign Traveler

Abbreviations On highway signs and in publications you'll often see New England states abbreviated. For example, Maine is "Me." and New Hampshire is "N.H." and Vermont is "Vt." All capital letters are used when addressing mail for the U.S. Postal Service.

Automobile Organizations Becoming a member of an automobile club is handy for obtaining maps and route suggestions and can be helpful should an emergency arise with your automobile. The nation's largest automobile club is the American Automobile Association (AAA), which has nearly 1,000 offices nationwide. AAA offers reciprocal arrangements with many overseas automobile clubs; if you're a member of an automobile club at home, find out whether your privileges extend to the United States. For more information on AAA, call **800/222-4357.**

Business Hours Businesses are typically open from 9am to 5pm Monday through Friday. Banks typically shut down at 3 or 4pm, although ATM machines operate 24 hours. Most restaurants and some shops stay open until 8 or 9pm. If you need something after hours, head to the nearest mall, which is typically open until 9pm or so.

Climate See "When to Go" in Chapter 2.

Currency See "Money," earlier in this chapter.

Drinking Laws You must be 21 years old to legally drink alcohol in most of the United States. No matter what your age, state laws in New England are notoriously harsh on those who drive drunk. Know your tolerance. If you plan to exceed that in an evening, allow enough time for the effects to wear off, or imbibe within walking distance of your hotel or inn.

Driving A current overseas license is valid on U.S. roads. If your license is in a language other than English, it's recommended that you obtain an International Drivers Permit from the American Automobile Association affiliate or other automobile organization in your own country prior to departure (see "Automobile Organizations," above).

Electricity Electrical incompatibility makes it tricky to use appliances manufactured for Europe in the United States. The current here is 110–120 volts, 60 cycles, compared to the 220–240 volts, 50 cycles used in many parts of Europe. If you're bringing an electric camera flash, portable computer, or other gadget that requires electricity, be sure to bring the appropriate converter and plug adapter.

Embassies/Consulates Embassies are located in Washington, D.C. Call directory assistance (☎ **202/555-1212**) and request the phone number. (Directory assistance calls are free from most pay phones.)

A handful of countries maintain consulates in Boston. Among English-speaking countries, these include **Australia,** 20 Park Plaza, Boston, MA 02116 (☎ 617/542-8655); **Canada,** 3 Copley Place, Suite 400, Boston, MA 02116 (☎ 617/262-3760); **Great Britain,** Federal Reserve Plaza, 600 Atlantic Ave. (25th floor), Boston, MA 02210 (☎ 617/248-9555); **Ireland,** 535 Boylston St., Boston, MA 02116 (☎ 617/267-9330); and **Israel,** 1020 Statler Office Building, 20 Park Plaza, Boston, MA 02116 (☎ 617/542-0041). For other countries, contact directory assistance (☎ 617/555-1212).

Emergencies In the event of any type of emergency, simply dial "911" from any phone. You do not need a coin to make this call. A dispatcher will immediately send medics, the police, or the fire department to assist you. If "911" doesn't work, dial "0" and report your situation to the operator. If a hospital is near when a medical emergency arises, look for the "Emergency" entrance, where you will be quickly attended to.

Gasoline   Gasoline is widely available throughout the region, with the exception of the North Woods region of Maine, where you can travel many miles without seeing a filling station. Gas tends to be cheaper further to the south and in larger towns and cities, where the competition is a bit stiffer; you're better off filling up before setting off into remote or rural areas. Gas is available in several different grades at each station; the higher the octane, the more expensive it is. Cars tend to run a bit smoother and more efficiently with higher grades of gasoline, but rental cars will take any grade.

Many of the filling stations in New England have both "self-serve" and "full-service" pumps; look for signs as you pull up. The full-service pumps are slightly more expensive per gallon, but an attendant will pump your gas and check your oil (you might have to ask for this). The self-serve pumps often have simple directions posted on them. If you're at all confused, ask anyone who happens to be around for instructions.

Holidays   With some important exceptions, national holidays usually fall on Mondays to allow workers to enjoy a three-day holiday. The exceptions are New Year's Day (January 1), Independence Day (July 4), Veterans' Day (November 11), Thanksgiving (last Thursday in November), and Christmas (December 25). Other holidays include Martin Luther King Jr. Day (third Monday in January), Presidents' Day (third Monday in February), Easter (first Sunday following a full moon occurring March 21 or later), Memorial Day (last Monday in May), Labor Day (first Monday in September), and Columbus Day (second Monday in October). In Maine and Massachusetts, Patriot's Day is celebrated on the third Monday in April. On these holidays, banks, government offices, and post offices are closed. Shops are sometimes open and sometimes not on holidays, but assume almost all will be closed on Thanksgiving and Christmas Day.

Languages   Some of the larger hotels may have multilingual employees, but don't count on it. Outside of the cities, English is the only language spoken. The exception is along the Canadian border and in some Maine locales (including Old Orchard Beach, Biddeford, Lewiston, and Van Buren), where French is commonly spoken or at least understood.

Legal Aid   If a foreign tourist accidentally breaks a law, it's most likely to be for exceeding the posted speed limit on a road (it's the law U.S. residents most frequently run afoul of). If you are pulled over by a police officer, don't attempt to pay the fine directly—that may be interpreted as a bribe, and you may find yourself in graver trouble. You'll be issued a summons with a court date and a fine listed on it; if you pay the fine by mail, you won't have to appear in court. If you are arrested for a more serious infraction, you'll be allowed one phone call from jail. It's advisable to contact your embassy or consulate.

Mail   Virtually every small town and village has a post office; ask anyone on the street where it is and you'll be directed there. Mail within the United States costs 32¢ for a one-ounce letter, and 23¢ for each additional ounce; postcards are 20¢. Overseas mail to Europe, Australia, New Zealand, Asia, and South America is 60¢ for a half ounce, 40¢ for a postcard. A half-ounce letter to Mexico is 35¢; a one-ounce letter to Canada is 40¢. If in doubt about weight or costs, ask the postal clerk. Mail may also be deposited at blue mailboxes with the inscription U.S. MAIL or UNITED STATES POSTAL SERVICE located on many streets. If you need to receive mail during your travels, have your correspondents address it to your name, "c/o General Delivery" at the city you are visiting. Go in person to the main post office to collect it; you'll be asked for identification (a passport is ideal) before it's given to you.

Newspapers/Magazines   Foreign newspapers and magazines are commonly found in the larger cities like Boston, but are harder to track down in northern New England. Your best bet is to go to Borders Bookstore (Portland and Bangor, Me.), or Barnes & Noble (Augusta, Me.; Salem, Nashua, and Manchester, N.H.; and South Burlington, Vt.) Both chains have large stores and offer a decent selection of the overseas press.

Taxes   Visitors to the United State are assessed a $10 customs tax upon entering the country, and a $6 tax on departure. The United States does not have a value-added tax (VAT). The tax you most commonly come across is a sales tax (usually 5% to 6%) added on to the price of goods and some services.

Telephone and Fax   Pay phones are not hard to find except in the more remote regions. Shops that have public phones inside usually display a blue sign featuring a bell inside a circle outside the store.

Telephone numbers beginning with "800" or "888" are toll-free. Press "1" before dialing a toll-free number.

Phone directories are divided between Yellow Pages (stores and services, listed by category) and the White Pages (names, listed alphabetically). Be aware that some White Pages are sometimes further split between commercial and residential listings. Phone books are sometimes found at pay phones; failing that, ask to see one at a friendly shop or restaurant. To find a specific local phone number, dial "411" (no coin needed) and an operator will take your request. The Yellow Pages section often features maps of the local area and other information of interest to travelers.

Local calls cost 10¢ or 25¢ (depending on the state) for a limited amount of time. You can use a quarter for a 10¢ phone call, but you won't receive change. How far you can call on a local call varies from place to place, and the boundaries will often seem arbitrary. If you're uncertain whether a call is long-distance or not, try it as a local call. If a recorded voice comes on telling you to deposit more money for the first three minutes, that means it's a long-distance call.

Long-distance calls at pay phones tend to be very expensive, and you'll need a lot of coins. There are other options. At some phones you can use your credit card. And prepaid phone cards are available at many convenience stores and other outlets, typically for $5 or $10. Follow the instructions on the card (you'll call a toll-free 800 number first, then punch in a code and the number you wish to call). Long-distance charges using the cards are usually about 30¢ per minute, and are less expensive and more convenient than feeding coins into a pay phone.

Be aware that many hotels (notably the more expensive chain hotels) tack on a surcharge for local and long-distance calls made from your room. Even toll-free "800" number calls can cost you $1 or more. Ask about these charges when you check in. If your hotel does add a high surcharge and you plan to make a number of phone calls, you're better off using a pay phone.

To charge the phone call to the person receiving your call, dial "0" then the area code and the number you're calling. An operator (or computer) will come on the line and ask your name, and will then call the number to ask permission to reverse the charges. If the person you're calling accepts, the call will be put through.

If you need to send or receive a fax (facsimile), ask at your hotel, or look in the Yellow Pages under "Fax Transmission Service." Many copy shops will provide this service for you.

Time All of New England is in the Eastern Time Zone—the same as New York, and the rest of the eastern seaboard. All states shift to Daylight Saving Time in summer, setting clocks ahead one hour in the spring (the first Sunday in April), and back again in the fall (the last Sunday in October).

Tipping Tipping is commonly practiced in the United States to recognize good service. Be aware that in restaurants, servers are typically paid a bare minimum and depend on tips for their wage. Tipping isn't considered optional, unless the service is unspeakably deplorable. For decent to good service tip 15%; for outstanding service 20%. Other suggestions for tipping include: bartenders, 10%–15%; bell-hops, $1 per bag; cab drivers, 10% of fare; chambermaids, $1 per day; checkroom attendants, $1 per garment; parking attendants, $1. No tipping is expected at gas stations or at fast-food or other self-service restaurants.

Toilets Public toilets (commonly called "rest rooms") are increasingly scarce in the United States, and where they do exist they're often not fit for use. Restaurants have rest rooms for their customers; some will let people off the street use them, but many have signs indicating "For Patrons Only." This is remedied by buying a pack of gum or a cup of coffee. Fast-food restaurants (like McDonald's or Burger King) are a good bet for reasonably clean toilets when traveling on the highways.

Boston 4

by Marie Morris

The Athens of America. The hub of the solar system. The capital of New England. The biggest college town in the world. America's walking city. As these immodest nicknames suggest, Bostonians are sitting on a good thing, and they know it. In a glorious waterfront setting that has attracted travelers for hundreds of years, Boston offers cosmopolitan sophistication on a comfortable scale. From the narrow, crowded streets near the harbor to the spacious boulevards along the Charles River, a sense of history permeates the city, where 18th-century landmarks sit alongside space-age office towers, and the leaders of tomorrow rush to lectures in redbrick buildings.

Boston manages to strike a careful balance between romantic celebration of the past and forward-looking pursuit of the future. Skyscrapers bear plaques describing the deeds and misdeeds of centuries past. The city's museums showcase the treasures of antiquity and cutting-edge technology. And the waterfront has been reclaimed from squalor and disrepair and restored to a condition that outshines its former glory.

It's not perfect, of course. Even a brief visit will confirm that the city's drivers have earned their terrible reputation, and the local accents are as ear-splitting as any in Brooklyn or Chicago. Wander into the wrong part of town and you may be ordered to "pahk yuh cah" (park your car) somewhere else—pronto. And college town or not, there isn't much of a late-night scene outside of convenience stores and photocopy shops, although the "blue laws" restricting the sale of alcohol on Sundays have been considerably relaxed.

Take a few days (or weeks) to get to know Boston, or use it as a gateway to the rest of New England. Here's hoping your experience is memorable and delightful.

1 Orientation

VISITOR INFORMATION The **Boston National Historic Park Visitor Center,** at 15 State St. (☎ 617/242-5642), across the street from the Old State House and the State Street "T" station, is a good place to start your excursion. National Park Service rangers staff the center, dispense information, and lead free tours of the Freedom Trail. The audiovisual show about the trail provides basic information on 16 historic sites. The center is accessible by stairs and ramps and has rest rooms and comfortable chairs. Open daily from 9am to 5pm except Thanksgiving, Christmas, and New Year's Day.

The Freedom Trail, a line of red paint or red brick on or in the sidewalk, begins at the **Boston Common Information Center,** at 146 Tremont St. on the Common. The center is open Monday to Saturday from 8:30am to 5pm and Sunday from 9am to 5pm. It's run by the Greater Boston Convention and Visitors Bureau (☎ 617/536-4100), as is the **Prudential Information Center,** in Center Court on the main level of the Prudential Center. It's open Monday through Friday from 9am to 6pm, Saturday from 10am to 6pm, and Sunday from 11am to 6pm.

PUBLICATIONS   The city's newspapers offer the most up-to-date information about events in the area. The "Calendar" section of the Thursday *Boston Globe* lists festivals, street fairs, concerts, films, speeches, and dance and theater performances. The Friday *Boston Herald* has a similar, smaller insert called "Scene." Both papers briefly list weekend events in their Saturday editions. The arts-oriented *Boston Phoenix,* published on Thursday, has extensive entertainment and restaurant listings.

Where, a monthly magazine available free at most hotels throughout the city, gives information about shopping, night life, attractions, and current shows at museums and galleries. Another freebie, *Quick Guide,* is published four times a year and offers entertainment and shopping listings, a restaurant guide, and maps.

The weekly *Tab,* which lists neighborhood-specific events information, the twice-monthly *Improper Bostonian,* with extensive event and restaurant listings, and the "Style" section of the *Phoenix,* are all available free from newspaper boxes around the city. *Boston* magazine (☎ 617/262-9700) is a lifestyle-oriented monthly with general interest stories on the city and listings on entertainment and dining.

CITY LAYOUT

When it was established as the first permanent European settlement in the region in 1630, Boston was one-third the size it is now. Parts of the city still reflect its original layout, a seemingly haphazard plan that leaves even longtime residents tearing their hair. Old Boston is littered with alleys, dead ends, one-way streets, streets that change names, and streets named after extinct geographical features. On the plus side, every "wrong" turn downtown, in the North End, or on Beacon Hill is a chance to see something interesting that you might otherwise have missed.

Much of the city's landscape was transformed by landfill projects of the 19th century that altered the shoreline and created the Back Bay, where the streets proceed in orderly parallel lines. After some frustrating time in the older part of the city, this simple plan will seem ingenious.

The most "main" street downtown is Washington Street. The causeway that connected the Boston peninsula to the mainland in the 17th and 18th centuries ran along this street, then called Orange in honor of the British royal family. By 1824 it had been renamed after George Washington; as another tribute, streets (except Massachusetts Avenue) change their names when they cross Washington Street: Bromfield becomes Franklin, Winter becomes Summer, Stuart becomes Kneeland. Off Washington Street in Chinatown, several blocks inland, is Beach Street, which used to be harborfront property.

Vestiges of the old waterfront crop up in other odd places. For example, Dock Square, at Congress and North streets, is a reminder of the days when ships could deliver their cargo directly to the market on the first floor of Faneuil Hall. Then there's Commercial Wharf North and South, between Commercial Street and Atlantic Avenue in the North End, and quite landlocked.

Beacon Hill is also named after a long-ago topographical feature. It seems like a big enough hill today—until you see the pillar behind the State House that rises 60 feet into the air, a reminder of its original height, before earth was taken from the top of the hill to be used as landfill. In their loftier days, Beacon, Copp's, and Fort hills gave the Shawmut peninsula the name Trimountain, known today as Tremont. Copp's and Fort hills sloped down to the town dock at Dock Square. Today, Copp's Hill is smaller, but still overlooks the North End; Fort Hill, which extended through downtown toward South Station, was leveled between 1869 and 1872. High Street, now quite flat, was once actually high.

When the hills were pulled down to fill in the coves that made up the shoreline, the layout of some new streets was somewhat willy-nilly. Not so in the Back Bay, where the streets not only line up but even go in alphabetical order, starting at the Public Garden with Arlington, then Berkeley, Clarendon, Dartmouth, Exeter, Fairfield, Gloucester, and Hereford (and then Massachusetts). In the South End, also mostly landfill, the grid is less pristine but still pretty logical. Streets change from West to East when they cross Washington Street, and many of the names are those of the towns with train service from South Station (such as Concord, Worcester, and Springfield), which was new when the streets were being christened.

MAIN ARTERIES & STREETS The most prominent feature of downtown Boston is Boston Common, whether in person, on a map, or from atop the John Hancock Tower or the Prudential Center. The land for the Common was set aside in 1640, when it had only three trees. The Common is bordered by Park Street, which is one block long (but looms large in the geography of the "T"), and four important thoroughfares. Tremont Street originates at Government Center and runs through the Theater District into the South End and Roxbury. Beacon Street branches off Tremont at School Street and curves around, passing the golden dome of the State House at the apex of Beacon Hill and the Public Garden at the foot, and slicing through the Back Bay and Kenmore Square on its way into Brookline. At the foot of the hill Beacon crosses Charles Street, the fourth side of the Common and the main street of Beacon Hill. Near Massachusetts General Hospital, Charles crosses Cambridge Street, which loops around to Government Center and turns into Tremont Street.

On the far side of Government Center, I-93 (a.k.a. the Fitzgerald Expressway) separates the North End from the rest of the city. Hanover Street is the main street of the North End; at the harbor it intersects with Commercial Street, which runs along the waterfront from the North Washington Street bridge (the route to Charlestown, a.k.a. the Charlestown Bridge) until it gives way to Atlantic Avenue at Fleet Street. Atlantic Avenue completes the loop around the North End and runs more or less along the waterfront past South Station.

Boylston Street is the fifth side of the Common. It runs next to the Public Garden, through Copley Square and the Back Bay, and on into the Fenway. To get there it has to cross Massachusetts Avenue, or "Mass. Ave.," as it's almost always called (you might as well get into the habit now). Mass. Ave. originates 9 miles away in Lexington, cutting through Arlington and Cambridge before hitting Boston at Storrow Drive, then Beacon Street, Marlborough Street, and Commonwealth Avenue. "Comm. Ave." starts at the Public Garden and runs through Kenmore Square, past Boston University, and into the western suburbs. Farther along Mass. Ave., Symphony Hall is at the corner of Huntington Avenue. Huntington begins at Copley Square and passes Symphony Hall, Northeastern University, and the Museum of Fine Arts before crossing into Brookline and becoming Mass. Route 9.

FINDING AN ADDRESS There's no rhyme or reason to the street pattern, compass directions are virtually useless, and there aren't enough street signs. The best way to find an address is to call ahead and ask for directions, including landmarks, or leave extra time for wandering around. If the directions involve a "T" stop, be sure to ask which exit to use—most stations have more than one.

STREET MAPS   Free maps of downtown Boston and the rapid transit lines are available at visitor information centers around the city. The Prudential Life Insurance Company (800 Boylston St.; ☎ 617/236-3318) distributes a neighborhood map of Boston at the Skywalk viewing platform, open daily from 10am to 10pm. It's helpful for walking trips of Beacon Hill, the North End, Chinatown, the South End, Charlestown, and Harvard Square. You can also write to the Greater Boston Convention & Visitors Bureau (P.O. Box 990468, Prudential Tower, Suite 400, Boston, MA 02199) for a visitor information kit that includes a city/subway/ Freedom Trail map. Enclose a $4.95 check or money order.

The Metropolitan District Commission (MDC) has an excellent map of the reservations, parks, and recreation areas in Greater Boston. It tells where to find salt- and freshwater beaches, swimming and wading pools, picnic areas, foot trails and bridge paths, playgrounds, tennis and golf courses, fresh- and saltwater fishing, bicycle paths, and outdoor ice-skating rinks. Contact Community Affairs at the MDC, 20 Somerset St., Boston, MA 02108 (☎ 617/727-5114, ext. 530) for a copy.

Gousha's Boston Fast Map ($4.95), Streetwise Boston ($5.95), and Artwise Boston ($5.95) are sturdy, laminated maps available at most bookstores. Less detailed but more fun is MapEasy's GuideMap to Boston ($5.50), a hand-drawn map of the central areas and major attractions.

NEIGHBORHOODS IN BRIEF

The Waterfront   Boston's harbor gained its excellent reputation from the fact that it's sheltered; this neighborhood faces not the ocean but the Inner Harbor. Although for purposes of city government (notably parking regulations) it's considered part of the North End, the Waterfront neighborhood has a different feel. The narrow area along Atlantic Avenue and Commercial Street, once filled with wharves and warehouses, now boasts luxury condos, marinas, restaurants, offices, and two hotels. Also on the waterfront are the New England Aquarium and piers where you can set out on harbor cruises and whale-watching expeditions.

The North End   Crossing under I-93 from downtown on the way to the waterfront brings you to one of the city's oldest neighborhoods, the North End. Home to waves of immigrants in the course of its history, it's been predominantly Italian for 70 years or so, but the balance is shifting. The best estimates say it's now about half Italian-American and half newcomers, many of them young professionals who walk to work in the Financial District. Nevertheless, you'll hear Italian spoken in the streets and find a wealth of Italian restaurants, cafes, and shops. Nearby, and technically part of the North End, is the North Station area. With the September 1995 opening of the FleetCenter to replace Boston Garden (which is slated for demolition but was still standing at press time), the restaurants and clubs in the part of the North End near Beacon Hill really started jumping. This commercial area is, at the moment, not a place to wander around alone at night.

Faneuil Hall Marketplace/Haymarket   Employees aside, actual Boston residents tend to be in short supply at Faneuil Hall Marketplace (also called Quincy Market after the central building). An irresistible draw for out-of-towners and suburbanites, the cluster of restored market buildings bounded by Government Center, State Street, the waterfront, and the North Station area is the city's most popular attraction. You'll find restaurants, bars, a food court, specialty shops, and Faneuil Hall itself.

Haymarket, just off the Central Artery, is home to an open-air produce and fish market on Fridays and Saturdays.

Government Center   Love it or hate it, Government Center introduces modern design into the redbrick facade of traditional Boston architecture. Flanked by Beacon Hill, Downtown Crossing, and Faneuil Hall Marketplace, it is home to state and federal office towers and to Boston City Hall.

Financial District   Bounded loosely by State Street, Downtown Crossing, Summer Street, and Atlantic Avenue, the Financial District is the banking, insurance, and legal center of the city. You'll find it frantic during the day and practically empty in the evening. Several impressive office towers now loom over the Custom House, once famous for its observation deck tower and now undergoing extensive renovations.

Beacon Hill   The tiny residential area in the shadow of the golden dome of the State House is made up of narrow, tree-lined streets and architectural showpieces, mostly in Federal style. Louisburg Square and Mount Vernon Street, two of the loveliest (and most exclusive) spots in Boston, are on Beacon Hill. Bounded by Government Center, Boston Common, and the river, it's also popular with employees of Massachusetts General Hospital, on the nominally less fashionable north side of the neighborhood.

Downtown Crossing   The intersection that gives Downtown Crossing its name is at Washington Street where Winter Street becomes Summer Street, and Filene's and Macy's face off across the pedestrian mall. The name applies roughly to the shopping and business district between the Common, the Theater District, the Financial District, and Government Center. It hops during the day and slows down considerably at night, after business hours.

Chinatown   The third-largest Chinese community in the country resides in a small but growing area near the Theater District. The narrow streets jammed with Chinese and Vietnamese restaurants, grocery stores, and gift shops have a real neighborhood feel. As the "Combat Zone," or red-light district, shrinks under pressure from the business community, Chinatown is expanding to fill the area between Downtown Crossing and the Mass. Turnpike extension. This is the only part of the city where you can definitely find food after midnight—some restaurants are open till 3 or 4am.

Back Bay   Perpetually fashionable since its creation out of landfill a century ago, the Back Bay overflows with gorgeous architecture and chic shops. It is bounded by the Public Garden (to the west), Massachusetts Avenue (to the east), the river (to the north) and Huntington Avenue (to the south), or St. Botolph Street, by some accounts. Students dominate the area near Mass. Ave. and grow scarce as property values rise the closer you get to the Public Garden. Commonwealth Avenue is largely residential, Newbury Street largely commercial; both are excellent places to walk around. In the Back Bay you'll find Trinity Church, the Boston Public Library, the John Hancock Tower, Copley Place, the Prudential Center, and the Hynes Convention Center.

Huntington Avenue   Not an actual neighborhood, but not an area you'll want to miss, Huntington Avenue starts at Copley Square, and separates Copley Place from the Prudential Center before heading south into the suburbs. A number of important landmarks are situated along it, including the Christian Science Center, Symphony Hall (at the corner of Massachusetts Avenue), Northeastern University, and the Museum of Fine Arts. Parts of Huntington can sometimes be a little risky, so if you're leaving the museum at night, stick to the car or the Green Line, travel in a group, or both.

The South End   Cross Stuart Street or Huntington Avenue heading south and you'll soon find yourself in a landmark district packed with Victorian row houses and little parks. Known for its ethnic, economic, and cultural diversity, and its galleries and boutiques, the South End has a large gay community and some of the best restaurants in the city. With the gentrification of the 1980s, Tremont Street (particularly the end closest to downtown) gained a cachet it hadn't known for almost a century. *Note:* Don't confuse the South End with South Boston, a predominantly Irish-American residential neighborhood.

Kenmore Square   The white-and-red Citgo sign that dominates the skyline above the intersection of Commonwealth Avenue, Beacon Street, and Brookline Avenue tells you you're approaching Kenmore Square. Its shops, bars, restaurants, and clubs are a magnet for students from adjacent Boston University. The college-town atmosphere goes out the window when the Red Sox are in town and baseball fans pour into the area on the way to historic Fenway Park, three blocks away (just follow the crowds).

Charlestown   One of the oldest areas of Boston, this is where you'll see the Bunker Hill Monument and USS *Constitution* (*"Old Ironsides"*), as well as one of the city's best restaurants, Olives. Off the beaten track, Charlestown is an almost entirely white residential neighborhood with a well-deserved reputation for insularity.

2 Getting Around

BY PUBLIC TRANSPORTATION

The **Massachusetts Bay Transportation Authority,** or **MBTA** (☎ 617/222-3200), is known as the "T," and its logo is the letter in a circle. It runs the subways, trolleys, and buses in Boston and many suburbs, as well as the commuter rail. The "T" has a web site (http://www.mbta.com) that gives you access to maps, schedules, and other information.

DISCOUNT PASSES   The **Boston Visitor Passport** (☎ 617/222-5218) is one of the best deals in town. You get unlimited travel for a one-, three-, or seven-day period on all subway lines and local buses and Zones 1A and 1B of the commuter rail system, plus discounts on museums, restaurants, and entertainment. The cost is $5 for one day, $9 for three days, and $18 for seven days. Passes are for sale at the Airport "T" station, North Station, South Station, and Back Bay Station, at the Government Center, Harvard, and Riverside "T" stations, the Boston Common information center, and Quincy Market. Your hotel might also be able to provide you with the Visitor Passport.

BY SUBWAY   The subways and Green Line trolleys will take you around Boston faster than any other mode of transportation except walking. You might find this hard to believe when you're trapped in a tunnel during rush hour, but it's true. The oldest system in the country, it dates to 1897, but recent and ongoing improvements have made it quite reliable. It's also packed with art—if your travels take you through the Kendall/MIT Red Line station and you're not in a hurry, hop off and play with the handles on either platform that control the "kinetic sculptures" between the sets of tracks. You'll be rewarded with the sound of thunder on the outbound side and the bell-like peal of a hammer striking metal on the other side.

The subways are color-coded and called the Red, Green, Blue, and Orange lines. The commuter rail to the suburbs shows up on system maps in purple (but it's rarely called the Purple Line). The local fare is 85¢ (you'll need a token) and can be as much

Boston MBTA Rapid Transit Lines

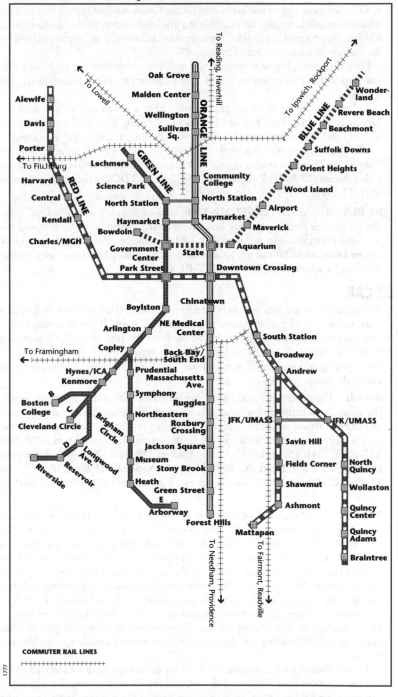

as $2.25 for some surface line extensions on the Green and Red lines. Route and fare information and timetables are available at Park Street station (under the Common), which is the center of the system. Signs reading "inbound" and "outbound" refer to the location in relation to Park Street.

Note that service begins at around 5am and shuts down between 12:30 and 1am, systemwide. The only exception is New Year's Eve, or First Night, when closing time is 2am.

Token vending machines are gaining popularity and can currently be found at Airport (Blue Line), Back Bay and Downtown Crossing (Orange Line), Prudential (Green Line), and South Station, Downtown Crossing, and Harvard (Red Line).

The Green Line is not wheelchair accessible, but most stations on other lines are. They are indicated on system maps. To learn more, call the **Office for Transportation Access** (☎ 800/533-6282 or 617/222-5123; TDD for the hearing impaired 617/222-5415).

BY BUS   The MBTA (☎ **617/222-3200**) runs buses and "trackless trolleys" (identifiable by their electric antennae but otherwise indistinguishable from buses) that provide service crosstown and to and around the suburbs. The local bus fare is 60¢; express buses are $1.50 and up. Exact change is required. Many buses are equipped with lifts for wheelchairs (☎ **800/LIFT-BUS**).

BY CAR

If you plan to confine your visit to Boston proper, there's absolutely no reason to have a car, and in fact, it's probably more trouble than it's worth. If you're driving to Boston, leave the car in the hotel garage and use it for day trips or to visit Cambridge, if you're feeling flush—you'll probably wind up paying to park there, too. If you're not motoring and you decide to take a day trip, you'll probably want to rent a car. Here's the scoop.

Rentals   The major car-rental firms have offices in Boston and at Logan Airport. (Be aware that a hefty drop-off charge is standard for most companies if you rent in one city and return in another.) If you're traveling at a busy time, reserve a car well in advance. Companies with offices at the airport include: **Alamo** (☎ 800/327-9633), **Avis** (☎ 800/831-2847), **Budget** (☎ 800/527-0700), **Enterprise** (☎ 800/325-8007), **Hertz** (☎ 800/654-3131), **National** (☎ 800/227-7368), and **Thrifty** (☎ 800/367-2277). Most companies have cars for nonsmokers, but you have to ask.

Parking   It's difficult to find your way around Boston and practically impossible to find parking in some areas. Most spaces on the street are metered (and patroled until 6pm on the dot every day except Sunday), and open to nonresidents for exactly two hours or less between 8am and 6pm. The penalty is a $20 ticket, but should you blunder into a tow-away zone, retrieving the car will take at least $50 and a lot of running around. Read the sign or the meter carefully. In some areas parking is allowed only at certain hours. Rates vary in different sections of the city (usually $1 an hour downtown), so bring plenty of quarters and dimes. Time limits range from 30 minutes to two hours. *Tip:* During the day, if you're visiting the eastern part of Cambridge, near MIT, parking on Memorial Drive is free and usually not terribly hard to find.

To save yourself a lot of aggravation, leave the car in a garage or lot and walk. Most will cost no more than $20 for a full day, and there's often a lower flat rate if you enter and exit before certain times or if you park in the evening. Some restaurants offer reduced rates at nearby garages; ask when you call for reservations.

The two largest garages are under Boston Common and under the Prudential Center. The reasonably priced city-run garage under the Common (☎ 617/954-2096) at Charles Street was renovated recently, and is limited to vehicles less than 6 feet, 3 inches tall. The garage at the Prudential Center (☎ 617/267-1002) has entrances on Boylston Street, Huntington Avenue, and Exeter Street, and at the Sheraton Boston Hotel & Towers. Parking is discounted if you make a purchase at the Shops at Prudential Center. A similar deal is offered at the garage at Copley Place (☎ 617/375-4488), off Huntington Avenue. The All Right lot off North Street under the Expressway (☎ 617/523-1719) offers a discount to patrons of many North End restaurants and shops—look for a sign in the window of the business.

Good-sized garages can be found at Government Center off Congress Street (☎ 617/227-0385), at the New England Aquarium (☎ 617/723-1731), at 75 State St. (☎ 617/742-7275), and near the Hynes Convention Center on Dalton Street (☎ 617/247-8006). There's also parking under the lovely park in Post Office Square, where another garage once stood. It's at Zero Post Office Square (☎ 617/423-1430), bounded by Milk, Pearl, Franklin, and Congress streets, across the street from Hotel Le Meridien, and near Faneuil Hall Marketplace and the New England Aquarium. It is open 24 hours with entrances on Pearl and Congress streets and is safe and easy to use.

Special Driving Rules   A right turn is allowed at a red light after stopping when traffic permits, unless a sign is posted saying otherwise (as it often is downtown). Seat belts are not mandatory for adults, but they are required for children, and infants and toddlers must be strapped into car seats. These laws are strictly enforced.

Two state laws to be aware of, if only because the frequency with which they're broken will take your breath away: Pedestrians in the crosswalk have the right of way, and vehicles already in a rotary (traffic circle or roundabout) have the right of way.

BY TAXI

Taxis are expensive and not always easy to find—try a hotel, or call a dispatcher. The fare structure is as follows: the first one-quarter of a mile (when the flag drops) costs $1.50, and each additional one-eighth of a mile is 20¢. "Wait time" is extra, and the passenger pays all tolls as well as the $1.50 airport fee (on trips leaving Logan only). Charging a flat rate is not allowed within the city; the Police Department publishes a list of distances to the suburbs that establishes the flat rate for those trips.

Cab drivers have a dress code established and enforced by the city. They must wear a shirt with a collar, be clean, and keep their beards neatly trimmed.

If you want to report a problem or have lost something in a cab, the Police Department runs a Hackney Hotline (☎ 617/536-8294).

To call ahead for a cab, try the Independent Taxi Operators Association, or ITOA (☎ 617/426-8700), Town Taxi (☎ 617/536-5000), or Checker Taxi (☎ 617/536-7000).

FAST FACTS: Boston

American Express   The main local office is at 1 Court St. (☎ 617/723-8400), close to the Government Center MBTA stop. It's open Monday through Friday from 8:30am to 5:30pm. The Cambridge office, just off Harvard Square at 39 John F. Kennedy St. (☎ 617/661-0005), is open Monday through Friday from 9am to 5pm and Saturday from 11am to 3pm.

Area Code For Boston and the immediate suburbs, it's 617; for other suburbs, 508. You sometimes must dial "1" and the area code before a number in the same area code (for example, when calling Marblehead from Boston).

Camera Repair Try **Bromfield Camera & Video** at 10 Bromfield St. (☎ 617/426-5230) or the **Camera Center** at 107 State St. (☎ 800/924-6899 or 617/227-7255).

Car Rentals See "Getting Around" earlier in this chapter.

Dentists The desk staff or concierge at your hotel may be able to provide the name of a dentist. The **Metropolitan District Dental Society** (☎ 508/651-3521) can point you toward a member of the Massachusetts Dental Society.

Doctors The desk staff or concierge at your hotel will probably be able to direct you to a doctor, but you can also try one of the many referral services run by Boston hospitals. Among them are: Beth Israel Healthcare Physician Referral (☎ 617/667-5356), Brigham and Women's Hospital Physician Referral Service (☎ 800/294-9999), Deaconess Hospital MediCall (☎ 800/472-4800), Massachusetts General Hospital Physician Referral Service (☎ 617/726-5800), and New England Medical Center Physician Referral Service (☎ 617/636-9700).

Driving Rules See "Getting Around" earlier in this chapter.

Embassies/Consulates See Chapter 3, "For Foreign Visitors."

Emergencies Call 911 for fire, ambulance, or the Boston, Brookline, or Cambridge police. This is a free call from pay phones. For the state police, call **617/523-1212.**

Eyeglass Repair **Cambridge Eye Doctors** has offices in downtown Boston at 100 State St. (☎ 617/742-2076) and 300 Washington St. (☎ 617/426-5536). In Cambridge, **For Eyes Optical** has a branch at 56 John F. Kennedy St. (☎ 617/876-6031).

Hospitals Here's hoping you won't need to evaluate Boston's reputation for excellent medical care. In case you do: Massachusetts General Hospital (55 Fruit St.; ☎ 617/726-2000, or 617/726-4100 for children's emergency services) and New England Medical Center (750 Washington St; ☎ 617/636-5000, or 617/636-5566 for emergency services) are closest to downtown Boston. At the Harvard Medical Area on the Boston-Brookline border are, among others, Beth Israel Hospital (330 Brookline Ave.; ☎ 617/667-8000, or 617/667-3337 for emergency services), Brigham and Women's Hospital (75 Francis St.; ☎ 617/732-5500), and Children's Hospital (300 Longwood Ave.; ☎ 617/355-6000, or 617/355-6611 for emergency services). In Cambridge are Cambridge Hospital (1493 Cambridge St.; ☎ 617/498-1000, or 617/498-1429 for emergency services) and Mount Auburn Hospital (330 Mount Auburn St.; ☎ 617/492-3500, or 617/499-5025 for emergency services).

Hotlines AIDS Hotline (☎ 800/235-2331 or 617/536-7733), Poison Information Center (☎ 800/682-9211 or 617/232-2120), Rape Crisis (☎ 617/492-7273), Samaritans Suicide Prevention (☎ 617/247-0220), Samariteens (☎ 800/252-8336 or 617/247-8050).

Information See "Visitor Information" earlier in this chapter.

Liquor Laws The legal drinking age is 21. In many bars, particularly near college campuses, you may be asked for ID if you appear to be under 30 or so. At sporting events, everyone purchasing alcohol is asked to show ID. Alcohol is sold in liquor stores and a few supermarkets and convenience stores. Liquor stores (and the liquor sections of supermarkets) are closed on Sundays, but alcohol may be served in restaurants. Some suburban towns are "dry."

Maps   See "City Layout" earlier in this chapter.

Newspapers/Magazines   The *Boston Globe* (☎ 617/929-2000) and *Boston Herald* (☎ 617/426-3000) are published daily. The *Boston Phoenix* (☎ 617/536-5390), a weekly, emphasizes arts coverage and publishes extensive entertainment and restaurant listings. *Boston* magazine (☎ 617/262-9700) is a lifestyle-oriented monthly.

Pharmacies (Late-Night)   The pharmacy at the **CVS** in the Porter Square Shopping Center, off Massachusetts Avenue in Cambridge (☎ 617/876-5519), is open 24 hours, seven days a week. The pharmacy at the CVS at 155–157 Charles St. in Boston (☎ 617/523-1028), next to the Charles "T" stop, is open until midnight. Some emergency rooms can fill your prescription at the hospital's pharmacy.

Police   Call **911** for emergencies.

Post Office   The main post office at 25 Dorchester Ave. (☎ 617/654-5326), behind South Station, is open 24 hours, seven days a week.

Radio   AM stations include: WBZ (news, Bruins games), 1030; WEEI (sports, Red Sox games), 850; WRKO (talk, sports, Celtics games), 680; WILD (urban contemporary, soul), 1090. FM stations include: WBCS (country), 96.9; WBOS (soft rock), 92.9; WBCN (rock, Patriots games), 104.1; WBUR (public radio, classical music), 90.9; WCRB (classical music), 102.5; WGBH (public radio, classical music, jazz), 89.7; WODS (oldies), 103.3; WJMN (pop, urban contemporary), 94.5; WFNX (alternative rock), 101.7; and WZLX (classic rock), 100.7.

Rest Rooms   The visitor center at 15 State St. has a public rest room, as do most hotels, department stores, and public buildings. There are rest rooms at the CambridgeSide Galleria, Copley Place, Prudential Center, and Quincy Market shopping areas, and one of the few public rest rooms in Harvard Square is in the Harvard Coop department store. Some public places are equipped with pay toilets, usually costing 10¢.

Safety   On the whole, Boston is a safe city for walking. As in any large city, stay out of the parks at night unless you're in a crowd, and in general, trust your instincts—a dark, deserted street is probably deserted for a reason. Specific areas to avoid at night include Boylston Street between Tremont Street and Washington Street, and Tremont Street from Stuart Street to Boylston Street. The "Combat Zone," or red-light district, has almost shrunk out of existence, but the neighborhood still isn't great. Public transportation in the areas you're likely to be is busy and safe, but service stops between 12:30 and 1am. Always be aware of your surroundings, keep a close eye on your possessions, and be particularly careful with cameras, purses, and wallets, all favorite targets of thieves and pickpockets.

Taxes   The 5% sales tax is not levied on food, prescription drugs, newspapers, or clothing worth less than $175, but there seems to be a tax on almost everything else. The lodging tax is 9.7%; the meal tax (which also applies to take-out food) is 5%; the gasoline tax (included on the price at the pump) is 10%. There is also a tax on alcohol based on alcoholic content.

Taxis   See "Getting Around" earlier in this chapter.

Transit Info   Call the MBTA at **617/222-3200**.

Useful Telephone Numbers   Travelers Aid Society (☎ 617/542-7286). Greater Boston Convention & Visitors Bureau (☎ 617/536-4100). Information Center for Individuals with Disabilities (☎ **800/462-5015,** MA only, or 617/450-9000). General Postal Service information (☎ **617/451-9922**). The correct time (☎ **617/637-1234**).

Weather Call **617/936-1234** for forecasts.

3 Accommodations

Rates at most area hotels are lower on weekends than on weeknights, when business and convention travelers fill rooms. Bargain-hunters who don't mind cold and the possibility of snow (sometimes *lots* of snow) will want to aim for January through March, when some great deals are offered, especially on weekends. Reserve well in advance during the busy spring and fall convention seasons, the vacation months of July and August, and the college graduation season of May and June. As with travel plans, it helps to be flexible when you're selecting dates—a hotel that's full of conventioneers one week may be courting business a few days later.

Boston charges a 9.7% tax on all hotel rooms (5.7% for the state, 4% for the city). To help you choose a hotel, the recommendations that follow are listed by location and then by price; within these categories the hotels are listed alphabetically. This chapter concentrates on hotels that are convenient to historic areas and transportation, those that provide special touches of luxury or service, and those that offer good value for the money.

MORE SUGGESTIONS The **Greater Boston Convention and Visitors Bureau** (☎ **800/888-5515** outside MA or 617/536-4100; fax 617/424-7664) publishes a free travel-planning guide, a comprehensive guidebook, and another children-focused guide called *Kids Love Boston;* all three are helpful in finding accommodations that will suit your needs and can offer substantial savings. To get the guidebook in advance of your trip, send $4.95 to the Greater Boston Convention & Visitors Bureau, P.O. Box 990468, Prudential Tower, Dept. TPO, Boston, MA 02199-0468. Also contact the **Massachusetts Office of Travel and Tourism** (100 Cambridge St., 13th floor, Boston, MA 02202; ☎ **800/447-6277** or 617/727-3201; fax 617/727-6525; e-mail vacationinfo@state.ma.us), which publishes a free "Getaway Guide" magazine. It's divided into six regional sections that list accommodations and attractions, and includes a map and a seasonal calendar.

BED & BREAKFASTS **Bed and Breakfast Associates Bay Colony Ltd.** (P.O. Box 57–166, Babson Park Branch, Boston, MA 02157; ☎ **800/347-5088** or 617/449-5302; fax 617/449-5958) lists more than 150 bed-and-breakfasts and inns in the metropolitan Boston area and throughout eastern Massachusetts, including the North Shore, South Shore, and Cape Cod. They also arrange long-term lodging and list furnished apartments and house-sharing opportunities. A member of the B&B National Network, they can also help arrange reservations elsewhere in the United States and in Canada.

Bed and Breakfast Agency of Boston (47 Commercial Wharf, Boston, MA 02110; ☎ **800/CITY-BNB** or 617/720-3540; fax 617/523-5761; from the United Kingdom, call 0800/89-5128) offers accommodations in waterfront lofts and historic homes (including Federal and Victorian townhouses) in Boston and Cambridge. Nightly, weekly, monthly, and special winter rates are available. Listings include 155 rooms and 60 suites as well as furnished studios and apartments, all within walking distance of downtown. Trolley tour discounts are available.

Host Homes of Boston (P.O. Box 117, Waban Branch, Boston, MA 02168; ☎ **617/244-1308;** fax 617/244-5156) lists 45 homes offering personalized hospitality and clean, comfortable accommodations. Many hosts speak foreign languages, and all provide breakfast. A two-night minimum stay is required.

Bed & Breakfast Reservations North Shore/Greater Boston/Cape Cod (P.O. Box 35, Newtonville, MA 02160; ☎ **800/832-2632** outside MA or 617/964-1606; fax 617/332-8572; e-mail bnbinc@ix.netcom.com) matches visitors with carefully inspected accommodations in Greater Boston and areas north of Boston, and on Cape Cod.

DOWNTOWN
VERY EXPENSIVE

✪ **Boston Harbor Hotel.** 70 Rowes Wharf (entrance on Atlantic Ave.), Boston, MA 02110. ☎ **800/752-7077** or 617/439-7000. Fax 617/330-9450. 230 rms, 26 suites. A/C MINIBAR TV TEL. $235–$385 double; from $350 suite. Children under 18 stay free in parents' room. Extra person $50. Weekend packages available. AE, DC, DISC, MC, V. Self-parking $21 weekdays; valet parking $23 daily. MBTA: Blue Line to Aquarium or Red Line to South Station.

The Boston Harbor Hotel is the prettiest in town, whether you approach from land or sea (the Airport Water Shuttle stops here). A dazzling six-story-high archway links the harbor and the city, and you'll forget about the Central Artery construction raging out front as soon as you glimpse the water. The hotel is within walking distance of downtown and the waterfront attractions, and it prides itself on offering top-notch service to travelers pursuing both business and pleasure. A museum-quality collection of paintings, drawings, and prints enhances the grand public spaces of the hotel, a 16-story redbrick structure that's part of a 10-year-old hotel-office-retail-condominium complex.

Guest rooms have a view of the harbor or the Boston skyline (rooms with city views are cheaper), and all have windows that open. Each is a luxurious bed- and living-room combination, decorated with mahogany furnishings that include armoire, desk, and comfortable chairs. Some suites have private terraces. Standard guest room amenities include hair dryers, bathrobes, slippers, and umbrellas.

Dining/Entertainment: Overlooking the harbor, the Rowes Wharf Restaurant (see "Dining" below for details) serves fresh seafood and American cuisine at breakfast, lunch, dinner, and Sunday brunch, and the Harborview Lounge offers afternoon tea and evening cocktails. The Rowes Wharf Bar serves cocktails and light fare from 11:30am to midnight. The Rowes Wharf Cafe offers outdoor dining from May to September.

Services: Concierge; 24-hour room service; valet service; nightly turndown; twice-daily maid service; baby-sitting; valet parking.

Facilities: Pay-per-view movies; health club and spa with 60-foot lap pool; whirl-pool; sauna, steam, and exercise rooms; and a salon for facials, massage, pedicures, and manicures. State-of-the-art business center with professional staff. Three floors for nonsmokers; 18 rooms for the disabled.

The Bostonian Hotel. 40 North St., Boston, MA 02109. ☎ **800/343-0922** or 617/523-3600. Fax 617/523-2454. 152 rms, 16 suites. A/C MINIBAR TV TEL. $245–$325 double; $335–$355 honeymoon or executive room; $450–$725 suite. Children under 12 stay free in parents' room. Extra person $20. Special weekend rates and other packages available. AE, DC, JCB, MC, V. Parking $20. MBTA: Green or Blue Line to Government Center, or Orange Line to Haymarket.

Across the street from Faneuil Hall Marketplace, the relatively small Bostonian Hotel is big on service and amenities. It's a unique building, with a round, cobbled parking area in a tiny courtyard outside the small but plush glass-walled lobby. The four- and seven-story red-brick hotel consists of two wings—one, an old warehouse

Boston Accommodations

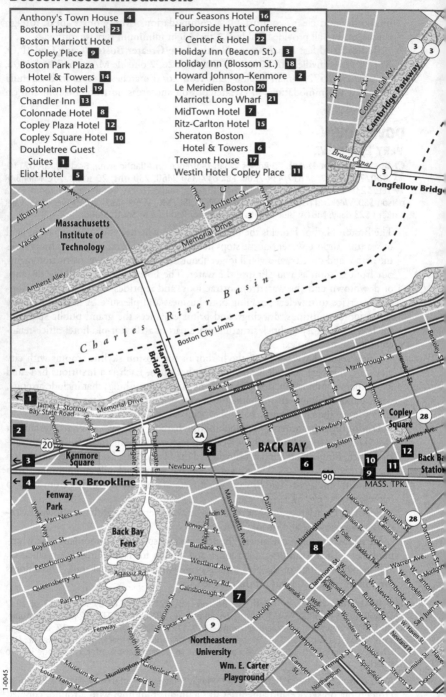

Anthony's Town House **4**
Boston Harbor Hotel **23**
Boston Marriott Hotel
  Copley Place **9**
Boston Park Plaza
  Hotel & Towers **14**
Bostonian Hotel **19**
Chandler Inn **13**
Colonnade Hotel **8**
Copley Plaza Hotel **12**
Copley Square Hotel **10**
Doubletree Guest
  Suites **1**
Eliot Hotel **5**

Four Seasons Hotel **16**
Harborside Hyatt Conference
  Center & Hotel **22**
Holiday Inn (Beacon St.) **3**
Holiday Inn (Blossom St.) **18**
Howard Johnson–Kenmore **2**
Le Meridien Boston **20**
Marriott Long Wharf **21**
MidTown Hotel **7**
Ritz-Carlton Hotel **15**
Sheraton Boston
  Hotel & Towers **6**
Tremont House **17**
Westin Hotel Copley Place **11**

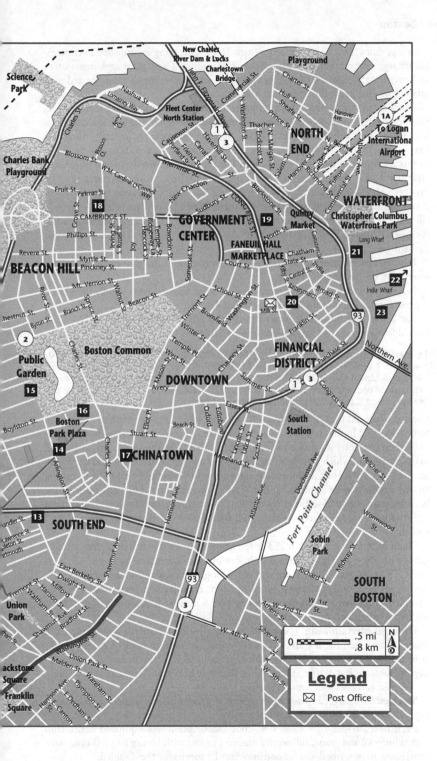

building, dates from 1824, the other from 1890. One wing is furnished in contemporary style, the other more traditionally. The interior is a pleasant agglomeration of architectural styles, with lots of glass and brass, and public spaces are decorated with artwork on loan from the Bostonian Society.

Guest rooms are furnished with armoires and tables, and many have French doors that open onto private balconies. Some suites have double vanities and separate dressing areas (terry-cloth robes are provided), working fireplaces, or Jacuzzis. All rooms have stereo VCRs, 26-inch TVs, safes, and two-line phones with dataports. Bathrooms are equipped with hair dryers, heat lamps, and both overhead and European-style hand-held shower sprays. This is one hotel where, in the interests of noise evasion, you really want to be as high up as you can afford, and away from the street if you can stand not having a nice view. Faneuil Hall Marketplace is busy from early till late, the Central Artery construction is nearby (and will be closer before it's farther away), and on Friday and Saturday, the noisy Haymarket vendors are in place by 7am.

Dining/Entertainment: On the fourth-floor rooftop is the glass-enclosed Seasons restaurant, one of Boston's finest.

Services: Concierge; 24-hour room service; newspaper delivery; nightly turndown; express checkout; limousine service to Logan Airport.

Facilities: VCRs; complimentary health club privileges at the excellent Sky Club four blocks away; rooms for nonsmokers available.

✪ **Le Meridien Boston.** 250 Franklin St. (at Post Office Sq.), Boston, MA 02110. ☎ **800/ 543-4300** or 617/451-1900. Fax 617/423-2844. 326 rms, 22 suites. A/C MINIBAR TV TEL. $285–$335 double; $450–$800 suite. Extra person $25. Weekend rates from $145 per night, including use of pool and health club plus parking. AE, CB, DC, MC, V. Parking $24. MBTA: Blue or Orange Line to State, or Red Line to Downtown Crossing.

Located in the old Federal Reserve Bank building, which was designed by R. Clipston Sturgis in 1922 in the style of a 16th-century Roman palace, this nine-story granite-and-limestone hotel is an architectural marvel. You'll see the bank's original grand marble staircase, which now leads to the dining areas; two murals by N. C. Wyeth on the walls of the bar; and ornately carved marble fireplaces and floor-to-ceiling arched windows. The location, in the heart of the Financial District, is perfect for business travelers, and vacationing visitors will be near the waterfront and downtown attractions. Whatever your mission, you'll find the service by the multilingual staff superb.

Guest rooms are arranged in 153 different configurations, including dramatic loft suites with first-floor living rooms, a bedroom in the loft area, and bathrooms on both levels. The glass mansard roof (not part of the original design) surrounds the top three stories, where a number of rooms have large sloped windows and extraordinary views. The already-plush guest rooms underwent a $5.5 million renovation in 1995. Each has two telephones (one in the bathroom).

Dining/Entertainment: The award-winning Julien restaurant serves lunch and dinner. The Julien Bar features live piano music six nights a week. A six-story glass atrium rises above the Café Fleuri, which serves breakfast, lunch, dinner, the Saturday "Chocolate Bar Buffet" (September through May), and Sunday jazz brunch. La Terrasse is the seasonal outdoor cafe.

Services: Concierge; 24-hour room service; dry cleaning and laundry service; weekday newspaper delivery; daily weather report.

Facilities: Pay-per-view movies; 40-foot indoor pool; well-equipped health club with whirlpool and sauna; full-service business center with library and full-time staff; conference rooms. Six floors for nonsmokers; 15 rooms for the disabled.

EXPENSIVE

In addition to the hotels in this price category listed below, Boston also has a Holiday Inn (5 Blossom St., Boston, MA 02114; ☎ 800/HOLIDAY or 617/742-7630) with all of the standard features you'd expect from the international chain.

Boston Marriott Long Wharf. 296 State St., Boston, MA 02109. ☎ **800/228-9290** or 617/ 227-0800. Fax 617/227-2867. 400 rms, 12 suites. A/C TV TEL. Apr–Nov $189–$269 double; Dec–Mar $159–$229 double. Extra person free. Weekend packages from $189 double; $450–$490 suite. AE, DC, DISC, JCB, MC, V. Parking $22. MBTA: Blue Line to Aquarium.

The terraced redbrick exterior of this long, narrow seven-story hotel looks nothing like the ocean liner it supposedly resembles, but it is one of the most recognizable sights on the harbor. A stone's throw from the New England Aquarium, it's convenient to all the downtown and waterfront attractions, and just two subway stops from the airport. A Rufus Porter harbor scene, one of the few remaining original frescoes painted by the 19th-century artist, dominates the lobby wall near the escalator. Although the locale is not identified, it is thought to be Boston Harbor in the early 1800s. It's worth seeing even if you're not a hotel guest.

Rooms face either side of Long Wharf, with views of Central Wharf and the aquarium or Mercantile Wharf and Waterfront Park. Rooms are large and decor varies, but all have in-room movies, a choice of king-size or double beds, and a table and chairs in front of the window.

The seventh floor is the Concierge Level, with fresh flowers in the guest rooms; complimentary continental breakfast, cocktails, and hors d'oeuvres served in a private lounge; and private exercise facilities.

Dining/Entertainment: The atrium-style Palm Garden, a cafe and lounge used for Sunday brunch, has a magnificent 420-foot ceiling mural; Oceana Restaurant features a 180-degree expanse of glass wall fronting the harbor; Waves Bar & Grill serves cocktails and light fare.

Services: Concierge; valet laundry; valet parking.

Facilities: Pay-per-view movies; indoor pool with an outdoor terrace; exercise room; whirlpools; saunas; game room; business center; conference rooms; 18 rooms for the disabled.

Harborside Hyatt Conference Center & Hotel. 101 Harborside Dr., Boston, MA 02129. ☎ **800/233-1284** or 617/568-1234. Fax 617/568-6080. 270 rms. A/C TV TEL. $220 double. Children under 12 stay free in parents' room. AE, CB, DC, DISC, JCB, MC, V. Parking $7 maximum for overnight guests. MBTA: Blue Line to Airport, then take shuttle bus. By car, follow signs to Logan Airport and take Harborside Dr. past the car-rental area and tunnel entrance.

This striking 14-story waterfront hotel, which opened in 1993, has unobstructed views of the harbor and city skyline. The turret at one end of the building is a lighthouse whose light is controlled by the Logan Airport control tower so it doesn't interfere with runway lights. Inside, fiber-optic stars change color in the skydome ceiling in the reception area. Public spaces are accented with nautical memorabilia, and the first-class guest rooms have all the amenities you'd expect from a deluxe hotel, plus such extras as irons and ironing boards in each room, luxury baths, fine wood furnishings, and excellent views.

Dining/Entertainment: The restaurant serves breakfast, lunch, and dinner. Floor-to-ceiling windows allow for spectacular views.

Services: Valet laundry; water taxi to Rowes Wharf from the hotel dock; 24-hour airport shuttle service.

Facilities: Pay-per-view movies; health club with indoor lap pool, whirlpool, and sauna; business center; conference rooms.

BACK BAY
VERY EXPENSIVE

The Colonnade Hotel. 120 Huntington Ave., Boston, MA 02116. ☎ **800/962-3030** or 617/424-7000. Fax 617/424-1717. 285 rms, 10 suites. A/C MINIBAR TV TEL. $240 standard double; $250 superior double; $270 deluxe double; $450–$1,400 suite. Children under 12 stay free in parents' room. AE, CB, DC, MC, V. Parking $20. MBTA: Green Line, E train to Prudential.

With Copley Place on one side and the Prudential Center across the street, the independently owned Colonnade is a slice of Europe in the all-American shopping mecca of the Back Bay. You might hear a dozen languages spoken by the guests and employees of this 10-story concrete-and-glass hotel, where the friendly, professional staff is known for giving every patron personalized VIP service. The elegance of the quiet, high-ceilinged public spaces is reflected in the guest rooms, which feature contemporary oak or mahogany furnishings, marble baths, pedestal sinks, bathrobes, and hair dryers. The newly designed suites have dining rooms and sitting areas, and the "author's suite" features autographed copies of the work of celebrated (or at least published) literary guests. And there's a pool on the roof.

Dining/Entertainment: Extremely popular before and after the symphony, the Cafe Promenade features seasonal menus and gourmet pizzas in a bistro setting. Every Friday and Saturday night, there's live entertainment and dancing in Zachary's Bar.

Services: Concierge; 24-hour room service; nightly turndown; valet parking.

Facilities: Seasonal "rooftop resort" with heated outdoor pool and fitness room; car-rental desk.

The Copley Plaza Hotel. 138 St. James Ave., Boston, MA 02116. ☎ **800/WYNDHAM** or 617/267-5300. Fax 617/247-6681. 373 rms, 61 suites. A/C MINIBAR TV TEL. $275–$374 double; $395–$1,400 suite. Extra person $25. AE, CB, DC, JCB, MC, V. Valet parking $22. MBTA: Green Line to Copley or Orange Line to Back Bay.

Built in 1912, the Copley Plaza faces Copley Square, with Trinity Church on one side and the Boston Public Library on the other. The Renaissance revival hotel has been synonymous with elegance since it opened. Renowned for its opulent decorative features, including crystal chandeliers, Italian marble columns, gilded vaulted ceilings, mirrored walls, and mosaic tile floors, the hotel has entertained royalty, statespeople, celebrities, and every U.S. president since William Howard Taft. Guest rooms and suites reflect the elegance of the public spaces and are furnished with reproduction Edwardian antiques. Additional in-room features include coffeemakers, phones with computer dataports, and movies. Bathrooms are equipped with hair dryers and heat lamps. After you settle into your room you can go on a walking tour that focuses on the hotel's art, architecture, and history with a member of the multilingual staff.

In 1996, the Fairmont hotel group announced plans to acquire the Copley Plaza. Fittingly, Fairmont's best-known property is the Plaza in New York, which had the same architect as the Copley Plaza, Henry Janeway Hardenbergh.

Dining/Entertainment: Options include the distinguished Plaza Dining Room, serving classic American cuisine; the Library Bar; the Plaza Bar, which serves light meals and features live entertainment; Copley's Restaurant (breakfast, lunch, afternoon tea, and dinner); and Copley's Bar.

Services: Concierge, 24-hour room service, dry cleaning and laundry service, nightly turndown, twice-daily maid service.

Facilities: Pay-per-view movies; fitness center; complimentary use of the nearby Le Pli Spa (with pool and sauna) at the Heritage; conference rooms; beauty salon. Four floors are reserved for nonsmokers, and rooms for the disabled are available.

✪ **Four Seasons Hotel.** 200 Boylston St., Boston, MA 02116. ☎ **800/332-3442** or 617/ 338-4400. Fax 617/423-0154. 288 rms, 80 suites. A/C MINIBAR TV TEL. $320–$495 double; from $650 1-bedroom suite; from $1,100 2-bedroom suite. Weekend packages available. AE, CB, DC, DISC, JCB, MC, V. Valet parking $22. MBTA: Green Line to Arlington.

Many other hotels offer exquisite service, beautiful locations, elegant guest rooms and public areas, a health club, and wonderful restaurants; but no other hotel in Boston combines every element you expect from a luxury hotel quite so seamlessly and pleasingly as the Four Seasons has since it opened in 1985. Overlooking the Public Garden, the 16-story redbrick-and-glass hotel combines traditional with contemporary, architecturally and in terms of attitude. Each room is elegantly appointed and has a striking view. Beds are large and comfortable, and breakfronts conceal the 19-inch remote-control TV and refrigerated minibar. The suites range from Four Seasons Executive Suites, which have enlarged alcove areas for entertaining or business meetings, to luxurious one-, two-, and three-bedroom deluxe suites, which are the utmost in elegance, privacy, and comfort. All rooms have bay windows that open, individual climate control, three two-line phones with computer and fax capability, hair dryers, terry-cloth bathrobes, and a safe. Children receive bedtime snacks and toys. Small pets are accepted and treated as well as their traveling companions, with a special menu and amenities.

Dining/Entertainment: The elegant restaurant Aujourd'hui, one of Boston's best, serves fine French cuisine; the Bristol Lounge is open for lunch, afternoon tea, dinner, and breakfast on Sunday, and features live entertainment nightly.

Services: In general, if you want it, you'll get it. Concierge; 24-hour room service; valet service; twice-daily maid service; valet parking; complimentary limousine service to downtown Boston addresses. If you lose your luggage en route, the staff will purchase new items and provide you with a full set of toiletries and other necessities.

Facilities: Pay-per-view movies; indoor heated pool and whirlpool with a view of the Public Garden; health spa with weight machines, StairMasters, treadmills, private masseuse, and sauna. (The pool and spa are shared with residents of the condominiums on the upper floors of the hotel.) Excellent business center; conference rooms. Five no-smoking floors; rooms for the disabled available.

The Ritz-Carlton. 15 Arlington St., Boston, MA 02117. ☎ **800/241-3333** or 617/536-5700. Fax 617/536-1335. 237 rms, 48 suites. A/C MINIBAR TV TEL. $270–$370 double; $500–$2,000 1-bedroom suite, $720–$2,100 2-bedroom suite. Ritz-Carlton Club $565–$795 1-bedroom suite, $830–$1,175 2-bedroom suite. Weekend packages available. AE, CB, DC, DISC, JCB, MC, V. Valet parking $20. MBTA: Green Line to Arlington.

Overlooking the Public Garden, the Ritz-Carlton has a tradition of gracious service that has made it famous since it opened in 1927, attracting both the "proper Bostonian" and the celebrated guest. The service and attention to detail are legendary. The 17-story hotel has the highest staff-to-guest ratio in the city, including white-gloved elevator operators.

The guest rooms have classic French provincial furnishings accented with imported floral fabrics and crystal chandeliers. Each room has two telephones (one in the bathroom), a refrigerator, a well-stocked honor bar, a safe, and an individual climate-control unit. The bathrooms are finished in Vermont marble, and terry-cloth robes are provided. All the guest rooms have closets that lock, and some have windows that open. Fresh flowers are provided in all suites. Many suites have wood-burning fireplaces.

The rooms on the top three floors have a panoramic view of the Public Garden and the city. Guests on those floors are invited to use the Ritz-Carlton Club, a pleasant lounge that has its own concierge and is open from 7am to 11pm, serving complimentary breakfast, afternoon tea, hors d'oeuvres, and after-dinner sweets.

Dining/Entertainment: The hotel has a superb Dining Room (see "Dining" later in this chapter for details), and the popular Ritz Bar, located off the street-level lobby. The second-floor Lounge is famous for afternoon tea, and from 5:30pm until midnight cigar and pipe smokers can relax over cognac, rare cordials, caviar, and desserts. The Café is open for breakfast, lunch, and dinner from 7am to midnight. The Roof, located on the 17th floor and open seasonally, offers a splendid view of the city with dinner and dancing to the Ritz-Carlton Orchestra. A famously strict dress code (the mayor of Boston was once turned away from the bar) is enforced.

Services: Concierge, 24-hour room service, dry cleaning and laundry service, complimentary newspaper delivery, nightly turndown, twice-daily maid service, baby-sitting available, secretarial services arranged, complimentary limousine service available, and complimentary shoeshine.

Facilities: Well-equipped fitness center with sauna and massage room; use of pool at nearby Le Pli Health Spa; conference rooms; beauty salon; flower and gift shop.

EXPENSIVE

Boston Marriott Copley Place. 110 Huntington Ave., Boston, MA 02116. ☎ **800/ 228-9290** or 617/236-5800. Fax 617/236-5885. 1,139 rms, 77 suites. A/C TV TEL. $199–$210 double; $250–$1,100 suite. Senior discount available. Children stay free in parents' room. Special packages available. AE, DC, DISC, JCB, MC, V. Valet parking $21; self-parking $17. MBTA: Orange Line to Back Bay or Green Line, E train to Prudential.

Yes, 1,139 rooms. You may not feel that you're asserting your individuality, but at least you'll feel comfortable. This 38-story tower has something for everyone— it's part of upscale Copley Place, with complete business facilities in the heart of Boston's shopping wonderland. Enter from the street or from Copley Place, and you'll find yourself in a giant lobby with a four-story-long chandelier, Italian marble floors, full-size trees, and a waterfall. Between guests, restaurant-goers, and pedestrians, the lobby is almost always so busy that a room anywhere else would be a nice break.

The guest rooms, which were renovated in 1995, are far more than just rooms and echo the finery of the lobby, with Queen Anne–style mahogany furniture, including a desk and table and either two armchairs or an armchair and an ottoman. Rooms are equipped with full-length mirrors, hair dryers, ironing boards, and phones with dataports. Ultrasuites feature individual whirlpool baths. One suite even holds a grand piano. Guests in Concierge Level rooms have, yes, their own concierge, and access to a private lounge where complimentary continental breakfast, cocktails, and hors d'oeuvres are served.

Dining/Entertainment: Champions Sports Bar is a fun place to watch sports on TV and eat bar food. Sunday brunch, with entertainment, is served in the Terrace Lounge. There are two Italian restaurants and a sushi bar as well.

Services: Concierge; 24-hour room service; valet laundry; valet parking.

Facilities: Pay-per-view movies; heated indoor pool; well-equipped health club with exercise room, whirlpools, saunas; full-service business center with personal computers; conference rooms; car-rental desk; tour desk. Rooms for nonsmokers and the disabled are available.

Boston Park Plaza Hotel & Towers. 64 Arlington St. (at Park Plaza), Boston, MA 02116. ☎ **800/225-2008** or 617/426-2000. Fax 617/426-1708. 960 rms, 10 suites. A/C TV TEL. Main hotel $175–$265 double; Towers $195–$245 double; $375–$2,000 suite. Extra person $20. Senior discounts and special packages available. Children 17 and under stay free in parents' room. AE, DC, MC, V. Valet parking $18. MBTA: Green Line to Arlington.

Built as the great Statler Hilton in 1927, the hotel is proud of its history and equally proud of its renovations. The lovely old features—such as the spacious lobby with its crystal chandelier, gilt trim, and red-carpeted corridors—have been retained, but the rooms have been updated with modern comforts. Room size and decor vary greatly (some rooms are quite small). The superior rooms offer extra services and access to a hospitality suite serving complimentary continental breakfast and evening wine and cheese. The location is central—just a block from Boston Common and the Public Garden, and about the same distance from the Theater District. The hotel lobby is a little commercial hub, with a travel agency, foreign currency exchange, Amtrak and airline ticket offices, and a pharmacy.

Environmentally conscious guests will be pleased to know that the Boston Park Plaza Hotel has initiated an environmental policy that is a model for the industry. All nonbiodegradable products have been eliminated from guest rooms, recycling programs are in effect, and stationery and forms are printed on dioxin-free recycled paper. A "Green Team" of hotel employees is attempting to conserve energy and water and to eliminate hazardous waste.

Dining/Entertainment: Guests can choose from the Cafe Rouge, which serves healthful cuisine prepared in consultation with the natural-foods supermarket chain Bread & Circus; the famous Legal Sea Foods restaurant; the Captains Bar; Cafe Eurosia; and Swans Court in the Grand Lobby.

Services: Concierge; 24-hour room service; valet laundry; secretarial services; valet parking.

Facilities: Pay-per-view movies; health club; kids' video/game room; hairdresser; beauty salon. Rooms for nonsmokers available.

✪ **Eliot Hotel.** 370 Commonwealth Ave. (at Massachusetts Ave.), Boston, MA 02215. ☎ **800/44-ELIOT** or 617/267-1607. Fax 617/536-9114. 16 rms, 78 suites. A/C MINIBAR TV TEL. $195–$225 double; $225–$265 suite. Extra person $20. Children under 12 stay free in parents' room. AE, DC, MC, V. Valet parking $18. MBTA: Green Line, B, C, or D train to Hynes/ICA.

This exquisite hotel combines the flavor of Yankee Boston with European-style service and amenities. Built in 1925 as a retirement residence for Harvard alumni (the Harvard Club is next door), the nine-story hotel underwent a complete renovation from 1990 to 1994. The cozy lobby is lit by a 5-foot-wide imported crystal chandelier and decorated with period furnishings and porcelain. Spacious suites are furnished with traditional English-style chintz fabrics, authentic botanical prints, and antique furnishings. French doors separate the living and bedrooms, and modern conveniences, such as Italian marble baths, dual-line telephones with modem capability, and two TVs are standard in suites. Many suites also have a pantry with a microwave.

The hotel is convenient to Boston University and MIT (across the river), and the location on tree-lined Commonwealth Avenue makes for a pleasant contrast with the urban bustle of Newbury Street, a block away.

Dining/Entertainment: Breakfast is served in the Charles Eliot Room.

Services: Concierge; room service and secretarial services available; valet parking.

Facilities: Smoke-free floor; rooms for the disabled; safe-deposit boxes. A health club is scheduled to open in 1997.

Sheraton Boston Hotel & Towers. 39 Dalton St., Boston, MA 02199. ☎ **800/325-3535** or 617/236-2000. Fax 617/236-1702. 1,208 rms, 85 suites. A/C MINIBAR TV TEL. $210–$255 double; from $255 suite. Children under 17 stay free in parents' room. 25% discount for students, faculty, and retired persons with ID, depending on availability. Weekend packages available. AE, CB, DC, DISC, JCB, MC, V. Parking $16. MBTA: Green Line, B, C, or D train to Hynes/ICA or E train to Prudential.

You might get lost once you're actually in this gigantic hotel, but you won't have trouble finding the 29-story towers attached to the Prudential Center. Neither does anyone else, apparently—this hotel is one of the most popular in the city. The location, lavish convention facilities, a range of accommodations, and huge pool make it a favorite with travelers pursuing both business and pleasure. It's connected directly to the Hynes Convention Center and the new Shops at Prudential Center, and by walkways to Copley Place.

Standard rooms are fairly large, with traditional furnishings in mahogany and cherrywood. Many suites have a phone in the bathroom, a wet bar, and a refrigerator. Executive Level guests get free local calls and no access charges on long-distance calls, and admission to the Executive Lounge, where complimentary breakfast and hors d'oeuvres are served. In-room amenities on this level include a desk, phone with dataport, morning newspaper, coffeemaker, and iron.

The luxurious Sheraton Towers, located on the 26th floor of the hotel and accessible via private elevator, features private check-in, an elegant atmosphere, some antique furnishings, and a wonderful view from the lounge, where Towers guests are offered complimentary breakfast, afternoon tea, and hors d'oeuvres and beverages. Rooms are outfitted with Egyptian cotton sheets, goose-down comforters, plush bathrobes, electric blankets, shoe trees, and phones in the bathroom (some even have a wall-mounted TV). Guests on this floor have their own butler.

Dining/Entertainment: The Mass. Bay Company and Turning Point Lounge serve light and full meals in clubby surroundings. The casual A Steak in the Neighborhood serves breakfast, lunch, dinner, and more than 70 varieties of beer in a fun, noisy setting that also serves as a sports bar with a dance floor.

Services: Concierge; 24-hour room service; valet laundry; valet parking.

Facilities: Pay-per-view movies, heated indoor/outdoor pool with retractable dome, pavilion, Jacuzzi, and sauna; well-equipped health club; conference rooms. Rooms for nonsmokers and the disabled available.

The Westin Hotel. 10 Huntington Ave., Boston, MA 02116. ☎ **800/228-3000** or 617/262-9600. Fax 617/424-7483. 800 rms, 46 suites. A/C MINIBAR TV TEL. $179–$250 double; $285–$1,500 suite. Extra person $20; $30 on Executive Club Level. Weekend packages available. AE, CB, DC, DISC, JCB, MC, V. Valet parking $21. MBTA: Green Line to Copley.

Looming 36 stories in the air above Copley Place, the Westin is popular with convention-goers, sightseers, and dedicated shoppers. Determined consumers don't even have to step outside—the hotel is linked by skybridges to Copley Place and the Prudential Center. Others may want to start exploring at Copley Square, across the street from the pedestrian entrance. The entrance is dominated by two-story-high twin waterfalls on either side of escalators that run to the Grand Lobby, where you'll find a multilingual staff that emphasizes quick check-in.

Upstairs, you might not notice the comfortable oak and mahogany furniture in the spacious guest rooms (at least at first), because you won't be able to take your eyes off the view. The qualms you might have had about choosing a huge chain hotel will fade as you survey downtown Boston, the airport and harbor, or the Charles River and Cambridge. Executive Club Level guests have private check-in and a private lounge where a complimentary continental breakfast and hors d'oeuvres are served.

Dining/Entertainment: The Palm, the newest branch of the famous New York–based chain, serves steak, chops, and jumbo lobsters at lunch and dinner. Turner Fisheries, a seafood restaurant known for its clam chowder, features live jazz nightly. Ten Huntington is a casual bar serving light meals. The Lobby Lounge is a relaxing spot for drinks and conversation that also serves coffee and pastries each morning.

Services: Concierge, 24-hour room service, valet service, in-room safes.

Facilities: Pay-per-view movies, indoor pool, health club with Nautilus equipment, saunas, business center with computer rentals and secretarial services, conference rooms. Forty guest rooms are designed for the disabled; they adjoin standard rooms to accommodate guests traveling with the disabled person.

MODERATE

Copley Square Hotel. 47 Huntington Ave., Boston, MA 02116. ☎ **800/225-7062** or 617/536-9000. Fax 617/236-0351. 143 rms, 12 suites. A/C TV TEL. $155–$185 double; $260 suite. Children under 17 stay free in parents' room. Packages and senior discount available. AE, DISC, JCB, MC, V. Parking available in adjacent lot for $16. MBTA: Green Line to Copley.

Although it was built in 1891 and is located in the shadow of the megahotels near Copley Place and the Prudential Center, the seven-story Copley Square Hotel, with attractively decorated rooms, good value, and excellent service, is definitely not over-shadowed. Each room has two double beds, a queen-size or king-size bed, and a unique layout. All rooms are equipped with hair dryers, coffeemakers, safes, and phones with modem hookups and guest voice mail. Rooms for nonsmokers are available, and there is a 24-hour currency exchange in the lobby. Guests are treated to afternoon tea and have access to the health club at the nearby Westin Hotel.

This hotel was one of the first in the country to institute an environmental policy, which includes energy and water conservation and waste reduction and recycling. Environmentally sound products are supplied in the guest rooms and are used throughout the hotel.

There are three dining options in the hotel: Pop's Place serves breakfast, and the Original Sports Saloon, a local landmark for its great barbecue, serves lunch and dinner, as does Café Budapest, one of Boston's finest restaurants.

☉ The MidTown Hotel. 220 Huntington Ave., Boston, MA 02115. ☎ **800/343-1177** or 617/262-1000. Fax 617/262-8739. 159 rms. A/C TV TEL. $109–$149 double. Extra person $15. Children under 18 stay free in parents' room. 10% senior discount with AARP card; government employees' discount subject to availability. AE, DC, DISC, MC, V. Free parking. MBTA: Green Line, E train to Prudential.

Even without free parking, this two-story hotel would be a good deal. It's on a busy street within easy walking distance of Symphony Hall, the Museum of Fine Arts, and the Back Bay attractions. The good-sized rooms are bright and attractively outfitted with contemporary furnishings, and some have connecting bedrooms for families. For business travelers, the phones have dataports, and photocopying and fax services are available at the front desk. The heated outdoor pool is open from Memorial Day through Labor Day. Tables of Content, an American cafe, is open from 7am to 10pm.

☉ Tremont House. 275 Tremont St., Boston, MA 02116. ☎ **800/331-9998** or 617/426-1400. Fax 617/482-6730. 281 rms, 34 suites. A/C TV TEL. $139–$199 double; $170–$270 suite. Children under 16 stay free in parents' room. Extra person $10. Weekend packages and 10% AAA discount available. AE, CB, DC, DISC, MC, V. Parking $15 in nearby garage or lot. MBTA: Green Line to Boylston or Orange Line to New England Medical Center.

The Tremont House is as close to Boston's theaters as you can be without actually attending a show, and convenient to downtown and the Back Bay.

This 15-story brick building, formerly the landmark Hotel Bradford, has been completely renovated to preserve the style that prevailed when the hotel was built in 1924. The original gold-leaf decorations and crafted ceilings in the huge lobby and ballrooms have been restored, the original marble walls and columns refurbished, and elegant, sparkling-new chandeliers installed.

The hotel, which has affordable rates and modern furnishings, is geared to travelers on a modest budget. That's not to say that there are no services—conference

👪 Family-Friendly Hotels

The moderately priced chain hotels are probably the ones in the area most accustomed to dealing with young guests, but their higher-end brethren put on a good show.

Boston Park Plaza Hotel & Towers (64 Arlington St.; ☎ 617/426-2000). The "Cub Club" can make life a joy for parents. The kids get a coupon book, Red Sox sundaes, environmental gifts, and swan boat rides. They can play in the video-game room or go to a story hour where milk and cookies are served. Picnic lunches/suppers, family movies, and bedtime snacks are also available. And there's a big bag of peanuts for feeding the ducks and swans in the Public Garden. Special family rates with free parking are also available.

Four Seasons Hotel (200 Boylston St.; ☎ 617/338-4400). Kids (and their parents) love the pool and spa and the executive suite, where they can get children's videos for the VCR, milk and cookies delivered by room service, child-size bathrobes, and any needed child accessories. The concierge has food packets for the ducks and squirrels at the Public Garden.

Le Meridien Boston (250 Franklin St.; ☎ 617/451-1900). The "Kids Love Boston" weekend program offers parents the chance to book a separate room next to their own for children under 12 for $60 a night (based on availability). Milk and cookies are served when you check in, and meals at the Cafe Fleuri include child-friendly options throughout the weekend.

The Ritz-Carlton (15 Arlington St.; ☎ 617/536-5700). This hotel pampers the kids with a video library, games and toys, snacks and beverages, all served up in a "Junior Presidential Suite" for a mere $495 a night. These lucky guests get a stuffed Carlton the Lion, too. The Ritz also has occasional special weekends (a nice way of saying lessons are involved) for young ladies and gentlemen, including "A Weekend of Social Savvy" and "The Junior Chef Debut." At Christmas there's a *Nutcracker* package.

rooms, secretarial services, and valet laundry are available. There are three top-of-the-line units that feature kitchenettes with a range, sink, and refrigerator (great for families who want to eat in). Four floors are reserved for nonsmokers, and there are 14 rooms for the disabled.

Weekend clubgoers have two options in the hotel. The upscale Roxy nightclub features Top 40 and international music, and the Jukebox club is a favorite with suburbanites. The Tremont Deli serves a casual menu at breakfast, lunch, and dinner.

INEXPENSIVE

Chandler Inn. 26 Chandler St. (at Berkeley St.), Boston, MA 02116. ☎ **800/842-3450** or 617/482-3450. Fax 617/542-3428. 56 rms. A/C TV TEL. Nov–Apr $79 double; May–Oct $99 double. Children under 12 stay free in parents' room. Rates include continental breakfast. AE, CB, DC, DISC, MC, V. Parking available in nearby garages. MBTA: Orange Line to Back Bay.

The Chandler Inn is technically in the South End, near the Boston Center for the Arts, but so convenient to the Back Bay and such a good deal that you won't mind the slightly lower-budget address. The guest rooms were recently redecorated, recarpeted, and, most importantly, air-conditioned. They're still nothing fancy, but if your needs are basic, you'll be fine. And the staff is friendly and helpful. This is a practical choice for bargain-hunters who don't care about a tony address and a lot of extras.

KENMORE SQUARE & ENVIRONS
EXPENSIVE

⑤ Doubletree Guest Suites. 400 Soldiers Field Rd., Boston, MA 02134. ☎ **800/222-TREE** or 617/783-0090. Fax 617/783-0897. 310 rms. A/C MINIBAR TV TEL. $169–$229 double. Extra person $20. Children 18 and under stay free in parents' room. Weekend packages from $109 per night. AAA discount available. AE, CB, DC, DISC, JCB, MC, V. Parking $14 Sun–Thurs, $7 Fri–Sat.

This hotel is one of the best deals in town—every unit is a two-room suite with a living room, bedroom, and bath. Business travelers can entertain in their rooms, and families can spread out, making this a good choice for both. Overlooking the Charles River near a Massachusetts Turnpike exit, the hotel isn't in an actual neighborhood, but complimentary van service to and from attractions and business areas in Boston and Cambridge is available.

The suites surround a 15-story sunlit atrium and can be reached via glass elevators. Rooms are large and attractively furnished, and most bedrooms have king-size beds and a writing desk. Living rooms feature full-size sofa beds, a dining table, and a good-sized refrigerator. Each suite has two TVs and three telephones (one in the bathroom).

Dining/Entertainment: Scullers Grille and Scullers Lounge serve meals from 6:30am to 11pm. Scullers Jazz Club has two nightly shows.

Services: Valet service; newspaper delivery; secretarial services; van service.

Facilities: Pay-per-view movies; heated indoor pool; exercise room; whirlpool; sauna; conference rooms; laundry room. Suites for the disabled on each floor.

MODERATE

Hotels in this price range in the Kenmore Square and Environs area mainly consist of chain hotels like the Holiday Inn Boston Brookline (1200 Beacon St., Brookline, MA 02146; ☎ **800/HOLIDAY** or 617/277-1200) and the Howard Johnson Hotel—Kenmore (575 Commonwealth Ave., Boston, MA 02215; ☎ **800/ 654-2000** or 617/267-3100), both of which offer the reliable but unremarkable accommodations and service that each chain is known for.

INEXPENSIVE

Anthony's Town House. 1085 Beacon St., Brookline, MA 02146. ☎ **617/566-3972.** 12 rms (none with bath). A/C TV. $45–$75 double. Extra person $10. Special weekly rates available. No credit cards. Free on-site parking. MBTA: Green Line, C train to Hawes St. (two stops past Kenmore).

Located one mile from Boston's Kenmore Square, about 10 minutes from downtown by subway, this turn-of-the-century restored four-story brownstone townhouse is listed in the National Register of Historic Places. Each floor has three rooms and a shared bath with enclosed shower. Rooms are decorated with Queen Anne– and Victorian-style furnishings, and the large front rooms have bay windows with comfortable lounge chairs. *Note:* Rates listed above cover all seasons. Rates during most of the year are generally on the higher end, dipping slightly in the dead of winter.

4 Dining

See also the listings for Cambridge restaurants in Chapter 5.

ON THE WATERFRONT
VERY EXPENSIVE

Rowes Wharf Restaurant. In the Boston Harbor Hotel, 70 Rowes Wharf (entrance on Atlantic Ave.). ☎ **617/439-3995.** Reservations recommended. Main courses $10–$16.75 at lunch,

$20–$31 at dinner. Breakfast $2–$12.75. AE, DC, DISC, MC, V. Mon–Sat 6:30–11am, Sun 7–10am; Mon–Sat 11:30am–2pm, Sun 10:30am–2pm; Mon–Sat 5:30–10pm, Sun 5:30–9pm. MBTA: Blue Line to Aquarium. REGIONAL AMERICAN.

Tucked away on the second floor of the Boston Harbor Hotel, the wood-paneled Rowes Wharf Restaurant feels almost like a private club. The richly upholstered chairs with arms encourage you to relax, and for service that puts you at ease and anticipates your every desire, the dining room staff is perfect (the employees at the door can be a bit chilly—hang in there). And that's not even mentioning the cuisine, which is among the best in the city, and the gorgeous china with the same border that's around the hotel's landmark archway.

The enormous picture windows afford a breathtaking harbor view, and the tables are far enough apart that you won't hear your neighbors admiring it. You might hear them exclaiming over the food, though. Chef Daniel Bruce uses local ingredients when possible, prepared in deceptively simple ways that accent natural flavors without overwhelming them. The signature appetizer is luscious Maine lobster meat seasoned and formed into a sausage, grilled, sliced, and served in a light cream sauce with lobster claw meat and lemon pasta. Spinach salad comes topped with oysters that taste of the sea, poached just enough to firm them up. Entrees range from pan-roasted Nova Scotia salmon to grilled chicken breast with a maple and chili glaze, to pecan-smoked filet mignon grilled and served with whiskey sauce. Desserts vary with the inspiration of the chef—there's usually an excellent sorbet sampler. The lunch menu indicates which items are low in fat, sodium, and calories.

EXPENSIVE

✪ **Cornucopia on the Wharf.** 100 Atlantic Ave. ☎ **617/367-0300.** Reservations recommended at dinner. Main courses $13.50–$23.95. AE, MC, V. Daily 5:30–10:30pm; Apr 15–Oct 15 daily 11:30am–2:30pm. Patio (seasonal) open daily 11:30am–9:30pm. MBTA: Blue Line to Aquarium. AMERICAN REGIONAL.

This festive spot is a great stop if you're visiting the waterfront and worth a trip if you're not. Jutting out into the harbor across a marina from Long Wharf, the dining room feels like the cabin of a ship, with lots of glass windows, polished wood trim, hand-painted columns, and a large bar. The popular outdoor patio is shielded from direct exposure to the street by a small park. The menu is short and changes regularly, offering the innovative seafood you might expect in this location as well as meat options. Menu items are accompanied by wine recommendations, a practice that makes many people secretly sigh with relief. Crispy calamari are usually available as an appetizer, ethereally fried and served in a white paper cone. The seafood pasta specials often available at lunch are outstanding. At dinner, the Thai fish stew with lobster, littlenecks, and mussels in a green curry broth and the baked scrod over roasted garlic mashed potatoes are excellent, but the pan-roasted lobster can be on the scrawny side. Events such as wine tastings are scheduled throughout the year—call to see if something's happening during your visit.

✪ **The Grill & Cue.** 256 Commercial St. ☎ **617/227-4454.** Reservations recommended at dinner. Main courses $6.95–$9.95 at lunch, $12.95–$16.50 at dinner; cafe fare $6.95–$9.95. AE, CB, DC, DISC, MC, V. Mon–Fri noon–2pm; Mon–Wed 5–10pm, Thurs–Fri 5–10:30pm; Sat–Sun 2pm–1am. MBTA: Blue Line to Aquarium. CONTEMPORARY AMERICAN.

The newest restaurant near the harbor is also one of the best in town. Across the street from the former home of the late, lamented Jasper's, the Grill & Cue scooped up many members of the displaced staff of that legendary New England seafood institution when it opened in 1995. One was chef Jon Dabelstein, who has a way with meat and pasta as well as fish. Everything is good here, and there's lots of it, starting with the great bread basket and excellent soups. At lunch, try the most sophisticated tuna melt ever, a focaccia sandwich with grilled tuna steak and onions, topped with fontina cheese. The cafe menu, available at lunch and dinner, offers casual fare such as feathery ricotta cavatelli with roasted plum tomatoes, and a mountain of steak tips with grilled peppers and onions. Dinner entrees are sturdy cuts of meat and fish with phenomenal side dishes—pan-roasted salmon with roasted vegetables, pesto-marinated grilled leg of lamb with artichoke-and-potato pie, or grilled sirloin with mashed potatoes and red onion rings.

The setting, like the food, is familiar yet daring, softly lit, with purple and black enamel accents, a tropical fish tank over the bar, and French doors that open to the street from the front dining room. The second floor is an upscale pool parlor (that's the "Cue" in the name), featuring a half-dozen imported slate tables with purple felt tops that go for as much as $18 an hour. You might prefer to splurge on dessert—anything with chocolate in it is excellent, and the ridiculous-sounding maple-ginger tiramisu is actually quite good.

MODERATE

Daily Catch. 261 Northern Ave. ☎ **617/338-3093.** Reservations not accepted. Main courses $10–$16.50. AE. Sun–Thurs noon–10:30pm, Fri–Sat noon–11pm. MBTA: Red Line to South Station. SOUTHERN ITALIAN/SEAFOOD.

Make sure your fellow travelers accompany you to this Fish Pier institution, because you're going to emanate garlic for at least a day and you might as well have someone to share it with. This is a basic storefront, where the waitstaff sometimes seems overwhelmed and it can take forever to get a table, but the food is terrific. There's Sicilian-style calamari (squid stuffed with bread crumbs, raisins, pine nuts, parsley, and tons of garlic), freshly shucked clams, mussels in garlic-flavored sauce, broiled and fried fish, and shellfish. Calamari is prepared at least eight ways—even the standard garlic-and-oil pasta sauce has ground-up squid in it. If you've never tasted it before, try the fried version as an excellent appetizer. And if you really want to try something different, order the squid ink pasta Alfredo. All food is prepared to order, and is usually served in the frying pans in which it was cooked.

The other two branches of this mini-chain don't accept credit cards. The original Daily Catch is in the North End, at 323 Hanover St. (☎ **617/523-8567**). Another is in Brookline at 441A Harvard St. (☎ **617/734-5696**). The hours are the same for all three.

INEXPENSIVE

Jimbo's Fish Shanty. 245 Northern Ave. ☎ **617/542-5600.** Main courses $6–$14. AE, DC, MC, V. Mon–Thurs 11:30am–9:30pm, Fri–Sat 11:30am–10pm, Sun noon–8pm. MBTA: Red Line to South Station. SEAFOOD.

Bring your sense of humor to this jam-packed restaurant, where model trains run overhead on tracks suspended from the fairly low ceiling, there are road signs everywhere, and the waitress will probably call you "honey." Under the same management as Jimmy's Harborside across the street, Jimbo's serves good, fresh seafood, skewers threaded with fish or beef, and pasta dishes (at dinner only) with varied sauces, including a lobster cream version. The truly decadent desserts generally involve ice cream and chocolate.

THE NORTH END
VERY EXPENSIVE

Mamma Maria. 3 North Sq. ☎ **617/523-0077.** Reservations recommended. Main courses $8–$14 at lunch, $14.50–$26 at dinner. AE, DC, DISC, MC, V. Tues–Sat 11:30am–2pm; daily 5:30–10pm. MBTA: Green or Orange Line to Haymarket. NORTHERN ITALIAN.

Boston Dining

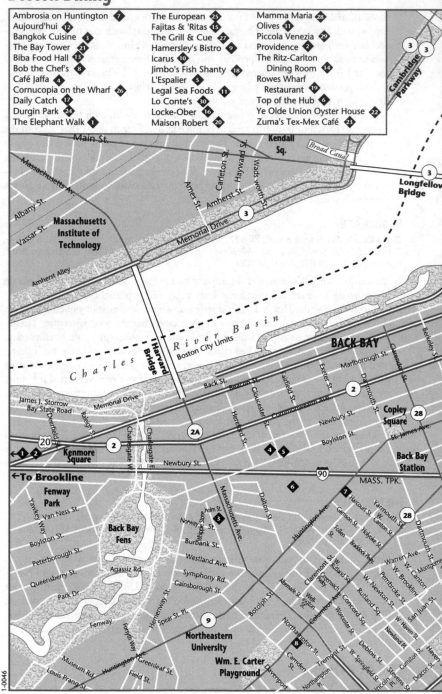

Ambrosia on Huntington **7**
Aujourd'hui **12**
Bangkok Cuisine **3**
The Bay Tower **21**
Biba Food Hall **13**
Bob the Chef's **8**
Café Jaffa **4**
Cornucopia on the Wharf **26**
Daily Catch **17**
Durgin Park **24**
The Elephant Walk **1**

The European **25**
Fajitas & 'Ritas **15**
The Grill & Cue **27**
Hamersley's Bistro **9**
Icarus **10**
Jimbo's Fish Shanty **18**
L'Espalier **5**
Legal Sea Foods **11**
Lo Conte's **30**
Locke-Ober **16**
Maison Robert **20**

Mamma Maria **28**
Olives **31**
Piccola Venezia **29**
Providence **3**
The Ritz-Carlton
  Dining Room **14**
Rowes Wharf
  Restaurant **19**
Top of the Hub **6**
Ye Olde Union Oyster House **22**
Zuma's Tex-Mex Café **23**

1-0046

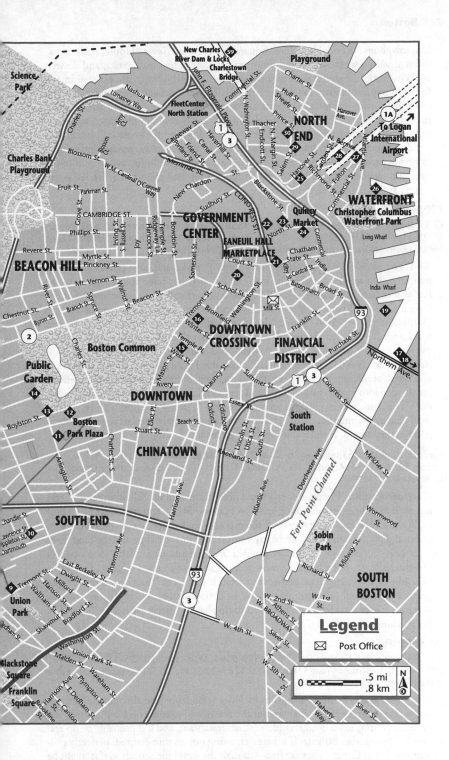

In a townhouse overlooking North Square and the Paul Revere House, this is a traditional setting where you'll find innovative cuisine. The bread, pasta, and desserts are homemade, the service is exceptional, and the cool, whitewashed rooms are among the most popular in town for getting engaged. The menu changes seasonally, but you can usually start with excellent pasta fagioli (bean-and-pasta soup) or the excellent risotto. The entrees are like nothing else in this neighborhood, presented so beautifully that it's hard to dig in. You'll be glad you did—try the roasted chicken with lightly steamed green beans, garlic poached to bring out its sweetness, and a hunk of potato casserole; the goat cheese ravioli with arugula, walnuts, oven-cured tomatoes, and capers; or the grilled salmon with beet-and-basil salad and artichoke pesto. Valet parking is available in the evening.

MODERATE

✪ Lo Conte's. 116 Salem St. ☎ **617/720-3550.** Reservations not accepted. Main courses $9.95–$14.95. AE, DC, DISC, MC, V. Sun–Thurs 11:30am–10pm, Fri–Sat 11:30am–11pm. MBTA: Green or Orange Line to Haymarket. SOUTHERN ITALIAN.

This is a real neighborhood place, with chummy service and large portions of excellent food. On weekend nights the wait can be long, but once your name is on the list, you're part of the gang—you'll be sent across the street to hang around at the Grand Cafe until your table is ready. When it is, you're seated in one of the two glorified-storefront dining rooms, decorated with photos of Italy on the walls and filled with the satisfied chatter of happy diners. Salads and appetizers aren't cheap, but portions are large and quality is high—the house salad dressing is a cheese-infused wonder; broccoli orata is battered and sautéed until it's both tender and crispy; and eggplant rolatini, when it's available as a special, is out of this world. Main dishes are divided into pasta, chicken, veal, and seafood, but you may not get past the specials. The house special chicken, broccoli, and ziti (a dish you'll find on more menus than chicken parmigiana) is the best in town, and the daily specials actually taste as good as they sound. If seafood is involved, go for it.

Piccola Venezia. 263 Hanover St. ☎ **617/523-3888.** Reservations not accepted. Main courses $9.95–$16.95. AE, DISC, MC, V. Daily 11:30am–10pm. MBTA: Green or Orange Line to Haymarket. ITALIAN.

Once upon a time, Piccola Venezia was a hole in the wall on Salem Street. In 1994 it moved to a larger, more inviting space on Hanover Street, and it's hardly had a slow night since. The glass front shows off the exposed-brick dining room, decorated with prints and photos and filled with happy patrons. Portions are large and the food tends to be heavy on red sauce, but more sophisticated specials are available. Some people feel the red sauce has a burned taste—you might want to try it as part of an appetizer (the excellent eggplant, perhaps) to see if it suits you. Then dig into your spaghetti and meatballs, chicken parmigiana, or pasta puttanesca. *Tip:* If you're dining as a pair, you're sometimes permitted to jump ahead of larger parties in line and be seated almost immediately.

INEXPENSIVE

The European. 218 Hanover St. ☎ **617/523-5694.** Main courses $7.95–$13. AE, CB, DC, DISC, MC, V. Sun–Thurs 11am–11pm, Fri–Sat 11am–12:30am. MBTA: Green or Orange Line to Haymarket. SOUTHERN ITALIAN.

The menu at this Boston institution includes reasonably priced complete dinners, among many, many other offerings, but the real reason to come here is the pizza. The European claims to be Boston's oldest Italian restaurant, and it'll probably be up and running for another 80 years if it keeps cranking out its thin-crusted, perfectly proportioned pies. Other dishes are fine—though the squid pie sounds as if it might be pizza, it's actually a turnover of pizza crust filled with calamari and served with marinara sauce—and if you're with a group, The European is a good choice because the dining rooms are huge. This is not the place to go for a romantic dinner, as it can get quite noisy, but that's part of the charm. Look for the famous clock above the front door—it's been there since the restaurant opened in 1917.

FANEUIL HALL/GOVERNMENT CENTER/FINANCIAL DISTRICT
VERY EXPENSIVE
The Bay Tower. 60 State St. ☎ **617/723-1666.** Reservations recommended. Main courses $17–$36. AE, CB, DC, MC, V. Mon–Thurs 5:30–10pm, Fri–Sat 5–11pm. MBTA: Blue or Orange Line to State. CREATIVE AMERICAN.

Let's cut to the chase: Would you pay this much at a restaurant with a view of a brick wall or a street corner? No. But is it worth it? Absolutely. One of the most beautiful dining rooms in Boston, the 33rd-floor Bay Tower has glass walls facing a glorious panorama of Faneuil Hall Marketplace, the harbor, and the airport. The terraced table area is arranged so that the view is visible from every seat, and it's reflected in many shiny (polished, not mirrored) surfaces that lend a casinolike air to the candlelit room.

Chef Raoul Jean-Richard's menu changes seasonally and includes a nice mix of traditional and contemporary preparations. You might start with a smoked-salmon napoleon, butternut squash ravioli, or shrimp cocktail. Entrees include the usual steaks, chops, chicken, and seafood, often with a twist. Baked haddock arrives in a mild horseradish crust on a bed of roasted vegetables with beet juice, and a generous portion of ratatouille is a good option for vegetarians. Special dietary preparations are available on request. As you might expect at a restaurant where many people come just for dessert, drinks, and dancing, desserts are wonderful, with an emphasis on chocolate. A $12 minimum is charged in the lounge after 9:30pm (on Friday and Saturday only dining room customers are exempt). Validated parking is available in the 60 State St. garage.

✪ Maison Robert. 45 School St. ☎ **617/227-3370.** Reservations recommended. Main courses $9–$22 at lunch, $17–$30 at dinner. Le Café has a fixed-price menu ($17 or $23) as well as à la carte selections. AE, CB, DC, MC, V. Mon–Fri 11:45am–2:30pm; Mon–Sat 5:30–10pm. MBTA: Green Line to Government Center or Red Line to Park Street. INNOVATIVE FRENCH.

Maison Robert is one of the finest French restaurants anywhere. Like many excellent restaurants, it's family-owned and -operated—proprietors Lucien and Ann Robert are the parents of executive chef André Robert, and Lucien's nephew Jacky Robert took over in the kitchen in 1996 after many years as a top chef in San Francisco (including 10 years at Ernie's).

A legend in Boston since it opened in Old City Hall in 1972, Maison Robert has only improved since Jacky Robert returned. The dining room was already spectacular, decorated in a formal style that complements the building's French Second Empire architecture, with majestic crystal chandeliers and tall windows overlooking the Old Granary Burying Ground (a gloomy thought, perhaps, but a peaceful spot in the hubbub of downtown). The food is every bit the equal of the setting, classic but dramatic. You might start with a tender, airy Roquefort soufflé, or a giant smoked-duck ravioli, which is indeed giant in both its size and the flavor of the filling and the luscious broth. Entrees include options you would expect and others that come as a pleasant surprise—steak au poivre is a meat-lover's delight, splendid roast rack of lamb is accompanied by an equally delicious potato cake, and the acorn squash of plenty overflows with crisp-tender vegetables and looks so beautiful you'll reach for your camera. Desserts are truly impressive, ranging from excellent soufflés to a selection of sorbets with a giant cookie (yes, "giant" again) to a heart-stopping chocolate-cake-and-mixed-berry concoction garnished with a chocolate Eiffel Tower too pretty to eat and too delicious not to.

The upstairs dining room is the formal counterpart of cozy Le Café on the ground floor, which has a more casual atmosphere and less expensive food, but is also thoroughly French in style. In the summer, cafe seating spills onto the lovely terrace next to the statue of Benjamin Franklin that you might have visited on the Freedom Trail. Valet parking is available for both restaurants.

MODERATE

⑤ Durgin-Park. 340 Faneuil Hall Marketplace. ☎ **617/227-2038.** Reservations not accepted. Main courses $4.95–$16.95, specials $15.90–$24.95. AE, MC, V. Daily 11:30am–2:30pm; Mon–Sat 2:30–10pm, Sun 2:30–9pm. MBTA: Green or Blue Line to Government Center, or Orange Line to Haymarket. NEW ENGLAND.

For huge portions of fresh, delicious food, a rowdy atmosphere where CEOs share tables with students, and famously cranky waitresses who can't seem to bear the sight of any of it, people have been flocking to Durgin-Park since 1827. It really is everything it's cracked up to be—a tourist magnet that also attracts hordes of local residents, where politicians rub shoulders with blue-haired grandmothers and everyone's disappointed when the waitresses are nice, as they often are. Approximately 2,000 people a day find their way to the end of the line that stretches down a flight of stairs to the first floor of the North Market building of Faneuil Hall Marketplace (look for the giant sign). The queue moves quickly, and you'll probably wind up seated at a long table with other people, although smaller tables are available.

The food is wonderful, and there's plenty of it—prime rib the size of a hubcap, giant lamb chops, piles of fried seafood, roast turkey that will fill you up till Thanksgiving. All steaks and chops are broiled on an open fire over wood charcoal. Seafood, including salmon, sole, haddock, shrimp, oysters, scallops, and lobster, is received twice daily, and fish dinners are broiled to order. Vegetables are served à la carte, and if you've been waiting to try Boston baked beans, now's the time. Homemade corn bread comes with every meal. For dessert, the strawberry shortcake is justly celebrated, and molasses-lovers (this is not a dish for dabblers) will want to try Indian pudding, a mixture of molasses and cornmeal slow-baked for hours and served with ice cream.

If you're going for "dinner" (otherwise known as lunch; the evening meal is called "supper"), beat the crowd by arriving when the restaurant opens. Or jump the line by starting out at the ground-floor Gaslight Pub, which has a private staircase that leads upstairs.

Ye Olde Union Oyster House. 41 Union St. (between North and Hanover Sts.) ☎ **617/227-2750.** Reservations recommended. Main courses $6.50–$13.95 at lunch, $8.95–$18.95 at dinner; lobster $21.95–$34.95. AE, CB, DC, DISC, MC, V. Sun–Thurs 11am–9:30pm, Fri–Sat 11am–10pm. Lunch served until 5pm Sun–Thurs, until 6pm Fri–Sat. Union Bar: 11am–3pm lunch, 3–11pm late-supper fare. Bar open until midnight. MBTA: Green Line to Government Center or Orange Line to Haymarket. NEW ENGLAND/SEAFOOD.

America's oldest restaurant in continuous service, the Union Oyster House opened in 1826, and the booths and oyster bar haven't moved since. At the crescent-shaped bar on the lower level of the cramped, low-ceilinged building, "where Daniel Webster drank many a toddy in his day," try the sampler, a mixed appetizer of about a dozen pieces each of oysters, clams, and scampi. The food is tasty, traditional New England fare. Oyster stew made with fresh milk and country butter makes a good beginning. Follow that with a broiled or grilled dish such as scrod or salmon, or perhaps seafood primavera, fried seafood, or a grilled veal chop. A complete shore dinner with chowder, steamers, broiled lobster, salad, corn, and dessert is an excellent introduction to local favorites. Low-calorie menu selections, introduced in 1994, are popular too. For dessert, try gingerbread with whipped cream. Ask to be seated at John F. Kennedy's favorite booth (number 18), which is marked with a plaque.

INEXPENSIVE

Zuma's Tex-Mex Café. 7 N. Market St., Faneuil Hall Marketplace. ☎ **617/367-9114.** Main courses $4.97–$13.99. AE, CB, DC, DISC, MC, V. Mon–Thurs 11:30am–11pm, Fri–Sat 11:30am–midnight, Sun noon–10pm. MBTA: Green or Blue Line to Government Center, or Orange Line to Haymarket. TEX-MEX.

Because of its great location on the lower level of the North Market building at Faneuil Hall Marketplace, Zuma's could probably get away with serving so-so food and still draw enormous crowds. Happily, its southwestern cuisine is excellent, with guacamole and salsa cruda made from scratch, and tortilla chips cut and fried throughout the day right in the dining room. This casual, friendly spot is somewhat dark, spotted with neon and small lights in the ceiling. Portions are large, especially considering the low prices. An appetizer of calamari fried in a spicy batter is big enough for three, and the noisy fajitas constantly flying out of the kitchen are substantial and delectable. The firecrackers, or fried jalapeños stuffed with shrimp and cheese, are marked with a skull on the menu and are not for the uninitiated. Tacos are just $1.97 each; the chimichangitas are also a bargain at $1.47. Owner Steve Immel boasts about the phenomenal key lime pie, the famous margaritas (including a neon version), and the most popular dish, enchiladas verdes. And you can order lunch to go.

DOWNTOWN CROSSING
VERY EXPENSIVE

Locke-Ober. 3 and 4 Winter Pl. ☎ **617/542-1340.** Reservations required. Main courses $8–$24.50 at lunch, $17–$40 at dinner. AE, DC, MC, V. Mon–Fri 11:30am–3pm; Fri 3–10pm, Sat 5:30–10:30pm, Sun 5:30–10pm. Closed Sundays in the summer. MBTA: Red or Orange Line to Downtown Crossing. AMERICAN.

"Locke's" is *the* traditional Boston restaurant, a favorite since 1875. Some Bostonians have the same lunch every day at the same table, and probably shudder when they see "lower fat specials" if they happen to look at a menu. In a tiny alley off the Winter Street pedestrian mall, this restaurant feels like a club, with carved paneling, stained-glass windows, crystal chandeliers, and silver buffet covers on the long, mirrored downstairs bar, which dates from 1880. The upstairs dining rooms are dark, elegant, and quiet. The food, once you get over the shock of seeing tofu on the menu in a place that looks like this, is magnificent, as is the service. Start with oysters (raw or Rockefeller) or the famous Jonah crabcakes, then immerse yourself in tradition—steak tartare, grilled salmon with horseradish sauce, Wiener schnitzel à la Holstein, lobster stew, and the most famous dish on the menu, lobster Savannah, for which the meat of a three-pound lobster is diced with pepper and mushrooms, bound with cheese-sherry sauce, stuffed into the shell, and baked. If your heart doesn't stop on the spot, you won't be hungry again for a long time. The dessert menu lists about two dozen items, and as you might expect, the chocolate mousse is a dish for the ages. Valet parking is available at dinner.

INEXPENSIVE

Fajitas & 'Ritas. 25 West St. (between Washington and Tremont Sts.). ☎ **617/426-1222.** Most dishes $8 and less. AE, DISC, MC, V. Mon–Sat 11:30am–9pm. MBTA: Red or Green Line to Park St. MEXICAN.

This entertaining storefront restaurant may not be the most authentic in town, but it's one of the most fun. You order by filling out a slip, checking off your choices of fillings and garnishes to go with your tacos, enchiladas, burritos, chimichangas, and, of course, fajitas. There's nothing exotic, just the usual beef, chicken, shrimp, beans, and so forth. A member of the somewhat harried staff relays your order to the kitchen and returns with huge portions of fresh food (this place is too busy for anything to be sitting around for very long). As the name indicates, margaritas, or 'ritas, are a house specialty, but this is closer to a family restaurant than a bar.

DIM SUM IN CHINATOWN

Many restaurants in Chinatown offer dim sum, the traditional midday meal featuring a wide variety of appetizer-style dishes, including dumplings filled with meats and vegetables; steamed buns filled with pork or bean paste; shrimp balls; spareribs; stewed chicken wings; and sweets such as coconut gelatin and sesame balls. Servers wheel carts laden with tempting snack-size morsels up to your table, and you order by pointing (unless you know Chinese). Your check is then stamped with the symbol of the dish, adding about $1 to $3 to your tab. Unless you're really ravenous or you decide to include à la carte dishes from the regular menu, the grand total won't be more than about $10 per person.

Dim sum varies from restaurant to restaurant and chef to chef; if something looks familiar, don't be surprised if it's different from what you're used to, and equally good. This is a great group activity, especially on weekends, when you'll see two and three generations of families sharing dishes and calling for more. Even picky children can usually find something they enjoy. If you don't like or can't eat pork and shrimp, be aware that many, but not all, dishes include one or the other.

Excellent choices include the **Golden Palace Restaurant** (14 Tyler St.; ☎ 617/ 423-4565) and **China Pearl** (9 Tyler St.; ☎ 617/426-4338). Although both specialize in Hong Kong–style food, the real reason to visit is for dim sum. Many people consider Golden Palace's the best dim sum in Boston, but this is an area where strong preferences develop quickly (maybe you'll have some of your own). Two other popular destinations are **Imperial Seafood Restaurant** (70 Beach St.; ☎ 617/426-8439) and **Dynasty Restaurant** (33 Edinboro St.; ☎ 617/350-7777).

AT THE PUBLIC GARDEN/BEACON HILL

✪ **Aujourd'hui.** In the Four Seasons Hotel, 200 Boylston St. ☎ 617/451-1392. Reservations recommended (imperative on holidays). Main courses $16.50–$19.50 at lunch, $29–$39 at dinner; Sun buffet brunch $39. AE, CB, DC, MC, V. Daily 6:30–10:30am; Mon–Fri 11:30am–2:30pm, Sun 11:30am–2:30pm (brunch); Mon–Sat 5:30–10:30pm, Sun 6–10:30pm. MBTA: Green Line to Arlington. INTERNATIONAL.

On the second floor of the city's premier luxury hotel, the most beautiful restaurant in town has floor-to-ceiling windows overlooking the Public Garden, but even if it were under a pup tent, the incredible service and food would make Aujourd'hui a hit. The executive chef, David Fritchey, uses regional products and the freshest ingredients available, and the wine list is one of the best in the country. The menu changes often. To start, you might try a perfectly balanced squash-and-apple soup or a huge salad of arugula and other greens so fresh they practically crackle. Entrees might include a juniper-roasted venison chop with a sweet potato, and turnip cake and cider-glazed chard; or grilled Atlantic salmon served with minted couscous and chicory salad. In addition, the crabcakes are among the best outside of Maryland. The dessert menu also changes, but might include a wonderful fruit tart or a decadent chocolate creation. A wonderful (to most) menu note asks that cellular phones not be used in the restaurant.

Biba Food Hall. 272 Boylston St. ☎ **617/426-7878.** Reservations recommended. Main courses $17–$34 at dinner; bar menu $3.50–$8.50. CB, DC, DISC, MC, V. Mon–Fri 11:30am–2pm, Sun 11:30am–2:30pm; Sun–Thurs 5:30–9:30pm, Fri–Sat 5:30–10:30pm. Bar menu offered until 2am. MBTA: Green Line to Arlington. ECLECTIC.

The mastermind behind Biba is Lydia Shire, a legend in culinary circles not just in Boston but in the United States. The menu here is well past the cutting edge, divided into categories that include "offal" (organ meats) and "legumina" (vegetables) as well as fish and meat. The restaurant, in the posh Heritage on the Garden complex across from the Public Garden, is decorated in bright geometric patterns based on Albanian kilim rug motifs. A grand spiral staircase with shiny red handrails leads from the bar (where you can have a light meal) to the second-floor dining room, which attracts a chic crowd, especially at dinner.

The food is as dynamic as the decor. Some of it is prepared in the brick wood-burning oven visible from the dining room or the tandoori oven used for roasting and baking. Everything is made on the premises, from bread and sausages to desserts. The menu is à la carte, changes regularly, and always includes the signature lobster pizza and steak au poivre. Sometimes those are the only dishes you'll recognize as they pass by, but exploring is half the fun. Try gray sole with baccala (salt cod) croquettes; beef carpaccio with warm crumbled Roquefort; or yam raviolis with sweetbreads dusted in white truffle flour. Desserts are luxurious; sticky toffee pudding comes with warm toffee sauce, and white chocolate cake with fresh berries is almost too rich.

Although Biba is hyped as a glamorous international bistro, there is no dress code (you can even come in shorts), and the price range is wide, so there is something on the menu for everyone, especially if you eat at the bar. Valet parking is available.

The Ritz-Carlton Dining Room. 15 Arlington St. ☎ **617/536-5700.** Reservations required. Jacket and tie required for men. Main courses $28–$43. Grand buffet (Sun) $46. AE, CB, DC, DISC, ER, JCB, MC, V. Sun–Thurs 5:30–10pm, Fri–Sat 5:30–11pm; Sat noon–2:30pm, Sun 10:45am–2:30pm (brunch). MBTA: Green Line to Arlington. FRENCH.

In proper blue-blooded Boston society, only one place will do when celebrating an occasion or a milestone like a graduation from Harvard Law School or the successful completion of a profitable corporate takeover: the magnificent second-floor restaurant of the elegant Ritz-Carlton, overlooking the Public Garden. Whether Sunday brunch or dinner under the crystal chandeliers with soft piano music playing in the background, a meal here is a memorable experience.

Less traditional dishes are available, but people come here for the French classics, such as rack of lamb with thyme, broiled sirloin steak in shallot sauce, and lobster "au whiskey," in a cream and bourbon sauce seasoned with tomatoes, thyme, and scallions. More than two dozen superb appetizers range from smoked north Atlantic salmon to lobster bisque with armagnac to beluga caviar with blinis. The wonderful desserts include chocolate and Grand Marnier soufflés and baked Alaska. Valet parking is available.

On Saturdays in the fall, winter, and spring, there's a series of Fashion Luncheons showcasing the designs of local designers and established boutiques.

BACK BAY
VERY EXPENSIVE

✪ **Ambrosia on Huntington.** 116 Huntington Ave. ☎ **617/247-2400.** Reservations recommended at dinner. Main courses $5–$12 at lunch, $16–$29 at dinner. AE, DISC, MC, V. Mon–Fri 11:30am–2:30pm; Mon–Thurs 5:30–10pm, Fri–Sat 5–11pm, Sun 5–9pm. MBTA: Orange Line to Back Bay or Green Line, E train to Prudential. FRENCH/ASIAN.

Felicitously named proprietors Tony and Dorene Ambrose (he's the chef) have turned the vacant ground floor of an office building into a dazzling room, where the dramatic architecture of the restaurant is matched only by the dramatic architecture of . . . the food. Every dish here is a feast for the eyes as well as the mouth and nose, with towering garnishes, accents of vegetables and pastry, and rich, unusual flavors that tie it all together. Starters are divided into exotic appetizers and shellfish, and simple salads. Peruvian purple potato spring roll in crispy paper with Cabernet truffle oil is a plump pocket of potato infused with winey flavor, and a green salad is served with a Champagne mustard-seed vinaigrette. An entree of Gulf Stream swordfish in sage Provençal broth with potato galette arrives already carved into five huge chunks, separated by upright fans of thinly sliced potato and resting comfortably on a mound of potatoes redolent with chives and garlic. A special pasta of shrimp in a light curry sauce on a bed of noodles is so pretty you just want to stare at it, but when you finally do taste it you'll be glad you did. There's an awful lot to look at inside, with contemporary art on the walls and, of course, the art on the plates, which provides more interesting scenery than the uninspiring view of a corner of the Prudential Center through the floor-to-ceiling windows. Service here, by teams rather than individuals, is excellent, and your water glass will never be empty. Valet parking is available.

Grill 23 & Bar. 161 Berkeley St. ☎ **617/542-2255.** Reservations recommended. Main courses $19–$30. AE, CB, DC, DISC, MC, V. Mon–Thurs 5:30–10:30pm, Fri–Sat 5:30–11pm, Sun 5:30–10pm. MBTA: Green Line to Arlington. AMERICAN.

In certain areas—delis, theater, late-night activity, sane drivers—Boston pales in comparison to New York. In the steakhouse category, Bostonians can point to Grill 23 and dare New Yorkers to top it. To be fair, Grill 23 is more than just a steakhouse. Slabs of beef and chops with all the trimmings are the stars of the show, but less aggressively carnivorous entrees attract equal attention from the kitchen and the diners. Steak au poivre and lamb chops are excellent examples of grilling done exactly right, crusty and juicy, so tender that your knife glides through the meat. Trout also arrives with a delectable crust of cornmeal and cumin, and the other grilled and roasted fish dishes rival those at any seafood restaurant. Side dishes, served à la carte, include huge plates of creamed spinach, home fries, and out-of-this-world garlic mashed potatoes, and could easily be entrees if your attention could be drawn away from the main dishes. Desserts show as little restraint as the meat offerings—try the deliriously good cappuccino cheesecake or flourless chocolate cake, or, if you insist on moderation, risk being called a wimp and request a dish of berries (not on the menu, but available if you ask).

On what was once the trading floor of the Salada Tea Building, Grill 23 is a wood-paneled, glass-walled, high-ceilinged room with a businesslike air. The service is exactly right for the setting, helpful but not familiar. *Two caveats:* Smoking is not only allowed but encouraged, as evinced by the humidor that makes the rounds of the dining room in the arms of a staff member. The ventilation is good, but you can smell smoke in your clothes and hair later. And the noise level grows louder in tiny increments as the evening progresses—you won't realize you're shouting until you're outside yelling about what a good time you had.

✪ **L'Espalier.** 30 Gloucester St. ☎ **617/262-3023.** Reservations required. Prix fixe dinner (4 courses) $62; vegetable dégustation menu (6 courses) $68; dégustation menu (7 courses) $78. AE, DISC, MC, V. Mon–Sat 6–10pm. MBTA: Green Line, B, C, or D train to Hynes/ICA. NEW ENGLAND/FRENCH.

Dinner at L'Espalier is a unique experience, certainly in Boston and perhaps anywhere. It's very much like eating at the home of a dear friend who has only your complete pleasure in mind . . . and happens to have a dozen highly trained helpers in the kitchen. Owners Frank and Catherine McClelland preside over the three dining rooms, on the second floor of an 1876 townhouse. Reached by a spiral mahogany staircase, the space is formal yet inviting, with fireplaces, ornately carved moldings, and bay windows. Service is beyond excellent, in that eerie realm where it seems possible that the waiter just read your mind.

The quality of the food, if anything, exceeds the trappings. Chef Frank McClelland has supervised the evolution of the restaurant from its original *nouvelle cuisine* identity into a regularly changing adventure, an exploration of the freshest and most interesting ingredients available. The breads, sorbets, ice creams, and desserts (many adapted from the family's heirloom cookbooks) are made on the premises. The prix fixe menu includes an *amuse geulle,* first course, main course, and dessert. There are five to seven choices in each category, always including a caviar selection (for an additional charge), hot or cold soup, fish, lamb, veal, beef, or venison. Flavors explode in your mouth. An appetizer of chimney-roasted Maine lobster, garnished with the shell, arrives standing in a pool of lemongrass, carrot juice, and star anise broth, accented with chickpea–sweet garlic puree. The salad offered as a first course sounds almost too trendy, with greens, chanterelles, apples, grilled radicchio, and Hubbardston blue goat cheese, but something this good should be more of a trend-setter. A main course of pan-roasted duck breast in fava bean crust with black quinoa and confit duck jambon and black cherry sauce is strong-flavored and savory; salmon in a sesame crust over noodles in a ginger-and-sesame broth is equally impressive. Desserts are alarmingly good—even if you have one of the superb soufflés, which are ordered with dinner, ask to see the tray.

The dégustation menus, both vegetarian and non, are available to entire tables only. The vintner's tasting of wines selected to go along with each course adds $45 to the cost of the regular dégustation menu. One course that's also available à la carte is the celebrated cheese tray (the Grand Fromage, with two local cheeses). The wine cellar is extensive, and wines can be ordered by the glass or bottle. Valet parking is available.

EXPENSIVE

✪ **Legal Sea Foods.** 800 Boylston St., in the Prudential Center. ☎ **617/266-6800.** Reservations recommended at lunch. Main courses $5.95–$12.95 at lunch, $13.95–$23.95 at dinner. AE, CB, DC, DISC, MC, V. Mon–Thurs 11am–10pm, Fri–Sat 11am–11pm, Sun noon–10pm. MBTA: Green Line, B, C, or D train to Hynes/ICA, or E train to Prudential. SEAFOOD.

The food at Legal Sea Foods ("Legal's," in Bostonian parlance) isn't the fanciest or the cheapest or the trendiest. What it is is the freshest, and management's commitment to that policy has produced a thriving chain. The family-owned business began as a small fish market in Cambridge in 1950 and opened its first restaurant in 1968. It has an international reputation for serving only top-quality fish and shellfish—broiled, baked, stir-fried, grilled, fried, steamed, and in casserole. The menu includes regular selections—scrod, haddock, bluefish, salmon, shrimp, calamari, and lobster, among others—plus whatever looked good at the market that morning, and it's all splendid. The clam chowder is a winner, and the fish chowder has its own appeal. Or start with creamy, salty smoked bluefish pâté. Entrees run the gamut from plain grilled fish to seafood fra'diavolo on fresh linguine. The seafood casserole—shrimp, scallops, whitefish, and lobster meat in a cream or butter sauce, topped with cheese—is sinfully good, as is salmon baked in parchment with vegetables and white wine.

The Prudential Center branch is suggested because it takes reservations (only at lunch), a deviation from a long tradition. There are also branches at the Boston Park Plaza Hotel & Towers (35 Columbus Ave.; ☎ 617/426-4444), Copley Place

(100 Huntington Ave.; ☎ **617/266-7775**), Kendall Square (5 Cambridge Center; ☎ **617/864-3400**), and eight other locations with the blue-and-white-checked decor and menu—for now. In 1996, legendary New England chef Jasper White came on board as executive chef. White, the person credited with revolutionizing the concept of both the hotel restaurant and the seafood restaurant (he owned and ran the renowned Jasper's restaurant, on the waterfront, until it closed in 1995), is expected to spruce up the menu and individualize the restaurants.

Top of the Hub. 800 Boylston St., Prudential Center. ☎ **617/536-1775.** Reservations recommended. Jacket advised for men. Main courses $7–$16 at lunch, $16–$29 at dinner. Menu dégustation $65 per person (2-person minimum). Sun brunch $29 adults, $14 children. AE, DC, DISC, MC, V. Mon–Fri 11:30am–2pm, Sat noon–3pm, Sun 11am–2:30pm (brunch); Sun–Thurs 5:30–10pm, Fri–Sat 5:30–11pm. MBTA: Green Line, B, C, or D train to Hynes/ICA, or E train to Prudential. CONTEMPORARY AMERICAN.

For many years, the answer to the question "How's the food at Top of the Hub?" was, "The view is spectacular." Since a complete overhaul of the space and the menu in 1995, the cuisine has been improved so dramatically that even if it's not quite a match for the 52nd-story panorama outside, you probably won't notice. Check the weather forecast and plan to eat here when it's clear out and you'll be able to see as much of Boston and the suburbs as is possible through the three glass-walled sides of the restaurant and lounge. At night the spectacle below is especially lovely. Consider coming before sunset and lingering over your meal until dark—it's the best of both worlds.

Executive chef Dean Moore emphasizes seafood and grilling, tastes that meet in the entree of north Atlantic sea scallops grilled and served with polenta, seasonal vegetables, and citrus. Lemon and garlic roasted chicken is another good choice at dinner. Lunch offerings include four pizzas and half a dozen tasty sandwiches served with sweet-potato fries. At either meal, the clam chowder is a standout, light and tasty, with more broth than cream. Salads are large and varied, but if you don't like your vegetables drowning in dressing, ask for it on the side.

Reduced parking rates are available in the Prudential Center garage after 4pm weekdays and all day on Saturday and Sunday. When you make your reservation, ask for a table by the window.

MODERATE

Bangkok Cuisine. 177A Massachusetts Ave. ☎ **617/262-5377.** Reservations not accepted. Main courses $4.75–$6.50 at lunch, $8–$13.50 at dinner. AE, DISC, MC, V. Mon–Sat 11:30am–3pm; Mon–Thurs 5–10:30pm, Fri 5–11pm, Sat 3–11pm, Sun 4–10pm. MBTA: Green Line, B, C, or D train to Hynes/ICA. THAI.

Bangkok Cuisine, opened in 1979, was the first Thai restaurant in Boston. It has set (and maintained) high standards for the many others that followed. The dishes run the gamut from excellent chicken and basil to all sorts of curry offerings, pan-fried or deep-fried whole fish, and hot and sour salads. The green curry in coconut milk and vegetables prepared with strong green Thai chili pepper are the most incendiary. You can order nonspicy food and, of course, pad Thai, the famous noodle dish. A rice plate special is served at lunch. The iced coffee and iced tea served Thai-style with sweetened condensed milk might be all the dessert you need, but there's also excellent homemade ice cream.

INEXPENSIVE

☉ Café Jaffa. 48 Gloucester St. ☎ **617/536-0230.** Reservations not accepted. Main courses $3–$8.75. AE, MC, V. Mon–Thurs 11am–10:30pm, Fri–Sat 11am–11pm, Sun 1–10pm. MBTA: Green Line, B, C, or D train to Hynes/ICA. MIDDLE EASTERN.

A long, narrow brick room with a glass front, Café Jaffa looks more like a snazzy pizza place than the wonderful Middle Eastern restaurant it is. Young people flock here, drawn by the low prices, excellent quality, and large portions of food, which includes burgers and steak tips as well as traditional Middle Eastern offerings such as falafel, baba ghanoush, and hummus. Lamb, beef, and chicken kebabs come with Greek salad and pita bread. If the desserts are fresh, try the baklava. There is a short list of beer and wine and (somewhat incongruously) many fancy coffee offerings.

CHARLESTOWN

✪ **Olives.** 10 City Sq., Charlestown. ☎ **617/242-1999.** Reservations accepted only for parties of 6 or more. Main courses $15.95–$30. AE, DC, MC, V. Tues–Fri 5:30–10pm, Sat 5–10:30pm. MBTA: Orange or Green Line to North Station; 10-minute walk. ECLECTIC.

This small, informal bistro near the Charlestown Navy Yard is one of the hottest spots in town. Patrons line up shortly after 5pm to get a table—you might be better off just making five friends and calling for a reservation. If you don't get there by 5:45, expect to wait at least an hour (at the bar if there's room) until a table opens. Once you're seated, you'll find many of the tables small and crowded, the service uneven, the ravenous customers festive, and the noise level high. The open kitchen in the rear of the restaurant, with a rotisserie and a huge brick oven, adds to the din.

Happily, the food is worth the aggravation. Todd English, chef and co-owner with his wife, Olivia, is a culinary genius. The menu changes regularly and always includes "Olives Classics," one of which is a meltingly delicious tart of olives, caramelized onions, and anchovies. Ginger spinach salad dressed with tahini arrives surrounded by shredded carrots with orange and cumin vinaigrette, a complex combination that works perfectly. Another Olives Classic, spit-roasted chicken flavored with herbs and garlic, oozes succulent juices into the old-fashioned mashed potatoes. Braised lamb shank with a sherry-and-olive sauce is so tender it falls off the bone, and the sweet lady celebrating her birthday at the next table (in other words, practically sitting with us) spoke highly of the Cuban steak. For dessert, when you order your entree you'll be asked if you want falling chocolate cake with raspberry sauce and vanilla ice cream. Say yes.

THE SOUTH END
VERY EXPENSIVE

Hamersley's Bistro. 553 Tremont St. ☎ **617/423-2700.** Reservations recommended. Main courses $18.50–$27. Menu dégustation varies. AE, DISC, MC, V. Mon–Fri 6–10pm, Sat 5:30–10pm, Sun 5:30–9:30pm. MBTA: Orange Line to Back Bay. ECLECTIC.

This is the place that made the South End a compass point on Boston's culinary map. The husband-and-wife team of Gordon and Fiona Hamersley presides over a long, narrow dining room decorated in cool yellow with lots of soft surfaces that absorb sound, so you can see but not hear what's going on at the tables around you. That means you'll have to quiz your server about the delicious-looking dish that just passed by—perhaps a marvelous appetizer of potato galette, smoked salmon, crème fraîche, and three caviars, or a celery root, apple, and beet salad with walnuts and mustard sauce. The menu changes seasonally and offers about a dozen carefully considered entrees (always including vegetarian dishes) noted for their emphasis on taste and texture. The signature roast chicken is flavored with garlic, lemon, and parsley and served with roast potato, roast onions, and whole cloves of sweet baked garlic. Oriental salmon roulade stuffed with jasmine rice and baby bok choy is wonderful, and grilled filet of beef is served with garlic mashed potatoes and a delectable red wine sauce. The wine list is excellent. There is valet parking.

✪ **Icarus.** 3 Appleton St. ☎ **617/426-1790.** Reservations recommended. Main courses $19–$28. Sun brunch main courses $5–$12.50. AE, CB, DC, MC, V. Sun–Thurs 6–10pm, Fri 6–11pm, Sat 5:30–11pm. Sun 11am–3pm (brunch). MBTA: Green Line to Arlington or Orange Line to Back Bay. ECLECTIC.

Every element that goes into a great dining experience is present at this subterranean restaurant, which manages to be both spacious and cozy. The upper level of the dining room overlooks the main floor, and the marble accents and dark wood trim lend an elegant air. Chef Chris Douglass, also an owner, prepares choice local seafoods, poultry, meats, and produce in a combination of styles to create imaginative menus that seem more like alchemy than cooking. The menu changes regularly—you might start with a salad of baked goat cheese, beets, endive, and lemon vinaigrette, or the daily "pasta whim." Move on to cod encased in a shredded potato cake and floating in grass-green herbal broth, or lamb shank served with lamb tenderloin and roast garlic whipped potatoes so good you'll want to ask for a plate of them. Don't—save room for one of the unbelievable desserts. Chocolate coconut cake with toasted coconut ice cream and cherry rum sauce was pronounced a favorite and instantly dethroned (in the estimation of an unregenerate chocoholic) by a trio of fruit sorbets. Valet parking is available.

MODERATE

Ⓢ **Bob the Chef's.** 604 Columbus Ave. ☎ **617/536-6204.** Breakfast $2.50–$7.50; dinners $7.50–$10.50; sandwiches $3–$6.50. AE, DC, MC, V. Mon–Thurs 11am–10pm, Fri–Sat 8am–11pm, Sun 8am–10pm. MBTA: Orange Line to Massachusetts Ave. SOUTHERN.

Where the South End meets Roxbury, Bostonians of every color meet for gargantuan portions of authentic soul food at this diner-style eatery. Perch at the Formica counter or take a booth or table and dig into "glorifried" chicken, alone or with barbecued ribs; pork chops; liver and onions; or "soul fish" (two whole pan-fried porgies). Dinners come with a tasty corn muffin and your choice of two delectable side dishes—black-eyed peas, macaroni and cheese, collard greens, rice with gravy or butter, and sweet potatoes—that could easily be a meal in themselves. If you're having trouble deciding, the warm-spirited staff will make a suggestion (and maybe call you "honey"). The vegetable plate is your choice of three vegetables and a corn muffin, and most of the main dishes are available in sandwich form. Whether it's a case of every little bit helps or closing the barn door after the horse is out, the frying medium has been changed from lard to vegetable oil, and everywhere you'd expect bacon for flavoring, as in collard greens and black-eyed peas, smoked turkey is used instead. Take a break and a deep breath and order dessert. The sweet-potato pie will ruin pumpkin pie for you from the moment you taste it.

This neighborhood is a parking nightmare, and after dark it can get a little scary. Come in a group, in a cab, or both, and make sure you're ravenous.

BROOKLINE & ENVIRONS

The Elephant Walk. 900 Beacon St., Boston. ☎ **617/247-1500.** Reservations recommended at dinner Sun–Thurs, not accepted Fri–Sat. Main courses $5.95–$18.50 at lunch, $9.50–$18.50 at dinner. AE, DISC, MC, V. Mon–Sat 11:30am–2:30pm; Mon–Thurs 5–10pm, Fri 5–11pm, Sat 4:30–11pm, Sun 4:30–10pm. MBTA: Green Line, C train to St. Mary's St. FRENCH/CAMBODIAN.

France meets Cambodia on the menu at the Elephant Walk, located four blocks from Kenmore Square on the Boston-Brookline border and decorated with lots of little pachyderms. This madly popular spot has a two-part menu (French on one side, Cambodian on the other), but the boundary seems quite porous. Many of the Cambodian dishes have part-French names, such as poulet phochani (chicken and green

⊕ Family-Friendly Restaurants

The **Bertucci's** chain of pizzerias appeals to children and adults equally, with wood-fired brick ovens that are visible from many tables, great rolls made from pizza dough, and pizza and pastas that range from basic to sophisticated. There are convenient branches in Faneuil Hall Marketplace (☎ 617/227-7889) and Harvard Square (21 Brattle St., Cambridge; ☎ 617/864-4748).

The **Bristol Lounge,** in the Four Seasons Hotel (200 Boylston St.; ☎ 617/351-2053), has a kids' menu featuring appetizers, plain main courses, desserts, and beverages. High chairs are available, the staff is unflappable and accommodating, and sticker fun books are available.

The **Ground Round** chain of suburban family restaurants has a branch at the Prudential Center (800 Boylston St.; ☎ 617/247-0500). There's free popcorn on the table, cartoons on a wall screen, video games, and crayons. On special days kids pay a penny a pound for their entree.

TGI Friday's (26 Exeter St., at Newbury St.; ☎ 617/266-9040) made its reputation by catering to singles, and all that pairing off apparently has led to children, who are courted as well. Available all day, the kids' package includes balloons and surprises wrapped in the chain's signature red and white stripes. Crayons, a coloring book, peanut butter, and crackers are included.

beans in a flavorful coconut milk–galangal sauce) and curry de crevettes (shrimp curry with picture-perfect vegetables). The Asian influence is evident on the French side, where you'll find pan-seared duck breast and leg confit served with scallion raviolis, and pan-seared tuna served over red and green chile cream sauces. There's a "challenging flavors" section on the Cambodian menu if you're feeling bold, and many dishes are available with tofu substituted for animal protein. Members of the pleasant waitstaff will help out if you need guidance. Ask to be seated in the plant-filled front room, which is less noisy than the main dining room and has a view of the street.

The original Elephant Walk is at 70 Union Sq., Somerville (☎ 617/623-9939). It keeps the same hours but is harder to get to than the Boston location, even from most places in Cambridge.

✪ **Providence.** 1223 Beacon St. ☎ **617/232-0300.** Reservations recommended. Main courses $10.95–$24.95. AE, DC, MC, V. Tues–Thurs 5:30–10pm, Fri–Sat 5:30–11pm, Sun 5–9:30pm. MBTA: Green Line, C train to St. Paul St. ECLECTIC.

Providence is not the city in Rhode Island, although the name can touch off a nice "who's on first"–type discussion. A glance around seems to reveal a typical American restaurant, until you look a little closer. There's a wood-paneled bar, but the light fixtures over it look like metal spaghetti. You're in a formal room, with columns and intricate moldings, but the warm tones of the paint on everything lend a casual air. Turning to the food, there are a lot of grilled meats and fish, but also a lot of vegetarian offerings. The courteous, helpful staff can help you navigate the list of specials, which is almost as long as the menu. It might include an appetizer of fresh fried Ipswich clams—standard stuff, until you taste the garlic-and-chipotle mayonnaise dribbled on top. The flatbread with eggplant puree and olives could be from any menu with Middle Eastern influences, but the flatbread is made of chickpeas, the eggplant exudes cardamom, and there's goat cheese on the plate. A main dish of tagliatelle pasta with prosciutto looks ordinary, but it's tossed with radicchio, smoked Maine shrimp, balsamic vinegar, and butter. There's even pastrami on the menu . . . veal pastrami, cured and smoked at the restaurant and served with sweet potato dumplings. And desserts are spectacular—for the signature warm chocolate fondant cake, it might even be worth going to Rhode Island. Chef Paul O'Connell is a wizard with flavors, combining ingredients in such a way that everything brings out the best in everything else. Including the stuffed, contented diners.

5 Seeing the Sights

THE FREEDOM TRAIL

Faced with flat attendance and competition from attractions that offer more innovative exhibits, in 1996 the city of Boston announced a massive overhaul of the Freedom Trail. The trail, which links 16 historical sights with a three-mile red line on the sidewalk first painted in 1958, may be starting to change by the time you visit, but the actual plots of land aren't going anywhere. Some of the major Freedom Trail sights are described here. For information on the others, visit the Visitor Center near the Park Street "T" stop.

If you continue along the trail into the North End, you'll come to the **Paul Revere House** (19 North Sq.; ☎ 617/523-2338). One of the most pleasant stops on the Freedom Trail, it presents history on a human scale. Revere set out for Lexington from here on the evening of April 18, 1775, a feat immortalized in Henry Wadsworth Longfellow's poem "Paul Revere's Ride" (*Listen my children and you shall hear / Of the midnight ride of Paul Revere . . .*). The house was built around 1680 (it's the oldest in downtown Boston), purchased by Revere in 1770, and put to a number of uses before being turned into a museum in the early 20th century. The $2^1/2$-story brown wood structure is filled with 17th- and 18th-century furnishings and artifacts, neatly arranged and identified. Many of them are the famous Revere silver, considered some of the finest anywhere. You can rush through the self-guided tour or linger over the objects that particularly interest you.

The Paul Revere House is open from November through April 14 from 9:30am to 4:15pm, and from April 15 through October from 9:30am to 5:15pm; it's closed Mondays in January, February, and March, as well as Thanksgiving, Christmas, and New Year's Day. Admission is $2.50 for adults, $2 for seniors and students, and $1 for children 5 to 17.

Across the cobblestone courtyard from Revere's house is the home of his Hichborn cousins, the **Pierce-Hichborn House.** This 1711 Georgian-style home is a rare example of 18th-century middle-class architecture. It's suitably furnished and shown only by guided tour. Call the Paul Revere House for schedules.

Paul Revere knew it was time to ride out because he saw a signal, a pair of lanterns in the steeple of the **Old North Church** (193 Salem St.; ☎ 617/523-6676). Formally known as Christ Church, this is the oldest church in Boston standing on its original site, where it has been since 1723. The building itself is in the style of Sir Christopher Wren, and the original steeple was the one where sexton Robert Newman hung two lanterns on the night of April 18, 1775, to indicate to Paul Revere that British troops were setting out for Lexington and Concord in boats across the Charles River, not on foot ("One if by land, two if by sea"). The impressive 175-foot "new" steeple (16 feet shorter than the original) was designed by the ubiquitous Charles Bulfinch after the original fell in a hurricane in 1804. The spire, long a reference point for sailors, appears on navigational charts to this day. The Revere family attended this church (their plaque is on Pew 54); famous visitors have included Presidents James Monroe, Theodore Roosevelt, Franklin D. Roosevelt, and Gerald R. Ford, and Her Majesty Queen Elizabeth II. There are markers and plaques throughout; note the bust of George Washington, the first memorial to the first president. The gardens on the north side of the church (dotted with more plaques) are open to the public. The Old North Church is open daily 9am to 5pm; Sunday services (Episcopal) are at 9 and 11am and 4pm. The quirky gift shop, in a former chapel, is open daily from 9am to 5pm, and proceeds go to support the church. Donations are appreciated.

The final stops on the Freedom Trail are in Charlestown. The **USS** *Constitution,* or *"Old Ironsides,"* one of the U.S. Navy's six original frigates, never lost a battle. It was constructed in the North End from 1794 to 1797 at a cost of $302,718 using bolts, spikes, and other fittings from Paul Revere's foundry. As the new nation made its naval and military reputation, the *Constitution* played a key role, battling French privateers and Barbary pirates, repelling the British fleet during the War of 1812, participating in 40 engagements, and capturing 20 vessels. It earned its nickname during an engagement on August 19, 1812, with the French warship HMS *Guerriere,* whose shots bounced off its thick oak hull as if it were iron. Retired from combat in 1815, it was rescued from destruction when Oliver Wendell Holmes's poem "Old Ironsides" launched a preservation movement in 1830.

It was completely overhauled in 1995 to 1996 in preparation for its bicentennial. The *Constitution* is towed into the harbor by tugs every Fourth of July and turned around to ensure that it weathers evenly. In honor of its 200th birthday in 1997, it is expected to be under sail for the first time since 1881 for the annual turnaround cruise.

Free tours (☎ 617/242-5670) are given by active-duty sailors in 1812 dress uniforms daily from 9:30am to 3:50pm.

The **USS** *Constitution* **Museum** (☎ 617/426-1812), just inland from the vessel, has several participatory exhibits that allow visitors to hoist a flag, fire a cannon, and learn more about the ship. The museum is open daily, June 1 to Labor Day 9am to 6pm; March to May and the day after Labor Day through November 10am to 5pm; December to February 10am to 3pm, and closed Thanksgiving, Christmas, and New Year's Day. Admission is $4 for adults, $3 for seniors, $2 for children 6 to 16, and free for children 5 and under. Discounted combination tickets are available if you plan to visit the Old State House on the same day.

Many people, especially those traveling with fidgety children, opt to skip the final stop on the Freedom Trail. If your party's not too close to the breaking point, it's an interesting excursion. Leave the Navy Yard, cross Chelsea Street, and climb the hill, following the Freedom Trail along Tremont Street. Your guidepost is also your destination, the **Bunker Hill Monument** (☎ 617/242-5644), a 221-foot granite obelisk built in honor of the men who died in the Battle of Bunker Hill on June 17, 1775. The colonists lost the battle, but nearly half of the British troops were killed or wounded, a circumstance that contributed to the decision to abandon Boston nine months later. The Marquis de Lafayette, the celebrated hero of both the American and French Revolutions, helped lay the monument's cornerstone in 1825. The top is at the end of a flight of 295 stairs—a long climb for a decent view that prominently features I-93.

In the lodge at the base of the monument there are dioramas and exhibits. It's staffed by National Park Service rangers and open from 9am to 5pm. The monument is open daily from 9am to 4:30pm. Admission is free.

Boston Attractions

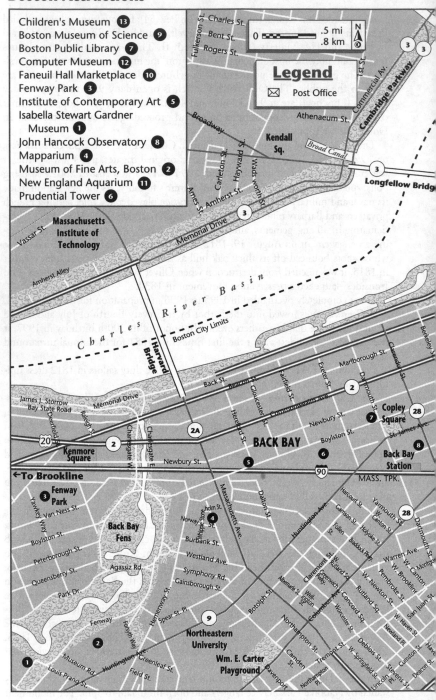

Children's Museum ⓭
Boston Museum of Science ⑨
Boston Public Library ⑦
Computer Museum ⑫
Faneuil Hall Marketplace ⑩
Fenway Park ❸
Institute of Contemporary Art ❺
Isabella Stewart Gardner Museum ❶
John Hancock Observatory ❽
Mapparium ❹
Museum of Fine Arts, Boston ❷
New England Aquarium ⑪
Prudential Tower ❻

0 [scale] .5 mi / .8 km   N

Legend
⊠ Post Office

Charles St.
Fulkerson St.
Bent St.
Rogers St.
1st St.
Commercial Av.
Cambridge Parkway
Athenaeum St.
Broadway
Kendall Sq.
Broad Canal
Longfellow Bridge
Carleton St.
Hayward St.
Wadsworth St.
Ames St.
Amherst St.
Memorial Drive
❸
Massachusetts Institute of Technology
Vassar St.
Amherst Alley

Charles River Basin

Boston City Limits
Harvard Bridge

James J. Storrow Bay State Road
Memorial Drive
Deerfield St.
Raleigh St.
Charlesgate W.
Charlesgate E.
20
❷
Kenmore Square
Back St.
Beacon St.
Fairfield St.
Gloucester St.
Exeter St.
Dartmouth St.
Clarendon St.
Berkeley St.
Marlborough St.
❷
Commonwealth Ave.
Newbury St.
⑦ Copley Square
28
2A
BACK BAY
Boylston St.
St. James Ave.
❽
Back Bay Station
Newbury St.
❺
❻
90
MASS. TPK.
←To Brookline
❸ Fenway Park
Yawkey Way
Van Ness St.
Boylston St.
Peterborough St.
Queensberry St.
Park Dr.
Back Bay Fens
Agassiz Rd.
Norway St.
Stoneholm St.
St. Germain St.
Burbank St.
Westland Ave.
Symphony Rd.
Gainsborough St.
❹
Massachusetts Ave.
Dalton St.
Harcourt St.
Huntington Ave.
Garrison St.
Cumberland St.
W. Canton St.
Holyoke St.
Follen St.
Braddock Pkwy.
Albemarle St.
Wellington St.
Greenwich St.
Rutland Sq.
Concord Sq.
Columbus Ave.
Worcester Sq.
28
Dartmouth St.
Warren Ave.
W. Canton
W. Brookline
Pembroke St.
W. Newton St.
Rutland Sq.
San Juan St.
W. Haven St.
Newland Pl.
❾
Northeastern University
Wm. E. Carter Playground
Hemenway St.
Forsyth Way
Spear St. Pl.
Fenway
Museum Rd.
Louis Prang St.
Huntington Ave.
Greenleaf St.
Field St.
Botolph St.
Camden St.
Davenport
Northampton St.
Tremont St.
W. Springfield St.
W. Dedham St.
Northampton Pl.
Deblois St.
Stevens St.
Lincoln St.
Cunston St.
Deacon St.
❷
❶

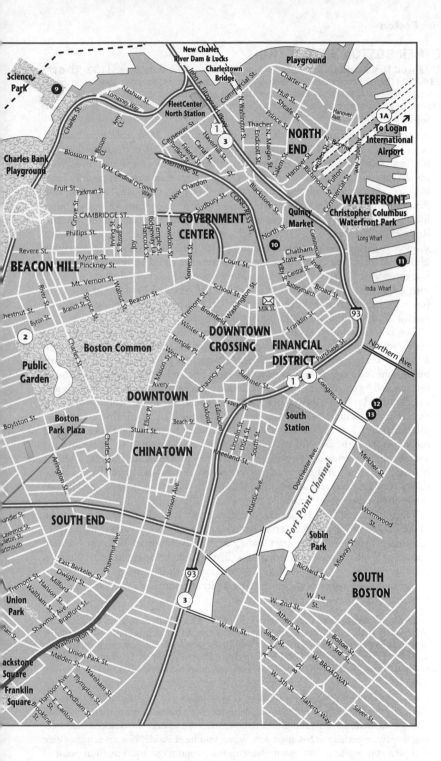

OTHER BOSTON ATTRACTIONS

✪ Faneuil Hall Marketplace. Between North, Congress, and State Sts. and I-93. ☎ 617/338-2323. Marketplace Mon–Sat 10am–9pm, Sun noon–6pm; Colonnade food court opens earlier; some restaurants open early for Sun brunch and remain open until 2am daily. MBTA: Orange Line or Blue Line to State St., Orange Line or Green Line to Haymarket, or Green Line to Government Center.

It's impossible to overestimate the effect of Faneuil Hall Marketplace on Boston's economy and reputation. A daring idea when it opened in 1976, the festival market has been widely imitated, but to good effect since each new complex of shops, food stands, restaurants, bars, and public spaces in urban centers around the country tends to reflect the city in which it is situated. Faneuil Hall Marketplace, brimming with Boston flavor and regional goods and souvenirs, is no exception. The marketplace includes five buildings—the central three-building complex is listed in the National Register of Historic Places—set on brick and stone plazas that teem with crowds shopping, eating, performing, watching performers, and just people-watching. Quincy Market itself (you'll hear the whole complex called by that name as well) is a three-level Greek revival–style building reopened after renovations turned it into a festival market on August 26, 1976, 150 years of hard use after Mayor Josiah Quincy opened the original market. The South Market Building opened on August 26, 1977, and the North Market Building in 1978 on, yes, August 26.

The central corridor of Quincy Market, known as the Colonnade, is the food court, where you can find anything from a bagel to a full Greek dinner, a fruit smoothie to a hunk of fudge. On either side, under the glass canopies, are pushcarts bearing the full range of crafts created by New England artisans and hokey souvenirs hawked by enterprising merchants. In the plaza between the South Canopy and the South Market Building is a visitor information kiosk, and throughout the complex, including the ground floor of Faneuil Hall, you'll find an enticing mix of chain stores and unique shops. On summer evenings the tables that spill out-doors from the bars fill with people unwinding, listening to or performing karaoke, or just enjoying the passing scene. One constant since the year after the market opened—after the *original* market opened, that is—is Durgin-Park, a traditional New England restaurant with traditionally crabby waitresses (see "Dining" earlier in this chapter for details).

Faneuil Hall itself sometimes gets overlooked, but it's well worth a visit. Known as the "Cradle of Liberty" for its role as a center of inspirational (some might say inflammatory) speeches in the years leading to the Revolutionary War, the building opened in 1742 and was expanded using a Charles Bulfinch design in 1805. National Park Service rangers give free 20-minute talks every half-hour from 9am to 5pm in the second-floor auditorium, which, after a recent refurbishment, is now in mint condition.

New England Aquarium. Central Wharf. ☎ 617/973-5200. Admission $8.75 adults, $4.75 children 3–11, $7.75 seniors. Children under 3 free. $1 off all fees Thurs 4–7:30pm. July 1–Labor Day Mon–Tues and Fri 9am–6pm, Wed–Thurs 9am–8pm, Sat–Sun and holidays 9am–7pm. Early Sept–June Mon–Wed and Fri 9am–5pm, Thurs 9am–8pm, Sat–Sun and holidays 9am–6pm. Closed Thanksgiving, Christmas, and until noon New Year's Day. MBTA: Blue Line to Aquarium.

Frolicking seals greet you from outdoor enclosures as you approach the Aquarium, the perfect welcome to an entertaining complex that's home to more than 7,000 fish and aquatic mammals. You might be tempted to settle in near the outdoor (and free) seal display, especially at feeding time. When you head inside, buy an exhibit guide and plan your route as you commune with the penguin colony. The focal point of

On Top of the World

Two of the city's top attractions are literally *top* attractions. From hundreds of feet in the air, you'll get an entirely different perspective on Boston.

The **John Hancock Observatory** (200 Clarendon St.; ☎ 617/572-6429) would be a good introduction to Boston even if it didn't have a sensational 60th-floor view. The multimedia exhibits include a multimedia show that chronicles the events leading to the Revolutionary War and demonstrates how Boston's land mass has changed. You'll see paintings, drawings, and photos and hear narration in a round room with a relief map of the Boston area on the floor. There's an illustrated time line, an interactive computer quiz about the city, and a display that allows you to ask for travel directions (by foot, car, and public transportation) to various points of interest. Telescopes and binoculars allow a close-up look at the faraway ground. Admission is $4.25 for adults and $3.25 for seniors and children ages 5 to 15. Hours are 9am to 11pm Monday through Saturday, 10am to 11pm on Sunday (May to October), and noon to 11pm on Sunday from November to April. The ticket office closes at 10pm. The nearest "T" stops are Copley on the Green Line (B, C, and D trains) and Back Bay on the Orange Line and the Commuter Rail.

The **Prudential Center Skywalk,** on the 50th floor of the Prudential Tower (800 Boylston St.; ☎ 617/236-3318), offers the only 360-degree view of Boston and beyond. From the enclosed observation deck you can see for miles, even (when it's clear) as far as the mountaintops of southern New Hampshire in the north or the beaches of Cape Cod to the south. Hours are 10am to 10pm daily. Admission is $4 for adults and $3 for seniors and children ages 5 to 15. On the 52nd floor the view can be enjoyed with food and drink at the Top of the Hub restaurant and lounge. The nearest "T" stops are Copley on the Green Line and Back Bay on the Orange Line and the commuter rail.

the main building is the aptly named Giant Ocean Tank. You'll climb four stories on a spiral ramp that encircles the cylindrical glass tank, which contains 187,000 gallons of saltwater, a replica of a Caribbean coral reef, and a conglomeration of sea creatures who seem to coexist amazingly well. Part of the reason for the prevailing calm may be that the sharks are fed five times a day by scuba divers who bring the food right to them. Other exhibits show off freshwater specimens, denizens of the Amazon, and jellyfish, and at the "Edge of the Sea" exhibit, you're encouraged to touch the starfish, sea urchins, and horseshoe crabs in the tide pool. A new installation, "Ponds: The Earth's Eyes," introduces you to the ecosystems and their resident reptiles, fish, and turtles. Be sure to leave time for a show at the floating marine mammal pavilion, "Discovery," where sea lions perform every 90 minutes throughout the day.

Note: The aquarium sponsors whale-watching expeditions (☎ 617/973-5281) daily from May through mid-October and on weekends in April and late October. You'll travel several miles out to sea to Stellwagen Bank, feeding ground for the whales as they migrate from Newfoundland to Provincetown. Tickets (cash only) are $24 for adults, $19 for seniors and college students, $17.50 for children age 12 to 18, and $16.50 for children age 3–11. Children must be 3 years old and at least 30 inches tall. Reservations are recommended and can be held with a MasterCard or Visa.

Mapparium. World Headquarters of the First Church of Christ, Scientist, 250 Massachusetts Ave. (at Huntington Ave.) ☎ **617/450-3790**. Free admission. Mon–Sat 10am–4pm. Mother Church Sun 11:15am–2pm, Mon–Sat 10am–4pm. Bible exhibit Sun 11:15am–2pm, Wed–Sat 10am–4pm. Closed major holidays. MBTA: Green Line or E train to Symphony, or Orange Line to Massachusetts Ave.

For a real insider's view of the world, step . . . inside. This unique hollow globe 30 feet across is a work of both art and history. The 608 stained-glass panels are connected by a bronze framework and surrounded by electric lights, and because sound bounces off the nonporous surfaces, the acoustics are as unusual as the aesthetics. As you cross the glass bridge just south of the equator, you'll see the political divisions of the world from 1932–35, when the globe was constructed.

Also in the 14-acre Christian Science complex are the Mother Church and the Bible exhibit "A Light Unto My Path." The Romanesque church, opened in 1894, is notable for its stained-glass windows; the domed Mother Church Extension, opened in 1906, is in Renaissance-Byzantine style and has one of the largest pipe organs in the world. Call for information on tours. The Bible exhibit includes a 30-minute film and slide program (shows every hour on the hour), an audiovisual time line, and a sculptured map where 12 journeys of figures from the Bible are illustrated and narrated.

Boston Public Library. 666 Boylston St., at Copley Sq. ☎ **617/536-5400**. Free admission. Mon–Thurs 9am–9pm, Fri–Sat 9am–5pm. Sun (Oct–May only) 1–5pm. Closed Sun June–Sept and legal holidays. MBTA: Green Line to Copley.

The central branch of the city's library system is an architectural as well as intellectual monument. The original 1895 building, a registered National Historic Landmark designed by Charles F. McKim, is an Italian Renaissance–style masterpiece that fairly drips with art. The front doors are the work of Daniel Chester French (who also designed the *Minute Man* statue in Concord); the murals are by John Singer Sargent and Pierre Puvis de Chavannes, among others; and you'll see notable frescoes, sculptures, and paintings. Visit the lovely courtyard or peek at it from a window on the stairs. The adjoining addition, of the same height and material (pink granite), was designed by Philip Johnson and opened in 1972. It's a utilitarian building with a dramatic skylit atrium. Visitors are welcome to wander throughout both buildings— the lobby of the McKim building alone could take half an hour—but you must have a library card (available to Massachusetts residents) to check out materials. The library has more than 6 million books and more than 11 million other items, such as prints, photographs, films, and sound recordings. It also has a web site (http://www.bpl.org).

Art & Architecture Tours are conducted Monday at 2:30pm, Tuesday and Wednesday at 6:30pm, Thursday and Saturday at 11am, and Sunday at 2pm, with additional tours scheduled for the weekend before the Boston Marathon, in mid-April.

MUSEUMS

✪ **Museum of Fine Arts, Boston.** 465 Huntington Ave. ☎ **617/267-9300**. Adults $10 when the entire museum is open, $8 when only the West Wing is open. Students and seniors $8 when the entire museum is open, $6 when only the West Wing is open. Children under 18 free. Free admission for all, Wed 4–9:45pm. No admission fee for those visiting only the Museum Shop, restaurants, library, or auditoria. Entire museum, Tues, Thurs–Fri, Mon holidays, Mon from Memorial Day through Labor Day 10am–4:45pm; Wed 10am–9:45pm; Sat–Sun 10am–5:45pm; West Wing only, Thurs–Fri 5–9:45pm. Closed Mon mid-Sept to late May and major holidays. MBTA: Green Line or E train to Museum of Fine Arts.

Not content with the MFA's reputation as the second-best museum in the country (after the Metropolitan Museum of Art in New York), the museum's management team works nonstop to make the collections more accessible and interesting.

Under new director Malcolm Rogers, in recent years the task of raising the museum's profile even higher has run the gamut from apparently little things, such as opening the Huntington Avenue entrance, to mounting even more top-notch exhibitions, expanding educational programs, and making admission free to children under 18.

The 121-year-old museum's not-so-secret weapon in its quest is a powerful one: its magnificent collections. Your visit is guided by the best sort of curatorial attitude, the kind that makes even those who go in with a sense of obligation leave with a sense of discovery and wonder. The MFA is especially noted for its Asian and Old Kingdom Egyptian collections, classical art, its Buddhist temple and medieval sculpture and tapestries, but the works you may find more familiar are American and European paintings and sculpture, notably the Impressionists. Some particular favorites: John Singleton Copley's 1768 portrait of Paul Revere, Gilbert Stuart's 1796 portrait of George Washington, Winslow Homer's *Long Branch, New Jersey*, a bronze casting of Edgar Degas's sculpture *Little Dancer*, Paul Gauguin's *Where Do We Come From? What Are We? Where Are We Going?*, Fitz Hugh Lane's *Owl's Head, Penobscot Bay, Maine*, and all 43 Monets. There are also magnificent print and photography collections, and that's not even touching on the furnishings and decorative arts, including the finest collection of Paul Revere silver in the world.

I. M. Pei designed the West Wing (1981), the latest addition to the original 1909 structure. It contains the main entrance, climate-controlled galleries, an auditorium, the excellent Museum Shop, and an atrium with a tree-lined "sidewalk" cafe. The Fine Arts Restaurant is on the second floor, and there's also a cafeteria. Pick up a floor plan at the information desk or take one of the free guided tours.

For a taste of what you'll see, the museum has a web site (http://www.mfa.org). The museum is located between Huntington Avenue and the Fenway. If you're driving, you can park in the garage or lot off Museum Road.

✪ **Boston Museum of Science.** Science Park. ☎ **617/723-2500.** Admission to the exhibit halls $8 adults, $6 seniors and children age 3–14, free for children under 3. To the Mugar Omni Theater, the Hayden Planetarium, or the laser theater, $7.50 adults, $5.50 seniors and children 3–14, free for children under 3. Tickets to 2 or 3 parts of the complex available at discounted prices. Daily 9am–5pm, Fri until 9pm. Closed Thanksgiving, Christmas. MBTA: Green Line to Science Park; the North Station commuter rail stop is a 10-minute walk from the museum.

For the ultimate pain-free educational experience, head to the Museum of Science. The demonstrations, experiments, and interactive displays introduce facts and concepts so effortlessly that everyone winds up learning something. Take a couple of hours or a whole day to explore the permanent and temporary exhibits. Some visitors who think they object to being here may prefer to pretend they're waiting for the rest of the group, but watch out—when they realize that they're mesmerized by, say, the visible inner workings of the escalator you just rode, they'll want to learn more.

Among the more than 450 exhibits, you might meet an iguana or a dinosaur, find out how much you'd weigh on the moon, or climb into a space module. If you've cooled your heels in traffic downtown, you'll probably want to check out the "Big Dig" exhibit, which allows you to try your hand at urban planning using an interactive computer display about the Central Artery project. And there's a Discovery Center especially for preschoolers. The newest permanent exhibit is an activity center called "Investigate!" The goal is to help visitors learn to think like scientists, formulating questions, finding evidence, and drawing conclusion through activities such as strapping on a skin sensor to measure reactions to stimuli or sifting through an archaeological dig. You can also visit the theater of electricity to see lightning manufactured indoors.

The separate-admission theaters are worth planning for. If you're making a day or a half-day of it (or even if you're skipping the exhibits), try to see a show. Buy all your tickets at once, not only because it's cheaper but because they sometimes sell out. Tickets for daytime shows must be purchased in person. Evening show tickets can be ordered over the phone using a credit card, but there's a service charge for doing so.

The **Mugar Omni Theater,** one of only 17 in the country, is an intense experience. You're bombarded with images on a four-story domed screen and sounds from a 12-channel sound system with 84 speakers. Even though you know you're not moving, the engulfing sensations and steep pitch of the seating area will have you hanging on for dear life, whether you're watching a film on Yellowstone, hurricanes and tornadoes, or the *Titanic.* The films change every four to six months.

The **Charles Hayden Planetarium** takes you deep into space with daily star shows and shows on special topics that change several times a year. On weekends, rock 'n' roll laser shows take over the planetarium—Pink Floyd fans, this is the place for you.

The museum has a web site (http://www.mos.org), a terrific gift shop where the toys and games promote learning without lecturing, and three restaurants. If you're driving, there's a garage on the premises.

✪ **Isabella Stewart Gardner Museum.** 280 The Fenway. ☎ **617/566-1401.** Admission $7 adults, $5 seniors and college students with valid ID, $3 children 12–17 and college students on Wed, free for children under 12. Tues–Sun 11am–5pm and some Mon holidays. Closed Mon. MBTA: Green Line, E train, to Museum of Fine Arts.

Isabella Stewart Gardner (1840–1924) was an incorrigible individualist long before such behavior was acceptable for a woman in polite Boston society, and her 19th-century eccentricity has proven a great boon to art lovers in contemporary Boston. "Mrs. Jack" designed her home in the style of a 15th-century Venetian palace and filled it with European, American, and Asian painting and sculpture, much chosen with the help of her friend and protégé Bernard Berenson. You'll see works by Titian, Botticelli, Raphael, Rembrandt, Matisse, and Mrs. Gardner's friends James McNeill Whistler and John Singer Sargent. The building, which was opened to the public after Mrs. Gardner's death, features furniture and architectural details imported from European churches and palaces. The *pièce de résistance* is a magnificent interior skylit courtyard filled year-round with fresh flowers (lilies at Easter, chrysanthemums in the fall, poinsettias at Christmas), stained-glass windows, and exquisite antique furnishings. A new special exhibition gallery, which opened in September 1992, features two or three changing exhibitions a year.

The Tapestry Room fills with music on weekends from September through April for the **concert series** (☎ **617/734-1359** for recorded information), which showcases soloists, chamber groups, and local students. The tiled floor and gorgeous wall hangings make a lovely setting for classical music. Concerts begin at 1:30pm on Saturday and Sunday. Tickets, which include museum admission, are $15 for adults, $9 for seniors and college students with valid ID, and $7 for youths ages 12 to 17.

Lunch and desserts are served in the museum cafe, and unique items are available at the gift shop.

The Computer Museum. 300 Congress St. (Museum Wharf). ☎ **617/426-2800** or 617/423-6758 for the "Talking Computer." Admission $7 adults, $5 students and seniors, free for children under 5. Tickets are half-price on Sun 3–5pm. Fall, winter, and spring Tues–Sun and Mon during Boston school holidays and vacations 10am–5pm; summer daily 10am–6pm. MBTA: Red Line to South Station. Walk north on Atlantic Ave. one block past the Federal Reserve Bank, and turn right onto Congress St.

As computer technology develops, the world's premier computer museum changes and grows with it. The exhibits at the Computer Museum tell the story of computers from their origins in the 1940s to the latest in PCs and virtual reality. The signature exhibit is the Walk-Through Computer 2000™, a networked multimedia machine 50 times larger than the real thing. When the computer's the size of a two-story house, the mouse is the size of a car, the CD-ROM drive is 8 feet long, the monitor is 12 feet high, and humans enjoying the 30 hands-on activities are the equivalent of crayon size. The exhibit is so cutting-edge that it even has a 7-foot-square Pentium processor, installed in 1995 during a million-dollar upgrade.

Computers don't exist in a vacuum, of course, and a permanent exhibit called "The Networked Planet" allows visitors to explore the information superhighway and its offshoots by logging on to real and simulated networks and learning about medicine, financial markets, and air-traffic control. There are also exhibits on robots, the history of the computer, and the practical and recreational uses of the PC—you might compose music, forecast the weather, or "drive" a race car. In all, you'll find more than 160 hands-on exhibits, three theaters, and countless ideas to try out on your home computer. For starters, you can check out the museum's web site (http://www.tcm.org).

Special activities, including Internet lessons, are offered on weekends. Call the Talking Computer for information about special programs and events. And before you leave, you can pick up some chocolate floppy disks or microchip jewelry at the Museum Store.

Boston Tea Party Ship & Museum. Congress St. Bridge. ☎ **617/338-1773**. Admission $6.50 adults, $5.20 students, $3.25 children 6–12, free for children under 6. Ship and museum, Mar 1–Nov 30 daily 9am–dusk (about 6pm in summer, 5pm in winter). Closed Dec 1–Feb 28 and Thanksgiving. MBTA: Red Line to South Station. Walk north on Atlantic Ave. 1 block past the Federal Reserve Bank, and turn right onto Congress St. The ship is docked at the Congress St. Bridge.

On December 16, 1773, a public meeting of independent-minded Bostonians led to the symbolic act of resistance that's commemorated here. The brig *Beaver II*, a full-size replica of one of the three merchant ships emptied by colonists poorly disguised as Indians on the night of the raid, is alongside a museum with exhibits on the "tea party." You can dump your own bale of tea into Boston Harbor (it will be retrieved by the museum staff), drink some complimentary tea (served iced in summer, hot in winter), and buy some tea to take home at the museum store.

✪ John F. Kennedy Presidential Library and Museum. Columbia Point, Dorchester. ☎ **617/929-4523**. Admission $6 adults, $4 seniors and students with ID, $2 children 6–16, free for children under 6. Daily 9am–5pm (last film begins at 3:50). Closed Thanksgiving, Christmas, and New Year's Day. MBTA: Red Line to JFK/UMass, then take the free shuttle bus, which runs every 20 minutes. By car, take the Southeast Expwy. (I-93/Rte. 3) south to Exit 15 (Morrissey Blvd./JFK Library), and follow signs to parking lot.

The Kennedy era springs to life at this dramatic library, museum, and educational research complex overlooking Dorchester Bay, where the 35th president's accomplishments and legacy are illustrated with sound and video recordings and fascinating displays of memorabilia and photos.

Your visit begins with a 17-minute film narrated by John F. Kennedy himself—a detail that seems eerie for a moment, then perfectly natural. Through skillfully edited audio clips, he discusses his childhood, education, war experiences, and early political career. Then you're turned loose to spend as much or as little time as you like on each museum exhibit. Starting with the 1960 presidential campaign, you're immersed in the period. In a series of connected galleries, you'll see 3¢ newspapers and campaign souvenirs, film of Kennedy debating Richard Nixon and being sworn in, gifts from foreign dignitaries, letters, and political cartoons. There's a film about the Cuban Missile Crisis, and displays on the civil rights movement, the Peace Corps, the space program, the First Lady, and the Kennedy family. Replicas of the Oval Office and the office of Attorney General Robert F. Kennedy, the president's brother, and a darkened chamber where news reports of John Kennedy's assassination and funeral play in a continuous loop leads to a room simply called "Legacy." Here you'll find books, archival documents, and interactive computers that explain the programs the president initiated and how they affect the world today.

From the final room, the soaring glass-enclosed pavilion that is the heart of the I. M. Pei–designed building, you have a glorious view of the water. Outside, JFK's boyhood sailboat, *Victura,* is on a strip of dune grass between the library and the harbor. Behind is the Archives Tower, nine stories of papers, books, films, and oral histories of John and Robert Kennedy. The material is available free to scholars and researchers.

The Sports Museum of New England. CambridgeSide Galleria, 100 CambridgeSide Place, Cambridge. ☎ **617/57-SPORT**. Admission $6 adults, $4.50 seniors and children 4–11, free for children under 4. Mon–Sat 10am–9:30pm, Sun 11am–7pm. The museum occasionally closes early for private functions. MBTA: Green Line to Lechmere, then walk 2 blocks; Red Line to Kendall, then take shuttle bus.

The Sports Museum of New England's collection highlights local sports history at every level of competition. Little Leaguers, professionals, Olympians, Special Olympians, and college stars are represented in displays of uniforms, equipment, newspaper clippings, and photographs. There are life-size statues of Larry Bird, Bobby Orr, Carl Yastrzemski, and Harry Agganis, small theaters modeled after Fenway Park, Boston Garden, and Harvard Stadium, and many interactive exhibits, including "Catching Clemens" (in which you find out what it's like to catch a Roger Clemens fastball—ouch), "In the Net" (in which you see what it's like to be hockey goalie), "Treadwall" (in which you try your hand at rock climbing), and "Stump Haggerty" (an interactive trivia contest). There's also a wall where you can see how you measure up against life-size photos of sports stars and an exhibit that spotlights memorabilia from a different New England town each month.

Institute of Contemporary Art. 955 Boylston St. ☎ **617/266-5152**. Admission $5.25 adults, $3.25 students, $2.25 seniors and children under 16; free to all Thurs 5–9pm. Thurs noon–9pm, Wed and Fri–Sun noon–5pm. Closed major holidays. MBTA: Green Line, B, C, or D train to Hynes/ICA.

Across from the Hynes Convention Center, the ICA showcases rotating exhibits of 20th-century art, including painting, sculpture, photography, and video and performance art. The institute also offers films, lectures, music, video, poetry, and an educational program for children and adults.

ORGANIZED TOURS
ORIENTATION TOURS

If you prefer not to explore on your own, **Boston By Foot** (77 N. Washington St.; ☎ 617/367-2345 or 617/367-3766 for recorded information) provides excellent tours. From May through October, Boston By Foot conducts historical and architectural tours that focus on particular neighborhoods or themes. The rigorously trained guides are volunteers (Boston By Foot is a nonprofit educational corporation), and questions are encouraged. The 90-minute tours take place rain or shine; call for offerings and schedules.

Rates for all tours are $7 for adults and $5 for children; reservations are not required. Tickets may be purchased from the guide.

The **Society for the Preservation of New England Antiquities** (☎ 617/227-3956) offers a fascinating tour that describes and illustrates life in the mansions and garrets of Beacon Hill in 1800. "Magnificent and Modest," a two-hour program, costs $10 and starts at the Harrison Gray Otis House, 141 Cambridge St., on Saturdays at 10am May through October, and Saturdays at 3pm from June through October. Reservations are recommended.

The **Historic Neighborhoods Foundation** (99 Bedford St.; ☎ 617/426-1885) offers several walking tours that focus on neighborhood landmarks, including Beacon Hill, the North End, Chinatown, the Waterfront, and the Financial District. Schedules change with the season, and the programs are based on themes, such as social history and topographical development. Write or call the Historic Neighborhoods Foundation for current schedules, fees, and meeting places.

The **Boston Park Rangers** (☎ 617/635-7383) offer free guided walking tours of the Emerald Necklace, a loop of green spaces designed by the first landscape architect, Frederick Law Olmstead. You'll see and hear about the city's major parks and gardens, including Boston Common, the Public Garden, the Commonwealth Avenue Mall, the Muddy River in the Fenway, Olmstead Park, Jamaica Pond, the Arnold Arboretum, and Franklin Park. The full six-hour walk includes a one-hour tour of any of the sites. Call for schedules.

You might want to take a narrated trolley tour for an overview of the sights before focusing on specific attractions, or you might want to use your all-day pass as a way to hit as many places as possible in eight hours or so. Whatever your approach, you'll have plenty of company. The business is competitive, with various companies offering different stops in an effort to distinguish themselves from the rest. All cover the major attractions and offer informative narratives and anecdotes in their 90- to 120-minute tours, as well as free reboarding if you want to visit the sites. Rates are between $16 and $18. Boarding spots are at hotels, historic sites, and tourist information centers.

Trolley companies are identified by the colors of their cars. **Old Town Trolley** (329 W. Second St.; ☎ 617/269-7010) has orange-and-green cars; **Boston Trolley Tours** (☎ 617/TROLLEY) uses blue cars; **Red Beantown Trolleys** (☎ 617/236-2148) are red; and the **Discover Boston Multilingual Trolley Tours'** (73 Tremont St.; ☎ 617/742-1440) vehicle is white. Boston Trolley Tours has ramps to make it handicapped-accessible, and the Red Beantown Trolleys are the only ones that stop at the Museum of Fine Arts and the Hard Rock Cafe. Only Old Town and the Red Beantown Trolleys stop at the Boston Tea Party Ship & Museum. Only Old Town offers a tour of Cambridge.

SIGHTSEEING CRUISES

Boston Harbor Cruises (1 Long Wharf; ☎ 617/227-4321) offers narrated trips around the harbor. From the white ticket center, you set out on either the 90-minute historic sightseeing cruise of the Inner and Outer Harbor, which departs every two hours beginning at 11am, or the 45-minute *Constitution* cruise, which takes you around the Inner Harbor and docks at Charlestown Navy Yard so you can go ashore and visit the USS *Constitution*. These tours leave every hour on the half-hour from Long Wharf, and on the hour from the navy yard. During the summer, the John F. Kennedy Library cruise leaves every two hours beginning at 10am. The cruise departs from the library at 10:45am, 12:45pm, 2:45pm, and 4:45pm. The 90-minute historic sightseeing and JFK Library cruises cost $8 for adults, $6 for seniors, and $4 for children. The *Constitution* cruise is $5 for adults, $4 for seniors, and $3 for children. And every evening at 7pm there's a sunset cruise, a wonderful way to unwind. It takes 90 minutes and features the lowering of the flag and a cannon blast at sunset. The fare is $8 for adults, $6 for seniors, and $4 for children.

Also on Long Wharf, at the red ticket office, **Bay State Cruise Company, Inc.** (☎ 617/723-7800) offers inner and outer harbor cruises. Ninety-minute cruises to the Outer Harbor with an optional stop at George's Island State Park depart several times a day; the price is $7 for adults, $6 for seniors, and $5 for children under 12. A 55-minute tour of the Inner Harbor is also available, with the option of going ashore at the Charlestown Navy Yard to see the *Constitution*; the fare is $5 for adults, $4 for seniors, and $3 for children. In addition, cruises to Provincetown are available. Call for exact dates and schedules.

Massachusetts Bay Lines (☎ 617/542-8000) offers 45-minute harbor tours from Memorial Day through Labor Day. Cruises leave from Rowes Wharf on the hour from 10am to 4pm, and at 5 and 6pm weekends and holidays; the price is $7.50 for adults, $5 for children 5 to 12 and seniors. The same company offers three-hour live-music cruises (blues, Wednesday at 7pm; rock, Thursday at 8pm) for $10. You must be at least 21 and have a photo ID.

The **Charles River Boat Company** (☎ 617/621-3001), offers 55-minute narrated cruises around the lower Charles River basin. Boats depart from the CambridgeSide Galleria on the hour from noon to 5pm; price is $7 for adults, $6 for seniors, $5 for children.

For almost a full day at sea, **Bay State Cruises' MV *Provincetown II*** (☎ 617/723-7800) sails from Commonwealth Pier daily from mid-June to Labor Day, and on weekends in May and September. Be at the pier by 9:30am (the water shuttle from Long Wharf leaves at 8:30am and costs $1) for the three-hour trip to Provincetown, at the tip of Cape Cod. The return trip leaves at 3:30pm, giving you a few hours for shopping and sightseeing. Same-day round-trip fares are $29 for adults, $22 for seniors, and $20 for children. Bringing a bike costs $5 extra each way.

Another day trip is offered by **A. C. Cruise Line** (☎ 800/422-8419 or 617/261-6633). The *Virginia C II* sails to Gloucester from Pier 7 (290 Northern Ave.) daily from late June through Labor Day at 10:30am and returns at 5pm. You'll have about 2¹/₂ hours to explore Gloucester. The round-trip charge is $18 for adults, $14 for seniors. A. C. Cruise Line also offers a three-hour country-western dance cruise ($12) with live entertainment Thursdays at 8pm.

The ***Spirit of Boston,*** a sleek 192-foot harbor-cruise ship operated by Bay State Cruises (☎ 617/457-1499), offers a New England lobster clambake luncheon cruise (daily, noon to 2:30pm) and a dinner dance cruise (nightly, 7 to 10pm). It sails from 60 Rowes Wharf near the Boston Harbor Hotel. Call for reservations.

WHALE WATCHING

The New England Aquarium (see listing above) runs its own whale watches.

Boston Harbor Whale Watch (☎ 617/345-9866) sends the 100-foot *Majestic* out to sea at speeds topping 20 knots and promises more time watching whales than trying to find them. Tours depart from Rowes Wharf beginning in mid-June and operate Friday, Saturday, and Sunday only through June. From July through early September there's daily service. Departure times are Monday through Friday at 10am, Saturday and Sunday at 9am and 2pm. Expect to spend about 4¹/₂ hours at sea. Tickets are $18 for adults, $15 for seniors and children under 13. Reservations are suggested, and discounted parking is available.

A. C. Cruise Line (☎ 800/422-8419 or 617/261-6633) offers a whale watch cruise Tuesday through Sunday, leaving at 10:30am and returning at 5pm. The fare

---

Duck, Duck, Loose

The newest and perhaps best way to see Boston is with **Boston Duck Tours** (☎ 617/723-DUCK). Sightseers board a "duck," a reconditioned Second World War amphibious landing craft, behind the Prudential Center at 101 Huntington Ave. The 80-minute narrated tour hits the high points, including Trinity Church, the Boston Public Library, the North End, Faneuil Hall, and the Old State House. The real high point comes when the duck lumbers down a ramp and splashes into the Charles River for a spin around the basin. Tickets are $18 for adults, $15 for seniors and students, and $9 for children 12 and under. Children 3 and under are free but need a ticket. Tours leave every hour or so starting at 9am and ending one hour before sunset. There are no tours from December through March; call for schedules.

---

is $19 for adults, $15 for seniors, $10 for children. Call for reservations and more information.

SPECIALTY TOURS

For Kennedy Buffs   The newest offering from Old Town Trolley (☎ 617/269-7150) is "JFK's Boston," a three-hour tour that stops at John F. Kennedy's birthplace in Brookline and the presidential library in Dorchester (a copresenter of the tour). The 3½-hour excursion starts at Atlantic Avenue and State Street and passes through the North End and Beacon Hill. Tickets are $22 for adults, $17 for seniors, and $12 for children, and include admission to the John F. Kennedy National Historic Site and the Kennedy Library. Tours start at 9:30am on Friday, Saturday, and Sunday from Memorial Day through Labor Day.

For Beer Nuts   Old Town Trolley stages a tour of three brewpub/restaurants twice a month. The three-hour journey includes stops at the Commonwealth Brewing Co. (see "The Bar Scene" later in this chapter for details) and Brew Moon Restaurant and Microbrewery in Boston, and John Harvard's Brew House (see "The Bar Scene" later in this chapter for details) in Cambridge. Food is served along with two 10-ounce beer samples at each location. Tickets are $38 and must be purchased in advance when you call (☎ 617/269-7150) for reservations.

ESPECIALLY FOR KIDS

If you're a parent traveling with your kids, you're asking, "What can children do in Boston?" A better question might be "What can't children do in Boston?" The answer: Not much. Just about every major destination in the city either is specifically designed to appeal to youngsters or can be easily adapted to do so. They're covered extensively elsewhere in this chapter; here's the boiled-down version for busy parents.

Hands-on exhibits are a big draw at several institutions: The **New England Aquarium** (☎ 617/973-5200), **The Computer Museum** (☎ 617/426-2800 or 617/423-6758), the **Boston Tea Party Ship & Museum** (☎ 617/338-1773), and **The Sports Museum of New England** (☎ 617/57-SPORT). Hard-core sports fans will enjoy a visit to a **Red Sox game** (see "Spectator Sports," below).

The **Boston Museum of Science** (☎ 617/723-2500) is not only a hands-on paradise but is also home to the **Hayden Planetarium** and the **Mugar Omni Theatre.**

For those in the mood to let other people do the work, take in the shows by the street performers at **Faneuil Hall Marketplace** (☎ 617/338-2323).

Under a new policy, admission is free for those under 18 at the **Museum of Fine Arts** (☎ 617/267-9300), which has special Sunday and after-school programs.

The allure of seeing people the size of ants draws young visitors to the **John Hancock Observatory** (☎ 617/572-6429) and the **Prudential Center Skywalk** (☎ 617/236-3318). And they can see actual ants—though they might prefer dinosaurs—at the Museum of Comparative Zoology, part of the **Harvard University Museum of Cultural and Natural History** (☎ 617/495-3045).

Older children who have studied modern American history will enjoy a visit to the **John F. Kennedy Presidential Library and Museum** (☎ 617/929-4523). And kids interested in cars will like the **Museum of Transportation** (☎ 617/522-6547).

Young visitors who have read Robert McCloskey's children's classic *Make Way for Ducklings* will relish a visit to the **Public Garden,** as will fans of E. B. White's *The Trumpet of the Swan,* who certainly will want to ride on the **swan boats** (☎ 617/ 522-1966 or 617/451-8558). Considerably less tame and much longer are **whale watches** (see "Organized Tours," above).

The walking-tour company **Boston By Foot** (77 N. Washington St.; ☎ 617/ 367-2345 or 617/367-3766 for recorded information) has a special program, **Boston By Little Feet,** geared to children 6 to 12 years old. The 60-minute walk gives a child's-eye view of the architecture along the Freedom Trail and of Boston's role in the American Revolution. Children must be accompanied by an adult, and a map is provided. Tours run from May through October and meet at the statue of Samuel Adams on the Congress Street side of Faneuil Hall, Saturday at 10am, Sunday at 2pm, and Monday at 10am, rain or shine. The cost is $5 per person.

The **Historic Neighborhoods Foundation** (99 Bedford St.; ☎ 617/426-1885) offers a 75-minute "Make Way for Ducklings" tour ($5 per person ages 5 or older). It's popular with children and adults, follows the path of the Mallard family described in Robert McCloskey's famous book, and ends at the Public Garden. Every year on Mother's Day, the HNF organizes the Ducklings Day Parade.

✪ **Children's Museum.** 300 Congress St. (Museum Wharf). ☎ **617/426-8855.** Admission $7 adults, $6 children 2–15 and seniors, $2 toddlers 1–2, free for infants under 1. Fri 5–9pm, $1 for all. Sept–June Tues–Sun 10am–5pm, Fri until 9pm; June–Aug daily 10am–5pm, Fri until 9pm. Closed Mon during school year, except Boston school vacations and holidays; Thanksgiving, Christmas, and New Year's Day. MBTA: Red Line to South Station. Walk north on Atlantic Ave. one block past the Federal Reserve Bank, and turn right onto Congress St. Call for information about discounted parking.

As you approach the Children's Museum, don't be surprised to see adults suddenly being dragged by the hand as their young companions realize how close they are and start running. You know the museum is near when you see the 40-foot-high red-and-white milk bottle out front. It makes both children and adults look small in comparison—which is probably part of the point. No matter how old, everyone behaves like a little kid at this delightful museum.

Not only is touching encouraged, it's practically a necessity if you're going to enjoy the exhibits. Children can stick with their parents or wander on their own, learning, doing, and role-playing. Some favorites: "Under the Dock," an environmental exhibit that teaches young people about the Boston waterfront and allows them to dress up in a crab suit; the "Kids' Bridge," where interactive videos allow a virtual visit to Boston's ethnic neighborhoods to learn about cultural differences and ways to combat racism; and the "Dress-Up Shop," a souped-up version of playing in Grandma's closet.

You'll also see "El Mercado," a marketplace that immerses children in Hispanic culture, surrounding them with Spanish newspapers, ethnic food products, and salsa music. The "Climbing Sculpture" is a giant maze designed especially for children (adults may get stuck). Another oversize display is a desk with a phone so big it doubles as a slide. "We're Still Here" concentrates on Northeast Native Americans and offers the chance to play in a wigwam. You can also explore a Japanese house from Kyoto (Boston's sister city) and learn about young adults in "Teen Tokyo." "Playspace" is a special room for children under 4 and their caregivers.

For bargain-priced craft supplies and materials for toys and games, check out the bags of industrial leftovers on sale at the RECYCLE Resource Center that can be used in many ways. Admission is free.

Note: When the kids get hungry, try the ice cream and sandwiches at the stand in the giant milk bottle, or go to the McDonald's adjoining the museum gift shop.

6 Sports & Outdoor Activities

SPECTATOR SPORTS

Boston's well-deserved reputation as a great sports town derives in part from the days when at least one of the professional teams was one of the world's best. None of them has done much lately, but passions still run deep—insult the local teams and be ready to defend yourself. This applies to some extent to college sports as well, particularly in hockey, where the Division 1 schools are evenly matched.

The biggest Boston sports story of the last few years was not about a team but an arena. In September 1995, the **FleetCenter** opened behind 67-year-old Boston Garden and the "Gah-den" was shut down (at press time, it's still standing as various corporate entities wrangle over who will pay for the demolition). The narrow, cramped seats and obstructed views in the incredibly steep Garden were replaced by cushy chairs in a wide-open bowl-shaped arena, and the feeling of being right on top of the action was replaced by the feeling of watching at a distance. One constant is the basketball floor, a collection of wood parquet tiles that made the trip to the new building.

The FleetCenter and the Garden History Center (☎ **617/624-1518**) are open for tours Monday through Saturday on the hour from 10am to 4pm, Sunday from 11am to 3pm, except during events. Tickets are $6 for adults, $5 for seniors and students, and $4.50 for children under 12.

BASEBALL   No experience in sports matches watching the **Boston Red Sox** play at **Fenway Park,** which they do from early April to early October, and later if they make the playoffs. The quirkiness of the oldest park in the major leagues (1912) and the fact that the team last won the World Series in 1918 only add to the mystique. A hand-operated scoreboard is built into the Green Monster, or left-field wall (watch carefully during a pitching change—the left fielder from either team may suddenly disappear into the darkness to cool off), and the wall itself is such a celebrity that it's often called simply The Wall. It's 37 feet tall, a mere 298 feet from home plate, and irresistibly tempting to batters who ought to know better. On two vertical white lines on the scoreboard you'll see Morse code for the initials of legendary owners Thomas A. and Jean R. Yawkey, now dead.

The crowds can be as interesting as the architecture. You'll see Cub Scouts on a field trip, positive that they're going to catch their first foul ball, and season-ticket-holders in their eighties, positive that this is finally the year. Fans are jammed together in narrow, uncomfortable seats close to the field, striking up conversations with total strangers, reminiscing, and making bold predictions. A recent fan-relations campaign called "Friendly Fenway" has produced better-mannered employees, a greater variety of concession items (but not lower prices), and expanded family-seating sections, but for the most part that's window dressing. You're in an intensely green place that's older than your grandparents, inhaling a Fenway Frank, and wishing for a home run—what could be better?

Practical concerns: Compared to its modern brethren, Fenway is tiny. Tickets go on sale in early December for the following season, and the earlier you order, the better chance you'll have of landing seats during your visit. Forced to choose between tickets for a low-numbered grandstand section (say, 10 or below) and less expensive bleacher seats, go for the bleachers. They can get rowdy during night games, but the view is better from there than from the deep right-field corner. If you plan to be in town around the same time as the Marathon, your chances of landing tickets for Patriots Day are poor (the game starts at 11am so that fans can, theoretically, be in Kenmore Square to watch the leading runners pass by), but don't despair. The next two or three games traditionally are scheduled for weekday afternoons, and they almost never sell out. Throughout the season, a limited number of standing room tickets go on sale the day of the game, and there's always the possibility that tickets will be returned. It can't hurt to check, especially if the team isn't playing well. The fans are incredibly loyal, but they're not all obsessed.

The Fenway Park ticket office is at 24 Yawkey Way, near the corner of Brookline Avenue. Call **617/267-8661** for information, 617/267-1700 for tickets. Tickets for the disabled and in no-alcohol sections are available. Smoking is not allowed in the park. Games usually begin at 7:05pm on weeknights and 1pm on weekends. Take the MBTA Green Line (B, C, or D train) to Kenmore.

BASKETBALL   The **Boston Celtics** have fallen on hard times in recent years, but their glorious history is illustrated by the 16 National Basketball Association championship banners hanging from the ceiling of the new FleetCenter (150 Causeway St.). They play from early October to April or May, and unless a top contender is visiting, you should have no trouble buying tickets. For information, call the FleetCenter at **617/624-1000;** for tickets, call TicketMaster at **617/931-2000.** To reach the FleetCenter, take the MBTA Green or Orange Line or commuter rail to North Station.

Other than being the site of the sport's creation (it was invented in Springfield, Mass., around the turn of the century), New England is not noted for its basketball history; but the local teams have all enjoyed a measure of success in recent years. Schools with teams include **Boston College** (Conte Forum, Chestnut Hill; ☎ **617/552-3000**), **Boston University** (Walter Brown Arena, 285 Babcock St.; ☎ **617/353-3838**), **Harvard University** (Lavietes Pavilion, N. Harvard St., Allston; ☎ **617/495-2211**), and **Northeastern University** (Matthews Arena, St. Botolph St.; ☎ **617/373-4700**).

FOOTBALL   The **New England Patriots** (☎ **800/543-1776**) play football from August through December (or maybe January if they make the playoffs) at Foxboro Stadium on Route 1 in Foxboro, about a half-hour drive south of the city. You can drive or catch a bus from the entrance of South Station, the Riverside "T" station, or Shopper's World in Framingham (west of the city). The team's fortunes have slowly improved over the last several years, and tickets ($23–$50) often sell out. Plan as far in advance as you can.

College football is played by **Boston College** (Alumni Stadium, Chestnut Hill; ☎ **617/552-3000**), **Boston University** (Nickerson Field, Commonwealth Ave.; ☎ **617/353-3838**), **Harvard University** (Harvard Stadium, N. Harvard St.,

Curses, Foiled Again

The most famous of all the famous numbers associated with Boston sports history—more famous than 16 (National Basketball Association championships won by the Celtics), 4 (legendary Bruins defenseman Bobby Orr's jersey), 46–10 (the score of the Super Bowl in 1986, when the Chicago Bears demolished the New England Patriots), or even .406 (Red Sox outfielder Ted Williams's batting average in 1941)—is 1918. In 1918, the Boston Red Sox won the World Series for the fifth time in the 15-year history of the event. They have yet to win another.

Fatalistic Red Sox fans attribute the team's disastrous luck to a transaction executed after the 1919 season. Team owner Harry Frazee, a theatrical producer who needed money to mount a production of the musical *No, No, Nannette,* accepted $100,000 from the New York Yankees in exchange for a promising young pitcher and outfielder—Babe Ruth. The "Curse of the Bambino" is believed to have prevailed ever since, leading to an exorcism, a book, and an uncanny number of postseason catastrophes.

Not that the Red Sox haven't come close. They lost one-game playoffs for the right to go to the World Series in 1948 and 1978. They actually went to the World Series in 1946, 1967, 1975, and 1986—and lost in the seventh and final game each time. The most agonizing loss (or at least the one most people remember best) was in 1986. The Red Sox led the New York Mets, 5 to 4, in the bottom of the 10th inning of the sixth game. They were one strike away from victory and the Champagne was already uncorked when a ground ball skipped through first baseman Bill Buckner's legs. The winning run scored, the demoralized Red Sox went on to lose the seventh game, and the curse lived on.

Allston; ☎ 617/495-2211), **Northeastern University** (Parsons Field, Kent St., Brookline; ☎ 617/373-4700).

HOCKEY Boston Bruins games are always exciting, especially if you happen to be in town at the same time as the archrival Montreal Canadiens. Tickets for many Bruins games (held at the FleetCenter, 150 Causeway St.) sell out early despite being among the most expensive in the league. For tickets ($43 to $70), call **617/624-1000** or call TicketMaster at 617/931-2000. To reach the FleetCenter, take the MBTA Green or Orange Line or commuter rail to North Station.

Economical hockey fans who don't have their hearts set on seeing a pro game will be pleasantly surprised by the quality of play at the college level in Boston. Even for sold-out games, standing-room tickets are usually available the night of the game. Colleges with teams include **Boston College** (Conte Forum, Chestnut Hill; ☎ 617/552-3000), **Boston University** (Walter Brown Arena, 285 Babcock St.; ☎ 617/353-3838), **Harvard University** (Bright Hockey Center, N. Harvard St., Allston; ☎ 617/495-2211), and **Northeastern University** (Matthews Arena, St. Botolph St.; ☎ 617/373-4700). These four are the Beanpot schools, who play a tradition-steeped tournament on the first two Mondays of February at the FleetCenter. The games generally sell out, but you can try to order early or wait till the day of the game and check for returned tickets.

HORSE RACING Suffolk Downs (111 Waldemar Ave., E. Boston; ☎ 617/567-3900) reopened under new management in 1992 after being closed for several years and ghastly for years before that. Today it's one of the best-run smaller tracks in the country, an excellent family destination (really), sparklingly clean, and the home of the Massachusetts Handicap, run in early June. Horse of the Year Cigar won the MassCap in 1995 and '96, conferring instant cachet on the event and the facility. There are extensive simulcasting options during and after the live racing season (the schedule may change dramatically in 1997; call for exact dates).

THE MARATHON   Every year on Patriots Day (the third Monday in April), the **Boston Marathon** is run from Hopkinton to Copley Square in Boston. Cheering fans line the entire route. An especially nice place to watch is tree-shaded Commonwealth Avenue between Kenmore Square and Massachusetts Avenue, but you'll be in a crowd wherever you stand, particularly near the finish line in front of the Boston Public Library. The centennial event in 1996 drew about 40,000 competitors, four times larger than a normal field, and there may be a residual effect for the 1997 race. For information about qualifying, contact the Boston Athletic Association (☎ 617/236-1652).

ROWING   In late October, the **Head of the Charles Regatta** attracts more rowers than any other crew event in the country to Boston and Cambridge. Some 4,000 oarsmen and oarswomen race against the clock for four miles from the Charles River basin to the Eliot Bridge in west Cambridge. Tens of thousands of spectators socialize and occasionally even watch the action.

Spring crew racing is far more exciting than the "head" format; the course is 2,000 meters and races last just five to seven minutes. Men's and women's collegiate events take place on Saturday mornings in April and early May in the Charles River basin. You'll have a perfect view of the finish line from Memorial Drive between the MIT boathouse and the Hyatt Regency. To find out who's racing, check the Friday *Globe* sports section.

OUTDOOR PURSUITS

BEACHES   The beaches in Boston proper are decent places to catch a cool breeze and splash around, but for real ocean surf, you'll need to head out of town. North Shore beaches are discussed in Chapter 6.

Closer to Boston are **Nahant Beach** (follow the signs from the intersection of Routes 1A and 129, near the Lynn-Swampscott border), which is large and extremely popular, and **Revere Beach.** Revere Beach is better known for its pick-up scene than its narrow strip of sand, but the cruising crowds are friendly and parking on the boulevard is free. The MBTA Blue Line has a Revere Beach stop; if you're driving, head north for smaller crowds at **Point of Pines**, which has its own exit off Route 1A. Across the street from the water is **Kelly's Roast Beef** (410 Revere Beach Blvd.; ☎ 617/284-9129), a local legend for its onion rings, fried clams, and, yes, roast beef sandwiches.

South Shore Beaches   The southern suburbs are riddled with private beaches, but there are a couple of pleasant public options. In Hull (take Route 3 or 3A to Route 228), **Nantasket Beach** (☎ 617/925-4905) is right in town. It's popular with families for its fairly shallow water and the historic wooden carousel in a building across the street from the main parking lot. Nine-mile-long **Duxbury Beach** (take Route 3A to Route 139 north and go right on Canal St.) makes an enjoyable stop on the way to Plymouth, if that's in your plans. **Plymouth Beach,** off Route 3A south of Plymouth at Warren Ave., is smaller, with mild surf.

Boston Beaches   The condition of Boston Harbor has improved considerably since its pollution was an issue in the 1988 presidential campaign, and the Metropolitan District Commission (☎ 617/727-9547) is working to restore the run-down beaches under its purview, but the MDC sometimes still has to fly red flags when swimming is not recommended (blue flags mean the water's fine). Be aware that these are very much neighborhood hangouts. In Dorchester, off Morrissey Boulevard, **Malibu Beach** and **Savin Hill Beach** are within walking distance of the Savin Hill stop on the MBTA Red Line. South Boston beaches are off Day Boulevard and accessible by taking the Red Line to Broadway or Green Line to Copley, then a bus marked "City Point" (routes 9, 10, and 11). Among them are **Castle Island, L Street,** and **Pleasure Bay.**

BIKING   Expert cyclists who feel comfortable with the layout of the city shouldn't have too much trouble navigating in traffic. If you don't fit that description, you're better off sticking to the many bike paths in the area and not tempting the blood-thirsty drivers. State law requires that children under 12 wear helmets. Bicycles are forbidden on MBTA buses and the Green Line at all times and during rush hour on the other parts of the system. You must have a permit (☎ 617/222-5799) to bring your bike on the Blue, Orange, and Red lines and commuter rail during non-rush hours.

Shops that rent require you to show a driver's license or passport and leave a deposit using a major credit card. They include **Earth Bikes** (35 Huntington Ave., near Copley Sq.; ☎ 617/267-4733), where rentals start at $12 for four hours; **Back Bay Bikes** (333 Newbury St., near Massachusetts Ave.; ☎ 617/247-2336), which charges $20 per day; and **Community Bicycle Supply** (496 Tremont St., near E. Berkeley St.; ☎ 617/542-8623), where rentals are $5 an hour or $20 a day.

The **Dr. Paul Dudley White Charles River Bike Path** is a 17.7-mile circuit that begins at Science Park (near the Museum of Science) and loops along both sides of the river to Watertown and back. You can enter and exit at many points along the way. Bikers share the path with lots of pedestrians, joggers, and in-line skaters, expecially in Boston near the Esplanade and in Cambridge near Harvard Square. The path is maintained by the Metropolitan District Commission, or MDC (☎ 617/727-9547), as is the 5-mile **Pierre Lallement Bike Path,** in Southwest Corridor Park. It starts behind Copley Place and runs for 5 miles through the South End and Roxbury along the route of the MBTA Orange Line to Franklin Park.

For additional information, call the **Bicycle Coalition of Massachusetts** (☎ 617/491-7433) or the **Charles River Wheelmen** (☎ 617/332-8546).

BOATING   Technically, riding a swan boat is boating. It's not exactly a transatlantic crossing, but it has been a classic Boston experience since 1877. The lagoon at the Public Garden turns into a fiberglass swan habitat every spring and summer and offers an excellent break in the midst of a busy day.

The pedal-powered swan boats (☎ 617/522-1966 or 617/451-8558) operate from the Saturday before Patriots Day (the third Monday in April) through September, 10am to 6pm in summer, 10am to 4pm spring and fall. The cost is $1.50 for adults, 95¢ for children.

There are also plenty of less tame options (see "Sailing," below). The **Charles River Canoe and Kayak Center** (☎ 617/965-5110) has two locations, on Soldiers Field Road in Allston and at 2401 Commonwealth Ave. in Newton. Both centers rent canoes and kayaks (the Newton location also rents sculls), and lessons are available. From April through October, they open at 10am on weekdays and 9am on weekends and holidays, and close at dusk.

Non-inflatable water craft are allowed on the Charles River and in the Inner Harbor. If you plan to bring your own boat, call the **Metropolitan District Commission** Harbor Master (☎ 617/727-0537) for information about launches.

ICE SKATING   The lagoons at the **Public Garden** and the **Frog Pond** on Boston Common freeze to smooth surfaces if the weather is exactly right, which happens only sporadically. The ongoing renovation of the Frog Pond is expected to help optimize conditions there, but for surfaces that are guaranteed to be frozen, you'll want to head indoors.

The **Skating Club of Boston** (1240 Soldiers Field Rd., Brighton; ☎ 617/782-5900) is a training center for many competitive skaters and was 1992 Olympic silver medalist Paul Wylie's headquarters when he was a Harvard undergrad. The well-maintained surface is open to the public at least twice a week, and skate sharpening and rentals are available all year ($6 adults, $4 children).

Grooming is less consistent at the rinks maintained by the Metropolitan District Commission, which are popular with recreational hockey leagues and don't all have services and concessions. If you've brought along your own sharpened skates, try **Steriti Memorial Rink** (☎ 617/727-4708), on Commercial Street in the North End, the only MDC rink convenient to downtown. It's open seasonally, and admission is $3 for public sessions; call for days and times.

SAILING   Community Boating, Inc. (21 Embankment Rd., on the Esplanade; ☎ 617/523-1038) offers sailing lessons and boating programs for children and adults from April to November. It runs on a co-op system; a 30-day adult membership is $65. The **Courageous Sailing Center** (Charlestown Navy Yard; ☎ 617/242-3821) offers youth program lessons year-round. A five-lesson program (one in the classroom, four on the water) is $125. The **Boston Sailing Center** (54 Lewis Wharf; ☎ 617/227-4198) offers lessons for sailors of all ability levels. The center is open all year (even for "frostbite" racing in the winter). Ten classes (five indoors, five outdoors) and a 35-day membership will run you $475. And the **Boston Harbor Sailing Club** (200 High St., at Rowes Wharf; ☎ 617/345-9202) offers rentals and instruction. A package of four classes, 16 hours of on-water instruction, and a 30-day membership is $414. Private lessons (three-hour minimum) are $20 an hour plus the rental of the boat (from $25 an hour) plus tax.

HARBOR ISLAND EXPLORATION   The **Boston Harbor Islands** were right under your nose if you arrived by plane, but their accessibility isn't widely known. There are 30 islands in the Outer Harbor, some open for exploring, camping, or swimming. Plan a day trip or even an overnight stay. The most popular is **George's Island,** home of Fort Warren (1834), where Confederate prisoners were kept during the Civil War. Tours are offered periodically. The island has a visitor center, refreshment area, fishing pier, place for picnics, and a wonderful view of Boston's skyline. From there, free water taxis run to **Lovells, Gallops, Peddocks, Bumpkin,** and **Grape islands,** which have picnic areas and campsites. For permits and reservations, call the Department of Environmental Management (☎ 617/740-1605), which administers **Bumpkin, Calf, Gallops, Grape, and Great Brewster islands;** or the Metropolitan District Commission (☎ 617/727-5290), which manages George's, Lovells, and Peddocks islands. Lovells Island also has the remains of a fort (Fort Standish), as well as a sandy beach; it's the only harbor island with supervised swimming. Boats to George's Island leave from Long Wharf and Rowes Wharf. The islands are part of the Boston Harbor Islands State Park. For more information, contact the Friends of the Boston Harbor Islands (☎ 617/740-4290).

FISHING   Freshwater fishing is permitted at **Turtle Pond** in the Stony Brook Reservation in Hyde Park, at **Jamaica Pond** in Jamaica Plain, and on the banks of the **Charles River** (eating your catch is not recommended.) For offshore saltwater fishing, the **Harbor Islands** are a good choice. You might also try fishing from the pier at **City Point** and the **John J. McCorkle Fishing Pier,** off Day Boulevard in South Boston.

For information on locations and regulations, call the **Sport Fishing Information Line** (☎ 800/ASK-FISH). Information is also available from the state **Division of Fisheries and Wildlife** (100 Cambridge St., Boston, MA 02202; ☎ 617/727-3151), and in the fishing columns in the *Globe* and *Herald* on Fridays in the spring, summer, and fall.

GOLF   You won't get far in the suburbs without seeing a golf course, and with the recent explosion in the sport's popularity, you won't be the only one looking. Given a choice, opt for the lower prices and smaller crowds you'll find on weekdays.

At **Newton Commonwealth Golf Course** (212 Kenrick St., Newton; ☎ 617/630-1971), an excellent 18-hole layout, greens fees are $20 on weekdays and $25 on weekends. At nine-hole **Fresh Pond Golf Course** (691 Huron Ave., Cambridge; ☎ 617/349-6282), it's $14, or $20 to go around twice, on weekdays, and $17 and $25 on weekends. Within the city limits there are two 18-hole courses: **Franklin Park Golf Course** (Dorchester; ☎ 617/265-4084), where greens fees are $17 on weekdays and $20 on weekends; and **George Wright Golf Course** (420 West St., Hyde Park; ☎ 617/361-8313), where fees are $21 on weekdays and $24 on weekends.

The **Massachusetts Golf Association** (175 Highland Ave., Needham, MA 02192; ☎ 617/449-3000) represents more than 270 golf courses around the state and will send you a list of courses on request. In addition, **Tee Times** (199 Wells Ave., Suite 9, Newton, MA 02159; ☎ 617/969-0638) organizes golf outings.

IN-LINE SKATING   As with biking, unless you're very confident of your ability and your knowledge of Boston traffic, staying off the streets is a good idea.

A favorite spot for in-line skaters is the **Esplanade,** between the Back Bay and the Charles River. It continues onto the bike path that runs to Watertown and back, but be aware that once you leave the Esplanade the pavement isn't totally smooth, which can lead to mishaps. Your best bet is to wait for a Sunday in the summer, when **Memorial Drive** in Cambridge is closed to traffic. It's a perfect surface.

If you didn't bring your skates, you have several options for renting. A former Olympic cyclist runs **Eric Flaim's Motion Sports** (349 Newbury St.; ☎ 617/247-3284). Or try the **Beacon Hill Skate Shop** (135 Charles St. South; ☎ 617/482-7400), **Earth Bikes** (35 Huntington Ave.; ☎ 617/267-4733), or **Ski Market** (860 Commonwealth Ave.; ☎ 617/731-6100).

The **InLine Club of Boston** recently brought out a book, *InLine Skating in Greater Boston,* that's available at skate and sporting goods shops and some bookstores for $8. The club has a web site (http://www.sk8net.com/icb) with up-to-date event and safety information and its extremely clever logo.

JOGGING   Check with the concierge or desk staff at your hotel for a map with suggested routes. The bridges across the Charles River allow for circuits of various lengths. Other sources of information include the **Metropolitan District Commission,** or MDC (☎ 617/727-1300) and the **Bill Rodgers Running Center** in Faneuil Hall Marketplace (☎ 617/723-5612). As in any large city, you're advised to stay out of park areas (including the Esplanade) at night.

TENNIS   Public courts are available throughout the city at no charge. They are maintained by the **Metropolitan District Commission** (☎ 617/727-1300). To find the one nearest you, call the MDC or ask the concierge or desk staff at your hotel. Well-maintained courts near downtown that seldom get busy until after-work hours are available at several spots on the Southwest Corridor Park in the South End (there's a nice one near W. Newton St.) and off Commercial Street near the N. Washington Street Bridge in the North End. The courts in Charlesbank Park, overlooking the river next to the State Police barracks on the bridge to the Museum of Science, are more crowded during the day.

7 Shopping

The other major shopping areas in Boston have been overshadowed recently by the **Back Bay,** which seems only fitting—the Prudential Center casts a long shadow over the neighborhood, and the Shops at Prudential Center are the hottest new retail destination in town. You could easily spend a day browsing the stores that the Back Bay has to offer, at the "Pru," upscale Copley Place (linked by a weatherproof walkway across Huntington Ave.), Neiman Marcus, Lord & Taylor, Saks Fifth Avenue, and the dozens of galleries, shops, and boutiques along Newbury Street.

If you're passionate or just curious about art, try to set aside a couple of hours for strolling along **Newbury Street.** You'll find an infinite variety of styles and media in the dozens of galleries at street level and on the higher floors (remember to look up). Twice a year, in late May and late September, the street is closed from the Public Garden to Massachusetts Avenue and more than 30 galleries are open for **Art Newbury Street,** a celebration of the area's galleries displaying work by regional and international artists with special exhibits and outdoor entertainment. Contact the Newbury Street League (158 Newbury St.; ☎ **617/267-7961**) or check the web site (http://www.newbury-st.tne.com).

Another popular destination is **Faneuil Hall Marketplace,** the busiest attraction in Boston, not only because of its smorgasbord of food outlets, but also because of its shops, boutiques, and pushcarts filled with everything from rubber stamps to costume jewelry.

If the prospect of the hubbub at Faneuil Hall is too much for you, stroll over to **Charles Street,** at the foot of Beacon Hill. It's a short but commercially dense (and picturesque) street noted for its antiques and gift shops.

One of Boston's oldest shopping areas is **Downtown Crossing.** Now a traffic-free pedestrian mall along Washington, Winter, and Summer streets near Boston Common, it's home to two major department stores—Filene's and Macy's—tons of smaller clothing and shoe stores, food and merchandise pushcarts, Woolworth's, and outlets of two major bookstore chains (Barnes & Noble and Borders). Next to Macy's on Washington Street is Lafayette Place, the forlorn shell of a mall that closed in the early '90s. In 1996 the city announced a project aimed at refurbishing Washington Street from Downtown Crossing to Chinatown, an undertaking that should be bearing fruit by the time you visit. Most stores are open weeknights and Saturday until 7pm, and Sunday until 5 or 6pm.

Note: Massachusetts has no sales tax on clothing (priced below $175) and food. All other items are taxed at 5%. Restaurant meals and food prepared for take-out are also taxed at 5%.

With the erosion of Sunday "blue laws," Massachusetts law no longer prohibits stores from opening before noon on Sunday, but many still wait till 12 or don't open at all—call ahead before setting out.

✪ **Filene's Basement.** 426 Washington St. ☎ **617/542-2011**.

This legendary Boston clothing store is probably the one store in the city that definitely deserves special mention. Follow the crowds to this Downtown Crossing institution, which has spoiled New England shoppers with retail discounts since

1908. Far from passing off their finds as pricey indulgences, true devotees boast about their bargains. Here's how it works: After two weeks on the selling floor, merchandise is automatically marked down 25% from its already discounted price. Check the boards hanging from the ceiling for the crucial dates; the original sale date is on the back of every price tag. Prices fall until, after 35 days, anything that hasn't sold (for 75% off) is donated to charity. Filene's Basement is no longer associated with Filene's, the department store upstairs from which it leases space. The independent chain, founded in 1978, has 47 branches in the Northeast and Midwest that offer great bargains, but the automatic markdown policy is in force only at the original store, which attracts 15,000 to 20,000 shoppers a day.

The crowds swell for the special sales, which come about when a store is going out of business or a classy designer, retailer, or catalog house (say, Neiman-Marcus, Barneys, Saks Fifth Avenue, Tweeds) finds itself overstocked. You'll see the unpredictable particulars, sometimes including an early opening time, advertised in the newspapers. Four times a year, the legendary $199 wedding dress sale sparks a truly alarming display of bridal hysteria usually documented by amused news camera crews; days are also set aside for dresses, men's and women's suits, raincoats, dress shirts, children's clothing, evening gowns, lingerie, cosmetics, leather goods, designer shoes, and anything else that looks promising to the store's eagle-eyed buyers. Two weeks later, leftovers wind up on the automatic-markdown racks, and the real hunting begins. Try to beat the lunchtime crowds, but if you can't, don't despair—just be patient. *Tip:* If you're not wild about trying on clothes in the open dressing rooms, slip them on over what you're wearing, an acceptable throwback to the days before there were dressing rooms. Or make like the natives and return what doesn't suit you, in person or even by mail.

If this is the sort of activity that gets your juices flowing, you haven't lived until you've clipped the original $225 price tag off a dress and responded to the first person who offers a compliment by saying, "Oh, do you like it? It was $17."

8 Boston After Dark

THE PERFORMING ARTS

For up-to-date entertainment listings, consult the "Calendar" section of the Thursday *Boston Globe,* the "Scene" section of the Friday *Boston Herald,* and the Sunday arts sections of both papers. The weekly *Boston Phoenix* (published on Thursday and available on newsstands all week) has especially good club listings, and the twice-monthly *Improper Bostonian* has extensive live music listings.

GETTING TICKETS   Two major ticket agencies serve Boston. TicketMaster (☎ 617/931-2000) and **Next Ticketing** (☎ 617/426-NEXT) both levy service charges that are calculated per ticket (not per order). To avoid the service charge, visit the venue in person. If you wait until the day before or the day of a performance, you'll sometimes have access to tickets that were held back for one reason or another and have just gone on sale.

Yankee thrift is artistically expressed at the **BosTix booths** at Faneuil Hall Marketplace and in Copley Square, where same-day tickets to musical and theatrical performances (subject to availability) are on sale for half-price. Credit cards are not accepted, and there are no refunds or exchanges. Check the board for the day's offerings. BosTix (☎ 617/723-5181) also offers full-price advance ticket sales, discounts on more than 100 theater, music, and dance events, as well as tickets to museums, historical sites, and attractions in and around Boston. Both locations are open Tuesday through Saturday from 10am to 6pm (half-price tickets go on sale at

11am), and on Sunday from 11am to 4pm. The Copley Square booth is also open Monday from 10am to 6pm.

You'll find most of the shows headed to or on hiatus from Broadway in the Theater District, at the **Colonial Theatre** (106 Boylston St.; ☎ 617/426-9366), the **Shubert Theatre** (265 Tremont St.; ☎ 617/426-4520), the **Wang Center for the Performing Arts** (270 Tremont St.; ☎ 617/482-9393), and the **Wilbur Theater** (246 Tremont St.; ☎ 617/423-7440).

✪ **Boston Pops.** Performing at Symphony Hall, 301 Huntington Ave. (at Massachusetts Ave.). ☎ **617/266-1492**, 617/CON-CERT for program information, or 617/266-1200 for Symphony Charge. Tickets $32–$43 for tables, $12–$27 for balcony seats.

From early May until early July, members of the Boston Symphony Orchestra lighten up, performing a repertoire that ranges from light classical to show tunes to popular music (hence the name), sometimes with celebrity guest stars. The floor seats at Symphony Hall are replaced with tables and chairs, and waitresses serve drinks and light refreshments. New conductor Keith Lockhart hit town in 1995 (he made his official debut in 1996) and quickly became so popular that he could almost give the orchestra its name all by himself. Performances are Tuesday through Sunday evenings, and a week of free outdoor concerts is given at the Hatch Shell on the Charles River Esplanade in early July, including the traditional Fourth of July concert, which features fireworks.

✪ **Boston Symphony Orchestra.** Performing at Symphony Hall, 301 Huntington Ave. (at Massachusetts Ave.). ☎ **617/266-1492** or 617/CON-CERT for program information, 617/266-1200 for Symphony Charge. Tickets $22–$67. Rush tickets $10 (on sale 9am Fri; 5pm Tues, Thurs). Rehearsal tickets $12.

The Boston Symphony Orchestra, one of the world's greatest, was founded in 1881 and has performed at acoustically perfect Symphony Hall since 1900. Music director Seiji Ozawa is the latest in a line of distinguished conductors presiding over an institution known for contemporary as well as classical music—the 1996 Pulitzer Prize in music was awarded to *Lilacs,* composed for voice and orchestra by George Walker and commissioned by the BSO.

The season runs from October through April. The orchestra performs most Tuesday, Thursday, and Saturday evenings, Friday afternoons, and some Friday evenings. A limited number of rush tickets (one per person) are available on the day of the performance for Tuesday and Thursday evening and Friday afternoon programs. Wednesday evening and Thursday morning rehearsals are sometimes open to the public.

Boston Ballet. 19 Clarendon St. ☎ **617/695-6950** or 617/931-ARTS (TicketMaster). Performing at the Wang Center; tickets can be purchased at the box office at 270 Tremont St., Mon–Sat 10am–6pm. Tickets $21–$65. Student rush tickets $12 (one hour before curtain).

Boston Ballet's reputation seems to jump up a notch every time someone says, "Oh, so it's not just *The Nutcracker.*" The country's fourth-largest dance company is a holiday staple, but during the rest of the season (October through May), it builds on 33 years of top-notch productions and a wide-ranging repertoire that includes classic story ballets as well as contemporary works.

FleetCenter. Causeway St. ☎ **617/624-1000** (events line) or 617/931-2000 (TicketMaster).

The state-of-the-art FleetCenter opened in September 1995, replacing legendary (but woefully outdated) Boston Garden as the home of the Bruins (hockey), the Celtics (basketball), and touring rock and pop artists. Concerts are presented in the round or in the arena stage format.

✪ Harborlights Pavilion. Fan Pier, Northern Ave. ☎ **617/374-9000** or 617/426-NEXT to order tickets. Web site http://www.harborlights.com.

Soft rock, pop, folk, and jazz performers draw crowds to a giant white tent on the waterfront that holds single-level seating for evening events from June through September. The pleasant, airy setting, convenient location, and reasonable size make Harborlights a wonderful place to spend a few musical hours.

THE CLUB & MUSIC SCENE

The club scene in Boston and Cambridge is multifaceted and constantly changing, but somewhere out there is a good time for everyone, regardless of age, clothing style, musical tastes, and budget. Check the *Phoenix,* the *Improper Bostonian,* the "Calendar" section of the Thursday *Globe,* the "Scene" section of the Friday *Herald,* or the *Tab* while you're making plans.

At most nightspots, unless otherwise specified, the admission or cover charge varies according to the night of the week and the entertainment offered, from up to $3 for a bar to more than $20 for a well-known jazz headliner.

COMEDY

✪ Comedy Connection at Faneuil Hall. Quincy Market, Upper Rotunda. ☎ **617/ 248-9700.** Cover $8–$30.

A large room with a clear view from every seat, the oldest original comedy club in town, established in 1968, draws top-notch talent from near and far. Big-name national acts lure crowds, and the openers are often just as funny but not as famous— yet. You can order munchies or come early for dinner (served only before the show). Shows are nightly at 8:30 with late shows on Friday and Saturday at 10:30pm. The cover charge seldom tops $12 during the week, but soars for a big name appearing on a weekend.

FOLK

Club Passim. 47 Palmer St., Cambridge. ☎ **617/492-7679.** Cover $5–$10.

Passim has launched more careers than the mass production of acoustic guitars—Joan Baez, Suzanne Vega, and Michelle Shocked started out here. Located in a basement on the street between buildings of the Harvard Coop, this coffeehouse is still building on a reputation for more than 30 years of nurturing new talent and showcasing established musicians. There's live music four to six nights a week and Sunday afternoons, and coffee and light meals are available all the time. Open Sunday to Thursday 11am to 11pm, Friday and Saturday 11am to 4am.

◉ Nameless Coffee House. 3 Church St., Cambridge. ☎ **617/864-1630.** Cover $3.

The Nameless represents a foot in the door for a wide range of musicians. The young crowd comes for the promising talent, the storytelling, and the free refreshments (coffee, cider, tea, cocoa, and cookies). Don't worry if half the patrons suddenly get up and leave—they're probably friends of the person who just finished performing. Open September to June, Friday and Saturday 7:30pm to midnight.

ROCK

Mama Kin and Mama Kin Music Hall. 41 Lansdowne St. ☎ **617/536-2100.** Cover for Music Hall only, $7–$25.

Members of the Boston-based band Aerosmith co-own Mama Kin and the adjacent music hall, which opened in December 1994 to wide acclaim and instant popularity. You probably won't see Steven Tyler, but you will see up-and-comers early in the week, and more established artists toward the weekend. Open seven nights; doors open at 8 or 9. Some shows are 19-plus (you must be 21 to drink alcohol).

✪ **The Rathskeller (The Rat).** 528 Commonwealth Ave. ☎ **617/536-2750** or 617/536-6508 (concert line). Cover downstairs only, $5–$7.

For 23 years, the Rathskeller (known far and wide as "the Rat") has been in the heart of Kenmore Square dispensing rock and riding out the fickle whims of musical fashion. There's nothing glamorous here—just live music Tuesday through Sunday nights and Sunday afternoons in the street-level room, tables and pool tables upstairs, and pretty good food. The menu features chicken and burgers and also includes vegetarian offerings and sandwiches. The restaurant is open 11am to 10pm, the bar until 2am.

T.T. the Bear's Place. 10 Brookline St., Central Sq., Cambridge. ☎ **617/492-0082** or 617/492-BEAR (concert line). Cover $6–$10.

T.T.'s admits people 18 and older (you must be 21 to drink alcohol), and its cutting-edge alternative music attracts a young crowd. Entertainment is offered from 9pm on. Monday night is Stone Soup Poetry night, and on Sunday Ethiopian food is served from 2pm to midnight.

JAZZ & BLUES

✪ **House of Blues.** 96 Winthrop St., Cambridge. ☎ **617/491-BLUE.** Cover $6–$15; $3 Sat matinees.

The original House of Blues packs 'em in for evening and weekend matinee shows, attracting big names and hordes of fans. Reservations are highly recommended. Call the above number for tickets and show times.

Regattabar. In the Charles Hotel, 1 Bennett St., Cambridge. ☎ **617/661-5000** or 617/876-7777 (Concertix). Tickets $5–$25.

The Regattabar features a selection of local and international artists considered the best in the area; Cassandra Wilson, Ellis and Branford Marsalis, Tito Puente, the Count Basie Orchestra, and Karen Akers have appeared within the past two years. The large third-floor room holds about 200 and has a 21-foot picture window overlooking Harvard Square. Buy tickets in advance from Concertix (there's a $2 per ticket service charge) or try your luck at the door one hour before the performance is scheduled to start. Open Tuesday through Saturday and some Sundays with one or two performances per night.

Ryles Jazz Club. 212 Hampshire St., Inman Sq., Cambridge. ☎ **617/876-9330.** Cover $5–$10.

During an evening at Ryles you can shuttle back and forth between the two levels or settle on one floor for the evening. True music buffs turn out here, for dining in the downstairs room with tunes in the background, and a wide variety of first-rate jazz, world beat, and Latin performances upstairs. Both levels offer good music and a friendly atmosphere. Open Tuesday through Sunday and some Mondays.

Scullers Jazz Club. In the Doubletree Guest Suites Hotel, 400 Soldiers Field Rd. ☎ **617/783-0811.** Cover $6–$23.

Overlooking the Charles River, Scullers books top jazz singers and instrumentalists in a comfortable, newly expanded room. Shows are usually Monday through Saturday. There's also an excellent monthly dinner/jazz show.

ECLECTIC

✪ **Johnny D's.** 17 Holland St., Davis Sq., Somerville. ☎ **617/776-2004** or 617/776-9667 (concert line). Cover $6–$10.

This family-owned and -operated restaurant and music club is one of the best in the area. You might catch acts on national and international tours, or acts that haven't been out of the 617 area code. The music ranges from zydeco to rock, rockabilly to jazz, blues to ska. The food's even good. Johnny D's is worth a long trip, but it's no more than 20 minutes from Harvard Square on the Red Line.

DANCE CLUBS

Axis. 13 Lansdowne St. ☎ **617/262-2437.** Cover $6–$8.

Progressive rock and "creative dress" attract a young crowd to Axis. There are special nights for hard rock, heavy metal, and alternative rock. Open Tuesday to Sunday 10pm to 2am.

✪ **Avalon.** 15 Lansdowne St. ☎ **617/262-2424.** Cover $5–$10.

A cavernous space divided into several levels, with a full concert stage, private booths and lounges, large dance floors, and a spectacular light show, Avalon is either great fun or a sensory overload. When the stage is not in use, you'll hear international music and, particularly on Saturday (suburbanites' night out), mainstream dance hits. The dress code calls for jackets, shirts with collars, and no jeans or athletic wear; the crowd is slightly older than at Axis. Open Thursday ("Euro night") to Sunday (gay night).

Zanzibar. 1 Boylston Pl. ☎ **617/351-2560.** Cover $5.

An atrium with a balcony and 25-foot-tall palm trees is the setting in which enthusiastic dancers gyrate to contemporary hits. The upscale clientele take breaks from dancing in the billiard room. The dress code (jackets and shirts with collars for men; no jeans or athletic wear) is strictly enforced. Open Wednesday to Saturday 9pm to 2am.

THE BAR SCENE

Boston Beer Works. 61 Brookline Ave. ☎ **617/536-2337.** No cover.

Across the street from Fenway Park, this cavernous microbrewery with vats right out on the floor is chaotic anyway, and before and after Red Sox games it's a madhouse. Visit during a road trip for excellent bitters and ales, seasonal concoctions such as Bambino Ale, lager with blueberries floating in it (not as dreadful as it sounds), hard cider, and particularly the cask-conditioned offerings, seasoned in wood till they're as smooth as fine wine. Sweet potato fries make a terrific snack, but don't plan on being able to hear anything your friends are saying. Open daily from 11:30am to 12:45am.

Bull & Finch Pub. 84 Beacon St. ☎ **617/227-9605.** No cover.

If you're out to impersonate a native, try not to be completely shocked when you walk into the Bull & Finch and realize it looks nothing like the bar on "Cheers" (the outside does, though). It really is a neighborhood bar, but today it's far better known for attracting legions of out-of-towners, who find good pub grub, drinks, and plenty of souvenirs. Food is served from 11am to 1:15am.

Commonwealth Brewing Company. 138 Portland St. ☎ **617/523-8383.** No cover.

Boston's first brewpub is still going strong 10 years after it started the trend. It doesn't hurt that the "Commonwealth Brewery," as you'll often hear it called, is a block from North Station and madly popular with the crowds heading to the FleetCenter (and before that, Boston Garden). The English-style brews are top-notch and served alone and in traditional combinations such as the snakebite (lager and hard cider) and shandy (ale and lemon soda). Here, too, the food is quite good—try the hummus plate. Open from 11:30am till midnight Sunday through Thursday, till 1am Friday and Saturday. There's live music and dancing downstairs Friday and Saturday nights.

Hard Rock Cafe. 131 Clarendon St. ☎ **617/353-1400.** No cover.

Still going strong since its establishment in London in 1971, the Hard Rock Cafe chain is perhaps the most successful restaurant network in the world, and this link in the chain is a fun one. The restaurant menu leans toward salads, burgers, and sandwiches (including the house specialty, "pig sandwich"). The bar is shaped like a guitar; the taped music bounces off all the hard surfaces and keeps the volume at a dull roar; stained-glass windows glorify rock stars; and the room is decorated with memorabilia of John Lennon, Jimi Hendrix, Elvis Presley, the local heroes from Aerosmith, and others. T-shirts and other goods are for sale at the Hard Rock store. Open daily 11am to 1am for food and until 2am at the bar.

John Harvard's Brew House. 33 Dunster St., Cambridge. ☎ **617/868-3585.** No cover.

This subterranean Harvard Square hangout pumps out English-style brews in a clublike setting (see if you can make out the sports figures in the stained-glass windows) and prides itself on its food. The selection of beers changes regularly, and aficionados will have fun sampling John Harvard's Pale Ale, Nut Brown Ale, Pilgrim's Porter, and brewmeister Tim Morse's other concoctions. Open daily 11:30am to 3:30pm and 5 to 10pm.

Cambridge & Eastern Massachusetts

5

by Marie Morris

In addition to being, as the saying goes, "the hub of the solar system," Boston is the hub of a network of wonderful day trips and longer excursions. Wherever you go, you'll find sights and attractions of great beauty and historical significance. All of the destinations described here make fascinating, manageable day trips and also offer enough diversions to fill several days. All are accessible by public transportation, but driving is preferable if you want to set your own pace.

If you have a few days to spend exploring eastern Massachusetts and history is your main motivation, consider approaching the area in roughly chronological order. Start in Plymouth with the Pilgrims, move on to Lexington and Concord to learn about the rebellious colonists, then acquaint yourself with the North Shore and Cape Ann and the prosperity of the Federal era.

WEST OF BOSTON Cambridge alone can take up a day or more, but if time is short, a visit can be combined with a trip to Lexington and Concord for a hefty dose of American history. Cambridge is about 15 minutes from Boston by subway (or longer by bus). Lexington is accessible by MBTA bus from Cambridge, and Concord can be reached by commuter rail from Boston and from Porter Square in Cambridge, north of Harvard Square.

NORTH OF BOSTON The years immediately following the Revolution brought great prosperity to eastern Massachusetts as the new nation took advantage of the lifting of British trade barriers. The spoils of the China trade can still be seen in the mansions and public edifices in the seaside towns and cities between Boston and the New Hampshire border. Fishing is still an important industry, but today this part of the world caters more to commuters and tourists than to those who make their living from the sea. The MBTA commuter rail and a network of bus lines run to and around the North Shore and Cape Ann.

SOUTH OF BOSTON The towns between Boston and Cape Cod are mostly suburban bedroom communities. The one that's famous on its own is Plymouth. One of the oldest permanent European settlements in North America, Plymouth is a lovely town where you can walk in the footsteps of the Pilgrims—and the countless out-of-towners who come in the summer and at Thanksgiving. Farther south, the old whaling port of New Bedford and the textile-industry center of Fall River make interesting detours. All three are accessible from Boston by bus.

1 Cambridge

Cambridge is so closely associated with Boston that many people believe they're the same city—a notion both cities' residents and politicians would be happy to dispel. Cantabrigians are often considered more liberal and better educated than Bostonians, which is another idea that's sure to get you involved in a heated discussion. Harvard dominates Cambridge's history and geography, but there's much more to see than just the university.

ESSENTIALS

GETTING THERE By public transportation from Boston, take the MBTA Red Line toward Alewife. Once in Cambridge, the subway stops at Kendall/MIT, and Central, Harvard, and Porter squares. If you're staying in or visiting the Back Bay, the longer and more colorful route is the number 1 bus (Harvard–Dudley), which runs along Massachusetts Avenue. It cuts through a wide variety of neighborhoods and affords a nice view of the Charles River but can be very slow at rush hour.

By car from Boston, follow Massachusetts Avenue, or take Storrow Drive along the south bank of the river to the Harvard Square exit. Or take Memorial Drive along the north side of the river to MIT, Central Square, or Harvard. From the Massachusetts Turnpike, take the Allston/Brighton exit, then turn left onto Storrow Drive or cross the bridge to reach Memorial Drive.

VISITOR INFORMATION At the main Harvard "T" entrance, there's an information booth run by **Cambridge Discovery, Inc.** (P.O. Box 1987, Cambridge, MA 02238; ☎ **617/497-1630**). It's in the middle of Harvard Square at the intersection of Massachusetts Avenue, John F. Kennedy Street, and Brattle Street. Trained volunteers dispense maps and brochures and answer questions Monday to Saturday from 9am to 5pm and Sunday from 1 to 5pm. From mid-June through Labor Day there are guided tours that include the entire old Cambridge area. Check at the booth about rates, meeting places, and times, or call ahead. If you prefer to sightsee on your own, you can purchase an old Cambridge or East Cambridge walking guide prepared by the Cambridge Historical Commission for $1.

GETTING AROUND Traffic in and around Harvard Square is almost as bad as in downtown Boston. Park the car and walk. If you prefer to ride, you can take a 75-minute narrated tour given by **Old Town Trolley** (329 W. Second St., Boston; ☎ **617/269-7010**). Tours leave from the middle of Harvard Square, near **Out of Town News** (a newspaper and magazine shop right outside the Harvard Square "T" stop), every 45 minutes between 9am and 4pm, and you may leave the trolley and reboard anywhere along the route. Tickets are $14 adults, $12 seniors, $7 children.

WHAT TO SEE & DO

Harvard Square offers something for almost everyone. It's a people-watching paradise of college and high school students, instructors, commuters, street performers, and sightseers. There are restaurants and stores along all three streets that radiate from the center of the square and the streets that intersect them. On weekend afternoons and evenings year-round, you'll hear music and see entertainers, and this is a great area for just walking around. To get away from the urban bustle, stroll down to the paved paths along the Charles River.

In case you want to see the world.

At American Express, we're here to make your journey a smooth one. So we have over 1,700 travel service locations in over 120 countries ready to help. What else would you expect from the world's largest travel agency?

do more

Travel

In case you want to be welcomed there.

We're here to see that you're always welcomed at establishments everywhere. That's why millions of people carry the American Express® Card – for peace of mind, confidence, and security, around the world or just around the corner.

do more

Cards

In case you're running low.

We're here to help with more than 118,000 Express Cash

locations around the world. In order to enroll, just call

American Express before you start your vacation.

do more

Express Cash

And just in case.

We're here with American Express® Travelers Cheques and Cheques _for Two_.® They're the safest way to carry money on your vacation and the surest way to get a refund, practically anywhere, anytime.

Another way we help you…

do more

AMERICAN EXPRESS

Travelers Cheques

ATTRACTIONS AT HARVARD UNIVERSITY

Harvard is the oldest college in the United States, with the most competitive admissions process, and if while visiting you suggest aloud that it's not the best, you may run up against the snobby attitude that inspired the saying "You can always tell a Harvard man, but you can't tell him much." Harvard includes the college and 10 graduate and professional schools located in more than 400 buildings around Boston and Cambridge.

During the school year, free, student-led tours leave from the **Holyoke Center Information Office** (1350 Massachusetts Ave.; ☎ 617/495-1573) twice a day during the week and once on Saturday, except during vacations; and during the summer, tours leave four times a day Monday through Saturday and twice on Sunday. Call for exact times; reservations aren't necessary, and you're also free to wander on your own. The information center has maps, illustrated booklets, and self-guided walking-tour directions, as well as a bulletin board where campus activities are publicized. See "A Stroll Around Cambridge," below.

Note that Harvard buildings are integrated into the community as well as set apart from it—structures in use by the school typically have plaques or other identifying features on the front.

Harvard University Museum of Cultural and Natural History. 26 Oxford St. ☎ 617/495-3045. Admission $5 adults, $4 students and seniors, $3 children 3–13, children under 3 free; free to all Sat 9am–noon. Mon–Sat 9am–5pm, Sun 1–5pm; closed New Year's Day, July 4th, Thanksgiving, and Christmas. MBTA: Red Line to Harvard. Cross Harvard Yard, keeping the John Harvard statue on your right, and turn right at the Science Center. The first street on the left is Oxford St.

This museum is actually four fascinating institutions: the Botanical Museum, the Museum of Comparative Zoology, the Mineralogical & Geological Museum, and the Peabody Museum of Archaeology & Ethnology. Under new director Cherrie Corey, a push began in 1995 to make the world-famous scholarly resource center even more accessible to the public, an initiative that should be bearing fruit by the time you visit. Even if the new interdisciplinary programs and exhibitions that tie in elements of all four collections don't appeal to you, you'll find something interesting here.

The best-known museum of the four is the **Botanical Museum**, and the best-known display there is the Glass Flowers, 3,000 models of more than 840 plant species devised between 1887 and 1936 by the German father-and-son team of Leopold and Rudolph Blaschka. You may have heard about them, and you may be skeptical, but it's true: they actually look real.

Children love the **Museum of Comparative Zoology**, where the dinosaurs share space with preserved and stuffed insects and animals that range in size from butterflies to giraffes. Young visitors also enjoy the dollhouse-like "Worlds in Miniature" display at the **Peabody Museum of Archaeology & Ethnology**, which capture people from all over the world in scaled-down homes. The Peabody also boasts the Hall of the North American Indian, where 500 Native American artifacts representing 10 cultures are on display, and where a terrific gift shop (☎ 617/495-2248) is packed with reasonably priced folk art and craftwork. The **Mineralogical & Geological Museum** is the most specialized of the four—unless there's an interesting interdisciplinary display or you're really into rocks, your time can be more productively spent elsewhere.

The complex also has a web site (http://fas-www.harvard.edu/~peabody museum_cult.html).

Around Boston

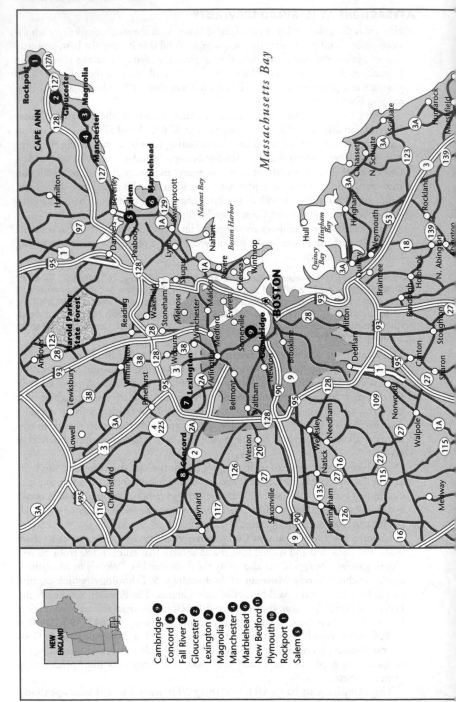

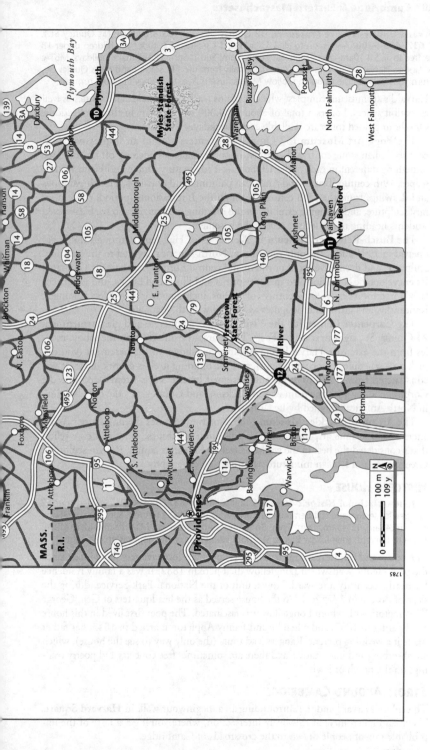

Harvard University Art Museums. 32 Quincy St. and 485 Broadway (at Quincy St.).
☎ **617/495-9400.** Admission to all 3 $5 adults, $4 seniors, $3 students, children under 18 free; free to all Sat 10am–noon. Mon–Sat 10am–5pm, Sun 1–5pm; closed major holidays. MBTA: Red Line to Harvard. Cross Harvard Yard diagonally from the "T" station and cross Quincy St., or turn your back on the Coop and follow Massachusetts Ave. to Quincy St., then turn left.

Harvard's art museum complex, which contains teaching and research facilities as well as exhibit spaces, houses a total of about 150,000 works of art in three collections. One-hour guided tours are available every weekday.

The **Fogg Art Museum** (32 Quincy St.) centers around an impressive 16th-century Italian stone courtyard, with two floors of galleries opening off it. You'll see something different in each of the 19 rooms—17th-century Dutch and Flemish landscapes, 19th-century British and American paintings and drawings, French paintings and drawings from the 18th century through the Impressionist period, contemporary sculpture, and changing exhibits. In the morning, you might also see bleary-eyed students heading to the lecture hall in the basement.

The **Busch-Reisinger Museum** in Werner Otto Hall (enter through the Fogg) opened in 1991 and is the only museum in North America devoted to the painting, sculpture, and decorative art of northern and central Europe—specifically Germany. Its encyclopedic collection also includes prints and illustrated books, and is particularly noted for its early 20th-century collections, including works by Klee, Feininger, Kandinsky, and artists and designers associated with the Bauhaus.

The **Carpenter Center for the Visual Arts** is a concrete and glass structure at 24 Quincy St., right next to the Fogg. There are art exhibitions in the lobby, movies from the extensive Harvard Film Archives are shown in the basement (you can pick up a schedule on the main floor), and the building itself is a work of art. It was constructed from 1961 to 1963 and designed by the Swiss-French architect Le Corbusier, along with the team of Sert, Jackson, and Gourley. It's the only building in North America designed by Le Corbusier.

The **Arthur M. Sackler Museum** (485 Broadway) houses the university's Asian, ancient, and Islamic art. Included are a collection of Chinese jades and cave reliefs that's considered the best in the world, as well as Korean ceramics, Roman sculpture, Greek vases, and Persian miniature paintings and calligraphy.

A HISTORIC HOUSE

Longfellow National Historic Site. 105 Brattle St. ☎ **617/876-4491.** Guided tour $2 adults, free for seniors and children under 16. Mid-May to mid-Oct to Wed–Sun 10am–4:30pm; tours at 10:45am, 11:45am, 1pm, 2pm, 3pm, and 4pm. Closed mid-Oct to mid-May. MBTA: Red Line to Harvard, then follow Brattle St. about seven blocks; the house is on the right.

The books and furniture at this ravishing yellow mansion have remained intact since the poet Henry Wadsworth Longfellow died here in 1882. It was a family residence for nearly a century afterward. Now a unit of the National Park Service, during the siege of Boston in 1775 to 1776 the house served as the headquarters of Gen. George Washington, with whom Longfellow was fascinated. The poet first lived in this house as a boarder in 1837, and when he and Fanny Appleton married in 1843, her father made it a wedding present. Rangers lead tours (the only way to see the house), which are absorbing and informative, and there are sometimes free concerts and poetry readings on the porch or lawn.

A STROLL AROUND CAMBRIDGE

To explore Harvard and the surrounding area, begin your walk in **Harvard Square.** Town and gown meet at this lively intersection, where you'll get a taste of the improbable mix of people drawn to the crossroads of Cambridge.

Locate the Au Bon Pain cafe between Dunster and Holyoke streets in the base of the **Holyoke Center,** an administration building designed by Josep Luis Sert with commercial space on the ground floor. It's easy to spot; the Holyoke Center is the tallest building in the vicinity. Standing with your back to the Au Bon Pain you'll be facing **Wadsworth House** (1341 Massachusetts Ave.), a yellow wood building across the street that was built in 1726 as a residence for Harvard's fourth president. Now the headquarters of the alumni association, its biggest claim to fame is a classic: "George Washington slept here."

Cross the street and enter the **Harvard Yard** through the gate to the left of Wadsworth House, walking along the path until you find yourself on the edge of a grassy plaza lined with paths and dotted with trees. "The Yard" was just a patch of grass with animals grazing on it when Harvard College was established in 1636 to train young men for the ministry. It wasn't much more when the Continental Army spent the winter here in 1775 to 1776. Now some of Harvard's most historic buildings are within this quadrangle, including **University Hall** (across the Yard to your right), the college's main administration building, constructed in 1812 to 1813 of granite quarried in nearby Chelmsford. In 1969 it was occupied by students protesting the Vietnam War, but it's best known as the backdrop of the **John Harvard Statue,** one of the most photographed objects in the Boston area. Designed by Daniel Chester French in 1884, it's known as the "Statue of Three Lies" because the inscription reads "John Harvard—Founder—1638." In fact, the college was founded in 1636; Harvard (one of many involved in its establishment) didn't really found the university—instead he donated money and his library; and this isn't John Harvard, anyway. No portraits of him survive, so the model was, according to various accounts, either his nephew or a student. This benevolent-looking bronze gentleman is occasionally doused with paint in the school color of a rival football team during the week before a big game, and almost instantaneously cleaned up. Luckily for him, Harvard's football team hasn't been very good recently, and the heated rivalries have cooled somewhat. Walk over to the statue and join the throng of tourists posing for pictures beside, in front of, or even in the lap of the famous monument.

John Harvard's statue faces a number of the Yard's most historic buildings. Facing them with your back to the statue, from the left they are **Matthews Hall,** a residence for first-year students; **Massachusetts Hall,** a National Historic Landmark which dates from 1720 and the university's oldest surviving building, now housing the office of the university president as well as freshmen; **Harvard Hall,** a classroom building constructed in 1765; and **Hollis** and **Stoughton halls,** matching side-by-side dormitories which date from 1763 and 1805, respectively. Hollis has been home to many students who went on to great fame, among them Ralph Waldo Emerson, Henry David Thoreau, and Charles Bulfinch.

Walk around University Hall into the adjoining quadrangle. This is still the Yard, but it's the "New Yard," sometimes called Tercentenary Theater because the college's 300th anniversary celebration was held here. This is where commencement and other universitywide ceremonies (most recently the 350th birthday party in 1986) are held. On your right is **Widener Library,** the centerpiece of the world's largest university library system. It was built in 1913 as a memorial to Harry Elkins Widener, a 1907 Harvard graduate who died when the *Titanic* sank in 1912 because he was unable to swim 50 yards to a lifeboat. His mother donated $2 million for the library on the condition that every undergraduate prove his ability to swim 50 yards or take swimming lessons. Today the library holds more than 3 million volumes, including 3,500 rare volumes collected by Harry Elkins Widener. It was designed by Horace Trumbauer of Philadelphia, whose primary design assistant was Julian Francis Abele,

Celebrity Cemetery

In addition to being the final resting place of many well-known people, **Mount Auburn Cemetery** in Cambridge is famous simply for existing. Dedicated in 1831, it was the first of America's rural, or garden, cemeteries. The establishment of burying places removed from city and town centers reflected practical and philosophical concerns. Development was encroaching on urban graveyards, and the ideas associated with the Greek Revival (the word "cemetery" derives from the Greek for "sleeping place") and Transcendentalism dictated that communing with nature take precedence over organized religion. Since the day it opened, Mount Auburn has been a popular place to retreat and reflect—in the 19th century, it was often the first place visitors from out of town were taken, and the first place they wanted to go.

A modern visitor will find history and horticulture coexisting with celebrity. The graves of Henry Wadsworth Longfellow, Oliver Wendell Holmes, Julia Ward Howe, and Mary Baker Eddy are here, as are those of Charles Bulfinch, James Russell Lowell, Transcendentalist leader Margaret Fuller, and abolitionist Charles Sumner. In season, you'll see gorgeous flowering trees and shrubs (the Massachusetts Horticultural Society had a hand in the design). Stop at the office or front gate to pick up brochures and a map or to rent the 60-minute audiotaped tour ($5; a $12 deposit is required), which you can listen to in your car or on a portable tape player. The **Friends of Mount Auburn Cemetery** (☎ 617/864-9646) conduct workshops and coordinate walking tours. Call for topics, schedules, and fees.

The cemetery (580 Mount Auburn St., Cambridge; ☎ 617/547-7105) is open daily from 8am to dusk. Admission is free. Animals and recreational activities such as jogging and picnicking are not allowed. MBTA bus routes 71 and 73 start at Harvard station and stop across the street; they run frequently on weekdays, less often on weekends. From Harvard Square by car (about 10 minutes) or on foot (at least 30 minutes), take Mount Auburn Street or Brattle Street west; just after they intersect, the gate is on the left.

a student of architecture at the University of Pennsylvania and the first black graduate of L'Ecole des Beaux Arts in Paris.

Facing the library is **Memorial Church,** built in 1931 and topped with a tower and weathervane 197 feet tall. You're welcome to look around this Georgian Revival–style edifice unless services are going on—or to attend them if they are. Morning prayers are said daily from 8:45 to 9, and the Sunday service is at 11am. The building is also used for private weddings and funerals. The entrance is on the left. On the south wall, toward the Yard, the names of the Harvard graduates who died in the world wars, Korea, and Vietnam are listed, including that of Joseph P. Kennedy Jr., the president's brother, class of 1938.

With Memorial Church behind you, turn left toward **Sever Hall,** a classroom building designed by H. H. Richardson (the architect of Trinity Church) and built from 1878 to 1880. Notice the gorgeous brickwork that includes roll moldings around the doors, and the fluted brick chimneys. The front door is set back in the "whispering gallery." Stand on one side of the entrance arch, station a friend or willing passerby on the opposite side, and speak softly into the facade. Someone standing next to you can't hear what you say, but the person at the other side of the arch can.

Harvard Square & Environs

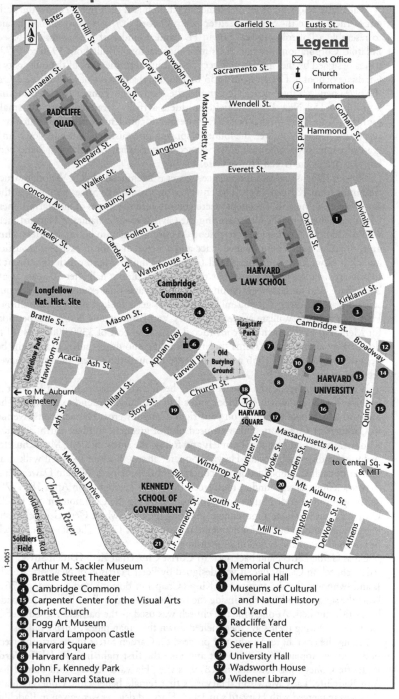

Legend

⊠ Post Office
† Church
(i) Information

RADCLIFFE QUAD

Longfellow Nat. Hist. Site

Cambridge Common

HARVARD LAW SCHOOL

Flagstaff Park

Old Burying Ground

HARVARD UNIVERSITY

HARVARD SQUARE

← to Mt. Auburn cemetery

to Central Sq. → & MIT

KENNEDY SCHOOL OF GOVERNMENT

Charles River

Soldiers Field

1-0051

Street labels: Bates, Avon Hill St., Garfield St., Eustis St., Linnaean St., Gray St., Bowdoin St., Avon St., Sacramento St., Massachusetts Av., Wendell St., Oxford St., Gorham St., Hammond, Langdon, Everett St., Divinity Av., Shepard St., Walker St., Concord Av., Chauncy St., Follen St., Berkeley St., Garden St., Waterhouse St., Kirkland St., Brattle St., Mason St., Cambridge St., Broadway, Longfellow Park, Hawthorn St., Acacia, Ash St., Appian Way, Farwell Pl., Church St., Hillard St., Story St., Quincy St., Memorial Drive, Ash St., Winthrop St., Dunster St., Holyoke St., Linden St., Mt. Auburn St., Eliot St., Plympton St., DeWolfe St., Athens, J.F. Kennedy St., South St., Mill St., Soldiers Field Rd.

- 12 Arthur M. Sackler Museum
- 19 Brattle Street Theater
- 4 Cambridge Common
- 15 Carpenter Center for the Visual Arts
- 6 Christ Church
- 14 Fogg Art Museum
- 20 Harvard Lampoon Castle
- 18 Harvard Square
- 8 Harvard Yard
- 21 John F. Kennedy Park
- 10 John Harvard Statue
- 11 Memorial Church
- 3 Memorial Hall
- 1 Museums of Cultural and Natural History
- 7 Old Yard
- 5 Radcliffe Yard
- 2 Science Center
- 13 Sever Hall
- 9 University Hall
- 17 Wadsworth House
- 16 Widener Library

Walk back across the front of Memorial Church and turn right. Follow the path out of the Yard to the **Science Center** (Zero Oxford St.), a 10-story monolith said to resemble a Polaroid camera (Edwin H. Land, founder of the Cambridge-based Polaroid Corporation, was one of its main benefactors). Built from 1970 to 1972, it was designed by the Spanish architect Josep Luis Sert, the dean of the university's Graduate School of Design from 1953 to 1969, and a disciple of Le Corbusier. On the plaza between the Science Center and the Yard is the **Tanner Rock Fountain,** a group of 159 New England field boulders artfully arranged around a small fountain. Since 1985 this has been a favorite spot for students to relax and watch unsuspecting passersby get wet; the fountain sprays a fine mist, which begins slowly and gradually intensifies. Step inside the Science Center to have a look around and perhaps a snack at the **Green House Cafe.**

To your right as you face the Science Center is **Memorial Hall,** a Victorian structure built from 1870 to 1874. The entrance on Cambridge Street puts you in the actual hall of memorials, a transept where you can read the names of the Harvard men who died fighting for the Union during the Civil War—the names of Harvard men who died for the Confederacy are absent. Memorial Hall also houses **Sanders Theater,** prized as both a performance space and a lecture hall for its excellent acoustics and clear views, and **Annenberg Hall** (originally Alumni Hall), which underwent a massive renovation in 1995 and was turned into a dining hall after 70 years as an open space used for class registration, blood drives, and final exams. It has gorgeous stained-glass windows that you might be able to get a look at if it's not mealtime. Harvard graduates William Ware and Henry Van Brunt won a design competition for Memorial Hall, which was constructed for a total cost of $390,000 (most of it donated by alumni). If it seems that the building should be taller, that might be because it once was. In 1956 a huge fire tore through the tower, and it was never rebuilt.

With the entrance to the Science Center behind you, turn right, and follow the walkway for the equivalent of a block and a half as it curves around to the right. The Harvard Law School campus is on your right. Carefully cross Massachusetts Avenue to **Cambridge Common.** This well-used plot of greenery and bare earth is dotted with memorials and plaques. Turn left and follow the sidewalk along Massachusetts Avenue, heading back toward Harvard Square; after a block or so you'll walk near or over horseshoes embedded in the concrete. This is the path William Dawes, Paul Revere's fellow alarm-sounder, took from Boston to Lexington on April 18, 1775. Turn right onto Garden Street and continue following the Common for one block. On your right you'll see a monument marking the place where Gen. George Washington took control of the Continental Army on July 3, 1775. The elm under which he assumed command is no longer standing.

Cross Garden Street and backtrack to **Christ Church** at Zero Garden Street. The oldest church in Cambridge, it was designed by Peter Harrison of Newport, Rhode Island (who was also the architect of King's Chapel in Boston), and opened in 1761. Note the square wooden tower. Inside the vestibule you can still see bullet holes made by British muskets. At one time the church was used as the barracks for Connecticut troops. During their stay, they melted down the organ pipes to make bullets.

Facing the church, turn right and proceed on Garden Street to the first intersection. This is Appian Way. Turn left and take the first right into **Radcliffe Yard.** Radcliffe College was founded in 1879 as the "Harvard Annex" and named for Ann Radcliffe, Lady Mowlson, Harvard's first female benefactor. Undergraduate classes were merged with Harvard's in 1943, Harvard degrees were given to Radcliffe graduates in 1963, and in 1977 responsibility for educating undergraduate women was officially turned over to Harvard. Today, Radcliffe remains an independent corporation within the university and has its own president, though its degrees, classes, and facilities are shared with Harvard. After you've strolled around, return to Appian Way and turn right. You'll emerge on Brattle Street; turn left, once again heading toward Harvard Square.

In about three blocks you'll find yourself in Brattle Square, part of Harvard Square. You may see street musicians or performers, a protest, a speech, or just more stores to explore. Cross Brattle Street at WordsWorth bookstore, turn right, and follow the curve of the building around the corner to Mount Auburn Street. Stay on the left-hand side of the street as you cross John F. Kennedy Street, Dunster Street, Holyoke Street, and Linden Street. The corner of Mount Auburn and Linden streets is a good vantage point for viewing the **Harvard Lampoon Castle,** designed by Wheelwright and Haven in 1909. Listed on the National Register of Historic Places, this is the home of Harvard's undergraduate humor magazine, the *Lampoon.* The main tower looks like a face, with windows as the eyes, nose, and mouth, topped by what looks like a miner's hat. The *Lampoon* and the daily student newspaper, the *Crimson,* share a long history of reciprocal pranks and harmless vandalism. Elaborate security measures notwithstanding, *Crimson* editors occasionally make off with the bird atop the castle (it looks like a crane but is actually an ibis), and *Lampoon* staffers have absconded with the huge wooden president's chair from the *Crimson,* which is less than a block away on Plympton Street.

Follow Mount Auburn Street back to John F. Kennedy Street and turn left. Cross the street at some point, and follow it toward the Charles River, almost to Memorial Drive. On your right is **John F. Kennedy Park.** This lovely parcel of land was an empty plot near the MBTA train yard in the 1970s (at that time the Red Line ended at Harvard), when the search was on for a site for the Kennedy Library. Traffic concerns led to the library's being built in Dorchester, but the Graduate School of Government and this adjacent park bear the president's name. Walk away from the street to enjoy the fountain, which is engraved with excerpts from the president's speeches. This is an excellent place to take a break and plan the rest of your day.

SHOPPING

Harvard Square is packed with bookstores, boutiques, and T-shirt shops. An aggressive neighborhood association has kept the area from being swallowed up by chain stores, and although the bohemian days of "the Square" are long gone, you'll find a mix of national and regional outlets as well as independent retailers. A walk along Massachusetts Avenue in either direction to the next "T" stop (Porter to the north, Central to the southeast) will take an hour or so, time well-spent for dedicated shoppers. If you just can't manage without a trip to a mall, head to East Cambridge or take the Red Line to Kendall/MIT, then the free shuttle bus to the **CambridgeSide Galleria** (100 CambridgeSide Place.; ☎ 617/621-8666).

Bookstore fiends flock to Cambridge—Harvard Square in particular caters to general and specific audiences. Check out the basement of the **Harvard Book Store** (1256 Massachusetts Ave.; ☎ 800/542-READ outside 617 or 617/661-1515) for great deals on remainders and used books; **WordsWorth** (30 Brattle St.; ☎ 800/899-2202 or 617/354-5201) for a huge selection, all discounted; and the **Coop** (1400 Massachusetts Ave.; ☎ 617/499-2000) for textbooks, academic works, and a large general selection.

WHERE TO STAY
VERY EXPENSIVE

❂ The Charles Hotel. 1 Bennett St., Cambridge, MA 02138. ☎ **800/882-1818** outside MA or 617/864-1200. Fax 617/864-5715. 252 rms, 45 suites. A/C MINIBAR TV TEL. $239–$259 double; $325–$1,500 suite. Children under 18 stay free in parents' room. Weekend and spa packages available. AE, CB, DC, DISC, JCB, MC, V. Parking $18. MBTA: Red Line to Harvard.

The Charles Hotel is a curious phenomenon—an instant classic. The nine-story brick hotel a block from Harvard Square has been *the* place to stay in Cambridge since it opened in 1985. Much of its fame derives from its excellent restaurants, jazz bar, and day spa, and the service is, if anything, equally exalted.

Antique blue-and-white New England quilts, handcrafted between 1865 and 1885, hang in the lobby's oak staircase and at the entrance to each floor. In the guest rooms, the style is contemporary country, with custom-designed adaptations of early American Shaker furniture and down quilts. Bathrooms are equipped with telephones, TVs, hair dryers, and scales. All rooms have large windows that open, incredibly comfortable beds, dataports, and state-of-the-art Bose wave radios equipped with powerful speakers for true audiophiles. And it wouldn't be Cambridge if your intellectual needs went unfulfilled—you can order books over the phone, and a Charles staffer will pick them up at the WordsWorth discount bookstore and bill your room.

Dining/Entertainment: Rialto, one of the best restaurants in greater Boston, serves Mediterranean cuisine by award-winning chef Jody Adams. Henrietta's Table offers New England country cooking at breakfast, lunch, dinner, and Sunday buffet brunch. The Regattabar features live jazz every night.

Services: Concierge, 24-hour room service, laundry service, turndown service, twice-daily maid service, valet parking.

Facilities: Pay-per-view movies; glass-enclosed pool; Jacuzzi; sun terrace; and exercise room at the Well Bridge Health and Fitness Center. Beauty treatments are available at the European-style Le Pli Day Spa. Facilities for teleconferencing. Seven floors for nonsmokers; 13 rooms for the disabled; rooms with special amenities for women travelers.

EXPENSIVE

Hyatt Regency Cambridge. 575 Memorial Dr., Cambridge, MA 02139. ☎ **800/233-1234** or 617/492-1234. Fax 617/491-6906. 469 rms. A/C TV TEL. $154–$239 double; $400–$575 suite. Extra person $25. Children under 18 stay free in parents' room. Weekend packages available. AE, DC, DISC, JCB, MC, V. Valet parking $16; self-parking $14.

This dramatic hotel, a prominent feature of the Cambridge skyline, is just as eye-catching inside. The terraced redbrick structure across the street from the Charles River encloses a 16-story atrium complete with diamond-shaped glass elevators, fountains, trees, and balconies. Rooms are nicely appointed, and some have breathtaking views of the river and the Boston skyline. Families are especially welcome. There are special reduced room rates for parents whose children sleep in a different room, and adult's and children's bicycles are available for rental.

The Hyatt Regency is about 10 minutes from downtown Boston and especially convenient for those visiting colleges, since it's halfway between Harvard and MIT and across the bridge from Boston University.

Dining/Entertainment: Jonah's Seafood Cafe, open to the atrium on one side and to a view of the river on the other, serves breakfast, lunch, dinner, and Sunday brunch. On the rooftop, the revolving, glass-enclosed Spinnaker restaurant serves dinner and Sunday brunch, and offers drinks and dancing until 12:30am during the week, 1:30am on Friday and Saturday. The Pallysadoe Sports Bar features billiard tables, darts, board games, and pinball machines.

Services: Concierge; shuttle service to points of interest; baby-sitting; currency exchange; laundry/valet service; room service; car rental service.

Facilities: Pay-per-view movies; junior Olympic-size swimming pool; full health club with steam room, sauna, and whirlpool. Floor for nonsmokers; 23 rooms for the disabled.

The Inn at Harvard. 1201 Massachusetts Ave., Cambridge, MA 02138. ☎ **800/458-5886** or 617/491-2222. Fax 617/491-6520. 109 rms, 4 suites. A/C TV TEL. $165–$249 double; $450 presidential suite. Extra person $10. Children 18 and under stay free in parents' room. Senior, AAA, and AARP discount and special packages available. AE, CB, DC, MC, V. Parking $18. MBTA: Red Line to Harvard.

At first glance, the Inn at Harvard looks almost like a dormitory. It's a stone's throw from Harvard Yard at the intersection of Massachusetts Avenue and Quincy Street, and its redbrick and Georgian-style architecture would fit nicely on campus. Step inside, though, and there's no mistaking it for anything other than an upscale hotel, popular with business travelers and university visitors. The four-story, skylit atrium opens from the "living room," where you'll find antique tables mixed with contemporary furniture, bookshelves stocked with current periodicals, newspapers, and Harvard University Press publications, and a small, upscale restaurant serving breakfast and dinner. (Guests can use the nearby Faculty Club for lunch.)

Guest rooms have cherry furniture and are elegantly decorated in neutral tones, and each room has a lounge chair or two armchairs around a table, windows that open, and an original painting from the Fogg Art Museum. Some have dormer windows and window seats. There are two phones with voice mail in each room, one of which has computer modem hookups. All rooms have night-lights.

Dining/Entertainment: The atrium restaurant serves seasonal New England fare.

Services: Business services with fax, courier, typing, copying, and package receiving and shipping; complimentary newspaper delivery; free shoeshine; room service.

Facilities: Pay-per-view movies; two floors for nonsmokers; six wheelchair-accessible rooms; safe-deposit boxes; backgammon and chess tables in the atrium library.

Royal Sonesta Hotel. 5 Cambridge Pkwy., Cambridge, MA 02142. ☎ **800/SONESTA** or 617/491-3600. Fax 617/661-5956. 400 rms, 28 suites. A/C MINIBAR TV TEL. $185–$235 double; $275–$635 suite. Children under 18 stay free in parents' room. AE, CB, DC, DISC, JCB, MC, V. Parking $15. MBTA: Green Line to Lechmere; 10-minute walk.

This hotel is in a curious location: It's close to only a few things, but it's convenient to everything. Across the street is the CambridgeSide Galleria mall, and the Boston Museum of Science is around the corner on the bridge to Boston (which is closer than Harvard Square). In the other direction, MIT is a 10-minute walk. Original contemporary artwork (including work by Andy Warhol and Frank Stella) is displayed throughout the public spaces, as well as in some guest rooms. Most rooms have a lovely view of the Charles River or the city. Everything is custom designed, with decorative furnishings, living-room and bedroom combinations, and luxurious bathrooms. Each room is equipped with a safe. Business-class rooms have personal computers, fax machines, and multiline phones. The hotel has seasonal promotions, such as free ice cream during the summer, with special rates, giveaways for children, and events for adults.

Dining/Entertainment: Davio's restaurant serves breakfast, lunch, and dinner and has an outdoor patio overlooking the Charles River that's great for warm-weather dining. The Gallery Cafe is casual.

Services: Room service (Sunday through Thursday 6am to 1am; Friday and Saturday 6am to 2am); baby-sitting service; secretarial services; courtesy van service to Boston and Cambridge.

Facilities: Heated indoor/outdoor pool with retractable roof; well-equipped health club; conference rooms. Rooms for nonsmokers and the disabled are available.

Sheraton Commander Hotel. 16 Garden St., Cambridge, MA 02138. ☎ **800/325-3535** or 617/547-4800. Fax 617/868-8322. 175 rms, 5 suites. A/C MINIBAR TV TEL. $165–$225 double; $225–$375 suite. Extra person $20. Children under 18 stay free in parents' room. AE, CB, DC, DISC, JCB, MC, V. Free parking. MBTA: Red Line to Harvard.

In the heart of the historic district of Cambridge, this six-story hotel opened in 1927, and it's exactly what you'd expect of a traditional hostelry a stone's throw from the Harvard campus. The colonial-style decor begins in the elegant lobby and extends to the guest rooms, which aren't huge but are attractively furnished. Each unique room features electronic locks, in-room coffeemakers, and phones with dataports and voice mail. The Executive Level offers additional amenities and a private lounge. Some rooms have refrigerators and whirlpools.

Dining/Entertainment: The 16 Garden Street Restaurant serves breakfast, lunch, dinner, and Sunday brunch. The 16 Garden Street Café serves lighter fare throughout the afternoon and evening.

Services: Concierge; room service until 11pm; valet parking.

Facilities: Pay-per-view movies; small fitness center; sundeck; conference rooms; laundry room.

MODERATE

A Cambridge House Bed & Breakfast Inn. 2218 Massachusetts Ave., Cambridge, MA 02140. ☎ **800/232-9989** or 617/491-6300 in U.S. and Canada, 800/96-2079 in the U.K. Fax 617/868-2848. 14 rms (10 with bath). A/C TV TEL. $109–$225 double. Extra person $35. Rates include breakfast. AE, DISC, MC, V. Free parking. MBTA: Red Line to Porter.

A Cambridge House is a beautifully restored 1892 colonial home listed in the National Register of Historic Places. The three-story building is on a busy stretch of Cambridge's main street (Massachusetts Ave.), set back from the sidewalk by a beautiful lawn. Rooms are warmly decorated with Waverly fabrics and antiques. Most have fireplaces and four-poster canopy beds with down comforters. Complimentary beverages and fresh pastries are served by the fireplace in the library or parlor. And a full breakfast, also complimentary, prepared by a professionally trained chef, is offered every morning. There's something different each day—omelets, crêpes, waffles, or fresh fruit. Every evening complimentary wine and cheese are also offered. Smoking is not allowed at the inn.

Harvard Square Hotel. 110 Mount Auburn St., Cambridge, MA 02138. ☎ **800/458-5886** or 617/864-5200. Fax 617/864-2409. 73 rms. A/C TV TEL. $125–$160 single or double. Children 16 and under stay free in parents' room. Corporate, AAA, and AARP rates available. AE, DC, DISC, JCB, MC, V. Parking $15. MBTA: Red Line to Harvard.

Smack in the middle of Harvard Square, this hotel is a great favorite with visiting parents and budget-conscious business travelers. In early 1996 the six-story brick hotel was completely refurbished and renamed (it used to be the Harvard Manor House), and the guest rooms were redecorated. Some rooms overlook Harvard Square, and the atmosphere is comfortable and unpretentious. Fax and copy services and complimentary newspapers (weekdays only) are available at the front desk, and there's same-day laundry service. Guests have dining privileges at the Inn at Harvard—like the Harvard Square Hotel, managed by Doubletree Hotels Corporation—and the Harvard Faculty Club.

Howard Johnson Hotel Cambridge. 777 Memorial Dr., Cambridge, MA 02139. ☎ **800/654-2000** or 617/492-7777. Fax 617/492-6038. 205 rms. A/C TV TEL. $85–$155 double.

Extra person $10. Free cribs. Children under 18 stay free in parents' room. Senior (with AARP card) and AAA discounts available. AE, CB, DC, DISC, JCB, MC, V. Free parking.

An attractive, modern hotel with a swimming pool and sundeck, this 16-story tower is near the major college campuses and the Massachusetts Turnpike, and just a 10-minute drive from downtown Boston. Each room has a picture window, giving guests who are up high enough a panoramic view of the Boston skyline. Rooms are large, with modern furnishings, and some have a private balcony. Prices vary with the size of the room, the floor, and the view. Valet laundry service and conference rooms are available.

WHERE TO DINE

The MBTA Red Line runs from downtown Boston to the heart of Harvard Square. Many of the restaurants listed here can be reached on foot from there. If inexpensive ethnic food is more your speed, head for Central and Inman squares, each a virtual United Nations of budget restaurants.

VERY EXPENSIVE

✪ **Rialto.** One Bennett St., in the Charles Hotel. ☎ **617/661-5050.** Reservations recommended. Main courses $19–$29. AE, DC, MC, V. Sun–Thurs 5:30–10pm, Fri–Sat 5:30–11pm. Bar Sun–Thurs 5pm–1am, Fri–Sat 5pm–1:30am. MBTA: Red Line to Harvard. MEDITERRANEAN.

If Rialto isn't the best restaurant in the Boston area, it's close. Every element is so carefully thought out that you might find yourself pausing during dinner to admire the end product as an intellectual as well as culinary masterpiece. You'll want to pause a lot, to look around the dramatic but comfortable room, with floor-to-ceiling windows overlooking Harvard Square, cushy banquettes, and standing lamps that cast a golden glow. Rialto attracts a chic crowd, but it's not a "scene" in the sense that out-of-towners will feel left behind. The staff is solicitous without being smothering, and chef Jody Adams's food eloquently speaks for itself.

The menu changes regularly, but you might start with a blue-cheese tart in a flaky crust with walnuts and a patch of green on the plate—the excellent "local simple greens," available as a salad on their own. Another outstanding appetizer is the *soupe de poisson* (Provençal fisherman's soup with rouille, Gruyère, and basil oil), the very essence of seafood. Main courses each sound so good that you might as well close your eyes and point. Vegetarians might come up with a plate of creamy potato slices and mushrooms so thick and juicy they're almost like eating meat. Seared duck breast with foie gras, squash raviolis, and quince is wonderful, and anything involving salmon is a guaranteed winner—even those who think they don't like it will fall for the perfectly flaky, orange-pink hunk, perhaps with sweet potatoes, dried cranberries, and pine nuts. Desserts are equally funky; a trio of seasonal sorbets is a great choice, as is *cassata* (Sicilian sponge cake with sweet ricotta, shaved chocolate, dried cherries, and Marsala).

Salamander. 1 Athenaeum St. (at First St.). ☎ **617/225-2121.** Reservations recommended. Main courses $18.50–$35. AE, DC, DISC, MC, V. Mon–Thurs 6–10pm, Fri–Sat 6–10:30pm. MBTA: Red Line to Kendall; 10-minute walk. AMERICAN/ASIAN.

Cambridge's hottest new restaurant, in every sense of the word, is Salamander. Chef-owner Stan Frankenthaler is a visionary, and this is his vision. You enter the Carter Ink Building, a block from the Charles River, through a four-story atrium to find Salamander humming on the ground floor, a foodie haven in a dimly lit room in the center of which is a grill over a wood fire. Seating spills into the courtyard, where it's brighter and less warm and smoky (from the fire), but also less cozy.

Cambridge Accommodations & Dining

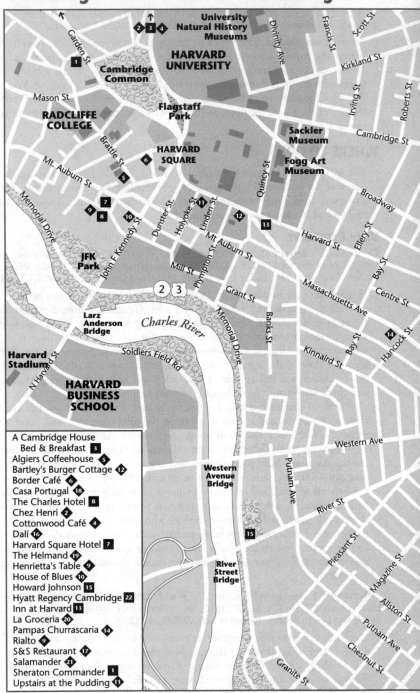

A Cambridge House
  Bed & Breakfast **3**
Algiers Coffeehouse **5**
Bartley's Burger Cottage **12**
Border Café **6**
Casa Portugal **18**
The Charles Hotel **8**
Chez Henri **2**
Cottonwood Café **4**
Dalí **16**
Harvard Square Hotel **7**
The Helmand **19**
Henrietta's Table **9**
House of Blues **10**
Howard Johnson **15**
Hyatt Regency Cambridge **22**
Inn at Harvard **13**
La Groceria **20**
Pampas Churrascaria **14**
Rialto **9**
S&S Restaurant **17**
Salamander **21**
Sheraton Commander **1**
Upstairs at the Pudding **11**

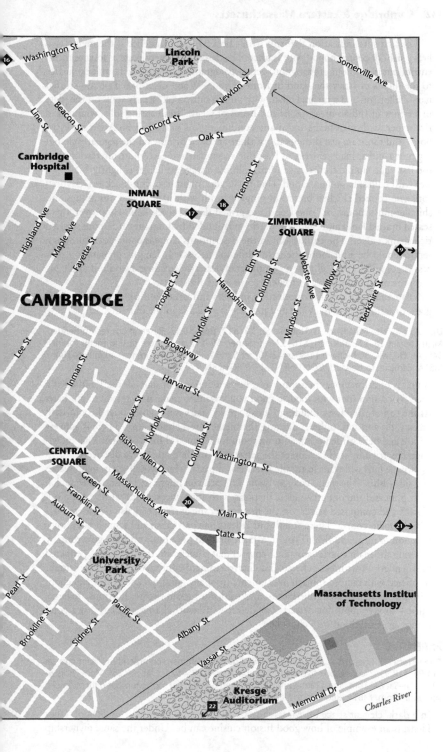

The first sure indication that this won't be a typical experience is the menu, two heavy slabs of copper bound with leather. The descriptions within are as long as menu entries can be without growing into actual paragraphs, and they still don't do justice to the flights of fancy that land in front of you. "Wood-oven-baked potato-stuffed nan, shallot jam and a mizuna salad; with cumin-saffron oil" nearly spills off the plate in a frenzy of Indian bread *(nan)* and heaps of salad; "fresh spring rolls, wrapped in rice paper, with torn herbs and many condiments" is practically an Asian smorgasbord. And those are just the appetizers; there are eight or nine on the regularly changing menu and as many entrees, at least one vegetarian and each more interesting than the last. The simplest (a relative term), almost always available, is lightly fried lobster with chiles, lemongrass, and Thai basil; you might also find black tea–flavored rotisserie-cooked chicken breast, in gingery broth with hand-rolled dumplings and shiitake mushrooms, or "one wood fire grilled double thick lamb chop over a pan seared braised lamb and eggplant 'pattie' surrounded by fragrant cardamom scented rich shank sauce." The enthusiasm in the descriptions alone is contagious, although service could be a bit more attentive while the necessarily lengthy preparation process is going on. After all this, a complicated dessert seems like overkill; if apple pie is on the menu, it makes an excellent contrasting finish.

Salamander is noted for its selection of beers and wine by the glass (and the half-glass, or tasting portion). Validated parking is available in the building.

Upstairs at the Pudding. 10 Holyoke St. ☎ **617/864-1933.** Reservations recommended. Main courses $8–$12 at lunch, $16–$27 at dinner, $9–$12 at brunch; tasting menu (dinner) $45. AE, DC, MC, V. Mon–Fri 11:30am–2:30pm; Sun 11:30am–2pm (brunch); nightly 6–10pm. MBTA: Red Line to Harvard. CONTINENTAL/NORTHERN ITALIAN.

An oasis of calm above the tumult of Harvard Square, Upstairs at the Pudding is a special-occasion spot with food so good you'll want to make up a reason to go there. At the top of the Hasty Pudding Club's creaky stairs is a high-ceilinged room with green walls and soft, indirect lighting that make it feel almost cozy. There is a lovely terrace and herb garden off the dining room for seasonal al fresco dining. The knowledgeable, friendly staff reinforces the sense that you've made a nice discovery.

Noodle fans will want to try the hand-rolled pasta, which you'll see in main dishes and side dishes. The menu changes daily. To start, you might try venison-filled ravioli with port and lingonberry sauce, or pizza with four cheeses and white truffle oil. Tossed and composed salads, on the menu after the entrees, can also be ordered before the main course. There you'll find at least one pasta dish and a small but choice selection of meat and fish. If you like garlic mashed potatoes, you can't go wrong by ordering the main course (any main course) that comes with them, perhaps peppered beef tenderloin with blue cheese and charred tomato coulis. Atlantic salmon might be offered with sautéed spinach over polenta (properly gummy), and grilled veal chops with maple demi-glaze, grilled leeks, and wild-mushroom risotto. Portions are large, but try to save room for dessert. Pot de crème (flavors change regularly) is a good choice, as is anything with chocolate.

EXPENSIVE

Chez Henri. 1 Shepard St. ☎ **617/354-8980.** Reservations recommended. Main courses $14.95–$18.95; 3-course prix-fixe menu $28; bar food $4.95–$7.95. AE, MC, V. Mon–Thurs 6–10pm, Fri–Sat 6–11pm, Sun 11am–2pm (brunch) and 6–9pm. Bar food Mon–Sat until midnight, Sun until 10pm. MBTA: Red Line to Harvard. FRENCH/CUBAN.

In a dark, elegant space off Massachusetts Avenue near Harvard Law School, Chez Henri is an example of how good fusion cuisine can be. Under the same ownership as Providence in Brookline, Chez Henri has a more focused menu that concentrates on French bistro–style food with Cuban accents. The menu changes regularly; it might include appetizers of frog's legs (the version with tamarind cream is silky and delicious) and pan-crisped sweetbreads served with warm arugula salad and straw-berries *au poivre,* a tantalizing assemblage of flavors and textures. Entrees include gen-erous portions of meat and fish—perhaps a juicy chicken breast served with black bean sauce, avocado slaw, and two spicy *empanadas* (turnovers) filled with potato and cheese; or halibut with plantains, roasted potatoes, mango coulis, and kiwi slices. The prix-fixe menu, a good deal, includes one of two appetizers and one of two entrees as well as dessert, of which the crème brûlée is a terrific choice.

Dalí. 415 Washington St., Somerville. ☎ **617/661-3254.** Reservations not accepted. Tapas $2.50–$7.50, main courses $14–$19. AE, DC, MC, V. Nightly 5:30–10:30pm. MBTA: Red Line to Harvard; follow Kirkland St. to intersection of Washington and Beacon sts. SPANISH.

Dalí casts an irresistible spell—it's noisy and crowded, it's on a grim corner not all that close to Harvard Square (though it's a short cab ride), it doesn't take reservations, and it still fills up with people cheerfully waiting more than an hour to get a table on weekends. The bar offers plenty to look at while you wait, including colorful paintings, dried flowers, sleeves of garlic, and a clothesline festooned with lingerie. The crowds come for the authentic Spanish food, especially the tapas, little plates of hot or cold creations that burst with flavor, perfect for sampling and sharing. There are about a dozen entrees (including excellent paella), but most people come in a group and cut a swath through the tapas offerings, 32 dishes on the regular menu and eight specials that change monthly. The *patatas ali-oli* (garlic potatoes) look like dull potato salad and taste so good you'll want to order more immediately. But hold off while you try the crunchy-tender *gambas con gabardina* (saffron-battered fried shrimp), the addictive *setas al ajillo* (sautéed mushrooms), and the rich but light *queso de cabra montañes* (goat cheese baked with tomato and basil). The waiters, in brightly embroidered vests, seem a bit overwhelmed but never fail to make sure there's enough bread for sopping up juices and sangria for washing it all down. If you want to experi-ment and order food in several stages, that's fine, too. Finish up with flan for a tradi-tional ending, or try the *tarta de chocolates.* Order your own if you like chocolate—it's so good the spirit of sharing will evaporate and you'll suddenly become terri-torial. Go early for a leisurely meal since it gets very crowded late in the evening.

⑤ Pampas Churrascaria. 928 Massachusetts Ave. ☎ **617/661-6613.** Reservations accepted only for parties of six or more. *Rodizio* $16.95, salad bar $7.99. AE, DC, MC, V. Mon–Fri 5:30–10:30pm, Sat 5–10:30pm, Sun 1–10:30pm. MBTA: Red Line to Harvard or Central. BRAZILIAN.

If you love meat, Pampas is a dream come true. Even if you don't eat meat at all, this rowdy spot between Harvard and Central squares still has a lot to offer in the form of a salad bar that nearly bows beneath the piles of pasta and potato salads, olives, bread, marinated vegetables, and other tasty morsels. The real reason to come here, though, is the *rodizio*. Meats of every description are marinated and threaded onto swords, then roasted in the giant fireplace (don't lean on anything brick here—it's hot). Waiters then shuttle back and forth with the giant skewers, stopping to offer each diner chicken, beef, pork, goat, ribs, and even, somewhat disconcertingly, chicken hearts. Then they come back again, and again. Soon you'll understand the true meaning of "all you can eat." If you can still move, you're doing something wrong. The location, a solid 20 minutes from the nearest subway stops, might seem inconvenient at first, but when you finish, you'll want to walk for at least that long just to make sure you still can.

MODERATE

Border Café. 32 Church St. ☎ **617/864-6100.** Reservations not accepted. Main courses $6–$12. AE, MC, V. Mon–Thurs 11am–1am, Fri–Sat 11am–2am, Sun noon–11pm. MBTA: Red Line to Harvard. SOUTHWESTERN.

When you first catch sight of this thoroughly southwestern restaurant your thoughts may turn to, of all people, Yogi Berra. The baseball Hall of Famer supposedly said, "No one goes there anymore—it's too crowded"; Yogi was talking about a popular New York club, but it's something people have been saying about this Harvard Square hangout for 10 years. The festival atmosphere is only enhanced by the fact that people hang around the bar for hours waiting to be seated for the generous portions of tasty, if not completely authentic, food. The menu features Cajun, Tex-Mex, and some Caribbean specialties. The beleaguered waitstaff keeps the chips and salsa coming, and if your order can be heard over the deafening roar of the crowd, try the excellent seafood enchiladas, any kind of tacos, Caribbean shrimp (dipped in coconut and spices before frying), or popcorn shrimp. The fajitas, served in the traditional way—good and loud—sizzling in a large iron frying pan, are also a popular choice. Set aside a couple of hours, be in a party mood, and ask to be seated downstairs if you want to be able to hear your companions. But beware: Your clothes will smell like the restaurant (smoky, greasy, and spicy) for hours after you leave, a small price to pay for one of the best deals in the area.

Casa Portugal. 1200 Cambridge St. ☎ **617/491-8880.** Reservations recommended on weekends. Main courses $7.95–$13.95. AE, DISC, MC, V. Daily 4:30–10pm. MBTA: Red Line to Harvard; from there take the Lechmere bus (no. 69) to Inman Sq./Cambridge St. PORTUGUESE.

To evaluate this restaurant we enlisted a friend of Portuguese descent, who kept glancing around and saying, "It looks like my grandmother's house." She apparently favored stucco, colorful decorations, and a low-ceilinged, cozy atmosphere, but we had to guess—after the food arrived the conversation ran to "Wow, this is good," and "Are you going to finish that?" Generous portions of hearty, inexpensive Portuguese fare draw the locals to this comfortable spot, where a soup of the day, rice, and traditional fried potatoes come with all entrees. Try a dish that includes the flavorful Portuguese sausages, linguiça, and chouriço. The tureens, which combine several types of shellfish, are excellent, as is the *bacalhau assado a cuca* (reconstituted salt cod, garlic, peppers, and potatoes baked with lots of olive oil).

✪ The Helmand. 143 First St. ☎ **617/492-4646.** Reservations recommended. Main courses $8.95–$14.95. AE, MC, V. Sun–Thurs 5–10pm, Fri–Sat 5–11pm. MBTA: Green Line to Lechmere. AFGHAN.

Even in cosmopolitan Cambridge, Afghan food is something novel, and if any competitors are setting their sights on the Helmand, they're contemplating a daunting task. The elegant setting belies the reasonable prices at this airy, spacious spot near the CambridgeSide Galleria mall. Knowing that this is probably all new to many diners, the courteous staff patiently answers questions about the food, which is distinctly Middle Eastern with Indian and Pakistani influences. Many vegetarian dishes are offered, and when meat appears it's often used as one element of a dish rather than the centerpiece. Every meal is accompanied by delectable bread made in the wood-fired brick oven in the dining room. To start, you might try the baked pumpkin topped with a spicy ground meat sauce, a good contrast of flavors and textures. Entrees include several versions of what Americans would call stew, including *deygee kabob,* an excellent mélange of lamb, yellow split peas, onion, and red peppers. Or try the *aushak,* pasta pockets filled with leeks and buried under a sauce of split peas and carrots.

Henrietta's Table. One Bennett St., in the Charles Hotel. ☎ **617/661-5005.** Reservations recommended. Main courses $2.25–$9.50 at breakfast; $7.50–$11.50 at lunch; $8–$12.50 at dinner. AE, MC, V. Mon–Fri 6:30–11am, Sat 7–11:30am, Sun 7–10:30am; Mon–Sat noon–3pm, Sun 11:30am–3pm (brunch); Sun–Thurs 5:30–10pm, Fri–Sat 5:30–11pm. Market Mon–Fri 6:30am–10pm, Sat–Sun 7am–10pm. MTBA: Red Line to Harvard. NEW ENGLAND.

The country-kitchen atmosphere here reflects the straightforward cooking style, which depends on the excellent quality of the produce for the daily menus. It's right there on the menu: "Fresh & Honest." You can see how fresh by pausing at the entrance to look around the little farmstand market filled with fruits, vegetables, breads, and condiments. The adjoining dining room, with its plain wood floor and white walls, green-and-white color scheme, and homey wooden tables and chairs, is a perfect match for the food—it looks like Grandma's house, but more sophisticated. The menu changes daily. You might start with a grilled portabella mushroom, topped with Vermont brie, and served over greens dressed with walnut vinaigrette. Maine rock crab and corn chowder is often available, the sprightly flavors contrasting nicely with the bacon in the soup. Entrees are limited in number but not in execution: roast chicken is flavorful and juicy, a grilled pork chop is smoked and served with chunky applesauce, and wood-smoked Maine salmon meshes perfectly with beach-plum vinaigrette. You can wash it all down with a New England microbrew from a long list. The incredibly fresh vegetables are served only à la carte, which can make the tab a bit higher than you might have expected. Even people who think they don't like bread pudding love the chocolate version here. The lunch menu features sandwiches, Yankee pot roast, and baked scrod, among other items. And at breakfast you can get hotcakes, waffles, farm-fresh eggs, and fresh-squeezed juice.

The restaurant's namesake, a 1,000-pound pig who belongs to the hotel owner and lives on Martha's Vineyard, is pictured in a photograph near the front desk, but (we couldn't resist asking) is not on the menu in any way, shape, or form.

House of Blues. 96 Winthrop St. ☎ **617/491-2583.** Reservations not accepted. Main courses $4.95–$14.95. AE, MC, V. Sun–Wed 11:30am–1am, Thurs–Sat 11:30am–2am. MBTA: Red Line to Harvard. CAJUN/PIZZA/INTERNATIONAL.

This is the original House of Blues, in a blue clapboard house near Harvard Square. Everything is blue here, and the walls and ceilings are dotted with whimsical pieces of folk art by various artists. On the ceiling near the bar area are plaster bas-reliefs of great blues musicians, and actual musicians play every night at 10 and on Saturday afternoon. The menu is essentially bar food, with enough variety to keep the legions of tourists who flock here contented. Try the buffalo legs (much bigger and meatier than buffalo wings), followed by jambalaya, a burger, or a pulled-pork sandwich. There's a wide selection of pizzas (try the one topped with feta cheese and garlic) that are baked in a wood-fired oven. The Sunday Gospel brunch requires reservations at least two weeks in advance.

☉ La Groceria. 853 Main St. ☎ **617/876-4162** or 617/547-9258. Reservations recommended at dinner. Main courses $5.95–$8.95 at lunch, $9.95–$17.95 at dinner. Pizzas $5.95–$8.95. Children's menu $4.95–$5.95. AE, DC, DISC, MC, V. Mon–Fri 11:30am–4pm; Mon–Thurs 4–10pm, Fri–Sat 4–11pm, Sun 1–10pm. MBTA: Red Line to Central Square. ITALIAN.

On a drab street just outside Central Square, this colorful, family-run restaurant has dished up large portions of delicious Italian food since 1972. At lunch you'll see business meetings, at dinner, family outings, and at all times, students. Cheery voices bounce off the stucco walls and tile floors, but it seldom gets terribly noisy, probably because everyone's mouth is full. Start with the house garlic bread, which overflows with chopped tomato, red onion, fennel seed, and olive oil. The antipasto platter is crowded with meats, cheeses, roasted vegetables, and whatever else the chef feels moved to include. Main dishes might include homemade pasta from the machine you see as you enter. Lasagna (a vegetarian version) is an excellent choice, as is the chicken marsala. Chicken is also available roasted, and the brick-oven pizzas are available in individual and large sizes.

S&S Restaurant. 1334 Cambridge St., Inman Sq. ☎ **617/354-0777.** Main courses $2.95–$10.95. No credit cards. Mon–Sat 7am–midnight, Sun 8am–midnight. Sat–Sun brunch 8am–4pm. MBTA: Red Line to Harvard; then bus no. 69 (toward Lechmere). DELI.

"Es" is Yiddish for "eat," and this Cambridge classic is as straightforward as its name ("eat and eat"). Founded in 1919 by the great-grandmother of the current owners, this wildly popular weekend brunch spot is northeast of Harvard Square, west of MIT, and worth a visit during the week, too. The menu includes such traditional deli items as corned beef, pastrami, tongue, and Reuben sandwiches; potato pancakes, blintzes, knockwurst, lox, and whitefish. The S&S is also a full-service restaurant with entrees of beef, chicken, and fish, plus quiche and croissants, and serves breakfast anytime during restaurant hours. Be early for brunch, or plan to spend a good chunk of your Saturday or Sunday standing in line people-watching and getting hungry.

INEXPENSIVE

Algiers Coffeehouse. 40 Brattle St. ☎ **617/492-1557.** Main courses $2.25–$7.95. AE, MC, V. Mon–Thurs 8am–midnight, Fri–Sat 8am–1am. MBTA: Red Line to Harvard. MIDDLE EASTERN.

This is an excellent place to take a break from rushing around Harvard Square and have a snack or a drink (try the special Algiers mint coffee), but you might find yourself lingering. That's the nature of coffeehouses, after all, and this is a particularly nice one. Long known as a dark, smoke-filled literary hangout, the new Algiers (which came about in the late 1980s as a result of a fire) is upstairs in Brattle Hall, and still a favorite with Cambridge intellectuals and would-be intellectuals. Smoking is allowed on the upper level. This a good spot to eavesdrop while you eat, and the soups, sandwiches, homemade sausages, falafel, and hummus are terrific.

✪ **Bartley's Burger Cottage.** 1246 Massachusetts Ave. ☎ **617/354-6559.** Most items under $8. No credit cards. Mon–Sat 11am–10pm. MBTA: Red Line to Harvard. AMERICAN.

A cross-section of Cambridge, from Harvard students to regular folks, makes this perennial favorite a regular stop for great burgers and the best onion rings anywhere. Burgers bear the names of local and national celebrities; the names change, but the ingredients stay the same. Anything you can think of to put on ground beef is available here, from American cheese to béarnaise sauce. There are also some good dishes that don't involve meat, notably the creamy, garlicky hummus. Bartley's is one of the only places in the area where you can still get a real raspberry lime rickey—raspberry syrup, lime juice, lime wedges, and club soda, the taste of summer even in the winter.

CAMBRIDGE AFTER DARK

For a full listing of clubs in the area, see "Boston After Dark" in Chapter 4.

The **Hasty Pudding Theatre** (12 Holyoke St.; ☎ 617/496-8400) is best known for the Hasty Pudding Theatricals—all-male shows put on every March with plenty of female characters and in-jokes. They gave the world Jack Lemmon and Fred Gwynne, among many others. The theater also features independent and student productions. Tickets range between $10 and $35, depending on the show.

Harvard University's **Loeb Drama Center** (64 Brattle St., at Hilliard St.; ☎ 617/547-8300) is the home of the American Repertory Theatre, which performs mainstream and more experimental works year-round, except when student productions are in the spotlight for about six weeks in the fall and spring. Tickets are $10 to $45, depending on the show.

Cambridge is no longer the revival-house paradise it once was, but there are a few good destinations for fans of nonmainstream cinema. The **Brattle Theater** (40 Brattle St.; ☎ 617/876-6837), one of the oldest independent movie houses in the country, features lectures and live performances in addition to foreign and classic films. For first-run independent films, head to East Cambridge and the **Kendall Square Cinema** (1 Kendall Square; ☎ 617/494-9800). Check the daily *Globe* for times, and the Thursday "Calendar" section for the coming week's schedule.

2 Lexington

6 miles NW of Cambridge, 9 miles NW of downtown Boston, 6 miles E of Concord

The shooting phase of the Revolutionary War started here, when British troops marching toward Concord to destroy the colonists' stockpiles of arms clashed with local militia members (known as Minutemen for their ability to assemble on short notice). News that eight Minutemen had died in the skirmish on Lexington's Town Green inspired their counterparts up the road to put up a fight—the Battle of Concord.

After the end of the French and Indian War, in 1763, the debt-laden British government increased taxes on the American colonies. The Crown's practical considerations ran headlong into the concerns of the notoriously independent-minded colonists, who had been exposed to the philosophical ideas of the Enlightenment, foremost among them opposition to perceived tyranny. From there it was a short jump to the cry of "no taxation without representation." Tensions rose throughout the early 1770s as British troops were quartered in colonists' homes and the "Intolerable Acts" of 1774 imposed new taxes. Mutual distrust ran high—Paul Revere wrote of helping form "a committee for the purpose of watching the movements of the British troops"—and when the British commander in Boston, General Gage, learned that the colonists were accumulating arms and ammunition, he dispatched men to destroy the stockpiles.

Troops marched from Boston to Lexington late on April 18, 1775 (no need to memorize the date; you'll hear it everywhere), preceded by Revere and William Dawes, who sounded the warning. They did their job so well that the alarm came well ahead of the advancing troops, who were forced to wade ashore in Cambridge. The Lexington Minutemen, under the command of Captain John Parker, got the word shortly after midnight, but the redcoats had taken so long to get out of Boston that they were still several hours away. The rebels repaired to their homes and the Buckman Tavern. John Hancock and Samuel Adams, who had left Boston several days earlier upon learning that the British were after them, slept at the Hancock-Clarke House nearby. Five hours later, some 700 British troops under Major Pitcairn arrived.

A tense standoff ensued. Three times Pitcairn ordered them to disperse, but the patriots—fewer than 100, and some accounts say 77—refused. Parker called: "Stand your ground. Don't fire unless fired upon, but if they mean to have a war, let it begin here!" Finally the captain, perhaps realizing as the sky grew light just how badly outnumbered his men were, gave the order to fall back. As the Minutemen began to scatter, a shot rang out. One British company charged into the fray, and the colonists attempted to regroup at the same time that Pitcairn tried unsuccessfully to call off his troops. Nobody knows who started the shooting, but when it was over, eight militia members were dead, including a drummer boy, and 10 wounded.

ESSENTIALS

GETTING THERE   Modern-day Route 2A approximates Paul Revere's path, but if you attempt to follow it during rush hour, you'll wish you had a horse of your own. Instead, take Route 2 from Cambridge through Belmont. Follow signs for Route 4/225 into the center of Lexington. Or take Route 128 (I-95) to Exit 31. Massachusetts Avenue runs through the center of town.

The MBTA (☎ 617/222-3200) runs bus routes 62, "Bedford," and 76, "Hanscom," from Alewife Station (the last stop on the Red Line) to Lexington every hour during the day and every half hour during rush periods. There is no Sunday service. There is no public transportation between Lexington and Concord.

VISITOR INFORMATION   Sketch maps and information about Lexington can be obtained at the Chamber of Commerce's **Visitor Center,** at 1875 Massachusetts Ave. (☎ 617/862-1450).

Some attractions are closed from November through March or mid-April—Patriots Day, a state holiday observed on the Monday closest to April 19. The anniversary is celebrated with a reenactment of the battle and other festivities. Make your Patriots Day reservations well in advance: it's the day of the Boston Marathon and the start of a school vacation week.

Before you set out, you might want to read "Paul Revere's Ride," Henry Wadsworth Longfellow's classic but historically questionable poem about the events of April 18 to 19, 1775.

GETTING AROUND   Downtown Lexington is easily negotiable on foot, and most of the attractions are within walking distance. If you prefer not to walk to the Munroe Tavern and the Museum of Our National Heritage, the 62 and 76 buses pass by on Massachusetts Avenue.

EXPLORING THE HISTORIC SITES

Start at the **Visitor Center,** on the Battle Green. It's open daily 9am to 5pm (9:30am to 3:30pm, from October through June). The most prominent and interesting display is the diorama and accompanying narrative that illustrate the Battle of Lexington. When you step back outside, you'll have a new perspective on the events of April 19, 1775, as you explore the Green. Its best-known feature is the **Minuteman Statue** (1900) of Captain John Parker, who commanded the militia. The **Old Revolutionary Monument** dates to 1799 and marks the grave of seven of the eight colonists who died in the conflict, which is commemorated by the **Line of Battle Boulder.** The **Memorial to the Lexington Minutemen** bears the names of the men who fell in the battle. Across Massachusetts Avenue, near Clarke Street, is the **Old Belfry,** a reproduction of the free-standing bell that sounded the alarm the day of the battle. **Ye Olde Burying Ground,** at the west end of the Green, dates to 1690 and contains the grave of Captain Parker. A stop at the visitor center and a walk around the monuments won't take more than about half an hour, and you'll get a good sense of what went on here and why the participants are still held in such high esteem.

Three important destinations in Lexington were among the country's first "historic houses" when their restoration began in the 1920s. All three are operated by the **Lexington Historical Society** (☎ 617/862-1703), which conducts guided tours from April through October, Monday through Saturday 10am to 5pm and Sunday 1 to 5pm. Admission is $4 per house, $10 for all three; children 6 to 16, $1 per house, $2 for all three; family (two adults, two children), $20 for all three. The last tour starts at 4:30; tours take 30 to 45 minutes.

The **Buckman Tavern,** at 1 Bedford St., is the only building still on the Green that was there on April 19, 1775, and the interior is restored to its appearance that day. You'll see the original bar and the original front door, which has a hole in it from a British musket ball. Built around 1710, the tavern is where the Minutemen gathered to wait for word of British troop movements, and where they brought their wounded after the conflict. Costumed guides describe the history of the building and its inhabitants, explain the battle, and discuss the colonial way of life. They are well versed in the social and culinary customs of the day, the use of ingeniously designed kitchen implements, and the derivation of many sayings that originated in that era. If time is short and you have to pick one house to visit, this is the one.

About one-third of a mile away, the **Hancock-Clarke House,** at 36 Hancock St., is where Samuel Adams and John Hancock were sleeping when Paul Revere arrived. They were evacuated to nearby Woburn. Built around 1698 by Hancock's grandfather and lavishly improved by his uncle Thomas Hancock, the house was the parsonage of the Reverend Jonas Clarke at the time of the Revolution. It has undergone many changes, and was even moved across the street for a time, but is restored and furnished in colonial style. The entrance hall display cases contain many artifacts that belong to the Historical Society, including a drum that was used to signal the Minutemen, and a set of pistols that belonged to Major Pitcairn and fell off his saddle during the battle.

The **Munroe Tavern,** about one mile from the Green at 1332 Massachusetts Ave., was taken over by the British on April 19, 1775. Under the command of Gen. Earl Percy, some 1,000 troops made the tavern their headquarters and, after the battle, infirmary. The ceiling in the tap room still has a bullet hole made by a careless British soldier. The building dates to 1690 and is packed with fascinating artifacts and furniture carefully preserved by the Munroe family, including the table and chair where President Washington dined in 1789. The grounds are beautifully planted and maintained.

If you continue on Massachusetts Avenue, you'll come to the **Museum of Our National Heritage** (33 Marrett Rd., Route 2A; ☎ **617/861-6559** or 617/861-9638), which mounts accessible exhibits that explore history through popular culture. The installations in the six exhibition spaces change regularly, but you can start with another dose of the Revolution, the permanent exhibit "Lexington Alarm'd." Other topics have ranged from gravestones to jigsaw puzzles, auto racing to George Washington. It's great fun, especially for children who are growing weary of nonstop colonial lore. Lectures, concerts, and family programs are also offered. The museum is open Monday through Saturday 10am to 5pm, and Sunday noon to 5pm. It's closed Thanksgiving, Christmas Eve, Christmas Day, New Year's Eve, and New Year's Day. Admission is free. It's sponsored by the Scottish Rite of Freemasonry.

WHERE TO STAY

Battle Green Motor Inn. 1720 Massachusetts Ave., Lexington, MA 02173. ☎ **800/343-0235** or 617/862-6100, or 800/322-1066 in MA. 96 rms (some with shower only). A/C TV TEL. Summer $65 room with 1 bed; $72 room with 2 beds. Winter rates are lower. AE, DC, DISC, MC, V.

Three blocks from the Minuteman Statue, this two-story motor inn surrounds an enclosed, L-shaped courtyard bordered with potted plants and trees. Rooms are basic and comfortable, and the units at the end farthest from the street overlook the pool, which is open all year. Park in the underground garage and explore on foot—the historic sites are within easy walking distance.

Sheraton Tara Lexington Inn. 727 Marrett Rd. (Exit 30B off I-95), Lexington, MA 02173. ☎ **800/THE-TARA** or 617/862-8700. Fax 617/863-0404. 119 rms, 2 suites. A/C TV TEL. $119–$155 double (varies seasonally); $165 suite. AE, DC, DISC, MC, V.

Lexington

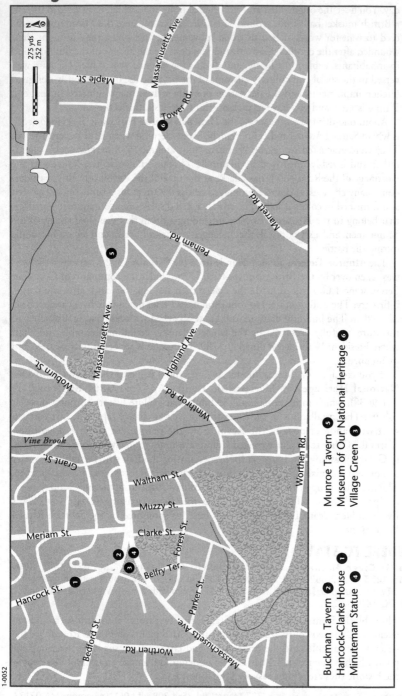

Buckman Tavern ②
Hancock-Clarke House ①
Minuteman Statue ④

Munroe Tavern ⑤
Museum of Our National Heritage ⑥
Village Green ③

1-0052

Overlooking the interstate, but sheltered from the noise by a stand of trees, this two-story hotel is the place to turn if you're staying in Lexington and need the amenities of a chain, including room service. Rooms have colonial-style furniture and are large enough to hold a wing chair or couch. All have cable TV and hair dryers, and some have balconies. An outdoor pool (seasonal) and exercise room are available. The historic attractions are a short drive away.

WHERE TO DINE

Bel Canto. 1709 Massachusetts Ave. ☎ **617/861-6556.** Main courses $5.50–$10.95; pizzas $5.75–$13.95; sandwiches and salads $4.50–$6.75. AE, DISC, MC, V. Mon–Thurs 11am–10pm; Fri–Sat 11am–11pm; Sun noon–10pm. ITALIAN/PIZZA.

One floor above the bustle of downtown Lexington, at peak times this local favorite can seem almost equally busy, but you won't feel rushed. The spacious, whitewashed room fills with the chatter of diners sharing garlic bread and pizza or generous servings of pasta. The antipasto plate of meats, cheeses, tuna, and marinated vegetables makes an excellent appetizer to share. Pizzeria Regina pizza is a recent addition to the menu, but you can get thin-crust pizza anywhere—go for the thick whole-wheat crust, with your choice of more than two dozen toppings. Or try the light, filling chicken lasagna. There's also a children's menu ($3.50–$3.95).

Lemon Grass. 1710 Massachusetts Ave. ☎ **617/862-3530.** Main courses $5.25–$6.50 at lunch, $6.50–$14.95 at dinner. AE, DISC, MC, V. Mon–Fri 11:30am–3pm; Mon–Thurs 5–9:30pm; Fri–Sat 5–10pm; Sun 4–9pm. THAI.

A welcome break: The only revolution going on here is in Americans' culinary habits. The space is a former coffee shop disguised with plenty of white paint, bamboo decorations, and the aromas of Asian spices. You might start with *satay,* skewers of meat served with a delectable peanut sauce, or chicken coconut soup, with a kick of pepper and plenty of chicken. Entrees range from a tasty rendition of traditional *pad thai* to excellent curry dishes, and the accommodating staff will adjust the heat and spice to suit your taste.

3 Concord

18 miles NW of Boston, 15 miles NW of Cambridge, 6 miles W of Lexington

Concord (say "conquered") revels in its legacy as a center of groundbreaking thought and its role in the country's political and intellectual history. After just a little time in this charming town, you may find yourself adopting the local attitude toward two of its most famous former residents: Ralph Waldo Emerson, who comes across as a well-respected uncle figure, and Henry David Thoreau, everyone's favorite eccentric cousin. Long before they wandered the countryside, the first official battle of the Revolutionary War took place at the North Bridge, now part of Minute Man National Historical Park. By the middle of the 19th century, Concord was the center of the Transcendentalist movement. Homes of Emerson, Thoreau, Nathaniel Hawthorne, and Louisa May Alcott are open to visitors, as is the authors' final resting place, Sleepy Hollow Cemetery.

ESSENTIALS

GETTING THERE   From Boston and Cambridge, take Route 2 into Lincoln. Where the road makes a sharp left, go straight onto the Cambridge Turnpike, and follow signs to "Historic Concord." From Lexington, take Route 2A west from Route 4/225 at the Museum of Our National Heritage and follow signs reading BATTLE ROAD.

There is no bus transportation to Concord, but **MBTA commuter trains** (☎ 617/222-3200) take about 45 minutes from North Station in Boston and stop at Porter Square in Cambridge. There is no public transportation between Lexington and Concord.

VISITOR INFORMATION   The **Chamber of Commerce** (2 Lexington Rd., Concord, MA 01742; ☎ 508/369-3120) maintains an information booth on Heywood Street, one block southeast of Monument Square. It's open weekends in April and daily May through October from 9:30am to 4:30pm. One-hour tours are available starting in May on Saturday, Sunday, and Monday holidays, or on weekdays by appointment. Group tours are available by appointment.

Concord also has a web site (http://www.concordma.com) containing information for visitors.

GETTING AROUND   From downtown Concord, the major attractions are within easy walking distance, but if you're trying to stop everywhere in a day or visiting Walden Pond or Great Meadows, you'll need a car.

SEEING THE SIGHTS

The town green, or **Monument Square**, at the confluence (it's not really an intersection) of Monument Street, Bedford Street, Lexington Road, Main Street, and Lowell Road, is a small green space in the middle of the sprawling town. The obelisk in the square reads FAITHFUL UNTO DEATH. At 2 Lexington Rd. is the **Wright Tavern,** which was built in 1747 and served as headquarters twice on April 19, 1775: for the Minutemen in the morning and the British in the afternoon. Today it plays the same role for the Chamber of Commerce and several businesses and is open to the public during business hours. Also overlooking the square is the **Colonial Inn,** which dates to 1716 (see "Where to Stay" below).

LITERARY LANDMARKS

The Old Manse. Monument St. at North Bridge. ☎ 508/369-3909. Guided tours $5 adults, $4 students and seniors, $2.50 children 6–12, $12 families (three to five people). Mid-Apr to Oct Mon–Sat 10am–5pm and Sun and holidays 1–5pm. From Concord Center, follow Monument St. about ³/₈ of a mile until you see signs for the North Bridge parking lot; the Old Manse is on the left.

The Reverend William Emerson built the Old Manse in 1770 and watched the Battle of Concord from the yard. He died during the Revolutionary War, and the house was occupied for almost 170 years by his widow, her second husband, their descendants, and two friends. Nathaniel Hawthorne and his bride, Sophia Peabody, moved in after their marriage in 1842 and stayed for three years. This is also where Ralph Waldo Emerson (William's grandson) wrote the essay "Nature." Today you'll see mementos and memorabilia of the Emerson and Ripley families and of the Hawthornes—more than anything you might read or hear, the notes they scratched on two windows with Sophia's diamond ring give a sense of the happy young couple.

Ralph Waldo Emerson House. 28 Cambridge Turnpike. ☎ 508/369-2236. Guided tours $4.50 adults, $3 seniors and children under 17. Call to arrange group tours (10 people or more). Mid-April to Oct Thurs–Sat 10am–4:30pm, Sun 2–4:30pm. Follow Cambridge Turnpike out of Concord Center; just before you reach the Concord Museum, the house is on the right.

A visit here is a must if you're interested in Emerson. The philosopher, essayist, and poet moved here in 1835, soon after his second marriage, to Lydia Jackson, and remained until his death in 1882. He called Lydia "Lydian," and she called him "Mr. Emerson," as the staff still does. You'll see original furnishings and some of Emerson's

Concord

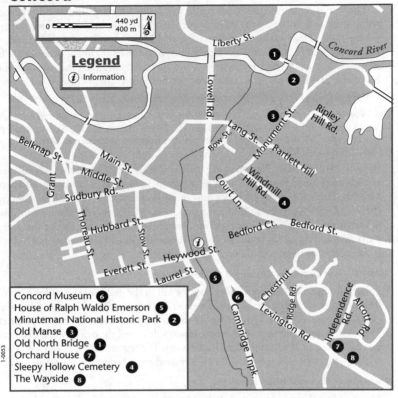

Legend
(i) Information

Concord Museum **6**
House of Ralph Waldo Emerson **5**
Minuteman National Historic Park **2**
Old Manse **3**
Old North Bridge **1**
Orchard House **7**
Sleepy Hollow Cemetery **4**
The Wayside **8**

1-0053

personal effects (the original contents of his study are in the Concord Museum), including his dressing gown.

Orchard House. 399 Lexington Rd. ☎ **508/369-4118.** Guided tours $5.50 adults, $4.50 seniors and students, $3.50 children 6–17, $16 families (up to 2 adults and 4 children). Apr–Oct, Mon–Sat 10am–4:30pm, Sun 1–4:30pm Nov–Mar; Mon–Fri 11am–3pm, Sat 10am–4:30pm, Sun 1–4:30pm. Closed Jan 1–15, Easter, Thanksgiving, Christmas. Follow Lexington Rd. out of Concord Center past the Concord Museum; the house is on the left.

With the theatrical and video release of the 1994 movie *Little Women* (which was filmed elsewhere), Louisa May Alcott's best-known and most popular work moved from the world of preadolescent girls back into the mainstream. The book, published in 1868, was written and set at Orchard House (though most of the actual events took place earlier—Louisa was in her mid-thirties when *Little Women* appeared), and seeing the Alcotts' home brings the family to life. Fans won't want to miss the excellent tour.

Louisa's father, Amos Bronson Alcott, was a writer, educator, philosopher, and leader of the Transcendentalist movement. He created the house by joining and restoring two early 18th-century homes already on the 12 acres of land he purchased in 1857. The family lived here from 1858 to 1877, and moved in the same circles as Emerson, Thoreau, and Hawthorne. Bronson Alcott's passion for educational reform eventually led to his being named superintendant of schools, and he ran the Concord School of Philosophy in Orchard House's backyard.

The rest of the Alcott family is equally well known for artistic and cultural contributions, and for being the models for the characters in *Little Women*. Anna ("Meg"), the eldest, was an amateur actress, and May ("Amy") was a talented artist. Elizabeth ("Beth") died before the family moved to Orchard House. Bronson's wife, Abigail May Alcott, was a social activist and frequently assumed the role of family breadwinner—Bronson, as Louisa wrote in her journal, had "no gift for money making."

The Wayside. 455 Lexington Rd. ☎ **508/369-6975.** Guided tours $3 adults, free for ages 16 and younger. Mid-Apr to Oct Thurs–Tues 10:30am–4:30pm. Closed Nov to mid-Apr. Follow Lexington Rd. out of Concord Center past the Concord Museum and Orchard House; the Wayside is on the left.

Part of Minute Man National Historical Park, the Wayside was Nathaniel Hawthorne's home from 1852 until his death in 1864. The Alcott family also lived here (the girls called it "the yellow house"), as did Harriett Lothrop, who authored the *Five Little Peppers* books under the pen name Margaret Sidney and owns most of the current furnishings. A new exhibit, housed in the barn, consists of audio presentations and figures of Louisa May and Bronson Alcott, Hawthorne, and Sidney. If you're already interested, this is a worthwhile stop.

Sleepy Hollow Cemetery. Entrance is on Rte. 62 West.

Follow the signs for "Author's Ridge" up the hill to the graves of some of the town's literary lights, including the Alcotts, Emerson, Hawthorne, and Thoreau. Emerson's grave, without religious symbolism, is marked by an uncarved quartz boulder. Thoreau's grave is nearby, and Emerson actually delivered the eulogy when his friend was laid to rest in 1862, concluding his tribute with these words: " . . . wherever there is knowledge, wherever there is virtue, wherever there is beauty, he will find a home."

Minute Man National Historical Park.

Minute Man National Historical Park preserves the scene of the first Revolutionary War battle at Concord on (all together now) April 19, 1775. Park in the lot off Monument Road and walk a short distance to the bridge (a reproduction), stopping along the path to read the narratives and hear the well-done audio presentations. Or start your visit at the **North Bridge Visitor Center** (174 Liberty St., off Monument St; ☎ **508/369-6993**), which overlooks the Concord River and the bridge. A diorama illustrates the battle, and exhibits include surprisingly tiny uniforms, weapons, tools of colonial and British soldiers, and a film about the battle, *April Fire.* Park rangers on duty lead programs and answer questions. Outside, picnicking is allowed, and the scenery (especially the fall foliage) is lovely. The bridge isn't far; you'll still want to see the displays there, too. The visitor center is open daily in summer from 9am to 5:30pm, in winter from 9:30am to 4pm, and is closed Christmas and New Year's.

Encouraged by their victory in Lexington, the British moved on to Concord, where the colonists were preparing to confront them. The Minutemen crossed the North Bridge, evading a group of British soldiers who were standing guard, and waited for reinforcements on a nearby hilltop. In Concord the British were searching homes for stockpiled arms (which had already been moved) and burning any guns they found along the way. The Minutemen saw the smoke and, mistakenly believing the British were burning the town, advanced against the men standing guard at the bridge. The redcoats opened fire and the colonists retaliated. At the North Bridge, the Minutemen fired what Ralph Waldo Emerson called "the shot heard round the world." (Bear in mind that he was from Concord, site of the first actual battle, but the shooting and bloodshed began in Lexington—as people there are quick to point out.)

On one side of the bridge you'll find a plaque commemorating the British soldiers who died in the Revolutionary War; on the other is Daniel Chester French's *Minute Man* statue, engraved with a stanza of the poem Emerson wrote for the dedication ceremony in 1876.

The park is open daily, year-round. At the Lexington end of the park, the **Battle Road Visitor Center** (off Route 2A, one-half mile west of I-95; ☎ 617/862-7753) is open from mid-April through October, daily from 9am to 5pm. The park includes the first four miles of the Battle Road, the route the defeated British troops took as they left Concord on the afternoon of April 19, 1775. They were harassed by colonial fire almost all the way back to Boston. Although this area is pretty built up, you'll still get a sense of how demoralizing the retreat must have been. At the visitor center, you can see displays about the Revolution, a diorama illustrating the path of the retreat, and a 22-minute film, *To Keep Our Liberty*, about the events leading up to the war. A pamphlet is available that describes a self-guided tour of a small part of the park near the visitor center; on summer weekends, park rangers lead tours.

Also on the park grounds, on Old Bedford Road, is the **Hartwell Tavern.** Costumed interpreters demonstrate daily life on a farm and tavern in colonial days. It's not Disney, but it is interesting. It's open daily from June through August and on weekends in April, May, September, and October, from 9:30am to 5pm. Admission is free.

OTHER ATTRACTIONS

✪ **Concord Museum.** Lexington Rd. and Cambridge Turnpike. ☎ 508/369-9763. Admission $6 adults, $5 seniors, $3 students and children 15 and under, $12 families. Apr–Dec Mon–Sat 9am–5pm, Sun noon–5pm; Jan–Mar Mon–Sat 11am–4pm, Sun 1–4pm. Follow Lexington Rd. out of Concord Center and bear right at the museum onto the Cambridge Turnpike; the entrance is on the left. Parking on the road is allowed.

Just when you're (understandably) suspecting that everything interesting that happened around here started on April 18, 1775, and ended the next day, a visit to the Concord Museum straightens you out. On the front lawn, what appears to be a shed is actually a replica of the cabin Henry David Thoreau lived in at Walden Pond from 1845 to 1847 (the furnishings are in the museum). Inside, the self-guided tour traces the history of the town and, in a way, of the country. You'll see Native American archaeological artifacts, silver pieces from colonial churches, a fascinating collection of embroidery samplers, and rooms furnished with period furniture and textiles, all with explanatory text that places the exhibits in context. One of the lanterns that signaled Paul Revere from the steeple of the Old North Church is on display, as are the contents of Ralph Waldo Emerson's study arranged the way it was just before he died in 1882, and a large collection of Thoreau's belongings. There are changing exhibits in the New Wing throughout the year. The new History Galleries are scheduled to open with an installation called "Why Concord?" in April 1997.

DeCordova Museum and Sculpture Park. 51 Sandy Pond Rd., Lincoln. ☎ 617/259-8355. Museum: $4 adults, $3 seniors, students, and children 6–12. Tues–Sun and Mon holidays noon–5pm. Sculpture park: free. Daily 8am–10pm. Closed July 4, Christmas, New Year's Day. From Rte. 2 East, take Rte. 126 to Baker Bridge Rd. (the first left after Walden Pond); when it ends, go right onto Sandy Pond Rd., and the museum is on the left. From Rte. 2 West, take I-95 to Exit 28B and follow Trapelo Rd. to Sandy Pond Rd., then follow signs.

Indoors and outdoors, the DeCordova shows the work of American contemporary and modern artists, with an emphasis on living New England artists. The main building, on a leafy hilltop, overlooks a pond and the area's only outdoor public sculpture park. Extensive renovations from 1995 to 1996 made the DeCordova even more cutting-edge, creating a video space for regular exhibitions and a sculpture terrace, where the work of one sculptor per year is on display. Picnicking is allowed in the sculpture park, and the **Store @ DeCordova** (☎ 617/259-8692) has an excellent selection of prints, jewelry, clothing, and other works by local artists, including instructors at the Museum School. The DeCordova also has a web site (http:/www.decordova.org).

Gropius House. 68 Baker Bridge Rd., Lincoln. Guided tours $5. Tours on the hour June–Oct Fri–Sun noon–4pm; Nov–May, first full weekend of the month, Sat–Sun noon–4pm. Take Route 2 to Route 126 south to left on Baker Bridge Rd.; the house is on the right. Or take I-95 to Exit 28B, follow Trapelo Rd. to Sandy Pond Rd., and go left onto Baker Bridge Rd.; the house is on the left.

The legendary German architect Walter Gropius (1883 to 1969), founder of the Bauhaus, accepted an appointment to teach at the Harvard Graduate School of Design in 1937 and built this home for his family on a hill in the prosperous suburb of Lincoln. The Society for the Preservation of New England Antiquities maintains the house, constructed of traditional materials such as clapboard, brick, and fieldstone, combined with materials then seldom used in domestic architecture, including glass block and welded steel. Many of the furnishings were designed by Marcel Breuer and made for the family at the Bauhaus. Decorated as it was in the last decade of Gropius's life, the house affords a revealing look at his life, career, and philosophy.

WILDERNESS RETREATS

The titles of Henry David Thoreau's first two published works can serve as starting points: *A Week on the Concord and Merrimack Rivers* (1849) and *Walden* (1854). To see the area from water level, there's no need to take a week; two hours or so should suffice. Rent a canoe at the **South Bridge Boat House** (496 Main St., ☎ 508/369-9438), west of the center of town, and paddle to the Old North Bridge and back. Rates are $8.50 per hour on weekends, $7.35 on weekdays; $39 per weekend day, $29 per weekday. Or opt for a small motorboat for $20 per hour, $80 per day.

At the **Walden Pond State Reservation** (Route 126; ☎ 508/369-3254), a pile of stones marks the site of the cabin where Thoreau lived from 1845 to 1847. Today the picturesque reservation is a popular destination for hiking (a path circles the pond), swimming, and fishing. Call for the schedule of interpretive programs. Take Walden Street (Route 126) south, away from Concord Center, cross Route 2 and look for signs directing you to the parking lot. From Memorial Day through Labor Day, the daily parking fee is $2.

Another Thoreau haunt, an especially popular destination for birders, is **Great Meadows National Wildlife Refuge** (Monsen Rd.; ☎ 508/443-4661). The Concord portion of the 3,400-acre refuge includes 2½ miles of walking trails around man-made ponds that attract abundant wildlife. More than 200 species of native and migratory birds have been recorded. The refuge is open daily, sunrise to sunset, and admission is free. Don't forget your camera and sunscreen.

To get there, follow Route 62 (Bedford St.) east out of Concord Center for 1.3 miles, then turn left onto Monsen Road.

WHERE TO STAY

Colonial Inn. 48 Monument Sq., Concord, MA 01742. ☎ 800/370-9200 or 508/369-9200. Fax 508/369-2170. 45 rms (some with shower only), 4 suites. A/C TV TEL. Apr–Oct $159–$165 main inn; $99–$159 Prescott wing; $200–$240 cottage. Nov–Mar $135–$139 main inn; $95–$135 Prescott wing; $170–$195 cottage. AE, DC, DISC, MC, V.

The Colonial Inn overlooks Monument Square and has since 1716, when the main building was constructed. Additions since it became a hotel in 1889 have left the inn large enough to offer modern conveniences and small enough to feel friendly. The 12 original colonial-era guest rooms (one of which is supposedly haunted) are in great demand, so reserve early if you have your heart set on staying in the main inn. Rooms in the three-story Prescott wing are a bit larger and have country-style decor. The public areas, including a sitting room and a front porch that's set back from busy Monument Square, are decorated in colonial style.

Two lounges that serve drinks and bar food, and a lovely restaurant offers salads, sandwiches, and pasta at lunch and traditional American fare at dinner.

✪ Hawthorne Inn. 462 Lexington Rd., Concord, MA 01742. ☎ **508/369-5610.** Fax 508/287-4949. 7 rms (some with shower only). TV. $95–$200 double. Extra person $15. AE, DISC, MC, V. Rates include continental breakfast. From Concord Center, take Lexington Rd. ³/₄ mile east; the inn is on the right.

Close your eyes and dream of a country inn. Open them and you may find yourself at this tree-shaded property, across the street from Hawthorne's home, the Wayside. The gorgeously decorated rooms are furnished with antiques and handmade quilts, and original art is on display throughout the two-story inn, which was built around 1870. Outside, relax in the garden, where there is a small pond. Gregory Burch and Marilyn Mudry have operated the inn for 20 years and will acquaint interested guests with the philosophical, spiritual, military, and literary aspects of Concord's history. No smoking is allowed at the inn.

North Bridge Inn. 21 Monument St., Concord, MA, 01741. ☎ **508/371-0014.** Fax 508/371-6460. 6 suites (one with shower only). A/C TV TEL. $135–$160 double. Extra person $15. AE, MC, V. Rates include continental breakfast.

A good choice for business travelers and families, the North Bridge Inn offers nicely appointed suites with kitchen facilities. The three-story inn is one building back from the street near the northwest corner of Monument Square, next to the Colonial Inn. The rooms are spacious and have contemporary and reproduction colonial furnishings, as do the breakfast room (where cookies are served nightly) and lobby.

A HISTORIC INN NEARBY

Longfellow's Wayside Inn. Wayside Inn Rd., Sudbury, MA 01776. ☎ **800/339-1776** or 508/443-1776. Fax 508/443-2312. 10 rms (some with shower only). A/C TEL. $70–$120 double. Extra person $15. AE, CB, DC, DISC, MC, V. Rates include full breakfast. Closed July 4, Christmas. From Main St. in Concord, follow Sudbury Rd., which becomes Route 20; 11 miles after passing I-95, bear right onto Wayside Inn Rd. The inn is on the right.

Worth a visit even if you're not spending the night or dining, this local institution dates to 1716 and got its name in 1863, when Henry Wadsworth Longfellow's *Tales of a Wayside Inn* was published. Henry Ford bought the property in 1923, and it has evolved into a private, nonprofit educational and charitable trust. A Ford Foundation grant helped fund the restoration of the inn in 1956 after a devastating fire, and today it's the country's oldest operating inn. A self-guided tour of the public rooms and historical artifacts is available.

All 10 guest rooms in the two-story inn are attractively decorated and furnished with antiques, but only two (the most popular, of course) are in the original building. Make your reservations as early as possible, especially for those rooms.

It's also the centerpiece of what amounts to a tiny theme park. On the 106 acres that surround it are a restored barn, the Redstone School of "Mary Had a Little Lamb" fame (built in Sterling, Massachusetts, in 1798 and moved to Sudbury in 1926), a wedding chapel, and a working grist mill. The mill, a reproduction built by Ford in 1929, stone-grinds the wheat flour and cornmeal that is used in the inn's baked goods and for sale at the gift shop. Old grindstones dot the pretty lawn out front, where you're welcome to sit and sunbathe. It's not very 18th-century, but the inn also has a web site (http://www.wayside.org).

Dining & Entertainment: Staff members in the inn's dining rooms wear colonial costumes and dish up hearty portions of traditional New England fare that might incorporate produce grown on the inn's property. The menu changes daily, but favorite choices include prime rib, lobster casserole, and, for dessert, strawberry shortcake. You'll see lots of families and retirees. Food is served Monday through Saturday from 11:30am to 3pm and 5 to 9pm, and Sunday noon to 8pm (dinner menu only). Main courses at lunch are $7.50–$14.50, at dinner $14 to $27, and portions are huge. Reservations are recommended.

WHERE TO DINE

✪ **Aïgo Bistro.** 84 Thoreau St. (Route 126), at Concord Depot. ☎ **508/371-1333.** Reservations recommended at dinner. Main courses $7–$9 at lunch, $14–$25 at dinner. Prix-fixe dinner (3 courses) $16.95. AE, MC, V. Daily 11:30am–2:30pm and 5–10pm. MEDITERRANEAN.

"Aïgo" is Provençal patois for "garlic," which perfumes the air half a block away from this delightful spot. It's pronounced "I go," and you'll want to, for scrumptious food and top-notch service in a sophisticated setting—one dining room overlooks the train tracks, the other is decorated with murals. Settle in on a tapestry banquette, play with the brightly colored salt and pepper shakers, and prepare to be delighted. The emphasis is on garlic and grilling, so you might start with the house special soup, aïgo bouïdo, a puree of roasted garlic, onion, and almond. Carnivores will relish the beef fillet au poivre, served in a cognac and roasted garlic glaze, or pork chop in sage jus with horseradish mashed potatoes. At least two vegetarian entrees (one a daily special risotto) are available. The lunch menu is heavy on salads and sandwiches, served on focaccia. Desserts are few but delectable—try the lavender mascarpone cheesecake.

4 Marblehead

15 miles NE of Boston, 4 miles SE of Salem

Like an attractive person with a great personality, Marblehead has it all. Scenery, history, architecture, and shopping combine to make it a wonderful place to spend a few hours or a few days. The narrow streets of the historic district, known as "Old Town," lead down to the magnificent harbor that helps make this the self-proclaimed "Yachting Capital of America." The homes along the way have plaques bearing the date of construction as well as the names of the builder and original occupant—a history lesson without any studying. Many of the houses have stood since before the Revolutionary War, when Marblehead was a center of merchant shipping. Two historic homes are open for tours, and you can shop for antiques, jewelry, clothing, and boating paraphernalia, just for starters. There is sailboat racing all summer and a Christmas celebration in early December.

None of this is secret, naturally, and in good weather visitors jam the streets and shops. If crowds aren't your cup of tea, try to visit on a weekday and definitely stay away during Marblehead Race Week at the end of July, when competitive sailors flock from all over the country.

ESSENTIALS

GETTING THERE From Boston, drive north on Route 1A until you see signs in Lynn for Route 129; follow that along the water through Swampscott into Marblehead. Or take I-93 or Route 1 to Route 128, then Route 114 through Salem into Marblehead.

MBTA (☎ 617/222-3200) bus route 441/442 runs from Haymarket Square (Orange and Green lines) in Boston to downtown Marblehead. The trip takes about an hour. The no. 441 bus detours to Vinnin Square shopping center in Swampscott; otherwise, both routes are the same.

VISITOR INFORMATION   The **Marblehead Chamber of Commerce** (62 Pleasant St., P.O. Box 76, Marblehead, MA 01945; ☎ 617/631-2868) is open daily from 9am to 3pm and operates an information booth (daily in season, 10am to 5:30pm) on Pleasant Street near Spring Street. It also publishes a 48-page visitor's guide, individual pamphlets that list dining, shopping, and accommodations options, and a map of the historic district with two well-plotted walking tours. The **North of Boston Convention & Visitors Bureau** (P.O. Box 642, Beverly, MA 01915; ☎ 800/742-5306 or 508/921-4990) also publishes a visitor's guide.

Marblehead has a web site (http://www.marblehead.com).

GETTING AROUND   Wear your good walking shoes—the bus can get you to Marblehead, but it can't negotiate many of the narrow streets of Old Town. You'll also be climbing hills, especially if you do a lot of exploring.

SEEING THE SIGHTS

An aimless stroll through the winding streets of Old Town invariably leads to shopping, snacking, or gazing at something picturesque, be it the harbor or a beautiful home. If you prefer more structure, follow the Chamber of Commerce's one- or two-mile walking tour. Even if you don't, stop outside the **Lafayette House,** at the corner of Hooper and Union streets. Legend has it that one corner of the first floor was chopped off in 1824 to allow Lafayette's carriage to negotiate the corner. In Market Square on Washington Street, near the corner of State Street, is the **Old Town House,** in use since 1727.

Be sure to spend some time in **Crocker Park,** on the harbor off Front Street. Especially in the warmer months, when boats jam the water nearly as far as the eye can see, the view is breathtaking. There are benches and a swing, and picnicking is allowed. You may not want to leave, but snap out of it—the view from **Fort Sewall,** at the other end of Front Street, is just as mesmerizing. The ruins of the fort, built in the 17th century and rebuilt late in the 18th, are another excellent picnic spot.

By car or bicycle, the swanky residential community of **Marblehead Neck** is worth a look. Follow Ocean Avenue across the causeway and visit the **Audubon Bird Sanctuary** (look for the tiny sign at the corner of Risley Avenue) or continue on to **Castle Rock** for another eyeful of scenery. At the end of "the Neck," at Harbor and Ocean avenues, is **Chandler Hovey Park,** where there's a (closed) lighthouse and a panoramic view.

Back in town, as promised, are several destinations of historical interest.

Abbot Hall. Washington Sq. ☎ **617/631-0528.** Free admission. Year-round Mon, Tues, and Thurs 8am–5pm, Wed 7:30am–7:30pm, Fri 8am–1pm; May–Oct Fri 8am–5pm, Sat 11am–6pm, Sun 9am–6pm. From the historic district, follow Washington St. up the hill.

The town offices and Historical Commission share Abbot Hall with Archibald M. Willard's famous painting *The Spirit of '76,* which is on display in the Selectmen's Meeting Room. The thrill of recognizing the ubiquitous drummer, drummer boy, and fife player is the main reason to stop here. The deed that records the sale of the land by the Native Americans to the Europeans in 1684 is also on view. The building's clock tower is visible from all over Old Town.

✪ **Jeremiah Lee Mansion.** 161 Washington St. ☎ **617/631-1069.** Guided tours $4 adults, $3.50 students, free for children under 10. Mid-May to Oct Mon–Sat 10am–4pm, Sun 1–4pm.

Closed Nov to mid-May. Follow Washington St. until it curves right and heads up the hill to Abbott Hall; the house is on the right.

The prospect of seeing original hand-painted wallpaper in an 18th-century home is reason enough to visit this house, built in 1768 for a wealthy merchant and considered an outstanding example of pre-Revolutionary Georgian architecture. Original rococo carving and other details complement historically accurate room arrangements, and ongoing restoration and interpretation by the Marblehead Historical Society place the 18th- and 19th-century furnishings and artifacts in context. The displays on the third floor draw on the Historical Society's collections of children's furniture, toys, and nautical and military memorabilia. A tip: On the hill between the mansion and Abbott Hall, the private homes at 187, 185, and 181 Washington Street are good examples of the architecture of this period.

King Hooper Mansion. 8 Hooper St., Marblehead. ☎ **617/631-2608.** Tour: Donation requested. Mon–Sat 10am–4pm, Sun 1–5pm. Call ahead; tours are not held during private parties. Where Washington St. curves right at the foot of the hill, bear left; the building is on the left.

Shipping tycoon Robert Hooper got his nickname because he treated his sailors so well, but it's easy to think he was called "King" because he lived like royalty. Located around the corner from the home of Jeremiah Lee (whose sister was the second of Hooper's four wives), the King Hooper Mansion was built in 1728 and gained a Georgian addition in 1747. The period furnishings, though not original, give a sense of the life of an 18th-century merchant prince, from the wine cellar to the third-floor ballroom. The building houses the headquarters of the Marblehead Arts Association, which stages monthly exhibits and runs a gift shop where members' work is for sale. The mansion also has a lovely garden; enter through the gate at the right of the house.

SHOPPING

Your own piece of history (contemporary or otherwise) may be waiting for you in one of Marblehead's galleries and antique, clothing, and jewelry shops. Old Town is the favored destination for shoppers, but don't forget that Atlantic Avenue and the south end of Pleasant Street are home to more mainstream businesses. This is just a selection—part of the fun of shopping, of course, is the thrill of discovery.

Along the square around the Old Town House are any number of delightful shops. Poke around in **Heeltappers Antiques** (134 Washington St.; ☎ 617/631-7722); the **Old Town Antique Co-op** (108 Washington St.; ☎ 617/631-8777), with four dealers under one roof; **Calico Country Antiques** (92 Washington St.; ☎ 617/631-3607), and **Cargo Unlimited** (82 Washington St.; ☎ 617/631-1112). **O'Rama's** (148 Washington St.; ☎ 617/631-0894) sells what it calls "miscellaneous elegancies," also known as jewelry, lingerie, accessories, and other high-end "girl stuff." At the **Marblehead Kite Company** (1 Pleasant St.; ☎ 617/631-7116), kites are outnumbered by greeting cards, T-shirts, stuffed animals, and toys (including some that children of the 1970s haven't seen since their youth). **Hector's Pup** (84 Washington St.; ☎ 617/631-5860), an excellent toy store, is best approached from State Street, where the corner windows overflow with dollhouse furniture. At the other end of State Street, **Brass and Bounty** (68 Front St.; ☎ 617/631-3864) specializes in marine antiques and antique lighting, and **Antiquewear** (82–84 Front St.; ☎ 617/639-0070) sells buttons ingeniously fashioned into jewelry.

Jewelry is known as "wearable art" at **Raven Gallery** (41 State St.; ☎ 617/639-3292), which also sells glass sculptures, paintings, and prints. **Arnould Gallery and Framery** (111 Washington St.; ☎ 617/631-6366) emphasizes Marblehead and New England themes. The **Art Guild Gallery** (78 Washington St.; ☎ 617/

631-3791), **Russian Gallery** (158 Washington St.; ☎ **617/639-2224**), and **Concetta's Gallery** (11 Pleasant St.; ☎ **617/639-2113**) are all worth a visit if you'd like to see what the local artists are up to.

WHERE TO STAY

The Chamber of Commerce accommodations listings include many bed and break-fasts. If you prefer to use an agency, try **Bed & Breakfast Reservations North Shore/Greater Boston/Cape Cod** (P.O. Box 35, Newtonville, MA 02160; ☎ **800/832-2632** or 617/964-1606 outside Massachusetts; fax 617/332-8572; e-mail bnbinc@ix.netcom.com).

Pleasant Manor Inn Bed and Breakfast. 264 Pleasant St. (Route 114), Marblehead, MA, 01945. ☎ **800/399-5843** or 617/631-5843. 12 rms (some with shower only; one room's bath is across the hall). A/C TV. $68–$80 double. Rates include continental breakfast. No credit cards.

Just outside the historic district, the Pleasant Manor Inn is a three-story Victorian mansion built as a private home in 1872 and operated as an inn since 1923. Innkeepers Richard and Takami Phelan took over in 1975. The spacious rooms open off a magnificent central staircase and are tastefully decorated with Victorian prints and some antiques. Aviation aficionados can request the room where Amelia Earhart stayed. Guests have the use of a tennis court in the backyard. Children are welcome, and smoking is not allowed.

Spray Cliff on the Ocean. 25 Spray Ave., Marblehead, MA 01945. ☎ **800/626-1530** or 617/631-6789. Fax 617/639-4563. 7 rms (some with shower only). Memorial Day weekend-late Oct $175–$205 double; lower rates off-season. Extra person $25. Rates include continental breakfast, evening refreshments, and use of bicycles. AE, MC, V. Take Atlantic Ave. (Route 129) to the lights at Clifton Ave. and turn east (right driving north, left driving south); parking area is at the end of the street.

Spray Cliff, a three-story Victorian Tudor built in 1910 on a cliff overlooking the ocean, is five minutes from town and a world away. Five of the large, sunny rooms face the water, three have fireplaces, and all are luxuriously decorated in contemporary style with brightly colored accents. Roger and Sally Plauché have run their "romantic, adult inn" on a quiet, residential street one minute from the beach since 1994. Smoking is not permitted.

WHERE TO DINE

Iggy's Bread of the World (5 Pleasant St.; ☎ **617/639-4717**) supplies many of the Boston area's top restaurants from its headquarters on a side street in Watertown. The Marblehead branch, though hardly a sit-down dining destination, smells so good that it's tough to leave empty-handed.

The Barnacle. 141 Front St., Marblehead. ☎ **617/631-4236.** Reservations not accepted. Main courses $3.95–$12.95 at lunch, $10.95–$15.95 at dinner. No credit cards. Daily 11:30am–4pm and 5–10pm. SEAFOOD.

This unassuming spot doesn't look like much from the street, but at the end of the gangplank-like entrance hall is a front-row seat for the action on the water. Even if you don't land a seat on the deck or along the counter facing the windows, you'll still have a shorebird's-eye view of the mouth of the harbor and the ocean from the jam-packed dining room. The food won't provide much of a distraction, but it's tasty and plentiful. The chowder and fried seafood, especially the clams, are terrific, and there's no better place to quaff a beer and watch the boats sail by.

Driftwood Restaurant. 63 Front St., Marblehead. ☎ **617/631-1145.** Main courses $1.60–$9.50. No credit cards. Summer daily 5:30am–5pm; winter daily 5:30am–2pm. DINER/SEAFOOD.

At the foot of State Street next to Clark Landing (the town pier) is an honest-to-goodness local hangout. Whether you're in the mood for pancakes and hash or chowder and a seafood "roll" (a hot dog bun filled with, say, fried clams or lobster salad), join the crowd at the counter or take a table. The house specialty, served on weekends and holidays, is fried dough, which is exactly as good-tasting and bad for you as it sounds.

King's Rook. 12 State St., Marblehead. ☎ **617/631-9838.** Reservations not accepted. Main courses $4.50–$8. MC, V. Mon–Fri noon–2:30pm; Tues–Fri 5:30–11:30pm; Sat–Sun noon–11:30pm. CAFE/WINE BAR.

There's no better place to complete the sentence "I'm thirsty and I'd like . . . " than this cozy spot, a favorite long before coffeehouses ruled prime-time television. Coffees, teas, hot chocolates, soft drinks, and more than two dozen wines by the glass are available, and the food has a sophisticated flair. The intimate atmosphere and racks of newspapers and magazines make this a great place to linger over a pesto pizza, a salad, or a sinfully rich dessert—and, of course, a beverage.

Kitchen Witch Eatery. 78 Front St., Marblehead. ☎ **617/639-1475.** Most items under $6. No credit cards. Summer Sun–Thurs 11am–10pm, Fri–Sat 11am–11pm. DELI.

Across the street from Clark Landing is this storefront oasis, where you can eat in the tiny dining area or order everything you need for a picnic. Sandwiches, salads, and soups are fresh and delicious, and the muffins and other baked goods are excellent. This is also the perfect place to grab some ice cream or frozen yogurt (in dozens of flavors) and set off to explore the town.

5 Salem

16 miles NE of Boston, 4 miles NW of Marblehead

Salem was settled in 1626 (four years before Boston) and later became known around the world as a center of merchant shipping and the China trade, but it's internationally famous today for a seven-month episode in 1692. The witchcraft trial hysteria led to 20 deaths, three centuries of notoriety, countless lessons on the evils of prejudice, and dozens of bad puns ("Stop by for a spell" is a favorite slogan). Unable to live down its association with witches, Salem has embraced it. The high school sports teams are called the Witches, and the logo of the *Salem Evening News* is a silhouette of a witch.

Visitors expecting wall-to-wall witches won't be disappointed, but they will be missing another important part of the city's history. Salem flourished in the 17th and 18th centuries as its merchant vessels circled the globe, returning with treasures and artifacts that can still be seen today. Its dominance peaked between the Revolutionary War and the War of 1812, when many overseas trading partners believed that Salem was an independent country. The shipping trade was on the decline in the 1840s when Salem native Nathaniel Hawthorne worked in the Custom House, where he found an embroidered scarlet "A" that set his imagination to work.

ESSENTIALS

GETTING THERE From Boston, take Route 1A north into downtown Salem, being careful in Lynn, where the road turns left and immediately right. Or take I-93 or Route 1 (if it's not rush hour) to Route 128, then Route 114 into downtown Salem. Keep left on 114 and ignore the signs for "Historic Salem," which lead you through downtown Peabody. In Salem, follow the signs—brown for the visitor center, blue for parking, and green for museums and historic sites.

From Boston, the MBTA (☎ **617/222-3200**) runs bus route 450 from Haymarket Square and commuter trains from North Station. They operate often on weekdays, less frequently on weekends. The bus takes about an hour, the train 30 minutes. At the Salem station, a long staircase runs from train level to street level.

VISITOR INFORMATION   An excellent place to start your visit is the **National Park Service Visitor Center** (2 New Liberty St., ☎ **508/741-3648**), where exhibits highlight early settlement, maritime history, and the leather and textiles industries. The center (open in summer daily 9am to 6pm; winter, daily 9am to 5pm) also has an auditorium where a free film on Essex County, *Where Past Is Present,* provides a good overview.

The **Salem Chamber of Commerce** in Old Town Hall (32 Derby Sq., Salem, MA 01970; ☎ **508/744-0004**) maintains an information booth (open in summer Monday through Saturday 9am to 5pm, Sunday noon to 5pm; winter, weekdays 9am to 5pm), and collaborates with the **Salem Office of Tourism & Cultural Affairs** (93 Washington St., Salem, MA 01970; ☎ **800/777-6848**) to publish a free visitor's guide. The **North of Boston Convention & Visitors Bureau** (P.O. Box 642, Beverly, MA, 01915; ☎ **800/742-5306** or 508/921-4990) also publishes a visitor's guide.

Salem has a web site (http://www.star.net/salem).

GETTING AROUND   In the immediate downtown area, walking is the way to go, but there's much more to Salem than just that. There's plenty of parking at meters and in lots and garages throughout the city. If you plan to spend the day and visit more than three or four places, consider buying an all-day trolley ticket (see below).

SEEING THE SIGHTS

Downtown Salem is spread out but flat, and the historic district extends well inland from the waterfront. Many 18th-century houses still stand, some with original furnishings. Ship captains lived near the water at the east end of downtown, in relatively small houses crowded close together. The captains' employers, the shipping company owners, built their homes away from the water (and the accompanying aromas). Many of them lived on **Chestnut Street,** which is preserved as a registered National Historic Landmark. Residents along the ravishingly beautiful thoroughfare must, by legal agreement, adhere to colonial style in their decorating and furnishings.

At the Essex Street side of the visitor center, you can board the **Salem Trolley** (☎ **508/744-5469;** daily, April through October, weekends March and November) for a one-hour narrated tour. Tickets ($8 adults, $7 seniors and students, $4 children 5 to 12; $20 family of two adults and two or more children) are good all day, and you can reboard as many times as you like at any of the 15 stops—a great deal if you're spending the day and don't want to keep moving the car or carrying leg-weary children. In December during **Holiday Happenings,** the Salem Trolley Players' traveling presentation of *A Christmas Carol* takes place on board. Call for reservations.

Should you find yourself in town at the end of October, you won't be able to miss **Haunted Happenings,** the city's two-week Halloween celebration. Parades, parties, and tours lead up to a ceremony on the big day.

The **Heritage Trail** is a 1.7-mile walking route that begins at the visitor center, near the two-block pedestrian mall on **Essex Street.** It's marked by a red line painted on the sidewalk and connects many of the major attractions.

Pickering Wharf, at the corner of Derby and Congress streets, is a cluster of shops, boutiques, restaurants, and condos adjacent to a marina. The waterfront setting makes it a good place for strolling, snacking, and shopping. The **Pickering Wharf Antiques Gallery** (☎ **508/741-3113**) collects 40 dealers of all stripes under one capacious roof. Leave at least an hour if your taste runs to antiques and collectibles. You can also take a harbor cruise or go on a whale watch organized by the **East India Cruise Company** (197 Derby St.; ☎ **800/745-9594** or 508/741-0434).

Three destinations on the outskirts of the historic district are worth the trip. By car or trolley, **Salem Willows,** a waterfront amusement park, is five minutes away (many signs point the way) and a wonderful place to bring a picnic. Admission and parking are free. To enjoy the great view without the arcades and rides, have lunch one peninsula over at **Winter Island Park.** Up-market gift shops throughout New England sell the chocolate confections of **Harbor Sweets,** and you can go to the source (Palmer Cove, 85 Leavitt St.; ☎ **508/745-7648**; open Monday through Friday 8:30am to 4:30pm, Saturday 9am to 3pm). The retail store overlooks the floor of the factory—call ahead to see if the machinery is running. Recent introductions to the product line include chocolates with equestrian motifs and two varieties made without sugar.

Finally, if you can't get witchcraft off your mind, several shops specialize in the necessary accessories, including crystal balls and tarot cards. The **Broom Closet** (3–5 Central St.; ☎ **508/741-3669**) and **Crow's Haven Corner** (125 Essex St.; ☎ **508/745-8763**) sell everything from crystals to clothing and cast a modern-day light on age-old customs—just bear in mind that Salem is home to many practicing witches who take their craft seriously.

The House of the Seven Gables. 54 Turner St. ☎ **508/744-0991.** Guided tours $7 adults, $4 children 13–17, $3 children 6–12. June 1–Labor Day daily 9am–6pm; off-season daily 10am–4:30pm. Closed Thanksgiving, Christmas, and New Year's Day. From downtown, follow Derby St. east 3 blocks past Derby Wharf; historic site is on the right.

Built by Capt. John Turner in 1668, this building was later occupied by a cousin of Nathaniel Hawthorne's, and Hawthorne's 1851 novel was inspired by stories and legends of the house and its inhabitants. If you haven't read the book, don't let that keep you away—begin your visit with the audiovisual program, which tells the story. The house holds six rooms of period furniture, including pieces referred to in the book, and a narrow, twisting secret staircase that will be the high point of the tour for most children and many adults. Costumed guides lead uncomplicated tours of the historic site, which include Hawthorne's birthplace (built before 1750 and moved to the grounds) and describe life when the houses were in use. Also on the grounds, overlooking Salem Harbor, are period gardens, the Retire Beckett House (1655), the Hooper-Hathaway House (1682), and a counting house (1830). Combination discounted tickets for Salem 1630 and the House of the Seven Gables are available at both sites.

✪ Peabody Essex Museum. East India Sq. ☎ **800/745-4054** or 508/745-9500. Admission (good on 2 consecutive days) $7 adults, $6 seniors and students, $4 children 6–16, $18 families (2 adults, 1 or more children). Free first Fri of each month 5–8pm. Mon–Sat 10am–5pm, Sun noon–5pm, Fri until 8pm. Closed Thanksgiving, Christmas, New Year's Day, and Mon Nov–Memorial Day. Take Hawthorne Blvd. to Essex St., following signs for visitor center. Plummer Hall (Essex Institute) is on the right; East India Hall (Peabody Museum) is at the corner of Liberty St., at the east end of the pedestrian mall.

The 1992 merger of the Peabody Museum and the Essex Institute combined fascinating collections that illustrate Salem's adventures abroad and its development at home. The Peabody Museum, the nation's oldest in continuous operation, was founded in 1799 by the East India Marine Society, a group of sea captains and merchants whose charter included provisions for a "museum in which to house the natural and artificial curiosities" brought back from their travels. The collection of the Essex Institute (1821), the county's historical society, encompasses American art, crafts, furniture, and architecture (including nine historic houses), as well as dolls, toys, and games.

This all adds up to the impression that you're in Salem's attic, but instead of opening dusty trunks and musty closets, you find all the work done for you and the treasures arranged in well-planned displays that help you understand the significance of each artifact. If you want to learn more, there are two research libraries, but you'll probably be more than happy wandering the galleries until you find something that interests you, as you surely will. Trace the history of the port of Salem and the whaling trade, study figureheads of ships or portraits of area residents (including Charles Osgood's omnipresent rendering of Nathaniel Hawthorne), learn about the witchcraft trials, immerse yourself in East Asian art and artifacts or the practical arts and crafts of the East Asian, Pacific Island, and Native American peoples. The Asian Export Art Wing displays decorative art pieces made in Asia for Western use from the 14th to 19th centuries. Be sure to sign up for a tour of one or more houses—the Gardner-Pingree House (1804), a magnificent Federal mansion, was the site of a notorious murder in 1830 and has been gorgeously restored. You can also sign up for a gallery tour or select from about a dozen pamphlets for self-guided tours on various topics.

Salem Maritime National Historic Site. 174 Derby St. ☎ **508/745-1470.** Free admission. Guided tours $3 adults, $2 seniors and children 6–16, $10 family. Summer daily 9am–5pm; winter Mon–Fri 10am–4pm, Sat–Sun 9am–5pm. Closed Thanksgiving, Christmas, and New Year's Day. Take Derby St. east; just past Pickering Wharf, the orientation center is on the right, at the head of Derby Wharf.

With the decline of the shipping trade, Salem's wharves fell into disrepair, a state the National Park Service began to remedy in 1938 when it took over a small piece of the waterfront. Derby Wharf is now a finger of parkland extending into the harbor, part of the nine acres, dotted with explanatory markers, that make up the historic site. The warehouse that houses the orientation center dates to around 1800 and was moved to the head of the wharf in the 1970s. Ranger-led tours, which vary according to seasonal schedules, expand on Salem's maritime history. They're well researched and quite interesting. Yours might include the Custom House (1819), where Nathaniel Hawthorne worked, and the Derby House (1762), a wedding gift to shipping magnate Elias Hasket Derby from his father. If you prefer to explore on your own, you can see the free film at the orientation center and wander around Derby Wharf, the West India Goods Store, the Bonded Warehouse, the Scale House, and Central Wharf.

Salem 1630: Pioneer Village. Forest River Park, off West Ave. ☎ **508/745-0525** or 508/744-0991. Admission $4.50 adults, $3.50 seniors and children 13–17, $2.50 children 6–12. Memorial Day–Halloween daily 10am–5pm. Closed Nov 1–late May. Take Lafayette St. (Routes 114 and 1A) south to West Ave., turn left and follow the signs.

A re-creation of life in Salem just four years after European settlement, this Puritan village is staffed by costumed interpreters who lead tours, demonstrate crafts, and tend to farm animals. As with any undertaking of this nature, it takes a while to get used to the atmosphere, but once you do, it's great fun. Don't wear your good shoes—the site is not paved.

When the 1996 film version of Arthur Miller's play about the witchcraft trials, *The Crucible*, was completed, the village inherited a large collection of authentic and reproduction props that have been put to use. Combination discounted tickets for Salem 1630 and the House of the Seven Gables are available at both sites.

Salem Witch Museum. 19¹/₂ Washington Sq. ☎ **508/744-1692.** Admission $4 adults, $3.50 seniors, $2.50 children 6–14. Sept–June daily 10am–5pm; July–Aug daily 10am–7pm. Closed

Trying Times

The Salem Witch Trials took place in 1692, a product of superstition brought to the New World from Europe, religious control of government, and plain old boredom.

The hysteria that led to the trials began in the winter of 1691 to 1692 in Salem Village (now the town of Danvers). The household of the Reverend Samuel Parris included his 9-year-old daughter, Elizabeth, her cousin Abigail, and a West Indian slave named Tituba who amused the girls and their friends during the long, harsh winter by telling them stories. Entertained by the tales of witchcraft, sorcery, and fortune-telling, the girls began acting as if they were under a spell, rolling on the ground and wailing. The superstitious settlers, aware that thousands of people in Europe had been executed for being witches in the previous two centuries, took the behavior seriously, and a doctor diagnosed Elizabeth, Abigail, and one of their friends as bewitched.

At first only Tituba and two other local women were accused of casting the spells, but the infighting that characterized the Puritan theocracy soon came to the fore, and an accusation of witchcraft became a handy way to settle a score. Anyone considered "different" was a potential target, from the elderly to the deaf to the poor. A special court was convened in Salem proper, and even though the girls soon recanted, the trials began. Defendants had no counsel, and pleading not guilty or objecting to the proceedings was considered the equivalent of a confession. Between March 1 and September 22, 27 of the more than 150 people accused had been convicted.

In the end, 19 people went to the gallows, and one man who refused to confess, Giles Corey, was pressed to death by stones piled on a board on his chest. Finally, cooler heads prevailed. Leading cleric Cotton Mather and his father, Harvard president Increase Mather, led the call for tolerance. With the jails overflowing, the trials were called off and the prisoners (including Tituba) freed.

The lessons of open-mindedness and tolerance that come down to us in this cautionary tale have been absorbed with varying degrees of success in the intervening years. Salem was the backdrop for the recent film version of Arthur Miller's *The Crucible*, a story of the witch trials and an allegory of the McCarthy Senate hearings of the 1950s—a time when those lessons could productively have been taught again.

Thanksgiving, Christmas, and New Year's Day. Follow Hawthorne Blvd. to the northwest corner of Salem Common.

Actually a three-dimensional audiovisual presentation with life-size figures, the Witch Museum is a huge room with displays along the walls that are lighted in sequence. The historically accurate 30-minute narration tells the story of the witchcraft trials and the accompanying hysteria. (One man was pressed to death by rocks piled on a board on his chest—smaller children may need to be reminded that he's not real.) The narrative makes a good introduction to the subject for adults and children alike.

On the traffic island across from the entrance is a statue, easily mistaken for a witch, of Roger Conant, who founded Salem in 1626.

WHERE TO STAY

Coach House Inn. 284 Lafayette St. (Routes 1A and 114), Salem, MA 01970. ☎ **800/ 688-8689** or 508/744-4092. 11 rms, 9 with bath (some with shower only). A/C TV. $65–$72 double with shared bath; $72–$95 double with private bath; $125–$155 suite with kitchenette. Extra person $15. Rates include continental breakfast. AE, MC, V.

Built in 1879 for a ship's captain, the Coach House Inn is a 20-minute walk or 5-minute drive from downtown Salem and two blocks from the harbor. The high-ceilinged rooms in the three-story mansion have elegant furnishings and fireplaces, many of marble or carved ebony. Breakfast arrives at your door in a basket. Smoking is not allowed.

Hawthorne Hotel. 18 Washington Sq. (at Salem Common), Salem, MA 01970. ☎ **800/729-7829** or 508/744-4080. Fax 508/745-9842. 83 rms, 6 suites. A/C TV TEL. $88–$145 double; $185–$225 suite. Lower rates off-season. Extra person $12. Children under 16 stay free in parents' room. Senior discount. AE, DC, DISC, MC, V.

This historic hotel, built in 1925 and nicely maintained—the lobby was remodeled in 1995—is as convenient as it is comfortable. The six-story building is centrally located, and some of the attractively furnished rooms overlook Salem Common. This is a busy neighborhood; ask to be as high up as possible. Guests have the use of an exercise room, and there are two restaurants on the ground floor.

Salem Inn. 7 Summer St. (Route 114), Salem, MA 01970. ☎ **800/446-2995** or 508/741-0680. Fax 508/744-8924. 31 rms (some with shower only). A/C TV TEL. Mid-Apr to mid-Oct, $109–$179 double; Halloween week $140–$175 double; Nov to mid-Apr $99–$169 double. Rates include continental breakfast. AE, DC, DISC, MC, V.

The hubbub of downtown falls away as you enter the two ship's captain's homes that make up the Salem Inn. The 1834 West House and the 1854 Curwen House (around the corner on Essex Street) are one block from historic Chestnut Street and offer guests large, tastefully decorated rooms, some with fireplaces, canopy beds, and whirlpool baths. Have breakfast in the Courtyard Cafe or wander out to the rose garden and brick patio at the rear of the main building.

WHERE TO DINE

In a Pig's Eye. 148 Derby St. ☎ **508/741-4436.** Reservations recommended at dinner. Sandwiches and salads $2.95–$6.50, main courses $3.75–$7.95 at lunch, $8.95–$12.25 at dinner Wed–Sat, $4.50–$9.95 at dinner Mon–Tues. AE, MC, V. Mon–Sat 11:30am–3pm and 6–10pm, Sun 11:30am–4pm. AMERICAN/MEXICAN.

Although it appears to be just a neighborhood bar, In a Pig's Eye is more silk purse than sow's ear—the food is wonderful. The lunch menu offers bar fare that's a step up from basic, with several vegetarian options, and Mexican food, including gigantic, delicious burritos. Mexican nights are Monday and Tuesday (the Mexican pizza, mounds of vegetables and salsa served on flour tortillas, is terrific), and the rest of the week sees a change to creative pasta dishes, beef, chicken, and at least half a dozen seafood choices.

✪ Lyceum Bar & Grill. 43 Church St. (at Washington St.). ☎ **508/745-7665.** Reservations recommended. Main courses $6–$9 at lunch, $9–$18 at dinner. AE, DISC, MC, V. Mon–Fri 11:30am–3pm, Sun 11am–3pm; daily 5:30–10pm. AMERICAN.

Alexander Graham Bell made the first long-distance telephone call at the Lyceum, and you may want to place one of your own, to tell the folks at home what a good meal you're having. The elegance of the Lyceum's high-ceilinged front rooms and glass-walled back rooms is matched by the quality of the food. Grilling is a favorite cooking technique here—be sure to try the marinated, grilled portabella mushrooms, even if you have to order a plate of them as an appetizer. They're also scattered throughout the menu, for example in delectable pasta with chicken, red peppers, and Swiss chard in wine sauce, or with beef tenderloin, red pepper sauce, and garlic mashed potatoes. Spicy vegetable lasagna is also tasty. Try to save room for one of the traditional yet sophisticated desserts. The brownie sundae is out of this world.

Ⓢ Red's Sandwich Shop. 15 Central St. ☎ **508/745-3527.** Most items under $6. No credit cards. Mon–Sat 5am–3pm, Sun 6am–1pm. DINER.

There's no telling what the Drivases, who run Red's, will do for their next trick— here they manage to run a no-frills place where locals and visitors feel equally comfortable. Hunker down at the counter or a table and be ready for your waitress to call you "dear" as she brings you pancakes and eggs at breakfast or soup (opt for chicken over chowder) and a burger at lunch. Under the same management, **Red's Winter Island Grille** (☎ **508/744-0203**) is open seasonally at Winter Island Park.

Stromberg's. 2 Bridge St. (Route 1A). ☎ **508/744-1863.** Reservations recommended at dinner. Main courses $3.95–$9.95 at lunch, $9.95–$14.95 at dinner; lobster priced daily. AE, DISC, MC, V. Tues–Thurs 11am–9pm, Fri–Sat 11am–10pm. Closed Tues on long holiday weekends. SEAFOOD.

For generous portions of well-prepared seafood and a water view, head to this wildly popular spot near the bridge to Beverly. You won't care that Beverly Harbor isn't the most exciting spot, especially if it's summer and you're out on the deck enjoying the live entertainment (weekends only). The fish and clam chowders are excellent, daily specials are numerous, and there are more chicken, beef, and pasta options than you'd think. Crustacean lovers in the mood to splurge will fall for the world-class lobster roll. There's also a children's menu ($2.50 to $3.95).

6 Gloucester, Rockport & Cape Ann

Gloucester, Rockport, Essex, and Manchester-by-the-Sea make up Cape Ann, a rocky peninsula so enchantingly beautiful that when you hear the slogan "Massachusetts' *other* Cape," you may forget what the first one was. Cape Ann and Cape Cod do share some attributes—scenery, shopping, seafood, traffic—but the smaller cape's proximity to Boston and manageable scale make it a wonderful day trip as well as a good choice for a longer stay. With the decline of the fishing industry that brought great prosperity to the area in the 19th century, Cape Ann has played up its long-standing reputation as a haven for artists. In addition to galleries and craft shops, you'll find historical attractions, beaches—and oh, that scenery!

The public transportation to and in this area is pretty good, but if you can, try to travel by car—you'll be able to set your own pace and take in more sights.

Be aware that this is anything but a four-season destination. Although plenty of people commute to Boston year-round and in recent years there's been a push to make Christmas a month-long celebration, many of the attractions that draw non-residents are closed from fall or early winter until April or May. Rockport in particular shuts up tighter than an Essex clam.

Cape Ann has a web site (http://wizard.pn.com/capeann).

BEACHES

Paradoxically, Cape Ann is almost as well known for its sandy beaches as for its rocky coastline. Two caveats: it's not Florida, so don't expect 70-degree water (the operative word is "refreshing"), and parking can be pricey—as much as $15 per car—and scarce, especially on weekends. If you can't set out early, wait till midafternoon and hope that the people who beat you to the beach in the morning have had enough. During the summer, lifeguards are on duty from 9am to 5pm at larger public beaches. Surfing is generally permitted outside of those hours.

Probably the best-known North Shore beach is **Singing Beach,** off Masconomo Street in Manchester-by-the-Sea. It's named for the sound the sand makes under your feet, and the legions of people walking six-tenths of a mile on Beach Street from the commuter rail station attest to both the beach's reputation and the difficulty (and expense) of parking. Save some cash and aggravation by taking the MBTA (☎ 617/222-3200) from Boston's North Station. **White Beach,** off Ocean Street, is another public beach in town.

Nearly as famous as Singing Beach and equally popular is **Crane Beach,** off Argilla Road in Ipswich, part of a 1,400-acre barrier beach reservation. Expanses of white sand and fragile dunes lead down to Ipswich Bay, with surf calmer than that at less sheltered Singing Beach, but still quite chilly. Also on Ipswich Bay is Gloucester's **Wingaersheek Beach,** on Atlantic Street off Route 133. It has its own exit (number 13) off Route 128, about 15 minutes away. When you finally arrive you'll find beautiful white sand, a glorious view, and more dunes. Across the bay, there's a beach at **Plum Island** that's part of the **Parker River National Wildlife Refuge** (see "Newburyport, Ipswich & Plum Island," below).

Watch out for the greenhead flies at Wingaersheek, Plum Island, and Crane beaches in late July and early August. They don't sting—they actually take little bites of flesh. Plan to bring or buy insect repellent.

Other nice beaches in Gloucester are **Good Harbor Beach,** off Route 127A at Thatcher Road in East Gloucester, **Coffin Beach,** just northwest of Wingaersheek, and **Half Moon Beach** and **Cressy's Beach,** at Stage Fort Park, off Route 127 near the intersection with Route 133. The park also contains a visitor information office (summer only), playgrounds, picnic and cookout areas, and the ruins of a Revolutionary War fort.

In Rockport, **Front Beach** and **Back Beach** are on Beach Street just a couple of blocks north of downtown, and **Old Garden Beach** is on Old Garden Road east of downtown. Heading south on Route 127A toward Gloucester, you can detour to **Pebble Beach** (which appears on some maps as "Pebbly Beach"), off Penzance Road, **Cape Hedge Beach,** off South Street, and **Long Beach,** off Thatcher Road.

If ocean beaches don't suit you, **Chebacco Lake** in Essex off Western Avenue is a freshwater option.

MANCHESTER-BY-THE-SEA

The scenic route from the south to Gloucester is Route 127, which runs through Manchester-by-the-Sea, a lovely village incorporated in 1645. Now a prosperous suburb of Boston, Manchester is probably best known for Singing Beach (see "Beaches," above). The MBTA commuter rail (☎ 617/222-3200) stops in the center of the compact downtown area, which boasts a number of shops and restaurants. Nearby **Masconomo Park** overlooks Manchester Harbor.

The home of the Manchester Historical Society is the **Trask House** (10 Union St.; ☎ 508/526-7230), a 19th-century sea captain's home with period furnishings and costume collections. It's open in July and August, Wednesday through Saturday from 2 to 5pm, from September through June on Thursday from 9am to 1pm, and by appointment. A donation is requested.

MAGNOLIA

Pay close attention as you head north from Manchester or south from Gloucester on Route 127—the signs for Magnolia are small and easy to miss, but the village is well worth a detour. Notable for its lack of waterfront commercial property, the village center is small and unremarkable, but the homes surrounding it, many of them one-time summer residences now occupied through the winter, are magnificent.

Less than a mile up the coast are two notable geological formations. **Rafe's Chasm** is a huge cleft in the shoreline rock, opposite the reef of **Norman's Woe,** which figures in Henry Wadsworth Longfellow's scary poem "The Wreck of the Hesperus."

ESSEX

If you approach or leave Cape Ann on Route 128, turn away from Gloucester at the Route 133 exit and head west to Essex, known for Essex clams, salt marshes, a long tradition of shipbuilding, an incredible number of antique shops, and one legendary restaurant.

Woodman's of Essex (Main St.; ☎ **800/649-1773** or 508/768-6451) supposedly was the birthplace of the fried clam in 1916. Today it's a great spot for lobster "in the rough," steamers, corn on the cob, onion rings, and (you guessed it) fried clams. Expect the line to be long, but it moves quickly and offers a good view of the regimented commotion in the food preparation area. Eat in a booth, upstairs on the deck, or out back at a picnic table. If this all sounds just plain uncivilized, call ahead for a reservation and head across the street to **Tom Shea's** (122 Main St.; ☎ **508/768-6931**) for table service, a more sophisticated menu, and a calmer atmosphere. You'll want to be well-fed before you set off to explore the numerous antique shops along Main Street.

The water views in town are of the Essex River, actually a saltwater estuary. Narrated 90-minute sightseeing tours that put you in prime bird-watching territory are available at **Essex River Cruises** (Essex Marina, 35 Dodge St.; ☎ **800/748-3706** or 508/768-6981) daily from April through October. The boats are screened, so you don't have to worry about being eaten alive by insects. Call for reservations.

GLOUCESTER

33 miles NE of Boston, 16 miles NE of Salem, 7 miles S of Rockport

ESSENTIALS

GETTING THERE   From Boston, the quickest route is I-93 (or Route 1, if it's not rush hour) to Route 128, which ends at Gloucester. The slower but prettier approach is to take Route 1A—all the way from East Boston, or from downtown Salem—across the bridge at Beverly and pick up Route 127. It runs through Manchester (near, not on, the water) to Gloucester. Route 128 is almost entirely inland; the exits for Manchester allow access to Route 127.

The MBTA (☎ **617/222-3200**) commuter rail line runs from North Station in Boston to Gloucester. The trip takes about an hour. The Cape Ann Transportation Authority, or CATA (☎ **508/283-7916**) runs buses from town to town on Cape Ann.

VISITOR INFORMATION   The **Gloucester Tourism Commission** (22 Poplar St., Gloucester, MA, 01930; ☎ **800/649-6839** or 508/281-8865) operates an excellent Visitors Welcoming Center that's open daily during the summer at Stage Fort Park, off Route 127 near the intersection with Route 133. Ask for a copy of the Tourism Commission's guide to the Gloucester Maritime Trail, a pamphlet that includes descriptions of four walking tours.

The **Cape Ann Chamber of Commerce** (33 Commercial St., Gloucester, MA 01930; ☎ **800/321-0133** or 508/283-1601) information center is open year-round (summer, weekdays 8am to 6pm, Saturday 10am to 6pm, Sunday 10am to 4pm; winter, weekdays 8am to 5pm).

The **North of Boston Convention & Visitors Bureau** (P.O. Box 642, Beverly, MA 01915; ☎ **800/742-5306** or 508/921-4990) publishes a visitor's guide.

Gloucester has a page on the Cape Ann web site (http://wizard.pn.com/capeann).

GETTING AROUND   The Cape Ann Transportation Authority (see above) serves most of Gloucester on its regular routes and operates special loops during the summer, but if you can possibly manage it, try to make this trip by car. You'll be able to make the best use of your time by making your own schedule.

EXPLORING THE TOWN

Start at the water, the city's lifeblood since long before the first European settlement in 1623. The French explorer Samuel de Champlain called the harbor "Le Beauport" when he came across it in 1604, some 600 years after the Vikings, and its configuration and proximity to good fishing gave it the reputation it enjoys to this day. Follow one or more of the Tourism Commission's walking tours, or explore on your own.

The fleet sets out early in the morning from the downtown part of the harbor, where processing plants—Clarence Birdseye invented the procedure for blast-freezing foods here—await the catch, which is unloaded on **State Fish Pier,** Parker Street. Although fishing is an important industry, it doesn't carry the economic clout it once did. The depletion of New England's fishing grounds has led to the rise of another important seagoing industry: whale watching (see below).

On Stacy Boulevard west of downtown is a reminder of the sea's danger. Leonard Craske's bronze statue of the **Gloucester Fisherman,** known as "The Man at the Wheel," bears the inscription "They That Go Down to the Sea in Ships 1623–1923." More than 10,000 fishermen lost their lives during the city's first 300 years, and a statue honoring the women and children who waited for them is currently in the works.

The fishing fleet enjoys some divine intervention every year during **St. Peter's Fiesta,** a colorful four-day event at the end of June. The Italian-American fishing colony's enormous festival features parades, music, food, sporting events, and, on Sunday, the blessing of the fleet.

During the feast, much of downtown is closed to traffic; if you visit on a bad traffic day, that will seem like a good idea all the time. One good reason to brave the congestion on Main Street is to visit the **Cape Ann Historical Museum** (27 Pleasant St.; ☎ 508/283-0455). The meticulously curated little museum makes an excellent introduction to Cape Ann's history and artists. An entire gallery is devoted to the wonderful work of Fitz Hugh Lane, the American Luminist painter whose light-flooded paintings show the best of his native Gloucester. The nation's single largest collection of his paintings and drawings is here, along with new galleries featuring 20th-century artists, and maritime and fishing galleries overflowing with everything from entire vessels (including one about the size of a station wagon that actually crossed the Atlantic) to photographs and models of the Gloucester waterfront. The Capt. Elias Davis House (1804) is part of the museum and decorated and furnished in Federal style with furniture, silver, and porcelains.

Admission is $3.50 adults, $3 seniors, $2 students, free for children 6 and under. The museum is open from March through January, Tuesday through Saturday from 10am to 5pm, and closed in February. Follow Main Street west through downtown and turn right onto Pleasant Street (at the Salvation Army store); the museum is one block up on the right. Metered parking is available on the street or in the lot across the street.

Moby Duck Tours (☎ 508/281-3825) are 50-minute sightseeing expeditions that travel on land before plunging into the water. The "amphibious" vehicles leave from **Harbor Loop** downtown, where tickets ($12 adults, $10 seniors, $8 children under 12) are available. Plan to take a tour if you have children along; as soon as they see the vessels, they'll want a ride. Also at Harbor Loop, you can tour the two-masted schooner *Adventure* (☎ 508/281-8079), a 121-foot fishing vessel built in Essex in 1926. The "living museum," a National Historic Landmark under continual restoration, is open to visitors from Memorial Day to Labor Day, Thursday through Sunday from 10am to 4pm. (Suggested donation $5 adults, $4 children.)

Stage Fort Park (off Route 127 near the intersection with Route 133) offers an excellent view of the harbor and is a good spot for a picnic, swimming, or just playing on the cannons in the Revolutionary War fort.

To reach East Gloucester, follow signs as you leave downtown or go directly from Route 128, Exit 9. On East Main Street, you'll see signs for the world-famous **Rocky Neck Art Colony,** the oldest continuously operating art colony in the country. Park in the lot on the tiny causeway and walk two blocks west to Rocky Neck Avenue, which is jammed with studios, galleries, restaurants, and people. The real draw is the presence of working artists, not just shops that happen to sell art. Some of the work winds up at the **North Shore Arts Association** (197 E. Main St., rear; ☎ 508/283-1857), founded in 1923 to showcase local artists' work. It's open June through September, Monday to Saturday 10am to 5pm, Sunday 1 to 5pm, and admission is free.

The high point of a trip to this part of town is a visit to **Beauport (Sleeper-McCann House),** at 75 Eastern Point Blvd. (☎ 508/283-0800). The Society for the Preservation of New England Antiquities, which operates it, describes Beauport as a "fantasy house," and that's putting it mildly. Interior designer Henry Davis Sleeper used his summer residence as a retreat and a repository for his vast collections of American and European decorative arts and antiques. From 1907 to 1934 he decorated the 40 rooms, 26 of which are open to the public, to illustrate literary and historical themes. You'll see architectural details rescued from other buildings, magnificent arrangements of colored glassware, an early American kitchen, the "Red Indian Room" (with a majestic view of the harbor), and "Strawberry Hill," the master bedroom.

If you're interested in interior design, it's worth scheduling your visit so you can see Beauport, which is closed on summer weekends. Tours are given on the hour from mid-May through mid-October on weekdays only from 10am to 4pm; and from mid-September through mid-October on weekdays from 10am to 4pm and weekends 1 to 4pm. The house is closed from mid-October through mid-May. Tickets are $6 adults, $5.50 seniors, $2.50 children 6 to 12. To get there, take East Main Street south to Eastern Point Boulevard (a private road), follow it one-half mile to the house, and park on the left.

Another fantasy house is now the **Hammond Castle Museum** (80 Hesperus Ave.; ☎ 508/283-7673, or 508/283-2080 for recorded information), off Route 127 near Magnolia. Although it's equally interesting, it suffers by comparison to Beauport because the tour is self-guided and all of the artifacts aren't as carefully labeled as they might be. Still, it's worth a visit for a look inside the mind of eccentric inventor John Hays Hammond, Jr. He spent more than $6 million on his brainchild, a medieval castle constructed of Rockport granite from 1926 to 1929. There are 85-foot towers, battlements, stained-glass windows, a great hall 60 feet high, and an enclosed "outdoor" pool and courtyard lined with foliage, trees, and medieval artifacts (including the whole wooden front of a butcher shop). The pipes in the ceiling "rain" on command. Many 12th-, 13th-, and 14th-century furnishings, tapestries, paintings, and architectural fragments fill the rooms. A pipe organ with more than 8,200 pipes is used for monthly concerts. Write for a copy of the events calendar.

The museum is open daily May through October from 10am to 5pm, weekends only November through April, and closed Christmas Day and New Year's Day.

Cape Ann

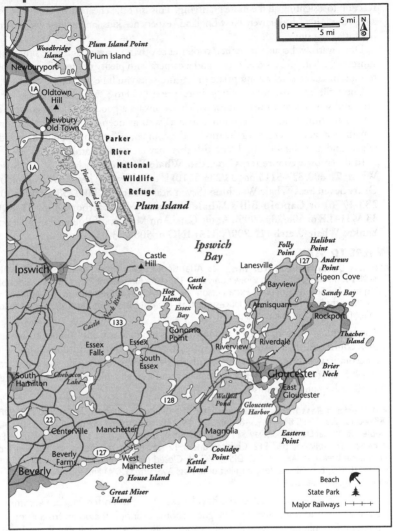

Admission is $6 adults, $5 seniors, $4 children 4 to 12. From Route 127, look for the tiny signs that point to Magnolia and the museum.

WHALE-WATCHING CRUISES

The waters off the coast of Massachusetts are prime whale-watching territory, and Gloucester is a center of whale-watching cruises. Stellwagen Bank, which runs from Gloucester to Provincetown about 27 miles east of Boston, is a rich feeding ground for the huge mammals, who feed on sand eels and other fish that gather along the ridge. The most commonly sighted species in this area are baleen whales, the finback, and the humpback. The whales often perform for their audience, too, by jumping out of the water, and occasionally dolphins join the show.

Once the novelty of putting out to sea is behind them, children tend not to be thrilled with the amount of time it takes to reach the bank, which makes their reaction to a sighting all the more gratifying. This isn't the cheapest way to spend half a day, but it is a "distinctively New England" experience kids (and adults) will remember for a long time.

Dress warmly, because it's much cooler at sea than in town, and take sunglasses, sunscreen, a hat, rubber-soled shoes, and a camera with plenty of film. If you're prone to motion sickness, take appropriate precautions, as you'll be out on the open sea.

Check the local marinas for sailing times, prices ($20 to $25 for adults, less for children and seniors), and reservations, which are always a good idea. Most companies offer a morning and an afternoon cruise as well as deep-sea fishing excursions. A naturalist on board narrates the trip for the companies listed here, pointing out the whales and describing the birds and fish that may cross your path.

In downtown Gloucester, **Cape Ann Whale Watch** (415 Main St., at Rose's Wharf; ☎ 800/877-5110 or 508/283-5110) is the oldest and best-known operation. Or try **Seven Seas Whale Watching** (Seven Seas Wharf; ☎ 800/238-1776 or 508/283-1776) or **Captain Bill's Whale Watching** (33 Harbor Loop; ☎ 800/33-WHALE or 508/283-6995). At the Cape Ann Marina, off Route 133, you'll find **Yankee Whale Watch** (☎ 800/WHALING or 508/283-0313).

WHERE TO STAY

Atlantis Oceanfront Motor Inn. 125 Atlantic Rd., Gloucester, MA 01930. ☎ 508/283-0014. 40 rms (some with shower only). TV TEL. Late June–Labor Day $100–$115 double; spring and fall $65–$95 double. Extra person $8. AE, MC, V. Closed Nov to mid-Apr. Follow Rte. 128 to the end (Exit 9, East Gloucester), turn left onto Bass Ave. (Rte. 127A) and follow 1/2 mile. Turn right and follow Atlantic Rd.

The stunning views from every window of this motor inn would almost be enough to recommend it; it also has a friendly staff and a heated outdoor pool. The redecoration of the guest rooms in comfortable, contemporary style was completed in 1995. Every room has a terrace or balcony and a small table and chairs, and there's a coffee shop on the premises.

Best Western Bass Rocks Ocean Inn. 107 Atlantic Rd., Gloucester, MA 01930. ☎ 508/283-7600. Fax 508/281-6489. 48 rms. A/C TV TEL. Mid-Apr to Memorial Day $90–$105 double; Memorial Day–Labor Day $115–$135 double; Labor Day–Oct $110–$125 double. Extra person $8. Rollaway bed $12. Children under 12 stay free in parents' room. Rates include continental breakfast. AE, CB, DC, DISC, MC, V. Closed Nov to mid-April. Follow Rte. 128 to the end (Exit 9, East Gloucester), turn left onto Bass Ave. (Rte. 127A) and follow a 1/2 mile. Turn right and follow Atlantic Rd.

A family operation since 1946, the Bass Rocks Ocean Inn offers modern accommodations in a traditional setting. The guest rooms overlook the ocean from a sprawling, comfortable motel, with the office and public areas in a Colonial Revival–style mansion built in 1899 and known as the "wedding-cake house." The rooftop sundeck, balconies, and swimming pool all offer excellent views of the surf. The large rooms have balconies or patios; each has a king-size bed or two double beds. Each morning a cold buffet breakfast is served, and each afternoon coffee and chocolate chip cookies are offered. A billiard room and library are available, and bicycles are at the disposal of the guests. Rooms for nonsmokers are available.

WHERE TO DINE

✪ **The Gull.** 75 Essex Ave. (Rte. 133), at Cape Ann Marina. ☎ 508/283-6565. Reservations recommended for parties of 8 or more. Main courses $5.95–$11.95 at lunch, $6.95–$20.95 at dinner. MC, V. Daily 5am–9:30pm. Take Rte. 133 less than 2 miles west of the intersection with Rte. 127, or approach along Rte. 133 eastbound from Rte. 128. SEAFOOD.

The Annisquam River is visible through the floor-to-ceiling windows from almost every seat at the Gull. This big, friendly restaurant specializes in seafood but is also known for its prime rib, and it draws locals, visitors, boaters, and families for large portions at reasonable prices. Ask about the daily specials. The seafood chowder is famous (with good reason), appetizers tend toward bar food, and fish is available in just about any variety and style—it seems unlikely, but the Cajun-style fish and chips is excellent. At lunch, there's an extensive sandwich menu. The Gull has a full bar.

The Rudder Restaurant. 73 Rocky Neck Ave., East Gloucester. ☎ **508/283-7967.** Reservations required for weekends. Main courses $12.95–$19.95. DISC, MC, V. Memorial Day–Labor Day, daily noon–10:30pm; call for open hours and days spring and fall. Closed Dec to mid-Apr. SEAFOOD/INTERNATIONAL.

A meal at the Rudder is not just a meal—it's a party. Overlooking Smith Cove, in the heart of the Rocky Neck Art Colony, the Rudder is jam-packed, floor to ceiling, with gadgets, colored lights, antiques, photos, menus from around the world, and other collectibles. Ask for a seat on the deck (if it's not low tide) and be prepared for anything, because the Rudder is known for its "spontaneous entertainment." You might hear live piano music or see Susan's invisible flaming baton twirling act. The chefs are creative (try the shrimp farcis for an appetizer), and main course offerings run the gamut from shrimp scampi over fresh linguini to chicken piccatta. There's also a children's menu ($7.95).

Square on Main. 272 Main St. ☎ **508/281-3951.** Reservations recommended (off-season, weekends only). Main courses $5.50–$8.50 at lunch, $9.50–$14.50 at dinner. AE, DC, DISC, MC, V. Mon–Sat noon–3pm; Mon–Sun 5–10pm. CONTINENTAL.

A reincarnation of East Gloucester's Square Cafe (whose sign hangs outside), Square on Main is an oasis of sophistication on a congested commercial-industrial strip of downtown that draws locals and out-of-towners alike. The plain brick building belies the spacious two-level interior, which has a sunny feel even at night because of the yellow, rag-painted walls and large windows. The food is equally unexpected—for one thing, it's not all seafood, and for another, each dish has a certain flair. Fresh clam chowder is a good rendition, made even better with the addition of crunchy corn, and jalapeño-lime mayonnaise has the same effect on fried oysters. Entrees include excellent roasted chicken served with "smashed" potatoes; scallops sautéed with ginger and red, yellow, and jalapeño peppers in a hot-sweet Hong Kong–style sauce; and vegetable lasagna so rich with pesto cream sauce and cheese that the health benefits of the vegetables are almost negated. You can also dine in the small, cozy bar.

ROCKPORT
40 miles NE of Boston, 7 miles N of Gloucester

This lovely little town at the tip of Cape Ann was settled in 1690 and over the years has been an active fishing port, a center of granite excavation and cutting, and a thriving summer community whose specialty seems to be selling fudge and refrigerator magnets to out-of-towners. There's more to Rockport than gift shops—you just have to look. For every year-round resident who seems genuinely startled when legions of people with cameras around their necks descend on Rockport each June, there are dozens who are proud to show off their town.

Take a little time to explore beyond the immediate downtown area, and you'll be reminded of what Winslow Homer, Fitz Hugh Lane, Childe Hassam, and other artists were getting at when they captured Rockport in magnificent seascapes. Peer down the alleyways between the waterfront buildings or walk out to a spot with a clear view of the ocean to get your own perspective. The views from **Halibut Point State Park** (see "A Side Trip to Halibut Point," below) are particularly dramatic. The town is still popular with painters, photographers, sculptors, and jewelry designers, and the

Rockport Art Association is active all year. Many galleries show the work of local artists. You'll also find a huge number of interesting places to stay—the number of beds seems to double from winter to summer—and some good restaurants.

ESSENTIALS

GETTING THERE   By car from Boston or anywhere else described here, Rockport is north of Gloucester along Route 127 or 127A. After the second Gloucester rotary at the end of Route 128, turn left at the signs for Rockport to take 127, or continue until you see the sign for East Gloucester and turn left onto 127A, which runs along the east coast of Cape Ann. Route 127 is a loop that cuts across the peninsula inland and swings around to follow Ipswich Bay.

The MBTA (☎ 617/222-3200) commuter rail line runs from North Station in Boston to Rockport. The trip takes about an hour. The Cape Ann Transportation Authority, or CATA (☎ 508/283-7916) runs buses from town to town on Cape Ann.

If you can schedule only one weekday trip, make it this one. For traffic and congestion, downtown Boston has nothing on Rockport on a summer Saturday afternoon. Whenever you go, circle the square once (mind the limits on many meters), and if there's no place to park, try the back streets, even if they're some distance from the center of town. Or use the parking lot on Upper Main Street (Route 127) on weekends. Parking from 11am to 6pm will cost about $6, and a free shuttle will take you downtown and back.

VISITOR INFORMATION   The **Rockport Chamber of Commerce and Board of Trade** (3 Main St., P.O. Box 67, Rockport, MA 01966; ☎ 508/546-6575) is open in summer daily from 9am to 5pm, and on winter weekdays from 10am to 4pm. The chamber also operates operate a seasonal (mid-May to mid-October) information booth on Upper Main Street (Route 127), about a mile from downtown. At either location, ask for the pamphlet "Rockport: A Walking Guide," which has a good map and descriptions of three short walking tours.

GETTING AROUND   Park and walk, especially downtown. The Cape Ann Transportation Authority (see above) runs within the town, but having your own car allows you to make your own itinerary.

SEEING THE SIGHTS

The most famous example of what to see in Rockport is surrounded by somewhat of an "Emperor's New Clothes" aura—it's a wooden fish warehouse on the town wharf, or T-Wharf, in the harbor. The barn-red shack (often rendered in bright red, but it's not), known as **Motif No. 1,** is far and away the most frequently painted object in a town filled with lovely buildings and surrounded by rocky coastline. The color certainly catches the eye in the neutrals of the surrounding seascape, but you may find yourself initiating or overhearing conversations about what the big deal is. Originally constructed in 1884 and destroyed during the blizzard of 1978, Motif No. 1 was rebuilt through donations from the local community and visitors. It stands again on the same pier, duplicated in every detail, and reinforced to withstand storms. Walk to the end of T-Wharf and look to the left so you can say you saw it, then move on.

Nearby is a phenomenon whose popularity is easier to explain—**Bearskin Neck** has perhaps the highest concentration of gift shops anywhere. It's a narrow peninsula with one main street (South Road) and several alleys lined—crammed—with galleries, snack bars, antique shops, and ancient houses. Bearskin Neck is named after an unfortunate bear who drowned and was washed ashore here in 1800. Today you'll find literally dozens of little shops carrying clothes, gifts, toys, inexpensive novelties, and expensive handmade crafts and paintings. Walk all the way to the end of the peninsula for a magnificent water view.

More than two dozen art galleries display the works of both local and nationally known artists. The **Rockport Art Association** (12 Main St.; ☎ **508/546-6604**), open daily year-round, sponsors major exhibitions and special shows throughout the year. Chamber music fans will want to check out the **Rockport Chamber Music Festival** (☎ **508/546-7391**), an early-summer highlight usually held on weekends in June.

Perhaps the mansions of Gloucester were too plush for you, or maybe you want some tips on what to do with old newspapers. Visit the **Paper House** (52 Pigeon Hill St., Pigeon Cove; ☎ **508/546-2629**). It was built in 1922 entirely out of 100,000 newspapers—walls, furniture, even a piano. Every item of furniture is made from papers of a different period. It's open from May through October daily from 10am to 5pm. Admission is $1.50 for adults and $1 for children. Follow Route 127 north out of downtown until you see signs pointing to the left.

And if you'd like to indulge the inexplicable craving for fudge that seizes mild-mannered travelers when they get their first whiff of saltwater, you can watch confections being made at **Tuck's Candy Factory** (7 Dock Sq.; ☎ **508/546-6352**), in the window of a retail store downtown.

WHERE TO STAY

Because the high season in Rockport is so short, reservations are essential in July and August—and they're not a bad idea in the spring and fall.

In Town

Addison Choate Inn. 49 Broadway, Rockport, MA 01966. ☎ **800/245-7543** or 508/546-7543 . 6 rms, 1 suite, 2 apts (some with shower only). Mid-June to Labor Day $95 double, $120 or $670 per week suite; spring and fall $85 double, $105 suite; winter rates are lower. Extra person $15. Rates include continental breakfast. DC, MC, V.

Long known as Rockport's most charming place to stay, the Addison Choate Inn is a Greek Revival–style house built in 1851 and beautifully restored. Innkeepers Shirley and Knox Johnson have furnished the nicely appointed rooms in a mix of period antiques and contemporary furnishings. They range from basic to plush—the "Celebrations Suite" on the third floor has a sitting room and a view of the harbor, and the apartment units in the stable house at the back of the property have loft bedrooms. Guests have the use of the outdoor pool. The suites have cable TV, and two units are air-conditioned.

Captain's Bounty Motor Inn. 1 Beach St., P.O. Box 43, Rockport, MA 01966. ☎ **508/546-9557.** 24 rms. TV TEL. Apr 1 to mid-May $65 oceanfront room, $68 oceanfront efficiency, $70 oceanfront efficiency suite; mid-May to mid-June and early Sept–Oct $78 oceanfront room, $82 oceanfront efficiency, $88 oceanfront efficiency suite; mid-June to early Sept $98 oceanfront room, $105 oceanfront efficiency, $115 oceanfront efficiency suite. Extra person $10. Rollaway bed $5. All rates based on double occupancy. DISC, MC, V. Closed Nov–Mar.

To get closer to the beach than this modern, well-maintained motor inn, you'd have to sleep on a houseboat. Ocean breezes provide natural air-conditioning—each room in the two-story building overlooks the water and has its own balcony and sliding glass door. Rooms are spacious and soundproofed, and kitchenette units are available.

۞ Inn on Cove Hill. 37 Mt. Pleasant St., Rockport, MA 01966. ☎ **508/546-2701.** 11 rms (9 with bath, some with shower only). A/C. $66–$102 double with private bath, $50 with shared bath. Extra person $25. Rates include continental breakfast. MC, V. Closed Nov to mid-Apr.

This three-story inn was built in 1791 from the proceeds of pirates' gold found a short distance away. Silly pirates—they could have used the money to stay here, in an attractive Federal-style home two blocks from the head of the town wharf. Although it's close to downtown, the inn is set back from the road and has a hideaway feel. Innkeepers Marjorie and John Pratt have decorated the guest rooms in period style, with at least one antique piece in each room. Most rooms have colonial furnishings and handmade quilts, and some have canopy beds. In warm weather, a continental breakfast with home-baked breads and muffins is served on china at the garden tables; in inclement weather, breakfast in bed is served on individual trays. No smoking is allowed.

If you're coming by train from Boston, the hosts will meet you at the station; if you drive, parking is provided.

Peg Leg Inn. 2 King St., Rockport, MA 01966. ☎ **800/346-2352** or 508/546-2352. 33 rms. TV. $80–$130 double; $150 2-bedroom unit mid-June to mid-Oct. Off-season rates are lower. Extra person $10. Rates include continental breakfast. MC, V.

The Peg Leg Inn is made up of five early American houses with front porches, attractive living rooms, and well-kept flower-bordered lawns that run down to a gazebo at the ocean's edge. Rooms are good-sized and neatly furnished in colonial style, and some have excellent ocean views. Guests at the inn may use the sandy beach across the road. The Peg Leg restaurant is next door.

On the Outskirts

Old Farm Inn. 291 Granite St. (Rte. 127) at Pigeon Cove, Rockport, MA 01966. ☎ **800/233-6828** or 508/546-3237. 10 rms. TEL. July–Oct $88–$125 double; Apr–June and Nov $78–$115 double. Room with kitchenette $115; 2-room suite $125; 2-bedroom housekeeping cottage $995 per week July–Aug. Extra person $10. Rollaway bed $15. Rates include buffet breakfast. AE, MC, V. Closed Dec to mid-Apr. Follow Rte. 127 north from the center of town until you see signs pointing to the right for Halibut Point State Park; the inn is in front of you.

This gorgeous bed-and-breakfast is a 1799 saltwater farm with antique-furnished rooms in the Inn, the Barn Guesthouse, and the Fieldside Cottage. Each room is uniquely decorated with country-style furnishings (many have beautiful quilts on the beds), and innkeepers Susan and Bill Balzarini are devoted to making your stay enjoyable and comfortable. The buffet breakfast, which includes fresh fruit, home-baked breads, a selection of hot and cold cereals, yogurt, and juices, is excellent. Nine of the rooms have air-conditioning, and most have a refrigerator. About $2\frac{1}{2}$ miles from the center of town, the inn is a stone's throw from Halibut Point State Park.

Ralph Waldo Emerson Inn. 1 Cathedral Ave., P.O. Box 2369, Rockport, MA 01966. ☎ **508/546-6321.** Fax 508/546-7043. E-mail emerson@cove.com. 36 rms. A/C TEL. July–Labor Day $96–$137 double; spring and fall $85–$125 double. Extra person $7. Crib or cot $7. Weekly rates available. DISC, MC, V. Closed Dec to mid-April; open weekends only in Apr and Nov. Follow Rte. 127 north from the center of town for 2 miles and watch for large sign; turn right at Phillips St.

Somewhere in the old guest register of the Ralph Waldo Emerson Inn you might find the name of Emerson himself, for the distinguished philosopher was a guest in the original (1840) inn in the 1850s. The oceanfront building was expanded in 1912 and still has an old-fashioned feel, with furnishings such as spool beds and four-posters in the nicely appointed, though not terribly large, rooms. There's no elevator—lower-priced rooms are those that require a climb and have indirect water views or face the street. A few flights of stairs seem a small inconvenience for the view from the top-floor rooms, however. Guests have the use of a heated outdoor saltwater pool or (for a fee) the indoor whirlpool and sauna. Recreation rooms include areas for playing cards, table tennis, or watching the wide-screen TV.

The dining room is open to the public on an availability basis for breakfast and dinner.

Sandy Bay Motor Inn. 173 Main St. (Rte. 127), Rockport, MA 01966. ☎ **800/437-7155** or 508/546-7155. Fax 508/546-9131. 79 rms. A/C TV TEL. April to mid-June $72–$126 double; mid-June to Sept 1 $92–$162 double; Sept 2–Oct $76–$130 double; Nov–Mar $64–$110 double. Extra person $6. AE, MC, V.

This is inn country, but if you're looking for something a bit more modern, pull off Route 127 on your way from Gloucester to downtown Rockport. This attractive motor inn on a hill overlooking the road boasts modern conveniences, including a heated indoor pool with a whirlpool and sauna, two tennis courts, a putting green, and a breakfast room. Some of the large rooms, furnished in contemporary style, have steam baths, and 25 are efficiencies. The highest room rates are for the six two-bedroom units. Rooms for the disabled are available.

Seaward Inn. 62 Marmion Way, Rockport, MA 01966. ☎ **800/648-7733** or 508/546-3471. 36 rms, 9 cottages (some with shower only). TV. Mid-May to Oct $115–$160 double per night, $850–$1,100 cottage per week; mid-Apr to mid-May and Nov to mid-Dec $100–$140 double, cottage $125–$155 cottage per night. Extra person $20. Rates include full breakfast. AE, DC, DISC, MC, V. Closed mid-Dec to Apr.

On five oceanfront acres, the Seaward Inn's three buildings and nine cottages make up a lovely complex where couples and families feel equally comfortable. The three-story main inn, two-story Carriage House, and two-story Breakers Lodge (facing the water) have comfortable rooms furnished in the summer-colony style you'd expect. The cottages, many of which have working fireplaces and kitchenettes, are perfect for families. Innkeepers Jane and Fred Fiumara bought the inn from the original owners four years ago and are constantly upgrading the 52-year-old property. There's a small pond for swimming, and bicycles are available if you want to explore, but you may just want to loll on the lawn and watch the ocean.

The SeaGarden Restaurant, on the first floor of the main inn, is open to the public for dinner. It features creative American cuisine with an emphasis on seafood.

WHERE TO DINE

Rockport is a "dry" community where restaurants are forbidden by law from serving alcoholic beverages, but you can brown-bag it with your own bottle. Top prices for main dishes may be as much as $5 more if lobster is involved.

Blacksmith Shop. 23 Mt. Pleasant St. ☎ **508/546-6301.** Reservations recommended. Main courses $7.95–$9.95 at lunch, $8.95–$16.95 at dinner. AE, DC, MC, V. Mid-Apr to Memorial Day, Thurs–Sun 11:30am–8pm; Memorial Day–Oct 31 Sun–Fri 11:30am–8pm, Sat 11:30am–9pm. Closed Nov 1 to mid-Apr. SEAFOOD.

For tasty food in a refined setting, walk one block from the town wharf to this cavernous restaurant set on stilts jutting into the harbor. The menu runs from basic seafood to more ambitious undertakings—lobster cakes, cheese tortellini with sun-dried tomatoes—but everything is fresh and good. The room is as pleasing as the food, with picture windows, wooden furnishings, paintings in the gallery, and an old forge, anvil, and bellows preserved from the shop where Rockport's village smithy stood. The main dining room has been enlarged many times since its establishment in 1927, and it now accommodates 200, but it still fills up. There is a children's menu ($3.95 to $4.95).

✪ **The Greenery.** 15 Dock Sq. ☎ **508/546-9593.** Reservations recommended at dinner. Main dishes $6.25–$11.95 at lunch, $9.25–$15.95 at dinner; breakfast items $1.25–$6.95. DISC, MC, V. Mid-Apr to Nov Mon–Fri 9am–10pm, Sat–Sun 8am–10pm. Closed Dec to mid-Apr. SEAFOOD/AMERICAN.

The cafelike front room of this restaurant at the head of Bearskin Neck gives no hint that at the back of the building is a cozy dining room with a great view of the harbor. Both rooms have large windows and are well-lit and plant-decorated. The terrific food ranges from crab salad quiche at lunch to grilled swordfish at dinner to steamers anytime, and there's a huge salad bar available on its own or with many entrees. Breakfast is served on weekends. All baking is done in-house, which explains the lines at the front counter for muffins and pastries. This is a good place to launch a picnic lunch on the beach, and an equally good spot for lingering over coffee and a delectable dessert and watching the action in the harbor.

My Place By-the-Sea. 68 Bearskin Neck. ☎ **508/546-9667.** Reservations recommended at dinner. Main courses $4.50–$12 at lunch, $12–$18 at dinner. AE, CB, DC, DISC, JCB, MC, V. Apr–Nov daily 11:30am–9:30pm. Closed Dec–Mar. SEAFOOD.

People travel to the very end of Bearskin Neck to dine at My Place By-the-Sea on Rockport's only outdoor oceanfront deck. There are excellent views of Sandy Bay from the two decks and shaded patio. Most menu choices depend on the daily catch, so everything is fresh. The baked fish and seafood pasta entrees are good choices, and you can also have chicken or beef. The dessert menu includes excellent homemade fruit pies.

⑤ Portside Chowder House. Bearskin Neck. ☎ **508/546-7045.** Reservations not accepted. Most menu items less than $8. No credit cards. Late June–Labor Day, daily 11am–8pm; Labor Day–late June, daily 11am–3pm. Closed Thanksgiving and Christmas. SEAFOOD.

Look to the left as you set out along Bearskin Neck; the crowds in front of the small brown wooden house on the first cross street are waiting for, yes, chowder—clam and whatever else looks good that day. It comes by the cup, pint, and quart, to go or to eat in the tiny, low-ceilinged dining room with partial water views. You can also get platters with seafood or surprisingly good burgers, but the real reason to come here is for tasty chowder to carry to the edge of the sea for a picnic.

A SIDE TRIP TO HALIBUT POINT

The very tip of Cape Ann is accessible to the public, and worth the trip north on Route 127 (turn right at the Old Farm Inn) to **Halibut Point State Park** (☎ **508/ 546-2997**). The point got its name not from the fish, but because sailing ships heading for the sheltered harbors in Rockport and Gloucester must "haul about" when they reach this jutting promontory.

Walk about 10 minutes from the parking area, being careful of the wildflowers, and you'll come to a huge water-filled quarry next to a visitor center where staffers dispense information, brochures, and bird lists. Scattered around the park are pieces of quarried granite. Swimming in the quarry is absolutely forbidden, but there are walking trails, tidal pools, and a rocky beach where you can climb around on giant boulders. Swimming is allowed there, but it isn't encouraged—the surf is rough and dangerous, and there are no lifeguards. Guided tours are available on Saturday mornings in the summer, and there are also bird, wildflower, and tidal-pool tours; call or write (Friends of Halibut Point State Park, P.O. Box 710, Rockport, MA 01966) for information. This is a also great place just to wander around, admire the scenery (on a clear day, you can see Maine), and perhaps do some bird-watching on your own.

7 Newburyport, Ipswich & Plum Island

The area between Cape Ann and the New Hampshire border is one of great beauty, with outdoor sights and sounds that can only be described as natural wonders, and enough impressive architecture to keep any city slicker happy. In a part of the world where the word "charming" is used almost as often as "hello," Newburyport is a singular example of a picturesque waterfront city. Downtown Newburyport is on the Merrimack River; on the town's Atlantic coast, Plum Island contains one of the country's top nature preserves, the Parker River National Wildlife Refuge. On the other side of Ipswich Bay, Ipswich itself is a lovely little town that's home to Crane Beach, on another wildlife reservation.

NEWBURYPORT   To go directly to Newburyport from Boston, take I-93 (or Route 1 if it's not rush hour) to I-95—not Route 128, which you'd take to most other destinations in this chapter—and follow it to Exit 57, a solid 45-minute ride. Signs lead you directly to downtown, where you can park on the street or in a lot (there's one on the waterfront at the foot of Green Street), and explore.

Perhaps because its distance from Boston makes the commute onerous (though not impossible), Newburyport has a substantial year-round population that lends it a less touristy atmosphere than its quaint appearance might suggest. Start your visit with a stop at the **Greater Newburyport Chamber of Commerce and Industry** (29 State St., Newburyport, MA 01950; ☎ **508/462-6680**), in the heart of the redbrick downtown shopping district. You can pick up maps, brochures, shopping directories, and accommodations listings.

Market Square, the area at the foot of State Street near the waterfront, is the center of a neighborhood packed with boutiques, gift shops, plain and fancy restaurants, and many antique stores. You can also just wander over to the water, take a stroll on the boardwalk, and enjoy the action on the river. Architecture buffs will want to climb the hill to High Street, where the Charles Bulfinch–designed building that houses the Superior Court (1805) is only one of the Federal-era treasures. Ask at the Chamber of Commerce for the walking-tour map. And if you haven't gone out to sea yet, **Newburyport Whale Watch** (Hilton's Dock, 54 Merrimac St.; ☎ **800/848-1111** or 508/465-7165) offers the same features as the companies out of Gloucester (see above). Reservations are suggested.

Or head in the opposite direction, to the ocean. From downtown, take Water Street south until it becomes Plum Island Turnpike and follow it to the:

PARKER RIVER NATIONAL WILDLIFE REFUGE   The 4,662-acre refuge (☎ **508/465-5753**) on Plum Island is a natural complex of barrier beaches, dunes, and salt marshes, one of the few remaining in the Northeast. There's an entrance fee for motorists, bikers, and pedestrians. The refuge is flat-out breathtaking, whether you're exploring the marshes or the seashore. More than 800 species of plants and animals (including more than 300 bird species) visit or make their home on the narrow finger of land with Broad Sound on one side and the Atlantic Ocean on the other. The seven parking lots fill up quickly on weekends when the weather is good. Plan to arrive early. South of lot 4 (Hellcat Swamp), the access road isn't paved; although it's flat and well-maintained and the speed limit is low, this isn't the place for your brand-new sports car.

It is the place for some of the best birding anywhere, and observation of mammals and plants as well as birds. Wooden boardwalks wind through the marshes and along the shore—most don't have handrails, so this isn't an activity for rambunctious children. You might see native and migratory species such as owls, hawks, martins, geese, warblers, ducks, snowy egrets, swallows, monarch butterflies, Canada geese, foxes, beavers, and harbor seals.

The ocean beach closes April 1 to allow piping plovers, listed by the federal government as a threatened species, to nest. The areas not being used for nesting reopen July 1, the rest in August when the birds are through with them. The currents are strong and can be dangerous, and there are no lifeguards—you may prefer to stick to surf fishing. Striped bass and bluefish are found in the area. A permit is required for night fishing and vehicle access to the beach. Call for information about fall and winter waterfowl hunting and the two-day deer hunt in the fall.

Across Ipswich Bay from Plum Island is the town of Ipswich. It's accessible from Route 1A (which you can pick up in Newburyport or at Route 128 in Hamilton) and from Route 133 (which intersects with Route 128 in Gloucester and I-95 in Georgetown). The **visitor center** in the Hall Haskell House on South Main Street (Route 133) is open daily in the summer, and visitor information is available from the **Ipswich Business Association** (P.O. Box 94, Ipswich, MA 01938; ☎ **508/356-4400**).

IPSWICH   Settled in 1630, Ipswich is dotted with 17th-century houses but is better known for two more contemporary structures. The **Clam Box** (206 High St., Route 1A/133; ☎ **508/356-5019**) is a restaurant shaped like—you guessed it—a red-and-white-striped takeout clam box. This is a great place to try Ipswich clams to stay or to go, and not an easy place to sneak past if you have children in the car. Heading south from Newburyport, it's on the right.

South of Ipswich Center, near the intersection of Routes 1A and 133, look carefully for the Argilla Road sign (on the east side of the street). If you're traveling west on Route 133 from Gloucester and Essex, keep your eyes peeled for a sign on the right pointing to Northgate Road, which intersects with Argilla Road. Follow it east to the end, where you'll find the 1,400-acre Richard T. Crane, Jr., Memorial Reservation. The property is home to **Crane Beach** and a network of hiking trails as well as **Castle Hill,** one of the Boston area's most popular wedding locations. The exquisite Stuart-style seaside mansion known as the Great House was built by Richard Teller Crane, Jr., who made his fortune in plumbing and bathroom fixtures early in this century. If you can't wangle an invitation to a wedding, tours of the house ($7 adults, $5 seniors and children) are given on Wednesday and Thursday in the summer and two Sundays a year, spring and fall. For more information, contact the Castle Hill/Crane Memorial Reservation (290 Argilla Rd., P.O. Box 563, Ipswich, MA 01938; ☎ **508/356-4351**).

Children (and adults) who can't get excited about a house tour can be sent on to the beach, or they might be pacified by a stop just before Castle Hill. **Goodale Orchards Store and Winery** (143 Argilla Rd.; ☎ **508/356-5366**) is open weekends in April and daily from May through Christmas Eve. There's a picnic area, farm animals to visit, and an excellent country store where apples and baked goods are always available. Depending on the season, you might go on a hayride or participate in a fruit-wine tasting. Whatever the season, be sure to try some cider and doughnuts.

8 Plymouth

40 miles SE of Boston

Everyone educated in the United States knows at least a little about Plymouth—about how the Pilgrims, fleeing religious persecution, left Europe on the *Mayflower* and landed at Plymouth Rock in 1620. Many also know that the Pilgrims endured disease and privation, and that just 51 people from the original group of 102 celebrated the first Thanksgiving in 1621 with Squanto, a Pawtuxet Indian associated with the Wampanoags, and his cohorts. What you won't know until you visit Plymouth is how small everything was—the *Mayflower* seems perilously tiny, and when you contemplate how dangerous life was at the time, it's hard not to be impressed by the settlers' accomplishments.

Cape Cod was named in 1602 by Capt. Bartholomew Gosnold, and 12 years later Capt. John Smith sailed along the coast of what he named "New England." Smith called the mainland opposite Cape Cod "Plymouth." The passengers on the *May-flower* had contracted with the London Virginia Company for a tract of land near the mouth of the Hudson River in "Northern Virginia"; in exchange for their passage to the New World, they promised to work the land for the company for seven years. However, on November 11, 1620, rough weather and high seas forced them to make for Cape Cod Bay and anchor there, at Provincetown. Subsequently, their captain announced that they had found a safe harbor, and he refused to continue the voyage farther south to their original destination. On December 16, Provincetown having proven an unsatisfactory location, the weary travelers landed at Plymouth. They had no option but to settle in New England, and with no one to command them, their contract with the London Virginia Company became void and they were on their own to begin a new world.

Today, Plymouth is a manageable day-trip destination particularly suited to families traveling with children. It also makes a good stopping-off point between Boston and Cape Cod. (For a map of Plymouth and the surrounding area, see Chapter 6, "Cape Cod.")

ESSENTIALS

GETTING THERE   By car, follow the Southeast Expressway (I-93) from Boston to Route 3 south. From Cape Cod, take Route 3 north. Take Exit 6 to Plymouth, then Route 44 east, and follow signs to the historic attractions. The trip from Boston takes about 45 minutes. Or take Route 3 to the Regional Information Complex at Exit 5. To go directly to Plimoth Plantation, take Exit 4.

Plymouth & Brockton (☎ 617/773-9401) buses leave from the terminal at Boston's South Station and from downtown Hyannis. You can also make connections at Logan Airport, where buses take on passengers at all airline terminals.

VISITOR INFORMATION   The **Visitor Center** (☎ 508/747-7525) is at 130 Water St., across from the town pier. To plan ahead, contact **Plymouth Visitor Information** (P.O. Box ROCK, Plymouth, MA 02361; ☎ 800/USA-1620 or 508/747-7525) or the **Plymouth Area Chamber of Commerce** (225 Water St., Suite 500, Plymouth, MA 02360; ☎ 508/830-1620). Off Exit 5 from Route 3 is the **Regional Information Complex,** where you can pick up maps, brochures, and information about Plymouth and the rest of eastern Massachusetts.

GETTING AROUND   The downtown attractions are accessible on foot, with a fairly shallow hill leading from the center of town to the waterfront. Note that Route 3A, which runs north to south through Plymouth, changes names as it goes, from Court to Main to Sandwich Street and finally to Warren Avenue.

If you plan a lot of stops, are traveling with young children, or both, consider purchasing an all-day ticket for the trolley, which serves downtown and Plimoth Plantation. **Plymouth Rock Trolley** (22 Main St.; ☎ 508/747-3419) offers a narrated tour and unlimited rebearding privileges daily from Memorial Day through October and weekends through Thanksgiving. Tickets are $7 for adults and $3 for children 3 to 12. Trolley markers indicate the stops, which are served every 20 minutes (except Plimoth Plantation, served once an hour in the summer).

DISCOVERING COLONIAL AMERICA

No matter how many elementary school pageants you suffered through wearing a big black hat and buckles on your shoes, you can still learn something about Plymouth and the Pilgrims.

The logical place to begin (good luck talking children out of it) is where the Pilgrims first set foot—at **Plymouth Rock.** The rock, accepted as the landing place of the *Mayflower* passengers, was originally 15 feet long and 3 feet wide. Time, in the form of erosion and mishandling, has left it much smaller. It was moved on the eve of the Revolution, when it broke in two, and several times thereafter. In 1867 it assumed its present permanent position at tide level, where the winter storms still break over it as they did in Pilgrim days. The McKim, Mead & White–designed portico around the rock was given in 1920 by the Colonial Dames of America. The rock itself is not much to look at, but the accompanying descriptions are interesting and the sense of history that surrounds it is curiously impressive.

At 6pm every Friday in August, citizens in Pilgrim costumes walk from Plymouth Rock to Burial Hill at Town Square, reenacting a trip to church by the survivors of the settlement's first winter. Fifty-one people might sound like a lot, but you'll be struck by the small size of the group.

To put yourself in the Pilgrims' footsteps, take a **Colonial Lantern Tour** offered by New World Tours (98 Water St.; ☎ 508/747-4161). Participants carry pierced-tin lanterns on a 90-minute walking tour of the original settlement under the direction of a knowledgeable guide. It might seem a bit hokey at first, but it's fascinating. Tours are given nightly from late March through Thanksgiving. The standard history tour leaves the New World office at 7:30pm; the "Legends and Lore" tour leaves from the lobby of the John Carver Inn (25 Summer St.) at 9pm. Tickets are $7 for adults, $5 for children, $5 per person for families of four or more.

A 40-minute harbor tour is another good introduction to Plymouth and a nice break from walking. You'll get a new perspective on Plymouth Rock and the *Mayflower II,* and learn about maritime history. **Capt. John Boats** (☎ 800/ 242-AHOY or 508/747-2400) runs tours on the hour from 11am to 7pm from June through September. They leave from State Pier, near the *Mayflower II.* Tickets are $5 for adults, $4 for seniors, $3 for children under 12. The same company operates whale-watching cruises narrated by a naturalist daily from mid-May through October and on weekends in April. They leave from Town Wharf, near the intersection of Water Street and Route 44. Tickets are about $23 for adults, less for seniors and children. Reservations are recommended. If you're interested in a deep-sea fishing excursion, ask about rates (they range from $16.50 to $28 for adults), schedules, and reservations.

To get away from the bustle of the waterfront, you might want to relax at **Town Brook Park** at Jenney Pond, across Summer Street from the John Carver Inn. The centerpiece of the park is a beautiful tree-lined pond with ducks and swans. Across from the pond is the **Jenney Grist Mill** (6 Spring Lane; ☎ 508/747-3715; admission $2.50 adults, $2 children 5 to 12), a working museum where you can see a reconstructed early American water-powered mill that operates in the summer, daily from 10am to 5pm. The specialty shops in the same complex, including the excellent Jenney Grist Mill Ice Cream Shoppe, are open year-round, daily from 10am to 6pm. There is plenty of parking.

Also removed from the waterfront is the **National Monument to the Forefathers** (Allerton St.; ☎ 508/746-1790), a granite behemoth inscribed with the names of the *Mayflower* passengers. Heading away from the harbor on Route 44, look carefully on the right for Allerton Street and climb the hill. The monument is 81 feet high, elaborately decorated with figures representing various moral and political virtues and scenes of Pilgrim history—a style of public statuary so unfashionable that it seems quite rebellious. The monument is somewhat incongruous in its little park in a residential neighborhood, but it's also quite impressive. It was proposed in 1820, designed by Hammet Billings of Boston in 1855, and dedicated in 1889. The view from the hilltop is excellent.

Mayflower II. State Pier. ☎ **508/746-1622.** Admission $5.75 adults, $3.75 children 6–17, children under 6 free. Apr–Nov 30 daily 9am–5pm.

Berthed only a few steps from Plymouth Rock, *Mayflower II* is a full-scale reproduction of the type of ship that brought the Pilgrims from England to America. Even at full scale, you'll probably be struck by how small it is. Although little technical information is known about the original *Mayflower,* William A. Baker, designer of *Mayflower II,* incorporated the few references in Governor Bradford's account of the voyage with other research to re-create as closely as possible the actual ship. Exhibits on board show what life was like during a 66-day voyage in 1620 on a vessel crowded with 102 passengers, 25 crewmen, and all the supplies needed to sustain the colony until the first crops were harvested.

Men and women in period costumes on board the ship talk about the ocean crossing, answer questions, and dispatch little-known but interesting pieces of information. You will probably want to tour the ship. The vessel is owned and maintained by Plimoth Plantation, which is three miles south of the ship. A combination ticket for *Mayflower II* and Plimoth Plantation is $18.50 for adults and $11 for children 6 to 17.

Alongside *Mayflower II* are museum shops that replicate early Pilgrim dwellings from 1620 to 1621.

Pilgrim Hall Museum. 75 Court St. ☎ **508/746-1620.** Admission $5 adults, $4 seniors, $2.50 children. Daily 9:30am–4:30pm. Closed Jan. From Plymouth Rock, walk north on Water St. and up the hill on Chilton St.

The Pilgrim Hall Museum, the oldest public museum in the United States, is listed on the National Register of Historic Places. It contains many original possessions of the early Pilgrims and their descendants, including a chair that belonged to William Brewster (alongside an uncomfortable modern-day model that can be sat on), one of Myles Standish's swords, and Governor Bradford's Bible. The building itself dates from 1824. Among the exhibits are a chunk of Plymouth Rock and the skeleton of the *Sparrow-Hawk,* a ship wrecked on Cape Cod in 1626, which lay buried in the sand and undiscovered until 1863. It's even smaller than the *Mayflower II.*

Plimoth Plantation. Rte. 3. ☎ **508/746-1622.** Plimoth Plantation and *Mayflower II* admission $18.50 adults, $11 children 6–17, children under 6 free. Apr–Nov daily 9am–5pm. From Route 3, take Exit 4, "Plimoth Plantation Highway." From downtown, take Rte. 3A south 2¹/₂ miles.

Plimoth Plantation is a re-creation of a 1627 Pilgrim village. You enter by the hilltop fort that protects the villagers and then walk down the hill to the farm area, visiting the homes and gardens along the way, which have been constructed with careful attention to historic detail. Once you get over the feeling that the whole operation is a bit strange (we heard someone mention Pompeii), it's great fun to talk to the "Pilgrims," who, in speech, dress, and manner, assume the personalities of members of the original community. You can watch them framing a house, splitting wood, shearing sheep, preserving foodstuffs, or cooking a pot of fish stew over an open hearth, all as it was done in the 1600s. And they use only the tools and cookware available at that time. Sometimes you can join in the activities—perhaps planting, harvesting, a court trial, or a wedding party. Leave at least half a day for your visit, because once you get into the spirit, you won't want to rush. And be sure to wear comfortable walking shoes.

The community is as accurate as research can make it: Accounts of the original Pilgrim colony were combined with archaeological research, old records, and the 17th-century history written by the Pilgrims' leader, William Bradford, who often used the spelling "Plimoth" for the settlement. There are daily militia drills with matchlock muskets that are fired to demonstrate the community's defense system. In fact, little defense was needed, because the local Native Americans were friendly. Local tribes included the Wampanoags, who are represented at a homesite near the village, where members of the museum staff show off native foodstuffs, agricultural practices, and crafts. The homesite is included in admission to the plantation.

At the main entrance to the plantation you'll find two modern buildings with an interesting orientation show, exhibits, gift shop, crafts center, bookstore, and cafeteria. There's a picnic area nearby.

✪ **Plymouth National Wax Museum.** 16 Carver St. ☎ **508/746-6468.** Admission $5.50 adults, $4.50 seniors, $2.50 children 5–12, children under 5 free. Mar–June and Sept–Nov daily 9am–5pm; July–Aug daily 9am–9pm. From Plymouth Rock, turn around and walk up the hill or the steps.

Across New England (and probably across the United States), adults who visited this museum as children can still tell you all about the history of the Pilgrims. There are more than 180 life-size figures and dramatic sound tracks that tell the story of the move to Holland to escape persecution in England, the harrowing trip across the ocean, the first Thanksgiving, and even the story of Myles Standish, Priscilla Mullins, and John Alden. This museum is a must if children are in your party, and adults will enjoy it, too. On the hill outside is a monument at the gravesite of the Pilgrims who died during the settlement's first winter.

Cranberry World. 225 Water St. ☎ **508/747-2350.** Free admission. May 1–Nov 30 daily 9:30am–5pm. Guided tours available; call for reservations. From Plymouth Rock, walk north for 10 minutes right along the waterfront.

Cranberries aren't just for Thanksgiving dinner, as Ocean Spray's interesting visitor center will remind you. Exhibits include outdoor demonstration bogs, antique harvesting tools, a scale model of a cranberry farm, and film and slide shows. There are daily cooking demonstrations and free cranberry refreshments. September and October are harvest time.

HISTORIC HOUSES

You can't stay at Plymouth's historic houses, but they're worth a visit to see the changing styles of architecture and furnishings since the 1600s. Costumed guides explain the homemaking details and the crafts of earlier generations. Most of the houses are open from Memorial Day through Columbus Day and during Thanksgiving celebrations; call for schedules. Especially if you're sightseeing with children, pretend the next sentence is written in capital letters: Unless you have a sky-high tolerance for house tours, pick just one or two from eras that you find particularly interesting. Each has something to recommend it; the Sparrow and Howland houses are most interesting for those curious about the original settlers.

The 1640 **Sparrow House** (42 Summer St.; ☎ **508/747-1240;** admission $1) is believed to be the oldest house still standing in Plymouth. It provides a fascinating look at the home life of the early residents. Pottery made on the premises is for sale in the craft gallery. The house is near Town Brook Park, across the street from the John Carver Inn. It's open Thursday through Tuesday from 10am to 5pm.

The 1666 **Howland House** (33 Sandwich St.; ☎ **508/746-9590;** guided tour $3 adults, 75¢ children 6–12) is the only house in Plymouth known to have been lived in by *Mayflower* passengers—owner Jabez Howland's parents, Elizabeth Tilley and John Howland. The tour tells about them and gives another good look at the Pilgrims' lives. The house is near the corner of Sandwich and Water Streets and is open daily from 10am to 4:30pm.

The next three houses are operated by the Plymouth Antiquarian Society (☎ 508/746-0012). At each house, admission is $3 for adults, 75¢ for children 6 to 12.

The 1677 **Harlow Old Fort House** (119 Sandwich St.) is staffed by costumed interpreters who demonstrate domestic crafts such as spinning and weaving amid period furnishings. By this time, the Pilgrims were settled, and you'll get a sense of life once mere survival stopped being a daily struggle. The house is about four blocks south of the center of town; call ahead for open hours, which usually are 10am to 4:30pm, Thursday through Saturday in July and August, and Friday and Saturday in June and September through mid-October.

The 1749 **Spooner House** (27 North St.) was a family residence for more than two centuries and is furnished with a wealth of heirlooms that illustrate the changes in daily life over that period. The house is a few steps up the hill from Plymouth Rock and keeps the same hours as the Harlow Old Fort House, plus Sundays in July and August. Call ahead to make sure the house is open.

The 1809 **Hedge House** (126 Water St.) is a Federal-style mansion next door to the visitor center near the Town Wharf. It has period furnishings as well as a gallery with regularly changing exhibits drawn from the Antiquarian Society's collections of textiles and decorative arts. The house keeps the same hours as the Spooner House, but call ahead to make sure it's open.

The 1754 (with an 1898 addition) **Mayflower Society Museum** (4 Winslow St.; ☎ 508/746-2590; admission $2.50, 75¢ children 6 to 12) was originally the home of Edward Winslow, a great-grandson of the Pilgrim of the same name who served as governor of Massachusetts. Today the furnishings span three centuries (17th, 18th, and 19th), there's a "flying" staircase that appears to defy gravity, and the formal gardens are a peaceful place to stroll. The museum is open from 10am to 5pm, daily in July and August, Friday through Sunday in June, September through mid-October, and Thanksgiving weekend. From Plymouth Rock, turn around, walk one short block up North Street, and turn right onto Winslow Street.

WHERE TO STAY

Lodgings fill up quickly on summer weekends. Try to make reservations well in advance.

Blue Anchor Motel. 7 Lincoln St., Plymouth, MA 02360. ☎ **508/746-9551.** 4 units (some with shower only). A/C TV. $48–$60 double. Rates include morning coffee. MC, V. Closed Nov–Apr. From downtown, take Rte. 3A (Sandwich St.) south; 3 blocks past the post office, turn left onto Lincoln St. The motel is on the right.

This mom-and-pop operation consists of four rooms around a courtyard, close to downtown. Look for the shutters with the anchors on the house next to Town Hall. Two of the comfortable, homey units have one double bed each, one has two double beds, and one has a bedroom with a double bed, a living room with daybeds, and a kitchenette.

Cold Spring Motel. 188 Court St. (Rte. 3A), Plymouth, MA 02360. ☎ **508/746-2222.** 31 rms. A/C TV TEL. $58–$78 double; $68–$88 cottage in season. Lower rates spring and fall. Extra person $5. AE, DISC, MC, V. Closed mid-Oct to Apr.

Convenient to the historic sights, this pleasant, quiet motel has plain, comfortable rooms with wall-to-wall carpeting. The two-story building is set back from the street two blocks inland, not far from Cranberry World, and there are two two-bedroom cottages. There's parking at your door.

Governor Bradford Motor Inn. 98 Water St., Plymouth, MA 02360. ☎ **800/332-1620** or 508/746-6200. Fax 508/747-3032. 94 rms. A/C TV TEL. $89–$124 double in season. Extra person $10. Rates lower in off-season. Children under 14 stay free in parents' room. AE, DC, DISC, MC, V.

The Governor Bradford is across the street from the waterfront and only one block from Plymouth Rock, the *Mayflower II*, and the center of town. The rooms, each with two double beds, are attractively furnished in a modern style, with wall-to-wall carpeting, refrigerator, and in-room coffee. More expensive rooms are higher up in the three-story building and have clearer water views. There's a small heated outdoor pool.

John Carver Inn. 25 Summer St. at Town Brook, Plymouth, MA 02360. ☎ **800/274-1620** or 508/746-7100. Fax 508/746-8299. 79 rms. A/C TV TEL. Apr 11–June 19 $69–$89 double; June 19–Oct 18 $85–$105 double; Oct 19–Nov 25 $75–$95 double; Nov 30–Apr 7 $65–$85 double. Children under 19 stay free in parents' room. Passport to History package rates change seasonally. Senior discount available. AE, CB, DC, DISC, MC, V.

This impressive colonial-style building offers comfortable, modern accommodations, a large pool, free cribs, and all the amenities. Many rooms are newly renovated and decorated in colonial style. Ask for a room on a higher floor, away from the road if possible. The inn is within walking distance of the main attractions. A **Hearth 'n' Kettle** restaurant is on the premises. The hotel offers a good deal (the John Carver Inn Passport to History packages) that includes a two-night, three-day stay for two, four breakfast tickets to the restaurant, two $10 discount dinner tickets at the restaurant, two Plimoth Plantation or whale-watch tickets, and two tickets to the trolley or wax museum.

Pilgrim Sands Motel. 150 Warren Ave. (Rte. 3A), Plymouth, MA 02360. ☎ **800/729-SANDS** or 508/747-0900. Fax 508/746-8066. 64 rms. A/C TV TEL. $90–$120 double, summer; $70–$95 double, spring and Indian summer; $60–$80 double, fall; $50–$70 double, winter. Higher rates for ocean view. Extra person $8. AE, CB, DC, DISC, MC, V.

This attractive, two-story motel is south of town, within walking distance of Plimoth Plantation. The ultramodern units, located right on the ocean, have individually controlled heating and air-conditioning, wall-to-wall carpeting, and tasteful furnishings. In the summer guests have access to the private beach, terraces, whirlpool spa, and outdoor and indoor pools. Most rooms have two double or two queen-size beds. Many rooms have refrigerators. One wing is reserved for smokers, the other for nonsmokers.

Sheraton Inn Plymouth. 180 Water St., Plymouth, MA 02360. ☎ **800/325-3535** or 508/747-4900. Fax 508/746-2609. 175 rms. A/C TV TEL. Apr–Oct $100–$160 double; Nov–Mar $85–$125 double. Children under 18 stay free in parents' room. Extra person $15. AE, CB, DC, DISC, JCB, MC, V.

Located at the Village Landing, this attractive hotel faces the harbor from a hill across the street from the waterfront. It's the place to stay in Plymouth for access to both the historic sights and the amenities of a chain. Guest rooms are tastefully furnished in contemporary style and have climate control and in-room movies. Some have balconies that overlook the indoor swimming pool and whirlpool, in a colorful garden setting. The hotel also has an exercise room and a restaurant, the **Harbor Grille,** which serves a delicious Sunday brunch, and the **Pub,** which serves lighter fare and has live entertainment on weekends.

WHERE TO DINE

Seafood is the specialty at almost all Plymouth restaurants, where much of the daily catch goes right from the fishing boat to the kitchen.

Lobster Hut. Town Wharf. ☎ **508/746-2270.** Fax 508/746-5655. Reservations not accepted. Luncheon specials $4.50–$7.95, main courses $4.95–$12.95 (lobster meat), sandwiches $1.75– $5.95. MC, V. Summer daily 11am–9pm; winter daily 11am–7pm. SEAFOOD.

The Lobster Hut is a clean, shiny, self-service restaurant. Take your order to an indoor table or out on the large deck that overlooks the bay. For starters, have some clam chowder or lobster bisque. The seafood "rolls" (hot dog buns with your choice of filling) are excellent. Or choose from a long list of fried seafood—including clams, scallops, shrimp, and haddock. Or you might prefer boiled and steamed items, burgers, or chicken tenders. Beer and wine are served, but only with a meal.

McGrath's Harbour Restaurant. Town Wharf. ☎ **508/746-9751.** Reservations recommended. Main dishes $9.95–$14.95. AE, MC, V. In season daily 11:30am–10pm. Closed Mon in winter. SEAFOOD.

McGrath's is big, busy, and the choice of many families, local businesspeople, and tour groups. In addition to fish and seafood dinners, the menu features chicken, prime rib, sandwiches, and children's selections. Ask for a table overlooking the water—the room facing inland is on the gloomy side—and be sure you're in good company, because service can be slow.

Run of the Mill Tavern. Jenney Grist Mill Village. ☎ **508/830-1262.** Reservations recommended at dinner. Main courses $6–$11. AE, MC, V. Mon–Sat 11am–10pm, Sun noon–10pm. AMERICAN.

You'll find the Run of the Mill Tavern near the water wheel at Jenney Grist Mill Village at Town Brook Park. It's an attractive setting, surrounded by trees, and the tavern offers good inexpensive meals. In a welcome surprise, the clam chowder here is fantastic. Other appetizers include nachos, potato skins, buffalo wings, and mushrooms. Entrees are standard meat, chicken, and fish, and there are also seafood specials. The children's menu is a great bargain, with burgers and fish and chips at $2.50 to $3.50.

9 New Bedford & Fall River

New Bedford's history is inextricably bound to the whaling industry, as Fall River's is to the textile industry. The decline of their respective lifebloods in the mid-19th and early 20th century led to the deterioration of the cities. Both have made great strides in recent years in a push to make themselves more attractive to the tourist trade, but it's a tough market. Almost anywhere else in the country, New Bedford and Fall River would probably be judged rousing successes. In southeastern Massachusetts, about an hour from Boston and even closer to Plymouth, Cape Cod, and Newport, they're better known for factory-outlet shopping than for historic attractions.

New Bedford and Fall River are 15 miles apart on I-195 and Route 6. From Boston, take the Southeast Expressway south to I-93 (Route 128), then Route 24 south. It runs directly to Fall River, where you can pick up I-195 or Route 6 east to New Bedford. To go straight to New Bedford, take Route 140 south off Route 24. From Plymouth, take Route 44 west to Route 24 south.

To get information before you go, contact the **Bristol County Convention & Visitors Bureau** (70 N. Second St., P.O. Box 976, New Bedford, MA 02741; ☎ **800/288-6263** or 508/997-1250), which distributes a factory-outlet guide; the **New Bedford Area Chamber of Commerce** (794 Purchase St., P.O. Box 8827, New Bedford, MA 02742; ☎ **508/999-5231**); or the **Fall River Area Chamber of Commerce** (200 Pocasset St., P.O. Box 1871, Fall River, MA 02722; ☎ **508/676-8226**).

In New Bedford, the downtown area near the waterfront has been nicely restored. The top attractions include the **Whaling Museum** (18 Johnny Cake Hill; ☎ 508/ 997-0046), where you can board a half-scale model of a whaling bark; the **Seamen's Bethel** (15 Johnny Cake Hill; ☎ 508/992-3295), a nondenominational chapel described in Herman Melville's classic novel *Moby Dick;* and the **New Bedford Fire Museum** (51 Bedford St.; ☎ 508/992-2162), with historic fire-fighting equipment and uniforms children can try on.

Fall River's most famous former resident wasn't a sailor but a teacher—and an accused murderer. Although Lizzie Borden was acquitted in 1893 of killing her father and stepmother the previous year, she is remembered because of the verse: *Lizzie Borden took an ax / And gave her mother forty whacks. / When she saw what she had done / She gave her father forty-one.*

On the Fall River waterfront, **Battleship Massachusetts** (Battleship Cove; ☎ 800/533-3194 or 508/678-1100) is a five-vessel complex where you can see and board the battleship USS *Massachusetts,* a destroyer, a submarine, and two PT boats. Also at Battleship Cove is the fully restored **Fall River Carousel** (☎ 508/324-4300), built in 1920 and moved here from a nearby park in 1992. The **Marine Museum** (70 Water St.; ☎ 508/674-3533) is best known for its one-ton model of the *Titanic,* with a great number of other models and exhibits about maritime history.

Lest you think Fall River emphasizes its seafaring legacy over its ties to the textile industry, don't forget the factory outlets. Clustered near I-195 (start at Exit 8A) in restored mill buildings, the outlets offer just about anything that can be manufactured from thread, including clothing, outerwear, linens, and curtains. And of course you'll also need accessories, hats, housewares, books, shoes, and more. It's all here, at excellent prices. Wear comfortable shoes and bring lots of money or credit cards (many outlets also accept personal checks with proper identification).

Now that you know your way around, let's move on to something simple.

For card and collect calls.

AT&T

Cape Cod 6

by Sandy MacDonald

Only 70 miles long, Cape Cod is a curling peninsula encompassing hundreds of miles of beaches, more freshwater ponds than there are days in the year, more than a dozen lovely, richly historic New England villages, scores of classic clam shacks and soft ice-cream stands—and just about everyone's idea of the perfect summer vacation. More than 17 million visitors flock from around the world to enjoy summertime's nonstop carnival.

The Cape is, if anything, perhaps a bit too popular at full swing: Cognoscenti are beginning to discover the subtler appeal of the off-season, when prices plummet along with the population. For some select travelers, the prospect of sunbathing *en masse* on sizzling sand can't hold a candle to the chance to take long, solitary strolls on a wind-swept beach, with only the gulls as company. Come Labor Day—Columbus Day, for stragglers—the crowds clear out, and the whole place hibernates till Memorial Day weekend, the official start of "the season." Several communities, though, such as Hyannis and Provincetown, are populous enough to weather the winter in style, and it's in this downtime that you're most likely to experience the "real" Cape—an elusive entity amid the summer madness. For some it may take a little resourcefulness to see the beauty in winter's sere, shuttered landscape (even the Pilgrims, who forsook this spot for Plymouth, didn't quite have the necessary mettle), but the people who do stick around are an interesting, independent-minded lot worth getting to know.

Towns like Sandwich and Falmouth will suit more conventional visitors to a T, whereas 20-somethings and adventurous types of all ages will probably feel more at home in an open-minded, forward-thinking setting such as Wellfleet or Provincetown (the atmosphere at this predominantly gay vacation capital is suffused with general *joie de vivre*). These are broad generalizations, because you're likely to find compatible company wherever you go. Families, in particular, are sure to have a fabulous time at whatever spot they choose, because all it takes is some splashing surf and an expanse of sand to keep kids happily absorbed all day.

The **Cape Cod Chamber of Commerce,** Routes 6 and 132, Hyannis, MA 02601 (☎ **508/362-3225;** fax 508/362-3698; web site www.capecod.com) is a clearinghouse of information about vacationing here.

1 The Upper Cape

Because Sandwich and the surrounding Upper Cape towns are so close to Boston by car (a bit over an hour), they've become bedroom as well as summer communities. They may not have the let-the-good-times-roll feel of more seasonal towns farther east, but then again they're spared the fly-by-night qualities that come with a transient populace. Shops and restaurants—many catering to an older, affluent crowd—tend to stay open year-round.

The college crowd tends to gravitate to the beaches of Falmouth Heights, a bluff covered with grand, shingled Victorians built during the first wave of touristic fever in the late 1800s. The tiny enclave of Woods Hole—home at any given time to several thousand research scientists—is developing a certain neo-Bohemian panache, with lively bars and an air of vigorous intellectual inquiry.

SANDWICH

3 miles (5km) E of Sagamore, 16 miles (26km) NW of Hyannis

The oldest town in this corner of the Cape (it was founded in 1637 by a contingent of Puritans who considered the environs north of Boston a mite crowded), Sandwich serves as a crash course in quaintness. A 1640 gristmill churns away at the mouth of a placid pond frequented by swans, geese, ducks, and canoeists, and the town square—more of a triangle, really—is presided over by two imposing early 19th-century churches and the columned Greek Revival Town Hall, in service since 1834.

On the whole, the pleasures that this region offers tend to be considerably quieter and more refined than the thrills offered elsewhere on the Cape; hence it tends to attract a more sedate, settled crowd. Older visitors, as well as young children, will find plenty to intrigue them. Those in-between, however, are likely to get restless and yearn for livelier climes.

ESSENTIALS

GETTING THERE   If you're driving, turn east on Route 6A toward Sandwich after crossing either the Bourne or Sagamore Bridge.

VISITOR INFORMATION   The **Cape Cod Canal Region Chamber of Commerce,** Main Street, Buzzards Bay (☎ **508/739-3122**), can provide literature on both Sandwich and Bourne. A consortium of Sandwich businesses have put together an excellent walking guide (with map): for a copy, contact the Summer House inn (see "Where to Stay," below).

SANDWICH HISTORY

✪ **Heritage Plantation of Sandwich.** Grove and Pine sts. (about ¹/₂ mile SW of town center), Sandwich. ☎ **508/888-3330.** Admission $8 adults, $7 seniors, $4 children 6–18. Mid-May to Oct daily 10am–5pm; no tickets sold after 4:15pm. Closed Nov to mid-May.

This is one of those rare museums equally appealing to adults and the children they drag along: The latter will leave clamoring for another visit. All ages have the run of 76 beautifully landscaped acres, crisscrossed with walking paths and riotous with color in late spring, when the towering rhododendra burst forth in blooms ranging from softest pink to gaudy orange. A scattering of buildings house a wide variety of collections, from Native American artifacts to Early American weapons. The art holdings, especially the primitive portraits, are outstanding. The high point for most children will be a calliope-accompanied ride on the 1912 carousel (safely preserved indoors), where the mounts are not horses but a menagerie of fancifully carved animals. Also sure to dazzle is the replica Shaker round barn packed with gleaming antique automobiles, including some celebrity vehicles. These motorcars were *massive*, and things of enduring beauty. Call ahead for a schedule of outdoor summer concerts, free with admission.

Sandwich Glass Museum. 129 Main St. (in the center of town), Sandwich. ☎ **508/ 888-0251.** Admission $3.50 adults, $1 children 6–12. Apr–Oct daily 9am–4:30pm, Feb–Mar and Nov–Dec Wed–Sun 9:30am–4pm. Closed Jan.

Even if you don't consider yourself a glass fan, make an exception for this fascinating museum, which captures the history of the town, and not only its legendary industry. A brief video introduces Deming Jarves's brilliant endeavor, which flourished from 1828 to 1888, bringing glassware—a hitherto rare commodity available only to the rich—within reach of the middle classes. Jarves picked the perfect spot, surrounded by old-growth forest to fuel the furnaces (the greenery has only recently recovered), with a harbor handy for shipping in fine sand from farther up the coast, and salt marsh hay with which to pack outgoing orders. Demand was such that Jarves imported hordes of immigrant workers, housing them in the rather shameful shanties of "Jarvestown." All went well (for him) until midwestern factories starting using coal; unable to keep up with their level of mass production, he switched back to handblown techniques just as his workforce was ready to revolt.

None of this turmoil is evident in the dainty artifacts displayed in a series of sunny rooms, and of course, the fact that the factory's output was finite makes surviving examples all the more valuable. Since the museum is run by the Sandwich Historical Society, one room is given over to changing exhibits highlighting other eras in the town's history, such as its stellar seafaring days. Anyone who goes in expecting not to be impressed is liable to leave dazzled. An excellent little gift shop stocks Sandwich glass replicas, as well as original glass works by area artisans.

Outdoor Pursuits

BEACHES For the Sandwich beaches listed, nonresident parking stickers—$20 for the length of your stay—are available at Sandwich Town Hall, 130 Rte. 130 (☎ 508/888-0340). Note that there's no swimming in the Cape Cod Canal: The currents are much too swift and dangerous.

- **Sandy Neck Beach,** off Sandy Neck Road in E. Sandwich: This 6-mile stretch of silken barrier beach with hummocky dunes is very popular with endangered piping plovers and, unfortunately, their nemesis, off-road vehicles. ORV permits ($80 per season for nonresidents) can be purchased at the gatehouse (☎ 508/ 362-8300) as long as it's not nesting season, but do this fragile environment a favor and walk. Parking costs $8 a day in season, and up to three days of camping is permitted at $10 a night.
- **Town Neck Beach,** off Town Neck Road in Sandwich: A bit rocky but ruggedly pretty, this narrow beach offers a busy view of passing ships, plus rest rooms and a snack bar. Parking costs $5 a day, or you could hike from town (about 1½ miles) via the community-built boardwalk spanning the salt marsh.
- **Wakeby Pond,** Ryder Conservation Area, John Ewer Road (off S. Sandwich Rd. on the Mashpee border): The beach, on the Cape's largest freshwater pond, has lifeguards, rest rooms, and parking ($4 a day).

BIKING/RECREATIONAL PATHS The Army Corps of Engineers (☎ 508/ 759-5991) maintains a **flat 14-mile loop** along the Cape Cod Canal that is equally suited to bicyclists and skaters, runners and strollers—even strollers pushing strollers. The most convenient place to park (free) is at the **Buzzards Bay Recreation Area** west of the Bourne Bridge, on the Cape side.

The closest bike rental shop is **P&B Cycles**at 29 Main St. in Buzzards Bay (☎ 508/759-2830), opposite the railroad station; they also offer free parking.

FISHING   Sandwich has eight fishable ponds; for details and a license, inquire at Town Hall in the center of town (☎ 508/888-0340). No permit is required for fishing from the banks of the Cape Cod Canal: Here your catch might include striped bass, bluefish, cod, pollock, flounder, or fluke. Local deep-water charters include the *Tigger Two*, docked in the Sandwich Marina (☎ 508/888-8372).

NATURE TRAILS   Shawme-Crowell State Forest, off Route 130 in Sandwich (☎ 508/888-0351), offers 280 camp sites and 742 acres to roam. Entrance is free; parking costs $2. The **Sandwich Boardwalk,** which the community rebuilt in 1991 after Hurricane Bob blew away the 1874 original, links the town and Town Neck Beach, by way of salt marshes that attract a great many birds, including great blue herons. The 57-acre **Green Briar Nature Center** in E. Sandwich (☎ 508/888-6870; free) has a mile-long path crossing marsh and stands of white pine. To request a map of other conservation areas in Sandwich (some 16 sites encompass nearly 1,300 acres), contact the **Sandwich Conservation Commission** at 270 Meeting House Rd. (☎ 508/888-4200).

WHERE TO STAY

Expensive

The Dan'l Webster Inn. 149 Main St. (in the center of town), Sandwich, MA 02563. ☎ 800/444-3566 or 508/888-3623. Fax 508/888-5156. Web: http://media3.com/dan'lwebsterinn/. 37 rms, 9 suites. A/C TV TEL. Summer $129–$199 double. MAP plan available. AE, CB, DISC, MC, V.

On this site there once stood a colonial tavern favored by the famous orator, who came to these parts to go fishing (silently, no doubt). It unfortunately burned to the ground in 1971, but the modern replacement, operated by the Catania family (owners of the Hearth 'N Kettle restaurants dotted about the Cape), will suit modern travelers perfectly. All the rooms are ample, and nicely furnished with reproductions. The eight suites located in nearby houses that *are* historic are especially appealing; they feature fireplaces and canopy beds. A small but prettily landscaped pool suffices for a quick dip, and those seeking a real workout can repair to a local health club, where admission is gratis for guests. The inn's common spaces are convivial, if bustling. This is a *very* popular place, among locals as well as travelers. The big draw is the restaurant, which turns out surprisingly sophisticated fare, especially considering the high volume (see "Where to Dine," below).

Moderate

The Belfry Inne. 8 Jarves St. (in the center of town), Sandwich, MA 02563. ☎ 508/888-8550. 8 rms. Summer (including full breakfast) $95–$165 double. MAP plan available. AE, MC, V.

You can't miss it: It's the gaudiest "painted lady" in town, recently restored to its original flamboyant glory after skulking for decades under three layers of siding. Newly liberated, this turreted 1879 rectory has turned its fancy to romance, with queen-size retrofitted antique beds, a clawfoot tub (or Jacuzzi) for every room, and a scattering of fireplaces and private balconies.

Isaiah Jones Homestead. 165 Main St. (in the center of town), Sandwich, MA 02563. ☎ 800/526-1625 or 508/888-9115. 5 rms. Summer (including full breakfast and afternoon tea) $100–$160 double. AE, DISC, MC, V.

When it's not being prissy, Victoriana can be, well, borderline kinky. That's definitely the case in the showier rooms to be found in this gingerbread 1849 captain's house.

The room named for industrial magnate Deming Jarves, for instance, boasts a plum-curtained half-canopy bed that could grace the cover of a bodice-ripper, and an oversize whirlpool tub clearly intended for bathing *à deux*. The gentility that prevails at the candlelight breakfast only serves to spice up the pleasures of the night.

Inexpensive

Pine Grove Cottages. 358 Rte. 6A (near the center of town), E. Sandwich, MA 02537. ☎ **508/888-8179.** 10 cottages. TV. Summer $240–$395 weekly, double. AE, DISC, MC, V. Closed Nov–Apr.

Cute as buttons, some of these one-room cottages are barely big enough to squeeze in a double bed. White walls make them seem a bit roomier, and stenciling adds a touch of romance—not that cottage-fanciers would need any added inducement. With lots of families in residence, and an above-ground pool to splash in, children enjoy good odds of finding a friend.

Spring Garden Motel. 578 Rte. 6A (about 2 miles E of town center), E. Sandwich, MA 02537. ☎ **800/446-4656** or 508/888-0710. Fax 508/371-1656. 11 units. A/C TV TEL. Summer $71–$75 double. AE, DISC, MC, V. Closed mid-Nov through Mar.

Looking like an elongated rose-covered cottage, this pretty double-decker motel overlooks the Great Sandwich Salt Marsh, and every room comes with a southern-oriented patio or porch that takes in the lush green landscape. With its spacious, tree-shaded backyard, the motel is understandably popular with families. Regular summerers also appreciate the complimentary homemade continental breakfasts.

☯ Summer House. 158 Main St. (in the center of town), Sandwich, MA 02563. ☎ **800/526-1625** or 508/888-4991. 5 rms (4 with shared bath). Summer (including full breakfast and afternoon tea) $65–$75 double. AE, DISC, MC, V.

The lack of private baths (only one room comes with its own) is the only possible explanation for the extremely reasonable rates at this elegant circa 1835 Greek Revival house. The bedrooms are all large corner rooms, brightened up with colorful home-stitched quilts and painted hardwood floors; four have working fireplaces, and a few overlook the English garden in back, in riotous bloom throughout the summer. It's here you'll find a hammock to hide away in, stirring only to be called in to breakfast (elaborate) or a bountiful tea.

WHERE TO DINE

The Belfry Bistro. 8 Jarves St. (in the center of town). ☎ **508/888-8550.** Main courses $7–$16. AE, MC, V. Late May to mid-Oct daily 11:30am–9:30pm; call for off-season schedule. NEW AMERICAN.

These are not "white tablecloth" prices, but the damask is indeed snowy and dense, the mood luxurious, the menu most ingratiating and geared to grazers. Selections change with the seasons, but among the trio of entrees you might find a superlative spring roll served in a pool of ginger tamari, or seared scallops in their shells, cloaked in Chardonnay cream sauce and served with herbed polenta. Desserts (offered independently as well, with specialty coffees) are designed to satisfy in and of themselves, as will the white chocolate cheesecake with morsels of meringue, in a pool of raspberry coulis.

The Dan'l Webster Inn. 149 Main St. (in the center of town). ☎ **508/888-3623.** Reservations recommended. Main courses $14–$20. AE, CB, DISC, MC, V. Daily 8am–9pm. INTERNATIONAL.

Though you have a choice of four main dining rooms—from a casual, colonial-motif tavern to a skylight-topped conservatory fronting a splendid garden—they're all served by the same kitchen, under the masterful hand of chef/co-owner Richard Catania. A devotee of fresh, local fruit and fish, he has gone so far as to build a model aquaculture farm that he can plunder at will. The results attest to his good taste. A restaurant on this scale could get away with ho-hum, middle-of-the-road food, but his output is on a par with that of the Cape's best boutique restaurants. Try a classicist dish like the *fruits de mer* in white wine, or entrust your palate to a seasonal highlight (the specials menu changes monthly). The desserts are as superb as all that precedes them.

✪ **The Dunbar Tea Shop.** 1 Water St. (in the center of town). ☎ **508/833-2485.** Main courses under $6. MC, V. Daily 10am–dark. BRITISH.

Choose the cozy confines of the tearoom or, in summer, a shady grove outside. Either way, you'll get to partake of hearty, authentic English classics such as savories, before moving on to sweets such as fresh-baked shortbread and seasonal pies. The Tea Shop also serves tea, of course, with all the traditional fixings and accompaniments.

FALMOUTH & WOODS HOLE

18 miles (30km) S of Sagamore, 20 miles (33km) SW of Hyannis

Often overlooked in the rush to catch the island ferries, Falmouth is a classic New England town, complete with white steeples encircling a town green. The area around the historic Village Green (given over to military exercises in the pre-Revolutionary days) is a veritable hotbed of B&Bs, with each vying to provide the most elaborate breakfasts and solicitous advice. Put yourself in the hands of your hosts, and you'll soon feel like a native.

Officially a village within Falmouth (one of nine), tiny Woods Hole has been a world-renowned oceanic research center since 1871, when the U.S. Commission of Fish and Fisheries set up a primitive seasonal collection station. Today the various scientific institutes crowded around the harbor—principally, the National Marine Fisheries Service, the Marine Biological Laboratory (founded in 1888), and the Woods Hole Oceanographic Institute (a newcomer as of 1930)—have research budgets in the tens of millions and employ thousands of scientists. Woods Hole's scientific institutions offer a unique opportunity to get in-depth—and often hands-on—exposure to marine biology.

Belying stereotype, the community is far from uptight and nerdy; in fact, it's one of the hipper communities on the Cape. In the past few decades, a number of agreeable restaurants and shops have cropped up, making the small, crowded gauntlet of Water Street (don't even bother fantasizing about parking here in summer) a very pleasant place to stroll.

West Falmouth (which is really more north of town, stretched alongside Buzzards Bay) has held onto its bucolic character and makes a lovely drive, with perhaps an occasional stop for the more alluring antique stores. Falmouth Heights, a cluster of shingled Victorian summerhouses on a bluff east of Falmouth's harbor, is as popular as it is picturesque; its narrow ribbon of beach is a magnet for all, especially the younger crowd. The Waquoit Bay area, a few miles east of town, has thus far eluded the overcommercialization that blights most of Route 28, and with luck and foresight will continue to do so. Several thousand acres of this vital estuarine ecosystem are now under federal custody, primarily at the instigation of the region's original residents, the Mashpee Wampanoags.

ESSENTIALS

GETTING THERE　After crossing either the Bourne or Sagamore Bridge, take Route 28 or 28A south.

The **Sea Line shuttle** (☎ 800/352-7155) connects Woods Hole, Falmouth, and Mashpee with Hyannis year-round (except Sundays and holidays); the fare ranges from 75¢ to $4, depending on distance, and children under 6 ride free.

VISITOR INFORMATION   Contact the **Falmouth Chamber of Commerce,** Academy Lane, Falmouth, MA 02541 (☎ **800/526-8532** or 508/548-8500; fax 508/540-4724).

OUTDOOR PURSUITS

BEACHES   Renters can obtain temporary beach parking stickers for Falmouth— $40 a week, $70 a month—at Falmouth Town Hall, 59 Town Hall Sq. (☎ **508/ 548-8623**), or at the Surf Drive Beach bathhouse in season. The town beaches for which a parking fee is charged all have rest rooms and a concession stand.

- **Old Silver Beach,** off Route 28A in W. Falmouth: Western-facing (great for sunsets) and relatively placid, this is a popular pick and therefore often crowded (parking costs $10 a day).
- **Nobska Beach,** by the Nobska Lighthouse in Woods Hole: Accessible by bike, via the Shining Sea Bicycle Path, this beach boasts a magnificent view.
- **Surf Drive Beach,** off Shore Street in Falmouth: About a mile from downtown and appealing to families, this is a serviceable choice with limited parking ($5 a day, $8 on weekends and holidays).
- **Falmouth Heights Beach,** off Grand Avenue in Falmouth Heights: Acknowledged college-kid turf, this is where teens and 20-somethings tend to congregate. Parking is sticker-only.
- **Menauhant Beach,** off Central Avenue in E. Falmouth: A bit off the beaten track, Menauhant is a little less mobbed than Surf Drive Beach, and better protected from the winds. Parking is $5 a day, $8 on weekends and holidays.

BIKING/RECREATIONAL PATHS   The **Shining Sea Bicycle Path** (☎ **508/ 548-8500**) is a 3.6-mile beauty skirting the Sound from Falmouth to Woods Hole, by way of the scenic Nobska Lighthouse; it also connects with a 23-mile scenic-road loop through pretty Sippewissett. You can park at the trailhead on Locust Street in Falmouth, or any nonmetered spot in town (parking in Woods Hole is scarce).

The closest shop—convenient to the main cluster of B&Bs, some of which offer "loaners"—is **Corner Cycle** at Palmer Avenue and N. Main Street (☎ **508/ 540-4195**). For a broad selection of vehicles—from six-speed cruisers to six-passenger "surreys"—and good advice on routes, visit **Holiday Cycles** at 465 Grand Ave. in Falmouth Heights (☎ **508/540-3459**).

FISHING   Falmouth has six ponds: licenses can be obtained at Falmouth Town Hall, 59 Town Hall Sq. (☎ **508/548-7611**). Surf Drive Beach is a great spot for surf-casting once the crowds have dispersed. To go after bigger prey, book the *Thank Abba* from the Little River Boat Yard on Seconset Island in Waquoit (☎ **508/ 447-1079**), or head out with a group on one of the Patriot Party Boats based in Falmouth's Inner Harbor (☎ **800/734-0088** or 508/548-2626): the clunky *Patriot Too*, with an enclosed deck, is ideal for family-style "bottom fishing," and the zippy *Minuteman* is geared to pros. Serious aficionados will want to go gunkholing with 30-year veteran Capt. John Christian on his Aquasport *Susan Jean* (☎ **508/ 548-6901**), moored in Woods Hole's Eel Pond, to hunt for trophy bass among the neighboring Elizabeth Islands.

NATURE TRAILS   Though hardly in its natural state, the **Ashumet Holly and Wildlife Sanctuary,** operated by the Massachusetts Audubon Society at 186 Ashumet Rd. off Route 151 (☎ **508/563-6390**), is an intriguing 49-acre collection of over

1,000 holly trees—spanning 65 species, culled worldwide—preserved by the state's first commissioner of agriculture, who was concerned that commercial harvesting might wipe out native species; they're flourishing here, along with over 130 species of birds and a carpet of Oriental lotus blossoms which covers a kettle pond come summer. The trail fee is $3 for adults, $2 for seniors and children under 13.

The 2,250-acre **Waquoit Bay National Estuarine Research Reserve,** at 149 Waquoit Hwy. in E. Falmouth (☎ 508/457-0495), charges a $2 fee in season to explore its one-mile, self-guiding nature trail. Also inquire about WBNERR's ferry over to Washburn Island (it's about a half-hour paddle via canoe) and its 10 primitive campsites—permits cost a mere $4 a night. The reserve offers a number of interpretive programs, including the popular "Evenings on the Bluff," geared to families.

WATER SPORTS   Falmouth is something of a sailboarding mecca, prized for its unflagging southwesterly winds. Both boards and boats can be rented at **Cape Water Sports,** 145 Falmouth Heights Rd., E. Falmouth (☎ 508/548-7700), or **Cape Cod Windsurfing Academy & Watersports Rentals** (☎ 508/495-0008), located at the Surfside Holiday motel on Maravista Beach in E. Falmouth; the latter also offers classes by appointment. Those already adept might consult **Cape Sailboards** (661 Main St., Falmouth; ☎ 508/540-8800) for advice on optimal boarding sites. Among the best is Old Silver Beach in N. Falmouth, where tyros can take lessons—again, by appointment—at the **New England Windsurfing Academy** (☎ 508/540-8016) located alongside the Sea Crest resort (see "Where to Stay," below) and the Trunk River area on the west end of Falmouth's Surf Drive Beach—the only public beach where windsurfers are allowed during the day. In addition, **Edward's Boat Yard,** 1209 E. Falmouth Hwy., E. Falmouth (☎ 508/548-2216) rents out canoes for exploring Waquoit Bay (see "Nature Trails," above). Thrill-seekers will want to hook up with **Cape Parasailing** (☎ 508/457-1900) out of Falmouth Harbor.

SEA SCIENCE

Marine Biological Laboratory. Water St. (at MBL St., in the center of town), Woods Hole. ☎ 508/289-7623. Free admission. June–Aug Mon–Fri at 1, 2, and 3pm. Closed to the public Sept–May.

A visit to this cutting-edge think tank, housed in an 1836 candle factory, requires a little forethought—the MBL prefers that reservations be made a week in advance—but will definitely reward the curious. After a slide presentation, a retired scientist leads a guided tour through the holding tanks, and then to the lab to observe actual research in progress. The MBL's area of inquiry is not limited to the aquatic, but encompasses the "biological process common to all life forms"; some of what you see may have an immediate bearing on your own life, or that of your descendants.

National Marine Fisheries Service Aquarium. Albatross St. (off the western end of Water St.), Woods Hole. ☎ 508/548-7684. Free admission. Mid-June to mid-Sept daily 10am–4pm; mid-Sept to mid-June Mon–Fri 10am–4pm.

A little beat-up after a century and a quarter of service and endless streams of eager schoolchildren, this aquarium—the first such institution in the country—is no longer what you'd call state-of-the-art, but a treasure nonetheless. The displays, focusing on local waters, might make you think twice before taking a dip. Children show no hesitation, though, in getting up to their elbows in the "touch tanks"; adults are also welcome to dabble. A key exhibit that everyone should see concerns the effect of plastic trash on the marine environment. You might time your visit to coincide with the feeding of two seals who summer here: The fish fly at 11am and 3pm.

OUT ON THE WATER

✪ **OceanQuest.** Water St. (in the center of town), Woods Hole. ☎ **800/376-2326** or 508/457-0508. Fee $14 adults, $10 children 3–12. Mid-June to early Sept daily at 10am, noon, 2, and 4pm.

A great family excursion, these 1½-hour harbor cruises actually accomplish real marine research, with passengers serving as bona-fide data collectors. Passengers divide into two teams at the outset. Up in the bow, company founder Kathy Mullin, a former grade school teacher, or a scientist borrowed from one of the institutes, trains the new crew in the niceties of reading water temperature, assessing turbidity, and taking other key measurements; in the stern, passengers get to examine the specimens hauled up by the dredger. Midway into the trip, the teams switch stations, so that everyone gets to ponder why the water looks blue (or the sky, for that matter) or, say, the sex life of a spider crab. Little kids get a real kick out of being addressed as "Doctor," and even adults who think they know it all will probably come away much better informed.

Patriot Party Boats. 227 Clinton Ave. (at Scranton Ave. on the harbor), Falmouth. ☎ **800/734-0088** or 508/548-2626. Fees vary. June–Aug 7:30am–7pm; call for off-season hours.

Offering one-stop shopping for would-be boaters, the Patriot fleet includes a high-speed fishing boat, the *Minuteman;* a poky fishing/sightseeing vessel, the *Patriot Too;* and a sleek replica 1750s Pinky schooner, the *LibeRoute.* Scenic cruises are offered on the last two, often with company founder Bud Tietje on board. While wending among the Elizabeth Islands, some privately owned by the Forbes family, he can give you the scoop on local gossip and lore spanning the past four decades. Even if the scenery weren't so lovely, his stories would make the time fly. The Patriot crew also offer ferry service directly to Edgartown on Martha's Vineyard.

WHERE TO STAY

Expensive

✪ **Inn at West Falmouth.** 66 Frazar Rd. (off Rte. 28A, in the center of town), W. Falmouth, MA 02574. ☎ **508/540-7696.** 9 rms. Summer $150–$185 double. No credit cards.

So thoroughly perfect is this opulent B&B that it made *Country Inns'* "Top 12 in the Country" list in 1994. The turn-of-the-century shingle-style mansion, set high on a wooded hill, with views to Buzzards Bay, had suffered some hard knocks in its day, serving at one point as a children's camp. Co-owner Lewis Milardo has purged it of the last trace of institutionalism: Welcoming your gaze at every turn are tableaux of rare, seemingly serendipitous beauty, from the spacious rooms lavished with custom linens and accented by a few judicious, unusual antiques, to the large living room set about with fresh flowers and heaps of best-sellers begging to be borrowed. After a leisurely continental breakfast highlighted by fresh-baked pastries, you might carry off a tome to the small, sparkling heated pool set in the deck or wander the beautifully landscaped grounds, seeking the optimal bower. There's a clay tennis court right at hand, and the beach is about a 10-minute walk down a country lane. On blustery days, you might take refuge in the tiny conservatory perfumed by lemon trees, sink into one of the voluminous couches by the fireplace, or retreat to your own private marble whirlpool bath. Whatever the weather, and whatever you do (or don't do), you're sure to come away refreshed.

Sea Crest. 350 Quaker Rd. (midway between N. and W. Falmouth), N. Falmouth, MA 02556. ☎ **800/225-3110** or 508/540-9400. Fax 508/548-0556. 266 rms. TV TEL. Summer $160–$225 double. AE, DC, MC, V.

Something of an anomaly in this part of the Cape, this sprawling two-story resort and conference center is undeniably a visual blight on beautiful Old Silver Beach. It might make a good choice, though, for those families who mostly want to bask on the beach. The complex is undergoing renovations, so be sure to ask for an updated room. All the services and facilities one could require are right on site: restaurant, indoor pool, health club, four tennis courts, a complimentary children's day camp. Perhaps most appealing is the opportunity to learn to windsurf (see "Water Sports," above) right outside your front door.

Moderate

Coonamessett Inn. Jones Rd. and Gifford St. (about ¹/₂ mile N of Main St.), Falmouth, MA 02540. ☎ **508/438-2300.** 24 suites, 1 cottage. A/C TV TEL. Summer $95–$120 double. AE, CB, DISC, MC, V.

A gracious, traditional inn that accrued around the core of a transplanted 1796 homestead (the river it originally flanked was named "place of the big fish"), the Coonamessett has been the social center of town since the century's teens. Its future was in question when the late Josiah K. Lilly, a local resident, funded it with a trust designed to keep its body and soul intact. Set on seven lushly landscaped acres overlooking a pond, it has the feel of a country club where all comers are welcome. Some of the rooms, decorated in reproduction antiques, can be a bit somber, so try to get one with good light.

The Coonamessett Inn Dining Room is unabashedly formal, and surprisingly good (see "Where to Dine," below). In the adjoining Eli's, a clubbily decorated tavern, a mellow jazz combo holds forth on weekends.

ⓢ Inn on the Sound. 313 Grand Ave. South (off Main St.), Falmouth Heights, MA 02540. ☎ **800/564-9668** or 508/547-9666. Fax 508/457-9631. 10 rms. Summer (including full breakfast) $95–$140 double. AE, DISC, MC, V.

The ambience here is as breezy as the setting, high on a bluff beside Falmouth's premier sunning beach, with a sweeping view of the Sound. The focal point of the living room is a handsome boulder hearth (nice for those nippy nights); a couple of bedrooms—most offer ocean views—have working fireplaces of their own. The breakfasts served, especially the banana-stuffed French toast or eggs Florentine, offer incentive to dawdle, but the outdoors exerts an even stronger attraction.

ⓞ Mostly Hall. 27 W. Main St. (W of the Village Green), Falmouth, MA 02540. ☎ **800/ 682-0565** or 508/548-3786. Fax 508/457-1572. A/C. Summer (including full breakfast) $95–$110 double. MC, V. Closed Jan to mid-Feb.

Built by a sea captain to please his New Orleans–born bride, this plantation-style house (unique on the Cape) exudes Southern graciousness as well as style. Longtime innkeepers Caroline and Jim Lloyd have pretty much mastered the art, providing memorable breakfasts (such as eggs Benedict soufflé), loaner bikes for exploring the Shining Sea Bikeway to Woods Hole, and plenty of valuable advice for making the most of your stay. The six stately corner bedrooms each boast a canopied four-poster bed, cheery floral wallpaper, and a lazily whirring ceiling fan (more for effect than function, since the inn is centrally air-conditioned). The gardens are lovely, and the gazebo makes a pleasant retreat—as does the house's cupola, a combo library/ videotheque.

Nautilus Motor Inn. 533 Woods Hole Rd. (about ¹/₂ mile W of town), Woods Hole, MA 02543. ☎ **800/654-2333** or 508/548-1525. Fax 508/547-9674. 54 rms. A/C TV TEL. Summer $92– $130 double. AE, DC, DISC, MC, V. Closed mid-Oct to mid-Apr.

A crescent-shaped complex poised above Woods Hole's picturesque Little Harbor, the Nautilus doesn't have to do much to make itself attractive: nature has already seen to that aspect. The two tiers of rooms are standard motelish, but each comes with a private balcony for taking in the view and/or sunning, and a very spacious wooden deck flanks the fair-sized pool. A rather curious restaurant, The Dome (see "Where to Dine," below), is right on the premises, and the Martha's Vineyard ferry is a very short stroll. Not so much a destination in and of itself, the Nautilus makes an ideal launching pad for various day trips.

Sands of Time Motor Inn & Harbor House. 549 Woods Hole Rd. (about ¹/₂ mile W of town), Woods Hole, MA 02543. ☎ **800/841-0114** or 508/548-6300. Fax 508/457-0160. 31 rms (2 with shared bath), 2 efficiencies. A/C TV TEL. Summer (including continental breakfast) $90–$125 double. AE, DC, MC, V. Closed Nov–Mar.

It's really two facilities in one: a two-story block of motel rooms (with crisp, above-average decor, plus private porches) and, next door, a shingled Victorian manse, where the quarters tend to be more lavish and romantic—four-posters, working fireplaces, wicker furnishings, the works. Both types of accommodation, though, afford the same charming harbor views and share the well-kept grounds and small pool. A couple of couples traveling together—one B&B-crazy, the other not—could both get their needs met here.

Woods Hole Passage. 186 Woods Hole Rd. (about 2 miles N of town center), Woods Hole, MA 02540. ☎ **508/548-9575.** Fax 508/540-9123. 5 rms. Summer (including full breakfast) $95–$105 double. AE, CB, DC, DISC, MC, V.

Credit the Euro-flair to Argentinean innkeeper Christina Mozo's other occupation as graphic artist. The decorative approach is ultratasteful, yet anything but quaint. In the main building, a former carriage house, she has painted the walls a somewhat shocking pink—which actually works quite well to frame the greenery of the extensive garden out back—and the elegant oatmeal-linen sofas redress any Bohemian leanings. The two cathedral-ceiling loft rooms in the adjoining 18th-century barn are definitely the most covetable, and seem custom-made for honeymooning (or otherwise cocooning) couples.

WHERE TO DINE

Very Expensive

✪ The Regatta at Falmouth-by-the-Sea. 217 Clinton Ave. (off Scranton Ave., about 1 mile S of Main St.), Falmouth. ☎ **508/548-5400.** Reservations recommended. Dress: "Attractively formal or informal." Main courses $19–$25. AE, MC, V. May–Sept daily 4:30–10pm. Closed Oct–Apr. INTERNATIONAL.

A dazzler since its very debut in 1970, this exemplary restaurant has it all: view (it's right on the harbor), polished yet innovative cuisine, and superb service. You're likely to find owner Brantz Bryan affably circulating: He's the one who seems to have wandered in off a golf course, hale and "attractively informal" in tastefully lurid preppy attire. His wife and partner, Wendy Bryan, designed the decor, from the rose petal–pale walls to the custom Limoges china, on which two roses entwine. The candlelight is muted so as to flatter, and scarcely strong enough to eat by. True connoisseurs, however, could track down these exquisite dishes in the dark, by aroma alone. Certain menu offerings are inviolable: Customers would rightfully squawk if they were to vanish. These include a celestial lobster-and-corn chowder, and the lamb *en chemise*—stuffed with chevre, spinach, and pine nuts, baked in puff pastry, and cloaked in a Cabernet Sauvignon sauce. Never ones to fall behind the wave, the

Brantzes have also ventured into fusion territory, with such dishes as grilled tamari-glazed shrimp and Szechuan duck served with sautéed Asian greens. If the dessert decision throws you into a tizzy, abandon all caution and order the "trilogy"—or several, with sufficient spoons.

Expensive

☼ Coonamessett Inn Dining Room. Jones Rd. and Gifford St. (see "Where to Stay," above), Falmouth. ☎ **508/548-2300.** Reservations recommended. Main courses $14–$21. AE, DC, MC, V. Daily 8–10am and 5–9pm; Mon–Sat 11:30am–2:30pm, Sun noon–3pm. NEW AMERICAN.

If the somewhat stuffy ambience has led you to expect bland country-club fare, you're in for a very pleasant surprise indeed. Chef David Kelley, an autodidact, has a masterful way with local provender. He cures his own salmon into superlative gravlax, and raids the inn's garden to create memorable seasonal variations on, say, lobster or lamb. Whimsical mermaid paintings, the work of local legend Ralph Cahoon, plus chandeliers shaped like hot-air balloons render the middle dining room (the largest of three, capable of accommodating 300 in toto) a semi-playful power spot.

☼ Fishmonger's Cafe. 56 Water St. (at the Eel Pond drawbridge), Woods Hole. ☎ **508/540-5376.** Main courses $10–$19. AE, MC, V. Mid-June to mid-Oct Mon–Thurs 7–11am, 11:30am–4pm, 5–10pm; Fri 7–11am, 11:30am–4pm, 5–10:30pm; Sat 7–11:30am, noon–4:30pm, 5:30–10:30pm; Sun 7am–noon, 12:30–4:30pm, 5:30–10:30pm. Call for off-season hours. Closed Dec to mid-Mar. NATURAL.

A cherished carryover from the early 1970s, this sunny cafe attracts local grungers and execs as well as Bermuda-shorted tourists with an ever-changing array of imaginatively prepared dishes. Regulars might grab a bite at the counter while schmoozing with staff bustling about the open kitchen. Newcomers usually go for the tables by the window, where you can watch the Eel Pond boats come and go. The menu ranges widely (lunch could be a tempeh burger, made with fermented soybeans, or ordinary beef), and long-time customers look to the blackboard for the latest innovations, which invariably include some delectable, albeit politically correct desserts, such as pumpkin-pecan pie. Many visitors, one suspects, must miss the Martha's Vineyard ferry on purpose, as an excuse to stop in for a bite.

Moderate

Cap'n Kidd. 77 Water St. (W of the Eel Pond drawbridge), Woods Hole. ☎ **508/548-9206.** Main courses $11–15. AE, CB, MC, V. Daily 11am–9pm. SEAFOOD.

The semi-official heart of town, this well-worn bistro really comes into its own once the tourist hordes subside. It's then that the year-round scientists and fishing crews can again belly up to the hand-carved mahogany bar (thought to date from the early 1800s), or huddle around the woodstove in the glassed back porch, beside the pond, and order up reasonably priced seafood, or drink to their heart's content—mostly the latter, judging from the degree of general bonhomie. The notorious 17th-century pirate, who is rumored to have debarked in Woods Hole on his way back to England to be hung, would probably get a warm reception were he to wander in today.

Peking Palace. 452 Main St. (in the center of town), Falmouth. ☎ **508/540-8204.** Fax 508/540-8382. Main courses $8–$12. AE, DC, MC, V. Jun–Aug daily 11:30am–2am; Sept–May Sun–Thurs 11:30am–midnight, Fri–Sat 11:30am–1:30am. CHINESE.

Incontrovertibly the best Chinese restaurant on the Cape, and among the top contenders in the state, this smallish restaurant has been infused with TLC at every turn. From the fringes of bamboo gracing the parking lot to the gleaming rosewood tables, no detail has been overlooked to create a cosseting, exotic environment. It's a wonder the staff finds the time, what with 300-plus items on the menu, spanning three regional cuisines (Cantonese, Mandarin, and Szechuan), as well as Polynesian. Sip a fanciful drink to give yourself time to take in the menu, and be sure to solicit your server's opinion: That's how we encountered some heavenly spicy chilled squid.

Shucker's World Famous Raw Bar & Cafe. 91A Water St. ($^1/_2$ block W of the Eel Pond drawbridge), Woods Hole. ☎ **508/540-3850.** Main courses $9–$15. AE, MC, V. Mid-May to mid-Oct daily 11am–11pm. Closed mid-Oct to mid-May. INTERNATIONAL.

A tight cluster of cafe tables hugging the edge of Eel Pond, this outdoor cafe has a loyal following, drawn by the well-priced, nonpareil seafood. The clam chowder is so thick with seafood (including the odd shrimp and crab) that it's truly a meal. Among the more unusual offerings are crabcaves (like a crab Welsh rarebit) and, for adventurous types, marinated grilled eel. Owner Kevin Murphy is also the force behind Falmouth's beloved local brew, Nobska Light, named for the resident lighthouse.

Inexpensive

Ⓢ Betsy's Diner. 457 Main St. (in the center of town), Falmouth. ☎ **508/540-0060.** Main courses $4–$8. AE, MC, V. May–Aug Sun–Thurs 5am–10pm, Fri–Sat 5am–11pm; call for off-season hours. AMERICAN.

Nothing could be finer than a resurrected diner—especially one offering time-travel food. Turkey dinner, breakfast all day, homemade pies—now, these are traditions worth maintaining. The original aluminum features dazzle as they surely did back then, and the jukebox is primed for retro-rock.

Ⓢ Cape Cod Chicken. 235 Main St. (in the center of town), Falmouth. ☎ **508/457-1302.** Main courses under $7. AE. Daily 11am–9pm. AMERICAN.

For a quick, cheap, delicious meal, duck into this tiny storefront restaurant, where you can custom-compose a platter of succulent rotisserie chicken plus such enticing sides as tarragon carrots and garlic-roasted bliss potatoes. While awaiting your order, check out the evocative flea-market artifacts decorating the walls.

The Clam Shack. 227 Clinton Ave. (off Scranton Ave., about 1 mile S of Main St.), Falmouth. ☎ **508/540-7758.** Main courses $5–$11. No credit cards. Daily 11:30am–7:45pm. Closed mid-Sept to late May. SEAFOOD.

"Shack" is the appropriate term. This tumble-down shanty clings to its pier like a barnacle, having weathered three decades of Nor'easters, not to mention the occasional hurricane. The fare has withstood the test of time, too: your basic fried clams (with belly intact, the sign of a joint that knows clams) and whatever else the nets have tossed up. Sitting at a postage-stamp table hinged to the wall, you can soak up a truly magnificent view.

FALMOUTH AFTER DARK

God knows who you'll meet in the rough-and-tumble old **Cap'n Kidd,** 77 Water St., in Woods Hole (☎ **508/548-9206**): maybe a lobsterwoman, maybe a Nobel Prize winner. Good grub, too—see "Where to Dine," above.

Casino by the Sea, at 281 Grand Ave. beneath the Wharf Restaurant (☎ **508/548-2772**), is essentially a dance hall catering to 20-somethings. The fun spills over from the sand; locally bred bands provide the beat. Cover $5. Closed October through April.

An alternative to rowdy bars is **The Coffee Obsession,** 110 Palmer Ave. near Route 28 (☎ **508/540-2233**), a *Friends*-style coffeehouse—something like a communal living room.

2 The Mid Cape

If the Cape could be said to have a capital, Hyannis would have to be it. It's a big sprawling mallified monstrosity (let's be blunt), where the Kennedy mystique of the 1960s had the unfortunate side effect of spurring heedless development over the next several decades—a period during which, not so incidentally, the Cape's year-round population nearly doubled, to approximately 200,000. The summer population is about three times that, and you'd swear every single person had daily errands to run in Hyannis. And yet even this overrun town has its pockets of charm. The waterfront area in particular, where the Island ferries dock, has benefited greatly from an influx of civic pride and attention, and Main Street, long eclipsed by the megastores along Route 132, is once again a pleasant place to stroll.

But the real beauty of the Mid Cape is to be found in the smaller towns: the old-money hideaways like Osterville to the west, and the historic preserve flanking the Old King's Highway (Route 6) along the bay shore. This entire stretch constitutes an enchanting itinerary. The whole architectural history of the Cape, from humble colonial saltboxes to ostentatious captains' mansions, unfurls as one meanders along the winding two-lane road. Intriguing antique shops—scores of them—subtly compete for a closer look, and each village seems a throwback to a kinder, gentler era.

BARNSTABLE & HYANNIS
15 miles (25km) E of Sagamore, 44 miles (71km) S of Provincetown

As the commercial center and transportation hub of the Cape, hyper-developed Hyannis—a mere "village"—grossly overshadows the actual seat of government in the bucolic village of Barnstable. The two locales couldn't be more dissimilar. As peaceful as Hyannis is hectic, the Bay area along historic Route 6A unfolds in a blur of greenery and well-kept colonial houses. No wonder many visitors experience "post-Camelot letdown" the first time they venture southward to Hyannis. The downtown area, sapped by the strip development that proliferated at the edges of town after the Cape Cod Mall was built in 1970, is making a valiant comeback, with attractive banners and a pretty public park flanking the wharf where frequent ferries depart for the Islands. If you were to confine your visit to this one town, however, you'd get a very warped view of the Cape. Along Routes 132 and 28, you could be visiting Anywhere, U.S.A.: They're lined by the standard chain stores, restaurants, and hotels, and enmired by maddening traffic.

Hyannis has more beds and better "rack rates" (in the travel industry jargon) than anywhere else on the Cape, but there's little rationale for staying right in town or along the highways—unless you happen to have missed the last ferry out. Even full resort facilities can't begin to compensate for the lack of local color.

The best strategy is to stay somewhere peaceful near the edge of town, in one of the moneyed villages—Centerville, Osterville, Marstons Mills, and Cotuit—to the west, or in the bayside villages of Barnstable due north, and just go into the "city" to sample the restaurants and nightlife. Hyannis and environs can offer plenty of both, to suit every palate and personality.

ESSENTIALS
GETTING THERE   After crossing either the Bourne or Sagamore Bridge, head east on Route 6 or 6A. The latter passes through Barnstable; Route 132 south of Route 6A leads to Hyannis.

The **Sea Line** (☎ 800/352-7155) makes a circuit of Barnstable, Mashpee, Falmouth, and Woods Hole daily except Sundays and holidays, and the fare is a reasonable 75¢ to $4 (depending on distance); children under 6 ride free.

VISITOR INFORMATION   For information, contact the **Hyannis Area Chamber of Commerce,** 1471 Rte. 132, Hyannis, MA 02601 (☎ **800/449-6647** or 508/362-5230).

OUTDOOR PURSUITS

BEACHES   Barnstable's primary Bay beach is **Sandy Neck,** accessed through East. Sandwich; see "Beaches" under "Sandwich," above. Most of the Sound beaches are fairly protected and thus not big in terms of surf. Beach parking costs $8 a day, usually payable at the lot; for a week-long parking sticker ($35), visit the Recreation Department at 141 Basset Lane, behind the Kennedy Memorial Skating Rink (☎ **508/790-6345**).

- **Craigville Beach,** off Craigville Beach Road in Centerville: Once a magnet for Methodist "camp" meetings (conference centers still line the shore), this broad expanse of sand boasts lifeguards and rest rooms. A magnet for the bronzed and buffed, it's known as "Muscle Beach."
- **Orrin Keyes Beach** (a.k.a. Sea Beach), at the end of Sea Street in Hyannis: This little beach at the end of a residential road is popular with families.
- **Kalmus Beach,** off Gosnold Street in Hyannisport: This 800-foot spit of sand stretching toward the mouth of the harbor makes an ideal launching site for windsurfers, who sometimes seem to play chicken with the steady parade of ferries. The surf is tame, the slope shallow—the conditions are ideal for little kids, too, and lifeguards, a snack bar, and rest rooms facilitate family outings.
- **Veterans Beach,** off Ocean Street in Hyannis: A small stretch of harborside sand adjoining the John F. Kennedy Memorial (a moving tribute from the town), this spot is not tops for swimming, unless you're very young and easily wowed. Parking is usually easy, though, and it's walkable from town. The snack bar, rest rooms, and playground will see to a family's needs.

FISHING   The township of Barnstable has 11 ponds for freshwater fishing; for **information and permits,** visit Town Hall at 367 Main St., Hyannis (☎ **508/790-6240**). Shellfishing permits are available from the Department of Natural Resources at 1189 Phinneys Lane (☎ **508/790-6272**). Surf casting, sans license, is permitted on Sandy Neck (see "Beaches," above). Among the charter boats berthed in Barnstable Harbor is the *Drifter* (☎ **508/398-2061**), a 35-foot boat offering half- and full-day trips. The **Tightlines Sport Fishing Service,** 65 Camp St., Hyannis (☎ **508/790-8600**), conducts saltwater fly-fishing expeditions. **Hy-Line Cruises** offers seasonal sonar-aided "bottom" or blues fishing from its Ocean Street dock in Hyannis (☎ **508/790-0696**). Also departing from that dock, **Hyannis Navigator Deep Sea Fishing** (☎ **800/771-9534** or 508/771-9500) claims the newest and fastest craft. **Helen H Deep Sea Fishing,** 137 Pleasant St., Hyannis (☎ **508/790-0660**), offers year-round expeditions aboard a 100-foot boat with a heated cabin and full galley. For a smaller, more personalized expedition, get in touch with Capt. Ron Murphy of **Stray Cat Charters** (☎ **508/428-8628**).

NATURE TRAILS   **Sandy Neck,** accessed through E. Sandwich (see "Beaches," above), is great for hiking; take care to avoid the endangered piping plovers.

WATER SPORTS   **Cape-Eco-Craft,** with offices at 605 Main St. in Hyannis (☎ **508/771-4009**), offers rentals, lessons, and tours via rowboats, canoes and sea kayaks, windsurfers, sunfish, Hobie cats, and sailboats; they'll even deliver to nearby launch spots. The **Goose Hummock Shop,** 2 Rte. 132 (☎ **508/778-0877**), rents the usual craft; **Eastern Mountain Sports,** 233 Stevens St. (☎ **508/755-1072**), offers rental kayaks—tents and sleeping bags, too—and sponsors occasional overnights to Washburn Island in Waquoit Bay, as well as free clinics.

For experienced paddlers, Barnstable's **Great Marsh**—one of the largest in New England—offers beautiful waterways out to Sandy Neck. For those who prefer to do their sightseeing underwater, **East Coast Divers,** 237 Rte. 28 (☎ **508/775-1185**), attends to all snorkeling and scuba needs, including instruction and charters; for the super-hardy, they're open year-round.

WHALE WATCHING   Provincetown is about an hour closer to the whales' preferred feeding grounds; then again, it would take you at least an hour (possibly *hours* on a summer weekend) to drive all the way down-Cape. If your time and itinerary are limited, hop aboard at **Hyannis Whale Watch Cruises,** Barnstable Harbor (about ½ mile north of Route 6A on Mill Way), Barnstable (☎ **800/287-0374** or 508/362-6088; fax 508/362-9739), for a four-hour voyage on a 100-foot high-speed cruiser. Naturalists provide the narration, and should you fail to spot a whale, your next trek is free. Tickets $22 adults, $19 seniors, $10 children 4 to 12 mid-June to mid-September; call for schedule and off-season rates. Closed November to March.

TOURING BY RAIL, STEAMER & SLOOP

Cape Cod Scenic Railroad. 252 Main St., Hyannis. ☎ **800/872-4508** or 508/771-3788. Ticket $11.50 adult, $7.50 children 3–12. Departures daily at 10am, 12:30pm, and 3pm June to late Oct; call for off-season hours. Closed Jan.

Offering a chance to get off the gridlocked roads and actually see the countryside, three vintage cars make a leisurely trip to Buzzards Bay, with a stop in Sandwich; round-trip, the 42 miles take a little under two hours. Occasionally, special "ecology" tours are scheduled, led by a local naturalist and including a half-hour stop for a guided marsh walk in Sandwich's Talbots Point Conservation Preserve. The dinner trains are also very popular (though the food's unremarkable for the prices).

Hyannisport Harbor Cruises. Ocean Street Dock, Hyannis. ☎ **508/778-2600.** Fee $8 adults, free–$3.50 children 12 and under. Late June to Aug 16 departures daily; call for schedule. Closed Nov to early Apr.

For a fun and informative introduction to the harbor and its residents, take a leisurely—one- to two-hour—narrated tour aboard the Hy-Line's 1911 steamer replicas *Patience* and *Prudence*. Five family trips a day in season offer free passage for children under 12, but for a real treat take them on the Sunday 3:30pm "Ice Cream Float," which includes a design-your-own Ben & Jerry's sundae, or the Thursday 9pm "Jazz Boat," accompanied by a Dixieland band.

The *Hesperus*. Pier 16, Ocean St. Dock, Hyannis. ☎ **508/790-0077.** Fee $22 adults, $15 seniors and children 12 and under. Late May to early Sept daily 12:30, 3, and 5:30pm; call for off-season schedule. Closed Nov–Apr.

Offering an elegant means of exploring the harbor (while sneaking a peak at the Kennedy compound), the 50-foot John Alden sloop accommodates only 22 passengers, who are welcome to help trim the sails or even steer. Most opt to luxuriate in the sparkling sun and cooling breezes. The sporadic moonlight sails are especially romantic.

THE KENNEDY LEGACY

For a lovely sightseeing drive, mosey around the moneyed Sound shore to the west. Don't even bother tracking down the Kennedy Compound in Hyannisport; it's effectively screened from view, and you'll see more at the John F. Kennedy Hyannis Museum (a mostly photographic display) in town. Or if you absolutely have to satisfy your curiosity, take a harbor cruise (see above).

John F. Kennedy Hyannis Museum. 397 Main St. (in the center of town), Hyannis. ☎ **800/ 492-6647** or 508/775-2201. Admission $3 adults, children under 16 free. June–Aug Mon–Sat 10am–4pm, Sun 1–4pm; Sept–May Wed–Sat 10am–4pm.

This primarily photographic display—supplemented by a brief video program narrated by Walter Cronkite—captures the Kennedys *en famille* during the glory days of 1934 to 1963. Those last three years were a bit chaotic (some 25,000 well-wishers thronged the roads when the senator and president-to-be returned from the 1960 Democratic Convention), but JFK continued to treasure the Cape as "the one place I can think and be alone." The candid shots included in this permanent display capture some of the quieter moments, as well as the legendary charm.

SHOPPING

Although Hyannis is undoubtedly the commercial center of the Cape, the stores you'll find there are fairly standard for the most part; you could probably find their ilk in Iowa. It's in the wealthy enclaves west of Hyannis, and along the antiquated King's Highway (Route 6A) to the north, that you're likely to find the real gems.

ANTIQUES/COLLECTIBLES   ✪ **The Farmhouse,** 1340 Main St. (about one mile south of Route 28), Osterville (☎ **508/420-2400**), is Carolyn and Barry Crawford's 1742 farmhouse set up like an adult-scale dollhouse, and the "lifelike" settings should lend decorative inspiration. Self-confident sorts will go wild in the barn; it's packed with intriguing architectural salvage.

Of the hundreds of antique shops scattered through the region, perhaps a dozen qualify as destinations for well-schooled collectors. ✪ **Harden Studios,** 3264 Rte. 6A (in the center of town), Barnstable (☎ **508/362-7711**), is one. Owner Charles M. Harden, ASID, used to supply to-the-trade-only dealers in the Boston Design Center. An architect by training, he renovated this deaconage, built around 1720, to display his finds. Some items, such as the primitive portraits and mourning embroidery, are all but extinct outside of museums.

Prince Jenkins Antiques, 975 Rte. 6A (at the intersection of Route 149), W. Barnstable (no phone), is one spooky shop, the piled-high kind that captivates scavengers. Wend your way (carefully) around the narrow path still discernible amid the heaped-up inventory, and you'll come across case upon case of vintage jewelry and watches, paintings, tapestries, urns and jade carvings, musty 18th-century garb, a Pilgrim chair or two, and all sorts of oddments, including—on our last visit—a glass-topped coffin complete with skeleton. The aged proprietor, Dr. Alfred King, D.F.A., claims that the admittedly ancient-looking house next door belonged to Gov. William Bradford in 1626—a dubious boast, given that the town wasn't settled until 1639, and Bradford was awfully busy in Plymouth. But what would you expect from a man whose card reads "In Business since 1773"? Closed mid-November to March.

ART/CRAFTS   The intricate, infinitely variable patterns of Jacquard weaving not only prompted the Industrial Revolution but prefigured the computer chip. Today there's only one weaver in the United States creating Jacquard designs by hand, and that's Bob Black, who began his trade at age 14 and refined it at the Rhode Island School of Design. He specializes in custom coverlets on commission; the double-sided designs can be used as blankets, throws, even tapestries. Customers often ask for special motifs to be worked in, with the ultimate goal a one-of-a-kind, commemorative artifact. **The Blacks' Handweaving Shop** is at 597 Rte. 6A (about one mile west of Rte. 149), W. Barnstable (☎ **508/361-3955**).

Ex-Nantucketer Bob Marks fashions the only authentic Nantucket lightship baskets crafted off-island, and as aficionados know, they don't come cheap (a mere handbag typically runs in the thousands). **Oak and Ivory** is at 1112 Main St. (about 1 mile south of Route 28), Osterville (☎ **508/428-9425**).

Believe it or not, weathervane theft is a real threat on the Cape, so valuable are some of these copper toppers. Some of Marilyn Strauss's prize specimens, displayed in an informal museum adjoining her shop, **Salt & Chestnut Weathervanes,** 651 Route 6A (about ¹/₃ mile west of Route 149), W. Barnstable (☎ **508/ 362-6085**), would fetch as much as $30,000, were she willing to part with them. Mostly she's in the business of creating replicas and custom orders, with the help of two dozen local artisans. Prices range from about $200 to $2,000.

WHERE TO STAY

Expensive

✪ **Ashley Manor Inn.** 3660 Rte. 6A (about 1 mile E of Hyannis Rd.), Barnstable, MA 02630. ☎ **508/362-8044.** 2 rms, 4 suites. A/C. Summer (including full breakfast) $115–$135 double, $160–$175 suite. AE, JCB, MC, V.

Nearly everyone has a vision in mind of the perfect country inn; this one could well fulfill it. The house is a much-modified 1699 colonial mansion that still retains many of its original features, including a hearth with beehive oven (the perfect place to sip port on a blustery evening), built-in corner cupboards in the wainscoted dining room, and wide-board floors, many of them brightened with Nantucket-style splatter-paint. The rooms, all but one of which boast a fireplace, are spacious and inviting, a true retreat. The two-acre property itself is shielded from the road by an enormous privet hedge, and fragrant boxwood camouflages a Har-Tru tennis court. (You'll find loaner bikes beside it, ready to roll.) Romantics can seek shelter in the flower-fringed gazebo, and breakfast on the brick patio is worth waking up for: you wouldn't want to miss the homemade granola, much less the main event—quiche, perhaps, or crêpes.

Inn at Fernbrook. 481 Main St. (about ¹/₂ mile S of Rte. 28), Centerville, MA 02632. ☎ **508/775-4334.** Fax 508/778-4455. 5 suites, 1 cottage. Summer (including full breakfast and afternoon tea) $125–$270 suite, $125 cottage. AE, DISC, MC, V.

An imposing 1881 showplace, set back from the street by a circular drive, this house has an unmistakable aura of grandeur, borne out by its pedigree and roster of former residents. Howard Marston, owner of Boston's Parker House hotel, commissioned no less a landscape architect than Frederick Law Olmsted (designer of New York's Central Park) to beautify his Queen Anne–style country retreat with a heart-shaped "sweetheart" rose garden, which remains intact and lovely. Among the subsequent owners were Dr. Herbert Kalmus, coinventor of Technicolor (his house guests included Gloria Swanson, Cecil B. DeMille, and Walt Disney), and the Catholic church, in the person of Cardinal Francis Spellman, who broke bread here with both Kennedy and Nixon. Current owners Brian Gallo and Sal DiFlorio restored the manse to not-too-fussy Victorian splendor, while retaining subsequent architectural quirks. The Spellman Room, which the Cardinal converted into a chapel, remains pretty much as revised—except for an elaborate and invitingly profane canopy bed where the altar once stood. The two-bedroom Olmsted Suite, occupying the entire third floor, boasts a fireplaced living room straight out of *Holiday* and steep stairs leading to a balcony and sundeck.

Moderate

Captain Gosnold Village. 230 Gosnold St. (off Ocean St., about 1 mile S of town center), Hyannis, MA 02601. ☎ **508/775-9111.** 33 rms, 8 efficiencies. A/C TV TEL. Summer $75 double, $250 efficiency. MC, V. Closed Dec–Mar.

A cluster of grizzled cottages with gay pink shutters, this little compound would make a pleasant family retreat. Far enough from the bustle of downtown, and a short walk from placid Kalmus Beach, the cottages—which can be rented by the room and day, as well as in toto or by the week—are remarkably cheery within, with fresh, modern decor. A lifeguard watches over the small outdoor pool, and lawn games and a play area keep kids happily occupied. For the inevitable rainy day, the office rents out videos.

✪ Charles Hinckley House. 8 Scudder Lane (at Rte. 6A about 1¹/₂ miles E of Rte. 132), Barnstable, MA 02630. ☎ **508/362-9924.** 4 rms. Summer (including full breakfast) $119–$149 double. No credit cards.

Set atop a riotous wildflower garden, this hip-roofed 1809 Federal manse hints at tasteful pleasures within—a promise on which it fully delivers. The period decor is almost stark, and deeply pleasing to those who prefer authenticity to misguided colonial clichés. Yet the comfort level is nonpareil: Fireplaces are a given in each room, and some have special features, such as a conservatory/sitting room with bay views (that's part of the Plum Suite) or a window seat flanked by walls of well-stocked bookshelves (the Library Room). Innkeeper Miya Patrick is a caterer of local renown, and her breakfasts are delightful eye-openers: They might begin with a fresh fruit plate (mangoes, raspberries, and bananas, for instance) adorned with edible flowers, and culminate in a crabcake variation on eggs Benedict. A five-minute walk down a historic lane lined with stone walls will bring you to the bay.

East Bay Lodge. 199 East Bay Rd. (about ¹/₂ mile SE of Main St.), Osterville, MA 02655. ☎ **800/933-2782** or 508/428-5200. Fax 508/428-5432. 18 rms. A/C MINIBAR TV TEL. Summer (including continental breakfast) $89–$149 double. AE, CB, DC, DISC, MC, V.

Well priced for its rarefied location (in a residential section of the Cape's wealthiest town), this modern, motel-like annex to a popular, historic restaurant is likely to disappoint those seeking the camaraderie of a real country inn. The reproduction-appointed rooms are perfectly pretty, though, and the grounds are inviting, with a croquet course, three tennis courts, and a photogenic gazebo. Best of all is the private bay beach within a few minutes' walk.

Hyannis Harborview Resort. 213 Ocean St. (opposite the Hy-Line Ferry dock), Hyannis, MA 02601. ☎ **800/676-0000** or 508/775-4420. Fax 508/775-7995. 126 rms, 10 suites. A/C TV TEL. Summer (including continental breakfast) $75–$125 double, $105–$170 suite. AE, CB, DC, DISC, MC, V. Closed Nov–Apr.

Situated right on the waterfront, this sprawling modern establishment makes a convenient stopover for the island-bound; it's also a good choice for those who select Hyannis as a base for sampling its nightlife: One of the livelier restaurant/bars, The Reach (see "Live and Loud" under "Barnstable After Dark," below), is right on the premises, and most of the others are within an easy walk. The rooms—those higher up afford nice harbor views—are done up in pleasing color schemes with contemporary blond-wood furniture. Among the other draws are outdoor and indoor pools, plus a whirlpool and exercise room.

Sea Breeze Inn. 397 Sea St. (about 1 mile S of the West End Rotary), Hyannis, MA 02601. ☎ **508/771-7213.** 14 rms. A/C TV TEL. Summer (including continental breakfast) $65–$130 double. AE, DISC, MC, V.

Within whistling distance of the beach, this classic shingled beach house has been decked out with the totems of small-town America: a picket fence, exuberant plantings, and even a wooden rocker built for two couples—or better yet, one. All this attention to the exterior is mirrored in the neat and cheerful interior. The coast used to be lined with superior guest houses of this sort, and to find one still in its prime is a real treat. Also on the intensively gardened grounds are three cottages that rent by the week, including one with a "honeymooners'" double Jacuzzi.

Simmons Homestead Inn. 288 Scudder Ave. (at W. Main St. about ¹/₄ mile W of the West End Rotary), Hyannis, MA 02601. ☎ **800/637-1649** or 508/778-4999. Fax 508/790-1342. 10 rms. Summer (including full breakfast) $110–$145 double. AE, DC, MC, V.

A former ad exec and race-car driver, innkeeper Bill Putman has a silly side and isn't afraid to show it. He started collecting animal artifacts—stuffed toys, sculptures, even needlepoint and wallpaper—to differentiate the rather traditional rooms in this rambling 1820s captain's manse and kind of got carried away. All the animalia, plus his general friendliness, serve as an icebreaker, though: This is an inn where you'll find everyone mulling around the hearth sipping complementary wine (served "sixish") while they compare notes and nail down dinner plans. Guests who prefer privacy may book the spiffily updated "servants' quarters," a spacious, airy cottage with its own private deck. Well-known athletes (such as O.J., in sunnier days, and Bruce Jenner) and performers from the nearby Cape Cod Melody Tent (e.g., Carly Simon) have sought refuge here over the years, and Putman promises every guest a special spot that's "ten million miles from anywhere, and two minutes from everything."

Inexpensive

ⓢ The Acworth Inn. 4352 Rte. 6 (near the Yarmouthport border), Cummaquid, MA 02637. ☎ **800/362-6363** or 508/362-3330. 6 rms. Summer (including full breakfast) $85–$95 double. AE, MC, V.

Cheryl Ferrell knows that it's the small touches that make a stay memorable, and anyone lucky enough to land in this sunnily rehabbed house is sure to remember every last one, from the cranberry spritzer offered on arrival to the handmade chocolates that take the place of pillow mints. She even grinds the whole grains that go into her home-baked breakfasts, in the form of cinnamon rolls or fruit-topped waffles. She or her husband, Jack, will gladly pick you up at the Hyannis airport, if you arrange it ahead of time, and from then on their complimentary bikes may be all you need in the way of wheels.

ⓞ Inn at the Mills. 71 Rte. 149 (at the intersection of Rte. 28), Marstons Mills, MA 02648. ☎ **508/428-2967.** 6 rms. Summer (including continental breakfast) $65–$100 double. No credit cards.

Unheralded by so much as a sign, this 1780 inn looks more like someone's enviable private estate—an illusion maintained once one ventures indoors, right into a rustic beamed kitchen. Beyond are further common rooms: a proper parlor with wingback chairs, and a sunporch harboring a white baby grand and comfy wicker couches. The view from here is of a small pool and below, beyond a sloping lawn, a good-sized pond occupied by gliding waterfowl and flanked by an inviting gazebo. The rooms are the picture of tasteful primness, too—except for the cathedral-ceilinged "hayloft" room, with dimensions fit for a medieval dining hall. This is where the honeymooners usually end up, after a picture-perfect gazebo wedding.

WHERE TO DINE

A couple of peripherals bear mention here: **Cape Cod Potato Chips,** on Breed's Hill Road at Independence Way, off Route 132 in Hyannis (☎ 508/775-7253), really *are* the world's best. Free factory tours are offered from Monday to Friday from 10am to 4pm. And **Country Store,** 877 Main St. in the center of Osterville (☎ 508/428-2097), is the essence of an old-fashioned general store: Proprietor Charlie Kalas, who grew up here, is now the grown-up dispensing penny candy and ice-cream pops.

Very Expensive

✪ Alberto's Ristorante. 360 Main St., Hyannis. ☎ **508/778-1770.** Reservations recommended. Main courses $13–$25. AE, CB, DC, DISC, MC, V. Daily 11am–11pm. ITALIAN.

By far the most sophisticated restaurant in town, Alberto's explores the full range of Italian cuisine, with a classicist's attention to components and composition. Owner-chef Felisberto Barreiro's sole Florentine, for instance, consists of gray sole fresh from Chatham, topped with lobster, spinach, and Fontina and enhanced with a *beurre blanc* flecked with sun-dried tomatoes. Hand-cut pasta is a specialty, including the ultrarich seafood ravioli cloaked in saffron cream sauce. Though the atmosphere is elegant, with sconces shedding a warm glow over well-spaced, linen-draped tables, the atmosphere is not one of hushed reverence: People clearly come here to have a good time, and the absolute assurance of friendly service and fabulous food ensures that they do. Indicative of the all-out approach is the fact that the restaurant offers limo service from area hotels. Locals who appreciate a bargain know to come between 4 and 6pm, when a full dinner, with soup, salad, and dessert, costs as little as $11.

✪ The Regatta of Cotuit at the Crocker House. 4613 Falmouth Rd. (Rte. 28, near the Mashpee border), Cotuit. ☎ **508/428-5715.** Reservations recommended. Main courses $18–$26. AE, MC, V. Daily 5:30–10pm. NEW AMERICAN.

The year-round cousin of the Regatta at Falmouth-by-the-Sea (see "Where to Dine" under "Falmouth," above) serves many of the same signature dishes—such as the stellar lamb *en chemise*—in a suite of charmingly decorated Federal-era rooms: This 1790 Cape was once a stagecoach inn. The wayfarers of old couldn't possibly have fared as well. The cuisine is at once exquisite and hearty, fortified by herbs and vegetables plucked fresh from the kitchen garden, and the mood is invariably festive.

Expensive

The Black Cat. 165 Ocean St. (opposite the Ocean St. Dock), Hyannis. ☎ **508/778-1233.** Main courses $9–$24. AE, DC, MC, V. Late May to early Sept daily 11:30am to 10pm; call for off-season hours. NEW AMERICAN.

Conveniently located less than a block from the Hy-Line ferries, this is a fine place to catch a quick bite or full meal while you wait for your boat to come in. The menu is pretty basic—steak, pasta, and of course fish—but attention is paid to the details; the onion rings, for instance, are made fresh. The dining room, with its bar of gleaming mahogany and brass, will appeal to chilled travelers on a blustery day; in fine weather, you might prefer the porch.

East Bay Lodge. 199 East Bay Rd. (¹/₂ mile SE of Main St.), Osterville. ☎ **508/428-5200.** Fax 508/428/5432. Reservations recommended; jacket requested. Main courses $14–$19. AE, CB, DC, DISC, MC, V. Late May to mid-Oct Tues–Fri 6–9pm, Sat 5:30–9pm, Sun 11am–2pm and 5:30–9pm; dinner only off-season. AMERICAN.

Straddling both traditional and innovative cuisine, this charming century-old restaurant is *the* place to eat in moneyed Osterville. The Sunday brunch segues into an evening shellfish buffet, both of which are impressive spreads, and a piano accompaniment adds panache to weekend suppers—as do the 400-plus wines in stock. The menu may look a little stodgy (there's even prime rib on weekends), but it's jazzed up by such grace notes as a garlicky red pepper coulis to accompany the sautéed jumbo shrimp, or ratatouille to go with grilled swordfish.

Ristorante Barolo. One Financial Place (297 North St., the West End Rotary), Hyannis. ☎ **508/778-2878.** Main courses $8–$20. AE, DC, MC, V. Jun–Sept Sun–Thurs 4–11pm, Fri–Sat 4pm–midnight; call for off-season hours. ITALIAN.

Part of a smart-looking brick office complex, this thoroughly up-to-date Italian restaurant does everything right, from offering extra-virgin olive oil for dunking its crusty bread to getting those pastas perfectly al dente. Patrons favor the filet Barolo, an Angus steak served with a reduction sauce of Barolo wine, with sun-dried tomatoes and wild mushrooms.

Moderate

✪ **Baxter's Boat House.** 177 Pleasant St. (near Steamship Authority ferry), Hyannis. ☎ **508/755-4490.** Main courses $8–$14. AE, MC, V. Late May to early Sept Mon–Sat 11:30am–10pm, Sun 11:30am–9pm; call for off-season hours. Closed mid-Oct through Mar. SEAFOOD.

A shingled shack on a jetty jutting out into the harbor, Baxter's has catered to the boating crowd since the mid-1950s, with Cape classics such as fried clams and fish virtually any way you like it, from baked to blackened.

⑤ **Fazio's Trattoria.** 586 Main St. (in the center of town), Hyannis. ☎ **508/771-7445.** Reservations recommended. Main courses $9–$12. AE, MC, V. Jun–Aug Mon–Thurs 5–10pm, Fri–Sun 5–11pm; call for off-season hours. ITALIAN.

This tiny storefront cafe, decorated with the traditional checkered tablecloths and Chianti bottles, delivers the old-world goods with new-wave brio. The oak-fired brick oven produces intelligently topped pizzas in the Neapolitan (regular) or rustic (thin-crusted) mode, as well as *boccacini*—enticing mouthfuls—of bruschetta and focaccia; it's also used to grilled ribeye steaks and fresh-caught fish. Pasta is a staple, of course, and there are usually a dozen or so handmade varieties, including *fusilli* Pavarotti, in a cream sauce flecked with olives and sun-dried tomatoes. Pace yourself: There's homemade cannoli and other treats still to come.

Joseph's Cafe. 825 Main St. (in the center of town), Osterville. ☎ **508/420-1742.** Main courses $10–$18. Daily 7am–2:30pm, 5–9pm. AE, MC, V. INTERNATIONAL.

A cool recess lined with bookshelves and ivy, with occasional splashes of Mediterranean color (in the appointments as well as the cuisine), chef/owner Joe Murray's place displays none of the glitz that this venue could get away with. From his low-fat Alfredo to spur-of-the-moment stir-fries and salads, this is *paisan* cooking: labor-intensive, based on the best seasonal produce, and festive at heart. The relatively proletarian prices are a surprise bonus.

Steamers Grill & Bar. 235 Ocean St. (opposite the Hy-Line dock), Hyannis. ☎ **508/778-0818.** Main courses $10–$19. AE, DC, MC, V. Late May to early Sept daily 11:30am–10pm; call for off-season hours. Closed mid-Nov through Mar. AMERICAN.

Around sunset, the deck starts to fill to overflowing. While the majority are imbibing and revving up for the night, a few will dally over the food: mesquite-grilled swordfish or steak, or maybe stuffed shrimp. Night owls need plenty of protein, after all.

Tugboats. 21 Arlington St. (at the Hyannis Marina, off Willow St.), Hyannis. ☎ **508/775-6433.** Main courses $11–$15. AE, DISC, MC, V. July–Aug daily 7:30am–10:30pm; call for off-season hours. Closed Nov to mid-Apr. AMERICAN.

Yet another harborside perch for munching and ogling, this one's especially appealing: The two spacious outdoor decks are angled just right to catch the sunset, with cocktail/frappes to match—or perhaps a bottle of Moët et Chandon. Forget fancy dining and chow down on blackened swordfish bites (topping a Caesar salad, perhaps) or lobster fritters, or the double-duty Steak Neptune, topped with scallops and shrimp. Among the "decadent desserts" (must we constantly be reminded?) are a shortbread-crusted bourbon pecan pie, and a key lime pie purportedly lifted straight from Papa's.

⑤ Up the Creek. 36 Old Colony Blvd. (about 1 mile S of Main St.), Hyannis. ☎ **508/ 771-7866.** Reservations recommended. Main courses $9–$13. AE, CB, DC, DISC, MC, V. Jun–Aug daily 11:30am–10pm; call for off-season hours. INTERNATIONAL.

Good luck finding it (tucked away in a residential area) and better luck getting in! Locals know a good deal when they see one, and dinner prices in the single digits draw an avid crowd. House specialties include a seafood strudel cloaked with hollandaise, and a broiled seafood platter comprising half a lobster, clams casino, scallops, scrod, and baked stuffed shrimp (that's the priciest entree at all of $13). Decorated like an Ivy League boathouse, the restaurant has grace and style, even when the occupancy maxes out.

Inexpensive

The Egg & I. 521 Main St. (in the center of town), Hyannis. ☎ **508/771-1596.** Most items under $10. AE, DC, DISC, MC, V. Daily 11pm–1pm. AMERICAN.

Yes, those are the correct hours. This Tudor-storefront diner *opens* at 11 at night, then serves past noon. A town with this many bars needs a place where patrons and staff alike can unwind and/or sober up after last call; a wholesome meal wouldn't hurt either. Breakfast is usually the meal of choice, especially the "create an omelette" option, but the pancakes—from chocolate-chip to fruit-loaded Swedish—are strong contenders. Children go gaga over the Mickey Mouse waffle (only $2, with bacon or sausage), and those who feel silly having breakfast before bed can order sandwiches or one of a dozen or so daily specials that change with the season.

BARNSTABLE & HYANNIS AFTER DARK

Low-Key Evenings

Baxter's Boat House. 177 Pleasant St. (see "Where to Dine," above), Hyannis. ☎ **508/ 755-4490.** No cover.

This congenial little lounge, with map-topped tables and low-key blues piano, draws an attractive crowd, including the occasional vacationing celebrity.

East Bay Lodge. 199 East Bay Rd. (see "Where to Dine," above), Osterville. ☎ **508/ 428-5200.** No cover.

For those who have yet to give up dinner dancing, a pianist playing jazz, cabaret, and oldies provides incentive to get up and sway or swing.

Roadhouse Cafe. 488 South St., Hyannis. ☎ **508/775-2386.** No cover.

If raucous rock is the last thing you seek in after-dinner entertainment, duck into this dark-paneled bar, decorated in burgundy leather like an English gentlemen's club. The bar stocks 48 boutique brews, in addition to all the usual hard, soft, and sweet liquors, and you won't go hoarse trying to converse over the soft jazz.

Live & Loud

Asa Bearse House. 415 Main St., Hyannis. ☎ **508/771-4444.** Cover $3–$5 in season.

You'd never suspect this dainty Victorian of harboring, under a peaked glass roof, a dance club that throbs to progressive rock. The "Reading Room" bar resembles a frat house in F. Scott Fitzgerald's day, complete with helter-skelter bookshelves, conversational nooks, and a moosehead as mascot.

Duval Street Station. 477 Yarmouth Rd. (about 1 mile NE of Main St.), Hyannis. ☎ **508/ 771-7511.** Nominal cover charge Fri–Sat in season.

Hyannis's first (and so far, only) gay bar occupies an old train station. The lower level is a comfortable lounge, and upstairs there's a dance bar complete with light show and DJ mixes that spin from Latin rhythms to New Wave to "gay disco classics" of the 1970s and 1980s.

Harry's. 700 Main St., Hyannis. ☎ **508/778-4188.** Cover Fri–Sat $1–$2.

There's hardly room to eat here, let alone rock, but the cramped dance floor makes for instant camaraderie. This kind of music—blues, jazz, rock, and blends thereof—really demands to be absorbed in an intimate space. Great southern kitchen at work here, too.

Pufferbellies Entertainment Complex. 183R Rte. 132 (at Yarmouth Rd.), Hyannis. ☎ **800/233-4301** or 508/790-4300. Cover about $5, season pass $10.

This rehabbed railroad roundhouse is huge enough to accommodate not only 1,500 revelers but three distinct styles of revelry. The Flashbacks section is a Top-40 dance club; Little Texas goes for country-western two-stepping; and the outdoors, summers-only Caribbean Cafe brings in steel bands to accompany the barbecue. For the weekly schedule, call the 800 number listed above.

✪ **The Reach Caribbean Grill.** 213 Ocean St. (see "Where to Dine," above), Hyannis. ☎ **508/778-1113.** No cover.

Nothing says "kick back" like the mellow rumble of steel drums, or the easy-going rhythms of reggae—except maybe a tall, cool tropical drink, perhaps prefaced by a raw cherrystone clam or oyster shooter. Pulling into shore as the evening advances, you can hear the merrymaking ripple across the water; it's hard to resist the urge to join in.

Sophie's Bar & Grill. 334 Main St., Hyannis. ☎ **508/775-1111.** Cover $3–$5 in season.

The dance bar in back is where buttoned-down preppies convene to cut loose. The live rock leans to such freaky extremes as the Strangemen out of Martha's Vineyard, a quintet of platinum-pompadoured alien-dandies who describe their sound as "sci-fi rockabilly surf rock." Above-average pub food is another draw.

Steamers Grill & Bar. 235 Ocean St. (see "Where to Dine," above), Hyannis. ☎ **508/778-0818.** No cover.

Everyone's glowing with the day's exertions as they cram onto the deck to enjoy a lingering sunset with liberal libations. It's a young, sporty crowd for the most part (despite the fuddy-duddy duffers' motif in the downstairs Putter's Pub), drawn by the live bands on weekends.

The Big Top

✪ **The Cape Cod Melody Tent.** West End Rotary, Hyannis. (☎ **508/775-9100**). July to early Sept, curtain 8pm nightly. Tickets about $13–$37. Call for schedule.

Built as a summer theater in 1950, this billowy blue big-top proved even better suited to variety shows. A nonprofit venture since 1990 (proceeds fund other cultural initiatives Cape-wide), the Melody Tent hosted the major performers of the past half-century, from jazz greats to comedians, crooners to rockers. Every seat is a winner in this grand oval, only 20 banked aisles deep. There's also a children's theater program Wednesday mornings at 11am.

THE YARMOUTHS

19 miles (31km) E of Sandwich, 38 miles (61km) S of Provincetown

This cross-section represents the Cape at its best—and worst. Yarmouthport, on the Bay, is an enchanting town, clustered with interesting shops and architectural pearls, whereas the Sound-side "villages" of West to South Yarmouth are an object lesson in unbridled development run amuck. This section of Route 28 is a nightmarish gauntlet of ticky-tacky accommodations and "attractions." Yet even here you'll find a few spots worthy of the name. You've got the north shore for culture and refinement, the south shore for kitsch. Take your pick, or ricochet schizophrenically, enjoying the best of both worlds.

ESSENTIALS

GETTING THERE   After crossing either the Bourne or Sagamore Bridge, head east on Route 6 or 6A. Route 6A (north of Route 6's Exit 7) passes through the villages of Yarmouthport and Yarmouth. The villages of West Yarmouth, Bass River, and South Yarmouth are located along Route 28, east of Hyannis; to reach them from Route 6, take Exit 7 south (Yarmouth Road), or Exit 8 south (Station Street).

VISITOR INFORMATION   Contact the **Yarmouth Area Chamber of Commerce,** 657 Rte. 28, W. Yarmouth, MA 02673 (☎ **508/778-1008**).

OUTDOOR PURSUITS

BEACHES   Yarmouth boasts 11 saltwater and 2 pond beaches open to the public. The body-per-square-yard ratio can be pretty intense along the Sound, but so's the social scene, so no one seems to mind. The beachside parking lots charge $7 a day; to obtain a week-long sticker ($30), visit Town Hall at 1146 Route 28 in S. Yarmouth (☎ **508/398-2231**).

- **Bass River Beach,** off South Shore Drive in Bass River: Located at the mouth of the largest tidal river on the eastern seaboard, this Sound beach offers all the usual features, plus a bonus—a wheelchair-accessible fishing pier.
- **Grays Beach,** off Centre Street in Yarmouth: Tame waters excellent for children; adjoins the Callery-Darling Conservation Area (see "Nature Trails," below).
- **Parker's River Beach,** off South Shore Drive in Bass River: The usual amenities, plus a 20-foot gazebo for the sun-shy.
- **Seagull Beach,** off South Sea Avenue in W. Yarmouth: Rolling dunes, a boardwalk, and all the necessary facilities attract a young crowd. Bring bug spray, though: greenhead flies get the munchies in July.

FISHING   Of the five fishing ponds in the Yarmouth area, Long Pond near S. Yarmouth is known for its large-mouth bass and pickerel; for details and a license (shellfishing is another option), visit Town Hall at 1146 Route 28 in S. Yarmouth (☎ **508/398-2231**). You can cast for striped bass and bluefish off the pier at Bass River Beach (see "Beaches," above).

NATURE TRAILS   Slightly east of Yarmouthport, follow Centre Street about a mile north and bear northeast on Homers Dock Road; from here a 2^1/2-mile trail through the Callery-Darling Conservation Area leads to Grays Beach, where you can continue across the Bass Hole Boardwalk for a lovely view of the marsh.

MUSEUMS

✪ **The Winslow Crocker House.** 250 Rte. 6A (about ¹/₂ miles E of town center), Yarmouthport. ☎ **508/362-4385**. Admission $4 adult, $3.50 seniors, $2 children 5–12. June to mid-Oct hourly tours Tues–Thurs and Sat–Sun noon–5pm (last tour at 4pm); closed mid-Oct through May.

The only property on the Cape currently preserved by the prestigious Society for the Preservation of New England Antiquities, this house built around 1780 deserves every honor. Not only is it a lovely example of the shingled Georgian style, it's packed with outstanding antiques—Jacobean to Chippendale—collected in the 1930s by Mary

Thacher, a descendant of the town's first land grantee. Anthony Thacher and his family had a rougher crossing than most: Their ship foundered off Cape Ann in 1635 (near an island that now bears their name), and though their four children drowned, Thacher and his wife were able to make it to shore, clinging to the family cradle. You'll come across a 1690 replica in the parlor. Thacher's son John, a colonel, built the house next door around 1680, and—with the help of two successive wives— raised a total of 21 children. All the museum-worthy objects in the Winslow Crocker House would seem to have similar stories to tell. For antique lovers, as well as anyone interested in local lore, this is a valuable cache and a very worthwhile stop.

KID STUFF

Children are likely to be enthralled by the rainy-day enticements of Route 28. Among the more enduringly appealing miniature golf courses clamoring for attention is **Pirate's Cove,** at 728 Route 28, S. Yarmouth (open daily 9am to 11pm in season), where the trap decor is strong on macabre humor. For something a little more wholesome, spend an afternoon at **Bray Farm,** a working 1800s farmstead maintained by the town of Yarmouth (☎ **508/778-1008**).

ZooQuarium. 674 Rte. 28 (midway between W. Yarmouth and Bass River), W. Yarmouth. ☎ **508/775-8883.** Admission $7.50 adults, $4.50 children 2–9. July–Aug daily 9:30am–8pm; off-season daily 9:30am–5pm. Closed late Nov to mid-Feb.

This slightly scruffy wildlife museum has made great strides in recent years toward blending entertainment with education. It's a little easier to enjoy the sea lion show once you've been assured that the stars *like* performing, have been trained with positive reinforcement only, and, furthermore, arrived with injuries that precluded their survival in the wild. The aquarium is arranged in realistic habitats, and the "zoo" consists primarily of indigenous fauna, both domesticated and wild (the pacing bobcat is liable to give you pause). Children will be entranced, and a very creditable effort is made to convey the need for ecological preservation.

SHOPPING

Route 6A through Yarmouthport and Yarmouth remains a rich vein of antique shops. Check them all out, if you're so inclined and have the time.

Most Cape antique stores offer plenty of "smalls" (decorative items such as glass, china, and silver) but scant the big stuff—major pieces of centuries-old furniture. There's plenty of the latter at ✪ **Nickerson Antiques,** 162 Rte. 6A (in the center of town), Yarmouthport (☎ **508/362-6426**), mostly imported from Great Britain and much of it skillfully refinished *in situ.*

The most colorful bookshop on the Cape (if not the whole East Coast) is ✪ **Parnassus Books,** 220 Rte. 6A (about ¼ mile east of town center), Yarmouthport (☎ **508/362-6420**). This jam-packed repository—housed in an 1858 Swedenborgian church—is the creation of Ben Muse, who has been collecting and selling vintage tomes since the 1960s. Relevant new stock, including the Cape-related reissues published by Parnassus Imprints, is offered alongside the older treasures, and don't expect much hand-holding on the part of the gruff proprietor. You'll earn his respect by knowing what you're looking for or, better yet, being willing to browse until it finds you. The outdoor racks, maintained on an honor system, are open 24 hours a day, for those who suffer from anbibliophobia—fear of lacking for reading material.

WHERE TO STAY

○ Captain Farris House. 308 Old Main St. (about ¹/₄ mile W of the Bass River Bridge), S. Yarmouth, MA 02664. ☎ **800/350-9477** or 508/760-2818. Fax 508/398-1262. 10 rms and suites. A/C TV TEL. $85–$175 double, $175–$225 suite. All rates include full breakfast. AE, MC, V.

"Sumptuous" is the only way to describe this small inn, improbably set amid a peaceful garden a block off bustling Route 28. Lavished with a blend of fine antiques and striking contemporary touches, this 1845 manse has been carved into lovely spaces designed for relaxing. Some suites are apartment-size, with fireplaced sitting rooms and whirlpool-tubbed bathrooms bigger than the average bedroom. Innkeeper Scott Toney whips up gourmet breakfasts replete with home-baked sweet breads, and can steer you to the best restaurants around. The central location puts the entire Cape, from Woods Hole to Provincetown, within a 45-minute drive, assuming you can bestir yourself from this pampering environment.

Ocean Mist. 97 South Shore Dr. (off Sea View Ave., E of the Bass River Bridge), S. Yarmouth, MA 02664. ☎ **800/248-MIST** or 508/398-2633. Fax 508/760-3151. A/C TV. Summer $135–$250 double. AE, DISC, MC, V.

If your children will settle for nothing less than a big motel on the water, this is among the more attractive ones chivvying for elbow room along the south shore. The rooms—some with duplex lofts and all with wet bars—are decorated in soothing sand tones, and the heated indoor pool, plus whirlpool, should compensate for the occasional cloudy day.

○ Wedgewood Inn. 83 Rte. 6A (in the center of town), Yarmouthport, MA 02675. ☎ **508/362-5157.** 9 rms. A/C. Summer (including full breakfast) $115–$160 double. AE, DISC, MC, V.

This elegant 1812 Federal house sits atop its undulating lawn with unabashed pride: The first house in town to be designed by an architect, it still reigns supreme as the loveliest home—one that happens to welcome strangers, though you won't feel like one for long. Innkeeper Gerrie Graham provides a warm welcome, complete with tea delivered to your room: one of the four formal front rooms (all with cherrywood pencil-post beds, Oriental rugs, antique quilts, and wood-burning fireplaces; some with private porches), the two romantic hideaways under the eaves, or the three spacious rooms, with canopy beds, fireplaces, and decks, wedged into the picturesque barn in back.

WHERE TO DINE

Don't miss **○ Hallet's,** on Route 6A in the center of Yarmouthport (☎ **508/362-3362**): Unsuspecting passersby invariably do a double-take when they happen upon this 1889 drugstore; Mary Hallet Clark, the granddaughter of town pharmacist (and postmaster and justice-of-the-peace) Thacher Taylor Hallet, is now the one dishing out frappes and floats from the original marble soda fountain.

○ Abbicci. 43 Main St. (near the Cummaquid border), Yarmouthport. ☎ **508/362-3501.** Reservations recommended. Main courses $13–$23. AE, DC, DISC, MC, V. Daily 11:30am–2:30pm and 5–10pm. ITALIAN.

Don't let the glaringly modernist ambience of this 1775 house turned upscale trattoria or the staff's citified attitude impinge on your enjoyment of this essentially rustic northern Italian cuisine. Just a taste of the veal *nocciole* (with toasted hazelnuts and a splash of balsamic vinegar), for instance, and you'll be transported straight to Tuscany. For a sampling of robust delicacies, don't miss the Sunday brunch.

⑨ Fiesta Grande. 737 Rte. 28 (midway between W. Yarmouth and Bass River), S. Yarmouth. ☎ **508/760-2924.** Main courses $5–$11. AE, DC, DISC, MC, V. June–Aug noon–10pm; call for off-season hours. MEXICAN.

Most of the Mexican food you'll encounter on the Cape is a well-intentioned approximation, but this is the real thing, whipped up by a hard-working chef from Mazatlán. Locally inspired specialties include shrimp fajitas and crabmeat enchiladas. The menu is so enticingly priced, it's tempting to try a bit of everything.

✪ Inaho. 157 Main St. (in the center of town), Yarmouthport. ☎ **508/362-5522.** Reservations recommended. Main courses $12–$20. MC, V. Early July to early Sept daily 5–11pm; call for off-season hours. JAPANESE.

What better use for the Cape's oceanic bounty than fresh-off-the-boat sushi? You can sit in communal awe at the sushi bar to watch chef/owner Yuji Watanabe perform his legerdemain or enjoy the privacy afforded by a gleaming wooden booth. An ordinary house on the outside, Inaho is a *shibui* sanctuary within, with minimalist decor (the traditional *shoji* screens and crisp navy-and-white banners) softened by tranquil music and service. On chilly days, opt for the tempura or a steaming bowl of *shabu-shabu*.

⑨ Jack's Outback. 161 Main St. (in the center of town), Yarmouthport. ☎ **508/362-6690.** Most items under $5. No credit cards. Daily 6:30am–2pm. AMERICAN.

This is a neighborhood cafe as Dr. Seuss might have imagined it: hyperactive (okay, semi-crazed) and full of fun. Chef/owner Jack Braginton-Smith makes a point of dishing out good-natured insults along with the home-style grub, which you bus yourself from the open kitchen, thereby saving big bucks as well as time. This is a perfect place for impatient children, who'll find lots of familiar, approachable dishes on the hand-scrawled posters that serve as a communal menu.

Lobster Boat. 681 Rte. 28 (midway between W. Yarmouth and Bass River), W. Yarmouth. ☎ **508/775-0486.** Main courses $10–18. AE, MC, V. May–Oct daily 4–10pm. SEAFOOD.

Just about every town seems to have one of these barnlike restaurants plastered with flotsam and serving the usual array of seafood in the usual manner, from deep-fried to boiled or broiled. True to its Sound-side setting, this tourist magnet advertises itself rather flamboyantly with a facade that features the hull of a ship grafted onto a shingled shack.

THE DENNISES

20 miles (32km) E of Sandwich, 36 miles (58km) S of Provincetown

If Dennis looks like a jigsaw puzzle piece snapped around Yarmouth, that's because it didn't break away until 1793, when the community adopted the name of Rev. Josiah Dennis, who'd ministered to Yarmouth's "East Parish" for close to four decades. His 1736 home has been restored and now serves as a local history museum.

In Dennis as in Yarmouth, virtually all the good stuff—pretty drives, inviting shops, restaurants with real personality—are in the north, along Route 6A. Route 28 is chockablock with more typical tourist attractions, RV parks, and family-oriented motels—some with fairly sophisticated facilities, but nonetheless undistinguished enough to warrant even a drive-by (the few exceptions are noted below). In budgeting your time, be sure to allocate the lion's share to Dennis itself and not its southern offshoots. It's as stimulating, yet unspoiled today as it was when it welcomed the Cape Playhouse, the country's oldest surviving straw-hat theater, in the anything-goes 1920s.

ESSENTIALS

GETTING THERE After crossing either the Bourne or Sagamore Bridge, head east on Route 6 or 6A. Route 6A passes through the villages of Dennis and East Dennis (which can also be reached via northbound Route 134 from Route 6's Exit 9). Route 134 south leads to the village of South Dennis; if you follow Route 134 all the way to Route 28, the village of West Dennis will be a couple of miles to your west, and Dennisport a couple of miles east.

VISITOR INFORMATION Contact the Dennis Chamber of Commerce, 242 Swan River Rd., W. Dennis, MA 02670 (☎ **800/243-9920** or 508/398-3568).

OUTDOOR PURSUITS

BEACHES Dennis harbors more than a dozen saltwater and two freshwater beaches open to nonresidents. The bay beaches are charming, and a big hit with families, who prize the uninsistent surf, so soft it won't bring toddlers to their knees. The beaches on the Sound tend to attract wall-to-wall families, but the parking lots are usually not too crowded, since so many beachgoers are billeted within walking distance. The lots charge $8 per day; for a week-long permit ($25), visit Town Hall on Main Street in S. Dennis (☎ **508/394-8300**).

- **Chapin Beach,** off Route 6A in Dennis: A nice, long bay beach pocked with occasional boulders and surrounded by dunes. No lifeguard, but there are rest rooms.
- **Corporation Beach,** off Route 6A in Dennis: Before it filled in with sand, this bay beach—with wheelchair-accessible boardwalk, lifeguards, snack bar, rest rooms, and a children's play area—was once a packet landing owned by a ship-building corporation comprised of area residents. It was donated to the town by Mary Thacher, owner of Yarmouthport's Winslow Crocker House (see "Museums" in "The Yarmouths," above).
- **Mayflower Beach,** off Route 6A in Dennis: This 1,200-foot bay beach has the necessary amenities, plus an accessible boardwalk. The tidal pools attract lots of children.
- **Scargo Lake** in Dennis: This large kettlehole pond (formed by a melting fragment of a glacier) has two pleasant beaches: Scargo Beach, accessible right off Route 6A, and Princess Beach, off Scargo Hill Road, where there are rest rooms and a picnic area.
- **West Dennis Beach,** off Route 28 in W. Dennis: This long (1½-mile) but narrow beach along the Sound has lifeguards, a playground, snack bar, rest rooms, and a special kite-flying area. The eastern end is reserved for residents; the western end tends, in any case, to be less packed.

BIKING/RECREATIONAL PATHS The 25-mile **Cape Cod Rail Trail** (☎ 508/896-3491) starts—or, depending on your perspective, ends—here, on Rte. 134, one-half mile south of Route 6's Exit 9. Once a Penn-Central track, this 8-foot-wide paved bikeway extends all the way to Wellfleet (with a few on-road lapses), passing through woods, marshes, and dunes. Sustenance is never too far off-trail, and plenty of bike shops dot the course. The shop closest to this trailhead is **All Right Bikes,** at 118 Route 28 in W. Dennis (☎ 508/394-3544), which stocks relevant paraphernalia (car racks, child trailers) and in-line skates as well. It's more than a mile away, but provides a free Chamber of Commerce booklet outlining several low-traffic routes. (Another paved bike path runs along **Old Bass Road** 3½ miles north to

Route 6A.) For joggers and fitness freaks in general, the 1 ¹/₂-mile **Lifecourse trail,** located at Old Bass River and Access roads in S. Dennis, features 20 exercise stations along its tree-shaded path. **Crow's Pasture,** accessible from South Street in the north-easterly corner of E. Dennis, offers 1 ¹/₂ miles of dirt roads leading through evergreen groves to marsh and beach.

FISHING   Fishing is allowed in Fresh Pond and Scargo Lake, where the catch includes trout and small-mouth bass; for a license (shell-fishing is also permitted), visit Town Hall on Main Street in S. Dennis (☎ 508/394-8300). Plenty of people drop a line off the Bass River Bridge along Route 28 in W. Dennis. Those with higher, or perhaps larger, aspirations, can head out from the bridge aboard a **Champion Line charter** (☎ 508/398-2266). Several charter boats operate out of the Northside Marina in E. Dennis's Sesuit Harbor, including the *Bluefin* (☎ 800/244-6464 or 508/697-2093).

NATURE TRAILS   Behind the Town Hall parking lot on Main Street in S. Dennis, a half-mile walk along the **Indian Lands Conservation Trail** leads to the Bass River, where blue herons and kingfishers often take shelter. Dirt roads off South Street in E. Dennis, beyond the Quivet Cemetery, lead to **Crow's Pasture,** a patch-work of marshes and dunes bordering the bay; this circular trail is about a 2 ¹/₂-mile round-trip.

WATER SPORTS   **Cape Cod Boats,** located on the eastern side of the Bass River Bridge along Route 28 in W. Dennis (☎ 508/394-9268) rents out canoes, sail-boards, sunfish, and motorboats, by the hour, day, or week. Located on the small and placid Swan River, Cape Cod Waterways, 16 Rte. 28, Dennisport (☎ 508/398-0080), rents canoes, kayaks, and paddleboats for exploring 200-acre Swan Pond (less than a mile north) or Nantucket Sound (2 miles south).

A Museum

Jericho House and Barn Museum. Trotting Park Rd. (at Old Main St., off Rte. 28 about ¹/₂ mile E of the Bass River Bridge), W. Dennis. ☎ 508/398-6736. Donations accepted. July–Aug Wed and Fri 2–4pm. Closed Sept–June.

For a century and a half, this classic 1801 Cape house remained in the family of its builder, Capt. Theophilus Baker, the model for Richard Henry Dana's *Two Years Before the Mast.* Its mostly Federal furnishings embody the understated elegance of the era. Out back is an 1810 barn housing assorted displays, from a miniature saltworks (the clearest possible depiction of one of the Cape's earliest and most lucrative industries) to an ingenious "driftwood zoo" improvised several decades ago by a playful summerer.

Kid Stuff

Dennisport boasts the best rainy-day—or any-day—destination for little kids on the entire Cape, the **Discovery Days Children's Museum & Toy Shop,** at 444 Rte. 6A (☎ 800/298-1600 or 508/398-1600). For a nominal admission fee ($4 adults, $4.50 children 1 to 18 and seniors), whole families can amuse themselves amid a vast edu-cational playspace equipped with a "bubble-ology" lab, a frozen-shadow wall, a trans-parent piano, and all sorts of other fun stuff. On Friday mornings in season, at 9:30 and 11:30am, the **Cape Playhouse** at 36 Hope Lane in Dennis (☎ 508/385-3911), hosts various visiting companies which mount musicals geared to children 4 and up; at only $5, tickets go fast.

Shopping

You can pretty much ignore Route 28. There's a growing cluster of antique shops in Dennisport, but the stock is flea-market level and requires more patience than most mere browsers—as opposed to avid collectibles collectors—may be able to muster. Save your time, and money, for the better shops along Route 6A, where you'll also find fine contemporary crafts.

More than 136 dealers stock the co-op **Antiques Center of Cape Cod,** 243 Rte. 6A (about one mile south of town center), Dennis (☎ **508/385-6400**); it's the largest such enterprise on the Cape. You'll find all the usual "smalls" on the first floor; the big stuff—from blanket chests to copper bathtubs—beckons above.

Eldred's, 1483 Rte. 6A (about ¹/₄ mile west of town center), E. Dennis (☎ **508/385-3116**), where the gavel has been wielded for more than 40 years, is the Cape's most prestigious auction house. Specialties include Oriental art, marine art, and Americana. Call for schedule.

With Eldred's (see above) so close, ✪ **Webfoot Farm Antiques,** 1475 Rte. 6A (about ¹/₄ mile west of town center), E. Dennis (☎ **508/385-2334**)—occupying most of an 1854 captain's house—gets the cream of the crop.

WHERE TO STAY

Expensive

✪ **Lighthouse Inn.** 4 Lighthouse Rd. (off Lower County Rd.), ¹/₂ mile S of Rte. 6A), W. Dennis, MA 02670. ☎ **508/398-2244.** Fax 508/398-5658. 34 rms, 27 cottages. A/C TV TEL. Summer (including full breakfast and dinner) $160–$240 double. MC, V. Closed mid-Oct to mid-May.

In 1938 Everett Stone acquired a decommissioned 1885 lighthouse and built a nine-acre cottage colony around it. Today his grandsons run the show, pretty much as he envisioned it: The light has even been resuscitated. As they have for at least two generations, families still gather at group tables in the summer camp–scale dining room to plot their day over breakfast and recap over dinner. With a private beach, heated outdoor pool, tennis courts, and motley amusements such as miniature golf and shuffleboard right on the premises, there's plenty to do. Most families pay a small daily surcharge to enroll their kids in "InnKids," the supervised play program, and many coordinate their vacations so that they can catch up with the same group of friends year after year. The rooms aren't what you'd call fancy, but they're adequate (some have great Sound views) and you'll probably be too busy to spend much time there anyway.

Dining/Entertainment: Serving three meals, the sail-loft-like dining room—decorated with state flags rippling from the rafters—is open to the general public. Of course, you'll have to take pot luck in terms of whom you have at your table, but that's half the fun. The prices are quite reasonable (entrees, for example, rarely exceed $16), and the menu isn't half as stuffy as you might expect: In fact, it's enlivened by reverberations of the New American revolution. Down the road, at the entrance to the complex, the Sand Bar serves as on-site night spot (see "The Dennises After Dark," below).

Moderate

Corsair & Cross Rip Resort Motels. 41 Chase Ave. (off Depot St., 1 mile SE of Rte. 28), Dennisport, MA 02639. 7 rms, 40 efficiencies. A/C TV TEL. Summer $89–$185 double. Special packages available. AE, DISC, MC, V.

Of the many family-oriented motels lining this part of the Sound, these two neighbors are among the nicest, with fresh contemporary decor, two heated beachview pools, and their own chunk of sand. As rainy-day backup, there's an indoor pool plus a game room, and even a toddler playroom equipped with toys.

Inexpensive

The Beach House Inn. 61 Uncle Stephen's Rd. (about ¹/₂ mile S of town center), W. Dennis, MA 02670. ☎ **508/398-4575.** 7 rms. TV. Summer (including continental breakfast) $85–$110 double. No credit cards.

Families will feel right at home in this breezy B&B, set right on the beach in a residential—i.e., motel-free—community. Whereas much of Dennis's southern shore is lined with big modern resorts, this untouched area, with a smattering of weather-silvered cottages, looks and feels like a carryover from the predevelopment decades. Some rooms feature private ocean-view decks, and all guests have access to a communal kitchen with two microwaves, a barbecue deck complete with grill, and a state-of-the-art climbing structure that should keep kids happily occupied should they ever tire of the beach (not likely).

The Four Chimneys Inn. 946 Rte. 6A (about ¹/₂ mile E of town center), Dennis, MA 02638. ☎ **800/874-5502** or 508/385-6317. Fax 508/385-6285. 7 rms, 1 suite. Summer (including continental breakfast) $75–$98 double. DISC, MC, V.

Scargo Lake is directly across the street and the village a brief walk away from this imposing 1881 Victorian, former home to the town doctor. Opulent tastes are evident in the high ceilings and marble fireplace of the front parlor. Rooms vary in size, but innkeeper Kathy Tomasetti has rendered them all quite appealing, with hand-painted stenciling and summery wicker furnishings. The breakfasts are knockouts, featuring such inspirations as blueberry blintz soufflé. The only element that doesn't seem to fit the overall aura of elegance is the surprisingly reasonable rates.

✪ **Isaiah Hall B&B Inn.** 152 Whig St. (1 block NW of the Cape Playhouse), Dennis, MA 02638. ☎ **800/736-0160** or 508/385-9928. Fax 508/385-5879. 11 rms (1 with shared bath). A/C. Summer (including continental breakfast) $81–$112 double. AE, MC, V. Closed mid-Oct through Mar.

So keyed-in is this Greek Revival farmhouse to the doings at the nearby Cape Playhouse that you might as well be backstage. Many stars have stayed here over the past half-century, and if you're lucky you'll find a few sharing the space. The "great room" in the carriage house annex is a virtual green room: It seems to foment late-night discussions, to be continued over home-baked breakfasts at the long plank table that dominates the 1857 country kitchen. Rooms range from retro-touristy (pine paneling, etc.) to spacious and spiffy.

WHERE TO DINE

Keep in mind the trendy offerings of **The Mercantile,** 766 Rte. 6A (at Mercantile Place, in the center of Dennis; ☎ **508/385-3877**)—picture a picnic starring shrimp salad sparked with fresh mango, perhaps, or a silky chocolate cake.

　　Tobey Farm, on Rte. 6A about ¹/₂ mile west of Dennis (☎ **508/385-2930**), is the place for produce, and **Woolfie's Home Baking,** 279 Lower County Rd. about ¹/₂ mile southwest of Dennisport (☎ **508/394-3717**), and **Gingersnaps,** Rte. 6A about ¹/₂ mile west of Dennis (☎ **508/385-4200**), make delicious muffins, bread, and pastries.

Expensive

The Ocean House. Depot St. (about 1 mile S of Rte. 28), Dennisport. ☎ **508/394-0700.** Reservations recommended. Main courses $10–$19. AE, DC, MC, V. Daily 5–10pm. NEW AMERICAN.

With the Sound as a glimmering backdrop, this brick bastion could have gotten away with bridge tables and lawn chairs; instead, the decor is all-out elegant (chandeliers, wood paneling, plush window treatments—the works) to match the ambitious cuisine. Chef Alain DiTomasso is similarly forthcoming, offering broccoli mousse and potato gratin, for example, alongside perfectly grilled lamb already enrobed in a rich reduction sauce graced with asparagus and baby carrots. Pan-seared scallops come accompanied with just as juicy porcini mushrooms, as well as fried leeks and crisp potato curls. At last, a compelling reason to venture Soundward!

✪ **The Red Pheasant.** 905 Main St. (about ¹/₂ mile E of town center), Dennis. ☎ **508/ 385-2133.** Reservations recommended. Main courses $13–$21. DISC, MC, V. Late May to early Sept daily 5–10pm; call for off-season hours. NEW AMERICAN.

An enduring Cape favorite since 1977, this handsome space—an 18th-century barn turned chandlery—has managed not only to keep pace with contemporary trends, but to remain a front-runner. Chef-owner Bill Atwood has a way with local provender: He transforms the ubiquitous zucchini of late summer, for instance, into homemade ravioli enfolding tasty *chevre*, and his signature cherrystone and scallop chowder gets its zip from fresh-plucked thyme. Two massive brick fireplaces tend to be the focal point in off-season, drawing in the weary—and delighted—wanderer. In fine weather the garden room exerts its own green draw.

Moderate

Jacob's Restaurant. 30 W. Main St. (Rte. 28 at Bass River Bridge), W. Dennis. ☎ **508/ 394-0331.** Main courses $8–$13. MC, V. Late Apr to mid-Oct 11:30am–9pm; closed mid-Oct to late Apr. AMERICAN.

Roll up your sleeves for a full-scale shore dinner, from chowder and steamers to lobster, chicken barbecue, and corn on the cob. If it's sunny out, grab a picnic table by the river.

Swan River Seafood. 5 Lower County Rd. (at Swan Pond River, about ²/₃ mile SE of town center), Dennisport. ☎ **508/394-4466.** Main courses $10–$15. AE, MC, V. Late May to Sept daily noon–3:30pm and 5–9:30pm. Closed Oct to late May. SEAFOOD.

Every town has its own version of the fish place with the fantastic view. Here the scenic vista is relatively low-key: a marsh punctuated by an old windmill. The fish—fresh from the adjoining market—is snapping fresh and available deep-fried, as it is everywhere, but also smartly broiled or sautéed. Go for the assertive shark steak au poivre and such specialties as scrod San Sebastian, fresh filets poached in a garlicky broth.

Inexpensive

Bob Briggs' Wee Packet. 79 Depot St. (at Lower County Rd., about ¹/₃ mile S of town center), Dennisport. ☎ **508/398-2181.** Main courses $6–$12. MC, V. Late June to early Sept daily 8am–11pm; call for off-season hours. Closed Oct–Apr. AMERICAN.

It's been Bob Briggs's place since 1949; otherwise, the name that might leap to mind would be "Mom's." This tiny joint serves exemplary diner fare, plus all the requisite seafood staples, fried and broiled.

⑤ Captain Frosty's. 219 Rte. 6A (about 1 mile S of town center), Dennis. ☎ **508/ 385-8548.** Main courses $2–$12. No credit cards. July–Aug daily 11am–9pm; call for off-season hours. Closed late Sept to early Apr. SEAFOOD.

We've had our share of tasteless deep-fried seafood seemingly dipped in greasy cement, thank you very much. Here the breading is light (thanks to healthy canola oil), and the fish itself is fresh off the local day boats. You won't find a more luscious lobster roll anywhere, and the clam cake fritters seem to fly out the door.

THE DENNISES AFTER DARK

The oldest continuously active straw-hat theater in the country and still one of the best, **The Cape Playhouse,** 36 Hope Lane (on Rte. 6A, in the center of Dennis; ☎ **508/385-3911,** fax 508/385-8162), was the 1927 brainstorm of Raymond Moore, who'd spent a few summers as a playwright in Provincetown and quickly tired of the strictures of "little theater." Salvaging an 1838 meetinghouse, he plunked it amid a meadow, and got his New York buddy, designer Cleon Throckmorton, to turn it into a proper theater. Even with a roof that leaked, it was an immediate success, and a parade of stars—both established and budding—trod the boards in the coming decades, from Ginger Rogers to Jane Fonda (her dad spent his salad days there, too, playing opposite Bette Davis in her stage debut), Humphrey Bogart to Tab Hunter. Not all of today's headliners are quite as impressive (many hail from the netherworld of TV reruns), but the theater—the only Equity enterprise on the Cape—can be counted on for a varied season of polished work. Performances late June to early September, Monday and Tuesday and Friday to Saturday 8pm, Wednesday and Thursday 2 and 8pm. Tickets $13 to 27.

Christine's Restaurant, 581 Rte. 28 (about one-quarter mile east of W. Dennis; ☎ 508/394-7333), features a 300-seat show room which draws some big acts nightly in season and weekends off-season, including local jazz great pianist Dave McKenna and all sorts of oldies bands; also on the roster are comedy acts and a Sunday night cabaret-cum-buffet. Cover varies.

The Sand Bar, at the Lighthouse Inn (☎ 508/398-2244; see "Where to Stay," above), was built in 1949, the very year Dennis went "wet." Rock King, a combination boogie-woogie pianist and comedian, still rules the evening and wows the crowd.

Sundancers, on Route 28 in W. Dennis (☎ 508/394-1600), is one of the larger dance clubs on the Cape, attracting a young clientele with an ever-changing roster of DJs and live bands, including Sunday afternoon reggae in season. Cover varies.

The ✪ Cape Cinema, 36 Hope Lane (off Route 6A in the center of Dennis; ☎ 508/385-2503 or 508/385-5644), part of the Cape Playhouse complex, is an art deco surprise, with a Prometheus-themed ceiling mural and folding curtain designed by artist Rockwell Kent and Broadway set designer Jo Mielziner. Independent-film maven George Mansour, curator of the Harvard Film Archive, sees to the art-house programming. That, plus the setting and seating—black leather armchairs—may spoil you forever for what passes for cinemas today. There are shows from early April to mid-November daily at 4:30, 7, and 9pm. Closed mid-November to early April.

3 The Lower Cape

Although the Cape's elbow makes a logical jumping-off point for those arriving by way of the Atlantic, by land it requires an intentional detour, which has helped to preserve Harwich and Chatham from the commercial depredations evident elsewhere along the Sound. The quaint village of Harwichport was all set for an upscale over-haul when the recession struck; faltering funds have left it in an agreeable limbo. Here, the beach is a mere block off Main Street, so the eternal summertime verities of a barefoot stroll capped off by an ice-cream cone can still be easily observed. Chatham, a larger, more prosperous community, is being touted by local realtors as "the Nantucket of the Cape," an apt sobriquet. Its Main Street, a gamut of appeal-ing shops and eateries, approaches an all-American, small-town ideal—complemented nicely by a scenic lighthouse and plentiful beaches nearby.

Occupying the easternmost portion of historic Route 6A, Brewster still enjoys much the same cachet that it boasted as a high roller in the maritime trade. But for a relatively recent incursion of condos, and of course the cars, it looks much as it might have in the late 19th century, its general store still serving as a social center-point. For some reason—perhaps because excellence breeds competition—Brewster has spawned several fine restaurants in recent years and become something of a mag-net for gourmets.

As the gateway to the Outer Cape, where all roads merge (most annoyingly), Or-leans is a bit too frantic to offer the respite most travelers seek. Its nearby cousin, East Orleans, is on the upswing as a destination, though, offering a couple of fun restaurants and—best of all—a goodly chunk of magnificent, unspoiled Cape Cod National Seashore.

BREWSTER

25 miles (40km) E of Sandwich, 31 miles (50km) S of Provincetown

Brewster still gives the impression of somehow setting itself apart. Mostly free of the commercial encroachments that have plagued the southern shore, this thriving community seems to go about its business as if nothing were amiss. It has even managed to absorb an intrusively huge development within its own borders, the 380-acre condo complex known as Ocean Edge, on what was once a huge private estate. The dust settles, the trees grow back, the buildings start to blend in, and it's life as usual, if a bit more closely packed. Brewster also welcomes the tens of thousands of transient campers and day trippers who arrive each summer to enjoy the nearly 2,000 sylvan acres of Nickerson State Park.

›ESSENTIALS

GETTING THERE   After crossing either the Bourne or Sagamore Bridge, head east on Route 6 or 6A. Route 6A passes through the villages of West Brewster, Brewster, and East Brewster. You can also reach Brewster by taking Route 6's Exit 10 north, along Route 124.

VISITOR INFORMATION   Contact the **Brewster Chamber of Commerce,** 74 Locust Lane, Brewster, MA 02631 (☎ **508/255-7045**), or the **Cape Cod Chamber of Commerce,** Route 6 and 132, Hyannis, MA 02601 (☎ **508/ 362-3225,** fax 508/362-3698, web site www.capecod.com).

OUTDOOR PURSUITS

BEACHES   Brewster's eight lovely bay beaches have minimal facilities, which make for a more natural experience. When the tide is out, the "beach" extends as much as two miles, leaving behind tide pools to splash in and explore, and vast stretches of rippled, reddish "garnet" sand. On a good day, you can see the whole curve of the Cape, from Sandwich to Provincetown. That hulking wreck midway, incidentally, is the USS *James Longstreet,* pressed into service for target practice in 1943 and used for that purpose right up until 1970; it's now a popular dive site. For a beach parking sticker ($8/day, $25/week), visit Town Hall at 2198 Rte. 6A (☎ **508/ 896-3701**).

- **Breakwater Beach,** off Breakwater Road, Brewster: Only a brief walk from the center of town, this calm, shallow beach (the only one with rest rooms) is ideal for young children. This was once a packet landing, where packet boats would unload tourists and load up produce—a system that saved a lot of travel time until the railroads came along.
- **Flax Pond** in Nickerson State Park (see "Nature Trails," below): This large freshwater pond, surrounded by pines, has a bathhouse and offers water-sports rentals. The park contains two more ponds with beaches—Cliff and Little Cliff. Access and parking are free.
- **Linnells Landing Beach,** on Linnell Road in E. Brewster: This half-mile bay beach is wheelchair-accessible and an ideal family location.
- **Paines Creek Beach,** off Paines Creek Road, W. Brewster: With 1 1/2 miles to stretch out in, this bay beach has something to offer sun lovers and nature lovers alike. Your kids will love it if you arrive when the tide's coming in—the current will give an air mattress a nice little ride.

BIKING/RECREATIONAL PATHS   The **Cape Cod Rail Trail** intersects with the 8-mile Nickerson State Park trail system at the park entrance, where there's plenty of free parking: you could follow the Rail Trail back to Dennis (about 12 miles) or onward toward Wellfleet (13 miles).

Idle Times (☎ **508/255-8281**) provides rentals within the park, in season. Another good place to jump in is on Underpass Road about ¹/₂ mile south of Route 6A. Here you'll find **Brewster Bicycle Rental** (442 Underpass Rd.; ☎ **508/896-8149**), flanked by a popular picnic purveyor, **Box Lunch** (☎ **508/896-6682**), which specializes in inventive "roll-up" pita sandwiches. Just up the hill is the well-equipped **Rail Trail Bike & Blade** (302 Underpass Rd.; ☎ **800/896-0120** or 508/896-8200).

FISHING   Brewster offers more ponds for fishing than any other town: 14 in all. Among the most popular are Cliff and Higgins ponds within Nickerson State Park, which are regularly stocked. For a license, visit Town Hall at 2198 Rte. 6A (☎ **508/896-3701**). Brewster lacks a deep harbor, so would-be deep-sea fishers will have to head to Barnstable or, better yet, Orleans.

NATURE TRAILS   Admission is free to the two trails maintained by the Cape Cod Museum of Natural History (see below). The **South Trail,** covering a ³/₄-mile round trip south of Route 6A, crosses a natural cranberry bog beside Paines Creek to reach a hardwood forest of beeches and tupelos; toward the end of the loop you'll come upon a "glacial erratic," a huge boulder dropped by a receding glacier. Before heading out on the ¹/₄-mile **North Trail,** stop in at the museum for a free guide describing the local flora, including wild roses, cattails, and sumacs. Also accessible from the CCMNH parking lot is the **John Wing Trail,** a 1¹/₂-mile network traversing 140 acres of preservation land, including upland, salt marsh, and beach. (*Note:* This can be a soggy trip. Be sure to heed the posted warnings regarding high tides, especially in spring, or you might very well find yourself stranded.) Keep an eye out for marsh hawks and blue herons.

As it crosses Route 6A, Paines Creek Road becomes Run Hill Road. Follow it to the end to reach **Punkhorn Park Lands,** an undeveloped 800-acre tract popular with mountain bikers; it features several kettle ponds, a "quaking bog," and 45 miles of dirt paths comprising three marked trails (you'll find trailguides at the trailheads).

Though short, the ¹/₄-mile jaunt around the **Stony Brook Grist Mill** (see below) is especially scenic: In spring you can watch the alewives (freshwater herring) vaulting upstream to spawn, and in the summer the millpond is surrounded and scented by honeysuckle. Also relatively small at only 25 acres, the **Spruce Hill Conservation Area** behind the Brewster Historical Society Museum (see below) includes a 600-foot stretch of beach, reached by a former carriage road reportedly favored by Prohibition bootleggers.

Just east of the museum is the 1,955-acre **Nickerson State Park** at Route 6 and Crosby Lane (☎ **508/896-3491**), the legacy of a vast, self-sustaining private estate that once generated its own electricity (with a horse-powered plant) and attracted notable guests, such as Pres. Grover Cleveland, with its own golf course and game preserve. Today it's an up-with-people, back-to-nature preserve encompassing 418 campsites (reservations pour in a year in advance, but some are held open for new arrivals willing to wait a day or two), eight kettle ponds, and eight miles of bicycle paths. The rest is trees—some 88,000 evergreens, planted by the Civilian Conservation Corps. This is land that has been through a lot but, thanks to careful management, is bouncing back.

WATER SPORTS   Various small sailboats, kayaks, canoes, and even aquabikes (a.k.a. seacycles) are available seasonally at **Jack's Boat Rentals** (☎ **508/896-8556**), located on Flax Pond within Nickerson State Park.

A NATURAL HISTORY MUSEUM

✪ **Cape Cod Museum of Natural History.** 869 Rte. 6A (about 2 miles W of town center). ☎ **800/479-3867** or 508/896-3867. Admission $4 adults, $2 children 6–14. Mid-Apr to mid-Oct Mon–Sat 9:30am–4:30pm, Sun 12:30–4:30pm; closed Mon off-season.

Long before "ecology" had become a buzzword, noted naturalist writer John Haye helped to found a museum that celebrates—and helps to preserve—Cape Cod's unique landscape. Open since 1954, the CCMNH was also prescient in presenting interactive exhibits. The display on whales, for instance, invites the viewer to press a button to hear eerie whale songs; the children's exhibits include an animal puppet theater. All ages are invariably intrigued by the "live hive"—like an ant farm, only with busy bees. The bulk of the museum, naturally, is outdoors, where 85 acres invite exploration (see "Nature Trails," above). Visitors are encouraged to log their bird and animal sightings upon their return. A new feature, introduced in 1995, is an ongoing, on-site archaeology lab on Wing Island, thought to have sheltered one of Brewster's first settlers—the Quaker John Wing, driven from Sandwich in the mid-17th century by religious persecution—and before him, summering native tribes dating back 10 millennia or more, when the Cape and Islands were still all of a piece. A true force in fostering environmental appreciation, the museum sponsors all sorts of activities to engage the public, from lectures and concerts to marsh cruises and "eco-treks"—including a sleepover on uninhabited Monomoy Island off Chatham.

BREWSTER HISTORY

Stony Brook Grist Mill and Museum. 830 Stony Brook Rd. (at the intersection of Satucket Rd. in the town center), W. Brewster. ☎ 508/896-6745. Free admission. July–Aug Thurs–Sat 2–5pm; May–June Fri 2–5pm. Closed Sept–Apr.

A rustic mill beside a stream. . . . It may not look it, but this was once one of the most active manufacturing communities in New England, cranking out cloth, boots, and ironwork for over a century, starting with the American Revolution. The one remaining structure was built in 1873, toward the end of West Brewster's commercial run, near the site of a 1663 water-powered mill, America's first. After decades of producing overalls and, later, ice cream (with ice dredged from the adjoining pond), the factory was bought by the town and fitted out as a cornmill, with period millstones. Volunteers now demonstrate, and urge onlookers to get in on the action. The second story serves as a repository for all sorts of Brewster memorabilia, including some ancient arrowheads. Recent archaeological excavations in this vicinity, sponsored by the Cape Cod Museum of Natural History, have unearthed artifacts dating back some 10,000 years. As you stroll about the millpond (see "Nature Trails," above), be on the alert—who knows what you'll stumble across?

WHERE TO STAY

Very Expensive

Ocean Edge Resort. 2660 Main St. (about 2¹/₃ miles E of town center), Brewster, MA 02631. ☎ **800/343-6074** or 508/896-9000. Fax 508/896-9123. 90 rms, about 125 condos (depending on the rental pool). A/C TV TEL. Summer $90–$275 double, $125–$275 condo. Golf, tennis, and holiday weekend packages available. AE, DC, DISC, MC, V.

If the price of admission strikes you as high, consider the built-ins: two fitness rooms and six pools (two indoor, four outdoor) scattered around an intensively landscaped 380-acre property, part of which fronts a private 1,000-foot stretch of bay beach. The entire tract, plus the nearby Nickerson State Forest, once belonged to a single family, whose prosperity appears to have been dogged by tragedy. Samuel Mayo Nickerson, a Chatham boy who made good as a Chicago banker, built the original mansion, Fieldstone Hall, in 1890 as a gift for his only son, Roland, who died two weeks after it burned down in 1906. His widow, Addie, built a 400-foot-long Renaissance Revival replacement—now a conference center and hotel—with an eye to meeting fire codes; it's rather homely, if grandiose, and not exactly enhanced by the accretion of dense condo accommodations begun in the building boom of the early 1980s. If you're up for the kind of stay-put vacation where every need is met right on the premises (for a price), this might make a good choice, but you're liable to miss out on the quirks that constitute a good portion of the Cape's charms.

Dining/Entertainment: There are four restaurants on the grounds: the refined Ocean Grille and British-style Bayzo's Pub within the mansion, and Mulligan's (New American) and the Reef Cafe (casual Caribbean) overlooking the golf course.

Services: "Kidstart," a supervised program for children 4 to 12.

Facilities: The 18-hole golf course features Scottish pot bunkers. There are 11 tennis courts on the grounds: 5 clay and 6 plexipave. Instruction and clinic packages are offered in both sports.

Expensive

✪ **Captain Freeman Inn.** 15 Breakwater Rd. (off Rte. 6, in town center), Brewster, MA 02631. ☎ **800/843-4664** or 508/896-7481. Fax 508/896-5618. 6 rms (3 with shared bath), 3 suites. A/C TV TEL. Summer (including full breakfast and afternoon tea) $90–$205 double. AE, MC, V.

The creation of an exemplary country inn is part business, part art, and Carol Covitz Edmondson—the ex-marketing director behind this beauty—poured plenty of both into her mint-green 1866 Victorian. The "luxury suites"—each complete with fireplace and a private porch with cloverleaf hot tub—incorporate every extra you could hope to encounter: a canopied, four-poster queen-size bed, a loveseat facing the cable TV/VCR (she has a store's worth of tapes available for loan), even a little fridge prestocked with cold soda, juices, and mineral water. The plainer rooms are just as pretty—one nice feature of the porch-encircled house is that the second-story windows reach almost to the floor. The three dormered third-floor rooms, though smallish, have enviable water views and are nicely priced; families often claim the whole floor. Delectable, yet healthy breakfasts—Edmondson, a culinary maven, hosts weekend cooking courses off-season—are served in bed (indulge yourself!), in the elegant parlor, or on a screened porch overlooking the heated pool and a lush lawn set up for badminton and croquet. Breakwater Landing is a bucolic 10-minute walk, or just moments away, if you avail yourself of a loaner bike. Bliss.

Moderate

The Bramble Inn. 2019 Rte. 6A (about ¹/₃ mile E of town center), Brewster, MA 02631. ☎ **508/896-7644.** Fax 508/896-9322. 12 rms, 1 suite. A/C TV. Summer (including full breakfast) $95–$125 double, $135 suite. AE, DISC, MC, V. Closed mid-Jan to mid-Mar.

This is really more of a compound than an inn per se. Cliff and Ruth Manchester oversee three lovely old buildings: two rambling mid-19th-century homes, decorated in a breezy, country-casual manner, and, across the street, a formal 1792 Federal manse done up in period style, with romantic canopied four-poster beds. Horse-lovers will love the rustic-beamed suite with its vintage riding gear. Ruth is a phenomenal chef (see "Where to Dine," below), so you know you'll be in good hands come breakfast time.

❂ **Old Sea Pines Inn.** 2553 Main St. (about 1 mile E of town center) Brewster, MA 02631. ☎ **800/843-4664** or 508/896-6114. Fax 508/896-2094. 19 rms (5 with shared bath), 2 suites. A/C TV. Summer (including full breakfast and afternoon tea) $50–$105 double, $85–$135 suite. AE, CB, DC, DISC, MC, V. Closed Jan–Mar.

In the early part of the century, this grand 1907 shingle-style mansion was the site of the Sea Pines School of Charm and Personality for Young Women. A great deal of that charm is still evident: In fact, the hosts, Michele and Steve Rowan, have done their best to re-create the gracious ambience of days gone by. The parlor and expansive porch lined with rockers are just as the young ladies might have found them, as are a handful of rather minuscule boarding-school-scale rooms on the top floor. This is one of the few places on the Cape where solo travelers can find a single room and pay no surcharge. The Rowans like to be able to offer a few lower-priced rooms, says Michele, because "It means we can get a real mix of people." Their inclusiveness is also evident in an added annex that's fully wheelchair-accessible (another rarity among historic inns). Whereas the main house has an air of exuberance muted by gentility, the annex rooms are outright playful, with colorful accoutrements, including—Steve got carried away—hot-pink TVs. He does double duty as the breakfast chef—dinner, too, in July and August—and prepares good old-fashioned food. You won't find any kiwis staring you down first thing in the morning.

WHERE TO DINE
Very Expensive
✪ **The Bramble Inn Restaurant.** 2019 Main St. (about ⅓ mile E of Rte. 124). ☎ 508/896-7644. Fax 508/896-9322. Reservations required. Prix fixe $38–$55. AE, DISC, MC, V. Jun to mid-Oct daily 6–9pm; call for off-season hours. Closed Jan–Apr. NEW AMERICAN.

There's an impromptu feel to this intimate restaurant, an enfilade of five small rooms each imbued with its own personality, from sporting (the "tack room") to best-Sunday-behavior (the elegant parlor). One-of-a-kind antique table settings add to the charm. Such niceties fade to mere backdrop, though, beside Ruth Manchester's extraordinary cuisine. A four-course (usually six-option) menu that evolves every month gives her free rein to follow fresh enthusiasms, as well as seasonal delicacies, and it's a thrill to be able to follow along. Any specifics are quickly history, but she has a solid grounding in Mediterranean cuisines and a gift for improvisatory cross-pollination.

Chillingsworth. 2449 Main St. (about 1 mile E of town center). ☎ **508/896-3640.** Reservations required; jacket requested. Prix fixe $40–$56. AE, DC, MC, V. July–Aug daily 11:30am–2:30pm and 6–9:30pm; call for off-season hours. Closed late Nov to mid-May. FRENCH.

A longtime contender for the title of best restaurant on the Cape, Chillingsworth is certainly the fanciest, what with antique appointments reaching back several centuries and a seven-course Francophiliac *table d'hote* menu that will challenge the most shameless of gourmands. There's a rote quality to the ritual, however, which can undercut what might otherwise amount to a transcendental culinary experience. See if you can ignore all the rigmarole and just focus on the taste sensations, which are indeed sensational. Or for a sampling, lunch or dine (sans reservations) in the à la carte Bistro.

✪ **High Brewster.** 964 Satucket Rd. (off Rte. 6A, about 2 miles SW of town center). ☎ **508/896-3636.** Reservations required. Prix fixe $28–$46. AE, MC, V. Late May to mid-Oct daily 6–9pm; call for off-season hours. Closed Jan–Mar. NEW AMERICAN.

By candlelight the close yet cozy keeping rooms and paneled parlors of this 1738 colonial Cape are irresistibly romantic, and Scott Anderson's sensual, sophisticated cuisine only serves to intensify the mood. His dishes tend to be bold in the modern manner—wild mushroom ravioli, for instance, with herb aïoli and candied shallots, or salmon encrusted in scallions and couscous—yet he's good at adapting local ingredients and traditional preparations to treats our ancestors could have imagined only in their dreams. What they would have given, heaven only knows, to be able to celebrate the harvest with apple crisp topped with homemade apple rum ice cream.

Expensive

✪ **The Brewster Fish House.** 2208 Main St. (about ¹/₂ mile E of town center). ☎ **508/896-7867.** No reservations. Main courses $12–$20. MC, V. June to early Sept Mon–Sat 11:30am–3pm and 5–10pm; Sun noon–3pm and 5–9:30pm; call for off-season hours. Closed mid-Dec to mid-Apr. NEW AMERICAN.

Spare and handsome as a Shaker refectory, this small eatery bills itself as a "nonconforming" restaurant and delivers on the promise. The approach to seafood borders on genius: Consider, just for instance, squid delectably tenderized in a marinade of soy and ginger, or silky-tender walnut-crusted ocean catfish accompanied by kale sautéed in Marsala. This are but two examples of the daily specials devised to take advantage of the latest haul. No wonder the place is packed: Better get there early if you want to get in.

Moderate

Beechcroft Bistro. At the Beechcroft Inn. ☎ **508/896-9534.** Reservations recommended. Main courses $8–$16. AE, CB, DC, DISC, MC, V. Mid-May to mid-Sept Tues–Sun 5:30–9pm; call for off-season schedule. INTERNATIONAL.

Generosity and warmth are the key ingredients of bistro fare, and you'll find plenty of both in the cozy fireplaced pub and more formal dining room. The fresh-seafood "bisque du jour" is just the ticket at the end of a blustery day. Lighter options include creatively sauced pastas and Boboli pizzas such as the "Mykonos" (eggplant and feta and olives, oh my), and there's usually a choice of at least five entrees, including sole Tivoli—wrapped around a core of seafood stuffing and artichoke heart, and topped with lemon butter. You're welcome, too, to stop in just for dessert, subject to the chef's whim but usually some fiendish delight: Beware the Chocolate Oblivion!

The Tower House Restaurant. 2671 Rte. 6A (about 1 mile E of town center). ☎ **508/896-2671.** No reservations. Main courses $8–$18. MC, V. Late May to mid-Oct daily 8am–9pm; call for off-season hours. INTERNATIONAL.

Every beach town needs a good cafe where the hours are as you like them (so you can sun at will). This one is unusually good-looking, and the food is reliable and competently done, if not exactly radical; the "fish market specials" are apt to be your best bet.

Inexpensive

Cobie's. 3260 Rte. 6A (about 2 miles E of Brewster center). ☎ **508/896-7021.** Most items under $10. No credit cards. Late May to mid-Sept daily 11am–9pm. Closed mid-Sept to late May. AMERICAN.

This picture-perfect clam shack has been dishing out exemplary fried clams, lobster rolls, foot-long hot dogs, black-and-white frappes, and all the other beloved staples of summer since 1948.

THE HARWICHES

24 miles (39km) E of Sandwich, 32 miles (52km) S of Provincetown

Harwichport is the quintessential sleepy seaside village, not too mucked up—as yet—by the creeping commercialization of Route 28. The town's main claim to fame was as the birthplace, in 1846, of commercial cranberry cultivation: The "bitter berry," as the Narragansetts called it, is now Massachusetts' leading agricultural product. The curious can find elucidating displays on this and other local distinctions at the Brooks

Academy Museum in the inland town of Harwich. The incurious, or merely vacation-minded, can loll on the beach.

ESSENTIALS

GETTING THERE From the Mid-Cape Highway, take Exit 10 south along Route 124. Harwich is located at the intersection of Route 39, where the two routes converge and head southwest to Harwichport and West Harwich, both located on Route 28. West Harwich is also on Route 28, several miles eastward, and East Harwich (more easily reached from Route 6's Exit 11), is inland, a few miles northeast.

VISITOR INFORMATION Contact the **Harwich Chamber of Commerce,** Route 28, Harwichport, MA 02646 (☎ **508/432-1600,** fax 508/430-2105).

OUTDOOR PURSUITS

BEACHES The Harwich coast is basically one continuous beach punctuated by the occasional harbor. Harwichport is so close to the Sound, it's a snap to walk the block or two to the water—provided you find a parking place in town (try the lot near the Chamber of Commerce booth in the center of town). Parking right at the beach is pretty much limited to residents and renters, who can obtain a weekly sticker for $25 at Town Hall, 732 Main St., Harwich (☎ **508/430-7513**). Also, a free trolley, the **Harwich Beach Shuttle** (☎ **800/352-7155**), heads up and down Route 28 in season, easing access for all.

- **Red River Beach,** off Uncle Venies Road south of Route 28 in S. Harwich, is the only Sound beach in town offering parking for day trippers (they still have to turn up early); the fee is $5 on weekdays or $10 weekends and holidays. Marked off with stone jetties, this narrow, 2,700-foot beach has full facilities.
- **Sand Pond,** off Great Western Road near Depot Street, honors the weekly beach sticker, as do the two parking lots at Long Pond.
- **Hinckleys Pond** and **Seymore Pond,** west of Route 124 and right off the Rail Trail, and **Bucks Pond** off Depot Road at Route 39 northeast of Harwich, welcome all comers.

BIKING/RECREATIONAL PATHS Transecting Harwich for about five miles, the **Cape Cod Rail Trail** skirts some pretty ponds in the western part before veering north and zigzagging toward Brewster along Route 124. For rentals and information, contact the **Harwichport Bike Co.,** 431 Rte. 28 (☎ **508/430-0200**), which can also provide in-line skates, kayaks, and canoes.

FISHING There are six ponds available for fishing in the Harwich area, as well as extensive shell-fishing in season; for details and a license, visit Town Hall at 732 Main St. in Harwich (☎ **508/430-7513**). For supplies and instruction, visit **Fishing the Cape,** at the Harwich Commons, Routes 137 and 39 (☎ **508/432-1200**); it's the official Cape headquarters for the **Orvis Saltwater Fly Fishing School** (☎ **800/ 235-9763**). Several deep-sea fishing boats operate out of Saquatucket Harbor (off Route 28, about ¹/₂ mile east of Harwichport), including the 33-footers *Fish Tale* (☎ **508/432-3783**) and *Arlie eX* (☎ **508/430-2454**), and the 65-foot *Yankee* (☎ **508/432-2520**). The *Golden Eagle* (☎ **508/432-5611**), offering evening blue fish trips several times a week, heads out from Wychmere Harbor.

NATURE TRAILS The largest preserve in Harwich is the 245-acre **Bells Neck Conservation** area north of Route 28 near the Dennis border. It encompasses the **Herring River,** ideal for birding and canoeing (see "Water Sports," below).

WATER SPORTS   Cape Water Sports 337 Rte. 28 in Harwichport (☎ 508/432-7079), offers lessons and rentals on several beaches: Available craft include canoes, sailboards, sunfish, and sailboats up to 42 feet. Meandering from a reservoir south to the Sound, West Harwich's Herring River—a natural herring run framed by cattail marsh—is ideal for canoeing. The **Harwichport Bike Co.,** 431 Main St. (☎ 508/430-0200), offers family tours, and rents out canoes and kayaks. **Cape Sail,** out of Saquatucket Harbor (☎ 508/896-2730), offers sailing lessons as well as private charters. **Cape Cod Divers,** 815 Main St. in Harwichport (☎ 800/348-4641 or 508/432-9035), is scuba central, offering rentals and lessons, a training pool, and charter trips to shipwreck sites.

WHERE TO STAY

۞ The Beach House Inn. 4 Braddock Lane. (off Bank St., S of Rte. 28 in the center of town), Harwichport, MA 02646. ☎ 800/870-4405 or 508/432-4444. 10 rms. A/C TV TEL. Summer (including continental breakfast) $145–$195 double. DISC, MC, V.

One of the few waterside hostelries to remain open throughout the year (a boon for solitary-minded beachcombers), this intensively renovated 1920s honey is a real find. The original rooms still boast their varnished pine paneling, as well as updated whirlpool baths, and the four glorious front rooms, added in 1995, each feature a fireplace or deck as well, plus sweeping views of Nantucket Sound.

The Commodore Inn. 30 Earle Rd. (about ¹/₂ mile S of town center, off Rte. 28), W. Harwich, MA 02671. ☎ 800/368-1180 or 508/432-1180. Fax 508/432-4634. 27 rms. A/C TV TEL. Summer (including full breakfast) $119–$175 double. AE, MC, V. Closed Jan–Feb.

From the outside, it looks like an especially nice motel encircling a heated pool; from the inside, the rooms resemble upscale condos, with cathedral ceilings and handsome, functional furniture. Guests are treated to a buffet breakfast, and special dinners (e.g., a barbecue or clambake) are offered regularly. This is one of the few small properties on the Cape that can accommodate meetings and provide business amenities.

Sandpiper Beach Inn. 16 Bank St. (S of Rte. 28 in the center of town), Harwichport, MA 02646. ☎ 800/432-2234 or 508/432-0485. 17 rms, 2 suites. A/C TV TEL. Summer (including continental breakfast) $110–$150 double, $225 suite. AE, MC, V. Closed Nov–Mar.

Plunked right on the beach, this motel looks far too tasteful to be a motel. The breezy rooms are further brightened by splashy fabrics and pretty wicker furniture. For those who appreciate country-inn aesthetics but prefer the freedom of movement afforded by a more impersonal atmosphere, this could be just the ticket.

WHERE TO DINE

The Cape SeaGrille. 31 Sea St. (S of Rte. 28 in the center of town). ☎ 508/432-4745. Reservations recommended. Main courses $11–$20. AE, MC, V. July–Aug daily 5–9pm; call for off-season hours. Closed Jan–Mar. NEW AMERICAN.

A pair of ambitious chef-owners are the power behind the stove of this relatively recent (1994) upscale enterprise occupying the pared-down, peach-toned shell of an ordinary beach house. The menu is under constant revision, the better to springboard off market finds, but among the keepers are a refreshing appetizer platter of marinated seafoods (from ceviche to salmon carpaccio), and grilled medley starring lobster, shrimp, and bacon-wrapped swordfish. City sophisticates who insist on creativity and innovation will find this the most consistently rewarding source in town.

Goucho's Mexican Restaurant and Bar. 403 Lower County Rd. (off Rte. 28 about ¹/₂ mile W of town center). ☎ 508/432-7768. Main courses $6–$14. MC, V. May–Sept Fri–Sat 4pm–midnight. Closed mid-Oct through Mar. MEXICAN.

Something about sultry summer nights seems to call for spicy Mexican fare—washed down with tart margaritas, *claro*. There's nothing about this buttoned-up country house to suggest authenticity, until you reach the interior—convincingly converted with adobe-style walls and strategic serapes. All the addictive traditional dishes are available, from fajitas to flautas, along with some peculiar cross-pollinations such as the "Philly burrito" (featuring sliced steak). It's a fun place, particularly once those golden margaritas start to glow.

L'Alouette. 787 Rte. 28 (about ¹/₂ mile E of town center). ☎ **508/430-0405.** Reservations recommended. Main courses $15–$23. AE, DC, DISC, MC, V. Tues–Sun 5–9pm, Sun noon–2:30pm. FRENCH.

Just as nothing can quite duplicate the delicate scent of a freshly washed Paris sidewalk, there's no way to fake the seductive aromas of an authentic French restaurant. The secrets are all in the stock, and chef Louis Bastres, formerly of Biarritz, of course makes his from scratch. He's a strict classicist (none of this *nouvelle* nonsense): specialties at this *auberge*-style restaurant include such time-honored tests of prowess as bouillabaisse and Chateaubriand.

Thompson's Clam Bar. 594 Rte. 28 (in the center of town). ☎ **508/430-1239.** No reservations. Main courses $15–$22. AE, DC, DISC, MC, V. Mid-June to mid-Sept daily noon–9:30pm. Closed mid-Sept to mid-June. AMERICAN.

Relocated from its perch on the harbor, where it had evolved from a fish market in 1949, this beloved local restaurant may have lost its view (and ambience) but retains its all-American menu. Why mess with success? Seafood—shucked, steamed, fried, baked, you name it—continues to be the main event, though carnivores are hardly ignored. Still craze-worthy after all these years are such classic New England desserts as Indian pudding and strawberry shortcake.

CHATHAM

32 miles (52km) E of Sandwich, 24 miles (39km) S of Provincetown

Sticking out like a sore elbow (and fortuitously removed from the tourist flow), Chatham was naturally one of the first spots to attract early explorers. Samuel de Champlain stopped by in 1606 but got into a tussle with the prior occupants over some copper cooking pots and had to leave in a hurry. The first colonist to stick around was William Nickerson, from Yarmouth, who befriended a local sachem (tribal leader) and built a house beside his wigwam in 1656. One prospered; the other—for obvious reasons—didn't. To this day, listings for Nickersons still occupy a half-page in the Cape Cod phone book.

Chatham, along with Provincetown, is the only area on the Cape to support a commercial fishing fleet—against increasing odds. Overfishing has resulted in closely monitored limits, to give the stock time to bounce back. Boats must now go out as far as a hundred miles to catch their fill. Despite the difficulties, it's a way of life few locals would willingly relinquish. As in Provincetown, there's surprisingly little animosity between the hard-working residents and summerers at play, perhaps because it's clear that discerning tourist dollars are what is helping to preserve this lovely town for all.

ESSENTIALS

GETTING THERE   After crossing either the Bourne or Sagamore Bridge, head east on Route 6 and take Exit 11 south (Route 137) to Route 28. From this intersection, the village of South Chatham is about ¹/₂ mile west, and West Chatham about 1¹/₂ miles east. Chatham itself is about 2 miles farther east on Route 28.

VISITOR INFORMATION   Contact the **Chatham Chamber of Commerce,** 533 Main St., Chatham, MA 02633 (☎ **800/715-5567** or 508/945-5199).

Outdoor Pursuits

BEACHES   Chatham has an unusual array of beach styles, from the peaceful shores of the Nantucket Sound to the treacherous, shifting shoals along the Atlantic. For information on beach stickers ($7/day, $35/week), call Town Hall (☎ **508/ 945-5100**).

- **Cockle Cove Beach, Ridgevale Beach,** and **Hardings Beach:** Lined up along the Sound, each at the end of its namesake road south of Route 28, these family-pleasing beaches offer gentle surf suitable for all ages, as well as full facilities.
- **Forest Beach:** No longer an officially recognized town beach (there's no life-guard), this Sound landing near the Harwich border is still popular, especially among surfboarders.
- **Oyster Pond Beach,** off Route 28: Only a block from Chatham's Main Street, this sheltered saltwater pond (with rest rooms) swarms with children.
- **Chatham Light Beach:** Located directly below the lighthouse parking lot (where stopovers are limited to 30 minutes), this narrow stretch of sand is easy to get to: just walk down the stairs. Currents here can be tricky and swift, though, so swimming is discouraged.
- **South Beach:** A former island jutting out slightly to the south of the Chatham Light, this glorified sandbar can be equally dangerous, so heed posted warnings and content yourself with strolling or, at most, wading.
- **North Beach:** Extending all the way south from Orleans, this five-mile barrier beach is accessible from Chatham only by boat; for a fee, you can hop a water taxi from the Chatham Fish Pier on Shore Road(☎ **508/430-2346**). Inquire about other possible dropoff points if you'd like to beach around.

BIKING/RECREATIONAL PATHS   Though Chatham has no separate recreational path per se, a demarcated bike/blading lane makes a scenic, eight-mile circuit of town, heading south onto "The Neck," east to the Chatham Light, up Shore Road all the way to N. Chatham, and back to the center of town. A descriptive brochure prepared by the **Chatham Chamber of Commerce** (☎ **800/715-5567** or 508/945-0342) shows the suggested route, and there are lots of lightly trafficked detours worth taking. Rentals are available at **Bikes & Blades,** 195 Crowell Rd., Chatham (☎ **508/945-7600**).

FISHING   Chatham has five ponds and lakes that permit fishing; Goose Pond off Fisherman's Landing is among the top spots. For saltwater fishing sans boat, try the fishing bridge on Bridge Street at the southern end of Mill Pond. First, though, get a license at Town Hall at 549 Main St. in Chatham (☎ **508/945-5101**). If you hear the deep sea calling, sign on with the *Booby Hatch* (☎ **508/430-2312**), a 33-foot sportfisherman out of W. Chatham, or the *Banshee* (☎ **508/945-0403**) or *Tiger Too* (☎ **508/945-9215**), both berthed in Stage Harbor. Shellfishing licenses are available at the Town Hall Annex on George Ryder Road in W. Chatham (☎ **508/ 945-5180**).

NATURE TRAILS   Heading southeast from the Hardings Beach parking lot (see "Beaches," above), the two-mile round-trip **Seaside Trail** offers beautiful parallel panoramas of Nantucket Sound and Oyster Pond River; keep an eye out for nesting pairs of horned lark. Access to 40-acre **Morris Island,** southwest of the Chatham Light, is easy: You can walk or drive across and start right in on a marked

³/₄-mile trail. Heed the high tides, as advised, though—it can come in surprisingly quickly, leaving you stranded.

Chatham's natural bonanza lies southward: the uninhabited **Monomoy Island,** 2,750 acres of brush-covered sand favored by some 285 species of migrating birds as the perfect pit stop along the Atlantic Flyway. Harbor and grey seals are catching on, too: Hundreds now carpet the coastline from late November through May. If you go out during that time, you won't have any trouble seeing them: They're practically unavoidable. Shuttle service to South Island is available aboard the *Rip Ryder* out of the Stage Harbor Marina (☎ **508/945-5450**), but you'll get a lot more out of the trip—and probably leave this unspoiled landscape in better shape—if you let a naturalist lead the way. Both the **Wellfleet Bay Wildlife Sanctuary** operated by the Audubon Society (☎ **508/349-2615**) and Brewster's **Cape Cod Museum of Natural History** (☎ **508/896-3867**) offer guided trips. About a dozen times each summer, the museum even organizes sleepovers in the island's only surviving structure, a clapboard "keeper's house" flanked by an 1849 lighthouse. It's just you and the birds and seals and lots of deer, plus various other species harder to spot.

WATER SPORTS   Sea-worthy vessels, from surf- and sailboards to paddle craft and Sunfish, can be rented from **Monomoy Sail and Cycle,** 275 Rte. 28 in N. Chatham (☎ **508/945-0811**). Pleasant Bay, the Cape's largest embayment, is the best place to play, for those with sufficient experience; if the winds don't seem to be going your way, try Forest Beach on the South Chatham shore.

Shopping

Chatham, with its tree-shaded Main Street lined with specialty stores, offers a nonpareil opportunity to shop and stroll. The goods tend to be on the conservative side, but every so often you'll happen upon a hedonistic delight.

Among the shops to check out are: ✪ **Amazing Lace,** 726 Rte. 28 (in the center of town; ☎ **508/945-4023**), offering one of the best collections of vintage clothing on the Cape; **Mildred Georges Antiques,** 447 Main St. (in the center of town; ☎ **508/945-1939**), a rewarding jumble of a shop; **The Spyglass,** 618 Main St. (in the center of town; ☎ **508/945-9686**), selling ancient nautical instruments; **1736 House Antiques,** 1731 Rte. 28 (about ¹/₂ mile east of Route 137; ☎ **508/945-5690**); ✪ **Chatham Glass,** 17 Balfour Lane (off Route 28 about one mile west of the Chatham rotary; ☎ **508/945-5547**), with outstanding handblown glassworks; **Chatham Pottery,** 2568 Rte. 28 (west of intersection with Route 137; ☎ **508/430-2191**), where Gill Wilson (potter) and Margaret Wilson-Grey (glazer) display their striking stoneware; the **Munson Gallery,** 880 Rte. 28 (about ¹/₈ mile northwest of the rotary; ☎ **508/945-2888**), a primarily contemporary gallery with a stellar track record; and ✪ **Midsummer Nights,** 471 Main St. (in the center of town; ☎ **508/945-5562**), purveyor of luxurious personal-care products and boudoir accessories.

Where to Stay

Very Expensive

Chatham Bars Inn. Shore Rd. (off Seaview St., about ¹/₂ mile NW of town center), Chatham, MA 02633. ☎ **800/527-4884** or 508/945-0096. Fax 508/945-5491. 132 rms, 20 suites. A/C TV TEL. Summer $170–$365 double, $385–$675 1-bedroom suite, $540–$1,000 2-bedroom suite. MAP and off-season packages available. AE, DC, MC, V.

A private hunting lodge built for a Boston family in 1914, this curved and colonnaded brick building—surrounded by 26 shingled cottages on 20 acres—has regained its glory days with recent renovations. The latest undertaking is a Victorian makeover, meant to lend the lovely behemoth a more imposing air. It still lends itself well to

Cape Cod

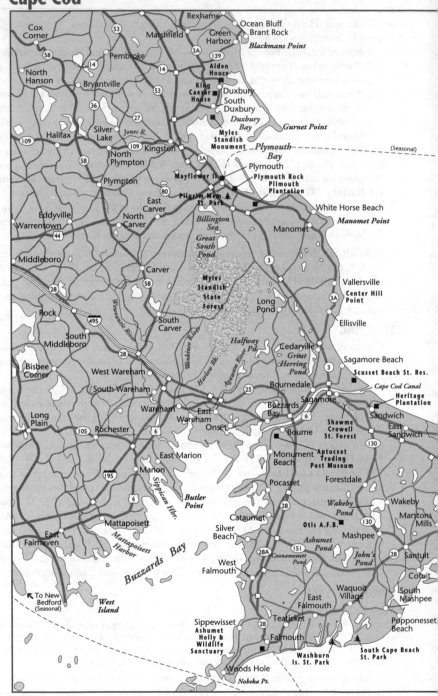

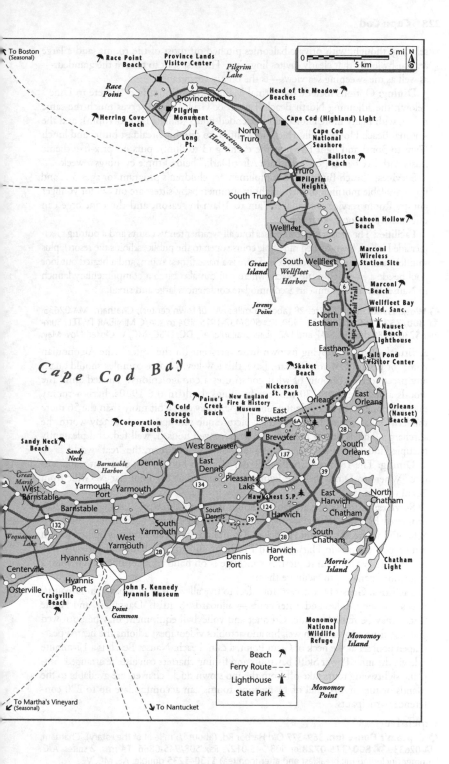

To Boston
(Seasonal)

Race Point
Beach

Province Lands
Visitor Center

*Pilgrim
Lake*

*Race
Point*

6

Provincetown

Head of the Meadow
Beaches

Herring Cove
Beach

Pilgrim
Monument

Cape Cod (Highland) Light

*Provincetown
Harbor*

North
Truro

Cape Cod
National
Seashore

Long
Pt.

Ballston
Beach

Truro
Pilgrim
Heights

South Truro

Cahoon Hollow
Beach

Wellfleet

Marconi
Wireless
Station Site

*Great
Island*

South Wellfleet

*Wellfleet
Harbor*

Marconi
Beach

*Jeremy
Point*

North
Eastham

Wellfleet Bay
Wild. Sanc.

Nauset
Beach
Lighthouse

Eastham

Salt Pond
Visitor Center

C a p e   C o d   B a y

Skaket
Beach

Nickerson
St. Park

Orleans

East
Orleans

Paine's
Creek
Beach

New England
Fire & History
Museum

Cold
Storage
Beach

East
Brewster

6A

Orleans
(Nauset)
Beach

Corporation
Beach

Brewster

137

South
Orleans

West Brewster

6

Sandy Neck
Beach

*Sandy
Neck*

East
Dennis

Pleasant
Lake

28

39

*Barnstable
Harbor*

Dennis

134

Hawksnest S.P.

East
Harwich

North
Chatham

*Great
Marsh*

West
Barnstable

Yarmouth
Port

Yarmouth

124

Harwich

Chatham

South
Dennis

39

Barnstable

6

South
Yarmouth

28

South
Chatham

132

West
Yarmouth

28

Dennis
Port

Harwich
Port

Chatham
Light

*Wequaquet
Lake*

Hyannis

*Morris
Island*

Centerville

Hyannis
Port

John F. Kennedy
Hyannis Museum

Osterville

Craigville
Beach

*Point
Gammon*

Monomoy
National
Wildlife
Refuge

*Monomoy
Island*

To Martha's Vineyard
(Seasonal)

To Nantucket

*Monomoy
Point*

0   5 mi
0   5 km

N

Beach	
Ferry Route	- - -
Lighthouse	
State Park	

relaxing, though, with private balconies pitched off most of the rooms, and a large and cushy lobby that clearly invites lingering. The best spot to take in the grandeur—as well as the sweeping sea views—is the breezy verandah.

Dining: Options include the formal Main Dining Room (see "Where to Dine," below); the adjoining North Beach Tavern & Grille, which serves much the same menu, with many more choices and extended hours (daily 11am to 10pm); and the seasonal Beach House Grill, which, in addition to offering breakfast buffet and lunch (7am to 3pm) and light fare into the evening (3 to 8pm), puts on prix-fixe theme feasts with live bands (see "Chatham After Dark," below) three evenings a week.

Services: "Beach Buddies," a complimentary children's program for ages 3 1/2 and up, is available morning through night in summer; baby-sitters are on call for younger guests. Room service is available 7am to 10am in season, and the concierge can offer advice on local excursions.

Facilities: The property encompasses four all-weather tennis courts and a putting green (Seaside Links, a town-owned nine-hole course open to the public, adjoins the resort), plus shuffleboard, croquet, and volleyball. There is a basic fitness room, and a heated outdoor pool beside a 1/4-mile private beach, where you can also catch a complimentary launch to Nauset Beach. The inn can accommodate conferences large and small.

۞ Wequassett Inn. 178 Rte. 28 (about 5 miles NW of town center), Chatham, MA 02633. ☎ **800/352-7169** or 508/432-5400. Fax 508/432-1915. 104 rms. A/C MINIBAR TV TEL. Summer $230–$480 double. MAP and FAP plans available. AE, DC, DISC, MC, V. Closed Nov–May.

A virtual village occupying its own little "crescent on the water" (the Algonquian name for Round Cove on Pleasant Bay), this low-key, 22-acre complex should quash any preconceived notions of what constitutes a cottage colony. Tucked amid the woods along the shore, 20 modest dwellings, built in the 1940s, harbor roomy quarters done up in an opulent country style: They cost a bit more than the 56 more modern "villa" rooms but, with their picturesque settings, are definitely worth the surcharge. This is one of those places where—well housed, well fed, and pleasantly occupied indeed—you're assured of a temporary respite from the "real" world.

Dining: The 18th-century Eben Ryder House is home to an excellent restaurant (see "Where to Dine," below); lighter fare is served at the Pool Bar & Grille from 10am to 6pm.

Services: Instruction is available in tennis (there are three pros on-site), sailing (co-ordinated by Cape Water Sports), and saltwater fly-fishing (a branch of the Orvis School); inquire about clinic packages. Complimentary van service is offered to two public golf courses in Harwich and Brewster, and to Chatham and Orleans; box lunches are available on request. A concierge is on hand to recommend activities; a recreation manager, to facilitate them.

Facilities: Guests have access (for a fee) to five all-weather plexipave tennis courts, plus a pro shop. Bikes and water crafts—sailboards, Sunfish, Daysailers, and Hobie Cats—may be rented on site. Croquet and volleyball equipment may be borrowed gratis. A fitness room (with weights and aerobics videotapes) adjoins the heated pear-shaped pool set at the neck of Clam Point, a calm beach. Nauset Beach is a 15-minute ride via the inn's Power Skiff; bay tours and fishing charters can also be arranged. Seaplane sightseeing tours take off from the inn's own dock; charters are available to the islands or the city. A total of 11 meeting rooms can accommodate up to 220 conference participants.

Expensive

۞ Captain's House Inn. 369–377 Old Harbor Rd. (about 1/2 mile N of the rotary), Chatham, MA 02633. ☎ **800/315-0728** or 508/945-0127. Fax 508/945-0866. 14 rms, 2 suites. A/C. Summer (including full breakfast and afternoon tea) $130–$235 double. AE, MC, V.

This 1839 Greek Revival house set—along with a cottage and carriage house—on two meticulously maintained acres is a shining example of its era and style. The rooms, named for Capt. Hiram Harding's ships, are richly furnished, with a preponderance of canopied four-posters, beamed ceilings, and, in some cases, brick hearths. One of the few B&Bs to serve the morning repast at noncommunal tables (a thoughtful touch for those of us slow to rev up, sociability-wise), the window-walled breakfast room is also the site of a traditional tea—presided over by innkeeper Jan McMasters, formerly of Bournemouth in Great Britain, who knows how to pour a proper cuppa.

✪ Chatham Wayside Inn. 512 Main St. (in the center of town), Chatham, MA 02633. ☎ 800/391-5734 or 508/945-5550. Fax 508/945-3407. 56 rms. A/C TV TEL. Summer $145–$310 double, $290–$325 suite. Off-season packages available. AE, DISC, MC, V.

Resurrected from the brink of dereliction, this former stagecoach stop dating from 1860 has reassumed its rightful stature. Don't expect any musty antique trappings: This is a thoroughly modern renovation, with lush carpeting, a warehouse's worth of Waverly fabrics, and polished reproduction furnishings, including four-posters. The restaurant serves sophisticated New American fare, indoors and out, and the prize rooms—for old-fashioned heavy-metal fans, at least—boast patios or balconies overlooking the town bandstand.

Pleasant Bay Village. 1191 Rte. 28 (about 3 miles N of Chatham center), Chathamport, MA 02633. ☎ 800/547-1011 or 508/945-1133. Fax 508/945-9701. 48 rms, 10 suites. A/C TV TEL. Summer (including full breakfast) $165–$195 double, $285–$355 1- or 2-bedroom suite (for 4 occupants). AE, MC, V. Closed Nov–Apr.

Owner Howard Gamsey is a prodigious gardener: Over the past quarter-century, he has transformed what was an ordinary motel into a playful Zen paradise, where a waterfall cascades through a colorful rock garden into a stone-edged pool dotted with lilypads and flashing koi. Actually, he has poured that kind of attention into the entire six-acre complex. The rooms and cottages, done up in restful pastels, are unusually pleasant, and the breakfast room features antique kilims, crewel curtains, and antique tables in lieu of shag carpeting and Formica. In summer, you can order lunch from the grill without having to bestir yourself from the heated pool.

Moderate

⑤ Inn Among Friends. 207 Main St. (on the shore, near the Chatham Light), Chatham, MA 02663. ☎ 800/750-0792 or 508/945-0792. 14 rms, 2 with shared bath. Summer (including a $4 breakfast credit at the Break-away Cafe) $95–$135 double. MC, V.

The flashy salmon awnings hint at high style lurking within this classic shingled cottage, and the living room has it in spades. The bedrooms are fairly subdued by comparison, but perfectly cozy. For those never quite satisfied unless they're practically in the water, this B&B is only steps from South Beach.

The Seafarer of Chatham. 2079 Rte. 28 (about ½ mile E of Rte. 137), W. Chatham, MA 02669. ☎ 800/786-2772 or 508/432-1739. 20 rms. A/C TV TEL. Summer $110–$125 double. AE, MC, V.

Convenient to Chatham's Sound-side beaches (Ridgevale Beach is about ½ mile due south), this personable Cape-style motel is shielded from the road by stately trees. Innkeeper Cathleen Houhoulis has decorated the spotless rooms with Early American–style stenciling, and both she and her husband, John, take pains to familiarize neophytes with the area. Behind the low-slung building you'll find a sheltered garden—sans pool, the better to celebrate the peace and quiet.

WHERE TO DINE
Very Expensive
✪ Eben Ryder House. Wequassett Inn on Pleasant Bay, 178 Rte. 28 (about 5 miles NW of town center). ☎ **800/352-7169** or 508/432-5400. Fax 508/432-1915. Reservations recommended; jacket requested. Main courses $15–$34. AE, DC, DISC, MC, V. Jun–Oct 7am–10pm. Closed Nov–May. NEW AMERICAN.

Reliably, season after season, Frank McMullen has proved himself to be a deft and often dazzling chef. Guests would surely squawk if some of his cherished dishes were ever supplanted: The saffron-suffused bisque of Nantucket scallops, for instance, is a definite keeper, as is the Lobster Sinclair—thoughtfully denuded and plumped atop a bed of saffron orzo. But it's always fun to see him kick up his heels with some world-beat concoction like duck and smoked pepper quesadilla or an incendiary Jamaican mixed grill of salmon, shrimp, and swordfish. All this, and dreamy cove views.

Expensive
Christian's. 443 Main St. (in the center of town). ☎ **508/945-3362.** Reservations recommended. Main courses $10–$20. AE, CB, DC, DISC, MC, V. Apr–Dec 11:30am–3pm and 5–10pm; call for off-season hours. NEW AMERICAN.

Owned by gifted, innovative chef Christian Schultz, this bi-level restaurant has a split personality: The summer-only downstairs dining rooms enjoy an *auberge*-like French country decor, whereas Upstairs at Christian's (open year-round) is British clubby, with leather couches, mahogany paneling, and a smattering of classic movie posters. The same cinematic-motif menu applies to both venues: Famous movie titles are accorded to such specialties as escargots in Marsala sauce—a.k.a. *Casablanca.*

The Main Dining Room. Chatham Bars Inn, Shore Rd. (about ⅓ mile NW of town center). ☎ **800/527-4884** or 508/945-0096. Fax 508/945-5491. Reservations and jacket required. Main courses $13–$20. AE, DC, MC, V. Mid-May to mid-Nov daily 8–11am; Sun–Fri 6–9pm, Sat 6:30–9pm; call for off-season schedule. NEW AMERICAN.

If it's grandeur you're after, the setting supplies a surplus. This water-view dining room is vast, of the ballroom dimensions all but lost in the modern age. In assuming the reins in the kitchen Al Hynes, formerly of Harwichport's HarborWatch Room (now a private club), has reined in the prices as well, while upping the portions. His roast rack of lamb Provençal—seasoned with three mustards, coated with herbed bread crumbs, and cloaked in a *vert pre* sauce—would set you back considerably more just about anywhere else, without presenting so interesting a twist.

Moderate
✪ Vining's Bistro. 595 Main St. (in the center of town). ☎ **508/945-5033.** No reservations. Main courses $12–$17. AE, DC, MC, V. Apr to early Sept 5:30–10pm; call for off-season hours. FUSION.

If you're looking for cutting-edge cuisine in a sophisticated setting, venture upstairs at Chatham's innocuous-looking mini-mall and into this ineffably cool cafe. The film-noirish wall murals suggest a certain Bohemian abandon, but the menu is up to the minute, and priced to suit Generation X. Warm lobster taco with salsa fresca and crème fraîche, a spit-roasted chicken suffused with achiote-lime marinade and sided with a salad of oranges and jicama—these are very intelligent juxtapositions, and reason enough to keep returning.

Inexpensive
❸ Crosswind Landing. Chatham Municipal Airport, off George Ryders Rd. (about ¼ mile N of Rte. 28), W. Chatham. ☎ **508/945-5955.** Most items under $6. No credit cards. Mid-May to mid-Oct Mon–Sat 7am–3pm, Sun 8am–1:30pm. Closed mid-Oct to mid-May. AMERICAN.

Basically the attic of Chatham's tiny airport, this playful cafe is smaller than a Cessna. Kids will enjoy watching the planes and rearranging the table settings—with everyone's blessing. Collages of postcards and customer doodles, they're meant to be messed with. Even the adults who come out here specially for a nonconformist business lunch can hardly keep their hands off. It's worth a special trip: Everything from the muffins and deep-dish breakfast quiches to the croissants that enfold the "CBLT" are baked fresh on the premises, and the special soups and sandwiches dreamed up daily are truly special.

CHATHAM AFTER DARK

While most towns boast some comparable event, Chatham's free band concerts 40 players strong—cruise incontrovertibly at the top of the charts, attracting crowds in the thousands. Held in Kate Gould Park (off Chatham Bars Avenue, in the center of town) from July through early September, they kick off at 8pm every Friday. Better come early to claim your square of lawn, and be prepared to sing—or dance—along. Call 508/945-0342 for information.

Live bands accompany the three weekly feasts held at **The Beach House Grill,** at Chatham Bars Inn (☎ **508/945-0096**): Western line-dancing to go with the Monday-night barbecue, Dixieland to accompany Wednesday's clambake, and Calypso for Thursday's Caribbean blowout.

A great leveler, **The Chatham Squire,** 487 Main St. (in the center of town; ☎ **508/945-0945**), is a local institution that attracts all the social strata in town. CEOs, seafarers, and collegiates alike convene to kibitz over the roar of a jukebox or band, and the din of their own hubbub. Cover varies.

Beloved of moneyed locals, **Upstairs at Christian's,** 443 Main St. (in the center of town; ☎ **508/945-3362**), is a sporting piano bar with the air of a vintage frathouse—it summons up young scions gracefully slumming it among scuffed leather couches and purloined movie posters. Cinematically themed nibbles are always available, to offset the generous movie-motif drinks. No cover.

ORLEANS

31 miles (50 km) E of Sandwich, 25 miles (40km) S of Provincetown

Orleans is where the "Narrow Land" (the early Algonquian name for the Cape) starts to get very narrow indeed: From here on up—or "down," in local parlance—it's never more than a few miles wide from coast to coast, and in some spots as little as one. All three main roads (routes 6, 6A, and 28) converge here, too, so on summer weekends it acts as a rather frustrating funnel.

But this is also where the oceanside beaches open up, into a glorious expanse some 40 miles long, framed by dramatic dunes and blessed—from a swimmer's or boarder's perspective—with serious surf. The thousands of ship crews who crashed on these shoals over the past four centuries could hardly be expected to assume so sanguine a view. Shipwrecks may sound like the stuff of romance, but in these frigid waters hitting a sandbar usually spelled a death sentence for all involved. So enamored were local inhabitants of the opportunity to salvage that some improved their odds by becoming "mooncussers" who prayed for cloudy skies and, lacking them, lured ships toward shore by tying a lantern to the tale of a donkey, so as to simulate the listing of a ship at sea.

Such dark deeds seem very far removed from the Orleans of today, a sedate town that shadows Hyannis as a year-round center of commerce. Lacking the cohesiveness of smaller towns and somewhat chopped up by the roadways coursing through, it's not the most ideal town to hang out in, despite some appealing restaurants and shops. The village of East Orleans, however, is fast emerging as a sweet little off-beach town with both family and singles allure. About 2 miles east is seemingly endless (nearly 10-mile-long) Nauset Beach, the southernmost stretch of the Cape Cod National Seashore preserve, and a magnet for the young and the buff.

ESSENTIALS

GETTING THERE　After crossing either the Bourne or Sagamore Bridge, head east on Route 6 or 6A; both converge with Route 28 in Orleans.

VISITOR INFORMATION　Contact the **Orleans Chamber of Commerce,** Post Office Sq., Orleans, MA 02653 (☎ **800/865-1386** or 508/255-1386).

OUTDOOR PURSUITS

BEACHES　From here on up, on the eastern side you're dealing with the wild and whimsical Atlantic, which can be kittenish one day and tigerish the next. While storms may whip up surf you can actually take a board to, less confident swimmers should definitely wait a few days until the turmoil and riptides subside. In any case, current conditions are clearly posted at the entrance. Week-long parking permits ($25 for renters, $30 for transients) may be obtained from Town Hall on School Road (☎ **508/240-3700**). Day-trippers who arrive early enough—better make that before 9am—can pay at the gate.

- **Nauset Beach** in East Orleans (☎ **508/240-3780**): Stretching southward all the way past Chatham, this 10-mile-long barrier beach—part of the Cape Cod National Seashore, but managed by the town—has long been one of the Cape's more gonzo beach scenes—good surf, big crowds, lots of young people. Full facilities can be found within the 1,000-car parking lot; the in-season fee is $10 per car, which is also good for same-day parking at Skaket Beach (below). Substantial waves make for good surfing in the special section reserved for that purpose, and boogie boards are ubiquitous.
- **Skaket Beach,** off Skaket Beach Road to the west of town (☎ **508/255-0572**): This peaceful bay beach is a better choice for families with young children. When the tide recedes (as much as a mile), little kids will enjoy splashing about in the tide pools left behind. Parking costs $8, and you'd better turn up early.
- **Pilgrim Lake,** off Monument Road about one mile south of Main St.: Because it's covered by a lifeguard in season, this small freshwater beach charges an $8 parking fee.
- **Crystal Lake,** off Monument Road about ³/₄ mile south of Main Street: Parking—if you can find a space—is free, but there are no facilities.

BIKING/RECREATIONAL PATHS　Orleans presents the one slight gap in the 25-mile off-road **Cape Cod Rail Trail** (☎ **508/896-3491**): Just east of the Brewster border, the trail merges with town roads for about one and one-half miles. The best way to avoid vehicular aggravation is to zigzag west to scenic Rock Harbor. Bike rentals are available at **Orleans Cycle,** 26 Main St. in the center of town (☎ **508/ 255-9115**), and there are several good places (see "Take-Out & Picnic Fare," below) to grab some comestibles.

FISHING　Fishing is allowed in Baker Pond, Pilgrim Lake, and Crystal Lake; the latter is a likely spot to reel in trout and perch. For details and a license, visit Town Hall at Post Office Square in the center of town (☎ **508/240-3700**). Surf casting— no license needed—is permitted on **Nauset Beach South,** off Beach Road. **Rock Harbor,** a former packet landing on the bay (about 1¼ miles northwest of the town center) shelters New England's largest sportfishing fleet: some 18 boats at last count.

One call (☎ **800/287-1771** or 508/255-9757) will get you information on them all. Or go look them over; the sunsets are sublime.

NATURE TRAILS   Inland there's not much, but on the Atlantic shore is a biggie, Nauset Beach. Once you get past the swarms of people near the parking lot, you'll have about nine miles of beach mostly to yourself. You'll see tons of birds (take a field guide) and perhaps some harbor seals off-season.

WATER SPORTS   **Arey's Pond Boat Yard,** off Rte. 28 in S. Orleans (☎ **508/255-0994**), offers sailing lessons. The **Goose Hummock Outdoor Center,** 15 Rte. 6A, south of the rotary (☎ **508/255-0455,** web site www.goose.com), rents out canoes, kayaks, sailboards, etc., and the northern half of Pleasant Bay is the perfect place to use them; inquire about guided excursions. The **Pump House Surf Co.,** 9 Rte. 6A (☎ **508/240-2226),** will meet all your scuba, sailboarding, and surfing needs, while providing up-to-date reports on where to find the best waves.

SHOPPING

Though the shops are somewhat scattered, the town is full of great finds for browsers and grazers.

Continuum Antiques, 7 S. Orleans Rd. (Rte. 28, south of the junction of Route 6A; ☎ **508/255-8513**), has some 400 vintage light fixtures here, from Victorian on down, along with a smattering of old advertising signs and venerable duck decoys. **Countryside Antiques,** 6 Lewis Rd. (south of Main Street in the center of East Orleans; ☎ **508/240-0525**), has a lode of stylish furnishings, mostly old, though age—and price—are evidently not criteria. ✪ **Pleasant Bay Antiques,** 540 Orleans Rd. (Route 28, about ¹/₂ mile south of town center in South Orleans; ☎ **508/255-0930**), is such that you'd have to head south to Sotheby's to find such a fine collection of Early American antiques.

The **Addison Holmes Gallery,** 43 Rte. 28 (north of Main Street; ☎ **508/255-6200**), represents such very diverse painters as Pat de Groot, whose decades' worth of Provincetown landscapes seem perennially fresh, and Susan Baker of North Truro, a deliberate primitivist with a wicked sense of humor. **New Horizons,** 35 S. Orleans Rd. (Route 28, north of Main Street; ☎ **508/255-8766**), shows a top-notch collection of contemporary crafts, including the output of such local standouts as Pewter Crafters of Cape Cod and Chatham Pottery. Also look in on **Kemp Pottery,** 9 Rte. 6A (about ¹/₈ mile south of the rotary; ☎ **508/255-5853**), and **Spindrift Pottery,** 37 Rte. 6A (about ¹/₄ mile south of the rotary; ☎ **508/255-1404**).

With Nauset Marsh and Monomoy Island so close at hand, it's great luck to have in town a place like the **Bird Watcher's General Store,** 36 Rte. 6A (south of the rotary; ☎ **800/562-1512** or 508/255-6974). It stocks virtually every birdwatching accessory under the sun, from basic binoculars to costly telescopes, modest birdhouses to birdbaths fit for a tiny Roman emperor.

WHERE TO STAY

The Barley Neck Inn Lodge. 5 Beach Rd. (in the center of town), E. Orleans, MA 02643. ☎ **800/281-7505** or 508/255-8484. Fax 508/255-3626. 18 rms. A/C TV TEL. Summer (with continental breakfast) $95–$115 double. Off-season MAP packages available. AE, DC, MC, V.

Having radically transformed the Barley Neck Inn restaurant (see "Where to Dine," below), new owners Kathi and Joe Lewis treated the adjoining motel to an equally intensive makeover. Every room is a little different, but all boast fluffy designer comforters and stylish appointments. There's a little pool within the complex, and Nauset Beach is less than two miles down the road.

The Cove. 13 S. Orleans Rd. (Rte. 28, N of Main St.), Orleans, MA 02653. ☎ **800/343-2233** or 508/255-1203. 39 rms, 7 suites, 1 efficiency. A/C TV TEL. Summer $93–$164 double, $139–$164 suite or efficiency. AE, CB, DC, DISC, MC, V.

Sensibly turning its back on busy Route 28, this well-camouflaged motel complex focuses instead on placid Town Cove, where guests are offered a free mini-cruise in season. The interiors are adequate, if not dazzling, and a small heated pool and a restful gazebo overlook the waterfront. Meeting facilities are available for those whose business just won't wait.

⑤ **Hillbourne House.** 654 Orleans Rd. (Rte. 28, near the Harwich border), S. Orleans. MA 02662. ☎ **508/255-0780.** 6 rms. Summer (including full breakfast) $60–$80 double. No credit cards. Closed Nov to late Apr.

Overlooking a pocket of Pleasant Bay once popular with pirates, this 1798 homestead has seen a lot of history: Innkeeper Barbara Hayes can show you the trap door that conceals a stone pit pressed into service for the Underground Railroad. The three carriage house rooms are beautiful examples of their era, and can be booked en masse, with their own kitchen and living room. The three more modern units carved out of the erstwhile paddocks are nearly as charming, with high ceilings countrified by wooden beams. All guests are offered a lavish breakfast and have access to the inn's little private beach and dock; in fact, some regulars arrive by sea.

Kadee's Gray Elephant. 212 Main St. (in the center of town), E. Orleans, MA 02643. ☎ **508/255-6184.** Fax 508/240-2976. 10 studio apts. A/C TV TEL. Summer $110–$120 double. Weekly rates available. MC, V.

Available short-term or long-, these exuberantly decorated units (Day-Glo wicker yet!) are extremely cheery and ideal for families. Nauset Beach is a few miles down the road, and meanwhile everything you'll need is right in town—or right on the grounds. There's a friendly restaurant/snack bar right next door, and the little mini-golf course out back is geared just right for mini-golfers.

✪ **Nauset House Inn.** 143 Beach Rd. (about 1¹/₂ miles E of town center), E. Orleans, MA 02653. ☎ **508/255-2195.** 14 rms (6 with shared bath). Summer $65–$105 double. Full and continental breakfast available for a surcharge. MC, V. Closed Nov–Apr.

Heathcliff would have loved this place, or at least the surrounding moors. Modern nature-lovers with a taste for creature comforts will, too. Several of the rooms located in greenery-draped outbuildings feature such romantic extras as a sunken bath or private deck. The most romantic hideaway here, though, is a 1907 conservatory appended to the 1810 farmhouse inn. It's the perfect place to lounge with a novel or lover (preferably both) as the rain pounds down, prompting the profuse camellias to waft their heady perfume. Breakfast would seem relatively workaday, were it not for the setting—a pared-down, rustic refectory—and innkeeper Diane Johnson's memorable muffins and pastries.

WHERE TO DINE

Very Expensive

✪ **The Barley Neck Inn.** 5 Beach Rd. (about ¹/₂ mile E of town center), E. Orleans. ☎ **800/281-7505** or 508/255-0212. Fax 508/255-3226. Reservations recommended. Main courses $15–$26. AE, DC, MC, V. Early July to early Sept daily 5:30pm–midnight; call for off-season hours. NEW AMERICAN.

Recently rescued from dereliction and tastefully restored, complete with fanlight door and mullioned windows, this 1857 captain's house immediately ascended into the first rank. The owners, enterprising ex-New Yorkers Joe and Kathi Lewis, have recruited a superb chef in Franck Champely, who came from Taillevent and Maxim's by way of New York's Four Seasons. His classical background shines in straightforward, yet subtle dishes such as grilled Atlantic salmon filet with a red-pepper coulis and basil vinaigrette, or sautéed shrimp in a sauce of sweet garlic and chablis atop lemon angelhair pasta and shiitake mushrooms. The cuisine may be worship-worthy, the wine list a connoisseur's delight, but the ambience is populist and festive, verging on boisterous. It's a very good mix.

Off the Bay Cafe. 28 Main St. (at Rte. 6A, in the center of town). ☎ **508/255-5505.** Reservations recommended. Main courses $18–$24. AE, CB, DC, DISC, MC, V. July–Aug 8–11am, 11:30am–4pm, and 5:30–10pm; call for off-season hours. NEW AMERICAN.

Admirably ambitious since its inception in the early 1980s, this snappy 19th-century storefront keeps delivering the goods. In light of the neo-nautical decor (lots of varnished wood and polished brass), one might expect passable seafood; instead, it's superlative, with such brilliant accompaniments as pineapple salsa or papaya hollandaise. The rotisseried game birds are every bit as well dressed, and superb.

Moderate

۞ Joe's Beach Road Bar & Grille. The Barley Neck Inn, 5 Beach Rd. (about ¹/₂ mile E of town center), E. Orleans. ☎ **800/281-7505** or 508/255-0212. Fax 508/255-3226. Reservations recommended. Main courses $7–$21. AE, DC, MC, V. Early July to early Sept daily 5:30pm–midnight; call for off-season hours. AMERICAN.

Joe Lewis's self-imposed mandate for his namesake bar is "good food, large drinks, and big fun." That's exactly what you'll find in this spacious tavern, built with rugged beams salvaged from a local saltworks. World War II posters (found in the inn's attic) and snazzy Roaring Twenties menswear ads (Joe's own collection, reflecting his previous occupation) adorn the barnboard walls. Off-season, a fire blazes in the huge fieldstone fireplace fronted by inviting navy-blue armchairs. Most everyone crowds around the 28-foot mahogany bar, though: It's mingling room only. Once you've secured your own table—the tablecloths are denim, the napkins bandannas—you have the run of a terrifically varied menu, which includes the exquisite dishes served in the more formal restaurant next door. If you just want to nosh, consider Joe's pizza (with goat cheese, roasted peppers, and spinach) or hifalutin fish and chips—beer-battered, with watercress aïoli.

Kadee's Lobster & Clam Bar. 212 Main St. (in the center of town), E. Orleans. ☎ **508/255-6184.** Fax 508/240-2926. No reservations. Main courses $7–$17. MC, V. Late June to Aug daily 11:30am–9:30pm; late May to late Jun Sat–Sun 11:30am–9:30pm. Closed early Sept to late May. AMERICAN.

Achieving an air of effortless authenticity, this atmospheric sea shanty has been rigged to improve on the climate. When the sun's out, the flower-print umbrellas pop up in the patio; as soon as the chilly sea-borne fog moves in, a curtained awning drops down. The menu is equally adaptable: There's nothing like the classic chowders and stews or a platter of sautéed "seafood simmer" to take the chill off; fine weather, on the other hand, calls for a lobster roll, or perhaps the obligatory (at least once a summer) shore dinner splurge.

۞ Land Ho! 38 Main St. (at Rte. 6A, in the center of town). ☎ **508/255-5165.** No reservations. Main courses $7–$15. AE, DISC, MC, V. Daily 11:30am–midnight. AMERICAN.

A longtime hit with the locals (who call it, affectionately, "the Ho"), this rough-and-tumble pub attracts its share of knowledgeable tourists as well, drawn by the reasonable prices and general bonhomie. The food may be nothing to write home about, but it's satisfying and easy on the budget. Just being there (provided you can find the door: it's around back) will make you feel like an imminent insider.

Inexpensive
Binnacle Tavern. 20 S. Orleans Rd. (Rte. 28, N of Main St.). ☎ **508/255-4847.** Most items under $12. AE, MC, V. Apr to mid-Oct daily 5–11:30pm; call for off-season hours. ITALIAN.

All sorts of strange nautical salvage adorns the barnboard walls of this popular pizzeria, where the pies—reputed to be the Cape's best—come with some very peculiar toppings, for those so inclined. More conservative combos are available, along with traditional Italian fare.

Take-Out & Picnic Fare
The Australians really are different from us, at least when it comes to their beloved "barbie." The charcoal-roasted chickens-to-go at **The Australian Chicken Shop,** 84 Rte. 6A (north of Main Street.; ☎ 508/240-3282)—"chooks" to the initiate— are crisp and intriguingly spiced. Even a devout vegetarian will find something to love in the healthy, ingenious side salads.

Pick your spot anywhere on the Cape—or within the continental United States, for that matter—and **Clambake Celebrations,** 9 West Rd. (at Skaket Beach Road, about one mile west of town center; ☎ **800/423-4038** or 508/255-3289), will pro- vide you with a coastal feast to go: lobsters, steamers, mussels, sausage, corn, pota- toes, all packed in a steamer pot and ready to boil. If you're in the vicinity, they'll even loan you a charcoal grill.

The charming little **Cottage St. Bakery,** Cottage Street (off Route 28, at the junc- tion of Route 6A; ☎ 508/255-2821), is the perfect place to grab a morning Danish (the family-size ones resemble pizzas) or indulge in a dessert.

✪ **Fancy's Farm,** 199 Main St. (in the center of E. Orleans; ☎ 508/255-1949), makes vegetables look unusually appealing. They're especially prime, to begin with, whether domestic or imported from halfway across the world. The charming barnlike setting helps, as do the extras—fresh breads, pastries, juices, and exotic salads and soups to go.

Longing for the real thing, a real mouth-wrestler? **New York Bagels,** 125 Rte. 6A (south of Main Street in Orleans; ☎ 508/255-0255), delivers the goods.

ORLEANS AFTER DARK
Joe's Beach Road Bar & Grille (☎ 508/255-0212; see "Where to Dine," above) is a big old barn of a bar that might as well be town hall: It's where you'll find all the locals exchanging juicy gossip and jokes. On Sunday evenings in season, the week- end warriors who survived in style can enjoy live "Jazz at Joe's." There's never a cover charge.

At the **Orleans Inn,** 3 Old County Rd. (on Town Cove, south of the rotary; ☎ 508/255-2222), blues, rock, and reggae, performed by popular local bands, rock the rehabbed Victorian manse throughout the summer. Call for schedule; cover varies.

4 The Outer Cape

Whereas the rest of the Cape may have its civilized enticements, it's only on the Outer Cape that the landscape, even the air, feels really *beachy*. Gradually the canopy of trees gives way to stands of stunted pine and scrub oak. You can smell the seashore just around the corner over the horizon—in fact, everywhere about you, because you're never more than a mile or two away.

And when you find it, it is a revelation. No high-rise hotels. No tacky amusement arcades. Not a whole lot of anything, other than dune grass rippling in the wind and the occasional cottage some lucky soul managed to get grandfathered before the seacoast succumbed to a federally-protected slumber back in the early 1960s. Henry David Thoreau witnessed virtually the same panorama when he came roaming in the 1850s. With any luck, it will still be here, unchanged, when your great-great-grand-children come to view this great natural wonder.

EASTHAM

35 miles (56km) E of Sandwich, 21 miles (34km) S of Provincetown

One thing you won't see in Eastham is tanned socialites clutching thousand-dollar Nantucket baskets as they peruse the latest shipment of distressed continental antiques. Despite its optimal location (the distance from bay to ocean is as little as one mile in spots), Eastham is one of the least pretentious locales on the Cape—and yet highly popular, as the gateway to the magnificent Cape Cod National Seashore.

The downside—or up, depending how you look at it—is that there aren't a whole lot of shops or attractions, or at least few worth checking out.

Most visitors won't bother. You can tell as soon as you pull into town: This is a place meant for kicking back—for letting the sun, surf, and sand dictate your day.

ESSENTIALS

GETTING THERE   After crossing either the Bourne or Sagamore Bridge, head east on Route 6 or 6A to Orleans, and north on Route 6.

VISITOR INFORMATION   Contact the **Eastham Chamber of Commerce,** Route 6 at Fort Hill Road, Eastham, MA 02642 (☎ **508/255-3444**).

OUTDOOR PURSUITS

BEACHES   From here on up, the Atlantic beaches are best reserved for strong swimmers: Waves are *big* (often taller than you) and the undertow can be treacherous. The flat, nearly placid bay beaches, on the other hand, are just right for families with young children. The sand slopes so gradually, you won't have to worry about them slipping in over their heads. When the tide recedes (twice daily), it leaves a mile-wide playground of rippled sand full of fascinating creatures, including horseshoe and hermit crabs.

- **Coast Guard** and **Nauset Light,** off Ocean View Drive: Connected to outlying parking lots by a free shuttle, these pristine National Seashore beaches have lifeguards and rest rooms. Parking is $5/day, $15/season.
- **First Encounter, Thumpertown, Campground,** and **Sunken Meadow:** These town-operated bay beaches generally charge $5 a day; permits ($20/week) can be obtained from the Highway Department on Old Orchard Road in N. Eastham (☎ **508/255-1965**).
- **Great Pond** and **Wiley Park:** These two town-run freshwater beaches are also open to the public, on the same terms as the bay beaches.

BIKING/RECREATIONAL PATHS   With plenty of free parking available at the Cape Cod National Seashore's Salt Pond Visitor Center (☎ **508/255-3421**), Eastham makes a convenient access point for the **Cape Cod Rail Trail** (☎ **508/896-3491**). Northward, it's about five wildflower-lined miles to Wellfleet, where the trail currently ends (further expansion is planned); Dennis is about 20 miles southwest. A 1.6-mile spur trail, winding through locust and apple groves, links the visitors center with glorious Coast Guard Beach: It's for bikes only (no blades).

Rentals are available at the **Little Capistrano Bike Shop** (☎ **508/255-6515**), on Salt Pond Road just west of Route 6, or **Idle Times,** 4550 Route 6 in the center of N. Eastham (☎ **800/924-8281** on the Cape, or 508/255-8281), which also carries in-line skates. The best trailside eatery—fried clams, lobster, and the like—is **Arnold's**

(☎ 508/255-2575), located on Route 6 about one mile north of the visitors center.

FISHING   Eastham has four ponds open to fishing: **Herring Pond** is stocked. For a freshwater fishing or shell-fishing license, visit the Department of Public Works on Old Orchard Road (☎ 508/255-1965). Surf-casting is permitted at **Nauset Beach North** (off Doane Road) and **Nauset Light Beach** (off Cable Road).

NATURE TRAILS   There are five "self-guiding nature trails"—for walkers only—with descriptive markers within this portion of the **Cape Cod National Seashore.** The 1¹/₂-mile **Fort Hill Trail** off Fort Hill Road (off Route 6, about one mile south of town center), takes off from a free parking lot just past the Captain Edward Penniman House, a fancy multicolored 1868 Second Empire manse maintained by the CCNS. The house is open daily from 1 to 4pm in season, but the exterior far outshines the interior, and more interesting sights await outside. Following the trail markers, you'll pass "Indian Rock" (bearing the marks of untold generations who used it to sharpen their tools) and enjoy scenic vantage points overlooking the channel-carved marsh—keep an eye out for egrets and great blue herons—and out to sea. The Fort Hill Trail hooks up with the one-half-mile **Red Cedar Swamp Trail,** offering boardwalk views of an ecology otherwise inaccessible.

Three relatively short trails fan out from the Salt Pond Visitor Center. The most unusual is the ¹/₄-mile **Buttonbush Trail,** specially adapted for the sight-impaired, with a guide rope and descriptive plaques in both oversize type and Braille. The **Doane Loop Trail,** a ¹/₂-mile woodland circuit about one mile east of the visitors center, is graded to allow access to wheelchairs and strollers. The one-mile **Nauset Marsh Trail** skirts Salt Pond to cross the marsh (via boardwalk) and open fields, before returning by way of a recovering forest.

WATER SPORTS   The best way to experience Nauset Marsh is by kayak or canoe. Rentals are available in neighboring towns: the closest source would be the **Goose Hummock Outdoor Center,** 15 Rte. 6A in Orleans (☎ 508/255-0455). **Jack's Boat Rentals** (☎ 508/349-9808) has a seasonal outlet on Wellfleet's Gull Pond, which connects to Higgins Pond by way of a placid, narrow channel lined with red maples and choked with yellow water lilies. In addition to watercraft to go, Jack's also offers guided paddle tours of Eastham's Herring River. For information about other excellent naturalist-guided tours, inquire about trips sponsored by the **Cape Cod Museum of Natural History** (☎ 800/479-3867 or 508/896-3867) and the **Wellfleet Bay Wildlife Sanctuary** (☎ 508/349-2615).

✪ SALT POND VISITOR CENTER   Since you're undoubtedly going to spend a fair amount of time on the beach, you might as well find out how it came to be, what other creatures you'll be sharing it with, and how not to harm them or it. I spent about five summers within a half-mile of the National Seashore's main visitor center, and never bothered to stop in, until 13 straight days of rain finally drove us there. Now I return at every opportunity: There's always more to learn.

Occupying more than half of the land mass north of Orleans and covering the entire 30-mile oceanfront, the 44,000-acre Cape Cod National Seashore was set aside as a sanctuary in 1961. Actually, it's not entirely free: If you're an American citizen, you part-own it, and contribute to its upkeep. Get your money's worth, and more, by taking advantage of the excellent educational exhibits and continuous film loops offered here. Particularly fascinating is a video about the accidental discovery, in 1990, of an 11,000-year-old campsite amid the storm-ravaged dunes of Coast Guard beach—which was about five miles inland when these early settlers spent their summers here. After absorbing some of the local history, be sure to take time to venture out— on your own or with a ranger guide—on some of the surrounding trails (see "Nature Trails," above).

The Center is on Salt Pond Road (east of Route 6; ☎ **508/255-0788**). Free admission. It's open daily from June through August from 9am to 6pm; call for off-season hours.

WHERE TO STAY

Over Look Inn. 3085 Rte. 6 (about ¼ mile N of town center, opposite Salt Pond Visitor Center), Eastham, MA 02642. ☎ **800/356-1121** or 508/255-1886. Fax 508/240-0345. 10 rms, 3 suites. A/C. Summer (including full breakfast and afternoon tea) $95–$145 double, $135 suite. AE, CB, DC, DISC, MC, V.

Henry Beston slept in this multicolored 1869 Queen Anne Victorian while planning his legendary sojourn at the Outermost House. You can bet it was a lot less cushy— and enchanting—before Scottish innkeepers Nan and Ian Aitchison took over in 1983. The house now reflects their many enthusiasms: The library, for instance, is dedicated to Winston Churchill, and the Ernest Hemingway Billiard Room is lined with trophies that would have done Papa proud. Their son Clive's colorful abstract canvases adorn many of the common spaces and rooms, some of which come enhanced with brass beds and clawfoot tubs. Pilgrims piking along the Rail Trail will appreciate the hearty breakfasts, including an authentic "kedgeree," whose contents are best left unlisted until you've had a taste.

The Penny House. 4885 Rte. 6, N. Eastham, MA 02651. ☎ **800/554-1751** or 508/255-6632. Fax 508/255-4893. 11 rms. Summer (including full breakfast) $95–$150 double. AE, DISC, MC, V.

Whizzing past on Route 6, you'd scarcely suspect there's a peaceful inn tucked away behind a massive hedge. This neat, comfortable B&B, graced with the warmth of Australian innkeeper Margaret Keith, is clustered around a 1751 saltbox, now the setting for rather rich homemade breakfasts. The rooms vary widely in terms of space and price, but all are nicely appointed and meticulously maintained. A communal phone and TV in the cathedral-ceilinged "gathering room" encourage socializing while leaving the rooms as distraction-free oases.

✪ **The Whalewalk Inn.** 220 Bridge Rd. (about ¾ mile W of Orleans rotary), Eastham, MA 02641. ☎ **508/255-0617.** Fax 508/240-0017. 7 rms, 5 suites, 1 cottage. A/C. Summer (including full breakfast) $125–$150 double, $165 cottage, $165–$180 suite and efficiency. MC, V. Closed Dec–Apr.

Regularly hailed as one of the Cape's prettiest inns, this 1830s Greek Revival manse— sequestered in a quiet residential area just a few blocks off the Rail Trail—fully deserves its reputation. Innkeeper Carolyn Smith has dressed up every last space in a tasteful, mostly pastel palette more suggestive of sunny California than dour New England; eclectic furnishings (many of them culled from Countryside Antiques in Orleans) cohabit harmoniously in the common rooms, where complimentary evening hors d'oeuvres are served. Both Carolyn and Dick, who is responsible for the indulgent gourmet breakfasts, can knowledgeably steer you to the best the area has to offer, and will lend you a bike if you like.

WHERE TO DINE

Old-timers convene at the counter of the **Hole-in-One Donut Shop,** 4295 Rte. 6A, about ¼ mile south of North Eastham; (☎ **508/255-9446**), to ponder the state of the world. You can join in—or scurry home with your haul of hand-cut doughnuts and fresh-baked muffins and bagels.

Arnold's. 3580 Rte. 6 (about 1¼ mile N of town center). ☎ **508/255-2575.** Main courses $7–$16. No credit cards. Daily 11am–10pm. Closed mid-Sept to mid-May. AMERICAN.

Offering a takeout window on the Rail Trail and a picnic grove for those who hate to waste vacation hours sitting indoors, this popular eatery dishes out all the usual seashore standards, from rich and crunchy fried clams (cognoscenti know to order whole clams, not strips) to foot-long chili dogs.

Eastham Lobster Pool. 4360 Rte. 6 (in the center of town), N. Eastham. ☎ **508/255-9706.** No reservations. Main courses $11–$25. AE, DC, DISC, MC, V. Early July to early Sept Sun–Thurs 11:30am–9pm, Fri–Sat 11:30am–10pm; call for off-season hours. Closed Nov–Mar. AMERICAN.

For three decades, the scrape of metal chairs against the cement floor of this no-frills dining hall has been synonymous with seafood feasts. You can eye your potential entree—scrabbling among a tankful of feisty lobsters—as you wait in line to gain admittance. (The locals, along with smarter tourists, know to show up in the early, early evening—i.e., late afternoon.) Beyond the lobsters, which come in some monster proportions, there's all sorts of fish, all available grilled, broiled, baked, fried, stuffed, or simply poached. As far back as the early 1980s, the specials were exhibiting harbingers of New American panache, and they still pack some sophisticated surprises: champagne-shallot butter, perhaps, to top a halibut steak. The bluefish, always affordable, is always fabulous. Some rather nice wines are available by the glass.

Mitchel's Bistro. At Lori's Family Restaurant, Main St. Mercantile (about ¼ mile S of town center), N. Eastham. ☎ **508/255-4803.** Main courses $10–$17. AE, DISC, MC, V. July–Aug daily 6–10pm; call for off-season hours. NEW AMERICAN/INDIAN.

Mitch Rosenbaum is a gifted chef (he used to run Wellfleet's Cielo) and Laxmi Venkateshwaran prepares some lovely and authentic Indian fare. However, it's hard to imagine how they'll ever make a go of this operation, which "moonlights" as a mall restaurant, the kind indifferently decorated with pseudo captain's chairs: The culture gap is just too glaring. But one wishes them luck. Anyone who can whip up grilled butterflied leg of lamb, much less grilled duck with fresh mango-pineapple glaze, at these prices deserves a round of applause, and steady patronage.

WELLFLEET

42 miles (68km) NE of Sandwich, 14 miles (23km) S of Provincetown

Wedged between tame Eastham and wild Truro, Wellfleet—with the well-tended look of a classic New England town—is the golden mean, the perfect destination for artists, writers, off-duty psychiatrists, and other contemplative types who hope to find more in the landscape than mere quaintness or rusticity. Distinguished literati such as Edna St. Vincent Millay and Edmund Wilson put this rural village on the map in the 1920s, in the wake of Provincetown's bohemian heyday. In her brief and tumultuous tenure as Wilson's wife, Mary McCarthy pilloried the pretensions of the summer population in her novel *A Charmed Life*, but had to concede that the region boasts a certain natural beauty: "steel-blue fresh-water ponds and pine forests and mushrooms and white bluffs dropping to a strangely pebbled beach."

To this day, Wellfleet remains remarkably unspoiled. Once you depart from Route 6, commercialism is kept to a minimum, though the town boasts plenty of appealing shops—including a score of distinguished galleries—and a couple of excellent New American restaurants. It's hard to imagine any other community on the Cape supporting so sophisticated an undertaking as the Wellfleet Harbor Actors Theatre, or hosting such a wholesome event as public square dancing on the adjacent Town Pier. And where else could you find, right next door to an outstanding nature preserve (the Wellfleet Bay Wildlife Sanctuary), a thriving drive-in movie theater?

ESSENTIALS

GETTING THERE   After crossing either the Bourne or Sagamore Bridge, head east on Route 6 or 6A to Orleans, and north on Route 6.

VISITOR INFORMATION   Contact the **Wellfleet Chamber of Commerce,** off Route 6, Wellfleet, MA 02663 (☎ **508/349-2510**).

OUTDOOR PURSUITS

BEACHES   Though the profiles are far from hard and fast, Wellfleet's fabulous ocean beaches tend to sort themselves demographically: LeCount Hollow is popular with families, Newcomb Hollow with high schoolers, White Crest with the college crowd (including surfers and off-hours hang-gliders), and Cahoon with 30-somethings. Alas, only the latter two beaches permit parking by nonresidents. To enjoy the other two, as well as Burton Baker Beach on the harbor and Duck Harbor on the bay, plus three freshwater ponds, you'll have to walk or bike in, or see if you qualify for a sticker ($25/week). Bring proof of residency to the seasonal Beach Sticker Booth on the Town Pier, or call the Wellfleet Recreation Department (☎ **508/349-0818**).

- **Marconi Beach,** off Marconi Beach Road in South Wellfleet: A National Seashore property, this cliff-lined beach (with rest rooms) charges an entry fee of $5 a day, or only $15 for the season. *Note:* The bluffs are so high, the beach lies in shadow by late afternoon.
- **White Crest** and **Cahoon Hollow** beaches, off Ocean View Drive in Wellfleet: These two town-run ocean beaches—big with surfers—are open to all. Both have snack bars and bathrooms. Parking costs $10 a day.
- **Mayo Beach,** Kendrick Avenue (near the Town Pier): Right by the harbor, facing south, this beach (with rest rooms) is hardly secluded but will please young waders and splashers. And the price is right: parking is free. You could grab a tasty, cheap bite at Painter's Lunch next to the Wellfleet Harbor Actor's Theatre: It's neo-Bohemian ramshackle, keeps odd hours, and has no phone, but it's fun.

BIKING/RECREATIONAL PATHS   The terminus (to date) of the 25-mile-and-growing **Cape Cod Rail Trail** (☎ **508/896-3491**), Wellfleet is also among its more desirable destinations: A country road off the bike path leads right to LeCount Hollow Beach. Located at the current terminus, the **Black Duck Sports Shop,** 1446 Rte. 6 in Wellfleet (☎ **508/349-9801**), stocks everything from rental bikes to "belly-boards" and inflatable boats; the deli at the adjoining **South Wellfleet General Store** (☎ **508/349-2335**) can see to your snacking needs.

FISHING   For a license to fish at Long Pond, Great Pond, or Gull Pond (all stocked with trout and full of native perch, pickerel, and sunfish), visit Town Hall at 300 Main St. (☎ **508/349-0300**). Surf casting, which doesn't require a license, is permitted at the town beaches. Shellfishing licenses—Wellfleet's oysters are world-famous—can be obtained from the Shellfish Department on the Town Pier off Kendrick Avenue. (☎ **508/349-0325**). Also heading out from here, in season, is the 60-foot fishing boat *Naviator* (☎ **508/349-6003**), and three smaller sportsfish-ermen: the *Erin-H* (☎ **508/349-9663**), *Jac's Mate* (☎ **508/255-2978**), and *Snoop* (☎ **508/349-6113**).

NATURE TRAILS You'll find five miles of very scenic trails lined with lupines and bayberries—Goose Pond, Silver Spring, and Bay View—within the **Wellfleet Bay Wildlife Sanctuary** in South Wellfleet (see below). Right in town, the short, picturesque boardwalk known as **Uncle Tim's Bridge,** off E. Commercial Street, crosses Duck Creek to access a tiny island crisscrossed by paths. The Cape Cod National Seashore maintains two spectacular self-guided trails. The 1¼-mile **Atlantic White Cedar Swamp Trail,** off the parking area for the Marconi Wireless Station, shelters a rare stand of the lightweight species prized by Native Americans as wood for canoes; red maples are slowly crowding out the cedars, but meanwhile the tea-tinted, moss-choked swamp is a magical place, refreshingly cool even at the height of summer. A boardwalk will see you over the muck (these peat bogs are 7 feet deep in places), but the return trip does entail a calf-testing half-mile trek through deep sand. Consider it a warmup for magnificent **Great Island,** jutting four miles into the bay (off the western end of Chequessett Neck Road) to cup Wellfleet Harbor. Before attaching itself to the mainland in 1831, Great Island harbored a busy whaling post; a 1970 dig turned up the foundations of an early 18th-century tavern. These days the "island" is quite uninhabited, and a true refuge for those strong enough to go the distance. Just be sure to cover up, wear sturdy shoes, bring water, and venture to Jeremy Point—the very tip—*only* if you're sure the tide is going out.

WATER SPORTS **Jack's Boat Rentals,** located on Gull Pond off Gull Pond Road about one-half mile south of the Truro border (☎ **800/300-3787** or 508/349-9808), rents out the usual craft—canoes, kayaks, sailboards, Sunfish—on Gull Pond, and also organizes guided paddle explorations of nearby kettle ponds and tidal rivers. A trip from Wellfleet's Town Pier across to the harbor to Great Island will get you beautifully nowhere, fast. **Surfing** is restricted to **White Crest Beach,** and **sailboarding** to **Burton Baker Beach** at Indian Neck during certain tide conditions; ask for a copy of the regulations at the Beach Sticker Booth on the Town Pier. The **Chequessett Yacht & Country Club** on Chequessett Neck Road in Wellfleet (☎ **508/349-3704**) offers sailing lessons for approximately $30 an hour. For those who already know how, **Wellfleet Marine Corp.** on the Town Pier (☎ **508/349-2233**) rents 14- to 20-foot sailboats in season.

WELLFLEET BAY WILDLIFE SANCTUARY A spiffy new eco-friendly visitor center serves as both introduction and gateway to this 1,000-acre refuge maintained by the Massachusetts Audubon Society. Passive solar heat and composting toilets are just a few of the waste-cutting elements incorporated in the seemingly simple $1.6 million building, which nestles into its wooded site like well-camouflaged wildlife. You'll see plenty of the latter—especially lyrical red-winged blackbirds and circling osprey—as you follow five miles of looping trails through pine forests, saltmarsh, and moors. To hone your observation skills, avail yourself of the naturalist-guided walks scheduled throughout the day, and sometimes into the night (see "Wellfleet After Dark," below): You'll see and learn so much more. Also inquire about special workshops for children (some, like the Japanese "fish-printing" session, are truly ingenious) and about canoeing, snorkeling, birding, and off-season seal-watching excursions. *Note:* It's worth joining the Massachusetts Audubon Society just for the chance—afforded only to members—to camp out here.

The center is located off West Road (about one mile north of Eastham border), in South Wellfleet (☎ **508/349-2615;** fax 508/349-2632). Trail use is free for Massachusetts Audubon Society members; the trail fee for nonmembers is $3 adults, $2 seniors and children. Trails are open July through August from 8am to 8pm, and September through June from 8am to dusk. The visitor center is open July and August daily from 8:30am to 5pm; during the off-season it's closed Mondays.

WELLFLEET HISTORY

Wellfleet Historical Society Museum. 266 Main St. (in the center of town). ☎ **508/ 349-9157.** Admission $1 adults, children under 12 free. Late June to early Sept Tues–Sat 2–5pm. Closed early Sept to late June.

Every last bit of spare Wellfleet memorabilia seems to have been crammed into this old storefront. The volunteer curators have taken pains to arrange the surfeit of artifacts so that visitors can follow up on a particular interest—the United Fruit Co., say, which got its start here in 1870 when one of Lorenzo Dow Baker's swift clipper ships delivered a cargo of exotic bananas, or Marconi's mysterious transoceanic experiments. Even restless children are likely to find something of interest, particularly among the antique toys in the attic. Inquire about the lecture schedule: The museum hosts some fascinating speakers, and sponsors a chowder supper once a summer.

SHOPPING

Boasting some two dozen arts emporia, Wellfleet has begun hailing itself as "the art gallery town." Though it may lag behind Provincetown in terms of quantity, the quality does achieve comparable heights. Crafts make a strong showing, too, as do contemporary women's clothing and eclectic home furnishings. Just one drawback: Unlike Provincetown, which has something to offer virtually year-round, Wellfleet pretty much rolls up its sidewalks come Columbus Day.

۞ Cherry Stone Gallery, 70 E. Commercial St. (about ⅛ mile south of E. Main Street; ☎ **508/349-3026**), is probably more influential than all the others put together. It got a head start, opening in 1972 and showing such local luminaries as Rauschenberg, Motherwell, and, more recently, Wellfleet resident Helen Miranda Wilson.

The smallish **Cove Gallery,** 15 Commercial St. (by Duck Creek; ☎ **508/ 349-2530**), carries the paintings and prints of many well-known artists, including Barry Moser and Leonard Baskin. Alan Nyiri, whose dazzling color photographs are collected in the coffee-table book *Cape Cod,* shows regularly, as does Carla Golembe, whose lively Caribbean-influenced tableaux have graced several children's books.

Crafts make a stronger stand than art at **Left Bank Gallery,** 25 Commercial St. (by Duck Creek; ☎ **508/349-9451**). The **Left Bank Print Gallery,** 3 W. Main St. (in the center of town; ☎ **508/439-7939**) features the spillover from the Left Bank Gallery, particularly prints.

Among the knockouts at **Swansborough Gallery,** 230 Main St. (in the center of town; ☎ **508/349-1883**), are Dennis sculptor Laura Baksa's dreamy alabaster figures and fragments thereof.

WHERE TO STAY

۞ Even'Tide. 650 Rte. 6 (about 1 mile N of Eastham border), S. Wellfleet, MA 02667. ☎ **800/368-0007** or 508/349-3410. Fax 508/349-7804. 28 rms, 3 apts. A/C TV TEL. Summer $72–$96 double, $96 efficiency. AE, CB, DC, DISC, MC, V.

Set back from the road in its own roomy compound complete with playground, this motel feels more like a friendly village centered around a large, heated indoor pool— a godsend in inclement weather. The Rail Trail goes right by it, and a ¾-mile footpath through the woods leads to Marconi Beach.

⑤ **The Holden Inn.** 140 Commercial St. (about ⅛ mile N of the Town Pier), Wellfleet, MA 02663. ☎ **508/349-3450.** 26 rms (14 with shared bath), 1 suite. Summer $58–$68 double, $110 suite (for 4). No credit cards. Closed mid-Oct to mid-Apr.

Run by the same family since 1924, this three-building complex—centered on an 1840 captain's house fronted by a welcoming porch and classic picket fence—projects the leisurely ease of a bygone era. Furnishings tend to be well-worn but homey, and the hospitality is genuinely gracious.

WHERE TO DINE

✪ **Aesop's Tables.** 316 Main St. (in the center of town). ☎ **508/349-6450.** Reservations recommended. Main courses $16–$23. AE, CB, DISC, MC, V. Jul–Aug Wed–Sun noon–3pm and 5:30–9:30pm; Mon–Tues 5:30–9:30pm; call for off-season hours. Closed mid-Oct to mid-May. NEW AMERICAN.

This delightful restaurant—offbeat and avant-garde enough to stay interesting year after year, since 1965—has it all: a handsome, historic setting (this was a 19th-century governor's summer house, the pride of a proud town), a relaxed and festive atmosphere, and utterly delectable food, reliably and artistically turned out by executive chef Peter Rennert. Brian Dunne is at once owner and host; it's he who sets the mood and oversees the sourcing of the superb local provender—even growing some of the edible flowers and delicate greens that go into the "Monet's Garden" salad. The scallops (served whole) and oysters come straight from the bay to be imaginatively treated. While some entrees have begun to show evidence of southwestern savvy and other welcome world-beat influences, the desserts are sacrosanct. Many fervid followers simply could not get through the summer without enjoying at least one encounter with "Clementine's Citrus Tart," a rich *pâté sable* offset by a piquant mousse blending fruit and white chocolate.

⑤ **Bayside Lobster Hutt.** 91 Commercial St. (about ¼ mile N of the Town Pier). ☎ **508/349-6333.** No reservations. Main courses $8–$20. No credit cards. July–Aug daily noon–10pm; late May–June and Sept daily 4:30–9pm. Closed Oct to late May. AMERICAN.

For your "dress-down" night (or several in a row), you couldn't do better than this classic, locally owned lobster joint, housed in a grizzled 1857 oyster shack—look for the life-size lobsterman on the roof. Streams of customers are willing to wait an hour or more to crowd into the communal mess hall at the height of summer. "Feeding frenzy" is the only way to describe the claw-cracking hordes at the long oilcloth-covered plank tables.

Finely JP's. 19 Freedjum Rd. (on Rte. 6, about 1 mile N of Eastham border), S. Wellfleet. ☎ **508/349-7500.** No reservations. Main courses $12–$15. MC, DISC, V. July–Aug daily 5–10pm; call for off-season schedule. Closed mid-Dec to mid-Jan. NEW AMERICAN.

The passing motorist who happens upon this roadside eatery will feel like a clever explorer indeed, even if locals have long been in on the secret. Were it not for the venue—a rather nondescript wood-paneled box right by the busy roadway—chef-owner John Pontius could charge a lot more for his polished cuisine. As it is, you could feast on baked oysters Bienville (doused with wine and cream and topped with a mushroom-onion *duxelle* and grated Parmesan) and an improvisatory "Wellfleet paella" having barely broken a twenty. Pass it on.

Flying Fish. 29 Briar Lane (off Main St.). ☎ **508/349-3100.** No reservations. Main courses $13–$19. MC, V. Late June to early Sept daily 7am–10pm; call for off-season hours. Closed Nov–Mar. NEW AMERICAN.

Just the thing: a deli/cafe catering to esoteric cravings (such as Jamaican jerk chicken, tabouli, Brie omelets) during the day, and loftier expectations (such as "lobster romantique" atop black pepper fettuccini with ginger-cinnamon beurre blanc) at night. Better yet, the on-site bakery means immediate access to such devilish confections as chocolate Chambord cake—plus the tourists who clog Main Street haven't yet caught on.

The Lighthouse. 317 Main St. (in the center of town). ☎ **508/349-3681.** Main courses $9–$13. DISC, MC, V. Daily 6:30am–10pm. AMERICAN.

Nothing special in and of itself, this bustling year-round institution is an off-season haven for locals, and a beacon to passing tourists year-round. Except on Thursday's "Mexican Night," the menu is all-American normal, from the steak-and-eggs breakfast to the native seafood dinners. Appreciative patrons usually keep up a dull roar throughout the day, revving up to a deafening roar as the Bass and Guinness flow from the tap.

✪ Painter's. 50 Main St. (near Rte. 6). ☎ **508/349-3003.** Reservations recommended. Main courses $10–$18. AE, MC, V. May–Oct Wed–Mon 5–11pm. Closed Nov–Apr. NEW AMERICAN.

The offspring of local literati, Kate Painter trained at some pretty fancy establishments: San Francisco's world-famous Stars, Boston top spot Biba, and Cape Cod's own Chillingsworth. Still, if she had her druthers—and now she does, having set up her own restaurant in a rambling 1750 tavern—she'd still prefer, in the words of her motto and mission statement, "simple food in a funky place." The modesty is misplaced, because although the setting is pretty low-key (a wood-beamed bistro dressed up with friends' artwork), her culinary skills are topnotch. Consider a warm duck breast salad with plum-balsamic vinaigrette, or Thai soup with pan-seared scallops and sunflower sprouts—that's just for starters. The hearty entrees include such robust dishes as clams Cataplana (like a sunnily spiced Portuguese bouillabaisse), flounder rubbed with roasted garlic, and an always-affordable *linguine aglio e olio*. Painter's sense of humor shows up in the desserts: "Something Chocolate" and "Something Lemon" are just that, an intriguing cross between cake and soufflé. Or you could just order a straight pint of Ben & Jerry's, served as if *chez vous*—in the carton, with bowls and a scoop.

Picnic & Take-Out Fare

Box Lunch, 50 Briar Lane (north of Main Street in town center; ☎ 508/349-2178)—its porch usually hemmed in by bicycles—is the original source of the Cape's signature "rollwiches": rolled pita sandwiches with unusual fillings.

✪ **Hatch's Fish Market/Hatch's Produce,** 310 Main St. (behind Town Hall, in the middle of town; ☎ 508/349-2810). This former fishing shack—plunked behind Town Hall—is the unofficial heart of Wellfleet. You'll find the best of local bounty from fresh-picked corn and fruit-juice popsicles to steaming lobsters and home-smoked local mussels and pâté. Virtually no one passes through without picking up a little something, along with the latest talk of the town. Closed late September to late May.

WELLFLEET AFTER DARK

Arguably the best dance club on Cape Cod, **The Beachcomber,** 1220 Old Cahoon Hollow Rd. (off Ocean View Drive south of Cahoon Hallow Beach; ☎ 508/349-6055)—"The Comber" in local parlance—is definitely the most scenic, and not just in terms of the barely legal-age clientele. It's right on Cahoon Hollow Beach—so close, in fact, that late beachgoers on summer weekends can count on a free concert: reggae, perhaps, or the homegrown "Incredible Casuals." Other nights, you might run into jazz, blues, hip-hop, or comedy, and often some very big names playing mostly for the fun of it. Cover $5 to $10.

Three eateries become evening roosts as the hour grows later: **Duck Creeke Tavern,** 70 Main St. (about ¹/₈ mile west of Route 6; ☎ 508/349-7369), hosts local talent to go with its light fare; **Painter's Upstairs,** 50 Main St. (near Route 6; ☎ 508/349-3003), features local jazz acts; and locally spawned blues and jazz usually suffuse the cozy attic at **Upstairs Bar at Aesop's Tables,** 316 Main St. (in the center of town; ☎ 508/349-6450).

Wednesday nights in summer, Wellfleet's workaday fishing pier (off Kendricks Avenue) resounds to the footfalls of avid amateur **square-dancers** of every age. Call **508/349-9382** for more information.

How about a night hike or bat walk? Both are offered at the **Wellfleet Bay Wildlife Sanctuary** (☎ 508/349-2615; see "Outdoor Pursuits," above). Fees vary; call for schedule and reservations. Just don't take in any vampire movies at the drive-in first.

The **Wellfleet Drive-In,** 51 Rte. 6 (just north of the Eastham border; ☎ 800/696-3532 or 508/349-2520), clearly deserves National Landmark status: Built in 1957, it's the only drive-in left on Cape Cod, and one of a scant half-dozen surviving in the state. The rituals are unbending, and every bit as endearing as ever: the playtime preceding the cartoons, the countdown plugging the allures of the snack bar, and finally, two full first-run features. The drive-in is open daily from late May through mid-September; showtime is at dusk. Admission is $6 adults, $3.50 seniors and children 5 to 11.

TRURO

46 miles (74km) E of Sandwich, 10 miles (16km) S of Provincetown

Truro is one of those blink-and-you'll-miss-it towns. With only 1,600 year-round residents (fewer than it boasted in 1840, when Pamet Harbor was a whaling and ship-building port), the town amounts to little more than a scattering of stores and public buildings, and lots of low-profile houses hidden away in the woods and dunes. Again, as in Wellfleet, writers, artists, and vacationing therapists are drawn to the quiet and calm. Edward Hopper lived in contented isolation in a South Truro cottage for nearly four decades.

If you find yourself craving cultural stimulation or other kinds of excitement, however, Provincetown is only a 10-minute drive (you'll know you're getting close when you spot the wall-to-wall tourist cabins lining the bay in North Truro). The natives manage to entertain themselves pretty well with get-togethers at the Truro Center for the Arts or, more simply, among themselves. However much money may be circulating in this rusticated community (a *lot*), inconspicuous consumption is the rule of the day. The culmination of the social season, tellingly enough, is the late-September "dump dance" held at Truro's recycling center.

ESSENTIALS

GETTING THERE   After crossing either the Bourne or Sagamore Bridge, head east on Route 6 or 6A to Orleans, and north on Route 6.

The **North Truro Shuttle System** (☎ 508/487-6870) connects the town with Provincetown in season, for only $2 one-way.

VISITOR INFORMATION   Contact the **Truro Chamber of Commerce,** Route 6A at Head of the Meadow Road, Truro, MA 02666 (☎ 508/487-1288).

OUTDOOR PURSUITS

BEACHES   Parking at all of Truro's exquisite Atlantic beaches, but for one Cape Cod National Seashore access point, is reserved for residents and renters. To obtain a sticker ($30 for two weeks), inquire at Town Hall on Town Hall Road

(☎ 508/349-3635). On your own power—walkers and bikers are welcome—visit such natural wonders as Ballston Beach, where all you'll see is silky sand and grass-etched dunes.

- **Head of the Meadow,** off Head of the Meadow Road: Among the more remote National Seashore beaches, this spot (equipped with rest rooms) is known for its excellent surf. Parking costs $5 a day, or $15 a season.
- **Corn Hill Beach,** off Corn Hill Road: Offering lifeguard supervision and rest rooms, this bay beach—near the hill where the Pilgrims found the seed corn that ensured their survival—is open to nonresidents for a parking fee of $5 a day.

BIKING/RECREATIONAL PATHS   Although it has yet to be linked up to the Cape Cod Rail Trail, Truro does have a stunning two-mile bike path of its own, the **Head of the Meadow Trail** off the road of that name (look for a right-hand turn about ¹/₂ mile north of where Routes 6 and 6A intersect). Part of the old 1850 road toward Provincetown—Thoreau traveled this route—it skirts the bluffs, passing Pilgrim Heights (where the Pilgrims found their first drinking water) and ending at High Head Road. Being fairly flat as well as short, this stretch should suit youngsters and beginners. Rentals can be arranged at **Bayside Bikes,** 102 Shore Rd., N. Truro (☎ 508/487-5735).

FISHING   Great Pond, Horseleech Pond, and Pilgrim Lake—flanked by parabolic dunes carved by the wind—are all fishable; for a license (inquire about shellfishing, too) visit Town Hall on Town Hall Road (☎ 508/349-3635). Surf casting is permitted at Highland Light Beach, off Highland Road.

GOLF   North Truro boasts the most scenic—and historic—nine-hole course on the Cape. Created in 1892, the minimally groomed, Scottish-style **Highland Links,** 10 Lighthouse Rd. off S. Highland Road (☎ 508/487-9201), shares a lofty bluff with the 1853 Highland Light, where Thoreau used to crash during his Outer Cape expeditions. Visible (but not visitable) to the south is the granite "Jenny Lind Tower," part of a Boston railroad depot where the celebrated Swedish nightingale sang to compensate her fans for an overbooked concert. Green fees at the federally owned, town-run Highland Links are quite reasonable, especially considering the spectacular setting.

NATURE TRAILS   The **Cape Cod National Seashore**—comprising 70 percent of Truro's land—offers three informative self-guided nature trails. The ¹/₂-mile **Cranberry Bog Trail** leads from the Little America youth hostel parking lot (see "Where to Stay," below) past a number of previously cultivated bogs reverting to their natural state. The **Pilgrim Spring Trail** and **Small Swamp Trail** (each a ³/₄-mile loop) head out from the CCNS parking lot just east of Pilgrim Lake. Pilgrim Spring is where the parched colonists sipped their first freshwater in months—with "much delight," according to a contemporary account. Small Swamp is named for Thomas Small, a rather overoptimistic 19th-century farmer who tried to cultivate fruit trees in a soil more suited to salt hay. Both paths overlook Salt Meadow, a freshwater marsh favored by hawks and osprey.

WATER SPORTS   The inlets of the **Pamet Harbor** are great for canoeing and kayaking; when planning an excursion, study the tides so you won't be working against them. The closest rentals are in Wellfleet.

AN ARTS CENTER & A MUSEUM
✪ **Truro Center for the Arts at Castle Hill.** 10 Meetinghouse Rd. (at Castle Rd., about ³/₄ mile NW of town center). ☎ **508/349-7511.** Fees vary; call for schedule. Closed Sept–June.

Plan ahead—that is, send for a brochure—and you could work some learning into your vacation. A great many celebrated writers and artists—from poet Alan Dugan to painter Edith Vonnegut—emerge from their summer hideaways to offer courses, lectures, and exhibits at this bustling little complex, an 1880s horse barn with windmill (now home to the administrative offices). The roster changes slightly from year to year, but you can rest assured that the stellar instructors will be at the top of their form in this stimulating environment.

The center also offers lots of children's workshops, from painting to silkscreening and assemblage, for artists age 7 and up.

✪ **Truro Historical Museum.** 6 Lighthouse Rd. (off S. Highland Rd., 2 miles N of town center on Rte. 6), N. Truro. ☎ **508/487-3397.** Admission $2 adults, $1.50 seniors, children under 12 free. Mid-June to mid-Sept daily 10am–5pm. Closed mid-Sept to mid-June.

Built as a hotel in 1907, the Highland House is a perfect repository for the odds and ends collected by the Truro Historical Society: ship's models, harpoons, primitive toys, a pirate's chest . . . be sure to visit the second floor, set up as if still occupied by 19th-century tourists.

SHOPPING

Susan Baker—rumors of whose death she herself has somewhat exaggerated so as to rate her own museum without croaking—is a definite character, as original as her work. ✪ **The Susan Baker Memorial Museum,** 46 Shore Rd. (Route 6A, ¹/₄ mile northwest of Route 6; ☎ **508/487-2557**), showcases her creative output, from fanciful/functional papier-mâché *objets* to primitivist landscapes. However, her main stock in trade—here, and at her Provincetown outlet—is humor in various media, from artist's books to very atypical T-shirts (among the more popular in Provincetown: TOO MEAN TO MARRY). Picture Nicole Hollander with a bit more bite. Call ahead October through May.

WHERE TO STAY

Ⓢ **Kalmar Village.** 674 Shore Rd. (Rte. 6A, about ³/₄ mile S of Provincetown border), N. Truro. ☎ **508/487-0585.** Fax 508/487-0585. 9 rms, 7 efficiency suites, 60 cottages. Summer $70 double, $110 suite; cottages $895–$1,495 weekly. MC, V. Closed mid-Oct to mid-May.

A lot spiffier than many of the motels and cottages lined up along this spit of sand between Pilgrim Lake and Pilgrim Beach, this 1940s complex resembles a miniaturized Edgartown, with little white cottages shuttered in black. The clientele—largely families—can splash the day away in the 60-foot freshwater pool or on the 400-foot private beach.

Outer Reach Motel. 535 Rte. 6 (midway between N. Truro center and Provincetown border), N. Truro, MA 02652. ☎ **800/942-5388** or 508/487-9090. Fax 508/942-5388. 59 rms. TV. Summer $79–$114 double. MC, V. Closed mid-Oct to mid-May.

The only tradeoff worth forfeiting a spot right on the beach is a fabulous view of the beach. This sprawling motel—the last development to sneak under the wire, pre–National Seashore—offers glorious vistas of Provincetown, where guests have privileges at another big (and equally unsightly) motel, the Provincetown Inn, on a narrow bay beach at the very western end of town. On site here in North Truro, you'll find an outdoor pool and tennis court; the ocean is one sylvan mile east. The rooms are standard-issue, but there's a terrific independent restaurant within the complex, Adrian's (see "Where to Dine," below).

✪ **South Hollow Vineyards Bed and Breakfast Inn.** 11 Shore Rd. (Rte. 6A, off Rte 6 ¹/₂ mile S of town center), N. Truro, MA 02652. ☎ **508/487-6200.** Fax 508/487-4248. 4 rms, 1 suite. Summer (including continental breakfast) $79–$89 double, $119 suite. MC, V.

You don't have to be a wine-lover to appreciate this beautiful 1836 B&B set amid five vine-covered acres. If you are, though, you'll be in your element. Each of the five bedrooms—including the Vintage Suite, with its double Jacuzzi—comes with a four-poster bed draped in a particular wine tone, ranging (imperceptibly, for all but the trained eye) from claret to burgundy. Horticulturalist/innkeepers Kathy Gregrow and Judy Wimer uncorked their first homegrown Chardonnay and Cabernet Franc in the fall of 1996, and the Muscadet is well on its way. The slate-floored living room, with its exposed beams, looks more French than Federal, and is decorated with interesting oenological artifacts. For the nonconnoisseur, the draw is likely to be the bucolic setting (this is one of the last working farms on the Outer Cape) only six miles from the center of Provincetown.

WHERE TO DINE

Seeing as this deli/bakery/grocery is basically *it* in terms of downtown Truro, and seasonal to boot, it's a good thing ✪ **Jams,** 14 Truro Center Rd. (off Route 6, in the center of town; ☎ **508/349-1616**), is so delightful. It's full of tantalizing aromas: fresh creative pizzas (from pesto to pupu), rotisseried fowl sizzling on the spit, cookies straight from the oven. The pastry and deli selections deserve their own four-star restaurant, but are all the more savory as part of a picnic. Closed early September to late May.

✪ **Adrian's.** 535 Rte. 6 (midway between N. Truro center and Provincetown border), N. Truro. ☎ **508/487-4360.** Fax 508/487-6510. Reservations recommended. Main courses $7–$17. AE, MC, V. Mid-June to early Sept Mon–Fri 8am–noon and 5:30–10pm; Sat–Sun 8am–1pm and 5:30–10pm; call for off-season hours. Closed mid-Oct to mid-May. NORTHERN ITALIAN.

Sharing a bluff with the Outer Reach Motel, Adrian Salcedo Cyr's stylish restaurant is greatly prized—not just for its knockout wood-fired *pizzette* and other creative fare, but for the superb breakfasts. Try for a table on the sunny deck overlooking all of Provincetown Harbor, and sample such eye-openers as orange-cinnamon French toast or huevos rancheros. Come back for the sunset and the Tuscan bread-and-tomato soup, the grilled eggplant salad, a thin-crusted "Quattro Stagioni" pizza, some masterful pasta—oh, and don't forget the tiramisu, heady with espresso brandy.

Terra Luna. 104 Shore Rd. (in the center of town), N. Truro. ☎ **508/487-1019.** Main courses $8–$16. AE, MC, V. Late May to mid-Oct daily 7am–1pm and 5:30–10pm. Closed mid-Oct to late May. FUSION.

People come from miles around to sample the outstanding breakfasts at this modest restaurant: The muffins and scones emerge fresh from the oven, and entrees such as the breakfast burrito or raisin French toast stuffed with cream cheese and walnuts call for a hearty appetite. You can start in again in the evening, on well-priced Pacific Rim and/or neo-Italian fare, such as penne in a fresh tomato-and-cream sauce splashed with vodka. The two-for-one pizzas, served nightly from 5 to 6:30, are a super deal and really hit the spot après-beach.

5 Provincetown

56 miles (90km) NE of Sandwich, 42 miles (68km) NE of Hyannis

You made it! To one of the most interesting, rewarding spots on the eastern seaboard. Explorer Bartholomew Gosnold must have felt much the same thrill in 1602 when he and his crew happened upon a "great stoare of codfysshes" here (it wasn't quite the gold they were seeking, but valuable enough to warrant changing the peninsula's name). The Pilgrims, of course, were ecstatic when they dragged into the harbor 18 years later: Never mind that they'd landed several hundred miles off-course—it was a miracle they'd made it round the treacherous Outer Cape at all. And Charles Hawthorne, the painter who "discovered" this near-derelict fishing town in the late 1890s and introduced it to the Greenwich Village intelligentsia, was besotted by this "jumble of color in the intense sunlight accentuated by the brilliant blue of the harbor."

He'd probably be aghast at the commercial circus his enthusiasm has wrought—though proud, perhaps, to find the Provincetown Art Association & Museum, which he helped found in 1914, still going strong. Although it's bound to experience the occasional off-year or dull stretch (as does the art world in general), the town is extraordinarily dedicated to creative expression, both visual and verbal, and right now it's on a roll. Some would ascribe the inspiration to the quality of the light (and it is particularly lovely, soft and diffuse) or the solitude afforded by long lonely winters. Still, the general atmosphere of open-mindedness certainly plays as pivotal a role in allowing a very varied assortment of individuals to pull together in pushing the boundaries of the avant-garde.

That same warm embrace of different lifestyles accounts in part for Provincetown's ascendancy as a gay and lesbian resort. During peak season, Provincetown's streets are a celebration of any individual's freedom to be as "out" as imagination allows. This isolated outpost has always been a magnet for the adventurous-minded: In fact, the tightly knit Portuguese community mostly descends from fishermen and whaling crews who set out from the Azores in centuries past. One might think that a culture so bound by tradition and religion would look askance at a way of life so antithetical to their own—but the term "family values" enjoys a very broad definition here. "Family" encompasses all the populace in its glorious diversity. Those who've settled here know they've found a very special place, and in that they have something precious in common.

ESSENTIALS

GETTING THERE   After crossing either the Bourne or Sagamore Bridge, head east on Route 6 or 6A to Orleans, then north on Route 6.

Bay State Cruises (☎ **617/723-7800** or 508/487-9274) makes round trips from Boston, daily in summer and weekends on the shoulder seasons. **Cape Cod Cruises** (☎ **508/747-2400**) connects Plymouth and Provincetown in summer.

VISITOR INFORMATION   Contact the **Provincetown Chamber of Commerce,** 307 Commercial St., Provincetown, MA 02657 (☎ **508/487-3424,** fax 508/487-8966, website www.capcodaccess.come/provincetownchamber); or the gay-oriented **Provincetown Business Guild,** 115 Bradford St., Provincetown, MA 02657 (☎ **800/637-8696** or 508/487-2313).

OUTDOOR PURSUITS

BEACHES   With nine-tenths of its territory (basically, all but the "downtown" area) protected by the Cape Cod National Seashore, Provincetown has miles of beaches. The three-mile bay beach that lines the harbor, though certainly swimmable, is not all that inviting compared to the magnificent ocean beaches overseen by the CCNS. The two official access areas (see below) tend to be crowded; however, you can always find a less densely populated stretch if you're willing to hike. *Note:* Local beachgoers have been mobilizing for "clothing-optional" beaches for years, but the rangers—fearful of voyeurs trampling the dune grass—are firmly opposed and routinely issue tickets, so stand forewarned (and fully clothed).

  • **Herring Cove** and **Race Point:** Both CCNS beaches are known for their spectacular sunsets: Observers often applaud. Race Point, on the ocean side, is

Provincetown

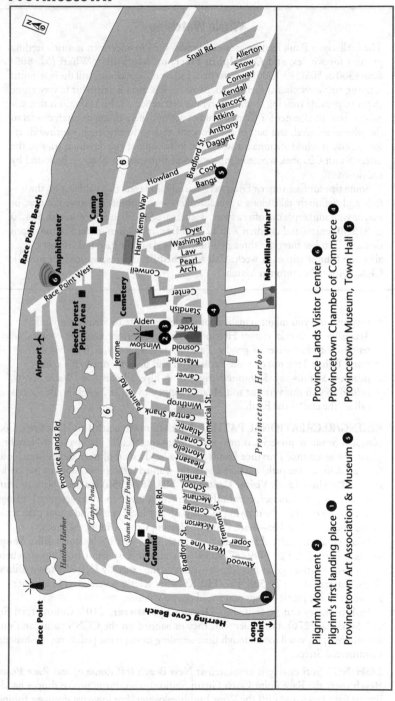

Snail Rd.

Allerton
Snow
Conway
Kendall
Hancock
Atkins
Anthony
Daggett
Bradford St.
Cook
Bangs **5**

Howland

Race Point Beach

Camp Ground

Amphitheater **6**

Race Point West

Harry Kemp Way

Dyer
Washington
Law
Pearl
Arch

Conwell

Cemetery

Center

Standish **4**

Beech Forest Picnic Area

Alden **2 3**

Ryder

Winslow

Jerome

Gosnold

Masonic

Carver

Court

Winthrop

Central Shank Painter Rd.

Shank Painter Pond

Commercial St.

MacMillan Wharf

Provincetown Harbor

Airport ✈

Province Lands Rd.

Clapps Pond

Atlantic

Conant

Montello

Pleasant

School

Franklin

Mechanic

Cottage

Nickerson

Creek Rd.

Camp Ground

Bradford St.

West Vine St.

Tremont St.

Soper

Atwood

Hatches Harbor

Race Point

Herring Cove Beach

Long Point →

Pilgrim's first landing place **1**

Pilgrim Monument **2**

Provincetown Art Association & Museum **3**

Provincetown Museum, Town Hall **3**

Provincetown Chamber of Commerce **4**

Provincetown Museum, Town Hall **3**

Province Lands Visitor Center **6**

Whale Watching

The Stellwagen Bank feeding area eight miles off Provincetown is a rich feeding ground for whales, and ✪ **Dolphin Fleet,** on MacMillan Wharf (☎ **800/ 826-9300** or 508/349-1900), was the first, and by most accounts still the best, outfit running whale watches at Stellwagen. Most cruises carry a naturalist (a very vague term) to provide running commentary; the difference on the Dolphin is that scientists from the Center for Coastal Studies are out there doing research crucial to the whales' survival, and part of the proceeds goes to further their worthwhile efforts. Serious whale aficionados will want to try one of the day-long trips to the Great South Channel, where humpbacks and finbacks are likely to be found by the dozen.

Some tips for first-timers: Dress very warmly, in layers (it's cold out on the water), and definitely take along a windbreaker—waterproof, if you've got one, or maybe your innkeeper can offer a spare. Tickets are $16.50 to $17.50 adults, $14.50 to $15.50 seniors and children 7 to 12, and free to children under 7. From April through October there are three 3½-hour trips daily; in July and August there's also one 8-hour trip each week. Call for schedule and reservations (required). Closed November through March.

rougher, and you might actually spot whales en route to Stellwagen Bank. Accessible by shuttle, calmer Herring Cove is a haven for same-sex couples, who tend to sort themselves by gender. Parking costs $5 a day, $15 a season.

- **Long Point:** Trek out over the Breakwater and beyond, or catch a water shuttle—$7 one-way, $10 round-trip—from Flyer's Boats (see "Water Sports," below) to visit this very last spit of land, capped by an 1827 lighthouse. Locals call it "the end of the Earth."

BIKING/RECREATIONAL PATHS   North of town, nestled amid the Cape Cod National Seashore preserve, is one of the more spectacular bike paths in New England, the seven-mile **Province Lands Trail,** a heady swirl of steep dunes (watch out for sand drifts on the path) anchored by wind-stunted scrub pines. With its free parking, the **Province Lands Visitor Center** (☎ 508/487-1256) is a good place to start: You can survey the landscape from the observation tower to try to get your bearings before setting off amid the dizzying maze. With any luck, you'll find a spur path leading to one of the beaches—Race Point or Herring Cove—lining the shore.

Bike rentals are offered seasonally, practically on-site, by **Nelson's Bike Shop,** 43 Race Point Rd. (☎ 508/487-0034). It's also an easy jaunt from town, where you'll find plenty of good bike shops—such as the centrally located **Ptown Bikes,** 306 Commercial St. (☎ 508/487-TREK:** better reserve several days in advance)— as well as all the picnic fixings you could possibly desire.

In-line skates can be rented at **Oceana Sportswear,** 210A Commercial St. (☎ 508/487-7276), but remember, they're banned on the CCNS paths, and unless you're a pro, you'll have a tough time wending through the pedestrian crush along Commercial Street.

FISHING   Surf casting is permitted at **New Beach** (off Route 6) and **Race Point Beach** (near the Race Point Coast Guard Station); also, many people drop a handline or light tackle right off the West End breakwater. For low-cost deep-sea fishing via party-boat, board the *Cee Jay* (☎ 508/487-4330) or *Captain Bill* (☎ 800/

675-6723). For serious fishing, sign on for the *Shady Lady* (☎ 508/487-1700). All three depart from MacMillan Wharf.

HORSEBACK RIDING   Nelson's Riding Stable on Race Point Road (☎ 508/487-1112) offers lessons and slow, guided trail rides through the dunes daily at 10am, noon, 2, 4, and 6pm April through October ($25); eperienced riders can enjoy a sunset sprint along the beach ($50). **Bayberry Holly Farm,** 17 W. Vine St. Extension (☎ 508/487-6584), offers pony rides for children—$5 a spin—in a paddock surrounded by flower gardens.

NATURE TRAILS   Within the Province Lands (off Race Point Road, ¹/₂ mile north of Route 6), the CCNS maintains the one-mile self-guided **Beech Forest Trail,** a shaded path which circles a shallow freshwater pond blanketed with water lilies— also look for sunning turtles—before heading into the woods. You can see the shifting dunes (much of this terrain is soft sand) gradually encroaching on the forest. Another wonderful walk (though only half "natural") is along the **West End breakwater** out to the end of Long Point, about three miles round-trip.

WATER SPORTS   In addition to operating a Long Point shuttle from its own dock and MacMillan Wharf (see "Beaches," above), **Flyer's Boat Rental** at 131 Commercial St. in the West End (☎ 508/487-0898)—established in 1945— offers all sorts of craft, from canoes and dinghies to sailboats of varying sizes; they also give sailing lessons and organize fishing trips and outings with aquaculturalists. Thrill-seekers might want to try **Aqua Ventures Para-Sailing** (☎ 800/300-3787 or 508/487-7386), off Macmillan Pier.

ORGANIZED TOURS

Art's Dune Tours. At the corner of Commercial and Standish sts. (in the center of town), Provincetown. ☎ 800/894-1951 or 508/487-1950. Fee $10 adults, $6 children under 12. Call for schedule and reservations.

In 1946 Art Costa started driving sightseers out to ogle the decrepit "dune shacks" where transient genii such as Eugene O'Neill, Jack Kerouac, and Jackson Pollock found their respective muses; in one such hovel, Tennessee Williams cooked up the steamy *Streetcar Named Desire.* The Park Service wanted to raze these eyesores, but luckily saner heads prevailed: They're now National Historic Landmarks. Art's tours, via Chevy Suburban, typically take about 1¹/₄ hours, and though he "narrates" straight through, his stories never seem scripted; one suspects (rightly) that he has scores more up his sleeve.

Bay Lady II. MacMillan Wharf (in the center of town), Provincetown. ☎ 508/487-9308. Fee $10–$13 adults, $5 children under 12. Mid-May to mid-Oct four 2-hour sails daily; call for schedule and reservations. Closed mid-Oct to mid-May.

In sightseeing aboard this 73-foot reproduction gaff-rigged Grand Banks schooner, you'll actually be adding to the scenery for those onlookers onshore. The sunset trip is especially spectacular.

MUSEUMS

✪ **The Expedition *Whydah* Sea Lab & Learning Center.** MacMillan Wharf (in the center of town), Provincetown. ☎ 508/487-3688. Fax 508/487-7955. Admission $5 adults, $3.50 children 3–12. July–Aug daily 9am–7pm; call for off-season hours. Closed Jan–Mar.

Cape Cod native Barry Clifford made headlines in 1984 when he tracked down the wreck of the 17th-century pirate ship *Whydah* (pronounced "WID-dah," like Yankee for "widow") 1,500 feet off the coast of Wellfleet, where it had lain undisturbed since 1717. Only 10 percent excavated to date, it has already yielded over 100,000 artifacts, including 10,000 gold and silver coins, plus its namesake bell, proving its authenticity. In this museum/lab, visitors can observe the reclamation work—involving electrolytic reduction—as it's done, and discuss the ship, its discovery, and its significance with the scientists and scholars on hand, while studying the many interpretive exhibits. You may never approach the beach in quite the same way again: Thousands more wrecks are out there, awaiting the patient and clever.

Province Lands Visitor Center. Race Point Rd. (about 1¹/₂ miles NW of town center), Provincetown. ☎ **508/487-1256.** Free admission. July–Aug daily 9am–6pm; call for off-season hours. Closed Dec–Mar.

Though much smaller than the Salt Pond Visitor Center, this satellite also does a good job of explicating this special environment, where plant life must fight a fierce battle to maintain its toehold amid shifting sands buffeted by salty winds. After perusing the exhibits, be sure to circle the observation deck, for great views of the "parabolic" dunes. Also inquire about any special events scheduled, such as guided walks and family campfires.

✪ **Pilgrim Monument & Provincetown Museum.** High Pole Hill Rd. (off Winslow St. N of Bradford St.). ☎ **800/247-1620** or 508/487-1310. Admission $5 adults, $3 children 4–12 (includes 2 hours' free parking). July to early Sept daily 9am–7pm, off-season daily 9am–5pm; last admission 45 minutes before closing. Closed Dec–Mar.

You can't miss it: Anywhere you go in town, this granite tower looms, ever ready to restore your bearings. Climb up the 60 gradual ramps interspersed with 116 steps—a surprisingly easy lope—and you'll get a gargoyle's-eye view of the spiraling coast and, in the distance, Boston against a backdrop of New Hampshire mountains. Definitely devote some time to the curious exhibits in the museum at the monument's foot, chronicling Provincetown's checkered past as both fishing port and arts nexus. Among the memorabilia, you'll find polar bears brought back from MacMillan's expeditions, and early programs for the Provincetown Players.

✪ **Provincetown Art Association & Museum.** 460 Commercial St. (in the East End). ☎ **508/487-1750.** Suggested donation $3 adults, $1 seniors and children under 12. Late May to early Sept daily noon–5pm, 7–9pm; call for off-season hours.

This extraordinary cache of 20th-century American art began with five paintings donated by local artists, including Charles Hawthorne, the charismatic teacher who first "discovered" this picturesque outpost. Founded in 1914, only a year after New York's revolutionary Armory Show, the museum was the site of innumerable "space wars" as classicists and modernists vied for square footage; an uneasy truce was finally struck in 1927 when each camp was accorded its own show. In today's more ecumenical atmosphere it's not unusual to see a tame still life hanging alongside a statement of GenX angst, or an acknowledged master sharing space with a less skilled upstart. Juried members' shows usually accompany the in-depth retrospectives, so there are always new discoveries to be made. Nor is there a hard and firm wall between creators and onlookers. Fulfilling its charter to promote "social intercourse between artists and laymen," the museum sponsors a full schedule of concerts, lectures, readings, and classes, in such disciplines as dance, yoga, and life-drawing.

SHOPPING

Of the several dozen art galleries in town, only a handful (noted below) are reliably worthwhile. (For in-depth coverage of the local arts scene, look to *Provincetown Arts,* a glossy annual sold at the Provincetown Art Association & Museum shop.) In season, most of the galleries and even some of the shops take a suppertime siesta so as to reopen later and greet visitors as late as 10 or 11pm. Shows usually open Friday evening, prompting a "stroll" tradition spanning the many receptions.

ANTIQUES/COLLECTIBLES   The second-story **Clifford-Williams Antiques,** 225 Commercial St. (in the center of town; ☎ 508/487-4174), is packed to the gills with substantial English furniture.

You'd have to go to Boston—or abroad—to view estate jewelry as fine as that at ✪ **Small Pleasures,** 359 Commercial St. (in the center of town; ☎ 508/487-3712). Virginia McKenna's hand-selected stock ranges from romantic Victorian settings to sleek silver for the 1920s-era male.

Two others: **Remembrances of Things Past,** 376 Commercial St. (in the center of town; ☎ 508/487-9443), is a fun kitsch-fest; **West End Antiques,** 146 Commercial St. (in the West End; ☎ 508/487-6723), is more of a nostalgia-fest.

ART/CRAFTS   Berta Walker is a force to be reckoned with, having nurtured artists such as Charles Hawthorne, Milton Avery, and Robert Motherwell. Whoever has her current attention—such as figurative sculptor Romolo Del Deo—warrants watching. ✪ **Berta Walker Gallery,** 208 Bradford St. (in the East End; ☎ 508/487-6411). Closed late October to late May.

A natural-born saloniste, Cortland Jessup has a knack for mixing medias and genres, and initiating interesting cross-pollinations. Ask to see *The Class of Forbidden Dreams* by photographer/performance artist Pat Delzell. **Cortland Jessup Gallery,** 432 Commercial St. (in the East End; ☎ 508/487-4479). Closed January.

Founded in 1994 by artist and publishing scion Nick Lawrence, ✪ **dna gallery,** 286 Bradford St. (in the East End; ☎ 508/487-7700), has attracted such talents as photographer Joel Meyerowitz (Provincetown's favorite portraitist, known for such tomes as *Cape Light*); sculptor Conrad Malicoat, whose free-form brick chimneys and hearths can be seen and admired about town; and painter Tabitha Vevers, who devises woman-centered shrines and "shields" out of goatskin vellum and goldleaf. Another contributor is local conceptualist/provocateur Jay Critchley, whose latest enterprise involves condoms adorned with an image of the Virgin Mary and whose ongoing *cause celebre* is to see the town declared a "cultural sanctuary." It's a very lively bunch, appropriately grouped under the rubric "definitive new art," and readings by cutting-edge authors add to the buzz. Closed mid-October to late May.

An artist herself, gallery director Bunny Pearlman has an eye for iconic art, such as the para-archaeological signage devised by the team of Nicholas Kahn and Richard Selesnick (you may remember their striking portrait of the pope as *Time*'s "Man of the Year"). **East End Gallery,** 349 Commercial St. (in the center of town; ☎ 508/487-4745). Closed late November to mid-April.

Julie Heller started collecting early Provincetown paintings as a child, and a tourist at that. She chose so incredibly well, her roster (shown in a rustic fishing shack) now reads like a *Who's Who* of local art. Hawthorne, Avery, Hofmann, Lazzell, Hensche—all the big names are here, as well as some contemporary artists who, in her view, "continue to carry on the tradition." ✪ **Julie Heller Gallery,** 2 Gosnold St. (off Commercial Street in the center of town; ☎ 508/487-2169).

Artists invited to show with the venerable ✪ **Long Point Gallery,** 492 Commercial St. (in the East End; ☎ 508/487-1795)—self-described as "an artists' place"—are indisputably among the elect. Paul Resika's Provincetown landscapes, for example, perfectly capture the intensity of color, the sense of suspension in time. Closed mid-September to mid-June.

The art shown at **Rice/Polak Gallery,** 430 Commercial St. (in the East End; ☎ 508/487-1052), has a decorative bent, which is not to say that it will match anyone's sofa, only that it has a certain stylish snap to it. Several gallery artists have fun with dimensions—such as painter Tom Seghi with his mammoth pears, and sculptor Larry Culkins with his assemblages of undersized, antique-look dresses. Photographer Karin Rosenthal's sculptural female nudes blend humor with utmost beauty. Closed December through April.

Playing "bargain basement" (relatively speaking) to the Long Point, **Rising Tide Gallery,** 494 Commercial St. (in the East End; ☎ 508/487-4037), cultivates the mid-career artists who have a good chance of ultimately moving upstairs. (The two galleries each occupy a floor in an 1844 schoolhouse.) An investment in the colorist landscapes of Don Beal or Noa Hall could prove a wise move in the long run. Closed mid-September to mid-June.

Splashy both in selection and in presentation, **UFO Gallery,** 424 Commercial St. (in the East End; ☎ 508/487-4424)—short for Universal Fine Objects—is not afraid to delve into the decorative and functional. Boston *fauve* Todd McKie, for instance, contributes colorful platters painted like tribal masks. The art for its own sake can be quite distinguished, with such respected figures as Michael Mazur *(Dante's Inferno)* and Helen Miranda Wilson delivering their latest musings. Closed early September to late May.

Not content to have cornered some of the best fine art around, Berta Walker (see above) has now opened a small storefront satellite gallery to showcase folk and functional art, including furniture, jewelry, and sundry "imaginative objects and special delights." **Walker's Wonders,** 153 Commercial St. (in the West End; ☎ 508/487-8794, web site: www.CapeCodAccess.com/WalkersWonders).

The **William-Scott Gallery,** 439 Commercial St. (in the East End; ☎ 508/487-4040), is so tiny that it may look, on the surface, like one of those roadside galleries geared to impulsive tourists. But take a closer look. John Dowd's straightforward house portraits are not as simple as they might seem: Still quite young, he's shaping up as Hopper's heir apparent. Closed November to late May.

DISCOUNT SHOPPING   **Adams' Pharmacy,** 254 Commercial St. (in the center of town; ☎ 508/487-0069), is Provincetown's oldest business (established in 1868), and still has an old-fashioned soda fountain. We—and apparently, a great many drag queens—like it for the cheapo makeup (two-for-$1 lipsticks) in outrageous colors.

Veteran scavengers won't be put off by the musty backstage aroma at the **Provincetown Second Hand Store,** 389 Commercial St. (in the center of town; ☎ 508/487-9153). There are prime pickings to be had here, including some extremely glam outfits and shoes in petite to he-man sizes, and an assortment of firsthand vintage lingerie culled from the owner's family business. Closed January and February.

WHERE TO STAY
EXPENSIVE

✪ **The Brass Key Guesthouse.** 9 Court St. (in the center of town), Provincetown, MA 02657. ☎ 800/842-9858 or 508/487-9005. Fax 508/487-9020. 10 rms, 2 cottages. A/C TV TEL. Summer (including continental breakfast) $155–$220 double, $190 cottage. AE, DISC, MC, V.

Michael MacIntyre and Bob Anderson could give lessons in how to set up and operate the ideal inn. They've inaugurated three so far: the original Brass Key in Key West, this beauty, and a new satellite on Bradford Street. What constitutes perfection? Take one lovely old captain's house on a quiet street, enhance its privacy with a decorative wooden fence, its beauty with intensive landscaping, and install a cerulean whirlpool large enough (at 17 feet) to swim laps in, if one were so inclined.

Most guests repair here after a night of hard dancing, to unkink while gazing up at the stars. The super-attentive service and topnotch amenities (every room has its own mini-fridge and VCR) reflect Michael's Ritz-Carlton background, and the tasteful country-style decor Bob's Greenwich, Connecticut, upbringing. Together, they're a powerful social force in town, sponsoring a series of winemaker dinners and importing the occasional cultural event. Staying here is like visiting rich relatives in Bar Harbor, except that they can't be counted on not to carp, and probably wouldn't provide a rooftop deck for nude sunbathing.

Hargood House at Bayshore. 493 Commercial St. (in the East End), Provincetown, MA 02657. ☎/fax: **508/487-9113.** 2 studios, 17 efficiencies. TV TEL. Summer $99–$103 studio, $132–$194 efficiency. AE, MC, V.

Recently taken over and "cheerified" by a trio of owners including Louise Walker Davy (whose twin sister is the eminent gallery director Berta Walker), this cherished beachfront complex is enjoying a new lease on life. While retaining some of their improvisatory charm, such as a few select antiques and salvaged architectural details, the rooms have been lightened up, the better to reflect the waterside setting. The prize rooms surround a flower-lined lawn, with pride of place going to a cathedral-ceiling loft right over the water; several more apartments, including a free-standing little house, can be found across the street. The decor is still not quite designer-level, but the big plus is the opportunity to live among artworks on loan from the Walker Gallery, many of which would rightly hang on a museum wall.

Land's End Inn. 22 Commercial St. (in the West End), Provincetown, MA 02657. ☎ **800/ 276-7088** or 508/487-0706. 17 rms (1 with separate bath), 2 apts, 1 suite. Summer (including continental breakfast) $85–$190 double, $140–$150 apt, $285 suite. No credit cards.

Enjoying a prime two-acre perch atop Gull Hill, this 1907 bungalow is stuffed to bursting with rare and often outlandish antiques. Some rooms would suit a 19th-century sheik, others your everyday hedonist. In the dark-paneled living room, it's always Christmas: the ornate decorations never come down. The place is quite unique, in other words, in a way that will delight some guests and overwhelm others. There's no denying that the octagonal loft suite, a virtual goldfish bowl poised to take in views in every direction, is a spectacular setting for romance (shy types need not apply). Though the inn is predominantly gay, cosmopolitan visitors will be made to feel welcome, regardless of gender or orientation.

✪ Watermark Inn. 603 Commercial St. (in the East End), Provincetown, MA 02657. ☎ **800/ 734-0165** or 508/487-0165. Fax 508/487-2383. 10 efficiencies. TV, TEL. Summer $130–$275 double. AE, MC, V.

If you'd like to experience Provincetown without being stuck in the thick of it (the carnival atmosphere can get tiring at times), this contemporary inn at the peaceful edge of town is the perfect choice. Resident innkeeper/architect Kevin Shea carved this beachfront manor into 10 dazzling suites: The prize ones, on the top floor, have peaked picture windows and sweeping views from their own 80-foot deck. Innkeeper/ designer Judy Richland, his wife, saw to the interior decoration—bold Marimekko quilts and plenty of primary colors. Even the lack of breakfast is a plus in its own way: You have an excuse to stockpile goodies from Martin's Market (467 Commercial St.; ☎ 508/487-4858), a gourmet grocery store nearby, or to brunch about town.

MODERATE

The Boatslip Beach Club. 161 Commercial St. (in the West End), Provincetown, MA 02657. ☎ **800/451-7547** or 508/487-1669. Fax 508/487-6021. 45 rms. TV TEL. Summer $120–$160 double. MC, V. Closed Nov to early Apr.

Better pack your party clothes. As the site of Provincetown's incomparable "tea dances," this modernized waterside motel is Party Central—mostly for gay men, but women, too, and anyone else who wants to hang around. There are some rather snazzy human specimens draped around the pool, the SRO sundeck, and one another. Just as you can expect to be scoped out, you can pretty much count on making interesting new friends.

✪ **The Tides.** 837 Commercial St. (near the Truro border), Provincetown, MA 02657. ☎ **800/ 528-1234** or 508/487-1045. 62 rms, 2 suites. Summer $132–$166 double, $221 suite. AE, DC, DISC, MC, V. Closed Nov–Apr.

Located on a peaceful six-acre parcel well removed both from Provincetown's bustle and North Truro's ticky-tacky congestion, this surprise oasis—part of the Best Western chain, which takes pride in individualized excellence—boasts every feature one might require of a beachfront retreat, including a nice wide beach you can literally flop onto from the ground-level units. Most of the rooms overlook Provincetown's quirky skyline, as does the generously proportioned outdoor pool. Every inch of this complex has been groomed to the max, including the ultra-green grounds, the Wedgewood-blue breakfast room which seems to have been lifted whole from an elegant country inn, and the spotless rooms decorated in a soothing palette of ivory and pale pastels. And the only sound you'll hear at night is the mournful refrain of a foghorn.

INEXPENSIVE

✪ **The Black Pearl Bed & Breakfast.** 11 Pearl St. (off Commercial St., near the center of town), Provincetown, MA 02657. ☎ **508/487-6405.** Fax 508/487-7412. 6 rms, 1 cottage. Summer (including continental breakfast) $70–$85 double, $150 cottage. MC, V. Closed Jan–Feb.

Every room in this cheerily updated captain's house has a look all its own, from bold southwestern to fanciful Micronesian, and several boast skylights and private decks. The Connemara Cottage takes the cake, with an antique bedstead, wood-burning fireplace, and double Jacuzzi, plus such niceties as air-conditioning and a cable TV with VCR.

The Fairbanks Inn. 90 Bradford St. (near the center of town), Provincetown, MA 02657. ☎ **800/324-7265** or 508/487-0386. 13 rms (4 with shared bath), 1 efficiency, 1 apt. Summer (including continental breakfast) $75–$95 double, $85 efficiency, $175 apt. AE, DC, MC, V.

Bargain-priced because of its Bradford Street location, this colonial mansion (built in 1776) looks its era without looking its age. Beautifully maintained, it boasts gleaming wooden floors softened by rich Orientals, and romantic bedding—sleigh beds and four-posters. A patio, porch, and rooftop sundeck lend themselves to pleasant socializing.

Holiday Inn. 6 Snail Rd. (at Rte. 6A, in the East End), Provincetown, MA 02657. ☎ **800/ 465-4329** or 508/487-1711. Fax 508/487-3929. 78 rms. A/C TV TEL. Summer $100 double. AE, CB, DC, DISC, MC, V. Closed Nov–Apr.

A good choice for first-timers not quite sure what they're getting into, this no-surprises motel-with-pool at the eastern edge of town is a bit far from the action but con-genial enough. Guests get a nice view of town, along with cable TV and free movies in the restaurant/lounge.

✪ **The Inn at Cook St.** 7 Cook St. (at Bradford St., in the East End), Provincetown, MA 02657. ☎ **888/COOK-655** or 508/487-3894. 3 rms, 2 suites, 1 cottage. TV. Summer (including continental breakfast) $85 double, $110–$120 suite, $100 cottage. MC, V.

A welcome addition to the B&B scene, this 1836 Greek Revival beauty, tucked away in a quiet neighborhood, positively exudes tasteful warmth, from its pale yellow exterior trimmed with black shutters to its hidden garden, complete with goldfish pool. All the handsomely appointed rooms are oriented to this oasis, with an assortment of private and shared decks, and the tiny rose-trellised cottage, with sleeping loft, is an integral part of its charm. Innkeepers Paul Church and Dana Mitton arrived at their dreamhouse by way of the elegant Cambridge House near Boston, and their enthusiasm is evident in every welcoming touch.

The Rose & Crown. 158 Commercial St. (in the West End), Provincetown, MA 02657. ☎ **508/487-3332.** Web site: ptown.com/ptown/rosecrown/. 6 rms (3 with shared bath), 1 apt, 1 cottage. Summer (including continental breakfast) $65–$95 double, $110 apt or cottage. DC, MC, V.

Follow the yellow brick road, over a tiny footbridge spanning a mini-lagoon full of disporting Barbies and Kens, to enter a world where, as the brochure brags, "Anything worth doing is worth overdoing!" That maxim is borne out at every turn, in the lace-draped lamps and movie-star dolls; even the resident cat, a magnificent Persian, seems to have gotten the message and shamelessly vogues. The kitschy front yard of this 1780s Georgian "square rigger" has secured, since its inception in 1989, the inn's title as Provincetown's most photographed, and any pennies you care to toss in Barbie's Dream Pool go toward the fight against AIDS.

Ⓢ **White Horse Inn.** 500 Commercial St. (in the East End), Provincetown, MA 02657. ☎ **508/487-1790.** 12 rms (9 with shared bath), 6 efficiencies. Summer $60–$70 double, $100–$110 efficiency. No credit cards.

The rates are a literal steal, especially given the fact that this inn is the very embodiment of Provincetown's Bohemian mystique. Frank Schaefer has been tinkering with this late 18th-century house since 1963. The rooms may be a bit austere, but each is enlivened by some of the artwork he has collected over the decades. A number of his fellow artists helped him out in cobbling together the studio apartments out of salvage: There's an aura of beatnik improv about them still.

WHERE TO DINE
VERY EXPENSIVE

✪ **Front Street.** 230 Commercial St. (in the center of town). ☎ **508/487-1145.** Reservations recommended. Main courses $17–$24. AE, MC, V. Jun–Oct daily 6–10:30pm; call for off-season hours. Closed Jan–Apr. NEW AMERICAN.

A long-time fave, this bustling little bistro—housed in the brick basement of a Victorian manse—continues to surprise and delight year after year. Chef Donna Aliperti revises her menu weekly, so aficionados know to check the latest posting, even if they've already reserved prime seating—the high-backed wooden booths—weeks in advance. Among the signature dishes that regularly surface in season are the grilled salmon splashed with raspberry balsamic vinegar, tea-smoked duck, and an unforgettable nectarine croustade.

✪ **Martin House.** 157 Commercial St. ☎ **508/487-1327.** Fax 508/487-4514. Reservations recommended. Main courses $14–$26. AE, CB, DC, DISC, MC, V. July–Oct Mon–Sat 6–11pm, Sun 3:30–11pm; call for off-season hours. Closed early Dec. FUSION.

Easily one of the most charming restaurants on the Cape—it occupies a house built around 1750 that is turned away from Commercial Street, for the simple reason that this thoroughfare didn't yet exist—this snuggery of rustic rooms also just happens to contain one of the Cape's most forward-thinking kitchens. Co-owner Gary Martin is the conceptualizer behind the inspired regional menu, and chef Alex Mazzocca the gifted creator. Both favor regional delicacies, such as the unusual *mizuma* (a Japanese bitter herb) that jazzes up a gingered dipping sauce for the Asian steamed buns, or the local littlenecks that appear in a kaffir lime-tamarind broth with green chili paste. By far the most esoteric item to turn up on any New England menu to date is the farm-raised organic ostrich filet, enhanced with rhubarb chutney. The dinners, pleasantly delivered, exceed every expectation: They're like nothing you've ever had before, and the peaceful, softly lit rooms make an optimal setting for exploring new tastes. On Sunday afternoons, the rose-choked garden terrace lends itself beautifully to a traditional Sunday afternoon tea, featuring faithful renditions of the customary savories and sweets.

EXPENSIVE

✪ **Cafe Edwige.** 333 Commercial St. ☎ **508/487-2008.** Reservations recommended. Main courses $15–$18. AE, DC, MC, V. July–Aug daily 8am–1pm and 6–11pm; call for off-season hours. Closed late Oct to Mar. NEW AMERICAN/FUSION.

The tourist throngs generally walk right on by this second-story eatery, little suspecting what they're passing up. To start: superlative breakfasts in a healthful mode, featuring everything from tofu frittatas to broiled flounder with stir-fried vegetables. The cathedral-ceilinged space, with hippie-era wooden booths and deco accents, is a great place to greet the day. At night it's commensurately romantic, with subdued lighting and the masterful cuisine of chef Steve Frappolli, a veteran of New York's New American landmark, An American Place. He's in his element here, dishing up the likes of planked codfish with ginger-carrot broth and wildberry shortcake.

The Flagship. 463 Commercial St. (in the East End). ☎ **508/487-4200.** Web site: ptownlib.com/users/ptown/flagship.html. Main courses $12–$23. AE, MC, V. July to early Oct Mon–Tues and Thurs–Fri 6–10pm, Sat–Sun 9am–1pm and 6–10pm; call for off-season hours. Closed Nov–Apr. NEW AMERICAN.

A dazzler from her days as Martin House's executive chef, Polly Hemstock enjoys free creative reign at the seaside restaurant she co-owns with partner/manager Susan Leven. Provincetown's oldest restaurant (Gertrude Stein and Anäis Nin are just two of the literati who flocked here after its early-1930s debut), this former sail loft is gung-ho nautical, right down to its Grand Banks dory bar. Hemstock does marvelous things with seafood, splashing oysters with tequila, lime, and jalapeños, wrapping ocean catfish into soft tacos, and pairing grilled tuna with a homemade cranberry catsup.

Gloria's. 269 Commercial St. (in the center of town). ☎ **508/487-0015.** Main courses $9–$23. DISC, MC, V. Daily 11am–10pm. PORTUGUESE.

Gloria Lomba's place, done up in very faux pink marble, is the perfect spot to celebrate Provincetown's Portuguese heritage. It's a boisterous, exuberant blend of *fado* refrains and piping-hot clay casseroles bearing mounds of *mariscada* (seafood stew), *bacalhau* (codfish in various guises), and even baked steak. On the delicate side, and superlative, are the *camarao a glorias*—marinated shrimp in a light saffron sauce. Better fast beforehand, or you may be overwhelmed.

The Lobster Pot. 321 Commercial St. (in the center of town). ☎ **508/487-0842.** No reservations. Main courses $14–$19. AE, DISC, DC, MC, V. Mid-June to mid-Sept daily 11:30am–10:30pm; call for off-season hours. Closed Jan. SEAFOOD.

Snobbish foodies might turn their noses up at a venue so flagrantly Olde Cape Coddish, but for Provincetown regulars, no season seems complete without at least one pilgrimage. Pilgrimage is the right word, because you have to suffer somewhat to get in: The line, which starts near the aromatic, albeit frantic kitchen, often snakes into the street. A lucky few will make it all the way to the outdoor deck; however, most tables, indoor and out, afford nice views of MacMillan Wharf.

✪ **The Mews Restaurant & Cafe Mews.** 429 Commercial St. ☎ **508/487-1500.** Reservations recommended. Main courses $15–$22. AE, CB, DC, DISC, MC, V. Mid-June to mid-Sept daily 11am–1pm; call for off-season hours. Closed late Dec (except New Year's Eve) to mid-Feb. NEW AMERICAN.

An enduring favorite since 1961, the Mews moved to its current location in 1992, carting along its century-old carved mahogany bar. You can still bank on fine food and suave service. The formal dining room, downstairs, is right on the beach—practically *of* the beach, with its sand-toned walls warmed by toffee-colored Tiffany table lamps. Standouts include the Marsala-marinated portabello mushrooms and a mixed seafood carpaccio. Among the showier entrees is "captured scallops": prime Wellfleet specimens enclosed with a shrimp and crab mousse in a crisp wonton pouch and served atop a petite filet mignon with chipotle aïoli. Desserts and coffees—you might take them upstairs in the cafe, to the accompaniment of improvisatory soft-jazz piano—are invariably delectable. Awash in sea blues which blend with the view, the Cafe serves a lighter menu and serves, almost year-round, as an elegantly informal community clubhouse.

Scruples World Bistro. 149 Commercial St. (in the West End). ☎ **508/487-1076.** Main courses $14–$22. AE, DISC, VC, V. Late June to early Sept 11am–1am; call for off-season hours. Closed Nov to mid-May. INTERNATIONAL.

HOSTESS WILL EAT YOU, reads the altered sign in the window, the site of many an alternative tourist photo. Actually, the hostess—often a drag performance artist—is more likely to entertain you, as will the wild mix of cuisines. Thai predominates, from classic coconut soup and chicken satay through lemongrass shrimp; other influences include Caribbean and Tex-Mex. All that spice makes an excellent foil for the bar's "beach cocktails": Blue Hawaii, Bahama Mama, and more.

MODERATE

Bubala's by the Bay. 183 Commercial St. (in the West End). ☎ **508/487-0773.** Main courses $9–$19. AE, DISC, MC, V. Apr–Oct daily 8am–1am. Closed Nov–Mar. ECLECTIC.

Once a nothing-special seaside restaurant, this trendy bistro—miraculously transformed with a gaudy yellow paint job and Picassoesque wall murals—promises "serious food at sensible prices." That it delivers, all day long—from buttermilk waffles with real maple syrup through lobster tarragon salad and creative foccacia sandwiches to fajitas, Cajun calamari, and pad Thai.

✪ **The Commons Bistro & Bar.** 386 Commercial St. ☎ **508/487-7800.** Reservations recommended. Main courses $9–$19. Late June to early Sept daily 8:30am–1pm; call for off-season hours. ECLECTIC.

It's a toss-up: The sidewalk cafe provides an optimal opportunity for studying Provincetown's inimitable street life, whereas the plum-colored dining room inside affords a refuge adorned with the owners' extraordinary collection of original Toulouse-Lautrec prints. Either way, you'll get to partake of chef Lea Forant's tasty and creative fare. At lunchtime, her overstuffed "lobster club" sandwich on lemon bread is nonpareil, and the grilled duck médaillons served atop soba, Asian greens, and shredded jicama is the ultimate summertime refresher. The Commons boasts the only wood-fired pizza oven in town to date, and the soft-crusted pizzette with various toppings—consider the crisped duck, scallions, chevre, and wild mushrooms—make a great snack whatever the hour. Another long overdue first for this seafaring town is a seasonal sushi bar.

⭘ **The Dancing Lobster Cafe/Trattoria.** 9 Ryder St. Extension (on Fisherman's Wharf, off Commercial St.). ☎ **508/487-0900.** No reservations. Main courses $10–$14. No credit cards. May–Oct daily 5:30–11pm. Closed Nov–Apr. MEDITERRANEAN.

One way or another, your jaw is bound to drop—whether at the scenic location of this glass-sided restaurant, or the easy-on-the-pocket prices that prevail. Native son Nils "Pepe" Berg has returned from stints at such top venues as Boston's Emporio Armani to treat the town in true prodigal style. It's worth lining up 90 minutes or more for one of 20 hotly contested tables to feast on the sunny output of this open kitchen. Where to begin? With the grilled-squid *bruscetta*, the saffrony Venetian *zuppa di pesce*, or perhaps the asparagus ravioli or steamed mussels with a basil aïoli? You'll appreciate the Italian tradition of *primi* and *secondi*, even if it curbs your craving for a *rustica* tiramisu—you could always take it with you, or better yet, use it as an excuse to come back.

Iguana Grill. 135 Bradford St. (in the center of town). ☎ **508/487-8800.** Fax 508/487-8267. Main courses $8–$14. AE, DISC, MC, V. July–Aug 10am–10pm; call for off-season hours. Closed Nov–Feb. LATIN AMERICAN.

Healthful Mexican? It might seem an oxymoron, except that co-owner Eric Ovalle insists on substituting low-fat updates for the rich fare he grew up on. You won't find a single fried food on the menu, and in fact not so much as a morsel of beef. Lean ground turkey fills in nicely for the usual *carne* in such traditional dishes as tacos, burritos, fajitas, and enchiladas. Be sure to try something cloaked in *mole*, a chocolate-based sauce that's spicy rather than sweet. And then, since you've been good, blow all your resolve on a *postre* like *go*, a Santo Domingan corn pudding.

INEXPENSIVE

Cafe Heaven. 199 Commercial St. (in the center of town). ☎ **508/487-9639.** No reservations. Most items under $10. No credit cards. Late May to early Sept daily 8am–3pm and 6:30–10pm; call for off-season hours. Closed Nov–Apr. AMERICAN.

Prized for its leisurely country breakfasts (served till mid-afternoon, for you reluctant risers), this modernist storefront—adorned with big, bold paintings, locally produced—also turns out substantive sandwiches, such as avocado and goat cheese on a French baguette. The salads are appealing as well—especially the "special shrimp," lightly doused with dilled sour cream and tossed with tomatoes and grapes. Innumerable "pasta possibilities," plus "heavenly" burgers with a choice of internationally inspired toppings, are the main event come evening.

BAKED GOODS & LATE-NIGHT DINING

One thing you absolutely have to do while in town is peruse the cases of *pasteis* (meat pies) and pastries at ⭘ **Provincetown Portuguese Bakery,** 299 Commercial St. (in the center of town; ☎ **508/487-1803**). Point to a few and take your surprise package out on the pier for delectation. Though perhaps not the wisest course for the whale watch–bound, it's the best way to sample the scrumptious international output of this beloved institution. Closed November through March.

A local landmark, **Spiritus,** 190 Commercial St. (in the center of town; ☎ **508/ 487-2808**), is an outré pizza parlor known for post-last-call cruising: It's open till 2am. The pizza's good, as are the fruit drinks, specialty coffees, and four brands of premium ice cream, from Emack & Bolio's to Coconut Joe's. For a peaceful morning repast—and perhaps a relaxed round of bocce—check out the little garden in back. Closed November through March.

PROVINCETOWN AFTER DARK

Note: There's so much going on in season on any given night, you might want to simplify your search by calling or stopping in at the **Provincetown Reservations System** office at 293 Commercial St. in the center of town (☎ **508/487-6400**).

THE CLUB SCENE

✪ **The Atlantic House.** 6 Masonic Place (off Commercial St., 2 blocks west of Town Hall). ☎ **508/487-3821.** Cover for the Big Room: $5.

Open year-round, the "A-house"—the nation's premiere gay bar—also welcomes straights of both sexes, except in the leather-oriented Macho Bar upstairs. Late in the evening, there's usually plenty going on in the Big Room dance bar. Check out the Tennessee Williams memorabilia, including a portrait *au naturel;* there's more across the street, in a new restaurant called Grand Central.

The Boatslip Beach Club.161 Commercial St. ☎ **508/487-2660.** Cover varies.

Come late afternoon, if you wonder where all the beachgoers went, it's a safe guess that a goodly number are attending at the gay-lesbian tea dance held daily in season from 3:30 to 6:30 on the hotel's pool deck. Later in the evening, after a post–tea dance dance at Pied Piper (see below), they'll probably be back for some disco or two-stepping.

Crown & Anchor. 247 Commercial St. (in the center of town). ☎ **508/487-1430.** Cover varies; call for schedule.

There's something for everyone at this warren of specialty bars, spanning leather (in "The Vault"), disco, comedy, drag shows (including headliner "Musty Chiffon" singing 1960s camp classics), and cabaret (such as the irresistable trio known simply as Betty). Facilities include a pool bar and game room.

Pied Piper. 293A Commercial St. (in the center of town). ☎ **508/487-1527.** Cover varies; call for schedule. Closed Nov to mid-Apr.

In season, a "parade" of gay revelers descends in early evening from the Boatslip to "the Pied," for its After Tea T-Dance. The late-night wave consists of a fair number of women, or fairly convincing simulacra thereof (Monday and Wednesday nights feature the "female illusionists" of the Drag Factory). For a glimpse of stars-in-the-making, check out "Putting on the Hits," a sampling of local talent held Tuesday nights at 10.

Vixen. Pilgrim House, 336 Commercial St. (in the center of town). ☎ **508/487-6424.** Cover varies; call for schedule.

Provincetown's oldest hotel was overhauled in 1995, yielding this chic new women's bar. On the roster are jazz, blues, and comedy acts—including the unabashedly butch (even in a prom dress) and very funny Lea Delaria, who resembles a punk Bud Costello.

THE BAR SCENE

Governor Bradford. 312 Commercial St. (in the center of town). ☎ **508/487-9618.** Cover varies; call for schedule.

It's a good old bar, featuring a summer-long lineup of blues acts, plus the inimitable home-grown, gender-bending rock group known as Space Pussy.

✪ **Larry's Bar.** At Sebastian's Waterside Restaurant. ☎ **508/487-3286.** No cover. Closed late Oct to mid-Apr.

Mrs. Wald did not raise a retiring child. The irrepressible Larry—perennial chair and chief cheerleader for Provincetown's campy Carnival Week—is a drink-dispensing one-man entertainment committee. Once he gets going on one of his riffs (usually centered on an assortment of mutant Barbie dolls), you can just sit back and enjoy the show. This tiny bar, wallpapered with classic paint-by-numbers *chef-d'oeuvres,* is the place to go when you need a good laugh.

The Islands

7

by Sandy MacDonald

For those who seek refuge here, from megastars and CEOs to middle-class families and impecunious students, the islands of Martha's Vineyard and Nantucket are the Cape's Cape—the ultimate escape. Time has a way of dropping away once you set off for these naturally isolated ports. Not that you'll be leaving the 20th century far behind: All the trappings of the modern age—laptops and cell phones, FedEx and satellite dishes—can be found in abundance. The difference is that you feel subtly encouraged to ignore them. Wouldn't it make much more sense to heed the gentle breezes stirring up the wild roses and bike out to a beach you can almost claim for your own?

Though geologically similar (both were once connected to the mainland, millennia ago), each island has a distinctive personality. Nantucket, flash-frozen mid-19th century through zealous zoning, has long been considered a Republican redoubt. It's rich, entrenched, and traditional, goes the stereotype, and if your great-grandparents didn't summer there, you might as well not bother: You'll just be roundly ignored. Perhaps, if you're of that vintage and are still harboring unfulfilled social aspirations. But the younger generations, many of whom did indeed grow up summering here among the old guard, tend to be more welcoming. There's a palpable creative buzz that's making itself heard in the form of brave new enterprises, especially shops and restaurants. True, prices tend to be steep (at least 150% the mainland norm), but if you've gone to the trouble and expense of getting here, you might as well enjoy yourself.

Martha's Vineyard, large enough to support a year-round population spanning a broader socioeconomic spectrum, is not quite so rarefied: Islanders pride themselves on their Democratic liberalism. True, a prime oceanside estate might fetch many millions, but the lucky denizens can't wait to dicker over zucchini at the local farmers' market. Whereas Nantucket is pretty much a unified whole, centered on one small town, the Vineyard, with its variegated villages, presents many facets. Edgartown comes closest to Nantucket in formality and architectural decorum. Oak Bluffs, with its gaudily painted cottages, is a religious community turned nightlife carnival. Bucolic Chilmark looks like a chunk of northern New England, complete with stone fences and idealistic back-to-landers. Commercially-oriented Vineyard Haven could be plunked back on the Cape, and no one would ever notice the difference.

In other words, there's something for everyone on both islands. It's fun to keep exploring and comparing until you happen upon a niche that feels just right.

1 Martha's Vineyard

5 miles (8km) S of Falmouth

For a place with such a chi-chi reputation—especially since the Clintons and Princess Diana put in well-publicized appearances—this good-sized island (it's New England's largest, at 100 square miles) can seem surprisingly dowdy at first glance, or at least those parts visible to ordinary mortals. It presents its showiest visage in the trim port of Edgartown, where impressive captain's mansions, almost uniformly white with black trim, bespeak the riches that prior generations wrested from the sea. Inland, you might forget you're on an island at all: The rolling meadows and dense forests are more reminiscent of landscapes back on the mainland.

Tourists typically cleave to the shore, usually making a circuit of Vineyard Haven (the main port, whose official name is Tisbury, and the only truly year-round town); Oak Bluffs, which started out as a rough-hewn revivalist "campground" in 1835 and soon grew into a colorful cluster of carpenter's gothic cottages; buttoned-down Edgartown, still the seat of money and power; and Gay Head, where the remarkable multicolored clay cliffs remain under the stewardship of their original caretakers, the Wampanoags. Visitors with a bit more time and latitude will also want to take in the rough-hewn fishing port of Menemsha and wander the rural back roads of Chilmark, where a loose-knit federation of artists, writers, actors, and musicians—some rather well known—seek and find inspiration.

ESSENTIALS

GETTING THERE & GETTING AROUND   Most visitors avail themselves of ferry service connecting the Vineyard to the mainland.

Oak Bluffs has the busiest harbor in season: It's served by the *Hy-Line* from Hyannis or Nantucket (☎ 508/778-2600), the *Island Queen* from Falmouth Heights (☎ 508/548-4800), and the state-run **Steamship Authority car ferry** from Woods Hole (☎ 508/477-8600).

Vineyard Haven welcomes Steamship Authority car ferries from Woods Hole year-round (you'll need a reservation, although there's limited standby space available, except during certain peak-demand stretches in summer, for those willing to wait around), and the *Cape Island Express* (☎ 508/997-1688) from New Bedford in summer. The *Island Queen* makes the quickest crossing, in about 40 minutes; the *Cape Island Express* takes about 1¹/₂ hours but spares travelers coming from New York the long drive onto the Cape. One-way fares range from about $5 to $11, depending on the distance, and the one-way rate for cars in season is $38. There are dozens of crossings a day in summer, but if the timing doesn't work out quite right, **Falmouth's Patriot Party Boats** (☎ 508/548-9400) will, for $100 per boatload, ferry passengers over to any of the ports, including Edgartown, which isn't keen on ferry traffic.

You can also fly into Katama Airport outside Edgartown. Carriers to Martha's Vineyard include **Cape Air** (☎ 800/352-0714 or 508/771-6944), **Island Airlines** (☎ 800/248-7779 or 508/775-6066), and **Nantucket Airlines** (☎ 800/635-8787 or 508/790-0300). Charter flights are offered by Cape Air and Nantucket Airlines as well as by **Air New England** (☎ 508/693-8899), Hyannis Air Service (☎ 508/775-8171), **Island Air Charter** (☎ 508/778-8360), **King Air Charters** (☎ 800/247-2427), and **Westchester Air** (☎ 800/759-2929).

Martha's Vineyard

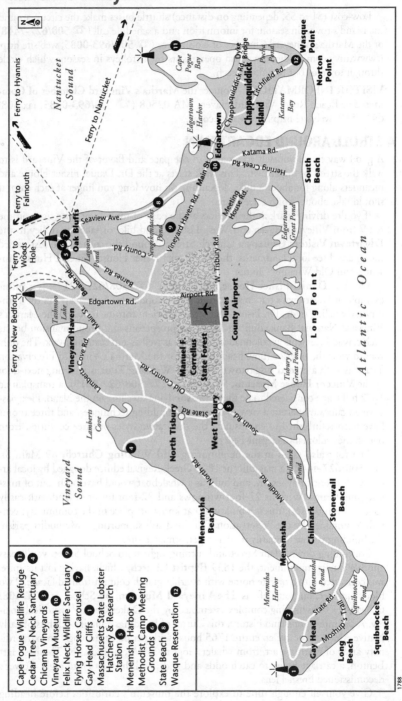

Nantucket Sound

Ferry to Hyannis

Ferry to Nantucket

Cape
Pogue
Bay

Dyke
Bridge

Pacha
Pond

Wasque
Point

Norton
Point

Edgartown Rd.
Chappaquiddick Rd.
Litchfield Rd.

Chappaquiddick
Island

Katama
Bay

Ferry to Falmouth

Ferry to Woods Hole

Edgartown
Harbor

Seaview Ave.

Edgartown

Katama Rd.

Herring Creek Rd.

South
Beach

Oak Bluffs

Lagoon
Pond

Main St.

Meeting
House Rd.

Edgartown
Great Pond

Ferry to New Bedford

Barnes Rd.

County Rd.

Sengekontacket
Pond

Vineyard Haven Rd.

W. Tisbury Rd.

Long Point

Atlantic Ocean

Tashmoo
Lake

Main St.

Edgartown Rd.

Airport Rd.

Dukes
County Airport

Vineyard Haven

Vineyard Cove Rd.

Lamberts Cove Rd.

Old County Rd.

Manuel F.
Correllus
State Forest

Tisbury
Great Pond

Lamberts
Cove

North Tisbury

State Rd.

West Tisbury

South Rd.

Vineyard Sound

North Rd.

Middle Rd.

Chilmark
Pond

Menemsha
Beach

Menemsha

Chilmark

Stonewall
Beach

Menemsha Harbor

Menemsha
Pond

State Rd.

Squibnocket
Pond

Gay Head

Moshup's Trail

Squibnocket
Beach

Long
Beach

Cape Pogue Wildlife Refuge ❶   ❹ Cedar Tree Neck Sanctuary
Chicama Vineyards ❸   ❿ Vineyard Museum
Felix Neck Wildlife Sanctuary ❼   ❾
Flying Horses Carousel ❶
Gay Head Cliffs ❺
Massachusetts State Lobster   ❷
Hatchery & Research
Station ❺   ❻
Menemsha Harbor ❷
Methodist Camp Meeting   ❻
Grounds ❻   ❽
State Beach ❽   ⓬
Wasque Reservation ⓬

1788

267

Low-cost ($1 to $5, depending on distance) shuttle buses make the circuit around the island's towns in season; for information and a schedule call (☎ **508/627-7448**) or the Martha's Vineyard Chamber of Commerce (☎ **508/693-0085,** web site http://www.mvy.com). Edgartown also operates its own trolleys in season, which circle through town or out to South Beach.

VISITOR INFORMATION   Contact the **Martha's Vineyard Chamber of Commerce** at Beach Road, Vineyard Haven, MA 02568 (☎ **508/693-0085,** fax 508/693-7589, web site http://www.mvy.com).

A STROLL AROUND EDGARTOWN

A good way to get yourself acclimated to the pace and flavor of the Vineyard is to walk the streets of Edgartown. This walk starts at the Dr. Daniel Fisher House and meanders along for about a mile; depending on how long you linger at each stop, it should take about two to three hours.

If you're driving, park at the free lots at the edge of town (you'll see signs on the roads from Vineyard Haven and West Tisbury) and bike or take the trolley to the **Edgartown Visitors Center** on Church Street. Around the corner (you just passed them) are three local landmarks: the Dr. Daniel Fisher House, Vincent House Museum, and Old Whaling Church.

The **Dr. Daniel Fisher House,** 99 Main St. (☎ **508/627-8017**), is a prime example of Edgartown's trademark Greek Revival opulence. A key player in the 19th-century whaling trade, Dr. Fisher amassed a sufficient fortune to found the Martha's Vineyard National Bank. Built in 1840, his prosperous-and-proud mansion boasts such classical elements as colonnaded porticos, as well as a delicate roofwalk. The only way to view the interior (now headquarters for the Martha's Vineyard Preservation Trust) is with a guided **Edgartown Historic Walking Tour** originating next-door at the **Vincent House Museum,** 99 Main St. (☎ **508/627-8619**), a transplanted 1672 full Cape considered to be the oldest surviving dwelling on the island. Plexiglas-covered cutaways permit a view of traditional building techniques, and three rooms have been refurbished to encapsulate the decorative styles of three centuries, from bare-bones colonial to elegant Federal.

The tour also takes in the neighboring **Old Whaling Church,** 89 Main St. (☎ **508/627-4442**), a magnificent 1843 Greek Revival edifice designed by local architect Frederick Baylies, Jr., and built as a whaleboat would have been, out of massive pine beams. With its 27-foot windows and 92-foot tower (a landmark easily spotted from the sea), this is a building that knows its place in the community: central. Maintained by the Preservation Trust and still supporting a Methodist parish, the building is now primarily used as a performance site.

Continuing down Main Street and turning right onto School Street, you'll pass another Baylies monument, the 1839 **Baptist Church,** which, having lost its spire, was converted into a private home with a rather grand, column-fronted facade. Two blocks farther, on your left, is **The Vineyard Museum,** 59 School St. (☎ **508/627-4441**), a fascinating complex assembled by the Dukes County Historical Society. A palimpsest of island history, this cluster of buildings contains exhibits of early Native American crafts; an entire 1765 house with period furnishings; an extraordinary array of maritime art, from whalers' logs to WPA-era studies by Thomas Hart Benton; a carriage house to catch odds and ends; and the Gay Head Light Tower's decommissioned Fresnel lens.

Give yourself enough time to explore the museum's curiosities before heading south one block on Cooke Street. Cater-corner across South Summer Street, you'll spot the first of Baylies's impressive endeavors, the 1828 **Federated Church.** One block left are the offices of the **Vineyard Gazette,** 34 S. Summer St. (☎ 508/627-4311). Operating out of a 1760 house, this exemplary small-town newspaper has been going strong since 1846: Its 14,000 subscribers span the globe.

Heading toward Main Street, you'll happen upon the **Charlotte Inn,** 27 S. Summer St. (☎ 508/627-4751), among the most charming on the entire East Coast. You don't have to be a guest to appreciate the English gardens, and in fact the in-house Edgartown Art Gallery provides a good excuse to explore the common rooms. Take a look at the restaurant, too—l'étoile, set in a lovely conservatory—if you're considering a dinner splurge.

Right now it's time to head down Main Street toward the water, stopping in at any inviting shops along the way. Veer left on Dock Street to reach the **Old Sculpin Gallery,** 58 Dock St. (☎ 508/627-4881). The output of the Martha's Vineyard Art Association displayed here tends to be amateurish, but you might happen upon a find. The real draw is the stark old building itself, which started out as a granary (part of Dr. Fisher's vast holdings) and spent the better part of the 20th century as a boat-building shop.

Keep an eye out for vintage beauties when you cross the street to survey the harbor from the dock at Town Wharf. It's from here that the tiny *On-Time* ferry makes its three-minute crossing to Chappaquiddick Island, hauling three cars at a time and a great many more sightseers—not that there's much to see on the other side. Just so you don't waste time tracking it down: The infamous Dyke Bridge, scene of the Kennedy/Kopechne debacle, has been dismantled and, at long last, replaced. However, the island does offer great stretches of conservation land that will reward the hearty hiker or mountain biker.

Mere strollers might want to remain in town to admire the many formidable captains' homes lining **North Water Street,** many of which have been converted into inns. Each has a tale to tell. The 1750 Daggett House (No. 59), for instance, expanded upon a 1660 tavern, and the original beehive oven is flanked by a "secret" passageway. Nathaniel Hawthorne holed up at the Edgartown Inn (No. 56) for nearly a year in 1789 while writing *Twice Told Tales*—and, it is rumored, romancing a local maiden who inspired *The Scarlet Letter.* You can make up stories of your own as you head back toward Main Street and the center of town.

Your last stop has got to be the **Truly Scrumptious Cafe,** 11 S. Summer St. (☎ 508/627-3990), offering top-notch noshing in the neo-Italian mode, with specialty coffees, of course. It's pretty much point-and-eat, in a stylish storefront setting where you'll also find a few select comestibles, gadgets, and cookbooks for sale.

OUTDOOR PURSUITS

BEACHES Most of the Vineyard's magnificent shoreline, alas, is privately owned or restricted to residents, and thus off-limits to the transient *hoi polloi.* Renters, however, can obtain a beach sticker by applying with a lease at the relevant town hall (Vineyard Haven, ☎ 508/696-4200; Oak Bluffs, ☎ 508/693-5511; Edgartown, ☎ 508/627-6180; West Tisbury, ☎ 508/693-9659; Chilmark, ☎ 508/645-2651; Gay Head, ☎ 508/645-9915). Also, many up-island inns offer the perk of temporary passes to such hot spots as Chilmark's Squibnocket and Lucy Vincent beaches (the latter features high bluffs and, to the left, bathers in the buff). In addition to the public beaches listed below, you might also track down a few hidden coves by requesting a map of conservation properties from the Martha's Vineyard Land Bank (☎ 508/627-7141).

- **Owen Park,** Main Street in Vineyard Haven: A tiny strip of sand adjoining a town green with swings and a bandstand will suffice for young children, who get lifeguard supervision.
- **Oak Bluffs Town Beach:** Swimming in the Sound, right in town, can be rather tame, but it's certainly convenient, and fine for undemanding little kids.
- **Joseph A. Sylvia State Beach,** midway between Oak Bluffs and Edgartown: Stretching a whole mile and flanked by a bike path, this placid beach is prized for its gentle and warm (relatively speaking) waves. Eastville Point, just past the drawbridge, offers especially calm water and scarce parking.
- **Lighthouse Beach,** off North Water Street, Edgartown: Tiny, unattended, lacking parking, and often seaweed-strewn, it's nonetheless terribly scenic.
- **Wasque Beach,** Wasque Reservation, Chappaquiddick: Surprisingly easy to get to (via the *On-Time*), this half-mile-long beach has all the amenities, without the crowds; in season, a $3 entrance fee is charged per car and per adult over 15.
- **East Beach,** Wasque Reservation, Chappaquiddick: Relatively few people go to the bother of biking and hiking (or four-wheel-driving) this far, so you should be able to find all the privacy you crave.
- **Katama Beach** and **South Beach,** about four miles south of Edgartown: This popular stretch of surf beach—three miles long in all—has parking lots that fill up very early in the day; it's also accessible by bike path or shuttle. Families tend to head to the left, college kids to the right.
- **Gay Head (a.k.a. Moshup) Beach:** Parking costs $10 a day at this half-mile beach just east of the colorful cliffs.
- **Lobsterville Beach,** at end of Lobsterville Road in Gay Head: This two-mile beauty boasts calm, shallow waters, ideal for children, but there's no parking.
- **Menemsha Beach,** next to Dutchers Dock: Despite its rough surface, this well-trafficked strand—with lifeguards and rest rooms—is quite popular, especially at sunset.
- **Seth's Pond,** off Lamberts Cove Road, W. Tisbury: A small freshwater pond attractive to families.
- **Lake Tashmoo,** off Herring Creek Road, Vineyard Haven: Limited parking and often brackish water mar what would otherwise be a prime location.

BIRDING   The Felix Neck Wildlife Sanctuary, a Massachusetts Audubon Society property, off Edgartown-Vineyard Haven Road (☎ **508/627-4850**), occupies 350 wet to wooded acres adjoining Sengekontacket Pond. Naturalist guides offer a great variety of programs, most notably a chance to observe nesting osprey, whose comeback the Sanctuary has helped to ensure. Fresh- and saltwater tanks enable visitors to view local aquatic life, including turtles and other reptiles. Admission is $3 adults, $2 children 1 to 12, seniors $1. July through August, the grounds are open daily from 8am to 7pm; the visitor center is open daily 8am to 4:30pm. Call for the off-season schedule.

FISHING   For shellfishing, you'll need to get information and a permit from the appropriate town hall (for the telephone numbers, see "Beaches," above). Popular spots for surf casting include Wasque Point on Chappaquiddick (see "Nature Trails," below), South Beach, and the jetty at Menemsha Pond. The party-boat *Skipper* (☎ **508/693-1238**), usually used for narrated celebrity sightings, offers half-day trips out of Oak Bluffs harbor in season. Deep-sea excursions can be arranged aboard the *Slapshot II* (☎ **508/627-8087**) or **Big Eye Charters** (☎ **508/627-3659**), both out of Edgartown, or **North Shore** (☎ **508/645-2993**) or **Conomo Charters** (☎ **508/ 645-9278**) in Menemsha, locus of the island's commercial fishing fleet; you may

Exploring the Vineyard on Two Wheels

A triangle of paved bike paths, roughly eight miles to a side, links the down-island towns of Oak Bluffs, Edgartown, and West Tisbury (the Sound portion, flanked by water on both sides, is especially enjoyable). The up-island roads leading to Chilmark, Menemsha, and Gay Head are often hilly and sometimes heavily trafficked; however, experienced cyclists shouldn't find them too difficult.

A word to the wise: By catching Creek Charters' informal bike ferry (☎ 508/645-9097) across the narrow mouth of Menemsha harbor—it runs daily on demand 8am to 6pm in July and August, with limited hours in the shoulder season—you can go straight to Gay Head and save yourself about 12 miles of backtracking, thereby making better use of your sightseeing time.

Bike-rental operations are ubiquitous near the ferry landings in Vineyard Haven and Oak Bluffs. If you'd prefer to get settled and unpacked first, **R. W. Cutler Bike** at 1 Main St. in Edgartown (☎ 508/627-4052), will gladly deliver a bike to your door.

You'll have no trouble finding sustenance in the down-island towns. Up-island, preferred pit stops include Alley's General Store in the center of West Tisbury (☎ 508/693-0088), the Chilmark Store (☎ 508/645-3739), and the Menemsha Bite on Basin Road (☎ 508/645-9329). Gay Head tends to be clogged with tourist buses, but you might try the fast-food booths lining the path: It's rumored that one boasts a Cordon Bleu chef.

---

recognize this weathered port from *Jaws*. IGFA world-record holder Capt. Leslie S. Smith operates **Backlash Charters** (☎ 508/627-5894, e-mail: backlash@tiac.net), specializing in light tackle and fly-fishing, out of Edgartown. Cooper Gilkes, III, proprietor of **Coop's Bait & Tackle** at 147 W. Tisbury Rd. in Edgartown (☎ 508/627-3909), which offers rentals as well as supplies, is another acknowledged authority; he's available as an instructor or charter guide, and even amenable to sharing hard-won pointers on local hot spots.

GOLF   President Clinton helped to publicize the nine-hole **Mink Meadows Golf Course,** off Franklin Street in Vineyard Haven (☎ 508/693-0600), which occupies a top-dollar chunk of real estate but is open to the general public, as well as the semi-private, championship-level 18-hole **Farm Neck Golf Club** off Farm Neck Road in Oak Bluffs (☎ 508/693-3057).

IN-LINE SKATING   In-line skates are evident everywhere: You'll find rentals at **Jamaikan Jam,** 154 Circuit Ave. (☎ 508/693-5003), or **M.V. Blade Runners,** Circuit Avenue Extension.(☎ 508/693-8852), both in Oak Bluffs; the latter offers renters complimentary introductory clinics twice daily in season. Other sources include **Sports Haven,** 13 Beach Rd., Vineyard Haven (☎ 508/696-0456), and the **Vineyard Sports Center,** at the Triangle in Edgartown (☎ 508/627-3933).

NATURE TRAILS   About a fifth of MV's land mass has been set aside for conservation. The **West Chop Woods,** off Franklin Street in Vineyard Haven, comprise 85 acres with marked walking trails. Midway between Vineyard Haven and Edgartown, the **Felix Neck Wildlife Sanctuary** (see below) includes a six-mile network of trails over varying terrain, from woodland to beach. Accessible by ferry from Edgartown, quiet Chappaquiddick is home to two sizable preserves: the **Cape Pogue Wildlife Refuge** and **Wasque Reservation** (☎ 508/627-7260), covering much of the island's eastern barrier beach, comprise 709 variegated acres that draw flocks of nesting or resting shorebirds. Also on the island, three miles east on Dyke Road, is another Trustees of the Reservations property, the distinctly "unnatural" but none-theless alluring **Mytoi**, a 14-acre Japanese garden.

A wilder alternative to South Beach, the 633-acre **Long Point Wildlife Refuge,** off Waldron's Bottom Road in West Tisbury (☎ 508/693-7392), lets you share the heath and dunes, the ponds and beach, with wildlife rather than human hordes; a $6 parking fee is charged in season. The 4,000-acre **Manuel F. Correllus Vineyard State Forest** occupies a sizable, if not especially scenic, chunk mid-island; it's riddled with mountain-bike paths and riding trails. Up-island, along the Sound, the **Menemsha Hills Reservation,** off North Road in Chilmark (☎ 508/693-7662), encompasses 210 acres of rocks and bluffs, with steep paths, lovely views, and even a public beach. The **Cedar Tree Neck Sanctuary,** off Indian Hill Road southwest of Vineyard Haven (☎ 508/693-5207), offers some 300 forested acres that end in a stony beach, where, alas, swimming and sunbathing are prohibited. It's still a re-freshing retreat.

WATER SPORTS   Wind's Up at 95 Beach Rd. in Vineyard Haven (☎ 508/ 693-4252), rents out canoes, kayaks, and various sailing craft, including windsurfers, and offers instruction on-site, on a placid pond; they also rent out surfboards and boogie boards. **John Moore** (☎ 508/693-1385), a Boston architect who commutes to Woods Hole from Lambert's Cove by kayak, is considered the Vineyard's top kayaking instructor: Contact him for lessons or tours, or just general guidance. For scuba equipment, visit **Vineyard Scuba** on South Circuit Avenue in Oak Bluffs (☎ 508/693-0288). Rank beginners may enjoy towing privileges at **M. V. Parasail and M. V. Ski** off Owen Park Pier in Vineyard Haven Harbor (☎ 508/693-2838): For the former you're airborne by parachute, for the latter you straddle waterskis, a kneeboard, or inner tube.

MUSEUMS & HISTORIC LANDMARKS

Cottage Museum. 1 Trinity Park (within the Camp Meeting Grounds), Oak Bluffs. ☎ 508/ 693-0525. Admission $1 (donation). Mid-June to mid-Sept Mon–Sat 10am–4pm. Closed mid-Sept to mid-June.

Oak Bluffs' famous "Camp Ground"—a 34-acre circle encompassing more than 300 multicolored, elaborately trimmed carpenter's Gothic cottages—looks very much the way it might have more than 100 years ago. These adorable little houses, loosely modeled on the revivalists' canvas tents that inspired them, have been handed down through the generations. Unless you happen to know a lucky camper, your best chance of getting inside one is to visit this homey little museum, which embodies the late 19th-century zeitgeist even as it displays representative artificacts: bulky black bathing costumes, for example, or a melodeon used for informal hymnal sing-alongs.

The compact architecture is at once practical and symbolic: The Gothic-arched French doors off the peak-roofed second-story bedroom, for instance, lead to a tiny balcony sited so that occupants could keep tabs on community doings. The daily schedule was in fact rather hectic. In 1867, when this cottage was built, campers typi-cally attended three lengthy prayer services daily. Today's denizens tend to blend in with the visiting tourists, though the opportunities for worship remain manifold: at the 1878 Trinity Methodist Church within the park or, just outside, on Samoset Avenue, at the nonsectarian 1870 Union Chapel, a magnificent octagonal structure with superb acoustics (posted signs give the lineup of guest preachers and musicians). At the very center of the Camp Grounds is the striking Trinity Park Tabernacle (1879), an open-sided chapel that is the largest wrought-iron structure in the country. Thousands can be accommodated on its long wooden benches, which are usually filled to capacity for the Sunday-morning services in summer, as well as for weekly community sings and occasional concerts.

✪ **Flying Horses Carousel.** 33 Circuit Ave. (at Lake Ave.), Oak Bluffs. ☎ 508/693-9481. Tickets $1 per ride, or $8 for 10. Late May to early Sept daily 10am–10pm; call for off-season hours. Closed mid-Oct to mid-Apr.

You don't have to be a kid—although it helps—to enjoy the colorful mounts adorning what is considered to be the oldest working carousel in the country. Built in 1876 at New York's fabled Coney Island, this National Historic Landmark maintained by the Martha's Vineyard Preservation Trust pre-dates the era of horses that "gallop": Lacking the necessary gears, these merely glide smoothly in place to the joyful strains of a calliope. The challenge lies in going for the gold ring—brass, actually—that entitles the lucky winner to a free ride. Some regulars, adults included, have grown rather adept: You'll see them scoop up several in a single pass. In between rides, take a moment to admire the intricate hand-carving and real horsehair manes, and gaze into the horses' glass eyes for a surprise: Tiny animal charms glint within.

✪ **The Vineyard Museum.** 59 School St. (2 blocks SW of Main St.), Edgartown. ☎ 508/627-4441. Fax 508/627-4436. Admission in-season $5 adults, $3 seniors and children 12–17. Early July to early Sept Tues–Sat 10am–4:30pm, Sun noon–4:30pm; call for off-season hours and rates.

All of Martha's Vineyard's colorful history is captured here, in a compound of historic buildings. To acclimate yourself chronologically, start with the pre-colonial artifacts—from arrowheads to colorful Gay Head clay pottery—displayed in the 1845 Captain Francis Pease House; there's also a small gift shop here, and a Children's Gallery to showcase the output of visiting children.

The Gale Huntington Reference Library houses rare documentation of the island's history, from genealogical records to whaleship logs. The library's holdings are extensive, and some extraordinary memorabilia, including scrimshaw and portraiture, is on view in the adjoining Francis Foster Museum. Outside, there's a reproduction "tryworks" to show the means by which whale blubber was reduced to precious oil.

To get a sense of daily life during the era when the waters of the East Coast were the equivalent of a modern highway, visit the Thomas Cooke House, a shipwright-built 1765 full Cape where the customs collector lived and worked (the trees in town having been cut back, he had a clear view of comings and goings in the harbor). A few of the house's 12 rooms are decorated as they might have been at the height of the maritime trade; others are devoted to special exhibits on other fascinating aspects of island history, such as the revivalist fever that enveloped Oak Bluffs. Further curiosities are stored in the nearby Carriage Shed: Among the vintage 19th-century vehicles are a painted peddlar's cart, a whaleboat, hearse, and fire engine, and the odds and ends include some touching mementos of early tourism.

The latest—and flashiest—addition to the museum's holdings is the Fresnel lens lifted from the Gay Head Lighthouse in 1952, after nearly a century of service. Though it no longer serves to warn ships of dangerous shoals (that light is automated now), it still lights up the night every evening in summer, just for show.

ORGANIZED TOURS

Arabella. Menemsha Harbor (at North Rd.), Menemsha. ☎ 508/645-3511. Fee $30 evening; day sail $50 adults, $27.50 children. Departures mid-June to mid-Sept daily 11am and 6pm. Reservations required. Closed mid-Sept to mid-June.

Hugh Taylor (James's equally musical brother) alternates with a couple of other captains in taking the helm of his swift 50-foot catamaran for daily trips to Cuttyhunk and sunset cruises around Naushon Island; you can book the whole boat, if you like, for a private charter. Zipping along at 15 to 25 knots, it's a great way to see lovely coves and vistas otherwise denied the ordinary tourist.

Edgartown Historic Walking Tours. From the Vincent House Museum, behind 99 Main St., Edgartown. ☎ **508/627-8619.** Fee $5 adults, children 12 and under free; inquire about combination passes including The Vineyard Museum (see above). June–Oct daily 11am–3pm; call for off-season schedule.

Laced with local lore, these hour-long tours provide access to the interiors of the 1672 Vincent House (the island's oldest surviving dwelling), the 1840 Dr. Daniel Fisher House (an elegant Greek Revival mansion), and the splendid Old Whaling Church, a town showpiece built in 1843.

Laissez Faire. Vineyard Haven Harbor, Vineyard Haven. ☎ **508/693-1646.** Rates $60–$100 per person; call for details and reservations. Closed Oct–May.

John and Mary Clarke, innkeepers at The Lothrop Merry House (see "Where to Stay, below), offer half-day and daylong sails aboard their 54-foot, 1962 Alden ketch— which serves as their summer bedroom. Refreshments—including wine and hors-d'oeuvres—are included.

The *Shenandoah*. Beach St. Extension (on the harbor), Vineyard Haven. ☎ **508/693-1699.** Day sails $50 July–Aug; call for schedule. Reservations required. Closed mid-Sept to mid-June.

Black Dog owner Robert Douglas's prized 110-foot topsail schooner, modeled on an 1849 revenue cutter and fitted out with period furnishings, spends most of the summer doing windjammer duty, transporting some 26 lucky souls wherever the wind happens to take them in the course of a week. With no engine to fall back on, it's very much a matter of the wind's whim—as well as of Douglas's considerable skill. Occasional day sails are offered at the height of the season—a great way to preview the full $750 cruise.

Vineyard Classic Cars. Circuit Avenue Extension (on the harbor), Oak Bluffs. ☎ **508/693-5551.** Rates range from $90–$250 per day; call for details and reservations. Closed Nov–Apr.

To reward yourself for having the sense to leave your own wheels back on the mainland, take a spin in a classy throwback—a 1964 Mustang convertible, perhaps, or a cherry 1971 'Vette.

SHOPPING

ANTIQUES/COLLECTIBLES   First off, there's **C.W. Morgan Marine Antiques,** Tisbury Wharf (at Beach Road just east of town center), Vineyard Haven (☎ **508/693-3622**). You don't have to be a bona fide collector to marvel over Frank Rapoza's nautical haul, encompassing paintings and prints, intricate ship models, venerable instruments, sailors' chests and scrimshaw, and anything remotely boating-related. Closed Wednesdays and January through March.

The **Chilmark Flea Market,** Chilmark Community Church, Menemsha Cross Road, Chilmark (☎ **508/645-3177**), convened Wednesday and Saturday mornings in summer, from 8:30am to 2pm, attracts a well-heeled crowd more accustomed to browsing Neiman-Marcus. No matter: Everybody loves a bargain, especially where nostalgia's involved.

ART/CRAFTS   The glorious seaside spread at **Allen Farm,** South Road (about ¹/₂ mile southeast of the village center), Chilmark (☎ **508/645-9064**), hasn't changed hands in three centuries. This stone-fenced farm shelters some 150

Corriedale sheep, some of whom end up in the island's better restaurants and all of whom contribute to the handsome sweaters, blankets, and whatnot knitted and woven on-site. Hours vary; call ahead.

Cheryl Stark started fashioning island-motif charms back in 1966 at **C. B. Stark Jewelers,** 126 Main St. (in the center of town), Vineyard Haven (☎ **508/693-2284**). The latest iconic accessory is jewelry fashioned from "wampum" (purple-shaded quahog shells) by Kate Taylor, James's sister and a fantastic singer/songwriter in her own right.

The **Chilmark Pottery,** off State Road (about four miles southwest of Vineyard Haven), W. Tisbury (☎ **508/693-6476**), also has a branch at 170 Circuit Ave., Oak Bluffs (☎ **508/693-5910**). If ever tableware was fashioned to suit its setting, Geoffrey Borr's is: He borrows his palette from the sea and sky and fashions highly serviceable stoneware with clean lines and a long lifeline.

One of my favorites is ◐ **The Field Gallery,** State Road (in the center of town), W. Tisbury (☎ **508/693-5595**). Marc Chagall meets Henry Moore in this rural pasture, where Tom Maley's playful figures have been enchanting locals and passersby for decades. The Sunday evening openings are high points of the summer social season.

The Granary Gallery at the Red Barn Emporium, Old County Road (off Edgartown–W. Tisbury Road, about ¼ mile north of intersection), W. Tisbury (☎ **800/472-6279** or 508/693-0455), showcases astounding prints by longtime summerer Alfred Eisenstaedt, dazzling color photos by local luminary Alison Shaw, and a changing roster of fine artists, some just emerging, some long since discovered.

World-renowned master glassblowers sometimes lend a hand at **Martha's Vineyard Glass Works,** State Road (in the village center), N. Tisbury (☎ **508/ 693-6026**) just for the fun of it. The three resident artists—Andrew Magdanz, Susan Shapiro, and Mark Weiner—are no slouches themselves, having shown to considerable acclaim all over the country. Their output is decidedly avant-garde and may not suit all tastes, but it's an eye-opening array in any case and all the more fascinating once you've seen the work involved. Closed mid-October to mid-May.

Another notable stop is the **Peter Simon Photography Gallery,** at The Feast of Chilmark, State Road (in the center of town), Chilmark (☎ **508/645-9575**). Singer Carly Simon's brother Peter has the family ear for music—he has produced two albums of local talent, called *Vineyard Sound*—but has made his own name behind a camera, chronicling island life since its great hippie heyday in the seventies. The Feast's smart black-and-white cafe/bar serves as a permanent gallery for his work, some of it hand-tinted by his wife, Ronni. Usually, one of them is on hand weekday mornings to greet curiosity-seekers as well as collectors.

Even if you're not in the market for a hand-crafted copper weathervane costing upwards of thousands of dollars, stop in to see **Travis Tuck,** 89 Main St. (in the center of town), Vineyard Haven (☎ **508/693-3914**), at his craft; visitors are always welcome. Of course, quite a few—like the Clintons and Beverly Sills—find themselves irresistibly placing an an order.

In the words of owner Doug Parker, the **Vineyard Studio/Gallery,** State Road, Vineyard Haven (☎ **508/693-1338**), offers "a glimpse of indigenous creativity few tourists get to see." Parker has transformed the barn of his summertime home into an artists' co-op, more or less as "a philanthropic gesture." As an artist and art-lover himself, he couldn't see the justice in galleries claiming a commission of 60%, so he charges none; here, artists pay only a nominal fee to cover overhead. The shows are ambitious, sophisticated ("No lighthouses or jetties," he promises), and worth a deliberate detour. Be sure to wander out back to admire the impressive perennial gardens. Closed November to April.

FASHION   Alley Cat, 66 Main St. (in the center of town), Vineyard Haven (☎ 508/693-6970), offers up-to-the-minute women's fashions, from Marigold's dresses in handscreened prints (the prints often have a 1940s feel—discreet martinis, for example) or Nomadic Collection clogs fashioned from antique Anatolian kilims. Definitely not your same old, same old. Closed February and March.

✪ **The Great Put On,** Mayhew Lane (in the center of town), Edgartown (☎ 508/ 627-5495), dates back to 1969 but stays right with the times, carrying Norma Kamali, Vivienne Tam, and BCBG, among other designers. Owner Ken Bilzerian is the brother of Boston couturier Alan Bilzerian; the pair share similar tastes. There's also a fine selection of shoes and men's fashions. Closed January through April.

Jamaikan Jam, 154 Circuit Ave. (in the center of town), Oak Bluffs (☎ 508/ 693-5003), one of the best ethnic shops along Circuit Avenue, carries colorful, comfortable clothes. The accoutrements of that other isle further south go over big on this one, and the bubbling reggae riddims definitely put the fun into shopping here. The shop sells Jamaican tchotchkes as well, and carries in-line skates for sale and rental, so you can take your new outfit for a road test. Closed January through April.

LeRoux, 89 Main St. (in the center of town), Vineyard Haven (☎ 508/ 693-6463), also has a branch at Nevin Square in Edgartown (☎ 508/627-7766). Treading a comfortable middle ground between functional and fashionable, the varied women's and men's labels here include some nationally known names, Patagonia and even lower-key Betsey Johnson, as well as Woodland Waders, an island-made line of sturdy woolen outerwear—everyday clothes for both sexes that are neither staid nor trendy.

GIFTS/HOME DECOR   ✪ Bramhall & Dunn, 61 Main St. (in the center of town), Vineyard Haven (☎ 508/693-6437), also has a branch at The Red Barn, Old County Road, W. Tisbury (☎ 508/693-5221). Owners Emily Bramhall and Tharon Dunn have a great eye for the kind of chunky, eclectic extras that lend character to country homes. Expect to find the requisite rag rugs, rustic pottery, a smattering of rugged antiques, sensuous linens, and even some "person furnishings" to match, from lacy lingerie to bulky knits.

Third World Trading Co., 14 Circuit Ave., Oak Bluffs (☎ 508/693-5550), offers well-priced clothing, accessories, and home accents gathered from the four corners of the globe.

WHERE TO STAY
VERY EXPENSIVE

✪ **Charlotte Inn.** 27 S. Summer St. (in the center of town), Edgartown, MA 02539. ☎ 508/ 627-4751. Fax 508/627-4652. 22 rms, 3 suites. A/C TV TEL. Summer (including continental breakfast and afternoon tea) $260–$450 double, $495–$650 suite. AE, MC, V.

Ask anyone to recommend the best inn on the island, and this is the name you're most likely to hear—not just because it's the most expensive, but because it's easily the most refined. Owners Gery and Paul Conover have been tirelessly fine-tuning this cluster of 18th- and 19th-century houses (five altogether, counting the Carriage House, a Gery-built replica) since 1971. Linked by formal gardens, each house has a distinctive look and feel, though the predominant mode is English country house, complete with hunting prints and quirky decorative accents. In the elegant 1860 Main House, the common rooms double as the Edgartown Art Gallery. Though the Carriage House was built much later, it blends right in and contains some of the more desirable quarters.

Dining/Entertainment: However sterling the accommodations at the Charlotte Inn, the restaurant may actually gather more laurels: l'étoile is one of Edgartown's finest. See "Where to Dine," below.

✪ **Harbor View Hotel.** 131 N. Water St. (about ¹/₂ mile NW of Main St.), Edgartown, MA 02539. ☎ **800/255-6005** or 508/627-7000. Fax 508/627-7566. 124 units. A/C TV TEL. Summer $225–$385 double, $400–$565 suite, $565 cottage. AE, DC, MC, V.

Grander even than a grand hotel, this shingle-style complex started out as two Gilded Age hotels, ultimately joined by a 300-foot veranda. Treated to a massive centennial makeover in 1991, it now boasts every modern amenity, while retaining its retro charm—and a lobby that looks lifted from an Adirondack lodge. Front rooms overlook little Lighthouse Beach; in back, there's a large pool surrounded by newer annexes. The hotel is located just far enough from "downtown" to avoid the traffic hassles, but close enough for a pleasant walk past impressive captains' houses.

Services: A concierge is on hand to lend advice and assistance; room service, overnight laundry, and baby-sitting are available, and guests enjoy privileges at the Farm Neck Golf Club.

Dining/Entertainment: The casual Breezes restaurant, headquartered in a vintage bar, is open continuously through the day, from 6:30am on; you can ask to be served on the veranda or by the pool, if you like. Starbuck's (see "Where to Dine," below) serves more formal meals in an elegant setting.

✪ **The Inn at Blueberry Hill.** North Rd. (about 4 miles NE of Menemsha), Chilmark, MA 02535. ☎ **800/336-3322** or 508/645-3799. Fax 508/645-3799. 25 rms. TV TEL on request. Summer (including continental breakfast) $150–$230 double, $225–$550 suite/cottage. AE, MC, V. Closed Jan–Mar.

Energetic young owners Bob and Carolyn Burgess bought this one-time white elephant while on their honeymoon, which may partly explain its runaway romanticism, wedded to high ideals. Their goal was to create a spa-like retreat of the utmost luxury without in any way compromising the lovely natural setting—56 acres of former farmland, surrounded by vast tracts of conservation forest. They've succeeded splendidly. The 1792 farmhouse has been spruced up to suit a more modern aesthetic—still simple, in the neo-Shaker mode, but suffused with light. The same is true of the scattered cottages (some tucked under towering spruces), where the decor has been kept intentionally minimal, so as to play up the natural beauty all around. Tasteful, hand-crafted furnishings and such gentle touches as fluffy comforters bespeak the general dedication to peace and well-being.

Facilities: The renovated barn contains a full-scale Cybex fitness center, overlooking a solar-heated outdoor lap pool and hot tub. Equipment is provided for croquet, horseshoes, and volleyball. Beyond the tennis court, miles of walking paths branch out through the woods. Carolyn Burgess, a personal trainer, can fashion a custom fitness program on request and oversee workouts, or arrange for massages and facials. Inn guests may avail themselves of complimentary passes and shuttles to Lucy Vincent and Squibnocket beaches, and local provender is showcased at Theo's (see "Where to Dine," below).

Kelley House. 23 Kelley St. (in the center of town), Edgartown, MA 02539. ☎ **800/225-6005** or 508/627-4394. Fax 508/627-4394. 51 rms, 8 suites. A/C TV TEL. Summer (including continental breakfast and afternoon tea) $215 double, $215–$525 suite. AE, CB, DC, MC, V. Closed Nov–Apr.

The setting couldn't be more central—plunk in the middle of prime shopping/strolling territory—and the rooms, many with harbor views, are large and airy, with handsome pine furnishings and low-key country accents. There's scarcely any vestige of the inn's origins as a 1742 tavern, except in its reconstituted cellar pub. If fresh decor and luxurious amenities (for example, a heated outdoor pool) are important to you, this place might win out over a more intimate B&B—and they do provide some nice personal touches, such as milk and cookies at bedtime.

Facilities: There's a small outdoor pool on the property, and guests are welcome to use the tennis courts at the Harbor View Hotel, under the same management. Overnight laundry and baby-sitting can be arranged.

✪ **Tuscany Inn.** 22 N. Water St. (in the center of town), Edgartown, MA 02539. ☎ **508/627-5999.** Fax 508/627-6605. 8 rms. A/C. Summer rates (including full breakfast): $185–$295. AE, DC, MC, V. Closed Feb.

Innkeepers Rusty Scheuer and Laura Sbrana-Scheuer have transformed a derelict captain's house into as winning a little inn as you'll find. Inside you'll find a decor that's straight from sunny Italy, with warm colors and an abundance of fine old paintings—anything but the usual Yankee austerity. Past a little library lined with leather-backed books is Laura's open kitchen, where she gives cooking classes off-season (she's from Florence and a formidable chef); lavish breakfasts (blueberry buttermilk pancakes, frittata with foccacia) are served here when the weather precludes a feast on the patio. Each of the eight rooms is a gem, with hand-painted antique armoires and fanciful beds—and, in some cases, skylights, marble whirlpools, and harbor views.

EXPENSIVE

Ashley Inn. 129 Main St. (at the eastern edge of town, ¹/₂ mile west of the harbor), Edgartown, MA 02539. ☎ **800/477-9655** or 508/627-9655. 8 rms, 2 suites. A/C TV TEL. Summer (including continental breakfast) $115–$150 double, $250–$275 suite. MC, V.

This 1860s captain's manse offers eight rooms and two suites, each one awash in grandmotherly comforts. The prices rise according to the height—third-floor rooms are especially spacious—but all have been cheerfully accoutred in a fresh country look, complete with quilts and dashes of brass and wicker. Some of the quarters boast a whirlpool bath and/or working fireplace, and the garden, where roses bloom behind a Chinese Chippendale fence, is especially restful—the hammock strung up in the spacious yard looks like an invitation to read a nice fat novel in one sitting.

Breakfast at Tiasquam. Off Middle Rd. (about 2 miles SW of W. Tisbury), Chilmark, MA 02535. ☎ **508/645-3685.** 8 rms (6 with shared bath). Summer (including full breakfast) $110–$195 double. No credit cards.

Unusual among B&Bs because it was actually built to be one (in 1987), this modern Cape stands amid parklike grounds. Owner Ron Crowe fell in love with the island while on a cycling vacation and decided to relocate in style. The eight-bedroom house, designed by Doug Richmond of Brunswick, Me., incorporates a two-story greenhouse atrium (one bedroom overlooks it), no fewer than 20 skylights, and a generous allotment of decks to make the most of the pastoral setting. The two heated outdoor showers are a treat after a trip to pretty and private Lucy Vincent Beach, to which Crowe provides passes. The interior is a veritable catalog of fine crafts, with burnished cherry woodwork, ceramic sinks created by local potter Robert Parrott, and minimalist Shaker-inspired furniture, some by Thomas Moser. For the morning meal, Crowe happily strives to satisfy virtually any craving; his specialties include corn-blueberry pancakes and freshly caught fish.

The Captain R. Flanders House. North Rd. (about 1 mile NE of Menemsha), Chilmark, MA 02535. ☎ **508/645-3123.** 5 rms, 2 cottages. Summer (including full breakfast) $130 double, $170 cottage. AE, MC, V. Closed mid-Nov to Apr.

Set amid 60 acres of rolling meadows crisscrossed by stone walls, this late 18th-century farmhouse, built by a whaling captain, has remained much the same over two centuries. The living room, with its broad plank floors, is full of astonishing antiques that look right at home—there's none of that "for show" feel prevalent in more self-conscious B&Bs. This is a working farm, so there's no time for posing (even if it *was* featured in Martha Stewart's *Wedding Book*). After fortifying themselves with home-made muffins, honey, and jam at breakfast, guests are free to fritter the day away however they like. Passes are provided to nearby Lucy Vincent Beach, or you might just take a long country walk. Whatever your choice, you're apt to find yourself echoing the sentiments of one regular visitor: "I hope this place never changes."

Colonial Inn. 38 N. Water St., Edgartown, MA 02539. ☎ **800/627-4701** or 508/627-4711. Fax 508/627-5904. 39 rms, 2 suites, 1 efficiency. A/C TV TEL. Summer (including continental breakfast) $140–$195 double, $225 suite or efficiency. AE, MC, V. Closed Jan–Mar.

Somewhat big and impersonal, this 1911 inn has been transformed into a fine modern hotel. It's been the unofficial center of town since its doors opened, and its lobby also serves as a conduit to the Nevins Square shops beyond. The lobby has a somewhat transient feel, hardly enhanced by a self-service breakfast cart—but the lack of ceremony is a plus if, like most tourists, you're bursting to get out and about. The 42 rooms, decorated in soothing, contemporary tones (with pine furniture, pastel fabrics, and brass beds), offer all one could want in the way of conveniences. Wherever you're billeted, be sure to visit the roof deck, ideally around sunset or, if you're up for it, sunrise over the water.

Daggett House. 59 N. Water St., Edgartown, MA 02539. ☎ **508/627-4600.** Fax 508/627-4611. 23 rms, 2 suites. TEL. Summer $145–$185 double, $230–$395 suite. AE, DC, MC, V.

Daggett House is a well-established property in the center of one of the Vineyard's most upscale towns. Exercise caution when reserving a room; some are large and luxurious, like the Widow's Walk suite, with its own deck and hot tub; others are penuriously small, and far from a bargain. Some units have terraces, fireplaces, or whirlpool baths. Beside the tavern's old beehive fireplace in the dining room is a revolving bookcase, which hides a secret stairway! It leads to a bedroom with a harbor view. Another plus is the secluded lawn, which stretches down to a private swimming dock.

Island Inn. Beach Rd. (about 1 mile S of town center), Oak Bluffs, MA 02557. ☎ **800/462-0269** or 508/693-2002. Fax 508/693-7911. 51 units. A/C TV TEL. Summer $125–$235. AE, DC, MC, V.

Sharing a verdant triangle of land between Nantucket Sound and Sengekontacket Pond with the popular Farm Neck Golf Club (see "Outdoor Pursuits," above), this modern complex is nicely situated amid seven acres shaded by tall trees. It's the kind of place where you'll feel comfortable letting children of a certain age wander about on their own (they'll head straight for the heated pool), while you hone your swing or serve. (The three Har-Tru tennis courts come with a resident pro.) All the units, from studios to a two-bedroom, two-fireplace cottage that sleeps six, contain all you could require for an extended stay, including a fully equipped kitchen.

Lambert's Cove Country Inn. Lambert's Cove Rd. (off State Rd., about 3 miles W of Vineyard Haven), W. Tisbury, MA 02568. ☎ **508/693-2298.** Fax 508/693-7890. 15 rms. A/C. Summer (including continental breakfast) $135–$175 double. AE, MC, V.

A dedicated horticulturalist created this haven in the 1920s, expanding on a 1790 farmstead. You can see the old adzed beams in some of the upstairs bedrooms. Among his more prized additions is the Greenhouse Room, a bedroom with its own conservatory. You'll find an all-weather tennis court on the grounds, and the namesake beach nearby. Brunch on the patio is a beloved island tradition, as are the skilled New

American dinners (see "Where to Dine," below). Set far off the main road and surrounded by apple trees and lilacs, this secluded estate suggests an age where time was measured in generations rather than nanoseconds: There's no better place to relax.

✪ The Oak House. Seaview Ave. (on the Sound), Oak Bluffs, MA 02557. ☎ **508/693-4187.** Fax 508/696-7385. 8 rms, 2 suites. A/C TV TEL. Summer (including continental breakfast and afternoon tea) $140–$180 double, $250 suite. AE, DISC, MC, V. Closed mid-Oct to mid-May.

An 1872 Queen Anne bayfront beauty, this one-time home of former Massachusetts governor William Claflin has preserved all the luxury and leisure of the Victorian age. Innkeeper Betsi Convery-Luce trained at Johnson & Wales; her pastries (served at breakfast and tea) are sublime. The rooms toward the back are quieter; then again, the front ones have Nantucket Sound views. The common rooms, like the 10 bedrooms (two are suites), are furnished in an opulent Victorian mode. Anyone intent on de-stressing is sure to benefit from this immersion course in the era that invented the leisure class.

Outermost Inn. Lighthouse Rd. (about ¼ mile NE of the lighthouse), Gay Head, MA 02535. ☎ **508/645-3511.** Fax 508/645-3514. 6 rms, 1 suite. TV on request. Summer (including full breakfast) $250–$285 double or suite. AE, DC, MC, V. Closed Nov to mid-Apr.

Location, location—you'd have to camp out at Gay Head lighthouse to enjoy a comparable panorama. Commanding a grassy bluff overlooking the Vineyard Sound, with the Elizabeth Islands off in the distance, this comfortable, shingled house was built by Jean and Hugh Taylor (James's sibling) in 1971 and embodies the artisanal ethos prevalent at the time. Each bedroom features floors of a distinctive wood, from cherry to ash, and all the furnishings—wool rugs, down comforters—are low-key and upscale-natural. The sitting room contains all sorts of musical instruments, ready for an impromptu improv ("We encourage guests to play if they know how—and not to, if they don't," says Jean with a laugh). Specializing in straightforward seafood, the dining room (see "Where to Dine," below) enjoys a splendid ocean view.

✪ Point Way Inn. 104 Main St. (at Pease's Point Way, in the center of town), Edgartown, MA 02539. ☎ **800/942-9569** or 508/627-8633. Fax 508/627-8579. 15 rms. A/C. Summer (including continental breakfast and afternoon tea) $110–$260 double. AE, MC, V.

Run by avid sailors and croquet players—the inn's little green serves as headquarters for the Edgartown Mallet Club—this homey inn really gives you a sense of what island life is all about. Ben and Linda Smith, who alighted here in 1979 after sailing about the Caribbean for 2½ years with their children (nautical charts and other happy mementos of their journeys adorn the walls), are real hands-on hosts. Ben likes to take guests clamming in his special spot, or give them croquet pointers (he's a championship-level player, and the well-tended course, shielded by arbor vitae hedges, stands at the ready)—visitors will feel like house guests who happen to be paying. You can even arrange to reserve the inn's loaner car to explore the environs. Days begin with the scent of Linda's delectable breakfast breads wafting from the cozy farmhouse-style kitchen and get a boost with afternoon lemonade and cookies served in the gazebo. The living room, featuring but one of the rambling inn's 11 fireplaces, is especially welcoming in the pre- and postdinner hours, when all but the most reclusive of guests tend to gravitate to the honor bar or perhaps the table occupied by a 500-piece custom-cut wooden puzzle. Rooms are not too fancy, but just fine—effortlessly, unshowily romantic.

MODERATE

Admiral Benbow Inn. 520 New York Ave. (about ½ mile NW of town center), Oak Bluffs, MA 02557. ☎ **508/693-6825.** 7 rms. Summer (including full breakfast and afternoon tea) $100–$150 double. AE, MC, V. Closed Jan.

Built for a minister at the turn of the century, this seven-bedroom house, topped by a cupola and encircled by a shady porch, has the dark, ornate woodwork typical of that time. Yet the B&B has a young, energetic feel to it, and it's owned by the Black Dog Tavern Co., which means for breakfast you can polish off piles of those pastries you've been eyeing in the display cases. There's no ocean view, and it's on a busy road somewhat removed from Oak Bluffs; by bike, however, it's a quick glide into town or to the Sound beaches.

✪ **The Arbor.** 222 Upper Main St. (on the western edge of town, about ³/₄ mile from the harbor), Edgartown, MA 02539. ☎ **508/627-8137.** 10 rms (2 with shared bath). A/C. Summer (including continental breakfast) $95–$145 double. MC, V. Closed Nov–Apr.

This unassuming-looking house hugging the bike path at the edge of town packs surprising style: Innkeeper/*antiquaire* Peggy Hall tacked a lovely cathedral-ceilinged living room onto her 1880 farmhouse to add light and liveliness. That you'll find, as you compare notes with other travelers or peruse a fine collection of coffee-table books from the comfort of an overstuffed chintz couch. The rooms range from tiny to spacious, but all are nicely appointed, largely with antiques, and the rates are singularly gentle, especially considering the fresh-baked breakfast served on fine china.

Edgartown Inn. 56 N. Water St., Edgartown, MA 02539. ☎ **508/627-4794.** 20 rms (5 with shared bath). A/C TV. Summer $80–$175 double. No credit cards. Closed Nov–Mar.

Nathaniel Hawthorne holed up here for nearly a year—secretly courting a Wampanoag maiden, it is rumored, who inspired *The Scarlet Letter.* It's also where a young and feckless Ted Kennedy sweated out that shameful night post-Chappaquiddick. Questionable karma aside, it's a lovely 1798 Federal manse, a showplace even here on captain's row, and the rooms are traditional but not overdone. Modernists might prefer the two cathedral-ceilinged quarters in the annex out back, which offer lovely light and a sense of seclusion.

The Lothrop Merry House. Owen Park (off Main St.), Vineyard Haven, MA 02568. ☎ **508/693-1646.** 7 rms (3 with shared bath). Summer (including full breakfast) $120–$195 double. MC, V.

You'll get more than the superficial Vineyard experience by opting to stay at this nicely weathered 1790 B&B overlooking the harbor, with its own little stretch of beach and a canoe and Sunfish to take out on the water. Innkeepers Mary and John Clarke also charter cruises aboard their ketch, the *Laissez Faire* (see "Organized Tours," above). A few of the simply furnished rooms have fireplaces (the island is especially lovely, and exceedingly private, in winter), and the two without waterviews compensate with air-conditioning.

⑤ **Menemsha Inn and Cottages.** Off North Rd. (about ¹/₂ mile NE of harbor), Menemsha, MA 02552. ☎ **508/645-2521.** 9 rms, 6 suites, 12 cottages. TV. Summer (including continental breakfast) $115–$170 double, $170 suite. $1,075–$1,475 cottage a week. No credit cards. Closed Dec–Apr.

There's an almost Quakerlike plainness to this weathered waterside compound, though many of the rooms are quite inviting. Mostly it's a place to revel in the outdoors (11 seaside acres), without needless distractions. The late *Life* photographer Alfred Eisenstaedt summered here for four decades, and the interior aesthetics would please any artist. There's no restaurant—just a restful breakfast room with a piano. The most luxurious suites are located in the Carriage House, which has a spacious common room with a fieldstone fireplace and inviting rattan-and-chintz couches. These rooms have private decks: If you just want to sit and gaze out to sea, you're all set.

The Oak Bluffs Inn. 167 Circuit Ave. (in the center of town), Oak Bluffs, MA 02557. ☎ **800/ 955-6235** or 508/693-7171. 9 rms. A/C. Summer rates (including continental breakfast): $115–$185 double. AE, DC, DISC, MC, V. Closed Nov–Mar.

Winsomely painted in a patchwork of mission rose, blue, green, and fuchsia, this cupola-topped Victorian contains all sorts of cozy spaces: eight rooms and a suite, all with bath, and some boasting handsome Mission furniture and private balconies. All guests are encouraged to enjoy the octagonal "viewing tower," up some steep nautical stairs, where the view takes in all of Oak Bluffs. Equally pleasant is the chance to while away the hours on one of the wicker rockers that grace the wraparound porch.

Wesley Hotel. 1 Lake Ave. (on the harbor), Oak Bluffs, MA 02557. ☎ **800/638-9027** or 508/ 693-6611. Fax 508/693-5389. 82 rms (20 with shared bath). A/C TV. Summer $90–$165 double. AE, CB, DC, DISC, MC, V. Closed mid-Oct to mid-May.

Recently treated to a rehab, this 1879 grand hotel, right on the harbor, hardly shows its age—unless you count the rockers (constantly in use) that line the spacious wraparound porch. Rooms are also nicely proportioned and come furnished with reproduction Victorian antiques. *Note:* The early bird—reservations-wise—gets the harbor view, sans surcharge.

INEXPENSIVE

🟊 **Attleboro House.** 11 Lake Ave. (on the harbor), Oak Bluffs, MA 02557. ☎ **508/ 693-4346.** 11 rms (all with shared bath). Summer (including continental breakfast) $60–$85 double. MC, V. Closed Oct–May.

As old-fashioned as the afghans that proprietor Estelle Reagan crochets for every bed, this harborside guest house—serving Camp Meeting visitors since 1874—epitomizes the simple, timeless joys of summer. None of the 11 rooms is graced with a private bath, but the rates are so retro, you may not mind. What was good enough for 19th-century tourists more than suffices today.

WHERE TO DINE

Note: Outside Oak Bluffs and Edgartown, all of Martha's Vineyard is "dry," so bring your own bottle; some restaurants charge a fee for uncorking.

EDGARTOWN

Very Expensive

✪ **l'étoile.** Charlotte Inn, 27 S. Summer St. (off Main St.), Edgartown. ☎ **508/627-5187.** Reservations required; jacket recommended. Prix fixe $62 and up. AE, MC, V. May to early Sept daily 6:30–9:45pm; call for off-season hours. Closed late Dec to Apr. FRENCH.

Every signal (starting, perhaps, with the price) tells you that this is going to be one very special meal. Having passed through a pair of ormolu-laden sitting rooms (which double as the Edgartown Art Gallery), one comes upon a conservatory sparkling to the light of antique brass sconces and fresh with the scent of potted citrus trees. Everything is perfection incarnate, from the table settings (gold-rimmed Villeroy & Boch) to a nouvelle cuisine menu that varies seasonally but is always exquisite. Chef Michael Brisson, who came up through the kitchen of Boston's famed L'Espalier, is determined to dazzle, and he does, with an ever-evolving menu of delicacies flown in from the four corners of the earth. Sevruga usually makes an appearance—perhaps as a garnish for chilled leek soup. A steamed lobster with champagne sauce might come with flying fish roe ravioli, or warm Mission figs might offset seared pheasant breast in an Armagnac-sage sauce accompanied by sautéed summer greens and quinoa. When dinner with a decent wine runs to $100 or so a head, you expect revelation, and you are very likely to find it at l'étoile.

Expensive

✪ **Savoir Fare.** 14 Church St. (Old Post Office Square, off Main St. in the center of town), Edgartown. ☎ **508/627-9864.** Reservations recommended. Main courses $18–$28. AE, MC, V. Late May to mid-Oct Mon–Sat 11:30am–2:30pm, daily 6–10pm; call for off-season hours. Closed Nov to mid-Apr. NEW AMERICAN.

Scott Caskey initially opened this stylish cathedral-ceilinged space as a gourmet deli/catering concern. Spurred by a rumor of impending competition (which never did materialize), he switched over to haute restaurateuring and has no regrets. He still gets to tend the garde-manger (salad and dessert station) in an open kitchen that enjoys the conviviality of a clubhouse. Some of the prettiest seating is outside, under the graceful pergola (you'd never guess you were surrounded by parking lot), where champagne and shellfish are always on ice. The mostly Mediterranean fare is both substantial and lyrical (for example, marrow-crusted T-bone with white-bean mashed potatoes), and Scott has a winning way with unusual desserts.

Starbuck's. At the Harbor View Hotel (see "Where to Stay," above), 131 N. Water St., Edgartown. ☎ **508/627-7000.** Reservations recommended. Main courses $18–$29. AE, MC, V. Mon–Sat 7–11am, noon–2pm and 6–9pm; Sun 8am–2pm and 6–9pm. NEW AMERICAN.

As befits its setting, Starbuck's is resolutely grand, lushly draped and formally accoutred with luteback chairs and tasseled curtains. The menu is far less stuffy, allowing sufficient latitude for, say, mussel soup Provençal, or a risotto binding wild mushrooms and artichokes. Most diners in this demographic group favor substantial slabs of fish and beef, and that's what they'll get, however they like it. The elaborate breakfast menu is also a highlight, featuring Yankee red flannel hash and choose-your-own-combo griddle cakes.

Moderate

The Newes from America. The Kelley House, 23 Kelley St., Edgartown. ☎ **800/225-6005** or 508/627-7900. Fax 508/627-8142. Main courses $7–$22. AE, DC, MC, V. Daily 11am–11pm. ECLECTIC.

The pub grub is better than average at this subterranean tavern, built in 1742 and only recently resurrected. The decor may be more Edwardian than colonial, but those who come to quaff don't seem to care. Try a "rack" of five esoteric brews, or let your choice of comestibles—from a wood-smoked oyster "Island Poor Boy" sandwich with linguica relish to an 18-ounce porterhouse steak—dictate your draft; the menu comes handily annotated. Other sandwich choices include Brazilian chicken salad and grilled eggplant—reliable and filling, if not especially distinguished.

Inexpensive

Among the Flowers. Mayhew Lane, Edgartown. ☎ **508/627-3233.** Main courses $9–$11. DC, MC, V. July–Aug 8am–11pm; call for off-season hours. Closed mid-Oct through April. INTERNATIONAL.

Everything's fresh and appealing at this outdoor cafe near the dock. Sit under the awning and you'll just catch a glimpse of the harbor. The breakfasts are the best around, and all the crêpes, waffles, and eggs are also available at lunch. The comfort-food dinners (lemon chicken, lobster Newburg crêpes and others) are among the most affordable options in this pricey town. There's almost always a wait, not just because it's so picturesque and appealing, but because the food is homey, hearty, and kind on the wallet.

Main Street Diner. Old Post Office Sq. (off Main St. in the center of town), Edgartown. ☎ **508/627-9337.** Most items under $6. MC, V. Daily 7am–9pm year-round. AMERICAN.

It's a little kitschy-cute, what with cartoon wallpaper decorated with vintage doodads, but tony Edgartown could use a place geared to small spenders. Kids and adults alike will enjoy this ersatz diner, where the food as well as the trimmings hearken back to the fifties. A one-egg breakfast with home fries and a buttermilk biscuit will set you back only two bucks; the burgers and sandwiches (including a classic open-face hot turkey with gravy, potatoes, and cranberry sauce) less than six. Grab a grilled cheese or BLT, wash it down with a cherry Coke, and head back out into the cool, cold world of the nineties.

⊗ **Truly Scrumptious Cafe.** 11 S. Summer St. (in the center of town), Edgartown. ☎ **508/627-3990.** Most items under $7. DISC, MC, V. Late May to early Sept daily 11am–8pm; call for off-season schedule. Closed Columbus Day–Memorial Day. ITALIAN/ECLECTIC.

With only five tiny tables, this storefront trattoria does more business as a takeout and catering concern. Once you've wandered in, though, you'll want to pull up a chair and plunder the deli cases for the likes of *panzanella* (the classic "bread salad" tossed with tomatoes and fresh mozzarella) plus handmade pastas and gourmet pizzas. Or plunge straight into dessert: a fresh pineapple torte, perhaps, or white chocolate biscotti to dip in espresso. The art you see—Chilmark sculptor Steve Loman shows his witty wire compositions here—is for sale.

OAK BLUFFS
Very Expensive

❂ **The Oyster Bar.** 162 Circuit Ave. (in the center of town), Oak Bluffs. ☎ **508/693-3300.** Fax 508/693-6439. Reservations recommended. Main courses $28–$44. MC, V. July–Aug daily 6pm–12:30am; call for off-season schedule. Closed Oct–Apr. NEW AMERICAN.

You'd never guess that this flashy venue—the Vineyard's most visible link to New York style—started out as a 19th-century grocery store. Squiggles of hot-pink neon are visible through a veritable forest of tropical plants, which turn the popular pastime of celebrity spotting into a spirited game of peekaboo (this is where summering big shots like Kevin Costner and Barbra Streisand invariably dine). Chef/owner Raymond Schilcher's creativity is considerable, yet the subliminal message is that the "O-Bar" output is meant not so much to be studied as savored. He'll whip up some white truffle polenta, or concoct a seafood couscous featuring wood-roasted monkfish and homemade lobster sausage. Desserts range from the trendy (tiramisu) to the feel-good (hot chocolate mousse).

Expensive

Jimmy Seas Pan Pasta Restaurant. 32 Kennebec Ave., Oak Bluffs. ☎ **508/696-8550.** No reservations. Main courses $13–$23. No credit cards. May to mid-Oct daily 5:30–10pm; call for off-season hours. Closed Jan–Mar. MEDITERRANEAN.

If you're wondering why the luncheonette-level decor at this restaurant where Frank Sinatra's crooning resounds at all times doesn't quite match up with menu prices, it's because chef Jimmy Cipolla gives his all to his one-pot pasta dishes, served right in the pan. Pasta comes in such intriguing guises as pumpkin tortellini in a cream sauce savory with sage, and everything's fair game for toppings, from chicken and shrimp with fresh pesto to swordfish in a balsamic vinaigrette. President Clinton ate it up, and you'll probably love it too.

Moderate

Isla/Cafe Luna. Circuit Ave. Extension (on the harbor), Oak Bluffs. ☎ **508/693-8078.** Main courses $5–$19. MC, V. Late May to mid-Oct daily noon–10pm. Closed mid-Oct to late May. LIGHT FARE.

Check out this gingerbread house for some primo snacking. The pizzas are made with the finest ingredients (some offered for sale), and a foccacia slathered with roasted vegetables and aged provolone makes an optimal lunch or light dinner. Those still peckish can head upstairs for tapas or desserts at the wine and coffee bar, which also occasionally features late-night jazz.

Zapotec. 10 Kennebec Ave. (in the center of town), Oak Bluffs. ☎ **508/693-6800.** No reservations. Main courses $10–$17. AE, MC, V. Mid-May to mid-Oct daily 11:30am–2pm and 5–10pm. Closed mid-Oct to mid-May. MEXICAN.

Look for the chili pepper lights entwining the porch of this clapboard cottage: They're a beacon leading to tasty regional Mexican cuisine, from Mussels Oaxaca (with chipotle peppers, cilantro, lime, and cream) to Crabcakes Tulum (mixed with codfish and grilled peppers, and served with dual salsas), plus the standard chicken and beef burritos. A good *mole* is hard to find; here you can accompany it with Mexico's unbeatable beers (including several rarely spotted north of the border), or perhaps a hand-picked, well-priced wine.

Inexpensive

Dee's Harbor Cafe. 1 Lake Ave. (on the harbor), Oak Bluffs. ☎ **508/693-6506.** Most items under $6. MC, V. May to mid-Oct daily 6:30am–3pm. Closed mid-October to Apr. ECLECTIC.

A tiny, cute, and bustling restaurant, Dee's gives you gourmet breakfasts on the cheap—how does Eggs Florentine for under $5 sound? The sandwiches, quesadillas, and salads are appealing, too, as are refreshing drinks such as the "southern fruit tea" (iced tea splashed with pineapple juice).

Papa's Pizza. 158 Circuit Ave., Oak Bluffs. ☎ **508/693-1400.** Most items under $8. MC, V. Jun–Aug 11am–11pm; call for off-season hours. PIZZA.

The pizza at this vintage-look parlor tend to be on the tame side (you won't have to pick off the arugula). For families with kids, it's ideal. Stop in if only to see the vintage photographs of erstwhile "campers."

Mad Martha's. 117 Circuit Ave (in the center of town), Oak Bluffs. ☎ **508/693-9151.** Fax 508/693-6335. Branches at 8 Union St., Vineyard Haven (☎ 508/863-9674) and 4 Main St., Edgartown (☎ 508/627-9768). Closed mid-Oct through Apr.

Vineyarders are mad for this locally made ice cream, which comes in two dozen enticing flavors. Clinton opted for a relatively restrained mango sorbet, which isn't to say you shouldn't go for a hot fudge sundae.

VINEYARD HAVEN
Very Expensive

Black Dog Tavern. Beach St. Extension (on the harbor), Vineyard Haven. ☎ **508/693-9223.** No reservations. Main courses $10–$25. AE, MC, V. June to early Sept Mon–Sat 7–11am, 11:30am–2:30pm and 5–10pm; Sun 7am–1pm and 5–10pm. Call for off-season hours. NEW AMERICAN.

How does a humble harbor shack come to be a national icon? Location helps. Soon after *Shenandoah* captain Robert Douglas decided, in 1971, that this hard-working port could use a good restaurant, influential vacationers, stuck waiting for the ferry, would wander in to tide themselves over with a bit of "blackout cake" or peanut butter pie. The rest is history, as smart marketing moves extrapolated on word of mouth. The smartest of these was the invention of the signature "Martha's Vineyard whitefoot," a black Lab whose stalwart profile now adorns everything from baby's overalls to doggy bandanas, golfballs, and needlepoint kits. Originally the symbol signaled Vineyard ties to fellow cognoscenti; now it merely bespeaks an acquaintance with mail-order catalogs. Still, tourists love this rough-hewn tavern, and it's not just hype that keeps them happy. The food is still home-cooking good—heavy on the seafood, of course (including grilled swordfish with banana, basil, and lime, and blue-fish with mustard soufflé sauce)—and the blackout cake has lost none of its impact. Though the lines grow ever longer (there can be a wait to get on the waitlist!), nothing much has changed at this beloved spot. Eggs Galveston for breakfast at the Black Dog Tavern is still one of the ultimate Vineyard experiences—go early, when it first opens, and sit on the porch, where the views are perfect.

✪ **Dry Town Cafe.** 70 Main St. (at the center of town), Vineyard Haven. ☎ **508/693-0033.** Reservations recommended. Main courses $24–$36. AE, MC, VC. June–Oct daily juice bar 10:30am–2:30pm, dinner 6–10pm; call for off-season schedule. Closed late Feb to late Mar. NEW AMERICAN.

This black-and-white bistro, transformed from a barber shop, has an uptown snap to it (boasting sleek woodwork under an elegant arched ceiling), matched by jazzy cuisine with a world-beat bent. Home-style cod cakes, for instance, get a kick with burnt-melon relish; grilled calamari might come with a fried corn tortilla and soy vinaigrette (that's at least four countries accounted for). Lunches feature such special-ties as native cod cakes with burnt melon relish, and the "dilla del dia" (quesadilla of the day). It's the kind of place where the distinguished regulars tend to know one another, but newcomers won't be made to feel like rubes. Do tuck a bottle of good wine under your arm when coming here.

Le Grenier. 96 Main St. (in the center of town), Vineyard Haven. ☎ **508/693-4906.** Reservations recommended. Main courses $18–$30. AE, DC, MC, V. July–Aug 11:30am–2pm and 6–10pm; call for off-season schedule. Closed mid-Oct to mid-Mar. FRENCH.

If Paris is the heart of France, Lyons is the belly, and that's where chef-owner Jean Dupon grew up on his maman's hearty cuisine (she now helps out here, cooking lunch). Dupon has the moves down, as evidenced in such classics as steak au poivre, calf's brains Grenobloise with beurre noir, and capers or lobster Normande flambéed with Calvados, apples, and cream. For an "attic" (the literal translation, and the ac-tual location), Le Grenier is rather romantic, especially when aglow with hurricane lamps.

Picnic Supplies & Take-Out

Black Dog Bakery. Water St. (near the harbor), Vineyard Haven. ☎ **508/693-4786.**

In need of a snack at 5:30am? That's when the doors to this fabled bakery open, and from mid-morning on, it's elbow room only.

TISBURY

Very Expensive

Lambert's Cove Country Inn. Lambert's Cove Rd. (off State Rd., about 3 miles W of Vine-yard Haven), W. Tisbury. ☎ **508/693-2298.** Fax 508/693-7890. Reservations recommended. Main courses $18–$23. AE, MC, V. Jun–Sept daily 6–8pm, Sun 11am–1pm; call for off-season hours. NEW AMERICAN.

Whether you choose to dine outdoors, canopied by wysteria, or indoors over candlelit lace tablecloths, the setting is sheer romance (see "Where to Stay," above), and the country house cuisine shows just enough quirks to tickle the tired palate. The do-mestic rack of lamb, for instance, is dressed with raspberry-blackberry mint vinegar, and the cheese and walnut ravioli in gorgonzola cream are bejeweled with asparagus and roasted red peppers. Sunday brunch is a beloved feast, with popular standards (eggs Benedict, Belgian waffles, French toast, and more) supplemented by a buffet of fresh-baked pastries.

✪ **Red Cat Restaurant.** 688 State Rd. (in the village center), N. Tisbury. ☎ **508/693-9599.** Reservations recommended. Main courses $17–$29. DISC, MC, V. Open through late Nov Tues–Sun 5:30–9:30pm. NEW AMERICAN.

Native son and chef Benjamin DeForest may have honed his chops at Boston's formidably sophisticated Four Seasons, but the laid-back island style comes naturally. At this few-frills roadside cafe, all the artistry is concentrated on the plate: in a tasty "fresca" of Thimble Farm tomatoes, corn, and basil, for instance, or a showy dish involving a hefty 14-ounce pork chop sauced with Calvados, pears, and blond raisins and topped with crispy sweet-potato curls. Among the more addictive desserts is a home-comfort chocolate bread pudding, and for a total treat, try the five-course tasting menu. The place is invariably mobbed: Come early, and midweek, if you can manage it.

Picnic Supplies & Take-Out

Alley's General Store. State Rd. (in the center of town), W. Tisbury. ☎ **508/693-0088.** Fax 508/693-3315.

That endangered rarity, a true New England general store, Alley's—in business since 1858—nearly foundered in the profit-mad eighties. Luckily the Martha's Vineyard Preservation Trust interceded to give it a new lease on life, along with a much-needed structural overhaul. The stock is still the same, though: Basically, everything you could possibly need, from scrub brushes to fresh-made salsa (sold, along with other appealing picnic fixings, from Back Alley's Bakery & Deli). Best of all, the no longer sagging front porch still supports a popular bank of benches, along with a blizzard of bulletin board notices. For a local's-eye view of noteworthy activities and events, this is the first place to check.

Farmer's Market. Old Agricultural Hall (in the center of town), W. Tisbury. ☎ **508/ 693-0100.** Wed 3–6pm, Sat 9am–noon.

This seasonal outdoor market is among the biggest and best in New England, and certainly the most rarefied, with local celebrities loading up on prize produce and snacking on pesto bread and other international goodies.

Thimble Farm. Stoney Hill Rd. (off State Rd. about 3 miles SW of town center), W. Tisbury. ☎ **508/693-6396.** Closed Mon and early Oct to mid-June.

It's a shame you have to be a near-adult (12 and up) to gather your own strawberries and raspberries at this working farm, but it wouldn't do to flout child labor laws—or to trample the goodies.

CHILMARK, MENEMSHA & GAY HEAD

Very Expensive

❂ **The Feast of Chilmark.** State Rd. (in the center of town), Chilmark. ☎ **508/645-3553.** Reservations recommended. Main courses $15–$29. AE, MC, V. Jul–Aug daily 6–10pm; call for off-season hours. Closed Nov–Apr. NEW AMERICAN.

Capturing the essence of "up-island,"this cored-out clapboard house conceals a sophisticated bi-level restaurant with lots of exposed wood and a menu to make jaded New Yorkers sit up and take notice. Chef Tony Saccocia's specialties include quahog chowder, lobster turnovers with shrimp and lemon cream, and rack of local lamb with a spinach-cognac glaze. On premises is the Peter Simon Photography Gallery, discussed under "Shopping," above.

Outermost Inn. Lighthouse Rd. (just east of the lighthouse), Gay Head. ☎ **508/645-3511.** Fax 508/645-3514. Reservations required. Prix fixe $38–$50. AE, DISC, MC, V. Late May through Oct daily seatings at 6 and 8pm. Closed Nov to late May. NEW AMERICAN.

Much as in this place's accommodations, simplicity is the order of the day in the seaview dining room. You'll find a straightforward prix-fixe menu, usually including dishes like a slab of grilled Menemsha swordfish or charbroiled sirloin filet, accompanied by homemade oatmeal rolls, a fresh garden salad, and steamed vegetables, followed by desserts like "brownies ecstasy" (with hazelnut ice cream), fruit shortcake, or white chocolate mousse. Every night the chef here provides proof that there's nothing tastier than "plain" food.

🟢 **Theo's.** At The Inn at Blueberry Hill, North Rd., Chilmark. ☎ **800/336-3322** or 508/645-3799. Fax 508/645-3799. Reservations required. Prix fixe $38–$50. AE, MC, V. Apr–Dec daily 7:30–9:30am, noon–1:30pm and 6–9pm. Closed Jan–Mar. NEW AMERICAN.

It's quite simply the perfect restaurant: sufficiently formal yet soothing and relaxed, satisfying to all the senses yet uninsistently health-conscious. Renowned local chef Robin Ledoux Forte plucks up each tender vegetable herself from the inn garden; her husband often hauls in the catch of the day. And while her preparations may be minimalist, all the better to bring out intrinsic flavors, she's awfully good at finding delicious combinations—surrounding noisettes of Menemsha swordfish, for instance, with sesame aïoli and a spicy Asian slaw. Chocolate, meet linguini: It's instant *amore*, with warm fudge sauce and cinammon-coffee ice cream. The lighting, cast by candles in blue goblets across rag-painted walls, creates an aura of unhurried comfort and a pervasive sense that all is as it should be, here in the unspoiled countryside.

Moderate

The Menemsha Bite. Basin Rd. (off North Rd., about ¼ mile NE of harbor), Menemsha. ☎ **508/645-9239.** Most items under $9. June to mid-Sept daily 11am–9pm. Closed mid-Sept to June. NEW ENGLAND.

It's usually places like "The Bite" that we crave when we think of New England: This is your quintessential "chowdah" and clam shack, flanked by picnic tables. Run by two sisters employing their grandmother's recipes, this place makes superlative chowder, potato salad, fried fish, and so forth. The food comes in graduated containers, with a jumbo portion of shrimp topping out at around $25.

Sweets

🟢 **Chilmark Chocolates.** State Rd. (in the town center), Chilmark. ☎ **508/645-3013.** Closed Mon–Tues and Jan–Mar.

Should you find a sample plumped on your B&B pillow (a delightful lagniappe), you'll want to hunt down the source. Friendly workers at this cottage industry—many of them coping with mental handicaps—will gladly demonstrate their edible artistry.

MARTHA'S VINEYARD AFTER DARK
Dance Clubs & Live Music

Atlantic Connection. 124 Circuit Ave. (in the center of town), Oak Bluffs. ☎ **508/693-7129.** Fax 508/696-8399. Cover varies; call for schedule.

Disco lives! As does—uh-oh—karaoke. Comedy, too, occasionally. Locals such as Spike Lee and Ted Danson seem to love the hodgepodge, and the unofficial house band, Entrain, has begun to attract a wide following with their reggae-laced rock.

🟢 **Hot Tin Roof.** Airport Rd. (at Katama Airport, 4 miles E of town center), Edgartown. (☎ **508/693-1137**). E-mail: mvhtr@aol.com. Web site: Http://mvhtr/homepage.htm. Cover varies; call for schedule. Closed mid-Sept through Apr.

Carly's back, and the joint is jumping. Simon first opened this nightclub-in-a-hangar in the early seventies and eventually lost interest (while it lost cachet). Now with multimillion-dollar backing from such high-rollers as hotelier Richard Friedman (who hosted the Clintons' first island visit), it's on a roll again. Notoriously stage-shy, she'll sometimes take the mike herself, but is mostly content to attract an eclectic roster including such notables as Jimmy Cliff, Peter Wolf, Hall & Oates, the

The Quintessential Lobster Dinner

When only a huge lobster and a sunset will do, visitors and locals alike head to **The Home Port** on North Rd. in Menemsha (☎ **508/645-2679;** fax 508/645-3119). At first glance, prices for the lobster dinners may seem a bit high, but they include an appetizer of your choice—go with the stuffed quahog—salad, amazing fresh-baked breads, a non-alcoholic beverage (remember, it's BYOB in these parts), and dessert. The decor is on the simple side, but who really cares? It's the scintillating harbor views that have drawn the faithful hordes to this family-friendly place for over 60 years. Locals who aren't keen on summer crowds prefer to order their lobster dinners for pick-up at the restaurant door, then mosey on down to Menemsha Beach for a private sunset supper that's half the price of eating in the restaurant. Reservations are highly recommended and the prix-fixe platters range from $19 to $30 (MasterCard, Visa, and American Express are all accepted).The Home Port is open June through September, daily 6-10pm; call for off-season hours. Closed mid-October through mid-April.

"Bacon Brothers" (including Kevin), and Kate Taylor, James's equally talented sister. Comedians command the stage on Tuesday, and on nonmarquee nights Carly's brother Peter—an accomplished photographer and music producer—often sits in as DJ. All in all, it's a family affair, where outsiders in sync with global-family values will feel right at home.

The Lampost/Rare Duck. 111 Circuit Ave. (in the center of town), Oak Bluffs. ☎ **508/ 696-9352.** Cover varies; call for schedule. Closed Nov–Mar.

Young and loud are the watchwords at this pair of clubs, the larger featuring live bands, the smaller (down in the basement) acoustic acts.

The Ritz Cafe. 1 Circuit Ave. (in the center of town), Oak Bluffs. ☎ **508/693-9851.** Cover varies; call for schedule.

Locals and tourists alike flock to this down-and-dirty blues club.

LOW-KEY EVENINGS

David's Island House. 120 Circuit Ave. (in the center of town), Oak Bluffs. ☎ **508/ 693-3416.** No cover; call for schedule. Closed Oct–Apr.

Pianist/proprietor David Crohan draws steady crowds—and occasional star collaborators—with his classical/pop music and winning personality.

Old Whaling Church. 89 Main St. (in the center of town), Edgartown. ☎ **508/627-4442.** Ticket prices vary; call for schedule.

This magnificent 1843 Greek Revival church functions primarily as a 500-seat performing arts center offering lectures and symposia, films, plays, and music and dance concerts. Such island luminaries as actress Patricia Neal and the late *Life* photographer Alfred Eisenstaedt have edified the populace from the pulpit.

THEATER

✪ **The Vineyard Playhouse.** 10 Church St. (in the center of town), Vineyard Haven. ☎ **508/ 696-6300.** Tickets $15–$25. Late June to early Sept Tues–Sun 8pm; call for off-season schedule.

In an intimate (112-seat) black-box theater carved out of an 1833 church turned Masonic lodge, Equity professionals put on a rich season of chestnuts and challenging new work—followed, on summer weekends, by musical or comedic cabaret in the gallery/lounge. Townspeople often get involved in the outdoor Shakespeare production, a three-week run starting in mid-July at the Tashmoo Overlook Amphitheatre about one mile west of town, where tickets for the 5:30pm performances Tuesday through Sunday run only $5 to $10.

ONLY ON THE VINEYARD

Gay Head Lighthouse. Off State Rd., Gay Head. ☎ **508/693-4922.** Donation requested; July–Aug Fri–Sun 7–9pm.

Though generally closed to the public, this 1856 lighthouse opens its doors on summer weekend evenings to afford an awe-inspiring view of the sunset over the Devil's Bridge shoals. The light has been automated since 1952 (the original lens lights up the night sky in Edgartown), but the experience is nonetheless romantic.

Wintertide Coffeehouse. Beach St. Extension, Vineyard Haven. ☎ **508/693-8830.** Cover varies; call for schedule.

This community-run, alcohol-free folkie haven not only helps keep the natives entertained through the long, lonely winters, it has been hailed by *Billboard* as one of the country's top 10 coffeehouses. The Wintertide has had a Bohemian spirit and presented live folk, blues, jazz, and comedy improv since its inception in 1978. About 80 people can squeeze in here and settle into the folding chairs to hear the likes of folk/jazz/blues headliners such as Tom Paxton, Dave Van Ronk, Patty Larkin, Robin Batteau, Flor de Cana, and islander Kate Taylor (James's very talented sister). In addition to music, you might catch some provocative dinner theater or the ad-libbed comedy of WIMP (the Wintertide Improv Troop). For a token fee, you could even perform yourself, by reserving an open-mike slot. Wintertide's high season actually peaks in late September, after the tourist influx has abated somewhat: It's then that the Wintertide mounts its Singer/Songwriter's Retreat and Concert Series. The players get to stay and hang out together at Oak Bluffs' Sea Spray Inn and partake in a series of workshops; audiences get to enjoy a parade of top names at their playing-for-the-fun-of-it peak. (The first such get-together, in 1992, resulted in a recording for Rounder Records: *Big Times in a Small Town.*) The Black Dog Bakery provides the nibbles.

Trinity Park Tabernacle. Trinity Park (within the Camp Meeting Grounds), Oak Bluffs. ☎ **508/693-0525.** July–Aug, Wed 8pm and occasional weekend evenings. Free; call for schedule.

Designed by architect J. W. Hoyt of Springfield, Mass., and built in 1879 for just over $7,000, this open-air church, now on the National Register of Historic Places, is the largest wrought-iron and wood structure in America. Its conical crown is ringed with a geometric pattern of amber, carmine, and midnight blue stained glass. Old-fashioned community sings take place Wednesdays at 8pm, and concerts are scheduled irregularly on weekends. James Taylor and Bonnie Raitt have regaled the faithful here, but usually the acts are more homespun—for example, the Parson's Plunkers, a local banjo band. The Martha's Vineyard Camp Meeting Association publishes a schedule of events open to the public, including interdenominational services and flea markets.

2 Nantucket

30 miles (48km) S of Hyannis

A lifetime removed from the bustle of big cities, Nantucket is a world unto itself. The name itself means "the faraway land," and although it's merely 30 miles offshore, stress and pressure melt away as you alight from the boat. Nantucket reigned as the

Nantucket

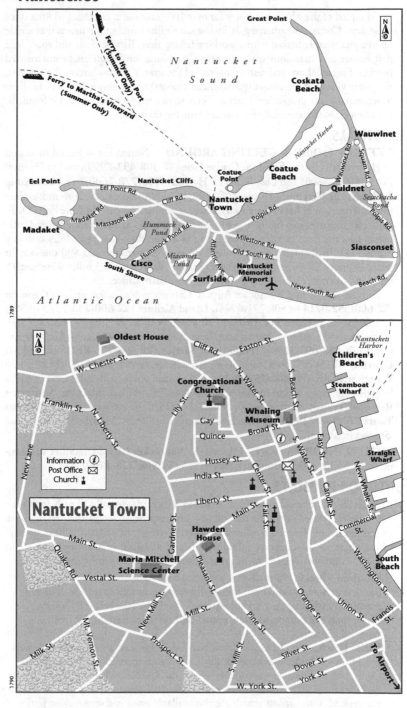

Ferry to Hyannis Port
(Summer Only)

Ferry to Martha's Vineyard
(Summer Only)

Nantucket Sound

Great Point

Coskata Beach

Wauwinet

Squam Rd.

Wauwinet Rd.

Quidnet

Nantucket Harbor

Coatue Point

Coatue Beach

Sesuchacha Pond

Polpis Rd.

Eel Point

Nantucket Cliffs

Eel Point Rd.

Cliff Rd.

Nantucket Town

Polpis Rd.

Madaket Rd.

Massasoit Rd.

Hummock Pond

Milestone Rd.

Siasconset

Hummock Pond Rd.

Old South Rd.

Madaket

Miacomet Pond

Atlantic Ave.

Cisco

South Shore

Nantucket Memorial Airport

New South Rd.

Beach Rd.

Surfside

Atlantic Ocean

1789

Oldest House

W. Chester St.

Cliff Rd.

Easton St.

Nantucket Harbor

Children's Beach

Franklin St.

Congregational Church

N. Water St.

S. Beach St.

Steamboat Wharf

N. Liberty St.

Lily St.

Gay

Whaling Museum

Broad St.

New Lane

Quince

Straight Wharf

Hussey St.

Center St.

S. Water St.

Easy St.

New Whale St.

Information ⓘ
Post Office ✉
Church ✝

India St.

Liberty St.

Candle St.

Nantucket Town

Gardner St.

Main St.

Fair St.

Commercial St.

Main St.

Hawden House

South Beach

Quaker Rd.

Maria Mitchell Science Center

Pleasant St.

Orange St.

Washington St.

Vestal St.

New Mill St.

Union St.

Milk St.

Mt. Vernon St.

Mill St.

S. Mill St.

Pine St.

Silver St.

Francis St.

Prospect St.

Dover St.

To Airport

W. York St.

York St.

1790

291

world capital of the whaling industry for over 100 years and it has changed little since those days. Cottages weathered gray by the salt air line cobblestone streets that amble up to a picturesque harbor with a working fishing fleet. Bicycle trails and roads lead past estates and mansions to open moors and dunes and then on to uncrowded beaches. Elegant shops and restaurants crowd the town's narrow streets. To the east, the pretty village of Siasconset (pronounced *scon*-set) has merely a clutch of facilities to accompany its sun-splashed beaches. Ferry service to Nantucket Island is frequent, but often crowded, especially for visitors bringing their cars.

ESSENTIALS

GETTING THERE & GETTING AROUND   Nantucket is linked in season to Harwichport by the **Freedom Cruise Line** (☎ 508/432-8999), and to Hyannis (☎ 508/477-8600) and Oak Bluffs by **Hy-Line** (**508/778-2600**). The **Steamship Authority car ferry** from Hyannis (☎ **508/477-8600**) operates year-round, as does the passengers-only **M/V *Grey Lady,*** a recent addition to the Hy-Line fleet. Ordinarily, it takes over two hours to get to Nantucket by boat, but this high-speed catamaran cuts the time in half, for more than twice the slow-boat price ($29 one-way versus $11). Incidentally, transporting a car costs an astronomical $90 one-way in season—pretty silly when you consider that the island is only 3 miles wide and 15 miles end to end. A bike ($5 one-way) will more than suffice.

You can also fly into Nantucket Airport. Carriers to Nantucket include **Cape Air** (☎ **800/352-0714** or 508/771-6944), **Island Airlines** (☎ **800/248-7779** or 508/ 775-6066), and **Nantucket Airlines** (☎ **800/635-8787** or 508/790-0300). Charter flights are offered by Cape Air and Nantucket Airlines, as well as by **Air New England** (☎ **508/693-8899**), **Hyannis Air Service** (☎ **508/775-8171**), **Island Air Charter** (☎ **508/778-8360**), **King Air Charters** (☎ **800/247-2427**), and **Westchester Air** (☎ **800/759-2929**). Free shuttle buses, with bike racks, make a loop through town and to certain outlying spots; for details, contact the **Nantucket Regional Transit Authority** (☎ **508/228-7025**). For a reasonable fee, **Barretts Tours** (☎ **508/228-0174**) runs beach shuttles to Jetties, Madaket, Surfside, and 'Sconset in season.

VISITOR INFORMATION   Contact the **Nantucket Island Chamber of Commerce** at 48 Main St., Nantucket, MA 02554 (☎ **508/228-1700**).

OUTDOOR PURSUITS

BEACHES   In distinct contrast to Martha's Vineyard, virtually all of Nantucket's 110-mile coastline is open to the public—on purpose. Though the pressures are sometimes intense (especially when four-wheel drivers insist on their right to go anywhere, anytime), islanders are proud that they've managed to keep the shoreline in the public domain. The following areas each tend to attract a different crowd.

- **Children's Beach,** Nantucket: A protected cove right on the busy harbor, to the west of Steamship Wharf, this small beach has family appeal, with its full amenities, including park and playground, snack bar (the beloved Downy Flake, source of homemade doughnuts), and even a bandstand for free weekend concerts.
- **Jetties Beach,** west of Brant's Point, Nantucket: Located about a half-mile west of Children's, Jetties is another family favorite with its mild waves, lifeguards, bathhouse, and relatively affordable restaurant, The Jetties Cafe & Grille. Facilities include the town tennis courts, volleyball nets, a skate park, and simple playground; water-sports rentals are also available on-site. Every August Jetties hosts an intense sandcastle competition.

- **Dionis Beach,** off Eel Point Road, Nantucket: A bit more remote, but easily accessed by bike, Dionis—featuring lifeguards and rest rooms—enjoys the same gentle Sound surf and a picturesque background of steep bluffs (stick to established paths to avoid further erosion).
- **Madaket Beach,** Madaket: Accessible by road or by a beautiful six-mile bike path traversing heathlands, this westerly beach—with lifeguards, rest rooms, and a food van—is narrow and subject to pounding surf and sometimes serious cross-currents. Unless it's a fairly tame day, you might content yourself with a wade. It's the best spot on the island for admiring the sunset, and a nearby restaurant, the Westender (see "Where to Dine," below) makes the most of the view.
- **Cisco Beach,** Cisco: A bit out of the way, in the southwestern quadrant of the island, unsupervised Cisco enjoys vigorous surf—great for the surfers who flock here, not so great for the waterfront homeowners.
- **Surfside Beach:** Three miles south of town via a popular bike/skate path, broad Surfside—equipped with lifeguards, rest rooms, and a surprisingly accomplished little snack bar—is appropriately named and commensurately popular; in fact, it's the island's most popular, drawing thousands of visitors a day in high season. There's free parking available for about 60 cars. You do the math—or better yet, ride a bike.
- **Siasconset Beach,** Siasconset: Reached by means of a less scenic and somewhat hilly (for Nantucket) seven-mile bike path, the easterly coast of 'Sconset is as pretty as the town itself and rarely, if ever, crowded, perhaps because of the water's strong sideways tow. There are usually lifeguards on duty, but the closest facilities (rest rooms, grocery store, cafe) are back in the center of the village. To enjoy every amenity, splurge on lunch at the Summer House (see "Where to Stay," below), which includes pool privileges.
- **Coatue,** Wauwinet: This fishhook-shaped barrier beach, on the northeastern side of the island, is Nantucket's outback, accessible to four-wheel-drive vehicles, watercraft, or the very strong of leg. Swimming is strongly discouraged, because of fierce tides.

BIKING/RECREATIONAL PATHS   Several lovely bike paths radiate out from the center of town to outlying beaches. The main thoroughfares run about six miles west to Madaket, three miles south to Surfside, and seven miles to Siasconset. Once you get out of town, with its jarring cobblestones and one-way streets (bikes must comply, too, and there's no riding on the sidewalks), the nonpath roads—such as Polpis Road, due to get a path of its own before long—are fairly relaxed. Strong riders could easily do a whole circuit in a half-day or less, though sometimes cyclists might prefer to plan on just one beach jaunt daily.

The best place for bike rentals, from basic three-speeds to high-tech suspension models, is **Young's Bicycle Shop,** in operation since 1931—check out the vintage vehicles they have on display—and conveniently located near Steamship Wharf (☎ **508/228-1151,** fax 508/228-3038, e-mail: bicycles@nantucket.net); they also deliver door-to-door. Cyclists share the paths with in-line skaters, who can gear up at **Nantucket Sports Locker on Wheels** (☎ **508/228-6610**).

FISHING   For shell-fishing you'll need a permit from the harbormaster's office at 38 Washington St. (☎ **508/228-7260**). You'll see surf casters all over the island (no permit is required); for a guided trip, try Mike Mont of **Surf & Fly Fishing Trips** (☎ **508/228-0529**). Deep-sea charters heading out of Straight Wharf include the *Albacore* (☎ **508/228-1439**) and *Monomoy* (☎ **508/228-6867**).

NATURE TRAILS　Through preservationist foresight, about one-third of Nantucket's 42 square miles are protected from development. Contact the **Nantucket Conservation Foundation,** 118 Cliff Rd. (☎ 508/228-2884), for a map of their holdings ($3), which include the 205-acre **Windswept Cranberry Bog** (off Polpis Road), where bogs are interspersed amid hardwood forests, and a portion of the 1,100-acre **Coskata-Coatue Wildlife Refuge,** comprising the barrier beaches beyond Wauwinet. The **Trustees of the Reservations** (☎ 508/228-6799), who oversee the bulk of this tract, offer three-hour naturalist-guided tours via truckbed out past the Great Point Lighthouse, a partly solar-powered replica of the 1818 original. The **Maria Mitchell Science Center** (see "Museums & Historic Landmarks," below) also sponsors guided birding and wildflower walks in season.

WATER SPORTS　**Force 5,** with its office at 37 Main St. (☎ 508/228-0700) and a seasonal satellite at Jetties Beach (☎ 508/228-5358), offers lessons and rents out kayaks, sailboards, sailboats, etc. **Sea Nantucket,** on tiny Francis Street Beach off Washington Street (☎ 508/228-7499), also rents kayaks; it's a quick sprint across the harbor to beautiful Coatue. **Nantucket Island Community Sailing** (☎ 508/228-6600) offers relatively low-cost lessons for adults (16 and up) and families; a seasonal adult membership covering open sail privileges costs $150. Scuba gear and lessons are available at the **Sunken Ship,** on S. Water and Broad streets, near the Steamship Wharf (☎ 508/228-9226).

MUSEUMS & HISTORIC LANDMARKS

Jethro Coffin House. Sunset Hill Rd. (off West Chester Rd., about ¹/₂ mile NW of town center), Nantucket. ☎ **508/228-1894.** Admission $3 adults, $2 children 5–14, or included in Nantucket Historical Association pass ($8 adults, $5 children). July–Aug daily 10am–5pm; call for off-season schedule. Closed mid-Oct to Apr.

This is the oldest building left on the island, a circa 1686 saltbox. A National Historical Landmark, it is also known as the Horseshoe House for the brick design on its central chimney. It was struck by lightning and severely damaged (in fact, nearly cut in two) in 1987, prompting a long-overdue restoration. Dimly illumined by leaded glass diamond-pane windows, it's filled with period furniture such as lathed ladderback chairs and a clever trundle bed on wooden wheels. Nantucket Historical Association docents will fill you in on all the related lore.

The Maria Mitchell Science Center. 2 Vestal St. (at Milk St., about ¹/₂ mile SW of town center), Nantucket. ☎ **508/228-9198.** Admission $5 adults, $3 children under 12, $2 seniors. Early June to late Aug Tues–Sat 10am–4pm; call for off-season hours.

This is a group of buildings organized and maintained in honor of distinguished astronomer and Nantucket native, Maria Mitchell (1818–89). The science center consists of astronomical observatories, with a lecture series, children's science seminars, and stellar observations (when the sky is clear). The Hinchman House at 7 Milk St. is home to the Museum of Natural Science, and offers evening lectures, bird watching, wildflower and nature walks, and children's nature classes. The Mitchell House at 1 Vestal St., the astronomer's birthplace, features a children's history series and adult artisans seminars, and has wildflower and herb gardens. The Science Library is at 2 Vestal St. and the aquarium at 28 Washington St.

Old Gaol. 15R Vestal St. (about ¹/₄ mile SW of town center), Nantucket. ☎ **508/228-1894.** Free admission. July–Aug daily 10am–5pm; call for off-season schedule. Closed mid-Oct to Apr.

The petty thieves, embezzlers, and murderers who did time here, from 1805 right up until 1933, had little hope of escaping this crude facility—the shingled facade, which seems right at home in this residential area, conceals a frame built of massive timbers bolted with iron. Cells have plank bunks, open privies, and iron grates for windows, but if you suspect the islanders of cruel and unusual punishment, keep in mind that most prisoners were allowed to go home at night, the risk of flight being slim. The Nantucket Historical Association keeps the building open, but there's rarely anyone on hand; you can poke about at your leisure.

Old Mill. S. Mill and Prospect sts. (about $^1/_2$ mile S of town center), Nantucket. ☎ **508/ 228-1894.** Admission $2 adults, $1 children 5–14, or included in a Nantucket Historical Association Pass ($8 adults, $4 children). July–Aug daily 10am–5pm; call for off-season schedule. Closed mid-Oct to Apr.

Originally one of four windmills that stood on the hills west of town, this 1746 structure is the only one remaining, and the only mill on the Cape and islands still in its original location. A 50-foot Douglas fir pole (the original was a mast) turns the 30-by-6-foot sailcloth-covered arms into the wind, setting in motion a wooden gear train that grinds corn between millstones weighing more than a ton apiece. You can buy some fresh meal after watching it (wind permitting) being made.

✪ **Whaling Museum.** 13 Broad St. (in the center of town). ☎ **508/228-1736.** Admission $5 adults, $3 children 5–14, or included in a Nantucket Historical Association pass ($8 adults, $3 children). Late May to mid-Oct daily 10am–5pm; call for off-season hours. Closed early Dec to mid-Apr.

Housed in a former spermaceti-candle factory, this museum is a must-visit; if not for the awe-inspiring skeleton of a 43-foot finback whale (stranded in the sixties), then for the exceptional collections of scrimshaw and nautical art (check out the action painting *Ship Spermo of Nantucket in a Heavy Thunder-Squall on the Coast of California 1876*, executed by a captain who survived). A map occupying one entire wall depicts the round-the-world meanderings of the *Alpha*, accompanied by related log entries. The price of admission includes several lectures, scheduled throughout the day, which give a brief and colorful history of the industry, starting with the beachside "whalebecue" feasts natives and settlers enjoyed when a cetacean happened to ground. Pursued to its logical conclusion, this booming business ultimately led to the tragic near-extirpation of some extraordinary species, but that story must await another museum; this one is full of the glories of the hunt. There's quite a nice gift shop, too.

ORGANIZED TOURS

Sparrow Yacht Charters. Slip 19, Straight Wharf, Nantucket. ☎ **508/228-6029.** Fees start at $25 per person (6-person maximum); call for reservations. Closed mid-Sept to early June.

Naval architect Randolph Watkins became so enamored of cruising aboard his 40-foot sailboat (modeled on a 1900s Norwegian North Sea pilot boat) that he took to the seas in 1983 and never stopped, except for his annual sojourn in Nantucket. In a brief cruise, perhaps out to Coatue, one can quickly get a taste for the good life.

Carried Away. Pick-up site to be arranged, Nantucket. ☎ **508/228-0218.** Fee $80 and up; call for reservations. Open year-round.

In most tourist haunts, you might feel like a yahoo taking a carriage ride, but here you'll blend in with the prevalent aesthetic and perhaps get a better feel for 19th-century life. The rides come with historical and architectural commentary, if desired.

The Endeavor/Nantucket Whaleboat Adventures. Slip 15, Straight Wharf, Nantucket. ☎ **508/228-5585.** Fee starts at $15 for a 1-hour sail; call for reservations. Closed Nov–Apr.

The *Endeavor* is a spirited 31-foot replica Friendship sloop, ideal for jaunts across the harbor to pristine Coatue; skipper James Genther will gladly drop you off for a bit of sunbathing or beachcombing, or even arrange for a treasure hunt. New to his fleet is a faithfully re-created whaleboat, the *Wanderer*, in which crews of six can recapture the arduous experience of chasing a whale—minus the target, of course, and without the traditional "Nantucket sleighride."

Gail's Tours. Departs from the Nantucket Information Bureau, 25 Federal St. (in the center of town), Nantucket, and from prearranged pickup sites. ☎ **508/257-6557.** Reservations required. Fee $10 adults, children 3 and under free. July–Aug departures at 10am, 1, and 3pm; call for off-season schedule.

If you're curious to dig up the dirt on the island's colorful residents, Gail Nickerson Johnson—a seventh-generation native whose mother started a tour business back in the 1940s—has the inside track, and the charm to keep a captive vanload aurally rapt throughout a 1 1/2–hour circuit of island highlights.

Nantucket Harbor Cruises. Slip 12, Straight Wharf, Nantucket. ☎ **508/228-1444.** Fee $22.50 adults, $17.50 for children 4–12; call for reservations. Closed May.

Adapting to the season, the *Anna W. II*, a lobster boat turned pleasure barge, offers lobstering demos in summer (passengers sometimes get to take home the proceeds) and seal-sighting cruises along the jetty in winter (no stowaways allowed). In between, Captain Bruce Cowan takes groups out just to view the lovely shoreline.

KID STUFF

The **Nantucket Park and Recreation Commission** (☎ 508/228-7213) organizes various free and low-cost activities for kids, from tennis clinics to tie-dye workshops (it's a bring-your-own-T-shirt proposition). **The Nantucket Historical Association** (☎ **508/228-1894**) sponsors two-hour adventures for children ages 6 to 10, which include grinding flour at the Old Mill, baking bread at the Oldest House, and trying your hand at knots and sailors' valentines. **The Actor's Theatre of Nantucket,** at the Methodist Church, 2 Centre St. (☎ **508/228-6325**), puts on theater for children by children late-July to mid-August Tuesdays through Saturdays at 5pm; tickets are $10. Little kids might like to get their hands on (and into) the touch tanks at the modest little **Maria Mitchell Aquarium** at 28 Washington St., overlooking the harbor from whence the creatures came (☎ **508/228-5387**); the cost is only $1, but hours are limited, so call ahead.

SHOPPING

All of the shops listed below are located right in the center of Nantucket Town.

ANTIQUES/COLLECTIBLES   Most tourists aren't looking to bring home a new living room set, but ✪ **Lynda Willauer Antiques,** 1 India St. (between Federal and Center sts.; ☎ **508/228-3631**), has such an exquisite selection of American and English furniture (plus paintings, quilts, porcelain, and accessories) that it's worth stopping by just to gawk. Closed late September to May.

Nantucket House Antiques, 1 S. Beach St. (☎ **508/228-4604**), is full of genuine treasures—some affordable, some with astronomical price tags.

Tonkin of Nantucket, 33 Main St. (☎ **508/228-9697**), has been an island fixture for decades. Brass and silver knickknacks are the specialty, and this is the place to find antique Nantucket lightship baskets, those peculiar woven purses you see dangling from tanned, moneyed arms.

ART/CRAFTS   Widely copied, the miniaturized jewelry version of Nantucket's trademark lightship basket was introduced at **The Golden Basket,** 44 Main St. (☎ **508/228-5977**), with another branch at Nantucket's Straight Wharf. The baskets, complete with gold penny, represent only a small portion of the offerings, which are exquisite.

Like many a seaside resort community, Nantucket tends to foster pretty landscape rather than serious art. But **Main Street Gallery,** 2 S. Water St. (☎ **508/228-2252**), offer more challenging and substantial work.

Appealing vintage prints are available from **Paul LaPaglia Antique Prints,** 38 Centre St. (☎ **508/228-8760**).

Two Rhode Island School of Design grads started **The Spectrum,** 26 Main St. (☎ **800/221-2472** or 508/228-4606), in a country schoolhouse in 1966 and quickly developed it into a premier showcase for crafts. The stock is accessible and appealing, from Josh Simpson's glass-marble "planets" to Thomas Mann's unique take on old-fashioned charms.

FASHION   **Force 5 Water Sports,** 37 Main St. (☎ **508/228-0700**), with a seasonal branch at Jetties Beach (☎ **508/228-5358**), is the place for wetsuits, Windsurfers, boogie boards, and more—but it also stocks the best bathing suit selection in town, plus Patagonia coverups and polar-fleece jackets for brisk off-season days.

Martha's Vineyard may have spawned Black Dog paraphenalia, but this island boasts the inimitable "Nantucket reds"—cotton clothing that starts out tomato-red and washes out to salmon pink. The fashion originated at the venerable **Murray's Toggery Shop,** 62 Main St. (☎ **800/368-2134** or 508/228-0437). Roland Hussey Macy, founder of Macy's, got his start here in the 1830s.

GIFTS/HOME DECOR   **Claire Murray,** 11 S. Water St. (☎ **800/252-4733** or 508/228-1923), designs and creates extraordinary hooked rugs. If you'd like to try your own hand at it, the store also sells kits, plus ready-made quilts, sweaters, hand-painted furniture, tableware, toiletries, and more.

Warm and welcoming, ✪ **Erica Wilson Needle Works,** 25–27 Main St. (☎ **508/ 228-9881**), spills over with needlepoint kits, richly textured sweaters, baby clothes, and home accessories.

Nantucket abounds in interior design shops promoting the lavish country look, but **Modern Arts,** 44 Main St. (☎ **508/228-1258**), features 1950s decor. Follow the vintage Cape Playhouse posters up to the second-story shop, where you'll find chenille bedspreads, art deco cocktail shakers, and more.

TOYS   Long a local fixture, **Pinwheel Toys,** 38 Centre St. (☎ **508/228-1991**), offers a great selection of playthings, both mass-market and customized.

✪ **The Toy Boat,** Straight Wharf (☎ **508/228-4552**), offers creative, educational playthings, including locally crafted items such as "mermaid's purses" and little working sailboats.

WHERE TO STAY
VERY EXPENSIVE
Cliffside Beach Club. Jefferson Ave. (off Spring St.), Nantucket, MA 02554. ☎ **508/ 228-0618.** Fax 508/325-4735. 19 rms, 8 apts, 1 cottage. A/C TV TEL. Summer (including continental breakfast) $270–$425 double, $525–$695 suite, $550 apt, $655 cottage. AE. Closed mid-Oct to late May.

The only lodging on the island located right on the dunes, this luxurious hotel has contemporary rooms decorated with diagonal wooden wainscoting and island-made modern furniture. The traditional, low-profile, shingled exterior gives no hint of the modern amenities concealed within the 27 units. The cathedral-ceilinged lobby is especially striking, its rafters hung with boldly patterned quilts to set off the white wicker furniture.

○ **Four Chimneys.** 38 Orange St. (about ¹/₄ mile E of Main St.), Nantucket, MA 02554. ☎ **508/228-1912.** Fax 508/325-4864. 10 rms. A/C. Summer (including continental breakfast) $150–$250 double. AE, DC, MC, V. Closed Nov to mid-May.

The Four Chimneys is a bed-and-breakfast of rare charm, stylishly outfitted with a grand piano in the front parlor and a dining room illumined by a crystal chandelier. For privacy-seekers, there's a beautiful little Japanese garden in back. Authentic antiques, including some stunning colonial chests, adorn the bedrooms, where beds have down comforters. Some rooms have fireplaces and/or terraces.

○ **Summer House.** 17 Ocean Ave. (¹/₈ mile S of village center), Siasconset, MA 02564. ☎ **508/257-4577.** Fax 508/257-4590. 10 rms. TEL. Summer (including continental breakfast) $275–$395 double. AE, MC, V. Closed Nov–Apr.

Romance incarnate, these former fishing shacks, entwined with roses, fragrant honeysuckle, and ivy, hug a bluff overlooking the sea. Adirondack chairs are scattered casually across the lush, shady lawn encircled by the cottages. At the bottom of the bluff is a small sparkling pool, where lunch is served, and beyond it, miles of scarcely populated beach. The cottages are outfitted with charming English country antiques and luxurious linens, and baths in all but one of the 10 rooms have a marble Jacuzzi. On the premises is a celebrated restaurant serving cutting-edge cuisine.

The Wauwinet. 120 Wauwinet Rd. (about 8 miles E of Nantucket center), Wauwinet, MA 02554. ☎ **800/426-8718** or 508/228-0145. Fax 508/228-712. 25 rms, 5 cottages. A/C TV TEL. Summer (including full breakfast and afternoon port) $270–$760 double, $610–$1,290 cottage. AE, DC, MC, V. Closed Nov to mid-Apr.

Stephen and Jill Karp renovated this ultradeluxe retreat in 1988 for roughly $3 million, and it has since earned several nicknames, including "The Ultimate," or, as the staff has been known to joke, the "We Want It." With 25 rooms in the main building (which started out as a restaurant in 1850) and 10 more in 5 modest-looking shingled cottages, the complex can only hold about 80 spoiled guests, tended to by 100 staffers. The lovely rooms—all provided with a cozy nook from which to gaze out across the water—each have a unique decorating scheme, with pine armoires, plenty of wicker, exquisite Audubon prints, handsome fabrics, and a lovely array of antique accessories.

Facilities: The staff will go to great lengths to please, jitneying you into town, for instance, in a 1936 "Woody," or dispatching you on a 21-foot launch across the bay to your own private strip of beach. The inn is the last stop on an eight-mile road to nowhere (actually, a wildlife sanctuary), contains several clay tennis courts with a pro shop and pro, a croquet lawn, a platform for nearly life-size "beach chess," and plenty of boats and bikes to borrow. Guests can dine in the highly acclaimed Topper's restaurant on the premises (see "Where to Dine," below.)

Westmoor Inn. Westmoor Lane (off Cliff Rd., about 1 mile W of town center), Nantucket, MA 02554. ☎ **508/228-0877.** 14 rms. Summer (including full breakfast) $140–$225 double. AE, MC, V. Closed early Dec to Mar.

This yellow 1917 Federal-style mansion has all its original delightful detailing—from the grand portico to the widow's walk—still intact, and a new interior design that maximizes the effect of the mansion's light-suffused hilltop setting. The spacious living room is full of thoughtful touches, such as the vase of magnificent gladiola on the baby grand, and a 1,000-piece puzzle of Nantucket arrayed as a work in progress. There's even a cozy little TV room (anathema at most B&Bs) sporting wicker couches and framed architectural blueprints. The 14 bedrooms, including a ground-floor suite with a full-size Jacuzzi and French doors leading to the lawn, are as fully romantic as one would expect. After breakfasting to classical music in the conservatory, one can head off down a sandy lane to a quiet stretch of bay beach or hop on one of the one-speed bikes provided and explore the island.

Wharf Cottages. New Whale St. (near South Wharf), Nantucket, MA 02554. ☎ **800/475-2637** or 508/228-4620. Fax 508/228-7197. 25 cottages. A/C. Summer $240–$525 cottage. Closed mid-Oct to late May.

These 25 charming cottages dot Old South and Swain's Wharves. Though tiny, each is nautically compact with crisp navy-and-white decor and a sitting area and garden. Each sleeps two to eight and you can bring your own boat; docking facilities are provided.

White Elephant Hotel. Easton and Willard sts., Nantucket, MA 02554. ☎ **800/475-2637** or 508/228-2500. Fax 508/325-1195. 72 rms, 8 cottages. A/C TV TEL. Summer $250–$475 double, $155–$595 cottage. AE, CB, DC, DISC, MC, V. Closed Nov–Apr.

Belying its name, this luxury property, right on the harbor, is the ultimate in-town lodging. Rooms (distributed among two buildings and 18 cottages) are big and airy, with picturesque views and country-chic decor. Every space is fresh and breezy, and none more so than the outdoor heated pool and hot tub surrounded by tasteful gray arbors. The hotel's location allows it to welcome "sail-in" guests.

EXPENSIVE

Beachside at Nantucket. 30 N. Beach St. (about ³/₄ mile W of town center), Nantucket, MA 02554. ☎ **800/322-4433** or 508/228-2241. Fax 508/228-8901. 90 rms. A/C TV TEL. Summer $185–$210 double. AE, DC, DISC, MC, V. Closed mid-Oct to mid-Apr.

Emphatically not an ordinary motel, the Beachside boasts bedrooms and a lobby lavished with Provençal prints and handsome rattan and wicker furniture; the patios and decks overlooking the central courtyard with its heated pool have been prettified with French doors and latticework. If you prefer the laissez-faire lifestyle of a motel to the sometimes constricting rituals of a B&B, you might find this the ideal base.

Fair Winds. 29 Cliff Rd. (about ¹/₂ mile W of town center), Nantucket, MA 02554. ☎ **508/228-1998.** 8 rms. Summer (including continental breakfast) $165–$185 double. Closed mid-Oct to mid-May.

A short walk from Nantucket Town is Fair Winds, an eight-bedroom B&B offering the peace many visitors are seeking: In fact, says innkeeper Kathy Hughes, a lot of first-time guests spot the house while out cycling and, after coming in for a look, make it their "second visit" destination. The light-drenched common rooms lead to a 50-foot deck with a panoramic view of the Sound; it's here that guests tend to bring their breakfast of fresh-baked breads and muffins. Four of the prettily decorated bedrooms enjoy that same priceless view.

Jared Coffin House. 29 Broad St. (at Centre St.), Nantucket, MA 02554. ☎ **800/248-2405** or 508/228-2405. Fax 508/228-8549. 60 rms. A/C TV TEL. Summer (including full breakfast) $150–$200 double. AE, DC, DISC, MC, V.

Built to the specs of the social-climbing Mrs. Coffin in 1845, this grand brick manse was abandoned for the big city after two years and left to take in boarders. Lovingly renovated to its original splendor by the Nantucket Historical Trust, it is the social center of town, as well as a mecca for tourists. Accommodations range from well-priced singles (rare in these parts) to roomy suites. Rooms in the neighboring annex houses are equally grand.

Periwinkle Guest House. 7–9 N. Water St. (in the center of town), Nantucket, MA 02554. ☎ **800/673-4559** or 508/228-9009. Fax 508/325-4045. 17 rms (2 with shared bath), 1 suite. A/C. Summer (including continental breakfast) $75–$195 double, $210 suite. AE, DISC, MC, V.

Just a couple of cobblestoned blocks away from the steamship wharf, this charming bed-and-breakfast is just enough removed from the hubbub of downtown, yet within easy walking distance of all its attractions. Most rooms are furnished with canopy beds and some have views of the harbor.

Roberts House. 11 India St. (in the center of town), Nantucket, MA 02554. ☎ **800/673-4559** or 508/228-0600. 22 rms, 1 suite, 1 cottage. A/C TEL. Summer (including continental breakfast) $95–$275 double, $275–$375 suite, $375 cottage. AE, DISC, MC, V.

An elegant parlor and rooms lavished with lace and colorful quilts characterize this large, centrally located bed-and-breakfast. For breakfast, you get a voucher good at a couple of nearby restaurants. Rooms vary greatly in terms of size, but all are sufficiently romantic.

The Woodbox Inn. 29 Fair St. (about 1/4 mile E of town center), Nantucket, MA 02554. ☎ **508/228-0587.** 7 rms, 2 suites. Summer (including full breakfast) $125 double, $160–$210 suite. Closed Jan to late May.

The oldest inn on the island, this shingled 1709 house is easily the most evocative. The sleeping quarters include seven queen-bedded rooms and two suites with fireplaces. Breakfasts in the keeping room feature delicious egg dishes and popovers.

MODERATE

Anchor Inn. 66 Centre St. (between Broad and Chester sts.), Nantucket, MA 02554. ☎ **508/228-0072.** 11 rms. Summer (including continental breakfast) $95–$155 double. AE, MC, V. Closed Jan–Mar.

A homey bed-and-breakfast flanking the Congregational Church (be sure to climb the spire for a bird's-eye view), this sea captain's home is graced by friendly hosts, who provide such thoughtful touches as beach towels and a communal refrigerator. Rooms have period furnishings.

India House. 37 India St. (about 1/8 mile W of Centre St.), Nantucket, MA 02554. ☎ **508/228-9043.** 9 rms. Summer (including continental breakfast) $85–$135 double. MC, V.

This wonderfully simple and spare nine-room B&B has wide plank floors and plenty of canopied four-posters. Guests are treated to one of the best breakfasts around, featuring such treats as blueberry-stuffed French toast and soft-shell crabs filled with scallop mousse, in addition to fresh juice and homemade breads and muffins. The private garden out back is a lovely spot to sip a cocktail.

✪ Martin House Inn. 61 Centre St. (between Broad and Chester sts.), Nantucket, MA 02554. ☎ **508/228-0678.** 13 rms (4 with shared bath). Summer (including continental breakfast) $85–$150 double. AE, MC, V.

One of the lower-priced B&Bs in town, but also one of the most stylish, double with a formal parlor and dining rooms and a spacious side porch, complete with hammock. The garret rooms with a shared bath are a real deal. Other higher-priced rooms have four-posters and fireplaces.

The Quaker House. 20 Chestnut St., Nantucket, MA 02554. ☎ **508/228-0400.** 8 rms. A/C. Summer (including full breakfast) $125–$160 double. Closed mid-Oct to late May.

This pretty B&B, built in 1847, is right in the center of town—a plus for those who like to be centrally located, maybe a minus for those who prefer to retire early. It's not that the street life is rowdy, but people do tend to stroll and socialize till all hours, and the houses are closely packed. All of the comfortable rooms have queen-size beds, and are simply but tastefully decorated.

Ships Inn. 13 Fair St. (about ¹/₈ mile E of town center), Nantucket, MA 02554. ☎ **508/ 228-0040.** Fax 508/228-6524. 12 rms. TV. Summer (including continental breakfast) $120–$150 double. AE, MC, V. Closed early Oct to May.

The Ships Inn is a simple, 1831 whaling captain's house, the only exterior decoration being the square-paned sidelights surrounding the door. The 12 rooms, all named for Starbuck's ships, are decorated like summerhouse guest rooms—they're not especially fancy but quite comfortable.

WHERE TO DINE
VERY EXPENSIVE

American Seasons. 80 Centre St. (at Chester St.), Nantucket. ☎ **508/228-7111.** Reservations recommended. Main courses $14–$24. AE, MC, V. Apr–Dec daily 6–10pm. Closed Jan–Mar. REGIONAL AMERICAN.

Exuberant in style, from the splashy murals to the artistry on the oversized plates, this stellar restaurant scours the four corners of the country—from New England to the Southwest—for inspiration. It's almost like four restaurants in one, and a boon to parties who can't agree on what cuisine they're craving.

Boarding House. 12 Federal St. (at India St.), Nantucket. ☎ **508/228-9622.** Fax 508/ 325-7109. Reservations recommended. Main courses $20–$27. AE, MC, V. June–Aug daily noon–10pm; call for off-season hours. Closed late Oct to mid-Nov. NEW AMERICAN.

The young chef has a deft hand with local ingredients and a world's worth of cuisines. His dishes range from sublimely rich (the lobster bisque) to light and healthy (soba noodles in a gingery broth) to tempt even the pickiest diner. Late in the evening, the outdoor cafe becomes a social magnet.

✪ Chanticleer Inn. 9 New St., Siasconset. ☎ **508/257-4154.** Reservations recommended; jacket required. Main courses $28–$35; prix fixe $65 and up. AE, MC, V. Mid-May to mid-Oct Tues–Sun noon–2:30pm and 6:30–9:30pm. Closed Mon and mid-Oct to mid-May. FRENCH.

Definitely the priciest restaurant throughout the Cape and Islands, this rose-covered cottage turned French *auberge* has fans that don't begrudge a penny. You'd have to cross an ocean to savor the likes of the classic cuisine that has been served here since the mid-seventies. To highlight just a few options on the prix-fixe menu (the dishes sound all the more glamorous in French): *gateau de grenouilles aux pommes de terre* (yes, a frogs' legs "cake" in a potato crust); *tournedos de lotte marinee au gingembre, sauce au rhum, croquettes d'ail* (a gingered monkfish scallopini with a lemon-rum sauce and sweet garlic fritters); and *pain perdu, glace au chocolat blanc, coulis d'abricots secs* (a very classy bread pudding with white-chocolate ice cream and apricot sauce). The restaurant also has a 1,500-vintage wine cellar with 38,000 bottles.

Cioppino's. 20 Broad St. (in the center of town), Nantucket. ☎ **508/228-4622.** Reservations recommended. Main courses $18–$30. DISC, MC, V. Daily lunch 11:30am–2:30pm, 5:30–10pm. Closed late Oct to mid-May. CONTINENTAL.

This elegant and popular restaurant features a pretty side patio and several handsome dining rooms painted the faintest of mauves; the lofty upstairs is especially nice. Aside from the namesake dish (a spicy San Franciscan shellfish stew), chef Matt Buckles' approach is mostly evolved continental: For example, he'll serve foie gras on a bed of crispy shredded potatoes, with a shallot confit and balsamic reduction sauce to add piquant depth, or roll a salmon filet in crushed hazelnuts and top it with a raspberry beurre blanc. The trellised garden is great for late-night drinks and desserts, whether a sensible, exotic sorbet or go-for-broke warm pecan pie with bourbon ice cream.

The Club Car. 1 Main St., Nantucket. ☎ **508/228-1101.** Reservations recommended. Main courses $20–$35. MC, V. June–Sept daily 11am–3pm and 6–10pm; call for off-season hours. Closed Nov and Jan–Mar. CONTINENTAL.

A perennial favorite, this elegant restaurant is flanked by a piano bar fashioned from an old narrow-gauge railroad car that used to transport fashionable tourists out to 'Sconset. Now they come here, for highly polished continental cuisine, prefaced, ideally, by a caviar fix. The "curry Bombay" makes for an unusual surf-and-turf combo: chicken and shrimp, with traditional accompaniments of basmati rice, masoor dal, and papadums.

✪ **Company of the Cauldron.** 7 India St. (between Federal and Centre sts.), Nantucket. ☎ **508/228-4016.** Reservations recommended. Prix fixe $42–$44. MC, V. Late May to mid-Oct Tues–Sun 7–11pm. Closed mid-Oct to late May. NEW AMERICAN.

A tiny space that's almost half kitchen, with the other half composed of odd architectural artifacts (such as a church pew serving as a banquette), this place has atmosphere in spades. The menu choices are limited (usually, two prix-fixe meals), so people call ahead to reserve the night when their favorites will surface, imaginatively conceived and exquisitely prepared. Menu items might include almond and hazelnut-crusted salmon served with beurre blanc, ginger carrots, and saffron rice.

✪ **DeMarco.** 9 India St. (bewteen Federal and Centre sts.), Nantucket. ☎ **508/228-1836.** Reservations recommended. Main courses $18–$30. AE, MC, V. June to mid-Sept daily 6–10pm; call for off-season hours. Closed Dec–Mar. ITALIAN.

Haute northern Italian cuisine hasn't quite swept the island as it has the mainland: So far, this frame house carved into a cafe/bar and loft is the only place to savor it in style. A forward-thinking menu and attentive service ensure a superior meal, which might include fettucine with grilled duck breast, porcini mushrooms, sun-dried tomatoes, and arugula.

The Galley on Cliffside Beach. Cliffside Beach Club, Jefferson Ave. (off Spring St., about 1 mile W of town center), Nantucket. ☎ **508/228-9641.** Reservations recommended for dinner. Main courses $23–$37. AE. Mid-June to mid-Sept daily 11:30am–2pm and dinner 6–10pm. Closed mid-Oct to late May. INTERNATIONAL.

A fine spot for a fine day: The Galley is surrounded by flower boxes and the gentle thrum of the surf. The restaurant serves up self-assured world-beat cuisine, from the Dungeness crab cake with roasted corn avocado relish and blood-orange butter sauce, to the grilled Nantucket striped bass with lobster risotto and mango salsa.

The Hearth. Harbor House, 7 S. Beach St., Nantucket. ☎ **800/475-2637** or 508/228-1500. Fax 508/228-7639. Reservations recommended. Main courses $12–$18. AE, DC, DISC, MC, V. Mid-June to mid-Sept daily 8–10am and 6–10pm; call for off-season schedule. Closed Jan–Mar. NEW ENGLAND.

One of the larger, more formal dining rooms in town, and a traditional spot for lavish Sunday brunches (followed, at night, with an all-you-can-eat prime rib buffet). While taking a firm meat-and-potatoes stance, the restaurant is not oblivious of culinary trends: The pan-roasted crab cakes come on a bed of corn salsa, with an apricot demi-glaze dipping sauce; the house-specialty steak comes enrobed in cracked pepper-corns and drizzled with a Jack Daniels reduction. The Hearth is one of the few island restaurants to offer an early-bird discount (labeled more tastefully as "sunset dinner specials"), and the prix-fixe menu is a very good deal. Local musicians, such as the engaging songster team of Phil and Elizabeth, hold fort evenings in the adjoining Hearth Lounge, a barnlike space with a carved whale hanging over the fireplace and a huge chandelier sporting brass weathervanes hung amid the massive beams.

✪ India House Restaurant. 37 India St. (about ¹/₈ mile W of Centre St.), Nantucket. ☎ **508/228-9043.** Reservations recommended. Prix fixe $44. MC, V. July–Aug Tues–Sun seatings at 7 and 9pm; call for off-season hours. Closed Mon and mid-Oct to late May. NEW AMERICAN.

At the India House three small dining rooms, with listing floors and low-slung ceilings, make a lovely, intimate setting for superb candlelit dinners. A longtime favorite dish is Lamb India House, enrobed in rosemary-studded breading and cloaked in béarnaise sauce, but new influences have surfaced of late: for example, Asian (as demonstrated in the 12-spice salmon sashimi with garlic and mint soy oil) and southwestern (Texas wild boar ribs with grilled pineapple barbecue sauce). The menu changes weekly, so you can be sure that this wonderful restaurant won't be resting on its well-deserved laurels.

✪ The Second Story. 1 S. Beach St. (in the center of town), Nantucket. ☎ **508/228-3471.** Reservations recommended. Main courses $18–$30. MC, V. May–Oct daily noon–2pm and 6–10pm. FUSION.

A carefully guarded secret among islanders, this intimate second-floor restaurant serves up an international menu that changes almost daily. Predominant influences are Asian, southwestern, and European; you might start, for instance, with an appetizer of rice noodles tossed with crab, peanuts, cucumbers, spinach, and mushrooms in a Singapore citrus curry vinaigrette, then move on to grilled lamb noisette with a Chianti, rosemary, and balsamic sauce, accompanied by goat-cheese lasagna. Desserts are classically inclined: to wit, a raspberry tart in a flaky pastry shell lined with bittersweet chocolate, then topped with a layer of white-chocolate buttercream.

✪ Topper's. The Wauwinet, 120 Wauwinet Rd. (off Squam Rd.), Wauwinet. ☎ **508/228-8768.** Fax 508/228-6712. Reservations recommended; jacket required. Main courses $26–$36. AE, DC, MC, V. May–Oct Mon–Sat noon–2pm and 6–9:30pm; Sun 10:30am–2pm and 6–9:30pm. Closed Nov–Apr. NEW AMERICAN.

The beneficiary of a multimillion-dollar makeover, this 1850 restaurant—part of a secluded resort—is a tastefully subdued knockout, with wicker armchairs, splashes of chintz, and a two-tailed mermaid to oversee a chill-chasing fire. Peter Wallace's cuisine is regionalism at its best: Lobster, in his hands, becomes a major event (it's often sautéed with champagne beurre blanc), and he also has a knack for unusual species such as Arctic char. Desserts are fanciful and fabulous: Consider the "chocolate boat."

✪ 21 Federal. 21 Federal St. (at Oak St.), Nantucket. ☎ **508/228-2121.** Fax 508/228-2962. Reservations recommended. Main courses $17–$25. AE, MC, V. June–Oct daily 11:30am–2:30pm and 6–10pm; call for off-season hours. Closed Jan–Mar. NEW AMERICAN.

This lovely restaurant, occupying a Greek Revival house, deserves its place in the vanguard of New American cuisine. Neatly skirting trendy extremes, it continues to serve the choicest possible ingredients in the manner that best brings out their intrinsic flavors—there's no exoticizing for novelty's sake. Best dish: thin-crusted pizza with Boursín, asparagus, and rock shrimp. The paneled dining rooms are spare and inviting, or you can choose to dine in the sheltered garden.

West Creek Cafe. 11 West Creek Rd. (about 1 mile E of town center), Nantucket. ☎ **508/228-4943.** Reservations recommended. Main courses $17–$26. MC, V. Apr–Jan Wed–Mon 6–10pm. Closed Feb–Mar. NEW AMERICAN.

For Nantucket, this recent (1995) arrival represents a real walk on the wild side. The decor actually features zebra-striped pillows—look out! The world-roaming cuisine is equally colorful and priced reasonably for international grazing.

The Woodbox. 29 Fair St. (3 blocks SE of Main St.), Nantucket. ☎ **508/228-0587.** Reservations required for dinner. Main courses $18–$24. No credit cards. Late May to mid-Oct daily 8:30–10am, 6:30 or 9pm (2 seatings); call for off-season schedule. Closed Jan.-Apr. CONTINENTAL.

How often do you get to eat in an authentic colonial setting, and not some gimmicky approximation? This is the real thing (1709), and the menu, though traditionalist at heart, is prepared with modern panache. Signature dishes include a toothsome beef Wellington, and justly famous popovers, which are also a big hit at breakfast.

EXPENSIVE

Obadiah's. 21 India St. (between Federal and Centre sts.), Nantucket. ☎ **508/228-4430.** Main courses $10–$20. AE, MC, V. Mid-June to late Sept Mon–Sat 12–3pm, daily 5:30–10pm. Closed late Sept to mid-June. REGIONAL AMERICAN.

Finding a reasonably priced restaurant in Nantucket is no mean feat. This one is a gem. You can eat outdoors on a lantern-lit patio, or in the atmospheric brick-walled basement of the 1840s house. The cuisine is not all that daring, but reliably and substantially good. Portions are generous; service swift and friendly.

RopeWalk. Straight Wharf, Nantucket. ☎ **508/228-8886.** No reservations. Main courses $17–$22. MC, V. Mid-May to mid-Oct 11:30am–1am. Closed mid-Oct to mid-May. NEW AMERICAN.

Making the most of its harborside setting, this open, airy cafe offers stellar seafood with interesting asides, such as polenta or risotto. The raw bar—which sometimes serves sushi—can't be beat.

'Sconset Cafe. Post Office Sq. (in the village center), Siasconset. ☎ **508/257-4008.** Reservations recommended. Main courses $17–$22. No credit cards. Mid-May to mid-Sept daily 8:30am–9:30pm. Closed mid-Sept to mid-May. NEW AMERICAN.

Chummy as a friend's kitchen, this small bistro turns out three great meals a day, starting with hearty waffles and ending, perhaps, with fork-tender veal or duck confit. Seafood is also a forté.

MODERATE

⑤ **Arno's.** 41 Main St., Nantucket. ☎ **508/228-7001.** Reservations recommended. Main courses $9–$18. AE, DISC, MC, V. Apr–Dec 8am–9pm; call for off-season hours. Closed Jan. ECLECTIC.

A storefront facing the passing parade of Main Street, this institution packs surprising style within its bare-brick walls (Molly Dee's mostly monochrome paintings, like vintage photographs, are especially nice). The internationally influenced menu yields tasty, bountiful platters.

❂ **The Brotherhood of Thieves.** 23 Broad St. (at Federal St.), Nantucket. No phone. No reservations. Main courses $8–$15. No credit cards. June–Sept daily 11:30am–12:30pm; apt to close early off-season. Closed Feb. AMERICAN.

An authentic 1840s whaling bar, this candlelit *boite* positively exudes ambience. But what keeps patrons lining up to enter is the well-priced, down-home food. The curly fries alone are certifiably addictive, and the warm soups, mulled ciders, and camaraderie help locals get through the off-season.

⑤ **Quaker House Restaurant.** 31 Centre St. (at Chestnut St.), Nantucket. ☎ **508/228-9156.** Fax 508/228-6205. Reservations recommended. Prix fixe $18–$25. AE, MC, V. Late May to mid-Oct daily 8–11:30am and 6–9:30pm. Closed mid-Oct to late May. INTERNATIONAL.

You might expect corners to be cut with a prix-fixe menu so well priced, with so many choices. But it's a complete white-tablecloth dining experience, every bit of it delicious. The breakfasts—comparatively pricier—are among the best in town.

INEXPENSIVE

Espresso Cafe. 40 Main St., Nantucket. ☎ **508/228-6933.** Most items under $7. No credit cards. Late May to early Sept daily 7:30am–11pm; call for off-season hours. INTERNATIONAL.

This reliable self-service cafe is in the heart of town. Pastries, sandwiches, and international dishes are affordably priced and delicious, and the cafe has some of the best coffee in town (the "Nantucket" and "Harvard" blends are perennial favorites). In good weather, enjoy a leisurely snack on the sunny patio out back.

✪ **Sushi by Yoshi.** 2 E. Chestnut St. (in the center of town), Nantucket. ☎ **508/228-1801.** Most dishes under $25. No credit cards. Apr to mid-Dec daily 11:30am–10pm. Closed mid-Dec through Mar. JAPANESE.

This place is Nantucket's best source for great sushi. The super-fresh local fish is artfully presented by Chef Yoshihisa Mabuchi, who also dishes up such healthy, affordable staples as miso or *udon* (noodle) soup. It's tempting to order a raft of Rhoda rolls (with tuna, avocado, and caviar), especially when a portion of the proceeds goes toward AIDS support.

TAKE-OUT & PICNIC FARE

Bartlett's Ocean View Farm. 33 Bartlett Farm Rd., Nantucket. ☎ **508/228-9403.** Truck on Main St. in season.

You can get fresh-picked produce right in town from Bartlett's traveling market, or head out to this eighth-generation farm where, in June, you might get to pick your own strawberries.

Claudette's. Post Office Sq. (in the village center), Siasconset. ☎ **508/257-6622.** Closed mid-Oct to mid-May.

Homebaked goodies spruce up the breakfasts and lunches prepared here, which can be enjoyed on the small terrace or carted straight to the beach.

SWEETS

✪ **The Juice Bar.** 12 Broad St. (in the center of town), Nantucket. ☎ **508/228-5799.** Closed mid-Oct through Mar.

This humble hole-in-the-wall scoops up some of the best ice cream around, complemented by superb homemade hot fudge. The pastries are also excellent, and yes, you can also get juice, from refreshing lime rickeys to healthful carrot cocktails.

NANTUCKET AFTER DARK

The **Nantucket Arts Alliance** (☎ **800/228-8118** or 508/228-8118) operates **Box Office Nantucket**—offering tickets for all sorts of cultural events around town—out of the Macy Warehouse on Straight Wharf in season Monday to Saturday 9am to 1pm, Sunday 11am to 3pm.

LIVE MUSIC & DANCE CLUBS

The Box. 6 Dave St. (off Pleasant St., about 1 mile E of town center), Nantucket. ☎ **508/228-9717.** Cover varies; call for schedule.

A little rougher than the Muse (sometimes a *lot* rougher), The Box is also more affordable and a favorite among the island's working classes, seasonal and otherwise. The sounds range from Irish rock to reggae, with a detour for Lobsterz from Mars, a group of Grateful Deadheads with a Dead-like sensibility and sound.

The Brotherhood of Thieves. 23 Broad St. (in the center of town). No phone. Closed Feb.

To be truthful, I tend to tune out the acoustic performers who hold forth in this atmospheric spot, however talented they may be: I'm usually too busy gobbling burgers and catching up on gossip. But they come from all over, and some are quite good.

The Hearth Lounge. Harbor House, 23 S. Water St., Nantucket. ☎ **508/228-1500.** No cover.

If a duo by the name of "Phil & Elizabeth" summons images of insipid folkies, think again. On weekend evenings in summer, these guys crank out stirring R&B.

The Muse. 44 Atlantic Ave. (about 1¹/₂ mile S of town center), Nantucket. ☎ **508/228-6873.** Cover varies; call for schedule. Closed Oct–Apr.

Midway to Surfside Beach, this club attracts hard-rocking bands and the island's *jeunesse doree* with salvage-yard decor and late-night pizza.

The Regatta. At the White Elephant, Easton and Willard sts., Nantucket. ☎ **800/475-2637** or 508/228-5500. No cover. Closed Oct–Apr.

At the Regatta a pianist regales well-heeled guests and well-dressed visitors with low-key show tunes.

THEATER

Actor's Theatre of Nantucket. Methodist Church, 2 Centre St. (in the center of town), Nantucket. ☎ **508/228-6325.** Tickets $15. Late May to mid-Sept Tues–Sun 8:30pm; call for off-season schedule. Children's production (tickets $10) mid-July to mid-Aug Tues–Sat 5pm. Closed Nov–Apr.

Drawing on some considerable local talent of all ages, this shoebox theater stages thought-provoking plays as readily as summery farces.

NANTUCKET LITERATI

✪ **Nantucket Atheneum.** Lower India St. (in the center of town), Nantucket. ☎ **508/228-1110.** Fax 508/228-1973. Free admission; call for schedule.

Continuing a 160-year tradition, the Nantucket Atheneum offers readings and lectures for general edification year-round, with such local literati as David Halberstam and Frank Conroy filling in for the likes of Henry David Thoreau and Herman Melville. The summer events are often followed by a charming garden reception.

Central & Western Massachusetts

8

by Herbert Bailey Livesey

While Boston and its maritime appendages of Cape Ann and Cape Cod face the sea and gingerly embrace it, inland Massachusetts turns in upon itself. Countless ponds and lakes pool in its folds and hollows, often hidden by deep forests and granite outcroppings, but the region grew linearly, along the north-south valleys of the Connecticut and Housatonic rivers. The heartland Pioneer Valley, embracing the first and greater watercourse, was just that in the early 18th century, when trappers and farmers began to push west from the colonies clinging to the edges of Massachusetts Bay. They were followed by visionary capitalists who erected redbrick mills along the river for the manufacture of textiles and paper. Most of those enterprises failed or faded in the post–World War II movement to the milder climate and cheaper labor of the South, leaving a diasma of economic hardship that has yet to be dispelled. But those industrialists also helped fund the establishment and growth of the several distinguished colleges for which the valley is now known, and those educated populations provide for much energy and a rich cultural life.

Roughly the same pattern applied in the Berkshires, the twin ranges of rumpled hills that define the western band of the state. There is only one college of note, however, and the development of the region in the late 18th and early 19th centuries owed more to the fact that it was accessible by railroad from New York as well as from Boston than it did to the institution itself. Artistic and literary folk made a favored summer retreat of it, followed, in the customary pattern, by wealthy people attracted by the delicious temblors of creativity and bohemianism. Their extravagent mansions, dubbed the "Berkshire Cottages," survive in great numbers, some converted to commercial use, but many still occupied by their spiritual and economic descendants. They support a vibrant summer schedule of the arts, then steal away as the crimson leaves fall and the Berkshires fall quiet beneath six months of snow.

1 Enjoying the Great Outdoors

Inland Massachusetts is rife with opportunities to partake of nature, whether by the mildly sedentary or the cut-and-toned hyper-fit visitor. A state park or forest is never more than minutes away, considering there are well over twoscore in the region and the entire width of the state from Worcester to the Berkshires can be traversed in an hour. Even the smallest and most undeveloped of these offer picnicking and walking trails, and most are available for camping, fishing, boating, hiking, and cross-country skiing as well. **October Mountain,** near Lee, and **Pittsfield State Forest,** both in the Berkshires, are especially comprehensive in their variety of possible pursuits.

The Pioneer Valley, with its generally low hills and under-used back roads close by the Connecticut River, is ideal for **biking,** and most of the larger towns have shops renting cycles. The 8 1/2-mile trail following an old railroad bed connecting Amherst and Northampton is especially convenient.

Birders and those who enjoy viewing native wildlife are served by local chapters of the Audubon Society and other organizations that set up preserves and sanctuaries with **observation trails,** as on the outskirts of Worcester, in Easthampton, and near Sheffield and Lenox, in the Berkshires.

While the state's **ski resorts** can't claim to match the vertical drops and numbers of trails found in Vermont and New Hampshire, they are nearer for New Yorkers and Bostonians, and often more family-friendly. Even the relatively flat Pioneer Valley has illuminated trails and a 3,600-foot run at Mt. Tom, and the Berkshires check in (from south to north) with Catamount (Egremont), Butternut Basin (Great Barrington), Bousquet (Pittsfield), Jiminy Peak (Hancock), and Bodie Mountain (New Ashford).

Most **golf courses** are private, but there are exceptions. Waubeeka Golf Links in South Williamstown, Pontoosuc Lake Country Club in Pittsfield, and the Egremont Country Club at the edge of Great Barrington are open to the public and greens fees are reasonable.

Those who most enjoy mildly strenuous outings on foot might want to contact **Berkshire Hiking Holidays,** P.O. Box 2231, Lenox, MA 01240 (☎ **800/877-9656** or 413/637-4442), which organizes **hikes** and **canoe trips** from May to October. These guided excursions can be as short as three days or as long as two weeks, with rates from $279 to $1,879. On their own, hikers are rewarded with 360° views at the summits of several peaks. Perhaps the most unexpected site of a scenic elevation is Joseph Skinner State Park, near South Hadley, which has been popular for leisure outings since the early 19th century. In the far southwestern corner, so near the border that it can be entered from New York State, is Bash Bish Falls. Its waters tumble between two peaks, affording a vista that stretches all the way across the Hudson River to the Catskill Mountains. The highest peak in the state, however, is Mt. Greylock, near Williamstown, a state reservation with a rustic overnight lodge near its top and a three-state panorama.

2 Worcester

43 miles W of Boston, 51 miles E of Springfield

There is a dispirited air clinging to Massachusetts' second-largest city, especially around the dilapidated edges. That observation applies to many of the region's cities, most of which reached their apogees in the late 19th century when the West was still wild and the Northeast had a hammerlock on the Industrial Revolution. Worcester has had various bootstrapping efforts with varying degrees of success, especially downtown around the towering Romanesque City Hall and the long green it fronts. And its citizens haven't given up. Those with the wherewithal bestowed by fortunes amassed a century ago have invested in a surprising number of social and political institutions, museums, historic buildings, and theatrical venues. Worcester (pronounced "Wuss-ter," or "Woos-tah" in local parlance) was the site of the first National Women's Rights Convention, held here in 1850 at Brinley Hall at 340 Main St., and the city's annual music festival claims to be the oldest in the country. While it can't be regarded as a "must" stop, the city offers enough diversion and enlightenment to fill a long day.

ESSENTIALS

GETTING THERE   Worcester is located near the juncture of the east-west Massachusetts Turnpike (I-90) and I-395, which runs south into Connecticut, connecting with I-95 to New Haven, New York, and points south.

Logan Airport in Boston, 50 miles away, is the nearest major airport. Car-rental agencies maintain offices there.

Amtrak's *Lake Shore Limited* runs daily each way through Worcester on its route between Boston and Chicago. In addition, Northeast Corridor trains run several times daily from Washington, D.C., Philadelphia, and New York, with intermediate stops, to Boston. Schedules change at least twice a year, so call (☎ **800/ 872-7245**) for up-to-date information and reservations.

VISITOR INFORMATION   Contact the **Worcester County Convention & Visitors Bureau** at 33 Waldo St., Worcester, MA 01608 (☎ **508/753-2924**). On the scene, you'll find it a block away from the Centrum. The Massachusetts Turnpike maintains marginally useful information centers on the westbound side before Exit 9 and on the eastbound side after Exit 9 (☎ **508/248-4581**).

MUSEUMS

Higgins Armory Museum. 100 Barber Ave. ☎ **508/853-6015.** Admission $4.75 adults, $4 seniors, $3.75 children 6–16. Tues–Sat 10am–4pm, Sun noon–4pm. Take I-190 to exit 1, onto MA 12 north, turn right on Barber Ave.

The steel-and-glass structure, one of the earliest of its kind, resembles a Gothic castle shining in its coat of aluminum paint. John W. Higgins was president of a company that processed steel, no doubt accounting for his interest in medieval and Renaissance armor and heraldry. He gathered many examples over his lifetime, supplementing his collection with ancient arms, paintings, stained glass, and tapestries. The results are displayed here, in a museum that opened in 1931. Sixty suits of armor, including one made for a dog, are arrayed in the main gallery, which is fashioned after an 11th-century castle. A sound-and-light show and various demonstrations bring the age of chivalry to life and there is a room in which visitors can try on armor and clothing of the period.

New England Science Center. 222 Harrington Way. ☎ **508/791-9211.** Admission $6 adults; $4 seniors, college students with ID, and children 3–16. Mon–Sat 10am–5pm, Sun noon–5pm. From Exit 14 of I-290, head east on Rte. 122 (Grafton St.), bearing left on Hamilton St., then left again on Harrington Way.

This retreat, an ambitious family-oriented institution enjoyed by children and adults alike, has brought together a planetarium, an observatory, an aquarium, and a zoo with hundreds of specimens, including the popular polar bears and eagles. Ponds and picnic areas dot the 60 acres of woods, which are traversed by a meandering nature trail. A narrow-gauge railroad is yet another attraction. Indoors, interactive displays and computers sugarcoat the somewhat diverse educational messages being addressed. In summer, a sunset jazz series is presented.

Salisbury Mansion. 40 Highland St. ☎ **508/753-8278.** Free admission; donation of $2 suggested. Thurs–Sun 1–4pm. Behind the Worcester Art Museum (below).

Dating from 1772, this historic large clapboard house has green shutters, cream trim, four chimneys, and a sizable widow's walk up top. Restoration continues, limiting the museum's open hours, with the intent of showing the interior as it would have looked in the 1830s.

✪ **Worcester Art Museum.** 55 Salisbury St. (corner of Tuckerman St.). ☎ **508/799-4406.** Admission $5 adults, $3 seniors and students with ID; children under 12 free. Wed–Fri 11am–3pm, Sat 10am–5pm, Sun 11am–5pm. Closed Sun in July and Aug, weekdays in Jan, first two weeks in Feb, and last two weeks in Aug. Museum Cafe Wed–Sun 11am–2pm when museum is open.

With a large modern concrete wing attached to the original building that faces Salisbury Street, the museum occupies most of a large city block and is therefore able to contain an unexpectedly large number of artworks. The diverse collections contain pieces from ancient Egypt and 20th-century America, a total of over 30,000 paintings, sculptures, and related objects. Particular strengths are the American wing, housing canvases by Sargent, Whistler, Ryder, and a few memorable works by anonymous colonial artists; the Europeans on the second floor, including works by Gauguin, El Greco, and Gainsborough; and the pre-Columbian artifacts on the fourth floor.

WHERE TO STAY

Pickings are slim for local lodgings, which are almost exclusively chain motels. If your itinerary includes accommodation-rich Sturbridge, under 20 miles away, consider making a day-trip to Worcester from there.

Beechwood Inn. 363 Plantation St., Worcester, MA 01605. ☎ **800/344-2589** or 508/754-5789. Fax 508/752-2060. 58 rms. A/C TV TEL. $109–$139 double. AE, CB, DC, DISC, MC, V. Free parking.

This fairly new brick building is readily identified by its round core structure, which resembles a medieval keep. The public spaces and guest rooms are adequately, not lavishly, furnished with pieces that use wood and fabric in nearly equal proportions. A hotel restaurant, The Harlequin, and an adjoining lounge are in the basement. The front desk might be willing to bargain on prices according to season and availability.

Crowne Plaza. 10 Lincoln Square (at the junction of I-290 and Rte. 9), Worcester, MA 01608. ☎ **800/227-6963** or 508/791-1600. Fax 508/791-1796. 243 rms, 7 suites. A/C TV TEL. $119–$139 double. AE, CB, DC, DISC, MC, V.

The new owners (this used to be a Marriott) undertook a year-long reconstruction that involved upgrading every part of the hotel, especially the guest rooms. In addition to the usual gadgets (TV, clock radio, hair dryers, etc.), they have added coffeemakers, magnifying makeup mirrors, and phones with dataports. The small fitness room and the indoor and outdoor pools remain, as do the two fireplaces in the lobby and adjacent dining area.

WHERE TO DINE

Bergamo's. 592 Main St. (off Franklin Square, W of City Hall). ☎ **508/753-2994.** Main courses $5.95–$11.95. AE, DC, DISC, MC, V. Mon–Wed 11:30am–9pm, Thurs 11:30am–10pm, Fri 11:30am–midnight, Sat 4pm–midnight. ITALIAN/AMERICAN.

Head here for the kind of pub grub that gets little attention from restaurant reviewers, but is nearly always satisfying. Big, bubbly, gooey, laden pizzas fit that description, as do most of the pasta variations and thickly layered sandwiches.

The atmosphere is fern bar sans greenery, with a handsome mahogany bar in front, exposed brick walls, fans turning overhead, and butcher paper over aqua tablecloths.

WORCESTER AFTER DARK

The annual **Worcester Music Festival** is only part of the cultural menu. The modern **Centrum** (50 Master St.; ☎ **508/798-8888**) and the 19th-century **Mechanics Hall** (321 Main St.; ☎ **508/752-5608**) host a variety of concerts by local and traveling solo performers and larger musical ensembles, from rock and pop to folk and classical.

A different comedy, drama, or the occasional musical is presented each month from October to April at the **Foothills Theatre Company** (Commercial Street, in the Worcester Common Fashion Outlets; ☎ **508/754-4018**).

3 Sturbridge

18 miles SW of Worcester, 32 miles E of Springfield

First things first. Sturbridge and Old Sturbridge Village aren't a single entity. The former is an organic community, populated by working people with real lives. But the presence of a greater number of motels and eating places than might be expected in a town of under 8,000 residents is owed to the latter, a fabricated early 19th-century village composed of authentic buildings moved here from other locations and peopled by docents pretending to pursuits of 170 years past. It is one of the two most prominent tourist destinations in central Massachusetts.

SPECIAL EVENTS Highly popular events in the area are the **Brimfield Antique and Collectible Shows,** when at least 3,000 dealers gather for up to six days in mid-May, mid-July, and mid-September. Brimfield is an otherwise sleepy village adjoining Sturbridge on the west. Since it has few lodging possibilities, most of the dealers and seekers stay in Sturbridge. Rooms for those periods must accordingly be reserved far in advance.

ESSENTIALS

GETTING THERE Leave the east-west Massachusetts Turnpike (I-90) at Exit 9, or the north-south I-84 at Exit 3B.

VISITOR INFORMATION The **Tri-Community Area Chamber of Commerce,** at 380 Main St. (Rte. 20) in Sturbridge (☎ **800/628-8379** or 508/347-2761), is open weekdays during regular business hours.

A 19TH-CENTURY VILLAGE

There is only one sight of significance in this otherwise pleasantly unremarkable town. Peak periods are consistent with those of the area—long holiday weekends in summer and the October foliage season in particular, but Thanksgiving and Christmas weeks at Old Sturbridge Village are special. Traditional New England dinners, concerts, and candlelit nights are only a few of the events brightening the calendar.

✪ **Old Sturbridge Village.** 1 Old Sturbridge Rd. ☎ **508/347-3362.** Admission (2-day pass) $15, $7.50 children 6–17. Apr–late Oct daily 9am–5pm; late Oct–Dec Tues–Sun 10am–4pm; Jan and first 2 weeks in Feb, weekends only 10am–4pm; mid-Feb to Mar Tues–Sun, 10am–4pm. Take exit 3B off I-84 or Exit 9 off I-90 and drive west on Rte. 20 to the entrance to the Village, on the left.

Only one of the over 40 restored structures in the complex stands on its original site—the Oliver Wight House, now part of the OSV Lodges, beside the entrance road. The rest were transported here from as far away as Maine, starting 50 years ago. All are authentic buildings, not re-creations, and they represent the living quarters and places of trade and commerce of a settlement of the 1830s. Among these are a Quaker meeting house, a sawmill, a bank, and a school. Costumed docents perform carefully researched demonstrations of blacksmithing, hearth cooking, glassmaking, printing, potting, and carpentry. Visitors are welcome to question them as they go about their daily tasks. These change with the seasons, and special events and activities mark such dates as Washington's Birthday, Mother's Day, and the 4th of July. Town meetings, weddings, militia drills, and a harvest fair are staged. Meals are available in Bullard Tavern, and a gift shop and bookstore are open during museum hours.

WHERE TO STAY

Old Sturbridge Village Lodges. Rte. 20 west, Sturbridge, MA 01566. ☎ **508/347-3362.** Fax 508/347-3018. 59 rms. A/C TV TEL. $110–$130 double, May–Oct; $65–$85 double, Nov–Apr. Extra person $5. AE, DISC, MC, V.

Apart from the over-200-year-old Oliver Wight House, which serves as a centerpiece, these six barnlike structures arranged around a common and a swimming pool are of post–World War II origin. Rooms are fresh, fairly spacious, and straightforward, with colonial reproductions. All have double or queen-size beds. Morning coffee is available in the office.

Publick House. Rte. 131 (Box 187), Sturbridge, MA 01566. ☎ **508/347-3313.** 17 rms. $85–$130 double (historic rooms), $55–$89 double (motel). AE, CB, DC, MC, V. From Exit 3B of I-84, drive 1.5 miles south of Rte. 20 on 131.

This four-building establishment is the high-profile lodging in the Sturbridge area. Apart from the main structure, built in 1771, additional accommodations are in the Colonel Ebenezer Crafts Inn, a 1786 Federalist farmhouse; the Chamberlain House, adjacent to the Publick House; and the Country Motor Lodge, which is what it sounds like. Go for the relatively peaceful eight-room Ebenezer Crafts Inn, a free-standing bed-and-breakfast a mile from the Publick House that has its own swimming pool and serves afternoon tea. Those who insist on room TVs need to look elsewhere, unless they can settle for the one in the common room. There are three adequate restaurants associated with the Publick House, serving mostly traditional New England dishes.

☉ **Sturbridge Coach Motor Lodge.** 408 Main St., Sturbridge, MA 01566. ☎ **508/347-7327.** 54 rms. A/C TV TEL. $60–$95 double, May–Oct; $45–$60 Nov–Apr. AE, MC, V.

You've seen it all before, from the avocado bathroom fixtures to the paper strip across the toilet seat to the wrapped plastic cups. But the rates are among the lowest in the area and the location is 200 yards from the entrance to Old Sturbridge Village. There's a pool next to the parking lot and free coffee in the office in the morning. Rates go higher over long weekends and during high-profile local events, like the Brimfield Antique Shows.

WHERE TO DINE

Rom's. Rte. 131 (2 miles south of Rte. 20). ☎ **508/347-3349.** Main courses $5.95–$8.75. AE, DISC, MC, V. Sun–Thurs 11:30am–9pm (until 10pm Fri–Sat). ITALIAN/AMERICAN.

This was once a hot dog and fried clam roadside stand that grew and grew over 40 years like a multigenerational New England farmhouse. Today it can seat 700 diners at a time on two levels, but remains a near-ideal family restaurant, with something to please everyone. Liquor is available, but only from a service bar, discouraging the hard-drinking crowd. The Wednesday night (5 to 9pm) and Thursday lunch (11:30am to 2pm) buffets are crowd-pleasers, as are the always low prices.

A takeout window shovels out "buckets of rigatoni," fish 'n' chips, and shrimp in a basket, among other favorites.

The Whistling Swan/Ugly Duckling. 502 Main St. (Rte. 20). ☎ **508/347-2331.** Reservations not accepted. Main courses $13.95–$21.95. AE, CB, DC, MC, V. Whistling Swan, Mon–Sat 11:30am–2:30pm and 5:30–9:30pm (until 10pm Sat), Sun noon–8pm; Ugly Duckling, Tues–Sun 11:30am–11pm (until 11:30pm Fri and Sat). CONTINENTAL/AMERICAN.

An 1855 Greek Revival mansion has been converted to house two restaurants that share a kitchen. On the main floor are the three rooms of the Whistling Swan, with widely-spaced tables, wall sconces, and Sheraton-style chairs. The menu lists conventional "continental" dishes—frog legs Provençal, sole with orange-lime sauce, even surf and turf. Their execution proves to be safe and careful, and the service is efficient, if rather unsophisticated, given the pretensions. Upstairs, the Ugly Duckling packs tables together under the rough-cut board roof and a big brass chandelier. Patrons strive to be heard over the live piano. It is loud, even boisterous. The food is simple and hearty. Which venue to choose? I'd mount the stairs, in a New York minute.

4 Springfield

89 miles W of Boston, 23 miles N of Hartford

Times have been stressful of late in this once-prosperous manufacturing city on the east bank of the Connecticut River. But its loyal citizens haven't given in to the consequences of job flight and high unemployment, and there is evidence of redevelopment throughout the downtown district, with recycled loft and factory buildings standing beside modern glass towers. It remains the most important city in the western part of Massachusetts not dominated by Boston, and has succeeded in attracting new enterprises, notably in plastics, toolmaking, and electronic equipment.

ESSENTIALS

GETTING THERE Springfield is located near the juncture of the east-west Massachusetts Turnpike (I-90), a toll highway, and north-south I-91, and is readily accessible from every city in the Northeast.

Bradley International (☎ **203/627-3000**) in Windsor Locks, Conn., is the nearest major airport, about 20 miles to the south. There are car-rental agencies and the Marriott and Sheraton hotels provide airport transportation for their guests.

Amtrak's *Lake Shore Limited* runs daily between Boston and Chicago and the *Vermonter* runs daily between Washington, D.C., and Burlington, Vt., with connecting buses from Montréal, Québec, and intermediate stops at New York and Hartford, among others. Schedules change at least twice a year, however, so call **800/872-7245** for up-to-date information and reservations.

VISITOR INFORMATION The **Greater Springfield Convention and Visitors Bureau** (☎ **413/787-1548**) is at 34 Boland Way, Springfield, MA 01103.

SPECIAL EVENTS A highlight of the annual calendar is the **Eastern States Exposition,** held on a fairground on the opposite side of the Connecticut River in West Springfield in mid-September. Also on the grounds is the **Old Storrowtown Village,** a collection of restored colonial buildings, accessible by guided tour, Monday to Saturday, from June to Labor Day.

MUSEUMS & HISTORIC SITES

Springfield has nurtured its share of wealthy benefactors, and enough of them gave back to their community to produce a number of museums of varying levels of interest. The more conventional are the four clustered around the grassy quadrangle behind the Springfield Library. In addition, there are three specialized museums that do their duty well but can easily be skipped by those who don't share those interests: the Springfield Armory and Basketball Hall of Fame are described below, and bikers real and imaginary will also want to check out the **Indian Motorcycle Museum** (33 Hendee St.; ☎ 413/737-2624).

Basketball Hall of Fame. W. Columbus Ave. (at Union St.). ☎ **413/781-6500.** Admission $8 adults 16 and over, $5 seniors and children 7–15. July 1–Labor Day 9am–6pm (until 5pm rest of year).

Dr. James Naismith invented basketball in Springfield in 1891, providing the logic for this memorial and entertainment center. A definite must for fans, it is painless even for those who regard the game as a blur of seven-foot armpits. Take the elevator to the third floor and work your way down. Up there are the inductees and displays recalling the history of the game. Descriptions of the early years are surprising. Remember the Waterloo Hawks? Pittsburgh Ironmen? Indianapolis Kautskys? Or the Philadelphia Hebrews? The Hall covers every aspect of the game, from high school to the NBA to the Olympics, as well as such offshoots as wheelchair leagues and the Harlem Globetrotters. An updated map of the United States announces the latest boys' and girls' champs in every state. No aspect of the sport is too small, attested by the collections of Topps cards and sneakers. On the ground floor is a shooting court with baskets at various heights, and next to it a virtual reality fantasy, in which visitors can insert themselves on a large viewing screen and play against the pros.

Matoon Street Historic District. Between Chestnut and Elliot sts.

Built between 1870 and the 1890s, this harmonious, largely unsullied block of Queen Anne Victorian and Romanesque Revival rowhouses is worth a short detour after visiting the Quadrangle Museums. One of the semi-famous residents was Lawrence O'Brien, postmaster general in the Kennedy administration and former Commissioner of the National Basketball Association. He lived at numbers 29 and 43. The street is dominated at the eastern end by a looming church designed by H. H. Richardson, the architect of Boston's Trinity Church. Turn south at the church onto Elliot Street, where there are a couple of impressively proportioned wooden Victorians.

Museums at the Quadrangle. 220 State St. (corner of Chestnut St.). ☎ **413/739-3871.** Admission $4 adults, $1 children 6–18; $1 more for the planetarium. Wed–Sun noon–4pm.

Four museums and a library surrounding a single inner quadrangle constitute this unusually rich resource, much of it resulting from the generosity of those who benefited from the industrial prosperity of the city during the 19th and early 20th centuries. A good way to begin a tour is to enter the library from State Street and walk through to the back. Out there, on the right, is the first museum, and the others can be visited around the quad in a counterclockwise circuit. A ticket bought in any of the museums is good for all the others. Before setting out, note the restricted open hours.

The **George Walter Vincent Smith Art Museum**'s eponymous donor, a wealthy carriage manufacturer, assembled an extensive, eclectic collection he installed in this 1896 Italian Renaissance–style mansion. Proceeding upstairs, you'll find a gallery of largely sentimental pastoral scenes, with a few small landscapes by George Inness,

Thomas Cole, and Alfred Bierstadt. Subsequent rooms house substantial numbers of Apulian red-figured vases and Chinese cloisonné, a form of pottery that employs metal, glass, and enamel. They are followed by rooms of Oriental carpets and prettily inconsequential Italian landscapes, many of Venice. On the main floor are cases of Japanese samurai armor and weaponry surrounding an arresting, heavily carved Shinto shrine dating from 1805.

Likely to be the biggest winner with children, the **Science Museum** contains a planetarium (showtime at 2:45pm), dioramas of large African animals, and downstairs, the Monsato Eco-Center. This new section strives for elusive cohesion with some interactive devices, aquariums with native and tropical fish, a boa and poisonous frogs, and scattered other exhibits.

You enter the **Connecticut River Valley Historical Museum** through a gateway that is a representation of the hat worn by Dr. Seuss's famous Cat in the Hat. (The children's author grew up in Springfield.) Inside are examples of weapons made by the city's firearms manufacturers, including a blunderbuss and an unusual 1838 rifle with a revolving cartridge chamber. Exhibits pertaining to local history and a genealogy library are of limited interest, but you may find the temporary exhibits upstairs appealing.

The strongest and most professionally organized repository of the lot is the **☉ Museum of Fine Arts,** which has 20 galleries with canvases by European and American artists. The latter are the most interesting, with examples of colonial paintings on through Gilbert Stuart and John Copley to early 20th-century realists George Bellows and Reginald Marsh and culminating with both magic realists and abstract expressionists of recent decades, sampling Frank Stella, Helen Frankenthaler, Don Eddy, and George Sugarman. Make a particular effort to view the remarkable seriograph of lower Manhattan by Richard Estes.

Springfield Armory. 1 Armory Sq. ☎ 413/734-8551. Free admission. Tues–Sun 10am–5pm. Take State St. east from downtown, turn left on Federal St., and left again onto the grounds of Springfield Technical Community College. Follow the signs.

A National Historic Site, the several buildings of the armory center around the Main Arsenal, constructed in the 1840s on a hillside site chosen by George Washington in 1777. The armory, which was government-funded and -operated, closed in 1966. Now a museum, it traces the evolution of weapons made here and by private manufacturers. Starting with rack after rack of flintlocks and percussion cap rifles, the collection proceeds with case after case of bolt-action and automatic weapons. One section illustrates the crafting of the guns with videos and actual machines. A small screening room runs a film on the history of the Armory.

WHERE TO STAY

Marriott Springfield. Boland and Columbus aves., Springfield, MA 01115. ☎ 413/731-8932. Fax 413/731-8932. 264 rms. A/C TV TEL. $139–$149 double. AE, DC, DISC, MC, V.

Easy to find just off the Springfield Center exit of I-91, this can be a reassuring treat after a few nights at often delightful but frequently quirky New England inns. Predictable, yes, but tuck into a room with all the standard goodies (cable TV with a score or two of hit movies on order, iron and board, hair dryer, coffeemaker, and phone with dataport) and lack of charm can suddenly seem unimportant. Especially when it's combined with room service, a handy parking garage, a friendly bar, a capable grill restaurant, and an executive floor with a private breakfast lounge.

Sheraton Monarch Place. 1 Monarch Place, Springfield, MA 01104. ☎ 413/781-1010. Fax 413/734-3249. 304 rms. A/C TV TEL. $89–$155 double. AE, DC, DISC, MC, V.

And to Think That I Saw It on Mulberry Street

The grandparents of Theodor Seuss Geisel lived on Springfield's Mulberry Street, and in 1937 the writer and illustrator later known as Dr. Seuss named the first of his dozens of children's books for the neighborhood. He followed up with such classics as *How the Grinch Stole Christmas* (1957), *Horton Hatches the Egg* (1940), and *The Cat in the Hat* (1957). Every last title is still in print, and over 100 million copies have been sold.

Geisel spent most of his adult life in California, the result of a nearly two-decade career in documentary films, during which he won two Academy Awards. But much of his inspiration for the children's books to which he returned can be traced to Springfield. His drawing of Bartholomew Cubbins's castle bears a strong resemblance to the Howard Street Armory, now a community center, and certain of his landscapes look as if they were recalled from his playtimes in Forest Park, near his boyhood home at 74 Fairfield St.

Mulberry Street is no longer the august avenue it once must have been, its Victorian manses now crowded by undistinguished apartment blocks and commercial strips. And the former Central High School from which Geisel graduated is now a condominium.

To get a sense of what this hotel has to offer, look at the description of the Marriott Springfield, directly above. The differences between the two hotels are too few to matter. Both have indoor pools and exercise rooms with saunas, both provide transportation to Bradley Airport. They're even directly across Boland Way from each other. Marriott rooms do have two phones while the Sheraton's rooms only have one.

WHERE TO DINE

Pioneer Valley Brew Pub. 51–59 Taylor St. (near Dwight St.). ☎ **413/732-2739.** Main courses $7.95–$18.95. Mon–Sat 11:30am–9pm (Thurs–Sat until 10pm), Sun 1–9pm. AE, MC, V. ECLECTIC AMERICAN.

Only open since March 1995, this sprightly brewpub is a welcome addition to a forlorn local dining scene. They describe the room as "Deco Diner," as close a description as is likely to be contrived. The main room is spacious, and a second one in the back overlooks a warm-weather dining terrace.

In addition to a regular slate of ales and lagers on tap (try Armory Amber), there are seasonal special brews (Spring Bok was a winner). They wash down such tasty dishes as Flemish stew in a sourdough boule and beer-battered chicken with a cashew dipping sauce. Even pedestrian sirloin is dressed up with a chili-cumin rub and a garlic-flavored custard.

Student Prince and The Fort. 8 Fort St. (west of Main St.). ☎ **413/734-7475.** Main courses $7.95–$19.75. Mon–Sat 11am–11pm, Sun noon–10pm. AE, DC, DISC, MC, V. GERMAN/AMERICAN.

In 1935, German immigrants opened a cafe they called the Student Prince and served beer in steins with schnitzels, sauerbraten, and hasenpfeffer. That might not have seemed the precise historical moment to ensure the success of such an enterprise, but it thrived. In 1946, they were able to add a large dining room next door, which they chose to call The Fort. The resulting complex is arguably the most popular eating place in town. Waitresses rush about in sensible shoes and frumpish uniforms, slapping plates down and tolerating no lip from playful patrons. They bring monster portions of everything—veal shanks as thick as a linebacker's forearm, a plate of wurst heaped high with sausages, boiled potatoes, and sauerkraut. Check out the enormous stein collection at the bar. Some are more than two feet tall.

Tavern Inn. 91 W. Gardner St. (on the corner of West Columbus Ave.). ☎ 413/736-0456. Main courses $5.95–$12.95. Mon–Fri 11:30am–2:30pm and 4:30–9pm (Thurs–Fri until 10pm), Sun 12–9pm. AE, MC, V. ITALIAN/AMERICAN.

Guileless as they come, this place is exactly what it seems to be. Two blocks south of the Basketball Hall of Fame, the Tavern has a sports bar–style atmosphere, with big TVs in both rooms, silently tuned to whatever game is on, but the mood is affable, not raucous. Meal options include manicotti and veal Florentine, and just about everything comes with a salad of iceburg lettuce and a choice of spaghetti, ziti, fries, or baked potato. None of it is so spectacular that it will interfere with conversation, but it is relatively cheap. Wines are available by the glass.

SPRINGFIELD AFTER DARK

The Springfield Symphony Orchestra offers performances at **Symphony Hall** (127 Main St.; ☎ 413/787-6610) from October to May. **Stagewest** produces a September-May theatrical series that concentrates on late 20th-century plays by such luminaries as A. R. Gurney and Edward Albee. The shows are mounted at **One Columbus Center** (☎ 413/781-2340) between Worthington and Bridge streets. The nearby **Paramount Performing Arts Center** (1700 Main St.; ☎ 413/734-5706) is a restored 1920s movie palace that hosts concerts by traveling pop, rock, comedy, and country performers.

5 The Pioneer Valley

In the Pioneer Valley, low billowing hills and quilted fields embrace the Connecticut River as it runs south to the Atlantic. The earliest pioneers came here for what proved to be uncommonly fertile soil, and were followed in the 19th century by men who harnessed the power of the river and became wealthy textile and paper manufacturers. They took the lead in initiating and funding the institutions of higher learning that are now the pride of the region. Prestigious Smith, Mt. Holyoke, and Amherst are here, as are innovative Hampshire College and the sprawling main campus of the University of Massachusetts, with its enrollment of over 25,000 students. All five contribute mightily to the cultural life of the valley and Northampton, Amherst, and South Hadley are invigorated by the vitality of thousands of college-age young people. In the north, near Vermont, the living village of Deerfield preserves the architecture and atmosphere of colonial New England, but without the whiff of sterility that afflicts artificial gatherings of old buildings with costumed docents.

Interstate 91 and Route 5 traverse the valley from south to north, and the trip from edge to edge on the Interstate can be accomplished in under an hour. That being the case, Route 5 tenders more of the flavor of pastoral vistas and colorful mill towns. There are ample numbers of motels along the way, but those who desire lodgings more representative of the character of the region may wish to contact the **Folkstone Bed & Breakfast Reservation Service** (☎ 800/762-2751 or 508/480-0380). They have listings throughout Central Massachusetts with rates of $50 to $150 a night and accept MasterCard and Visa.

ESSENTIALS

GETTING THERE   From Boston and upstate New York, take the Massachusetts Turnpike (I-90), a toll highway, to Springfield, then follow I-91 or Route 5 north. While there are local buses, a car is by far the most convenient way to travel the valley.

The nearest major airport is **Bradley International** (☎ 203/627-3000) south of Springfield, in Connecticut. A private service called **Valley Transporter** (☎ 800/872-8752 or 413/549-1350) offers van shuttles between Bradley and Amherst, Northampton, Hadley, Holyoke, and Deerfield.

Amtrak's *Vermonter* stops in Amherst and Northampton on its daily trips between Burlington, Vt. and Washington, D.C., but schedules change at least twice yearly, so call **800/872-7245** for up-to-date information and reservations.

VISITOR INFORMATION   The **Pioneer Valley Tourist Information Center** (☎ 413/665-7333) is at the intersection of Routes 5 and 10 in South Deerfield.

HOLYOKE

8 miles N of Springfield, 88 miles W of Boston

Once an important paper manufacturing center, Holyoke has suffered a long economic slide since the flight of industry to warmer, cheaper climes after World War II. Abandoned brick factories and a dissolute air to the commercial center don't bolster first impressions. Still, there are a couple of modestly worthwhile sights and a pleasant inn for a meal or an overnight stay.

A HALL OF FAME & A HOUSE MUSEUM

Volleyball Hall of Fame. 44 Dwight St. (next to Heritage Park). ☎ **413/536-0926.** Free admission. Tues–Fri 10am–5pm, Sat–Sun noon–5pm.

The valley abounds with specialized museums that needn't detain any traveler who doesn't harbor the specific interests they address, and this is one of them. Volleyball was invented in Holyoke by one William Morgan in 1895, an event commemorated by this one room in a converted mill shared with a **children's museum**. If you're a passionate volleyball fan, you'll find this place fascinating; if you barely know the difference between volleyball and basketball, you'll be more than underwhelmed. It's your call.

Wistariahurst Museum. 238 Cabot St. ☎ **413/534-2216.** Free admission for tours; special musical events $5–$10. Apr–Oct Wed and Sat–Sun 1–5pm; Nov–Mar Wed and Sat–Sun noon–4pm. Closed last 2 weeks Aug.

Skinner is a name that pops up with some regularity in these parts. This was once the home of William Skinner, a silk manufacturer, and though it looks a little the worse for wear of late, it retains a fine marble vestibule, coffered ceilings, and Tiffany windows. This is essentially a house museum, with paintings, objects, and furnishings of the late 19th century. The museum's great hall is a venue for frequent musical events.

OUTDOOR PURSUITS

Canals dug during the city's heyday as a paper manufacturing center still cut through the downtown area, intended to allow access to its mills and a bypass around a dam in the Connecticut River. Linear **Heritage State Park** (221 Appleton St.; ☎ 413/534-1723) runs beside one of the canals, and has an interpretive center that offers walking tours and exhibits limning the history of the industrial glory days. On most Sundays from mid-June to late August, the ancient locomotive of the **Heritage Park Railroad** pulls three cars of train buffs on a two-hour, five-mile trip downriver from the park to Holyoke Mall at Ingleside. Times and fares vary, since demand and funds fluctuate. Call Heritage State Park for more information.

For **skiing,** hit **Mt. Tom** (two miles north of the city center off MA 5; ☎ 413/536-0416), which, at 1,150 feet, won't remind anyone of the Jungfrau, but still has 15 mostly intermediate trails, and a long run of 3,600 feet. They are illuminated at night and snowmaking equipment is at hand. Rentals are available. All-day lift tickets are $29 adults, $25 seniors and children 9 to 12. Summer recreational facilities include an artificial wave pool and water slide as well as hiking trails.

WHERE TO STAY & DINE

Yankee Pedlar Inn. 1866 Northampton St. (MA 5), Holyoke, MA 01040. ☎ **413/532-9494.** 30 rms. A/C TV TEL. $65–$100 double. Rates include breakfast. AE, CB, DC, DISC, MC, V. Five blocks east of Exit 16 off I-91.

A detailed description will be out-of-date before this ink is dry, for a vigorous young manager has big plans for this Victorian inn, and renovations and new construction continue at a brisk pace. Of the five buildings in the complex, the 1850 house has the most modern rooms. Some rooms have canopied beds, and four of the 15 suites have kitchenettes. The main dining room, with its breezy menu and lively bar, is popular with locals as well as travelers.

SOUTH HADLEY

15 miles N of Springfield, 7 miles S of Amherst

Pioneer educator Mary Lyon founded Mt. Holyoke Female Seminary in 1836 and presided over it for 12 years. One of the "Seven Sisters" group of prestigious women's colleges, it emphasizes liberal arts and preparation for the service professions. Strung along the eastern side of Route 116 (College Street), the college is the essential reason for the existence of this small town (population 13,600), although it was settled in the late 17th century.

On the campus is an admirable **Art Museum** (☎ **413/538-2245**), which focuses on art of the Orient, Egypt, and the Mediterranean, but also mounts temporary exhibits on a considerable range of topics. Admission is free. Hours are Tuesday to Friday from 11am to 5pm, Saturday and Sunday from 1 to 5 pm. To find it, take Park Street from the east side of the "Y" intersection in the center of town and follow the signs.

Joseph Skinner State Park (☎ **413/586-0350**) straddles the border between South Hadley and Hadley. On its 390 acres are miles of walking trails, picnic grounds, and the historic Summit House. The building (open weekends only from May to October) was erected in a single day in 1821 by a group of energetic male friends who wanted a place to party with copious quantities of gin, rum, cigars, and panoramic views of the valley.

A tastefully designed mall called **The Village Commons** (☎ **413/532-3600**) stands alongside Route 116 opposite the Mount Holyoke campus. Over 30 shops, including a movie theater, three eating places, and the admirable **Odyssey Bookshop,** are clustered in white clapboard buildings suggesting a classic New England village.

NORTHAMPTON

21 miles N of Springfield, 16 miles S of Deerfield

Smith College, with its campus sprawling along Main Street slightly west of the commercial center, is Northampton's dominating physical and spiritual presence. One of the original "Seven Sisters" before that informal league of women's colleges was broken up by coeducation, Smith is the largest female liberal-arts college in the United States.

Northampton was long the home of Calvin Coolidge, who pursued his law practice here before and after his monosyllablic occupancy of the Oval Office. (At a White House dinner, the laconic Silent Cal was seated next to a woman who said she had made a bet she could get three words out of him. "You lose," he said.) He lived in houses at 21 Massasoit St. and on Hampton Terrace, but the homes are privately owned and not open to the public. A room containing many of his papers is maintained by the **Forbes Library** (20 West St.; ☎ 413/584-8399).

SEEING THE SIGHTS

Museum Houses. 46 Bridge St. (east of the railroad bridge). ☎ **413/584-6011.** Admission $3 adults, $1 children 7–12. Tours Mar–Dec, Wed–Sun noon–4pm.

Some of Northampton's most popular attractions are the Museum Houses, a clutch of expertly restored and maintained houses that include some eyecatching Victorians and the three historic houses that constitute *Historic Northampton.* They are the 1712 Parsons House, the 1796 Shepherd House, and the 1812 Isaac Damon House. The last contains a furnished parlor true to 1820, while the Parson House stages exhibits of furniture and the decorative arts.

Smith College

To a considerable extent, the campus buildings that line Elm Street are a testament to the excesses of late 19th-century architecture. Their often egregious admixtures of Gothic, Greco-Roman, Renaissance, and medieval esthetic notions lend a Teutonic sobriety to the west end of town.

That aside, one of those ponderous brown monoliths houses a worthwhile **Museum of Art** (76 Elm St. at Bedford Terrace; ☎ 413/584-2700). Included in its permanent holdings of over 24,000 works of the late 19th and 20th centuries are paintings by Degas, Monet, Picasso, and Winslow Homer. Admission is free. It's open September to June Tuesdays, Fridays, and Saturdays from 9:30am to 4pm, Wednesdays and Sundays noon to 4pm, and Thursdays noon to 8pm; in July and August hours are Tuesday to Sunday from noon to 4pm.

Words & Pictures Museum. 140 Main St. ☎ **413/586-8545.** Admission $3 adults, $1 children under 18. Tues–Wed and Sat–Sun noon–5pm, Thurs noon–8pm.

Don't let the fact that funding is provided in part by a creator of the Teenage Mutant Ninja Turtles lead to the conclusion that this repository of comic-book illustrations is just the place to take the kiddies. Most of the work on display, while expertly rendered, is of the decidedly adult variety, with action characters demonstrating a predilection for violence as well as for costumes of an S&M persuasion displaying more than just a few bared breasts and buttocks. Parents with children should escort their charges through the mock "cave" entrance onto the elevator directly to the second floor, where there are interactive computer games and a replica of a Ninja Turles movie set.

OUTDOOR PURSUITS

Three miles southwest of town on Route 10 in Easthampton is the **Arcadia Nature Center and Wildlife Sanctuary** (☎ 413/584-3009), a 625-acre preserve operated by the Audubon Society. It contains a mixed ecology of marshes and woods bordering the Connecticut River. Over five miles of well-tended trails provide access to a variety of flora and fauna. The Sanctuary is open dawn to dusk, Tuesday to Saturday. Admission is $3 for nonmember adults, $2 for children.

Cyclists make good use of the **Norwottuck Trail Bike Path,** an 8¹/₂-mile trail that follows a former railroad bed running between Northampton and Amherst, reached by an old bridge across the river. Access can be made on Damon Road and at Mt. Farms Mall. Bikes can be rented at **Valley Bicycles** (319 Main St.; ☎ 413/256-0880) across the river in Amherst. **Look Memorial Park** (300 N. Main St.; ☎ 413/584-5457) is northwest of town off Route 9, with 157 acres of woods, a

5-acre lake, picnic grounds, and a small zoo of native animals. Boats are available for rent. There are musical and theatrical events, including puppet shows, in summer.

SHOPPING

One of the pleasures of college towns for bibliophiles and browsers are the larger-than-usual numbers of bookstores, often dealing in exotica not found in the big national chains. Northampton has those, in abundance, but also enjoys the most diverting shopping in the valley. All of the following stores are open seven days a week.

The **Antique Center of Northampton** (9½ Market St.; ☎ 413/584-3600) contains the stalls of over 60 independent dealers on three floors. **Pinch Pottery and the Ferrin Gallery** (179 Main St.; ☎ 413/586-4509) offers superb contemporary jewelry, glassware, and ceramics, and represents elite craftspeople whose works are found in the distinguished White House Collection. There are no bargains, but there are affordable pieces. CDs, greeting cards, and stationery supplement the extensive stock of the two-level **Beyond Words Bookshop** (189 Main St.; ☎ 413/586-6304). The store motto is "Book lovers never go to bed alone." A former department store has been reconfigured into **Thorne's Marketplace** (150 Main St.; ☎ 413/584-5582), which now contains over 30 specialty boutiques on five floors. The enthusiastic owner of **Tianguis** (7 Old South St.; ☎ 413/586-6723; pronounced "tee-AHN-gees") regularly travels to Mexico to flesh out her colorful stock of ceramics, textiles, and folk crafts. Most of the items are from Puebla, Oaxaca, and Guanajuato, and are quite fairly priced.

WHERE TO STAY

This being a college town, with frequent influxes of parents and alumnae during graduations, homecomings, and other events, anticipate higher rates and limited vacancies at times in addition to the usual holiday weekends.

Autumn Inn. 259 Elm St., Northampton, MA 01060. ☎ 413/584-7660. Fax 413/586-4808. 28 rms, 2 suites. A/C TV TEL. $96 double. AE, CB, DC, MC, V.

A genteel hotel in remotely Georgian style, the Autumn is conveniently situated opposite the quieter northern end of the Smith College campus. Most rooms have two double beds. There is a restaurant with a huge woodburning fireplace serving breakfast and lunch (not dinner). In summer, an unheated pool beckons. Smoking isn't permitted on the second floor, in the lobby, or in the dining room.

Hotel Northampton. 36 King St., Northampton, MA 01060. ☎ 413/584-3100. Fax 413/584-9455. 77 rms. A/C TV TEL. $83–$180 double. AE, CB, DC, DISC, MC, V.

Built in 1927, this five-story brick building at the center of town looks older. An admirable restoration and modernization has brought it up to date, with rooms containing lots of wicker and colonial reproductions, floral prints, feather duvets, and assorted Victoriana. Many front rooms have balconies overlooking King Street, some have canopied beds, a few have Jacuzzis. This is a nonsmoking hotel.

Service in the hotel's Coolidge Park Cafe is pleasant enough, but glacial in execution. Downstairs, Wiggins Tavern is an authentic colonial watering hole that predates the hotel by a couple of centuries, with dark beams and stone fireplaces. If you value your limited time, eat elsewhere.

Inn at Northampton. Rte. 5 and I-91, Northampton, MA 01060. ☎ 413/586-1211. Fax 413/586-0630. 124 rms. A/C TV TEL. $90–$130 double. AE, DISC, MC, V.

Easily accessible just west of Exit 18 off I-91, this inn is hidden behind a Mobil gas station, and the entrance isn't clearly marked. Renovations have elevated it from a standard motel to something less readily categorized, closer to a modest resort, with its lighted tennis court and two swimming pools, one of them indoors. Though the recreational amenities are impressive, they need to work on their breakfasts, which primarily consist of canned juice and boxed cereals.

Eastside Grill. 19 Strong Ave. (1 block south of Bridge St.). ☎ **413/586-3347.** Main courses $9.95–$14.95. AE, MC, V. Mon–Sat 11:30am–2:30pm and 5–10pm (until 11pm Fri–Sat); Sun 4–9pm. REGIONAL AMERICAN.

The consensus choice for tops in town, this white clapboard building with a nautical look is small for the amount of business it does. The long, far-reaching menu has noticeable bayou riffs, such as chicken etouffée and shrimp and andouille jambalaya. But while the Cajun/Creole canon obviously absorbs much of the kitchen's attention, there are ample alternatives. The seafood is impressive, as is the blackened scallops appetizer. And you'd do well to end your meal with New Orleans pudding—pecans, coconut, and raisins in a bread custard doused with a bourbon sauce.

Fitzwilly's. 21 Main St. (near Pleasant St.). ☎ **413/584-8666.** Main courses $9.95–$13.95. AE, DC, DISC, MC, V. Daily 11:30am–1am. AMERICAN.

Occupying a historic building constructed in 1898, this ingratiating pub makes the most of its high stamped-tin ceilings and ample space. Big copper brewing kettles constitute much of the decor, a signal that there is an intriguing selection of beers on tap, some of them from regional microbreweries. Beyond the two long bars are curtained booths where patrons dive into grilled pizzas, burgers, ribs, or maybe the club sandwich on slabs of warm focaccia bread. There are also low-cal, low-fat "spa" dishes, like the vegetable stir-fry.

La Cazuela. 7 Old South St. (down the hill from Main St.). ☎ **413/586-0400.** Main courses $9.75–$11.95. AE, DISC, MC, V. Mon–Thurs 5–9pm, Fri 5–10pm, Sat 3–10pm, Sun 3–9pm. SOUTHWESTERN/MEXICAN.

The menu at this restaurant mixes recipes of the American Southwest with those of Mexico, and the kitchen takes its job quite seriously. In addition to the predictable flautas, enchiladas, and chimichangas, frequently changed special dinners explore the cuisines of less known gastronomic regions, such as the Yucatán in such dishes as *pollo asado de Yucatán,* a chicken roasted in a banana leaf.

   La Cazuela is one of several businesses in a rustic 1850 building, and earth tones and Mexican artifacts give the interior a Santa Fe look. Smoking is not permitted.

La Veracruzana. 31 Main St. (near Pleasant St.). ☎ **413/586-7181.** Main courses $5.45–$7.95. No credit cards. Daily 11am–10pm (until 11pm Thurs, until midnight Fri–Sat). SOUTHWESTERN/MEXICAN.

Choose from the big handwritten menu over the counter next to the kitchen in back—lunch or snack items like burritos, tostadas, tacos, and fajitas, or more serious plates in the order of *pechuga de pollo en mole poblano:* chicken breast in the famous Mexican chocolate-based (but spicy, not sweet) sauce. If you go with a friend, share the six-taco package deal (in any style or combination) for only $7.95. There's a free salsa bar, and beer and wine are also now available.

Vermont Country Deli & Cafe. 48 Main St. (near Pleasant St.). ☎ **413/586-7114.** Main courses $5.50–$7.95. MC, V. Daily 7:30am–7pm. ECLECTIC.

The eye-catching sign out front only says "French Bakery," but the appetizing sights glimpsed through the window drag people inside. On the right is a long case crowded with platters of tantalizing salads and main courses, so many they can barely be cataloged. A partial list: Hunan orange chicken, sesame noodles, grilled vegetables,

Vietnamese pasta salad, and spinach knishes. Fat focaccia sandwiches are made to order, including one with "Cajun" turkey, lettuce, and tomato with a coriander horseradish dressing. On the opposite side of the room are plump sticky buns, lemon poppy muffins, sourdough baguettes, and several urns of various coffees. Eat at one of the few tables in back, or keep it in mind for takeout picnics.

NORTHAMPTON AFTER DARK

The presence of Smith College only partially accounts for the large number of music bars and clubs in town, making Northampton the nightlife magnet of the valley. In April, the **Loud Music Festival** rattles walls with over 250 alternative rock bands from around the country. For a rundown of what's happening, pick up a copy of the *Optimist*, a weekly handout. Here are only three of over a dozen possibilities.

Academy of Music. 74 Main St. ☎ **413/584-8453.**

This fine old music hall—104-years-old and thriving—serves several functions, and has done so since the Barrymores (actors John, Ethel, and Lionel) came through town. It shows big-screen films as well as providing a venue for opera, ballet, and stellar pop performers on tour. The hall operates irregularly, and attractions and prices vary, so call ahead for details.

Iron Horse Music Hall. 20 Center St. ☎ **413/584-0610.**

This old favorite has played host to an enormous variety of artists, from famous folkies Bonnie Raitt, Tom Rush, and Richie Havens, to obscure but no less gratifying Celtic fiddlers, blues belters, and grunge rockers. It's open nightly, but covers vary, so call ahead.

Pearl Street Nightclub. 10 Pearl St. ☎ **413/584-7771.**

Live alternative bands alternate with DJ dance parties at this two-floor club. There are often dance party nights targeted at teenagers or gays (usually Wednesdays). Call ahead for details on specific events. The club is closed on Mondays.

AMHERST

7 miles E of Northampton, 16 miles SE of Deerfield

Winter naturally suppresses the street activity of this otherwise lively college town, but any hint of a break in the weather has students, faculty members, and townspeople jogging, bounding, strolling, and greeting each other as they gravitate toward the shops and cafes clustered around the downtown intersection of Pleasant, Amity, and Main streets. Yet another Pioneer Valley town that would be deeply diminished by the absence of its educational institutions, this one would have even more to lose than most, with distinguished Amherst College occupying much of its center, the large University of Massachusetts campus to its immediate northwest, and Hampshire College off South Pleasant Street.

HISTORIC HOMES & COLLEGES

Most of the historic homes are within a few blocks of the Amity/Main/Pleasant Street crossing. Amherst College, which has two museums of interest, lies mostly along the east side of the town common. At the northeast corner of the green is the Town Hall, another fortresslike Romanesque Revival creation of Boston's H. H. Richardson. Across the way, a block south, is a seasonal information booth. Its hours vary, and when it is closed, visitors can consult the **Chamber of Commerce** office (☎ **413/ 253-0700**) in the Lord Jefferey Inn (entrance at 11 Spring St.).

Amherst College. South Pleasant & College sts. ☎ **413/542-2000.**

Named for Baron Jefferey Amherst, a British general during the last of the French and Indian Wars, the illustrious liberal-arts college for men maintains an active cooperative relationship with Smith, Mount Holyoke, the University of Massachusetts, and the experimental Hampshire College. It was founded in 1821, with Noah Webster on its first board of trustees. Robert Frost was a member of the faculty for over a decade. Its large campus cuts through the heart of the town, and contains two museums open to the public. The **Pratt Museum of Geology** (☎ 413/542-2165), at the southeast corner of the main quadrangle, boasts a large number of dinosaur tracks and fossils, a mastadon skeleton, a meteorite, and rocks and minerals indigenous to the valley. The **Mead Art Museum** (☎ 413/542-2335), at the intersection of Routes 116 and 9, displays varied collections of sculptures, paintings, photographs, and antiquities. Its strengths lie in the works of 19th- and 20th-century American artists and French Impressionists. Admission to both museums is free.

Amherst History Museum at the Strong House. 67 Amity St. (1 block west of the main intersection). ☎ **413/256-0678.** Admission $2. Mid-May to mid-Oct Wed–Sat 12:30–3:30pm; mid-Oct to mid May Thurs only 12:30–3:30pm.

Built around 1744, this is one of the oldest houses in town. That's its principal appeal, for the collection of furniture, clothing, and accessories it contains are in need of a firm curatorial hand and the funds to pull it all together in an organized fashion. Volunteers gamely lead the required guided tours.

Emily Dickinson Homestead. 280 Main St. (2 blocks east of the Town Hall). ☎ **413/542-8161.** Admission $3. Tours by appointment, May–Oct, Wed–Sat 1:30–3:45pm; Mar–Apr and Nov to mid-Dec, Wed and Sat 1:30–3:45pm. Reservations recommended.

Designated as a National Historic Monument, this house was where Emily Dickinson was born in 1830 and where she lived until her family moved in 1840. They returned in 1855, and the famous poet stayed here from then until her death 31 years later. The "Belle of Amherst" was the granddaughter and daughter of local movers and shakers, the source of her support while she produced the poetry that was to be increasingly celebrated even as she withdrew into near-total seclusion.

University of Massachusetts. Visitors Center (MA 116). ☎ **413/545-4237.** Free admission. Campus tours, intended primarily for prospective students and their parents, are available by appointment.

Though the university was founded in 1863, this 1,200-acre campus north of the town center is relatively young, dating from the 1960s. Its 25,000 students study for degrees in 90 academic fields. In recent years, the university's success in intercollegiate basketball (the team made it to the Final Four in March of 1996) has provoked the enthusiasm of sports fans all over the state.

Art is given a high priority by the administration, with six galleries scattered around the campus. Foremost among these is the **University Gallery** (☎ 413/545-3670) in the Fine Arts Center beside the pond in the quadrangle. Its permanent collection and frequent temporary exhibitions focus on works of 20th-century artists. The center also mounts productions in dance, music, and theater. Call the box office (☎ 413/545-2511) for information about current and upcoming performances.

BICYCLING

An 8¹/₂-mile bicycle trail following a former railroad bed between Amherst and Northampton is well-used by residents of both towns. Bicycles can be rented at **Valley Bicycles,** 319 Main St. (☎ 413/256-0880) in Amherst.

SHOPPING

Atticus/Albion Bookstore, at 8 Main St. (☎ 413/256-1547), has a rumpled, disorganized aspect that is catnip for readers who like to poke among the piles of new and used books and take a seat on the window sofa to skim their finds. The nearby **Jefferey Amherst Bookshop,** at 26 South Pleasant St. (☎ 413/253-3381), is tidier, emphasizing paperbacks and specializing in Emily Dickinson and academic texts.

WHERE TO STAY

Allen House. 599 Main St. (5 blocks east of the Town Hall), Amherst, MA 01430. ☎ 413/253-5000. 7 rms. A/C. $45–$95 double. Rates include breakfast. AE, DISC, MC, V.

A Queen Anne–style Victorian built in 1886, the colorful exterior paint job makes it easy to spot. The interior is fitted out in the manner of the eyeblink moment of the Aesthetic artistic movement, which had Oscar Wilde as one of its boosters but barely lasted 10 years. In any event, the parlor and bedrooms are lovingly decorated and highly visual, embellished with tracery and curlicues that are somehow Arabic in feel. The Eastlake Room is the prize. The house was built on Dickinson family land, and Emily's former home is a short walk away. Free pick-up service from the Amtrak station is provided. Children must be 10 or older to stay here, and smoking is not permitted.

Lord Jefferey Inn. 30 Boltwood Ave. (next to the Town Hall), Amherst, MA 01002. ☎ 800/742-0358 or 413/253-2576. Fax 413/256-6152. 50 rms. A/C TV TEL. $68–$118 double. AE, DC, MC, V.

Perhaps it is inevitable that the principal lodging in a college town is going to look a little battered and threadbare. The Lord Jeff does, and not just because it's been around since 1926, which isn't *that* old anyway. Despite being slightly worn after over 70 years of graduations, homecomings, and conferences, the inn offers an environment that is as warm as the several working fireplaces it has in its public and private rooms. The warmth was enough to draw Robert Frost to stay here for two of his last years as an English professor at the college. The main dining room is open for all meals, including Sunday brunch, and the less formal Boltwood's Tavern, with its own entrance, serves plain food from 11:30am to 10pm.

WHERE TO DINE

Judie's. 51 N. Pleasant St. (north of Amity and Main sts.). ☎ 413/253-3491. Main courses $4.95–$14.95. AE, DC, MC, V. Daily 11:30am–10pm (until 11pm Fri–Sat). ECLECTIC AMERICAN.

As popular as any place in town, Judie's does its best to suit every taste. Just to keep things ticking, for example, they push a "Munchie Madness" period from 3 to 6pm Monday to Friday, with a half-price snacks menu. Throughout the day, folks drop by for just a cup of soup and one of the trademark popovers. A glass-enclosed porch fronts the converted house, which has several interior rooms. Typical of the posted lunch specials is sautéed chicken with broccoli, mushrooms, and onions in a Bordelaise sauce, with a baked stuffed potato on the side—all for just $4.99.

Rasa Sayang. 13 N. Pleasant St. (near intersection of Amity and Main sts.). ☎ 413/253-7888. Main courses $3.95–$8.95. AE, CB, DC, DISC, MC, V. Mon–Sat 11:30am–10pm (until 11pm Fri–Sat), Sun noon–10pm. MALAYSIAN.

Opened in August of 1995 at a site that has seen several failed ventures, this operation appears to possess the ingredients for survival. Prices are reasonable, service is warm and efficient, and the food is just different enough to pique jaded taste buds. Malaysia is at that Asian cultural crossroads that brings together the curries of India and the variegated cooking styles of China, and the food attests to it. There is a lengthy menu to sample, with 15 varieties of "noodles in soup," 8 with pork, 16 with seafood, and 13 with chicken and duck, not to mention the daily specials. Start, perhaps, with the excellent hot-and-sour soup, a rich brown broth dense with mushrooms, tofu, scallions, and enough hotness to perk it all up. Follow with satay chicken, a toss of onions, carrots, zucchini, and chicken nubbins touched with sesame and mild fire. Beer and wine are available, and the restaurant has plans to add a full bar.

AMHERST AFTER DARK

Students and young adults tend to gravitate toward the livelier music scene in Northampton, but Amherst itself does have some nightime entertainment to offer. Close at hand is the **Black Sheep Cafe**, at 79 Main St. (☎ **413/253-3442**), which is active nightly, with folk and blues singers, poetry readings, chamber music . . . a broad, unpredictable selection. Entrance is usually free. Throughout the school year, Amherst College's **Buckley Recital Hall** (☎ **413/542-2195**) and **The Millins Center** (☎ **413/545-0505**) at UMass mount a variety of pop, classical, dance, and theatrical performances which might include, for example, the Cincinnati Symphony, Mummenschantz, or Elton John.

DEERFIELD

16 miles N of Northampton, 16 miles NW of Amherst

Meadows cleared and plowed over 300 years ago still surround this historic town between the Connecticut and Deerfield rivers. Every morning tobacco and dairy farmers leave houses fronting the main street to work their land nearby. Students attend the distinguished prep school, Deerfield Academy, founded in 1797. Lawyers maintain offices here, while other residents commute to and from jobs elsewhere. Deerfield is an invaluable fragment of American history, and it isn't one of those New England village exhibits with costumed performers who go home to their condos at night.

A town still exists here because the earliest English settlers were determined to thrive despite their status as a frontier pressure point in the wars that tormented colonial America. Massacres of Deerfield's settlers by the French and Indian enemies of the British nearly wiped out the town in 1675 and again in 1704. In the latter raid, 49 people were killed and over 100 were taken prisoner and marched to French Québec.

The main avenue, simply called The Street, is lined with over 80 houses built in the 17th, 18th, and 19th centuries. Most are private, but 14 of them can be visited through tours conducted by Historic Deerfield, a local tourism organization (see entry below). And all along The Street there is not a single tube of neon nor a commercially franchised intrusion.

MUSEUMS & HISTORIC HOMES

"The Street" is a mile long, with most of the museum houses concentrated along the long block north of the central town common. There are two buildings operated by organizations other than Historic Deerfield. One is Memorial Hall Museum, east of the town common on Memorial Street, for which a separate admission is charged. (For the slightly larger fee of $12 adults, $5 children 6 to 21, tours of the 14 museum houses can be combined with a visit to Memorial Hall through Historic Deerfield.) The other is the Indian House Memorial, north of the Deerfield Inn, also maintained by a separate organization. A tepee is pitched in the front yard, rather chummily considering the historical depth of hostility between the colonists and Native Americans in this region. As it is only a 1929 reproduction of an earlier house, it is of less interest than the other structures.

Special celebrations in the town are held on Patriots Day (the third Monday in April), Washington's Birthday, Thanksgiving, and over the Christmas holidays. In summer, there is an antique and classic car show.

Memorial Hall Museum. Memorial St. (between The Street and MA 5 and 10). ☎ **413/ 774-3768.** Admission $5 adults, $3 children 6–21. May 1–Nov 3 daily 10am–4:30pm.

Deerfield Academy's original 1798 classroom building was converted into this museum of village history in 1880. A popular exhibit, for understandably grisly reasons, is the preserved door of a 1698 home that shows the gashes made by weapons of the French and Indian raiders in 1704. Should the point be too muted, a hatchet is imbedded in the door. Five period rooms are also on view, and 14 other exhibition rooms, constituting a substantial collection of colonial furniture, vintage clothing, quilts, paintings, pottery, and pewter, as well as examples of Native American weapons and tools.

Historic Deerfield. Information Center, Hall Tavern, The Street. ☎ **413/774-5581.** Admission (good for 1 week) $10 adults, $5 children 6–21. Daily 9:30am–4:30pm.

Begin with a visit to the Hall Tavern, opposite the post office, where tickets are sold and maps and brochures are available. This is also the departure point for guided tours, which customarily leave on the half hour during busier seasons (April through October), and according to demand during the slower months.

While there are no charges for simply strolling The Street, anymore than in any other village, the only way to get inside the museum houses is by tour. One attraction that is also free is the new Channing Blake Meadow Walk. Open from 8am to 6pm in good weather, the trail begins beside the Rev. John Farwell Moors House, a relatively recent Historic Deerfield acquisition on the west side of The Street. The walk is marked by interpretive tablets, and goes through a working farm, past the playing fields of Deerfield Academy, and through pastures beside the Deerfield River. Along the trail you can see sheep and cattle up close (which will delight the kids), but for that reason, dogs aren't allowed on the trail. Wheelchairs should be able to negotiate the trail in most seasons.

The 14 houses on the tour were constructed between 1720 and 1850. They contain over 20,000 furnishings, silver and pewter pieces, textiles, ceramics, and implements used from the early 17th century to 1900. Included are imports from China and Europe as well as items made in the Connecticut River Valley during its prominence as an industrial center. The objects are all tidily arranged and displayed to good effect, and the tour guides provide interesting descriptions and background.

SHOPPING

Historic Deerfield's **Museum Store** (☎ 413/774-5581) is in a weathered shack between the post office and the Deerfield Inn. While it does stock a few T-shirts, the general run of its merchandise is a cut above most similar enterprises. Judicious selections include weathervanes, hand-dipped candles, relevant books, fruit preserves, and reproductions of light fixtures found in the village houses. It's open during museum hours.

WHERE TO STAY & DINE

Deerfield Inn. 81 The Street, Deerfield, MA 01342. ☎ **800/926-3865** or 413/774-5587. Fax 413/773-8712. 23 rms. A/C TV TEL. $122–$156 double. Rates include breakfast. AE, DC, MC, V.

Even if it had any significant local competition, this inn would attract more than its share of guests. Built in 1884, the Deerfield is conveniently located in the middle of The Street, with all the historic houses in easy walking distance, and is one of the stellar stopping places in the valley. The restless innkeepers continually scour their establishment in its excellent upkeep, recently replacing all the bathroom fixtures, refinishing the older furniture, and installing new carpeting. Bedrooms, named after people who lived in the village, have combinations of kings, queens, doubles—six of them four-posters—and a few sofa beds, to accommodate different family configurations.

Stacks and shelves of books and magazines in every room prompt leisurely afternoons, perhaps with high tea (included). A modern south wing is constructed to resemble a tobacco barn. The full-service Stenciled Horse dining room and an informal cafeteria are on the premises. Smoking isn't permitted.

6 The Berkshires

They are more than hills, but less than mountains, so the Taconic and Hoosac ranges that define this region at the western end of the state go by the collective name of "The Berkshires." The hamlets, villages, and two small cities that have long drawn energy and sustenance from the region's kindly Housatonic River and its gentle tributaries are as representative an evocation of greater New England as can be found.

Mohawks and Mohegans lived and hunted here, and while white missionaries established settlements at Stockbridge and elsewhere in an attempt to Christianize the native tribes, the Indians eventually moved on west. Farmers, drawn to the narrow but fertile floodplains of the Housatonic, were supplanted in the 19th century by manufacturers, who erected the brick mills that drew their power from the rushing river. Many of these factories survive, largely abandoned or converted to perform other functions.

At the same time, artists and writers came here for the mild summers and seclusion that these hills and many lakes offered. Nathaniel Hawthorne, Herman Melville, and Edith Wharton were among many who put down temporary roots. By the last decades of the 19th century and the arrival of the railroad, wealthy New Yorkers and Bostonians had discovered the region and began to erect extravagant summer "cottages" with dozens of bedrooms on scores of tailored wooded acres. With their support, culture and the performing arts found a hospitable reception. By the 1930s, theater, dance, and concerts had established themselves as sturdily regular summer fixtures. Tanglewood, Jacob's Pillow, and the Berkshire and Williamstown Theatre Festivals are events that draw tens of thousands of visitors every July and August.

When making reservations, note that the many inns in the region routinely stipulate minimum two- or three-night stays in summer and over holiday weekends and often require advance deposits.

ESSENTIALS

GETTING THERE The Massachusetts Turnpike (I-90) runs east-west from Boston to the Berkshires, with an exit near Lee and Stockbridge. From New York City, the scenic Taconic State Parkway connects with I-90 not far from Pittsfield.

Amtrak's *Lake Shore Limited* runs daily between Boston and Chicago, stopping in Pittsfield.

VISITOR INFORMATION Pittsfield's **Berkshire Visitors Bureau** (☎ 800/ 237-5747 or 413/443-9186), Berkshire Common, Pittsfield, MA 01201 (off South Street, near the entrance to the Hilton) provides brochures and answers questions for the entire region. In addition, local chambers of commerce and other civic groups maintain information booths at central locations in Great Barrington, Lee, Lenox, Stockbridge, and Williamstown. Internet surfers can find online information on what's happening in Berkshire County on the World Wide Web at: http://berkcon.com.

SHEFFIELD

11 miles S of Great Barrington

The first settlement of any size that you'll encounter after crossing the Connecticut border north on Route 7 (if you're approaching from the south), Sheffield occupies a floodplain beside the Housatonic River, with the Berkshires rising to the west. Agriculture has been the principal occupation of its residents, and still is, to a large degree. Everyone else sells antiques, or so it might seem while continuing along Route 7 (a.k.a. Main Street or Sheffield Plain). The wide road and generously spaced, well-maintained houses cultivate an impression of prosperous tranquillity.

A PIONEER'S HOME

May through October, you can make a short excursion to see the **Colonel Ashley House** (Cooper Hill Road; ☎ 413/229-8600) in Ashley Falls. Built in 1735, this small, gray, modified saltbox is believed to be the oldest house in Berkshire County. It was built by a Colonel Ashley, a person of considerable repute in colonial western Massachusetts, a pioneer in the area, an officer in one of the French and Indian Wars, and later a lawyer and a judge. Furnishings and farm tools appropriate to the period inform the interior. To find it, drive south on Route 7, watching for Route 7A on the left toward Ashley Falls. After a short distance on 7A, bear right on Rannappo Road. At the Y intersection, turn right on Copper Hill Road and drive for about 200 yards. Visiting times are sharply restricted. The house is open 1 to 5pm on Saturday, Sunday, and holiday Mondays in June, September, and October; Wednesday to Sunday July through Labor Day.

OUTDOOR PURSUITS

The 278-acre nature reservation called **Bartholomew's Cobble** (Route 7A; ☎ 413/229-8600) lies beside an ox-bow bend in the Housatonic. It is latticed with six miles of trails suitable for gentle hiking in the warmer months and for cross-country skiing in winter. They cross pastures and penetrate forests and provide a fine vista of the river and its valley from the area's high point, Hurlburt's Hill. Picnicking is permitted. A sign near the entrance claims there are 700 varieties of plants, 125 types of trees, and 450 kinds of wildflowers. Birders should take their binoculars, for many species are attracted to the flora and the feeders set up near the the administrative cabin. The requested donations are $3 adults, $1 children 6 to 12. To get to Bartholomew's Cobble, follow the directions for the Colonel Ashley House (see above), except at the end of Rannappo Road, bear left on Weatogue Road and follow it to the reservation entrance.

ANTIQUING

Sheffield can legitimately lay claim to the title of antiques capital of the Berkshires, no small feat, given what seems to be an effort by half the population to sell collectibles, treasures, and near-antiques to the other half. These are canny, knowledgeable dealers who know exactly what they have, so expect high quality and no bargains. Of the many, many possibilities, here is a slender sampling.

Driving north on Route 7, the jumbled display of birdhouses on the right drag the eye to the **Antiques Center of Sheffield** (33 S. Main St.; ☎ 413/229-3400). The garrulous owner claims it has been an antiques store since 1860. His stock is not afflicted by excessive tidiness, but it is diverse, including railroad lanterns, military mementoes, and wildly varied Americana.

Across the street is **Darr Antiques** (Main St., P.O. Box 130; ☎ 413/229-7773), a well-ordered shop in pristine contrast to its neighbor—one of the owners is an interior designer. Darr specializes in formal 18th- and 19th-century English and American furniture, with some Chinese accessories, accummulated on frequent buying trips abroad. Open year-round, they close on Tuesday and Wednesday in winter.

Farther north along Route 7, on the right, is **Dovetail Antiques** (440 Sheffield Plain; ☎ 413/229-2628), specializing in American clocks, especially those made in Connecticut in the last century. Some have gears, cogs, and other internal parts made of wood.

Continuing along Route 7, on the left at the edge of town, is **Susan Silver** (Route 7; ☎ 413/229-8169). On display are meticulously restored 18th- and 19th-century English library furniture—desks, reading stands, cabinets—and French accessories of comparable age.

There are at least two dozen other dealers along this route. Most of them have available the free directory of the Berkshire County Antiques Dealers Association, which lists and briefly describes member dealers from Sheffield to Cheshire and across the border in New York. Look, too, for the pamphlet, "The Antique Hunter's Guide to Route 7," covering 81 dealers along that road in both Massachusetts and Vermont.

WHERE TO STAY

Ivanhoe Country House. 254 S. Undermountain Rd. (Rte. 41), Sheffield, MA 01257. ☎ **413/229-2143.** 9 rms. $55 double, winter, $95 double, summer. Rates include breakfast. No credit cards.

Apart from the unheated pool out back, a stay at this inn most resembles a visit to a gregarious country aunt, the one who has her rules. No decorator had a hand in assembling the stolid, comfortable furnishings. Rooms have either double beds or twins (no queens) and each is assigned a refrigerator so guests can keep beer, wine, or soft drinks. Three have working fireplaces and access to porches. Tray breakfasts are left outside guests' doors each morning. The only TV is in the common "Chestnut Room." Those rules? No children under 15 on weekends in July and August. Dogs are accepted, for an extra $10 a day, but must be leashed at all times and cannot be left alone in guests' rooms.

SOUTH EGREMONT

5 miles SW of Great Barrington

As the larger, busier half of the town of Egremont, this enjoyably diverting village borders Route 23, the most-used gateway to the southern Berkshires from Route 22 and the Taconic Parkway in New York State. It was once a stop on the stagecoach route between Hartford and Albany, and retains many structures from that era, including mills that utilized the stream that still rushes by. Those circumstances make it a magnet for antique dealers, restaurateurs of varying levels of ambition, and refugee urban professionals who have made the precarious leap into innkeeping and retailing.

OUTDOOR PURSUITS

HIKING   In warmer months, scenic ✪ **Bash Bish Falls State Park** (Route 23; ☎ 413/528-0330) makes a rewarding day outing for hiking, birding, and fishing. (No camping or picnicking, though.) Getting there from South Egremont isn't too complicated. Drive west on Route 23 from the town center, turning south on Route

The Berkshires

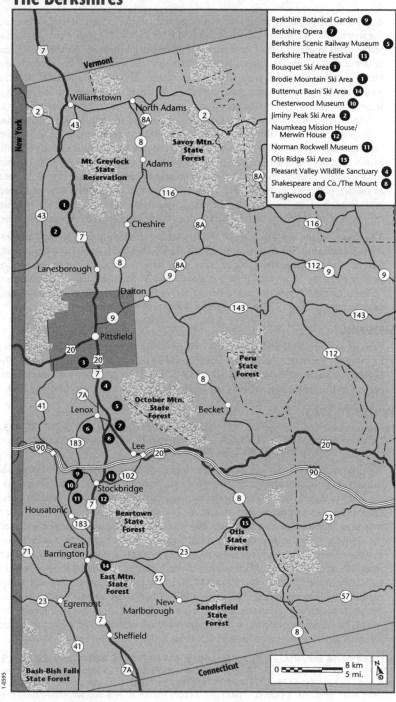

Berkshire Botanical Garden **9**
Berkshire Opera **7**
Berkshire Scenic Railway Museum **5**
Berkshire Theatre Festival **13**
Bousquet Ski Area **3**
Brodie Mountain Ski Area **1**
Butternut Basin Ski Area **14**
Chesterwood Museum **10**
Jiminy Peak Ski Area **2**
Naumkeag Mission House/
Merwin House **12**
Norman Rockwell Museum **11**
Otis Ridge Ski Area **15**
Pleasant Valley Wildlife Sanctuary **4**
Shakespeare and Co./The Mount **8**
Tanglewood **6**

41, and immediately right on Mt. Washington Road. Keep alert for signs directing the way to Mt. Washington State Forest and Bash Bish Falls. After eight miles, past fallow fields, summer houses, and groves of white birch bright against the deep green of dense pine, a sign indicates a right turn toward the falls. Look for it opposite a board-and-batten church with an unusual steeple. The road begins to follow the course of a mountain stream, going downhill. In about three miles, on the left, is a large parking place next to a craggy promontory and a sign prohibiting alcohol, camping, and fires. The sign also points off to a trail down to the falls, which should only be negotiated by reasonably fit adults. First, mount the promontory for a splendid view across the plains of the Hudson Valley to the pale blue ridgeline of the Catskill Mountains, between two rounded peaks off to the west. You'll hear the falls, but not see them yet, down to the left. If the trail seems too steep, continue down the road to another parking area, on the left. From here, a gentler trail a little over a mile long leads in to the falls. The falls themselves are quite impressive, crashing down from over 50 feet into a deep pool. The park is open from dawn to dusk. Admission is free.

SKIING At the western edge of the township, touching the New York border, is the **Catamount Ski Area** (Route 23; ☎ **413/528-1262**). About two hours from Manhattan, it is understandably popular with New Yorkers, who must drive twice as long to get to Vermont's higher peaks. It has 24 trails, including the daunting "Catapult," the steepest run in the Berkshires (to be attempted by experts only), and four double chairlifts. There is also night skiing on 13 of the area's trails.

SHOPPING

Fans of weathervanes and other folk arts, or of the recently chic painted country furniture of America, Québec, and Bavaria, will be delighted by the offerings of **The Splendid Pheasant** (Route 23; ☎ **413/528-5755**). Evidently, they have much company, for the owners have recently expanded their galleries into a second building.

WHERE TO STAY

Egremont Inn. Old Sheffield Rd. (P.O. Box 418), South Egremont, MA 01258. ☎ **413/528-2111.** Fax 413/528-3284. 18 rms. A/C TEL. July–Aug $90–$165 double; lower the rest of the year. Rates include breakfast. AE, DISC, MC, V.

Slip into this friendly former stagecoach stop as easily as into a pair of beloved old slippers. Tens of thousands have preceded you, since the Egremont has been a tavern and inn since 1780. That longevity shows, in tilting floors and lintels and a grand brick fireplace constructed over an ancient blacksmith hearth. The present owners have been on the scene for a little over two years, and their renovations have included the merging of smaller bedrooms to create five suites. The Egremont is a restaurant as well—dinner is served Wednesday to Sunday all year, and there's Sunday brunch from July to mid-October. Main courses of the "Country American" food go for $15 to $22.50 in the dining room, $9 to $12.50 in the informal tavern. A guitar player performs on Thursdays and a jazz ensemble on Saturdays and at Sunday brunch. There are no TVs in the rooms, but there's a satellite-fed set in one of the common rooms. Children are welcome, and they can make use of videos and games stockpiled for them as well as the swimming pool out back. There are also two tennis courts.

Weathervane Inn. Rte. 23, South Egremont, MA 01258. ☎ **800/528-9580** or 413/528-9580. Fax 413/528-1713. 12 rms. A/C. Sun–Thurs $95–$135 including breakfast and afternoon tea; Fri–Sat $175–$205 double including breakfast, tea, and dinner. MAP (breakfast and lunch or dinner included in rate) and 2-night minimum required weekends; no dinner Mar–Apr.

"Screw the Golden Years" reads a sampler pillow in the sitting room, an apparently accurate reflection of the owners' nose-thumbing views on life. An affectionate cat is more welcoming, as are the bedrooms, many of which have four-poster beds with quilts. The core of the building was a 1735 farmhouse, but the Greek Revival appearance of the property dates to an 1835 renovation. An unheated pool is available. Smoking isn't permitted indoors.

WHERE TO DINE

☼ John Andrew's. Rte. 23. ☎ **413/528-3469.** Reservations recommended on weekends. Main courses $12–$20. MC, V. June–Aug Mon–Sat 5:30–10pm, Sun 11am–3pm; Sept–May Thurs–Tues 5:30–10pm. ECLECTIC AMERICAN.

Entering the front door of this made-over farmhouse, you'll encounter appetizing but not instantly recognizable aromas adrift in the air. This is no barbecue or fish joint. A fertile imagination is at work behind the kitchen doors, one that conjures such refreshing culinary departures as wilted beet greens with artichoke hearts and sun-dried tomato vinaigrette, or seared sea scallops with couscous and sweet-pea mint coulis. A choice of breads arrive with the generous martinis—rosemary focaccia, pita, and sourdough. Rows of windows in the rear dining room let in the fading summer light, which falls on Parsons chairs, bare-wood floors, and sponged walls of dusky rose. Espresso and brandies are available, and desserts feature homemade ice cream. All is very near countrified faultlessness. Quibbles? Well, okay, the focaccia was a little doughy.

Mom's Cafe. Main St. ☎ **413/528-2414.** Main courses $4.95–$12.95. MC, V. Daily 6:30am–9:30pm. ECLECTIC.

"Mom" is Rich Altman, who keeps his informal drop-in place perking from early breakfast to late cappuccino. Logically, his menu runs from omelets and pancakes to pizzas with toppings as diverse as avocado and pineapple. A couple of years ago, he added Spanish tapas in the evening, and credits such standards as *mejillones a la vinegreta* (mussels in vinaigrette), *gambas en salsa verde* (shrimp in green sauce), and sangría as key to his best summer in the seven years he's owned the cafe. In good weather, elect to eat on the deck over the stream that runs behind the building. The restaurant also serves beer and wine.

GREAT BARRINGTON
7 miles S of Stockbridge

Even with a population well under 8,000, this pleasant commercial and retail center is the largest town in the southernmost part of the county. Rapids in the Housatonic provided power for a number of mills in centuries past, most of which are now gone, and in 1886, it was one of the first communities in the world to have electricity on its streets and in its homes. More recently, it was spared by the killer tornado of Memorial Day 1995 that hopped over Great Barrington only to touch down again a few miles east around Monterey, tearing off hundreds of trees halfway up their trunks. That devastation will be seen along Route 23 for decades to come.

Great Barrington has no sights or monuments of significant interest, leaving ample time to browse its many antique galleries and a growing number of specialty shops. Convenient as a home base for excursions to such nearby attractions as Monument Mountain, Bash Bish Falls, Butternut Basin, Tanglewood concerts, and the museums and historic houses of Stockbridge, it has a number of unremarkable but entirely adequate motels along Route 7 north of the town center that tend to fill up slower on weekends than the better-known inns in the area. It is something of a dining center, too, compared to other Berkshire towns.

The **Southern Berkshire Chamber of Commerce** maintains an information booth at 362 Main St. (☎ 413/528-1510), near the town hall. It's open Monday to Friday 9:30am to 12:30pm and 1:30 to 4:30pm, Saturday and Sunday noon to 3pm.

OUTDOOR PURSUITS

The **Egremont Country Club** (Route 23; ☎ 413/528-422) is open to the public. Its facilities include an 18-hole golf course, tennis courts, and an Olympic-size pool.

Butternut Basin (Route 23; ☎ 413/528-2000), two miles east of town, is known for its strong family ski programs. A children's center provides day care for kids 2^1/$_2$ to 6 daily from December 23rd to the end of the season, and the SKIwee program offers full and half-day programs for children 4 to 12 that include lunch, ski instruction, and a lift ticket. Six double and quad chairlifts provide access to 22 trails, the longest of which is a 1^1/$_2$-mile run. There are also 5 miles of cross-country trails.

A little over 4 miles north of town, west of Route 7, is **Monument Mountain,** with two hiking trails to the summit. The easier one is called the Indian Monument Trail, about an hour's hike to the top; the more difficult route, the Hickey Trail, isn't much longer, but takes the steep way up, and should probably be avoided by novice hikers. The summit, called Squaw Peak for an Indian maiden who allegedly leapt to her death from the spot, offers splendid panoramic views. Nathaniel Hawthorne and Herman Melville, two members of the remarkable mid-19th-century literary set that summered in the Berkshires, first met here on a hiking trip.

Camping and hiking equipment, as well as free advice on area trails, are available at **Appalachian Mountain Gear** (777 S. Main St.; ☎ 413/528-881). The owner guides free hikes on Sundays.

SHOPPING

Shoppers will want to take a turn off of Main Street onto Railroad Street, the town's best shopping strip. Start on the corner, at **T. P. Saddle Blanket & Trading Co.** (304 Main St.; ☎ 413/528-6500), an unlikely but fascinating emporium that looks like it was lifted whole from the Colorado Rockies. Packed to the walls with western gear—boots, hats, plates, Indian jewelry, pitchers, jars of salsas, rugs, blankets—it's open every day. Down the left side of Railroad Street is **Bleu Lavande** (Route 7; ☎ 413/528-1618), whose French Canadian owner parades her good taste with a stock of Gallic tableware, bed linens, country furniture, and nightwear. Open daily.

Several antique and art galleries and other enterprises mingle kitsch and class at **Jennifer House Commons** (Route 7; ☎ 413/528-2690), on the right, north of town, on Route 7. In town, just before Route 7 turns right across a short bridge, Route 41 goes straight, toward the village of Housatonic. In about four miles is a long, low shed that houses the kiln, workrooms, and showroom of **The Great Barrington Pottery** (Route 41; ☎ 413/274-6259). Owner/master Richard Bennett has been throwing pots for over 30 years according to ancient Japanese techniques.

WHERE TO STAY

✪ **The Old Inn on the Green & Gedney Farm.** Rte. 57, New Marlborough, MA 01230. ☎ 413/229-3131. 8 rms, 5 suites. TEL. $120–$285 double. Rates include breakfast. MC, V. Take Rte. 23 east from Great Barrington, picking up Rte. 57 after 3.4 miles. After 5.7 miles, you'll see the The Old Inn on the left. Continue another ^{1}/$_4$ mile to the barns on the left. Registration is in the ground floor of the gray barn.

A two-part establishment comprised of a former 1760 tavern/general store/ post office on the village green and two converted dairy barns down the road, its reputation has been built on the creativity of its admirable kitchen and the comely decor of its guest rooms. The restaurant is in the Old Inn, open only for dinner (Thursday to Sunday from November through June, Wednesday to Monday from July through October). While the baths in the Old Inn have recently been redone, the most desirable rooms are in the barn, combining contemporary furnishings and accessories with Oriental rugs. Given the steep prices, guests might reasonably expect television and air-conditioning. They don't get them.

Windflower Inn. 684 S. Egremomt Rd. (P.O. Box 25), Great Barrington, MA 01230. ☎ **800/ 992-1993** or 413/528-2720. Fax 413/528-5147. 13 rms. A/C TV. $170–$220 double, MAP; $100–$160 with breakfast and afternoon tea. AE.

A roadside lodging for decades—veteran Berkshire lovers might remember it as the Fairfield Inn—the Windflower has attained its highest order of quality under the current owners, who have operated it since 1980. Built in the middle of the last century in Federal style, it commands a large plot of land opposite the Egremont Country Club on Route 23 between Great Barrington and South Egremont. All rooms have small black-and-white televisions, six have fireplaces, and four have canopied beds. Dinner is served Thursday to Sunday in summer. Out back is an unheated pool. Smoking is allowed only in the living room. Children are welcome, but pets are not.

WHERE TO DINE

Barrington Brewery. Rte. 7 (in the Jennifer House complex, north of town). ☎ **413/ 528-8292.** Main courses $7.95–$13.95. AE, MC, V. Daily 11:30am–10 or 11pm (depending on business). ECLECTIC AMERICAN.

This converted barn hasn't been "done" to death, and retains its rough siding and beams. All beers and ales are made on premises (in the brewery upstairs), and they are good enough to distract even devoted oenophiles (although wines are also available). A fun gimmick is the selection of three-ounce shot glasses of currently available brews, produced in the visible tanks upstairs. Grub is of the bratwurst, burger, and nacho variety, but good pot pies and grilled strip steaks are also on the card. The restaurant bakes its own breads and desserts as well. The ground floor is all nonsmoking, even at the bar. In summer, a tented dining area is erected outside.

Boiler Room Cafe. 405 Stockbridge Rd. (Rte. 7). ☎ **413/528-4280.** Main courses $9–$21. MC, V. Tues–Sat 5–10pm. ECLECTIC/INTERNATIONAL.

They need a new sign out front, for you can sail past on the way to Stockbridge without spotting the current one (on the left). What's more, the menu describes the fare as "cuisine locale," but it's hard to say where that "locale" might be, given that the menu is replete with such items as raclette, tuna marinated in soy sauce with sesame noodles, and Mexican braised lamb shanks with avocado salsa. Whatever. The only real problem here is deciding what to order, since everything sounds good. One recent possibility—the menu is changed once or twice a month—was a "Mediterranean Platter," which included homemade sausage of lamb, pork, and fennel, white beans, shrimp, asparagus, goat cheese, olives, smoked mussels, and grilled bread. The decor is as offbeat and amusing as the food, with dried tree branches scrambling over rust-red walls.

✪ **Castle Street Cafe.** 10 Castle St. (near the Town Hall). ☎ **413/528-5244.** Main courses $9–$21. AE, DISC, MC, V. Wed–Mon 5–9pm (until 10pm Fri–Sat). NEW AMERICAN.

This storefront bistro has ruled the Great Barrington roost for some time now, with such Francophilic fare as grilled veal chop with roast garlic sauce and "homemade" mashed potatoes or roast duck with black-currant sauce. Pastas are so big that half portions are available. There's a short bar at the back of the room to have a drink while checking out the night's menu.

GREAT BARRINGTON AFTER DARK

Baroque and classical music performed on period instruments constitute the **Aston Magna Festival,** held on five Saturdays in July and August at the St. James Church (Main Street and Taconic Avenue; ☎ **413/528-3595**).

STOCKBRIDGE

7 miles N of Great Barrington, 6 miles S of Lenox

Stockbridge's ready accessibility to Boston and New York, each about 2½ hours away by today's highways and reachable by rail since the second half of the 19th century, transformed the original frontier settlement into a Gilded Age summer retreat for the super-rich and the merely wealthy. The town has long been popular among artists and writers as well, including Norman Rockwell, who lived here for 25 years and who rendered the Main Street of his adopted town in a famous painting. Along and near Main Street are a number of historic homes and other attractions, enough to fill the hours of a long weekend, even without the Tanglewood concert season in nearby Lenox.

    The chamber of commerce maintains a self-service seasonal information booth opposite the row of stores Rockwell depicted. It is open 24 hours a day from May through October, with stocks of pamphlets and notices about area attractions and lodgings.

WHAT TO SEE & DO

Berkshire Botanical Garden. Rtes. 102 and 183. ☎ **413/298-3926.** Admission $5 adults, $4 seniors, children under 12 free. May–Oct daily 10am–5pm. Drive west from downtown Stockbridge on Main St., picking up Church St. (Rte. 102) northwest and driving about 2 miles.

These 15 acres of flower beds, shrubs, ponds, and raised vegetable and herb gardens are an inviting destination for strollers and picnickers. The first weekend in October is devoted to a harvest festival, which features jugs of cider, displays of pumpkins, and hayrides.

Chesterwood. 4 Williamsville Rd. ☎ **413/298-3579.** Admission $6 adults, $3 children 13–18, $1 children 6–12. May 1–Oct 31 daily 10am–5pm. Drive west on Main St., south on Rte. 183 about 1 mile to the Chesterwood sign.

Sculptor Daniel Chester French used this estate as his summer home and studio for over 30 years. His famous sculpture of the Minute Man at the Old North Bridge in Concord, completed in 1875 at the age of 25, launched his highly successful career. Subsequent commissions included a bust of Ralph Waldo Emerson at Harvard, the statue of *Alma Mater* at Columbia University, and one of the most moving monuments in America, the Abraham Lincoln Memorial in Washington, D.C. His house and studio here were designed by his friend and collaborator on the Lincoln Memorial, Henry Bacon. A visit can easily be combined with one to the Rockwell Museum, under a mile away.

Children's Chime Bell Tower. Main St. No phone. Free admission.

West of the town center, the Greek Revival Town Hall and a mid-19th century red-brick Congregational church face the old village green. The campanile out front is the Children's Chime Bell Tower. Dating from 1878, its bells are tolled every evening from spring to first frost.

Merwin House. 14 Main St. ☎ **413/298-4703.** Admission $4. June to mid-Oct Tues, Thurs, Sat, Sun noon–5pm.

A small, brick Federalist house with a later wood frame extension, this 1825 residence contains furnishings true to the period. The lawn runs down to the Housatonic. Admission is by guided tour only.

Mission House. Main and Sergeant sts. (Rte. 102). ☎ **413/298-3239.** Admission $5 adults, $2.50 children. Daily Memorial Day–Columbus Day 10am–5pm.

The Reverend John Sergeant had the most benevolent, if paternalistic, of intentions: He sought to build a house among the Stockbridge Indians of the Housatonic tribe, hoping to convert them to civilized (i.e., English) ways through proximity to his godly self and his small band of settlers. The Mission House, built in 1739, was the site of this Christianizing process, and it was moved here, understandably weathered, in 1928. A few of the furnishings were owned by Sergeant. Visits are by guided tour, and include a stroll around the herb garden.

Naumkeag. Prospect Hill. ☎ **413/298-3239.** Admission $7 adults, $2.50 children. Daily Memorial Day–Columbus Day 10am–5pm. From the Cat & Dog Fountain in the intersection next to the Red Lion Inn, drive north on Prospect Hill Rd. about 2 miles.

Architect Stanford White of the celebrated New York firm of McKim, Mead & White designed this 26-room house for Joseph Hodge Choate and his family in 1886. A classic Berkshire cottage of the Gilded Age, his client dubbed it "Naumkeag," an Amerindian name for Salem, Mass., which was his childhood hometown. Choate was a lawyer and served as U.S. ambassador to the Court of St. James. His many-gabled and chimneyed house is largely of the New England Shingle style, surrounded by impressive gardens. Admission is by guided tour only, but worth it for the glimpses of the rich interior, fully furnished and decorated in the manner of the period, including many paintings and an extensive collection of Chinese export porcelain.

✪ Norman Rockwell Museum. Rte. 183. ☎ **413/298-4100.** Admission $9 adults, $2 children 6–18, $20 family. May 1–Oct 31 daily 10am–5pm; Nov 1–Apr 30 Mon–Fri 11am–4pm, Sat–Sun 10am–5pm. Take Main St. (Rte. 102) west to the junction with Rte. 183, with its traffic signal. Turn left (south). In about ¹/₂ mile, the entrance to the museum is on the left.

This striking building of generous proportions was erected at a cost of $4.4 million in 1993 to house the works of Stockbridge's favorite son. The beloved illustrator used both his neighbors and the town where he lived for the last third of his life to tell stories about an America rapidly fading from memory. Most of Rockwell's paintings adorned covers of the weekly *Saturday Evening Post,* warm and often humorous depictions of homecomings, first proms, visits to the doctor, and the marriage license bureau. He displayed serious concerns, too, notably with his series on the "Four Freedoms" and his poignant portrait of a little African-American girl in a white dress being escorted by U.S. marshals into a previously segregated school. Art critics and intellectuals routinely denounced his work as saccharine and sentimental, but the self-effacing artist didn't fire back, instead expressing his admiration for the work of the Abstract Expressionists. Selections of his illustrations are rotated into view from the large permanent collection, the pity being that none of his ingenious April Fool's covers are included. A couple of galleries show the works of other illustrators of the past hundred years, including Howard Pyle, Charles Dana Gibson, and N. C. Wyeth. The lovely 36-acre grounds also contain Rockwell's last studio, moved here to a point overlooking a bend in the Housatonic. Picnic tables are provided.

WHERE TO STAY

Inn at Stockbridge. 30 East St. (Rte. 7; Box 618), Stockbridge, MA 01262. ☎ 413/298-3337. Fax 413/298-3406. 8 rms. A/C TEL. June–Oct $100–$235 double; Nov–May $98–$190 double. Rates include breakfast. AE, MC, V.

A mile north of Stockbridge center, this 1906 neoclassical building, with its grandly columned porch, is set well back from the road on 12 landscaped acres. The former New Yorkers who own and run the inn are almost painfully anxious to please, serving full breakfasts by candlelight and afternoon spreads of cheese and wine (hot cider in cold weather). Carafes of brandy are in each room. They intend to add another four rooms, but the best of the existing accommodations is the "Terrace Room," with a deck, a private entrance, Jacuzzi, and the only bedroom TV. There is also a pool. While they own a hand-licking poodle, they don't allow other pets. Children must be 12 or over. Smoking isn't permitted.

The Red Lion. Main St., Stockbridge, MA 01262. ☎ 413/298-5545. Fax 413/298-5130. 111 rms. A/C TEL. $94–$159 double, late Apr–late Oct, $87–$123 the rest of the year. AE, CB, DC, DISC, MC, V.

So well-known it serves as a virtual all-inclusive symbol of the Berkshires, this eternally busy inn had its origins as a stagecoach tavern in 1773. That original building is long gone, and the summer hotel that grew up on the site burned to the ground in 1896. Quickly rebuilt, that is essentially the structure extant today, with the later addition of private baths and an outdoor pool. Many of the antiques arranged in both public and private rooms survived the fire, including a collection of colonial table china. Most rooms have TVs. Guests can take sustenance in the moderately formal dining room (main courses $16.50 to $26.50), in the casual Widow Bingham Tavern (main courses $9.95 to $15.95), in the basement Lion's Den (main courses $6.95 to $12.95), and, in good weather, in the courtyard out back. Many of the guests pass a daily hour or two in rocking chairs on the long porch, chatting and people-watching in a New England version of a sidewalk cafe. This place is quite popular, so make reservations even further in advance than is recommended for other Berkshire inns.

The Taggart House. Main St., Stockbridge, MA 01262. ☎ 413/298-4303. 4 rms. A/C. $300–$355 July–Oct, $235–$255 the rest of the year. Rates include breakfast. Two- and three-day minimum stays apply on summer and fall weekends. AE, CB, DC, DISC, MC, V.

Ordinarily, an inn with only four guest rooms wouldn't merit space here. But what rooms! The decor and furnishings of this outwardly sedate 1850 Victorian/Colonial mansion only a block west of the Red Lion are breathtaking. Start with the theatrical main floor—the dining room, perhaps. The inlaid mahogany table is over a century old, once a centerpiece in an Argentine palace and now the site of candlelight breakfasts that more nearly resemble brunch. Wallpapers and fabrics throughout the house are mostly of the complex arts-and-crafts variety. A birchbark canoe hangs above the billard table, only the largest item of an intriguing collection of Amerindian arts and artifacts. There is a paneled library, a ballroom that is often the scene of weddings, a handsome harpsichord, and nine beguiling fireplaces. And upstairs, beds with fur throws or East Indian silk coverlets or velvet canopies and chests painted with turtleshell and bois effects . . . it would take many more pages than this to adequately describe this immersion in the Gilded Age.

WHERE TO DINE

Michael's. Elm St. (off Main St.). ☎ 413/298-3530. Main courses $10.95–$15.95. AE, CB, DC, MC, V. Mon–Sat 11:30am–11pm, Sun noon–10pm (bar until 1am). ITALIAN/AMERICAN.

Admittedly unremarkable, this tavern with a decided sports flavor and its adjoining dining room are one of the few nearby alternatives to the Red Lion Inn. Bar snacks served around the 60-inch TV are nachos and fried mozzarella sticks, as expected in these environs as the surf 'n' turf and fettucine Alfredo. But the execution of such reliables is pretty good, the greeting off-handed but friendly, and the place stays open throughout the day for those times when throats go dry and the munchies attack. Upstairs are pool tables and video games.

STOCKBRIDGE AFTER DARK

The Lion's Den in the Red Lion Inn has nightly live entertainment, usually of the folksy variety. In summer, the **Berkshire Theatre Festival** (P.O. Box 797, Main St.; ☎ 413/298-5536) holds its annual late June to late August season of classic and new plays, often with marquee names starring or directing, Dianne Wiest and Joanne Woodward among them. Its venue is a "casino" built in 1887 to plans by Stanford White.

WEST STOCKBRIDGE

5 miles NW of Stockbridge

The hills around this Stockbridge satellite are alive with the sounds of creativity. Potters, painters, writers, sculptors, weavers, and glassblowers pursue their compulsions summers or year-round, selling the results from their studios and several galleries. A pamphlet called *The Art of West Stockbridge* is available in display racks throughout the area and describes the work of some of the most important artisans and where it can be found.

One of the most ambitious new creative enterprises is the **Berkshire Center for Contemporary Glass** (6 Harris St.; ☎ 413/232-4666). The spanking-new building has ample space for a showroom and a large work area, including a viewing area for spectators. Kids find the process fascinating and are even allowed to participate. Classes and workshops are scheduled, and artisans can rent studio time. The Center, located in the heart of the village, is open 10am to 10pm May through October, 10am to 6pm November through April.

WHERE TO STAY & DINE

Williamsville Inn. Rte. 41, West Stockbridge, MA 01266. ☎ 413/274-6118. Fax 413/274-3539. 16 rms. A/C. $120–$185 double July–Oct, $105–$160 double Nov–June. AE, MC, V. About 5 miles south of West Stockbridge center.

Rooms are in the 1797 main house, the coverted barn, or in the no-frills cottages. Some have woodstoves or fireplaces or four-posters; some have full baths, others only shower stalls; and some are more expensive than they should be. The kitchen has received good notices for its "eclectic country cuisine," and the two dining rooms are open for dinner from 5:30 to 9pm—daily from May to October, Thursday to Sunday from November to April. On the grounds are a clay tennis court and a pool. Wild turkeys and deer are often seen grazing out near the treeline.

LEE

45 miles W of Springfield, 5 miles SE of Lenox

While Stockbridge and Lenox were developing into luxurious recreational centers for the satraps of Boston and New York, Lee was a thriving paper mill town. That inevitably meant it was shunned by the wealthy summer people and thus essentially remained a town of workers and merchants. It has a somewhat raffish, although not unappealing, aspect, its center clustered with shops and offices, and few of the stately homes and broad lawns that characterize the neighboring communities. The town's contribution to the Berkshire cultural calendar is the Jacob's Pillow Dance Festival, which first thrived on a fabled alliance between founder Ted Shawn and Martha Graham.

The Lee Chamber of Commerce operates an **information center** during summer and early fall on Railroad Street (Route 20; ☎ 413/243-0852). They can assist in obtaining lodging in the area, often in modest guest houses and B&Bs that are rarely as grand as those in Lenox, but nearly always significantly cheaper. That's something to remember when every other place near Tanglewood seems to be fully booked or quoting prices of $200 a night or more.

A BERKSHIRE ART GALLERY

With no immediate obligatory historic homes or museums, visitors in search of touristic attractions routinely make the short excursion to the hamlet of Tyringham. To get there, take Route 20 south to Route 102, near the #2 interchange of the Massachusetts Turnpike. Following the signs through the complicated intersection, pick up Tyringham Road and drive south about four miles.

You'll know when you get where you're going. It's on the left, an odd fairytale structure often called the "Gingerbread House." At the front wall are jagged limestone outcroppings, in back are conical turrets topping towers, and the shingled roof rolls like waves on the ocean. Erected at the turn of the century as a studio for sculptor Henry Hudson Kitson, it now houses the **Tyringham Art Galleries** (☎ 413/243-0654), showcasing the works of competent, if not breathtaking, Berkshire artists. Open daily 10am to 5pm, Memorial Day to Columbus Day. Admission is $1 adults, children free.

CAMPING

October Mountain State Forest offers 50 campsites (with showers) and over 16,000 acres for hiking and walking, canoeing and other nonmotorized boating, cross-country skiing, and snowmobiling. To get there, drive northwest on Route 20 into town, turn right on Center Street, and follow the signs.

JACOB'S PILLOW

Jacob's Pillow (George Carter Road, Becket; ☎ 413/243-0745) is to dance what Tanglewood is to classical music, each showcasing talent of equal stature in each field. Known as a regular summer venue for famed dancer and choreographer Martha Graham, who died in 1991 after a 70-year career, the theater has long welcomed troupes of international reputation. In 1995, for example, it enjoyed appearances by the Mark Morris Dance Group, the Paul Taylor Company, and Feld Ballet/NY, as well as repertory companies whose work is based on jazz, flamenco, and Indian and Asian music. The season is from late June to late August, and tickets go on sale May 1st. The more prominent companies are seen in the main Ted Shawn Theatre, where tickets are in the $27 to $43 range; other troupes are assigned to the Studio/Theatre, where tickets are $12 to $15.

WHERE TO STAY

✪ **Applegate.** 279 W. Park St., Lee, MA 01238. ☎ 800/691-9012 or 413/243-4451. 6 rms. A/C. $85–$225 double. MC, V. From Stockbridge, drive north on Rte. 7. In about ¹/₂ mile, take a right on Stockbridge Rd. The inn is 2 miles ahead, on the right.

This paradigm of the B&B trade utilizes a gracious 1920s Georgian colonial manse to full advantage. The most desirable lodging has a huge canopied bed with a puffy comforter, Queen Anne reproductions, sunlight filtering through gauzy curtains, a walk-around steam shower, and a fireplace with real wood instead of pressed logs. Two robes hang ready for guests' use, and a complimentary carafe of brandy is also waiting. Wing chairs have good reading lights. Other rooms are similar, albeit somewhat smaller. Breakfast is by candlelight, and the innkeepers set out wine and cheese in the afternoon. There's also a swimming pool. There are no room TVs, but there's a large set with VCR on the sunporch. Welcoming as this all is, the inn doesn't accept children 12 and under or pets, even though five cats call the Applegate home.

LENOX & TANGLEWOOD
7 miles S of Pittsfield, 23 miles S of Williamstown

Even more so than in Stockbridge, stately homes and fabulous mansions mushroomed in this former agricultural settlement from the 1890s until around 1910. By 1913, the 16th Amendment, which authorized income taxes, put a severe crimp in that impulse. But Lenox remains a repository of extravagent domestic architecture surpassed only in such fabled resorts of the wealthy as Newport and Palm Beach. And since many of the cottages have been converted into inns and hotels, it is possible to get inside some of these beautiful buildings, if only for a cocktail or a meal.

In a town with a permanent population of barely 5,000, the reason for so many hostelries—over two dozen post signs and others take in guests through B&B networks—is Tanglewood, a series of concerts presented by the Boston Symphony Orchestra every summer on a nearby estate. While the weekend performances of the BSO are the big draw, there are also solo recitals, chamber concerts, and appearances by the privileged young musicians who study at the prestigious Tanglewood Music Center.

The **Lenox Chamber of Commerce** operates an information center in the Lenox Academy Building (75 Main St.; ☎ **413/637-3646**). It has public rest rooms, and attendants can assist in obtaining lodgings.

OPEN-AIR CONCERTS, A MUSEUM & A LITERARY HOME
Berkshire Scenic Railway Museum. Housatonic St. and Willow Creek Rd. ☎ **413/637-2210**. Guided tours, June–Oct Sat, Sun, holidays.

Housed in a deactivated and restored train station, the Berkshire Scenic Railway Museum has displays of model railroads, a gift shop, and a real caboose. Fifteen-minute train rides are also offered. This is one of the few attractions in Lenox likely to appeal to children.

Edith Wharton Restoration. Plunkett St. (intersection of rtes 7, 20, and 7A). ☎ **413/637-1899**. Guided tours in May, Labor Day–Oct Sat–Sun 10am–3pm; June–Aug Tues–Sun 9am–3pm, July–Aug also Mon noon–3pm. Admission $6 adults, $4.50 children 13–18, children under 13 free.

Wharton, who won a Pulitzer Prize for her novel *The Age of Innocence,* was singularly equipped to write this subtle and deftly detailed examination of the upper classes of the Gilded Age and the first decades of this century. She was born into that stratum of society in 1862 and traveled in those circles that made the Berkshires a regular stop on their restless movements between New York, Florida, Newport, and the Continent. She had her own "cottage" built on this 130-acre lakeside property in 1902 and lived there 10 years before leaving for France, never to return. Far from a passive client, she took an active hand in both the overall design and the execution of its details. She was, after all, the author of an upscale 1897 how-to guide called *The Decoration of Houses.* Grand by today's standards, it wasn't especially large for that time in Lenox history. Called "The Mount," it is often used by the actors of the

Shakespeare & Co. troupe (see "Tanglewood & the Performing Arts Scene," below) to stage on-site productions based on the author's works. Restoration is ongoing, but tours continue as scheduled.

✪ **Tanglewood.** West St., Stockbridge, MA 01262. ☎ **413/637-1940** (box office for concerts, June–Aug). Admission to grounds is free, except for concerts (prices vary). Drive 1¹/₂ miles southwest on Rte. 183.

This estate of over 500 gorgeous acres of manicured lawns, gardens, and groves of ancient trees, much of it overlooking Stockbridge Bowl lake, was put together starting in 1849 by William Aspinwall Tappan. At the outset, the only structure on the property was a modest something referred to as the Little Red Shanty. In 1851, it was rented to Nathaniel Hawthorne and his wife Sophia. The author of *The Scarlet Letter* and *The House of the Seven Gables* stayed there long enough to write a children's book, *Tanglewood Tales*, and meet Herman Melville, who lived nearby in Dalton and became a close friend. The existing Hawthorne Cottage is a replica, now serving as practice studios. It isn't open to the public. On the grounds is the original Tappan mansion, with fine views, and the 1938 Koussevitsky Music Shed, an open-ended auditorium seating 5,000 where the Boston Symphony performs every summer. Two smaller structures of more recent vintage provide space for recitals, lectures, and chamber concerts. Although Tanglewood is associated with Lenox, it lies within Stockbridge township.

OUTDOOR PURSUITS

Pleasant Valley Wildlife Sanctuary (West Mountain Road; ☎ **413/637-0320**) has a small museum and seven miles of hiking and snowshoeing trails crossing its 1,000 acres. Beaver lodges and dams can be glimpsed from a distance and waterfowl and other birds are found in abundance, rewarding targets for those who come equipped with binoculars. Open Tuesday to Sunday, dawn to sunset. Admission is $3 adults, $1 children 6 to 12. To get there, drive north three miles on routes 7 and 20 and turn left on West Mountain Road.

In town, **Main Street Sports & Leisure** (48 Main St.; ☎ **413/637-4407**) rents bicycles, canoes, in-line skates, snowshoes, cross-country skis, tennis rackets, and related equipment. They can also advise you on routes and trails. Kennedy Park, right down the street from the store, is a lovely spot for cross-country skiing in winter, or for a ramble in any season.

WHERE TO STAY

While it may seem that every other house in town puts up guests—the long list below is only partial—most can only accommodate small numbers. The Tanglewood concert season is a powerful draw, so prices are highest in summer and reservations must be made far in advance. This also applies to the brief fall foliage season, usually around Columbus Day. Rate schedules are marked by their Byzantine complexity, with tariffs set according to wildly varying combinations of seasons and days of the week, as well as specific facilities, including private or shared baths, fireplaces, views, air-conditioning, and size of quarters. Minimum two- or three-night stays are required during the Tanglewood weeks, October foliage, and long holiday weekends. None of this forewarning will matter if you don't make your reservations well in advance.

Not all the bed-and-breakfasts hang signs out front. Some aren't permitted to, due to zoning restrictions, while others prefer to operate through a referral service. One of these is **Berkshire B&B Homes** (Main St., Box 211, Williamsburg, MA 01096; ☎ **413/268-7244,** fax 413/268-7243.)

Given the substantial numbers of lodging inns and hotels and the limited space to describe them, admittedly arbitrary judgments have been made to winnow the list. Some inns, for example, are so rule-ridden and facility-free they come off as crabby and cranky—no smoking, no children, no pets, no phones, no TV, no credit cards, no breakfast before 9am, shared bathrooms, check-out at 11am, check-in after 3pm—and cost twice as much as nearby motels that have all those conveniences. Let them seek clients elsewhere. Others are open only six or seven months a year, and charge the world for a bed or a meal. In this category, though, two places deserve at least a mention. **Blantyre** (16 Blantyre Rd.; ☎ **413/637-3556** in summer, or 413/298-3806 in winter), in its 1902 Tudor-Norman mansion, bestows its guests with a soak in undeniable luxury, while the only somewhat less expensive **Apple Tree Inn** (334 Lenox St.; ☎ **413/637-1477**) has a hilltop location almost directly opposite the entrance to Tanglewood, but has new owners and an uncertain future.

When all the area's inns are fully booked or if you want to be assured the full quota of 20th-century comforts and gadgets, Routes 7 and 20 north and south of town harbor a number of conventional motels. Among the possibilities are the **Mayflower Motor Inn** (☎ **413/443-4468**), **Susse Chalet** (☎ **413/637-3560**), and the **Lenox Motel** (☎ **413/499-0324**).

Very Expensive

Canyon Ranch in the Berkshires. 165 Kemble St., Lenox, MA 01240. ☎ **800/742-9000** or 413/637-4100. Fax 413/637-0057. 120 rms. 3-night packages from $1,600–$2,360 double. Rates include 3 meals daily. Taxes and 18% service charge extra. AE, DC, MC, V.

Welding turn-of-the-century opulence to the twin contemporary impulses for dietary deprivation and masochistic physicality isn't the way most people choose to spend their leisure time, at least not at these prices. But for the too-rich and too-thin set or for those who'd care to splurge just once, this is the place. A polite but firm security guard turns away the unconfirmed at the gate, so there's no popping in for a drink and a look around. Alcohol isn't served, anyway. Instead, sweat away the pounds in the huge spa complex, with 40 exercise classes a day, weights, an indoor running track, raquetball, squash, and indoor and outdoor pools and tennis. But first have a consultation with the staff of the Health & Healing Center, who "can help you enhance your wellness opportunities." After being steamed, exhausted, massaged, and showered, the real events of each day are mealtimes, "nutritionally balanced gourmet," natch. The core facility is the 1897 extravaganza of a mansion, Bellefontaine, said to be modeled after Le Petit Trianon at Versailles. While it has been painstakingly restored, it is difficult to say what was lost in the disastrous fire of 1949, which left only the magnificent library untouched. Guest rooms are certainly pleasant, but no more so than might be expected of an upper-level chain hotel.

Cranwell Resort & Golf Club. 55 Lee Rd., Lenox, MA 01240. ☎ **800/272-6935** or 413/637-1364. Fax 413/637-4364. 65 rms. A/C TEL TV. $99–$239 double Jan–May, $199–$389 double June–Labor Day, $99–$329 double Sept–Dec. Rates include breakfast. 3-night minimum stay July–Aug. AE, DC, DISC, MC, V. From Lenox Center, go north to Rte. 20 east. The resort is on the left.

Yet another century-old mansion, this one in modified Tudor style is at the center of this 380-acre resort. That's where the most expensive rooms are; the rest are in a number of surrounding smaller buildings. Some of the latter have wet bars or kitchenettes. The lovely grounds and the 18-hole, par-71 golf course are the best features, but there are two tennis courts and a large heated pool, too. In winter, the gentle slopes serve as cross-country ski trails. Three dining rooms range from formal to pubby, and there is live musical entertainment on weekend nights.

⚙ Wheatleigh. W. Hawthorne Rd., Lenox, MA 01240. ☎ **413/637-0610.** Fax 413/637-4507. 17 rms. A/C TEL TV. $155–$535 double. AE, DC, MC, V.

On my first stay at Wheatleigh, years ago, a bevy of glamorous young New Yorkers, all dressed in white, draped themselves in Gatsbyesque poses around the lavishly appointed Great Hall. They all contrived to look elaborately bored, no easy feat in this persuasive 1893 replica of a 16th-century Italian palazzo that equals or surpasses the highest standards of the monied Berkshires. Wheatleigh was very expensive then, and still is. But other places are catching up, and the new French manager is striving to give requisite value for the rates he asks. He has added TV sets, for example, with stands that don't clash with the superb decor. (Innkeepers are fond of saying that people don't visit them to watch *Seinfeld*, but at these prices, guests should be able to at least catch the evening news if they wish.) An exercise room is being added as well, with the usual exercycles and Stairmasters. A pool and tennis court are also available. The dining room admirably rounds out the experience, with immaculate floral arrangements on white napery, original contemporary art on the walls, muted chamber music playing just below recognition level. The year-round prix-fixe menu is $68; reservations recommended on weekends. In paradoxical summation, the cheapest rooms are too expensive, averaging only 11 by 13 feet, while the priciest are almost reasonable.

Expensive

Brook Farm Inn. 15 Hawthorne St., Lenox, MA 01240. ☎ **800/285-7638** or 413/637-9750. 12 rms. $100–$175 double July–Labor Day, $65–$140 double Sept–Oct, $65–$110 double Nov–June. Rates include breakfast. DISC, MC, V. From the town center, go south 1 block on Old Stockbridge Rd. Turn right.

"There is poetry here," insist the owners of this picture-pretty 1870 farmhouse, and an afternoon idle in the hammock overlooking the pool or a curled-up read by the fireplace will have you agreeing. Breakfast is an ample buffet, and the afternoon tea is complimentary. Only five of the rooms have air-conditioning, a huge plus if it's a hot summer, as the last few have been, and none of them have phones. Smoking isn't permitted indoors and the inn doesn't accept pets or children under 12.

Gables Inn. 103 Walker St., Lenox, MA 01240. ☎ **413/637-3416.** 15 rms, 3 suites. A/C. $70–$195 double. Rates include breakfast. DISC, MC, V.

Edith Wharton, who spent over two decades in Lenox, made this Queen Anne mansion her home for two years while her house, The Mount was being built. That may be enough to interest fans of the novelist, but there is much more about the Gables that will appeal to potential guests, including the canopied four-poster and working fireplace in Edith's bedroom, which was recently redone. Meticulously maintained Victoriana and related antiques are found in every corner, most notably in the eight-sided library. No rooms have phones, but suites have TVs, VCRs, and refrigerators. A heated indoor pool and tennis court are available. Children under 12 are not made welcome.

Gateways Inn. 71 Walker St., Lenox, MA 01240. ☎ **413/637-2532.** Fax 413/637-1432. 12 rms. A/C TEL TV. $85–$295 double. Rates include breakfast. AE, DC, DISC, MC, V.

Harley Proctor, who hitched up with a man called Gamble and made a bundle, had this built as his summer home in 1912. Christened "Orleton," its most impressive feature is the eye-catching staircase that winds down into the lobby. You'll probably hear the oft-repeated myth that it was designed by Stanford White, but that would have been quite a trick—White died in 1906. Still, whoever did it, it's a stunner, just the thing for a grand entrance. Equally as impressive is the suite named for conductor Arthur Fiedler, with not one but two fireplaces and a big four-poster on the sunporch.

While the kitchen has long been regarded as very capable, the tone in the dining room went beyond formal to stuffy. It's loosened up of late, and dining here is one of Lenox's greater pleasures. (Dinner entrees run $12.50 to $21.50; reservations recommended on weekends.) No smoking, no pets, no children 12 or under.

Whistler's Inn. 5 Greenwood St., Lenox, MA 01240. ☎ **413/637-0975.** 14 rms, 3 suites. TEL TV. $90–$200 double and suites July–Oct, 20–35% lower rest of year. Rates include breakfast. AE, DISC, MC, V.

Both innkeepers are compulsive travelers, hitting every continent, but with particular fondness for India and Africa. They bring things back from every trip, filling the cavernous rooms of their Tudor mansion with clusters of cut glass, painted screens, assorted Victoriana, grandfather clocks, Persian rugs, landscape paintings, ormolu candelabras, a grand piano, shelf after shelf of books (both of them are writers), and lavish furniture. The result is rooms that are not so much decorated as gathered, without a single visually boring corner. A little white ragmop of a dog called Pushkin races around demanding attention. Breakfast is suitably proportioned (to the surroundings, not the dog) and a bottle of sherry or port is kept in the library for guests to pour themselves a drink to sip with tea and cookies. Concerts are often held in the music room in summer. Ten of the guest rooms are air-conditioned.

Moderate

Amadeus House. 15 Cliffwood St. (near corner of Main St.), Lenox, MA 01240. ☎ **800/ 205-4770** or 413/637-4770. 8 rms (6 with private bath). $60–$175 double July–Labor Day, $60–$150 double mid-May to June and Sept–Oct, $60–$125 double Nov to mid-May. Rates include breakfast. AE, DISC, MC, V.

As can be assumed from the name, the owners are lovers of classical music. That theme carries through with the names given the guest rooms—Bach, Bernstein, and Brahms, for instance—and the fact that the usual common room TV is replaced by a stereo and stacks of CDs. "Beethoven" is a two-bedroom suite with a sitting area and fully-stocked kitchen. Only one room has air-conditioning; most of the rest have ceiling fans. The central part of the house dates from 1820, and the graceful bannister on the main staircase was built by a Shaker carpenter. Breakfast incorporates a hot entree and afternoon tea is served. No smoking, children 10 or under, or pets, though there is a resident Labrador retriever named "Bravo."

Candlelight Inn. 53 Walker St., Lenox, MA 01240. ☎ **413/637-1555.** 8 rms. A/C. $70–$155 double. Rates include breakfast and taxes. AE, MC, V.

A folksy gathering place for locals as well as guests, the inviting bar at the end of the center hall in this 1885 country Victorian sees a friendly, not raucous, nightly trade, and the four dining rooms are often full. In winter, clink glasses beside a crackling fire; in summer, reserve a table in the courtyard beneath Campari umbrellas. Main courses are $13.95 to $22.95. Dinner is served all year, lunch from Memorial Day to late October. While the Candlelight does most of its business on the restaurant side, the upstairs rooms are comfortable, if not memorable, and all have private baths. No pets, no smoking, and no kids under 10.

Cornell Inn. 203 Main St., Lenox, MA 01240. ☎ **800/637-0562** or 413/637-0562. 30 rms. A/C TV TEL. $99–$199 double. Rates include breakfast. AE, DC, MC, V.

This underpublicized three-building inn about a mile north of Lenox Center has much to commend, even if one or two staffers could use warmth lessons. Versatility is a particular virtue. All but two rooms have TVs, and those two are among the most attractive, both with fireplaces, one with a four-poster and the other with a brass bed. Others have twins, doubles, queens, and kings in various combinations, and lodgings in the new building have whirlpools, fireplaces, wet bars, and decks. One has a kitchenette as well. The restaurant, with a full-service bar, offers terrace dining in summer. There is a cramped "spa" with modest exercise equipment, a sauna, and a Jacuzzi, but its musty basement location isn't very inviting. No pets are allowed, but kids under 12 are permitted in one of the buildings. Smoking is only allowed in bedrooms and the tavern.

Village Inn. 16 Church St., Lenox, MA 01240. ☎ **800/253-0917** or 413/637-0020. 32 rms. A/C TEL. $80–$195 double summer–fall, $60–$110 double winter–spring. AE, DC, DISC, MC, V.

An inn since 1775, with occasional periods when it was put to other uses, this populist stopping place hasn't a whiff of pretense. Its unusually large number of rooms come in considerable variety, and are categorized as "Superior," "Standard," or "Economy." That means four-postered kings or queens in the high-end rooms, some of which have working fireplaces and/or whirlpool baths, and constricted quarters with double beds in the low-end rooms. Claw-foot tubs are common in rooms in all categories. Afternoon tea and dinner are served June to October in the restaurant, light meals in the downstairs tavern (which is the only room where smoking is allowed). Small combos play on some weekends, and there have been poetry readings. No pets are permitted, but children over 6 are welcome.

WHERE TO DINE

✪ Church Street Cafe. 65 Church St. ☎ **413/637-2745.** Reservations recommended on weekends. Main courses $14.95–$17.95. MC, V. Daily 11:30am–2pm and 5:30–10pm (closed Mon in winter). ECLECTIC AMERICAN.

The most popular eatery in town got that way by delivering fanciful combinations of victuals that alert the eyes and pique the taste buds without scaring off timid or conservative diners. Such innovative cuisine includes the lunchtime "cafe sandwich," a layered production of grilled disks of eggplant, roasted sweet red peppers, goat cheese, watercress, red onion slices, and tomato on nubby wholegrain bread. So many powerful flavors seep and mingle here, even meat-eaters hardly notice the absence of cooked flesh (though the cafe is not exclusively a vegetarian restaurant, it does specialize artfully in meatless dishes). Similar creativity informs the dinner plate of potato cake, roast ratatouille, sautéed mixed greens, and grilled bread drizzled with oil. Surroundings are unembellished, plain wood chairs and tables and crocks of flowers. The large dining deck fills up whenever the weather allows.

Lenox 218. 28 Main St. (Rte. 7A). ☎ **413/637-4218.** Main courses $12.95–$21.95. AE, CB, DC, DISC, MC, V. Mon–Sat 11:30am–2:30pm and 5–9:30pm. ITALIAN/AMERICAN.

Largely black-and-white, with hanging pots of ivy, the decor at this unremarkable restaurant falls short of the urban sophistication it evidently seeks. So does the food, which mainly consists of simple, familiar fare like veal piccata, chicken cacciatore, and meatloaf with peas, carrots, and mashed potatoes. But that's okay. It's cooked and assembled well enough, and the service is at least pleasant. Lunch might be the better time, when the bar in front is quiet, and the meatloaf goes for $7.95, not the $12.95 it costs at night.

TANGLEWOOD & THE PERFORMING ARTS SCENE

Lenox is filled with the beautiful strains of music every July and August, and the undisputed headliners are Seiji Ozawa and the Boston Symphony Orchestra, of which he is music director. Their concerts are given at the famous ✪ **Tanglewood** estate, usually beginning the last weekend in June and ending the weekend before Labor Day. While the BSO is Tanglewood's 800-pound cultural gorilla, the program features a menagerie of other performers and musical idioms. These run the gamut from popular artists (past performers have included James Taylor and Peter, Paul & Mary) and jazz vocalists and combos (including Dave Brubeck, Betty Carter, Joe Williams, and George Shearing), to choral groups like the Robert Shaw choral troupe and guest soloists and conductors such as André Previn, Itzak Perlman, and Jessye Norman. Large visiting ensembles like the Kirov Orchestra and Chorus and the Boston Pops are also featured.

Such prominent groups and individual artists usually appear in "The Shed," an open-ended auditorium that seats 5,000, and also plays to a huge surrounding lawn, where an outdoor audience lounges on folding chairs and blankets. Less-known performers and chamber groups appear in Ozawa Hall and the separate theater. Seats in The Shed range from $20 to $63, while lawn tickets are usually $11.50 to $15.50. (Higher prices apply for some special appearances.) For information on programs, call **617/266-1492** (Boston) or 413/637-5165 (Lenox). For weekly updates on the performance schedule call 413/637-1666. To order tickets by mail before June, write the Tanglewood Ticket Office at Symphony Hall, Boston, MA 02115. After the first week in June, write the Tanglewood Ticket Office, Lenox, MA 01240. Tickets can be charged by phone through Symphonycharge (☎ **800/274-0808** outside Boston, or 617/266-1200 in Boston).

As consuming as the events at Tanglewood are, there's even more. **Shakespeare & Company** uses buildings and outdoor amphitheaters on the grounds of The Mount to stage its late May to end of August season of plays by the Bard himself, works by Edith Wharton, and new American playwrights. Performances by dance troupes, student actors, and even puppets flesh out the schedule. The venues are the outdoor amphitheaters, Mainstage and Oxford Court, and two indoor stages, Stables and Wharton. Staggered performances take place Tuesday through Sunday, from as early as noon to 8:30pm. Tickets range from $12.50 to $27.50. Call the box office at **413/637-3353.** Lunch and dinner picnic baskets can be purchased on site.

In addition, the **Berkshire Opera Company** (17 Main St.; ☎ **413/243-1343**) mounts two operas in English in July and August. From June to September, the **National Music Center** (70 Kemble St.; ☎ **413/637-1800** for information, 413/637-4718 for tickets) is home to the **Berkshire Performing Arts Theatre,** which presents a June to September season of music—jazz, pop, folk, and blues—in its 1,200-seat hall. And, on selected Saturdays between October and May, chamber music recitals are presented at the Lenox Town Hall by **Armstrong Chamber Concerts** (P.O. Box 367, Washington Depot, CT 06794; ☎ **860/868-0522**).

PITTSFIELD
137 miles W of Boston, 7 miles N of Lenox

Berkshire County's largest city (in 1990 the population was over 48,000) gets little attention in most tourist literature, and there's good reason. A commercial and industrial center—Martin Marietta is the largest employer—it presents little of the charm that marks such popular destinations as Stockbridge and Lenox. Still, it is a convenient base for day excursions to attractions elsewhere in the region, including several ski centers, the summer concert season at Tanglewood, and Hancock Shaker Village, a few miles to the west. Pittsfield is also home to the house where Herman Melville wrote *Moby Dick*, and an eccentric little museum with a theater showing art films much of the year.

The **Berkshire Visitors Bureau** (☎ 413/443-9186) is located in the same block of buildings as the Hilton, on Berkshire Common.

A MUSEUM & HISTORIC HOME

Arrowhead. 780 Holmes Rd. ☎ **413/442-1793.** Admission $4.50 adults, $4 seniors, $3.50 children 6–16. Late May–Labor Day 10am–5pm; Labor Day–end of Oct Fri–Mon 10am–5pm; rest of year, by appointment only. Drive east from Park Square on East St., turn right on Elm St. and right again on Holmes Rd.

Herman Melville, just one prominent member of the literary and artistic community that kept summer homes in the Berkshires, bought this house in 1850 and lived here until 1863. It was during this time that he wrote his masterpiece, *Moby Dick,* and a number of lesser works. One of his best friends was Nathaniel Hawthorne, and they conversed regularly in the upstairs study and at a table beside the large fireplace in the kitchen. In truth, however, the house is only likely to be interesting to literature students and avid readers. Visits are by guided tour only.

Berkshire Museum. 39 South St. (1 block south of Park Square). ☎ **413/443-7171.** Admission $3 adults, $2 seniors and students, $1 children 12–18. Tues–Sat 10am–5pm (open Mon July–Aug), Sun 1–5pm.

It began in 1903 as the "Museum of Natural History and Art," the words chiseled in stone above the entrance. The holdings bounce from Babylonian cuneiform tablets to stuffed birds to mineral displays to tanks of live fish in the basement aquarium. An auditorium seating 300 serves as the "Little Cinema," which has a season of art and foreign films during the warmer months. Apart from the aquarium, the greatest interest may be generated by the art and archaeological artifacts assembled on the second floor. A sculpture gallery has full-size casts of important 16th-century Italian sculptures and a 19th-century *Diana* by American Augustus Saint-Gaudens. While those looking for "name" artists will generally be disappointed, there are a number of canvases and sculptures by contemporary artists that deserve attention, and here and there are minor Alexander Calders, a Reginald Marsh, and a couple of landscapes by Alfred Bierstedt. Among cases of 2nd-century Mediterranean glassware and Roman funerary busts are pieces of pre-Christian Egyptian jewelry and pottery and a delicate necklace from Thebes dating to at least 1500 B.C. Kids will love the mummy, of course, and the tropical and native fish and amphibians in the basement.

OUTDOOR PURSUITS

CAMPING   A prime recreational preserve is **Pittsfield State Forest** (Cascade Street; ☎ 413/442-8992), a little over three miles west of the center of town on West St. Its 10,000 acres have 31 campsites, boat ramps, streams for canoeing and fishing, and trails for hiking, horseback riding, and cross-country skiing. Open daily 8am to 8pm. Admission is $2 per car.

GOLFING, BOATING & BICYCLING   A useful Pittsfield store to know is **Plaine's Bike Golf Ski Golf** (55 W. Housatonic St.; ☎ 413/499-0294), which rents bikes by the day and week and carries equipment for all the sports its name suggests. It's on Route 20, west of the city center, at the corner of Center Street. **Onota Boat Livery** (463 Peck Rd.; ☎ 413/442-1724) rents canoes and motorboats for use on Onota Lake, conveniently located at the western edge of the city. Nonmember golfers are welcome on the 18-hole course at **Pontoosuc Lake Country Club** (Kirkwood Drive; ☎ 413/445-4217) for reasonable greens fees.

SKIING   South of the city center, off Route 7 near the Pittsfield city limits, is **Bousquet Ski Area** (Dan Fox Drive; ☎ 413/442-2436). It has 21 trails, the longest over one mile and with a vertical drop of 750 feet, with two double chairlifts and two rope tows. Night skiing is on Monday to Saturday; equipment can be rented for moderate rates.

About nine miles in the other direction, off Route 7 in the town of New Ashford, is **Bodie Mountain Ski Area** (☎ 413/443-4752), with a vertical drop of 1,250 feet and a long run of 2¹/₂ miles. Midweek ski school packages are attractive, and in summer they offer raquetball, tennis, and campsites.

Alternatively, turn west a mile short of Bodie on Brodie Mountain Road and continue about three miles to **Jiminy Peak** (Hancock, MA 01237; ☎ 413/738-5500, or 413/738-7325 for 24-hour ski reports). This expanding resort aspires to four-season activity, so **skiing** on 28 trails (18 are open at night) with seven lifts is supplemented the rest of the year with horseback riding, trapshooting, fishing in a stocked pond, six tennis courts, mountain biking, pools, and golf at the nearby Waubeeka Springs course. Ample lodging is available (see "Where to Stay," below.)

WHERE TO STAY

Hilton Inn Berkshire. West St., Pittsfield, MA 01201. ☎ **800/445-8667** or 413/499-2000. Fax 413/442-0449. 175 rms. A/C TV TEL. $79–$189 double. AE, CB, DC, DISC, MC, V.

The tallest building in town at 14 stories, this Hilton isn't hard to find, although it takes a little round-the-block maneuvering to get to the front door. (Look for signs to Berkshire Common, west of South Street, the main drag.) It has most of the bells and whistles expected of a first-class chain hotel, and is more family-friendly than many lodgings in the region. Three advantages: (1) With all those rooms, chances are better for copping a bed for Tanglewood weekends; (2) Unlike nearly all the inns in the Lenox area, children are not only welcome, they stay for free when occupying the same room as their parents, and most rooms have two double or queen-sized beds, with sleep sofas; (3) There is a newly outfitted fitness room and a heated indoor pool to keep the kids occupied. Some rooms have hair dryers and fully stocked minibars. Clock radios, cable TV, and in-room movies are standard. Seven floors are nonsmoking, but that leaves five more for nicotine-dependents. Management is in the process of replacing all the mattresses and carpeting.

The Country Inn at Jiminy Peak. Brodie Mountain Rd. (near Rte. 43), Hancock, MA 01237. ☎ **800/882-8859** or 413/738-5500. Fax 413/738-5513. 105 suites. A/C TV TEL. $95–$195 suite. Rates include breakfast. AE, CB, DC, DISC, MC, V.

The "Jiminy Peak" moniker might suggest some cutesy mock-Alpine enclave with rapacious singles and indefatigable social directors in Tyrolean pants. On the contrary, this is one of the better lodging deals in the Berkshires, especially if your idea of luxury is space. All units are one-bedroom suites with full kitchens and pull-out sofas, suitable for families or two couples traveling together. A buffet breakfast is served in the Founders' Grill in season, meaning late June to mid-October and mid-December to April. The inn has its drawbacks: Some signs of the robust use to which ski resorts are subject can be seen in the nicks on furniture legs and around elevators, though maintenance is otherwise relatively good. And most guests could probably live without the constant reminders that they, too, "could be part of the Jiminy Peak family" by buying a condo. But these shortcomings pale beside the two pools and abundant recreational facilities (mentioned above in the description under "Outdoor Pursuits"), and Tanglewood is less than 30 minutes away.

WHERE TO DINE

Giovanni's. Rte. 7N (north of the center). ☎ **413/443-2441.** Main courses $7–$17. AE, DC, DISC, MC, V. Mon–Thurs 4:30–9pm, Fri–Sat 4:30–10pm, Sun noon–8pm. ITALIAN/AMERICAN.

Four rows of 30 hanging fake Tiffany lamps date the room to about the middle of the disco decade, and don't provide much illumination. The menu is as retro as the decor, hearkening back to an era when iceberg lettuce was still salad king and cocktails came in egg cup–size glasses. Despite these reservations, Giovanni's does have its high points. For one, the dishes served here aren't for peckish appetites. Portions are gargantuan, opportunities for enough carbo-loading to propel a marathon runner five miles past the finish line. And though you've seen this veal amandine and these baked stuffed shrimp before, that doesn't mean they don't taste good. A self-designated house specialty is chicken ricco with shrimp, broccoli, mushrooms, onions, and strips of roast bell peppers all heaped on at least a half-pound of linguine and showered with oregano and parmesan. It'll serve two—without appetizer, bread, or dessert. Seniors have a fondness for the early-bird specials, served from 4:30 to 6pm and priced at $9.75, including a glass of wine.

ON THE SHAKER TRAIL: A DRIVING TOUR

Mother Ann arrived in near-revolutionary New York State in 1774 with eight disciples. The former Ann Lee, previously imprisoned for her excess of religious zeal, had proclaimed a vision that anointed her the leader of the United Society of Believers in Christ's Second Coming. That austere Protestant sect was popularly known as "The Shakers" for their spastic movements when in the throes of religious ecstasy.

Mother Lee established their first communal settlement in Watervliet, near Albany, N.Y. By the time of her death in 1784 she had made many converts, who then fanned out across the country to form colonies from Maine to Indiana. Two of the most important communities straddled the Massachusetts–New York border, within miles of each other near Pittsfield and New Lebanon, N.Y. Farther west, a Shaker Museum has been established at Old Chatham.

Shaker society produced highly disciplined farmers and craftspeople, whose products were much in demand in the outside world. They sold seeds, invented early agricultural machinery and handtools, and erected large buildings of several stories and exquisite simplicity. Their spare, clean-lined furniture and accessories anticipated the so-called "Danish Modern" style by a century, and in recent years have drawn astonishingly high prices at auction.

All of these accomplishments required a verve owed at least in part to sublimation of sexual energy—a fundamental Shaker tenet was total celibacy. They kept going with converts and adoptions, but by the 1970s the inevitable result of that shortsighted policy left the movement with a bare handful of adherents. The string of Shaker settlements and museums that remain is testament to their dictum, "Hands to work, hearts to God."

To tour the region's Shaker attractions, start out in Pittsfield, heading west on Route 20. In about five miles, on the left, is Hancock Shaker Village.

Hancock Shaker Village. Rtes. 20 and 41, Pittsfield, MA 01202. ☎ **800/817-1137** or 413/443-0188. Admission $12.50 adults, $5 children 6–17, $25 families. Apr–Memorial Day and late Oct to late Nov (guided tours only) daily 10am–3pm, Memorial Day–3rd week in Oct daily 9:30am–5pm. Also open 1st weekend in Dec, Christmas weekend, and 3rd week in Feb (call ahead for times and events).

Of the 20 restored buildings that make up the village, the signature structure is clearly the 1826 round stone barn. The Shaker preoccupation with primacy of functionalism and purity of line and material is no more clear than here, the purpose of the shape being to expedite the chores of feeding and milking livestock (arranging the cows in a circle instead of in rows makes it easier to milk and feed them). The precise joinery of the roof beams and support pillars is a joy to examine. The second "must-see" on the grounds is the brick dwelling that contained the communal dining room, kitchens, and upstairs sleeping quarters. Sexes were separated at meals, work, and religious services, and equality was served by such features as the opposing staircases leading to male and female "retiring rooms." Other buildings of note include the Meeting House, where religious services were held, and the laundry and machine shop. While present-day artisans and docents labor in herb and vegetable gardens and in shops demonstrating Shaker crafts and techniques, they are not in costume, nor do they pretend to be Shaker inhabitants. They are knowledgeable about their subject in varying degrees, however, and dispense such nuggets as explanations of the Shaker discipline that required members to dress the right side first, to button from right to left, and to step with the right foot first.

The museum shop is excellent, with books and replicas of Shaker baskets, boxes, and small furniture. A cafe serves lunches during the main Memorial Day to October season, with some dishes based on Shaker recipes. On Saturday nights in July, August, September, and October, the Village presents tours and Shaker four-course dinners by candlelight at a cost of $38 per person. Reservations are essential (☎ 413/443-0188).

Mount Lebanon Shaker Village. Rte. 20, New Lebanon, NY 12125. ☎ **518/794-9500.** Admission $6 adults, $3 children 7–18. Memorial Day–Labor Day weekends (and some Mon holidays) 10–4pm. Continue to the far end of the village, taking the rutted gravel road down to the red barn on the left.

From Hancock, turn left (west) on Route 20. In about five miles, on the left, is the private Darrow School, which has taken over most of the buildings that were once part of one of the Shaker movement's most important communities. They're easy to spot after a visit to Hancock Shaker Village, with their sober, simple dimensions and utter lack of ornamental detailing. Some of the buildings have been set aside as the Mount Lebanon Shaker Village.

This was the first self-contained Shaker community in America, established in 1787. In the red barn is a gift shop and a small museum of tools, furniture, farm implements, and related items. Guided tours are available (on a sporadic basis) of buildings not in use by the school, the most interesting of which are the meetinghouse and a stone dairy barn. Past fund-raising auctions held on the school grounds helped send prices for antique Shaker furniture and artifacts into the stratosphere, especially after enthusiasts Oprah Winfrey and Bill Cosby showed up and added their figurative two cents to the bidding.

Shaker Museum and Library. 88 Shaker Museum Rd., Old Chatham, NY 12136. ☎ **518/794-9100.** Admission $6 adults, $5 seniors, $3 children 8–17. Late April–early Nov Wed–Mon 10am–5pm. About a mile on County 13, on the right.

Leaving the museum, turn left (west) again on Route 20. After Brainard (about eight miles), watch for the turn south on Route 66. Continue to the hamlet of Old Chatham, where you'll pick up County Road 13. This is tricky, so watch closely for the sign next to the general store pointing to the Shaker Museum and Library.

Obviously better-funded and pampered than the Mount Lebanon Shaker Village, this concentration of barns and outbuildings contains a substantial collection of about 8,000 Shaker tools, pieces of furniture, machinery, and smaller items, such as the famous oval boxes that held everything from seeds to sewing materials. They fill 24 galleries, most of which offer illuminating essays, reproductions of Shaker writings, and helpful descriptive labels. Many of the galleries are arranged as period rooms, including living quarters, kitchen areas, weaving shops, a classroom, and a blacksmith's shop. All is displayed with curatorial taste and painstaking care, and, except when school groups are about, can be contemplated at leisure and in rural calm. Periodic special events are mounted, which have included, in the recent past, antiques fairs, apple harvest breakfasts, herb and plant sales, concerts, and kite-flying demonstrations.

After a visit, the perfect overnight retreat is directly at hand . . . right across the road.

WHERE TO STAY & DINE

Old Chatham Sheepherding Company Inn. 99 Shaker Museum Rd., Old Chatham, NY 12136. ☎ **518/794-9774.** Fax 518/794-9779. 8 rms. A/C TEL. $150–$325 double. Rates include breakfast. AE, DC, MC, V.

Bounding—tastefully—out of the chute in late 1995, this newcomer demanded instant recognition as one of the most accomplished inns in the Northeast. The 1790 Georgian manor in which it is housed may seem too grand and sumptuously appointed for association with the stringently ascetic Shakers, but there are connections. A previous owner, John S. Williams, was a collector of Shaker artifacts and gave his accumulated holdings to the museum across the street. And the new owners, who have put together an estate of 500 acres of gorgeous rolling farmland, built vast barns in the spare Shaker style, even furnishing the offices with reproductions of Shaker designs. In no time, they have assembled and nurtured a flock of 2,000 sheep, with more to come. Their prime interest is in developing sheep's milk products—cheeses, ice cream, and yogurt—and guests are welcome to witness the operation of the 48-station milking parlor. In the adjoining barn, newborn lambs cavort and gambol around their mothers, no less adorable than those depicted in children's books. That might make it hard for sensitive folk to dine at night on leg of lamb and spicy lamb sausage in the 48-seat dining room, but there are always options on a menu that is changed daily. The head chef makes maximum use of the farm's products and of produce from the upper Hudson Valley. She is a Culinary Institute graduate who has worked with such star chefs as Alice Waters and Larry Forgione. Rooms in the main house and in adjoining cottages are faultlessly decorated in manners unique to each. Four-poster beds have mattresses covered with fleece-filled pads, the baths have etched glasses and more thick, wraparound towels than any two people are likely to need. Most rooms have views of the flocks whirling across the meadows; three have working fireplaces. At night, as part of the turndown service, a sheepskin is laid beside the bed to cuddle the feet upon arising. Smoking isn't allowed and they discourage bringing children under 12.

WILLIAMSTOWN

145 miles W of Boston, 23 miles N of Lenox

Entering the town on Route 7 or intersecting Route 2, you'll see a central green shaded by tall trees. In the middle is a weathered building that looks authentic, but turns out to be a replica of a 1753 dwelling. It was made with period tools in celebration of the town's bicentennial. The town and its prestigious liberal-arts college were named for Col. Ephraim Williams, who was killed in 1755 in one of the French and Indian Wars. He bequeathed the land for creation of a school and a town. His college grew, spreading east from the central common along both sides of Main Street (Route 2). Since it has been around for over 200 years, every new building was erected in one of the styles popular at the time of construction. That makes Main Street a virtual museum of institutional architecture, with representatives of the Georgian, Federalist, Gothic Revival, Romanesque, and Victorian modes and a few that are yet to be labeled. They stand at dignified distances from each other, so what might have been a tumultuous visual hodge-podge is a stately lesson in historical design.

A free weekly newspaper, *The Advocate,* produces a useful *Guide to the Northern Berkshires* that mainly covers Williamstown. For a copy, send a check for $3.50 to *The Advocate,* P.O. Box 95, 38 Spring St., Williamstown, MA 01267. An unattended **information booth** at the corner of North Street (Route 7) and Main Street (Route 2) has an abundance of pamphlets and brochures free for the taking.

ART MUSEUMS

✪ **Sterling and Francine Clark Art Institute.** 225 South St. ☎ **413/458-9545.** Free admission. Tues–Sun (and some Mon holidays) 10am–5pm.

The eponymous Mr. Clark was an art lover. He was also an heir to the Singer fortune, which allowed him to pursue his avocation and bestow this remarkable repository upon his community. Clark's donation funded the modern wing to the original white marble neoclassical building and covered all acquisitions, upkeep, and recent renovations; in addition, he specified in his bequest that no admission fees be charged. It is a remarkable gift, for this is not the collection of an undisciplined, self-absorbed millionaire. Within these walls are canvases by Renoir (several), Degas, Gauguin, Toulouse-Lautrec, Pissaro, and their predecessor Corot. While they are the stars, there are also 15th- and 16th-entury Dutch portraitists, English and European genre and landscape painters, and Americans Sargent and Homer, as well as fine porcelain, silverware, and antique furnishings. This qualifies as one of the great cultural resources of the Berkshires and the state.

Williams College Museum of Art. Main St. ☎ **413/597-2429.** Free admission. Tues–Sat (and some Mon holidays) 10am–5pm, Sun 1–5pm.

The second, lesser leg of Williamstown's two prominent art repositories exists in large part due to the college's collection of almost 400 paintings by the American modernists Maurice and Charles Prendergast. Some of their works are always rotated into view, and while they are of moderate interest, visitors are more likely to be drawn to such names as Juan Gris, Fernand Leger, Giorgio de Chirico, James Whistler, and Pablo Picasso. These are salted with more contemporary pieces by Andy Warhol and Edward Hopper and supplemented by frequently changed temporary exhibitions. The striking three-story entrance atrium was designed by prominent architect Charles Moore.

OUTDOOR PURSUITS

Waubeeka Golf Links (Rtes. 7 and 43, South Williamstown, MA 01267; ☎ **413/458-5869**) is open to the public, with highest weekend greens fees of only $22. The clubhouse can seat 150 people in three dining rooms.

    Mt. Greylock State Reservation contains the highest peak (3,487 feet) in Massachusetts and a section of the Appalachian Trail. A road allows cars to be driven almost to the summit, where the War Memorial Tower is located—even the sedentary visitor can enjoy 360-degree vistas of the Taconic and Hoosac ranges, far into Vermont and New York. More active people will find hiking trails radiating from the parking lot near **Bascom Lodge** (P.O. Box 1800, Lanesborough, MA 01237; ☎ 413/743-1591), a grandly rustic creation of the Civilian Conservation Corps in the New Deal thirties. Simple dormitory beds and four private rooms are available by the night from mid-May to late October. Dinners are available by reservation. Look for Greylock Road off Route 7 in New Ashford.

SHOPPING

In South Williamstown, the white frame building on the right (going north on Route 7) looks like a recycled general store, and it is. Once a basic small town emporium, **The Store at Five Corners** (Routes 7 and 43; ☎ **413/458-3176**) now stocks more upscale merchandise like stylish takeouts and picnics comprised of pâtés, baguettes, French cheeses, wines, deli meats, and salads. Meals can also be eaten on premises. Open daily 7am to 8pm.

Saddleback Antiques (1395 Cold Spring Rd.; ☎ 413/458-5852) features country, wicker, and Victorian furniture and a variety of collectibles, while **Collectors Warehouse** (105 North St.; ☎ 413/458-9686) has a little bit of almost everything—jewelry, books, dolls, furniture, glassware. Both are on Route 7, the first to the south of the town center, the second slightly to the north. Both accept MasterCard and Visa.

WHERE TO STAY

This is a college town, so remember that in addition to the usual peak periods of July, August, and the October foliage season, lodgings fill up during graduation (late May to early June) and on football weekends.

Field Farm Guesthouse. 554 Sloan Rd., Williamstown, MA 01262. ☎ 413/458-3135. 5 rms. TEL. $90 double. MC, V. Follow Rte. 7 to its intersection with Rte. 43. Turn west, then make an immediate right turn on Sloan Rd. Continue 1 mile to the Field Farm entrance, on the right.

After an extended vacation of B&B-hopping, there may come a time when one more tilted floor or wobbly Windsor chair will send even a devout inn-lover over the edge. Here's one antidote. In 1948, this pristine example of postwar modern architecture rose in the middle of a spectacularly scenic 294-acre estate. Most of the rooms look over tidy meadows in the foreground and on up to the summit of Mount Greylock. The living room is equipped with a telescope to view the beavers and waterfowl on the the lake a hundred yards away.

The setting is so lovely actor Christopher Reeve used it as a backdrop for his wedding, and other couples have followed suit. Most of the furniture, of the then avant-garde Scandinavian Modern school, was designed and made to order for the house. All rooms are spare, utterly free of clutter, decorated in muted colors. A pool and tennis court are available to guests. Breakfast has been upgraded from continental to hearty meals of waffles and five-cheese omelets utilizing fruits, herbs, and vegetables grown on the property. A pantry is open for guests to help themselves to beverages and snacks. Smoking is forbidden, as are pets, but well-behaved children are welcome.

Orchards Inn. 222 Adams Rd., Williamstown, MA 01267. ☎ 800/225-1517 or 413/458-9611. Fax 413/458-3273. 49 rms. $125–$225 double. AE, CB, DC, MC, V.

Most guests seem entirely satisfied with this small hotel at the eastern edge of town, although little about it will quicken your heartbeat. The management certainly tries hard, though, providing a fully equipped exercise room with Jacuzzi and sauna, an outdoor pool, and access to nearby tennis and golf. Rooms are decorated with reproductions of English furniture, attractively enough, but with fewer antiques than claimed in the brochures. Room fridges are stocked with soft drinks, the TVs have VCRs attached, and many rooms have working fireplaces. Terry-cloth robes are provided, and the nightly turndown service includes a plate of cookies. The restaurant kitchen seeks no new frontiers, with fairly typical offerings like veal marsala and broiled salmon with broccoli and wild rice (main courses $16.50 to $23).

Williams Inn. 1090 Main St. (Rtes. 7 and 2), Williamstown, MA 01267. ☎ 800/828-0133 or 413/458-9371. Fax 413/458-2767. 100 rms. A/C TV TEL. $100–$150 double. AE, CB, DC, DISC, MC, V.

Despite the name, this is a standard motel, built in 1974 and not in the least memorable, but containing most of the gadgets and conveniences today's traveler has come to expect. Even the smallest rooms are ample in dimension, and children under 14 stay free in the same room with their parents. Guests have access to an indoor kidney-shaped pool, and to a Jacuzzi and saunas as well. Pets are permitted on the first floor. The main dining room trafficks in such expectables as veal scallopine and chicken amandine (main courses $13.95 to $19.95) and there is also a tavern menu with burgers and such ($4.95 to $9.95). Weekend nights there are live groups playing forties music. They accept many bus tours, for which they are eminently suited, by size and disposition.

WILLIAMSTOWN AFTER DARK

Williamstown's premier attraction each summer, in contrast to that of the southern Berkshires, is the **Williamstown Theatre Festival** (Adams Memorial Theatre, Main Street, P.O. Box 517, MA 01267; ☎ 413/597-3400). Staging classic and new plays during its performance season (late June through August), the festival attracts many top actors and directors. The are two venues: the Main Stage showcases works by major playwrights, while the Other Stage features more experimental works. Ticket prices range from $14 to $32, depending upon venue and performance date.

All college towns nurture music, from classical to rock and all stops in between, and Williamstown is no exception. Bars and restaurants provide the space. One such in the area is the **Night Shift Cafe** (87 Marshall St., North Adams; ☎ 413/663-7646), often a scene for jazz, blues, and funk. The Williams College Department of Music sponsors diverse concerts and recitals, from choral groups to jazz ensembles. Call their 24-hour recorded **Concertline** at 413/597-3146 to learn of upcoming events. In addition, the Clark Art Institute (see "Art Museums," above) hosts frequent classical music events.

9
Connecticut

by Herbert Bailey Livesey

Connecticut is a place that resists generalization and confounds spinners of superlatives. It doesn't rank at the top or bottom of any major chart of virtues or liabilities, which makes it impossible to stuff into pigeonholes. Certainly compact—only 90 miles from west to east and 55 miles south to north—it is still three times the size of the smallest state, right next door. While parts of it are clogged with humanity, there are three other states even more congested, and much of it is as empty and undeveloped as inland Maine.

By some measures, its citizens are as wealthy as any in the country, but dozens of its cities and large towns are hollow shells of their prosperous 19th-century selves, beset by crime and poverty as bleak and intractable as it gets. It can boast no dramatic geographical feature—no Smuggler's Notch, no Cape Cod—and its highest elevation is only 2,380 feet, a hill so far north it almost tips into the next state. Established in 1635 by disgruntled English settlers who didn't like the way things were going at the Plymouth Colony, it has long seemed spiritually divorced from the rest of New England, an appendage of New York, or a place to be traversed on the way from there to Boston.

That might seem like a hopelessly unresolvable identity crisis, and hardly makes Connecticut seem like an appealing vacation destination. But a closer look reveals an abundance of reasons to slow down, to linger. To a great extent, the state owes its existence to the presence of water. Drought isn't a word that comes up very often here. In addition to having Long Island Sound off of its southern coast, several significant rivers and their tributaries lace the hills and coastal plain—the Housatonic, Naugatuck, Qunnipiac, Connecticut, and Thames. They provided power for the mills along their courses and the towns and cities that grew around them. Industry still drives most of the economy, despite the bucolic image that mention of the state often conjures, but the pollution of the water that it helped cause is being cleaned up, both in the rivers and the Sound. Development, too, has slowed, helping to preserve a little longer the scores of classic colonial villages from the Litchfield Hills to the Mystic coast. They are as placid and timeless as they have been for over three centuries or as polished and sophisticated as transplanted urbanites can make them. And the state's salty maritime heritage is palpable in the old boatbuilding and fishing villages at the mouths of its rivers, especially those to the east of New Haven. Connecticut is New England's front porch. Pull up a chair and stay awhile.

1   The Gold Coast

Mansions, marinas, and apartment blocks elbow for space right up to the deeply indented shoreline of this southwestern corner of the state bordering Long Island Sound. This is one of the most heavily developed stretches of the coast, and, in terms of family incomes, one of the wealthiest (hence the name "Gold Coast"). As the land rises slowly inland from the water's edge, woods thicken, roads narrow, and pockets of New England unfold. Yacht country becomes horse country.

The first suburbs started to form in the middle of the last century, when train rails started radiating north and east from New York's Grand Central Terminal into the countryside. That made this part of the state accessible for warm-weather refugees from the big city, and eventually—inevitably—the summer homes were made permanent. Corporate satraps liked the life of gentry, so after World War II, they started moving their companies closer to their new homes. Stamford became a city; Greenwich, New Canaan, Darien, and Westport were their bedrooms of choice—pricey, haughty, redolent of the good life. Of course, Fairfield County also contains Bridgeport, a depressed city that once considered filing for bankruptcy and may yet do so. But for visitors, the fashionable exurbs are the draw, along with the villages farther north, especially Ridgefield, that hint of Vermont within an hour and a half of Times Square.

ESSENTIALS

GETTING THERE   From New York and points south, take I-95 or the Merritt Parkway. From eastern Massachusetts and northern Connecticut, take I-84 south to Danbury, then Route 7 south into Fairfield County.

The **Metro North** commuter line (☎ **800/223-6052** or 212/532-4900) has many trains daily to and from New York's Grand Central Terminal, with stops at Greenwich, Stamford, Darien, Norwalk, Westport, and additional stations all the way to New Haven. Less frequent trains connect Danbury with Norwalk.

VISITOR INFORMATION   An information booklet for the northern part of the county is available from the **Housatonic Valley Tourism District** (Box 406, Danbury, CT 06813; ☎ **800/841-4488**).

STAMFORD

38 miles NE of New York City, 40 miles SW of New Haven

A trickle of corporations started moving their headquarters from New York to Stamford in the 1960s, an outflow that became a steady stream, if not exactly a flood, by the 1980s. The trend was cut short by the recession at the end of that decade, but signs of recovery are strong, and almost two dozen Fortune 500 companies continue to direct their operations from here. They have erected shiny mid-rise towers that give the city of 108,000 an appearance closer to that of the new urban centers of the Sun Belt than to those of the Snow Belt.

One result is a lively downtown that other, weaker, Connecticut cities must sorely envy. Roughly contained by Greylock Place, Tressler Boulevard, and Atlantic and Main streets, it has two theaters offering live entertainment, tree-lined streets with many viable shops and a large mall, pocket parks and plazas, and a growing number of stylish restaurants, sidewalk cafes, and nightclubs. Spotted throughout the area are realistic life-sized bronze sculptures by J. Seward Johnson, Jr.

For further information, contact the **Greater Stamford Convention & Visitors Bureau,** One Landmark Square, Stamford, CT 06902; ☎ **203/359-4761.**

AN ART MUSEUM

Whitney Museum of American Art at Champion. One Champion Plaza (Atlantic St. and Tresser Blvd.). ☎ **203/358-7630** or 203/358-7652. Free admission. Tues–Sat 11am–5pm.

This outpost of the generous parent institution in New York is housed on the ground floor of one of Stamford's shiny new downtown office towers. It displays the kinds of cutting-edge contemporary art that routinely infuriates and amuses critics, artists, and devout art-lovers at the mother museum. With no permanent collection, the artworks on view are traveling exhibitions, changed every five or six weeks.

OUTDOOR PURSUITS

A fine family-oriented resource is the **Stamford Museum & Nature Center** (39 Scofieldtown Rd.; ☎ **203/322-1646**), a mile north of Exit 35 of the Merritt Parkway (Route 15) and about five miles north of the city center. The Center has a large lake with mallards and Canada geese who brazenly waddle out of the water to beg tidbits from the picnickers at the nearby tables. Farther along is an open pen with a pair of river otters, and beyond that, the edge of the Hecksher Farm, a real, not re-created, complex of weathered barns and zigzag rail fences housing goats, sheep, chickens, dairy cattle, and—an exotic surprise!—peacocks. May and June are good months to go, when the nonhuman population expands with the arrival of newborn chicks, kids, calves, and lambs. Feeding time is 9am. The farm has a country store stocked with souvenirs and snacks, and that's not all—also on the grounds are nature trails, an imaginative playground, a small planetarium, and an oddball Tudor-Gothic main house that has an art gallery. Open Monday to Saturday and holidays 9am to 5pm. Admission $4 adults, $3 seniors and children under 14.

The **Bartlett Arboretum** (151 Brookdale Rd.; ☎ **203/322-6971**) is less compelling, perhaps, but quieter and as soothing as only a garden in the woods can be. Operated by the University of Connecticut, which has an adjoining campus, the horticultural preserve has several walking trails, none of them strenuous, and gardeners working with their blossoming charges are happy to chat with visitors about techniques and choices.

Recreational sailors might want to consider the bareboat fishing charters at **Yacht Haven** (Washington Boulevard; ☎ **203/359-4500**), while less experienced or venturesome folk may prefer joining the professional crew of the *SoundWaters* (☎ **203/323-1978**), an 80-foot three-masted schooner. The three-hour sailing trips are intended to be educational lessons on the ecology of the Sound. There are, however, sunset dinner cruises and singles sails, a total of 10 or so each summer. Fees are $10 to $25, depending on the event.

SHOPPING

Dedicated antiquers and the simply curious will want to make time for **United House Wrecking** (535 Hope St.; ☎ **203/348-5371**). The name may not sound promising, but the company got its start selling architectural remnants salvaged from demolitions. When these pillars and mantelpieces were increasingly augmented with large decorative garden fixtures and then used as antique furniture and accessories, they had to move here to contain the exploding inventory. Hankering for a stone pig? A two-foot *David?* A pagoda? A 1930s gas pump? An amusement park bumper car? Or perhaps a chandelier with monkeys in frock coats holding candlesticks? They're here. Open Monday to Saturday 9:30am to 5:30pm, Sunday noon to 5pm. It's tough to find. From exit 9 of I-95, pick up Route 1, then Route 106 north, make a left on Glenbrook Road, which becomes Church Street, then turn right on Hope Street. Be sure you have a map, or detailed directions.

WHERE TO DINE

Hacienda Don Emilio. 222 Summer St. (north of Main St.). ☎ **203/324-0577.** Main courses $11.95–$16.95. AE, CB, DC, DISC, MC, V. Mon–Fri 11:30am–2:30pm and 5–10pm (Fri until 11pm); Sat noon–11pm; Sun 1–9pm. MEXICAN.

Expect no surprises on the menu, but aficionados of mainstream Mexican cookery aren't necessarily looking for invention. More important is the pronounced quality of ingredients, preparation, and presentation, no doubt the result of the supervision of the cookbook author and executive chef who spend about 20 weeks a year on-site training and directing the kitchen staff. Specialties are the *pollo en mole poblano* and *puerco en salsa bruja*—chicken in chocolate-based sauce and pork simmered with to-matoes, onions, and hot peppers. A tasty bar menu has carefully executed smaller dishes, appetizers, essentially, just the thing for a light lunch. Skip the ordinary com-bination plates. With two cavernous rooms and a bar in between, reservations shouldn't be necessary.

Kathleen's. 25 Bank St. (between Park and Atlantic sts.). ☎ **203/323-7785.** Reservations rec-ommended. Main courses $15.50–$22. AE, MC, V. Mon–Thurs 11:30am–3pm and 5–10pm; Fri–Sat 5–11pm. NEW AMERICAN.

This popular restaurant was named after the chef-owner's mother and has all the warm, relaxed, and informal ambience of a family-oriented place. In warm weather, tables with umbrellas take up the sidewalk outside, facing a leafy triangular plaza across the street. When the snow flies, the interior has a warm, clubby atmosphere, with a panelled ceiling above the bar, a Hoosier cabinet serving station, baskets of dried flowers, and a couple of shelves with books and bottles. At lunchtime, the shirt-sleeved regulars at the bar banter with the female barkeep, doing more eating than drinking, and garden club ladies mingle with executives in suits in the back. The menu ranges around the Hemisphere for inspiration, grilled Jamaican jerk pork chop with black-bean salsa sharing menu space with charred sirloin rubbed with Creole spices and laced with Jack Daniel's sauce and plum chutney. If it's available, go for the Tabasco-fired seafood gumbo, crowded with whole clams and plump shrimp (but no okra). With the Palace Theatre, Rich Forum, and a new cineplex nearby, Kathleen's does brisk business at night, too. Reserve or expect a short wait.

STAMFORD AFTER DARK

Community and corporate leaders have long supported the cultural and popular per-forming arts in the city, the presence of which gives rise to commercial performance spaces and nightclubs. The **Rich Forum** of the **Stanford Center for the Arts** (At-lantic Street and Tressler Boulevard; ☎ 203/325-4466) presents professional pro-ductions with name actors of such successful Broadway and Off-Broadway plays as *After-Play* and Edward Albee's *Three Tall Women*, while the **Palace Theatre** (61 At-lantic St.; ☎ 203/325-4466) offers rotating appearances by the Stamford Symphony Orchestra, Connecticut Grand Opera and Orchestra, and the Connecticut Ballet, with one-night stands by solo acts and traveling troupes like George Carlin, Harry Belafonte, Judy Collins, and the Alvin Ailey Dance Theater.

Of the several downtown clubs showcasing live music, two that can be easily sampled are **The Grille on Park Place** (78 W. Park Place; ☎ 203/348-7878), which has blues and jazz acts Friday and Saturday and the **Art Bar** (84 W. Park Place; ☎ 203/973-0300), which has rock for dancing and jazz in a smaller room Thursday to Saturday. Another possibility is the **Terrace Club** (1938 W. Main St.; ☎ 203/961-9770), which alternately features live acts and DJ dance nights.

NORWALK
45 miles NE of New York City, 79 miles SW of New Haven

Given the despair that grips too many crime-ridden New England cities, the evident improvement of this city's once notorious South Norwalk neighborhood gladdens the heart. The rehabilitation of several blocks of 19th-century row houses is effectively transforming the T-shaped waterfront district into an increasingly prosperous and trendy area that has come to be called, inevitably, "SoNo." The transformation is far from complete, and decay still festers around the edges, but new shops, restaurants, and night spots open weekly, a process that looks to be self-generating. The opening of the Maritime Aquarium was a prime motivation, and the district—bounded by Washington, Water, and North and South Main streets—is readily accessible from the East Norwalk railroad station.

For further information, contact the **Coastal Fairfield County Tourism District** (297 West Ave.; ☎ **800/866-7925** or 203/854-7825) located in the gatehouse in front of the Lockwood-Mathews Mansion (see below).

SEEING THE SIGHTS
Lockwood-Mathews Mansion Museum. 295 West Ave. (Exit 15, I-95). ☎ **203/838-1434.** Admission $5 adults, $3 seniors and children 12 and under. Feb to mid-Dec Tues–Fri 11am–3pm, Sun 1–4pm. Closed Sat.

Erected in 1864 for a financier by the unlikely name of LeGrand Lockwood, the four-story granite mansion covered with peaked and mansard slate roofs has 50 rooms arranged around a stunning skylit octagonal rotunda. Marble, gilt, intricately carved wood, marquetry, etched glass, and frescoes were commissioned and incorporated with abandon. It cost $1.2 million, back when that was real money. Visits are by one-hour guided tour only.

✪ **Maritime Aquarium.** 10 Water St. (Rte. 136). ☎ **203/852-0700.** Admission $7.50 adults, $6.50 seniors and children 2–12; IMAX $6 adults, $4.50 seniors and children; packages $11.75 adults, $9.50 seniors and children. July–Labor Day daily 10am–6pm; Labor Day–June 10am–5pm.

Formerly the Maritime Center at Norwalk, the name has changed, but this remains the centerpiece of revitalized SoNo. In fact, the earlier name seems more inclusive, since part of the complex includes exhibits of dive suits, model ships, and full-sized vessels, including the *Tango,* which was *pedaled* across the Atlantic Ocean. The main attractions, admittedly, are the marine creatures and mammals on view. On the ground floor is an indoor-outdoor tank of harbor seals, which are found in nearby Long Island Sound. They are fed at 11:45am, and 1:45 and 3:45pm, when they wriggle up on the rocks and all but rest their heads in their handler's lap. A new exhibit features a pair of river otters, and the small and large tanks beyond focus on fishes and sea creatures found in Sound waters, from monster lobsters, flounder, and pollack to the more exotic sea robin, skate, and bristling sea ravens. And to make sure no one's expectations are unmet, there is a large tank of tiger sand sharks, swimming silently and eerily in unending circles, their fearsome mouths inches away from onlookers. There are frequent, but palatable, ecological messages. The giant IMAX screen shows nature films that aren't necessarily confined to the seven seas. One recent show, for example, was *Africa: The Serengeti.*

CRUISES
Refreshing cruises to **Sheffield Island** and its historic lighthouse are offered by the **M/V** *Island Girl* (☎ 203/838-9444), a 60-passenger vessel that departs from Hope Dock, near the Maritime Aquarium at Washington and North Water streets.

Weather permitting, the boat sets out two to four times daily, weekends from late May to late September and weekdays from late June to Labor Day. The round-trip takes about 1¹/₂ hours, with a 15-minute layover on the island. Fares are $9 adults, $8 seniors, $7 children under 12. Special outings at extra cost include Thursday evening clambakes and occasional Sunday picnics. Call ahead.

Similarly, the oyster sloop *Hope* has "creature cruises" in winter to spot seals and birdlife, and marine study cruises at other times, a service of the Marine Aquarium. Fares are $15 per person. Inquire and reserve ahead at **203/852-0700,** ext. 206.

SHOPPING

Don't make a special trip, but **Stew Leonard's** (100 Westport Ave. (Route 1); ☎ **203/847-7213**) is worth a quick look in passing. They say so themselves, with humongous signs reading WORLD'S LARGEST DAIRY STORE AS FEATURED IN *RIPLEY'S BELIEVE IT OR NOT.* The store's general jokey tone is established by a sign at the door, "Rule #1: The customer is always right. Rule #2: If the customer is ever wrong, re-read rule #1." Inside, you'll find a wall of signed photos of celebrity visitors, most of them holding Stew Leonard shopping bags, and model trains running around the walls. Otherwise, those expecting a Disneyland of dairy and produce will be disappointed (talking, singing barnyard figures notwithstanding).

Bulk quantities are held to be greater virtues than diversity, and most shoppers will find less variety than they expect of their neighborhood supermarket, despite the hoopla.

Serious shoppers have several choices. Mainstream goods are on sale at the **Factory Outlets** (East Avenue; ☎ **203/838-1349**), with discounted items from Dress Barn, Bed Bath & Beyond, and Royal Doulton, among others. It's about ¹/₂-mile from Exit 16 of I-95, opposite the East Norwalk railroad station and is open daily. And poking among the boutiques and galleries along Washington and Main streets may produce a bargain or at least a surprise.

WHERE TO DINE

✪ **Amberjacks Coastal Grill.** 99 Washington St. (between Broad and Main sts.). ☎ **203/853-4332.** Main courses $16.95–$19.95. AE, MC, V. Daily noon–3pm and 5:30–10pm (until 11pm Fri–Sat). NEW AMERICAN.

The Grill's owner/chef used to run a restaurant in Key West and it looks like he could have brought this room with him intact from Duval Street. There's the bar, shaped like the prow of a boat, the large, colorful paintings with watery motifs, and the spidery Italianate lights. And there's the food—bold, distinctive flavors, with liberal use of tropical fruits and pronounced Asian spices. A simple example is the yellowfin tunaburger with ginger and mango-papaya "ketchup" on a Portuguese onion roll, accompanied by an Oriental vegetable salad with a pile of taro chips. The chef also offers what he calls "small plates"—essentially large appetizers costing $5.95 to $8.95—perfect for a light lunch or as side orders to be shared at dinner. There is a jazz combo Thursday night, outdoor tables on pleasant days, and a lively Friday happy hour of 30-ish singles.

Lucky Luke/Barcelona Wine Bar. 63 N. Main St. (east of Washington St.). ☎ **203/899-0088** or 203/854-9088. Main courses $3.50–$7.50. MC, V (Barcelona Wine Bar only). Lucky Luke Tues–Fri 11:30am–10pm (until 11pm Sat–Sun); Barcelona Wine Bar daily 5:30–10pm (until midnight Sat–Sun).

The owners call themselves the Two-Faced Restaurant Group, a name that fits this schizophrenic operation to a double-T. One side, Lucky Luke, is basically a burger and sandwich joint, but it departs from the greasy roadstand norm with fresh beef ground daily and rolls baked on the premises. Jazzier sandwiches include the grilled tuna filet with basil pesto and the grilled chicken and veggie sandwich with olive mayonnaise. "Triple-thick" milk shakes are the classic drink. But the lion's share of attention goes to the other half of the building, which has been dressed up to look like a cutting-edge designer bar from Barcelona's tony Eixample district. Tapas, the appetizer-sized Spanish bar snacks, are featured. Or at least, the concept is. The kitchen isn't doctrinaire about recipes, which range all over the Mediterranean for inspiration, from *antipasti* to *meze*. The back bar is lined with cracked ice, the bed for platters of the night's delectables. They might include grilled lamb with mint on slices of focaccia, "serrano" ham with papaya, or the chorizo and green lentil casserole. Fixed-price dinners of three to eight plates cost from $17.50 to $49.50, the most expensive feeding at least four people. Barcelona is fully licensed, with 8 beers on draft and 12 red and white wines sold by the glass.

WESTPORT

47 miles NE of New York City, 29 miles SW of New Haven

After World War II, the housing crunch had young couples scouring the metropolitan area for affordable housing lying along the three main routes of what is now known as the Metro North transit system. Some of them wound up in this pretty village beside the Saugatuck River, several miles inland from Long Island Sound. Most of the new commuter class thought it too far away from Manhattan—three hours a day on the train plus additional transport at either end—and it was deemed the archetype of the far-out bedroom communities that were dubbed the "exurbs"— beyond suburban. Notable for its large contingent of people in the creative crafts, primarily commercial artists, advertising copywriters, art directors, and their fellows, the city was also appealing to CEOs and higher-level executives, many of whom solved their commuting problem by moving their offices to nearby Stamford. The result is a bustling community with surviving elements of its rural New England past wrapped in a sheen of Big Apple panache.

For further information contact the **Westport Chamber of Commerce,** 15 Imperial Ave., P.O. Box 30, Westport, CT 06880 (☎ **203/227-9234**).

A TRIBUTE TO A CHARLATAN

The Barnum Museum. 820 Main St. (Frontage St.), Bridgeport, CT 06604. ☎ **203/ 331-9881.** Admission $5 adults, $4 seniors and students, $3 children 4–18. Open Tues–Sat 10am–4:30pm, Sun noon–4:30pm; in July–Aug, also Mon 10am–4:30pm.

Phineas T. Barnum was Bridgeport's most colorful citizen, even though his career as huckster extraordinaire took him around the world. While this museum doesn't contain all his collections of circus art and memorabilia, there's enough here to justify an in-and-out trip to seedy downtown Bridgeport. See the famous Fiji "mermaid"! A two-headed calf! A detailed scale model of the Barnum & Bailey Three-Ring Circus! And more mementos of Barnum's two New York museums. A thorough renovation was completed in 1989, and a new wing by architect Richard Meier contains temporary exhibits.

OUTDOOR PURSUITS

One of several state parks making the most of their Soundside locations, **Sherwood Island State Park** (P.O. Box 188, Green Farms, CT 06436; ☎ **203/226-6983**), has two long swimming beaches separated by a grove of trees sheltering dozens of picnic tables with grills. Surf fishing is a possiblity from set-aside areas, and the park has concession stands and rest rooms. Don't make a special effort to check out the amateurish "nature center." Open from 8am to sunset. Pets aren't allowed April 15 to September 30. Get there from Exit 18 of I-95 or US 1, following the road called the Sherwood Island Connector. Admission $8 for out-of-state cars.

West of the town center is **The Nature Center for Environmental Activities** (10 Woodside Lane; ☎ **203/227-7253**). Its 62 acres have several walking trails, a wildlife rehab center, and a building with live animals and an aquarium. Admission is $1 adults, 50¢ children 3 to 14. Open Monday to Saturday 9am to 5pm, Sunday 1 to 4pm.

Sailboats can be rented and lessons arranged at **Longshore Sailing School** (Longshore Club Park, 260 S. Compo Rd.; ☎ **203/226-4646**), about two miles south of the Boston Post Road (US 1).

SHOPPING

Window-shopping along Main Street is diverting, although most of the shops are outlets of the chains most often seen in middling to upscale malls, including **Brooks Brothers, Talbots, The Gap, Eddie Bauer, Banana Republic, Williams-Sonoma, Crabtree & Evelyn, Ann Taylor,** and **Barney's New York.** Less conventional is **Lillian August** (17 Main St.; ☎ **203/629-1539**), a large collection of paintings, rugs, overstuffed chairs and sofas, and related accessories. Owing allegiance to no specific style, it looks as if it might have been put together by Laura Ashley on speed.

WHERE TO STAY & DINE

✪ **Inn at National Hall.** 2 Post Rd. (west end of the Saugatuck Bridge), Westport, CT 06880. ☎ **800/628-4255** or 203/221-1351. 15 rms, 7 suites. A/C TV TEL. $195–$450 double. Rates include breakfast. AE, DC, MC, V.

It's nearly impossible to go wrong choosing a member of the international Relais & Chateaux association for a celebratory night's stay, assuming expense isn't a serious consideration. This riverside hotel was offered virtually instant membership, and, if anything, it stands above the already high standards. You know something special is going on as soon as you enter the elevator, which turns out to be a trompe l'oeil representation of an estate library, complete with a skulker betwixt the volumes. There is, in fact, a playful elegance on display throughout. It isn't possible to detail the voluptuous furnishings, baroque canopied beds, and the rarely seen antiques that fill the public rooms and bi-level suites. But it's improbable that you've seen anything like it elsewhere. The Inn's 1873 brick building was a furniture store, bank, town hall, and office building before it finally realized its destiny as an exquisitely decorated and furnished hotel. On top of all that, the in-house restaurant, **Zanghi,** is acknowledged to be superior to anything within miles. Its cuisine is updated French/Italian, with unrepentantly lavish use of foie gras and similar ingredients. Main courses are $16.50 to $28.50. Both inn and restaurant are nonsmoking.

WESTPORT AFTER DARK

One of the oldest theaters on the straw-hat circuit, the **Westport Playhouse** (25 Powers St.; ☎ **203/227-4177**) is nearing its 70th year. Outdoor musical performances are offered at **Levitt Pavilion** (off Jesup Green; ☎ **203/226-7600**). Both are near the center of town.

RIDGEFIELD

58 miles NE New York City, 8 miles S of Danbury

No town in Connecticut has a more imposing main street—Ridgefield's is almost 100 feet wide, lined with ancient towering elm, maple, and oak trees and bordered by massive 19th-century houses set well back on plush carpets of lawn. Impressive at any

The Greatest Flack on Earth

Bombast, jest, hyberbole, and boggling fabrication were the tools of his trade, and Phineas Taylor Barnum wielded them with whatever surgical or blunderbuss skill the situation required. His name is forever linked to the Barnum & Bailey Circus— "The Greatest Show on Earth"—but he didn't get into that relatively respectable business until he was past 60. He was one of the most flamboyant figures of the last tumultuous century, and his life spanned most of it.

Born in Bethel, Conn., in 1810, he is most often associated with New York, where he fashioned a career based largely upon his ability to grab the spotlight and bang the drums until everyone wanted to believe his latest outrageous tale.

There was his trumpeted exhibit of the "Fiji Mermaid," a monkey's upper body sewn to the stuffed tail end of a fish. And his copy of the 10-foot stone creature called the "Cardiff Giant," the original of which proved to be a sculpture, not a fossil, making P.T.'s version a hoax of a fraud. Tom Thumb was real, though, if not his name (which was Charles Stratton) or the title of "General" that Barnum bestowed upon him. Thumb was 33 inches tall, and Barnum took him around the world, making them both rich. Chang and Eng, Siamese twins, were genuine, too, but are said to have hated P.T. for adding them to his horde of bearded ladies and other "freaks." Barnum's greatest coup may have been arranging the wildly successful tour of the Swedish singer Jenny Lind, whom he dubbed "The Swedish Nightingale," even though he had never seen or heard her.

Retiring from show biz in 1855, Barnum served terms as a Republican representative from Fairfield in the Connecticut legislature and a one-year term as mayor of Bridgeport. He also spent some time in the Danbury jail, for libel. It wasn't until he lost his fortune through bad investments that he created his circus, in 1871. After becoming partners with James A. Bailey, he procured the services of one of his greatest attractions, Jumbo, a 6½-ton elephant. Jumbo was hit by a freight train in 1885. His corpse was stuffed and presented to the Barnum Museum at Tufts University in Medford, Mass. Barnum outlived his prized pachyderm, but only by a few years; he died in 1891, one of the greatest showmen and hucksters the world had ever seen.

time of the year, it is in its glory during the short blaze of foliage season. Only a little over an hour from New York City, the town is nonetheless a true evocation of the New England character, a popular weekend getaway for stressed Manhattanites.

There was a settlement here as early as 1709—and at least one building, the Keeler Tavern, survives from those years. In 1777, Benedict Arnold, who was to cause mischief all over this state and nearby New York, was still on the side of the rebels. That April he commanded American troops against a British force retreating from Danbury, to the north. After a fierce skirmish, the Redcoats smashed through Arnold's barricades and escaped to the coast. It remains known as the Battle of Ridgefield.

AN ART MUSEUM & HISTORIC TAVERN

Aldrich Museum of Contemporary Art. 258 Main St. ☎ **203/438-4519.** Admission $3 adults, $2 seniors. Tues–Sun 1–5pm. Near the intersection of Rtes. 35 and 33 at the south end of Main St.

The eponymous patron of the arts is past 90 now, but his superb collection of paintings and sculptures of the second half of the 20th century continues to grow.

The original white clapboard structure has been more than doubled in size with a harmonious addition, and a professional curator now oversees the permanent holdings and organizes frequent temporary exhibitions, concerts, films, lectures, and other events. The outdoor sculptures set up in the side and back yards can be viewed anytime, as compensation when the museum itself is closed, often the case with hours that fluctuate with the season and current exhibitions.

Keeler Tavern. 132 Main St. ☎ **203/438-5485.** Admission $3 adults, $2 seniors, $1 children. Wed, Sat, and Sun 1–5pm.

This 1715 tavern was providing sustenance to travelers between Boston and New York long before the Revolutionary War, but that conflict provided it with its object of greatest note. A British cannonball is imbedded in one of its walls, presumably fired during the Battle of Ridgefield in 1777. Period furnishings have been installed to set the tone, and costumed guides tell the story. The tavern has another claim to fame: It was long the summer home of architect Cass Gilbert (1849 to 1934), who designed New York's landmark Woolworth Building and the Supreme Court Building in Washington, and was a key figure in the construction of the George Washington Bridge.

SHOPPING

Apart from the usual antique shops and the funk of strip malls and franchise enterprises north of the town center on Route 35, one of the most interesting stops for devoted foodies is the **Hay Day Market** (21 Governor St.; ☎ **203/438-2344**) in a shopping center behind the shops that line Main Street. It is about as upscale a food market as exists outside of Beverly Hills or Manhattan, with sections devoted to excellent produce, prepared foods, baked goods, charcuterie, cheeses, and fresh flowers. Check out items like Camembert en brioche and platters of pasta primavera.

WHERE TO STAY

The Elms. 500 Main St., Ridgefield, CT 06877. ☎ **203/438-2541.** 20 rms. A/C TV TEL. $99–$130 double. Rates include breakfast. AE, CB, DC, MC, V. Main St. is Rte. 35; the inn is at the north end of town.

A pair of buildings constitute Ridgefield's oldest (1799) operating inn. Facing them from the street, the one on the right has the reception desk and most of the rooms. Inside, it has the ambience of a contemporary small hotel—that is, comfortably unremarkable, but with the conveniences many travelers desire. And as an extra bonus, the rooms have canopied four-poster beds. The restaurant is in the other building, where a slick 1996 renovation has retained hints of the tavern it once was. Food served is essentially of the "continental" variety, with American infusions. A dining porch is inviting in good weather. No pets are allowed.

West Lane Inn. 22 West Lane (off Rte. 35), Ridgefield, CT 06877. ☎ **203/438-7323.** Fax 860/438-7323. 20 rms. A/C TV TEL. $115–$165 double. Rates include breakfast. AE, CB, DC, MC, V. Driving north from Wilton on Rte. 7, turn west on Rte. 35 at the edge of town.

An inn to fit most people's notions of a country getaway, this one also works for businesspeople, since it offers modem jacks in every room as well as voice mail and 24-hour phone service. For romantics, several rooms have fireplaces and all have queen-size four-poster beds. The 1849 house sports a fine oak staircase and stands on a multiacre property blessed with giant shade trees.

While there is no formal dining room, just next door is the **Inn at Ridgefield** (☎ **203/438-8282**), which serves lunch and dinner daily. (Reservations are required on weekends, and men are expected to wear jackets at dinner.)

2 The Litchfield Hills

When the Hamptons got too pricey and too visible and too chi-chi back in the 1980s, a lot of stockbrokers, CEOs, and celebs started discovering the Litchfield Hills, arguably the most fetchingly rustic yet sophisticated part of Connecticut. The topography and, to a considerable extent, the micro-culture of the region are defined by the river that runs through it, the Housatonic. Broad but not deep enough for vessels larger than canoes, it waters farms and villages and forests along its course, provides recreational float trips and angling, and, over the millenia, has helped to shape these foothills into the Berkshires of Massachusetts.

Men in overalls and CAT caps still stand on the porches of general stores, their breath steaming in the bracing autumn air. Others wade into the river, working the riffs and rills with long looping casts of trout flies hand-tied over the winter. Churches hold pancake breakfast fundraisers, neighbors squabble about development. That's one side of these bucolic hills, less than two hours from Times Square. Increasingly, the other side is fashioned by refugees, permanent and temporary, from New York and its workaholic suburbs. These terminally chic seekers of tranquillity and real estate fled to pre-Revolutionary saltboxes and Georgian colonials on Litchfield's warren of back roads and brought Manhattan-bred expectations with them. Boutiques fragrant with designer coffees and flowery cachets opened in spaces once occupied by luncheonettes and feed stores. The *New York Times* and *Wall Street Journal* appeared on racks next to local weeklies. Restaurants discovered sushi and sun-dried tomatoes and just how much money they could get away with charging the newcomers. Compromises and city-country conflicts aside, the Litchfield Hills remain a satisfying all-season destination for day trips and overnights from metropolitan New York and Connecticut.

ESSENTIALS

GETTING THERE   From New York City, take the Hutchinson River Parkway to I-684 north to I-84 east, taking Exit 7 onto Route 7 north. Continue on Route 7 for New Milford, Kent, West Cornwall, and Canaan. Or, pick up Route 202 at New Milford for Washington Depot, New Preston, and Litchfield. An especially attractive entrance into the region is Route 44 from the Taconic Parkway, through Millerton and into Lakeville and Salisbury. From Boston, take the Massachusetts Turnpike west to the Lee exit, picking up Route 7 south from nearby Stockbridge.

VISITOR INFORMATION   A useful 40-page brochure is produced by the **Litchfield Hills Travel Council** (P.O. Box 968, Litchfield, CT 06759; ☎ **860/ 567-4506**). When making telephone calls to this region, note that the area code has recently been changed from 203 to 860. The old code still appears on much printed material.

NEW MILFORD

This town, a gateway to the Litchfield Hills, was founded by immigrants from the older Milford, down on the coast, in 1703. It functions as a commercial center for the smaller villages that surround it—Roxbury, Bridgewater, Washington, and Brookfield—and as host for such industrial entities as Kimberly-Clark and Nestle. Several rivers and streams run through it, dammed Lake Candlewood is nearby, and it is at the edge of the Hills themselves. It is also at the high end of a long stretch of the egregiously overdeveloped Route 7, which is clogged with mini-malls, auto dealerships, and ill-conceived enterprises dealing in plastic lawn ornaments and hubcaps.

For those reasons, it is a welcome stop on the drive north, if only for lunch and a short stroll. Turn right on Route 202 where it splits from Route 7 and crosses the Housatonic River and a railroad track. Up on the left is one end of the long town green, marked by an early World War II tank and a bandstand. A fire in 1902 destroyed many of the buildings around the green, so this isn't one of those picture-book New England settings. Rather, it is a somewhat pleasant mix of late Victoriana, early Greek Revival, and mid-Eisenhower architecture, not to ignore the requisite First Congregational Church.

Otherwise, there are no sights of an obligatory nature, so a walk down Bank Street, west of the green and along Railroad Street, is diverting, with crafts shops, a bookstore, and an Arte Moderne moviehouse, but won't take long. There are also almost a dozen unheralded restaurants of various levels of accomplishment (from pizza-and-brew to ambitious storefront fusion), and at least half of them family-friendly.

OUTDOOR PURSUITS

Candlewood Lake (☎ **860/354-6928**) is the third largest man-made lake in the eastern United States. It has a finger that pokes into New Milford, but the area with the most recreational facilities is a few miles to the east. From New Milford, drive north on Route 7 about $2^{1}/_{2}$ miles, turn west on Route 37 toward and through Sherman, then south on Route 39 to the unfortunately named **Squantz Pond State Park** (☎ **860/424-3200**). With over 170 acres along the lakeshore, it offers swimming, ice skating, fishing, hiking and cycling trails, picnic grounds, rental canoes, and a boat launch.

SHOPPING

When conductor Skitch Henderson and his wife Ruth decided to put together **The Silo** (44 Upland Rd.; ☎ **860/355-0300**), they didn't allow themselves to be hemmed in by conventional categories. Housed in their old farm buildings are an arts and crafts gallery, a store selling kitchen implements and packaged food products, and a cooking school where noted chefs and food critics give classes most weekends. Open daily from 10am to 5pm. You'll find it off Route 202, four miles north of New Milford center; watch closely for the unobtrusive sign on the right.

WHERE TO STAY

There are good reasons for families to consider making New Milford their base for explorations of the Litchfield Hills. Inns in the towns farther north typically exclude children under 12, not to mention pets. Smokers are restricted, too, and room rates fluctuate wildly according to the day of the week and season. The following inn welcomes children and smokers and is relatively inexpensive. Because it does good business during the week as well as on weekends, its rates are stable.

⑤ **Heritage Inn**. 34 Bridge St. (opposite Railroad Station), New Milford, CT 06776. ☎ **860/354-8883**. Fax 860/350-5543. 20 rms. A/C TV TEL. $79–$94 double. Rates include breakfast. AE, DISC, MC, V.

This sky-blue building started life as a tobacco warehouse in 1870, but after the conversion to an inn over a century later, it looks more like a railroad hotel in the Old West, with its ultrahigh ceilings and long central hall that runs all the way from front to back. The heavy old beams were left exposed, a nice touch, for the decor is otherwise uninspired and a trifle gloomy, though perfectly comfortable and hardly claustrophobic. The somewhat more spacious upstairs rooms pull together better visually, and several have sitting areas. Breakfast goes well beyond the continental standard, with French toast, pancakes, and eggs any way, including made-to-order omelets with a variety of fillings. Fresh copies of the *New York Times* are on hand.

While the inn stands hard by the railroad tracks, only an occasional freight train rumbles past, since commuter service was ended years ago. Children under 5 stay free; older kids sharing their parents' room cost $15. In deference to the inn's many business guests, smoking is permitted. Pets are accepted.

WHERE TO DINE

There are abundant dining choices along Bank and Railroad streets (Salsa for Mexican food and the hangout called Rock's Station Café) and out along Route 7 (consider ribs in the red barn called Riley's or beef at the North Country Steak House).

The Bistro Café. 31 Bank St. (west of the town green). ☎ 860/355-3266. Main courses $13.95–$17.95. AE, MC, V. Mon–Sat 11am–3pm and 4:30–10pm; Sun noon–4pm and 4:30–10pm. THAI/NEW AMERICAN.

Consensus points to this redundantly named eatery as the pick of the local litter. The late 19th-century structure has served many functions, including funeral parlor. Now, its walls are stripped to the brick and the tables are dark polished wood, each set with a cork extractor and a blue flask of olive oil. The lunch menu runs to soups, salads, and sandwiches, most of it given interesting twists, as with the chicken club with spicy andouille sausage. At night, there are a few southern flourishes—oven-roasted catfish and Cajun fries, for example—but no fervid culinary allegiances. In fact, one member of the squad of chefs specializes in Thai dishes, making it necessary to add a special page of his creations to the already eclectic menu. Upstairs is the Tap Room, with a convivial bar at its center, open only in the evenings and offering a menu of light dishes. It's closed Monday.

WOODBURY

The chief distinction of this attractive town strung along several miles of Route 6, west of the city of Waterbury, is the number of antique stores it contains—at least 30, by rough count. That means that weekends in good weather the main road is clogged with cars trolling for treasures and progress can be slow.

About the only scrap of surviving history worth mentioning is the 1770 **Glebe House** (Hollow Rd.; ☎ 203/263-2855) ¼ mile west of Route 6 on a street of fine 18th-century houses. The original home of an Episcopal bishop, a *glebe* was a property of land given to a preacher as partial compensation for his services. Inside are furnishings true to the period; outside is the **Gertrude Jekyll Garden,** named for a prominent landscape gardener of this century. Open April to November Wednesday to Sunday 1 to 5pm.

North of Woodbury on Route 6, watch for Flanders Road forking to the left. Three miles along, on the right, is the office building for **Flanders Nature Center** (☎ 203/263-3711). The organization that runs it is also a land trust, keeping its 1,300 acres in four different towns out of the hands of developers. The people in the office have trail maps of the various properties. One woman there is a wildlife rehabilitator, and keeps her charges in cages near her desk. On one occasion, they included a pair of baby screech owls no bigger than tennis balls. The office is open Monday to Friday 9am to 5pm; the trails, dawn to dusk.

Shoppers are drawn here for—what else?—antiques of every sort, funky to obscure to elegant, with a few contemporary crafts thrown in. Pick up a copy of the directory of shops produced by the Woodbury Antiques Dealers Association at one of the member stores to winnow the list.

Two to check are at the intersection of Routes 6 and 317. **Rosebush Farm** (289 Main St.; ☎ 860/266-9114) trafficks in the kinds of outsized unusual

Litchfield Hills

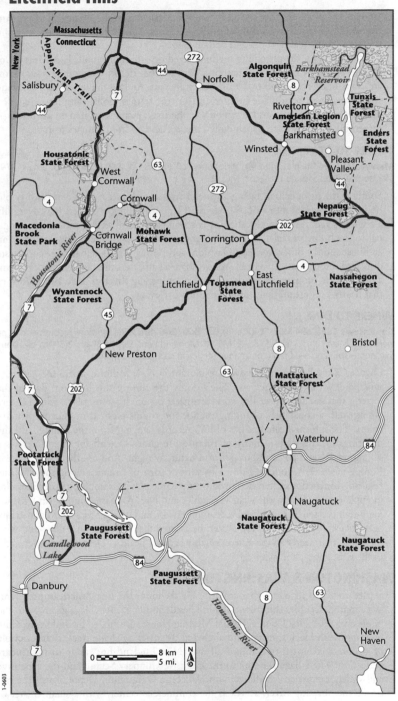

1-0603

"statement" pieces that are catnip for interior designers, while **Nancy Fierberg Antiques** (289 Main St.; ☎ **860/263-4957**) carries American country furniture and folk art such as weathervanes and barber poles.

A variation on the prevailing menu of aged or collectible goods is **A Merry-Go-Round of Fine Crafts** (319 Main St.; ☎ **860/263-2920**). Crowding its six rooms are crafts of every sort, all by Connecticut artisans. Among the items on display are wheat weavings, handmade picture and mirror frames, dolls, samplers, stenciled floorcloths, and, for reasons known only to the artist, pictures painted on sawblades—something for every taste. Open daily except Tuesdays from January to Easter.

WHERE TO STAY

Merryvale. 1204 Main St. (Rte. 6), Woodbury, CT 06798. ☎ **860/266-0800.** 5 rms. $79–$99 double. Rates include breakfast. MC, V.

South of the town center, facing a quieter stretch of Route 6, this two-century-old house was converted into a B&B back in 1951, but the present owners took over only a few years ago. A striking focal point is a wall painting of an American eagle, original to the house, revealed during the renovation process. One of the owners is an architect and the other worked in fashion, accounting for the remarkably good taste displayed throughout. Two of the rooms share a bath, the others each have their own. The four-acre property slopes down to the Pomperaug River in back. Breakfast is of that hearty proportion that can make lunch irrelevant.

WHERE TO DINE

Good News Café. 694 Main St. (Rte. 6). ☎ **860/266-4663.** Reservations recommended on weekends. Main courses $17–$18. AE, MC, V. Mon and Wed–Sat, 11:30am–2:30pm, 5–10pm; Sun noon–3pm and 5–10pm (continuous service in cafe bar). FUSION.

Owner Carole Peck used to have a restaurant in New Milford, where she packed a scrapbook with glowing reviews. She's doing the same at this location. Part of the secret is that she doesn't see her work as nuclear fission. It's a fun place, with a cheery young staff, a constantly changing menu, and rooms painted in blazing primary colors. The informal cafe-bar has old 45 records hanging from the ceiling, and the paintings on the walls—many of them quite good—are all for sale. There is a dining terrace and jazz combos perform Saturday night. And oh, the food? Make it Europe meets Asia, touching down in various parts of America along the way, the resulting concoctions often deployed on the same plate. Examples: curried linguini in apple-carrot sauce with Asian vegetables and basil or roasted monkfish with tomato-fennel essence, carmelized red-onion ravioli, and wilted Swiss chard and crispy beet garnish. If that sounds too clever, be assured that it works—usually—and with the bonus that nearly all the entrees qualify as heart-healthy. Desserts, however, tend to the rich, gooey, and caloric.

WASHINGTON & WASHINGTON DEPOT

Settled in 1734, its name changed in 1779 to honor the first American president, Washington occupies the crown of a hill beside Route 47. Its village green, with the impressive 1802 First Congregational Meeting House surrounded by uniformly white buildings with black shutters and sheltered by towering shade trees, is an example of a municipal institution found all over New England but rarely to such near-perfection. The village is home to the exclusive Gunnery School and the expensive and widely renowned Mayflower Inn. Adjacent Washington Depot, down the hill beside the Shepaug River, serves as the commercial center, with a small cluster of mostly upscale shops. Nearby **Steep Rock Reservation** is a lovely spot for hiking, fly fishing, or cross-country skiing.

The traveling series of musical events known as the **Armstrong Chamber Concerts** usually alights in Washington on four Sunday afternoons in spring and fall (other appearances are in Greenwich and Lenox, Mass.). Performances are in the Congregational Church.

A worthwhile detour takes drivers down Curtis Road, past the private gunnery School to **The Institute for American Indian Studies** (Route 199; ☎ 860/868-0518). The small repository of Native American crafts and artifacts is presented with sensitivity and, in the main, without polemics. A sound track of birdsong and running water plays in the galleries of permanent and temporary exhibits. These baskets, pots, tools, and artworks are fascinating in themselves, but they are used to tell the story of Amerindians past and present, mostly of those who lived and still live in this region. Displays are supplemented by workshops, performances, films, and storytelling sessions. Down a nearby path is a re-creation of an Algonquian Village, which, while accurate, suffers visibly from exposure to the elements. Open Monday to Saturday 10am to 5pm, Sunday noon to 5pm (closed Monday and Tuesday January through March). Admission is $4 adults, $2 children 6 to 12.

In Washington Depot, consider putting together the components of a delectable picnic from the array of quiches, pizzas, and salads at **The Pantry** (5 Titus Rd.; ☎ 860/868-0258). Also available are an abundance of cookware and other kitchen gizmos and necessities. Nearby is the beguiling **Hickory Stick Bookshop** (Titus Square; ☎ 860/868-0525). Don't worry if you're running low on cash—there is an ATM in the bank next door.

WHERE TO STAY & DINE

✪ Mayflower Inn. 118 Woodbury Rd. (Rte. 47), Washington, CT 06793. ☎ **860/868-9466.** Fax 860/868-1497. 25 rms. A/C TV TEL. $230–$535 double. AE, MC, V. Take Rte. 202 north 2 miles past New Preston, turning south on Rte. 47 through Washington Depot and up the hill past Washington Common. The entrance is on the left.

These words can do little to burnish the reputation of Connecticut's courtliest (and most expensive) manor inn. Galaxies of stars, diamonds, and flags have already been showered upon it by the usual arbiters of taste. The main building is almost entirely new, but some elements survive from the 1894 structure that has served as an inn since 1920. The most delightful of these is the richly paneled library, nearly intact from the days before the present owners took over in 1990. Porches look out across manicured lawns to flower beds and deep woods, from which white-tailed deer routinely emerge. Furnishings throughout reflect a sensibility honed by knowledge of sumptuous English country houses and French provincial *auberges*—a genuine Joshua Reynolds portrait hangs in the parlor, and Tabriz carpets lie on gleaming wood floors. Unlike lesser inns that cut corners on conveniences with the justification that their patrons want to escape the late 20th century, the Mayflower makes available everything that a superior urban hotel might offer, with extras. That includes minibars in all rooms and gas fireplaces in most; baths with tapestry rugs, Limoges fittings, and mahogany wainscotting; a heated outdoor pool, a tennis court, and a fully-equipped fitness center. Three dining rooms of differing styles present the light-touch eclectic dishes created by the Culinary Institute of America–trained chef. He transforms humble tapioca into something rivaling crème brûlée. Service is intelligent and alert. In sum, this is as close to perfection as any such enterprise is likely to be, almost justifying the breathtaking prices ($75 for a massage?). The fact that the clientele is drawn from the martini-and-manhattan generation may not endear it to affluent younger people who aren't on honeymoons, and there are restrictions: no children 12 or under, no smoking in the bedrooms, and no pets.

NEW PRESTON

Never more than a few houses and retailers at the juncture of two country roads, this hamlet long served primarily as a supplier for local residents and, starting in the middle of the 19th century, the large families who summered each year on nearby Lake Waramaug (which is named, by the way, for a Chief Waramaug, whose daughter Lillinoah was one of the countless Indian maidens alleged to have leapt off numerous ledges across North America). More recently, New Preston's small grocery and hardware stores have been converted to antiques emporia of high order, and they and a couple of casual cafes find themselves surrounded on weekends by BMWs and Volvos.

At the northwest tip of the L-shaped lake, **Lake Waramaug State Park** (Lake Waramaug Road; ☎ 860/868-0220) gives the public access to a beautiful body of water that is otherwise monopolized by the private homes and inns that border it. Canoes and paddleboats are for rent, there is a swimming beach, picnic tables, food concessions, and a total of almost 80 RV- and campsites.

In no time, the intersecting streets that form the center of the village have gone from sleepy to spiffy, catering to all those *nouveau* Nutmeggers from Manhattan and weekend tourists from all over the Northeast. Among the dozen antique shops, especially notable are **Black Swan Antiques** (Main Street; ☎ 860/868-2788), specializing in English provincial furniture and accessories; **J. Seitz & Co.** (Main Street; ☎ 860/868-0119), featuring trendy southwestern painted furniture; and the more generalized offerings of **Grey Squirrel Antiques** (Main Street; ☎ 860/868-9750).

A former dairy farm on a wide promontory above Lake Waramaug was converted into the **Hopkins Vineyard** (Hopkins Road; ☎ 860/868-7954) in 1979. Headquartered in a 19th-century barn across the street from the Hopkins Inn (below), its tasting and sales rooms are open January through April Friday and Saturday 10am to 5pm, Sunday 11am to 5pm; May through December Monday to Saturday 10am to 5pm, Sunday 11am to 5pm.

The 10 or so bottlings range from a sparkling white to a surprising hard cider, with Chardonnays and a Pinot Noir in between. They won't make anyone forget the Napa Valley, but prices are fair and the wines make worthy mementos of a good weekend.

WHERE TO STAY

The Boulders. East Shore Rd. (Rte. 45), New Preston, CT 06777. ☎ **860/868-0541.** Fax 860/868-1925. 17 rms. A/C TEL. $200–$250 double ($50 lower Nov–Apr, $50 higher Fri–Sat June–Oct). Rates include full breakfast. AE, MC, V. Drive north from New Preston about 2 miles on Rte. 45.

This once rustic, folksy, lakeside inn has been nudged upward in both price and quality. Part of the improvement lies with the outlying "guest houses," four relatively new buildings with two spacious units each that all enjoy private decks, fireplaces, cassette players, and refrigerators. These have contemporary furnishings, while the tone of the rooms in the 1895 main house is set by antiques and reproductions of country styles. Juice and cookies await arriving guests, and the *New York Times* is provided on weekdays. Great views are bonuses of the main sitting and dining rooms. Down by the shore is the private boathouse with canoes, rowboats, and paddleboats available free to guests. A serious wine cellar complements the acclaimed cuisine (entrees $18.50–$22), which arrives in such intriguing combinations as duck breast with gingered black-bean salad, vegetable strudel, and a star-anis and orange reduction. Guests are encouraged to take the Modified American Plan, which includes breakfast and dinner and costs only $50 more per room than the B&B rate, a bargain of sorts.

Ⓢ Hopkins Inn. 22 Hopkins Rd., New Preston, CT 06777. ☎ **860/868-7295.** Fax 860/
868-1768. 12 rms. $61–$78 double. No credit cards. From New Preston, take Rte. 45 north
about 2¹/₂ miles, and look for the sign on the left.

A family named Hopkins started farming this land in 1787, and its descendants were
still around in 1979, when they turned the farm into a vineyard and winery. The
yellow frame farmhouse with black shutters that is now the inn sits atop a hill with
the best views of the lake and a dining terrace that takes maximum advantage of that
virtue. Food is the main event (entrees $16.25 to $19.25), since the guest rooms are
on the Spartan side, with no phones, air-conditioning, or TV. The continental menu
features Germanic dishes of the Swiss and Austrian Alps, like backhendl with lingon-
berries, supplemented with such dishes as trout bleu or meunière, the central
ingredient of which is netted live on order from a tank. Now pay attention: The inn
is open for lodging from late March through December. Breakfast, lunch, and dinner are served Tuesday to Sunday May through October, but only breakfast and
lunch are offered in April, November, and December. Two rooms share a bath. No
pets are allowed, and reservations are required for meals.

Inn at Lake Waramaug. 107 N. Shore Rd., New Preston, CT 06777. ☎ **800/525-3466** or
860/868-0563. Fax 860/868-9173. 23 rms. A/C TEL TV. $156–$229 double, MAP. Rates include
breakfast and dinner. 15% service charge. AE, MC, V. Drive north on Rte. 45 from New Preston
about 2¹/₂ miles to sign on left, then 1 mile to the inn.

In recent years, guests could never be sure what they might find here, the result of
many ownership changes. For the moment, at least, its operation has settled into a
reassuring steady hum, with most facets running smoothly. The reputation of the
kitchen has jumped, too, so the mandatory MAP (breakfast and dinner) isn't the
straitjacket it might be. The many public and private rooms ramble through several
buildings, some old, some fairly new, from the high end of a slope down to the waterside cafe called The Boathouse. Canoes and a sailfish are available for launching
off the inn's beach. A kidney-shaped indoor pool in the basement of the main house
is being upgraded; the nearby sauna already has been. There is also a tennis court.
The dining room and some guest rooms are nonsmoking. Note that a 15% service
charge is added to the bill, so tipping isn't necessary.

LITCHFIELD

Possessed of a long common with stately trees reconfigured around the turn of the
century by the Frederic Law Olmsted landscaping firm (designers of New York's
Central Park), Litchfield is testimony to the taste and prosperity of the Yankee entrepreneurs who built it in the late 18th and early 19th centuries from a colonial farm
community to an industrial center. The factories and mills were dismantled during
the second half of the 19th century, and the men who built them settled back to enjoy
their riches, now more often compounded through investment than with iron and
leather.

Their uncommonly large homes, either authentic Federalists and Greek Revivals
or later remodeled to look that way, are set well back from the streets. The commercial district is a single block of late 19th-century houses facing the common, with
gaudier enterprises kept to the outskirts. Litchfield has produced its share of notables,
including Harriet Beecher Stowe, author of *Uncle Tom's Cabin,* and her abolitionist
preacher brother, Henry Ward Beecher. In recent decades, the town has become fashionable with chic New Yorkers, who find it a less frenetic weekend and vacation retreat than The Hamptons of Long Island. Their influence is seen both in the quality
of store merchandise and restaurant fare and the lofty prices they command.

A WALK THROUGH HISTORY

Litchfield's houses and broad tree-lined streets reward leisurely strolls, whether you're kicking through piles of fallen leaves in autumn or passing through shafts of sunlight piercing the canopy of arching trees. From the stores and restaurants along West Street, walk east (that's to the right when you're facing the common), then turn right on South Street. On the opposite corner is the **Litchfield Historical Society** (South and East streets; ☎ 860/567-4501), containing exhibits outlining life in the area during the late colonial and post-Revolution periods, with paintings, furniture, and household utensils. Inquire here about tours of private homes conducted every July. It's open mid-April to November Tuesday to Saturday 11am to 5pm, Sunday 1 to 5pm. Walking down South Street, on the right behind a white picket fence, is one of the few historic houses regularly open to the public, the 1773 **Tapping Reeve House & Law School** (☎ 860/567-4501). It was the earliest American law school, established before this was a country, and counted among its students Aaron Burr, Noah Webster, and three Supreme Court justices. The house was Mr. Reeve's, who taught his classes in the small building to the left. Hours are the same as the Litchfield Historical Society, which maintains it.

When the street starts to peter out into more modern houses, cross over and walk back toward the common and cross to the north side. Over there on the right is a magisterial First Congregational Church, built in 1828. Turn left, then right on North Street, where the domestic architecture matches the quiet splendor of South Street.

OUTDOOR PURSUITS

The **White Memorial Foundation** (Route 202; ☎ 860/567-0857) is a 4,000-acre wildlife sanctuary and nature conservancy about five miles southwest of Litchfield. It has campsites and 35 miles of trails for hiking, cross-country skiing, and horseback riding. On the grounds is a small museum of natural history with a few stuffed native animals and a gift shop.

This is horse country, so a canter across the meadows and along the wooded trails of **Topsmead State Park** (☎ 860/567-5694) is a logical diversion. The park has a wildlife preserve and a Tudor-style mansion that can be toured in the summer. Follow Route 118 one mile east of town. Horses can be hired nearby at **Lee's Riding Stables** (☎ 860/868-7954).

SHOPPING

Most of the interesting shops are in the row of late 19th-century brick buildings on the south side of the town green. In the front of **Barnidge & McEnroe** (7 West St.; ☎ 860/567-9499) is a coffee bar for espressos and lattes, fueling browses through an uneven but entertaining selection of books, gifts, and ceramics at the rear of the store. Open daily.

It isn't often that a commercial nursery becomes a tourist attraction, but **White Flower Farm** (Route 63; ☎ 860/567-8789) is special. For avid gardeners across the country, this is the L.L. Bean of the mail-order plant and seedling trade. The four main sections strung out along Route 63 (three miles south of Litchfield center) display perennials, flats of seedlings, bulbs, herbs, florals, potted plants, and shrubs. A featured attraction is the greenhouse full of rare tuberous Begonias. The operation is large enough that some staffers must stay in touch by walkie-talkie. It is usually closed from December through March, but days and hours vary, so call ahead.

Chardonnays and Merlots don't spring to mind as likely Connecticut products, but the **Haight Vineyard** (29 Chestnut Hill Rd.; ☎ 860/567-4045) corrects that impression. Established in 1978, it has grown and prospered, presently offering 10 drinkable bottlings, including a respectable Riesling, a couple of sturdy picnic-style reds, and a traditional apple wine. They range in price from $6.98 to $10.98 per bottle. The tasting room is open all year Monday to Saturday 10:30am to 5pm, Sunday noon to 5pm. There is a second winery in Mystic.

WHERE TO STAY

✪ **Tollgate Hill Inn.** Rte. 202 (Tollgate Rd.), Litchfield, CT 06759. ☎ **800/445-3903**, 860/567-4545, or 860/567-3821. Fax 860/567-8397. 21 rms. A/C TV TEL. $90–$175 double. Rates include breakfast. AE, DC, DISC. 2¹/₂ miles northeast of Litchfield on Rte. 202.

Three barn-red buildings on 10 wooded acres, including the 1745 tavern that is the main house, constitute the liveliest, most atmospheric lodging in Litchfield. The busy restaurant may have wavy wide-board floors and high-backed wooden booths in its oldest room, but the food is thoroughly contemporary, of the New American variety (main courses $18 to $24). Shellfish pie—puff pastry encasing lobster chunks, crabmeat, scallops, and shrimp—is one delectable possibility. A Bloody Mary at the table in front of the fireplace in the bar is a treat on a frosty Sunday. Weekends from mid-June to September, jazz combos perform on variable schedules in the cellar or for Sunday brunch. No sacrifices need be made in the bedrooms, with their private baths and all the electronic conveniences. Morning coffee is free for the pouring at the registration desk, next to the parrot. Note that the gruff, no-nonsense proprietor refuses to accept MasterCard or Visa.

WHERE TO DINE

The County Seat. 3 West St. (on the green). ☎ **860/567-8069.** Main courses $3–$6. No credit cards. Sun–Thurs 7am–10pm, Fri–Sat 7am–midnight. ECLECTIC.

Not easy to describe, but a pleasure to experience, this new establishment has a store in front selling kitchenware, candles, coffee beans, baskets, and espresso machines. In back is a soda fountain featuring ice cream, and in between is a coffee bar/lunch counter offering soups, sandwiches, salads, and light dishes. Soups include a tomato-based minestrone with shredded spinach, and one featured sandwich is a smoked mozzarella quesadilla with mixed greens and olive mayonnaise. There's no table service, but upholstered chairs and sofas are available for lounging and chatting.

Spinell's Litchfield Food Company. West St. (on the green). ☎ **860/567-3113.** Main courses $3.95–$8.95. Daily 8am–6pm. ECLECTIC.

Ensconsed in one of a row of late 19th-century buildings facing the town green, the Spinnell is essentially a takeout shop with a cafe attached, but its proprietor has infused it with a sensibility honed in some of New York's most celebrated restaurants. The cold case has the makings of a marvelous picnic, displaying such appetizing platters as seasonal fiddlehead salad, wild rice with dried cranberries, and black bean and corn salad. Supplement those with some exotic French and Spanish cheeses, Thai chicken sausage, salmon cakes, and soups of squash and onion or fennel with ham. There are house-made pies, breads, and tarts, and just about anything can be ordered up for an eat-in lunch. Breakfast possibilities include buttermilk pancakes and three-egg omelets with fillings of your choice and big or bigger cups of espresso or cappucino.

The Stone House Cafe & Gallery. 637 Bantam Rd. (Rte. 202, 5 miles south of town). ☎ **860/567-3326.** Main courses $12.95–$18.95. AE, MC, V. Tues–Thurs 11:30am–2:30pm and 5:30–9pm; Fri–Sat 11:30am–2:30pm and 5:30–10pm; Sun 10am–4pm and 6–9pm. NEW AMERICAN.

It stands on nine acres beside a swift-running stream, a handsome 1849 house that is part art gallery and all restaurant. A graduate of the Culinary Institute of America ("the other CIA") and Boston's Ritz-Carlton shakes the skillets, cranking out such wintry delectables as leg of lamb stuffed with herbed feta and spinach propped beside a white bean ragout, and summery fare along the lines of pan-seared sea bass with a tumble of Mediterranean veggies. A cheerful young staff brings it all, upstairs, downstairs, and out on the deck. Mostly Californian and French wines are available by the glass. The photos and paintings on the wall are for sale.

West Street Grill. 43 West St. (on the green). ☎ **860/567-3885.** Reservations required on weekends. Main courses $14.95–$24.95. AE, MC, V. Mon–Thurs 11:30am–3pm and 5:30–9pm; Fri–Sun 11:30am–4pm and 5:30–10pm. NEW AMERICAN.

Known as an incubator for some of Connecticut's best chefs, several of whom have gone off to open their own places, this sprightly contemporary bistro hasn't lost a perceptible step, despite the frequent changes. Entrees tend towards Asian-tinged Cal-Tal renditions of meats, fowl, and grilled fish dressed with innovative sauces and garnishes. The trendiest spot for miles, it attracts the weekend celebrity set, with vaguely familiar faces exchanging confidences at every other table. Some patrons complain that people not known to the staff get short shrift, but that seems more likely due to insecurity or excess sensitivity than reality.

Litchfield After Dark

No one goes to Litchfield for its pounding nightlife, but movie-lovers might consider the **Bantam Cinema** (☎ 860/567-0006) in the otherwise unremarkable village of Bantam, about three miles southeast on Route 209. Don't expect the latest Schwartzenegger action flick, since the managers concentrate on the kinds of art and foreign films that don't get wide distribution.

Kent

A prominent prep school of the same name, a history as an iron-smelting center, and a reputation as a gathering place of artists define this town of fewer than 2,000. Noted 19th-century landscape painter George Inness helped establish the last facet of that estimation, and several galleries represent the works of his creative descendants. They are joined by a multiplicity of antiques shops and bookstores, most of them strung along Route 7. South of town on the same road is the hamlet of Bull's Bridge, named for one of the two remaining covered bridges in the state that can be crossed by cars.

North of Kent center, near Kent Falls (below), is the double-duty **Sloane-Stanley Museum & Kent Furnace** (Route 7; ☎ 860/927-3849). Fans of the books of illustrator-author Eric Sloane, who celebrated the work and crafts of rural America, will enjoy this replica of his studio, exhibits of tools he depicted, and the drawings and paintings that adorn the walls. On the grounds are the ruins of an iron furnace that was in operation for much of the 19th century, one of many once-active ironworks in the Kent area. Open mid-May through October Wednesday to Sunday 10am to 4pm. Admission is $3 adults, $1.50 seniors and children.

Four miles north of Kent is the handily accessible **Kent Falls State Park** (Route 7; ☎ 860/927-3238). Its centerpiece, a 250-foot cascade, is clearly visible from the road, and picnic tables are set about the grounds. A path mounts the hill beside the falls, and there are a total of 295 wooded acres to explore. Rest rooms are available. A parking fee of $8 per car is charged on weekends and holidays, June through October. Serious hikers have a greater challenge nearby, should they choose to undertake it: On the opposite side of Route 7, the Appalachian Trail follows a stretch of the Housatonic River north toward Cornwall Bridge and West Cornwall and all the way into Massachusetts.

WEST CORNWALL

Not be be confused with Cornwall, about four miles to the southeast, nor Cornwall Bridge, about seven miles to the south, this tiny hamlet is best known for its picturesque covered bridge, one of only two in the state that still permit the passage of cars. The bridge connects Routes 7 and 128, crossing the Housatonic. With a state forest to the north and a state park to its immediate south, Cornwall, a cluster of houses and a handful of commercial enterprises, enjoys a piney seclusion that remains welcoming to passersby.

Housatonic Meadows State Park (Route 7; ☎ **860/672-6772** in summer, 860/927-3238 the rest of the year) is comprised of 452 acres bordering both sides of the Housatonic immediately south of West Cornwall, and provides access to fishing, canoeing, and picnicking. A couple of local organizations offer equipment and guidance. One is **Housatonic Anglers** (P.O. Box 282, Cornwall, CT 06796; ☎ **860/672-4457**), whose owners offer float trips, weekend fly-fishing schools, and half- and full-day guided fishing trips (lunch is included). The other is **Clarke Outdoors** (163 Rte. 7, Cornwall, CT 06796; ☎ **860/672-6365**), which provides rentals of river craft, including kayaks and rafts, as well as instruction and guided white-water trips.

Just outside Cornwall proper, off Route 4, is **Mohawk Mountain Ski Area** (46 Great Hollow Rd.; ☎ **800/895-5222** or 860/672-6100). "Mountain" is an overstatement, but this is the state's oldest ski resort, with 5 chairlifts, 23 trails, and snowmakers. Rentals and instruction are provided.

Apart from a couple of antiques shops, shoppers are drawn to **The Cornwall Bridge Pottery Store** (Route 128; ☎ **860/672-6545**), catercorner from the Brookside Bistro (below). In addition to handmade and manufactured ceramics, the store has counters and shelves of lamps, copper pots, windchimes, kitchen gadgets, and even knitwear.

WHERE TO DINE

Brookside Bistro. Rte. 128 (near the covered bridge). ☎ **860/672-6601.** Reservations recommended on weekends. Main courses $10.75–$19.95. MC, V. Daily noon–2:30pm and 6–9:30pm (closed Mar, Mon–Wed in winter). COUNTRY FRENCH.

More truly a bistro than most that so describe themselves, this nicely situated eatery trafficks in such classic Gallic recipes as coq au vin, lamb shank, and eggplant tart. None of that tricky *nouvelle* gimmickry, just carefully rendered, very tasty food. Portions are sizable, so large, in fact, that perhaps a third of the patrons leave with their leftovers in plastic containers. This should lead us to suggest that appetizers and/or desserts be avoided, but who can resist the herbed chicken sausage in brioche with mustard-cream sauce? Or the airy cheesecake or earthy tarte tartin? The screened dining deck thrusts out over a tumbling brook, the seating area of choice in good weather. Closings aren't always predictable, so call ahead.

SHARON

Early on, this attractive hamlet near the New York border established a reputation for its industries, which included plants that manufactured mousetraps and cannon shells. The industries no longer exist, and Sharon is now primarily residential, a highly picturesque village, with many houses made of brick or fieldstone in an area where wood-frame houses prevail.

The **Sharon Audubon Center** (Route 4; ☎ 860/364-0520) is a 684-acre nature preserve with herb and flower gardens, a shop and interpretive center, and 11 miles of hiking and nature trails. Injured birds are brought to the center for rehabilitation, and there are usually several raptors—birds of prey—on display. The grounds are open dusk to dawn, the main building Monday to Saturday 9am to 5pm and Sunday 1 to 5pm, while the trails can be accessed from sunup to sundown. Admission to trails is $3 adults, $1.50 seniors and children.

WHERE TO DINE

West Main Cafe. 13 W. Main St. ☎ **860/364-9888.** Main courses $12.95–$16.95. AE, DC, MC, V. Wed–Sun 11:30am–3pm and 5:30–10pm (until 9pm Sun). NEW AMERICAN.

One of the most celebrated of the chefs who have passed through the West Street Grill in Litchfield, Matthew Fahrner has recently taken a flier on this formerly scorned eatery in his hometown. There are only eight tables, and decor is minimal, with butcher paper over white napery and a few unremarkable paintings on the walls. That leaves the spotlight on Fahrner's fancies of the moment, which bound around the culinary map, but seem most often to play on southwestern and Asian themes. Caribbean and European touches also sneak onto the menu, though, so there can be no guarantees of what will next capture his imagination. Arrive in expectation of gustatory adventure.

LAKEVILLE & SALISBURY

These two attractive villages share a common history and a main street lined with 19th-century houses stretching along Route 44. The "lake" in question is Lake Wononscopomuc, slightly south of the town center, its shoreline dotted with summer homes.

The discovery in the area of a particularly pure iron ore led to the development of mines and forges as early as the mid-1700s. One of the ironworkers was the eccentric Ethan Allen, later to become the leader of the Green Mountain Boys and a hero for his capture of Fort Ticonderoga from the British in 1775. The forges of the area supplied Washington's army with many cannons in the critical early years of the Revolution.

One wealthy forge owner and manufacturer, John Milton Holley, bought a 1768 mansion and doubled its size in 1808. The result is known as the **Holley-Williams House** (Upper Main Street; ☎ **860/435-2878**), a Federalist and Greek Revival architectural mix. One of the few historic houses in the area open to the public, it contains furnishings and collections of china, silverware, and glass collected by Holley and his descendants over the continuous 173 years the family lived there. Open July through September Saturday and Sunday 1 to 5pm. Admission is $3, children under 12 free.

Not far from Lakeville center (south on Rte. 41, then east on Rte. 112) is **Lime Rock Park** (☎ **860/435-2571** or 860/435-0896), one of the premier auto racing courses in the northeast. It has garnered even greater attention since Paul Newman, a Connecticut resident, started piloting his own car around the turns. While sports cars are the central attraction, there are special races with vintage vehicles, and the famous Skip Barber racing and driving schools are located here. Races are held late April through mid-October, Saturday and Monday holidays.

In Salisbury, **Three Ravens** (1 E. Main St.; ☎ 860/435-9602) deals in rustic furniture and amusing/charming examples of American folk art, while the **Salisbury Antiques Center** (46 Library St.; ☎ 860/435-0424) specializes in more exalted forms of English and American furniture and accessories.

WHERE TO STAY & DINE

White Hart. The Village Green (P.O. Box 385), Salisbury, CT 06068. ☎ **860/435-0030.** Fax 860/435-0040. 26 rms. A/C TV TEL. $75–$190 double. AE, CB, DC, MC, V.

Fortunes have fluctuated in the White Hart's 180-plus years, but lately this white clapboard inn at the end of Salisbury's main street seems to be on the rise. The front porch with its voluptuously curved wicker furniture is the prime summertime site, and the ambitious main restaurant, June's New American Sea Grill, has gathered deserved kudos for its creative way with shellfish and swimmers. Informal meals and snacks are served in the Tap Room, and a front parlor with fireplace long ago replaced a cheesy gift shop. Apart from the three suites and the large Ford Room (these are included in the 26-room tally above and go for around $190), most of the rooms are on the small side.

NORFOLK

Founded in 1758, Norfolk was long popular as a summer vacation destination for industrialists who owned mills and factories along Connecticut's rivers. At the very least, drive into the center for a look at the visually arresting village green. It is highlighted by a monument that involved the participation of two of the 19th century's most celebrated creative people—sculptor Augustus Saint-Gaudens and architect Stanford White.

At the opposite corner is the 90-year-old "Music Shed," a closed auditorium on the Ellen Battell Stoeckel Estate that is the venue for an eagerly awaited series of summer events, the **Norfolk Chamber Music Festival** (Box 545, routes 44 and 272, Norfolk, CT 06058-0545; ☎ **860/542-3000**). Held from late June to mid-August, it hosts evening performances by such luminaries as the Tokyo String Quartet and the Vermeer Quartet. These are augmented by morning recitals by young musicians in training.

Two prime recreational areas are near each other on Route 272, north of town. One mile from the village green is **Haystack Mountain State Park** (☎ **860/482-1817**). Its chief feature is a short trail leading up from the parking lot to a stone tower at the 1,715-foot crest. The splendid views from the top, on the proverbial clear day, take in a panorama stretching from the Catskill Mountains in New York to Long Island Sound. Picnicking is allowed. Another five miles further north, on the Massachusetts border, is **Campbell Falls** (☎ **860/482-1817**), which enjoys an abundance of streams, rapids, and cascades. Fishing is a possibility, as are hiking and picnicking.

3 New Haven

The approach to New Haven via Interstate 95 isn't a paean to positive urban planning. What is first seen, at the waterfront, are acres of railroad switchyards, oil storage tanks, warehouses, and grimy factories. Inland are a few half-hearted efforts at mid-rise office buildings that look less like a skyline than a jaw of broken teeth. The streets approaching the downtown district are dissolute, untended, radiating a sense of hopes unfulfilled. It is easy to think that a better idea might be to continue on to Mystic. But that would only shortchange both the city and the prospective visitor. For while New Haven suffers the routine roster of afflictions of most of Connecticut's cities—nearly a quarter of its citizens live at or below the poverty line and street crime is high—it also has a great deal to offer the leisure traveler. Ready and waiting to fill out a rewarding weekend are four active performing-arts centers and theaters with September to June seasons of first-rate professional caliber, three outstanding small museums, autumn renewals of college football rivalries that date back 120 years, and a variety of ethnic restaurants that will drive foodies mad with the abundance of choices.

Much of what is worthwhile about New Haven can be credited to the presence of one of the world's most prestigious universities. That it both enriches its community and exacerbates the usual town-gown conflicts is a paradox with which the institution and civic authorities have struggled since the colonial period. But there can be no denying that the city would be reduced to a lump of queasy urban malaise were the university to evaporate.

Relatively little serious history has happened here. But there are a number of amusing "firsts" that boosters love to trumpet. Yale rewarded the first Doctor of Medicine degree in 1729 to a man who never practiced medicine. The first hamburger was allegedly made and sold here, as was, even less certainly, the first pizza. Noah Webster compiled his first dictionary here, and Eli Whitney perfected his cotton gin. A resident invented the corkscrew in 1860, and a candy company came up with the name "lollipop" for one of its products. The first telephone switchboard was made here, necessitated by a Reverend John E. Todd, who was the first person in the world to request telephone service. Charles Goodyear of New Haven came up with a way to vulcanize rubber, and a local man named Colt invented a revolver in 1836.

Important seasonal events are the new International Festival of Arts & Ideas, held at many sites around the city in late June, and a free jazz festival on the green in late July through early August.

ESSENTIALS

GETTING THERE Interstate 95 between New York and Providence skirts shoreline New Haven and I-91 from Boston and Hartford ends there. Connections can also be made from the south along the Merritt and Wilbur Cross parkways. Downtown traffic isn't too congested, except at the usual rush hours, and there are ample parking lots and garages near the green and Yale University, where most visitors spend their time. Even on-street spots aren't difficult to find most of the day.

Tweed–New Haven Airport (☎ 203/946-8283) receives feeder flights connecting with several major airlines, including Continental, USAir, and United. It's located southeast of the city, near exits 50 and 51 of I-95.

Amtrak (☎ 800/523-8760 for Metroliners, 800/872-7245 for all other trains) has several trains daily that run between Boston and New York and stop in New Haven. **Metro-North** (☎ 800/METRO-INFO) commuter trains make many daily trips between New Haven and New York. The trip to or from New York takes $1^{1}/_{2}$ hours, to or from Boston, about 3 hours. Metro-North tickets are much cheaper than Amtrak's.

VISITOR INFORMATION The **Greater New Haven Convention & Visitors Bureau** maintains an attended office at One Long Wharf Drive, CT 06511 (☎ 203/777-8550), visible and easily reached from Exit 46 of I-95. It's open from Memorial Day to Labor Day. The visitors bureau also has a hotel reservation service (☎ 800/332-7829). An especially useful detailed map of New Haven that even points out restaurants and store locations is *Professor Pathfinder's Yale University & New Haven,* available in bookstores.

EXPLORING YALE & NEW HAVEN

The major attractions are all associated with Yale University, and except for the Peabody Museum, are within walking distance of each other near the New Haven green.

Peabody Museum of Natural History. 170 Whitney Ave. (at Sachem St.). ☎ **203/ 432-5050** (recording). Admission $5 adults, $3 seniors and children 3–15. Mon–Sat 10am– 5pm, Sun noon–5pm.

Start on the third floor and work your way down, especially if a school group has just entered—the assault on adult eardrums can be fearsome, for this is probably the most popular field-trip destination in town. Up on the third floor there are dioramas with stuffed animals in various environments, abetted by quite effective backdrop paintings. There are bighorn sheep, wading marsh birds, a leopard, Alaska brown bear, southwestern javelina, mule deer, bison, musk oxen, and the assorted birds, snakes, and rodents with which they share their natural settings of desert, jungle, or tundra. An adjoining gallery has mounted birds purportedly representing every species found in Connecticut. Quite a number it is, too, and most of them look perkily lifelike. On the same floor is a small but illuminating collection of ancient Egyptian artifacts, including pottery, funerary objects, and fragments of reliefs and hieroglyphics. The second floor doesn't hold a great deal of general interest, but down on the first is a "bestiary" of large stuffed animals, from a single-wattled cassowary to a type of needle-nosed Indian crocodile called a gavial. This display leads logically into the Great Hall of Dinosaurs, its assembled fossils ranging from a pea-brained stegosaurus and mastodons to the fearsome brontosaurus. Remaining galleries deal with animal and human evolution, including displays of the weapons, headdresses, clothing, and body ornaments of Polynesian, Plains Indian, and pre-Columbian cultures.

New Haven Green. Bounded by Elm, Church, Chapel, and College sts.

The flat green, about one-third the size of Boston Common, is divided into two unequal parts by north-south Temple Street. It was set aside by town elders in earliest colonial days as a place for citizens to graze their livestock, bury their dead, and spend leisure hours strolling its footpaths. Government and bank buildings border it on the east, a retail district on the south, and some older sections of the vast Yale campus to the north and west. Facing Temple Street are three historic churches, all dating from the early 19th century. Next to Chapel Street is **Trinity Episcopal,** a brownstone Gothic Revival structure, the Georgian **First Church of Christ/ Center Congregational,** and the essentially Federalist **United Congregational.** The First Church of Christ is of the greatest interest, built atop a crypt with tombstones inscribed as early as 1687. Tours are conducted Tuesday to Friday 10:30am to 2:30pm.

Yale Center for British Art. 1080 Chapel St. (High St.). ☎ **203/432-2800** or 203/ 432-2850. Free admission. Tues–Sat 10am–5pm, Sun noon–5pm.

What looks like a parking garage from outside is a great deal more impressive once you step inside. The museum claims to be the most important collection of British art outside the United Kingdom, and there is no obvious reason to dispute it. Confirm this by taking the elevator to the fourth floor, where the bulk of the permanent collection is exhibited. It is arranged chronologically, from the 16th century to the early 19th, so turn right from the elevator to enter the Elizabethan Age and proceed in a clockwise direction. The paintings—portraits, in the main—are carefully hung and illuminated by many translucent skylights. It's a dazzling progression, some 250 canvases in all, by such luminaries as Hogarth, the landscapist Antonio Canal, Gainsborough, Sir Joshua Reynolds, Benjamin West, and the glorious Turner, from his early realistic seascapes to the lyrical visions that anticipated Impressionism toward the end of his life (1851). On the third floor are temporary exhibits, and on the second floor the visual narrative is picked up with works from the second half of the 19th century and the 20th, culminating with such familiar contemporary artists as Barbara Hepworth and Henry Moore. On the ground floor is the museum shop and a lecture hall.

Yale University. Visitor Information Center, 149 Elm St. (near College St.). ☎ 203/ 432-2300. Mon–Fri 9am–4:45pm, Sat–Sun 10am–4pm.

The oldest house in New Haven is now the **Yale Information Center,** a white colonial facing the north side of the green. While its primary mission is to familiarize prospective students and their parents with the university, anyone can stop by and arrange to take a one-hour guided walking tour (Monday to Friday 10:30am and 2pm, Saturday and Sunday 10am to 4pm). They have an introductory video and maps for self-guided tours.

It is impossible to imagine New Haven without Yale, so pervasive is its physical and cultural presence, nor, for that matter, the United States without it. After all, it helped educate our last two presidents, as well as Gerald Ford, William Howard Taft, Noah Webster, Nathan Hale, and Eli Whitney. Established in 1702 in the shoreline town now known as Clinton, the young college was eventually moved here in 1718 and named for Elihu Yale, who made a major financial contribution. It has many prestigious schools and divisions, including those devoted to medicine, law, theology, architecture, and engineering. The most evocative quadrangle of the sprawling institution is the Old Campus, which can be entered from College, High, or Chapel streets. Inside, the mottled green is enclosed by Victorian Gothic and Federalist buildings and dominated by Harkness Tower, a 1920 Gothic Revival campanile that looks much older. Sculptures of notable Yale alumni constitute much of the exterior ornamentation.

Yale University Art Gallery. 1111 Chapel St. (York St.). ☎ 203/432-0600. Admission $3 (suggested donation). Tues–Sat 10am–5pm, Sun 2–5pm. Closed Aug.

This last of the triad of distinguished university museums allocates space to artworks of many epochs and regions, but is most noted for its collections of the work of French impressionists and American realists of the late 19th and early 20th centuries. Architect Louis I. Kahn, responsible for the nearby Center for British Art, also designed the larger of these two buildings. Following our standard recommendation, take the elevator to the fourth floor and work your way down. Asian arts and crafts command the top floor, a permanent core of them surrounded by temporary displays. The tiny Netsuke ivories at the center bear close examination, as do the bronze, porcelain, and ceramic vessels in nearby cases. On the third floor, to the right, are 14th to 18th century Gothic ecclesiastical panels, mainly tempera on wood with prodigious amounts of gilt. To the left are 16th-century Italian and Dutch portraits and allegorical scenes, among them paintings by Rubens and Frans Hals. In sharp contrast are adjoining galleries of avant-garde 20th-century Americans of the abstract expressionist school—Rothko, Rauschenberg, Reinhardt, Stella, Ellsworth Kelly, and Kenneth Noland—as well as Europeans Braque, Brancusi, Klee, Picasso, Mondrian, Duchamp, and Miró. It is as satisfying a collection of the sort as might be found, yet without testing the patience of most teenagers and those adults who aren't regular museum-goers.

SHOPPING

A retail time machine, **Group W Bench** (1171 Chapel St.; ☎ 203/624-0683) celebrates an eyeblink epoch that lasted about 3 years in real time but has had a half-life that has survived five presidents. Started in 1968, the store is packed with beads, chimes, peace emblems, peacock feathers, Mexican yo-yos, rubber chickens, and bumper stickers reading "Thank You, Jerry" (as in "Garcia"). You can get a sixties-nostalgia-contact high just walking in the door. The bearded founder also owns the **Gallery Raffael** (1177 Chapel St.; ☎ 203/772-2258), right next door, which showcases mostly American arts and crafts, including his own.

Farther east on the same street is **WAVE** (1046 Chapel St.; ☎ 203/782-6212), a more upscale operation with a wealth of handblown glassware, brightly colored ceramics, candles, fragrances, toiletries, mirrors with handpainted frames—in short, just the sort of place that invites browsing.

Atticus Bookstore & Café (1082 Chapel St.; ☎ 203/776-4040) might as easily be listed under "Where to Dine," for one end of this bookstore consists of an always occupied lunch counter and takeout section. Famous for their scones, they also sell delectable pastries, crusty loaves of bread, soups like black bean and gazpacho, and hero sandwiches suffed with meats, cheeses, and vegetables. The New Orleans–style muffeletta is especially good. Cafe lattes and cafe au lait complete the bill. The rest of the space is devoted to what many call the best bookstore in town. It's open daily from 7am to midnight.

WHERE TO STAY

New Haven lodgings are both limited and, with one notable exception, devoid of either charm or distinctiveness. A monument to this miasmic condition is the **Park Plaza,** a large downtown hotel that closed its doors a couple of years ago and remains shuttered, its future uncertain. The remaining motels and hotels fill up far in advance for such university-related events as football weekends, alumni reunions, and graduation. One establishment reports reservations for graduation weeks into the next century.

Among the national chains are the **Holiday Inn** (30 Whalley Rd.; ☎ 203/777-6221), **Howard Johnson** (400 Sargent Dr.; ☎ 203/562-1111), and the **Marriott Residence Inn** (3 Long Wharf Dr.; ☎ 203/777-5337).

The Colony. 1157 Chapel St. (between Park and York sts.), New Haven, CT 06511. ☎ 800/458-8810 or 203/776-1234. Fax 203/772-3929. 86 rms. A/C TV TEL. $92–$103 double. AE, CB, DC, MC, V.

A conventional hotel that looks a little dated and worn, the Colony's chief value is its location, on a decent stretch of one of the city's better streets within easy walking distance of the green, the Yale campus, theaters, most of our recommended restaurants, and two of the Yale museums. It provides room service, bellhops, a concierge, and a restaurant—Charlie B's Steakhouse—that serves decent food (including seafood from a raw bar) and features jazz combos on weekend nights.

✪ **Three Chimneys Inn.** 1201 Chapel St. (between Park and Howe sts.), New Haven, CT 06511. ☎ 203/789-1201. Fax 203/776-7363. 10 rms. A/C TV TEL. $150 double. Rates include breakfast. AE, DISC, MC, V.

This 1870 mansion with its arresting paint job and formal front garden long did business as the Inn at Chapel West. Then, quite unexpectedly, it plunged into bankruptcy, and many of its furnishings and fixtures were ripped out to placate creditors. A vibrant new management has resurrected this favorite inn of Yalies and their parents. The parking lot was repaved, a new roof was added, and all rooms were reoutfitted with massive custom-made medicine cabinets, armoires to hide the TVs, and four-poster kings and queens, some with canopies. Many rooms have stuffed chaises, and all have at least two reading chairs. And for the executives who prefer it to the chain hotels, two-line phones with dataports have been installed. In the morning, a selection of newspapers waits outside the dining room. The "enhanced" continental breakfast is different each day, but typically includes cereal, fresh fruit, yogurt, and eggs or another hot dish. In the parlor across the hall, a tray of postprandial cordials is set out for guests to pour themselves. No children under 6 or pets are allowed.

WHERE TO DINE

The Brü Rm at BAR. 254 Crown St. (between High and College sts.). ☎ 203/495-1111. Pizzas $5–$11. MC, V. Mon 5pm–1am, Tues–Wed 11:30am–2:30pm and 5pm–1am, Thurs 11:30am–1am, Fri 11:30am–2am, Sat 5pm–2am, Sun 2pm–1am. PIZZA.

Yes, those spellings and capitalizations are correct. This place is a 1996 brewpub tacked onto a slightly older nightclub ("BAR"). What it also is is a naked challenge in the eternal New Haven pizza wars. If Frank Pepe's (see below) is the champ, as local consensus insists, this whippersnapper takes over as the new no. 1 contender. This of course assumes that one agrees with the local conviction that the thinner the crust the better. The pizzas here easily meet that requirement—if they were any thinner you could read this page through them. Basic categories are red, red with cheese, and white (cheese only), with 20 additional toppings to choose from. The smallest size can feed two people, especially if they start with the house salad, an unusual concoction of pears and pecans atop mixed greens in vinaigrette with crumpled blue cheese scattered over all. The shiny chrome and copper vats on the ground floor and open mezzanine produce five beers and ales, from the BAR Blonde to the Damn Good Stout. They are drawn as half-pints, pints, and pitchers.

🅢 **Caffé Adulis.** 228 College St. (near Crown St.). ☎ 203/777-5081. Main courses $8.95–$12.95. AE, MC, V. Sun–Wed 5–10pm, Thurs noon–3pm and 5–10pm, Fri noon–3pm and 5–11:30pm, Sat 5–11:30pm. ERITREAN.

Talk about specialization. Eritrea recently won its independence from Ethiopia after a 30-year civil war, and the Eritrean owners insist that there are significant differences in their cuisines, too. Maybe so, but whatever its other virtues, this successful ethnic eatery rewards the slightly venturesome diner with novel taste experiences at soothingly low prices. There is, for example, *injera,* a spongy, sour flatbread made of millet that figures in most of these dishes, including *tsebhe Derho* (chicken simmered with hot peppers) and shrimp *barka,* the jumbo crustaceans pan-seared and tumbled together with tomato-basil sauce, coconut, and dates ladled over fragrant basmati rice. About half the dishes are vegetarian, and most, not all, are spicy-hot, but the chef will adjust the seasonings if you ask. A familiar culinary touchstone is the authentic presence of pasta, introduced by the Italians during their long colonial rule of the region. Beer goes better with this peppery food than wine. Local Elm City Ale is a good choice, one of several regional microbreweries represented.

🅢 **Claire's Corner Copia.** 100 Chapel St. (at College St.). ☎ 203/562-3888. Main courses $4.50–$6.75. No credit cards. Sun–Thurs 8am–10pm, Fri–Sat 8am–11pm. VEGETARIAN.

Few college towns are without at least one cheap vegetarian restaurant. This one has ruled in New Haven since 1975, long enough for the founder to produce her own cookbook, copies of which she happily sells to satisfied customers. Dining options include curried couscous, eggplant rollatini, and a number of Mexican entrees, but the stars might well be the veggieburgers and the four different pizzettes. Meateaters can still partake, especially at breakfast, with the bounty of plump scones and massive muffins. A big blackboard lists many choices for all three meals and in-between snacks. On occasion the restaurant has live entertainment. All this, and the kitchen keeps kosher, too. A quibble: The Mexican and Indian dishes could use a little more zip.

Frank Pepe's. 157 Wooster St. (between Olive and Brown sts.). ☎ 203/865-5762. Pizzas $4.95–$10. No credit cards. Mon and Wed–Thurs 4–10:30pm, Fri–Sat 11:30am–midnight, Sun 2:30–10:30pm. PIZZA.

On the scene for most of this century, Pepe's has been accorded the pizza crown while fighting off perpetual challenges throughout its history. In exchange for truly super, almost unimaginably thin-crusted pies, pilgrims put up with long lines, minimal decor, and a perpetually sullen staff that brooks no hesitancy or questioning from the paying supplicants.

If the wait looks to be especially long, you can do about as well, quality and personnel-wise, at **Sally's** (237 Wooster St.; ☎ **203/624-5271**), just down the street.

By the way, the local spelling for the tomato and cheese pie in question is the old-fashioned "apizza," often pronounced "abeetz."

☉ Louis' Lunch. 261–263 Crown St. (between High and College sts.). ☎ **203/562-5507.** Hamburgers $2.30–$3.10. No credit cards. Mon–Thurs 11am–4pm, Fri–Sat 11am–1am. AMERICAN.

Here's history on a bun. The claim, unprovable but gaining strength as the decades roll on, is that America's very first hamburger was sold in 1900 at this boxy little brick luncheonette with the shuttered windows. Louis' Lunch wasn't always at this location—it was moved a few years ago to escape demolition—but not much else has changed. The tiny wooden counter and tables are incised with the carved initials of a century of patrons. The beef is freshly ground each day, formed into crude patties, squeezed into vertical grills, thrust into gas-fired ovens almost as old as the building, and then served (medium rare, usually) on two slices of white toast on paper plates. The only allowable garnishes are slices of tomato and onion—add cheese and you'll have a Louis burger with "the works." There's no mustard and no ketchup, so don't even ask. And no fries, either, just potato chips. They usually have three or four kinds of pie, though, and if they have time, they might make a tuna sandwich. But don't expect history to make compromises.

Pika Tapas Café. 39 High St. (south of Chapel St.). ☎ **203/865-1933.** Main courses $9–$14. MC, V. Mon–Thurs 11:30am–10:30pm, Fri–Sat 11:30am–11:30pm. SPANISH.

Tapas, for those still uninitiated, are the tasty snacks served in Spanish taverns as accompaniments to wine or beer. Comparable to hors d'oeuvres or antipasti, they come in an infinite variety of tastes and combinations. Among the most common are *tortilla*, a firm potato-and-egg omelet; *pan Catalan*, thick slices of bread moistened with tomato pulp and topped with cured ham; *croquetas de bacalao*, cod croquets with garlic mayo; and *gambas al ajillo*, shrimp sautéed with garlic. All these and at least 20 more are offered at the big semicircular bar in front of the Miró-like mural at this sprightly new enterprise. Keep it in mind for light meals before or after curtain at the nearby theaters. There are also larger portions of such classics as paella and clams with chorizo sausage and white beans.

✪ Union League Café. 1032 Chapel St. (between High and College sts.). ☎ **203/562-4299.** Main courses $14–$17. AE, MC, V. Mon–Fri 11:30am–2:30pm and 5:30–9:30pm (until 10pm Fri), Sat 5:30–10pm, Sun 4–8:30pm. CREATIVE FRENCH.

These grand salons with high arched windows opening onto Chapel Street retain an air of their aristocratic origins, which date back to 1854. Even the name fairly shrieks—with genteel Yankee reticence, of course—of its former status as a bastion of WASP privilege, the Union League Club. Now, however, it has loosened up considerably, and jeans-clad Yalies, their doting parents, philosophizing profs, and deal-making execs are all equally comfortable. The atmosphere is now closer to that of an updated Provençal brasserie than to that of a gentlemen's sanctuary, with waiters in aprons and butcher paper on the tables. Dinner entrees routinely tinker with tradition; witness the *osso buco de lotte aux pâtés fraîches*—monkfish with fresh pasta—or *poulet grillé aux éspices*—grilled marinated chicken with curry, ginger, and cumin over a basmati risotto. You could almost make a meal of the basket of superbly crusty, chewy bread. Also, the welcoming bar in back has a menu of light snacks. Lunch is mostly salads and sandwiches, but with twists, as in the leaves of roast lamb dressed with pesto and tomatoes on toasted slabs of that great bread.

NEW HAVEN AFTER DARK

The presence of Yale and a highly educated faction of the general population ensures a cultural life the equal of many larger cities. Within a couple of blocks of the green are the **Shubert Performing Arts Center** (247 College St.; ☎ **800/955-5566** or 203/562-5666), which presents such touring troupes as the Bolshoi Ballet and the Alvin Ailey Dance Theater, musical plays, and miscellaneous musical organizations; and the **Palace Performing Arts Center** (248 College St.; ☎ **203/789-2120**), with a more erratic schedule of pop singers and bands. A deconsecrated church is the home of the **Yale Repertory Theatre** (Chapel and York streets; ☎ **203/432-1234**), west of the green, which mounts an October through May season of lesser-known plays by known playwrights as diverse as David Mamet and George S. Kaufman. Away from downtown, but worth the taxi fare, is the **Long Wharf Theatre** (222 Sargent Dr; ☎ **203/787-4282**), known for its success in producing new plays (October through June) that often make the jump to Off-Broadway and even Broadway.

  Sprague Memorial Hall (470 College St.; ☎ **203/432-4157**) and **Woolsey Hall** (College and Grove streets; ☎ **203/432-2310**) are two important additional venues on the Yale campus that host the performances of many resident organizations, including the New Haven Symphony Orchestra, the New Haven Civic Orchestra, the Yale Concert Band, the Yale Glee Club, the Bach Society, and the Yale Jazz Ensemble.

  Bars and clubs also thrive, in considerable variety. The biggest and best for live rock and pop is **Toad's Place** (300 York St.; ☎ **203/624-8623**), which has welcomed the likes of the Rolling Stones, U2, Phoebe Snow, Bob Dylan, and Johnny Winter. Admission charges can get up to $15 or more for the top acts, but are much less most of the time. The club usually features live music Wednesday to Sunday, with dancing (to a band or DJ) on most Saturday nights.

  A less frenetic evening of music and conversation can be spent at **Xando** (338 Elm St.; ☎ **203/495-7166**). A bi-level postmodernist environment with brick walls and track lighting, it has an espresso bar and a segregated smoking section downstairs and less crowded tables on the upper level, where folk singers often perform. For something in between, there's **BAR** (254 Crown St.; ☎ **203/495-1111**), which has a lounge in front—open to the street on warm nights—and a pool table, a terrace, and a dance floor with another bar in back. Connected to BAR is the Brü Rm, described above in "Where to Dine."

  A reliable source of information about cultural events and nightlife is the free weekly newspaper, the *New Haven Advocate,* widely available at hotels, bookstores, and restaurants.

4 Hartford

115 miles NE of New York City, 103 miles SW of Boston

The second largest city of the Constitution State shares with its urban sisters a visible malaise that it can't seem to shake, even with its status as state capital and the presumed political clout to prop it up. It is not, after all, a Worcester sharing territory with a Boston, nor an Albany with a New York. Yet even while straining to focus on its grand edifices—the divinely overwrought gold-domed Capitol, the Mark

Twain House, the emblematic Travelers Insurance Tower, the august Wadsworth Athenaeum—it is impossible to ignore the miles of distressed housing, hollow-eyed office and industrial structures, and weed-strewn lots that radiate out from the center. Unattended grime, street crime, youth gangs, and abundantly apparent poverty are persistent thorns in the civic hide. On top of all that, the bedrock insurance business has been in the doldrums and companies have been dispersing to the suburbs and farther away, taking jobs and taxes with them. Conceding that none of this grief is unique to Hartford, and without making comparisons to cities far worse off, it is sufficient to note that this is not a place likely to retain for long the attention of people who don't have business here.

It isn't as if they don't try. A civic center was completed in 1975 in an attempt to attract business downtown, and an above-street walkway connects it with the newer, 39-story CityPlace. Both venues offer special concerts and art exhibits, and the 489-seat Hartford Stage Company has a 10-month theatrical season in its own 1977 building catercorner from the center. A block away, the gracious Old State House recently reopened after four years of careful renovation, and across Main Street a shed has been provided for a daily farmers' market and a local paper sponsors noontime rock concerts during the summer. All these efforts have encouraged the establishment of a few cosmopolitan restaurants and a couple of good hotels, so most of a day trip or overnight visit will be contained within only a few square blocks.

Hartford was founded in 1636 by dissidents fleeing the rigid religious dictates of the Massachusetts Bay Colony. Three years later, they drafted what were called the "Fundamental Orders," the basis of a subsequent claim that Connecticut was the first political entity on earth to have a written constitution. From 1701 until 1875, Hartford shared the status of capital with New Haven, undergirding the municipal rivalry that continues today.

ESSENTIALS

GETTING THERE   Interstate routes 84 and 91 intersect in central Hartford. Route 9 connects with coastal I-95 at Old Saybrook, west of Mystic, while Route 44 runs northwest to the Litchfield Hills.

Several major U.S. airlines provide direct or feeder line service to **Bradley International Airport** (☎ 860/292-2000) in Windsor Locks, about 12 miles north of the city. Buses, cabs, and limousines shuttle passengers into the city and to other points in the state. Major airlines serving Hartford include: **American** (☎ 800/433-7300), **Continental** (☎ 800/525-0280), **Delta** (☎ 800/221-1212), **Northwest** (☎ 800/225-2525), **United** (☎ 800/241-6522), and **USAir** (☎ 800/247-8786).

Amtrak (☎ 800/872-7245) has several trains daily following the inland route between New York City and Boston, stopping at Hartford and Windsor Locks. The trip to either New York or Boston takes about 2½ hours.

VISITOR INFORMATION   A sporadically attended desk in the basement of the Old State House (800 Main St.; ☎ 203/522-6766) has a limited number of informational brochures. A counter on the main floor of the Civic Center (Trumbull, Asylum, and Church streets.) has most of the same materials, but is manned by members of the **Hartford Guides.** Quite knowledgeable about their city, they not only provide information about sightseeing, shopping, restaurants, and hotels, they conduct walking tours and can provide escort service for women and seniors from lodgings or eating places to their cars or buses. To obtain their assistance or suggestions, call **860/293-8105.**

SEEING THE SIGHTS

The Old State House. 800 Main St. (Asylum Ave.). ☎ **860/522-6766.** Free admission. Jan–Oct Mon–Fri 10am–4pm, Sat 10am–3pm; Nov–Dec Mon–Sat 10am–5pm, Sun noon–5pm.

After closing for a four-year $12-million renovation, the 1796 State House opened in time to celebrate its bicentennial. Costumed "interpreters" stand ready, even eager, to answer questions. Upstairs, on the right, is the restored Senate chamber, with an original full-length painting of the first president by the indefatigable Washington portraitist, Gilbert Stuart. Across the hall is the room that housed the city council after the state government moved to a larger facility. These days, the plan is to use the building for temporary art exhibitions, changed two or three times yearly. If subsequent shows live up to the standard of the opening exhibit—contemporary paintings by Latino artists—this will become a must stop on the local cultural circuit. There is a museum shop in the basement.

✪ **Mark Twain House.** 351 Farmington Ave. ☎ **860/247-0998.** Admission $7.50, $7 seniors, $3.50 children 6–12. Memorial Day–Columbus Day and Dec Mon–Sat 9:30am–5pm, Sun noon–5pm; rest of the year closed Tues. Visits by guided tour only. Take Exit 46 off I-84, turn right onto Sisson Ave., then right onto Farmington Ave. The house is on the right, in less than a half-mile. From downtown, drive west on Asylum St., bearing left on Farmington Ave. The house is on the left.

Hartford makes the most of its association with one of America's most beloved and honored authors. His image is seen everywhere, and the city puts on three "Mark Twain Days" in mid-August, packed with such events as frog jumping and fence painting, sack races and riverboat rides, and performances of plays based on Twain's life or works. Most activities are free.

The 19-room house is a fascinating example of the late 19th-century style sometimes known as "Picturesque Gothic," with several steeply peaked gables and brick walls whose varying patterns are highlighted by black or orange paint. Samuel Clemens, whose pseudonym was a term used by Mississippi River pilots to indicate a water depth of two fathoms, lived here with his wife Olivia and three daughters from 1873 to 1897. The high Victorian decor of the interior was the result of Twain's enthusiasm for newfangled gadgets—there is a primitive telephone in the entrance hall—and distinguished designers of the time—Louis Comfort Tiffany provided advice and stained glass. Much of the first and second floors of the 19-room house is embellished with what looks like wallpaper but is actually stenciled with silvery paint. The adjoining drawing room is brighter than the dim foyer, intentionally so, to illuminate the activities that took place there—piano-playing, singing, chatting with visitors. The guided tour takes about an hour, and proceeds through the dining room and library (which has a magnificent carved mantelpiece that reaches to the ceiling), and then up through the bedrooms on the second floor. Note the picture in the playroom titled *Life And Death,* which looks like two people in a window up close, but becomes a skull when viewed from a distance. On the top floor is the writer's main workroom, a large space that also has a pool table. Twain would often walk across the hall in the middle of the night and wake up his butler to play a few games.

On the same property, about 60 yards across the lawn from the porte cochere of the Twain residence, is the **Harriet Beecher Stowe House** (73 Forest St.; ☎ **860/525-9317**). A smaller, "cottage" version of its neighbor, built in 1871, Stowe lived in it for most of the time Twain resided in his. This author of *Uncle Tom's Cabin* was hardly a great writer, despite the fact that her antislavery novel is regarded as the first international best-seller. Perhaps that is why Twain regarded the older woman with neighborly equanimity. He was not so disposed toward many of his contemporary and earlier rivals. Of an acclaimed novel by Henry James, Twain expressed the

Hartford

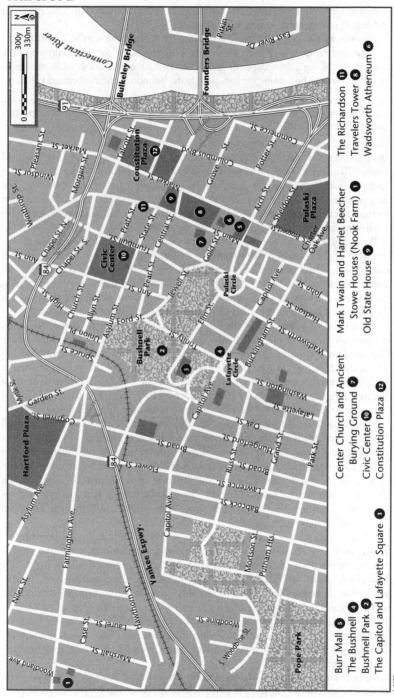

Burr Mall ⑤
The Bushnell ④
Bushnell Park ②
The Capitol and Lafayette Square ③

Center Church and Ancient
Burying Ground ⑦
Civic Center ⑩
Constitution Plaza ⑫

Mark Twain and Harriet Beecher
Stowe Houses (Nook Farm) ①
Old State House ⑨

The Richardson ⑪
Travelers Tower ⑧
Wadsworth Atheneum ⑥

1-0602

sentiments of countless university students when he commented that "Once you put it down, it isn't possible to pick it up again."

Prices and policies for the Stowe House are similar to those for the Twain House. Couples and families may want to skip the resulting high cost, especially since the competence of the guides depends greatly on the luck of the draw. Most are admirably well-versed, but others are lost outside the bounds of their rehearsed spiels.

✪ **Wadsworth Athenaeum.** 600 Main St. (Gold St.). ☎ **203/278-2670.** Admission $6 adults, $4 seniors and students, $3 children 6–17 (free all day Thurs). Tues–Sun 11am–5pm (until 8pm 1st Thurs of month).

Opened in 1842, this is the first public art museum in the United States. It looks its age from the outside, its wings and additions a hodgepodge of ineptly executed Gothic, Renaissance, and Victorian Revival styles. The refurbished interior is another story, with its soaring atrium courts ringed with open galleries and balconies. The only problem lies with the confusion of varying levels and the installation of frequent temporary exhibitions that not only close off large spaces but make movement difficult from one part of the second floor to the other.

Persevere, for this is a noteworthy repository with few equals in New England. The strengths of the collection lie primarily in its American paintings, spanning the period from the Hudson River landscapists of the first half of the 19th century through luminaries of the New York School of the mid-20th to the provocative work of contemporary young artists active in these last years before the millenium. Less space is devoted to 17th- and 18th-century European artworks of lesser magnitude.

For an overview, proceed by elevator to the top floor. In a far corner is a room devoted to Thomas Cole, accorded a leadership role among native artists of the Hudson River School. Adapting the then-prevailing romanticism of European artists to lush depictions of American landscapes, he was one of the most restrained in his use of color but didn't neglect the drama of the Catskill Mountains and the Hudson Highlands. In the next gallery are works by Frederick Church, a Hartford native, and the flamboyant Albert Bierstadt, who devoted himself to huge, sumptuous portrayals of the Rocky Mountains and the West. At the other end are three small Winslow Homers in a room of academic post–Civil War pictures. Outside that section, on the balcony that borders the Avery Court, are more Americans, many of whom fudged the border between art and illustration—Frederic Remington, Andrew Wyeth, Ben Shahn, Reginald Marsh, Milton Avery, even Norman Rockwell. Watch for the shadow box by Joseph Cornell. These lead naturally to a gallery of the so-called American impressionists, whose work bore resemblances to their European colleagues but never achieved their acclaim.

The highlights of the second floor are room after room of early Connecticut furniture, most of it chairs and chests extensively and elaborately carved in the English manner of the period, a form of utilitarian folk art. Continuing down to the first floor, look for the MATRIX Gallery, full of rule-bending multimedia works by current artists. It makes the adjacent rooms of large canvases by abstract expressionists and Pop and Op artists of the 1950s and 1960s look cozily familiar and accessible, hardly the reactions they provoked at their first exposures. Here, find stellar examples by de Kooning, Rauschenburg, Frankenthaler, Albers, and Kline, as well as sculptures by Donald Judd and David Smith. Looking right at home is a splendid desk by Frank Lloyd Wright.

On the same floor is the **Museum Café,** which has surprisingly good light items that alone are reasons enough for a visit. There are tables out on the terrace in good weather. Lunch is served Tuesday to Saturday, brunch on Sunday, and dinner on the first Thursday of each month, when the museum is open until 8pm.

WHERE TO STAY

✪ **The Goodwin Hotel.** 1 Haynes St. (Asylum St.), Hartford, CT 06103. ☎ **800/922-5006** or 860/246-7500. Fax 860/247-4576. 124 rms. A/C TV TEL. $131–$153 double. AE, CB, DC, DISC, MC, V.

In a state with few luxury hotels, this quiet hostelry opposite the Civic Center stands out. It is housed in a Queen Anne–style Victorian built in 1881 as a residence for J.P. Morgan, the 19th-century industrialist, financier, and railway tycoon. While its understated public areas are lovely, the bedrooms are not as plush as one might hope and the air conditioning isn't always sufficient during a real heat wave. Valet parking is a blessing along this crowded block, but don't expect your car to arrive promptly if you need it at a busy time—waits can be long. I found the staff cordial but have heard serious complaints from others about service. Pierpont's is the capable in-house restaurant, serving New American cuisine that is creative and satisfying without being too startling. Work off the calories in the health club.

Sheraton. 315 Trumbull St. (Civic Center Plaza), Hartford, CT 06103. ☎ **860/728-5151.** Fax 860/522-3356. 388 rms. A/C TV TEL. $120 double. AE, CB, DC, DISC, MC, V.

You can spot it from just about anywhere, highways or downtown. The 22-story slab is everything you'd expect of a Sheraton. Its rates are no bargain, but aren't a rip-off, either. The standard Sheraton conventionalities are observed in service and facilities, which include a health club, an indoor pool, and garage parking.

WHERE TO DINE

Bombay's. 89A Arch St. (corner Columbus Blvd.). ☎ **860/724-4282.** Main courses $8.95–$17.95. MC, V. Daily 11:30am–2:30pm and 5–9:30pm. INDIAN.

Hartford's burgeoning population of immigrants from the Indian subcontinent is responsible for several exotic restaurants, including this one, thought by many to be the best of the lot. An unpromising exterior and an interior made gaudy by fanned crimson napkins in every water glass don't raise high hopes. Pictures of camels and caravans and an acoustical tile ceiling complete what amounts to decor. But wait! Even if Indian menus seem to you only a blur of *tikka* this and *tandoori* that, there's no mistaking the tantalizing aromas issuing from the curtained kitchen. It would be no deprivation to lunch only on one or two of the appetizers and a big basket of *nan,* the puffy flatbread warm from the oven, its bigger bubbles nicely singed. (This chef doesn't coat the bread in oil, as some do.) But that would mean missing such flavor-packed entrees as chicken *tikka sang*—chunks of tandoor-reddened chicken in a lush sauce of spinach, tomatoes, green peppers, and onions—or lamb *dhansak*—tender cubes of lamb cooked with lentils in a stew seasoned with ginger and curries. Dishes are authentically spicy enough to pop a few beads of sweat, but won't take the top of your head off. If you like your food *really* hot, they'll oblige. Prices are about 40% less at lunch than in the evening.

Civic Café. 150 Trumbull St. (near Asylum St.). ☎ **860/493-7412.** Main courses $14.95–$22.95. AE, CB, DC, MC, V. Mon–Tues 11am–2:30pm, 5–10pm, Wed–Thurs 11am–2:30pm and 5–11pm, Fri–Sat 11am–2:30pm and 5pm–midnight. ECLECTIC.

The prosperous, self-satisfied bunch who frequent this restaurant would be at ease in Boston or New York, and they have found a place that looks like it belongs in a hipper city. Up above, it's postindustrial ducts, pipes, and whirring fans.

Air-conditioning is glacial, and so, sometimes, is the service. No one seems to mind, so busy are they watching the collisions of egos. Suits dominate at lunch, when the raw bar near the front is a big draw, and at happy hour, when patrons down fruit-colored martinis around the rectangular bar. It's all so very . . . *happening* . . . lesser food might go unnoticed. But this fare gets your attention, not least for the gobs of salsas and garnishes and dustings of herbs cast over each plate. "Lemon herb-rubbed rotisserie chicken with buttermilk mashed potatoes and roast garlic" is as simple as things get, and of course tuna is served rare, in one case sandwiched between crisp wontons. T-shirts and shorts are no-nos.

A markedly similar formula and clientele is evident at the even newer **Max Downtown** a block away on Asylum Street, opposite the Civic Center.

Hot Tomato's. 1 Union Place (corner Asylum St.). ☎ **860/249-5100.** Main courses $13.95–$19.95. AE, CB, DC, MC, V. Sun–Mon 5:30–9:30pm, Tues–Thurs 5:30–10pm, Fri–Sat 5:30–11pm. ITALIAN.

The admirable renovation of Union Station spawned this popular trattoria in one wing. Walk from the host's podium past the ordered frenzy of the open kitchen and down into a large glass-sided dining room or out onto the dining terrace. A knowing crowd, most of it casually dressed, tucks into big black bowls of pasta, which they are usually unable to finish. Many of the avowedly authentic recipes are infrequently available this side of Bologna. Especially spicy dishes are marked with a star, the hot pepper flakes provided at each table hardly necessary with flavors this powerful. One such is ziti tossed with grilled chicken strips, olive oil, whole roasted garlic cloves, and bitter broccoli rabe (admittedly an acquired taste). Another blends a zippy marinara sauce with shrimp, hot sausage, olives, and pepperoncini and lays the mixture over a bed of linguini. Main courses come with a house salad, which may be replaced with a "petite" Caesar salad for $1.95 extra. The waitress will produce a pepper grinder from a pouch on her belt or a wedge of Parmesan for fresh gratings to order. Garlic bread will be suggested, but the basket of plain chewy bread slabs that comes with every meal is entirely satisfying.

HARTFORD AFTER DARK

The **Bushnell Performing Arts Center** (166 Capitol Ave.; ☎ 860/246-6807) is the venue for the **Hartford Ballet,** a classical and contemporary troupe that doesn't neglect to stage the obligatory Christmas season *Nutcracker.* It is also home to the **Hartford Symphony** and the **Hartford Pops,** when it isn't hosting visiting orchestras or road companies of Broadway plays like *Miss Saigon.* **Hartford Stage** (50 Church St.; ☎ 860/527-5151) mounts a variety of traditional and mainstream plays, occasionally interspersed with introductions of new productions, while **Theatreworks** (233 Pearl St.; ☎ 860/527-7838) explores new frontiers. In late July, there is a **Festival of Jazz** with free performances at the pavilion in Bushnell Park.

Several downtown clubs and bars put on live bands, usually Thursday to Saturday. Assuming they're still in operation, never something to be assumed, check out the **bar with no name** (115 Asylum St.; ☎ 860/522-4646), **The Russian Lady** (191 Ann St.; ☎ 860/525-3003), and **Arch Street Tavern** (85 Arch St.; ☎ 860/246-7610). For beer by the pint or pitcher and Monday Night Football with the guys (and the women who put up with them), where better than **Coach's** (187 Allyn St.; ☎ 860/522-6224). It has 32 TVs and serves such dainty delectables as chili in scooped-out loaves of bread. A similar sports bar is **Huskies** (356 Asylum St.; ☎860/278-4747), which has various drink and food promotions as well as a patio overlooking Bushnell Park.

A widely available free weekly paper, the *Hartford Advocate,* provides much useful info on cultural, sports, and musical events.

5   The Way East: Guilford to Old Saybrook

Usually ignored by vacationers anxious to get on to Mystic and Essex and such gaudy attractions as the Foxwoods Casino, the stretch of coast between New Haven and the Connecticut River known simply as the Shoreline has its gentle pleasures, enough to justify a short detour for lunch, a walk on a beach, a spell of shopping, or even a proper British high tea. When lodgings are difficult to find at the flossier destinations, Shoreline's inns and resorts are logical alternatives within easy driving distance.

ESSENTIALS

GETTING THERE   The Shoreline can be accessed by taking Exit 57 of I-95 and picking up Route 1 (a.k.a. Boston Post Road), which serves as the main street of several Shoreline towns.

Several daily **Amtrak** trains stop at Old Saybrook, and the **Shoreline East** (☎ **800/255-7433**) commuter line uses the same tracks to service towns between there and New Haven, but only Monday through Friday.

VISITOR INFORMATION   Informational materials can be obtained in advance from the **Connecticut River Valley and Shoreline Visitors Council** (393 Main St., Middletown, CT 06457; ☎ **800/486-3346** or 860/347-0028).

GUILFORD

13 miles E of New Haven

One of the state's oldest colonial settlements (1639), this village embraced by the West and East rivers has an uncommonly large green bordered by churches, shops, and public buildings.

There are dozens of historic houses to see in town, most of them privately owned and a few others open to the public on a limited seasonal basis, typically Memorial Day weekend to Labor Day or Columbus Day. **Hyland House** (84 Boston St.; ☎ **203/453-9477**), built around 1660, and **Thomas Griswold House** (171 Boston St.; ☎ **203/453-3176**), from 1774, are two of these. The Whitfield House (below) is open all year.

Henry Whitfield State Museum. 248 Whitfield St. (east of the green). ☎ **203/453-2457.** Admission $3 adults, $1.50 seniors and children 6–17. Feb–Dec 14 and Wed–Sun 10am–4:30pm; Dec 15–Jan 30 by appointment only.

The Whitfield Museum's billing as the "oldest house in Connecticut and the oldest stone house in New England" is misleading. In addition to undergoing frequent alterations over the years, the house was devastated by a major fire in 1860 that left little more than the granite walls. After reconstruction, it was inhabited until the turn of the century, and by the 1930s it had deteriorated from neglect, and had to be rebuilt once again. Most of what is seen now, including the leaded windows, dates from that time, not from the mid-1600s, when the original structure went up. It is instructive, nonetheless, and is presented as a museum, not a historic home. The furnishings inside are authentic to the period, and there are displays of powder horns, flintlock rifles, spinning wheels, and a loom. The settlers of Guilford were Puritans, and they were fearful of hostile action from nearby English and Dutch colonies. This building was one of four that served as part of a fortification system. As evidence, look for the unusual corner window on the second floor, which was used as a lookout over Long Island Sound, though the water is no longer visible due to tree growth.

WHERE TO DINE

The Stone House. 506 Whitfield St. (east of the Whitfield Museum). ☎ **203/458-1311.** Main courses $11.95–$18.95. AE, MC, V. Daily 11:30am–10pm. ITALIAN/SEAFOOD.

Recently reopened and renovated by new owners, this low stone building has agreeable views of the ocean and a marina. The location only partially influences the menu, which has as many meat as fish dishes. Presumably, that's just to accommodate the varied tastes of its patrons, since the self-proclaimed specialties of the house are lobster bisque and baked lobster stuffed with crabmeat and fish. The provocative wine list includes selections from vintners, largely Californian, not seen everywhere—including Meridian, Ferrari-Carano, and Hess Select. To the left of the entrance is a spacious lounge with a bar, a circular fireplace, and tables for diners who smoke. They sit beneath two hanging racing sculls. To the right are the understated main dining rooms, including an area in back usually reserved for groups on bus tours, who frequently fill the restaurant.

MADISON

19 miles east of New Haven

Madison is home to a historic architectural district that stretches west of the business district along the Boston Post Road, from the main green to the town line, and boasts many examples of 18th- and 19th-century domestic styles and few commercial intrusions. Prosperous Madison has completed the transition from colony to seaside resort to year-round community, a process begun when the first house was built in 1651. Today there are two dwellings from the early years that can be visited on limited summer schedules. **Deacon John Grave House** (581 Boston Post Rd.; ☎ 203/245-4758) dates from 1685, and the **Allis-Bushnell House** (853 Boston Post Rd.; ☎ 203/245-4567) from 1785.

Off the Boston Post Road east of the town center, also reached from Exit 62 off I-95, is **Hammonasset Beach State Park** (☎ 203/245-1817), a more than 900-acre peninsula jutting into Long Island Sound that has the only public swimming beach in the area. The park also has a nature center, picnic areas, and campgrounds, and offers boating, too. Cars with Connecticut license plates get in for $5 Monday to Friday and $7 weekends; out-of-state plates cost $8 and $12, respectively.

Madison's central commercial district may look ordinary at first glance, but several specialty shops along Boston Post Road and intersecting Wall Street provide for entertaining browsing. These are the remaining holdouts against the magnetic pull of the monster outlet malls recently opened in neighboring Clinton and Westbrook. One of the most visible as well as highly active stores in the community is **R.J. Julia Booksellers** (768 Boston Post Rd.; ☎ 203/245-3959), which holds frequent author readings and even poetry slams, readings in which competing poets face off in mock lyrical battles. Many books on the store's two levels have annotation cards offering the specific observations of obviously well-read staff members. There is a large, separate children's section.

A few steps east is **Walker-Loden** (788 Boston Post Rd.; ☎ 203/245-8663), which inadequately describes its wares as "gifts, antiques, and artwork." On hand are diverse souvenir and household items, such as straw hats, cookbooks, nonmechanical toys, greeting cards, pillboxes, prayer rugs, silk ties and scarves, and much more.

Cross the street and proceed north, and you'll come across several other shops. One of them, in a 1690 plum-colored saltbox, could also be listed under eating places. **The British Shoppe** (45 Wall St.; ☎ 203/245-4521) stocks such English favorites as "kippers" (fish), "bangers" (sausages), pork pies, boxes of various teas, and several sublime cheeses, all imported from Blighty. (The breads are from Old Saybrook, down the road.) Gifts and housewares of British origin are on sale, many of them of the sort used in the Front Parlor, the dining room where lunches and afternoon teas are served. "Ploughman's Lunches" of cheese, bread, tomato, lettuce, and pickled onions recall those in classic English pubs, unfortunately without pints of cool English beer, licensing requirements being too tough to meet. Afternoon teas are Monday to Saturday 2 to 4pm and Sunday 12:30 to 4pm, offering properly brewed loose teas with finger sandwiches and cakes.

WHERE TO STAY

Tidewater Inn. 949 Boston Post Rd. (east of the business district), Madison, CT 06443. ☎ **203/245-8457.** 9 rms. A/C TV TEL. $80–$160 double. AE, MC, V.

The bland exterior isn't promising, but impressions change once inside. The new owners have lowered rates and upgraded facilities, and the inn is now as useful to business travelers as it is comforting to vacationers. Despite the new management, the decor has not changed much, retaining its intriguing combinations of New England decorative conventions: floral wallpapers and four-poster beds alongside collections of Chinese porcelains, Japanese prints, and related Orientalia. It is as if the New England wife of a long-absent merchant captain had embellished the house's standard trimmings with all of the gifts and souvenirs he carried back from his trade in Asia. Most of the rooms have two reading chairs and desks with utilitarian brass office lamps. Breakfasts are fairly substantial, with fresh fruit followed by waffles, pancakes, or other hot items. A fridge with soft drinks and an iron and ironing board are available to guests. A gentle suggestion, though: The inn would do well to lose the fake wreaths, lacy padded hearts, and most of the silk flowers.

WESTBROOK

28 miles E of New Haven

In Westbrook, a roadside sprawl markedly more plebian in character than Guilford and Madison, intermittent houses share space with strip malls, fish shanties, cookie-cutter franchises, marinas, and enterprises dedicated to boating services. Only the town center preserves a touch of its New England character.

Giving a boost to the local economy is the new outlet mall, **Westbrook Factory Stores** (Flat Rock Place; ☎ **860/399-8656**), north of town at Exit 65 of I-95. Expected to eventually house 80 or more outlets, the complex observes an architectural style that might be described as Rural Railroad Revival, actually a pleasant change from the more common "cellblock" design of most malls. "Name" dealers include Reebok, Timberland, Dockers, Blu Boy, Olga/Warner's, Haggar, Corning/Revere, American Tourister, Nordic Track, Springmaid/Wamsutta, J. Crew, Jockey, and Oshkosh B'Gosh. Open daily.

WHERE TO STAY

Water's Edge. 1525 Boston Post Rd. (Rte. 1), Westbrook, CT 06498. ☎ **800/222-5901** or 203/399-5901. Fax 203/399-6172. 32 rms. A/C TV TEL. $110–$280 double. AE, CB, DC, DISC, MC, V.

Water's Edge started out as Bill Hahn's Resort, a shambling family getaway spot that had the feel of a Catskills vacation resort transplanted on the Connecticut coast. It grew and grew into what is now a full-service holiday hotel with time-share condo units as well. Oft-used for corporate conferences as well as by families and couples, it has sacrificed a reputed former coziness in favor of efficiency and a measure of gloss. The hotel restaurant, for example, is a tony, multilevel, pink-and-buff affair with terraces overlooking the lawn and the wide sandy beach. While the kitchen is capable, the best deal is the generous Sunday brunch. All manner of recreational facilities are available, including two pools (one indoor), a supervised summer play program for kids, paddleboats and sailboats, a full fitness center, and tennis courts. Weekend entertainment involves live music and dancing. Families may wish to rent one of the unoccupied units of the 68 villas, which are in addition to the hotel rooms mentioned above.

WHERE TO DINE

⑤ **Lenny & Joe's Fish Tale.** 86 Boston Post Rd. (Rte. 1). ☎ **203/669-0767.** Main courses $6.75–$13.95. No credit cards. Sun–Thurs 11am–10pm, Fri–Sat 11am–11pm. SEAFOOD.

"The new T-shirts have arrived," announces a sign at the door, setting this restaurant's casual tone. Inside, it is a rough-and-ready fish shack with low ceilings, little pretense of decor, and waitresses in shorts, aprons, and sneakers. On each bare table is a ketchup bottle and a canister of sea salt. And believe it or not, this place is actually classier than the other Fish Tale branch in Madison (1301 Boston Post Rd.; ☎ **860/ 245-7289**), which suffers from the lack of a liquor license. Fish is the thing, of course, most of it fried. And while it is sure to elevate tryglyceride counts, the nutty, crunchy coating on super-fresh whole clams, oysters, shrimp, or calamari is hard to resist, especially on a summer evening when the air carries the scent of oceans and distant islands. The menu is printed daily to reflect market prices and availability.

OLD SAYBROOK

35 miles E of New Haven, 26 miles W of Mystic

Its location at the mouth of the Connecticut River is this otherwise nondescript town's principal lure, and it is necessary to get off Route 1 to see it at its best. Pick up Route 153 south at the western edge, following its nearly circular route as it touches the shore and passes through the hamlets of Knollwood and Fenwick and across the causeway to Saybrook Point before ending up back in the main business district.

Movie buffs will get an extra kick out of cruises on *The African Queen* (Saybrook Yacht Basin, Ferry Road; ☎ **860/388-2007**), the actual steam-powered launch from the 1951 film of the same name starring Humphrey Bogart and Katherine Hepburn. It makes daily voyages from May to October.

WHERE TO DINE

Cuckoo's Nest. 1712 Boston Post Rd. (Rte. 1). ☎ **860/399-9060.** Main courses $10.95–$15.95. AE, DC, MC, V. Daily 11:30am–10pm (until 11pm Fri–Sat). TEX-MEX.

"Mexican Food Plus Cajun & Creole," crows the ecumenical menu, so sanctimonious sticklers for gastronomic authenticity need look elsewhere. The rest of us can have a good time at moderate cost at this unabashedly raffish roadhouse complete with wooden chairs, tables, and floors that haven't seen fresh coats of shellac since the 1976 opening. On the walls are old advertising signs and English street markers, pierced-tin lamps hang over some of the tables, and fans rotate lazily overhead. A jazz duo performs Thursday nights. As for the food, corn-crusted codfish with yellow rice and roasted garlic salsa may or may not be truly Mexican, but it tastes mighty good. So do the pork loin fajitas with veggies and rice, topped with shredded cheese, pico de gallo, and sour cream. As for the "Cajun & Creole" offerings, check out the New Orleans popcorn shrimp or the catfish Creole. A little jambalaya couldn't hurt, either. Begin your visit with a mango margarita, out on the terrace if it's a warm night.

6 The Connecticut River Valley

New England's longest river originates in the far north near the Canadian border, 407 miles from Long Island Sound. It separates Vermont from New Hampshire, splits Massachusetts in half, then takes a 45° turn at Middletown, south of Hartford, to make its final run to the sea. Native Americans of the region called the river *Quinnehtukqut,* which, to the linguistically dead ears of the English settlers, sounded like "Connecticut." The colonists encroached upon Indian territory as far north as present-day Windsor, which ignited a brief war with the Pequot, who occupied the land.

Since the river was navigable by relatively large ships as far as Hartford, the sheltered lower Connecticut became important for boatbuilding, for transporting provisions to oceangoing clipper ships, and to industries associated with that worldwide trade. The Connecticut retains that nautical flavor, but the valley has miraculously avoided the industrialization, land development, and predictable decay that afflicts most of the state's other rivers.

There aren't a great many motels to be found between Haddam and Old Lyme, the southernmost segment of the valley that is of greatest interest to tourists, but there are several excellent full-service inns and many bed-and-breakfasts, both of the independent variety and those that can only be found through referral agencies. Two such B&B referral companies are **Bed & Breakfast, Ltd.** (P.O. Box 216, New Haven, CT 06513; ☎ **203/469-3260**) and **Nutmeg Bed & Breakfast Agency** (P.O.Box 1117, West Hartford, CT 06127; ☎ **800/727-7592** or 860/236-6698.)

ESSENTIALS

GETTING THERE   Limited-access state highway 9 runs parallel to the river, along the west side of the valley, connecting I-91 south of Hartford with I-95 near Old Saybrook. The lower valley is therefore readily accessible from all points in New England and from the New York metropolitan area and points south.

Amtrak (☎ **800/872-7245**) trains stop at Old Saybrook, at the mouth of the river, several times daily on their runs between New York and Boston. In addition, **Shoreline East** (☎ **800/255-7433**) commuter trains operate Monday to Friday between New Haven and Old Saybrook.

VISITOR INFORMATION   The **Connecticut River Valley and Shoreline Visitors Council** (393 Main St., Middletown, CT 06457; ☎ **800/486-3346** or 860/347-0028) is a source of pamphlets, maps, and related materials.

OLD LYME
40 miles E of New Haven, 21 miles W of Mystic

As quiet a town as the coast can claim, with tree-lined streets largely free of traffic, Old Lyme was the favored residence of generations of seafarers and ship captains. Many of their 18th- and 19th-century homes have survived, some as summer residences of the artists who established a colony here around the turn of the century, a few as inns and museums.

A MANSION OF ART
Florence Griswold Museum. 96 Lyme St. (Rte. 1). ☎ **860/434-5542.** Admission $4 adults, $3 seniors and students, children under 12 free. June–Nov Tues–Sat 10am–5pm, Sun 1–5pm; Dec–May Wed–Sun 1–5pm.

Once the shipbuilding and merchant trade had all but flickered out at the end of the last century, artists who came to be known as the "American impressionists" took a fancy to the area. Encouragement, patronage, and even food and shelter were offered them by Ms. Griswold, the wealthy daughter of a sea captain. Her 1817 Federalist mansion was the temporary home for a number of painters, most of whom left samples of their work in gratitude, including pictures painted directly on the walls of the dining room. Visitors can walk across the mansion's six acres to the Lieutenant River, a brief course that flows slightly to the west of the Connecticut.

Rotating temporary exhibits are held on the first and second floors. The restored studio of impressionist William Chadwick is also on view.

A SEASIDE PARK

One of several state parks located at the edge of Long Island Sound, **Rocky Neck State Park** (Route 156; ☎ 860/739-5471), east of Old Lyme, has a half-mile, scimitar-shaped beach and over 560 acres for camping, picnicking, fishing, and hiking. Reach it from Exit 72 of I-95, picking up Route 156 south.

WHERE TO STAY & DINE

Bee and Thistle Inn. 100 Lyme St. (Rte. 1), Old Lyme, CT 06371. ☎ **800/622-4946** or 860/ 434-1667. Fax 860/434-3402. 12 rms. $69–$195 double. Rates include breakfast. A/C. Approaching from the south, take Exit 70 from I-95, turn left, then right on Rte. 1 north.

The core structure of the inn dates from 1756, with the usual wings and additions. A small detached cottage is the best lodging, with the only room TV and a fireplace. Two of the bedrooms in the main house share a bathroom, the rest have their own. Every corner of the place is an enjoyable clutter of antiques and collectibles. A skilled professional kitchen staff prepares three meals a day, served on dining room tables near fireplaces by an eager-to-please but inexperienced waitstaff. Musicians are on hand weekend evenings. Guests are asked to appear for the evening meal in a jacket or the female equivalent—no jeans or shorts—and children must be over 12. No pets.

Old Lyme Inn. 85 Lyme St. (Rte. 1), Old Lyme, CT 06371. ☎ **800/434-5352** or 860/ 434-2600. Fax 860/434-5352. 13 rms. A/C TV TEL. $99–$158 double. Rates include breakfast. AE, CB, DC, DISC, MC, V. To get there, follow the directions for the Bee and Thistle, above.

Most of the bedrooms in this 1850s farmhouse are spacious, mostly furnished with Victorian chairs, loveseats, and four-poster, or so-called "cannonball" beds. The dining rooms are even more impressive, especially the Grill, which features an entire antique bar and marble-manteled fireplace—admirers of Victorian taverns might not want to leave. The Grill offers a light dinner menu, and live music on weekends. The other dining rooms are more formal—which isn't to say that they're stuffy—and serve more substantial fare, creative American meals prepared by a highly competent chef. Entrees in the Grill are $15.65 to $16.75, in the main rooms $20.95 to $26.95.

ESSEX

35 miles E of New Haven

It is hard to imagine what improvements might be made to bring this dream of a New England waterside village closer to perfection. In fact, one recently published survey book, *The 100 Best Small Towns in America,* ranked Essex Number One. The criteria were lowest crime rates, per-capita income, proportion of college-educated residents, and the number of physicians in towns with populations between 5,000 and 15,000, and Essex was among the leaders in every category. Residents insist they can still walk away from their homes leaving their doors unlocked. Tree-bordered streets are lined with shops and homes that retain an early 18th-century flavor without the unreal frozen-in-amber quality that often afflicts other towns as postcard-pretty as this. People live and work and play here, and bustle busily along a Main Street that runs down to Steamboat Dock and its flotilla of working vessels and pleasure craft.

SEEING THE SIGHTS

Clustered along the harbor end of Main Street are three historic houses that can be visited on limited schedules. Number 40 is the **Richard Hayden House,** an 1814 brick Federalist that was home to the namesake merchant and shipbuilder. During the War of 1812, British raiders burned Hayden's entire fleet. He was ruined, and died soon after, still a young man. Next door, at no. 42, is a mid-1700 center-hall colonial that was also the home of a boatbuilder, the **Noah Tooker House.** And at no. 51 is the **Robert Lay House,** completed about 1730 and thought to be the oldest original structure in town. These historic buildings are a short stroll from the:

Connecticut River Museum. Steamboat Dock (foot of Main St.). ☎ **860/767-8269.** $4 adults, $3 seniors, $2 children 6–12. Tues–Sun 10am–5pm.

Anglers wet their lines from the dock, gulls and ducks hang around hoping for a discarded tidbit. Steamboat service was fully operational here from 1823, and the existing dock dates from 1879. Designated as a National Historic Site, the museum proper is a converted warehouse, which has two floors of intricately detailed model ships, marine paintings, and various artifacts. They relate the story of shipbuilding in the valley, which began in 1733 and helped make this a center of world trade far into the 19th century. Essex had as many as nine boatyards, and the first American warship constructed for the War of Independence, the *Oliver Cromwell,* was finished here in 1775. Also in the museum is a replica of the first submersible vessel deployed in wartime, the *Turtle.* The museum usually has walking maps ($1) of Essex, making this a good first stop on a visit.

Essex Steam Train. Railroad Ave. (Rte. 154). ☎ **860/767-0103.** Fares, train and boat $14 adults, $7 children 3–11; train only $10 adults, $5 children 3–11. Daily trips June–Labor Day, less frequently Sept–Apr.

Steam locomotives from the 1920s chuff along a route from this station on the road between Essex center and Ivoryton to a boat landing in the hamlet of Deep River, a mildly engrossing excursion of about an hour. It can be combined with an optional additional cruise on the river, for a total of 2¹/₂ to 3 hours. Special events include a Halloween "ghost" train, a Christmas express with Santa Claus, a jazz festival in June, and dinner trains.

WHERE TO STAY & DINE

✪ **Griswold Inn.** 36 Main St. (center of town), Essex, CT 06426. ☎ **860/767-1776.** 30 rms. A/C TEL. $90–$175 double. Rates include breakfast. AE, MC, V.

Gloss over the assertion that "The Griz" is the oldest inn in America (there are other claimants). What's more important to locals and regular guests from out of town is that the inn has been rescued from a rumored takeover by foreign and domestic entrepreneurs harboring dark plans for its transformation. Three brothers who grew up in town with the inn as a focal part of their lives (as it is for every Essex native) have bought it, and the new managing partner Doug Paul vows that there will be no dramatic changes, and that maintenance and modest alterations will proceed at a measured pace. That's a relief, for it is difficult to imagine this corner of New England without The Griz. Rumpled, cluttered, folksy, and forever besieged by drop-in yachtspeople, anglers, locals, guests, and tourists, the main building dates to 1776.

The taproom, one of the most atmospheric taverns north of Key West, started life as a schoolhouse, and was moved here in 1800. Its vaulted ceiling is said to be made of crushed shells and horsehair, seemingly held up there by the centuries' worth of wafting tar and nicotine that turned it a deep tobacco brown. The walls are layered with nautical memorabilia, as are most of the public rooms, and there is live entertainment almost every night, be it only a man with a banjo or a comedian spouting one-liners. The dining rooms (The Library, The Gun Room, etc.) are nearly as colorful, named for their displays of books, antique weapons, or marine paintings. The food doesn't set off any gastronomic alarms, but it is hearty, no-foolin' victuals—turkey with stuffing, roast loin of pork, mixed grill with sauerkraut, venison sausage. Creative risks are restricted to the menu's descriptive prose, which features titles like "The Awful Awful NY Sirloin"—"awful big and awful good." Forgive them their excesses, for servings are large, the cooking is straightforward, and prices are fair.

When the Brothers Paul get around to careful renovation, their efforts might best be directed to the rather plain and unadorned bedrooms, scattered through six buildings, that are rarely more than a place to lay one's head. Otherwise, viva Griz!

IVORYTON

32 miles E of New Haven

Once a center for the ivory trade, where factories fabricated piano keys and hair combs—hence the name—Ivoryton has since subsided into a residential quietude. A virtual suburb of the only slightly larger Essex, a few miles east, the town perks up a bit in the summer, when the **Ivoryton Playhouse** (☎ **860/767-3075**) opens its June to August theatrical season. The Playhouse's repertoire runs to revivals of Broadway and Off-Broadway comedies and mysteries.

WHERE TO STAY & DINE

✪ **Copper Beach Inn.** 46 Main St., Ivoryton, CT 06442. ☎ **860/767-4330.** 13 rms. A/C TV TEL (Carriage House only). $105–$170 double. Rates include breakfast. AE, CB, DC, MC, V. Take Exit 3 from Rte. 9 and head west on Main St.

Comparisons with the Griswold Inn in nearby Essex are inevitable, but they are two very different animals. Where the Griz is decidedly populist, perennially busy, and well into its third century, the Copper Beach has much less traffic, and is stately in its pace, without a single figurative hair out of place. The previous owners rescued this 19th-century home of an ivory importer hours before it was to be burned to the ground in a fire department training exercise. It was gutted and rebuilt from the studs out, and the present innkeepers have expanded on the earlier effort. The nine rooms in the converted barn they call the "Carriage House" have ample elbow room, cushy chairs, expensive reproductions of 19th-century furniture styles, and not much character. They compensate with whirlpool tubs, phones, and TV. The four rooms in the main room tuck right into country-inn stereotypes, with original turn-of-the-century bath fixtures and a plentitude of antiques. They have phones but no TVs, and staying here can be as nostalgic as a visit to Aunt Edna's. Obviously, which to book is a matter of taste.

The dining choice is easier—the Copper Beach is home to one of the most honored kitchens in the region. "New Traditionalist" might describe the chef's take on French recipes and techniques as applied to his fresh, high-quality ingredients. Service is seamless in the three formal dining areas, with rolled napkins in the water glasses standing as alert as rabbit ears in a meadow. The restaurant is closed Mondays from April to December, and Mondays and Tuesdays January to March. Smoking isn't allowed anywhere on the property.

CHESTER

Hardly more than a three-block business center with a few side streets that straggle off into the woods and stone fences of the encompassing countryside, Chester can be dismissed easily enough. After all, it's small enough to barely require downshifting. That's too bad, for this is a classic riverside hamlet that deserves savoring. Along Main Street are antique shops and art galleries, the post office, a library, and several eating places that range from sandal-informal to dressy-casual. The two small streams that once provided power for early grist- and sawmills are canalled and all but hidden.

Downtown Chester doesn't have much room for shops, but it squeezes in at least a couple that deserve a closer look. At **Naturally, Books and Coffee** (16 Main St.; ☎ 860/526-3212) a small selection of books occupies the front of the store, and there's an espresso bar in the back. Naturally. They have outdoor tables on warm days and live acoustic jazz, folk, and pop performers on weekends. **Ceramica** (36–38 Main St.; ☎ 860/526-9978), an outlet of a small chain with branches in SoHo (Manhattan), West Hartford, and Scarsdale, N.Y., carries a line of mostly Italian and uniformly gorgeous handpainted platters, bowls, pitchers, vases, cups, tureens, and teapots. Open daily.

WHERE TO DINE

Fiddlers. 4 Water St. (behind Main St.). ☎ **860/526-3210.** Main courses $12.50–$18.95. MC, V. Tues–Sat 11:30am–2pm and 5:30–9pm (until 9:30pm Fri, until 10pm Sat); Sun 4–9pm. SEAFOOD.

Here you can have your fish any way you want—poached, sautéed, broiled, baked, or grilled over mesquite—or you can leave it up to the skillful kitchen, for they can come up with some eye-openers. Topping that list is the "lobster au pêché"—fat chunks of lobster meat married to peach nubbins, shallots, mushrooms, cream, and peach brandy. Not for lobster purists, certainly, but a downright revelatory example of what an imaginative chef can do. All entrees come with a starch, vegetable, and garlic bread with an aïoli dip. The rooms are cheerfully unremarkable, with bentwood chairs, marine prints, and ruffled curtains.

The Wheatmarket. 4 Water St. (next to Fiddlers, above). ☎ **860/526-9347.** Soups, salads, sandwiches $3.19–$4.99. MC, V. Mon–Sat 9am–6pm. DELI.

Eat out or eat in at this upwardly mobile country delicatessen. They're anxious to please, and will even make up full picnic baskets for $9.50 to $16 per person. "The Gourmet" version includes smoked salmon with capers, cream cheese, and red onion; mousse truffée with toast points, chicken and grape salad, caesar salad, cheesecake, and sparkling cider. Or put together your own from the appetizing array of breads, cheeses, pâtés, cold cuts, soups, salads, and sandwiches (daily specials). Shelves are stocked as well with bottled jams, olive oils, a variety of coffee beans, mustards, and vinegars.

EAST HADDAM

39 miles E of New Haven

Hardly more than a wide spot in a country road surrounded by woods and meadows, Hadlyme (a jurisdiction of the town of East Haddam) wouldn't attract much attention at all if a wealthy thespian hadn't decided to build his hilltop redoubt here.

To get there, take the **Chester-Hadlyme Ferry,** at the end of Route 148, slightly less than two miles from Chester. A ferry has operated here since 1769, and if the Toonerville Trolley of "Blondie" fame had one at track's end, this would be it. The current version takes both cars and pedestrians ($2.25 for vehicles plus $1.50 for trailers, 75¢ for walk-on passengers). It operates (when it feels like it) from 7am to 6:45pm in the warmer months. If it is closed down, they post a sign out at the intersection of Routes 148 and 154, in which case you have to drive north on 154 to Haddam and take the bridge.

AN ECCENTRIC'S CASTLE

Gillette Castle State Park. River Rd. ☎ **860/526-2336.** Admission $4 adults, $2 children 6–11. Grounds open daily 8am–sunset; castle Memorial Day–Columbus Day daily 10am–5pm, Columbus Day–end of Nov weekends 10am–4pm.

William Gillette was a successful actor and playwright known primarily for his repeated theatrical portrayals of Sherlock Holmes. He took the money and ran to this hill rearing above the Connecticut River, where he had his castle built. It's difficult to believe that he really thought the result resembled the Norman fortresses that allegedly were his inspiration. Rock gardens by roadside eccentrics in South Dakota or Death Valley are closer relations. His castle has two dozen oddly-shaped rooms, partly due to the fact that Gillette felt it was necessary to design a dining-room table that slid into the wall, an inexplicable space-saving effort by a bachelor rattling around in 24 rooms. Whatever Gillette's deficiencies as an architect and designer, no one can argue with his choice of location. The castle sits atop a hill above the east bank, with superlative vistas upriver and down. Nowhere else is the blessed underdevelopment of the estuary more apparent. Since the terrace of the "castle" can be entered for free, many visitors choose to avoid the fees for entrance to the interior. The 184-acre grounds have picnic areas, nature trails, and fishing sites. There is a snack bar at the edge of the parking lot.

RIVER CRUISES

A voyage on the river is a near-irresistible outing. Cruises of a variety of lengths, times, and themes are offered by **Camelot Cruises** (1 Marine Park, Haddam, CT 06438; ☎ **860/345-8591**). The pride of their small fleet is the M/V *Camelot,* a 160-foot vessel carrying as many as 500 passengers. In addition to dinner and mystery cruises (in which the passengers solve a staged "murder"), there are summer and fall excursions to Sag Harbor, Long Island.

EAST HADDAM AFTER DARK

From the Gillette State Park, turn north on Route 82, and make the short drive to East Haddam proper. The dominant building is a restored six-story Victorian of splendid proportions that opened in 1877 and is now the **Goodspeed Opera House** (Goodspeed Landing; ☎ **860/873-8668**). A century ago, it presented such productions as *All is Not Gold that Glitters* and *Factory Girl.* Now it mostly stages revivals of Broadway musicals on the order of *Sweeney Todd* and *Annie,* but has made room for more experimental shows that have eventually made it all the way to the Big Apple. The Goodspeed's season is usually from April to December.

7 Mystic & the Southeastern Coast

If a whirlwind driving tour of New England leaves only two or three days for all of Connecticut, plan to spend them in this section of the coast that segues into the mainland beach resorts of Rhode Island. And go soon, because it's impossible to predict the eventual effects that the gushers of money produced by two new and immensely successful gambling casinos will have on the character of this precious region. The town of Mystic and its singular attraction, the living, working museum that is Mystic Seaport, are clearly the prime reasons for a stay—the Seaport alone can easily occupy most of a day and the two-part town itself sustains a delightful nautical air, with fun shops and restaurants to suit most tastes and every budget. But that is far from a complete list. The tranquil neighboring village of Stonington is home to an active commercial fishing fleet, the last in the state; nearby Groton, on the Thames River, offers tours of the world's first nuclear submarine; there are several enchanting inns in the area; many companies and individuals offer their vessels for whale watching, dinner cruises, and deep-sea fishing excursions; and for those with a taste for the adrenaline rush of a winning streak, there are those two casinos.

If at all possible, avoid July and August, when the crowds are oppressive, restaurants are packed, and motels and inns are reserved months in advance. Motels do abound, especially in clusters around the several exits off I-95, and can handle the load the other 10 months of the year. But travelers who seek lodgings of a more intimate and sometimes less expensive nature can contact the Southeastern Connecticut Tourism District (see below) to request a folder describing the loosely affiliated **Bed & Breakfasts of Mystic Coast,** which lists 23 establishments in the area, including four just across the Rhode Island state line. Most are in the $50-to-$110 range and accept credit cards.

ESSENTIALS

GETTING THERE   From New York City, take I-95 to exits 84 (New London), 86 (Groton), 90 (Mystic), or 91 (Stonington). Or, to avoid the heavy truck and commercial traffic of the western segment of I-95, use the Hutchinson River Parkway, which becomes the Merritt Parkway (Rte. 15) and merges with the Wilbur Cross Parkway. Continue to Exit 54, connecting with I-95 for the rest of the trip. From Boston, take the Massachusetts Turnpike to I-395 south to Exit 75, then south on Route 32 to New London and I-95 west.

Amtrak (☎ 800/872-7245) has six trains daily (three each way) on its Northeast Direct route between New York, Providence, and Boston, with intermediate stops at New Haven, Old Saybrook, New London, and Mystic.

The regional bus company **SEAT** (☎ 860/886-2631) connects the more important towns and villages of the district, except for North Stonington.

VISITOR INFORMATION   The **Southeastern Connecticut Tourism District** (P.O. Box 89, New London, CT 06320; ☎ 800/863-6569 or 860/444-2206) can provide free vacation kits. Note that the local area code changed from 203 to 860 in 1995, although some materials still carry the old code.

NEW LONDON

46 miles E of New Haven, 45 miles SE of Hartford

Founded in 1646 and first known by the Pequot name Nameaug, New London's protected deep-draft harbor at the mouth of the Thames River was responsible for its long and influential history as a whaling port. That heritage lingers, but its years of great prosperity are behind it. Possessed of an architecturally interesting but somnolent downtown district, New London's touristic importance lies primarily in its standing as a transit point for three ferry lines connecting Block Island, R.I., and Long Island, N.Y., with the mainland. **Connecticut College** has a large campus at the northern edge of the city, along Route 32 and Williams Street. The **U.S. Coast Guard Academy** is also here, but while it welcomes visitors, it is mainly only of interest to alumni, prospective students, and their parents.

An attended **visitor information booth** is located in downtown New London at the corner of Eugene O'Neill Drive and Golden Street (there's no telephone). It's open June through August daily 10am to 4pm; May, September, and October Friday to Sunday 10am to 4pm.

SEEING THE SIGHTS

Coast Guard Academy. 15 Mohegan Ave. ☎ 860/444-8270. Free admission. Grounds, Mon–Fri 10am–5pm; Visitors Pavilion May 1–Oct 31 10am–5pm; Apr Sat–Sun 10am–5pm. Located off Williams St., north of Exit 84 of I-95.

A guard takes names at the gate, and directs cars to the Visitors Pavilion on the other side of the base, overlooking the Thames. The Pavilion doesn't offer much except views of the river and shores; the short film run on request is a public-relations exercise designed to recruit students, not enlighten the public. A full-rigged sailing vessel, the *Eagle*, is the Academy's principal attraction, available to visitors only on a limited basis. The latest in a line of Coast Guard cutters that goes back to 1792, it was built as a training ship for German Naval cadets in 1936 and taken as a war prize after World War II. Renamed the *Eagle*, the barque continues that instructional function at the Academy. When in port, usually only in April and May, it can be boarded Monday to Friday from 4pm to sunset, Saturday and Sunday from noon to sunset. Its dock can be seen from the Visitors Pavilion. If it is a Friday in spring or early fall, there might be a dress parade by the corps of cadets.

Lyman Allyn Art Museum. 625 Williams St. ☎ 860/443-2545. Admission $3 adults, $2 seniors and students, children under 12 free. July–Labor Day Tues–Sat 10am–5pm, Sun 1–5pm; Labor Day–June Tues–Sun 1–5pm. From Exit 84 of I-95, proceed north on Rte. 32 to the first exit, following brown signs to the museum.

This imposing neoclassical granite pile stands on a hill looking across Route 32 toward the Coast Guard Academy. Its holdings are the results of the enthusiasms of private collectors, and therefore hold to no particular curatorial or scholarly vision. Its various parts are interesting, however, even if they don't belong to a harmonious whole. The basement contains highly detailed room settings of Victorian dollhouse furniture, right down to tiny ladles on the kitchen counter and buttonhooks on the bureau. On the main floor are American paintings and furnishings dating to the colonial period, including landscapes by Hudson River School artists Frederic Edwin Church, George Inness, and Albert Bierstadt. Upstairs are galleries with exhibits as diverse as Asian temple castings, African carvings, Japanese lacquerware, and paintings related to New London's past.

OUTDOOR PURSUITS

Not far from the downtown area is **Ocean Beach Park** (south end of Ocean Ave., ☎ 800/510-7263 or 860/447-3031), a 40-acre recreational facility with a broad sand beach, boardwalk, 50-meter-long freshwater pool, miniature golf course, and triple water slide. Also available are a bathhouse with lockers and showers, concession stands, and a lounge. Live entertainment is scheduled throughout the summer. Open Saturday before Memorial Day through Labor Day, daily 9am to 10pm. The parking fee also covers admission for all occupants of the car.

From June to September, waterborne excursions run by **Thames River Cruises** (P.O. Box 1673, New London, CT 06320; ☎ 860/444-7827) carry passengers up past the *Nautilus* submarine base (see "Groton," below). Daily departures are made hourly from 9am to 5pm; $10 adults, $6 children 6 to 13. Home dock is the City Pier at the foot of State Street, behind the railroad station.

The ferries that ply Long Island Sound from New London have a recreational aspect, as well as simply serving as transport between Block Island and Long Island. Year-round service to Orient Point on Long Island is provided by **Cross Sound Ferry** (☎ 860/443-5281). Departures are every hour or two during the day, and the one-way voyage takes about an hour and 20 minutes. Call ahead both to confirm departure times and make reservations, especially when taking a car. The **Fishers Island Ferry** (☎ 860/443-6851) also has daily departures for Long Island. **Nelseco Navigation Co.** (☎ 860/442-7891 or 860/442-9553) operates its ferry once a day (with an extra trip Friday evenings) from mid-June to early September between New London and the Old Harbor on Block Island. The one-way trip takes about two hours. An advance reservation for cars is essential, but a call ahead is also important to determine fares and current sailing times.

WHERE TO STAY

Queen Anne Inn. 265 Williams St. (east of Rte. 32), New London, CT 06320. ☎ **800/347-8818** or 860/447-2600. 10 rms. A/C. $89–$175 double. Rates include breakfast. AE, CB, DISC, DC, MC, V.

Parents visiting their kids at the area colleges are frequent guests at the Queen Anne, as are businesspeople who prefer to avoid the anonymity of highway motels. This relatively steady occupancy flow is the reason why rates don't fluctuate as much as at many inns. The inn's name refers to the building's late Victorian architectural style. An oak staircase reaches up three floors (there's no elevator) to the Tower Room, probably the best of the lot. It is equipped with a TV and phone as well as a kitchen with stove, fridge, and coffeemaker. These extras are not features of all the rooms, however—two rooms share a bath, and only some have phones and TV, so make your needs known when reserving. A couple of rooms have fireplaces, and most have four-posters or canopy beds.

Breakfast is an extravaganza of Mexican quiches, chocolate waffles, and citrus French toast with strawberry cream sauce. That treat is complimented with high teas (3 to 9pm) of coffee cakes, scones, and delicate sandwiches. You may not care to eat a single meal out during your stay.

WHERE TO DINE

✪ **Don Juan's.** 405 Williams St. (near Exit 84 of I-95). ☎ **860/437-3791**. Main courses $7.95–$14.75. DISC, MC, V. Tues–Fri 11:30am–2pm; daily 5pm–closing (usually 11pm).

A surprising meal at this unusual storefront eatery may be the most fun you've had for the least expense in a long time. The walls are covered with closely spaced paintings by one of the owners and his friends. They underscore the inventiveness of the food, described as "international combat style cuisine." What that means is subject to interpretation, but in practice, the kitchen's concoctions draw from the old Southwest, Louisiana, Jamaica, Mexico, Italy, and New England. They don't do battle on the plate, happily, even though the possibilities range from jerk chicken to tingas to tempura to Portuguese clams to dessert burritos. Spring for the "Combat Platter" to get a taste of just about everything. Tables are plain, service gives new depth to the term "laid-back," and patrons must bring their own booze or plonk. (There's a package store next door.) Don't let the drawn curtains fool you into thinking the place is closed. It always looks like that.

GROTON

The future is uncertain for this naval-industrial town on the opposite side of the Thames from New London, for it has long been dependent on the presence of the Electric Boat division of General Dynamics and the Navy's Submarine Base, and cutbacks in military budgets show no signs of reversal. Whatever happens, the principal touristic attraction will probably remain the famous **USS** *Nautilus,* the world's first nuclear-powered vessel.

After a visit to the submarine museum, history buffs may wish to stop for a stroll around **Fort Griswold Battlefield State Park** (Monument Street and Park Avenue; ☎ **860/445-1729** or 860/449/6877). It was here, in 1781, that the traitor Benedict Arnold led a British force against American defenders, ruthlessly ordering the massacre of his 88 prisoners after they had surrendered. Museum open Memorial Day to Labor Day daily 10am to 5pm, Labor Day to Columbus Day Saturday and Sunday 10am to 5pm. Free admission.

Submarine Force Library & Museum. Submarine Base. ☎ **800/343-0079** or 860/449-3174. Free admission. Mid-Apr to mid-Oct Wed–Mon 9am–5pm, Tues 1–5pm; mid-Oct to mid-Apr Wed–Mon 9am–4pm. Take Exit 86 from I-95, driving north on Rte. 12 and following signs to the museum.

Outside the museum are battered minisubs used by the Axis powers in World War II. The entry hall and adjoining galleries display models of submarines, torpedoes, missiles, deck guns, hands-on periscopes, and a full-scale cross-section of Bushnell's *Turtle,* the "first submersible ever used in a military conflict" in 1776—unsuccessfully, as it happens.

Continuing out the back and across a set of railroad tracks, the USS *Nautilus* itself stands at its mooring, ready for inspection. Before descending into the sub, keep in mind that large people or those with arthritis or similar afflictions might find it difficult to negotiate some of the hatchways and steep staircases. The somewhat claustrophobic walk through the control rooms, attack center, galley, and sleeping quarters is aided by listening devices handed out to each visitor that click on with audio descriptions at appropriate points along the tour. The self-guided tour only takes about 10 minutes.

FISHING TRIPS

A number of companies offer full- and half-day fishing trips. Typical of the party boats is the 114-foot *Hel-Cat II* (181 Thames St.; ☎ 860/535-2066 or 860/535-3200), operating from its own pier about two miles south of Exit 85N or 86S.

Both charter and party boats are available from the **Sunbeam Fleet** based at **Captain's John's Sport Fishing Center** (15 First St., Waterford; ☎ **860/443-7259**). Fishing party boats sail twice daily Friday to Sunday in June, Thursday to Tuesday July through Labor Day. The same firm has day-long whale-watching voyages Sunday, Tuesday, and Thursday in July and August. Rates for the half-day fishing trips and 9am to 4pm whale watches are $30 for adults, $27 seniors, $17.50 to $20 children 4 to 12. Fishing rods are included. The whale-watch boat has a galley and bar. Waterford is the town immediately south of New London; the dock is next to the Niantic River Bridge.

NORWICH

There is touristic potential here, where the Yantic and Shetucket rivers converge to form the Thames. Blocks of Broadway and Union Street are lined with substantial mansions in styles ranging from the Federalist and Classical Revival of the first half of the 19th century to the Italianate, French Second Empire, and Eclectic Victorian conceits of the second. They survive from the city's golden era, when the abolitionist preacher Henry Ward Beecher was inspired to compare the hills of Norwich to the petals of a rose, prompting the oft-repeated reference to the city as the "Rose of New England."

There is no pretending, however, that this historic old mill town isn't in the doldrums. Until efforts to reverse that decline take hold, the principal reason for a visit is described immediately below.

WHERE TO STAY & DINE

✪ **Norwich Inn & Spa.** 607 W. Thames St. (Rte. 32), Norwich, CT 06360. ☎ **800/267-0525** or 860/886-2401. Fax 860/886-9483. 65 rms. A/C TV TEL. $115–$245 double. AE, DC, MC, V. From New Haven and New York, take Exit 76 off I-95 onto I-395 north, Exit 79A onto Rte. 2A east, then exit onto Rte. 32 north and drive 1.5 miles to the inn entrance.

There is none of the tone of rigidly enforced self-denial here that exists at many places that call themselves "spas." It would be entirely possible to spend a long weekend here without experiencing a whiff of deprivation. The complex is set among woods on a

40-acre property, the main building augmented by outlying clapboard "villas" with 160 condo units, about half of which are available for overnight guests. (These are in addition to the 65 inn rooms.) A typical villa has a full kitchen with crockery and utensils, a large sitting area with logs and paper at the ready in the fireplace, two double beds in the separate bedroom, and a deck overlooking the woods and a pond. Inn rooms aren't as expansive and don't have fireplaces, but they are hardly Spartan. And everyone has access to two outdoor pools, an indoor pool, a golf course, and a gym with brand-name stationary bikes, treadmills, Stairmasters, and weight machines, as well as steam rooms and saunas. Massages are available, too, at $69 a 50-minute hour. Make reservations for fitness classes when arranging for lodging. The dining room is called the Prince of Wales, blessed with a versatile kitchen staff capable of producing meals either conventional or fitness-minded, both uncommonly satisfying. The property is now owned by the Pequot tribal organization, but that association isn't noticeable. Foxwoods Casino is about 15 minutes away, making this a soothing and convenient respite from the glitz.

MYSTIC

55 miles E of New Haven

The spirit and texture of the maritime life and history of New England are captured in many ports along its indented coast, but nowhere more cogently than along the Mystic River estuary, its harbor nearly enclosed by Mason Island. This was a highly active whaling and shipbuilding center during the colonial period and into the last century, but the discontinuation of the first industry and the decline of the second haven't adversely affected the community. No derelict barges nor rotting piers degrade the views and waterways, or at least not many.

Mystic and West Mystic are stitched together by a drawbridge, the raising of which, mostly for sailboats, causes traffic stoppages at a quarter past every hour but rarely shortens tempers, except for visitors who don't leave their urban impatience behind. There are complaints by some that the two-part town has been commercialized, but the incidence of T-shirt shops and related tackiness is limited, and the more garish motels and attractions have been restricted to the periphery, especially up near Exit 90 of Interstate 95.

The town is home to one of New England's most singular attractions, the Mystic Seaport museum village. Far more than the single building the name might suggest, it is a re-created seaport of the mid-1800s, with dozens of buildings and watercraft of that romantic era of clipper ships and the China trade. The spidery webs of full-rigged sailing ships beckon visitors almost as soon as they leave the highway, and the briny tang of the ocean air draws them on.

A **visitor information center** is located in the Olde Mistick Village shopping center (Route 27 and Coogan Boulevard; ☎ **860/536-1641**) near the Interstate.

SEEING THE SIGHTS

✪ **Mystic Seaport.** 75 Greenmanville Ave. (Rte. 27). ☎ **800/572-5319** or 860/572-5331. Admission $16 adults, $8 children 6–15 (2nd day included with validation). AE, MC, V. Jan–Mar, and Oct–Dec daily 9am–4pm; Apr–June and Sept–Oct daily 9am–5pm; July–Aug daily 9am–8pm. Take Exit 90 from I-95, driving about 1 mile south on Rte. 27 toward Mystic. Parking lots are on the left, the entrance on the right.

Few visitors fail to be enthralled by this evocative museum village, easily one of the paramount attractions in New England. Far more than a single building of maritime artifacts, this is an entire waterfront settlement, over 60 buildings on and near a 17-acre peninsula poking into the Mystic River. With all there is to see and do, and considering the hefty admission charges, plan to set aside at least two or three hours minimum for a visit. In truth, most of an entire day can easily be occupied here, especially for those who thrill at the sight of full-rigged tall ships standing at their wharves as if readying for voyages to Cathay and the Spice Islands.

Deciding where to start and what to see is something of a challenge. A useful map and guide is available at the ticket counter in the Visitor Center in the building opposite the Museum Stores (which can be saved for later, since they stay open later than the village most of the year). A recommended route, exiting the Center, is to bear right along the path leading between the Galley Restaurant and the village green. It bends to the left, intersecting with a street of shops, public buildings, and houses. At that corner, for example, is an 1870s hardware and dry goods store. Turning right there, pass a one-room schoolhouse, a chapel, a furnished 1830s home, and a **children's museum.** The museum, which invites youngsters to play games characteristic of the seafaring era, faces a small square that is the starting point for horse-drawn wagon tours of the village. From there, one of the proudest possessions of the seaport fleet of over 400 craft is only a few steps away—the three-masted barque *Charles W. Morgan.* It was built in 1841, a whaler that called New Bedford home. (If you are curious about ship nomenclature but all you know for sure is that the pointy end is the bow, you might want to stop by the bookstore later and ask if they still have the sheet that defines basic riggings.) Facing the *Morgan* is a row of shops and services that bore particular commercial association with the whalers and clipper ships that put in at ports such as this. Bearing left along the waterfront, they include a tavern (nonfunctional), an 1833 bank with an upstairs shipping office, a house with a garden, a cooperage (where barrels and casks were made), and a print shop.

By this point, visitors will have started picking up hints about the origins of English words and phrases, even if they haven't tried. A "mainstay," for example, is the line that stabilizes the main mast on a sailing ship. And when entering the print shop, they might hear the printer complaining that she is "out of sorts," meaning she has run out of the lead letters she needs to complete setting a page. The friendly docents in the village are highly competent at the crafts they demonstrate and are always ready to impart as much information as visitors care to absorb. They aren't dressed in period costumes, which paradoxically lends to the authenticity of the village, perhaps because it avoids the unreal, contrived air of too many such enterprises.

Continuing along the waterfront, the next vessel encountered is the iron-hulled square-rigger, *Joseph Conrad,* which dates from 1881 and has spent most of its life as a training ship, and still serves that function. Up ahead is a small lighthouse at the point of the peninsula, which looks out across the water toward the large riverside houses that line the opposite shore. Following the water's edge, you'll pass boat sheds and fishing shacks and the smaller ketches and sloops that are moored along here in season. Finally comes a dock for the perky 1908 **SS** *Sabino,* which provides half-hour river rides from 11am to 4pm ($3.50 adults, $2.50 children 6 to 15) and $1 \frac{1}{2}$-hour evening excursions leaving at 5pm ($8.50 adults, $7 children). A few steps away is the 1921 fishing schooner, *L.A. Dunton.*

And still the village isn't exhausted. A few steps south is the Henry B. Du Pont Preservation Shipyard, where the hundreds of boats in the collection are painstakingly restored and the work can be observed in progress. At the other end of the village, back near the *Morgan,* is the Stillman Building, which contains fascinating exhibits of scrimshaw and intricate ship models.

Exiting the grounds, ask the gatekeeper to validate your ticket if you wish to return the next day for no additional charge. Across the brick courtyard with the requisite giant anchor is a building containing several museum stores and a maritime art

Mystic Seaport

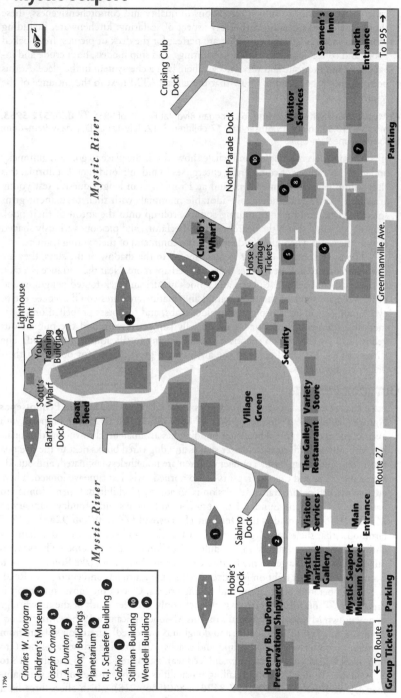

Charles W. Morgan **4**
Children's Museum **5**
Joseph Conrad **3**
L.A. Dunton **2**
Mallory Buildings **8**
Planetarium **6**
R.J. Schaefer Building **7**
Sabino **1**
Stillman Building **10**
Wendell Building **9**

Mystic River

Lighthouse Point

Scott's Wharf
Bartram Dock
Youth Training Building
Boat Shed

Chubb's Wharf

Cruising Club Dock

North Parade Dock

Seamen's Inne

North Entrance

To I-95 →

Visitor Services

Parking

7

10

9 **8**

5

6

Horse & Carriage Tickets

Security

Village Green

The Galley Restaurant

Variety Store

Greenmanville Ave.

Hobie's Dock

Sabino Dock

1

2

3

4

Visitor Services

Main Entrance

Mystic Maritime Gallery

Mystic Seaport Museum Stores

Henry B. DuPont Preservation Shipyard

Route 27

← To Route 1
Parking
Group Tickets

1796

gallery. Far superior to similar operations in quality and comprehensiveness, these shops stock books dealing with every aspect of seafaring; kitchenware, including enameled metal plates and cups that are perfect for the deck or picnics; fresh-baked goods and coffee; nautical prints and paintings; and ship models, both crude and inexpensive and exquisite and very pricey. There isn't a cheesy item in the place. At this point, it might be useful to know that there is an ATM next to the entrance of the Visitors Center.

✪ **Mystic Marinelife Aquarium.** 55 Coogan Blvd. (at Exit 90 of I-95). ☎ **860/572-5955.** Admission $10.50 adults, $9.50 seniors, $7 children 3–12. July–Labor Day daily 9am–6pm, Labor Day–June 9am–5pm.

If you've never seen a dolphin and whale show, this is the place to go. Less gimmicky and glitzy than those of commercial enterprises found in Florida and California, this show illuminates as it entertains, and at 15 minutes in length doesn't test young attention spans. The undeniably adorable mammals with their permanent grins squawk, click, and make thumping sounds, roll up onto the apron of their pool, tailwalk, joyously splash the nearer rows of spectators, and pick out variously shaped toys in the water when blindfolded, all at the command of their young trainers.

While the rest of the exhibits necessarily fall in the shadow of the stars, they are enough to occupy at least another hour and perhaps more. Near the entrance is a tank of fur seals, out back are sea lions and a flock of African black-footed penguins, and in between are some of the most remarkable marine creatures you'll ever see eye to eye. Among them are scorpionfish, spider crabs, and seahorses propelled on gossamer fins; billowing, translucent moon jellyfish; sea ravens; and the pugnacious yellowhead jawfish, which spends its hours digging fortifications in the sand. The shrieks of excited children rend the air, not too great a price for observing their delighted discoveries.

Outdoor Pursuits

For a change from salt air and ship riggings, drive inland to the **Denison Pequotsepos Nature Center** (109 Pequotsepos Rd.; ☎ **860/536-1216**), a 125-acre property with over seven miles of trails. The center building has an amateur, thrown-together quality, with stuffed birds next to plaster snakes and dog-eared books next to the live boa constrictor and worm farm. Younger children are nonetheless fascinated, and outside are picnic tables and cages of raptors—two horned owls, last time we looked. There are five marked nature trails. Admission is $3 adults, $1 children. Open Monday to Saturday 9am to 5pm, Sunday 1 to 5pm (closed Sundays and Mondays January to March). Across the road is the **Denison Homestead** (☎ **860/536-9248**), a 1717 farmhouse that sheltered 11 generations of Denisons and is filled with that family's antique furnishings. Admission $4 adults, $1 children under 16. Open Thursday to Sunday 1 to 5pm. To get to the Nature Center and Homestead, take Route 27 north from Mystic, make a right on Mistuxet Avenue, then turn left on Pequotsepos Road.

Several operators offer sailing and fishing cruises. One of the most convenient is the *Argia* (☎ **860/536-0416**), which docks only 100 feet south of the drawbridge in downtown Mystic. Morning sails on this 81-foot replica of a 19th-century schooner are from 10am to 1pm (coffee and doughnuts are served), afternoon sails are from 1 to 5pm (complete with soft drinks and snacks), and evening cruises are from 6 to 8pm (and feature cheese, crackers, and iced tea). Fares are $28 to $55 adults, $18 to $27 children under 18. Longer sailing possibilities are the outings of the windjammer *Mystic Whaler* (☎ **800/697-8420** or 860/536-4218), which offers three-hour dinner and twilight cruises, overnight trips, and extended cruises that can last from three to five days. Corresponding rates go from as little as $50 per passenger to $675.

Voyages set out from a pier on Holmes Street, off Route. 27, one mile south of Mystic Seaport.

SHOPPING

Olde Mistick Village (Route 27 and Coogan Boulevard; ☎ 860/536-4941) is essentially a conventional mall, but in new buildings simulating a colonial village with fluctuating degrees of efficacy. More than 60 shops and eating places are on site, including two bank branches, cinemas, and a winery. The Village is open daily, year-round.

Downtown Mystic has a limited variety of shopping opportunities, one of the most engaging of which is **Bank Square Books** (53 W. Main St.; ☎ 860/536-3795). Maybe they don't really have any volume you want in the jumble of shelves and racks, but it's fun looking.

WHERE TO STAY

There are plenty of ho-hum, adequate independent and chain motels in the area that can soak up the traffic at all but peak periods, meaning weekends from late spring to early fall and high season weekdays in July and August, when it is necessary to have reservations. Within a block north and south of Exit 90 are the **Best Western Sovereign** (☎ 800/528-1234), **Comfort Inn** (☎ 800/228-5150), **Howard Johnson Motor Lodge** (☎ 800/654-4656), **Days Inn** (☎ 800/325-2525), and **Residence Inn** (☎ 800/331-3131). But for more distinctive accommodations with New England charm, try one of the inns listed below.

The Inn at Mystic. Rtes. 1 and 27, Mystic, CT 06355. ☎ **860/536-9604.** 67 rms. A/C TV TEL. $55–$250 double. AE, DC, DISC, MC, V.

A splendid variety of lodgings and prices are offered at this inn occupying 13 hillside acres overlooking Long Island Sound, and the complex also incorporates one of the finest restaurants in the region. At the crest of the hill is the desirable Inn, an impressive 1904 Classical Revival mansion with rooms as grand as the exterior, enhanced by whirlpool baths, fireplaces, and canopied beds. Bogart and Bacall spent part of their honeymoon here. Down the hill a ways is the intimate Gatehouse, similarly accoutered, and furnished with a scattering of antiques. Some of the rooms in the new motel sections are equally as well-appointed, including a few with balconies; others are modest and conventional. All rooms have hair dryers, clock radios, and basic cable. A tennis court and an outdoor pool are on the premises, and guests have access to a health club ¼ mile away and to paddleboats and canoes down on the water.

Even if you find dinner at the Flood Tide (see below) too expensive, don't miss the bounteous and relatively inexpensive breakfasts, which feature stuffed crêpes, three-egg omelets, Belgian waffles, and eggs Benedict . . . with lobster! (The Inn also supplies discount coupons for various establishments around town.) A complimentary afternoon tea is served as well.

Mystic Hilton. 20 Coogan Blvd., Mystic, CT 06355. ☎ **800/445-8667** or 860/572-0731. Fax 860/572-0328. 184 rms. A/C TV TEL. $125–$205 double. AE, CB, DC, DISC, MC, V. Take Exit 90 of I-95 and drive south 1 block to Coogan Blvd.

This hotel is your basic Hilton. For those who don't get out much, that means generally crisp efficiency, not much personality, a site-specific theme restaurant (The Moorings), room service until 1am, a piano player in the evenings, in-room movies and hair dryers . . . you get the picture. This one also has an indoor pool and fitness equipment. The reluctance of the front desk to quote tariffs bespeaks a willingness to negotiate on prices according to season and demand.

✪ **Steamboat Inn.** 73 Steamboat Wharf, Mystic, CT 06355. ☎ **860/536-8300.** 10 rms. A/C TV TEL. $95–$275 double. Rates include breakfast. AE, MC, V. Look for the inn sign pointing down an alley on the west bank of the Mystic River, just before the drawbridge.

Mystic's most appealing lodging is easily overlooked from land, but readily apparent from the river. Perched daintily on the riverbank, the yellow clapboard structure first served as a warehouse in the early part of this century. Converted to a luxury bed-and-breakfast only a few years ago, its four downstairs rooms are larger, with double whirlpool baths, wet bars, and some kitchen facilities, while the upstairs six have smaller whirlpools and wood-burning fireplaces. That makes the choice of which to request in summer or winter easy, and while every room is decorated differently, they are uniformly Laura Ashley–attractive, and all but one have water views. Antique armoires hide the TVs. Breakfast in the fetching common room is what is often described as "hearty continental," with ample quantities of plump homemade muffins, fresh bagels, granola, and fruit compote. Sherry is left out all day for guests to pour themselves. The sailing ship *Argia* is moored outside, enhancing the nautical aspect of the inn. There are some restrictions, however: The inn is totally nonsmoking, children under 9 are not permitted, and no pets are allowed.

Taber Inne. 66 Williams Ave. (Rte. 1), Mystic, CT 06355. ☎ **860/536-4904.** 25 rms. A/C TV TEL. $85–$310 double. AE, MC, V. Two blocks east of the intersection of Rtes. 27 and 1.

This hotel has something to suit almost all tastes and budgets, with six buildings containing both simple motel units and hedonistic two-bedroom duplex suites with whirlpool baths, decks, and fireplaces. For larger family groups, the homey "Little House" has two bedrooms, a sitting room, and kitchen with coffeemaker, microwave oven, and dishwasher. While it can't be described as glamorous, it will sleep up to six in relative comfort for only $195 in high season. In addition to cable TV and phones, some accommodations have porches, some have gas- or wood-burning fireplaces, and some have canopied beds. While breakfast isn't served, there's a coffeepot waiting in the reception area, and the manager hands out discount coupons for village restaurants. Guests also have access to a community center with indoor pool, tennis, racquetball, and a fitness room.

Whaler's Inn. 20 E. Main St., Mystic, CT 06355. ☎ **800/243-2588** or 860/536-1506. Fax 860/572-1250. 41 rms. A/C TV TEL. $82–$210 double. AE, MC, V.

The most commendable aspects of this downtown inn are its restaurant, Bravo Bravo (see below) and its relatively low rates. (The high price above is for a suite. Doubles run only to $135 in summer.) Decor slips from bleakly old-fashioned to gaudy faux Victorian, and the reception staff could apply a touch more warmth. Those quibbles aside, this hotel is a good value. The rooms are deployed in four adjacent buildings, one of which is a house contructed in 1865, another a three-story building dating from 1917 that was once the "U.S. Hotel." The rooms are comfortable enough, if not particularly pleasing to the eye, and can be useful to businesspeople on a tight budget as well as leisure travelers. Phones have dataports, beds are queens or doubles, half the bathrooms only have showers, and most rooms are nonsmoking. Children under 16 stay free in their parents' rooms. No pets are allowed.

WHERE TO DINE
Abbott's Lobster in the Rough. 117 Pearl St., Noank. ☎ **860/572-9128.** Main courses $15–$23 (but subject to market fluctuations). MC, V. First weekend in May–Labor Day daily noon–9pm; Labor Day–Columbus Day Fri–Sun noon–7pm. SEAFOOD.

It's as if a wedge of the Maine coast had been transplanted to the Connecticut shore. What has been wrought here is a nitty-gritty lobster shack at the edge of the Sound, with plenty of indoor and outdoor picnic tables and not a frill to be found. While there are many options and combinations, including hot dogs and chickens for the crustaceaphobic, the classic shore dinner rules. That means clam chowder, a mess of boiled shrimp in the shell, a bowl of steamed clams and mussels, and a small but tasty lobster. That'll be $21.95 (or thereabouts), with coleslaw, potato chips, and drawn butter thrown in. Smaller appetites might settle for selections from the raw bar, clams and oysters shucked to order. Dessert can be cheese or carrot cake. Bring your own beer or wine.

Finding Abbott's can be an adventure: Drive south from downtown Mystic on Route 215, alert for signs to Noank, and cross a railroad bridge. At Main Street in Noank, turn left, then take an immediate right on Pearl Street. Be prepared to ask for directions anyway.

Bravo Bravo. 14 E. Main St. (in the Whaler's Inn). ☎ **860/536-3228.** Main courses $13.95–$24.95. AE, MC, V. Sun and Tues–Thurs 5–9pm, Fri–Sat 5–10pm. NEW ITALIAN/AMERICAN.

Ask locals about the best restaurant in town and often as not, they'll enthusiastically send you to this trattoria. In warm weather, Bravo Bravo has an adjoining tented deck, and the resulting combination is a money machine for the owners, even on a nondescript Tuesday evening. Inside and out, it is filled with men in suits, polo shirts and khakis, families, and couples. As the night wears on, it can get as noisy as a disco, and the waitstaff is asked to cover too many tables, so getting refills of wine or water is nigh impossible. A basket of marvelous bread arrives with the drinks, along with a ramekin of a spread comprised of emulsified white beans, sun-dried tomatoes, and roasted garlic. That will have to keep you happy until someone shows up for your order. When the time finally comes, keep it simple. Some of the dishes sound appealing—say, the tomato fettuccine with lobster nubbins, scallops, mussels, tomato, and asparagus, for example—but are simply overloaded with ingredients. The daily specials are apt to be better choices. And, note that prices out on the deck are lower, for less complicated dishes.

Flood Tide. Rtes. 1 and 27 (in The Inn at Mystic). ☎ **860/536-8140.** Main courses $16.95–$24.95. AE, DC, DISC, MC, V. Mon–Thurs 7–10:30am, 11:30am–2:30pm, and 5:30–9:30pm (until 10pm Fri and Sat); Sun 11am–2:30pm and 5:30–9:30pm. CONTINENTAL.

Peel back about three decades and this place looks more familiar. In the 1960s elaborate tableside preparations were popular, and they're still doing them here, especially with Caesar salad and fettuccine Alfredo, but also with beef Wellington, chateaubriand, rack of lamb, and roast pheasant, which is carved before your eyes with a sense of showy melodrama. The performance is unabashedly retro, but reminds me why I used to relish this celebratory stuff in the years before Nouvelle-Pan-Asian-Italo-Southwestern-Fusion firecracker pseudo-food was invented. Flood Tide even has a pianist plinking at the baby grand nightly and at Sunday brunch. The two dining rooms look out over the Sound, and smoking is confined to the handsome bar. Lunch is cheaper and less fussy, and breakfast is a particular treat (see The Inn at Mystic, above).

⑤ PizzaWorks. 12 Water St. (Rte. 215, south of Main St.) ☎ **860/572-5775.** Pizzas $5–$11.95. MC, V. Daily 4–9 or 10pm. PIZZA.

Mystic Pizza is still on Main Street, much gussied-up since Julia Roberts made her debut there in the movie of the same name. But if a good pizza is more important to you than dimly reflected Hollywood glory, get here fast. PizzaWorks is your basic pizza parlor—complete with checked oilcloth on the tables, brick walls, and neon beer signs on the walls—and the pies are excellent. Pizzas are "red"—with tomato sauce—or "white"—without. Toppings are inventive but well short of gimmicky (none of that Hawaiian pineapple foolishness), but while extras can be piled on, the regular recipes stand alone. The "white" clams casino and the barbecued chicken with onion and bacon are super, and the "red" sausage cacciatore matches them. But then, almost any of the 25 possible toppings make eyeballs roll in pleasure. The long list of premium beers includes such lesser-knowns as Pete's Wicked Honey Wheat, Nantucket Amber, Lightship, and Elm City Ale. This is brew-and-pie nirvana. There is another PizzaWorks branch in Old Saybrook.

STONINGTON & NORTH STONINGTON

Not much seems to happen in these slumbering villages, only lightly brushed by the 20th century despite all the thrashing about over in heavily touristed Mystic. That suits most of the residents just fine, explaining why they are not thrilled by rumors that a giant theme park might be erected in their midst, another project of the powerful Pequot tribe. Inland North Stonington is as peaceful a New England retreat as can be found, with hardly any commercialization beyond a couple of inns. Soundside Stonington has a pronounced maritime flavor, sustained by the presence of the state's only remaining fishing fleet. Its two lengthwise streets are lined with well-preserved Federalist and Greek Revival homes.

For an introduction, drive south to Cannon Square along Stonington's Water Street, which has most of the town's shops and restaurants. Standing in the raised grassy square are two 18-pound cannons that were used to fight off an attack by British warships during the War of 1812. Opposite is a lovely old granite house, on the corner, a neoclassical bank.

Continue south to the end of Water Street, where there is a parking lot and the small **town beach** (admission $2 to $3 per person, $5 to $6 per family). From there, the misty blue headland directly south across the Sound is Montauk Point, the eastern extremity of New York's Long Island. Return along Main Street, which is almost exclusively residential except for a few government buildings.

A SEASIDE MUSEUM

Old Lighthouse Museum. 7 Water St. ☎ **860/535-1440.** Admission $3 adults, $1 children 6–12. Open May–Oct Tues–Sun 11am–5pm.

Built of stone in 1823, this two-story lighthouse with its short tower was moved here from a hundred yards away and deactivated. Most of the exhibits inside relate to the maritime past of the area, with scrimshaw tusks, a whalebone wool-winding wheel, a tortoiseshell serving dish, and export porcelain that constituted much of the 19th-century China trade. There are also weapons and relics of the Revolutionary period and the War of 1812, but the most interesting item might be the carved ivory pagoda. Upstairs are kitchen tools and Shaker boxes and trays, and the tower can be climbed for a view of coast and sea.

A PUBLIC GOLF COURSE

Duffers who feel overwhelmed by all the nautical talk and activity of the area can retreat to the fairway familiarity of their favorite game at the **Pequot Golf Club** (Wheeler Road, Stonington; ☎ **860/535-1898**). It has a par-70, 18-hole course and is fully open to the public, including the restaurant. Cart and club rentals are available. Call ahead to make reservations for weekend tee times. Take Exit 91 from I-95 north to Taugwonk Road, turn west on Summers Lane, and south on Wheeler Road.

SHOPPING

One of the Nutmeg State's handful of earnest wineries, **Stonington Vineyards** (523 Taugwonk Rd., Stonington; ☎ 860/536-1222) has a tasting room in a barn beside its fields of vines. There are usually six or seven pressings to be sampled, from a blush to a reisling, with a chardonnay leading the pack, at least according to most tastebuds. Bottles cost from $7.99 to $15.99. Open daily from 11am to 5pm, with a cellar tour at 2pm. To get there, take Exit 91 from I-95 and drive north 2¹/₂ miles.

WHERE TO STAY

Antiques & Accommodations. 32 Main St., North Stonington, CT 06359. ☎ 860/ 535-1736. 7 units. A/C. $99–$189 double. Rates include breakfast. MC, V. Take Exit 92 of I-95, drive west on Rte. 2 for 2¹/₂ miles, then turn right onto Main St. at the sign.

Gardens, porches, and patios invite lounging and ambling at this converted 1820 farmhouse in a peaceful isolated hamlet. Rooms and suites vary substantially in dimension and fixtures. The largest has three bedrooms with a dining room and kitchen; another has two bedrooms sharing a kitchen and sitting room; the "bridal suite" has a canopied queen-size bed. Four rooms have cable TV, and three have working fireplaces, but none have phones. Obviously, it is necessary to make your wishes known at the outset. Everyone, though, shares the four-course candlelit breakfast, with such surprises as cantaloupe soup and walnut-and-banana waffles. Guests who take a liking to any of the antique silver or crystal pieces or furnishings, which tend to have Federalist and Victorian origins, will be pleased to know that just about everything is for sale.

Randall's Ordinary. Rte. 2, North Stonington, CT 06320. ☎ 860/599-4540. Fax 860/ 599-3308. A/C. $55–$195 double. Rates include breakfast. AE, MC, V. Take Exit 92 from I-95, head north on Rte. 2.

The oldest structure on this 27-acre estate dates from 1685, which provides the rationale for the central gimmick of the inn: Meals are cooked at an open hearth and served by a staff in period costumes. Considering the primitive circumstances under which the food is prepared, it turns out to be hearty and tasty, if a tad too simple for refined tastes. There are three to five choices of entree, often including duck breast, leg of lamb, and pork loin, but main courses are changed daily. Reserve ahead for dinner, which is price-fixed at $30. This nightly event takes place on the ground floor of the John Randall House, the farm house that has been occupied continuously by members of the Randall family for over 200 years.

The three rooms upstairs in the old building have fireplaces and are charmingly furnished with four-poster and canopied beds, but have no phones or television. Those amenities are found in most of the rooms of the nearby barn, moved here from upstate New York and converted for this purpose. While the barn interior is dramatic, with heavy hand-cut beams and banisters made of stripped logs, the furnishings are, well, ordinary, albeit comfortable enough, if you don't mind bare floors. Coffee is set out in the lobby, near the parrot. Randall's Ordinary was sold to the Pequot tribal organization for a reported $1.4 million in 1995, but that affiliation isn't noticeable.

WHERE TO DINE

Harbor View. 66 Water St. (near Cannon Square), Stonington. ☎ 860/535-2720. Main courses $14.95–$25.95. AE, DC, MC, V. Daily 11:30am–11pm. SEAFOOD.

Long the area's most popular eatery, not least due to its atmospheric tavern, the Harbor View went into sharp decline after its sale a few years back. Viktor Baker, who has a solid background in the dining industry as a force behind New York's Rainbow Room and Dallas' celebrated Mansion at Turtle Creek, took over the foreclosed

A Casino in the Woods

What has been wrought in the woodlands north of the Mystic coast is nothing less than astonishing. There was very little there when the Mashantucket Pequot tribe received clearance to open a gambling casino on their ancestral lands in rural Ledyard. Virtually overnight, the tribal bingo parlor was expanded into a full-fledged casino and a hotel was built. That was in 1992. Within three years, it had become the single most profitable gambling operation in the world. Money cascaded over the Pequot (pronounced "Pee-kwat") in a seemingly endless torrent. Expansion was immediate—another hotel, then a third, more casinos, plans for a $13 million museum of Native American arts and culture, golf courses, a monorail, perhaps even a new Disneyesque theme park. The tribe bought up adjacent lands, at least a couple of nearby inns, and contemplated opening casinos in other cities.

All this prosperity came to a tribe of only 350 acknowledged members, many of them of mixed ethnicity. Residents of surrounding communities—indeed, of the whole state—were ambivalent, to put the best face on it. When it was learned that one of the tribe's corporate entities was to be called Two Trees Limited Partnership, a predictable query was, "Is that all you're going to leave us? Two trees?" But while there is a continuing danger of damage to the fragile character of this most authentically picturesque corner of Connecticut, it is also a fact that due to the recent development, thousands of non-Pequots have found employment at a time of economic stagnation and corporate and military downsizing throughout the region.

The complex can only be reached through forested countryside and quiet hamlets that give little hint of the growing behemoth rising above the trees in Ledyard township. There are no signs screaming "FOXWOODS." Instead, watch for plaques with the symbols of tree and fire above the word "Reservation." The widening of Route 2 is one of the first indications that something is up. As you enter the property, platoons of attendants point the way to parking and hotels. Ongoing construction surrounds the dark glassy tower of the hotel and sprawling casino. Though busy and bustling, it doesn't look like Vegas from the outside—happily, there are no Sphinxes, no pyramids, no 20-story neon palm trees—yet.

---

property (along with the nearby Skipper's Dock, reviewed below) and now runs the restaurant. After gutting and rehabilitating much of the building (the beloved barroom was renovated rather gingerly) at considerable expense, he and his wife reopened in July 1996. It is essentially two restaurants, with a cheaper, more casual menu in the tavern, a more elaborate and costlier version in the more formal dining rooms. Seafood remains the primary focus, with sophisticated culinary twists fusing French and Asian techniques and ingredients. At least that was the expectation when the place first reopened. Allow for the inevitable changes in staff and direction that characterize every restaurant start-up. The Harbor View was also planning to have live jazz on Sundays, and perhaps every night, and will hopefully have sorted out the logistics in time for your visit.

Skipper's Dock. 66 Water St. (behind Harbor View), Stonington. ☎ **860/535-2000.** Main courses $14.95–$25.95 (subject to market fluctuations). AE, DC, MC, V. Mar 1–Oct 30 daily 11:30am–10pm. SEAFOOD.

Diners are entertained by the frequent passage of sloops and motor yachts that power out between the breakwaters of Stonington Harbor and past this salty waterside lobster shanty. Outdoor tables are set out on the pier, the place to be in shade or sun.

Inside, the glitz gap narrows, but it is still relatively restrained as such temples to chance go. The gambling rooms have windows, for example, when the prevailing wisdom among casino designers is that they should not give customers any idea what time of day or night it is. And no one is allowed to forget that this whole eye-popping affair is owned and operated by Native Americans. Prominently positioned around the main buildings are larger-than-life sculptures by Alan Houser and Bruce LaFountain, of Chiricahua and Chippewa descent respectively, depicting Amerindians in a variety of poses and artistic styles. One other Indian-oriented display is *The Rainmaker*, a glass statue of an archer shooting an arrow into the air. Every hour on the hour, he is the focus of artificial thunder, wind-whipped rain, and lasers pretending to be lightning bolts, and the action is described in murky prose by a booming voice-of-Manitou narrator. That's as close as the chest-thumping gets to going over the top, although some visitors might reflect upon the political correctness of the non-Indian cocktail waitresses outfitted in skimpy Pocahontas mini-dresses with feathers in their hair.

The pace of all this might be slowing, at least temporarily, for another tribe has obtained the necessary certification and has built a casino in Uncasville, barely six miles away as the crow flies. **Mohegan Sun Resort** has 155,000 square feet of space for 170 gambling tables, 3,000 slot machines, dining areas, and showrooms. It's not as big as Foxwoods—yet—and doesn't have a hotel, but the casino is hard by exits 78 and 79 of I-395. That makes for easy on-and-off access for gamblers who don't want to deal with that onerous 20-minute drive to Ledyard before emptying their bank accounts. The Pequots are waiting to see what this will do to their business, and are ready to make adjustments to sustain the flow.

Two dozen bus companies provide daily service to Foxwoods from Boston, Hartford, Providence, New York, Philadelphia, and Albany, among many other cities—too many to list here. For information about transit from particular destinations, call **860/885-3000**.

There's an interior, but it's rather gloomy, despite the windows revealing boat traffic. Skipper's Dock Serves lobster prepared at least 10 different ways, including Thermidor, Savannah, and "Lazy," meaning they do the work for you. The shore dinner consists of clam chowder, a pint of steamers, a whole lobster, corn-on-the-cob, fries, and hot apple pie—all for $32.50, and worth it. Also a winner, at $25.95, is the munificent bouillabaisse, a stew brimming with clams, oysters, fish chunks, mussels, shrimp, scallops, and, yes, a whole lobster. At lunch, the hot lobster roll is as good as that delectable New England standby gets, with what seems like the flesh of an entire small lobster heaped between two halves of a focaccialike roll. And at the end of the meal, chocolate addicts won't want to miss the "Nationally Acclaimed Chocolate Torte," dense wedges of which arrive floating on a puddle of strawberry coulis. A six-piece Dixieland band plays on weekends.

FOXWOODS RESORT CASINO

The casino-hotel complex (☎ **860/885-3000**) is a moving target, forever changing, adding, renovating, and expanding. There are, in fact, several cavernous gambling rooms, one of the most popular being the hall containing the 4,500 slot machines, the most recent a smoke-free casino, small now but due to get bigger. A high-tech horse parlor, with toteboards and live feeds from tracks around the country, is an impressive newcomer. All the usual methods of depleting wallets are at hand—blackjack, bingo, chuck-a-luck, keno, craps, baccarat, roulette, acey-deucy, money wheel, and several variations of poker. To keep players at tables, there is tableside food service in the poker parlor and complimentary drinks are served at craps and blackjack tables. Even while the management uses the word "gaming" to gloss over the reality of the enterprise, there are notices set around the rooms offering counseling to those who "have a problem" with gambling.

WHERE TO STAY

When last seen, the resort had only the two hotels described below, but a new one, then unnamed, was under construction and will probably be operational by the time you read these words. With over 900 rooms, it will more than double the resort's housing capacity. Unlike Las Vegas and other gambling centers, room rates aren't kept artificially low as an inducement to visit, although that policy may change depending upon competitive pressures from such looming rivals as the Mohegan Sun Resort.

Foxwoods Resort Hotel. Rt 2, Ledyard, CT 06339. ☎ **800/369-9663** or 860/885-3000. Fax 860/885-4040. 312 rms. $190–$300 double. AE, DISC, MC, V. From Boston, take I-95 south to exit 92 onto Rte. 2 west. From New Haven and New York, take I-95 to I-395 north to Exit 79A onto Rte. 2A east, picking up Rte. 2 east.

Don't even bother trying to park your car in the huge garage by yourself. It will take forever, and the valet parking at the front door is free. Spanking new and well-maintained despite the heavy foot traffic, this hotel has eight floors adjoining the several casinos. Rooms are colorful, but not too gaudy (except for the suites for high-rollers on the top floor), and are provided with the usual amenities. There are no premium channels or in-room movies on the TV, though; the management doesn't want you lolling around your room watching the tube when you could be downstairs losing money. They do provide a spa and indoor pool to relax those neck muscles knotted from hours spent hunched over a card game.

Two Trees Inn. 240 Lantern Hill Rd. (off Rte. 2), Ledyard, CT 06339. ☎ **800/369-9663** or 860/885-3000. Fax 860/885-4050. 280 rms. $140–$200 double. Rates include breakfast. AE, DISC, MC, V. Follow directions for Foxwoods Resort Hotel above, continuing past the entrance to the casino on Rte. 2 to Lantern Hill Rd.

This was the first Foxwoods hotel, built in less than three months, now a short shuttle bus ride or 10-minute walk from the casino complex. Essentially a conventional motor hotel with a heated indoor pool and fitness room but few other extras, it attracts large numbers of bus tours. A skimpy continental breakfast is set out each morning in the small woody lobby, an occasion to contemplate your fellow guests' taste in white pants and hot pastel tops . . . in January. There is a busy middling restaurant, Branches. A nonsmoking floor is available. No pets.

WHERE TO DINE

Nine sit-down restaurants and five fast-food operations situated throughout the casino complex cover the most popular options. Only a couple aspire to even moderately serious culinary achievement. **Cedars Steak House** (☎ 860/885-3000, ext. 4252) grills beef and seafood that are supplemented by a raw bar, while **Al Dente** (ext. 4090) does designer pizzas and pastas. Both expect their guests to be dressed at least a notch better than tank tops and shorts. They are the only ones that accept reservations. The most popular dining room is the **Festival Buffet** (ext. 3172), which charges $10 for an all-you-can-eat spread that usually includes five or six main courses plus soups, salads, sides of vegetables and starches, and desserts. Other self-explanatory possibilities are **Han Garden** (ext. 4093), **Pequot Grill** (ext. 2690), and **The Deli** (ext. 5481).

FOXWOODS AFTER DARK

Just as in Vegas and Atlantic City, big showbiz names are whisked onto the premises, usually on weekends, in an effort to drag players up to the tables. Expect no surprises. Even Wayne Newton makes the scene, as do the likes of Tony Bennett, Paul Anka, Loretta Lynn, Donna Summer, Luther Vandross, Willie Nelson, Tom Jones, and the usual testaments to nostalgia—The Monkees, Frankie Avalon, and Fabian. For information about current headliners, call **800/200-2882.**

For a break from the whirring of the slots and the insistent chatter of the croupiers, and to occupy underage kids, Foxwoods has created **Cinetropolis,** an entertainment center that looks like a cleaned-up futuristic Gotham back alley. This is the electronic age at its most playfully frantic. *Turbo Ride* lets you pretend you are experiencing the rumbling takeoffs and powerful G-forces of jets taking off, this by way of giant films and machinery that makes your seat rock and roll as if in a cockpit. *Fox Giant Screen Theatre* is an IMAX-like production that features front-row rock concerts and exploding volcanoes, and *Virtual Adventures* lets you take control of an undersea vessel slipping past the dangers and challenges of the ocean depths. Once all that is exhausted, the *Fox Arcade* has pinball and video games that might seem a little pallid after the rest of these diversions.

10 Rhode Island

by Herbert Bailey Livesey

Water defines "Little Rhody" as much as mountain peaks characterize Colorado. The Atlantic thrusts all the way to the Massachusetts border, cleaving the state into unequal halves, filling the geological basin that is Narragansett Bay. That leaves 400 miles of coastline and several large islands. Despite the statistical fact that no state is more densely populated, half of inland Rhode Island is forest, little of it given to agriculture. But that isn't where its substantial interest to visitors lies. A string of coastal towns runs in a northeasterly arc from the Connecticut border up to Providence. The governmental and business capital is at the point of the Bay, 30 miles from the open ocean. It was here that Roger Williams, banned from the Massachusetts Bay Colony in 1635 for his outspoken views on religious freedom, established his colony. While little survives from that first century, a large section of the city's East Side is composed almost entirely of 18th- and 19th-century dwellings and public buildings.

Rhode Island isn't. An island, that is. Another group of Puritan exiles established their settlement a couple of years after Providence on an island known to the Narragansett as Aquidneck. Settlers thought their new home resembled the Isle of Rhodes in the Aegean, so the official name became "Rhode Island and Providence Plantations," subsequently applied to the entire state. The most important town on the island is Newport, arguably the best reason for an extended visit. Its first era of prosperity was during the colonial period, when its ships not only plied the new mercantile routes to China but engaged in the reprehensible "Triangular Trade" of West Indies molasses for New England rum for African slaves. Their additional skill at smuggling and evading taxes brought them into conflict with their British rulers, whose occupying army eventually all but destroyed Newport during the Revolution. After the Civil War, the town began its transformation from commercial outpost to resort with the arrival of the millionaires of what Mark Twain sneeringly described as the "Gilded Age." They built astonishingly extravagent mansions, their contribution to Newport's bountiful architectural heritage. With their winning of the America's Cup and subsequent defenses of yachting's most famous trophy, the town became a recreational sailing center with a packed summer cultural calendar. The happy result is that those whose idea of a successful vacation is a deep tan by Monday can coexist with those who find pleasure in excursions through recent and distant history and concerts held within hearing of waves hissing across packed sand.

Finally, there is Block Island, a one-hour ferry ride from Point Judith. A classic summer resort, it has avoided the imposition of Martha's Vineyard chic and Provincetown clutter. It has also sidestepped history, even though it was first settled in 1661, so there are few mandatory sights. That leaves visitors free simply to walk its beaches, explore its lighthouses, and hike its cliffside trails.

1 Providence

45 miles S of Boston, 55 miles NE of New London

Roger Williams knew what he was doing. Admired for his fervent advocacy of religious and political freedom in the early colonial period, he obviously had good instincts for town-building, as well. He planted the seeds of his settlement on a steep rise overlooking a swift-flowing river at the point where it widened into a large protected harbor. That part of the city, called the East Side and dominated by the ridge now known as College Hill, remains the most attractive district of a New England city second only to Boston in the breadth of its cultural life and rich architectural heritage.

College Hill is so-called because it is the site of Rhode Island College, which started life in 1764 and was later renamed Brown University. A member of the elite Ivy League, it is further enhanced by the presence of the highly regarded Rhode Island School of Design, whose buildings are wrapped around the perimeter of the Brown campus. In and around these institutions are several square miles of 18th- and 19th-century houses, colonial to Victorian, lining often gas-lit streets. At the back of the Brown campus is the funky shopping district along Thayer Street, while at the foot of the Hill is the largely commercial Main Street.

While most of what there is to be seen and experienced in Providence is found on the East Side, the far larger collection of neighborhoods west of the river has its own attractions. The level downtown area is the business, governmental, and entertainment locus, with City Hall, a new convention center, the two best large hotels, some small parks and historic buildings, and several theaters for music, dance, and theatrical productions. To its north, across the Woonasquatucket River, is the imposing State House and the Amtrak railroad station. And to its west, on the other side of Interstate 95, is Federal Hill, a residential area bearing a strong ethnic identity, primarily Italian, but increasingly leavened by numbers of more recent immigrant groups.

This is a city of manageable size—the population is about 170,000—that can easily occupy two or three days of a Rhode Island vacation. Locals are proud of its burgeoning reputation as an achiever in the gastronomic arena, pointing to several ambitious new restaurants that are nearly always less expensive than their counterparts in Boston and New York. College Hill is only one of 26 National Historic Districts, the calendar is full of concerts and special events, and the presence of so many young people promotes a lively nightlife. Thanks, Rog.

ESSENTIALS

GETTING THERE I-95 runs right through the heart of the city, the logical route from either Boston or New York. From Cape Cod, pick up I-195 west.

Rhode Island Airport Corp. (☎ 401/737-8222) in Warwick, south of Providence (Exit 13, I-95) handles all national flights. Major airlines serving this airport include: **American** (☎ 800/433-7300), **Continental** (☎ 800/525-0280), **Delta** (☎ 800/221-1212), **Northwest** (☎ 800/225-2525), **United** (☎ 800/241-6522), and **USAir** (☎ 800/247-8786). The Rhode Island Public Transit Authority (RIPTA) provides transportation to and from the city center. Taxis are also available, costing about $20 for the 20-minute trip.

Amtrak (☎ 800/872-7245) runs several trains daily along the shore route between Boston and New York, stopping at the attractive new station at 100 Gaspee St., near the State House.

VISITOR INFORMATION   In advance of a visit, contact the **Greater Providence Convention and Visitors Bureau** of the Chamber of Commerce (30 Exchange Terrace, Providence; RI 02903, ☎ **401/274-1636**). Once in Providence, you can consult a visitor information center at that address, or check the center at the Roger Williams National Park at the corner of Smith and North Main streets.

EXPLORING PROVIDENCE

Two leisurely walks, one short, another longer, will take curious visitors past most of the prominent attractions as well as bestow a palpable sense of the city's evolution from a colony of dissidents to a contemporary center of commerce and government. Downtown, chart a route from the 1878 City Hall on Kennedy Plaza along Dorrance Street one block to Westminster, turning left past The Arcade (see "Where to Dine," below), then right on Weybosset. Better still, cross the Providence River and walk down South Water Street as far as James, turn left, then left again on Benefit Street. This is the start of the so-called "Mile of History." Lined with restored or carefully preserved 18th- and 19th-century houses, it is a feast for aficionados of early American domestic architecture, enhanced by sections of brick herringbone sidewalks and gas streetlamps. Along the way are opportunities to visit, in sequence, the 1786 John Brown House, the First Unitarian Church (1816), the Providence Athenaeum, and the Museum of Art of Rhode Island School of Design. Two of our recommended inns are also on this lovely street, and an uphill detour on College Street leads to the handsome campus of Brown University.

Those who prefer expert direction to the sudden discoveries of haphazard rambling may want to take advantage of the walking tours provided by the **Providence Preservation Society** (21 Meeting St.; ☎ **401/831-7440**). Two 90-minute audio-cassette tours are available, in addition to booklets describing several historic neighborhoods. The cassettes can be rented (with your driver's license as hostage), the booklets purchased. The office is open Monday to Friday 9am to 5pm.

Brown University. Office of Admissions, 45 Prospect St. (near Angell St.). ☎ **401/863-2378.** Free admission. Mon–Fri 9am–5pm.

The nation's seventh oldest college was founded in 1764, and has a reputation as being the most experimental among its Ivy League brethren. The evidence of its pre-Revolutionary origins is seen in University Hall, built in 1771 and serving as a barracks for American and French troops in the war against the British. Tours of the campus, with buildings from every period in its history, are intended primarily for prospective students, but anyone can join, most readily by calling ahead.

Gov. Henry Lippitt House Museum. 199 Hope St. (Angell St.). ☎ **401/453-0688.** Admission $4 adults, $2 seniors and students. Apr–Dec Tues–Fri 11am–3pm, Sat–Sun 1–3pm; Jan–Mar by appointment only.

Visits to the museum are by guided tour only, and these leave on the hour, so plan your trip accordingly, for this house is as magnificently true to its grandiose Victorian era as any residence on the Continent. Its style is technically Renaissance Revival,

Providence

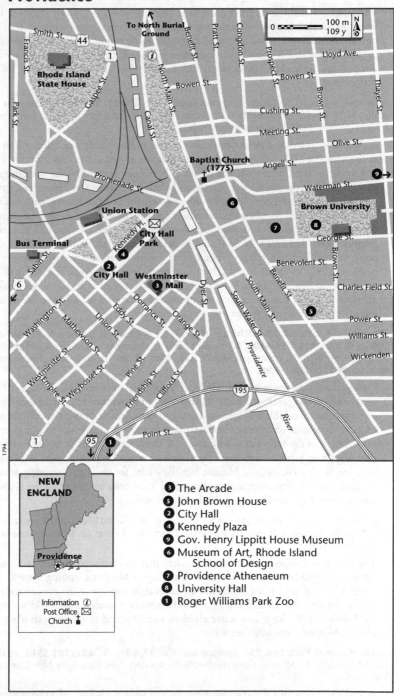

❸ The Arcade
❺ John Brown House
❷ City Hall
❹ Kennedy Plaza
❾ Gov. Henry Lippitt House Museum
❻ Museum of Art, Rhode Island
   School of Design
❼ Providence Athenaeum
❽ University Hall
❶ Roger Williams Park Zoo

Information ⓘ
Post Office ✉
Church ⛪

which really meant the architect brought to bear any motif or conceit that took his fancy. Meticulously detailed stenciling, expanses of stained glass, ornately framed mirrors, inlaid floors, wood intricately carved or made to look like marble combine to make this mansion one of the treasures of College Hill. The fact that the governor and his descendants lived in the house until 1981 helped enormously in its preservation.

John Brown House. 52 Power St. (corner Benefit St.). ☎ **401/331-8575.** Admission $5 adults, $3.50 seniors and students, $2 children 7–17. Tues–Sat 10am–4:30pm, Sun noon–4:30pm (Mon–Fri Jan–Feb by appointment only).

A three-story mansion made of brick, in contrast to the mostly wood-frame houses of the same late 18th-century era, this was the home of a man who made his fortune as a master of the China trade. He is said to have been responsible for the burning of a British warship, the *Gaspee*, four years before the start of the Revolution. John was also a slave-trader, in contrast to his industrialist brother Moses, who was an abolitionist. The style of the house is Georgian, although no doubt the owner preferred to think of it as Federalist after the war was won. His widow, children, and grandchildren lived here until 1846. Subsequent owners made additions and redecorated in the Victorian fashion. Their efforts were reversed after the house was bequeathed to the Rhode Island Historical Society in 1941, which restored it to its original condition and colors. Brown University was named in honor of the family, members of which were generous contributors. The mansion faces Power Street, laid out in 1638 for Roger Williams's town.

Museum of Art, Rhode Island School of Design. 224 Benefit St. (between Waterman and College sts.). ☎ **401/454-6100.** Admission $2 adults, $1 seniors, 50¢ students and children 5–18. Summer Wed–Sat noon–5pm; winter Tues, Wed, Fri, Sat 10:30am–5pm, Thurs noon–8pm, Sun and holidays 1–5pm.

Prestigious RISD (pronounced "RIZ-dee") supports this relatively compact but ingratiating center housing the 65,000 artworks of the permanent collection and frequent temporary exhibitions. Demonstrating its considerable breadth, on display are Chinese terra-cotta sculptures, Greek statuary, French Impressionist paintings, and early American decorative arts, with frequent illuminating stops in between. Probably of greatest general interest are the rooms of works by such masters as Monet, Cezanne, Rodin, Picasso, and Matisse, but allow time for the American wing, which contains not only fine antique furnishings and accessories but paintings by Gilbert Stuart, John Singleton Copley, and John Singer Sargent.

The Providence Athenaeum. 251 Benefit St. (College St.). ☎ **401/421-6970.** Free admission. Mon–Fri 8:30am–5:30pm, Sat 9:30am–5:30pm, Sun 1–5pm (In summer, Wed until 8:30pm, closed Sat).

The Providence Athenauem, a learned society that was founded in 1753, commissioned this granite 1838 Greek Revival building to house its lending library, the fourth oldest in the United States and an innovative concept at the time. Random glances through the old card catalog reveal handwritten cards dating well back into the 1800s. It has a large and active children's section and is a marvelous place in which bibliophiles can lose themselves.

Roger Williams Park Zoo. 950 Elmwood Ave. (Exit 17, I-95). ☎ **401/785-3510.** Admission $3.50 adults, $1.50 seniors and children 3–12. Apr–Oct daily 9am–5pm; Nov–Mar daily 9am–4pm.

In a 430-acre park that also contains a museum of natural history and a planetarium, the zoo is divided into habitats—Tropical America, The Farmyard, Plains of Africa.

Of over 150 species, the most popular are the polar bears, giraffes, penguins, the birds of the walk-through rain forest, and the cuddly critters of the petting zoo. Ongoing renovations have removed the prisonlike structures of the Victorian era in which the zoo was created, replacing them with concealed moats and hidden fences so that the animals can be viewed with less obvious barriers. Children can also be treated to rides on the carousel, a little train, on real ponies, and in paddleboats on the lake. Families might want to take a picnic and make a day of it.

Rhode Island State House. 82 Smith St. (between Francis and Hayes sts.). ☎ **401/ 277-2357.** Free admission. Mon–Fri 8:30am–4:30pm.

Constructed of Georgian marble that blazes in the sun, the stunning 1900 Capitol building dominates the city center by virtue of its hilltop location and superior esthetic. This near-flawless example of neoclassical governmental architecture is given room to flaunt, with open spaces all around. Its self-supported dome is one of the largest in the world, reminding many viewers of that on St. Peter's Cathedral in Rome. The gilded figure on top represents *Independent Man,* the state symbol. Inside, a full-length portrait of George Washington is given pride of place, one of many depictions of the Father of His Country by Gilbert Stuart, one of Rhode Island's own. Guided tours by appointment.

OUTDOOR PURSUITS

Boosters are proud of their new **Waterplace Park & Riverwalk,** which encircles a tidal basin and borders the Woonasquatucket River down past where it joins the Moshassuck to become the Providence River. It incorporates an amphitheater, boat landings, landscaped walkways with benches and trees, and vaguely Venetian bridges that cross to the East Side. Summer concerts and other special events are held here. If you can ignore the rubbish that floats in the local waterways, **Baer's River Workshop** (222 South Water St.; ☎ **401/453-1633**) offers canoe and kayak tours and rentals.

SHOPPING

Thayer Street, which is the main commercial district for the university, has the official **Brown Bookstore** (no. 244, corner Olive Street), open daily, but not in the evenings, and the **College Hill Bookstore** (no. 252), funkier and wider-ranging in its selections, and open daily until midnight. In the vicinity are **Urban Cargo** (no. 224), with casual clothes and jewelry for college-age women, and **Hillhouse** (no. 135), long in the business of providing male Brownies with Ivy dress-up clothes for interview weeks and parent days.

WHERE TO STAY

Assuming charm and character aren't paramount criteria in lodging, the clusters of motels around most of the exits from I-95 and I-195 are routinely comfortable and offer decent value, especially since the average visit is likely to be no more than one or two nights. Alternatives are provided by B&B referral agencies, such as **Bed & Breakfast of Rhode Island** (P.O. Box 3291, Newport, RI 02840; ☎ **800/828-0000** or 401/849-1298). These are rooms in private homes, so sometimes quirky rules and limitations apply, to be ascertained at the time of booking. Remember, too, that they are rarely as inexpensive as local units of economy motel chains.

HOTELS

🅢 **Days Hotel.** 220 India St., Providence, RI 02903. ☎ **800/325-2525** or 401/272-5577. 140 rms. A/C TV TEL. $80–$125 double. AE, CB, DC, DISC, MC, V.

Don't demand a room with a view. Representative of the chain's efforts to upgrade its image—slightly—this vertical motel has an expressway on one side and an unsightly section of waterfront on the other. The usual conveniences are in place, and there is a serviceable dining room as well as a modest exercise room with a whirlpool. Keep asking for cheaper rooms, for even on a weeknight in summer they can be had for $60 or less, depending upon the occupancy rate. Most of Providence's attractions are within a 10-minute drive. In addition, the hotel has a 24-hour shuttle service to and from the airport and bus and train stations. Make arrangements when booking.

Providence Biltmore. Kennedy Plaza, Providence, RI 02903. ☎ **800/294-7709** or 401/421-0700. Fax 401/455-3050. 217 rms. A/C TV TEL. $114–$199 double. AE, CB, DC, MC, V.

The former Omni is now part of something called the Grand Heritage group. A grand staircase beneath an impressive Deco-ish bronze ceiling dates the building to the 1920s, and a plaque on a column in the lobby shows the nearly 7-foot-high water level of the villainous 1938 hurricane. A dramatic new feature is the glass elevator that starts in the lobby and exits outdoors to scoot up the side of the building. Phone service includes voice mail and modem ports, which, combined with the central location and 24-hour fitness center, make it the equal of the newer Westin (nearby), with which it shares honors as the capital's prime business hotel. Given its relatively moderate rates, vacationing couples and families might be inclined to splurge.

Westin Providence. 1 W. Exchange St., Providence, RI 02903. ☎ **800/228-3000** or 401/598-8000. Fax 401/598-8200. 363 rms. A/C TV TEL. $140–$195 double. AE, DC, MC, V.

With its luxurious interior and central downtown location next to the convention center, this is a business hotel of high order at rates considerably lower than siblings in Boston and New York. Only a couple of years old, its rotunda lobby is filled with oversized chairs set around a white piano. To one side is a lounge with the buffed glow of a venerable men's club, and upstairs are adjoining bars featuring sports and live jazz. Bedrooms have minibars, cable TV with in-house movies, and phones with dataports and voice mail. Upgraded executive floors are available, and there is a health club and heated indoor pool on the roof, along with two restaurants. The chilly grandeur of the architectural spaces hasn't seemed to afflict the sunny personalities of most of the staff.

INNS

Lodging places in historic districts are required to provide off-street parking—free, in these three cases.

⑤ C.C. Ledbetter. 326 Benefit St., Providence, RI 02903. ☎/fax **401/351-4699.** 5 rms. A/C TV. $75–$115 double. Rates include breakfast. No credit cards.

There's no sign out front, because that's the way the eponymous owner wants it. She doesn't want to attract a boozy football weekend crowd or to bother her Benefit Street neighbors. Look for the 1780 clapboard building with the olive-green exterior. Things are a lot more colorful inside, with a substantial collection of contemporary artworks, much of it of museum quality. Two rooms share a bath, another might be the only one in the state to contain a rowing machine. A hearty continental breakfast is served around a common table on the ground floor. The two dogs—one is blind and deaf—are usually there, too. While the owner isn't enthusiastic about accepting children and pets, she'll consider both or either. And she makes no bones about the fact that she ups her rates on parents and alumni weekends and at graduation (booked through the end of the century).

The Old Court. 144 Benefit St., Providence, RI 02903. ☎ **401/751-2002** or 401/351-0747. 10 rms. A/C TEL. $75–$135 double. Rates include breakfast. DISC, MC, V.

This was once a rectory, built in 1863, and the furnishings reflect that period in surprising diversity. There are examples of Rococo Revival and Eastlake styles, as well as secretaries embellished with marquetry and Oriental rugs on bare floors, standouts amid more familiar Victoriana. Most traces of the building's tenure as a boardinghouse for college students have been expunged. Breakfast is a production, always with a hot entree, and served in a room with eight tables so guests don't have to deal with strangers first thing in the morning. Only three rooms have TV, so far, but they expect to add more. Families or longer-term visitors may be interested in the apartment across the street. It has one bedroom, a living room, and a full kitchen with dining nook. Rather dowdy and a little musty, it does offer a good deal of space and the opportunity to save money on meals.

State House Inn. 43 Jewett St., Providence, RI 02908. ☎ **401/785-1235.** 10 rms. A/C TV TEL. $99–$109 double. Rates include breakfast. AE, MC, V. From the easily identified State House, drive west on Smith St., over I-95, then left on Holden and right on Jewett.

The neighborhood isn't the best, but the owners compensate with lower rates and hotel conveniences not present in many inns, including cable TV, hair dryers, and clock radios. Weekday corporate rates are further discounted, and guests have access to a fax and copier. Some rooms have canopy beds or fireplaces. Breakfast is substantial, with at least one hot dish. Children are welcome, but not pets. No smoking. Reserve well in advance for special events at local colleges. All the better downtown restaurants are only minutes away.

WHERE TO DINE

Providence has a sturdy Italian heritage resulting in a profusion of tomato sauce and pizza joints, especially on Federal Hill, the district west of downtown and I-95. Since they are so many and so obvious, the suggestions below focus—a bit perversely, perhaps—on restaurants that have broken away from the red sauce imperative. One fruitful strip to explore for dining options is that part of **Thayer Street** that borders the Brown University campus, which counts Thai, Tex-Mex, barbecue, Indian, and even Egyptian eating places among its possibilities.

Adesso. 161 Cushing St. (off Thayer St.). ☎ **401/521-0770.** Main courses $9.95–$23.95. AE, MC, V. Mon–Thurs 11:45am–10:30pm, Fri–Sat 11:45am–11:30pm, Sun 4:30–10pm. FUSION.

They call it a "California Café," and follow through with Wolfgang Puck–ish designer pizzas from the wood-burning grill in the obligatory open kitchen along one wall of the long middle room. Go for them, or the entree-sized salads or creative main courses, but not the view, which is of the parking lot. One typical pizza combines strips of smoked chicken breast, curls of bacon, sun-dried tomatoes, mozzarella, and blanched garlic and scallions in a mustard-dill sauce. Alternatively, there is a grilled Chilean sea bass with a port wine cream sauce and Portabello mushrooms. No one goes hungry, not with portions large enough to quell the raging metabolism of a Brown defensive end. In back is a recently added liquor and espresso bar. Adesso is all but hidden down unmarked Cushing Street, off Thayer.

Cafe Nuovo. 1 Citizens Plaza. ☎ **401/421-2525.** Main courses $14.50–$23.95. AE, DC, DISC, MC, V. Daily 11:30am–2:30pm and 5–10pm (until 11pm Fri–Sat). MEDITERRANEAN FUSION.

This sleek relative newcomer occupies part of the ground floor of a postmodernist office tower that looks out at the confluence of the Moshassuck and Woonasquatucket rivers. Its reputation as a see-and-be-seen hotbed shortchanges the skill of its capable chefs. While grounded in the Italian repertoire, they skip lightly among other inspirations—Thai, Greek, and Portuguese among them. That restlessness brings them to dishes like lamb shank baked in a clay pot with orzo and rosemary and a cioppino of lobster chunks, shrimp, littlenecks, calamari, and whitefish in a ragout of tomatoes, leeks, and herbs. If that isn't enough, start with an appetizer-size pizza while casting an eye around the room of glass and marble and burnished wood. There are tables outside in warm weather. Access is from the Steeple Street bridge.

✪ **The Gatehouse.** 4 Richmond Square (east end of Pitman St.) ☎ **401/521-9229.** Reservations recommended on weekends. Main courses $16.95–$22.95. AE, DC, MC, V. Mon–Fri noon–2:30pm and 5:30–10pm, Sat 5:30–10pm, Sun 10am–2pm and 5:30–10pm. NEW AMERICAN.

At the Gatehouse you'll step inside a refined taproom with a green marble bar on the left, a working fireplace and elegantly set tables over to the right. Downstairs is a candlelit lounge and an outdoor deck perched above the Seekonk River. Jazz pianists or duos perform down there Wednesday to Saturday, and a pub menu offers burgers and pastas. Service and edibles are more polished on the main floor. Just imagine the signature appetizer: A fig wrapped in a crispy phyllo husk combines a number of rare tastes, including Stilton cheese, toasted pine nuts, prosciutto, cream, and port with a balsamic glaze. It's a perfect marriage, unlikely as it may sound, although it might as well be listed as dessert. Most of the entrees are grilled, at least in part, as with roasted tomato polenta, portabello mushrooms, and julienned vegetables cooked over hickory and rolled in a warm burrito. Presentation is careful but unfussy. The clever wine list sweeps from Australia's Hunter Valley to the Rhone and on to the Napa—don't ignore a selection from Rhode Island's own Sakonnet Vineyard. Despite other claimants, this is my choice for the one meal to have in Providence.

Pot au Feu. 44 Custom St. (off Webosset St.) ☎ **401/273-8953.** Main courses, salon $19.50–$26.50; bistro $13.95–$19.95. AE, CB, DC, MC, V. Salon Tues–Fri noon–1:30pm and 6–9pm, Sat 6–9:30pm; bistro Mon–Thurs 11:30am–2pm and 5:30–9pm, Fri 11:30am–2pm and 5:30–10pm, Sat 5:30–10pm. TRADITIONAL FRENCH.

Named for the classic boiled dinner of chicken, beef, onions, and root vegetables, this is, remarkably, one of only two French restaurants in town. They do it up right, and if English weren't being spoken all around, you'd think the restaurant was off a Lyonnaise side street. Dishes like steak au poivre, suprême de volaille Colbert, sole Indienne, and lotte à la niçoise are all exactly as they should be, remembrances of what made Gallic cooking memorable long before the excesses of the food revolution set in sometime around the first Reagan administration. Unless someone else is paying or you absolutely must have a tablecloth, there's no good reason not to head straight downstairs, especially at dinner, when the price gap widens between the salon and the basement bistro. The stone walls and bare floors do nothing to muffle the din down there, but that deliciously earthy food comes from the same kitchen. There are daily changes in soups, crêpes, quiches, and omelets. Smoking is confined to the bar.

Quick Bites & Lowbrow Treats

A bona-fide National Historic Landmark is an unlikely venue for snaffling up cookies, salads, fries, souvlaki, doughnuts, and egg rolls. But **The Arcade** (65 Weybosset St.; ☎ 401/456-5403) is a 19th-century progenitor of 20th-century shopping malls, an 1828 Greek Revival structure that runs between Weybosset and Westminster streets. Its main floor is given over largely to fast-food stands and snack counters of the usual kinds—yes, the Golden Arches, too—while the upper floor is primarily clothing and jewelry boutiques and toy and souvenir shops. Open daily.

Another local culinary institution arrives in Kennedy Plaza on wheels every afternoon around 4:30. The grungy aluminum-sided, trailer-sized **Haven Bros.** (☎ **401/ 861-7777**) food truck deals in decent burgers and better fries from its usual parking space next to City Hall. No new frontiers here, except that it hangs around until way past midnight to dampen the hunger pangs of clubgoers, overworked lawyers, assorted nightpeople, and workaholic pols (the mayor is a regular).

PROVIDENCE AFTER DARK

College towns propagate get-down music and partying venues, as well as more elevated entertainments. In the latter category are the **Ocean State Light Opera** (P.O. Box 603117, Providence, RI 02906; ☎ **401/331-6060**), which often performs at the Wheeler School Theater, and the **Rhode Island Philharmonic** (222 Richmond St.; ☎ **401/831-3123**), usually appearing at the Providence Performing Arts Center.

The southern end of Water Street has four bar/restaurants functioning essentially as nightspots. **The Hot Club** (575 S. Water St.; ☎ **401/861-9007**) opens at noon and keeps its door open past midnight, with live jazz two or more nights a week. Other nearby possibilities, last I looked, are **Steam Alley, Fish Co.,** and **Grappa** (all on South Water Street). Around the corner on South Main Street, **Clef no. 580** has live jazz most nights. Concerts by star acts like Joe Cocker and B.B. King, as well as mainstreamed and upcoming alternative bands are held at **The Strand** (79 Washington St.; ☎ **617/423-6398**). For art-house films and midnight cult movies, there is the **Avon Repertory Cinema,** on Thayer Street, near Meeting.

2 Between Providence & Newport: A Bucolic Detour

As a break from the rushed urbanity of Providence or the concentration of sights and activities that is Newport, a sidetrip down the length of the oddly isolated southeastern corner of the state is as soothingly diverting as an excursion can be. No one has thought to throw a bridge or run a ferry across the water between Newport and Sakonnet Point, prospects the reclusive residents would no doubt resist to the last lawsuit. They have been known to steal away with road signs to discourage summer visitors, and there are almost no enterprises geared to attract tourists. Things are quiet in these parts, and they intend to keep it that way.

To get there from Providence or Boston, pick up I-195 east, then I-24 south, toward Newport. Take Exit 3 for Route 77 south, just before the Sakonnet River Bridge. From Newport, take Route 138 toward Fall River, and exit on Route 77 south immediately after crossing the bridge.

After a welter of small businesses, most of them connected in some way to the ocean, Route 77 smooths out into a pastoral Brigadoon, not quite rural, but more rustic than suburban. Colonial farmhouses, real or replicated, bear sidings and roofs of weathered shakes the color of wood smoke. They are centered in tidy lawns, with fruit trees and firs as sentinels, bordered by miles and miles of low stone walls assembled with a sculptural sense of balanced shapes and textures. No plastic deer, no faded flamingoes, no tomato plants in the front yard, none of those cute little banners hung from porches to herald seasons and holidays. It is as if a requirement of residence were attendance at a school of good taste. There are a few antique shops and roadside farm stands, of both the permanent and card-table variety, as well as a snack shop or two and a garden store, but nothing even remotely intrusive to sour the serenity.

One of the few good reasons to pull off the road is **Sakonnet Vineyards** (162 W. Main St.; ☎ **401/635-8486**), with an entrance road on the left, about 3 miles south of the traffic light in Tiverton Four Corners. In operation over 20 years, it is one of New England's oldest wineries, and produces 40,000 cases of creditable wines annually. Types range from a popular pinot noir to a dry gewürztraminer, abetted by such whimsical bottlings as their Eye of the Storm blush, commemorating the 1985 arrival of Hurricane Gloria. With the foresight of bringing along a picnic lunch, visitors can buy a bottle or two and retire to one of the tables beside the pond near the tasting room. The "hospitality center" is open daily, from 10am to 6pm in summer.

Continuing south on Route 77, the road skirts what passes for the population center of Little Compton (to which we will return) and on to **Sakonnet Point,** where the inland terrain gives way to stony beaches and coastal marshes. There's a wetlands wildlife refuge where snowy egrets and herons might be glimpsed, a small harbor with working boats, and not much else.

Return, then, along Route 77, shortly noting the entrance to the **Stone House Club** (122 Sakonnet Point Rd., Little Compton, RI 02837; ☎ 401/635-2222). A restaurant/tavern/inn that is in fact open to the public, it must observe the wink-wink subterfuge of being a private club because it serves spirits and there is a church next door. That means a $20 membership fee for individuals and $36 for couples, in addition to room rates that range from $58 to $125 depending on season and type of accommodation. Rates include breakfast. MasterCard and Visa are accepted. The cellar Tap Room and more formal dining room upstairs traipse all over the gastronomic map—traditional, nouvelle, Italian, Asian—with a predisposition to seafood. They are open Tuesday to Sunday in summer, Friday to Sunday November to April. No TV, no room phones (but an intercom), and 4 of the 13 rooms share baths. Furnishings are worn and unstylish, but look oddly right for the location. Two private swimming beaches are available to guests. Children are welcome, pets aren't.

Driving north on Route 77, watch for the sign pointing toward Adamsville (if the natives haven't made off with it). Take the second right turn from the club, onto a road that doesn't appear to have a name. Shortly, it arrives at a T-intersection surrounded by a Congregational church, a few small shops, a post office, law and real estate offices, and the Commons restaurant. That's downtown **Little Compton.** Turn left (north) and you're back in the country before you shift into third gear. In about four miles, the road ends at Peckham Road. Turn right, in the faith that you are heading toward **Adamsville;** you'll arrive there in about eight miles.

The claimed birthplace of the Rhode Island red chicken is a less pristine hamlet than its neighbor, with a disheveled aspect and more pickup trucks than sports utility vehicles. At its center is **Abraham Manchester's** (Main Road; ☎ 401/635-2700), as much social center as restaurant, the gregarious owner and her staff greeting almost everyone by name and bantering as old friends do. The building is a former general store, but not much attention is paid the niceties of historic preservation. There are splintery beams of indeterminate age, and the mounted stag head and wagon wheel are typical of the decor. The menu is unexpectedly imaginative, with, for example, a smoked chicken Alfredo over spinach fettuccine, and a production called the "Manchester Medley Platter." That's a jumble of shrimp marinated in red wine, blackened swordfish, pieces of barbecued chicken, and a slab of sautéed tenderloin, an assemblage fragrant with garlic, herbs, and balsamic vinegar. Portions are daunting. Main courses are $6.85 to $21.95. The place is open daily, 11:30am to 10pm, and accepts American Express, MasterCard, and Visa. If it's before 11:30am, the owner's daughter runs **The Barn** on the other side of the parking lot, offering freshly baked breads and pastries with her elaborate breakfasts.

From Adamsville, return to Route 77 via Route 179 to Tiverton Four Corners to get back to Newport, or take Route 81 to Route 24 if returning to Providence or Boston.

3 Newport

75 miles S of Boston, 115 miles NE of New Haven

"City by the Sea" is the singularly unimaginative nickname an early resident unloaded on Newport. At least it was accurate, since for a time during the colonial period it rivaled Boston and even New York as a center of New World trade and prosperity. It occupies the southern tip of Aquidneck Island in Narragansett Bay, connected to the mainland by three bridges and a ferry. The perimeter of the city resembles a heeled boot, its toe pointing west. Wealthy industrialists, railroad tycoons, coal magnates, financiers, and robber barons made respectable by political connections and vast fortunes were drawn to the area in the 19th century, especially between the Civil War and World War I. They bought up property at the ocean's rim, building summer mansions patterned after the palaces of Europe that they used as summer "cottages." Their toys were equally extravagant yachts meant for pleasure, not commerce, and competitions between them established Newport's reputation as a sailing center. In 1851, the sporting schooner *America* defeated a British ship in a race around the Isle of Wight. The prize trophy became known as the America's Cup, which remained in the possession of the New York Yacht Club (with an outpost in Newport) until 1983. In that shocking summer, *Australia II* snatched the Cup away from *Liberty* in the last race of a four-out-of-seven series. Though the cup was regained by an American team in 1987, it was won by New Zealand in 1995 and remains down under. The strong U.S. yachting tradition has endured despite the Cup's loss, and Newport continues as a bastion of world sailing and a destination for long-distance races.

The downtown business and residential district is up where the "laces" of the "boot" would be. Several wharves push into the bay, providing support and mooring for flotillas of pleasure craft, from stubby little inboards and character boats to graceful sloops and visiting tall ships. Much of the strolling, shopping, eating, quaffing, and gawking is done along this waterfront and its parallel streets, America's Cup Boulevard and Thames Street. (The latter used to be pronounced "Tems," in the British manner, but was Americanized to "Thaymez" after the Revolution.) The navy has pulled out its battleships, causing a decline in the local economy, but hardly the disaster predicted by some. And this area has thus far been spared the coarser intrusions that afflict so many coastal resorts. Monster RVs and motorcycle gangs rarely arrive to complicate the heavy traffic of July and August, and T-shirt emporia have kept within reasonable limits. Considering it has over 3.7 million visitors a year, that's remarkable.

Immediately east and north of the business district are blocks of colonial, Federal, and Victorian houses of the 18th and 19th century, many of them restored and bearing plaques designating them as National Historic Sites. Happily, they are not frozen in amber, no-touch museum pieces, but are very much in use as residences, eating places, offices, and shops. In the aggregate, they are as visually appealing in their way as the 40-room cottages of the super-rich.

So despite Newport's prevailing image as a collection of stupefyingly ornate mansions and rarefied regattas of sailing ships inaccessible to all but the highest-income 2% of the population, the city is, for the most part, middle-class and moderately priced. Summer evenings are often cool enough for a cotton sweater.

Scores of inns and bed-and-breakfasts assure lodging even during festival weeks, at rates and fixtures from budget to luxury level. In nearly every regard, this is the "First Resort" of the New England coast.

ESSENTIALS

GETTING THERE   From New York City, take I-95 to the third exit, picking up Route 138 east (which joins briefly with Route 4) and crossing the Newport toll bridge slightly north of the downtown district. From Boston, take Route 24 through Fall River, picking up Route 114 into Newport.

Rhode Island Airport Corp. (☎ 401/737-8222) in Warwick, south of Providence (Exit 13, I-95), handles national flights into the state. Major airlines serving this airport include: **American** (☎ 800/433-7300), **Continental** (☎ 800/525-0280), **Delta** (☎ 800/221-1212), **Northwest** (☎ 800/225-2525), **United** (☎ 800/241-6522), and **USAir** (☎ 800/247-8786). A few of the larger Newport hotels provide shuttle service, as does **Cozy Cab** (☎ 401/846-2500). **Pineapple Beantown Express** (☎ 401/841-8989) has shuttle service between Newport and Boston's Logan Airport.

The **Interstate Navigation Company** (☎ 401/783-4613) ferries between Providence, Block Island, and Newport's Fort Adams.

VISITOR INFORMATION   In advance of a visit, call **24-hour visitor information line** (☎ 800/263-4636 outside Rhode Island, or 401/848-2000 in Rhode Island). On site, check in at the excellent **Newport Gateway Visitors Center** (23 America's Cup Ave.; ☎ 800/326-6030 or 401/849-8040). Open daily 9am to 5pm (until 6pm Friday and Saturday), it has several attendants on duty to answer questions, rest rooms, brochures for attractions and accommodations, a lodging availabilty service, and panoramic photos showing the locations of mansions, parks, and other landmarks. They even validate parking in the adjacent lot for up to the first half-hour.

SPECIAL EVENTS   Arrive any day between Memorial Day and Labor Day and expect to find at least a half-dozen festivals, competitions, or other events in progress. Following is only a partial list of some of the more prominent. (Specific dates often change from year to year, so it is necessary to call ahead to confirm (☎ 800/263-4636 outside Rhode Island, or 401/848-2000 in Rhode Island). In February: Newport Winter Festival. June: Secret Garden Tour, Great Chowder Cook-Off, Outdoor Arts Festival. July: Newport 12-Meter Regatta, the Small Boat Regatta, the Miller Lite Hall of Fame Tennis Championship played on grass courts, Hall of Fame Invitational Tournament for women, Newport Music Festival, classical music at several mansions and similar sites, the Newport Flower Show at Rosecliff, and the Black Ships Festival, celebrating the city's long association with Japan. August: Newport Classic Yacht Regatta, Newport Folk Festival, the Rhythm and Blues Festival, and the JVC Jazz Festival at Fort Adams State Park. September: Newport International Boat Show and the Newport Irish Music Festival at the Newport Yachting Center. October: Bowen's Wharf Waterfront Seafood Festival. December: Christmas in Newport, with traditional celebrations throughout the city.

TOURS & CRUISES

Most of Newport's attractions can be reached on foot, except for the mansions. Leaving the car parked at your downtown hotel or inn is wise. Lots and garages aren't cheap, especially at the waterfront, and many streets are too narrow. The metered parking slots along Thames Street are closely monitored by police and fines are steep.

Newport

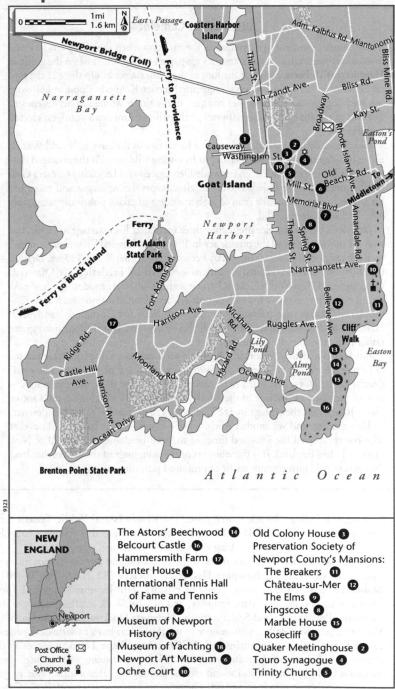

0 | 1mi
1.6 km

N

East Passage

Coasters Harbor Island

Newport Bridge (Toll)

Ferry to Providence

Narragansett Bay

Third St.

Adm. Kalbfus Rd. Miantonomi

Bliss Mine Rd.

Van Zandt Ave.

Bliss Rd.

Kay St.

Broadway

Kempear

Rhode Island Ave.

Easton's Pond

① Causeway

Washington St.

② ③

④

⑲ ⑤

Old Beach Rd.

Goat Island

Mill St.

⑥

Memorial Blvd.

⑦

To Middletown

Newport Harbor

Ferry

Fort Adams State Park

⑱

Thames St.

⑧

Spring St.

⑨

Narragansett Ave.

⑩

†

⑪

Ferry to Block Island

Fort Adams Rd.

⑰

Harrison Ave.

Wickham Rd.

Bellevue Ave.

Ruggles Ave.

Cliff Walk

⑫

Annandale Rd.

Ridge Rd.

Moorland Rd.

Hazard Rd.

Lily Pond

⑬

Easton Bay

Castle Hill Ave.

Harrison Ave.

Ocean Drive

Ocean Drive

Almy Pond

⑭

⑮

⑯

Brenton Point State Park

Atlantic Ocean

9323

NEW ENGLAND

Newport

Post Office ⊠
Church †
Synagogue ☆

The Astors' Beechwood ⑭
Belcourt Castle ⑯
Hammersmith Farm ⑰
Hunter House ①
International Tennis Hall of Fame and Tennis Museum ⑦
Museum of Newport History ⑲
Museum of Yachting ⑱
Newport Art Museum ⑥
Ochre Court ⑩

Old Colony House ③
Preservation Society of Newport County's Mansions:
  The Breakers ⑪
  Château-sur-Mer ⑫
  The Elms ⑨
  Kingscote ⑧
  Marble House ⑮
  Rosecliff ⑬
Quaker Meetinghouse ②
Touro Synagogue ④
Trinity Church ⑤

Summers in Camelot

There comes a moment in every tour of the mansion when the group lets loose an involuntary sound that is part starstruck gasp, part sad sigh. It is when the guide at **Hammersmith Farm** pauses at the foot of the main staircase. Up there at the top, on September 12, 1953, she says, Jaqueline Bouvier Kennedy stood in her ivory silk wedding gown and tossed her bouquet to the single women at her reception. She was in the first day of her 10 years as the wife of America's youngest elected president.

Jack Kennedy had wasted no time after his service in the navy in World War II, either in ascending the political ladder or in sowing wild oats. At the arranged dinner where he first met Jackie, an erstwhile Deb Queen and Inquiring Camera Girl, Washington's most eligible bachelor "reached across the asparagus and asked her for a date." It was time for a man of high ambition to take a politically acceptable wife, and soon after, he did.

Jack lost a bid for the vice presidency three years after his marriage to Jackie, but won the nomination and the presidency in 1960. The shingled Victorian "cottage" on a hill overlooking Narragansett Bay became his summer White House. Despite its 28 rooms and the extensive gardens designed by Frederic Law Olmsted, the designer of New York's Central Park, it seems a relatively modest residence. At least it does after visits to a few of Newport's other fabled mansions, such as the 70-room neo-Renaissance palazzo, The Breakers, built for Cornelius Vanderbilt. Hammersmith has antiques, but not all that many, and its other furnishings are rather ordinary, in rooms of no great size.

But here is a history we know. The president's desk is on display, as are photos of Jacqueline and her children. They lived and worked and played here. The presidential yacht, *Honey Fitz,* used to be moored down at the dock. Also seen are images of members of her side of the family, the aristocratic Auchinclosses. One of them, John, built the cottage in 1887. His son Hugh married Janet Lee Bouvier, Jackie's mother, and yet another Auchincloss—Louis—is the lawyer and novelist who has chronicled the lives and times of the well-bred and well-heeled of New York and New England. It is the whispers of the minglings of those lives that lend the cottage at Hammersmith an air of profound purpose and loss.

Renting or bringing a bicycle is an option. The **Rhode Island Public Transit Authority** (RITPA; ☎ **401/781-9400**) has a free shuttle bus that follows a roughly circular route through town, making stops at prominent sites.

Several organizations conduct tours of the mansions and the downtown historic district. In summer, the **Newport Historical Society** (82 Touro St.; ☎ **401/846-0813**) has two itineraries. Tours of Historic Hill leave at 10am and 3pm Thursday and Friday and 10am Saturday, and of Cliff Walk at 10am and 3pm on Saturdays. Prices are $5 and $7 respectively. **Newport On Foot** leaves the Gateway Visitor Center twice daily on 90-minute tours. If your car has a cassette deck or you have a portable player, a company called **CCInc Auto Tape Tours** produces a 90-minute recorded tour of the mansions for $12.95. It is well-done, with an intelligent narration backed by music and sound effects, although it takes a little while to get the hang of when to turn it on and off. The tapes are available at a booth in the Gateway Visitor Center (see above) for $12.95 each or directly from the company at P.O. Box 227, 2 Elbrook Dr., Allendale, NJ 07401 (☎ **201/236-1666**).

Viking Tours (Gateway Visitors Center; ☎ 401/847-6921) has narrated bus tours of the mansions and 1- and 2¹/2-hour harbor cruises, the longer version including a guided tour of Hammersmith Farm. **Yankee Boat Peddlers** (Bannister's Wharf; ☎ 401/847-0298) schedules several daily departures of its 72-foot schooner *Madeleine* and its classic powerboat *RumRunner II*. One-hour cruises of the bay and harbor are given by **Newport Navigation** on its *Spirit of Newport* (Newport Harbor Hotel & Marina; ☎ 401/849-3575), twice daily Monday to Friday, three times on weekends. And the **Old Newport Scenic Railway** (19 America's Cup Ave.; ☎ 401/624-6951) has three-hour excursions in vintage trains along the edge of the bay to the Green Animals Topiary Gardens in Portsmouth, at the northerly end of the island.

THE COTTAGES

That's what wealthy summer people called the almost unimaginably sumptuous mansions they had built in Newport in the last decades before the 13th Amendment to the Constitution, the one that allowed the imposition of an income tax. Say this for the wealthy of the Gilded Age, many of whom obtained their fortunes by less than honorable means: They knew a good place to put down roots when they saw it. These are the same ones, after all, who developed Palm Beach in winter, the Hudson Valley in spring, the Berkshires in autumn, and Newport in summer, sweeping from house to luxurious house with the insouciance of a bejeweled matron dragging her sable down a grand staircase. They were Vanderbilts and Astors and their blueblooded friends and rivals, and they rarely stayed in any one of their mansions for more than a few weeks a year.

When driving or biking through the cottage district (walking is impractical for most people), the fact that most of these astonishing residences are still privately owned is almost as remarkable to contemplate as are the grounds and interiors of the nine that are open to the public. When setting out, ask if the fabled mansion of Doris Duke, recently protected by high walls topped with barbed wire, has begun to welcome visitors, too, as it is slated to sometime in the near future. Also, resolve to ration visits to one or two a day. The sheer opulence of the mansions can soon become numbing, an effect not unlike touching down in five European countries in a week and touring the most lavish palaces in each. Each residence requires 45 minutes to an hour for its guided tour. The aptitude and personality of individual docents is generally good, apart from their understandable tendency to take on a robotic tone. If at all possible, go during the week. Weekend foot and vehicular traffic can resemble Times Square at curtain time.

Six of the mansions are maintained by the **Preservation Society of Newport County** (118 Mill St.; ☎ 401/847-6543), which also operates the 1748 Hunter House and the Green Animals Topiary Gardens in Portsmouth. They sell a combination ticket, good for a year, to all eight properties; it's $35.50 for adults, $10 for children 6–11. Tickets for individual mansions are $6.50 to $10 for adults, $3 to $3.50 for children. Strip tickets for two to six mansions are also available. They can be purchased at any of the properties. The cottages are open daily from 10am to 5pm from late May to Labor Day; November to April they're open Saturday and Sunday 10am to 4pm. The mansions that aren't operated by the Preservation Society but are open to the public are Belcourt Castle, Beechwood, and Hammersmith Farm. Following are descriptions of the nine in the order they are encountered when driving south from Memorial Boulevard along Bellevue Avenue, then west on Ocean Avenue.

Kingscote. Bowery St. (west of Bellevue Ave.) See "Preservation Society" above for admission details.

Built in 1839, this mansion (on the right-hand side of the avenue) is a reminder that well-to-do southern families often had second homes north of the Mason-Dixon line to avoid the sultry summer months of the deep South. Richard Upjohn was the architect, and Kingscote reflects the Gothic Revival style he used for Trinity Church in New York. Although considered one of the Newport "cottages," the mansion's existence precedes the Gilded Age to which the others belong, a period usually delineated as starting around 1875 and ending with the outbreak of World War I, and its inclusion in the group is largely due to its acquisition in 1864 by the sea merchant William Henry King. His family's furnishings are those now on view, many of them porcelains and textiles accumulated as a result of his participation in the China trade. Shortly after the purchase, he went mad and spent the rest of his life in an asylum. The New York architectural firm of McKim, Mead & White was commissioned to design the 1881 dining room, notable for its Tiffany glass panels.

The Elms. Bellevue Ave. See "Preservation Society" above for admission details.

Architect Horace Trumbauer is said to have been inspired by the Chateau d'Asnieres outside Paris, and a first look at the ornate dining room of The Elms, suitable for at least a marquis, buttresses that claim. So, too, do the sunken gardens, laid out and maintained in the formal French manner. The owner was a first-generation millionaire, a coal tycoon named Edward J. Berwind. His cottage was completed in 1901, and he filled it with genuine Louis XIV and XV furniture and paintings and accessories true to the late 18th century.

Château-sur-mer. Bellevue Ave. See "Preservation Society" above for admission details.

William S. Wetmore was yet another Rhode Island merchant who made his fortune in the lucrative China trade. The entrance to this "Castle by the Sea" is on the left-hand side of Bellevue, driving south. High Victorian in style, which means it drew from many inspirations, Italian Renaissance and French Second Empire among them, the Château features a central atrium four stories high with a glass skylight and balconies at every level.

✪ The Breakers. Ochre Point Ave. (east of Bellevue Ave.) ☎ **401/847-6543.** See "Preservation Society" above for admission details. After Château-sur-mer, turn left on Ruggles Ave., then left again on Ochre Point Ave. The Breakers is on the right, a parking lot on the left.

If you only have time to see one of the "cottages," make it this one. Architect Richard Morris Hunt was commissioned to create this replica of a generic Florentine Renaissance palazzo, and was apparently unrestrained by mere considerations of cost. The high iron entrance gates alone weigh over seven tons. Such mind-numbing extravagance shouldn't really be surprising—Hunt's patron was, after all, Cornelius Vanderbilt II, grandson of railroad tycoon Commodore Vanderbilt and a superstar spender of the Gilded Age. Had he been European royalty, The Breakers would have provided motive for a peasant revolt. Vanderbilt's small family, their guests, and their staff of 40 servants had 70 rooms in which to roam. Nearly three years in construction, completed in 1892, the mansion's foundation is approximately the size of a football field. The furnishings are original, and platoons of artisans were imported from Europe to apply gold leaf and carve wood and marble and provide mural-size baroque paintings.

Rosecliff. Bellevue Ave. See "Preservation Society" above for admission details. From The Breakers, return to Bellevue Ave. and turn left (south). Rosecliff is on the left.

Stanford White of McKim, Mead & White thought the Grand Trianon of Louis XVI at Versailles a suitable model for this 1902 commission for Mr. Hermann Oelrichs.

With a middling 40 rooms, it doesn't overwhelm, at least not on the scale of The Breakers. But it has the largest ballroom of all the cottages—the crossbar in the "H" layout of the house—not to mention a storied heart-shaped grand staircase. All this was made possible by one James Fair, an immigrant who made his fortune after unearthing the thickest gold and silver vein of Nevada's Comstock Lode and bought the property for his daughters, Theresa and Virginia (a.k.a. Tessie and Birdie). Theresa was the sister who married Hermann Oelrichs, a highly successful New York businessman. In 1941, the mansion and its contents were sold for $21,000. It was used as a setting for some scenes in the Robert Redford movie of Fitzgerald's *The Great Gatsby* and for a ballroom scene in Arnold Schwarzenegger's *True Lies*.

Beechwood. 580 Bellevue Ave. ☎ **401/846-3772.** Admission $8 adults, $6 seniors and children under 12. Daily 10am–5pm (tours on the half-hour, except at 12:30pm).

Mrs. William Backhouse Astor—*the* Mrs. Astor, as every brochure and guide feels compelled to observe—was, during her active life, the arbiter of exactly who constituted New York and Newport society. "The 400" list of socially acceptable folk was influenced or perhaps even drawn up by her, and that roster bore meaning, in some quarters, well into the second half of the 20th century. Being invited to Beechwood was absolutely critical to a social pretender's sense of self-worth, and elaborate machinations were set in motion to achieve that lofty goal. It may be of some comfort to the descendants of the failed supplicants that Mrs. Astor spent her last few years at the cottage greeting imaginary guests. Built in 1852, the mansion isn't as large or impressive as some of its neighbors. But unlike those managed by the Preservation Society, it provides a little theatrical pizzazz with a corps of actors who pretend to be friends, children, and servants of Mrs. Astor.

✪ **Marble House.** Bellevue Ave. See "Preservation Society" above for admission details.

Architect Richard Morris Hunt, another favorite of the cottage-builders, outdid himself for his clients, the Vanderbilts, William and Alva. Several types of marble were used both outside and inside in a lush opulence that rivals the palaces of the Sun King, reaching its apogee in the ballroom, encrusted with three kinds of gold. It cost William $2 million to build Marble House and another $7 million to decorate it, but Alva divorced him four years after the project was finished. She got the house, which she soon closed after marrying William's friend and neighbor, Oliver Hazard Perry Belmont. When her second husband died, Alva discovered the cause of female suffrage, and reopened Marble House in 1913 to hold a benefit at the Chinese Teahouse in the growing campaign for women's right to vote.

Belcourt Castle. Bellevue Ave. ☎ **401/846-0669.** Admission $6.50 adults, $5 seniors and college students, $4 children 13–18, $2 children 6–12.

This was the only slightly less grand mansion to which Alva Vanderbilt repaired after her second marriage. While the Vanderbilts were avid yachtsmen, her new husband Oliver was a fanatical horseman. His 62-room house, also a design by Richard Morris Hunt, actually contained stables on the ground floor, where his beloved steeds slept under monogrammed blankets (the Belmonts were instrumental in building New York's Belmont Racetrack). Alva and Oliver entertained frequently, and counted among their guests Kaiser Wilhelm and the Duke of Windsor. The castle, meant to resemble a royal hunting lodge, contains a large collection of European Gothic stained glass, scores of Oriental carpets, and French Renaissance furniture and artifacts. Thomas Edison designed the lighting.

Continuing south on Bellevue, on the left just before a sharp turn west along what becomes Ocean Drive, is Rough Point, the home of tobacco heiress Doris Duke. She died in October 1993 and her 1887 Tudor mansion is expected to be opened to the public in the next year or so.

Continue west on Ocean Drive to reach the last mansion, below.

Hammersmith Farm. Ocean Dr. (past Castle Hill Ave.). ☎ **401/846-0420** or 401/846-7346. Admission $8 adults, $3 children 6–12. Memorial Day–Labor Day daily 10am–7pm; Apr–May and Sept to mid–Nov 10am–5pm.

Built for John W. Auchincloss in 1887 on a farm established in the 17th century, the house was used for the wedding reception of one of his descendants, Jacqueline Bouvier, in 1953. Set on a rise with an unimpeded view across 50 acres of manicured lawns and gardens to Narragansett Bay, it subsequently became the unofficial Summer White House of the short Kennedy presidency. John-John and Caroline played here in a small outbuilding near the gardens that is now the gift shop. Out in the meadows beyond you can see the miniature horses and equally diminutive donkey that are descendants of animals raised by the Auchinclosses.

Despite an impressive porte cochere, its substantial size, and its superb setting, the cottage is hardly pretentious, managing to seem as homey as the Hudson Valley residence of another millionaire and inspiration to Jack Kennedy, Franklin D. Roosevelt. There is a certain irony in the location of the Kennedy Summer White House, for on the adjoining property, Fort Adams State Park, was the Dwight D. Eisenhower Summer White House. It makes concrete the symbolism mentioned by Kennedy in his inaugural address, the passing of power from men born in the last century to those born in this one.

Admission fees are not by the carload, the way most people arrive, but by individual, which means that a car with five adults will cost $40. That will separate true Kennedy lovers from the merely curious. Even though it is open to the public, Hammersmith is privately owned, and it is said to be up for sale for $9.5 million. There is no way to tell whether it will remain open or in what ways it will be changed after that future change in ownership.

ANOTHER HISTORIC HOME

Hunter House. 54 Washington St. (at Elm St.). ☎ **401/847-6543.** Admission $6 adults, $3 children 6–11. May–Sept daily 10am–5pm; Apr and Oct Sat–Sun 10am–5pm.

Another property of the Preservation Society, this 1748 to 1754 colonial with its gambrel roof and widow's walk is one of the most impressive dwellings in the lightly touristed neighborhood known as The Point, north of downtown. Above the doorway, within the broken pediment, is a carved wooden pineapple. This symbol of welcome derived from the practice of placing a real pineapple at the door to announce that the sea captain owner had returned from his long voyage and was ready to receive guests. The interior is furnished with furniture crafted by Newport's famed 18th-century cabinetmakers, Townsend and Goddard.

OTHER ATTRACTIONS

International Tennis Hall of Fame. 194 Bellevue Ave. (corner of Memorial Dr.). ☎ **401/ 849-3990.** Admission $6 adults, $3.50 seniors, $3 children under 12; $12 family. Daily 10am–5pm (except during tournaments).

On Bellevue Avenue there was (and is) an exclusive men's club called the Newport Reading Room. One member was James Gordon Bennett, Jr., the wealthy publisher of the *New York Herald*. He persuaded a friend to ride a horse into the club. The outraged members reprimanded Bennett, who had an instant snit that they hadn't enjoyed his little jest. He went right out and bought a property on the other side of Memorial Boulevard, and ordered a structure built for his own social and sports club.

The New York architectural firm of McKim, Mead & White, a favorite of Gilded Age millionaires, was hired. They produced a shingle-style edifice of lavish proportions with turrets and verandahs and an interior piazza for lawn games, equestrian shows, concerts, and a new game called tennis. As Bennett hoped, his Newport Casino swiftly became the premier gathering place of his privileged compatriots. Now, those grass courts not only host important professional tournaments, but are open to the public for play (phone ahead to make reservations, May to October). The building itself houses the Hall of Fame, recently renovated at a cost of $6 million, containing trophies, memorabilia, and computerized interactive exhibits. The Hall will be of interest primarily to fans of the game, but has photographic highlights recognizable to casual observers.

Museum of Newport History. Washington Square (Thames and Touro sts.). ☎ **401/ 841-8770.** Admission $5 adults, $4 seniors, $3 children 6–13. Mon and Wed–Sat 10am–5pm; Sun 1–5pm.

One of five properties maintained by the Newport Historical Society, this museum is in the refurbished 1772 Brick Market (not to be confused with the nearby shopping mall, Brick Marketplace). The architect was Peter Harrison, also responsible for the Touro Synagogue (below), and the market was only recently refurbished and reconfigured to contain this professionally installed illumination of the city's history. The museum houses boat models, paintings, antique silverware, old photos, a ship figurehead, and features videos and occasional audio commentaries on Newport history. A printing press used by Benjamin Franklin's brother James is also on display.

Newport Art Museum. 76 Bellevue Ave. (corner Beach Rd.) ☎ **401/848-8200.** Admission $4 adults, $3 seniors, free for children under 18. Memorial Day–Labor Day daily 10am–5pm; Sept–May Tues–Sat 10am–4pm, Sun 1–5pm.

Standing across the avenue from Touro Park, this was the first Newport commission of Richard Morris Hunt, who went on to design many of the Cottages along Bellevue Avenue. Unlike most of his later Newport houses, this 1862 structure is in the Victorian Stick style, a wood construction that had origins in earlier Carpenter Gothic. This, the former Griswold Mansion, is often cited as a supreme example of the style. Now a museum and headquarters of the local art association, it mounts exhibitions of the works of Newport artists and offers classes and lectures, and serves as a venue for concerts of the city's frequent music festivals.

Spring Street. Between Memorial Blvd. and Touro St.

Historic Hill is the large district of colonial Newport that rises from America's Cup Boulevard, along the waterfront, to Bellevue Avenue, the beginning of Victorian Newport. Spring Street serves as the Hill's main drag, a trove of colonial, Georgian, and Federal structures serving as residences, inns, and antique and other shops. There are no 20th-century architectural intrusions. Chief among its visual delights is the 1725 Trinity Church, at the corner of Church Street. Said to be fashioned in the manner of the legendary British architect Christopher Wren, it certainly reflects that inspiration in its belfry and distinctive spire, seen from all over downtown Newport and dominating Queen Anne Square, a greensward that runs down to the waterfront. The church is sheathed in clapboard recently painted beige and has two stained-glass windows by Tiffany.

Touro Park. Bellevue Ave. (between Pelham and Mill sts.)

This small park is opposite the Newport Art Museum. Its central feature, apart from providing a shaded respite from shopping, is the Old Stone Mill. Dreamers like to believe that the eight columns of the roughly circular structure were erected by

Vikings. Realists say it was built by Benedict Arnold, a governor of the colony long before his great-great-grandson committed his infamous act of treason during the War for American Independence.

Touro Synagogue. 72 Touro St. (Spring St.) ☎ **401/847-4794.** Free admission. July 4–Sept 1 Sun–Fri 10am–4pm. Guided tours on the half-hour.

This is the oldest existing synagogue in the United States, dating from 1763. A Sephardic Jewish community existed in Newport from the mid-17th-century, largely refugees from Portugal, but it was over a hundred years before the building was erected. It was designed by Peter Harrison, who was also responsible for the Brick Market, which now houses the Museum of Newport History. The synagogue was closed at the end of its first century for lack of a congregation of sufficient size. It had come back into use in yet another hundred years and was designated a National Historic Site in 1946. On display inside is a 500-year-old Torah.

Next door is the Newport Historical Society (82 Touro St.; ☎ **401/846-0813**). In addition to its displays of colonial Newport furnishings and decorative arts, the Society sponsors walking tours (details in "Tours & Cruises," above).

OUTDOOR PURSUITS: THE BEACH AND BEYOND

Fort Adams State Park (Harrison Ave.; ☎ **401/847-2400**) is on the thumb of land that partially encloses Newport Harbor. It can be seen from the downtown docks and reached by driving or cycling south on Thames Street, west on Wellington Avenue (a section of Ocean Drive, which becomes Harrison Avenue). The fort for which the park is named is being restored. Boating, ocean swimming, fishing, and sailing are all available on its 105 acres. Open Memorial Day to Labor Day; admission is $2 per car (state residents, seniors); $4 for nonresidents. Also on the grounds is the **Museum of Yachting** (☎ **401/847-1018**), housed in a stone barracks of the early 19th century. Photographs, videos, paintings, and models chart the history of competitive sailing. Mid-May to October 31 daily 10am to 5pm. Admission is $3 for adults, free for children under 12.

Farther along Ocean Drive, past Hammersmith Farm (described above) is **Brenton Point State Park.** The dramatically scenic preserve borders the Atlantic, with nothing to impede the waves rolling in and collapsing on the rock-strewn beach. These aren't the towering breakers of the West Coast, but are usually high enough for rather sedate surfing. Scuba divers are seen surfacing offshore and anglers enjoy casting from the long breakwater. In one part of the park, inshore of Ocean Drive, folks fly kites in such numbers they are in danger of crashing into each other.

There are other beaches more appropriate for swimming. The longest and most popular is **Easton's Beach,** which lies along Route 138A, the extension of Memorial Boulevard, east of town. It has a carousel, picnic areas, a large bathhouse, and the **Newport Aquarium** (☎ **401/849-9430**). On Ocean Drive, less than two miles from the south end of Bellevue Avenue, is **Gooseberry Beach,** privately owned, but open to the public.

✪ **Cliff Walk** skirts the edge of the southern section of town where most of the Cottages were built, and provides better views of many of them than can be seen from the street. Traversing its length, high above the crashing surf, is more than a stroll, but less than an arduous hike. Think of it as a highly scenic fitness walk. For the full 3.5-mile length, start at the access point near the intersection of Memorial Boulevard and Eustis Avenue. For a shorter walk, start at the Forty Steps, at the end of Narragansett Avenue, off Bellevue. Leave the walk at Ledge Road and return via Bellevue Road. Figure two to three hours for the round-trip, and be warned that there are some rugged sections to negotiate.

Biking is one of the best ways to get around town, especially out to the mansions and along Ocean Drive, about 18 miles in a circular route from downtown and back. Among several rental agencies are **Firehouse Bicycle** (25 Mill St.; ☎ **401/ 847-5700**), **Ten Speed Spokes** (18 Elm St.; ☎ **401/847-5609**), and **Fun Rentals** (1 Commercial Wharf; ☎ **401/846-3474**). The last firm also rents mopeds.

Adventure Sports Rentals (Inn on Long Wharf, 142 Long Wharf; ☎ **401/ 849-4820**), not only rents bikes and mopeds, but outboard boats, kayaks, and sailboats, and arranges parasailing outings and fishing trips.

SHOPPING

At the heart of the downtown waterfront, Bannister's Wharf, Bowen's Wharf, and Brick Marketplace have about 60 stores between them, none of them especially compelling. More interesting, if only for their quirky individuality, are the shops along Lower Thames Street. For example, **Aardvark Antiques** (no. 475), specializes in salvaged architectural components and larger items rescued from old houses. Books, nautical charts, and sailing videos are offered at **Armchair Sailor** (no. 543), and for vintage clothing, visit **Cabbage Rose** (no. 493).

Spring Street is noted for its antique shops, but purveyors of crafts, jewelry, and folk art are also scattered among them. One of these is **MacDowell Pottery** (no. 140), which has carvings from Indonesia and the Philippines and ceramics by Rhode Island artisans; another, the nearby **J.H. Breakell & Co.** (no. 135) is a good source for handcrafted sterling and gold jewelry. Antique boat models, including mounted half-hulls and miniatures in bottles, are displayed along with charts and navigational instruments at **The Nautical Nook** (no. 86). For a pricey memento of Newport's Gilded Age history, check out **The Drawing Room/The Zsolnay Store** (no. 152– 154), which stocks 19th-century furnishings and accessories, many from local estates. Folk art and furniture are primary goods at **Liberty Tree** (no. 104).

Spring intersects with Franklin Street, which harbors even more antique shops in its short length, alongside the post office. **Newport China Trade Co.** (no. 8) deals in export porcelain and objects associated with 19th-century China. Take a fat wallet to **The John Gidley House** (no. 22) for European antiques of high order. **Patina** (no. 32) is another dealer in Americana and folk art.

Note that most of these dealers have their own notions about what are appropriate operating hours and may not be open when other stores are.

WHERE TO STAY

The **visitor information office** (☎ **401/849-8040**) provides a useful service to those who arrive in town without reservations. All the motels, hotels, and inns that have vacancies that night are listed on a frequently updated board. Most have a number next to their names, to be called from the free direct-line phones located nearby. With dozens of possibilities, there is nearly always something available, even in summer, but less impulsive travelers will want to make reservations in advance to be certain of getting what they want, especially for weekends from June through Labor Day. **Newport Reservations** (☎ **800/842-0102** or 401/842-0102, fax 401/842-0104) is one free service representing a number of hotels, motels, inns, and B&Bs. **Anna's Victorian Connection** (☎ **401/849-2489**) is similar, but charges a fee and doesn't represent hotels or motels. They accept credit cards.

EXPENSIVE

Doubletree Islander. Goat Island, Newport, RI 02840. ☎ **800/222-8733** or 401/849-2600. Fax 401/846-7210. 253 rms. A/C TV TEL. $105–$254 double. AE, CB, DC, DISC, MC, V.

More than 25 years old, previously a Hilton and then a Sheraton, the Doubletree is notable primarily for its full hotel services and its intriguing location on an island on the northern end of Newport Harbor. There are delightful views from most of its rooms (some of which have balconies), a fitness center, indoor and outdoor pools, two tennis courts, racquetball courts, formal and casual eating places, and a lounge. Most of the staff endeavor to be pleasant, which helps to counter the inherent impersonality of such establishments.

✪ **Cliffside Inn.** 2 Seaview Ave. (near Cliff Ave.), Newport, RI 02840. ☎ **800/845-1811** or 401/847-1811. Fax 401/848-5850. 15 rms and suites. A/C TV TEL. $165–$325 double. Rates include breakfast. AE, DISC, MC, V.

Assuming that cost is not of paramount concern, there are really only two places to stay in Newport—this and the Francis Malbone House (below). It is difficult to imagine what further improvements might be made in these accommodations. Taking it from the top, 11 of the 15 units have whirlpool baths and working fireplaces; all have nightly turndown service and terry-cloth robes. Antiques and admirable reproductions are generously deployed, including Eastlake originals and entrancing Victorian fancies. Two-headed partner showers are common, and in one room there's an amusing "birdcage" shower from 1890. Favorite units are the "Garden Suite," a duplex with private garden and a big double bath with radiant heat beneath the Peruvian tile floors, and the "Tower Suite," with a green marble bath, a mini-fireplace next to the step-up window seat, and a cedar-lined steeple above the bed. A young, conscientious staff anticipates most needs, as with coffee and juice delivered to rooms in anticipation of the full breakfast.

✪ **Francis Malbone House.** 392 Thames St. (east of Memorial Dr.), Newport, RI 02840. ☎ **800/846-0392** or 401/846-0392. Fax 401/848-5956. 18 rms. A/C TV TEL. $135–$325 double. Rates include breakfast. AE, MC, V.

Nine new rooms have just been added in an attached wing of the original 1760 Colonial house. Very nice, they are, with king-size beds, working fireplaces, and excellent reproductions of period furniture. Four of them share two sunken gardens and three have whirlpool baths built for two. But given a choice, take a room in the old section. There, antiques outnumber repros, glowing Oriental rugs lie upon buffed wide-board floors, and silks and linens are deployed unsparingly. (There are no TVs in the main building, though. They'd destroy the effect.) In the front hall is a print of a painting by Gilbert Stuart of shipping merchant Francis Malbone and his brother. A full breakfast is served in the morning and afternoon refreshments are set out. The most interesting parts of the waterfront are right outside the door. No smoking, no pets, and no children under 12.

Wynstone. 232 Spring St. (near Memorial Blvd.), Newport, RI 02840. ☎ **800/524-1386**, 401/848-5300, or 401/849-7397. 5 rms. A/C TV. $195–$285 double. Rates include breakfast. MC, V.

When last seen, the paint was still drying on this restored Greek Revival house and the first official guests weren't to arrive for two days. Obviously, the service couldn't be evaluated, but the owners have a track record, with three other operating inns in town. (The reservation numbers above are used for all four properties.) They let out the stops here, with Ralph Lauren bed linens, double Jacuzzis, robes in every room, working fireplaces, green marble or terra-cotta tile baths, and gorgeous oak mantlepieces. In one room, the massive custom-made California king-size bed is so high off the floor a guest sitting in the bathtub can see *under* it to the fireplace on the other side. Rooms all have cable TV and some have VCRs. Breakfasts are substanial. It remains to be seen whether the Wynstone will eventually compete on an equal footing with the Francis Malbone or the Cliffside, but it strives mightily.

MODERATE

Admiral Fitzroy. 398 Thames St. (east of Memorial Blvd.), Newport, RI 02840. ☎ **800/343-2863** or 401/848-8000. Fax 401/848-8006. 18 rms. A/C TV TEL. $85–$195 double. Rates include breakfast. AE, CB, DC, DISC, MC, V.

The largest of another group of four local inns, this one attracts a substantial foreign clientele, most of them Europeans and Australians drawn to the many international yachting events that begin or end in Newport. Despite the current name, the antique barometers, and the ship model at the end of the reception desk, this used to be a nunnery. That isn't meant to suggest Spartan gloom. Rehabilitating old domestic and commercial structures is a central interest of the owners, whose attention to detail is seen in the hand-painted walls with floral renderings found in every room. Many rooms have "peek" harbor views, but better still, take a glass of wine up to the roof deck, which offers a 360° panorama. In addition to the breakfast buffet, the kitchen serves a choice of three or four hot dishes each morning. The staff is unfailingly pleasant, although they have a tendency to absent themselves with some frequency. Since they accept children, as many inns do not, lots of families make this home base. Pets are discouraged, however.

If the 1854 Fitzroy is full, reservations can be made through the same telephone numbers for the similar Admiral Benbow (93 Pelham St.) and the Admiral Farragut (31 Clarke St.). They rotate two- to four-week closings each winter.

Beech Tree. 34 Rhode Island Ave., Newport, RI 02840. ☎ **401/847-9794.** 8 rms, 1 apt. A/C TV TEL. $79–$215 double. Rates include breakfast. AE, DISC, MC, V. Drive north on Broadway from downtown and turn right on Rhode Island Ave. It's the eighth house on the left.

Arrive here on a Friday evening and the avuncular owner will sit you down to a bowl of Newport chowder, fresh bread, and a glass of wine. After that, a lot of guests skip dinner and go straight upstairs to soak away their road trip in a whirlpool bath. On the dining room wall are photos of the owner with Sandy Dennis and Soupy Sales and one of their sons with George Bush. They are brief distractions from the other big event of the day—perhaps the most elaborate and filling breakfast served by any B&B in Newport. There are bagels, muffins, pastries, fruit bowls, and five juices to pave the way for plates heaped with eggs to order, waffles, pancakes, sausages, and/or bacon. Lunch will be irrelevant. The owners even leave out bottles of brandy and cordials and invite guests to help themselves. Except for one of the two bedrooms of the upstairs apartment, all the rooms have king- or queen-size beds and good reading chairs. The flowery decor won't be to everyone's taste, but the value is so good, it can easily be ignored (the $215 rate quoted above is for the inn's single suite in summer). A family atmosphere prevails.

Castle Hill. Ocean Dr., Newport, RI 02840. ☎ **401/849-3800.** Fax 401/849-3838. 40 rms. TEL. $65–$200 double. Rates include breakfast. AE, MC, V.

With 40 beautiful oceanfront acres on a near-island with its own lighthouse, it isn't difficult to forgive the management for the sorely needed but agonizingly piecemeal renovation of the 1874 Victorian mansion. The venerable taproom and its handsome bar are sheathed in wood, with a riveting view of sailing ships on Narragansett Bay that is shared with the dining room and deck. So far, so good. It is in the bedrooms that the impression of genteel shabbiness is most evident. Furnishings are mostly old, not antique, and artlessly arranged. There are no televisions and only two air conditioners to justify the high summer tariffs (the $200 quoted above is the summer rate for the inn's most expensive double), although they are promised soon, as are private marble baths for all rooms, king- or queen-size beds, and more air conditioners. If any of those items are important to you, be sure to confirm their installation when booking. Primitive lodgings are deemed a virtue by some guests, who reserve the separate "Beach Cottages" down the hill. Lacking central heating and just about everything else invented since Edison, they are furnished in yard-sale remnants—bunk beds, rudimentary chairs and tables—and are available only in summer. Some of them have kitchens, though, and children and smoking are acceptable, which are not in the main house. Weekly rentals are $750 to $850. Breakfasts are expansive; main courses at dinner cost $16 to $28.

Clarkeston. 28 Clarke St., Newport, RI 02840. ☎ **800/524-1386,** 401/846-8242, or 401/849-7397. 9 rms. A/C TEL. $95–$245 double. Rates include breakfast. MC, V.

The charcoal gray exterior enhances the house, built around 1705, one of the oldest in town. Its age means that rooms tend to be small, but not oppressively so. They are named for famous Newport residents—Doris Duke, Ms. Astor, Harry Belmont—none of whom stayed here, as far as is known. The owners have dressed it up with his-and-her walkaround shower stalls and feather-padded mattress covers. Whirlpools and name-brand Jacuzzis have also been installed, and there are a few working fireplaces. Hot water comes up almost instantly, which seems not all that important unless you have waited 10 minutes in other inns for that to happen. All guests are welcome to store food in a fridge in the ground-floor lobby, and a full breakfast is served in the front parlor.

If the inn is full, the same owners have the less elegant **Cleveland House,** directly across the street. Built in 1885, this former rooming house has been perked up with marble baths and four-poster beds, but is well short of memorable. The best rooms are in back. Breakfast is skimpier than across the street. Prices are as low as $55 for a double. Both inns are on Clarke Street, a short block toward the waterfront off Mary Street, west of Spring Street.

Elm Tree Cottage. 336 Gibbs Ave., Newport, RI 02840. ☎ **800/882-3356** or 401/849-1610. Fax 401/849-2084. 5 rms, 1 suite. A/C. $115–$225 double. Rates include breakfast. AE, MC, V.

Only a couple of blocks from the beach, this B&B gets enough laudatory magazine ink to elevate it among Newport's best-known inns. The flamboyant Victorian manse is a pleasure to behold, inside and out. In an agreeable deviation from local convention, many of the furnishings, especially the beds, are French in origin, albeit of, or reflecting, the Victorian time period. Louis XV is a central inspiration, but much of the decor was obtained at estate auctions. All but one of the rooms have fireplaces, in which only Duraflame logs may be burned. One of the owners creates stained-glass panels and plays musical instruments in the spare time that only busy innkeepers seem to be able to find. Look for the bar with silver dollars imbedded in its surface in the sitting room, where she has two pianos and puts out refreshments in the afternoon. Breakfasts are ample. Children must be 14 or over. No pets, no smoking.

Inntowne. Thames and Mary sts., Newport, RI 02840. ☎ **800/457-7803** or 401/846-9200. Fax 401/846-1534. 26 rms. A/C TEL. $95–$179 double. AE, MC, V.

Location is paramount here, since it is at the edge of one of the most active strips of Thames Street and in walking distance of everything appealing along the waterfront. Parking is a bummer—$12.25 a night across the street in a municipal lot. Some visitors find the reception cordial, others judge it unresponsive. Either way, rooms are comfortable, most with four-poster or canopied beds. Breakfast is a little skimpy, but afternoon tea is an agreeable extra. TV is available only in the common room. My recommendation is less than wholehearted, but the Inntowne surpasses many equally visible operations along the waterfront, and has more available rooms than most.

Mill Street. 75 Mill St., Newport, RI 02840 (2 blocks east of Thames). ☎ **800/392-1316** or 401/849-9500. Fax 401/848-5131. 23 suites. A/C TV TEL. $65–$295 suite. Rates include breakfast. Children under 16 stay free in parent's room. AE, CB, DC, MC, V.

Something different from most Newport inns, this turn-of-the-century sawmill was scooped out and rebuilt from the walls in. Apart from exposed expanses of brick and an occasional wood beam, all of it is new. The designers chose to create an all-suite facility, each with a queen-size bed in the bedroom and a convertible sofa in the sitting room. It's a good deal for families. The more expensive duplexes have private balconies, but everyone can use the rooftop deck, where breakfast is served on warm days. A new manager has been brought in to upgrade the inn to the luxury level it already pretends to have achieved. While the staff doesn't prohibit smoking on premises, they don't put out ashtrays, either.

INEXPENSIVE

Jailhouse. 13 Marlborough St. (east of Thames St.), Newport, RI 02840. ☎ **401/847-4638.** Fax 401/849-3023. 21 rms. A/C TV TEL. $45–$215 double. AE, MC, V.

They claim that this was once a colonial jail, although it doesn't look as if it's that old or served that purpose. In any case, the management hams up the incarceration theme, with references to its "prison staff," the "cell block" rooms, legal notices, and speed limit signs. Someone thinks this is cute and clever. It isn't, but there are compensations. Price, primarily. Even during a festival week in July, a room can be had here for as little as $55 (the high rate noted above is for a two-bedroom "maximum security" suite.) And that includes motel conveniences like cable TV with HBO, as well as continental breakfasts, afternoon tea, and a mini-fridge in every room. Listless efforts at decor have pegboards instead of closets, but also new baths and carpeting. It's on the same block as the White Horse Tavern. Children and smoking are okay, but not pets. And maybe they'll think better of the barred reception desk before you get there.

Pilgrim House. 123 Spring St. (between Mary and Church sts.), Newport, RI 02840. ☎ **800/525-8373** or 401/846-0040. 11 rms. A/C. $60–$175 double. MC, V.

This narrow, four-story, elevator-less mid-Victorian has as its most notable feature a rooftop deck with unobstructed harbor views. On good days, the "enhanced" continental breakfast can be taken out there. Afternoon refreshments might be sherry and shortbread. While rooms are without phones or TV, they do have clock radios, and the cozy common room has a fireplace, TV, and VCR. The two cheapest rooms share a bath, logical for a family of three or four. Smoking isn't allowed and children must be over 12. Their brochure says they're open all year, but they usually close in January.

WHERE TO DINE
EXPENSIVE

Canfield House. 5 Memorial Blvd. (behind the Tennis Hall of Fame). ☎ **401/847-0416.** Main courses $9.95–$25.95. AE, DC, DISC, MC, V. Daily 5–10pm. NEW AMERICAN.

Named for the gambler who ran a casino in this house from 1897 to 1907, this restaurant possesses the grandeur of dimension and decor suitable for the society swells who were his customers. That still applies. The main room has a high-vaulted mahogany ceiling, and the lounge, a fireplace and leaded glass panels above the bar. Male patrons are often sockless in Guccis, with green trousers and blue blazers carrying about 30 gold buttons each. They are with bronzed and shiny women who look as if they spend 10 months of the year in San Diego. Sprinkled among them are officers attending the Navy War College and yachtsmen just in from Bermuda. The restaurant closed for a while for retooling and opened again in spring of 1996, with lowered prices and an improved kitchen. The word went out fast, and it was doing hefty business in a few weeks, not months. The food isn't haute, by any means, despite some of the fevered hoorahs it has received. But it is prepared to order and attractively presented, things like grilled tuna with mango salsa ringed with garlic mashed potatoes, baby carrots, asparagus, roasted tomatoes, dressed greens, and yellow squash. On one plate. Obviously, appetizers and desserts can be skipped.

There are four spacious bedrooms upstairs renting for $80 to $100 a night, but they share a lone bathroom.

Le Bistro. Bannister's Wharf (near America's Cup Ave.). ☎ **401/849-7778.** Main courses $13.95–$33.95. AE, DC, DISC, MC, V. Daily 11:30am–11pm. FRENCH.

One night last July, the people at the next table suddenly dropped their menus and left. Whether they thought the service too slow or the cost too high, they were about 50% right. The lone waitress was required to cover too many tables and some of the prices did slip over the edge of reason, given the fairly routine surroundings on the second and third floors of the building. Still, the kitchen might well be the most capable in town, assembling lightened versions of French country standards. A rough country pâté is worth the wait, which can be spent nibbling at the crusty bread while checking out fellow guests. They are a prosperous and congenial lot, Rolexes peeking out from the cuffs of Ralph Lauren sweats when they lean over to strike up conversations with their neighbors. (It helps if you have a 50-footer moored in the harbor.) Once they get caught up in seeing and being seen, they barely notice the excellent bouillabaisse, the Burgundian sausage with hot potato salad, the spicy fettuccine with fresh fat clams and big chunks of tomato. By then, they have forgotten the lapses.

✪ White Horse Tavern. Marlborough and Farewell sts. ☎ **401/849-3600.** Main courses $25–$33. AE, DC, DISC, MC, V. Wed–Mon noon–3pm, daily 6–10pm. NEW AMERICAN.

It may not be the oldest operating tavern in America, as is claimed, but since it's still going strong after 324 years, there can't be too many other healthy claimants. It was once the two-story residence of Francis Brinley, a pirate turned tavernkeeper, and while it has obviously undergone many alterations and renovations, it retains its authenticity. On the ground floor are a bar and two dining rooms, one small, one large, with a big fireplace once used for cooking. The upstairs has a similar arrangement. Given the setting, the kitchen could have chosen to coast on boiled dinners and baked apples. But the food is quite good, from the daily soup-and-sandwich lunch specials to the thick, mesquite-grilled veal chop with an ancho rub and applejack reduction sauce. About a third of the dishes involve seafood. They wouldn't be so gauche as to call it "surf 'n' turf," but the grilled lobster and veal paillard braised in a roasted garlic and lemon broth scented with rosemary is a highly refined version of the same. Prices are significantly lower at lunch and at Sunday brunch. Men must wear jackets at night.

MODERATE TO EXPENSIVE

Black Pearl. Bannister's Wharf. ☎ **401/846-5264.** Reservations required for dinner in Commmodore's Room. Main courses, tavern $13.50–$22.50; Commodore's Room $17.50–$35. AE, MC, V. Tavern daily 11am–11pm, Commodore daily 11:30am–2:30pm and 6–11pm. SEAFOOD/AMERICAN.

This long building near the end of the wharf is divided into two sections. The "Tavern" has an atmospheric bar of indeterminate age and a room painted mostly in black with framed marine charts on the walls. The "Commodore's Room" isn't all that different, except it's green, more formal, and a two-pound lobster goes for $35, with trimmings. The simpler preparations of fish, duck, and beef are the ones to order. In the Tavern, don't miss the definitive Newport chowder, followed by a Pearlburger or one of the other overstuffed sandwiches. And in summer, the menu is similar at the dining patio and an open-air bar out on the wharf. Men are required to wear jackets at dinner in the Commodore's Room.

Cooke House. Bannister's Wharf. ☎ **401/849-2900.** Main courses, Candy Store and Grill $11.95–$21.95; Dining Room $21–$30. AE, DC, DISC, MC, V. Candy Store and Grill daily 11:30am–10:30pm; Dining Room daily 6–10pm. ECLECTIC.

For many, this is the quintessential Newport eating place. Most of its several levels are open to the air in summer and glassed-in in winter, with overhead fans dispersing the sea breezes. Several bars lubricate conversation, the one on the main floor with a five-foot model of a schooner on the back wall and the real thing straining at hawsers right outside. The 19th-century structure was moved to the wharf from America's Cup Boulevard in the 1970s. Up on the formal third floor, they sauté your lobster out of the shell while you put away appetizers of lobster ravioli and wild mushroom with leeks and morels bound with mushroom butter ($9.50) or duck foie gras terrine with black mission fig compote ($17.50). If that seems too rich for wallet or liver, spare the walk upstairs and opt for swordfish with red pepper coulis or the Thai-style whole-wheat spaghetti with jalapeño, bean sprouts, shrimp, cilantro, and peanuts. At one side is an espresso bar, and people stop in throughout the day for a latte or a beer or sandwich.

Scales & Shells. 527 Lower Thames St. ☎ **401/846-3474.** Reservations not accepted. Main courses $6.95–$17.95. No credit cards. Sun–Thurs 5–10pm, Fri–Sat 5–11pm. SEAFOOD.

That graceless name is an accurate reflection of the uncompromising character of this clangorous fish house. Diners who insist upon a modicum of elegance should cross this off their list, or at least head for the upstairs room, called "Upscales," which is less boisterous, if hardly sedate. Fans of Boston's Legal Sea Foods will recognize the drill, if not the more rugged surroundings. A waiting list lengthens at the door as the evening wears on. Lots of different fish and shellfish at mid-range prices are listed on the big blackboard in back. An open kitchen with a low counter starts almost at the door—no secrets there. They put together ingredients in guileless preparations that allow the natural tastes to prevail. Salmon with a puddle of crab dill butter and bluefish with black olives and grilled yellow peppers are typical. Also in front is a three-sided bar, where the stressed bartender not only pours every drink, but opens every clam and oyster served. Ask him for a New England brew called smuttynose, and give the man a good tip.

INEXPENSIVE TO MODERATE

Ⓢ **Anthony's Seafood.** Waites Wharf (off Thames St.). ☎ 401/848-5058. Reservations not accepted. Main courses $5.95–$14.95. AE, MC, V. Daily 11am–9pm. Closed Dec to mid-Apr. AMERICAN/SEAFOOD.

It couldn't be less casual, with paper plates of food set down on wooden picnic tables. The star meal combo is a New England shore dinner, encompassing chowder, steamed clams, Portuguese sausage, corn-on-the-cob, and lobster. Or you can choose from an extensive list of sandwiches (such as lobster or clam rolls), salads, pastas, and fried dinners of shrimp, scallops, oysters, and combo plates. A free cup of chowder comes with every entree. The restaurant is now fully licensed.

Brick Alley Pub. 140 Thames St. ☎ **401/849-6334.** Reservations recommended. Main courses $8.95–$17.95. Mon–Fri 11:30am–midnight, Sat–Sun 11am–midnight. ECLECTIC.

So you know what you're getting into, the cab of a red Chevy pickup truck is next to the soup and salad bar. Walls are covered with old advertising posters and a room in back has a pool table, pinball machine, and video games. Families, tourists, working stiffs, and yachtsmen squeeze through the doors into the thronged front dining rooms, the bar in the middle, and out onto the tree-shaded terrace in back. They're big on frozen daiquiris. The 18-page menu doesn't leave much out: baked stuffed clams, six Caesar salads, hot cherry peppers stuffed with prosciutto and provolone, Cajun catfish, nachos, 20 kinds of burgers, seven pizzas, chicken teriyaki, and "triple hot buffalo shrimp pasta," whatever that might be, accompanied by the admonition, "No crybabies!" Tuesdays are Mexican Fiesta Days. It's loud and good-natured and prices are palatable if you avoid lobster. The bars stay open later than the kitchen.

Music Hall Café. 250 Thames St. ☎ **401/848-2330.** Main courses $9.50–$17.50. AE, DISC, MC, V. Daily noon–2:30pm and 5:30–10pm. TEX/MEX.

Named for the 1894 building in which it is located, this restaurant seems straight from Santa Fe. Windows and arches painted on one wall suggest haciendas, and there are carvings of howling coyotes, a kiva ladder, bleached skulls, and hand-painted Mexican tiles on the bar. Under the hard-to-miss tri-colored awning out front is a row of green tables, ideal for evaluating the Thames Street scene. Barbecue is prominent, be it chicken, pork, ribs, or a combination. Along with the usual enchiladas, tamales, and assemble-your-own soft tacos are a number of grilled items, including crabcakes and chicken marinated with roasted red peppers and chipolte sauce. Vegetarian fare with a kick is also on the card. Even when every chair is occupied, the place isn't crowded.

NEWPORT AFTER DARK

While the Basque sport of jai alai is proclaimed the fastest in the world, the real reason for the existence of **Newport Jai Alai** (150 Admiral Kalbfus Rd.; ☎ **401/849-5000**) is gambling. In addition to the game itself, and its highly complicated scoring and odds systems, there are 432 video slot machines and simulcasts of horse races from around the country. Slots are open daily from 10am until 1am, and jai-alai games, from May to October, start at 7pm Wednesday to Friday, at noon Monday and Saturday, and at 1pm on Sunday.

The most likely places to spend an evening of elbow-bending, conversation, or listening to music lie along Thames Street. Bars are unthreatening, with casual places prevailing. The **Candy Store** of Cooke House (Bannister's Wharf) has a classic waterside bar. Nearby, two of the most obvious possibilities are **The Red Parrot** (Memorial Boulevard and Thames Street), which has the passing look of an Irish saloon and jazz combos Friday to Sunday all year, and **One Pelham East** (Thames and Pelham streets), with a cafe to one side, a small dance floor, and a stage for rockers at the front. A full schedule of live music is on the plate at the **Newport Blues Café** (Thames and Green streets) with bands and shouters Monday to Saturday evenings in season (Thursday to Saturday off-season) and a Sunday gospel brunch. Meals are available 5 to 10pm.

4 South County: From Wickford to Watch Hill

Travelers rushing along the Boston–New York corridor inevitably choose I-95 to get from Providence to the Connecticut border. They do not have the time for a detour or do not know that the nearby shore has some of the best beaches and most congenial fishing and resort villages of New England. This is called "South County," a designation that has no official status, but refers to the coast that is the southerly edge of Bristol County. Definitions are fuzzy, but for our purposes, South County runs from Wickford, near Providence, to Westerly, nudging Connecticut. Times to avoid are weekends in July and August, when the crush of day-trippers can turn these two-lane roads into parking lots. Worst of all is arriving on a Friday afternoon and departing on a Sunday evening. If those are your only options, however, lock in lodging reservations at least a few days in advance.

To get to South County from Providence or Boston, pick up I-95 south, leaving it at Exit 9 to pick up Route 4, also a limited-access highway. In about seven miles, exit onto Route 102 east, and you'll soon arrive in Wickford. From Newport, cross the Newport and Jamestown bridges on Route 138 to Route 1A north, and take it to Wickford. Narragansett, at the center of South County's beach country, is 32 miles southwest of Providence, and 14 miles west of Newport.

Apart from those summer weekends, a day or two in South County is as stress-free and laid-back as an outing can be. There is nothing that can be regarded as a must-see sight, hardly any museums to speak of, and only a couple of historic houses to divert from serious cafe-sitting, sun-soaking, and shop-browsing, the chief pursuits in **Wickford,** a tidy village that crowds the cusp of a compact harbor. Sailors and fishermen, artists and craftspeople are among the inhabitants, all of them evident within a block on either side of the Brown Street bridge that crosses the narrow neck of the waterway connecting Academy Cove with the harbor. Most of the shopping of interest is there, slipping over to adjoining Main Street. Buildings in the area are largely survivors from the 18th and 19th century. Parking is usually easy to find, for this is the quiet end of South County. One place that catches the eye is **The Shaker Shop** (16 West Main St.; ☎ 401/294-7779), which features handcrafted replicas of the clean-limbed furniture of the eponymous religious sect. Quilts, baskets, and boxes are also displayed. Next to the shop, at the same street address, is **Peaches** (☎ 401/294-5771), a self-described tearoom that is just the spot for a snack, a light meal, or simply a glass of iced tea. The basket of garlic-and-paprika-dusted pita triangles with a bowl of hummus hits the spot, as does the "tugboat" of chili served in a bowl made from a round of sourdough bread. Salads and sandwiches are available, too.

A mile north of town is **Smith's Castle** (Route 1; ☎ 401/294-3521). It isn't a castle at all, but a farmhouse on a site where Roger Williams once had a trading post. The property was sold to Richard Smith in 1651, while the core of the present structure, a clapboard farmhouse, went up in 1678. It is presently undergoing an extensive renovation, so don't make a special trip. Tours are limited to weekends, June through September, and only from noon to 4pm.

Proceed south on Route 1A, known through here as Boston Neck Road. About a mile south of Hamilton, watch for the side street on the right marked for the **Gilbert Stuart Birthplace** (815 Gilbert Stuart Rd.; ☎ 401/294-3001). This may be the one historic homestead in South County that is worth a detour, not because the painter famous for his portraits of George Washington was born here. After all, he left for good in young adulthood, and none of his original art is on display. Rather, it is the setting and the two preserved buildings that reward a visit. First is a weathered gristmill dating from the late 1600s; second, the Stuart birthplace itself, built over his father's snuff mill. The undershot waterwheel and millstones still work, powered by controlled discharges from the adjacent pond. Admission is $3 for adults, $1 for children 6 to 12, and you have to go on the guided tour. Open from April 1 to November 1, Thursday to Monday from 11am to 4:30pm.

Still on Route 1A, on the right, south of Saunderstown, is the **Casey Farm** (☎ 401/295-1030). Owned by the Society for the Preservation of New England Antiquities, the still-working 300-acre farmstead is a handsome 18th-century complex of barns and houses. Free-ranging chickens hop along carefully laid stone walls that section the fields. Unfortunately, the farm is only open to visitors June 1 to October 15 Tuesday, Thursday, and Saturday from 1 to 5pm.

Continuing south on 1A, the pace quickens, at least from late spring to foliage season. After crossing the Narrow River Inlet, the road bends toward the series of consecutive beaches around Narragansett Pier, the name of which derives from a 19th-century amusement wharf that no longer exists.

Since ocean waves break upon the sand at an angle, there is enough action to permit decent surfing at **East Matunuck State Beach.** In the middle of it all is **The Towers,** a massive stone structure that spans the road between cylindrical towers with conical roofs. It is all that remains of the Gilded Age Narragansett Casino, which was designed by the New York firm of McKim, Mead & White. In the seaward tower is the **Narragansett Tourist Information Office** (☎ 401/783-7121), run by the local chamber of commerce, which can help you find lodging. Nearby, on the left, the 1888 **Coast Guard House** (40 Ocean Rd.; ☎ 401/789-0700) is now a highly regarded restaurant. It has recovered from a devastating 1991 hurricane, and enjoys unobstructed views of beach and ocean from its wraparound picture windows. There are several inns and hotels in the vicinity, many of them looking out over the water across wide lawns. McKim, Mead & White had yet another commission in what is now a B&B, **Stone Lea** (40 Newton Ave.; ☎ 401/783-9546). Situated near the crest of a cliff that falls into the ocean, it is an antique-filled delight to wander through, if a bit formal in tone. Seven rooms rent for $85–$125 double, including breakfast. MasterCard and Visa are accepted.

A few blocks before The Towers, Route 1A makes a sharp right turn (west), but stick to the shore, proceeding south on Ocean Road. Soon you'll pass **Scarborough State Beach,** a favorite destination of veteran beachgoers, although often jammed with frolicking young people. Following that road to the end, you'll reach the **Point Judith Lighthouse** (1460 Ocean Rd.; ☎ 401/789-0444). Built in 1816, the brick beacon is a photo op that can be approached but not entered. Backtrack along Ocean Road, turning left on Route 108, then left again on Sand Hill Cove Road, past the dock of the only year-round ferries to Block Island, and into the Port of Galilee.

The impulse to drive as far as you can without winding up in the drink may account for the popularity of **George's of Galilee** (250 Sand Hill Cove Rd.; ☎ 401/783-2306). It can't be the food, which is ordinary, nor the service, which is slap-dash. Anyway, prices aren't exorbitant, and while it can be brassy on weekends, its decks give good vantage to watch the heavy boat and ferry traffic on the adjacent channel. As for food, any of the nearby eating places are likely to do as well. Beyond George's parking lot is the redundantly named **Salty Brine State Beach.** Though small, it is protected by a long breakwater that blunts the waves produced by the passing vessels, and is a good choice for families with younger children.

To get a better sense of the area from the water, consider the 1³/₄-hour tour on the ***Southland*** (State Pier, Galilee; ☎ 401/783-2954), a Mississippi riverboat that hugs the coast as it moves past fishing villages and beaches. Prices are $6 for adults, $4 for children 4 to 12. Reservations aren't necessary and there's a bar and snack counter on board. Another possible excursion is a **whale-watching cruise** on the three boats of the ***Frances Fleet*** (2 State St., Point Judith; ☎ 800/662-2824 or 401/783-4988). Cruises are made July 1 through Labor Day Monday to Saturday from 1pm to about 6pm, depending on the location of the whales. It's isn't cheap, at $30 for adults, $27

Rhode Island & the South County

MASS.
R.I.

CONN.

Woonsocket

Pascoag
Pascoag Res.
Glendale

Smithfield

Manville

Valley Falls

N. Providence
PROVIDENCE ★
Pawtucket

E. Providence

Fran Lake
Scituate Res.
Cranston

Westconnaug Res.

Flat River Res.
Quidnick Res.

W. Warwick
Anthony

Barrington
Warren

FALL RIVER

Warwick

Bristol

E. Greenwich

Carr Pond

Arcadia State Park

Arcadia

Prudence Island

Tiverton
Portsmouth

Wickford
Narragansett Bay
Conanicut Island
Saunderstown
Middletown

R.I.

Sakonnet River

Jamestown
Newport Bridge

NEWPORT

Kingston

Worden Pond
Wakefield

Westerly

Point Judith

Ferries to Block Island

Rhode Island Sound

Atlantic Ocean

Watch Hill

South County

CONN.

Kingston

Worden Pond
Wakefield

Narragansett Pier

East Matunuck State Beach
Galilee
Scarborough State Beach

Westerly

Matunuck

Point Judith

Misquamicut State Beach
Misquamicut
Watch Hill

Block Island Sound

for seniors, and $20 for children under 12, but the sight of a monster humpback leaping from the water is unforgettable. Numerous party and charter boats leave for fishing expeditions from Point Judith.

Leaving Galilee, drive north on 108 to Route 1, turning west on Route 1, toward Connecticut. Before long, it joins Route 1A and enters the township of **Westerly,** although the immediate area remains semi-rural. If it is time to stop for the night, or for dinner, watch for the entrance on the left to the **Shelter Harbor Inn** (10 Wagner Rd.; ☎ 401/322-8883). Parts of the main building date to 1810, and a genteel tone prevails thoughout. Several of the 23 rooms in three buildings have fireplaces, decks, or both. A rooftop whirlpool, two paddle tennis courts, and a croquet green are available and a shuttle takes guests to the private beach a mile away. A creative restaurant and honored wine cellar round out the picture. No pets. Rates are $72 to $126 double. American Express, MasterCard, and Visa are accepted.

Follow Route 1A west toward **Watch Hill,** a beautiful land's-end village that achieved its desirable resort status during the post–Civil War period and has retained it ever since. Many grand shingled summer mansions and gingerbread Queen Anne houses remain from that time. The north side of the point is the harbor, packed with pleasure boats, and along the south shore is **Misquamicut State Beach,** a long but often crowded strand. South of town on Watch Hill Road is the picturesque **Watch Hill Lighthouse** (viewable only from outside). Back in town at the small **Watch Hill Beach,** kids are sure to get a kick out of the nearby carousel, which dates to 1867. Shoppers have more than 50 boutiques to explore.

And for a rare East Coast treat, find a seat to watch the sun drop into the ocean. A good place to do that would be the **Watch Hill Inn** (38 Bay St.; ☎ 401/ 348-8912). All meals are served, largely in the unsurprising New England tradition, but with superb sunset views.

From Watch Hill, take Route 1A toward the Westerly Airport and pick up the Route 78 bypass around Westerly to Route 2 in Connecticut, following signs onto Interstate 95.

5 Block Island

Viewed from above or on a map, the island resembles a pork chop or a lumpy pear with a big bite out of the middle. Only 7 miles long and 3 miles wide, it is edged with long stretches of beach lifting at points into dramatic bluffs. The interior is dimpled with undulating hills, only rarely reaching above 150 feet in elevation. Its hollows and clefts cradle an alleged 365 sweetwater ponds, some no larger than a backyard swimming pool. That "bite" out of the western edge of the chop/ pear is **Great Salt Pond,** which almost succeeds in cutting the island in two, but, as it is, serves as a fine protected harbor for fleets of pleasure boats.

The only notable concentration of houses, businesses, hotels, and people is at **Old Harbor,** on the lower eastern shore, where the ferries from the mainland dock and where most of the few remaining commercial fishing boats moor. For the record, the island was named for Adrian Block, a Dutch explorer who briefly stepped ashore in 1641. The earliest European settlement was in 1661, and the island has since attracted the kinds of people who nurture fierce convictions of independence fueled in part by the streaks of paranoia that leads them to live on a speck of land with no physical connection to the mainland. That has meant farmers, pirates, fishermen, smugglers, scavengers, and entrepreneurs, all of them willing to deal with the realities of isolation, lonely winters, and occasional killer hurricanes. Today, that means about 800 permanent residents who tough it out nine months a year waiting for the sun to stay a while.

The challenges of island living aren't readily apparent to the tens of thousands of visitors who arrive every summer for a day or a season. They are wont to describe this as paradise, a commendation that seems to be assigned only to islands. And they are correct, at least if sun and sea and zephyrs are paramount considerations. Those elements transformed the island from an offshore afterthought into an accessible summer retreat for the urban middle-class after the Civil War, America's first taste of mass tourism. Unlike other such regions throughout the country that have lost their sprawling Victorian hotels to fire or demolition, Block Island has preserved many of its buildings from that time. They crowd around Old Harbor, providing most of the lodging base. Smaller inns and bed-and-breakfasts add more tourist rooms, most in converted houses built at the same time as the great hotels. There are only a bare handful of establishments that even look like motels, and building stock is marked, with few exceptions, by tasteful Yankee understatement. Angular structures covered in weathered gray shingles prevail.

Away from the sand and surf, it is an island of peaceful pleasures and gentle observations. Police officers wear Bermuda shorts. Children tend semi-permanent lemonade stands in front of picket fences and low hedges. Old-timers work their morning route along Water Street, barely making it to the other end in time for lunch, so many are the opportunities to exchange views and news.

ESSENTIALS

GETTING THERE   The Interstate Navigation Company (P.O. Box 482, New London, CT 06320; ☎ **401/783-4613**) provides most of the surface service, including passengers-only ferries on daily triangular routes between Providence, Newport, and Block Island from June 22 to September 2. Bicycles may be taken on board for a small extra fee. While reservations aren't required for passengers, get to the dock early, because the boats fill up quickly.

Getting a car to Block Island is something of a hassle and considerably more expensive. Car ferries of the **Nelseco Navigation Company** (same address and telephone as above) depart from the Port of Galilee at Point Judith, R.I. Apart from blacked-out days from Christmas to New Year's Day, there are daily departures all year, as few as one or two a day in winter to as many as 10 a day from early June to late August. Sailing time is usually 1 hour, 10 minutes.

Ferries leave New London, Conn., daily from early June to Labor Day at 9am (extra trips at 7:15pm Fridays) and return daily at 4:30pm. Sailing time is a little over two hours. Since the round-trip fare for a two- or three-day weekend for a car and a driver can total nearly $80—more, with additional passengers—consider parking in one of the nearby garages at Point Judith or New London. Block Island is small, rental bicycles and mopeds are readily available, there are cabs for longer distances, and most hotels and inns are within a few blocks of the docks. If you intend to take a car anyway, please understand that it is important to make reservations well in advance—a month or two isn't too early for weekend departures.

Service is also provided between Block Island and Montauk, at the eastern end of New York's Long Island, by **Viking Ferry Lines** (RD 1 Box 159, West Lake Drive, Montauk, NY 11954; ☎ **516/668-5700**). From late May to mid-October, there are daily departures at 9am, returning from Block Island at 4:30pm. Trips take about 1 hour 45 minutes. Only passengers and bicycles can be accommodated; parking is available in Montauk. As emphasized above, advance reservations are advised.

Westerly State Airport, near the Connecticut border, is the base for over a dozen regular daily flights to and from Block Island by **New England Airlines** (☎ **800/ 243-2460,** 401/596-2460 in Westerly, or 401/466-5881 on Block Island). Flights take 12 minutes, and are more frequent in the summer. They are supplemented by the June to October service of **Action Air** (☎ 800/243-8623 or 860/448-1646) from Groton, Conn. In either case, make advance reservations and allow for the possibility that not-infrequent coastal fogs will delay or cancel flights.

VISITOR INFORMATION If taking a car to the island, fill up before boarding the ferry. There is a rudimentary gas station—no signs, just a trailer office and nameless pumps—next to the post office. On the other side of the post office is a bank with an ATM, the only one on the island, last I checked.

The **Block Island Chamber of Commerce** (Water Street; Block Island, RI 02807; ☎ 401/466-2982) has knowledgeable attendants, many brochures, and can help you find lodging. It is open daily 10am to 5pm from April to mid-October, Monday to Saturday 10am to 4pm from mid-October to March. In addition, an information booth opens during ferry arrivals at the dock.

GETTING AROUND THE ISLAND Cars are allowed on the island, but roads are narrow, winding, and without shoulders, and drivers must contend with flocks of bicycles and mopeds, many of which are piloted by inexperienced riders. So assuming your physical condition is up to the task, it is recommended that you leave the car on the mainland and join the two-wheelers.

Several in-town shops and stands rent bikes and/or mopeds, most of them within a couple of blocks of the main ferry dock at Old Harbor. Rates for mountain bikes are typically $18 a day, with widely available discount coupons lowering that to $15. Mopeds rates vary, but are usually about $75 a day. One convenient source is **The Moped Man** (435 Water Street; ☎ 401/466-5011), on the main business street facing the dock. They rent both bikes and mopeds at the prices mentioned above. Similar outlets are **Island Moped and Bike** (behind Harborside Inn on Water Street; ☎ 401/466-2700) and **Esta's Bike Rentals** (Water Street; ☎ 401/466-2651). Several inns also rent bicycles, so a possible plan is to take a taxi from the ferry or airport to one of them, drop off luggage, and get around by bike after that. Two such inns are the **Seacrest** (207 High Street; ☎ 401/466-2882) and **Rose Farm** (Roslyn Road; ☎ 401/466-2034), but inquire about rentals when making room reservations—most hotels and inns have ready sources.

EXPLORING THE ISLAND

Little on the island distracts from the central missions of most visitors—sunning, cycling, lolling, and inhaling copious quantities of lobster, clams, chowders, and alcohol. There is only one museum, and it takes only about 20 minutes to cover, even for those enamored of local history. Add a couple of antique lighthouses, a wildlife refuge, and three topographical features of note, and that's about it, enough to provide destinations for a few cycling outings. A driving tour of every site on that list takes no more than two hours.

A couple of miles south of Old Harbor on what starts out as Spring Street is the **Southeast Lighthouse.** By the road is a tablet that claims that in 1590 a war party of 40 Mohegans was driven over the bluffs by the Manisseans, the Indians of Block Island. An undeniably appealing Victorian structure, the lighthouse's claim for attention lies primarily in the fact that it had to be moved 100 feet back from the eroding precipice a couple of years ago to save it. There is a free small exhibit on the ground floor, but the admission fee to the top is as steep as the stairs ($5). Continuing a hundred feet or so along the same road to the **Edward S. Payne Overlook,** paths from the small parking lot lead out to a promontory with views of the 160-foot-high **Mohegan Bluffs,** cliffs plunging down to the ocean. Pretty, yes; stunning, no.

Continuing in the same direction along the same road, which goes through other names and soon makes a sharp right turn inland, watch for the left (west) turn onto

Block Island

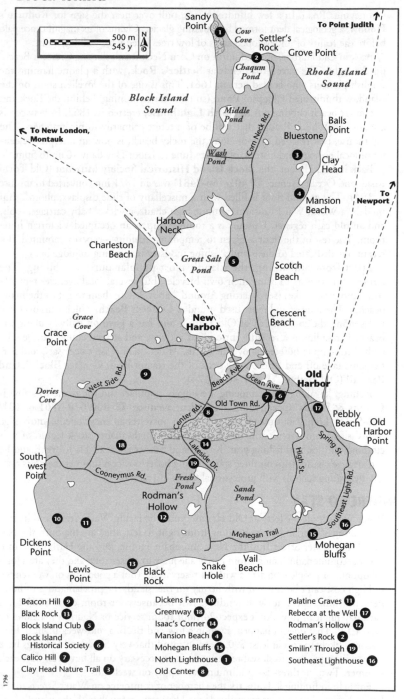

0 — 500 m
— 545 y
N

To Point Judith

To New London, Montauk

To Newport

Sandy Point
Cow Cove
Settler's Rock
Grove Point
Chaqum Pond
Rhode Island Sound
Block Island Sound
Middle Pond
Corn Neck Rd.
Balls Point
Bluestone
Wash Pond
Clay Head
Mansion Beach
Harbor Neck
Charleston Beach
Great Salt Pond
Scotch Beach
Crescent Beach
Grace Cove
Grace Point
New Harbor
Dories Cove
West Side Rd.
Beach Ave.
Ocean Ave.
Old Harbor
Old Town Rd.
Pebbly Beach
Old Harbor Point
Center Rd.
Lakeside Dr.
High St.
Spring St.
Southwest Point
Cooneymus Rd.
Fresh Pond
Rodman's Hollow
Sands Pond
Southeast Light Rd.
Dickens Point
Mohegan Trail
Mohegan Bluffs
Lewis Point
Black Rock
Snake Hole
Vail Beach

Beacon Hill **9**
Black Rock **13**
Block Island Club **5**
Block Island Historical Society **6**
Calico Hill **7**
Clay Head Nature Trail **3**
Dickens Farm **10**
Greenway **18**
Isaac's Corner **14**
Mansion Beach **4**
Mohegan Bluffs **15**
North Lighthouse **1**
Old Center **8**
Palatine Graves **11**
Rebecca at the Well **17**
Rodman's Hollow **12**
Settler's Rock **2**
Smilin' Through **19**
Southeast Lighthouse **16**

1796

455

Cooneymus Road. In a few hundred yards, pull over near the sign for **Rodman's Hollow,** a geological dent formed by a passing glacier. Claims of its magnificence pale before the reality of undeveloped acres of low trees laced with walking trails.

Back in Old Harbor, proceed north on Corn Neck Road, skirting Crescent Beach, on the right. The paved road ends at **Settler's Rock,** with a plaque naming the English pioneers who landed here in 1661. This is one of the loveliest spots on the island, with mirrored **Chaqum Pond** (suitable for swimming) behind the Rock and a scimitar beach curving out to **North Lighthouse,** erected in 1867. In between is a National Wildlife Refuge that will be of interest primarily to birdwatchers. The lighthouse, best reached by foot along the rocky beach, is now an interpretive center of local ecology and history, open late June to Labor Day daily 10am to 5pm.

Back in Old Harbor, the **Block Island Historical Society Museum** (Old Town Road. and Ocean Avenue; ☎ 401/466-2481) was an 1871 inn converted to this use in 1941. The ground floor is filled with a miscellany of slide displays, photos, ship models, a World War I uniform, antique high chairs, a wicker baby carriage, tools, and an old cash register. Upstairs is a room set up as an occupied Victorian hotel room. The rest of the floor is given to temporary exhibits—expertly mounted, if a recent one dedicated to the island's fishing industry is anything to judge by.

Apart from sunbathing, the island's most popular pursuit is biking. The ferries allow visitors to bring their own bicycles, but several local agencies rent 21-speed mountain bikes (see "Getting Around," above). Use them to get to the many beaches. The longest and most-used strand is **Crescent Beach,** which runs over two miles along the shore north of Old Harbor and has a pavilion halfway along the beach. Parasailing is a recently introduced activity, and striped chutes can be seen daily, lifting up to 600 feet above the ocean. Athletic ability isn't necessary, and participants take off and land on the deck of the tractor boat. Contact **Block Island Parasail** (Old Harbor; ☎ 401/466-2474).

Fishing, kayaking, and canoeing are hugely popular, and the name to know is **Oceans & Ponds** (Ocean and Connecticut avenues; ☎ 800/678-4701 or 401/466-5131). Loquacious owner Bruce Johnson possesses an encyclopedic knowledge of his island and doesn't stint on sharing it. His high-quality stock features Orvis clothing, duffles, and fishing gear. Kayaks and canoes are available for rent, and he can arrange charter trips on three sport-fishing boats. Twice a summer, he hosts one-day fly-fishing schools with professional Orvis instructors.

WHERE TO STAY

When you get off the ferry at Old Harbor, you'll be facing Water Street and its row of looming Victorian hotels. Reading from right to left, they are the Surf, the National, the Water Street Inn, the New Shoreham House, and the Harborside Inn. Their accommodations range from barely adequate to satisfactory, and they are a logical option for people who arrive without reservations (not a good idea on weekends).

High cost can't be equated with luxury on the island, the proclamations of hoteliers and innkeepers notwithstanding. Just because your room costs $225 for a Saturday night in July, don't expect 24-hour room service or Nautilus machines or even a TV. That doesn't happen. Even in a low-end B&B, a mid-week night in high season is likely to cost at least $90. Keep in mind that very few island lodgings have air-conditioning, but fresh seabreezes make it unnecessary on all but a few days each summer. Two- or three-day minimum stays apply on weekends.

For help in finding lodging, try the chamber of commerce on Water Street, to the left and around the corner from the dock. They stay in touch with the island's inns and B&Bs and can offer suggestions.

Anchor House Inn. 253 Spring St., Block Island, RI 02807. ☎ **800/730-0181** or 401/466-5021. 4 rms. TV TEL. $99–$130 double. Rates include breakfast. AE, MC, V.

A huge anchor out front marks this former eyesore, transformed into a virtually new B&B in 1996. For the moment, the available rooms are upstairs, while the owners decide what to do with the ground floor. Room decor is spare and restful, avoiding the frou-frou that afflicts too many other inns. Quilts on the beds and a few pictures by island artists are about it. All rooms have ceiling fans and private bathrooms with showers, not tubs. Breakfasts are of the hearty continental variety, typically including fruits, juices, bagels, fresh muffins, and quiche. No pets, no smoking, and children should be older than 12. Parking is limited.

✪ Atlantic. High St., Box 188, Block Island, RI 02807. ☎ **800/224-7422** or 401/466-5883. Fax 401/466-5678. 21 rms. TEL. $99–$210 double. Rates include breakfast. AE, MC, V.

Perched upon six rolling acres south of downtown, the 1879 Atlantic has a beguiling verandah. Drawn by the promise of spectacular sunsets and a special menu of nibbles and drinks, including the most diverse beer and wine selection on the island, guests and others start assembling from 3:30pm on. The flowers that brighten the many public and private rooms are grown on the property. Bedrooms are decorated almost entirely with antiques, a departure from the common practice at other inns of sprinkling a token few among the many reproductions. Note, for example, the magnificent grandfather clock in the lobby. The Atlantic shines most in its dining room, where they serve six-course fixed-price dinners ($45) whose components are changed weekly. The primary chefs are CIA-trained, so ingredients are the freshest available and presentations are as eye-pleasing as the food is gratifying.

The restlessly well-versed chef might decide on sea scallops marinated in citrus juices, swiftly seared, tossed in an orange-lime butter and surrounded by a whole-wheat pastry shell garnished with baby asparagus on one night, then move on to herb-encrusted game hen served with lingonberry sauce, red onion jam, and grilled polenta the next. Try to work it off on the two all-weather tennis courts. Children are welcome. Smoking isn't permitted. The hotel is open mid-April through October.

✪ Champlin's. Great Salt Pond, P.O. Box J, Block Island, RI 02807. ☎ **800/762-4551** or 401/466-2641. 30 rms. A/C TV. $125–$225 double. AE, MC, V. From Old Harbor, drive west on Ocean Ave., turn left on West Side Rd. The entrance road to Champlin's is on the right.

Families with kids are welcome at this all-inclusive resort, and there are 220 transient slips in the marina (for reservations call **800/762-4541**) for visiting yachtspeople. Those who can live without the tilted floors and idiosyncratic adornments of the Victorian inns will be pleased by the clean lines and muted fabrics of the bedrooms and the standard microwave ovens and compact fridges. Once you're unpacked, there isn't much to compel you to leave. On the premises are a large freshwater pool with Tiki bar, two tennis courts, a mini-mart, snack shop, Laundromat, restaurant, even a theater showing first-run movies. Cars, mopeds, bicycles, kayaks, and paddleboats are all available for rent. Live music is provided on weekends. The ferry from Long Island docks nearby; a shuttle van is provided for trips to other parts of the island.

Manisses. 1 Spring St., Block Island, RI 02807. ☎ **800/626-4773** or 401/466-2063. Fax 401/466-2858. 25 rms. TEL. $80–$265 double. Rates include breakfast. AE, MC, V.

Pulling into the parking space up the hill from Old Harbor, many guests are delightedly surprised to see llamas grazing in the meadow down to the left. There are emus, goats, geese, and a Scottish Highland ox down there, too, an inevitable draw for adults as well as children. They are part of the hotel, which itself is only the most

Real Island Fables

Close quarters and long winters provoke neighborly disputes, diverting myths, and giddy controversies on every island. They also tend to promote an overindulgence in drink, especially in the days when this was populated in large part by fishermen long at sea. Their behavior when resting up on land after long voyages, their pockets full from the sale of catches arduously hauled on board, inspired one Lucretia Mott Ball to found the island's chapter of the Women's Christian Temperance Union. Ms. Ball was descended from the earliest settlers and was of fittingly sturdy stuff. Her most enduring project was to purchase and place a monument to the WCTU conviction that water was "the most desirable drink for both human and beast." It was a statue erected in 1896 at the end of Water Street and dubbed "Rebecca at the Well," which depicts a lady in a toga holding an urn standing on a pedestal with water basins at various levels to serve horses, people, and dogs.

The message didn't take. During Prohibition, one of the largest rum-running fleets on the East Coast put in regularly at the island, defying the Coast Guard patrols. Speakeasies flourished, and not many visitors have taken the abstinence creed to heart in the decades since, judging from the nightly gatherings to celebrate the sunset. They go so far as to lubricate the event with an appalling concoction called a "Mudslide." This involves chocolate liqueur and related substances amounting to a malt with a kick, just the thing for people who don't like the taste of alcohol.

Rebecca does serve a purpose. Ask directions to almost anywhere and sooner or later you'll hear, "Go to Rebecca and turn right." She got a new paint job for her 100th birthday. All white.

Another sequence of events has recently captured the interest of natives. A fishing boat called the *Mad Monk* hauled in a 14-foot-long skeletal cartilage of an unidentified marine creature. The remains were stuffed in a freezer while specialists tried to figure out what it was. Sharks, rays, or sturgeons were the rational guesses, but romantics wanted more. They wanted it to be their very own Block Ness Monster.

Now they may never know. The skeleton was stolen from the freezer and pleas to return it "no questions asked" were unavailing. Block Nessie lives on, however. On T-shirts produced by the first mate of the *Mad Monk*.

---

visible of a small hospitality empire. Other properties include the 1661 Inn, further up the hill, and the Dodge, Sherman, and Nicholas Ball Cottages. Reception personnel are gracious and helpful, and are kept aware of vacancies at the other houses. Over to the side of the front desk are two inviting rooms, one with a fully stocked bar. In the evening, it serves as a dessert parlor, where they also go in for flaming coffees. Upstairs rooms use oak antiques and lots of wicker. They are of widely varying dimensions, the largest situated at the building's corners, with whirlpool tubs. Each room has a tray of soft drinks, cordials, and snacks next to a carafe of sherry. All meals are served, often extracting such superlatives as "impressive" and "sophisticated" from restaurant reviewers. Children over 12 are okay, pets aren't. Smoking is permitted. Some rooms share baths.

Rose Farm. Roslyn Rd., Box E, Block Island, RI 02807. ☎ **401/466-2034.** 19 rms. TV TEL. $65–$160 double. Rates include breakfast. AE, DISC, MC, V. Closed at least 2 months in winter. From Old Harbor, drive south on Spring St. and turn left at the entrance to the Spring House Hotel. Follow the road around the back of the hotel to Rose Farm.

The remodeled 1897 farmhouse that was the original inn has now been joined by an additional house across the driveway. Four of the rooms in the new building have large whirlpool baths and decks. One room is fully accessible for disabled guests, some have canopied beds, most have ocean views, all have Victorian reproduction furnishings with a few antiques, including a handsome Eastlake bedstead. A separate shed contains the inn's bicycle rental shop, with a stock of bright new 21-speed mountain bikes. The continental-plus breakfast is followed by afternoon refreshments, usually iced tea and pastries. Children over 12 are welcome, pets are not, and smoking is limited to the decks.

Spring House. 902 Spring St., P.O. Box 902, Block Island, RI 02807. ☎ **800/234-9263** or 401/466-5844. 49 rms. TEL. $89–$275 double. Rates include breakfast. AE, MC, V.

Marked by its red mansard roof and wraparound porch, the island's oldest hotel (1852) has been host to the Kennedy clan, Mark Twain, Ulysses S. Grant . . . and Billy Joel. The young staff is congenial, if occasionally scatter-brained. A considerable attraction for guests and drop-ins are the all-you-can-eat barbecue lunches next to the bar on the verandah. Alert to trends, the management now boasts of its large portable humidor with expensive cigars that it trots out in the spacious lounge, Victoria's Parlor. On the other side of the lobby is a sitting area with a fireplace, not common at island hostelries, and from there stretches the light, bright, white dining room. The menu and its execution is conventional and competent. There are three styles of bedrooms, most of quite decent size, with dusky rose carpeting, queen-size beds, and pullout sofas. They don't have TVs or air-conditioning, but wet bars are standard. Swimming is allowed in the freshwater pond on the property. Kids are accepted, pets aren't.

Water Street. Water Street, Block Island, RI 02807. ☎ **800/825-6254** or 401/466-2605. 10 rms. TV TEL. $65–$179 double. Rates include breakfast. AE, MC, V. Closed a few months in winter.

Less conspicuous than the larger Victorians lining Water Street, but of the same era, this inn is known more for its ground-floor restaurant, Mohegan Café, than for the comfortable rooms and suites upstairs. Even the cheapest (and noisiest) room at the top of the stairs is large enough to walk around in and has a pullout sofa. Baths are a little primitive, with dim lighting and toilets that tend to tilt on the sloping floor, but all rooms have clock radios and ceiling fans, and some have air-conditioning and harbor views. A coupon provided at check-in entitles bearers to breakfast at the Portfolio Coffeehouse around the corner. Children are welcome, but not pets. The entire building is nonsmoking, except for the bar of the cafe. Show up an hour or so after the last ferry and they might lower the rate if they still have rooms left. Find the reception on the right side of the building, in what amounts to a converted closet.

WHERE TO DINE

Apart from a couple of kitchens that aspire to more rarefied levels of achievement, expect boiled or broiled lobsters, lots of fried and grilled fish and chicken, and the routine varieties of burgers and beef cuts. Chowders are usually surefire, especially but not exclusively the creamy New England version. Clam cakes are ubiquitous. Actually deep-fried fritters containing more dough than clams, they are still fun eating, especially when dipped in tartar sauce.

Ballard's. Old Harbor. ☎ **401/466-2231.** Main courses $9.50–$21.95. MC, V. May to mid-Oct daily 11:30am–11:00pm. AMERICAN.

Sooner rather than later, everyone winds up at Ballard's, so we might as well mention it. Behind the long porch is a warehouselike interior hung with nautical flags that was once a monster clambake hall that would be hard to fill if every one of the island's permanent populace showed up. Beyond that are a cement terrace with white resin tables and chairs shaded by umbrellas and a long, crowded beach. Several bars fuel the late-evening crowd that piles in for frequent live entertainment, much of which was in style 50 years ago. The menu ranges all over the map, with something for everyone. Execution is ordinary. One surprising appetizer is "Ballard's Clam Cake Special," comprised of a bowl of chowder, six clam cakes, and a wedge of watermelon. At only $5.50, it makes an ample and inexpensive lunch.

Dead Eye Dick's. Payne's Dock, New Harbor. ☎ **401/466-2654.** Main courses $13.95–$19.95. AE, MC, V. Memorial Day to mid-Sept daily noon–3pm and 5pm–midnight. SEAFOOD/AMERICAN.

Its name and chosen logo—a shark with an eyepatch—suggest the kind of waterside joint that sponsors wet T-shirt contests. It doesn't. Feel free to take the kids . . . and the grandparents. Neither picky appetites nor touchy stomachs will have trouble finding something suitable on the menu. Appetizers include conventional clams casino and Maryland crabcakes, but also special daily designer pizzas and bruschettas. Follow with grilled or blackened fish steaks, often accompanied by jalapeño jelly. Salads that precede entrees are ordinary, but come with good crusty bread and a garlicky dipping sauce. While seafood is their focus, they also do well by beef and pork cuts, grilled to juicy near-perfection. The bar has some offbeat brews on tap or in bottle, including a microbrew from Vermont, Otter Creek.

Ernie's. Water St. ☎ **401/466-2473.** Main courses $2.95–$5.50. AE, MC, V. May to mid-Oct daily 6:30am–noon. AMERICAN.

Breakfast, and nothing but breakfast, is what they've been doing for over 35 years. That means an early-morning crowd of serious anglers and insomniacs and a much later, stumble-in clutch of visitors so relaxed they can barely move. They have choices of low-fat plates of scrambled chemical-tasting egg substitutes and turkey sausages or Texas-thick dipped-in-batter French toast drenched with maple syrup and heaped with hash browns and rashers of bacon. Guess which the regulars pick. Tables are inside for the cool mornings, outside on the deck as the sun starts to rise.

The Oar. West Side Rd. ☎ **401/466-8820.** Sandwiches and salads $2.75–$11.75. AE, MC, V. Late Apr to mid-Oct daily 6:30–midnight. AMERICAN.

The Oar is more good-time bar than eating place. I think the best reason to seek this place out (at the B.I. Marina) is the view of the Great Salt Pond and the myriad pleasure boats that cover its surface all summer. It can be taken in at leisure from either the deck or the cool bar, with its wide picture window. The restaurant's name should be plural, since the ceiling and walls are hung with scores of oars—all of them painted with cartoons, graffiti, names, and assorted messages of obscure or ribald intent. Commemorating races, anniversaries, important events, or simply some really great parties, they provide such idle diversions as "find the oldest" (1965). The menu is largely unchanging old reliables, from Buffalo wings and fried calamari to bacon cheeseburgers and lobster rolls. The only things resembling an actual dinner are plates and buckets of fried chicken, which come with coleslaw and fries or rice and beans. The 20-piece bucket costs $32. There were no plans to add a proper dinner menu at last visit, but that might change. The menu shortens after 9pm and drinks are served until 1am.

BLOCK ISLAND AFTER DARK

Nightlife isn't of the guzzling, rollicking south Florida variety, but neither do they close the bars at sunset. Prime candidates for a potential rockin' good time are

Captain Nick's (Ocean Avenue; ☎ 401/466-5670), with pool tables and live bands supplemented by disco, and **McGovern's Yellow Kittens** (Corn Neck Road; ☎ 401/466-5855), also presenting live bands in high season. **Ballard's** (see "Where to Dine" above) has music nightly, often of the accordion or "big band" variety. Pitchers of beer, pool tables, pinball, and foozeball are the attractions at **Club Soda** (Connecticut Avenue; ☎ 401/466-5912), but there is live music once or twice a week. Find it under the Highview Inn, off Ocean Avenue. Another live music venue is the lounge of the **National Hotel** (Water Street; ☎ 401/466-2901).

Two cinemas show current films: **Oceanwest** (Champlin's Marina, New Harbor; ☎ 401/466-2971) and the **Empire** (Water Street, Old Harbor; ☎ 401/466-2555), which also has a video game room.

11 Vermont

by Wayne Curtis

A pair of East Coast academics raised a ruckus recently with a proposal to turn much of the Great Plains into a national park, and let the buffalo roam free again.

With all due respect, if there's any state that should be turned wholesale into a national park, it's Vermont. This would preserve a classic American landscape of rolling hills punctuated with slender white church spires and covered bridges (Vermont has more than 100). It would preserve the perfectly scaled main streets in towns like Woodstock and Bennington and Middlebury and Montpelier. It would save the dairy farms that fan across the shoulders of verdant ridges. But most of all, it would preserve a way of life that, one day, America will wish it had retained.

Without feeling in the least like a theme park, Vermont captures a sense of America as it once was. Vermonters still share a strong sense of community, and they respect the ideals of thrift and parsimony. They still prize their small villages and towns, and they understand what makes them special. In his 1996 state-of-the-state address, Gov. Howard Dean said that one of Vermont's special traits was in knowing "where our towns begin and end." That alone speaks volumes.

Of course, it's not likely that Vermont residents would greet a national park proposal with much enthusiasm or equanimity. Meddlesome outsiders and federal bureaucrats don't rank high on their list of folks to invite to Sunday supper. At any rate, such a preservation effort would ultimately be doomed to failure. Because Vermont's impeccable sense of place is tied to its autonomy and independence, and any effort to control it from above would certainly cause it to perish.

Happily for travelers exploring the state, it's not hard to get a taste of Vermont's way of life. You'll find it in almost all of the small towns and villages. And they are small—the suburbs *of suburbs* of some East Coast cities are far larger. Let the numbers tell the story: Burlington, Vermont's largest city, has just 39,127 residents; Montpelier, the state capital, 8,247; Brattleboro, 8,612; Bennington, 9,532; Woodstock, 1,037; Newfane, 164. (All these figures are from the 1990 census.) The state's entire population is just 560,000—making it one of a handful of states with more senators than representatives in Congress.

Of course, the numbers don't tell the whole story. You have to let the people do that. One of Vermont's better-known residents, Nobel Prize–winning author Sinclair Lewis, wrote 70 years ago: "I like Vermont because it is quiet, because you have a population that is solid and not driven mad by the American mania—that mania which considers a town of four thousand twice as good as a town of two thousand . . . Following that reasoning, one would get the charming paradox that Chicago would be ten times better than the entire state of Vermont, but I have been in Chicago and not found it so."

Thankfully, that still holds true today.

1 Enjoying the Great Outdoors

BACKPACKING The **Long Trail,** running 262 miles from Massachusetts to the Canadian border, was the nation's first long-distance hiking path and remains one of the best. This high-elevation trail follows Vermont's gusty ridges and dips into shady saddles, crossing federal, state, and private lands. Open-sided shelters are located about one day's hike apart, making this a convenient way to traverse the backcountry. The trail can be quite demanding in parts, and to hike the entire length requires stamina and experience. Shorter excursions of two or three days are, of course, entirely possible.

The best source of information about the Long Trail and other backcountry opportunities in Vermont is the **Green Mountain Club,** R.R. #1, Box 650, Route 100, Waterbury Center, VT 05677 (☎ **802/244-7037**), which publishes the *Guidebook of the Long Trail.* Club headquarters is located on Route 100 between Waterbury and Stowe, and is open weekdays until about 4:30pm.

BIKING Vermont's back roads offer some of the most superb biking in the Northeast. Even Route 100 is spectacular along stretches; especially appealing is Route 100 north of Killington to Sugarbush. While sheer hills on some back roads can be excruciating for those who've spent too much time behind a desk, close scrutiny of a map should reveal routes that follow rivers and offer less gruelling pedaling.

Vermont also lends itself to superb mountain biking. Numerous county and town roads have been abandoned and offer superior backcountry cruising. Most Green Mountain National Forest trails are also open to mountain bikers (but not the Appalachian or Long trails). Mountain bikes are prohibited from state park and state forest hiking trails, but are allowed on the gravel roads through these lands. There's also a 10-mile pilot trail for mountain bikers in the Little River area of Mt. Mansfield State Forest that's worth checking out. Mt. Snow and Jay Peak ski areas, among others, will bring you and your bike to blustery ridges via lift or gondola, allowing you to work with rather than against gravity on your way down. The Craftsbury Center is your best best if you're looking for back road cruising through farmland rather than forest.

Organized inn-to-inn bike tours were invented in Vermont, and they remain a great way to see the countryside by day while relaxing in luxury at night. Tours are typically self-guided, with luggage transferred for you each day by vehicle. Try **Vermont Bicycle Touring** (☎ **802/453-4811**), **Country Inns Along the Trail** (☎ **802/247-3300**), **Bike Vermont** (☎ **800/257-2226**), and **Cycle-Inn-Vermont** (☎ **802/228-8799**).

CANOEING Vermont offers exceptionally pleasant canoeing on a number of rivers and lakes. Lake Champlain offers protected canoeing on the east side of North Hero Island and Grand Isle; outside these waters, be aware that sudden winds can come up unexpectedly with disastrous results. Numerous small ponds within the Green Mountains lend themselves to a lazy afternoon's paddle.

Good paddling rivers include the Battenkill in southwest Vermont, the Lamoille near Jeffersonville, the Class II Winooski near Waterbury, and the Missisquoi from Highgate Center to Swanton Dam. The whole of the historic Connecticut River, while frequently interrupted by dams, offers uncommonly scenic paddling through rural farmlands. Especially beautiful is the seven-mile stretch between Moore and Comerford Dams near Waterford. Rentals are easy to come by near Vermont's major waterways; just check the local Yellow Pages.

In the early 1990s the **Upper Valley Land Trust** (☎ 603/643-6626) set up a network of primitive campsites along the Connecticut River, allowing canoeists to paddle and portage its length and camp along the riverbanks at night. Two of the campsites are accessible by car. Call for a brochure.

Vermont also offers a novel way to explore the state: canoeing inn-to-inn. These trips can usually be tailored for most ability levels, and offer leisurely touring at a pace that's perfect for Vermont. **Vermont Waterways** (☎ 800/492-8271) offers weekend and five-day tours by canoe and sea kayak on the Connecticut River, Lake Champlain, and the Lamoille and Winooski rivers. Prices start at $380 per person for a weekend trip, which includes all meals and lodging at inns or B&Bs.

A helpful guide is Roioli Schweiker's *Canoe Camping Vermont & New Hampshire Rivers,* published by Countryman Press.

FISHING   Vermont attracts anglers from all over the eastern United States, who flock to its banks with spinners and flies. Both lake and river fishing can be excellent—if you know what you're doing. Vermont has 288 lakes of 20 acres or larger, hundreds of smaller bodies of water, and nearly countless miles of rivers and streams.

Novice fly fishermen would do well to stop by the sizable **Orvis Catalog Store** (☎ 802/362-3750) in Manchester to ask for some friendly advice, then perhaps try out some of the famed tackle on the store's small ponds. If time permits, sign up for one of the Orvis fly-fishing classes and have an expert critique your technique and offer some pointers.

Vermont's rivers and lakes are home to 14 major species of sports fish, including landlocked salmon, four varieties of trout (rainbow, brown, brook, and lake), and large and smallmouth bass. The 100-mile-long Lake Champlain attracts its share of enthusiasts angling for bass, landlocked salmon, and lake trout. In the south, the Battenkill is perhaps the most famed trout river (thanks in part to the proximity of Orvis), although veteran anglers contend that it's lost its luster. The Walloomsac and West rivers have also been rumored to give up a decent-sized trout or two. And don't overlook the Connecticut River, which the Fish and Wildlife Department calls "probably the best-kept fishing secret in the Northeast."

Fishing licenses are required and are available by mail from the state or in person at many sporting goods and general stores. License requirements and fees change from time to time, so it's best to write or call for a complete list: **Vermont Fish & Wildlife Dept.,** 103 South Main St., Waterbury, VT 05671 (☎ 802/241-3700).

Two invaluable guides are *The Atlas of Vermont Trout Ponds* and *Vermont Trout Streams,* both published by Northern Cartographic, 4050 Williston Rd., South Burlington, VT 05403 (☎ 802/860-2886).

HIKING   Vermont offers a spectacular range of hiking trails, from undemanding woodland strolls to lengthy treks along rugged, windswept ridges.

The two premier long-distance pathways in Vermont are the **Appalachian and Long trails,** which traverse some of the most dramatic terrain the state has to offer.

Day hikes are easily carved out of these longer treks; see "Backpacking" above for information on the Green Mountain Club, which is the best source of advice on Vermont's trails.

The **Green Mountain National Forest** offers a total of 500 miles of hiking trails, from the Long Trail to pathways through lowland valleys. There is no single best area for hiking; just head to any of those big green areas on the state map and search out local information on trails. Any of the four Green Mountain offices will make a good stop for picking up maps and requesting hiking advice from rangers. The main office is in Rutland (☎ 802/747-6700). District ranger offices are in Middlebury (☎ 802/388-6688), Rochester (☎ 802/767-4261), and Manchester (☎ 802/362-2307).

In addition to the national forest, Vermont has in excess of 80 state forests and parks, many of which set the stage for superior hiking. Guides to hiking trails are essential to get the most out of a hiking vacation in Vermont. Recommended guides include the Green Mountain Club's *Day Hiker's Guide to Vermont,* and *50 Hikes in Vermont,* published by Countryman Press. Both are widely available in bookstores throughout the state.

SKIING Vermont has been eclipsed by upscale western and Canadian ski resorts in the past few decades, but in many minds Vermont is *still* the capital of downhill skiing in the United States. The nation's first ski lift—a rope tow—was rigged up off a Buick engine in 1933 near Woodstock. The first lodge to accommodate skiers was built in Vermont at Sherburne Pass.

Ski areas in Vermont vary widely, but each has its appeal. For those looking for the allure of big mountains, steep faces, and a lively ski scene, there's Killington, Sugarbush, Stratton, and Stowe. Families and intermediates find their way to Mount Snow, Pico, Okemo, Bolton Valley, and Smuggler's Notch. For old-fashioned New England ski mountain charm, there's Mad River Glen, Ascutney, Burke, and Jay Peak. Finally, those who prefer a small mountain with a smaller price tag make tracks for Middlebury Snow Bowl, Bromley, Maple Valley, and Suicide Six.

Vermont is also blessed with about 50 cross-country ski areas throughout the state. These range from modest mom-and-pop operations to elaborate destination resorts with snowmaking that extends the season and tides skiers over during snow droughts. The general advice is to head north, and head to higher elevations, where the best snow is usually found. Among the snowiest, best-run destinations are the Trapp Family Lodge in Stowe, the Craftsbury Nordic Center in the Northeast Kingdom, and Mountain Top near Killington. For a free brochure listing all the cross-country facilities, contact the **Vermont Dept. of Travel and Tourism** (☎ 800/837-6668). The state also updates a recorded cross-country ski report every Thursday (☎ 802/828-3239). A fax of the report is available by calling **800/833-9756.**

Inn-to-inn ski touring is catching on; contact the Trapp Family Lodge or the Craftsbury Center for information.

SNOWMOBILING Vermont boasts a lengthy, well-developed network of snowmobile trails throughout the state. That's the good news. The bad news is that out-of-staters must pay their pound of flesh for the privilege of riding in Vermont. Nonresidents pay $22 to register their sled, and an additional $25 to join the Vermont Association of Snow Travelers (VAST). Snowmobilers must also join a local snowmobile club, with fees of $7 to $10. The fine for ignoring these rules is currently $117.50.

The best source of information on snowmobiling in Vermont is **VAST,** P.O. Box 839, Montpelier, VT 05601 (☎ 802/229-0005), which produces a great newsletter and can help point you and your machine in the right direction.

Snowmobile rentals are hard to come by in Vermont, although guided tours are common. In southern Vermont, **High Country Snowmobile Tours,** located eight and a half miles west of Wilmington (☎ **800/627-7533** or 802/464-2108) offers tours between one hour and overnight. If you've never been on a snowmobile before but want to give it a whirl, rides around a 1¹/₂-mile track are offered just south of Stowe at **Nichols Snowmobile Rentals** (☎ **802/253-7239**).

2 Bennington, Manchester & Southwestern Vermont

Southwestern Vermont is the turf of Ethan Allen, Robert Frost, Grandma Moses, and Norman Rockwell. As such, it may feel familiar to you even if you've never been here before. Over the decades, it's subtly become ingrained in America's cultural and geographic psyche.

The region is sandwiched between the Green Mountains to the east and the rolling hills of the Vermont–New York border to the west. The first town you're likely to hit is Bennington—a commercial center that offers up a selection of goods for locals and tourists alike. Northward toward Rutland the terrain is more intimate than intimidating, with towns clustered in gentle valleys along rivers and streams. Former 19th-century summer colonies and former lumber and marble towns exist side by side, with both offering pleasant accommodations, delightful food, and, in the case of Manchester Center, world-class shopping.

These outposts of sophisticated culture are within easy striking distance of the Green Mountains, allowing you to enjoy the outdoors by day and goose-down duvets by night. The region also attracts its share of weekend celebrities, as well as shoppers, gourmands, and those simply looking for a brief fantasy detour in the elegant inns and B&Bs.

Keep in mind when traveling here that two Route 7s exist. Running high along the foothills is the new Route 7, which offers limited access and higher speeds, resulting in a speedy trip up the valley toward Rutland. Meandering along the valley floor is Historic Route 7A, a more languorous route with plenty of diversions (antique shops, historic views) along the way. If you've got the time, take the slow road from Bennington to Manchester.

BENNINGTON

Bennington owes its fame (such as it is) to a handful of eponymous moments, places, and things. Like the Battle of Bennington, fought in 1777 during the American War of Independence. And Bennington College, a small but prestigious liberal-arts school that's produced a bumper crop of well-regarded novelists in recent years. And Bennington pottery, which traces its ancestry back to the first factory here in 1793, and is today prized by collectors for its superb quality.

Bennington is a pleasant, no-nonsense town with a handful of restaurants and stores still selling things that people actually need. The surrounding countryside, while defined by rolling hills, is afflicted with fewer abrupt inclines and slopes than many of Vermont's towns. The downtown is compact, low, and handsome, and boasts a fair number of architecturally striking buildings. In particular, don't miss the stern marble Federal building (formerly the post office) with its six fluted columns at 118 South St.

ESSENTIALS

GETTING THERE   Bennington is located at the intersection of Route 9 and Route 7. The nearest interstate access from the south is via the New York Thruway at Albany, N.Y. From the east, I-91 is about 40 miles distant at Brattleboro.

VISITOR INFORMATION   The **Bennington Area Chamber of Commerce,** Veterans Memorial Drive, Bennington, VT 05201 (☎ **802/447-3311**), maintains an information office on Route 7 north near the veterans' complex. The office is open during business hours; after hours, you can pick up a map of Bennington and a list of attractions from the box outside the front door.

EXPLORING THE TOWN

Bennington's claim to history is the fabled Battle of Bennington, which took place August 16, 1777. While a relatively minor skirmish, it had major implications for the outcome of the war.

The British had devised a grand strategy to defeat the impudent colonies: Divide the colonies from the Hudson River through Lake Champlain, then concentrate forces to defeat one half followed by the other. As part of the strategy, British general John Burgoyne was ordered to attack the settlement of Bennington and capture the military supplies that had been squirreled away there by the Continental militias in anticipation of hostilities. There, he came upon the colonial forces led by Gen. John Stark, a veteran of Bunker Hill. After a couple of days playing cat and mouse, Stark ordered the attack on the afternoon of August 16, proclaiming, "There are the redcoats, and they are ours, or this night Molly Stark sleeps a widow!" (Or so the story goes.)

The battle was over in less than two hours—the British and their Hessian mercenaries were defeated, with more than 200 enemy troops killed; the colonials lost but 30 men. This cleared the way for another vital colonial victory at the Battle of Saratoga, ended the British strategy of divide and conquer, and set the stage for a colonial victory in the War of Independence.

That battle is commemorated by northern New England's most imposing monument. You can't miss the **Bennington Battle Monument** if you're passing through the surrounding countryside. This 306-foot obelisk of blue limestone atop a low rise was dedicated in 1891. It resembles a shorter, paunchier Washington Monument. Note also that it's actually about six miles from the site of the actual battle; the monument actually marks the spot where the munitions were stored.

The monument's viewing platform, which is reached by elevator, is open 9am to 5pm daily from April through October. A small fee is charged.

Along the highway between Old Bennington and the current town center is the **Bennington Museum** (☎ **802/447-1571**). This intriguing collection traces its roots back to 1875; the museum has occupied the current stone-and-column building overlooking the valley since 1928. Nine galleries feature a wide range of exhibits, including furniture, glass, oil paintings, and pottery. Of special interest are the colorful, primitive landscapes by Grandma Moses (1860–1961), who lived much of her life nearby, and a glorious luxury car called the Wasp, 16 of which were crafted in Bennington between 1920 and 1925. The museum is open 9am to 5pm daily (until 7pm Friday through Monday in summer). Admission is $5 for adults, $4.50 for students and seniors, and $12 for a family with children under 18. Children under 12 enter free.

Bennington College was founded as an experimental women's college in the 1930s. It's since gone co-ed, and has garnered a national reputation as a leading liberal-arts schools (it also claimed the title of most expensive college in the United States for a time). Bennington has a reputation for teaching writing; W.H. Auden, Bernard Malmud, and John Gardner have all taught here. In the 1980s, Bennington produced a number of prominent young authors, including Donna Tartt, Bret Easton Ellis, and Jill Eisenstadt. The pleasant campus north of town is well worth wandering about.

Southern Vermont

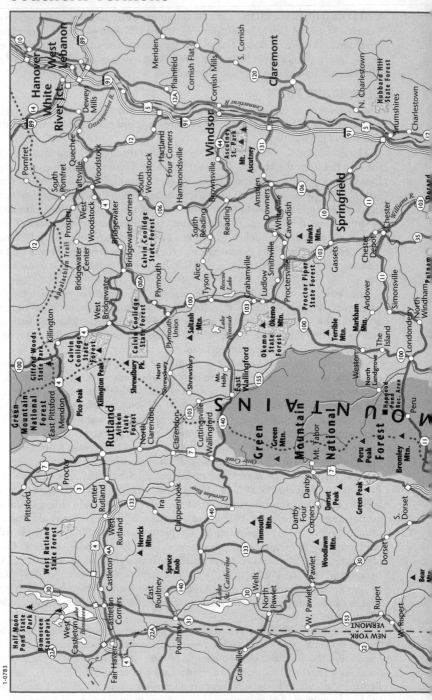

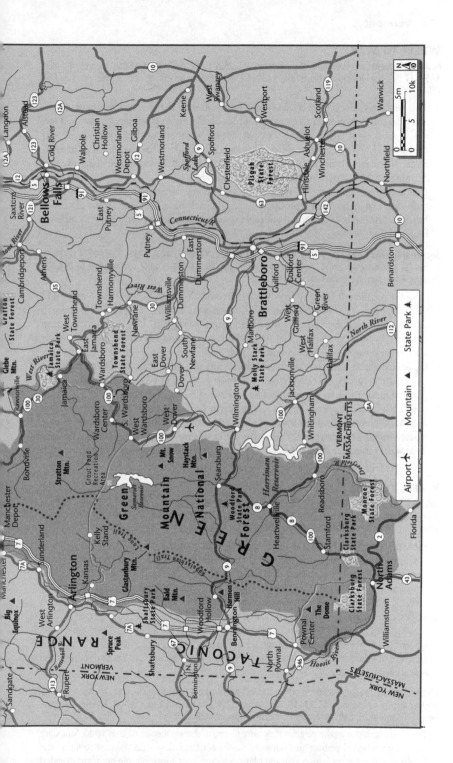

WHERE TO STAY

Four Chimneys. 21 West Rd., Bennington, VT 05201. ☎ **802/447-3500.** 11 rms. TV TEL. $85–$175 double including breakfast; $170–$250 including breakfast and dinner. AE, CB, DC, DISC, MC, V.

This striking Colonial Revival building will be among the first to catch your eye as you arrive in Bennington from the west. Set off Route 7 on a large, landscaped lot, it's an imposing white, three-story structure with, naturally, four prominent chimneys. (Local secret: The third chimney's a fake, added for the purposes of symmetry.) The inn, built in 1912, is at the edge of Old Bennington; the towering Bennington Monument looms above the backyard.

The carpeted guest rooms are inviting and homey, decorated in a casual country style with early American reproductions. About half have fireplaces; most also offer Jacuzzis. The inn is in the process of making over its rooms; ask for one that's recently been redone.

South Shire Inn. 124 Elm St., Bennington, VT 05201. ☎ **802/447-3839.** Fax 802/442-3547. 9 rms (1 with shower only). A/C TEL. Peak season $95–$150 double; off-season $80–$130 double. Rates include breakfast. AE, MC, V.

A locally prominent banking family hired architect William Bull to design and build this impressive Victorian home in 1880. It was an era when architects knew how to use big space, and their patrons were willing to foot the bill. Today, guests can reap the benefits of that vision at Bennington's finest bed-and-breakfast, located a short walk from downtown. The downstairs is spacious and open, with detailing including leaded glass on the bookshelves and intricate plasterwork in the dining room.

The guest rooms are richly hued, and most have canopy beds and working fireplaces (Duraflame-style logs only). The best of the bunch is the old master bedroom, which has a king-size canopy bed, a tile-hearth fireplace, and a beautiful bathroom with hand-painted tile. Four more modern guest rooms are in the old carriage house, where the innkeepers spared little expense in the makeover. The carriage house's downstairs rooms are slightly more formal; the upstairs rooms are more intimate, with low eaves and skylights over the tubs.

WHERE TO DINE

Alldays & Onion. 519 Main St. ☎ **802/447-0043.** Reservations accepted for dinner, but not often needed. Sandwiches $2.25–$6.95; dinner $10.95–$14.95. AE, DC, DISC, MC, V. Mon–Tues 8am–6pm, Wed–Sat 8am–8pm. ECLECTIC.

First off, the name. For reasons that are not entirely clear, this eminently casual place is named after a turn-of-the-century British automobile manufacturer. Locals flock here to enjoy the wholesome, tasty sandwiches, the filling deli salads (like Cajun chicken and pasta salads), and tasty quiches and soups. More ambitious dinners are served later in the week, with entrees ranging from Southwest cowboy steak with skillet corn sauce to a more politically correct soba and stir-fried vegetables. The atmosphere is that of a small-town restaurant gussied up for a big night out—the fluorescent lights are bright, but the dark hues of the walls knock down the intensity a notch, and folk-rock background music mellows it further still. In summer, enjoy the airy screened-in patio.

Ⓢ **Blue Benn Diner.** North St. (Rte. 7). ☎ **802/442-5140.** Breakfast $1.25–$5.95; sandwiches and main courses $1.95–$5.75; dinner $7.95. No credit cards. Mon–Tues 6am–5pm, Wed–Fri 6am–8pm, Sat 6am–4pm, Sun 7am–4pm. AMERICAN.

Diner aficionados make pilgrimages here to enjoy the ambience of this 1945 Silk City classic, with barrel ceiling and copious amounts of stainless steel. Blue stools line the laminate counter, on which you see plain evidence that more people are right-handed than left-handed by the wear marks. But even folks who don't give a fig for diners flock here for the tremendous value on food. The printed menu is vast, but don't overlook the specials scrawled on paper and taped all over the walls. Blue-plate dinner specials are $7.95, and include vegetables, rice, soup or salad, rolls, and Indian pudding for dessert. There's also a great selection of pies, like blackberry, pumpkin, and chocolate cream, that sell for $2.50 a slice (add 25¢ if you want it à la mode).

ARLINGTON, MANCHESTER & DORSET

Vermont's rolling Green Mountains are rarely out of view in this cluster of hamlets. And in mid-summer the lush green hereabouts gives Ireland a good run for its money—verdant hues are found in the forests blanketing the hills, the valley meadows, and the mosses along the tumbling streams, making it obvious how these mountains earned their name.

These quintessential Vermont villages make ideal destinations for romantic getaways, aggressive antiquing, and serious outlet shopping. Each of the towns is worth visiting, and each has its own peculiar charm. Arlington has a quaint town center that borders on microscopic (U-turns are a popular pastime among travelers). To the north, Manchester and Manchester Center share a blurred town line, but maintain distinct characters. The more southerly Manchester has an Old-World, old-money elegance with a campuslike town center centered around the columned Equinox Hotel. Just to the north, Manchester Center is a major mercantile center with dozens of outlets offering discounts on brand-name clothing, accessories, and housewares. A worthy detour off the beaten track is Dorset, an exquisitely preserved town of white clapboard architecture and marble sidewalks.

ESSENTIALS

GETTING THERE   Arlington, Manchester, and Manchester Center are located north of Bennington on Route 7A, which runs parallel to and west of the more modern, less interesting Route 7. Dorset is north of Manchester Center on Route 30, which intersects with Route 7A in Manchester Center.

VISITOR INFORMATION   The **Manchester and the Mountains Chamber of Commerce,** R.R. 2, Box 3451, Manchester Center, VT 05255 (☎ **802/362-2100**), maintains two information centers in Manchester Center in the summer. One is in a gray house two blocks north of the blinking light (open year-round). The other (open summer through foliage season only) is four blocks north of the blinking light in a white house on Adam Park Green. Hours are daily from 9am to 5pm (Sunday 9am to 2pm).

For information about outdoor recreation, the Green Mountain National Forest maintains a district **ranger office** (☎ **802/362-2307**) in Manchester on routes 11 and 30 west of Route 7 on Routes 22 & 30. It's open 8am to 4:30pm Monday through Friday.

EXPLORING THE AREA

Arlington owes its closest brush with fame to its association with painter and illustrator Norman Rockwell, who resided here from 1939 to 1953. Arlington residents were regularly featured in Rockwell covers for the *Saturday Evening Post.*

Arlington maintains a small monument to its Rockwell legacy. Housed in a 19th-century Carpenter Gothic–style church in the middle of town, **The Norman Rockwell Exhibition** (☎ **802/375-6423**) features displays including many of those famous covers, along with photographs of the original models. Sometimes you'll find the models working as volunteers. Reproductions are available at the gift shop. Open

9am to 5pm daily in summer; open in the off-season 10am to 4pm weekdays and 10am to 5pm weekends. Admission is $1.

Between Arlington and Manchester you'll pass the entrance to **Skyline Drive** (☎ 802/362-1113), a looping toll road that takes you to the summit of 3,835-foot **Mount Equinox**—which, incidentally, is the highest peak in Vermont not traversed by the Long Trail. The toll is $5 per car for the five-mile trip to the top, which affords open views of the Green Mountains to the east. Don't expect wilderness; there's even a modest inn up top that's open May to October. The mountaintop is also accessible by hiking trail.

Manchester has long been one of Vermont's moneyed resorts, attracting prominent summer residents like Mary Todd Lincoln and Julia Boggs Dent, the wife of U.S. Grant. This town is well worth visiting just to wander its quiet streets, bordered with distinguished homes dating from the early Federal period. It feels a bit like you've entered a time warp here, and the cars driving past the green seem like anachronisms. Be sure to note the sidewalks made of irregular marble slabs. The town is said to have 17 miles of such sidewalks, made from the castoffs of Vermont's marble quarries.

Seven miles north of Manchester on Route 30 is the village of Dorset. Fans of American architecture owe themselves a visit. While not nearly as grand as Manchester, this quiet town of white clapboard and black and green shutters has a quiet and appealing grace. The elliptical green is fronted by early homes that are modest by Manchester standards, but nonetheless are imbued with a subtle elegance. In fact, Dorset feels more like a Norman Rockwell painting than most Norman Rockwell paintings. The main action here is at **Peletier's Store,** which has been provisioning villagers for more than 175 years, although the product line is decidedly more upscale these days.

Museums & Historic Homes

✪ **Hildene.** Rte. 7A, Manchester. ☎ **802/362-1788.** $7 adults, $2 children 6–14. Tours daily from mid-May through Oct 9:30am–4pm. Special holiday tours Dec 27–29.

Robert Todd Lincoln was the only son of Abraham and Mary Todd Lincoln to survive to maturity. But he also achieved plenty on his own, earning millions as a prominent corporate attorney and serving as secretary of war and ambassador to Britain under three presidents. He also served as president of the Pullman Company (makers of deluxe train cars) from 1897 to 1911, stepping in after the death of company founder George Pullman.

What did one do with millions of dollars in an era when that was still something more than pocket change? Build lavish summer homes, for the most part. And Lincoln was no exception. He summered in this stately, 24-room Georgian Revival mansion between 1905 and 1926, and delighted in showing off its remarkable features, including a spectacular sweeping staircase and a 1908 Aeolian organ with its 1,000 pipes (you'll hear it played on the tour). And what summer home would be complete without formal gardens? Lincoln had gardens designed after the patterns in a stained-glass window and planted on a gentle promontory with outstanding views of the flanking mountains.

A tour of the estate will give you a good sense of life here—descendants of Lincoln occupied the home until 1975, when they donated the property to the Church of Christ, Scientist, which later sold the property to the Friends of Hildene. Many of the furnishings are original, and a number of family mementos are on display.

Special Christmas candlelight tours are held at the end of December, and in winter nine miles of cross-country skiing trails are maintained on the property, with the carriage house serving as a warming hut. Visitors pay a $7 skiing fee.

American Museum of Fly Fishing. Rte. 7A (a block north of the Equinox Hotel), Manchester. ☎ **802/362-3300.** $3 Adults, children free. May–Oct daily 10am–4pm; Nov–Apr Mon–Fri 10am–4pm.

Warning: This is not the place to take diffident teenagers who complain that adults do boring things on vacation. It is, however, the place for serious anglers interested in the rich history and delicate art of fly-fishing. The museum includes exhibits on the evolution of the fly-fishing reel, paintings and sculptures of fish and anglers, displays of creels, and dioramas depicting fishing at its best. You can see the fly-fishing tackle of some of the nation's more notable anglers, including Herbert Hoover, Andrew Carnegie, and Ernest Hemingway. And, naturally, there are extensive exhibits of beautifully tied flies, displayed in oak and glass cases.

SHOPPING

Manchester Center is one of several upscale factory outlet meccas in northern New England. Retailers include (take a deep breath) Pendleton, Bass Shoes, Timberland, Burberry's, Polly Flinders, Christian Dior, J. Crew, Seiko, Donna Karan, Coach, Van Heusen, Giorgio Armani, and Dansk. The shops conveniently cluster along a "T" intersection in the heart of Manchester Center. Most are readily accessible on foot, while others are a bit further afield, requiring scuttling from one to the next by car.

A couple of local shops are worth seeking out amid the high-fashion names. Orvis, which has crafted a worldwide reputation for manufacturing topflight fly-fishing equipment, is based in Manchester. The **Orvis Catalog Store** (☎ 802/362-3750) is located between Manchester and Manchester Center, and offers rustic housewares, sturdy outdoor clothing, and, naturally, fly-fishing equipment. Two small ponds just outside the shop allow prospective customers to try before they buy.

Near the middle of Manchester Center at the intersection of Route 7A and Route 30 is the **Northshire Bookstore** (☎ 802/362-2200), one of the best bookshops in a state where reading is a popular pastime. In addition to great browsing, the store sponsors frequent readings by prominent authors, both local and from away.

SUMMER SPORTS

HIKING & BIKING   Superb hiking trails ranging from challenging to relaxing can be found in the hills a short drive from town. Get acquainted with what's where at the Green Mountain District Ranger Station (see "Visitor Information," above). Ask for the free brochure "Day Hikes on the Manchester Ranger District."

The Long Trail and Appalachian Trail (they overlap in southern Vermont) run just east of Manchester; one of the more popular day treks runs along these trails to **Spruce Peak.** Five miles east of Manchester Center on Routes 11 and 30 look for parking where the Long Trail/Appalachian Trail crosses the road. Strike out southward on foot over rocky terrain for 2.2 miles to the peak, looking for the blue-blazed side trail to the open summit with its breathtaking views of the Manchester Valley.

A scenic drive northwest of Manchester Center you'll come to the **Delaware and Hudson Rail-Trail,** of which 20 miles have been built in two sections in Vermont. (Another 14 miles will eventually be developed across the state line in New York.) The southern section of the trail runs about 10 miles from West Pawlet to the state line at West Rupert, over trestles and past vestiges of former industry, such as the old Vermont Milk and Cream Co. Like most rail-trails, this is perfect for exploring by mountain bike. To reach the trailhead, drive north on Route 30 from Manchester Center to Route 315, then continue north on Route 153. In West Pawlet, park across from Duchie's General Store (a good place for refreshments), then set off on the trail southward from the old D&H freight depot across the street.

ON THE WATER   For a duck's-eye view of the rolling hills, stop by **Battenkill Canoe Ltd.** (☎ 800/421-5268 from out of state, or 802/362-2800) in Arlington. This friendly outfit offers daily canoe rentals on the scenic Battenkill and surrounding areas. Trips range from two hours to a whole day, and multiday inn-to-inn canoe packages are also available.

Aspiring anglers can sign up for fly-fishing classes taught by skilled instructors affiliated with **Orvis** (☎ 800/548-9548), the noted fly-fishing supplier and manufacturer. The two-and-a-half-day classes include instruction in knot tying and casting; students practice catch-and-release fishing on the company pond and the Battenkill River. Classes are held from mid-April through Labor Day.

SKIING

Bromley. P.O. Box 1130, Manchester Center, VT 05255. ☎ **800/865-4786** or 802/824-5522 for lodging. Vertical drop: 1,334 feet. Lifts: 6 chairlifts, 3 surface lifts. Skiable acreage: 175. Lift tickets: $39 weekends, $19 weekdays.

Bromley is a great place to learn to ski. Gentle and forgiving, the mountain also features long, looping intermediate runs that are tremendously popular with families. The slopes are mostly south-facing, which means some protection from the winter winds and the warmth of the sun. (Of course, it also means that the snow melts here first.) The base lodge scene is more mellow than at many resorts, and your experience here is likely to be very relaxing.

Stratton. Stratton Mountain, VT 05155. ☎ **800/843-6867** or 802/297-2200 for lodging. Vertical drop: 2,003 feet. Lifts: 1 gondola, 9 chairlifts (including 1 six-person high-speed), 2 surface lifts. Skiable acreage: 478. Lift tickets: $48 weekends, $42 weekdays.

Stratton is striving to reinvent itself. Founded in the 1960s, it labored in its early days under the belief that Vermont ski areas had to have a Tyrolean flair. Hence, a Gothic clock tower, Swiss Chalet Nightmare architecture, and the overall feel of being Vail's younger, less affluent sibling. Stratton is working to leave the image of Alpine quaintness behind in a bid to attract a younger, edgier set. The jury is still out, but the resort appears to be heading in the right direction. The slopes are especially popular with snowboarders, a sport that was invented here when bartender Jake Burton slapped a big plank on his feet and aimed down the mountain. Expert skiers should seek out Upper Middlebrook, a fine, twisting run off the summit.

WHERE TO STAY & DINE

✪ **Arlington Inn.** Rte. 7A (P.O. Box 369), Arlington, VT 05250. ☎ **800/443-9442** or 802/ 375-6532. 18 rms (some with showers only, one with detached bath). A/C. Summer, Christmas, Thanksgiving, Presidents' and Memorial Day weekends $80–$160 double; foliage season $90–$185 double; late fall through spring $70–$150 double. All rates include breakfast. AE, CB, DC, DISC, MC, V.

This stout, cream-colored Greek Revival home, built in 1848 for a railroad baron, seems better suited to the Virginia countryside. But it anchors the village well here, set back from the road on a lawn bordered with sturdy maples. Inside, the inn boasts a similarly courtly feel, with unique wooden ceilings adorning the first floor rooms, and a tavern that borrows its atmosphere from an English hunt club.

Innkeepers Deborah and Mark Gagnon, Boston refugees who acquired the inn in 1994, have taken strides to improve the inn's regal decor. Room rates vary widely, but even the least expensive rooms are well-appointed with period reproductions. The quietest rooms are in the detached carriage house, which many guests specifically request.

The Gagnons recently purchased the equally handsome 1830 Federal-style house next door, and have converted this into five more guest rooms, all of which have TVs and telephones, and three of which have wood-burning fireplaces. No smoking.

Dining/Entertainment: Dinners, served in the main dining room, include native produce and meats when available. Dinner choices change frequently, but might include an appetizer of duck, wild mushroom and sun-dried cranberry strudel, followed by a grilled veal chop served on a bed of artichokes, shallots, and fresh herbs. Entrees are priced from $18 to $24.

Barrows House. Rte. 30, Dorset, VT 05251. ☎ **800/639-1620** or 802/867-4455. Fax 802/867-0132. 28 rms (1 with shower only). A/C. $185–$245 double, including breakfast and dinner. B&B rates also available. Discounts available in midwinter and midweek. AE, CB, DC, DISC, MC, V.

Within easy strolling distance of the village of Dorset stands this compound of eight early American buildings, set on nicely landscaped grounds studded with birches, firs, and maples. The main house was built in 1784, and it's been an inn since the early 1900s. Some of the guest rooms have gas or wood fireplaces, and all share a small, country-style common area in the main inn. The inn offers limited rooms for smokers, and only some rooms have telephones.

Dining/Entertainment: Enjoy a before-dinner drink in the casual and cozy tavern with the trompe l'oeil bookshelves. The main dining area is a happy marriage of classical and contemporary. Sit in either the traditional country inn room, or the more modern greenhouse addition. The cuisine is contemporary New England, with entrees like Atlantic salmon with a sun-dried tomato pesto cream, or pan-roasted chicken breast with roasted peppers, shiitake mushrooms, and artichoke hearts. Entrees range from $9.95 to $18.75.

✪ 1811 House. Rte. 7A, Manchester Village, VT 05254. ☎ **800/432-1811** or 802/362-1811. 14 rms, including 3 cottage rms. A/C. $160–$200 double. Rates include full breakfast. AE, DISC, MC, V.

This historic Manchester Village home, the first part of which was built in the mid-1770s, started taking in guests in 1811 (hence the name). And it often seems that not much has changed here in the intervening centuries. The warrenlike downstairs common rooms are rich with history—the pine floors are uneven, the doors out of true, and everything is painted in earthy, colonial tones. Even the exterior is painted a pheasant-brown color. The antique furniture re-creates the feel of the house during the Federal period, and a delightful English-style pub lies off the entryway, complete with tankards hanging from the beams. For aficionados of early American culture, this is without question the place to be. This is a bed-and-breakfast; no evening meals are served.

The Equinox. Rte. 7A (P.O. Box 46), Manchester Village, VT 05245. ☎ **800/362-4747** or 802/362-4700. Fax 802/362-1595. 180 rms (8 with shower only). A/C TV TEL. $159–$289 double; $369–$549 suite. AE, DC, DISC, MC, V.

A blue-blood favorite, The Equinox dominates Manchester Village with its gleaming white clapboard and trim rows of columns. And make no mistake, its historic lineage notwithstanding (it was established in 1769), this is a full-blown resort with sports facilities, two dining rooms, and all the in-room amenities. As is fitting for its faux-Anglo charm, there's a even a British school of falconry affiliated with the inn that offers introductory classes at princely fees ($65 per person for a 45-minute introductory lesson).

Guest rooms, which were extensively renovated in 1991, are by and large decorated similarly in a country pine motif. The suites are a bit richer hued. Room prices vary widely based on size, but there's really not all that much difference between the largest and smallest rooms.

Next door is the grand Charles Orvis Inn, an 1812 home renovated by The Equinox in 1995. It offers nine elegantly appointed suites for $649 to $888 per night, including breakfast. Early reports suggest that this annex, while quite pleasant, is more than slightly overpriced.

Dining/Entertainment: Choose the dining room to fit your mood: There's the continental elegance of The Colonnade, where men are requested to wear jackets at dinner, or the more relaxed, clubby comfort of Marsh's Tavern.

Services: Room service, concierge, valet parking, baby-sitting, dry-cleaning and laundry, express check-out, and nightly turndown.

Facilities: Golf course, indoor and outdoor pools, room, and a falconry school.

Inn at Ormsby Hill. Rte. 7A (near Hildene, south of Manchester Village), Manchester Center, VT 05255. ☎ **800/670-2841** or 802/362-1163. Fax 802/362-5176. 10 rms. A/C. $115–$205 double. Rates include full breakfast. Discounts midweek and off-season. AE, MC, V. Closed briefly in Apr.

Chris and Ted Sprague put themselves on the culinary and innkeeping map after opening the delightful Newcastle Inn in coastal Maine some years ago. Well, they're at it again. In September 1995 they sold the Newcastle, bought this historic inn, doubled the number of guest rooms, and polished the place to a lustrous splendor. The oldest part of the inn dates to 1764 (Ethan Allen was said to have hidden here), with a harmonious addition put on by Edward Isham, a prominent 19th-century Chicago attorney. His addition to the back of the house, designed to look like the interior of a steamship, now houses the dining room and offers guests wonderful morning views as they enjoy Chris's otherworldly breakfasts.

Guest rooms vary in size and style. Among the best are the Taft Room, with its vaulted wood ceiling, and the first-floor library, with many of Isham's books still lining the shelves. The newer rooms, in what used to be a dormitory when the inn housed a home for underprivileged boys, are somewhat smaller, but still tastefully done. All newer rooms feature whirlpools and gas fireplaces.

Dining/Entertainment: Chris offers guests a light supper upon arrival on Friday nights (at $15 per couple), and an optional four-course dinner Saturday night ($60 for two). Go with the dinner. You won't be disappointed.

The Reluctant Panther. West Rd. (P.O. Box 678), Manchester Village, VT 05254. ☎ **800/822-2331** or 802/362-2568. Fax 802/362-2586. 16 rms (some with showers only). A/C TV TEL. $165–$275 double, $210–$235 double during foliage season and Christmas week. Rates include breakfast and dinner. AE, MC, V. No children under 14.

The Reluctant Panther, located a short walk from the Equinox, is easy to spot: It's painted a pale eggplant color and has faded yellow shutters, making it stand out in this staid village of white clapboard. It's run with couples in mind. This 1850s home is elegantly furnished throughout (as are guest rooms in an adjacent building, built in 1910), and features nice touches, including goose-down duvets and a split of wine in every room. Ten of the rooms have fireplaces, and one, the Mark Skinner suite, even features a wood-burning fireplace and a double Jacuzzi in the bathroom. Smoking is permitted in the lounge only.

Dining/Entertainment: As nice as the inn is, the Reluctant Panther is perhaps better known locally for its excellent dining. The first-floor dining room, decorated with floral prints, achieves the feat of being intimate without feeling crowded. (There's also a greenhouse with slate floor, which is very pleasant in summer.) The cuisine is European, prepared by Swiss-German chef Robert Bachofen, the former director of food and beverage at the Plaza Hotel in New York. The menu changes frequently, but expect entrees like grilled veal chops with ragout of shiitake and white mushrooms, or tuna steak with a minted cilantro-walnut salsa. Entree prices range from $18.95 to $24.95.

West Mountain Inn. River Rd., Arlington, VT 05250. ☎ **802/375-6516.** Fax 802/375-6553. 18 rms (2 with shower only). Spring weekends, summer, and winter $152–$184 double; foliage season $172–$204 double; spring midweek $139 double. All rates include breakfast and dinner. AE, DISC, MC, V.

The West Mountain Inn is a handsome, rambling, white clapboard building dating back a century-and-a-half. Sitting atop a steep, grassy bluff at the end of a dirt road one-half mile from the center of Arlington, it's a perfect place for travelers seeking sanctuary from the hectic modern age. The guest rooms, named after famous Vermonters, are nicely furnished with country and Victorian reproductions. The rooms vary widely in size and shape, but even the smallest has a surplus of charm and character. If the weather is uncharacteristically steamy, ask for one of the rooms on the top floor, which is air-conditioned. No smoking.

Dining/Entertainment: The inviting dining room is furnished in a hearty rather than cloying country style, with maple floors, pine walls, and green-and-white plaid tablecloths. Dinners include regional fare prepared and served with flair. Typical entrees are roasted quail with an orange-kiwi glaze, and steak au poivre in a mushroom merlot demi. Dinner for nonguests is by reservation only, and is $30 fixed price.

WHERE TO DINE

✪ **Chantecleer.** Route 7A, 3¹/₂ miles north of Manchester Center. ☎ **802/362-1616.** Reservations recommended. Main courses $18.75–$27.50. Wed–Mon 6–9:30pm. Closed Mon in winter and for 2–3 weeks in Nov and Apr. CONTINENTAL.

If you like superbly prepared continental fare but are put off by the stuffiness of high-brow Euro-wannabe restaurants, this is the place. Rustic elegance is the best description for the dining experience in this century-old dairy barn. The oddly slick exterior, which looks as if it could house a Ponderosa-style chain restaurant, doesn't offer a clue to just how pleasantly romantic the interior is. Heavy beams define the soaring space overhead, the walls are appropriately of barnboard, and the small bar is crafted of a slab of pine. A rooster motif predominates (predictably enough, since *chantecleer* is French for rooster), fresh flowers decorate the tables, and, when the weather's right, a fire blazes in the arched fieldstone fireplace. Swiss-born chef Michel Baumann, who's owned and operated the inn since 1981, changes his menu every three weeks, but his selections might feature entrees such as veal sweetbreads in a Madeira morel sauce, grilled prime veal chop, or frog legs Provençal. Arrive expecting an excellent meal; you won't go away disappointed.

3 Brattleboro & the Southern Green Mountains

The southern Green Mountains are New England writ large. If you've developed a preconception of what New England is but haven't ever visited here, this is probably the place you're thinking of.

The hills and valleys around the bustling town of Brattleboro, in Vermont's southeast corner, contain some of the state's best-hidden natural treasures. Travel along the main valley floors—along the West or the Connecticut rivers, or on Route 100—tends to be fast and quick. To really soak up the region's flavor, turn off the main roads and wander up and over rolling ridges, and into narrow folds in the mountains that hide peaceful villages. If it suddenly seems to you that the landscape hasn't changed all that much in the past two centuries, well, you're right. It hasn't.

This region is well known for its pristine and historic villages. You'll stumble across them as you explore—you can't help but find them. And no matter how many other people have found them before you, there's almost always a sense that these are your own private discoveries.

A good strategy is to stop for a spell in Brattleboro to stock up on supplies or sample some local music. Then set off for the southern Green Mountains, settle in to a remote inn, and continue your explorations by foot, bike, or canoe. In winter, you can plumb the snowy white hills by cross-country ski or snowshoe.

The single best source of regional travel information in the region is the **state visitors' center** (☎ **802/254-4593**) on I-91 in Guilford, south of Brattleboro.

BRATTLEBORO

Set in a scenic river valley, Brattleboro is not only a good spot for last-minute provisioning, but also has a funky, slightly dated charm that's part 1940s, part 1970s. The rough brick texture of this compact, hilly city has aged nicely, its flavor only enhanced with its adoption by "feral hippies" (as a friend of mine calls them), who live in and around town and operate many of the best local enterprises.

While Brattleboro is very much part of the 20th century, its heritage runs much deeper. In fact, Brattleboro was Vermont's first permanent settlement. (The first actual settlement, which was short-lived, was at Isle la Motte on Lake Champlain in 1666.) Soldiers protecting the Massachusetts town of Northfield built an outpost here in 1724 at Fort Dummer, about a mile and a half south of the current downtown. The site of the fort is now a small state park. In later years, Brattleboro became a center of trade and manufacturing, and was the home of the Estey Organ Co., which once supplied countless home organs carved in an ornate Victorian style to families across the nation.

Brattleboro remains the commercial hub of southeast Vermont, located at the junction of I-89, routes 5 and 9, and the Connecticut River. It's also the most convenient jumping-off point for those arriving from the south via the interstate.

ESSENTIALS

GETTING THERE   From the north or south, Brattleboro is easily accessible via Exit 1 or 2 on I-91. From the east or west, Brattleboro is most easily reached via Route 9.

VISITOR INFORMATION   The **Brattleboro Chamber of Commerce,** 180 Main St., Brattleboro, VT 05301 (☎ **802/254-4565**), next to the Dunkin Donuts, dispenses travel information year-round between 8am and 5pm weekdays.

EXPLORING THE TOWN

Here's an easy strategy for exploring Brattleboro: Park. Walk.

The commercially vibrant downtown is blessedly compact, and strolling around on foot is the best way to appreciate its very human scale and handsome commercial architecture. Even if you're en route to a destination to the north, it's well worth a stop for a bite to eat and some light shopping.

Enjoyable for kids and curious adults is the **Brattleboro Museum & Art Center** (☎ **802/257-0124**) at the Union Railroad Station. Founded in 1972, the center offers wonderful exhibits highlighting the history of the town and the Connecticut River Valley, along with paintings and sculpture by artists of local and international repute. The museum is open daily except Mondays from noon to 6pm from mid-May through October. It's located downtown near the bridge to New Hampshire. Admission is $2 for adults, $1 for seniors and college students, free for children under 18.

North of town on Route 5, where the highway crosses the West River (a Connecticut River tributary), you can sign up for a guided river tour on the **Belle of Brattleboro** (☎ 802/254-1263). This sturdy, wood-decked riverboat, which may recall the *African Queen* among incurable romantics or those with poor vision, seats about 50 at picnic table–style seating under a yellow canopy. A variety of cruises is offered, but all offer a glimpse of Brattleboro's wildlife and small-town allure from the languid West and Connecticut rivers. Tours run frequently in summer, and cost $7 for adults and $4 for children; there's an additional fee for cruises featuring meals or on-board entertainment.

OUTDOOR PURSUITS

A soaring aerial view of Brattleboro might be had by hiking **Wantastiquet Mountain,** which is just across the Connecticut River in New Hampshire. You can drive to the trailhead, but somehow it's more adventurous to walk from downtown (figure on a round trip of about three hours). To reach the base of the "mountain" (a term that's just slightly grandiose), cross the river on the two green steel bridges, then turn left on the first dirt road; go two-tenths of a mile to a parking area on your right. The trail begins here; trekkers ascend via a carriage road (stick to the main trail and avoid the side trails) that winds about two miles through forest and past open ledges to the summit, which is marked by a monument dating from 1908. From here, you'll be rewarded with sweeping views of the river, the town, and the landscape beyond. Retrace your steps back to town or your car.

Canoeists stuck in Vermont without their canoe will find salvation at **Connecticut River Safari** (☎ 802/257-5008 or 802/254-3908) where Route 5 spans the West River north of town. Located in a shady riverside glen, this is a fine spot to rent a canoe or kayak to poke around for a couple of hours ($10 for two people), a half day ($15), or a full day ($20). Explore locally, or arrange for a shuttle upriver or down. The owners are exceedingly helpful about providing information and maps to keep you on track. Among the best areas for snooping, especially for bird-watchers, are the marshy areas along the lower West River and a detour off the Connecticut River locally called "The Everglades." Pack a lunch and make a day of it.

WHERE TO STAY

40 Putney Rd. 40 Putney Rd., Brattleboro, VT 05301. ☎ **800/941-2413** or 802/254-6268. Fax 802/258-2673. 4 rms. A/C TEL. $80–$95 double. Rates include breakfast. AE, DISC, MC, V.

This stately home of white brick and gray slate sits off Route 5 at the northern edge of downtown Brattleboro. Built in the early 1930s as a home for the superintendent of the nearby Brattleboro Retreat, this small French chateau–style mansion was converted to a B&B in 1991 and now offers Brattleboro's most elegant accommodations. The common rooms have hardwood floors and dark wood detailing, which nicely offsets the pale muted colors of the walls. Wingback chairs and a bowback sofa face the fireplace; there's always a decanter of port set out for guests. Innkeepers Joan and Pete Broderick are gracious hosts, offering complimentary juices in an upstairs refrigerator, and the *New York Times* and *Boston Globe* on Sundays.

Guest rooms are well-appointed with country modern furnishings, including hooked and chenille rugs. The best of the four rooms is the two-room suite, which features built-in bureaus and a large tiled bathroom. Guests are welcome to enjoy the landscaped backyard along the West River, or stroll into town on a riverside path. Breakfasts are at the gourmet end of the scale, and are served on the pleasant backyard patio in summer. No smoking.

Latchis Hotel. 50 Main St., Brattleboro, VT 05301. ☎ **802/254-6300.** Fax 802/254-6304. 30 rms. A/C TV TEL. $49–$98 double. AE, MC, V.

This wonderful downtown hotel fairly leaps out in Victorian-brick Brattleboro. Built in 1938 in an understated art deco style (it's one of only two genuinely art deco buildings in Vermont), the Latchis was once the cornerstone for a small chain of hotels and theaters. It no longer has its own orchestra or commanding dining room (although the theater remains), but it's still owned by the Latchis family and has an authentic if slightly dated flair.

Guests enter through a narrow lobby decorated with subtle art deco detailing, then walk or ride the elevator to guest rooms on the three upstairs floors. The colorful hallways are reminiscent of a film noir piece—you can't help but wonder what's going on behind all the doors. For the most part, the guest rooms are comfortable, not luxurious, with simple maple furniture and old-time radiators that keep the place toasty in winter. From the hotel, it's easy to explore the town on foot, or you can wander the first-floor hallways to take in a first-run movie at the Latchis Theatre or quaff a pint at the Windham Brewery.

WHERE TO DINE

🟢 **Common Ground.** 25 Eliot St. ☎ **802/257-0855.** Reservations not accepted. Lunch $2.25–$7.50; dinner $3–$7. No credit cards. Mon and Wed–Thurs 11:30am–8pm, Fri–Sat 11:30am–9pm, Sun 10:30am–2pm and 5:30–9pm. WHOLE FOODS.

The Common Ground, which opened two years after the Woodstock Music Festival, is now a well-established culinary landmark occupying a funky, hectic space on the second floor of a downtown building. The tone is set walking up the stairway, where business cards tout trauma touch therapy, astrological readings, and meditation and movement services. At the top of the stairs, diners choose from a well-worn interior space, or a pleasant greenhouse addition. The Common Ground is operated as a worker-owned cooperative, and service is cordial if not always brisk.

There's little variation between the lunch and dinner menu; both draw heavily from local and organic ingredients. A meal might include grilled tofu with tahini, brown rice with tamari ginger sauce, or a marinated sea vegetable salad. Or stick with the basics: a bowl of brown rice, beans, and a tortilla costs just $2.50. Sandwiches include tempeh reuben, Vermont cheddar, and the classic peanut butter and jelly (made with organic Valencia peanut butter and cider jelly and served on whole-wheat bread). There's often live entertainment in the evenings.

Curtis Bar-B-Q. Rte. 5, Putney. ☎ **802/387-5474.** Main courses $4–$20. No credit cards. Wed–Sun 10am–dark. Closed Nov–spring. BARBECUE.

Just uphill from Exit 4 off I-91 (about 9 miles north of Brattleboro) you suddenly smell the delicious aroma of barbecue sizzling over open pits. Do not pass this place by, because you will change your mind later and waste a lot of time and gasoline backtracking. After all, this is the best barbecue in Vermont, and possibly in New England.

This classic roadside food joint, situated on a scruffy lot next to a Mobil station, has a heap of charm despite itself. (The five signs commanding "All dogs must be leashed" set a strangely appropriate mood for dining here.) This self-serve restaurant consists of two blue school buses and a tin-roofed cooking shed; guests take their booty to a smattering of picnic tables scattered about the lot. Place your order, grab a seat, dig in, and enjoy.

Peter Havens. 32 Eliot, Brattleboro. ☎ **802/257-3333.** Reservations strongly recommended. Main courses $15–$21. MC, V. Tues–Sat 6–9pm. REGIONAL/AMERICAN.

Peter Havens has been serving up the most consistently reliable fine dining in Brattleboro since it opened in 1989. Situated downtown in an upscale, contemporary building, Peter Havens doesn't offer a creative menu. You won't find towering appetizers that defy architectural principles, or wheelbarrow-loads of this year's trendy herb in your meal, but you will get choice ingredients served with panache and flair. The restaurant has but a handful of tables, so make a reservation if you have your heart set on dining here.

All appetizers are priced at $6.50 (except for soup at $4), and range from pâté to gravlax to a smoked filet of lemon-peppered trout. Fewer than 10 entrees are on the menu, but among these you'll find a grilled filet mignon served with a green peppercorn bourbon sauce, and duck breast roasted with a black currant and port sauce. For seafood, there's scallops with roasted peppers and crabmeat in a light cream sauce, and salmon with a delicately sweet Zinfandel and shallot sauce. Wines are limited, but the selection is decent.

WILMINGTON REGION

Set high in the hills on the winding mountain highway midway between Bennington and Brattleboro, Wilmington has managed to retain its charm as an attractive crossroads village despite its location on two busy roads. The town draws its share of tourists (especially from New York and New Jersey) but still has the feel of a gracious mountain village.

From Wilmington, the ski resorts of Haystack and Mt. Snow are easily accessible to the north via Route 100, which is brisk, busy, and close to impassable on sunny weekends in early October. Heading north, you'll first pass through West Dover, a very attractive, classical New England town with a prominent steeple and acres of white clapboard.

Between West Dover and Mt. Snow, it becomes increasingly evident that developers and entrepreneurs discovered the area in the years following the founding of Mt. Snow in 1954. Some regard this stretch of highway as a monument to lack of planning. While the development isn't dense (this is no North Conway, N.H.), the buildings represent a not-entirely-savory mélange of architectural styles, the most prominent of which is Tyrolean Chicken Coop Nightmare. Many of these buildings began their lives as ski lodges and have since been reincarnated as boutiques, inns, and restaurants. The silver lining is this: The unsightly development prompted Vermont to later pass a progressive and restrictive environmental law, which has saved many other areas from degradation.

Much of the development along Route 100 ceases just north of Mt. Snow. Also, remember that you're not restricted to Route 100, no matter what the locals tell you. The area is packed with smaller roads, both paved and dirt, that make for excellent exploring.

ESSENTIALS

GETTING THERE Wilmington is located at the juncture of Routes 9 and 100. Route 9 offers the most direct access from both Bennington and Brattleboro. The Mt. Snow area is located north of Wilmington on Route 100.

VISITOR INFORMATION The **Mt. Snow/Haystack Region Chamber of Commerce,** Main Street, P.O. Box 3, Wilmington, VT 05363 (☎ **802/464-8092**), maintains an information booth May through September at the intersection of Route 9 and Route 100. The **Mt. Snow Lodging Bureau and Vacation Service** (☎ **800/ 245-7669**) can assist with booking rooms in the area.

THE MARLBORO MUSIC FESTIVAL

The renowned Marlboro Music Festival offers classical concerts performed by highly talented student musicians on weekends from July through mid-August in the agreeable town of Marlboro, east of Wilmington on Route 9. Concerts take place in the 700-seat auditorium at Marlboro College, and advance ticket purchases are strongly recommended. Call or write for a schedule and ticket forms. Between September and June contact the festival's winter office at Marlboro Music, 135 S. 18th St., Philadelphia, PA 19103 (☎ 215/569-4690). In summer, write Marlboro Music, Marlboro, VT 05344, or call the box office (☎ 802/254-2394).

WHAT TO SEE & DO

Mountain Biking

Mt. Snow was one of the first resorts to foresee the growing appeal of mountain biking, and the region remains one of the leading destinations for those whose vehicle of choice has knobby tires. Mt. Snow established the first mountain bike school in the country, and remains one of the best places to be formally introduced to the sport. The **Mountain Bike Center** (☎ 800/245-7669) at the base of the mountain offers equipment rentals, maps, and advice.

Independent mountain bikers can also explore some 140 miles of trail and abandoned road that lace the region. For a small fee, you can take your bike to the mountaintop by chairlift and coast your way down along marked trails, or earn the ride by pumping out the vertical rise to the top. Fanning out from the mountain are numerous abandoned town roads that make for less challenging but no less pleasant excursions.

Alpine Skiing

Mt. Snow/Haystack. Mt. Snow, VT 05356. ☎ 800/245-7669 or 802/464-3333 for lodging. Vertical drop: 1,700 feet. Lifts: 21 (1 high speed), 3 surface lifts. Skiable acreage: 650. Lift tickets: $47 weekends, $42 weekdays.

These two former ski resorts, once competitors, are now both owned by American Skiing Company, which also owns numerous other New England resorts. Bear in mind that the figures above are for the combined ski areas—neither one is all that big. The main mountain is noted for its widely cut runs, and is an excellent destination for intermediates and advanced intermediates. Advanced skiers head to the North Face, which is its own little world. Because it's the most southerly of the Vermont ski areas and the closest to the Boston–New York megalopolis, it can become quite crowded at times. Haystack, which is 10 miles distant by car (it's much closer if you're a crow) is a classic older New England ski mountain, with challenging, narrow runs. Lift lines are typically much shorter at Haystack.

Mt. Snow's village is attractively arrayed along the base of the mountain. The most imposing structure is the balconied hotel overlooking a small pond, but the overall character is shaped more by the unobtrusive smaller lodges and homes. While once famed for its groovy singles scene, Mt. Snow's postskiing activities today tend to center around families and downtime in the condo. With its conscientious landscaping and agreeable location, Mt. Snow is among the most aesthetically appealing New England ski areas in summer, a season when few resorts lavish much attention on their facilities.

Cross-Country Skiing

The Mt. Snow area offers several excellent cross-country ski centers. **Timber Creek Cross Country Touring Center** (☎ 802/464-0999) in West Dover near the Mt. Snow access road is a popular area with beginners and holds snow nicely thanks to its high elevation. The **Hermitage Ski Touring Center** (☎ 802/464-3511) attracts more advanced skiers to its varied terrain and 30 miles of trails. The **White House Ski Touring Center** (☎ 802/464-0999), at the inn by the same name on Route 100, offers the easiest access to the Vermont woods and a good range of terrain. And the **Sitzmark** ski center (☎ 802/464-3384) maintains 24 miles of cross-county trails that covers terrain with 550 feet of elevation gain.

WHERE TO STAY

Inn at Sawmill Farm. Rte. 100 (P.O. Box 367), West Dover, VT 05356. ☎ **802/464-8131.** Fax 802/464-1130. 21 rms. A/C. $340–$400 double. Rates include breakfast and dinner. AE, MC, V. Closed last week of Apr and first week of May.

"Interior designers say you can't mix plaid with floral," says innkeeper Rodney Williams as he walks through his barn turned common room at Sawmill Farm. "But this works," he says, indicating the bright floral upholstered couch on the bold tartan carpet. Well, whatever. But rest assured, the fashion police won't find anything else to fault at this very elegant, very cordial, and very expensive inn, which is part of the exclusive Relais & Chateaux chain. Many guests book rooms just to be close to the restaurant (see "Where to Dine," below), which serves memorable meals.

The rooms in this old farmhouse, parts of which date back to 1797, are each different, but all share a similar contemporary country styling and colonial reproduction furniture. The rooms are generally spacious; among the best are Cider House no. 2, with its rustic beams and oversized canopy bed, and the Woodshed, a quiet cottage with a beautiful brick fireplace and a cozy loft. After 6pm, men are requested to wear jackets in all public areas of the inn.

Facilities: Guests have the run of the 28-acre grounds, set near the quintessential New England village of West Dover, and can fish for rainbow trout in the two ponds or lounge by the swimming pool.

Trail's End. 5 Trail's End Lane ($^{1}/_{2}$ mile off Rte. 100 between Haystack and Mt. Snow), Wilmington, VT 05363. ☎ **802/464-2727.** 15 rms (2 with shower only). Summer $90–$140 double, fall $100–$160 double, winter $110–$170 double. Rates include full breakfast. AE, MC, V. Closed Easter to late May.

When the current innkeepers bought Trail's End in 1985, it was a rough ski lodge 30 years old, with bunk beds nailed into the walls. Since acquiring it, Bill and Mary Kilburn have carved out an inviting, friendly spot that attracts repeat visitors who come for the instant camaraderie with other guests and their gregarious hosts.

Trail's End's carpeted guest rooms are spotlessly clean, styled in a light country fashion with pine and wicker furniture. But few guests seem to spend much time in their rooms. They congregate around the 22-foot stone fireplace in the main common room, in the stone-floored library and game room, or in the informal second-floor loft—or they hang out in the kitchen with Bill as he obsessively polishes his gleaming stove. At breakfast, the congregating continues around three massive round tables. Introverts, it should go without saying, will not be happy here. Others will.

Facilities: In summer, guests enjoy the heated outdoor pool and a clay tennis court set amid 28 acres of forest owned by the inn.

White House of Wilmington. Rte. 9, Wilmington, VT 05363. ☎ **800/541-2135** or 802/464-2135. 23 rms. $108–$178 double. Rates include full breakfast. Fireplace rms are $30 less in summer. AE, MC, V.

The White House of Wilmington, a fanciful Greek Revivial–style home with two prominent porticos (built in 1915 by a wealthy lumber baron), sits impressively on the crest of an open hill just east of Wilmington. The interior is spacious and open, with hardwood floors, arched doorways, and superb detailing throughout. Formal without being stuffy, the inn has an especially appealing bar on its enclosed porch, which can't be beat as a spot to sip something soothing while watching the sun sink over the Vermont hills.

Dining/Entertainment: The inn's restaurant is well regarded for its continental cuisine, served in an attractive dining room with hardwood floors, dark wood trim, pink tablecloths, and an intricate fireplace mantel. Entrees include duck stuffed with walnuts, apples, and grapes (the chef's specialty); veal piccata; and filet mignon au poivre.

Facilities: The inn boasts an attractive swimming pool, tennis courts, and, for winter travelers, 27 miles of groomed cross-country ski trails. The inn also accommodates snowmobilers.

WHERE TO DINE

✪ **Inn at Sawmill Farm.** Rte. 100, West Dover. ☎ **802/464-8131.** Reservations strongly recommended. Men requested to wear jackets. Main courses $27–$32. AE, MC, V. Daily 6–9:30pm. Closed the last week of Apr to the first week of May. CONTINENTAL.

Let's talk wine. About 36,000 bottles of wine. That's what's lurking in the inn's custom-made wine cellar, and what garnered it a coveted "Grand Award" from *Wine Spectator* magazine.

But that's the least of the reasons diners flock here. The food is deftly prepared by innkeeper/chef Brill Williams (son of innkeepers Ione and Rodney Williams), with entrees ranging from pan-seared salmon in saffron sauce to breast of pheasant with a forestiere sauce. For a little foreign intrigue, you might opt for the sautéed breast of chicken, served with a surprisingly delicate Indonesian curry sauce and caramelized banana.

The atmosphere is near perfect. While the garden dining room is less posh than the popular formal dining room (housed in a portion of an old barn), the soft tones, wide pine planks in the floors, and live piano music filling the air lend the whole dining room a soft and romantic feel. Beautiful silverware and glassware accent the mood. The service is superb, although the slavish attention and overall formality instantly makes informal folks somewhat edgy.

Le Petit Chef. Rte. 100, Wilmington. ☎ **802/464-8437.** Reservations recommended. Main courses $15–$25 (mostly $19–$22). AE, MC, V. Wed–Thurs and Sun–Mon 6–9pm, Fri–Sat 6–10pm. FRENCH.

Situated in an old Cape Cod–style house on Route 100, Le Petit Chef has attracted legions of satisfied customers who flock here to sample Betty Hillman's superb and creative cooking. The interior has been updated and modernized at the expense of some character, and the service can be spotty at times, but the quality of the food typically overcomes these shortcomings. By all means, start with the signature "Bird's Nest," an innovative mélange of shiitake mushrooms and onions cooked in a cream sauce and served in a basket of deep-fried potatoes. The main courses are equally succulent, with selections like a filet of salmon baked in a horseradish crust, loin of venison sautéed and served with sun-dried cherry sauce, and spicy shrimp sautéed with leeks and peppers and served on crispy noodles.

NEWFANE & TOWNSHEND

For many travelers, these two villages about five miles apart on Route 30 are the epitome of Vermont. Both are set deeply within the serpentine West River Valley, and both are built around open town greens. Both towns consist of impressive white clapboard homes and public buildings that share the grace and scale of the surrounding homes. Both towns boast striking examples of early American architecture, notably Greek Revival.

Don't bother looking for strip malls, McDonald's, or garish video outlets hereabouts. Newfane and Townshend feel as if they've been idled on a sidetrack for decades while the rest of American society steamed blithely ahead. That's not to say these villages have the somber feel of a mausoleum. On recent visits in autumn, a swarm of teenagers was skateboarding off the steps of the courthouse in Newfane, and a lively basketball game was under way at the edge of the green in Townshend. There's life here.

For visitors, inactivity is often the activity of choice. Guests find an inn or lodge that suits their temperament, then spend the days strolling the towns, undertaking aimless back-road driving tours, soaking in a mountain stream, or striking off on foot for one of the rounded, wooded peaks that overlook villages and valleys.

ESSENTIALS

GETTING THERE   Newfane and Townshend are located on Route 30 northwest of Brattleboro. The nearest interstate access is off Exit 3 from I-91.

VISITOR INFORMATION   There's no formal information center serving these towns. Brochures are available at the **state visitors center** (☎ 802/254-4593) on I-91 in Guilford, south of Brattleboro. Visitors might also try the Townshend Country Store for local advice.

EXPLORING THE AREA

Newfane was originally founded on a hill a few miles away in 1774; in 1825 it was moved down to the valley floor. Some of the original buildings were dismantled and rebuilt, but most date from the early- to mid-19th century. The **National Historic District** is comprised of some 60 buildings around the green and scattered on nearby side streets. You'll find styles ranging from Federal through Colonial Revival, although Greek Revival appears to predominate. A strikingly handsome courthouse—where cases have been heard for 170 years—sets on the edge of the shady green. This structure was originally built in 1825; the imposing portico was added in 1853. For more detailed information on area buildings, obtain a copy of the free walking tour brochure at the Moore Free Library on West Street.

About a dozen **antique shops** line Route 30 through the West River Valley, as well as on Route 35 north of Townshend. They provide good grazing on lazy afternoons, and are a fine resource for serious collectors. The **Newfane Antiques Center** (☎ 802/365-4482) houses 20 dealers on three floors and offers a broad selection ranging from bric-a-brac to quality furniture. Other dealers include the **A. Richter Gallery** (☎ 802/365-4549) in Townshend, which specializes in early prints and posters, and **Schommer Antiques** (☎ 802/365-7777) in Newfane Village, which carries a good selection of 19th-century furniture and accessories.

Hard-core treasure hunters should time their visit to hit the **Newfane Flea Market** (☎ 802/365-4000), which features 100-plus tables of assorted stuff. The flea market is held Sundays May through October on Route 30 just north of Newfane village.

OUTDOOR PURSUITS

Three miles outside of Townshend is **Townshend State Park** (☎ 802/365-7500) and **Townshend State Forest.** Located at the foot of Bald Mountain, the park consists mostly of a solidly built campground constructed by the Civilian Conservation Corps in the 1930s. But you can park here to hike **Bald Mountain,** one of the better short hikes in the region. A 3.1-mile loop trail begins behind the ranger station, following a bridle path along a brook. The ascent soon steepens, and at 1.7 miles you'll arrive at the 1,680-foot summit, which turns out not to be bald at all. But open ledges offer views toward Mt. Monadnock to the east, and Bromley and Stratton mountains to the west. The descent is via a steeper 1.4-mile trail that ends behind the campground. The park is open early May through Columbus Day; the day use fee is $1.50 for adults, $1 for children. Ask for trail maps at the park office. The park is reached by crossing the Townshend Dam (off Route 30), then turning left and continuing to the park sign.

For more swimming, continue northwest on Route 30 to the photogenic town of Jamaica. **Jamaica State Park** (☎ 802/874-4600) offers campsites and picnicking along the West River (there's good swimming and splashing in the river), and a trail to Ball Mountain Dam. Some of New England's premier white-water canoeing and kayak racing takes place on the river below the dam in the spring and fall; races are scheduled around controlled releases from the dam.

WHERE TO STAY

Four Columns Inn. West St. (P.O. Box 278), Newfane, VT 05345. ☎ **800/787-6633** or 802/ 365-7713. 15 rms. A/C TEL. $110–$175 double, including full breakfast; foliage season $200– $275 double, including breakfast and dinner. AE, MC, V.

You can't help but notice The Four Columns Inn in Newfane: It's the regal, white clapboard building with four Ionic columns, setting just off the green. The inn is decorated in a light country style throughout, and is located on lushly landscaped grounds. It's a great base for exploring the village. If you've stayed here in the past and found the management to be a little impersonal and haughty, give it another try; new innkeepers Pam and Gorton Baldwin acquired the inn in early 1996.

Dining/Entertainment: Perhaps the inn's greatest attraction is the well-respected dining room, which serves creatively prepared meals such as scallops and shrimp with vegetables in a green curry, and grilled duck with a sour cherry and rosemary sauce.

West River Lodge. R.R. 1 (P.O. Box 693), Newfane, VT 05345. ☎ **802/365-7745.** 8 rms (2 with private bath; 6 others share 3 baths). $70–$80 double. Rates include full breakfast. DISC, MC, V. Closed during mud season.

This is as close as you'll come to a dude ranch vacation in the East—and you can enjoy it without the early morning wake-up call. Situated in a beautiful, broad valley with views of farmland and countryside, the West River Lodge caters to equestrians in the summer and cross-country skiers in the winter. This is not the place to be if you prefer to be left alone on your vacation. Guests become part of the family here, with everyone sitting down to eat at 7pm, and sharing stories in cluttered and cozy common rooms after the meal. Many guests couple their stay with horseback riding classes or tours at the adjacent West River Stables. The stables, which have been offering English riding instruction since 1948, are run by Roger Poitras and his staff, who know the hidden bridle trails well and are happy to share their knowledge with you. If you're not a horse person, you can just enjoy farm life (there are also dogs, cats, and cows), or walk down the dirt lane to a fine swimming hole.

✪ Windham Hill Inn. Windham Hill Rd., West Townshend, VT 05359. ☎ **800/944-4080** or 802/874-4080. 18 rms, including 5 in nearby barn. A/C TEL. $195–$230 double, including breakfast and dinner. AE, DC, DISC, MC, V. Closed Apr and Thanksgiving weekend through Christmas. Turn uphill across from the country store in West Townshend and climb 1¹/₄ mile up a demanding hill to a marked dirt road; turn right and continue to end.

The Windham Hill Inn is one of the most elegant, quiet, and remote inns you'll find in Vermont. Situated at the end of a dirt road in a high upland valley, the inn was originally built in 1823 as a farmhouse, and remained in the same family until the

1950s, when it was converted to an inn. Under the new ownership of innkeepers Pat and Grigs Markham, the Windham Hill has ratcheted up several notches in quality as costly and extensive renovations have managed to meld the best of the old and the new. The guest rooms are wonderfully appointed in elegant country style. Ask to see the five rooms in the barn, which are a bit more rustic but marvelous examples of adaptive reuse.

Windham Hill is at the pricey end of the scale, but it's a guaranteed treat for those with limited leisure time who don't wish to take a chance on their vacation. This is a no-smoking inn.

Dining/Entertainment: The newly expanded dining room is still the picture of elegant simplicity, with light ash flooring and simple table settings. The views of the small pond are lovely, but not enough to distract from the delicious meals, which feature creative French cooking with a strong emphasis on local and seasonal ingredients.

Facilities: The inn is located on 160 acres, with 6 miles of cross-country ski trails groomed in the winter, and fine hiking through mixed forest and meadows in the summer.

WHERE TO DINE

Townshend Corner Store. Corner of rtes. 30 and 35, Townshend. ☎ **802/365-4624.** Breakfast $1.55–$4.25, lunch and dinner items $1.60–$4.05. No credit cards. Daily 6:30am–7pm. LUNCHEONETTE.

"Sit long—talk much" reads the sign behind the counter. It's posted over the day's ice-cream selections, which, quite frankly, don't vary much from yesterday's selections. Or tomorrow's. But the sign offers good advice for getting the most out of this classic country store, located on the green in Townshend. The dining area takes up about half the room, and in summer is likely to be occupied by a mix of locals and tourists, each eyeing the other warily. But don't fret it. Just sidle up to the worn, red laminate counter with the red toadstool-shape stools, and enjoy the simple, filling luncheonette fare. Particularly good are the old-fashioned milk shakes and pies, and the thick slabs of bacon that come with breakfast.

GRAFTON & CHESTER

When I first visited Grafton, I was fully prepared to dislike it. I'd heard from others that it was pristine and quaint, the result of an ambitious preservation plan by wealthy benefactors. I figured it would be too precious, too fussy, too much an overwrought picture-book re-creation of New England as envisioned by the D.A.R.

But it only took me about a half-hour of aimless wandering to come away a serious booster of the place. It's not a museum like Sturbridge Village or Colonial Williamsburg, but an active town with some 600 residents. It just happens to have dozens of museum-quality homes and buildings.

More commercial Chester, in contrast, is less pristine and feels more lived in. The downtown area has a pleasant neighborly feel to it, along with a handful of intriguing boutiques and shops set along the long, narrow green. Chester is a great destination for antiquing, with several good dealers in the area. When heading north of town on Route 103, be sure to slow enough to enjoy the Stone Village, where a neighborhood of well-spaced, austere stone homes line the roadway. Many of these homes were said to be major stopping points on the Underground Railroad.

ESSENTIALS

GETTING THERE The most direct route to Bellows Falls is via I-91; get off at either Exit 5 or 6 and follow signs to town via Route 5. Grafton is 12 miles west of

Bellows Falls on Route 121, at the intersection of Route 35. *Tip:* The trip north on Route 35 from Townshend to Grafton is exceedingly scenic and pastoral.

VISITOR INFORMATION The **Grafton Information Center,** Grafton, VT 05146 (☎ **802/843-2255**), is located on Route 35 just south of the village. For information about Chester, contact the **Chester Chamber of Commerce,** P.O. Box 623, Chester, VT 05143 (☎ **802/875-2939**).

EXPLORING GRAFTON

Grafton is best seen at a languorous pace, on foot, when the weather is welcoming. Don't expect to be overwhelmed with grandeur. Instead, keep a keen eye out for telling historical details.

Start at the **Grafton Information Center** (see above), which offers parking and access to the rest of the village. Exhibits in the main center provide some background on the village's history. Barns nearby house other informative exhibits.

From here, follow a footpath past the barns and through a small covered bridge to the **Grafton Cheese Co.** (☎ **800/472-3866**), a small, modern building where you can buy a snack of award-winning cheese and peer through plate-glass windows to observe the cheesemaking process. (*Note:* Outwardly, it's not very complicated or interesting.)

Cross back over the covered bridge and bear right on the footpath along the cow pasture to the **Kidder Covered Bridge,** then head into town via Water Street, continuing on to Main Street. Toward the village center, white clapboard homes and shade trees abound. Appreciate it. This is about as New England as New England gets.

On Main Street, stop by the **Grafton Historical Society Museum** (☎ **802/ 843-2344**; open weekends only) for photographs, artifacts, and memorabilia of Grafton. The nearby **Grafton Museum of Natural History** (☎ **802/843-2347**; open weekends only) offers intriguing displays on Vermont wildlife.

Afterwards, stop by the **Old Tavern at Grafton,** the impressive building that anchors the town and has served as a social center since 1801, and enjoy a beverage at the rustic Phelps Barn Lounge, or a meal in one of the dining rooms (see below). From here, you can make your way back to the information center by wandering on pleasant side streets. If you'd like to expand your range and cruise the outlying areas by bike, ask about rentals at the tavern. Horse and buggy rides are also available here.

If you're visiting in winter, Grafton offers superb cross-country skiing at the **Grafton Ponds Cross-Country Ski Center** (☎ **802/843-2400**), located just south of the cheese factory on Route 35. Managed by the Old Tavern, Grafton Ponds has 18 miles of groomed trails (with snowmaking on 3 miles) and a warming hut near the ponds where you can sit by a fire and enjoy a steaming bowl of soup. Ski and snowshoe rentals are available; a trail pass costs $12 for adults, $8 for seniors, and $6 for children 12 and under.

WHERE TO STAY & DINE

Inn at Long Last. Rte. 11 (P.O. Box 589), Chester, VT 05143. ☎ **802/875-2444.** 30 rms (some with shower only). $160 double, including breakfast and dinner; $110 double on Mon, including breakfast only. MC, V. Closed Apr and mid-Nov.

"This place succeeds where others are just cutesy," wrote one recent guest in the hotel's guest book. And that about sums it up. This three-story downtown hostelry, originally built in 1923, has a low-key charm and quirky ambience. Owned by Jack Coleman, formerly the president of Haverford College in Pennsylvania, the inn features eclectically furnished guest rooms, each decorated with a theme. The

Frederick Law Olmsted Room, for instance, features prints of Olmsted-designed parks and two books about the landscape architect on the bedside table. The Charles Dickens Room has volumes by the author, and a regal Victorian veneer. Take a look around and find a room that suits you. Downstairs the lobby has the feel of a bustling stagecoach stop, with highly polished floors, braided and Oriental rugs, a stone fireplace, and a tidy collection of miniature soldiers in lighted cases. Guests are made to feel like family here, and it's a fun family to be part of.

Dining/Entertainment: The dining room at the Inn at Long Last has a formal setting with an informal character. The meals are creative and professionally prepared by chef Russ Jones. You might start with slices of grilled smoked pork tenderloin with apple-pistachio butter, or a mushroom and Gruyère tortellini. Then graduate to a grilled breast of chicken with a fennel-artichoke ratatouille, or salmon served with a Thai-melon salsa.

✪ **The Old Tavern at Grafton.** Rtes. 35 and 121, Grafton, VT 05146. ☎ **800/843-1801** or 802/843-2231. 66 rms (2 with shower only). $115–$165 double. Rates include continental breakfast. Discounts available May–June and midweek in summer. MC, V. Closed Apr.

Countless New England inns seek to replicate the service and gracious style of a far larger resort, but fall short because of understaffing and a woeful lack of capital. But the Old Tavern at Grafton succeeds, and wildly so. It should be noted this is called Old Tavern, not "Ye Olde Taverne," a good reflection of the understated quality and professional service that has pervaded the establishment since a management change a few years ago. Note also that the Old Tavern advertises only lightly, yet still draws capacity crowds through word of mouth.

The inn seems more intimate than its 66 guest rooms would suggest, since the rooms are spread throughout the town. Fourteen are in the exceptionally handsome colonnaded main building, 22 are across the street in the Homestead Cottage, and the remaining rooms are scattered among seven historic guest houses in and around the village. All rooms are decorated with antiques and an upscale country elegance, but the rooms in the Homestead Cottage (which is actually two historic homes joined together) have a more modern, hotel-like character.

The common areas in the inn are formal in a Federal-style sort of way, but those determined to relax can still do so. And, of course, there's the village of Grafton to reconnoiter, which requires but a few steps from the front door.

Dining/Entertainment: "Appropriate dinner attire" is requested, but there's still a fairly loose, relaxed air to the three dining rooms in the evening. The menu features classic New England fare, updated for more adventurous palates and with healthier choices in mind. Dinner features entrees like roasted rack of lamb, panéed mignons of venison, and a house favorite, lobster pie. Lighter entrees include grilled chicken breast and vegetarian pizza.

Facilities: As for recreation, the inn boasts swimming in an attractive sand-bottomed pool, hiking, bike rentals, two tennis courts, and, in winter, ice-skating, cross-country skiing, and platform tennis.

LUDLOW & OKEMO

Ludlow is home to Okemo Mountain, a once-sleepy ski resort that's been nicely upgraded and updated in the past decade. Ludlow is also notable as one of the few Vermont ski towns that didn't go through one of those unfortunate Tyrolean identity crises. Centered around a former mill that produced fabrics and, later, aircraft parts, Ludlow has an unpretentious made-in-milltown-Vermont character that seems quite distant from the prim grace of white-clapboard Grafton. Low-key and unassuming, it draws skiers by the busload in winter (it's especially popular with travelers from the New York City metropolitan area); in summer, it's a good place to put your feet up on the rail and watch the clouds float over the mountaintops.

ESSENTIALS

GETTING THERE   Ludlow is situated at the intersection of Route 193 and Route 100. The most direct route from an interstate is Exit 6 off I-93; follow Route 103 westward to Ludlow.

VISITOR INFORMATION   The **Ludlow Area Chamber of Commerce,** P.O. Box 333, Ludlow, VT 05149 (☎ 802/228-5830), staffs a helpful information booth at the Okemo Marketplace, at the foot of Mountain Road.

SKIING

Okemo. Ludlow, VT 05149. ☎ **800/786-5366** or 802/228-4041 for lodging. Vertical drop: 2,150 feet. Lifts: 10 chairlifts (2 high-speed), 2 surface lifts. Skiable acreage: 470. Lift tickets: $47 weekend, $43 weekday.

Okemo fans like to point out a couple of things. First, this is one of the few family-owned mountains remaining in Vermont (it's been owned by Tim and Diane Mueller since 1982). Second, it now offers some good advanced trails on the newly cut south face, ridding it of the accusations that it's just an intermediate's mountain. Okemo still doesn't attract the yahoos, who gravitate to way-gnarlier Killington to the north. As such, it's still first and foremost a mountain for families, who not only like the varied terrain but the friendly base area that's of a scale not too intimidating for kids.

WHERE TO STAY

During ski season, contact the **Okemo Mountain Lodging Service** (☎ 800/ 786-5366 or 802/228-5571) for reservations at a variety of area accommodations, including slopeside condos. Those looking for a longer stay should check with **Strictly Rentals** (☎ 802/228-3000), which can arrange for stays of a weekend or longer.

Black River Inn. 100 Main St. (Rte. 103), Ludlow, VT 05149. ☎ **802/228-5585.** 10 rms, 2 with shared bath (6 with shower only). Weekend $105–$125 double with private bath, from $95 double with shared bath; midweek $85–$105 double with private bath. AE, DISC, MC, V.

The centerpiece of the Black River Inn is in the Lincoln Room, the only first-floor guest room. It contains a four-poster walnut bed made in 1794 and slept in by none other than Abraham Lincoln himself—there's even documentation (of sorts) framed on the wall. The rest of this brick Federal home is equally historic, including the vibrant, zebralike wood floors in the dining room and kitchen, and a countrified living room with working fireplace. The guest rooms are decorated in a Victorian country style, with a mélange of antiques including oak, maple, walnut, and brass; many have handsome pine floors. Most of the rooms are very small, but seem large compared to their Lilliputian bathrooms. Two rooms share a bath, but several others have private "detached baths" requiring a walk down the hall. In those rooms, robes are provided.

The Castle. Rte. 103 (at Rte. 131; P.O. Box 207), Proctorsville, VT 05153. ☎ **800/697-7222** or 802/226-7222. Fax 802/226-7853. 10 rms (2 with shower only). $135–$185 double, including breakfast; $190–$240 double, including breakfast and dinner. Off-season discounts available. AE, MC, V. Closed 2 weeks in Apr.

Sit in the lobby long enough and you'll hear someone walk in and exclaim, "*Look* at this place!" And the first floor of this stunning stone mansion on a rise overlooking Route 103 *is* exquisite. The original owner had an obvious thing for wood, and the house, built in 1901, is opulent with dark, chocolatey woodworking throughout.

Somewhat paradoxically, this makes the house a little gloomy during the day, but it glows with a golden luster at night, warmly lit by burning logs in the fireplaces.

The upstairs guest rooms, six of which feature wood-burning fireplaces, have come a long way since Boston corporate refugees Erica and Richard Hart bought the place in early 1995. Out went the 1950s-era furniture and design aesthetic; in came a truck-load of antiques, handsome carpets, updated bathrooms, and CD players in all the rooms. There's still a ways to go—some of the old details are nice, like the spherical glass doorknobs; others aren't, like cracked and discolored tiles in some of the bathrooms, and outdated electrical fixtures. And be forewarned that some of those bathrooms are quite small. The innkeepers are amid a six-year plan to restore the place; look for improvements with each visit. In summer, guests can also avail themselves of the swimming pool and tennis court.

WHERE TO DINE

The Castle. Rte. 131 (at Rte. 103, just south of Ludlow), Proctorsville. ☎ **802/226-7222.** Reservations recommended weekends and peak seasons. Main courses $14.25–$24. AE, MC, V. Wed–Sun 5:30–9pm. FRENCH.

The Castle's dining area occupies two rooms of exquisite woodworking on the first floor of this grand 1901 stone mansion. (Guest rooms are upstairs; see above.) The mood is set with candles on the tables, diffuse lighting, and jazz playing softly in the background. Chef Mark Dickerson, a New England Culinary Institute grad who's also worked in New Orleans and the Virgin Islands, prepares straightforward meals with a classical French touch. You might start with crab-stuffed prawns or a baked Roquefort and pear tart, then graduate to veal with artichoke and capers, or a delicious brook trout stuffed with prawns and served with a citrus buerre blanc sauce. When I last visited, the desserts gracefully ushered guests back from France to New England, with offerings such as lemon tartlet, apple-cranberry cobbler, and maple crème brûlée.

Harry's Cafe. Rte. 103 (4 miles north of Ludlow), Mount Holly. ☎ **802/259-2996.** Reservations recommended on weekends. Main courses $10.95–$16.95. AE, MC, V. Wed–Sun 5–10pm. ECLECTIC.

Along a dark stretch of road north of Ludlow you'll pass a brightly lit roadside cafe with a red neon "Harry's" over the door. This isn't a hamburger joint, as you might assume, but a highly creative restaurant that serves up some of the tangiest sauces in Vermont. Inside, the atmosphere seems more fast-food restaurant than cozy bistro, and that's obviously not what draws the crowds here. It's the food, which seems to span the globe.

Entrees are a veritable culinary United Nations, with New York sirloin, jerk pork, flautas, spicy Thai curry, fish and chips, Portuguese seafood stew, and chicken breast stuffed with ricotta cheese, basil, and sun-dried tomatoes. All dishes share the menu with apparent harmony. If you like the sauces you can take some home; owner Trip Pearce bottles and sells six different sauces, and does a brisk mail-order business as well.

4 Woodstock

In 1847 Woodstock native and noted sculptor Hiram Powers unveiled his statue of a nude, entitled "Greek Slave." It caused a huge uproar nationwide, not only because of Powers's depiction of nudity, but because of his depiction of slavery at a time when slavery was emerging as the nation's most divisive issue.

Woodstock seems an odd spawning ground for someone who would foment a national scandal. Because today Woodstock is dedicated to preserving the mannered past, not to challenging the unsettled future. Travelers simply can't drive to Woodstock on a route that *isn't* pastoral and scenic, putting one in mind of an earlier, more peaceful era. The superb village green is surrounded by handsome homes, creating what amounts to a comprehensive review of architectural styles of the 19th and early 20th centuries.

Much of the town is on the National Register of Historic Places, and 500 acres surrounding Mt. Tom (see "Warm-Weather Sports," below) has been deeded to the National Park Service by the Rockefeller family and is in the process of becoming a National Historic Park (it's expected to open by the year 2000).

In fact, some joke that downtown Woodstock might as well be named Rockefeller National Park, given the attention and cash the Rockefeller family has lavished upon the town in the interest of preservation. (For starters, Rockefeller money built the faux-historic Woodstock Inn and paid to bury the unsightly utility lines around town.)

Woodstock, which sits on the banks of the gentle Ottauquechee River, was first settled in 1765, rose to some prominence as a publishing center in the mid-19th century (no fewer than five newspapers were published here in 1830), and began to attract wealthy families who summered here in the late 19th century. To this day, Woodstock just feels as if it should have a prestigious prep school just off the green, and it comes as some surprise that it doesn't.

Wealthy summer rusticators were instrumental in establishing and preserving the character of the village, and today the very wealthy have turned their attention to the handsome farms outside of town. Few of these former dairy farms still produce milk; barns that haven't been converted to architectural showcase homes more than likely house valuable collections of cars or other antiques.

Woodstock is also notable as a former center of winter outdoor recreation. The nation's first ski tow (a rope tow powered by an old Buick motor) was built in 1933 at the Woodstock Ski Hill near today's Suicide Six ski area. While no longer the skiing center of Vermont, Woodstock remains a worthy destination during the winter months for skating, cross-country skiing, and snowshoeing.

One caveat: Woodstock's excellent state of preservation hasn't gone unnoticed, and it draws hordes of travelers. During the peak of foliage season, it can even be hard to view the green for all the tour buses driving around it.

ESSENTIALS

GETTING THERE   Woodstock is 13 miles west of White River Junction on Route 4 (take Exit 1 off I-89). From the west, Woodstock is 20 miles east of Killington on Route 4.

VISITOR INFORMATION   The **Woodstock Area Chamber of Commerce,** 18 Central St., Woodstock, VT 05091 (☎ **802/457-3555**), staffs an information booth on the green between June and October. Ask about the guided village walking tours.

EXPLORING THE REGION

IN TOWN   I've got plenty of company when I say that Woodstock is one of my favorite New England villages. Few others can top it for sheer grace and elegance. The heart of the town is the shady, elliptical Woodstock Green. Admiral Dewey spent his later years in Woodstock, which may help explain the canard promulgated by some that the green was laid out in the shape of Dewey's flagship. In fact, the town's basic design was more or less laid out by 1830, well before Dewey made his mark on history.

At the east end of the green is Woodstock's compact commercial area, with a small but good selection of boutiques and restaurants. To the south is the regal Woodstock Inn (see "Where to Stay," below). To the north is **Middle Covered Bridge,** one of three in town and I'd argue the most photographed covered bridges in existence; it was built in 1969 by one of the few master craftsmen still living. Around the rest of the green and along the shady side streets are architecturally outstanding buildings where you can neatly trace the evolution of American architecture.

For a simple, 20-minute walking tour of the village, leave from the green through the covered bridge over the Ottauquechee River and make a right on River Street. You'll follow along the river past trim homes, then past a shady forest before connecting within a few minutes to Elm Street. Turn right into town, taking the time to admire the remarkable homes along the route. You'll soon walk into Woodstock's downtown; veer right at the T-intersection and you're soon back at the green.

While en route, stop by the **Woodstock Historical Society,** 26 Elm St. (☎ 802/ 457-1822). Housed in the 1807 Charles Dana House, this beautiful home has rooms furnished in Federal, Empire, and Victorian styles, and offers displays of dolls, costumes, and examples of early silver and glass. The Dana House is open from May through October. Hours are Monday through Saturday 10am to 5pm and Sunday from noon to 5pm. Admission is free.

OUTSIDE WOODSTOCK Less than a half-mile north of town on Route 12 (Elm Street) is the **Billings Farm and Museum** (☎ 802/457-2355), a working farm well worth visiting for a glimpse of life in a grander era. The farm was built by Frederick Billings, the man who is credited with completing the Northern Pacific Railroad, then saving the rail during the Panic of 1873. (The town of Billings, Mont., is named after him.) This dairy farm was renowned late in the last century for its scientific breeding of Jersey cows and its fine architecture, especially the gabled 1890 Victorian farm house. Now owned by Billings's grandaughter and her husband, Laurence Rockefeller, the farm includes hands-on demonstrations of farm activities, exhibits of farm life, an heirloom kitchen garden, and active milking barns.

The museum is open daily May through October from 10am to 5pm, and on weekends in November and December. The farm is also open for special events in winter, including sleigh rides. Admission is $6.50 adults, $5.50 seniors, $5 children 13 to 17, $3 children 5 to 12, and $1 children 3 to 4.

Bird watchers will enjoy a trip to the **Vermont Institute of Natural Science** (☎ 802/457-2779), which also houses the Vermont Raptor Center. The center is home to 25 species of birds of prey that have been injured and can no longer survive in the wild. The winged residents change from time to time, but typically range from majestic bald eagles to the diminutive saw-whet owl. Serious birders might also choose to spend some time in the institute's Pettingill Ornithological Library. Other attractions include an herbarium, nature trails, and exhibits of live animals, including snakes, bees, and tarantulas. The institute is located $1^{1}/_{2}$ miles south of the village on Church Hill Road. It's open daily 10am to 4pm, but is closed Sundays from November through April. Admission is $5 adults, $2 for children.

About five miles east of Woodstock is the riverside village of **Quechee.** Formerly a town of prosperous woolen mills, Quechee is emerging as a huge, low-key resort community. Some 6,000 acres of the surrounding countryside is owned by the Quechee Lakes Corporation, which has developed second homes and other amenities, including a golf course and polo field.

The small village, with a handful of boutiques and restaurants, still revolves spiritually and economically around the restored brick mill building along the falls. **Simon Pearce Glass** (☎ 802/295-2711), which makes exceptionally fine and exceptionally pricey glassware, occupies the former Downer's Mill, where it houses its glassmaking operation, a retail store, and a respected restaurant (see below). Visitors can watch glassblowing take place weekdays and on summer weekends from a catwalk viewing gallery. Open daily from 9am to 5pm.

WARM-WEATHER SPORTS

Outdoor activities in the Woodstock area aren't as rugged as those you'll find in the Green Mountains to the west, but they'll easily occupy you for an afternoon or two.

Don't leave the village without climbing **Mt. Tom,** the prominent hill that overlooks Woodstock. Start your ascent from Faulkner Park, named after Mrs. Edward Faulkner, who created the park and had the mountain trail built to encourage healthful exercise. (To reach the trailhead from the Woodstock Green, cross Middle Covered Bridge and continue straight on Mountain Avenue. The road bends left and soon arrives at a grassy park at the base of Mt. Tom.)

The trail winds up the hill, employing one of the most lugubrious sets of switchbacks I've ever experienced. Designed after the once-popular "cardiac walks" in Europe, the trail sometimes seems to require hikers to walk for miles only to gain a few feet in elevation. But persevere. This gentle trail eventually arrives at a clearing overlooking the town. A steeper, rockier, and more demanding trail continues 100 yards or so from there to the summit. At the top, a carriage path encircles the summit like a friar's fringe of hair, offering fine views of the town and the Green Mountains to the west. You can follow the carriage path down to Billings Farm, or retrace your steps back to the park.

Experienced and aspiring equestrians should head to the **Kedron Valley Stables** (☎ **802/457-1480**), about 4¹/₂ miles south of Woodstock on Route 106. A full menu of riding options is available, ranging from a one-hour beginner ride ($30) to a five-night inn-to-inn excursion ($1,350 per person including all meals and lodging, double occupancy). The stables rent horses to experienced riders for local trail rides, offers sleigh and carriage rides, and has an indoor riding ring for inclement weather. It's open every day except Thanksgiving and Christmas.

Five miles east of town, Route 4 crosses **Quechee Gorge,** a popular if somewhat overrated tourist attraction. The sheer power of the glacial runoff that carved the gorge some 13,000 years ago must have been dramatic, but the 165-foot gorge itself isn't all that impressive. More impressive is the engineering history. This chasm was first spanned in 1875 by a wooden rail trestle, when 3,000 people gathered along the gorge to celebrate the achievement. The current steel bridge was constructed in 1911 for the railroad, but the tracks were torn up in 1933 and replaced by Route 4.

The best view of the bridge is from the bottom of the gorge, which is accessible by a well-graded gravel path that descends south from the parking area. The round-trip requires no more than a half-hour. If the day is warm enough, you might also follow the path northward along the gorge's rim, then descend to the river to splash around in a fine, rocky swimming hole near the spillway.

SKIING

The area's best cross-country skiing is at the **Woodstock Ski Touring Center** (☎ **802/457-2114**) at the Woodstock Country Club, just south of town on Route 106. The center maintains 36 miles of trails, including 12 miles of trail groomed for skate-skiing. And it's not all flat; the high and low points along the trail system vary by 750 feet in elevation. Lessons and picnic tours are available. The full-day trail fee is $11 for adults and $8 for children under 14.

Suicide Six ski area (☎ **802/457-6661**) may have an intimidating name, but at just 650 vertical feet it doesn't pose much of a threat to either life or limb. Owned and operated by the Woodstock Inn, this venerable family ski resort (it first opened in 1934) has two double chairs, a complimentary J-bar for beginners, and a spiffy new base lodge. Beginners and intermediates will be content here. Lift tickets are $32 for adults, $21 for seniors and children under 14. The ski area is located two miles north of Woodstock on Pomfret Road.

WHERE TO STAY

Jackson House Inn. Rte. 4, Woodstock, VT 05091. ☎ **802/457-2065.** 12 rms, all with shower only. A/C. $135–$250 double. Rates include full breakfast. No credit cards.

The graceful aesthetic inside the Jackson House Inn, just outside of Woodstock on Route 4, is unrivaled anywhere in New England, if not the United States. Everything in this pale yellow 1890 Victorian is immaculate and perfectly chosen, from the Oriental rugs and 300-year-old tallcase clock in the first-floor common room, to cherry and maple floors so beautiful you'll feel guilty for not taking off your shoes. The guest rooms, which are each decorated in different period styles (Empire, Federal, etc.), are equally well appointed. The inn features the elegant touches you'd expect for the high price, like decanters of sherry and Bose speakers in the rooms. But there are others you wouldn't expect, like the small fitness room in the basement with steam room, tanning bed, and juice bar; the video library; and the three-acre backyard with formal English gardens and a pond stocked with rainbow trout.

The sole disadvantage of the Jackson House is its location just off Route 4—not far from the sound of traffic—which somewhat detracts from the rural tranquillity the innkeepers have otherwise succeeded in achieving. No smoking.

✪ **Kedron Valley Inn.** Rte. 106, South Woodstock, VT 05071. ☎ **800/836-1193** or 802/457-1473. Fax 802/457-4469. E-mail kedroninn@aol.com. 27 rms, 2 with shower only. TV. $119–$191 double; foliage season and Christmas week $180–$275 double. Rates include full breakfast. Discounts available spring and midweek. DISC, MC, V. Closed Apr and briefly prior to Thanksgiving.

This is a stand-out inn. Located in a complex of Greek Revival buildings at a country crossroads about five miles south of Woodstock, the inn is run by Max and Merrily Comins, a cordial couple who offer guests a bit of history, a bit of country style, and a whole lot of good food and wine. The attractive guest rooms in all three buildings are furnished with a mix of antiques and reproductions, and all have heirloom quilts from Merrily's collection; 14 feature wood-burning fireplaces. Don't be alarmed if you're put in the newer, motel-like log building by the river. The rooms are equally well appointed, with canopy beds, custom oak woodwork, and fireplaces. Room 37 even has a private streamside terrace. All guests can share in the inn's pond located above and behind the main house. *Editor's note:* My dog Lucy loves this place.

Dining/Entertainment: The country-elegant dining room has two fireplaces and a nice view of the grounds, and features a menu of contemporary American cuisine built on a classical French foundation. You might start with fresh spinach agnolotti filled with pesto and served with a dressing of sun-dried tomato, then move on to salmon stuffed with a scallop, shrimp, and salmon mousse and wrapped in a puff pastry.

✪ **Twin Farms.** Barnard, VT 05031. ☎ **800/894-6327** or 802/234-9999. Fax 802/234-9990. 14 rms and cottages. A/C TV TEL. $700–$850 double; $850–$1,500 cottage. Rates include all meals, liquor, and many amenities. Children under 18 not accepted. AE, MC, V. Closed Apr.

Twin Farms offers uncommon luxury at an uncommon price. Housed on a 300-acre farm that was once home to Nobel Prize–winning novelist Sinclair Lewis and his wife, journalist Dorothy Thompson, Twin Farms has carved out an international reputation as a low-key, exceptionally tasteful small resort. The clientele includes royalty and corporate chieftains looking for simplicity and willing to pay dearly for it. The inn consists of the main inn with 4 guest rooms, and 10 outlying cottages, including 4 that opened in 1995. The rooms are impeccable, designed by talented interior decorators who commissioned craftsmen and artisans to create much of the furniture and adornment. The inn is owned by the Twigg-Smith family, who are noted art collectors in Hawaii. Some of the work on display at the inn and in guest rooms includes originals by David Hockney, Roy Lichtenstein, Milton Avery, and William Wegman.

Dining/Entertainment: Meals are understatedly sumptuous affairs served at locations of your choosing—at your cottage, along a stream, or in one of the dining areas around the estate. Don't go looking for a menu; the gourmet chefs serve what's fresh, and your meal is likely to include ingredients from the organic vegetable and herb gardens on the property.

Woodstock Inn & Resort. 14 The Green, Woodstock, VT 05091. ☎ **800/448-7900** or 802/457-1100. 143 rms, 2 town houses. A/C TV TEL. $145–$279 double. AE, MC, V.

The Woodstock Inn, an imposing white brick structure behind a garden off the Woodstock Green, appears a venerable and long-established institution at first glance. But it's not—at least not *this* building. Constructed from 1968 to 1969, the inn happily shunned the more unfortunate trends in sixties architecture for a dignified look suitable for Woodstock. Everyone's the better for it. Inside, guests are greeted by a broad stone fireplace, and sitting areas are tucked throughout the lobby in the manner of a 1940s-era resort. Guest rooms are tastefully decorated in either country pine or a Shaker-inspired style. The best rooms are in the new wing (built 1991), and feature rich carpeting, refrigerators, fireplaces, and built-in bookshelves.

Dining/Entertainment: The dining room is classy and semiformal, with continental and American dishes served on elegant green-bordered custom china. Entrees are in the $20-to-$25 price range.

Facilities: There's a Robert Trent Jones golf course at the inn-owned Woodstock Country Club, two swimming pools (indoor and out), hiking trails, putting greens, and a fitness center with tennis, squash, racquetball, and steam rooms. In winter, the resort maintains 36 miles of groomed cross-country ski trails.

WHERE TO DINE

Bentley's. 3 Elm St. ☎ **802/457-3232.** Reservations recommended for parties of 4 or more. Lunch items $4.50–$8.25; main dinner courses $12.95–$18.50; brunch items $6.25–$7.75. AE, CB, DC, DISC, MC, V. Mon–Thurs 11am–9:30pm, Fri–Sat 11am–10pm, Sun 10:30am–9:30pm. Open later for drinks and dancing on weekends. AMERICAN.

There's a famous photo of Winston Churchill with his elbow on a bar, glowering at a photographer. That photo could have been shot at the bar at Bentley's, with its affluent, English-gentleman's-club feel. Beyond the bar, the dining room affects a Victorian elegance, but not ostentatiously so. The menu offers American standards with a twist (stuffed clams, steak flambéed with Jack Daniels, champagne trout), but also opens its doors to international fare, like focaccia, Mediterranean-style sauté of mixed vegetables, and chorizo quesadillas. There's a fine brunch on Sunday; spite your doctor and go for the New England corned-beef hash with poached eggs and hollandaise sauce.

Stick around late enough on weekend evenings and witness a transformation: The tables get swept off a dance floor, the ceiling rolls back to reveal high-tech lighting, and Bentley's becomes Woodstock's hot place (did someone say *only* place?) to dance the night away.

✪ **The Prince and the Pauper.** 24 Elm St. ☎ **802/457-1818.** Reservations recommended. Dinner $32 fixed price. DISC, MC, V. Sun–Thurs 6–9pm, Fri–Sat 6–9:30pm. NEW AMERICAN/ CONTINENTAL.

It takes a bit of sleuthing to find The Prince and the Pauper, located down Dana Alley (next to the Woodstock Historical Society's Dana House). But it's worth the effort. This is Woodstock's best restaurant, with an intimate but informal setting. Ease into the evening by starting off in the lounge with its taproom atmosphere (it's open an hour before the restaurant), then move over to the rustic-but-edged-with-elegance dining room. Start with an appetizer of lobster ravioli or smoked Coho salmon, then enjoy the grilled boneless rack of grilled lamb baked in a puff pastry with spinach and mushroom duxelles, or a grilled swordfish with spicy Thai ginger sauce. The $32 fixed-price dinner offers good value, but if that's out of your budget, head to the lounge and order off the bistro menu ($10.95 to $15.95), with selections like barbecue pork, Maryland crabcakes, and Indonesian curried lamb. There's also a selection of pizzas at $9.95.

Simon Pearce Restaurant. The Mill, Quechee. ☎ **802/295-1470.** Reservations recommended for dinner. Lunch items $6.75–$11.50; dinner main courses $16–$24. AE, DC, DISC, MC, V. Daily 11:30am–2:45pm and 6–9pm. REGIONAL/AMERICAN.

The setting can't be beat. Housed in a restored 19th-century woolen mill with wonderful views of a waterfall (spotlit at night), the Simon Pearce is a collage of exposed brick, buttery yellow pine floorboards, and handsome wooden tables and chairs. Meals are served on Simon Pearce pottery and glassware (if you like your setting, you can buy it afterward at the sprawling retail shop). The restaurant atmosphere is a wonderful concoction of formal and informal, ensuring that everybody feels comfortable here whether in white shirt and tie or (neatly pressed) jeans.

You might start off your evening with Maine crabcakes with roille, or cheese croquettes with tomato chutney. Then move on to the chile-cured roast tenderloin of pork with grilled corn salsa, or perhaps the seared tuna with sesame, noodle cakes, wasabi, and pickled ginger. Simon Pearce is also open for lunch, when the menu lightens to include delectable entrees like warm goat cheese salad, grilled chicken sandwich with roasted peppers and Parmigiana aïoli, and tarragon chicken salad with scallions and toasted almonds.

5 Killington

In 1937 a travel writer described the town near Killington Peak as "a small village of a church and a few undistinguished houses built on a highway three corners." The area was rugged and remote, isolated from the commercial centers to the west by imposing mountains, and accessible only through the challenging Sherburne Pass.

That was before Vermont's second-highest mountain was developed as the Northeast's largest ski area. And before a wide, five-mile-long access road was slashed through the forest to the mountain's base. And before Route 4 was widened and improved, easing access to Rutland. In fact, that early travel writer would be hard-pressed to recognize the region today.

Since the mountain was first developed for skiing in 1957, dozens of restaurants, hotels, and convenience stores have sprouted along Killington Road to accommodate the legions of skiers who descend on the area during the long skiing season, which typically runs October through May.

Killington Road is a brightly lit, highly developed modern ski resort access road. There's not much to remind visitors of classic Vermont between the highway and the base lodge. Suburban-style theme restaurants dot the route (The Grist Mill has a waterwheel; Casey's Caboose has a red caboose), along with dozens of hotels and condos ranging from high-end fancy to low-end dowdy.

It's also become a choice destination for those who ski for the nightlife as much for the moguls. With some 60 bars within striking distance, Killington cultivates a hard-partying personality. The area has a frenetic, where-it's-happening feel in winter. (That's not the case in summer, when the empty parking lots can trigger mild melancholia.) Those most content here are skiers who like their skiing BIG, and travelers who want a wide selection of amenities and are willing to sacrifice charm for choice.

ESSENTIALS

GETTING THERE   Killington Road extends southward from routes 4 and 100, just east of the intersection with Route 100 north. It's about 12 miles east of Rutland on Route 4. Many of the inns offer shuttles to the Rutland airport.

VISITOR INFORMATION   The **Killington & Pico Areas Association,** P.O. Box 114, Killington, VT 05751 (☎ 802/773-4181), supplies seasonal travel information from the Killington Ltd. Ski Shop on Route 4 just west of Route 100. It's open May through October from 10am to 6pm. For winter information, contact the **Killington Travel Service** (☎ 800/372-2007) or the **Killington Lodging Bureau** (☎ 800/621-6867). For the Pico Mountain area, try the **Pico Lodging Bureau** (☎ 802/775-9140).

ALPINE SKIING

Killington. Killington, VT 05751. ☎ **800/621-6867** or 802/422-3261 for lodging. Vertical drop: 3,150 feet. Lifts: 2 gondolas, 16 chairlifts (2 high-speed), 2 surface lifts. Skiable acreage: 935. Lift tickets: $48.

Killington is the Northeast's largest ski area, and it's been likened to a huge mall that's run with brisk efficiency if not much of a personal touch. That's a bit unfair, because Killington's personality is not found in its service, but in its trails, which range from long, old-fashioned, narrow trails with almost no discernible downhill slope to killer bump runs high on its flanks.

Skiers new to Killington are in a bit of a quandary. The two-sided trail map is virtually worthless since it's impossible to follow. But make one wrong turn and you'll end up on a no-slope green trail practically walking back to the bottom.

My advice: At the outset, focus on one lift and follow the lift signs—don't even try to figure out the trail signs. After a couple of runs, the layout will start to make sense. Then move on to another lift. And if you're reasonably competent on skis, don't be intimidated by the black diamonds. Many of these expert slopes are intersected by beginner or intermediate escape trails, but this isn't always indicated at the major intersections. Take some chances.

Killington is a superb mountain for both experts and beginners. Intermediates might find the lack of blue trails a bit frustrating, and may be more content at Pico. Also bear in mind that Killington's trails are heavily congested on weekends; I'd advise moving over to Pico for at least Saturday and possibly Sunday.

Pico. Sherburne Pass, Rutland, VT 05701. ☎ **800/898-7426** or 802/775-4345 for lodging. Vertical drop: 1,967. Lifts: 7 chairlifts (2 high speed), 3 surface lifts. Skiable acreage: 200. Lift tickets: $41 weekends, $37 weekdays.

Pico claims to offer skiing on five peaks; the casual observer will discern three, maybe four. But they're fine peaks, with a good variety of terrain and with trails maintained in good condition. The lower mountain has fine, open intermediate cruising runs that are served by a detachable quad. The upper mountain offers some beautiful glade skiing; the Outpost double chair serves serious expert slopes. Among its greatest charms, Pico rarely inconveniences its guest with lift lines, even on weekends.

Pico's "village" at the base is modest, subdued, and quietly appealing. It's fairly sleepy at night (nightlife mavens head over to Killington Road), which makes it a good choice for families looking for a tranquil stay near the slopes.

CROSS-COUNTRY SKIING

The intricate network of trails at the **Mountain Top Inn** (☎ 800/445-2100 or 802/ 483-2311) has had a loyal local following for years, but it's now attracting considerable attention from far-flung skiers as well. The 66-mile trail network runs through mixed terrain with fabulous views, and is nicely groomed for both traditional and skate-skiing. The area is often deep with snow owing to its high ridgetop location in the hills east of Rutland, and snowmaking along key portions of the trail ensure that you won't have to walk across bare spots during snow droughts. The resort maintains three warming huts along the way, and lessons and ski rentals are available. The trails cover a wide variety of terrain, with a elevation gain of 670 feet. Trail passes are $13 adult, $10 children.

SUMMER ACTIVITIES

MOUNTAIN BIKING   Mountain bikers challenge themselves on Killington's five mountains as they explore 50 miles of trails. The main lift is equipped to haul bikes and riders to the summit, delivering spectacular views. Riders then give their forearms a workout applying breaks with some vigor and frequency while bumping down the slopes. Explore on your own, or sign up for a full- or half-day tour.

The **Mountain Bike Shop** (☎ 802/422-6232) is located at the Killington Base Lodge and is open from June through mid-October from 9am to 6pm daily. A trail pass is $5; trail pass with a one-time chairlift ride is $15; unlimited chairlift rides are $25 per day. Bike rentals are also available, starting at $20 for two hours, or $32 for a day. Helmets are required ($3 per day).

HIKING   Those who'd like to explore the rocky highlands but are a bit unsure of themselves in the wilds should head for the **Merrell Hiking Center** (☎ 802/ 422-6708) at the Killington Base Lodge. The center's staff can offer helpful recommendations on area trails based on your experience and inclinations. Five dollars gets you a trail pass for hiking on Killington Peak, a map, and a pocket field guide. Another $5 will allow you to cut to the chase by taking the chairlift to the 4,195-foot summit to explore the ridgeline before hiking down. (This also offers a way for hikers with bad knees to stay active: Hike to the summit, then avoid the knee-jarring descent by riding the chairlift down.) Guided nature hikes and other specialized tours are available on request, as are rentals of boots and backpacks.

Hikers on their own might set their sights on **Deer Leap Mountain** and its popular three-hour loop to the summit and back. The trail departs from the Inn at Long Trail off Route 4 at Sherburne Pass. Park across from the inn, then head north through the inn's parking lot onto the Long Trail/Appalachian Trail and into the forest. Follow the white blazes (you'll return on the blue-blazed trail you'll see entering on the left). In one-half mile, you'll arrive at a juncture. The Appalachian Trail veers right to the New Hampshire's White Mountains and Mt. Katahdin in Maine; Vermont's Long Trail runs to the left. Follow the Long Trail, and after some rugged climbing over the next 1.9 miles, turn left at the signs for Deer Leap Height. Great views of Pico and the Killington area await you in four-tenths of a mile. After a break here, continue down the steep, blue-blazed descent back to Route 4 and your car. The entire loop is about 2.5 miles.

BIRD WATCHING   Vermont Ecology Tours (☎ 800/368-6161 or 802/422-3500) offers breakfast with the birds from its headquarters on Killington Road. Guests meet at the office (or are picked up at their hotel) at 7:30am for a two-hour tour of local habitats, including lake, woodland, and marsh. The tour, on a 13-passenger minibus, includes coffee and use of binoculars; bring something to eat. The cost is $12.

AN ADVENTURE IN HISTORY

President Calvin Coolidge State Historic Site. Rte. 100A, Plymouth. ☎ 802/672-3773. $4.50 adults, children under 14 free. Late May to mid-Oct daily 9:30am–5:30pm; closed late Oct to Apr.

When told that Calvin Coolidge had died, literary wit Dorothy Parker is said to have responded, "How can they tell?" Even in his death, the nation's most taciturn president rarely got the respect even Dan Quayle received. A trip to the Coolidge Historic District should at the least raise Silent Cal's reputation among visitors, who'll get a strong sense of the president raised in this mountain village, a man shaped by harsh weather, unrelieved isolation, and a strong sense of community and family.

Situated in a high upland valley, the historic district consists of a group of about a dozen unspoiled buildings open to the public, and a number of other private residences that may be observed from the outside only. It was at the Coolidge Homestead (open for tours) that in August 1923 Vice President Coolidge, on a vacation from Washington, was awoken in the middle of the night and informed that President Warren Harding had died unexpectedly. His father, a notary public, administered the oath of office.

With sloping, open meadows surrounding the village, visitors can plainly see the distinct patterns of life in an early Vermont town, where commerce and residential life clustered tightly and barn animals roamed the rest. A new mile-long walking trail offers access to the area's meadows and woods.

Be sure to stop by the **Plymouth Cheese Factory** in a trim white shop just uphill from the Coolidge Homestead. Founded in the late 1800s as a farmer's cooperative by President Coolidge's father, the shop is now run by the president's son, who in his nineties still stops by daily in summer. Excellent cheeses are available here, including a spicy pepper cheddar. "It's got some authority," an elderly clerk warned me, and she was right.

WHERE TO STAY

Killington offers hundreds of guest rooms along the access road between Route 4 and the mountain. Prospective visitors can request lodging information from the **Killington and Pico Areas Association** (☎ 802/773-4181). Or they can line up a vacation with a single phone call to the **Killington Lodging Bureau** (☎ 800/621-6867). The accommodating staff will take care of all your travel needs, including air or train reservations.

EXPENSIVE

Cortina Inn. Rte. 4 (1.5 miles west of Pico), Killington, VT 05751. ☎ 800/451-6108 or 802/773-3333. Fax 802/775-6948. E-mail cortina1@aol.com. 97 rms. A/C TV TEL. Winter and foliage season $175–$275 double; summer $140–$240 double. Rates higher during holidays. Rates include breakfast. AE, DISC, MC, V.

Travelers seeking modern amenities within striking distance of Vermont's wilds and ski mountains will be content at Cortina Inn. The original lodge, situated on Route 4 between Pico and Rutland, was built in 1966, with additions in 1975 and 1987.

The interior still feels a bit like a private ski chalet—albeit one with *really* long hallways. Why, there's even a sunken conversation pit with a two-sided fireplace, and a spiral staircase up to the second level.

Guest rooms vary slightly in their modern country style, but all are comfortably furnished. Especially nice is Room 201 (the priciest of the bunch) with a loft, fan window, refrigerator, and Adirondack-style log furniture. Innkeepers Bob and Brenda Harnish do a good job making this inn, with nearly 100 rooms, feel like a smaller and more intimate place. Especially appealing is the attention paid to detail—the hotel staff even brushes off the car windows of guests each morning after a snowstorm.

Dining/Entertainment: Evening meals are available on premises at Zola's Grill. There's also a tavern, and afternoon tea is served in winter.

Services: Free shuttles to both Killington and Pico during ski season.

Facilities: Extras include a brick-walled indoor pool, a fitness room, a mountain biking center, eight tennis courts, and a small pond along the highway that's just big enough to practice a few canoe strokes. There's also a game room for kids, and another game room for adults (with pool and darts) off the downstairs tavern.

Inn of the Six Mountains. Killington Rd. (P.O. Box 2900), Killington, VT 05751. ☎ **800/ 228-4676** or 802/422-4302. Fax 802/422-4321. 103 rms. TV TEL. Winter $139–$179 double midweek, $179–$219 double weekend, $229–$269 double holidays. Off-season discounts available. Rates include full breakfast. AE, DC, DISC, MC, V.

With its profusion of gables and dormers, the Inn of the Six Mountains stands as the most architecturally dramatic of the many hotels along Killington Road. The lobby is welcoming in a modern, Scandinavian sort of way, with lots of blonde wood and stone, and the location is convenient to Killington's base lodge, just a mile up the road. But for a luxury hotel that offers only "deluxe rooms" and suites, and charges accordingly, the attention to detail comes up short. While the guest rooms are tastefully decorated in a Shaker-inspired sort of way, many have scuffed walls, weary carpeting, and bruised and gouged furniture. This might be expected in a ski dorm, but not in a luxury inn.

Facilities: There's a handsome restaurant, a festive lounge, an attractive indoor pool, and a well-equipped fitness center.

Mountain Top Inn. Mountain Top Rd., Chittenden, VT 05737. ☎ **800/445-2100** or 802/ 483-2311. Fax 802/483-6373. 35 rms, 20 units with 1–4 bedrooms. A/C TEL. Summer and fall $176–$216 double; winter $176–$206 double midweek, $196–$246 double weekends and holidays; off-season $98–$168 double. AE, MC, V.

The Mountain Top Inn was carved out of a former turnip farm in the 1940s, but has long since left its root-vegetable heritage behind. Situated on 1,300 ridgetop acres with expansive views of the Vermont countryside, the inn has the feel of a classic, small Pocono resort hotel, where the hosts make sure you've got something to do every waking minute. Overall, the Mountain Top doesn't offer good value to those only looking for simple room and board. But those who like to be active outdoors and who prefer to stay put during their vacation will be kept plenty busy for their money.

Dining/Entertainment: The pleasant dining room, with heavy beams and rustic, rawhide-laced chairs, features regional American cuisine with a continental flair. Entrees, which range from $12.95 to $20.95, might include pork tenderloin served with apples and an applejack brandy sauce, or New England seafood pie.

Facilities: In winter, excellent cross-country skiing on 66 miles of trails is included in the room rates. Come summer, horseback riding reigns supreme as the activity of choice.

MODERATE

Inn at Long Trail. Rte. 4, Killington, VT 05751. ☎ **802/775-7181.** 22 rms, some with showers only. Midweek $78–$98 double, including full breakfast. Two-night minimum on weekends and during foliage season at $300–$398 double, including two nights, two dinners, and two breakfasts. AE, MC, V. Closed late Apr to late June.

The Inn at Long trail, situated in an architecturally undistinguished building at the intersection of busy Route 4 and the Long and Appalachian trails, is not a drive-by. The interior of this rustic inn is far more charming than the exterior. "Rustic" can be a travel-guide code word for "shabby," but that's not the case here. Tree trunks support the beams in the lobby, which sports log furniture and bannisters of yellow birch along the stairway. The older rooms in this three-floor hotel (built in 1938 as an annex to a long-gone lodge) are furnished simply in ski-lodge style. Comfortable, more modern suites with fireplaces, telephones, and TVs are offered in a motel-like addition.

Just off the lobby is a relaxing, woody pub—an ideal place to knock back a pint of Guinness after a day on the trails. The back dining room maintains the Keebler elf theme, with a stone ledge that juts through the wall from the mountain behind. Innkeepers Murray and Patty McGrath (along with their children Connor and Brogan) emphasize the Gaelic in both atmosphere and cuisine. The menu features a selection of hearty meals popular with hungry hikers and skiers, including the inn's famed Guinness stew, corned beef and cabbage, and Irish poached salmon. Delicious homemade bread accompanies the meals. And there's live Irish music in the pub on weekends during the busy seasons.

WHERE TO DINE

Charity's. Killington Rd. ☎ **802/422-3800.** Reservations not accepted. Lunch items $5.95–$6.75; main dinner courses $12.95–$15.95. AE, DC, MC, V. Daily 11:30am–11pm. PUB FARE.

Rustic, crowded, bustling, and boisterous, Charity's is the place to head after a day on the slopes if you like your food big and your company to be young. (Lunchtime in summers is a decidedly more mellow affair.) The centerpiece of this barnlike restaurant adorned with stained-glass lamps and turn-of-the century prints is a handsome old bar crafted in Italy, then shipped to West Virginia, where it completed a run of nearly a century before being dismantled and coming to Vermont in 1971. The menu offers a good selection of burgers, plus a half-dozen vegetarian entrees, like veggie stir-fry and red-pepper ravioli.

✪ Hemingway's. Rtes. 100 and 4. ☎ **802/422-3886.** Reservations recommended. Summer main courses $22–$28; winter fixed-price menu $42–$45; vegetarian menu $36.50; tasting menu $60–$65 (with wines). AE, MC, V. High season Tues–Sun 6–10pm, off-season Wed–Sun 6–9pm. Closed briefly in mid-Apr and early Nov. AMERICAN/ECLECTIC.

Hemingway's is an unusually elegant spot. Opened by Linda and Ted Fondulas in 1982, the restaurant has become recognized nationally, and was named one of the nation's 25 top restaurants by *Food & Wine* magazine in 1992, and one of 50 most distinguished U.S. restaurants by *Condé Nast Traveler* in 1993. It's continued to improve since then.

Located in the 1860 Asa Briggs House, a former stagecoach stop now fronting a busy stretch of highway between Killington and Woodstock, Hemingway's offers dining in three formal areas. The wine cellar has an Old-World intimacy and is suited for groups out for a celebration; the two upstairs rooms are elegant with damask linen, silver flatware, crystal goblets, fresh flowers, and white gloves on the waiters. Fellow diners tend to be dressed casually but neatly (no shorts or T-shirts). The food is superior, and dinner comes at a price that's actually quite reasonable given the quality of the cooking and the superb presentation. (And just compare the cost of dining here with the cost at any other of the *Food & Wine* 25.)

The menu changes frequently to reflect available stock. Guests might start with a salmon carpaccio with coconut, seaweed, and brioche toast, or a wild mushroom and truffle soup, then move on to risotto with lobster, shrimp and grilled asparagus, or a Napoléan of beef tenderloin with Roquefort pastry. For dessert, guests might conclude their feast with a citrus tart with Grand Marnier, or cappuccino ice cream in a caramel cage.

Mother Shapiro's. Killington Rd. ☎ **802/422-9933.** Reservations not accepted. Breakfast $2.99–$8.75; lunch/munchies $3.95–$7.25; main dinner courses $9.95–$13.95. AE, DISC, MC, V. Daily, breakfast 7am–1pm, lunch and munchies 11:30am–2am, dinner 4:30–10pm. PUB FARE/AMERICAN.

Mother Shapiro's motto is "Such a nice place." That understated approach sets the tone for this funky, locally popular establishment. "Mother" is actually Jay Shapiro, a mustachioed entrepreneur who founded the restaurant in 1980. He's made this a fun, relaxed place, done up in a sort of Victorian vaudeville/brothel look. The menu nags ("no whining," "don't make a mess," "no substitutions concerning this menu unless it's not too busy, then we'll talk") while offering a broad if not overly creative selection of dishes. Individual breakfasts are nearly large enough for two. Dinners include teriyaki steak and pot roast, and a more-than-filling all-you-can-eat rib dinner for $13.95. This spot is often tremendously busy with locals (especially at breakfast), and offers a good bar menu afterhours for those whose hunger catches up with them long after the sun has set.

6 Middlebury

Middlebury is a gracious college town set amid bucolic countryside. The town center is idyllic in a peculiarly New-England-as-envisioned-by-Hollywood sort of way. It's centered around a slightly awkward, sloping green; above the green is the commanding Middlebury Inn; shops line the downhill sides. In the midst of the green is a handsome chapel, and the whole scene is lorded over by a fine, white-steepled Congregational church built between 1806 and 1809. Otter Creek tumbles dramatically through Middlebury, flanked by a historic district where you can see the intriguing vestiges of former industry. In fact, Middlebury has 300 buildings listed on the National Register of Historic Places. About the only disruption is the constant growl of trucks downshifting as they drive along the main routes through town.

Historic Middlebury College, which is within walking distance of downtown, doesn't so much dominate the village as coexist nicely alongside it. The college has a sterling reputation for its liberal-arts educations, but may be best known for its intensive summer language programs. Don't be surprised if you hear folks conversing in exotic tongues while walking through town. Students commit to total immersion, which means no lapsing by gossiping in English while they're enrolled in the program.

ESSENTIALS

GETTING THERE Middlebury is located on Route 7 about midway between Rutland and Burlington.

VISITOR INFORMATION The **Addison County Chamber of Commerce,** 2 Court St., Middlebury, VT 05753 (☎ **800/733-8376** or 802/388-7951), is located in a handsome, historic white building just off the green facing the Middlebury Inn. Brochures and assistance are available weekdays during business hours. Ask also for the map and guide to downtown Middlebury, published by the Downtown Middlebury Business Bureau, which lists shops and restaurants around town. Downstairs is the **Vermont Folklife Center,** offering exhibits on the crafts, arts, and culture of Vermont.

WHAT TO SEE & DO

The best place to begin a tour of Middlebury is the Addison County Chamber of Commerce (see above), where you can request the chamber's self-guided walking tour brochure.

The historic **Otter Creek** district, set along a steep hillside by the rocky creek, is well worth exploring. While here, you can peruse top-flight Vermont crafts at the **Vermont State Crafts Center at Frog Hollow,** 1 Mill St. (☎ 802/388-3177). The center, picturesquely situated overlooking tumbling Otter Creek, is open daily and features the work of some 300 Vermont craftspeople, with exhibits ranging from extraordinary carved wood desks to metalwork to glass and pottery. The Middlebury center also features a pottery studio and a resident potter who's often busy at work. The Crafts Center also maintains shops in Manchester Village and at the Church Street Marketplace in Burlington.

Beer hounds should schedule a stop at the **Otter Creek Brewing Co.,** 85 Exchange St. (☎ 800/473-0727), for a tour and free samples of their well-regarded beverages, including the Copper Ale and Stovepipe Porter. The brewery is open Monday through Saturday 10am to 6pm and Sunday 11am to 4pm.

Located atop a flat ridge with beautiful views of both the Green Mountains and farmlands rolling toward Lake Champlain, prestigious **Middlebury College** has a handsome, well-spaced campus of gray limestone and white marble buildings that's best explored by foot. The architecture of the college, founded in 1800, is primarily Colonial Revival. Especially appealing is the prospect from the marble Mead Memorial Chapel, built in 1917 and overlooking the campus green.

At the edge of campus is the **Middlebury College Center for the Arts,** which opened in 1992. This architecturally engaging center houses the **Middlebury College Museum of Art** (☎ 802/388-3711, ext. 5007), a small museum with a selective sampling of European and American art, both ancient and new. Classicists will savor the displays of Greek painted urns and vases; modern art aficionados should head for the powerful "Imagem da Minha Revolta," a 1988 installation by Brazilian artist Franz Krajcberg that deftly depicts the tragedy of the destruction of the rain forest. The museum is located on Route 30, and is open Tuesday to Friday 10am to 5pm, and weekends noon to 5pm. Admission is free.

Horse fans should head 2¹/₂ miles outside of Middlebury to the **Morgan Horse Farm** (☎ 802/388-2011), which is owned and administered by the University of Vermont. The farm has roots dating back to the late 1800s, and was for a time owned by the federal government, which in turn gave the farm to the university in 1951. The farm is credited with preserving the Morgan breed, a horse of considerable beauty and stamina that served admirably in war and exploration, and are now prized as show horses. The farm and its 70 registered stallions, mares, and foals is open for guided tours daily May through October daily from 9am to 4pm. There's also a picnic area. Admission is $3.50 for adults, $2 for teens, and free for children under 12. To reach the farm, head past the college on Route 125 to Weybridge Street (Route 23); turn right and follow signs for approximately 2.5 miles.

OUTDOOR PURSUITS

HIKING The Green Mountains roll down to Middlebury's western borders, making for easy access to the mountains. Stop by the **U.S. Forest Service's Middlebury**

Ranger District office, south of town on Route 7 (☎ 802/388-4362), for guidance and information on area trails and destinations. Ask for the brochure "Day Hikes on the Middlebury & Rochester Ranger Districts," which lists 14 hikes.

One recommended stroll for people of all abilities—and especially those of poetic sensibilities—is the **Robert Frost Interpretive Trail,** dedicated to the memory of New England's poet laureate. Frost lived in a cabin on a farm across the road for 23 summers. (The cabin is now a National Historic Landmark.) Located on Route 125 about 6 miles east of Middlebury, this relaxing loop trail is just a mile long, and excerpts of Frost's poems are placed on signs along the trail. Also posted is information about the trail's natural history. The trail, which is managed by the Green Mountain National Forest, offers pleasant access to the gentle woods of these lovely intermountain lowlands.

SKIING Downhill skiers looking for a low-key, low-pressure mountain invariably head to **Middlebury College Snow Bowl** (☎ 802/388-4356), near Middlebury Gap on Route 125 east of town. This historic ski area, founded in 1939, has a vertical drop of just over 1,000 feet served by three chairlifts. The college ski team uses the ski area for practice, but it's also open to the public at rates of about half what you'd pay at Killington.

There's also cross-country skiing nearby at the **Rikert Ski Touring Center** (☎ 802/388-2759) at Middlebury's Bread Loaf Campus on Route 125. The center offers 25 miles of machine-groomed trails through a lovely winter landscape.

WHERE TO STAY

Middlebury offers a handful of motels in addition to several inns. Two well-kept, inexpensive motels are located south of town on Route 7: The **Blue Spruce Motel** (☎ 802/388-4091) and the **Greystone Motel** (☎ 802/388-4935).

Middlebury Inn and Motel. 14 Courthouse Square, Middlebury, VT 05753. ☎ **800/842-4666** or 802/388-4961. 80 rms (3 with shower only). A/C TV TEL. Midweek $68–$134 double; weekends $75–$144 double; $122–$210 suite. MC, V.

The historic Middlebury Inn traces its roots back to 1827, when Nathan Wood built a brick public house he called the Vermont Hotel. It's come a long way since then, and now contains 80 modern guest rooms equipped with most conveniences. The rooms are a good size and most come furnished with a sofa or upholstered chairs in addition to the bed; rooms are decorated in rich, dark hues and colonial reproduction furniture. The eight guest rooms in the Porterhouse Mansion next door also have a pleasant, historic aspect. An adjacent motel is decorated in an early American motif, but it feels like veneer—underneath it's still a motel.

The inn's spacious lobby is decorated in an aggressive colonial American style, but has a nice feel with a creaky floor, leather chairs, and bowback sofas. Late in the day, the lobby is filled with the rich golden glow of the setting sun, making the wonderful colors come even more alive. Two dining rooms offer breakfast, lunch, and dinner, and a plan including breakfast and dinner is available at $34 per person additional.

Swift House Inn. 25 Stewart Lane, Middlebury, VT 05753. ☎ **802/388-9925.** Fax 802/388-9927. 21 rms (1 with shower only). A/C TEL. $75–$165 double. Rates include continental breakfast. AE, CB, DC, DISC, MC, V.

The Swift House Inn is a compound of three graceful old homes set in a residential area just a few minutes' walk from the town green. The main Federal-style inn dates back to 1814; inside, it's splendidly decorated in a simple, historical style that still bespeaks a modern crispness.

There's a dining room and tiny pub (see "Where to Dine," below), and common rooms that are comfortable if not terribly cozy. Guest rooms are uncommonly well designed with antique and reproduction furnishings. Especially appealing is the Swift Room, with its oversize bathroom, whirlpool, and private terrace. About half of the 21 rooms have fireplaces or whirlpools or both; all but two rooms have televisions. Light sleepers may prefer the main inn or the Carriage House rather than the Gatehouse down the hill; the latter is on Route 7 and the truck noise can be a minor irritant at night. The Swift House offers lodging at reasonable prices for what guests receive, and the less expensive rooms are among the better deals in the state.

WHERE TO DINE

Swift House Inn. 25 Stewart Lane. ☎ **802/388-9925.** Reservations recommended during peak seasons, weekends, and college events. Main courses $10–$22 (most $15–$17). AE, CB, DC, DISC, MC, V. Thurs–Mon 5:30–9:30pm. REGIONAL.

Guests here are likely to feel as if they're having an exceedingly pleasant dinner in the house of an elderly, wealthy relative—one with the good taste to hire a creative cook who understood when and where to borrow from the Orient. The dining room on the first floor of this wonderful inn is divided among three rooms, some of which are detailed with lustrous cherry woodwork and 12-over-12 windows. In the cooler seasons, request a seat near the fireplace with its gorgeous mantel of polished cherry and marble. If time permits, arrive early for a single-malt Scotch at the cozy pub. Then, to food.

For starters, you might opt for the grilled duck sausage with polenta and a tomato-caper chutney, or spicy pork wontons with a pickled-ginger and lime vinaigrette. Next, it's on to roasted venison with a fried fruit compote, or dill-crusted salmon with caviar and a ham and white-bean sauce. Desserts flirt with the sublime; the crème brûlée is among the best in the state.

Woody's. 5 Bakery Lane (on Otter Creek just upstream from the bridge in the middle of town). ☎ **802/388-4182.** Reservations recommended on weekends and during college events. Lunch items $3.95–$6.95; main dinner courses $9.95–$16.95. AE, MC, V. Mon–Sat 11:30am–3pm and 5–10pm; Sun 10:30am–3pm and 5–9pm. Closed Tues in winter. PUB FARE/PASTA.

Woody's is not Olde New Englande. Set down a small alley in the middle of town, Woody's features dining on three levels overlooking the creek in an exuberantly retro interior with a huge neon clock, lots of brushed steel, soaring windows, and red-and-black-checkered linoleum floors. It's the kind of fun, hip place destined to put you in a good mood the moment you walk in. Lunches include burgers, sandwiches, and salads, along with burritos and pita melts. Dinner is heavy on the pasta selections (try the fettuccine with sea scallops sautéed and served with a sauce of sun-dried tomatoes, leeks, basil, and cream), but also features appetizing selections from the grill, like Cajun-grilled salmon and a char-roasted leg of lamb with a poached garlic flan.

7 Montpelier & Barre

Montpelier is easily the most down-home, low-key state capitol in the United States. There's a hint of that in every photo of the glistening gold dome of the state capitol. Rising behind it isn't a bank of mirror-sided skyscrapers, but a thickly forested hill. Montpelier, it turns out, isn't a self-important center of politics, but a small town that happens to house the state government.

The state capitol is worth a visit, as is the local art museum and historical society. But more than that, it's worth visiting just to experience a small, clean, New England town that's more than a little friendly. Barre is more commercial and industry-oriented, but shares an equally vibrant past. Between the two towns is a six-mile stretch of road with motels, fast-food restaurants, and many of the other conveniences sought by travelers.

Montpelier centers around two main boulevards: State Street, which is lined with state government buildings, and Main Street, where many of the town's shops are located. It's all very compact, manageable, and cordial. If you so much as think about crossing the street, the drivers of the next car will probably stop and wave you across.

Lots of people I know have visited Montpelier and come away thinking, "Hey, I could live here!" The downtown has two hardware stores next door to one another (one had this sign posted on its front door recently: "We just oiled our floor and it may be slippery when wet until it gets wore in."), and two movie theaters, including the **Savoy** (☎ 802/229-0509), arguably the best art house in northern New England. At the Savoy, a large cup of cider and a small popcorn slathered with real, unclarified butter cost me $2.20.

Nearby Barre (pronounced "Barry") has a more commercial, blue-collar demeanor than upscale Montpelier. The historic connection to the thriving granite industry is seen here and there, from the granite curbstones lining its long Main Street, to the signs for commercial establishments carved out of locally hewn rock. (The absence of any imposing granite buildings is a bit odd, however.) Barre attracted talented stone workers from Scotland and Italy (there's even a statue of Robert Burns), which gave turn-of-the-century Barre a lively, cosmopolitan flavor.

ESSENTIALS

GETTING THERE   Montpelier is accessible via Exit 7 off I-89. For Barre, take Exit 8.

VISITOR INFORMATION   The **Central Vermont Chamber of Commerce,** P.O. Box 336, Barre, VT 05641 (☎ 802/229-5711), is located on Airport Road (Exit 7 off I-89). From Montpelier, head toward Barre on Route 62 and look for signs.

EXPLORING THE TOWNS

Start your exploration of Montpelier with a visit to the gold-domed **State House** (☎ 802/828-2228). If you're in a hurry, you can take a self-guided tour, admiring the statue of Ethan Allen guarding the doors, and the long, stately halls with marble floors. If time allows and you're here in the right season, take one of the free guided tours, which are offered July through mid-October. The tours leave on the half-hour Monday to Friday 10am to 3:30pm, and on Saturdays from 11am to 2pm.

A short stroll from the State House, at 109 State St., is the **Vermont Historical Society** (☎ 802/828-2291). This is a great spot to admire some of the rich tapestry of Vermont's history. The museum is housed in a replica of the elegant old Pavilion House, a prominent Victorian hotel, and contains a number of intriguing artifacts, such as the gun once owned by Ethan Allen. The Governor's Corridor offers a rotating series of artwork from the collection. The museum is open Tuesday through Saturday from 9am to 4:30pm, and Sundays from noon to 4pm. Admission is $2 adults, $1 for students and seniors.

FOR ROCK FANS

Rock of Ages Quarry. Graniteville. ☎ 802/476-3119. Tours $4 adults, $3.50 seniors, $1.50 children 6–12. Mon–Fri 8am–3:30pm. Closed Nov–Apr. Drive south on Rte. 14 from Barre; watch for signs to quarry.

When in or around Barre, listen for the deep, throaty hum of industry. That's the Rock of Ages Quarry, set on a rocky hillside high above town near the aptly named hamlet of Graniteville. A free visitors center presents informative exhibits, a video about quarrying, a glimpse at an old granite quarry (no longer active), and a selection of granite gifts.

For a look at the active quarry, sign up for a guided half-hour tour of the world's largest quarry. An old bus groans up to a viewer's platform high above the 500-foot, man-made canyon (it looks like something sculpted by Picasso in his cubist period), where workers cleave huge slabs of fine-grained granite and hoist them out using 150-foot derricks anchored with a spider's web of 15 miles of steel cable. It's an operation to behold. Afterwards, visitors are invited to stop by the nearby manufacturing plant to see the granite carved into memorials, architectural adornments, and other pieces.

For a more poignant, less staged display of the local stonecutters craft, head to **Hope Cemetery,** located on a hillside in a wooded valley north of Barre on Route 14. The cemetery is filled with columns, urns, and human figures carved of the fine-grained grey granite. It's more than a memorial park—it's a remarkable display of the talent of area stonecutters.

WHERE TO STAY

Capitol Plaza Hotel. 100 State St., Montpelier, VT 05602. ☎ **800/274-5252** or 802/223-5252. Fax 802/229-5427. 42 rms. A/C TV TEL. Midweek $82 double; weekends (May–Sept) $92 double; foliage season $102 double. AE, DISC, MC, V.

The Capitol Plaza is Montpelier's business and conference hotel, but is well located (across from the state capitol) to serve travelers planning to explore the town. This solid brick building was originally constructed in the late 1950s, but underwent a makeover with a change of ownership to a family-run business in 1993. The carpeted lobby is small and has a colonial cast to it; the rooms on the three upper floors also adopt a light, faux-colonial tone, and feature the usual hotel amenities, including in-room coffeemakers. The hotel is nothing fancy, but it is clean, comfortable, and very convenient. A simply decorated restaurant on the first floor is open for all three meals.

Inn at Montpelier. 147 Main St., Montpelier, VT 05602. ☎ **802/223-2727.** Fax 802/223-0722. 19 rms (4 with showers only). A/C TV TEL. $99–$153 double. Rates include continental breakfast. AE, DC, DISC, MC, V.

Two historic in-town homes house guests at the Inn at Montpelier, and both offer superb accommodations with most major amenities. The main cream-colored Federal-style inn, built in 1827, features a mix of historical and up-to-date furnishings, along with a sunny sitting room and deck off the rear of the second floor. The larger front rooms are nicely appointed, but so too are the much smaller rooms in the former servants' wing. If you'd prefer not to catch the wafting scents of dinner cooking, ask for a room at the adjacent house, built in 1807, and decorated with comparable flair. Room 27 is especially pleasant, and features a large private deck. The inn tends to be a shade more antiseptic and Spartanly furnished than other historic inns, but it's more intriguing and comfortable than any chain hotel.

Dining/Entertainment: The inn's restaurant is very well regarded, with appealingly prepared entrees featuring pheasant breast, salmon filets, and hand-rolled fettuccine. Entrees are priced from $13 to $21.

WHERE TO DINE

A creation of the New England Culinary Institute, **La Brioche Bakery & Cafe** (☎ 802/229-0443) occupies the corner of Montpelier's State and Main streets. It's a little bit of Europe in one of New England's more continental cities (Montpelier could slip into the Black Forest or the Vienna Woods without causing much of a stir).

A deli counter offers baked goods like croissants and baguettes. Get them to go, or settle into a table in the afternoon sun outdoors.

☉ Horn of the Moon. 8 Langdon St., Montpelier. **☎ 802/223-2895.** Reservations not accepted. Breakfast $2.50–$4.50; lunch/dinner items $3.95–$5.25. No credit cards. Tues–Sat 7am–9pm, Sun 9am–7pm. VEGETARIAN.

This relaxed, informal, and inexpensive restaurant overlooking a tributary of the Winooski was the first vegetarian restaurant in Vermont, and it remains one of the best. In fact, it's appealing enough to attract plenty of meat eaters, drawn by the Middle Eastern platter, the tasty sandwiches made on whole-wheat flatbread, and the Mexican-style dishes like burritos and tostadas. If you're looking for a full three-course meal with dinner rolls and linens, you're better off around the corner at the Main Street Grill. But if you want wholesome, inexpensive food, get here early and get here often.

Main Street Grill & Bar. 118 Main St., Montpelier. **☎ 802/223-3188.** Reservations usually not needed. Lunch items $3.75–$6.50; main dinner courses $5.95–$12.75. AE, DC, DISC, MC, V. Mon–Fri 7–10am, Sat 8–10am; Mon–Sat 11:30am–2pm, Sun 10am–2pm; daily 5:30–10pm. AMERICAN/ECLECTIC.

This airy, modern grill serves as a classroom and ongoing exam for students of the New England Culinary Institute, which is located just down the block. It's not unusual to see knots of students, toques at a rakish angle, walking between the restaurant and class. Diners can eat on the first level dining room, watching street life through the broad windows (in summer, there's seating on a narrow porch outside the windows), or burrow in the homey bar downstairs. Dishes change with the semester, but might include a vegetarian chili, vegetable stir-fry, portobello mushroom sandwich, or a robust penne with chicken, artichokes, and sun-dried tomatoes in a fennel cream sauce. The breakfast burrito is served with a tangy corn salsa, and is nearly large enough for two.

For fancier, more formal dining, head for the second-floor Chef's Table, which is also part of the culinary institute. Entrees here range from $15.25 to $18.75.

8 Mad River Valley

The Mad River Valley is one of Vermont's best-kept secrets, and has something of a Shangri-la quality to it. In places it appears to have changed little since it was first settled in 1789 by Gen. Benjamin Wait and a handful of early Revolutionary War veterans, including half a dozen said to have served as Minutemen at the battles of Concord Bridge and Lexington.

Since 1948, ski-related development has joined the early farms that were the backbone of the region for two centuries, but the newcomers haven't been too pushy or overly obnoxious. Save for a couple of telltale signs, you could drive Route 100 through the sleepy villages of Warren and Waitsfield (it's hard to tell where one stops and the other begins) and not realize that you've passed close to some of the choicest skiing in the state. The region happily hasn't fallen prey to condo or strip mall developers, as have some other ski areas in Vermont, and it still maintains an aggressively friendly and informal feel.

The region's character becomes less pastoral along the Sugarbush Access Road, but even then, development isn't heavily concentrated, not even at the base of Sugarbush, the valley's preeminent ski area. The better lodges and restaurants tend to be tucked back in the forest or set along streams, and it behooves travelers to make sure they have good directions before setting out in search of accommodations or food.

Hidden up a winding valley road, Mad River Glen, the area's older ski resort, has a pleasantly dated quality that eschews glamour in favor of the rustic. Its slogan is: "Ski it if you can."

ESSENTIALS

GETTING THERE   Warren and Waitsfield straddle Route 100 between Killington and Waterbury. The nearest interstate access is from Exit 10 (Waterbury) on I-89; drive south on Route 100 for 14 miles to Waitsfield.

VISITOR INFORMATION   The **Sugarbush Chamber of Commerce,** P.O. Box 173, Waitsfield, VT 05673 (☎ **800/828-4748** or 802/469-3409), on Route 100, is open Monday through Saturday 9am to 5pm.

SKIING

Mad River Glen. Waitsfield, VT 05763. ☎ **802/496-3551.** Vertical drop: 2,000 feet. Lifts: 4 chairlifts. Skiable acreage: 90. Lift tickets: $26 midweek, $30 weekends.

Mad River Glen is the George Burns of the Vermont ski world—it's been around forever, it's curmudgeonly, and it does what it does very well. High-speed detachable quads? Forget it. The main lift is a circa-1950 *single*-chair lift that creaks its way to the summit. Snowmaking? Don't count on it. Only 15% of the terrain benefits from the fake stuff; the rest is dependent on unreliable Mother Nature. Mad River's slopes are twisting and narrow, and hide some of the steepest drops you'll find in New England. Mad River Glen has long since attained the status of a cult mountain among serious skiers, and its fans seem bound and determined to keep it that way.

But how long it stays that way remains to be seen. Longtime owner Betsy Pratt sold the ski area to a cooperative of about 1,000 Mad River skiers in late 1995. It's said that most of the new owners are adamant about retaining the rough-hewn character of the mountain, but another faction is pushing for changes and modernization.

Sugarbush. Warren, VT 05674. ☎ **800/537-8427** or 802/583-2381 for lodging. Vertical drop: 2,600 feet. Lifts: 14 chairlifts (4 high-speed), 4 surface lifts. Skiable acreage: 412. Lift tickets: $45.

After absorbing nearby Glen Ellen Ski Area to create Sugarbush South and Sugarbush North in 1979, this sprawling but low-key resort struggled with solvency under several owners. Noted for its often icy and rocky runs, the mountain tended to attract young kids and older skiers who prized the classic New England ski trails. The neon-ski-suit and grunge-snowboard crowd stuck with Killington, one hour south.

With the purchase of Sugarbush by Les Otten in 1995—and a quick $28 million in improvements—Sugarbush aims to add some flash and zip to broaden its appeal. The "new" Sugarbush got under way by linking the two areas with a 2-mile, 10-minute high-speed chairlift (no more irksome shuttle buses), and adding three other high-speed, detachable quad chairlifts. Snowmaking has been significantly upgraded (Otten is a master of snowmaking, if nothing else), and the improved slopes are generating a buzz among ski bums far and wide. Sugarbush is still a family-friendly area at heart with great intermediate cruising runs on the north slopes and some challenging expert slopes to the south, but expect a harder and glossier edge as the resort races to make up for lost time.

HIKING & BIKING

A rewarding 14-mile bike trip along paved roads begins at the village of Waitsfield. Park your car near the covered bridge, and follow East Warren Road past the Inn at Round Barn Farm and into the farm-filled countryside. Near the village of Warren, turn right at Brook Road to connect back to Route 100. Return north on bustling but generally safe and often scenic Route 100 to Waitsfield.

Bike rentals, repairs, and advice are available in Waitsfield at **Mad River Bike Shop** (☎ 802/496-9500). The shop is located on Route 100 just south of the junction with Route 17, and is open daily 9am to 6pm (until 5pm on Sunday).

Hikers in search of good exercise and a spectacular view should strike for **Mt. Abraham,** west of Warren. Drive west up Lincoln Gap Road (it leaves Route 100 just south of Warren Village), and continue until the crest, where you'll cross the intersection with the Long Trail. Park here and head north on the trail; about two miles along you'll hit the Battell Shelter, which can sleep eight hikers. (There's also a spring nearby.) Push on another eight-tenths of a mile up a steep ascent to reach the panoramic views atop 4,006-foot Mt. Abraham. Enjoy. Retrace your steps back to your car. Allow four or five hours for the round-trip hike.

For a less demanding adventure that still yields great views, head *south* from Lincoln Gap Road on the **Long Trail.** In about six-tenths of a mile, look for a marked spur trail to Sunset Rock with open vistas of the Champlain Valley. A round-trip hike requires about one hour.

OTHER OUTDOOR PURSUITS

Without a doubt the most unique way to explore the region is atop an Icelandic pony. The **Vermont Icelandic Horse Farm** (☎ 802/496-7141) specializes in tours on these small, sturdy, strong horses. Day and half-day rides are available, but to really appreciate both the countryside and the horses, you should sign up for one of the multiday treks. These tours range from one to five nights, and include lodging at area inns, all your meals (lunches are either picnics or enjoyed at a local restaurant), your mount, and a guide to lead you through the lush hills around Waitsfield and Warren. In winter, there's also skijoring, which can best be described as waterskiing behind a horse. The overnight trips range from $355 (based on double occupancy) for the two-day trip, to $1,095 for the six-day trip. Call for information and reservations for day and half-day trips.

The classic **Warren General Store** (☎ 802/496-3864) anchors the former bustling timber town of Warren. Set along a tumbling stream, the store has uneven wooden floorboards, a potbellied stove, and a shelf stock fully updated for the 1990s with a good selection of gourmet foods and wines. Get a coffee or a sandwich at the back deli counter, and enjoy it on the deck overlooking the water. Afterwards, browse the crafts gallery upstairs, which features local pottery, leather goods, and candles. The store is located in Warren Village just off Route 100 south of the Sugarbush Access Road.

Visitors can explore local rivers or lakes with the help of **Clearwater Sports** (☎ 802/496-2708) on Route 100 in Waitsfield, just north of the covered bridge. These outgoing guides rent canoes and kayaks, and offer shuttle services for intrepid paddlers looking for adventures ranging from whitewater (best in the spring) to a placid summer afternoon paddle on the Waterbury Reservoir. Rates are $35 per day for canoe rental; guided tours run from 9am to 3pm and cost $45 per person, including transportation, equipment, and instruction (bring your own picnic lunch). In a romantic mood? Ask about Clearwater's moonlight cruises.

Also in Waitsfield is the **Mad River Canoe Factory Showroom** (☎ 802/496-3127). Experienced canoeists will recognize the name of this respected canoe manufacturer, which makes fiberglass and other canoes of complex laminates suitable for running raging rivers and poking around placid ponds. The showroom, located on Mad River Green, is open weekdays from 10am to 4pm. Paddling accessories (and some good advice) are also available here.

Central Vermont & the Champlain Valley

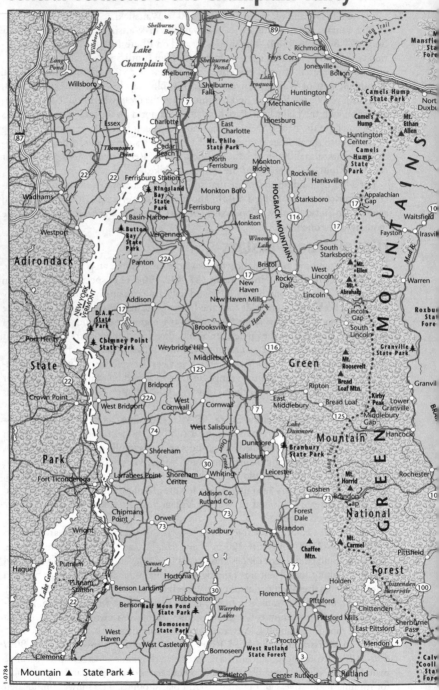

Mountain ▲ State Park ⚑

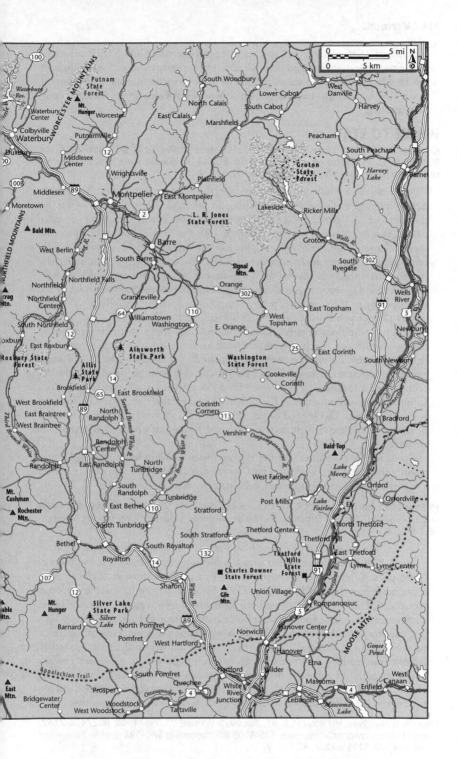

513

South of Warren, Route 100 pinches through **Granville Gulf,** a wild and scenic area of tumultuous streams and sheer hillsides. The highway twists and winds through this troll-like defile, which stands in contrast to the more open vistas along most of Route 100. Look for the roadside pull-off at **Moss Glen Falls,** one of the state's loveliest cascades.

WHERE TO STAY

✪ **Inn at Round Barn Farm.** East Warren Rd., Waitsfield, VT 05673. ☎ **802/496-2276.** Fax 802/496-8832. 11 rms (some with shower only). $100–$185 double. Rates include full breakfast. $5 surcharge during holidays and foliage. AE, MC, V.

"We're basically for romantics," says Jennifer, the assistant manager of this extraordinary inn. And that's the all-encompassing definition of "romantic." Those seeking the romance of Vermont will find it here in spades. You arrive at the inn after passing through a covered bridge off Route 100; a mile later you come upon this spectacular structure, set along a sloping hill with views of fields all around. The centerpiece of the inn is the eponymous Round Barn, a strikingly beautiful 1910 structure that's used variously for weddings, arts exhibits, and Sunday church services. Owners Jack, Doreen, and AnneMarie Simko have improved the grounds bit by bit since opening in 1987, and they're now beautifully landscaped with stone walls, gardens, and duck ponds—the next project is a sculpture garden.

Elegant, pine-floored guest rooms will appeal to couples looking to kindle their own romance. Each is furnished with an impeccable country elegance so deft that it doesn't overstay its welcome. Particularly wonderful is the Dana Room, a peaceful retreat set privately down a narrow corridor, with gas fireplace, cathedral ceilings, and a luxurious steam shower. It's $155 a night—and a good deal at that. Common rooms downstairs are furnished with comparable flair. Especially inviting is the library with its Oriental carpet, grandfather clock, and always-full decanter of sherry. A breakfast solarium overlooks some of the inn's pastoral 85 acres. No smoking.

Facilities: In the winter you can explore the inn's 18 miles of groomed crosscountry trails, and then work the knots out in what's perhaps the inn's best surprise: a modern 58-foot indoor lap pool hidden partially beneath the barn.

♦ **Mad River Barn.** Rte. 17 (R.R. #1; P.O. Box 88), Waitsfield, VT 05673. ☎ **800/631-0466** or 802/496-3310. 15 rms. Summer $65 double; winter $95 double. Rates include breakfast. AE, DISC, MC, V.

The Mad River Barn, run by former Mad River Glen Ski area owner Betsy Pratt, is a classic, 1940s-style ski lodge that attracts a clientele nearly fanatical in its devotion to the place. While half of the rooms have TVs and steam showers, it's best not to come here expecting anything fancy. Do come expecting to have some fun once you're settled in. It's all knotty pine, with Spartanly furnished guest rooms, and rustic common rooms where visitors feel at home putting their feet up. Most guests stay in a two-story barn behind the white clapboard main house; some stay at the annex up the lawn. In winter, guests can elect to get their dinners on the premises, served in boisterous family style. In summer, the mood is slightly more sedate (only breakfast is offered), but enhanced by a beautiful pool a short walk away in a grove of birches. The Mad River Barn isn't so much an institution or accommodation as a big family, and guests who approach it in that spirit won't go away disappointed.

West Hill Inn. West Hill Road (R.R. #1, Box 292), Warren, VT 05674. ☎ **802/496-7162.** 7 rms (4 with shower only). Summer $85–$105 double; spring $80–$95 double; foliage and ski seasons $90–$115 double. AE, MC, V.

Eating Your Way Through Nearby Waterbury

Waterbury is the home to a number of food emporia, and is developing a reputation as a sort of factory outlet center for deluxe comestibles. Most shops are located along Route 100 north of I-89.

Start a tour with the "anchor store"—**Ben & Jerry's factory**—that started it all. The saga of Ben & Jerry's has been repeated enough in the national press that it doesn't need much elaboration here. It all began when school buddies Ben Cohen and Jerry Greenfield went into the ice-cream business in a garage in Burlington in 1978, using just $8,000 in capital and a culinary education acquired from a $5 correspondence course. Today, the pair sells millions of pints of their rich, creamy ice cream, has set up scoop shops all around the world, and their factory has become the top tourist attraction in Vermont.

The factory, about a mile north of I-89 on Route 100, has a festival marketplace feel to it, despite the fact that there's no festival and no marketplace. During peak summer season vast crowds wait for the 30-minute, $1 tours (the afternoon tours fill up quickly, so get there early if you want to avoid a long wait). Once you've got your ticket, browse the small ice-cream museum (learn the long, strange history of Cherry Garcia), buy a cone of your favorite flavor at the scoop shop, or lounge on the promenade, which is scattered with Adirondack chairs and picnic tables. For kids, there's the "Stairway to Heaven," which leads to a playground, and a "Cow-Viewing Area," which needs no explanation. The tours are informative and fun, and conclude with a sample of the day's featured product. For more information on the tours, call **802/244-8687.**

A short drive north of Ben & Jerry's on Route 100 is a modern outlet featuring the products of three other area food producers: **Green Mountain Chocolates** (☎ **802/244-1139**), **Cabot Cheese** (☎ **802/244-6334**), and **Green Mountain Coffee Roasters** (☎ **802/244-8430**). All three have set up under one roof, and it's a good spot for free-range grazing. Cabot is the most generous with its samples; Green Mountain Chocolates, alas, is quite stingy. But try the truffles and other handcrafted chocolates, and don't forget a steaming coffee for the road. The outlets are open daily 9am to 6pm (until 8pm on Fridays). Ask the Cabot clerks about tours of their cheese factory.

Yet farther north on Route 100 is **Cold Hollow Cider Farm** (☎ **802/244-8771**), a tremendously popular attraction. Despite its claim to be "New England's Most Famous Cider Mill," it's really just a sprawling gift shop housed in a very un-Vermont red, mauve, and purple farm complex. Tempting samples of various foods are arrayed around the shop, but ubiquitous signs nag shoppers against taking too much, thereby inducing unwarranted guilt with every bite. The vaunted cider-making operation is in the back and observers are welcome, but it's not a very compelling display. My advice: Look for one of the dozens of less commercial, unheralded cider houses in the small towns around the state if you want to find the flavor of a real cider farm.

Nestled on a forested hillside along a lightly traveled country road, the West Hill Inn offers the quintessential New England experience with an easy commute to the slopes at Sugarbush. Built in the 1850s, this farmhouse was expanded in the summer of 1995 with a modern common room, which offers a handsome fireplace for warmth in winter and an outdoor patio for summer lounging. The guest rooms vary, but all are well-appointed in an updated country stylc. A room with a fireplace sits atop a spiral staircase; two Hobbitlike rooms are tucked under the eaves above a narrow staircase in the old part of the home.

Guests often linger amid the rich, colorful tones of the library, with its woodstove and walls of books, or borrow a VCR and one of the 80 movies before retreating to their rooms. Country breakfasts are served around a large dining room table, and the day's first meal tends to be an event as much as it is nourishment. It often takes some effort to pry yourself away from the good company to get outdoors before lunchtime rolls around.

WHERE TO DINE

☉ The Common Man. German Flats Rd., Warren. ☎ **802/583-2800.** Reservations highly recommended in season. Main courses $9.50–$19. AE, DISC, MC, V. Daily 6:30–9pm. Open at 6pm on Sat and till 10pm on busier nights. Closed Mon from mid-Apr to mid-Dec. CONTINENTAL.

Dapper proprietor Mike Ware personally greets guests arriving at The Common Man, and it's clear by the warm response from returning patrons that he and chef Patrick Matecat are doing something *very* right. It's spectacularly located in a century-old barn moved here in 1987 (the original barn was destroyed in a fire), and the interior is soaring and dramatic, but manages to be intimate as well. Chandeliers, floral carpeting on the walls (weird, but it works), and candles on the tables meld successfully and coax all but coal-hearted guests into a relaxed frame of mind.

The menu is as ambitious and appealing as the decor. Guests might start with an appetizer of salmon filet dressed with green peppercorns and spices, or cheddar and walnut raviolis with basil-marinated sweet peppers. The feast continues with dishes ranging from braised rabbit served with a creamed Dijon sauce, to rainbow trout sautéed with pine nuts and sage.

The Den. Junction of rtes. 100 and 17, Waitsfield. ☎ **802/496-8880.** Reservations not accepted. Lunch items $3.50–$6.95; main dinner courses $8.50–$13.95. AE, MC, V. Daily 11:30am–4pm and 5–10:30pm. AMERICAN.

Jonesing for a juicy burger without frills or fancy service? Look no further: The Den is your destination. A local favorite with a comfortable, neighborly feel, it's the kind of place where you can plop yourself down in a pine booth, help yourself to the salad bar while waiting for your main course, and cheer on the Red Sox on the tube over the bar. The menu offers pub fare, with all manner of burgers, plus reubens, roast beef sandwiches, chicken in the basket, and even pork chops with apple sauce and french fries.

☉ John Eagan's Big World Pub. In Madbush Falls Country Motel, Rte. 100, Warren. ☎ **802/496-3033.** Reservations not accepted. Main courses $9.50–$16.25; burgers and sandwiches $6.25. AE, MC, V. Daily 5:30–9:30pm. GRILL/INTERNATIONAL.

Extreme skier John Eagan starred in 10 Warren Miller skiing films over the years, but *really* took a risk when he opened his own restaurant in December 1994. Located in a 1970s-style motel dining room that's sorely lacking in charm or élan (save for the bar made of ski sections signed by skiing luminaries like Tommy Moe), the Big World Pub compensates with a small but above-average pub menu that the chef pulls off with unexpected flair. Dishes include wood-grilled chicken breast glazed with Vermont cider, ginger, and lime; pan-roasted pork loin brushed with Dijon; and a delicious fresh tortellini with tossed shrimp and sausage. Try the unique "dog bones" appetizer—Polish sausage wrapped in puff pastry and served with sauerkraut and mustard. Wash your meal down with a pint of custom Eagan's Extreme Ale, brewed by Vermont's Catamount Brewery.

9 Stowe

There's no getting around it: Stowe is a tourist destination. That's even evident in summer, when telltale ski racks don't grace every car. After all, how else to explain the shop called "Everything Cows" that sells bovine-themed giftware?

But Stowe, which bills itself as the "Ski Capital of New England," has managed the juggernaut of steady growth reasonably well and with good humor. There are condo developments and strip mall–style restaurants, to be sure. But there are still spectacular views of the mountains, and wonderful vistas across fertile farmlands of the valley bottom. And the village of Stowe has retained its charm and small-town feel.

Stowe is quaint, compact, and contains perhaps Vermont's most gracefully tapered church spire, located atop the Stowe Community Church. Most of the recent development has taken place along Mountain Road (Route 108), which runs northwest of the village to the base of Mt. Mansfield and the Stowe ski area. Here you'll find an array of motels, restaurants, shops, bars, and even a three-screen cinema. A free trolley connects the village with the mountain during ski season, so you can let your car get snowed in and still not miss out on anything.

ESSENTIALS

GETTING THERE   Stowe is located on Route 100 north of Waterbury and south of Morrisville. In summer, Stowe may also be reached via Smugglers Notch on Route 108. This pass, which squeezes narrowly between the rocks, is closed in winter.

VISITOR INFORMATION   The **Stowe Area Association,** P.O. Box 1320, Stowe, VT 05672 (☎ 802/253-7321), maintains a handy office in the village center. Ask for advice, pick up brochures, or make lodging reservations at dozens of area inns and hotels. This is a good first stop if you show up in town without a place to stay.

Stowe's homepage on the Internet may be found at http://www.stowe.com/smr.

The **Green Mountain Club,** a venerable statewide association devoted to building and maintaining backcountry trails, has a visitor's center on Route 100 between Waterbury and Stowe. This is a good place to buy detailed hiking guides, and to ask the staff for hiking and camping suggestions and ideas.

WARM-WEATHER OUTDOOR ACTIVITIES

Stowe's forte is winter (see the sections on skiing, below), but it's also an outstanding fair-weather destination, surrounded by lush, rolling green hills and open farmlands, and towered over by craggy **Mt. Mansfield,** Vermont's highest peak at 4,393 feet.

Deciding how to get up Mt. Mansfield is half the fun. The **toll road** (☎ 802/253-7311) traces its lineage back to the 19th century, when it served horses bringing passengers to the old hotel sited near the mountain's crown. (The hotel was demolished in the 1960s.) Drivers now twist their way up this road and park below the summit of Mansfield; a two-hour hike along well-marked trails will bring you to the summit and unforgettable views. The toll road is open from late May through mid-October. The fare is $12 per car with up to six passengers, $2 per additional person; $7 per motorcycle (two people). Ascending by foot or bicycle is free.

Another option is the **Stowe gondola** (☎ 802/253-7311), which whisks ski-less travelers to within striking distance of the summit at the Cliff House Restaurant— it's about a half-hour hike farther beyond. Hikers can explore the rugged, open ridgeline, then descend just before twilight. The gondola runs mid-June through mid-October and costs $9 for adults, $4 for children 6 to 12.

The budget route up Mt. Mansfield, and to my mind the most rewarding, is by foot, and you have at least nine options for the ascent. The easiest but least pleasing route is up the toll road. Other options require local guidance and a durable map. Ask for information from knowledgeable locals (your inn might be of help), or stop by the Green Mountain Club headquarters, open weekdays, on Route 100 about four miles south of Stowe. GMC can also assist with advice on other area trails.

A short drive from Waterbury is **Camel's Hump,** the state's fourth highest peak at 4,083 feet. (It's also the highest Vermont mountain without a ski area.) Once the site of a popular Victorian-era summit resort, the mountain still attracts hundreds of hikers who ascend the demanding, highly popular trail to the barren, windswept peak. It's not the place to get away from crowds on sunny summer weekends, but it's well worth the effort for the spectacular vistas and to observe the unique alpine terrain along the high ridge.

The round-trip loop hike is about 7.5 miles (plan on six hours or more of hiking time), and departs from the Couching Lion Farm eight miles southwest of Waterbury on Camel's Hump Road. (You're best off asking locally for exact directions.) At the summit, seasonal rangers are on hand to answer questions and to admonish hikers to stay on the rocks to avoid trampling the delicate alpine grasses, found in Vermont only here and on Mt. Mansfield to the north.

One of the most understated, most beloved local attractions is the **Stowe Recreation Path,** which winds 5.3 miles from behind the Stowe Community Church up the valley toward the mountain, ending behind the Topnotch Tennis Center. This exceptionally appealing pathway, completed in 1989, is heavily used by locals for transportation and exercise in the summers; in the winter, it serves as a cross-country ski trail. You can connect to the pathway at either end, or at points where it crosses side roads connecting to Mountain Road. No motorized vehicles or skateboards are allowed.

Bikes are available for rent ($10 to $25 for four hours) at **The Mountain Bike Shop** (☎ 802/253-7919), located in the Big Red Building along the Rec Path.

Fisherfolk should allow ample time to peruse **The Fly Rod Shop** (☎ 800/535-9703 or 802/253-7346), located on Route 100 two miles south of the village. This well-stocked shop offers fly and spin tackle, along with camping gear, antique fly rods, and rentals of canoes and fishing videos.

ALPINE SKIING

Stowe Mountain Resort. Stowe, VT 05672. ☎ 800/253-4754 or 802/253-3000 for lodging. Vertical drop: 2,360 feet. Lifts: 1 gondola, 8 chairlifts (1 high-speed), 2 surface lifts. Skiable acreage: 487. Lift tickets: $45.

Stowe's been knocked from its perch as the ski capital of New England in recent years (Killington, Sunday River, and Sugarloaf all can make more substantial claims). But this historic resort, first developed in the 1930s, still has lots of funky charm and plenty of good runs. Especially notable are its legendary "Front Four" trails (National, Starr, Lift Line, and Goat), which have humbled more than a handful of skiers attempting to claw their way from intermediate to expert. The majority of the slopes are located on Mt. Mansfield; other trails are on adjacent Spruce Peak, which has a vertical drop of 1,550 feet. Other facilities include eight restaurants and limited night skiing.

CROSS-COUNTRY SKIING

Stowe is an outstanding destination for cross-country skiers, offering no fewer than four groomed ski areas with a combined total of 93 miles of trails traversing everything from gentle valley floors to challenging mountain peaks.

The **Trapp Family Lodge Cross-Country Ski Center,** on Luce Hill Road, two miles from Mountain Road (☎ **800/826-7000** or 802/253-8511), was the nation's first cross-country ski center. It remains one of the most gloriously sited in the Northeast, set atop a ridge with views across the broad valley and into the folds of the mountains flanking Mt. Mansfield. The center features 36 miles of groomed trails on its 2,200 acres of rolling forestland.

The **Edson Hill Manor Ski Touring Center** (☎ **800/621-0284** or 802/253-7371) has 25 miles of wooded trails (15 miles groomed) just off Mountain Road. Also offering appealing ski touring are the **Stowe Mountain Resort Cross-Country Touring Center** (☎ **800/253-4754** or 802/253-7311), with 30 miles at the base of Mt. Mansfield, and **Topnotch Resort** (☎ **800/451-8686** or 802/253-8585), with 12 miles of groomed and ungroomed trails in the forest off Mountain Road.

WHERE TO STAY

✪ **Green Mountain Inn.** Main St. (P.O. Box 60), Stowe, VT 05672. ☎ **800/253-7302** or 802/253-7301. Fax 802/253-5096. 65 rms. A/C TV TEL. Winter and summer $109–$250 double. Higher rates on holidays, lower during off-season. Ask about packages. AE, DISC, MC, V.

This tasteful, historic structure is the only inn right in the village. It's a big place with 65 rooms spread through three buildings, but it feels far smaller, with personal service and cozy rooms. The rooms are all decorated with an early 19th-century motif that befits the 1833 vintage of the main inn. Primitive art, braided rugs, and stenciling on the wall in the guest rooms all blend nicely to create a mood that's pleasantly historic but not overzealously so. (About half the rooms are carpeted, so if you want the buttery golden wood floors, be sure to ask when you book.) Even the annex rooms, built some 25 years ago, have a pleasantly antiquarian flair.

Dining/Entertainment: The Green Mountain offers a raft of welcome amenities, including a beautiful outdoor pool set amid gardens, a fitness club, a library and game room, and two dining rooms. (See "Where to Dine," below).

Stowehof. 434 Edson Hill Rd. (P.O. Box 1139), Stowe, VT 05672. ☎ **800/932-7136** or 802/253-9722. Fax 802/253-7513. 50 rms, 2 guest houses. A/C TV TEL. $70–$190 double. Rates include full breakfast. AE, DC, DISC, MC, V.

Stowehof's exterior architecture is mildly alarming in that aggressive neo-Tyrolean ski chalet kind of way. But inside, the place comes close to magic—it's pleasantly woodsy, folksy, and rustic in an Alpine way, with heavy beams and pine floors, ticking clocks, and massive maple tree trunks carved into architectural elements. Guests may feel a bit like characters in *The Hobbit.* The guest rooms are furnished simply, each decorated individually: some are bold and festive with sunflower patterns, others subdued and quiet.

Dining/Entertainment: Diners are are served in a cozy dining room, with entrees like Vermont venison stew, smoked pork chop, and the house specialty, Wiener schnitzel. Entrees range from $14.95 to $21.95.

Facilities: The inn has all-weather tennis courts and a beautiful pool outside the cantilevered sitting room. In the winter, sign up for a sleigh ride or a naturalist-led snowshoe hike.

✪ **Topnotch.** 4000 Mountain Rd. (P.O. Box 1458), Stowe, VT 05672. ☎ **800/451-8686** or 802/253-8585. Fax 802/253-9263. 90 rms. A/C TV TEL. Ski season $186–$570 double; off-season $130–$496 double; Christmas week $198–$685 double, with 5-night minimum. Townhome accommodations $185–$695 depending on season and size. AE, DC, DISC, MC, V.

A boxy, uninteresting exterior hides a creatively designed interior at this upscale resort and spa. The main lobby is imaginatively conceived and furnished, with lots of stone and wood and an absolutely huge moosehead hanging on the wall. There's even a telescope to watch skiers schuss down the slopes across the valley. The guest rooms, linked by long, motel-like hallways, are nicely appointed if basic; ask for one of the top-floor rooms with cathedral ceilings.

Dining/Entertainment: Well-prepared, healthy dishes are offered in the inn's handsome stone-walled dining room (entrees $18 to $26).

Facilities: The spa facilities are the real draw here. Fitness classes are offered throughout the day, and guests spend much of their time around the exceptionally appealing 60-foot indoor pool with bubbling fountain and 12-foot whirlpool. There's an outdoor pool for summer use as well. Other activities include horseback riding, tennis (indoor courts provide for tennis all year), and cross-country skiing on the inn's property.

Trapp Family Lodge. Luce Hill Rd., Stowe, VT 05672. ☎ **800/826-7000** or 802/253-8511. Fax 802/253-5740. 93 rms. TV TEL. Winter $138–$188 double (higher during school vacation); summer $118–$168 double. Breakfast $10 extra per person. Discounts available in spring and late fall. AE, DC, DISC, MC, V. Depart Stowe village westward on Rte. 108; in 2 miles bear left at fork near white church; continue up hill following signs for lodge.

The Trapp Family of *Sound of Music* fame bought this sprawling farm high above in Stowe in 1942, just four years after fleeing the Nazi takeover of Austria. Maria and Baron von Trapp's family continue to run this Tyrolean-flavored lodge. The original lodge burned in 1980, and guests still complain that its replacement lacks the character of the old place. But it's still a comfortable resort hotel, if designed more for efficiency than elegance. The guest rooms are a shade or two better than your standard hotel room, and most come with fine valley views and balconies.

Common areas with blonde wood and comfortably upholstered chairs abound, and make for comfortable idling. Especially nice is the second-floor library with fireplace.

Dining/Entertainment: The restaurant offers wonderful views for the lucky few with tables along the window, and well-prepared continental fare for all.

Facilities: Stowe's best cross-country skiing is just outside the door in winter.

WHERE TO DINE

The **Harvest Market,** 1031 Mountain Rd. (☎ 802/253-3800), is the place for gourmet-to-go. The market offers basics like fruit and dairy products, but this isn't the place for the mundane. Browse the Vermont products and exotic imports (they've got eight different kinds of olives), then pick up some of the fresh-baked goods, like the pleasantly tart raspberry squares, to bring back to the ski lodge or take for a picnic along the bike path. There's also a great selection of wine and beer.

Cliff House. Atop Mt. Mansfield (gondola access). ☎ **802/253-3665.** Reservations required. Fixed-price dinner $39. AE, DC, DISC, MC, V. Open in winter on nights when night skiing is offered 5:30–9pm. Open irregularly in summer, but typically Thurs–Sun; call first. REGIONAL/AMERICAN.

The setting is a somewhat stark, modern ski lodge. The food is well prepared if not quite worthy of a standing ovation. But talk about the views! Those are reason to hop the gondola to this high-altitude restaurant on the shoulders of Mt. Mansfield. Plan to arrive early enough to stroll the deck outside the restaurant; in summer, you can even come up in the late afternoon for the sunset atop Mansfield, then hike down to the Cliff House for dinner. The restaurant offers a fixed-price dinner daily, with the charge including appetizer, salad, entree, dessert, *and* the gondola ride. Entrees draw on regional products, and might include spinach ravioli with Vermont chevre, native trout with forest mushrooms, or pan-seared tournedos of beef with roasted walnut spaetzle.

ⓢ Miguel's Stowe-Away Lodge. Mountain Rd. ☎ **802/253-7574.** Reservations recommended weekends and peak ski season. Main courses $9.50–$12.50. AE, MC, V. Summer daily 5:30–10pm; other seasons daily 5–10pm. MEXICAN.

Located in an old, dark-red farmhouse midway between the village and the mountain, Miguel's packs in the locals who come for the most authentic Mexican food in the valley, if not in all of Vermont. Just like the big national chains, Miguel's has grown sufficiently popular to offer its own brand of chips, salsa, and other products in shops throughout New England. Start off with a killer margarita, then try out one of the appetizers like the queso fundido made with lamb sausage. Follow with dreamy crab enchiladas or the zesty zulu crisp—which includes just about everything they could scrounge up in the kitchen. Miguel's offers superb quality for the money, and the kitchen pays attention to the little things, like using only Hass avocadoes for its guacamole rather than their watery Florida counterparts. Miguels also operates a branch on the Sugarbush Access Road in Warren.

The Shed. Mountain Rd. ☎ **802/253-4364.** Reservations recommended weekends and holidays. Lunch items $4.50–$7.95; main dinner courses $8.75–$15.95. AE, DC, DISC, MC, V. Daily noon–midnight (light fare only 10pm–midnight); Sun brunch 9am–11:30am. PUB FARE.

When The Shed burned down in early 1994, the gnashing of teeth and the tearing of sackcloth could be heard throughout the valley. Since opening three decades earlier, this friendly, informal place won converts by the sleighload with its solid pub food and feisty camaraderie. The good news is that the replacement structure has recaptured much of the original charm—especially the bar, with its barnlike interior that's already been worn to a nice patina. (The main dining room, alas, has the somewhat more sterile atmosphere of a chain restaurant.) The best news is that a new brewery was built along with the restaurant, and The Shed is cranking out some fine brews. Especially excellent is the dark Mountain Ale. The bar also serves up some fairly toxic West Indian rum drinks.

Whip Bar & Grill. Main St. ☎ **802/253-7301.** Reservations recommended. Sandwiches $4.95–$7.95; burgers and main dinner courses $5.50–$17.95. AE, DISC, MC, V. Mon–Thurs 11:30am–9:30pm, Fri–Sat 11:30am–10pm, Sun 11am–9:30pm (brunch served 11am–2pm). UPSCALE PUB FARE.

The Whip is located beneath the historic Green Mountain Inn in the village center, and management is quick to boast that it had the first liquor license in Stowe. This small, classy grill still has loads of pubby charm, and it's not hard to relax here after a day outside—even when facing the wall of antique whips (for horses, that is) that lends the bar its name. It's a good destination if you're hungry for something quick and fairly light. The menu offers a good selection of salads, sandwiches and burgers. Slightly more ambitious meals include a lime and tequila marinated chicken quesadilla, and sesame-ginger stir fry.

10 Burlington

Burlington is a vibrant college town that's continually, valiantly resisting the onset of middle age. It's the birthplace of hippies turned mega-corporation Ben & Jerry's. It elected a socialist mayor in 1981, Bernie Sanders, who's now Vermont's representative to the U.S. Congress. Burlington is also home to the eclectic rock band Phish, which has been anointed by some as the heirs to the Grateful Dead tradition. And just look at the signs for offices as you wander downtown—an uncommonly high number seem to have the word "polarity" in them.

It's no wonder that Burlington has become a magnet for those seeking alternatives to big city life with its big city problems. The city has a superb location overlooking Lake Champlain and beyond to the Adirondacks of northern New York. To the east, visible on your way out of town, the Green Mountains rise dramatically, with two of the highest points (Mt. Mansfield and Camel's Hump) soaring above the undulating ridge.

In this century, Burlington turned its back for a time on its spectacular Lake Champlain waterfront (dubbed "New England's West Coast" by hyperactive marketers). Urban redevelopment focused on parking garages and high-rises; the waterfront lay fallow, open to development by light industry. In recent years the city has sought to regain a toehold on the waterfront, acquiring and redeveloping parts for commercial and recreational use. It's been successful in some sections, less so in others.

In contrast, the downtown is thriving. The pedestrian mall (Church Street) works here as it has failed in so many other towns. As a result, the scale is skewed towards pedestrians in the heart of downtown. It's best to get out of your car as soon as feasible.

ESSENTIALS

GETTING THERE   Burlington is at the junction of I-89, Route 7, and Route 2.

Burlington International Airport, about three miles east of downtown, is served by **Continental Express** (☎ 800/732-6887), **United Airlines** (☎ 800/241-6522), **USAir** (☎ 800/428-4322), and **Delta Connection** (☎ 800/345-3400).

Amtrak's *Vermonter* offers daily departures for Burlington from Washington, Baltimore, Philadelphia, New York, New Haven, and Springfield, Mass. Call **800/872-7245** for more information.

Vermont Transit Lines (☎ 802/864-6811), with a depot at 135 St. Paul St. facing City Hall Park, offers bus connections from Albany, Boston, Hartford, New York's JFK Airport, and other points in Vermont, Massachusetts, and New Hampshire.

VISITOR INFORMATION   The **Lake Champlain Regional Chamber of Commerce,** 60 Main St., Burlington, VT 05401 (☎ 802/863-3489), maintains an information center in a handsome brick building on Main Street just up from the waterfront and a short walk from Church Street Market. The center is open weekdays from 8:30am to 5:30pm.

A seasonal information booth is also staffed summers on the Church Street Marketplace at the corner of Church and Bank streets. There's no phone.

Burlington has three free weeklies that keep residents and visitors up to date on local events and happenings. (To confuse matters somewhat, the *Free Press* is the one paper that costs money.) *Seven Days* carries topical and lifestyle articles along with listings. *The Vermont Times* emphasizes local politics. And "Vox," a Vermont Times product, has an extensive cultural and nightlife calendar. All three are widely available at downtown stores and restaurants.

ORIENTATION   Burlington is comprised of three distinct areas: the UVM campus atop the hill, the waterfront along Lake Champlain, and the downtown area flanking the popular Church Street Marketplace.

University of Vermont   The University of Vermont was founded in 1791, funded by a state donation of 29,000 acres of forestland spread across 120 townships. In the two centuries since, the university has grown to accommodate 7,700 undergraduates and 1,200 graduate students, plus 300 medical students. The school is set on 400 acres atop a hill overlooking downtown and Lake Champlain to the west, and offers a glorious prospect of the Green Mountains to the east. The campus has more than 400 buildings, many of which were designed by the most noted architects of the day, including H.H. Richardson and McKim, Mead & White. (By the way, UVM stands for "Universitas Virdis Montis," which translates as University of the Green Mountains.)

UVM doesn't have a college neighborhood with bars and bookstores immediately adjacent to the campus, as is common at many universities. Downtown serves that function. The downtown and the campus are five long blocks distant, connected via aptly named College Street. A shuttle, which looks like an old-fashioned trolley, runs daily on College Street between the Community Boathouse on the waterfront and the campus. It's in operation year round between 11am and 9pm, and it's free.

Church Street Marketplace   The downtown centers around the Church Street Marketplace, which is alive with activity throughout the year. (See "Shopping," below.) Fanning from Church Street are a number of side streets, containing an appealing amalgam of restaurants, shops, offices, and malls. This is the place to wander without purpose and watch the crowds; you can always find a cafe or ice-cream shop to rest your feet. While the shopping and grazing are good here, don't overlook the superb historic commercial architecture that graces much of downtown.

Waterfront   The biggest project on the waterfront these days is the $6 million renovation centered around Union Station at the foot of Main Street. In 1995 two new buildings opened. The Wing Building, an appealingly quirky structure of brushed steel and other offbeat materials, blends in quite nicely with the more rustic parts of the waterfront. (A little too nicely, some of the tenants complain, noting the lack of foot traffic to date.) Next door is the new Cornerstone Building, with a restaurant and offices, which offers better views of the lake from its higher vantage. Nearby is the city's Community Boathouse, which is an exceptionally pleasant destination on a summer's day (see "Outdoor Pursuits," below).

Bear in mind that Burlingtonians accept a fairly liberal definition of the adjective "lakeside." In some cases this might mean the shop or restaurant is 100 yards or so from the lake.

EXPLORING BURLINGTON

Ethan Allen Homestead. Rte. 127. ☎ **802/865-4556.** Admission $3.50 adults, $3 seniors, $2 children 6–16. Mid-May to mid-June Tues–Sun 1–5pm; mid-June to mid-Oct daily 10am–5pm (Sun opens at 1pm). Take Rte. 127 northward from downtown; look for signs.

A quiet retreat on one of the most idyllic, least developed stretches of the Winooski River, the Ethan Allen Homestead is a shrine to Vermont's favorite son. While Allen wasn't born in Burlington, he settled here later in life on property confiscated from a British sympathizer during the Revolution. The reconstructed farmhouse is an enduring tribute to this Vermont hero; an orientation center offers an intriguing multimedia accounting of Allen's life and other points of regional history. The Homestead is located in a sizeable park, which is open year-round. Admission to the park is free.

Lake Champlain ferries. King Street Dock, Burlington. ☎ **802/864-9804.** One-way fare for car and driver from Burlington to Port Kent $12; round-trip $5.50 for adult passengers; $1.50 children 6–12; children under 6 free. Burlington ferry operates mid-May to mid-Oct. Departures hourly in summer between 7:45am and 7pm. Schedule varies in spring, fall, and foliage season; call for current departures.

Car ferries chug across the often placid, sometimes turbulent waters of Lake Champlain from Burlington to New York State between late spring and foliage season. It's a good way to cut out miles of driving if you're heading west toward the Adirondacks. It's also a good way to see the lake and the mountains on a pleasant, inexpensive cruise. Take a round-trip from Burlington with your binoculars; bring a bite to eat.

Ferries also cross Lake Champlain between Grande Isle, Vt. and Plattsburgh, N.Y. (year-round), and Charlotte, Vt. and Essex, N.Y. (April through early January).

✪ Shelburne Museum. Rte. 7 (P.O. Box 10), Shelburne, VT 05482. ☎ **802/985-3346.** Summer admission (good for two consecutive days), $15 adults, $9 students, $6 children 6–14; winter tours, $7 adults, $3 children. Mid-May to late-Oct daily 10am–5pm. Nov to mid-May daily tours at 1pm (reservations recommended).

If you've allotted time to visit only one museum while in northern New England, this is the one. Established in 1947 by Americana collector Electra Havenmeyer Webb, the museum contains one of the most outstanding collections of American decorative, folk, and fine art. The museum is spread over 45 beautiful acres seven miles south of Burlington; the collections occupy some 37 buildings. The more mundane exhibits include quilts, early tools, decoys, and weathervanes. But the museum also collects and displays *whole buildings* from around New England and New York State. These include an 1890 railroad station, a lighthouse, a stagecoach inn, an Adirondack lodge, and a round barn from Vermont. There's even a 220-foot steamship, eerily landlocked on the museum's grounds. Spend a few hours here and you're bound to come away with a richer understanding of regional culture. The grounds also contain a museum shop, cafeteria, and picnic area.

In the winter, much of the museum is closed but tours of selected collections are offered daily at 1pm. Dress warmly.

The Spirit of Ethan Allen II. Burlington Boathouse, Burlington. ☎ **802/862-8300.** Narrated cruises (1¹/₂ hours) $7.95 adults, $3.95 children 3–11. Sunset cruises (2¹/₂ hours) $8.95 adults, $4.95 children. Specialty cruises (dinner, brunch, mystery theater) priced higher. Late May to mid-Oct.

The Spirit of Ethan Allen II is Burlington's premier tour boat. Accommodating 500 passengers on three decks, this sleek ship provides a good way of seeing Burlington, Lake Champlain, and the Adirondacks. The views haven't changed much since the area was explored by Samuel de Champlain, who first reached here in 1609. Food is available on all cruises, including all-you-can-eat buffets at dinner and on Sunday brunch. The scenic cruise departs daily every other hour beginning at 10am through 4pm. The sunset cruise departs at 6:30pm.

SHOPPING

The **Church Street Marketplace** is one of the more notable success stories of downtown development anywhere in the U.S. Situated along four blocks between Main Street and Pearl Street, and extending southward from the austerely elegant 1816 Congregational Church, the marketplace buzzes with the sort of downtown energy that urban planners everywhere are seeking. While decidedly trendy (there are Banana Republic and The Nature Company stores), the marketplace still makes room for a used-book store and a $10 astrological reading joint. In summer, leave time to be entertained by buskers, sidewalk vendors, and knots of young folks just hanging out. In winter, there's the warm comfort of the **Burlington Square Mall,** an adjacent enclosed mall that's doing an admirable job of beating the suburbs at their own game.

Burlington

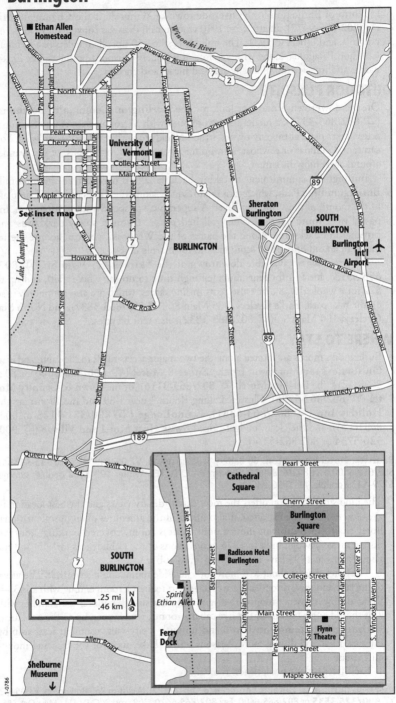

Ethan Allen Homestead

Route 127 Beltline

North Avenue

Winooski River

Riverside Avenue

East Allen Street

Mill St.

North Street

Park Street

N. Champlain St.

N. Union Street

N. Winooski Ave.

N. Prospect Street

Mansfield Ave.

Colchester Avenue

Grove Street

Pearl Street

Cherry Street

University of Vermont

College Street

Main Street

University Pl.

East Avenue

Lake Champlain

Battery Street

Church Street

S. Winooski Avenue

S. Union Street

S. Willard Street

S. Prospect Street

Maple Street

See inset map

St. Paul St.

Sheraton Burlington

SOUTH BURLINGTON

Burlington Int'l Airport

BURLINGTON

Howard Street

Williston Road

Hinesburg Road

Pine Street

Ledge Road

Shelburne Street

Spear Street

Dorset Street

Patchen Road

Flynn Avenue

Kennedy Drive

Queen City Park Rd.

Swift Street

Pearl Street

Cathedral Square

Cherry Street

Burlington Square

Bank Street

SOUTH BURLINGTON

Radisson Hotel Burlington

College Street

Lake Street

Battery Street

S. Champlain Street

Pine Street

Saint Paul Street

Church Street Market Place

Center St.

S. Winooski Avenue

Spirit of Ethan Allen II

Main Street

Flynn Theatre

0   .25 mi
    .46 km

N

Ferry Dock

King Street

Allen Road

Maple Street

Shelburne Museum

1-0786

525

North of Burlington in the riverside town of Winooski is the **Champlain Mill** (☎ 802/655-9477), an attractive 1910 woolen mill that was converted to shops, restaurants, and offices in 1981. The mill hosts some 40 upscale retailers like Kenneth Cole and Patagonia, along with vendors of uniquely Vermont products, like Dakin Farms and its selection of locally smoked meats and cheeses.

OUTDOOR PURSUITS

On the downtown waterfront look for the **Burlington Community Boathouse** (☎ 802/865-3377), a modern structure built with Victorian flair. A lot of summer action takes place at this city-owned structure and along the 900-foot boardwalk. You can rent a sailboat or rowboat, sign up for kayak or sculling lessons, or just wander around and enjoy the sunset.

Burlington's commitment to taking back its lake is best seen in the nine-mile **Burlington Bike Path,** which runs picturesquely along the shores of Lake Champlain to the mouth of the Winooski River. A superb way to spend a sunny afternoon, the paved bike route over a former rail bed passes through shady parklands and Burlington's backyards. Along the banks of the Winooski, you can admire the remains of an old bridge and scout around for marble chips.

Bike rentals are available downtown at the **Skirack,** 85 Main St. (☎ 802/658-3313), for $14 for four hours (enough time to do the whole trail), and up to $22 for a whole day. Skirack also rents in-line skates, which are also commonly used on the bike path. **Earl's Cyclery,** 135 Main St. (☎ 802/863-3832), and **North Star Cyclery,** 100 Main St. (☎ 802/863-3832), also rent bicycles.

WHERE TO STAY

Burlington's motels are located along the two major access roads to the south and east. On Route 7 south of town, try the **Super 8 Motel** (☎ 800/800-8000 or 802/862-6421), the **Bel-Aire Motel** (☎ 802/863-3116), or the **Town & Country Motel** (☎ 802/862-5786). Clustered along Route 2 near I-89 and the airport are the **Holiday Inn** (☎ 802/863-6361), **EconoLodge** (☎ 800/371-1125 or 802/863-1125), and the clean, budget-priced **Swiss Host Motel and Village** (☎ 800/326-5734 or 802/862-5734).

Radisson Hotel Burlington. 60 Battery St., Burlington, VT 05401. ☎ **800/333-3333** or 802/658-6500. Fax 802/658-4659. 255 rms. A/C TV TEL. Winter $92–$102 double; summer $129–$139 double. AE, DISC, MC, V.

The nine-story Radisson offers the most extraordinary views and the best location in the city. As might be expected, it also offers all the amenities of an upscale national hotel chain, including an indoor pool, fitness room, covered parking, and two dining areas. Though built in 1976, renovations of the public areas in 1993 and the guest rooms in 1995 have kept the weariness at bay.

The hotel charges about $10 more for a lakeside room, and it's worth it. The views of the lake and the Adirondacks are spectacular; request a room ending with a "43"— these southwest corner rooms are bright and offer superb panoramas. Families with kids should angle for one of the five cabana rooms, which open up to the pool area.

Dining/Entertainment: If you end up with a city-view room, at least stop by the tiered bar and dining room, Seasons on the Lake, to savor the lake and mountain vistas.

Facilities: Indoor pool, fitness rooms.

Sheraton Burlington Hotel & Conference Center. 870 Williston Rd., Burlington, VT 05403. ☎ **800/325-3535** or 802/865-6600. Fax 802/865-6670. 308 rms. A/C TV TEL. May–Oct $85–$140 double; Nov–Apr $69–$125 double. AE, DISC, MC, V.

The largest conference facility in Vermont, the Sheraton also does a commendable job catering to individual travelers and families. This sprawling complex just off the interstate and a few minutes' drive from downtown features a sizeable indoor garden area. The guest rooms all have two phones and in-room Nintendos (families take note); rooms in the newer addition (built in 1990) are a bit nicer, furnished in a simpler, lighter country style. Ask for a room facing the west (no extra charge) to enjoy the views of Mt. Mansfield and the Green Mountains.

Dining/Entertainment: The informal restaurant boasts its own gazebo.

Facilities: Indoor pool with retractable skylights for summer, two Jacuzzis, a fitness room, and an outdoor sundeck.

✪ **The Inn at Shelburne Farms.** Harbor Rd., Shelburne, VT 05482. ☎ **802/985-8498.** 24 rms (17 with private bath). TV. Spring $85–$210 double; summer $90–$220 double; fall $95–$250 double. Closed mid-Oct to mid-May. AE, DC, MC, V.

The numbers behind this exceptional turn-of-the-century mansion on the shores of Lake Champlain tell the story: 60 rooms, 10 chimneys, 1,000 acres of land. Built in 1899 by William Seward and Lila Vanderbilt Webb, this sprawling Edwardian "farmhouse" is the place to fantasize about the lifestyles of the *truly* rich and famous. From the first glimpse of the mansion as you come up the winding drive, you'll realize you've left the grim world behind. That's by design. Noted landscape architect Frederick Law Olmsted had a hand in shaping the grounds, and noted forester Gifford Pinchot helped with the planting.

The 24 guest rooms are also splendidly appointed. Meals aren't included in the rates, but a restaurant on the property offers outstanding breakfasts and dinners. If you're traveling on a restricted budget, do this: Camp for a few nights, stay in a cheap motel, whatever it takes to free up a few dollars. Then pool your savings and book the least expensive room with the shared bath just to gain access to the mansion and the grounds. You'll feel like American royalty for a day.

WHERE TO DINE
MODERATE

Daily Planet. 15 Center St. ☎ **802/862-9647.** Reservations recommended for parties of more than four. Lunch items $4.95–$6.50; main dinner courses $10.75–$18.25 (mostly $12–$14). AE, DC, DISC, MC, V. Mon–Fri 11:30am–3pm; Sun–Thurs 5–9:30pm, Fri–Sat 5–11pm. Sept–May Sat–Sun brunch 11am–3pm. ECLECTIC/GLOBAL.

This hugely popular, uncommonly creative spot is usually brimming with college students and downtown workers evenings and weekends. But it's worth putting up with the mild mayhem for some of the better food in town. The restaurant consists of several informal, comfortable dining rooms, including a solarium (pleasant during the winter brunch) and an adjacent bar, which has a loud, smoky saloon atmosphere with a stamped tin ceiling and a judicious use of neon.

The menu is wildly eclectic, and the dishes far better than the usual pub fare you might expect from a spot like this. For lighter appetites, the Planet enchilada, made with spiced beans, corn, and sweet potatoes is remarkably flavorful. Full entrees include grilled tuna on Tuscan white beans, Moroccan vegetable sauté, and filet of beef in a port sauce served with wild mushrooms and roast potatoes.

✪ **Five Spice.** 175 Church St. ☎ **802/864-4045.** Reservations recommended on weekends and in summer. Lunch items $5.25–$7.95; main dinner courses $9.95–$14.95. AE, CB, DC, MC, V. Sun–Thurs 11:30am–10pm, Fri–Sat 11:30am–11pm. PAN-ASIAN.

Five Spice is the best of Burlington's bumper crop of Asian restaurants. Located upstairs and down in an intimate setting with rough wood floors and aquamarine wainscoting, Five Spice is a popular draw among college students and professors. But customers pour in for the exquisite food, not for the scene. The cuisine is multi-Asian, drawing on the best of Thailand, Vietnam, China, and beyond. Try the excellent hot and sour soup. Then gear up for Indonesian beef or the superior kung pao chicken. The dish with the best name on the menu—Evil Jungle Prince with Chicken—is made with a light sauce featuring a winning combination of coconut milk, garlic, and lemongrass. If you're looking to save money, come for lunch rather than dinner. The menu's the same but the prices are about half the dinner menu.

Mona's. 3 Main St. (in the Cornerstone Building). ☎ **802/658-6662.** Reservations recommended. Lunch items $5.25–$7.95; main dinner courses $8.95–$21.95 (mostly $10–$14). AE, CB, DC, MC, V. Mon–Fri 11:30am–11pm, Sat 11:30am–midnight, Sun 11:30am–10:30pm. NEW AMERICAN.

This restaurant overlooking the waterfront opened in late 1995 to great local acclaim, and quickly started attracting Burlington's business folk and grooverati. Located next to the train station, Mona's is an uptempo, contemporary kind of place rich with copper tones throughout. The first-floor ceiling is even made of copper, and seemingly emits a lurid, unearthly glow at sunset. Glimpses of Lake Champlain and the Adirondacks might be had out the first-floor windows; for better views, head upstairs and ask for a seat on the open deck.

The bustling open kitchen on the first floor produces some creative surprises. Appetizers include mushrooms baked with sun-dried tomato, artichoke, and cheddar; mussels steamed with lemongrass, ginger, and hot peppers; and a vegetable strudel with a port wine and fruit sauce. Entrees run the gamut, from a shellfish stew over linguini to polenta-crusted catfish to some mighty beefy steaks, including a 24-ounce porterhouse.

INEXPENSIVE

Al's. 1251 Williston Rd. (Rte. 2, just east of I-89), South Burlington. ☎ **802/862-9203.** Sandwiches 75¢–$3.55. No credit cards. Mon–Wed 10:30am–11pm, Thurs–Sat 10:30am–midnight, Sun 11am–10pm. BURGER JOINT.

Two words: french fries.

BURLINGTON AFTER DARK

There's always something going on in the evening in Burlington, although it might take a little snooping to find it in the slow season. Check the papers (see "Visitor Information," above).

Burlington has a thriving local music scene, one that's been infused with a bristling energy since Phish put the city on the map. The city government, recognizing a potential economic boon when it sees one, has worked to help incubate this scene. Check the local free weeklies for information on festivals and concerts during your visit, and to find out who's playing at the clubs.

The most popular clubs are located near the juncture of Main and College streets. At 188 Main St., **Nectar's** (☎ 802/658-4771), half of which is a funky cafeteria-style restaurant, features live bands seven days a week and no cover charge. On weekends it's packed with UVM students and abuzz with a fairly high level of hormonal energy. Look for the revolving neon sign.

One flight above Nectar's is **Club Metronome** (☎ 802/865-4563), a loud and loose nightspot that features a wide array of acts with a heavy dose of world beat. This is a no-frills place with tomato-red walls and disco mirror ball where you can dance or shoot a game of pool (or do both at once, as seems popular). The cover is generally less than $5, although national touring acts might run $12 or so.

Around the corner at 165 Church St. is **Club Toast** (☎ 802/660-2088), which is a little rougher around the edges than the other two and often showcases local alternative rock bands. Cover charge is typically less than $5.

Other nightime options include the **Comedy Zone** (☎ 802/658-6500) at the Radisson Hotel, and **CB's Dance Club** (☎ 802/878-5522) in Essex, which features country dancing most nights. Call for the evening line-up and directions.

For gay nightlife, head to **135 Pearl** (☎ 802/863-2343), Burlington's leading gay club, located naturally enough at 135 Pearl St. Get a bite to eat, dance, or listen to live music Wednesday through Saturday. Open noon until 2am, it's a friendly place that attracts a diverse clientele.

11 The Northeast Kingdom

Vermont's Northeast Kingdom is one of northern New England's most spectacularly remote regions. Consisting of Orleans, Essex, and Caledonia counties, the region was given its memorable name in 1949 by Sen. George Aiken, who understood the area's allure at a time when few others paid it much heed.

Contrasts with southern Vermont aren't hard to find. Rather than pinched, narrow valleys, the Kingdom's landscape is far more open and spacious, with rolling meadows ending abruptly at the hard edge of dense boreal forest. The leafy woodlands of the south give way to spiky forests of spruce and fir. And rather than Saabs and Volvos, you'll see pickup trucks dominating the roads, and plenty of them.

Accommodations and services for tourists aren't as plentiful or easy to find here as in the southern reaches of the state, but some superb inns are tucked among the hills and in the forests.

This section includes a loose, slightly convoluted driving tour of the Northeast Kingdom, along with some suggestions for outdoor recreation. If your time is limited, make sure you at least stop in St. Johnsbury, which in the Fairbanks Museum and St. Johnsbury Athenaeum has two of the most remarkable indoor attractions in the state.

Visitor information is available from the **Northeast Kingdom Chamber of Commerce** in St. Johnsbury (☎ 800/639-6379 or 802/748-3678). Other helpful **chambers of commerce** in the region include Barton (☎ 802/525-1137), Lake Willoughby (☎ 802/525-4496), Hardwick (☎ 802/472-6894), Island Pond (☎ 802/723-4326), Lyndon (☎ 802/626-9696), and Newport (☎ 802/334-7782).

TOURING THE NORTHEAST KINGDOM

Your first stop should be **Hardwick,** a small town with rough edges, set along the Lamoille River. It has an attractive, compact commercial main street, and some quirky shops.

From here, head north on Route 14 a little over seven miles to the turn-off toward Craftsbury and **Craftsbury Common.** An uncommonly graceful village, Craftsbury Common is home to a small academy and large number of historic homes and buildings spread along a sizeable green and the village's broad main street. The town occupies a wide upland ridge, and offers sweeping views to the east and west. Be sure to stop by the old cemetery on the south end of town, where you can wander among historic tombstones of the pioneers, some of which date back to the 1700s. Craftsbury is an excellent destination for mountain biking and cross-country skiing, and is home to the region's finest inn (see "Where to Stay," below).

From Craftsbury, continue north to reconnect to Route 14. You'll wind through the towns of Albany and Irasburg as you head north. At the village of Coventry, veer north on Route 5 to the lakeside town of **Newport.** This crusty commercial center (pop. 4,400) is set on the southern shores of Lake Memphremagog, a spectacular 27-mile-long lake that's but 2 miles wide at it broadest point, and the bulk of which is located in Canada. Newport, improbably enough, has a small outlet zone on Main Street. Look for discounted outdoor gear from **Bogner** (☎ 802/334-0135), **Louis Garneau** (☎ 802/334-5885), and **Great Outdoors** (☎ 802/334-2831).

Newport's only lakeside restaurant is **The East Side,** located at 25 Lake Rd. (☎ 802/334-2340). It's a good spot for lunch or a refreshing beverage while admiring shimmering, hill-encased Lake Memphremagog.

From Newport, continue north on Route 5, crossing under I-91, for about seven miles to the town of **Derby Line** (pop. 2,000). This border outpost has a handful of restaurants and antique shops; you can park and walk across the bridge to poke around the Canadian town of Rock Island without much hassle. (The weaker Canadian dollar will likely yield a cheap lunch if you've held out this long.) Back in Derby Line, look for the **Haskell Free Library and Opera House,** at the corner of Caswell Avenue and Church Street (☎ 802/873-3022). This handsome neo-classical building contains a public library on the first floor, and an elegant opera house on the second that's modeled after the old Boston Opera House. The theater opened in 1904 with the advertisements promoting a minstrel show featuring "new songs, new jokes, and beautiful electric effects." The theater is attractive in the extreme, with a scene of Venice painted on the drop curtain and carved cherubim adorning the balcony.

What's most notable about the structure, however, is that it lies half in Canada and half in the United States. (The Haskell family donated the building jointly to the towns of Derby Line and Rock Island.) A thick black line runs through the seats of the opera house, indicating who's in the U.S. and who's in Canada. Because the stage is set entirely in Canada, stories abound from the early days of frustrated U.S. officers watching fugitives perform on stage. More recently, the theater has been used for the occasional extradition hearing.

From Derby Line, retrace your path south on Route 5 to Derby Center and the juncture of Route 5A. Continue south on Route 5A to the town of Westmore on the shores of **Lake Willoughby.** This glacier-carved lake is best viewed from the north, with the shimmering sheet of water pinching between the base of two low mountains at the southern end. There's a distinctive Alpine feel to the whole scene, and this underappreciated lake is certainly one of the most beautiful in the Northeast. Route 5A along the eastern shore is lightly traveled and well-suited to biking or walking. To ascend the two mountains by foot, see the "Outdoor Pursuits" section, below.

Head southwest on Route 16, which departs from Route 5A just north of the lake. Follow Route 16 through the peaceful villages of Barton and Glover. A little over a mile south of Glover, turn left on Route 122. Very soon on your left look for the farmstead that serves as home to the **Bread and Puppet Theater.** For the past three decades, Polish artist and performer Peter Schumann's Bread and Puppet Theater has staged elaborate summer pageants at this farm, attracting thousands of attendees who participate, watch, and lounge about the hillsides. The multi-day fest takes place in a grown-over former quarry on the farm's property, and features huge, lugubrious, brightly painted puppets crafted of fabric and papier-mâché. (For the exact dates, call 802/525-3031.) The theme of the pageant is typically rebellion against tyranny of one form or another, and visitors get a distinct sense of reliving the 1960s. Think of it as Woodstock without the loud music.

Maple Syrup & How It Gets That Way

Maple syrup is at once simple and extravagant: Simple because it's made from the purest ingredients available, extravagant because it's an expensive luxury.

Two elemental ingredients combine to create maple syrup: sugar maple sap and fire. Sugaring season slips in between northern New England's long winter and short spring; it usually lasts around four or five weeks, typically beginning in early to mid-March. When warm and sunny days alternate with freezing nights, the sap in the maple trees begins to run from roots to the branches overhead. Sugarers drill shallow holes into the trees, and insert small taps. Buckets (or plastic tubing) are hung from the taps to collect the sap that drips out bit by bit.

The collected sap is then boiled off. The equipment for this ranges from a simple backyard fire pit cobbled together of concrete blocks, to elaborate sugar houses with oil or propane burners. It requires between 32 and 40 gallons of sap to make one gallon of syrup, and that means a fair amount of boiling. The real cost of syrup isn't the sap; it's in the fuel to boil it down.

Vermont is the nation's capital of maple syrup production, producing some 570,000 gallons a year. The fancier inns and restaurants all serve native maple syrup with breakfast. Other breakfast places will charge $1 or so for real syrup rather than the flavored corn syrup that's so prevalent elsewhere. (Sometimes you have to ask if the real stuff is available.)

You can pick up the real thing in almost any grocery store in the state, but it somehow tastes better if you buy it right from the farm. Look for handmade signs touting syrup posted at the end of farm driveways around the region throughout the year. Drive right on up and knock on the door.

A number of sugarers invite visitors to inspect the process and sample some of the fresh syrup in the early spring. Ask for the brochure "Maple Sugarhouses Open to Visitors," available at information centers, from the **Vermont Travel Division** (134 State St., Montpelier, VT 05602), or from the agriculture department at **802/828-2416.**

Between June and October the venerable, slightly tottering barn on the property contains the **Bread and Puppet Museum,** housing many of the puppets used in past pageants. This is a remarkable display, and shouldn't be missed if you're anywhere near the area. Downstairs in the former cow-milking stalls are smaller displays, such as King Lear addressing his daughters, and a group of mournful washerwomen doing their laundry. Upstairs, the vast hayloft is filled to the eaves with soaring, haunting puppets, some up to 20 feet tall. The style is witty and eclectic; the barn seems a joint endeavor of David Lynch, Red Grooms, and Hieronymous Bosch. Admission is free, although donations are encouraged.

From Glover, continue south through serene farmlands to Lyndonville, where you pick up Route 5 south to **St. Johnsbury.** This town of 7,600 inhabitants is the largest in the Northeast Kingdom, and is the major center of commerce. First settled in 1786, the town enjoyed a buoyant prosperity in the 19th century, largely stemming from the success of platform scales, which were invented here in 1830 by Thaddeus Fairbanks and are still manufactured here. The town, which has not suffered from the depredations of tourist boutiques and brewpubs, has an abundance of fine commercial architecture in two distinct areas, which are joined by steep Eastern Avenue. The more commercial part of town lies along Railroad Street (Route 5) at the base of the hill. The more ethereal part of town, with the library, St. Johnsbury Academy, and a grand museum, is along Main Street at the top of the hill. The north end of Main Street is also notable for its grand residential architecture.

Those with a literary-caffeine bent should strike for the **Northern Lights Café and Bookstore,** 79 Railroad St. (☎ **802/748-4463**). This shop has the best selection of reading matter in town (local works are especially well represented), and serves up delicious snacks and light meals, including sandwiches, homemade muffins, and a delectable blueberry coffee cake.

At the corner Main and Prospect streets in St. Johnsbury, ○ **The Fairbanks Museum** (☎ **802/748-2372**) is an imposing Romanesque red sandstone structure constructed in 1889 to hold the collections of obsessive amateur collector Franklin Fairbanks, the grandson of the inventor of the platform scale. Fairbanks was once described as "the kind of little boy who came home with his pockets full of worms." In adulthood, his propensity to gather and accumulate continued unabated. His artifacts include four stuffed bears, a huge moose with full antlers, art from Asia, and 4,500 stuffed native and exotic birds. And that's just the tip of it.

The soaring, barrel-vaulted main hall, reminiscent of an old-fashioned railway depot, embodies Victorian grandeur. Among the assorted clutter look for the unique mosaics by John Hampson. Hampson crafted scenes of American history—such as Washington bidding his troops farewell—entirely of mounted insects. In the Washington scene, for instance, iridescent green beetles form the epaulets, and the regal great coat is comprised of hundreds of purple moth wings. Words fail me here; you must see them.

There's also a planetarium and weather station. The museum is open Monday to Saturday from 10am to 4pm, and Sunday from 1 to 5pm, with longer hours in summer. Admission is $4 for adults, $3 for seniors, and $2.50 for children 5 to 17.

Also in town, at 30 Main St., ○ **The St. Johnsbury Athenaeum** (☎ **802/ 748-8291**) is a quirky brick building with a truncated mansard tower and prominent keystones over the windows. This is the town's public library, but it also houses an extraordinary art gallery dating to 1873. It claims to be the oldest, unadulterated art gallery in the nation, and I see no reason to question the claim. Your first view of it is spectacular: After winding through the intimate library with its ticking regulator clock, you round a corner and find yourself gazing across Yosemite National Park. This luminous 10-by-15-foot oil was created by noted Hudson River School painter Albert Bierstadt, and the gallery was built specifically to accommodate this work. ("Now 'The Domes' is doomed to the seclusion of a Vermont town, where it will astonish the natives," groused the *Boston Globe* at the time.) The natural light flooding in from the skylight above nicely enhances the painting. Some 100 other works fill the walls. Most are painted reproductions of other paintings (a common teaching tool in the 19th century), but look for originals by other Hudson River School painters including Asher B. Durand, Thomas Moran, and Jasper Cropsey.

The Athenaeum is open Monday and Wednesday 10am to 8pm; Tuesday, Thursday, and Friday from 10am to 5:30pm; and Saturday 9:30am to 4pm. Admission is free, but donations are encouraged.

OUTDOOR PURSUITS
HIKING

At the southern tip of Lake Willoughby, two rounded peaks rise above the lake's waters. These are the biblically named Mt. Hor and Mt. Pisgah, both of which lie within Willoughby State Forest. Both summits are accessible via footpaths that are somewhat strenuous but yield excellent views.

Northern Vermont

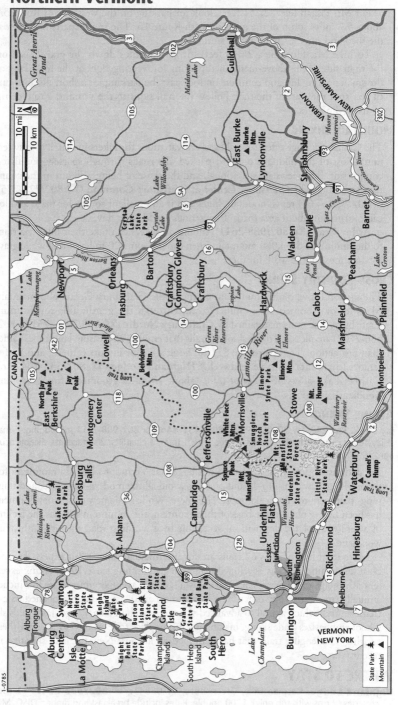

For Mt. Pisgah (elev. 2,751 feet), look for parking on the west side of Route 5A about 5.7 miles south of the junction with Route 16. The trail departs from across the road and runs 1.7 miles to the summit.

To hike Mt. Hor (elev. 2,648 feet), drive 1.8 miles down the gravel road on the right side of the above-mentioned parking lot, veering right at the fork. Park at the small parking lot, and continue on foot past the parking lot a short distance until you spot the start of the trail. Follow the trail signs to the summit, a round trip of about 3.5 miles.

MOUNTAIN BIKING

The Craftsbury ridge offers several excellent variations for bikers in search of easy terrain. Most of the biking is on hard-packed dirt roads through sparsely populated countryside. The views are sensational, and the sense of being well out in the country very strong. The **Craftsbury Center at Craftsbury Common** (☎ 800/729-7751 or 802/586-7767) rents mountain bikes and is an excellent source for maps and local information about area roads. Bike rentals are $12 per day.

At **Jay Peak** (☎ 802/988-2611), mountain bikers can take their bikes via tram to the summit of the 3,968 mountain, then explore some 20 miles of trail while gravity does most of the work for them.

CROSS-COUNTRY SKIING

The same folks who offer mountain biking at the Craftsbury Center also maintain 61 miles of groomed cross-country trails through the gentle hills surrounding Craftsbury. The trails maintained by **Craftsbury Nordic** (☎ 800/729-7751 or 802/586-7767) are pleasant, old-fashioned trails that emphasize pleasing landscapes rather than fast action. Trail passes are $11 for adults, $5 for juniors 6 to 12, and $7 for seniors (discounts available midweek.) **Highland Lodge** (☎ 802/533-2647) on Caspian Lake offers 36 miles of trails (about 10 miles groomed) through rolling woodlands and fields.

ALPINE SKIING

Jay Peak. Rte. 242, Jay, VT 05859. ☎ **800/451-4449** or 802/988-2611 for lodging. E-mail skijayvt@aol.com. Vertical drop: 2,153 feet. Lifts: 1 tram, 4 chairlifts, 2 surface lifts. Skiable acreage: 300+. Lift tickets: $38.

Located just south of the Canadian border, Jay is Vermont's best ski mountain for those who get away just to ski and prefer to avoid all the modern-day glitter and trappings that seem to clutter ski resorts elsewhere. While some new condo development has been taking place at the base of the mountain, the mountain still has the feeling of a remote, isolated destination, accessible by a winding road through unbroken woodlands.

More than half of Jay's 62 trails are for intermediate skiers. But experts haven't been left behind. Jay has developed extensive glade skiing since 1994, taking excellent advantage of its sizeable natural snowfall, which averages more than 300 inches annually (more than any other New England ski area). Jay has also reopened its extreme chutes, which appeal to advanced skiers in search of a challenge. Jay Peak's ski school emphasizes glade skiing, making it a fitting place to learn how to navigate these exciting, challenging trails that have cropped up at most New England ski areas in recent years.

WHERE TO STAY

Highland Lodge. Caspian Lake, Greensboro, VT 05841. ☎ **802/533-2647.** 11 rms, 11 cottages (2 rms with tub only). $200 double. Rates include breakfast and dinner. DISC, MC,

V. Closed mid-Mar to May and mid-Oct to Christmas. From Hardwick, drive on Rte. 15 east 2 miles to Rte. 16; drive north 2 more miles to East Hardwick. Head west and follow signs to inn.

The Highland Lodge was built in the mid-19th century, and has been accommodating guests since 1926. It's a great destination for a relaxing, old-fashioned holiday. Located just across the road from lovely Caspian Lake, this lodge has 11 rooms furnished in a comfortable country style. A wide porch runs the length of the inn, and white Adirondack chairs are well placed for shady reading or dozing.

Facilities: The main activities here tend to be relaxing rather than hectic: There's swimming and boating in the lake in summer, along with tennis on clay courts; in winter, the lodge maintains its own cross-country ski area with 30 miles of groomed trail. Behind the lodge is a nature preserve, which makes for quiet exploration. Bored? There's also badminton, croquet, and horseshoes.

✪ Inn on the Common. Craftsbury Common, VT 05827. ☎ **800/521-2233** or 802/586-9619. Fax 802/586-2249. 16 rms (3 with shower only). $200–$230 double; foliage season $250–$270 double. Rates include breakfast and dinner ($30 less for breakfast only). AE, MC, V.

This exceedingly handsome complex of three Federal-style buildings anchors the charming ridgetop village of Craftsbury Common. Innkeepers Penny and Michael Schmitt have been running this place with panache since 1973, and have created a beautiful, comfortable inn that offers just the right measures of history and luxury. Guests can unwind in the nicely appointed common rooms, or stroll the 15 acres of beautifully landscaped grounds.

Dining/Entertainment: Dinner starts with cocktails at 7pm, then guests are seated amid elegant Federal-era surroundings at 8pm. The menu changes nightly, but includes well-prepared dishes like venison ravioli and jumbo shrimp stuffed with scallops and served with a sherry sauce.

Facilities: There's a pool, clay tennis court, and croquet in the back gardens; in winter, cross-country skiing and snowshoeing are popular activities. If the weather turns sour, the inn has a collection of 250 videos to peruse.

12 New Hampshire

by Wayne Curtis

There are two ways to get old-time New Hampshirites riled up and spitting vinegar. First, tell them you think that Vermont is a really great state. Then tell them you think it's weird that they still don't have a state income tax or sales tax.

At its most basic, New Hampshire defines itself by what it isn't, and that, more than not, is Vermont—a state regarded by local old-timers as one of the few Communist republics still remaining. No, New Hampshire is not Vermont, and they'll thank you not to confuse the two.

Keep in mind that New Hampshire's state symbol is the Old Man of the Mountains, which is an actual site you can visit in the White Mountains. You'll see this icon just about everywhere you look— on state highway signs, on brochures, on state police cars. And it's an apt symbol for a state that relishes its cranky-old-man demeanor. New Hampshire has long been a magnet for folks who talk of government with tones normally reserved for scabies. That "Live-Free-or-Die" license plate? It's for real. New Hampshire stands behind its words. It hasn't quite accepted state planning as a legitimate task. Nor does New Hampshire have a bottle deposit law, or a law banning billboards. (Godless Vermont has both, as does its other heathen neighbor, Maine.)

New Hampshire savors its reputation as an embattled outpost of plucky, heroic conservatives fighting the good fight against intrusive laws and irksome bureaucrats. Without a state sales tax or state income tax, it's had to be creative. Many government services are funded through the "tourist tax" (an 8% levy on meals and rooms at restaurants and hotels) along with a hefty local property tax (the mere mention of which is another way to get local folks riled up). In fact, candidates for virtually every office with the possible exception of dogcatcher must take "The Pledge," which means they'll vow to fight any effort to impose sales or income tax. To shirk The Pledge is tantamount to political suicide.

The state's cranky spirit is perhaps best captured by its leading newspaper, the *Manchester Union Leader*. This conservative powerhouse has made and broken candidates in their quest for the White House during New Hampshire's influential first-in-the-nation primary. The paper's attitude has mellowed somewhat since the demise of cantankerous editor William Loeb, and it's dropped the vitriolic front-page editorials. But it still delivers plenty of fire and brimstone in its editorial section. (The newspaper also has the policy of printing all letters to the editor it receives. As such, it has become the outlet of choice for conspiracy theorists and people who believe the government is beaming radio waves at their brain.)

Get beyond New Hampshire's affable crankiness, and you'll find pure New England. Indeed, New Hampshire may represent the New England ethic distilled to its essence. At its core is a mistrust of those from outside the state, a premium placed on independence, a belief that government should be frugal above all else, and a laconic acceptance that, no matter what, you just can't change the weather. Travelers exploring the state with open eyes will find these attitudes in spades.

Travelers will also find wonderfully diverse terrain—from ocean beaches, to the broad lakes, to the region's most impressive mountains. Without ever leaving the state's borders you can play Frisbee on a sandy beach, ride bikes along quiet country lanes dotted with covered bridges, hike rugged granite hills blasted by some of the most severe weather in the world, and canoe on a placid lake in the company of moose and loons. You'll also find good food and country inns you won't want to ever leave. But most of all, you'll find vestiges of that feisty independence that has defined New England since the first settlers ran up their flag three and a half centuries ago.

1 Enjoying the Great Outdoors

Visitors coming from the West scoff at the low elevations of New England's peaks. ("Four thousand feet? *Four thousand feet?* That's not even a foothill where we come from!")

Savvy eastern hikers indulge their guests with good humor. Then they take them to the White Mountains' brutally rugged, steep trails to snap their will and force them to beg for mercy—never mind the plentiful oxygen at these low elevations. After that, they tend to stay quiet.

The White Mountains' famed network of hiking trails will test anyone's mettle. The hard granite hills of the ancient mountains of New England resist the sort of gently graded trail through the crumbly earth found so often in the American West. And the White Mountains' early trailblazers were evidently a humorless lot, who found it amusing to build trails straight up sheer pitches and through tortuous boulder fields.

Despite (or perhaps because of) these trails, the White Mountains are *the* destination in New England for serious outdoorspeople heading north from Boston and New York. There's superb hiking in the summer, and fine skiing (both cross-country and alpine) in the winter. It's also a good place to test your meteorological acumen—the weather can change almost instantly on the high ridges, so backcountry explorers have to keep a keen eye out. A pleasant afternoon picnic can turn into a harrowing, cold experience for the unwary. Atop Mt. Washington, the region's highest peak, it's not unusual to see snow any time of the year—mid-summer flurries aren't that uncommon.

More gentle outdoor recreation is found throughout much of the rest of New Hampshire, from canoeing on the meandering Connecticut River (which forms the border with Vermont), to sailing on vast Lake Winnipesaukee. If you're so inclined, come prepared for outdoor recreation, because it doesn't take much to find it.

An excellent general source of information is the **Appalachian Mountain Club,** 5 Joy St., Boston, MA 02108 (☎ **617/523-0636,** or 603/466-2727 in N.H.). The group sponsors outings and instructional workshops throughout the year throughout New England, but especially in the White Mountains. Signing up for a trip is an excellent way to get to know the area under the leadership of someone who knows the area well.

New Hampshire

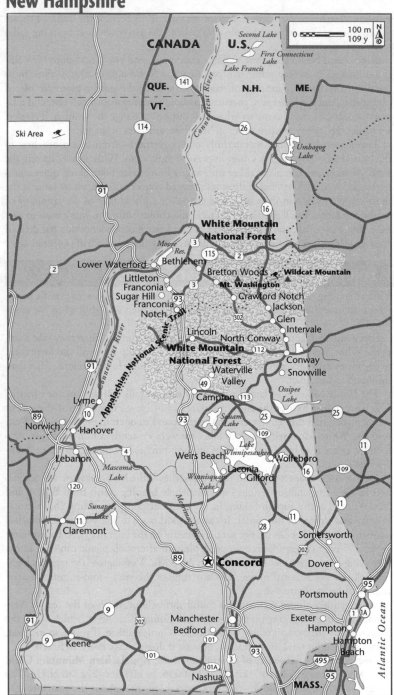

BACKPACKING   The White Mountains of northern New Hampshire offer the most extensive, most challenging, most beautiful backpacking in the Northeast. The bulk of the best trails are located within 773,000-acre **White Mountain National Forest,** which encompasses several 5,000-plus foot peaks and more than 100,000 acres of designated wilderness. Trails range from easy lowland walks along bubbling streams to demanding ridgeline paths buffeted by fierce winds. AMC huts offer shelter in eight dramatically situated cabins that boast a high degree of comfort. (Reservations are essential; call **603/466-2727.**)

In addition, a number of three-sided Adirondack-style shelters are located throughout the backcountry on a first-come, first-served basis. Some are free; at others a small fee is collected. Pitching a tent in the backcountry is free subject to certain restrictions (for example, no camping within a certain distance of a trail or river), and no permits are required. It's best to check with the **forest headquarters** (☎ **603/ 528-8721**) or a district ranger station for current rules and regulations.

The ridges around Mt. Washington attract the densest crowds. Backpackers in search of a more remote experience should head for trails in the Mt. Moosilauke/ Kinsman Notch area west of I-93, and the northern unit of the forest just west of Berlin.

The **Appalachian Trail** passes through New Hampshire, entering the state at Hanover, running along the highest peaks of the White Mountains, and exiting into Maine along the Mahoosuc Range northeast of Gorham. The trail is well-maintained, although it tends to attract teeming crowds along the highest elevations in summer.

Rental equipment—including sleeping bags and pad, tents, and packs—is available at **Eastern Mountain Sports** (☎ **603/356-5433**) in North Conway at reasonable rates.

BIKING   There's superb road biking throughout the state. The best advice is to sacrifice the direct-line convenience of the major roads for the winding, twisting back roads. Southwest New Hampshire near Mount Monadnock offers a multitude of shady back roads for exploring, especially around Hancock and Greenfield.

In the White Mountains, my favorite one-day loop (bring lunch) is on the east side of the mountains outside of North Conway. Start in Conway and follow the Kancamagus Highway (Route 112) to Bear Notch Road. Turn right, then climb Bear Notch before descending to the town of Bartlett; turn right and follow busy Route 302 (the worst part of the trip) to River Road, which connects to West Side Road and continues back to Conway.

The White Mountains also offer plenty of opportunities for mountain bikers; trails are open to bikers unless otherwise noted. Bikes are not allowed in wilderness areas. The upland roads outside of Jackson offer some superb country biking. **Great Glen Trails** (☎ **603/466-2333**), near Mt. Washington, and **Waterville Valley Base Camp** (☎ **800/468-2553**), at the southwest edge of the park, both offer bike rentals and maintained mountain bike trails at a fee.

Mountain Road Tours (☎ **603/532-8708**) in southern New Hampshire can arrange inn-to-inn biking tours in the state.

CAMPING   Campers shouldn't have any problem finding a place to pitch a tent or park an RV in New Hampshire, especially in the northern half of the state.

The **White Mountain National Forest** maintains 20 campgrounds (no hook-ups), some very small and personal, other quite large and noisy. Sites tend to be fairly easy to come by midweek, but on summer and early fall weekends you're taking your chances if you arrive without reservations. Reservations are accepted by the **Forest Service** (☎ **800/280-2267**) at 11 of the campgrounds from 14 to 180 days before arrival.

Fifteen of New Hampshire's **state parks** allow camping (two of these offer camping for RVs only). About half of these parks are located in and around the White Mountains. In 1995 the New Hampshire state park system began accepting reservations for many of the campgrounds it manages. Between January and May call **603/271-3627;** during the summer season, call the campground directly to reserve. Not all campgrounds participate; some remain first-come, first-served. A list of parks and phone numbers is published in the *New Hampshire Visitor's Guide*, which is distributed widely through information centers, or by contacting the **Office of Travel and Tourism Development,** P.O. Box 1856, Concord, NH 03302 (☎ **603/271-2343**).

New Hampshire also has more than 150 private campgrounds. For a free directory, get in touch with the **New Hampshire Campground Owners' Association,** P.O. Box 320, Twin Mountain, NH 03595 (☎ **603/846-5511**).

CANOEING   New Hampshire has a profusion of river and lakes suitable for paddling, and canoe rentals are available widely around the state. Good flat-water paddling may be found along the **Merrimack and Connecticut rivers** in the southern parts of the state. Virtually any lake is good for dabbling about with canoe and paddle, although beware of stiff northerly winds when crossing vast **Winnipesaukee.** In the far north, 8,000-acre **Lake Umbagog** is home to bald eagles and loons, and is especially appealing to explore by canoe. In general the farther north you venture, the wilder and more remote your experience will be.

In the north, the **Androscoggin River** offers superb Class I–II white water and swift flat water upstream of Berlin; below, the river is fetid with paper mill pollution and is best avoided.

Serious white-water enthusiasts head to the upper reaches of the **Saco River** during spring run-off, where the Class III–IV rapids are intense if relatively short-lived along a 6.5-mile stretch paralleling Route 302.

FISHING   New Hampshire ponds, streams, and rivers offer good fishing throughout the state. A vigorous stocking program keeps the waters active with fish. Brook trout account for about half of all trout stocked in the state's waters; lake and rainbow trout are also stocked. Other sport fish include small and largemouth bass, landlocked salmon, and walleye.

Fishing licenses are required for freshwater fishing throughout the state, but not for saltwater fishing. For detailed information on regulations, request the free "Freshwater Fishing Digest" from the **New Hampshire Fish and Game Department,** 2 Hazen Dr., Concord, NH 03301 (☎ **603/271-3211**). Fishing licenses for nonresidents range from $18.50 for three days to $35.50 for the season. Another helpful booklet, also available free from the fish and game department, is "Fishing Waters of New Hampshire."

HIKING   New Hampshire has hiking trails in abundance. The White Mountains alone offer 1,200 miles of trails; state parks and forests add considerably to the mileage.

Serious hikers will want to bypass much of the state and beeline for the Whites. The essential guide to hiking trails is the Appalachian Mountain Club's *White Mountain Guide,* which contains up-to-date detailed descriptions of every trail in the area. The guide is available at most book and outdoor shops in the state. See the section on the White Mountains later in this chapter for further suggestions on hikes.

In southwest New Hampshire, the premier hike is **Mt. Monadnock,** said to be one of the world's two most popular hikes (second only to Mt. Fuji in Japan). This lone massif, rising regally above the surrounding hills, is a straightforward day hike accessible via one of several trails.

For other hiking opportunities outside the Whites, two recommended guidebooks are *50 Hikes in New Hampshire* and *50 More Hikes in New Hampshire,* both written by Daniel Doan and published by **Backcountry Publications,** P.O. Box 175, Woodstock, VT 05091 (☎ **800/245-4151**).

SKIING While New Hampshire doesn't offer the sprawling, brawny mountains found in Vermont or Maine, it does offer everything from challenging slopes to gentle runs at 22 downhill ski areas.

New Hampshire's forte may be the small ski area that caters to families. These include Gunstock, Temple Mountain, Mt. Sunapee, King Pine, and Pats Peak, all with vertical drops of 1,500 feet or less. The more challenging skiing is in the White Mountains region; the best areas are Cannon Mountain, Loon, Waterville Valley, Wildcat, and Attitash. These all have vertical drops of around 2,000 feet, and feature the services one would expect at a professional ski resort.

Ski NH (☎ **800/343-2250,** or 603/745-9396 in N.H.) distributes a ski map and other information helpful in ski trip planning. To check on current downhill ski conditions, call **800/258-3608.**

The most impressive ski run in New Hampshire is one not served by a lift. **Tuckerman Ravine** drops 3,400 feet from a lip on the shoulder of Mt. Washington down to the valley floor. Skiers arrive from throughout the nation to venture here in the early spring (it's dangerously avalanche-prone during the depths of winter), first hiking to the top then flying to the bottom of this dramatic glacial cirque. The slope is sheer and unforgiving; only very advanced skiers should attempt it. Careless or cocky skiers are hauled out every year on stretchers, and few years seem to go by without at least one skier's death. Contact the AMC's **Pinkham Notch camp** (☎ **603/ 466-2725**) for information on current conditions.

Ample cross-country skiing opportunities also exist. The state boasts some 26 cross-country ski centers, which groom a combined total of more than 500 miles of trails. The state's premier cross-country destination is the town of **Jackson** (☎ **603/ 383-9355**), with 55 miles of groomed trail in and around an exceptionally scenic village in a valley near the base of Mt. Washington. Other favorites include **Bretton Woods** (☎ **800/232-2972** or 603/278-5181) at the western entrance to Crawford Notch, also with more than 50 miles of groomed trail, and the spectacularly remote **Balsams/Wilderness cross-country ski center** (☎ **800/255-0600** or 603/ 255-3951) in the farthest reaches of the state.

My favorite inn with its own cross-country ski center is the **Franconia Inn** (☎ **800/473-5299** or 603/823-5542), which has nearly 40 miles of groomed trail on the scenic western edge of Franconia Notch.

SNOWMOBILING Sledders will find nearly 6,000 miles of groomed, scenic snowmobile trails lacing the state, connected via an intricate trail network maintained by local snowmobile clubs. All sleds must be registered with the state; this costs $29 and can be done through any of the 200 off-highway recreational-vehicle agents in the state. More information about snowmobiling in the state may be obtained from the **New Hampshire Snowmobile Association,** 722 Rte. 3A, Bow, NH 03304 (☎ **603/224-8906**).

The state's most remote and spectacular destination for snowmobilers is that nubby finger that thrusts up into Canada. It also happens to be the snowiest part of the state.

The **Connecticut Lakes Tourist Association** (☎ 603/538-7405) can provide information on services and lodging in the area. Your best bet for rentals or snow-mobile tours of the area is **Pathfinder Sno-Tours,** based at Timberland Lodge in Pittsburg (☎ 603/538-6613).

2 Portsmouth

Portsmouth is a civilized seaside city of bridges and brick and seagulls, and is far and away one of the most attractive small cities on the whole of the eastern seaboard. Filled with elegant architecture that's more intimate than intimidating, this bonsai-sized city projects a strong and proud sense of its heritage without being overly precious about it.

Part of the city's appeal is its variety. Upscale coffee shops and fancy leather-goods stores exist alongside old-fashioned barber shops and tattoo parlors. There's been a steady gentrification in recent years, which has brought a surfeit of twee shops, but the town still has a fundamental earthiness that serves as a tangy vinegar for the hand-ful of overly saccharine spots. Portsmouth's humble waterfront must actually be sought out, and when found it's rather understated.

Portsmouth's history runs deep, which is instantly evident when walking through town. For the past three centuries, the city has served as a hub for the region's mari-time trade. In the 1600s, Strawbery Banke (it wasn't renamed Portsmouth until 1653) was a center for the export of wood and dried fish to Europe. In the 19th cen-tury, it grew as a center of regional trade. Across the river in Maine, the Portsmouth Naval Shipyard was founded in 1800, and evolved into a prominent base for the building, outfitting, and repair of U.S. Navy submarines. Today, Portsmouth's mari-time tradition continues with a lively trade in bulk goods (look for scrap metal and minerals stockpiled along the shores of the Piscataqua River on Market Street); the city's de facto symbol is the tugboat, one or two of which are almost always tied up near the waterfront's picturesque "tugboat alley."

Visitors to Portsmouth will find there's a whole lot to see in a little space. There's good shopping in the boutiques that now occupy much of the historic district, good eating at the many small restaurants, and plenty of history to explore among the his-toric homes and museums that crop up on almost every block.

ESSENTIALS

GETTING THERE   Portsmouth is served by Exits 3 through 7 on I-95. The most direct access to downtown is via Market Street (Exit 7), which is the last New Hamp-shire exit before crossing the river to Maine. By bus, Portsmouth is served by Concord Trailways and Vermont Transit.

VISITOR INFORMATION   The **Greater Portsmouth Chamber of Commerce,** 500 Market St., Portsmouth, NH 03802 (☎ 603/436-1118), operates a very helpful tourist information center year-round between Exit 7 and downtown. The office is open daily in summer, weekdays only the remainder of the year. In summer the chamber staffs a second information booth at Market Square in the middle of the historic district.

ORIENTATION   Portsmouth consists of two main areas of interest to travelers. First, there's the historic commercial district, located around Market Square and ex-tending to the shores of the Piscataqua River. Second, there's Strawbery Banke, the city's premier historic museum/neighborhood (admission charged), which is near the public gardens and a waterfront park.

PARKING   Most of Portsmouth can be easily reconnoitered on foot, so you need park only once. Parking can be tight in and around the historic district in summer. Happily, the municipal parking garage costs just 25¢ per hour; look for signs pointing you there just west of Market Square off Congress Street. Strawbery Banke also offers limited parking for visitors.

A "MUSEUM" NOT TO MISS

✪ **Strawbery Banke.** P.O. Box 300, Portsmouth, NH 03802. ☎ **603/433-1100.** $10 adults, $9 seniors, $7 children 7–17, $25 families. Early May to late Oct daily 10am–5pm. Special events held around Thanksgiving and the first 2 weekends of Dec; otherwise closed Nov–Apr. Look for directional signs posted around town.

If Portsmouth were a festival of historic homes and buildings, Strawbery Banke would be the main stage. In 1958 the city planned to raze this venerable neighborhood, first settled in 1653, to make way for urban renewal. A group of local citizens fought the tides of progress and won, establishing an outdoor history museum that's grown to be one of the largest in New England. The museum today consists of 10 downtown acres and 42 historic buildings, 10 of which have been restored to 10 different eras and are open to the public. (One admission fee buys access to all homes and exhibits.) While Strawbery Banke employs staffers to assume the character of historic residents (including Thomas Bailey Aldrich, a frequent early contributor to the *Atlantic Monthly*), the emphasis is more on the buildings, architecture, and historic accoutrements, and less on "living history" at practiced at Sturbridge Village or Plimoth Plantation in Massachusetts.

The neighborhood surrounds an open lawn (formerly a tidal creek), and has a settled, picturesque quality to it. You'll find three working crafts shops on the grounds, where you can watch coopers, boatbuilders, and potters at work. The most intriguing home may be the split-personality Drisco House, half of which depicts life in the 1790s, and half of which shows life in the 1950s, nicely demonstrating how houses grow and adapt to each era. In 1997, the museum will open another home, which will depict the life of a Russian Jewish immigrant family in 1919.

A MAGICAL HISTORY TOUR

Portsmouth's 18th-century prosperity can be plainly seen in the regal Georgian-style homes that dot the city. A walking tour of the city will take in the most significant homes, many of which are maintained by various historical or colonial societies and are open to the public. A helpful map and brochure describing the key historic homes entitled "The Portsmouth Trail: An Historic Walking Tour" is available free at the city's information centers (see above). If you plan to tour more than one home, ask about the **Portsmouth Passport,** which offers a small discount.

John Paul Jones House. 43 Middle St. ☎ **603/436-8420.** $4 adults, $2 children 6–14. June to mid-Oct Mon–Sat 10am–4pm, Sun noon–4pm. Closed late Oct–May.

Revolutionary War hero John Paul Jones ("I have not yet begun to fight") was a boarder in this handsome 1758 home during the Revolutionary War, when he oversaw the construction of his sloop, *Ranger,* believed to be the first ship to sail under the U.S. flag (there's a model of it on display here). The home has been immaculately restored and maintained by the Portsmouth Historical Society; costumed tour guides offer tours of 45 minutes to an hour, providing a raft of information along the way about Jones and Sarah Wentworth, the widow who opened this large, Georgian-style home to boarders to support her sizable family. The house, which was built by six carpenters working six days a week for two years, contains a handsome collection of

Portsmouth

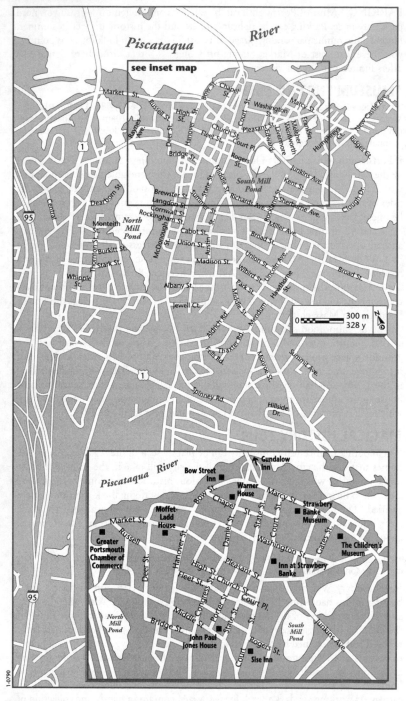

period furniture; there are also collections of china and period clothing, including elaborate wedding gowns.

Moffatt-Ladd House. 154 Market St. ☎ **603/436-8221.** $4 adults, $1 children under 12. June 15–Oct 15 Mon–Sat 10am–4pm, Sun 2–5pm; closed mid-Oct to mid-June.

The Moffatt-Ladd House, built for a family of prosperous merchants and traders, is as notable for its elegant garden as for the 1763 home, with its Great Hall and elaborate carvings throughout. Remarkably, the home remained in one family between 1763 and 1913, when it became a museum. Many of the furnishings have never left the house. The home will especially appeal to aficionados of early American furniture and painting; it's hung with portraits of some 15 family members. The terraced garden's design dates to the mid-19th century, but some of the roses can be traced back to plantings in 1768 and 1776. The home is owned by the National Society of The Colonial Dames of America in the State of New Hampshire.

Warner House. 150 Daniel St. ☎ **603/436-5909.** $4 adults, $2 children 7–12. Early June–Oct Tues–Sat 10am–4pm, Sun 1–4pm. Closed Nov–May.

The Warner House, built in 1716, was the governor's mansion in the mid-18th century when Portsmouth served as state capital. This stately brick home with graceful Georgian architectural elements (note the alternating arched and triangular pediments above the dormer windows) is a favorite among architectural historians for its circa 1716 wall murals (said to be the oldest murals still in place in the United States), the early wall marbleizing, and the original white pine paneling. Benjamin Franklin visited the house in 1763 to personally supervise the installation of a lightning rod on the west wall.

Wentworth-Gardner House. 50 Mechanic St. ☎ **603/436-4406.** $4 adults, $2 children 6–14. Mid-June to mid-Oct Tues–Sun 1–4pm. Closed late Oct to early June.

The Wentworth-Gardner is arguably the most handsome mansion in the entire Seacoast region, and is widely considered to be one of the best examples of Georgian architecture in the country. Built in 1760, the home features many of the classic period elements, including very pronounced quoins (the blocks on the building's corners), pedimented window caps, plank sheathing (this was meant to make it appear as if made of masonry), and an elaborate doorway featuring Corinthian pilasters, a broken scroll, and a paneled door topped with a pineapple, the symbol of hospitality. The inside is no less impressive, with hand-painted Chinese wallpaper and a vast fireplace in the kitchen featuring a windmill spit. This waterfront house was once owned by Wallace Nutting, the noted chronicler of old New England ways, and at one point was owned by the Metropolitan Museum of Art in New York, which had considered moving the house to Central Park.

BOAT TOURS

Portsmouth is especially attractive when seen from the water. A small fleet of tour boats ties up at Portsmouth, offering scenic tours of the Piscataqua River and the historic Isle of Shoals throughout the summer and fall.

The **Isle of Shoals Steamship Co.** (☎ **800/441-4620** or 603/431-5500) sails from Baker Wharf on Market Street and is the most established of the tour companies. The firm offers a variety of tours on the 90-foot, three-deck *Thomas Laighton* (it's a modern replica of a turn-of-the-century steamship) and the 70-foot *Oceanic,* which was especially designed for whale watching. Among the most popular excursions are to the Isle of Shoals, allowing passengers to disembark and wander about **Star Island,** a dramatic, rocky island that's part of an island cluster far out in the offshore swells. Star Island has a rich history and today serves as the base for a summer religious institute. Reservations are strongly encouraged for this trip. Other popular trips include six-hour whale-watching voyages and a sunset lighthouse cruise. Fares range from $9 to $17 for adults, $5 to $15 for children.

Portsmouth Harbor Cruises (☎ 800/776-0915 or 603/436-8084) specializes in tours of the historic Piscataqua River aboard the *Heritage,* a 49-passenger cruise ship with lots of open deck space. Cruise by five old forts during the harbor cruise, or enjoy the picturesque tidal estuary of inland Great Bay, a scenic trip upriver from Portsmouth. Trips run daily, and reservations are suggested. Fares are $7.50 to $15 for adults, $5 to $8 for children.

SHOPPING

Portsmouth's compact historic district has dozens of unique boutiques that sell items you won't find at the mall, including many hand-crafted products. The selection ranges from urban funky to country casual, so few are likely to leave disappointed. If you're serious about browsing, allow at least a couple of hours to wander through town. The following are just a sampling of the more intriguing places.

Choozy Shooz. 19 Market St. ☎ **603/433-4455.**

The most creative shoe store in the city, Choozy Shooz offers a wide selection of hip as well as eminently practical footwear.

City & Country. 50 Daniel St. ☎ **603/433-5353.**

This contemporary housewares store—a sort of Pottery Barn Lite—has a small but intriguing selection of glasses, table settings, flatware, and cooking implements, along with a mix of furniture and wrought-iron accessories.

Harbor Treats. 4 Market Sq. ☎ **603/431-3228.**

This is a chocoholic's paradise, with a good selection of homemade fudges, chocolates, and truffles. Don't leave without trying the chocolate turtles.

Macro Polo. 89 Market St. ☎ **603/436-8338.**

Macro Polo takes retro and makes it retro chic. This pleasantly cluttered shop stocks pink flamingos, refrigerator magnets, movie kitsch, candies, coffee mugs, and T-shirts, most of which are embellished with off-beat humor. It's a popular spot with teens.

N.W. Barrett Gallery. 53 Market St. ☎ **603/431-4262.**

A contemporary gallery featuring the work of area craftspeople, this elegant shop offers up a classy selection of creative, exuberant crafts, including ceramic sculptures, glassware, lustrous woodworking, and a wide array of handmade jewelry.

Paradise Garage. 63 Penhallow St. ☎ **603/431-0180.**

Packed to the eaves with small stuff, this shop offers up an array of clever postcards, greeting cards, a good selection of car models (the kind you put together with glue), and vintage automobile bric-a-brac.

Slackers. 51 Ceres St. ☎ **603/427-1425.**

This appealing shop tucked away near Tugboat Alley features a selection of casual, contemporary clothing and footwear, including plenty from Patagonia. It's a draw for college students and young professionals.

WHERE TO STAY

Portsmouth has a good selection of places to stay within walking distance of the downtown historic area. Less expensive, less stylish options include several chain hotels at the edge of town near I-95. Among them are the **Anchorage Inn,** 417 Woodbury Ave. (☎ **603/431-8111**); **Susse Chalet,** 650 Borthwick Ave. (☎ **603/ 436-6363**); and the **Holiday Inn of Portsmouth** (☎ 603/431-8000), also on Woodbury Avenue.

Bow Street Inn. 121 Bow St., Portsmouth, NH 03801. ☎ **603/431-7760.** Fax 603/433-1680. 9 rms. A/C TV TEL. Aug to mid-Sept $105–$139 double; mid-May to July $99–$130 double; off-season $89–$119 double. Rates include continental breakfast. AE, DISC, MC, V.

This is a fine spot for travelers willing to give up charm to gain convenience. This former downtown brewery was made over in the 1980s in a bit of inspired adaptive reuse—condos occupy the top floor, and the respected **Seacoast Repertory Theatre** (☎ 603/ 433-4472) occupies the first.

The second floor is the Bow Street Inn, a modern nine-room hotel that offers superb access to historic Portsmouth. The guest rooms, set off a somewhat sterile hallway, are clean, comfortable, and for the most part unexceptional, although rooms 6 and 7 both feature fine views of the harbor. A couple of quibbles: The elevator may be the slowest in the western world, and this is one of the very few lodgings in northern New England that doesn't offer free and easy parking. (Parking is on the street or at a nearby paid lot.) But the theater's right downstairs, and all of historic Portsmouth lies right outside your door. That's where the Bow Street's value lies.

Inn at Strawbery Banke. 314 Court St., Portsmouth, NH 03801. ☎ **800/428-3933** or 603/436-7242. 7 rms (5 with shower only). Peak season $90–$95 double; off-season $70–$75 double. Rates include full breakfast. AE, DISC, MC, V.

The Inn at Strawbery Banke, located in a home built in the early 1800s on historic Court Street, is ideally located for exploring Portsmouth. Strawbery Banke is but a block away, and Market Square is just two blocks. Innkeeper Sarah O'Donnell is a young and friendly host, and has done a nice job taking this antique home and making it comfortable for her guests. Rooms are small but bright, and feature stencilling, wooden interior shutters, and beautiful pine floors; one has a bathroom down the hall. There are two sitting rooms with televisions, and a dining room where a full breakfast is served between 8 and 9am.

✪ **Sise Inn.** 40 Court St., Portsmouth, NH 03801. ☎ **603/433-1200.** Fax 603/433-1200. 34 rms. A/C TV TEL. Late May–Oct $89–$175 double; Nov–early May $79–$150 double. Rates include continental breakfast. AE, DC, MC, V.

The Sise Inn is basically a modern, elegant, small hotel in the guise of a country inn. This solid gray Queen Anne–style home with jade and cream trim overlooks the busy intersection of Court and Middle streets, but inside it's peaceful and a world removed from the bustle of town. The original home was built for a prominent merchant in 1881; the hotel addition was constructed about a decade ago. The effect is surprisingly harmonious, with the antique stained glass and copious oak trim meshing well with the more contemporary elements. An elevator serves the three floors and there's modern carpeting throughout, but many of the rooms and suites feature antique armoires and an updated Victorian styling. Among the most appealing rooms is #302, a two-level room with an upstairs bedroom and a private downstairs living room. (The sofa folds out and there are two bathrooms, making this a good choice for families.)

An elaborate continental breakfast is served in the huge old kitchen and adjoining sunroom, and there's usually something to snack on in the afternoon. Be sure to admire the lustrous butternut trim surrounding the fireplace in the parlor.

WHERE TO DINE

The **Ceres Street Bakery,** 51 Penhallow St. (☎ 603/436-6518), is Portsmouth's original funky bakery, set off on a quiet side street. It's less trendy than the more upscale Cafe Brioche smack downtown, and is a better place for local flavor and good home baking. It's a tiny space with just a handful of tables, so you're better off getting a cookie or slice of cake to go, then walking the couple of blocks to the waterfront rose gardens.

✪ **Blue Mermaid World Grille.** The Hill (between Hanover and Deer sts. near the municipal parking garage). ☎ 603/427-2583. Reservations recommended for parties of 6 or more. Lunch items $4.95–$8.75; main dinner courses $8.95–$16.95. AE, DC, DISC, MC, V. Sun–Thurs 11:30am–9pm, Fri–Sat 11:30am–10pm. Open 1 hour later in summer. ECLECTIC.

This place ranks among my favorites in Portsmouth for its good food, good value, and good attitude. Blue Mermaid is a short walk from Portsmouth's mainstream tourist destinations in a historic area called The Hill, whose main feature today is a large parking lot. Sited in an old house with lots of exterior charm, inside there's a certain Zenlike grace to the spare bar downstairs and dining room upstairs. It's not a pretentious place—bottles of hot sauce sit on the table, and Tom Waits drones on in the background. More locals than tourists congregate here.

The simple surroundings contrast nicely with the adventurous menu, which creatively builds on cuisines from around the world. You might try the spicy grilled Yucatán sausages served over pasta in a cilantro cream sauce; or pan-seared haddock in a coconut cream sauce served with plantain fritters; or skewered shrimp and scallops served with a watermelon salsa. More mainstream entrees include barbecue ribs, lamb with couscous, and salmon filet, but why not be adventurous?

Muddy River Smokehouse. 21 Congress St. ☎ 603/430-9582. Reservations not accepted Fri–Sat. Sandwiches $4.95–$6.95; main courses $7.95–$17.95 (mostly $9–$12). AE, MC, V. Sun–Wed 11am–9pm, Thurs 11am–10pm, Fri–Sat 11am–11pm. BARBECUE.

"So authentic you'll get a notion to marry your sister," claims the Muddy River T-shirt. And that's not far from the mark, if a bit cruel. This fun, lively restaurant, which opened in 1995, is a bit deceptive, like a speakeasy. The entrance is through an unremarkable, narrow storefront just down the block from historic Market Square. Guests pass through a long, open, brick-walled bar area decorated with neon and garbage-can lampshades, then suddenly arrive in a surprisingly cavernous, cacophonous dining room that has a cafeteria-like feel to it. Done up in a festive, faux-bayou atmosphere (there's an impressive wall mural), the dining room offers an appealingly wide-ranging menu. There's a superb assortment of mouth-watering barbecued beef ribs, pork ribs, chicken, and sausage (they're slow-smoked over hickory or apple wood), and there's also sandwiches, burgers, and chili. This is definitely the place for the carnivore in your life. A limited menu is offered through midnight weekends downstairs in the lounge.

Portsmouth Brewery. 56 Market St. ☎ 603/431-1115. Reservations accepted only for parties of 10 or more. Lunch items $4.50–$8.95; main dinner courses $8.95–$12.95. AE, CB, DC, DISC, MC, V. Mon–Sat 11:30am–12:30am, Sun 10am–12:30am (Sun brunch served until 2pm). PUB FARE.

Located in the heart of the historic district (look for the tipping tankard suspended over the sidewalk), the Portsmouth Brewery opened in 1991 and quickly attracted a young, hip clientele drawn by the superb beers. The high-ceilinged, brick-walled dining room is open, airy, echoey, and redolent of hops. Alberta Hunter is playing in the background. The brews are made in 200-gallon batches, and include specialties like Old Brown Ale, a hearty Murphy's Law Red Ale, and the delightfully creamy Black Cat Stout. The eclectic menu complements the robust beverages, with selections including burgers (try the "murder burger" with Cajun spices), stir-fry, burritos, white or red pizza, and beer-marinated beef kabobs. The food's okay; the beer is well above average.

Ⓢ **Press Room.** 77 Daniel St. ☎ **603/431-5186.** Reservations not accepted. Sandwiches $3.25–$5.25; main courses $5.25–$8.25. AE, DC, DISC, MC, V. Tues–Sat 11:30am–1am, Sun–Mon 5pm–1am. PUB FARE.

Diners flock here more for the convivial "Cheers"-like atmosphere and the easy-on-the-budget prices than for creative cuisine. Opened in 1976, The Press Room likes to boast that it was the first in the area to serve Guinness Stout, and so it's appropriate that the atmosphere reflects a certain Gaelic charm. It's the sort of place where locals like to gather to discuss the issues of the day ("BMWs? I *hate* BMWs!") and feel at home. As for character, it's got plenty. During winter and cool coastal days, a fire burns in the woodstove and quaffers flex their elbows at darts amid brick walls, pine floors, and heavy wooden beams overhead. Choose your meal from a basic bar menu, with inexpensive selections including a variety of burgers, nachos, fish and chips, stir-fries, and a selection of salads.

PORTSMOUTH AFTER DARK

Portsmouth's nightlife typically takes place in downtown bars over a pint or two of locally brewed beers. If you're geared up for something more active, check out the following options.

Dolphin Striker. 15 Bow St. ☎ **603/431-5222.**

Live jazz, classical guitar, and low-key folk rock is offered most Wednesday through Sunday evenings.

Elvis Room. 142 Congress St. ☎ **603/436-9189.**

The Elvis Room has fought battles against The King's lawyers (they didn't like the name) and unruly local teens who adopted the place as their own. They prevailed in both instances, and today this smoky, relaxed coffeehouse is a fine place to read a book, play some chess, or listen to eclectic live music. It's open later than anyplace else in the city.

Muddy River Smokehouse. 21 Congress St. ☎ **603/430-9582.**

Blues are the thing at Muddy River's downstairs lounge, which is open evenings Thursday through Saturday. Thursday nights draw the region's aspiring blues artists to open-mike night; weekends offer wrenching blues with well-known performers from Boston, Maine, and beyond.

The Music Hall. 28 Chestnut St. ☎ **603/433-2400.**

This historic theater dates back to 1878, and was recently brought back to its former glory by a nonprofit arts group. A variety of shows are staged here, from magic festivals to comedy revues to concerts by the visiting symphonies and pop artists. Call for the current line-up.

The Press Room. 77 Daniel St. ☎ **603/431-5186.** Cover charge usually under $10.

A popular local bar and restaurant (see "Where to Dine," above), The Press Room offers casual entertainment most evenings, either upstairs or down. Tuesday nights are the popular Hoot nights, with an open mike hosted by local musicians. Friday nights are typically set aside for contemporary folk, starring name performers from around the region. But The Press Room might be best known for its live jazz on Sunday night, when the club brings in quality performers from Boston and beyond.

3　Hanover & Environs

If your notion of New England involves a sweeping green edged with stately brick buildings, be sure to head to Hanover, a thriving university town agreeably situated in the Connecticut River Valley. First settled in 1765, the town was home to the early pioneers who were granted a charter by King George III to establish a college. The school was named after the second earl of Dartmouth, the school's first trustee. Since its founding, Dartmouth College, the most northerly of the Ivy League schools, has had a large hand in shaping the community. One alumnus has aptly said of the school, "Dartmouth is the sort of place you're nostalgic for even if you've never been there."

Dartmouth has produced more than its share of illustrious alumni, including poet Robert Frost, Nelson Rockefeller, Supreme Court justice Salmon P. Chase, and children's book author Dr. Seuss. Perhaps the most famous son of Dartmouth was the renowned 19th-century politician and orator Daniel Webster. In arguing for the survival of Dartmouth College in a landmark case before the U.S. Supreme Court in 1816 (when two factions vied for control of the school), Webster offered his famous closing line: "It is a small college, gentlemen, but there are those who love it." This has served as an informal motto for the school alumni ever since.

Today, a handsome, oversized village green marks the permeable border between college and town. In the summer, the green is an ideal destination for strolling and lounging. In the winter, look for the massive, intricate ice sculptures from the winter carnival. The best way to explore Hanover is by foot, so your first endeavor is to park your car, which can be trying during peak seasons. Try your hand at the municipal lots west of Main Street.

The town boasts a compact and prosperous commercial area, offering great browsing and shopping. While the area clearly caters to the affluent with its shops like Simon Pearce, The Gap, and several excellent bookshops, there's a good selection of small stores that are light on frills and fluff.

Just south of Hanover is the working-class town of **Lebanon,** another commercial center, which in many ways has a less artificial New England air to it. This colorful community has a village green to be proud of, a decent variety of shops, some surprising restaurants, and a quirky mall carved out of an old brick powerhouse. If you're looking for the *New York Times*, head to Hanover; if you need a wrench, head for Lebanon.

ESSENTIALS

GETTING THERE　Lebanon and its sibling West Lebanon are located on I-89 (Exits 17 to 20), and just across the river from I-91 (Exit 10). Hanover is north of Lebanon on Route 10 or Route 120.

Amtrak serves White River Junction, Vt., just across the river.

VISITOR INFORMATION　Dartmouth College alumni and other volunteers maintain an **information center** (☎ 603/643-3512) on the green in the summer and fall. Good sources of local information in the off-season are the **Hanover Chamber of Commerce,** P.O. Box 5105, Hanover, NH 03755 (☎ 603/643-3115), located on Main Street across from the post office, and the **Lebanon Chamber of Commerce,** 2 Whipple Place, Lebanon, NH 03766 (☎ 603/448-1203).

SPECIAL EVENTS   The **Dartmouth Winter Carnival,** held annually in mid-February, is the best way to make the most of the region's notorious cold weather. The festival features winter sporting competitions such as ski jumping, but it may be best known for the ice sculpture contest, in which elaborate if ephemeral artworks and cartoon characters grace the green. The festival is not necessarily family-oriented—it traditionally presents an opportune time for college kids to break the winter doldrums with the copious consumption of alcohol. Contact Dartmouth College (☎ 603/646-1110) for more information.

EXPLORING HANOVER

Hanover is a superb town to explore by foot or on bike. Start by picking up a map of the campus, available at the Dartmouth information center on the green or at the Hanover Inn. (Free guided tours are also offered in the summer.) The expansive, leafy campus is a delight to walk through; be sure to stop by the **Baker Memorial Library** to view the **murals** by Latin American painter José Orozco. He painted *The Epic of American Civilization* while teaching here between 1932 and 1934. Given the school's current renown as a hotbed of conservativism, it's a bit surprising these paintings by the renowned leftist have gone unscathed.

On the south of the green next to the Hanover Inn is the modern **Hopkins Center for the Arts** (☎ 603/646-2422). The center attracts national acts to its 900-seat concert hall, and stages top-notch performances at the Moore Theater. Call for information on current shows. If the building looks vaguely familiar, there may be a reason for that. It was designed by Wallace Harrison, the architect who later went on to design New York's Lincoln Center, and it seems that this could have been a trial run for his later masterwork.

Adjacent to the Hopkins Center is the **Hood Museum of Art** (☎ 603/646-2426). Although it houses one of the oldest college museums in the nation, it's in a decidedly contemporary, open building, constructed in 1986. The austere, three-story structure displays selections from the permanent collection, including a superb selection of 19th-century American landscapes and a fine grouping of Assyrian reliefs dating from 883 to 859 B.C. The museum is open Tuesday through Saturday from 10am until 5pm (open until 9pm on Tuesday), and Sunday from noon to 5pm. Admission is free.

THE MONTSHIRE MUSEUM: A FUN FAMILY OUTING

The nearby **Montshire Museum of Science** (Montshire Road, Norwich, Vermont; ☎ 802/649-2200) is not your average New England science museum of dusty stuffed animals in a creaky building in need of attention. Located on the border between New Hampshire and Vermont (hence the name), the Montshire is a new, architecturally engaging, hands-on museum that draws kids back time and again. The Montshire took root in 1976, when area residents gathered up the leavings of Dartmouth's defunct natural history museum and put them on display in a former bowling alley in Hanover. The museum grew and prospered, largely owing to the dedication of hundreds of volunteers. In 1989, the museum moved to this beautiful 100-acre property sandwiched between I-91 and the Connecticut River.

Exhibits are housed in a open, soaring structure inspired by the region's barns. The museum contains some live animals (don't miss the leaf cutter ant exhibit on the second floor), but it's mostly fun, interactive exhibits that involve kids deeply, teaching them the principles of math and science on the sly. Even preschoolers are entertained here at "Andy's Place," a play area with aquariums, bubble-making exhibits, and other magical things. Outside, there's a science park masquerading as a playground, and four nature trails that wend through this riverside property of tall trees and chirpy birds. Admission is $5 adults, $3 children 3 to 17, under 3 free. Daily 10am to 5pm. To get there, use Exit 13 off I-91 and head east; look for museum signs almost immediately.

WHERE TO STAY

Several hotels and motels are located off the interstate in Lebanon and West Lebanon, about five miles south of Hanover. Try the **Airport Economy Inn** (☎ 800/ 433-3466 or 603/298-8888), **Days Inn** (☎ 603/448-5070), the **Radisson Inn North Country** (☎ 603/298-5906), or **The Sunset** (☎ 603/298-8721). Another area option is the **Norwich Inn,** a short hop across the river in Vermont (see Chapter 11).

Hanover Inn. Wheelock St. (P.O. Box 151), Hanover, NH 03755. ☎ 800/443-7024 or 603/ 643-4300. Fax 603/646-3744. E-mail hanover.inn@dartmouth.edu. 92 rms. A/C TV TEL. $197– $256 double. AE, DC, DISC, MC, V. Parking $5 per day.

The Hanover Inn has been owned and operated by Dartmouth College for more than a century, which helps explain all the rich forest-green hues throughout (it's Dartmouth's signature color). Housed in a handsome Colonial Revival building facing the green, this exceptionally well-maintained inn is the destination of choice for parents and dignitaries visiting the college. (It's also where performers appearing at the adjacent Hopkins Center stay, so you might bump into musical celebrities in the halls.) For such a large inn the common areas are quite limited (the ground floor is mostly occupied by two restaurants) but the hotel connects via tunnels and enclosed walkways to the student center and the Hood Museum, so it's easy to stretch your legs, even in winter.

Rooms are priced according to size (there are three different sizes), and each is nicely furnished in a contemporary country style. Most have canopy or four-poster beds and down comforters. Ask for a view of the green, if available, since there's no extra charge. Also note that the fourth-floor rooms seem a bit smaller owing to lower ceilings and dormer windows.

Mary Keane House. Lower Shaker Village, Enfield, NH 03748. ☎ 603/632-4241. 7 rms. TV. $59–$99 double; foliage season $89–$149 double. AE, DC, MC, V.

Situated at Lower Shaker Village about 25 minutes from Dartmouth, the Mary Keane House is an ideal spot for quiet relaxation and gentle recuperation of a harried soul. Built in 1929 (two years after the Shakers had abandoned the village), this two-story yellow Georgian Revival doesn't share much with the Shaker village in architecture or spirit—in fact, it's filled with lovely Victorian antiques, which seem anathema to the Shaker sensibility. But it's kept immaculately clean (something the Shakers would appreciate), and it's right in the Shaker village, so guests can explore the buildings and museum by day (the grounds are especially peaceful at twilight), paddle one of the inn's canoes on Lake Mascoma, or swim at the small private beach. Room 3 is a particular gem, with Corinthian columns, a formal sitting room, plenty of space to unwind, and a refined country-Victorian elegance.

WHERE TO DINE

Café Buon Gustaio. 72 South Main St. ☎ 603/643-5711. Reservations recommended. Main courses $8–$19. AE, CB, DC, DISC, MC, V. Tues–Thurs 5:30–9:30pm, Fri–Sat 5:30–10pm. ITALIAN.

Four words sums up Café Buon Gustaio: simple setting, elegant fare. Tucked away on the quiet end of Hanover's Main Street in a 19th-century home, the cafe is a trattoria-style restaurant with a menu that changes frequently and a kitchen staff with the proven ability to pull off a good meal night after night. A handsome bar occupies part of one parlor; diners adjourn to the second, more intimate parlor. Begin your meal with a grilled portobello mushroom with artichoke salad, or a lobster ravioli with roasted red pepper cream. Then feast on spaghettini served with tuna, capers, olives, and beans; or canneloni of smoked chicken, peppers, scallions, and ricotta in a d'Abruzzi sauce. If you don't pine for pasta, there's usually a selection of pizzettas and grilled dishes, such as Black Angus steak with a five-peppercorn butter, and swordfish with a spicy shrimp salsa.

✪ Daniel Webster Room. In the Hanover Inn, Wheelock St. ☎ **603/643-4300.** Reservations recommended. Breakfast items $4.25–$9.50; lunch items $6.95–$13.50; main dinner courses $15–$23. AE, DC, DISC, MC, V. Daily 7:30–10:30am, 11:30am–1pm, and 6–9pm. CONTINENTAL.

The neoclassical Daniel Webster Room of the Hanover Inn will appeal to those looking for exceptionally fine dining amid a formal New England atmosphere. The inn's proper dining room is reminiscent of a 19th-century resort hotel, with fluted columns, floral carpeting, and regal upholstered chairs. The only concession to frivolity are the Tavern-on-the-Green-style white lights adorning the potted plants. The dinner menu isn't extensive, but that doesn't make it any less appealing. Entrees range from filet mignon with foie gras and truffled potatoes, to a more exotic Moroccan-spiced tuna with couscous. The restaurant has a commendable wine list, and is one of only two restaurants in New Hampshire to receive AAA's four-star rating.

Next door is the more informal **Ivy Grill,** set in retro, Miami Vice–like surroundings that come as a bit of a surprise at this staid inn. It's open daily from 11:30am to 10pm, and serves up lunches for under $10 and dinners like chicken with wild mushrooms and barbecue ribs with corn bread. Most entrees are $11 to $14.

❸ Lou's. 30 S. Main St. ☎ **603/643-3321.** Breakfast items $2.10–$5.95; lunch items $3.85–$5.95. Mon–Fri 6am–3pm, Sat–Sun 7am–3pm. Bakery open for snacks until 5pm. BAKERY/DINER.

Lou's is a Hanover institution, attracting large crowds for breakfast on weekends and a steady clientele for lunch throughout the week. The mood is no-frills New Hampshire, with a black-and-white linoleum checkerboard floor and maple-and-vinyl booths updated with a modern country look. Breakfast is served all day here (real maple syrup on your pancakes is $1 extra), and the sandwiches are huge and delicious, served on fresh-baked bread. If you're inclined to blow your calorie budget, the baked goods are a fine temptation. The macaroons are especially good.

A SIDE TRIP SOUTH TO CORNISH

Artists flocked to the quiet Cornish area in the late 19th century, and the subtle beauty of the region, still prevalent today, makes it abundantly clear why. The first artistic immigrants to arrive were the painters and sculptors, who showed up in the late 1880s and early 1890s, building modest homes in the hills. They were followed by politicians and the affluent, who eventually established a thriving summer colony. Among those who populated the rolling hills that looked across the river toward Ascutney were sculptor Daniel Chester French, painter Maxfield Parrish, and *New Republic* editor Herbert Crowley. Prominent visitors included Ethel Barrymore and presidents Woodrow Wilson and Theodore Roosevelt. A 1907 article in the *New York Daily Tribune* noted that artists made their homes in Cornish not "with the idea of converting it into a 'fashionable' summer resort, but rather to form there an aristocracy of brains and keep out that element which displays its lack of grey matter by an expenditure of money in undesirable ways."

The social allure eventually peaked, and the area has lapsed into a peaceful slumber. Those who come here now do so for the beauty and seclusion, not for the gatherings and parties. Indeed, the country's most famous recluse (J.D. Salinger) lives in Cornish today.

The region lacks obvious tourist allure—there are no fancy hotels, no five-star restaurants—but it's well worth visiting and exploring. At twilight, you can see where Maxfield Parrish found his inspiration for the rich, pellucid azure skies for which his prints and paintings are so noted.

The region's premier monument to its former arts colony is the **St. Gaudens National Historic Site** (☎ 603/675-2175), located off Route 12A. Noted sculptor Augustus St. Gaudens first arrived in this valley in 1885, shortly after receiving an important commission to create a statue of Abraham Lincoln. His friend Charles Beaman, a lawyer who owned several houses and much land in the Cornish area, assured him he would find a surfeit of "Lincoln-shaped men" in the area. St. Gaudens came, and pretty much stayed the rest of his life.

His home and studio, which he called "Aspet" after the village in Ireland where he was raised, is a superb place to learn more about this extraordinary artist. A brief tour of the house, which is kept pretty much as it was when St. Gaudens lived here, provides a brief introduction to the man. Visitors learn about St. Gaudens the artist at several outbuildings and on the grounds, where many replicas of his most famous statues are on display.

The 150-acre grounds also feature short nature trails, where visitors can explore the hilly woodlands, passing along streams and a millpond.

The historic site is open daily 9am to 4:30pm from late May through October. Admission is $2 for adults 17 and over; children under 17 are free.

Covered bridge aficionados will want to seek out the **Cornish-Windsor Covered Bridge,** which is the nation's longest covered bridge. Spanning the Connecticut River between Vermont and New Hampshire, this bridge has an ancient and interesting lineage. A toll bridge was first built here in 1796 to replace a ferry; the current bridge was built in 1866, and extensively restored in 1989. When the late afternoon light hits it just right, this vies for the title of most handsome covered bridge in New England.

For a fisheye view of the bridge and the scenic, forested shores of the Connecticut River, rent a canoe a few miles downstream from the bridge at **Northstar Canoe Livery** (☎ 603/542-5802). For $17 per person, Northstar will shuttle you 12 miles upstream, allowing a leisurely paddle back to your car over the next few hours. Or just rent by the hour and dabble in the currents.

4 The Lake Winnipesaukee Region

Unless you're bobbing in a canoe in the middle of New Hampshire's largest lake when a squall comes up, it rarely seems all that huge. That's because Lake Winnipesaukee's 180-mile shoreline is convoluted and twisting, warped around dozens of inlets, coves, and bays, and further fragmented with some 274 islands. As a result, intermittent lake views from the shore give the illusion you're viewing a chain of smaller lakes and ponds rather than one massive body of water that measures 12 miles by 20 miles at its broadest points. (Incidentally, there's no agreement on the meaning of the lake's Indian name. Although "beautiful water in a high place" and "smile of the great spirit" are the most poetic interpretations, the more commonly accepted translation is "good outlet.")

How to best enjoy the lake? If you've got kids, settle in at Weirs Beach for a few days and take in the gaudy attractions. If you're looking for isolation, consider renting a lakeside cabin for a week or so on the eastern shore, find a canoe or sailboat, then explore much the same way travelers did a century ago. If your time is limited, a driving tour around the lake with a few well-chosen stops will give you a nice taste of the region's woodsy flavor.

THE WEST SHORE

Lake Winnipesaukee's west shore has a more frenetic and congested atmosphere than its sibling shore across the lake. That's partly for historic reasons (the main stage and rail routes passed along the west shore), and partly for modern reasons—I-93 runs west of the lake, serving as a sluice for hurried visitors streaming in from the megalopolis to the south. The west shore offers the most diversions for short attention spans. It also has more tourist amenities, including hotels, restaurants and shops, especially in Laconia and Meredith.

ESSENTIALS

GETTING THERE   Interstate access to the west shore is from I-93 at Exit 20 or Exit 23. From Exit 20, follow Route 3 north through Laconia to Weirs Beach. (It's less confusing and more scenic to stay on Business Route 3.) From Exit 23, drive nine miles east on Route 104 to Meredith, then head either south on Route 3 to Route 11, or strike northwest on Route 25.

VISITOR INFORMATION   The **Greater Laconia/Weirs Beach Chamber of Commerce,** 11 Veterans Square, Laconia, NH 03246 (☎ 800/531-2347), maintains a seasonal information booth on Business Route 3 about halfway between Laconia and Weirs Beach. It's open daily in summer from 10am to 6pm. Information is also available year-round at the chamber's office at the old railway station in Laconia. It's open Monday through Friday from 9am to 5pm and on Saturdays from 10am to 2pm.

The **Lakes Region Association,** P.O. Box 1545, Center Harbor, NH 03226 (☎ 800/605-2537 or 603/253-8555), doesn't maintain an information booth but is happy to send out a handy vacation kit with maps and extensive information about local attractions.

ENJOYING WEIRS BEACH

Weirs Beach is a compact resort town that reflects its Victorian heritage. Unlike beach towns that sprawl for miles, Weirs Beach clusters in that distinguished turn-of-the-century fashion along a boardwalk, just north of a sandy beach. At the heart of the town is a railroad that connects to the steamship line—a nice throwback to an era when summer vacationers weren't dependent on cars. The town attracts a mix of visitors, from history and transportation buffs, to beach nuts and young video-game warriors.

But most of all, it attracts families. Lots of families. In fact, Weirs Beach is an ideal destination for parents with kids possessed by an insatiable drive for novelty and flashing lights. Families might start the morning at **Endicott Beach** (named after the Royal Governor of Massachusetts Bay Colony, who sent surveyors here in 1652), swimming in the clear waters of Winnipesaukee. Arrive early if you want to find public parking, which costs 50¢ an hour with a five-hour maximum.

Afterwards stroll along **the boardwalk** into town, which offers penny arcades, bumper cars, jewelry outlets, leather shops, and delicious if unnutritious fare like crispy caramel corn.

Along the access roads to Weirs Beach are a number of activities that delight young kids and parents desperate to take some of the energy out of them. **The Surfcoaster** (☎ 603/366-4991) has a huge assortment of wave pools, water slides, and other moist diversions. It's on Route 11B just outside of Weirs Beach. Also on Route 11B is **Daytona Fun Park** (☎ 603/366-5461), which has go-karts, mini-golf, and batting cages. The **Weirs Beach Waterslide,** on Route 3 (☎ 603-366-5161), has four slides that produce varying levels of adrenaline. And the **Funspot** (☎ 603/366-4377) will keep kids (and uninhibited adults) occupied with video games, candlepin bowling, and a driving range.

Nearby **Laconia** is a good destination for drying out after the water rides or venturing on a rainy day. The town has a trim, miniature downtown that's been coming back bit by bit since the ill-fated pedestrian mall was torn up in 1994. Enjoy the eclectic architecture (there's a handsome white-spired church across from a Richardson-inspired train station), then quaff a home-brewed porter or ale at the **Winnipesaukee Pub and Brewery,** downtown at 546 Main St. (☎ 603/527-1300), which has an open, modern layout.

EXPLORING BY LAND & LAKE

Scenic train rides leave from town on the **Winnipesaukee Scenic Railroad** (☎ 603/279-5253), which offers one- and two-hour excursions from Weirs Beach throughout the day during the summer. It's a unique way to enjoy a view of the lake and forest; kids are provided a hobo lunch packed in a bundle on a stick. Fares for adults are $7.50 for the two-hour ride, and $6.50 for the one-hour ride. Children ages 4 to 11 are charged $5.50 and $4.50.

After riding the rails, head out onto the waters on the stately **M/S *Mount Washington,*** an exceptionally handsome 230-foot-long vessel with three levels and a capacity of 1,250 passengers (☎ 603/366-2628). This ship, by far the largest of the lake tour boats, is the best way to get to know Winnipesaukee, with excellent views of the winding shoreline and the knobby peaks of the White Mountains rising over the lake's north end. As many as four cruises a day are offered in summer, ranging from a 2¼-hour excursion ($12 adults, $5 children 4 to 12) to a 3½-hour dinner cruise ($32) that includes dinner and live music with two bands. The dinner cruises offer different themes, but don't look for alternative rock; most are along the lines of oldies nights and country-and-western. The ship operates from the end of May through mid-October, departing from the train station in Weirs Beach. (You can't miss it when it's at the dock.)

SKIING

Gunstock, on Route 11A between West Alton and Gilford (☎ 800/486-7862), is a fine destination for families and intermediate skiers who like good views and great grooming as part of their ski experience. This venerable state-run ski area, with a vertical drop of 1,420 feet, has the comfortably burnished patina of a rustic resort dating from a much earlier era—no garish condos, no ski-theme lounges, no forced frivolity. But the mountain managers pride themselves on maintaining excellent ski conditions throughout the day on its 45 trails, and even closes several during lunch for mid-day grooming. Gunstock skiers have a choice of two double chair lifts, two triples, and a quad (plus two surface lifts); from the slopes, the views of iced-over Winnipesaukee and the White Mountains to the north are superb. Gunstock also offers night skiing on 12 trails served by three chairlifts. Adult lift tickets from 1995 to 1996 were $28 midweek and $37 weekends and holidays. For juniors (ages 6 to 12) and seniors (65+), rates are $20 midweek and $22 weekends and holidays.

WHERE TO STAY

Creeping condomania has reduced the number of guest rooms in the lake area, but Business Route 3 (which runs picturesquely along Paugus Bay) still offers a good

Hog Heaven!

Laconia and Weirs Beach get VERY LOUD in mid-June, when some 150,000 motorcyclists descend on the towns to fraternize, party, and race during what's become the legendary Motorcycle Week.

This bawdy event dates back to 1939, when motorcycle races were first staged at the newly built Belknap Gunstock Recreation Area. The annual gathering gained some unwelcome notoriety in 1965, when riots broke out involving bikers and locals. The then-mayor of Laconia attributed problems to the Hell's Angels, claiming he had evidence that they had trained in Mexico before coming here to foment chaos. This odd episode was documented in Hunter S. Thompson's 1966 work, *The Hell's Angels*.

Laconia and Weirs Beach eventually recovered from that unwanted publicity, and today bike races take place at the Loudon Speedway just north of Concord, and at the Gunstock Recreation Area, which hosts the Hill Climb. But the whole of the Weirs Beach area takes on a leather-and-beer carnival atmosphere throughout the week, with bikers cruising the main drag and enjoying one another's company until late at night. Many travelers would pay good money to avoid Weirs Beach at this time, but they'd be missing out on one of New England's more enduring annual phenomena.

---

selection of motels, cottages, and motor courts, including many that will delight aficionados of 1950s-style architecture and neon. Try the **Naswa Lakeside Resort** (☎ 603/366-4341), which offers simple cottages and motel-style rooms on the water and features a popular restaurant and bar. The **Hi-Spot Motor Court** (☎ 603/524-3281) has its own beach and rowboats for guests, who choose from housekeeping cottages and motel rooms. If you'd prefer to be within walking distance of Weirs Beach attractions, the **Half Moon Motel and Cottages** (☎ 603/366-4494) is perfectly situated on a hillside overlooking the town and the lake beyond.

Inn at Mill Falls. Rtes. 3 and 25, Meredith, NH 03253, ☎ 800/622-6455 or 603/279-7006. Fax 603/279-6797. 78 rms in 2 buildings. A/C TV TEL. Summer and fall $79–$235 double; winter and spring $68–$195 double. AE, CB, DC, DISC, MC, V.

Located in the middle of Meredith, the Inn at Mill Falls is part of a complex of two dozen shops and restaurants in a renovated and expanded mill built around a small waterfall. The inn, which opened in 1985, has loads of architectural integrity, but it's best suited for those who prefer the amenities of a modern hotel to the charm of a country inn. It's a thoroughly up-to-date hotel with nicely decorated guest rooms (the maple and pine furniture is by New Hampshire craftsmen), an indoor pool, and views across the highway to the Meredith Bay. Fifty-four of the guest rooms are at the old mill site; another 24 are across the way at Bay Point, a four-story building with superior lake views and turn-of-the-century boathouse styling.

Ⓢ Red Hill Inn. Rte. 25B (P.O. Box 99), Center Harbor, NH 03226. ☎ 800/573-3445 or 603/279-7001. Fax 603/279-7003. 21 rms (some with shower or tub only). TEL. $85–$125 double at inn and farmhouse; $125–$150 cottage. Rates include breakfast. AE, CB, DC, DISC, MC, V. From Center Harbor, drive NW 2.9 miles on Route 25B.

The Red Hill Inn is tucked in the rolling hills between Winnipesaukee and Squam Lake (where *On Golden Pond* was filmed), but borrows more of its flavor from the mountains than the lakeshore. Housed in an architecturally austere, three-story brick home dating from the turn of century, the inn looks down a long meadow toward a small complex of elegant green-and-red-shingled farm buildings at the foot of a hill. (Two of these have been converted to well-appointed guest quarters.)

The rooms and common areas in the main inn are handsomely furnished in low Victorian style with floral wallpaper and maple floors. Room prices are based on views and size, but my favorite room (the Kearsarge) is one of the least expensive, with a very private brick and chocolatey-brown panelled sitting room, off which lies a small bathroom with clawfoot tub.

Despite a price that may seem average-to-high at first glance, the Red Hill delivers more for the dollar than most any other inn in New Hampshire. For an even better deal, ask about the inn's three-night midweek packages.

Dining/Enteratainment: The inn's dining room serves lunch and dinner, with entrees such as médaillons of venison au poivre, or rack of lamb with a feta cheese and Dijon mustard topping.

WHERE TO DINE

Kellerhaus (☎ 603/366-4466) is *the* classic house of sweets. Located in a storybook-like stone and half-timber structure on Route 3 a third of a mile north of Endicott Beach, this old-fashioned place with bull's-eye windows on a hillside overlooking the lake features a diet-busting ice-cream buffet, where fanatics can select from a battery of toppings including macaroon crunch, butterscotch, chocolate, and whipped cream. The smorgasbord is $3.25 to $5.95, depending on the number of scoops you begin with. There's also a sizable gift shop with homemade candies providing snacks for the road.

Hart's Turkey Farm Restaurant. Rte. 3, Meredith. ☎ **603/279-6212.** Reservations recommended during peak season. Main courses $9.50–$17.75. AE, CB, DC, DISC, MC, V. Summer daily 11:15am–9pm; fall through spring daily 11:15am–8pm. POULTRY/AMERICAN.

Hart's Turkey Farm Restaurant is not good news if you're a turkey. On a typically busy day, this popular spot dishes up more than a ton of America's favorite bird, along with 4,000 dinner rolls and 1,000 pounds of potatoes. And let's not even talk about Thanksgiving.

Judging by name alone, Hart's Farm sounds more rural than it is. In fact, there are no turkeys to be seen nearby. It's in a nondescript roadside building on a busy, nondescript part of Route 3. Inside, it's comfortable in a faux Olde New Englande sort of way, and the service has that brisk efficiency found only in places where waitresses have been hoisting heavy trays for years. But diners don't flock to Harts for the charm. They come here for filling meals that range from fried fish to filet mignon. And most off all, they come for turkey that's cooked right every time.

Hickory Stick Farm. 60 Bean Hill Rd., Belmont. ☎ **603/524-3333.** Reservations recommended. Main courses $10.95–$18.95. AE, DISC, MC, V. Memorial Day to Columbus Day Tues–Sun 5–8pm; limited schedule remainder of the year. Ask for directions when making reservations. AMERICAN.

The Hickory Stick Farm is well off the beaten path in the countryside outside of Laconia, but has managed to attract and keep happy diners since it first opened its doors in 1950. Ask for a seat on the screened-in gazebo room during balmy weather. When it turns chilly, angle for a table near the fireplace in the brick-floored dining room.

The restaurant is famous for its distinctive duck dishes, served with an orange-sherry sauce. The duck is slow-roasted for four to five hours, and the fatty layer is removed from beneath the skin. This method yields delicate and crispy skin, but moist meat. The duck attracts gourmands from Boston and beyond, but tasty country fare like vegetable lasagne, sirloin, and roast rack of lamb keeps the locals coming in night after night.

S Las Piñatas. 9 Veteran's Square, Laconia. ☎ **603/528-1405.** Reservations suggested for parties of 5 or more. Lunch items $3.75–$7.99; main dinner courses $7.99–$9.99. MC, V. Daily 11am–2pm; Mon–Fri 5–8pm, Sat–Sun 5–9:30pm. MEXICAN.

Armando Lezama first came to Laconia from Mexico City in 1979 as a high school exchange student. He liked it, so he moved here with his family, opening what's most certainly the most authentic Mexican restaurant in New Hampshire. Housed in the stone railroad station on the edge of Laconia's downtown, Las Piñatas has a good menu of genuine Mexican dishes and frozen margaritas that seem especially tasty after a long day at the lake. While diners might gripe about the lackadaisical service or the overabundance of iceberg lettuce, the entrees boast authentic spicing—the beans are earthy and the salsa tangy. Everything is uniformly well-prepared, and offered at excellent prices. The menu includes Mexican regulars like empanadas, tacos al carbón, and fajitas. Among the specialities are the delicious enchiladas de mole, made with the Lezamas' homemade mole sauce. For dessert, try the coconut flan, or a buñuelo with maple syrup.

THE EAST SHORE

For some travelers, Winnipesaukee's east shore might recall Gertrude Stein's comment about Oakland: "There's no there there." Other than the low-key town of **Wolfeboro,** the east shore is mostly islands and coves, mixed forests and rolling hills, rocky farms and the occasional apple orchard. While it's a large lake, its waters are also largely inaccessible from this side. Old summer homes and new gated condominium communities occupy some of the best coves and points. But narrow roads do touch on the lake here and there, and most roads are nicely engineered for leisurely cruising. The secret to getting the most out of the east shore is to take it slow and enjoy the small villages and quiet forests as if they were delicately crafted miniatures, not vast panoramas.

ESSENTIALS

GETTING THERE Lake Winnipesaukee's east shore is best explored on Route 28 (from Alton Bay to Wolfeboro) and Route 109 (from Wolfeboro to Moultonborough). From the south, Alton Bay can be reached via Route 11 from Rochester, or from Route 28, which intersects Routes 4 and 202 about 12 miles east of Concord.

VISITOR INFORMATION The **Wolfeboro Chamber of Commerce,** P.O. Box 547, Wolfeboro, NH 03864 (☎ **603/569-2200**), offers regional travel information and advice from a converted railroad station at Depot Square, one block off Main Street in Wolfeboro (turn on Railroad Avenue).

EXPLORING WOLFEBORO

The town of Wolfeboro claims to be the first summer resort in the United States, and the documentation makes a pretty good case for it. In 1763, John Wentworth, the nephew of a former governor, built a summer estate on what's now called Lake Wentworth, along with a road to it from Portsmouth. Wentworth didn't get to enjoy his holdings for long—his Tory sympathies forced him to flee when the political situation heated up in 1775. The house burned in 1820, but the site now attracts archaeologists. Tourists are lured to **Wentworth State Beach** (☎ **603/ 569-3699**) not so much because of history but because of the attractive beach, refreshing lake waters, and shady picnic area. The park is located five miles east of Wolfeboro on Route 109.

The town of Wolfeboro (pop. 2,800) has a vibrant, homey downtown that's easily explored on foot. Park near Depot Square and the gingerbread Victorian train station, and stock up on brochures and maps at the Chamber of Commerce office inside. Behind the train station, running along the former tracks of the rail line, is the **Russell C. Chase Bridge-Falls Path,** a rail-trail that (so far) runs pleasantly about one-half mile along Back Bay to a set of small waterfalls. (Plans call for extending the pathway much further in coming years.)

The ponderous **M/S *Mount Washington*** docks in Wolfeboro on its cruises from Weirs Beach, but if you'd like a more intimate tour of the lake, sign up for a cruise on the ***Blue Ghost,*** an open, 19-foot U.S. mail boat that serves a handful of island communities around the lake. The three-hour tour departs from the Wolfeboro waterfront at 9:50am, and covers some 60 miles of the lake. Reservations are essential (call **603/569-1114**), and capacity is limited to eight passengers. The fare is $16 adults, $8 for children under 12.

A QUIRKY CASTLE

Castle in the Clouds. Rte. 171 (4 miles south of Rte. 25), Moultonborough. ☎ **800/729-2468** or 603/476-2352. $10 adults, $9 seniors, $7 students. (Grounds only, $4.) Mid-May to mid-June Sat–Sun 9am–5pm; mid-June to Labor Day daily 9am–5pm; Labor Day to third week of Oct daily 9am–4pm; closed Nov to Apr.

Cranky millionaire Thomas Gustav Plant built this eccentric stone edifice high atop a mountain overlooking Lake Winnipesaukee early in this century. Completed in 1913 at a cost of $7 million, the home is a sort of rustic San Simeon East, with orange roof tiles, cliff-hugging rooms, stained-glass windows, and unrivaled views of the surrounding hills and lakes. Visitors drive as far as the carriage house (nicely converted to a snack bar and restaurant), where they park and are taken in groups through the house by knowledgeable guides.

Even if the castle holds no interest, the 5,200-acre grounds themselves are worth the admission price (there's a discount for those visiting the grounds only). The long access road is harrowingly narrow and winding (kids, don't try this in your mobile home), with wonderful vistas and turnouts for stopping and exploring along the way. I'd advise taking your time on the way up; the exit road is fast, straight, and uninteresting.

Equestrians can rent horses to explore the hills at $25 for a one-hour ride. (Reservations required.)

On your way out you're invited to visit the modern bottling plant, where Castle Springs Water is packaged for shipment to shops throughout the Northeast.

WHERE TO STAY & DINE

Wolfeboro Inn. 90 N. Main St., Wolfeboro, NH 03894. ☎ **800/451-2389** or 603/569-3016. Fax 603/569-5375. 44 rms. A/C TV TEL. $109–$219 double. Rates include breakfast. Add $20 on weekends. AE, DISC, MC, V.

This small, elegant hotel strives to mix modern and traditional, and succeeds admirably in doing so. Located a short stroll from downtown Wolfeboro, the inn dates back to 1812 but was extensively expanded and updated from 1985 to 1986. The modern lobby features a small atrium with wood beams, slate floor, and a brick fireplace, and has managed to retain an Old World elegance and grace. Comfortable guest rooms vary in size, and most are furnished with early American reproductions. Some have fireplaces; others have views of Wolfeboro Bay. The inn also has some nice extras, including its own 75-passenger excursion boat (a free trip is included in room rates). On the downside, for an inn of this elegance and price it has only a disappointing sliver of lakeshore and a miniature beach for guests.

Dining/Entertainment: The main dining room has two areas to suit your mood: Sit near the fireplace in a low-ceilinged room decorated in a traditional early American style, or choose the upper, gazebo-like room, which is airy and summery. In the inn's early wing is the atmospheric Wolfe's Tavern, with pewter tankards hanging from the low beams, 60 brands of beer, and a selection of basic pub fare, including salads, burgers, and a variety of pasta dishes.

5 The White Mountains

The White Mountains are northern New England's undisputed outdoor recreation capital. This cluster of ancient mountains is a sprawling, rugged playground that attracts kayakers, mountaineers, rock climbers, skiers, mountain bikers, bird watchers, and hikers.

Especially hikers. The **White Mountain National Forest** encompasses some 773,000 acres of rocky, forested terrain, more than 100 waterfalls, dozens of remote backcountry lakes, and miles of clear brooks and cascading streams. An elaborate network of 1,200 miles of hiking trails dates back to the 19th century, when the urban gentry took to the mountains in droves to build character, build trails, and experience the raw sublimity of nature. Trails ranging from easy and extraordinarily demanding lace the hillside forests, run along remote valley rivers, and traverse barren, windswept ridgelines where the weather can change dramatically in less time than it takes to eat lunch.

The spiritual center of the White Mountains is its highest point: 6,288-foot **Mt. Washington,** an ominous, brooding peak that's often cloud-capped, and often mantled with snow early and late in the season. This blustery peak is accessible by train, car, and foot, making it one of the most popular spots in the region. You won't find wilderness here, but you will find a surfeit of natural drama.

Flanking this colossal peak are the brawny **Presidential Mountains,** a series of fractured granite peaks named after U.S. presidents and offering spectacular views. Surrounding these are numerous other rocky ridges that lure hikers looking for challenges and a place to experience nature at its more elemental and raw.

As for **camping,** simple but comfortable "huts" (managed by the Appalachian Mountain Club) and three-sided lean-tos are scattered throughout the White Mountains, providing overnight shelter for campers. Meals are included at the huts, but it's surprisingly pricey. Shelters are sometimes free, sometimes a backcountry manager will collect a small fee. Backcountry tent camping is free throughout the White Mountains (no permit needed). Check with one of the ranger stations for restrictions.

Travelers whose idea of fun doesn't involve steep cliffs or icy dips in mountain streams still have plenty of opportunities for milder adventure. A handful of major arteries provide easy access to mountain scenery. **Route 302** carries travelers through North Conway and Crawford Notch to the pleasant villages of Bethlehem and Littleton. **Route 16** travels from southern New Hampshire through congested North Conway before twisting up dramatic Pinkham Notch at the base of Mt. Washington. Wide and fast **Route 2** skirts the northern edge of the mountains, offering wonderful views en route to the town of Jefferson. **I-93** gets my vote for the most scenic interstate in northern New England, passing through spectacular Franconia Notch as it narrows to a two-lane road in deference to its natural surroundings (and local political will). And finally, there's the **Kancamagus Highway,** linking Conway with Lincoln, and providing some of the most scenic White Mountain vistas in the region. Along the way, frequent roadside pull-offs and interpretive exhibits allow casual explorers to admire cascades, picnic along rivers, and enjoy sweeping mountain views. Several less demanding nature hikes are also easily accessible from various roadside turnouts.

Keep in mind that the White Mountains are a *national forest*, not a *national park*, a distinction that's sometimes lost on urbanites and foreign travelers. There's a big difference. National forests are managed for multiple uses, which includes timber harvesting, wildlife management, recreational development, and the like. This may disappoint those offended by clearcutting and logging roads. Fortunately, the level of cutting is not as excessive as in many western forests, and the regrowth here also tends to be more rapid than in the arid West. Also bear in mind that about 15% of the White Mountains is designated as wilderness areas, from which mechanical devices (including mountain bikes) are prohibited. Strike for these areas if you're looking to step deep into the wilds.

As for accommodations, it's easy to find an area to suit your mood and inclinations. North Conway is the motel capital of the region, with hundreds of rooms, many quite charmless, but at very reasonable rates. The Loon Mountain and Waterville Valley area have a sort of planned condo village graciousness that delights some travelers and creeps out others. Jackson, Franconia Notch, Crawford Notch, and the Bethlehem-Littleton area are the best destinations for old-fashioned hotels and inns.

RANGER STATIONS & INFORMATION

Guidance for outdoor adventures can be obtained at the national forest visitor centers, which are located in various locations around the White Mountains. The **Saco Ranger Station** (☎ 603/447-5448) in Conway is on the Kancamagus Highway just 100 yards west of Route 16. The **Androscoggin Ranger Station** (☎ 603/466-2713) is at 80 Glen Rd. in Gorham. The **Evans Notch Ranger Station** (☎ 207/824-2134) covers the Maine portion of the White Mountains (about 50,000 acres) and is located on Route 2 just north of Bethel. The **Ammonoosuc Ranger Station** (☎ 603/869-2626) is on Trudeau Road in Bethlehem. The **Forest Service's** central White Mountains office is in Laconia at 719 Main St. (☎ 603/528-8721).

General information and advice about recreation in the White Mountains is available at the **AMC's Pinkham Notch Camp** (☎ 603/466-2721) on Route 16 between Jackson and Gorham. The center is open daily from 6am to 10pm.

SPECIALIZED GUIDES

If you're serious about exploring the wind-scoured crags and mossy ravines of the White Mountains, you'll need supplemental guides and maps to keep you on track in the great outdoors. Here's a short list of recommended guides, most of which are available at area bookstores:

- *AMC White Mountain Guide* (Appalachian Mountain Club, 1992, $16.95). This compact, 638-page book (no, that's not an oxymoron) is chock-full of detailed information on *all* the hiking trails in the White Mountains. It's printed in small type in a format suitable to throwing in your pack, and comes with a handy set of maps. This is the hiker's bible for the region.
- *Mount Washington: A Guide and Short History* (Countryman Press, 1992, $9.95). Peter Randall originally wrote this handy and informative guide in 1983, updating it in 1992. The guide will appeal to those interested in the history and hiking of the Northeast's tallest peak.
- *Fifty Hikes in the White Mountains* (Backcountry Publications, 1994, $14). The fourth edition of this popular guide, written by John Doan, offers a good selection of mountain rambles ranging from easy strolls to overnight backpack trips.

- *Ponds & Lakes of the White Mountains* (Backcountry Publications, 1993, $16). The White Mountain high country is studded with dramatic tarns (many left by retreating glaciers). This 350-page guide by Steven D. Smith offers 68 trips to help get you there.
- *Waterfalls of the White Mountains* (Backcountry Publications, 1990, $17). Water lovers will get their money's worth from Bruce and Doreen Bolnick's guide to 100 mountain waterfalls, including roadside cascades and backcountry cataracts.

NORTH CONWAY & ENVIRONS

North Conway is the commercial heart of the White Mountains. Shoppers adore it because of the profusion of outlets, boutiques, and restaurants along Routes 302 and 16. (The two state highways overlap through town.) Outdoor purists abhor it, considering it a garish interloper to be avoided at all costs, except when looking for pizza.

No doubt, North Conway itself won't strike anyone as nature's wonderland. The shopping strip south of the village is basically one long turning lane flanked with outlet malls of every architectural stripe, motels, and chain restaurants. On rainy weekends and during the foliage season the road can resemble a linear parking lot.

Regardless, North Conway is beautifully situated along the eastern edge of the broad and fertile Saco River Valley (often called the Mt. Washington Valley by local tourism boosters). Gentle, forest-covered mountains, some with sheer cliffs that suggest the distant, stunted cousins of Yosemite's rocky faces, border the bottomlands. Northward up the valley, the hills rise in a triumphant crescendo to the blustery, tempestuous heights of Mt. Washington.

The village itself is trim and attractive (if often congested), with an open green, quaint shops, Victorian frontier-town commercial architecture, and a distinctive train station. It's a good place to park, stretch your legs, and find a cup of coffee or a snack.

Visitors who'd prefer a more scenic, less commercial route bypassing North Conway's strip malls should detour to **West Side Road.** Arriving from the south, turn north at the light in Conway Village on to Washington Street. One-half mile farther, bear left on West Side Road. The road passes near two covered bridges in the first half-mile, then dips and winds through the broad farmlands of the Saco River Valley. You'll pass working farms and farmstands, and some architecturally distinctive early homes.

You'll also come upon dramatic views of the granite cliffs that form the western wall of the valley. Stop for a swim at **Echo Lake State Park** (it's well-marked, on your left). At the first stop sign, turn right for North Conway Village, or turn left to connect to Route 302 in Bartlett, passing more ledges and cliffs.

ESSENTIALS

GETTING THERE North Conway and Mt. Washington Valley are on Route 16 and Route 302. Route 16 connects to the Spaulding Turnpike outside of Portsmouth, N.H. Route 302 begins in Portland, Me.

VISITOR INFORMATION The **Mt. Washington Valley Chamber of Commerce,** P.O. Box 2300, North Conway, NH 03860 (☎ **800/367-3364** or 603/ 356-3171), operates a seasonal information booth opposite the village green with brochures about attractions and inns. The staff can arrange for accommodations. It's open daily in summer (Monday to Friday 9am to 6pm, and weekends 9am to 8pm). In winter it's open weekends only.

The state of New Hampshire also operates an **information booth** with rest rooms and telephones at a vista with fine views of Mt. Washington on Routes 16 and 302 north of North Conway.

The White Mountains & Lake Country

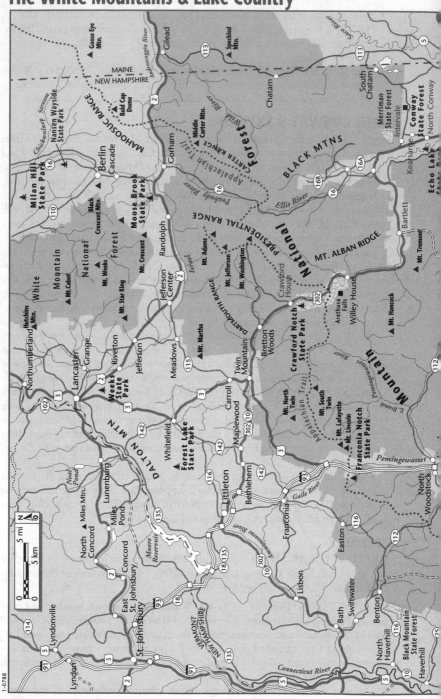

1-0788

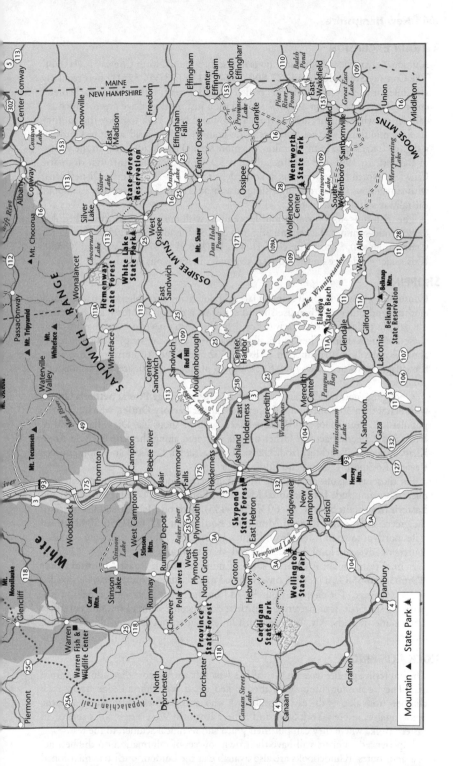

Mountain ▲   State Park ✦

A Train Excursion

A unique way to view the mountainous landscape around North Conway is via train. The **Conway Scenic Railroad** (☎ **800/232-5251** or 603/356-5251) offers regularly scheduled trips in comfortable cars pulled by either steam train or sleek early diesel engine. Trips depart from an 1874 train station just off the village green, which recalls an era when tourists arrived from Boston and New York to enjoy the country air for a month or two each summer. One-hour excursions head south to Conway; a slightly longer (and in my opinion, far more scenic) trip heads north to the village of Bartlett. In 1995 the rail line added a 5^{1}/$_{2}$-hour excursion through dramatic Crawford Notch (I think of this as equivalent to the old "A" ticket at Disneyland), with stupendous views from high along this beautiful glacial valley. Ask also about the railway's dining excursions.

The train runs April through mid-December, with more frequent trips scheduled daily in mid-summer. Tickets are $8.50 to $16.50 for adults ($31.95 to $36.95 for Crawford Notch), $5 to $7 for children 4 to 12 ($16.95 to $21.95 Crawford Notch). Kids under 4 ride free on the Conway trip only. Reservations are advised.

Shopping

Consumers who get themselves into a lather about saving a few bucks on name-brand clothing and other merchandise should schedule a day or two for raking through the bargain racks of North Conway's outlets. You won't have to search hard to find these 200-plus shops. They're readily apparent along "the strip," which extends about 3 miles from the junction of Route 302 and Route 16 north of Conway to the village of North Conway itself. It's a town planner's nightmare, but a shopper's paradise.

Among the more notable outlet clusters are **Outlet Village Plus at Settler's Green,** with better than 30 name-brand shops; the **Tanger Factory Outlet,** which hosts the popular L.L. Bean shop; and **Willow Place,** with 11 shops like Dress Barn, Bed & Bath, and Lingerie Factory. Other outlets scattered along the strip include Anne Klein, American Tourister, Izod, Dansk, Donna Karan, Levi's, Polo/Ralph Lauren, Reebok/Rockport, J. Crew, and Eddie Bauer.

For those setting out on a White Mountain expedition, outdoor equipment suppliers in town include **International Mountain Equipment** (☎ **603/356-7013**) and **Eastern Mountain Sports** (☎ **603/356-5433**), both on Main Street just north of the green. There's also **Ragged Mountain Equipment** (☎ **603/356-3042**), three miles north of town in Intervale on Routes 16 and 302. All three shops are excellent sources of advice on local destinations and weather conditions.

A final testimonial: A favorite shop of mine is **Chuck Roast Mountainwear** (☎ **603/356-5589**), a North Conway–based manufacturer of outerwear, backpacks, and soft luggage. The daypack I purchased from them five years ago has held up superbly despite constant battering. All their goods come with a lifetime guarantee. Their outlet is at the Mt. Washington Outlet Center, not far from the L.L. Bean outlet.

Rock Climbing

The impressive granite faces on the valley's west side are for more than admiring from afar. They're also for climbing. Cathedral Ledge and Whitehorse Ledge attract rock climbers from all over the eastern seaboard, who consider these cliffs (along with the Shawangunks in New York State and Seneca Rocks in West Virginia) as sort of an eastern troika where they can put their grace and technical acumen to the test.

Experienced climbers will have their own sources of information on the best access and routes. (Guidebooks are also available at the outdoor outfitters mentioned above.) Inexperienced climbers should sign up for a class taught by one of the local outfitters, whose workshops run from one day to one week. Try the **Eastern Mountain Sports Climbing School** (☎ 603/356-5433), the **International Mountain Climbing School** (☎ 603/356-7064), or the **Mountain Guides Alliance** (☎ 603/356-5310).

To tone up or keep in shape on rainy days, the **Cranmore Sports Center** (☎ 603/356-6301) near the Mt. Cranmore base lodge has an indoor climbing wall open weekdays 5 to 9pm and weekends 2 to 8pm. The fee is $12, plus a one-time $5 belay test for newcomers. Private, semi-private, and group lessons are also available.

SKIING

Mt. Cranmore. North Conway Village, NH 03860. ☎ **603/356-5544.** Vertical drop: 1,200 feet. Lifts: 6 chairlifts (1 high-speed quad), 4 surface lifts. Skiable acreage: 190. Lift tickets: Adults $39 weekend, $29 midweek; $20 and $15 for children under 12.

Mt. Cranmore is within walking distance of downtown North Conway, although I wouldn't dare try it in ski boots. The oldest operating ski area in New England, Mt. Cranmore is unrepentantly old-fashioned, and doesn't display an iota of pretense. It's not likely to challenge advanced skiers, but it will delight beginners and intermediates, as well as those who like the old-style New England cut of the ski trails.

In a bit of disingenuous hype, Mt. Cranmore is being marketed jointly with **Attitash Bear Peak** as "New Hampshire's largest ski area," despite the fact that Attitash Bear Peak is 10 miles from Cranmore. (The brochures make it look as if you can practically ski from one to the other.) Lift tickets from Attitash are transferable, however, so you can begin at the more challenging peaks of Attitash Bear Peak, take a few cruiser runs at Cranmore in the afternoon, then set out for outlet shopping in the pretwilight hours.

WHERE TO STAY

Route 16 through North Conway is packed with basic motels that are reasonably priced in the off-season, but may be pricey during peak travel times such as fall foliage. Fronting the commercial strip, these motels don't offer much in the way of a pastoral environment, but most are comfortable and conveniently located. Try the **School House Motel** (☎ 603/356-6829), with a heated outdoor pool; **The Yankee Clipper Motor Lodge** (☎ 800/343-5900 or 603/356-5736), with a pool and mini-golf; or the slightly more pricey **Green Granite Motel** (☎ 800/468-3666 or 603/356-6901), with whirlpool suites, 88 rooms, and a free continental breakfast.

Expensive

Four Points Hotel. Rte. 16 at Settler's Green (P.O. Box 3189), North Conway, NH 03860. ☎ **800/648-4397** or 603/356-9300. 200 rms. A/C TV TEL. Summer $89–$179 double; foliage season $105–$215 double; off-season $69–$149 double. AE, CB, DC, DISC, MC, V.

If you're looking for convenience, modern amenities, and easy access to outlet shopping, this Sheraton-run hotel is your best bet. Built in 1990 on the site of North Conway's old airfield, the Four Points is a four-story, gabled hotel adjacent (and architecturally similar) to Outlet Village Plus, one of the two or three million outlet centers based in North Conway. The Four Points offers impeccably clean, comfortable, basic hotel rooms.

Facilities: Guests have access to a pleasing brick-terraced indoor pool and Jacuzzi. Other extras include tennis courts, an outdoor pool, a fitness room, an above-average restaurant and tavern, and kids' karaoke nights.

Red Jacket Inn. Rte. 16 (P.O. Box 2000), North Conway, NH 03860. ☎ **800-752-2538** or 603/356-5411. Fax 603/356-3842. 164 rms. A/C TV TEL. $89–$154 double, depending on season, time of week, and view. AE, DC, DISC, MC, V.

Set high on a grassy ridge overlooking the Saco Valley, the Red Jacket Inn is a 1970s-era resort that avoided that dated disco-era look through constant renovations. A modern, two-story building with two wings flanking a reception area, dining room, and indoor pool, the Red Jacket presents a quiet oasis on 30 acres above the hubbub of the highway. The spacious guest rooms are nicely furnished with colonial reproductions, and many offer private patios or balconies. If the weather's nice, splurge on a mountain-view room and enjoy the vistas of the Moat Mountains across the valley.

Dining/Entertainment: As for food, you're better off exploring locally. The resort's Champey's Restaurant is a rather dim and gloomy affair overdue for renovation. Not even wonderful views and a decent menu can enliven the atmosphere.

Facilities: The grounds are handsomely landscaped, and guests can entertain themselves at the swimming pool and tennis courts.

Stonehurst Manor. Rte. 16 (1.2 miles north of North Conway village; P.O. Box 1937), North Conway, NH 03860. ☎ **800/525-9100** or 603/356-3271. 24 rms (2 with shared bath, some with showers only). A/C TV. $75–$125 double ($20–$30 surcharge during foliage season); $96–$156 double with breakfast and dinner included. MC, V.

The Stonehurst Manor seems determined to confound expectations. This imposing, eclectic Victorian stone-and-shingle mansion, set amid white pines on a rocky knoll above Route 16, wouldn't seem at all out of place in the south of France or on the moors of Scotland. The immediate assumption is that it caters to the stuffy and affluent. But don't assume. The main focus here is on outdoor adventure vacations, and it attracts a youngish crowd. The restaurant makes the best wood-fired pizza in the area (see "Where to Dine," below). And the rates aren't nearly as prohibitive as you might expect.

My advice is to request one of the 14 rooms in the regal 1876 mansion itself (another 10 are in a comfortable but less elegant wing built in 1952). These mansion rooms are all unique and furnished appropriately to the building's era. Room 21A, for instance, one of the nicest in the inn, has stained-glass windows and a wicker-furnished private porch with sunset views toward Humphrey's Ledge. It's easy to slip into a fantasy that you're the guest of the Bigelow carpet tycoons—the wealthy Victorians who originally built this endearing edifice. Relax and enjoy it.

✪ **White Mountain Hotel and Resort.** West Side Rd. (5.4 miles W of North Conway; P.O. Box 1828), North Conway, NH 03860. ☎ **800/533-6301** or 603/356-7100. 80 rms. A/C TV TEL. Summer $89–$179 double; foliage season $109–$189 double; winter $69–$139 double; off-season $59–$119 double. AE, DISC, MC, V.

This modern, upscale resort has the best location of any choice in the North Conway area. Sited at the base of dramatic White Horse Ledge near Echo Lake State Park and amid a new golf course community, the White Mountain Hotel was built in 1990 but borrows from the rich legacy of classic White Mountain resorts. Its designers have managed to take some of the more successful elements of a friendly country inn—a nice deck with a view, comfortable seating in the lobby, a clubby tavern area—and incorporate it into a thoroughly modern resort. The tones throughout are muted and rich, and overall sensibility seems more influenced by a European elegance than early American rusticity.

Guest rooms are comfortably appointed with dark wood and an earthy maroon carpeting, and are a solid notch or two above standard hotel furnishings. Mini-suites offer a bit more elbow room and small refrigerators.

Facilities: Fitness center, heated outdoor pool, and Jacuzzi.

Moderate

🅢 **Cranmore Inn.** 80 Kearsarge St., North Conway, NH 03860. ☎ **800/526-5502** or 603/356-5502. 18 rms, 14 with private bath (some hall baths, some with showers only). Summer

$56–$74 double; foliage season and ski weekends $69–$84 double; off-season $44–$59 double. Rates include full breakfast. AE, MC, V.

The Cranmore Inn has the feel of a 19th-century boarding house—which is appropriate, since that's what it is. Open since 1863, this three-story Victorian home is hidden on a side street a short walk from North Conway's main attractions. Its distinguished heritage (it's the oldest continuously operating hotel in North Conway) adds considerable charm and quirkiness, but comes with some minor drawbacks, like uneven water pressure in the showers and some sinks with cracked or stained enamel. During my last visit, I had a window that wouldn't stay up and a windowshade that wouldn't stay down. You should ask to see your room before you hand over your credit card.

That said, I'd return here in a second because of its charm, its graciousness, and the good humor of the innkeepers (all the more remarkable since they've been running the place for more than a dozen years, which is about 175 in innkeeper's years). The inn also has nice details like guests' names on placecards at breakfast in the dining room. The old-fashioned downstairs parlors are great for cribbage or mingling with other guests; the front porch allows you to monitor the rather sedate comings and goings of Kearsarge Street.

Inexpensive

Albert B. Lester Memorial Hostel. 36 Washington St., Conway, NH 03818. ☎ 603/447-1001. 45 beds. $16 per person. Rates include continental breakfast. JCB, MC, V. Closed Apr 1–15; Nov 20–26; Dec 18–25. Turn N at the light in Conway on Washington St.; it's the third house on the left.

Conveniently situated near the center of Conway Village, the Lester Hostel is the best choice for those traveling on a shoestring but not enamored of camping. Rooms in this gracious black-and-white farmhouse are set up hostel-style and accommodate 45 people (some family rooms are available), but guests, many of whom are young Europeans, generally spend their time in the yard knocking around a volleyball or availing themselves of the barbecue. Not only will you save money here, but the congenial atmosphere is a great way to swap tips on area trails and attractions with newfound friends. The hostel is open for check-in or check-out daily 7:30am to 9:30am, and 5 to 10pm.

WHERE TO DINE

Bellini's. 33 Seavey St., North Conway. ☎ 603/356-7000. Reservations not accepted. Main courses $9.95–$18.95. AE, DC, DISC, MC, V. Sun–Thurs 5–10pm, Fri–Sat 5–11pm. Closed 2 weeks in Nov and 2 weeks during mud season. ITALIAN.

Bellini's has a fun, quirky interior that's more informal than its Victorian exterior might suggest. Inside it features Cinzano umbrellas and striped awnings, black-and-white checkerboard floors, and huge potted plants—it's the kind of place to put you in a good mood right off. And the food, which runs the Italian gamut from fettuccini chicken pesto to braciola, can only but further improve your spirits. The pleasantly garlicky marinara sauce is only a notch above average, but much of the rest of the fare shines brighter. Particularly good are the toasted raviolis. This is a great place to sup with a gaggle of friends or your extended family, but a moon-eyed couple might also find a quiet niche to make a romantic evening of it.

Stonehurst Manor. Rte. 16 (1.2 miles N of the village), North Conway. ☎ 800/525-9100 or 603/356-3113. Reservations recommended. Main courses $7.75–$21; pizza $8.95–$12.95. MC, V. Daily 6–10pm. AMERICAN/PIZZA.

It's likely these are the most elegant surroundings in which you'll ever consume a pizza. Wood-fired pizza was added to the menu about a decade ago, just ahead of the national trend, when the restaurant noticed inn guests arriving late from Boston didn't feel up to a full meal. So they added pizza in a number of elegant variations (chicken sausage and wild mushrooms; lobster, shrimp and calamari), and the word spread. The pizza became a local institution, complementing the other superb dishes served here.

Diners have a choice of four dining areas on the first floor of this sumptuous 1876 mansion, and each area is decorated informally and comfortably. (In the summer, head for the screened patio overlooking the garden.) In addition to pizza, the chef serves up a raft of other creative dishes, including wood-fired roast duck with blackberry sauce, and baked haddock in parchment with vegetables. If you have a lighter appetite, try the slightly bizarre but tasty crab and artichoke sandwich served on a soft pretzel.

JACKSON & ENVIRONS

Situated in a picturesque valley just off Route 16 about 15 minutes' drive north of North Conway, Jackson is an eddy swirling gently on its own, just out of the flow of the tourist mainstream. You enter Jackson, somewhat tentatively, on a single-lane covered bridge. The village center is tiny, but touches of Old World elegance remain here and there—vestiges of a time when Jackson was a premier destination for the East Coast affluent, who fled the summer heat in the cities to board at rambling wooden hotels or retire to shingled country estates.

With the depression and the subsequent rise of the motel trade in the 1940s and 1950s, Jackson and its old-fashioned hostelries slipped into a decades-long quiet slumber. Then along came the 1980s, which brought developers winging in and out of the valley in private helicopters, condo projects sprouting in fields where cows once roamed, and the resuscitation of a few vintage wooden hotels that didn't burn or collapse during the dark ages.

Thanks to a new golf course and one of the most elaborate and well-maintained cross-country ski networks in the country, Jackson is today again a thriving resort in summer and winter. It's still out of the mainstream, and a peaceful spot quite distant in character from more commercial North Conway. Settle into one of the old summer homes converted to an inn, park your feet on a porch rail, and you'll notice that not all that much has changed in the intervening century.

ESSENTIALS

GETTING THERE   Jackson is just off Route 16 about 11 miles north of North Conway. Look for the covered bridge on the right when heading north.

VISITOR INFORMATION   The **Jackson Chamber of Commerce,** P.O. Box 304, Jackson, NH 03846 (☎ **800/866-3334** or 603/383-9356), can answer your questions about lodging and attractions.

EXPLORING MT. WASHINGTON

Mt. Washington is home to a number of superlatives. At 6,288 feet it's the highest mountain in the Northeast. (Mt. Mitchell in North Carolina is slightly higher, robbing Mt. Washington of the "highest in the east" title.) It's said to have the worst weather in the world outside of the polar regions. And it holds the world's record for the highest surface wind speed—231 miles per hour, set in 1934. Consider also that winds over 150 miles per hour are routinely recorded every month except June, July, and August, the result of the mountain's location at the confluence of three major storm tracks.

Mt. Washington may also be the mountain with the most routes to the summit. Visitors can ascend by cog railroad (see the "Crawford Notch" section, "Where to Stay & Dine"), by car, by van, or by foot. There's an annual bike race and foot race to the summit, and each year winter mountaineers test their mettle by inching their way to the top equipped with crampons and ice axes.

The summit of Mt. Washington is a well-developed place, and not the best destination for those seeking brutish wilderness. There's a train platform, a parking lot, a snack bar, a gift shop, a museum, and a handful of outbuildings, some of which house the weather observatory, which is staffed year-round. And there are the crowds, which can be thick on a clear day. Then again, on a clear day the views can't be beat, with vistas extending into four states and to the Atlantic Ocean.

The best place to learn about Mt. Washington and its approaches is the **Pinkham Notch Camp** (☎ 603/466-2721), operated by the Boston-based Appalachian Mountain Club. Located at the crest of Route 16 between Jackson and Gorham, Pinkham Notch offers overnight accommodations and meals (see "Where to Stay & Dine," below), maps, a limited selection of outdoor supplies, and plenty of advice from helpful staff. A number of hiking trails depart from Pinkham Notch, allowing for several loops and side trips.

About a dozen trails lead to the mountain's summit, ranging in length from 3.8 to 15 miles. (See Peter Randall's *Mount Washington: A Guide and Short History,* mentioned in the "Specialized Guides" section, for details.) The most direct and, in many ways, most dramatic trail is the **Tuckerman Ravine Trail,** which departs from Pinkham Notch. Healthy hikers should allow four to five hours for the ascent, an hour or two less for the return trip. Be sure to schedule in time to enjoy the dramatic glacial cirque of **Tuckerman Ravine,** which attracts extreme skiers to its snowy chutes and sheer drops as late as June, and often holds patches of snow well into summer.

The **Mt. Washington Auto Road** (☎ 603/466-3988) opened in 1861 as a carriage road, and since then has been one of the most popular White Mountain attractions. The steep, winding 8-mile road (it has an average grade of 12%) is partially paved and incredibly dramatic; your breath will be taken away at one turn after another. The ascent will test your iron will; the descent will test your car's brakes. If you're nervous at all, consider that there have been only two fatalities in more than a century, attesting to the road's sound engineering.

If you'd prefer to leave the driving to some one else, custom vans ascend regularly allowing you to relax, enjoy the views, learn about the mountain from informed guides, and leave the fretting about overheating brakes to someone else.

The **Auto Road,** which is on Route 16 north of Pinkham Notch, is open mid-May to late October from 7:30am to 6pm (shorter hours early and late in the season). The cost for cars is $15 for vehicle and driver, and $6 for each additional passenger ($4 for children 5 to 12). The fee includes use of an audiocassette featuring a narrator pointing out sights along the way. Van rates are $20 for adults; $10 for children 5 to 12.

One additional note: The *average* temperature atop the mountain is 30 degrees. (The record low was –43 degrees, and the warmest temperature *ever* recorded atop the mountain, in August, was 72 degrees.) Even in summer visitors should come prepared for blustery, cold conditions.

If you'd prefer to observe Mt. Washington from a safe and respectful distance, head up **Wildcat Mountain** (☎ 800/255-6439 or 603/466-3326) on the enclosed gondola for a superb view of Tuckerman Ravine and Mt. Washington's summit. The lift operates weekends from Memorial Day to mid-June, then daily through October. The base lodge is located just north of Pinkham Notch on Route 16.

CROSS-COUNTRY SKIING

Jackson regularly makes rankings of the top five cross-country ski resorts in the nation, and there's one reason for that: the nonprofit **Jackson Ski Touring**

Foundation (☎ 603/383-9355), which created and now maintains the extensive trail network. The terrain around Jackson is wonderfully varied, with 93 miles of trails maintained by the foundation (56 miles are regularly groomed).

Start at the foundation headquarters in the middle of Jackson, then head right out the back door and ski through the village. Gentle trails traverse the valley floor, with more advanced trails heading up the flanking mountains. Snowmaking blankets 2.6 acres in the valley, helping to extend the season and keep conditions up to par. One-way ski trips with shuttles back to Jackson are also available; ask if you're interested. Trail fees are $10 for adults, $5 for children 10 to 15, and free for children under 10. Ski rentals are available at the Jack Frost ski shop adjacent to the ski center.

ALPINE SKIING

Black Mountain. Jackson, NH 03846. ☎ 800/475-4669 or 603/383-4490. Vertical drop: 1,100 feet. Lifts: 4. Skiable acreage: 98. Lift tickets: Weekend $30 adult, $20 junior; weekdays $14 all.

Dating back to the 1930s, Black Mountain is one of the White Mountains' pioneer ski areas. It remains the quintessential family mountain—modest in size, entirely non-threatening, and perfect for beginners. It offers some great views from the top to boot. It feels a bit like you're skiing in a farmer's unused hayfield, which just adds to the charm. The original lift was a tow where skiers held on to shovel handles to get to the top.

Wildcat. Rte 16, Pinkham Notch, NH 03846. ☎ **800/255-6439** or 603/466-3326. Internet http://www.skiwildcat.com. Vertical drop: 2,100 feet. Lifts: 1 gondola, 5 chairlifts. Skiable acreage: 120. Lift tickets: Weekends and holidays $37 adults, $22 juniors (6–12); midweek $25 adults, $19 juniors (6–12).

Wildcat Mountain has a strong heritage as a venerable New England ski mountain. It also happens to offer the best mountain views of any ski area in the Whites. Situated on national forest land just across the valley from Mt. Washington and Tuckerman Ravine, Wildcat has strong intermediate trails and some challenging expert slopes, including a newly cut double diamond with 60% drops. This is skiing as it used to be—there's no base area clutter, just a simple ski lodge. While there's no on-slope accommodations, you've got an abundance of choices within 15 minutes' drive. Spend the night bunkhouse-style just up the road at AMC's Pinkham Notch Camp, or enjoy the luxury comforts of Jackson's inns. A short trip to the north is the unassuming town of Gorham, which offers several good motels at accommodating rates and a handful of basic-fare restaurants.

KID STUFF

Parents with young children who find majestic mountains only slightly less interesting than veal aspic can buy brief peace of mind at two area attractions. **Story Land,** at the northern junction of Routes 16 and 302 (☎ 603/383-4293), is filled with improbably leaning buildings, magical rides, fairy-tale creatures, and other enchanted beings. Kids can take a ride in a Pumpkin Coach, float in a swan boat, ride the watery "Bamboo Chute," or spin on a lively carousel. A new "sprayground" opened in 1996, featuring a 40-foot happy octopus—if they're so inclined, kids can get a good summer soaking. Live shows and snacks easily fill out an afternoon. Story Land is open mid-June through Labor Day daily 9am to 6pm, and Labor Day to Columbus Day on weekends from 10am to 5pm. Admission, which includes all rides and entertainment, is $16 for visitors over 4 years old.

Next door is **Heritage New Hampshire** (☎ 603/383-9776), which endeavors to make state history easily digestible for both adults and kids. It's an indoor theme park in a Georgian-style building with a theme of old-time New Hampshire. Visitors learn about the famous Concord Coach and hear prominent politician Daniel Webster "speak" about his life and times. You'll come away with some context for the rest of your stay in the state. The museum is open mid-May to mid-October daily 9am until 5pm (until 6pm mid-June to Labor Day). Admission is $8 adults, $4.50 children 6 to 12, and free under 6.

WHERE TO STAY & DINE

Eagle Mountain House. Carter Notch Rd., Jackson, NH 03846. ☎ **800/966-5779** or 603/383-9111. Fax 603/383-0854. 93 rms. TV TEL. $79–$149 double; $109–$169 suite. AE, DC, DISC, MC, V.

The Eagle Mountain House is a fine and handsome relic that happily survived the ravages of time, fire, and the capricious tastes of tourists. Built in 1916 and fully renovated in 1986, this five-story wooden classic is set in an idyllic valley above the village of Jackson. The lobby is rich with earth tones, polished brass, and oak accenting.

The guest rooms, set off wonderfully wide and creaky hallways, are furnished with a country pine look and feature stencilled blanket chests, pine armoires, and feather comforters. There's a premium for rooms with mountain views, but it's not really worth the extra cash. Just plan to spend your free time lounging on the wide porch with the views across the golf course toward the mountains beyond.

Dining/Entertainment: There's a handsome oak tavern off the lodge. The spacious, formal dining rooms seat about 150 guests, and provoke a distinct "well-here-we-are!" sense of glee when you first settle in for dinner under the high ceilings. The menu features creative New England classics, with offerings like Maine lobster pie and roasted cranberry duck.

Facilities: Other amenities include a nine-hole golf course, lighted tennis courts, a heated outdoor pool, and a small health club.

✪ **Inn at Thorn Hill.** Thorn Hill Rd. (P.O. Box A), Jackson, NH 03846. ☎ **603/383-4242.** 19 rms (some with showers only). $140–$200 double; peak season (foliage and Christmas) $176–$232 double, $230–$275 cottage. All rates include breakfast and dinner. AE, DC, DISC, MC, V.

This is a truly elegant inn. Housed in a classic shingle-style home designed by Stanford White in 1895 (although now swathed in yellow siding), the Inn at Thorn Hill is just outside of town, surrounded by wooded hills that seem to greet it in a warm embrace. Inside, there's a comfortable Victorian feel, although mercifully sparing on the frilly stuff. The two sitting parlors are well-designed for lounging—one boasts a woodstove, piano, and views toward the mountains (cookies and tea are served here in the afternoon). There's also a TV room with jigsaw puzzles and a decent selection of books on the shelves. Classical music is piped throughout.

Dining/Entertainment: The dining room is decorated in what might be called Victorian great-aunt style, with rich green carpeting, press-backed oak chairs, and pink tablecloths. The inn serves some of the best meals in the valley.

The Lodge at Pinkham Notch. Rte. 16, Pinkham Notch, NH (Mailing address: AMC, 5 Joy St., Boston, MA 02108). ☎ **603/466-2727.** 108 beds in bunkrooms of 2, 3, and 4 beds. All have shared bath. Sun to Fri (except Aug) $45 per adult, $27 per child, (discount for AMC members); Sat and Aug, $50 adult, $32 child; all rates include breakfast and dinner. MC, V.

Guests flock to the Pinkham Notch Camp for the camaraderie as much as for the accommodations. Situated spectacularly at the base of Mt. Washington and with easy access to numerous hiking trails, the lodge is operated like a Scandinavian youth hostel, with guests sharing bunk rooms with new friends, and enjoying boisterous, filling meals at long family-style tables in the main lodge. A zealous warden even walks the hallways near dawn beating a pot with a wooden spoon to ensure no slackers try to shirk their obligation to GET UP AND HIKE!

The accommodations are Spartan and basic, but that's overcome by the often festive atmosphere. Think of it as a field trip with a bunch of excitable teens—although the teens in this case often happen to be hardy mountain veterans in their sixties or seventies. In the winter I've been awoken in the predawn darkness by eager mountaineers preparing their ascents in the parking lot to blaring Grateful Dead tapes. In the summer, I've spent hours swapping late-night tips on hiking destinations with grizzled hikers twice my age. It's not a place to be an introvert, but it *is* a place to feel part of the rich heritage of local mountain recreation.

Wentworth Resort Hotel. Jackson, NH 03846. ☎ **800/637-0013** or 603/383-9700. Fax 603/383-4265. 58 rms. A/C TV TEL. Weekdays $59–$119 double; weekends $89–$159 double. Higher rates during foliage season and Christmas week; discounts available Mar to mid-June. AE, MC, V.

The venerable Wentworth sits in the middle of Jackson Village, all turrets and eaves and awnings. Built in 1869, this Victorian shingled inn edged to the brink of deterioration in the mid-1980s, but was pulled back by a plucky entrepreneur, who added a number of condominiums clustered around the golf course. The large guest rooms are good value for the money, decorated with a Victorian grace and elegance. Some rooms feature fireplaces, whirlpools, or clawfoot tubs.

Dining/Entertainment: The dining room is well-respected, serving up regional favorites like garlic and herb chicken and char-grilled salmon.

Facilities: It's no challenge to find something to do in the area. The inn has its own century-old, 18-hole PGA golf course, clay tennis courts, billiards (on an enclosed porch), and close proximity to hiking. For swimming, there's an outdoor heated pool, or you can stroll just up the road and plunge into the cold waters of Jackson Falls. In winter, you can cross-country ski out the door.

Wildcat Inn & Tavern. Rte. 16A, Jackson, NH 03846. ☎ **800/228-4245** or 603/383-4245. 15 rms, some with shower only, 2 with hall bathrooms. $84–$114 double. Rates include breakfast. AE, DC, MC, V.

The Wildcat Inn occupies a three-story farmhouse-style building in the middle of Jackson, directly across from the cross-country ski center. It's a comfortable, informal kind of place, better known for its restaurant and tavern than for its accommodations. Most guest rooms are cozy, two-room suites, carpeted and furnished eclectically. Sitting rooms typically contain contemporary sofas, chairs, and pine furniture, and offer cozy sanctuary after a day of hiking or skiing.

Dining/Entertainment: The downstairs dining room is in country farmhouse–style, with old wood floors and pine furniture. Country-style meals are prepared with considerable flair, and include a tenderloin of beef topped with lobster, asparagus, and Hollandaise sauce (main courses are $14.95 to $20.95). In the winter, the smart money stakes out a toasty spot in front of the tavern fireplace—one of the most popular gathering spots in the valley—to sip soothing libations and order from the bar menu, which has lighter fare like chicken quesadillas and spanakopita ($6.95 to $8.95).

CRAWFORD NOTCH

Crawford Notch is a wild, rugged mountain valley that runs through the heart of the White Mountains. Within the notch itself lies a lot of legend and history. For years after its discovery by Timothy Nash in 1771, it was an impenetrable wilderness, creating a barrier to commerce by blocking trade between the upper Connecticut River

Valley and commercial harbors in Portland and Portsmouth. That was eventually surmounted by a plucky crew who hauled the first freight through.

As the traffic picked up, the Crawford family offered lodging to the first teamsters, and later to the tourists who flocked here to experience the sublime feelings of raw nature. The Crawfords also led tours to the summit of Mt. Washington, and built the first horseback trail.

Nathaniel Hawthorne immortalized the notch with his short story about a real-life 1826 tragedy, in which the Willey family fled their home during a tempest when they heard an avalanche roaring toward the valley floor. The avalanche divided above the inn and spared the structure; the seven who fled were killed in tumbling debris. The only survivors were the family dog and two oxen. (You can still visit the site of the Willey home today.)

The notch is accessible along Route 302, which is wide and speedy on the lower sections, and becomes challenging only in its steepness as it approaches the narrow defile of the notch itself. (Modern engineering has taken most of the kinks out of the road.) The views up the cliffs from the road can be spectacular on a clear day; on an overcast or drizzly day, the effect is slightly foreboding and medieval.

ESSENTIALS

GETTING THERE   Route 302 runs through Crawford Notch about 25 miles from the towns of Bartlett and Twin Mountain.

VISITOR INFORMATION   **Twin Mountain Chamber of Commerce,** P.O. Box 194, Twin Mountain, NH 03595 (☎ **800/245-8946** or 603/846-5407), offers general information and lodging referrals at their information booth near the intersection of Routes 302 and 3. Open year-round, but hours are shorter in the off-season.

WATERFALLS & SWIMMING HOLES

Much of the land flanking Route 302 falls under the auspices of **Crawford Notch State Park,** which was established in 1911 to preserve land that elsewhere had been decimated by aggressive logging. The headwaters of the Saco River form in the notch, and what's generally regarded as the first permanent trail up Mt. Washington also departs from here. Several turnouts and trail heads invite a more leisurely exploration of the area. The trail network on both sides of Crawford Notch is extensive; consult the *AMC White Mountain Guide* for detailed information.

Engorged by snowmelt in the spring, the Saco River courses through the notch's granite ravines and winds past sizable boulders that have been left by retreating glaciers and crashed down from the mountainsides above. It's a popular destination among serious white-water boaters, and makes for a good spectator sport if you're here early in the season. During the lazy days of summer, the Saco offers several good swimming holes just off the highway. They're unmarked, but where you see cars parked off the side of the road for no apparent reason, you should be able to find your way to a good spot for soaking and splashing.

Up the mountain slopes that form the valley, hikers will spot a number of superb waterfalls, some more easily accessible than others. A day spent exploring the falls is a day well spent. A few to start with:

Arethusa Falls has the highest single drop of any waterfall in the state, and the trail to the falls passes several attractive smaller cascades en route. These are especially beautiful in the spring or after a heavy rain, when the falls are at their fullest. The trip can be done as a 2.6-mile round-trip to the falls and back on Arethusa Falls Trail, or as a 4.5-mile loop hike that includes views from stunning Frankenstein Cliffs.

If you're arriving from the south, look for signs to the trail parking area shortly after passing the Crawford Notch State Park entrance sign. From the north, the trail head is one-half mile south of the Dry River Campground. At the parking lot, look for the sign and map to get your bearings, then cross the railroad tracks to start up the falls trail.

Another hike begins a short drive north on Route 302. Reaching tumultuous **Ripley Falls** requires an easy hike of a little more than one mile round-trip. Look for the sign to the falls on Route 302 just north of the trailhead for Webster Cliff Trail. (If you pass the Willey House site, you've gone too far.) Drive in a bit and park at the site of the Willey Station. Follow trail signs for the Ripley Falls Trail, and allow about a half-hour to reach the cascades. The most appealing swimming holes are at the top of the falls.

Two attractive falls may be seen from the roadway at the head of the notch, just east of the crest. **Flume Cascades** and **Silver Cascades** tumble down the hills in white braids that are especially appealing during a misty summer rain. These falls were among the most popular sites in the region when tourists alighted at the train station about one mile away. They aren't nearly as spectacular as the two mentioned above, but they're accessible if you're in a hurry. Travelers can park in the lots along the road's edge for a better view.

A HISTORIC RAILWAY

Mt. Washington Cog Railway. Rte. 302, Bretton Woods. ☎ 800/922-8825 or 603/846-5404. Fare $35 adults, $24 children 6–12, under 5 free. Runs daily Memorial Day through late Oct, plus weekends in May. Frequent departures; call for schedule. Reservations recommended during peak season.

The cog railway was a marvel of engineering when it opened in 1869, and it remains so today. Part moving museum, part slow-motion roller-coaster ride, the cog railway steams to the summit with a determined "I think I can" pace of about four miles per hour. But there's still a frisson of excitement on the way up and back, especially when the train crosses Jacob's Ladder, a rickety-seeming trestle 25 feet high that angles upward at a grade of more than 37%. Passengers enjoy the expanding view in relative comfort on this three-hour round-trip (there are stops to add water to the steam engine, to check the track switches, and to allow other trains to ascend or descend). There's also a 20-minute stop at the summit to browse around.

It's hard to imagine anyone not enjoying this trip—from kids marveling at the ratchtety-ratchety noises and the thick plume of black smoke, to curious adults trying to figure out how the cog system works, to naturalists who get superb views of the boney, brawny uplands leading to Mt. Washington's summit.

SKIING

Attitash Bear Peak. Rte. 302, Bartlett, NH 03812. ☎ 800/223-7669 or 603/374-2368. Vertical drop: 1,750 feet. Lifts: 10 chairlifts (including 1 high-speed quad), 1 surface lift. Skiable acreage: 214. Lift tickets: $43 weekends and holidays, $35 weekdays.

Attitash expanded in 1994 to include the adjacent 1,000-foot-high Bear Peak. The new area includes five trails and some new base facilities, which has taken some pressure off the main lift lines. Attitash is a good intermediate-to-advanced skier mountain with a selection of great cruising runs and a few that are somewhat more challenging. The base lodge is modern if unexciting. There's not much happening locally at night, so those still looking for action typically head to North Conway.

The ski area also offers a smart ticket program, which allows skiers to buy as many "points" as they'd like on a ticket. Points are deducted for each run (more points on weekends and on longer lifts). The advantage? If conditions deteriorate or if you're seized by the urge to shop in North Conway, you can do so then use up the rest of your points the next day. Points can also be transferred to others and are good for two years from date of purchase.

Bretton Woods. Rte. 302, Bretton Woods, NH 03575. ☎ **800/232-2972** or 603/278-5000. Vertical drop: 1,500 feet. Lifts: 4 chairlifts (including 1 high-speed quad), 1 surface lift. Skiable acreage: 150. Lift ticket: Adults $38 weekends and holidays, $31 weekdays; children 6–15 $25 weekends and holidays, $15 midweek.

Bretton Woods is a solid beginner-to-intermediate mountain with great views of Mt. Washington and a pleasant family atmosphere. The resort does a good job with kids, and offers some nice intermediate cruising runs and limited night skiing. There's even a speedy detachable quad chair, which skiers don't often find at resorts of this size. Accommodations are available on the mountain and nearby, but evening entertainment tends to revolve around hot tubs, TVs, and going to bed early. There's also an excellent cross-country ski center nearby.

WHERE TO STAY & DINE

The Bernerhof. Rte. 302, Glen, NH 03838. ☎ **800/548-8007** or 603/383-4414. Fax 603/383-0809. 9 rms. A/C TV TEL. $69–$139 double including full breakfast; $119–$189 double including breakfast and dinner. Two-night minimum during peak season. AE, MC, V.

Situated off busy Route 302 en route to Crawford Notch, The Bernerhof occupies a century-old home that's all gables and turrets on the outside. Inside, the guest rooms are equally eclectic and fun, crafted with odd angles and corners. All are tastefully furnished in an elegant country style that's sparing with the frou-frou. Head for the roomy suites on the third floor—Room 8 is especially wonderful, with a Jacuzzi under a skylight, wood floors, a brass bed, and a handsome cherry armoire.

Dining/Entertainment: Downstairs, the rustic Black Bear Pub is all oakey and mellow—the type of place where you can relax with aplomb. There's a bearskin on the wall and 63 varieties of beers. The decor in the adjacent dining room is less inspired, but the food is superb and draws gourmands for miles. (The inn also hosts regular cooking schools.) Middle European fare, including several delicious veal dishes, is the specialty, but other creative entrees are available, like the chicken wallbanger, the inn's "moderately famous" dish of chicken breast layered with pesto, ham, and smoked gouda cheese. Dining is open to the public nightly, with entrees ranging from $15.95 to $21.95.

Mount Washington Hotel. Rte. 302, Bretton Woods, NH 03575. ☎ **800/258-0330** or 603/278-1000. 195 rms (6 with shower only). TEL. Midweek $185–$280 double, up to $585 suite; weekends and holidays $225–$315 double, up to $585 suite. All rates include breakfast and dinner. AE, DISC, MC, V. Closed mid-Oct to mid-May.

Your first response to the Mount Washington Hotel will likely be one of disbelief. It seems as if some bizarre Edwardian glacier had flowed down from the mountains and settled resolutely in the valley. This five-story wooden resort, with its gleaming white clapboard and cherry-red roof, seems something out of a fable. Built in 1902 by railroad and coal magnate Joseph Stickney ("Look at me gentlemen . . . for I am the poor fool who built all this," he said at the grand opening), the resort attracted luminaries in its glory days like Babe Ruth, Thomas Edison, Woodrow Wilson, and silent screen star Mary Pickford.

After large resorts fell out of fashion, the Mount Washington went through a succession of owners and fell on hard times. Threatened with demolition and put on the auction block in 1991, it was purchased for just over $3 million by a group of dedicated local business folks who launched the long process of bringing it back from the brink. Being frugal Yankees, they're renovating with operating profit, not with borrowed money, but the improvements are moving along nicely.

The guest rooms are furnished simply but comfortably (TVs are available only on request), but as at most other grand resorts, the Mount Washington was designed around public areas. Wide hallways and elegant common areas on the first floor invite strolling and indolence. A broad 900-foot wraparound veranda makes for relaxing afternoons.

The main hotel is open only seasonally, but three other properties—including a smaller 1896 inn, a motor inn, and contemporary townhomes—are open year-round. All in all, a trip to the Mount Washington is a fanciful trip back in time.

Dining/Entertainment: Meals are enjoyed in the impressive octagonal dining room, which was designed such that no guest would be slighted by being seated in a corner. (Jackets are requested for men at dinner.) In the evening, there's dancing to the house orchestra.

Facilities: 27-hole golf course, 12 red-clay tennis courts, indoor and outdoor pools, stables, game room, gift shop.

✪ **Notchland Inn.** Rte. 302, Hart's Location, NH 03812. ☎ **800/866-6131** or 603/374-6131. Fax 603/374-6168. 11 rms, 7 with shower only. Midweek $150–$170 double, including breakfast and dinner; weekends $170–$190 double; foliage season and holidays $180–$230 double. AE, DISC, MC, V.

The Notchland Inn appears just off the road in a wild, remote section of the valley, looking every bit like a redoubt in a Sir Walter Scott novel. Built of hand-cut granite between 1840 and 1862 by a prosperous Boston dentist, Notchland is today a superior inn perfectly situated for exploring the wilds of the White Mountains by day and basking in luxury at night. All 11 guest rooms are well-appointed with antiques and traditional furniture, and all feature fireplaces, high ceilings, and individual thermostats.

A stay here typically begins with a brief tour of the home, including the common rooms, one of which was remodeled at the turn of the century by Gustav Stickley himself, the father of the Mission style. There are other treasures to be found, like an original oil painting by George L. Frankenstein, the prominent 19th-century artist whose name graces nearby cliffs, and a wood-fired hot tub in a gazebo overlooking a small pond. The Notchland is a no-smoking inn.

Dining/Entertainment: Dinners in the newly renovated dining room are as eclectic as they are well-prepared, and might feature Thai curries, gado-gado (a savory Malaysian salad), or three-pepper-crusted roast beef. Dinners are served at 7pm, and are available to the public (space permitting) at a prix fixe of $30.

WATERVILLE VALLEY & LINCOLN

On the southwestern edge of the White Mountains are two ski resorts tucked away in mountain valleys. Both have blossomed in recent years, not always with favorable results. Waterville Valley, which lies at the end of a 12-mile dead-end road, was the first to be developed. Incorporated as a town in 1829, Waterville Valley became a popular destination for summer travelers during the heyday of mountain travel late in the 19th century. Skiers first started descending the slopes in the 1930s after a few ski trails were hacked out of the forest by the Civilian Conservation Corps and local ski clubs. But it wasn't until 1965, when a skier named Tom Corcoran bought 425 acres in the valley, that Waterville began to assume its current modern air.

While the village has a decidedly manufactured character (it easily has as many parking lots as the average regional mall), Corcoran's vision has kept the growth within bounds. There's not much in the way of sprawl here; the village is reasonably compact, with modern lodges, condos, and restaurants clustered around the "Town Square," itself a sort of mall complex. The architecture is inspired by New England vernacular; there's not a Swiss chalet to be found. The village is also quite pleasant in summer, when the place abounds with outdoor activities like mountain biking, hiking, and swimming.

Some 25 miles to the north is Loon Mountain, which is located just outside the former paper mill town of Lincoln. (That's the distance by major roads in winter; it's shorter in summer by crossing Thornton Gap on Tripoli Road.) The resort was first conceived in the early 1960s by Sherman Adams, a former New Hampshire governor and Eisenhower administration official. The mountain opened in 1966 and was quickly criticized for its mediocre skiing, but continual upgrading and expanding since then has brought the mountain greater respect.

Loon has since evolved from a friendly intermediate mountain served by a few motels to a friendly intermediate mountain served by dozens of condos and vast, modern hotels. Lincoln seems to embrace sprawl with the same zeal Waterville Valley shuns it. At times it seems that Lincoln underwent not so much a development boom in the 1980s as a violent development spasm. Clusters of chicken coop–style homes and condos now blanket the lower hillsides of this narrow valley, and fast-food restaurants and strip mall–style shops line Route 112 from I-93 to the mountain.

The Loon area includes the adjacent towns of Lincoln and North Woodstock on either side of I-93. North Woodstock has more of the feel of a town that's lived in year-round. The Lincoln and Loon Mountain base villages are both lively with skiers in the winter, but in the summer the area can have a post–nuclear fallout feel to it, with lots of homes but few people in evidence despite efforts to stage special events like lumberjack shows. The ambience is also compromised by that peculiar style of resort architecture that's simultaneously aggressive and bland.

ESSENTIALS

GETTING THERE   Waterville Valley is located 12 miles northwest of Exit 29 on I-93 via Route 49. Lincoln is accessible off I-93 on Exits 32 and 33.

VISITOR INFORMATION   The **Waterville Valley Chamber of Commerce,** RFD #1, Box 1067, Campton, NH 03223 (☎ **800/237-2307** or 603/726-3804), staffs an information booth on Route 49 in Campton, just off I-93. The **Lincoln-Woodstock Chamber of Commerce,** P.O. Box 358, Lincoln, NH 03251 (☎ **800/ 227-4191** or 603/745-6621), has an information office open business hours at Depot Plaza on Route 112 in Lincoln.

The most comprehensive place for information about the region from Lincoln northward is the **White Mountains Visitor Center,** P.O. Box 10, North Woodstock, NH 03262 (☎ **800/346-3687** or 603/745-8720), located just east of Exit 32 on I-93. They'll send a visitor's kit, and they offer brochures and answer questions from their center, which is open daily 8:30am to 5pm.

HIKING & MOUNTAIN BIKING

Impressive mountain peaks tower over both Lincoln and Waterville Valley, making both areas great for hiking and mountain biking. As always, your single best source of information is the Appalachian Mountain Club's *White Mountain Guide,* which offers a comprehensive directory of area trails. Also check with Forest Service staff at the White Mountains Visitor Center for information on local outdoor destinations.

From Waterville Valley, a popular four-hour hike runs to the summit of **Mt. Tecumseh,** the shoulders of which host skiers in winter. The hiking trail starts about 100 yards north of the ski lodge, and offers wonderful views as you climb. From the 4.003-foot summit, you can return via the **Sosman Trail,** which winds its way down beneath the ski lifts and along ski runs closed for summer.

The Kancamagus Highway: A Scenic Byway
Through the White Mountains

The Kancamagus Highway—locally called "The Kanc"—is the White Mountain's most spectacular road. Officially designated a national scenic byway by the U.S. Forest Service, the 34-mile roadway joins Lincoln with Conway through 2,860-foot Kancamagus Pass. When the highway was built in 1960 to 1961, it opened up 100 square miles of wilderness—a move that irked preservationists but has proven wildly popular with more casual tourists.

The route begins and ends along wide, tumbling rivers on relatively flat plateaus. The two-lane road, which is almost entirely within the boundaries of the national forest, rises steadily to the pass. Several rest areas with sweeping vistas allow visitors to pause and enjoy the mountain views. The highway makes a good destination for hikers also; any number of day and overnight trips may be launched from the roadside. One simple, short hike along a gravel pathway (it's less than one-third mile each way) leads to **Sabbaday Falls,** a cascade that's especially impressive after a downpour. Six national forest campgrounds are also located along the highway.

Be sure to take your time and stop frequently. Think of it as a scavenger hunt as you look for a covered bridge, cascades with good swimming holes, a historic home with a fascinating story behind it, and spectacular mountain panoramas. All these things and more are along the route.

The highway is popular with serious bikers in training, but it's also a strong draw for casual peddlers in reasonable physical shape. The shoulders are wide enough to accommodate both bikes and RVs, and the grade is reasonably forgiving, especially on the eastern slope. Make sure your brakes are in good working order before setting off down the long descent.

Outdoor novices who prefer their adventures neatly packaged will enjoy the **Waterville Valley Base Camp** (☎ 800/468-2553). The "camp," located at the Waterville Valley Town Square, offers mountain bike rentals, in-line skates, guided tours, lift access for bikers and hikers, and information on area trails. Rates start at $5 for a single ride on the lift, to $55 for a private four-hour guided hike.

In the Lincoln area, a level trail that's excellent for hikers in any physical shape is the **Wilderness Trail** along the East Branch of the Pemigewasset River. Head eastward on Route 112 (the Kancamagus Highway) from I-93 for five miles then watch for the parking lot on the left just past the bridge. Both sides of the river may be navigated; the Wilderness Trail on the west side runs just over three miles to beautiful, remote Black Pond; on the east side, an abandoned railroad bed makes for smooth mountain biking. The two trails may be linked by fording the river where the railbed is crossed by a gate.

The **Loon Mountain Bike Center** (☎ 603/745-8111 ext. 5566) offers more than 70 mountain bikes for rent at its facility at the mountain's base. There's also in-line skating at Loon's **skating center** (☎ 603/745-8111, ext. 5568), which features a skate arena and half-pipe.

Additionally, hikers will find easy access to various trail heads along the Kancamagus Highway (see below).

SKIING

Loon Mountain. Lincoln, NH 03251. ☎ **800/227-4191** or 603/745-8111 for lodging. Internet: http://www.mainstream.net/~loon/. Vertical drop: 2,100 feet. Lifts: 6 chairlifts

(1 high-speed), 1 high-speed gondola, 1 surface lift. Skiable acreage: 250. Lift tickets: $43 weekends, $36 weekdays.

Located on U.S. Forest Service land, Loon has been stymied in past expansion efforts by environmental concerns regarding land use and water withdrawals from the river. Loon finally got the go-ahead for limited expansion in 1994, and is now in the midst of a $12 million, six-year effort to expand and reshape the ski mountain, add uphill capacity, and improve snowmaking. That should reduce some of the congestion of this popular area and open up more room to roam. Today, most of the trails still cluster toward the bottom, and most are solid intermediate runs. Experts head to the north peak, which has a challenging selection of advanced trails served by a triple chairlift.

Waterville Valley. Waterville Valley, NH 03215. ☎ **800/468-2553** or 603/236-8311. Vertical drop: 2,020 feet. Lifts: 9 chairlifts (1 high speed), 4 surface lifts. Skiable acreage: 255. Lift tickets: $43 weekends, $37 weekdays.

While Waterville Valley has some good, steep drops, it's known mostly as a superb intermediate's mountain. There's been a recent effort to upgrade the mountain and offer more challenging trails. In 1995 to 1996 the mountain opened a skiing glade (called Wide Weald), just off a double-diamond bump trail.

The ski resort has also taken strides to accommodate snowboarders—management built a snowboard playground called The Boneyard on Mt. Tecumseh (it features a bus buried up to its roof in snow and some hairy jumps), and it decreed that Snow Mountain (the beginners' mountain) is open *only* to snowboarders on weekends. (Snowboarders are welcome anywhere else on the mountain as well, of course.) There's also a good snowboard shop in the base complex.

WHERE TO STAY

In Waterville Valley

Golden Eagle Lodge. Snowsbrook Rd., Waterville Valley, NH 03215. ☎ **800/910-4499** or 603/236-4600. Fax 603/236-4947. 118 rms. TV TEL. Winter $89–$239 per unit; summer $117–$177 per unit; spring $78–$138 per unit. Rates vary according to season and time of week. Premium charged on holidays. All rates subject to 7% "resort fee." Children stay free in parent's room. AE, DC, DISC, MC, V.

This sprawling, contemporary condominium project is centrally located in the village and is the most regal of the bunch. The lodge can accommodate two to six people in one- and two-bedroom units, all of which have kitchens and basic cookware. The five-story resort strives for a modern-meets-rustic-lodge appearance, generally to good effect. But guests don't travel great distances for the decor here; they come for the resort's amenities and location (an easy shuttle-bus ride to the slopes).

Facilities: There's an indoor pool and whirlpool on site. Room rates also include unlimited access to a nearby $2 million athletic facility, which features steam rooms, fitness room, indoor jogging track, and indoor racquet courts (an additional charge applies for the courts). In summer, guests also get 18 holes of free golf (midweek only) and the use of clay tennis courts.

Snowy Owl Inn. Village Rd., Waterville Valley, NH 03215. ☎ **800/766-9969** or 603/236-8383. Fax 603/236-4890. 80 rms. TV TEL. $89–$239 double. Discounts in off-season and summer. Rates include continental breakfast. AE, DISC, MC, V.

The Snowy Owl will appeal to those who like the amiable character of a country inn, but demand all the modern conveniences. Another modern resort project near Town Square, it offers a number of pleasant extras like a towering fieldstone fireplace in the lobby and a rooftop observatory that offers a fine panorama of the surrounding hills. The rooms are basic motel-style rooms decently furnished and featuring pine accenting; about half have whirlpools and wet bars, and a few feature air-conditioning.

Facilities: There are indoor and outdoor pools and a game room, and rates include access to the valley athletic club and its numerous amenities.

In Lincoln & Woodstock

In addition to the places listed below, Lincoln offers a range of motels that will appeal to budget travelers. Among those worth seeking out are the **Kancamagus Motor Lodge** (☎ 800/346-4205 or 603/745-3365), the **Mountaineer Motel** (☎ 800/356-0046 or 603/745-2235), and **Woodward's Motor Inn** (☎ 800/635-8968 or 603/745-8141).

Mountain Club at Loon. Rte. 112 (R.R. 1; Box 40), Lincoln, NH 03251. ☎ **800/229-7829** or 603/745-2244. Fax 603/745-2317. 234 rms. A/C TV TEL. Winter midweek $109–$399 double, weekend $189–$499 double; summer and off-season starting at $79 double. AE, DC, DISC, MC, V.

Set at the edge of Loon Mountain's slopes, the Mountain Club is a huge, contemporary resort built during the real-estate boom of the 1980s. It was managed for several years as a Marriott, and the decor tends to reflect its chain-hotel heritage. The lobby is done up in dark green tones with leather-like couches arrayed before a polished granite fireplace, and the rooms are adorned with copious oak veneer. Guest rooms are designed to be rented either individually or as a two-room suite; each pair features one traditional hotel-style bedroom with king-size bed, and one studio with a kitchen, sitting area, and a fold-down queen-size bed.

Facilities: The prime attraction of the resort (second to the ski-out-the-door access to the slopes) is the superb athletic facilities, which are connected via an enclosed walkway. There's an indoor and outdoor pool, small indoor basketball court, volleyball court, aerobics rooms, two outdoor tennis courts, a well-equipped fitness room, game room, and a heated outdoor whirlpool that's especially enjoyable during the deep freeze of winter. The free covered parking will be appreciated during heavy snowstorms, as will the resort's in-house restaurant and lounge.

Woodstock Inn. Main St. (P.O. Box 118), North Woodstock, NH 03262. ☎ **800/321-3985** or 603/745-3951. Fax 603/745-3701. 19 rms (11 with private bath). A/C TV TEL. Summer and winter $54–$135 double; foliage season $75–$140 double; off-season $39–$95 double. Rates include breakfast. AE, DC, DISC, MC, V.

Woodstock Station shares some qualities with Dr. Jekyll and Mr. Hyde. In the front, it's a fusty white Victorian with black shutters amid Woodstock's downtown commercial area. In the back, it's a modern, boisterous brewpub that serves up tasty fare along with its robust ales (see below). The inn features 19 guest rooms spread among three houses. If you're on a tight budget, go for the shared bathrooms in the main house and the nearby Deachman house; the slightly less personable Riverside building across the street offers rooms with private baths, but at a premium. Rooms are individually decorated in a country Victorian style, furnished with both reproductions and antiques. There's a pervasive aroma of sachet and cedar in the main building that adds to the period mood. Woodstock Station is a fun place to hang your hat, and is the best local alternative to modern, oversized hotels.

WHERE TO DINE

Woodstock Station. Main St. ☎ **603/745-3951.** Reservations accepted for Clement Room only. Breakfast items $3.95–$9.50; lunch and dinner items $5.49–$15.99 (dinner in Clement Room $11.95–$19.95). AE, DC, DISC, MC, V. Serving 7:30–11:30am, 11:30am–10pm (Woodstock Station), 5:30–9:30pm (Clement Room). PUB FARE/AMERICAN.

You've got a choice here: dine amid the Victorian frippery of the Clement Room on the enclosed porch of the Woodstock Inn. Or head to the relaxed brewpub in the back, housed in a heavily doctored old train station. In the Clement Room, you can enjoy elegant American and continental fare like chicken breast with wild mushrooms, shrimp stuffed with clams, or beef Wellington.

The pub is far more informal, with high ceilings, knotty pine, and decorations consisting of vintage winter recreational gear. There's a large-screen TV, and live local music is featured some nights. The menu rounds up the usual pub suspects, like nachos, chicken wings, burgers, and pasta, all of which is prepared decently if without much creative flair. A new craft brewery opened on the premises in March 1995, and serves up tasty porters, stouts, and brown and red ales.

FRANCONIA NOTCH

Franconia Notch is rugged New Hampshire writ large. As travelers head north on I-93, the Kinsman Range to the west and the Franconia Range to the east begin to converge, and the road angles upward. Soon, the parallel mountain ranges press in on either side, forming tight and dramatic Franconia Notch, which offers little in the way of civilization but a whole lot in the way of natural grandeur. Most of the notch is included in a well-run state park that for practical purposes is indistinguishable from the national forest. Travelers seeking the sublime should plan on a leisurely trip through the Notch, allowing enough time to get out of the car and explore forests and craggy peaks.

ESSENTIALS

GETTING THERE   I-93 runs through Franconia Notch, gearing down from four lanes to two (where it becomes the Franconia Notch Parkway) in the most scenic and sensitive areas of the park. Several roadside pullouts and scenic attractions dot the route.

VISITOR INFORMATION   Information on the park and surrounding area is available at the state-run **Flume Information Center** (☎ **603/823-5563**) at Exit 1 off the Parkway. The center is open during the summer from Monday through Saturday 9am to 4:30pm. North of the Notch, head to the **Franconia/Eaton/Sugar Hill Chamber of Commerce,** P.O. Box 780, Franconia, NH 03580 (☎ **800/866-3334** or 603/823-5661) on Main Street next to the town hall. It's open Monday through Saturday 9am to 5pm.

EXPLORING FRANCONIA NOTCH STATE PARK

Franconia Notch State Park's 8,000 acres, nestled within the surrounding White Mountain National Forest, hosts an array of scenic attractions easily accessible from I-93 and the Franconia Notch Parkway. For information on any of the follow attractions, contact the park offices (☎ **603/823-5563**).

Without a doubt, the most famous park landmark is the **Old Man of the Mountains,** located near Cannon Mountain. From the right spot on the valley floor, this 48-foot-high rock formation bears an uncanny resemblance to the profile of a craggy old man—early settlers said it was Thomas Jefferson. If it looks familiar, it's because this is the logo you see on all the New Hampshire state highway signs. The profile, which often surprises visitors by just how tiny it is when viewed from far below, is best seen from the well-marked roadside viewing area at Profile Lake. In years past, harried tourists craning their necks to glimpse the Old Man while speeding onward resulted in some spectacular head-on collisions. Take your time and pull over. It's free.

The Flume is a rugged, 800-foot gorge through which the Flume Brook tumbles. The gorge, a hugely popular attraction in the mid-19th century, is 800 feet long, 90 feet deep, and as narrow as 20 feet at the bottom; visitors explore by means of a network of boardwalks and bridges. If you're looking for simple and quick access to natural grandeur, it's worth the money. Otherwise, set off into the mountains and seek your own drama with fewer crowds. Admission is $6 adults, and $3 for children 6 to 12.

Echo Lake is a picturesquely situated recreation area, with a 28-acre lake, a handsome swimming beach, and picnic tables scattered about all within view of Cannon Mountain on one side and Mt. Lafayette on the other. This is the best spot for a relaxing afternoon when the weather's in an agreeable mood. A bike path runs along the lake and continues onward both north and south.

Admission to the park is $2.50 for visitors over 12 years old.

For a high-altitude view of the region, set off for the alpine ridges on the **Cannon Mountain Tramway.** The old-fashioned cable car serves skiers in winter; in summer, it whisks up to 80 travelers at a time to the summit of the 4,180-foot mountain. Once at the top, you can strike out by foot along the Rim Trail for superb views. Be prepared for cool, gusty winds. The tramway costs $8 for adults, $4 for children 6 to 12. It's located at Exit 2 of the parkway.

HIKING

Hiking opportunities abound in the Franconia Notch area, ranging from demanding multiday hikes high on exposed ridgelines to gentle valley walks. Consult the *AMC White Mountain Guide* for a comprehensive directory of area hiking trails.

A pleasant woodland detour of two hours or so can be found at the **Basin-Cascades Trail** (look for well-marked signs for The Basin off I-93 about 1¹/₂ miles north of the Flume). A popular roadside waterfall and natural pothole, the Basin attracts teeming crowds, but few visitors slip away from the masses by continuing on the trail to a series of other cascades beyond. Look for signs for the trail, then head off into the woods. After about one-half mile of easy hiking you'll reach **Kinsman Falls,** a beautiful 20-foot cascade. Continue on about six-tenths of a mile beyond to **Rocky Glen,** where the stream plummets through a craggy gorge. Retrace your steps back to your car.

For a more demanding hike, set off for rugged **Mt. Layfayette,** with its spectacular views of the western White Mountains. Hikers should be well-experienced, well-equipped, and in good physical condition. Allow six to seven hours to complete the hike. A popular and fairly straightforward ascent begins up the **Old Bridle Trail,** which departs from the Lafayette Place parking area off the parkway. This trail climbs steadily with expanding views to the AMC's **Greenleaf Hut** (2.9 miles). From here, continue to the summit of Lafayette on the **Greenleaf Trail.** It's only 1.1 miles further, but it covers rocky terrain and can be demanding and difficult, especially if the weather turns on you. If in doubt about conditions, ask advice of other hikers or the AMC staff at Greenleaf Hut.

SKIING

Cannon Mountain. Franconia Notch Parkway, Franconia. ☎ **603/823-5563.** Vertical drop: 2,146 feet. Lifts: 1 80-person tram, 6 chairlifts. Skiable acreage: about 200. Lift tickets: $37 weekend, $28 weekday.

Cannon Mountain, a state-run ski area, was once *the* place to ski in the East. One of New England's first ski resorts, Cannon remains famed for its challenging runs and exposed faces, and the mountain still attracts skiers serious about getting down the hill in style. Many of the old-fashioned New England–style trails are narrow and fun (if sometimes icy, scoured by the notch's winds), and the enclosed tramway is an elegant way to get to the summit. There's no base scene to speak of; skiers tend to retire to inns around Franconia or retreat southward to the condo villages around Lincoln.

WHERE TO STAY & DINE

Franconia Inn. 1300 Easton Rd., Franconia, NH 03580. ☎ **800/473-5299** or 603/823-5542. Fax 603/823-8078. 30 rms (2 with shower only), 2 suites. Midweek $75–$115 double; weekends $90–$130 double. Rates include breakfast. MAP rates also available. Closed Apr to mid-May. AE, MC, V.

This is a pleasant inn that's well-priced for what you get. Owned by Alec and Richard Morris, two brothers who bought the inn in 1981, the Franconia Inn is set along a quiet road in a bucolic valley two miles from the village of Franconia. A grass airstrip lies across the road, used by glider pilots (you can sign up for an hour-long soaring excursion over dramatic Franconia Notch).

The inn itself, built in 1934 after a fire destroyed the original 1886 inn, has a welcoming, informal feel to it, with wingback chairs around the fireplace in one common room, and jigsaw puzzles half completed in the paneled library. Families are always welcome; kids tend to gravitate to the basement game room for pinball, video games, and Ping-Pong. Guest rooms are nicely appointed in a relaxed country fashion.

Facilities: At the barn next door guests can rent horses to tour the network of scenic bridle trails. There's also an outdoor hot tub, clay tennis courts, bikes for guests to use free of charge, a heated pool, and golf courses nearby. In winter, guests ski on 38 miles of groomed ski trails that start right outside the front door.

BETHLEHEM & LITTLETON

A century ago, Bethlehem was about the same size as North Conway to the south, boasting an impressive number of sprawling resort hotels, summer homes, and even its own semi-professional baseball team. (Joseph Kennedy, patriarch of the Kennedy clan, played for the team.) Bethlehem subsequently lost the race for the riches (or won, depending on your view of outlet shopping), and today is again a sleepy town high on a hillside.

Famous for its lack of ragweed and pollen, Bethlehem was once teeming with vacationers seeking respite from the ravages of hay fever. When antihistamines and air-conditioning appeared on the scene, the sufferers stayed home. Empty resorts burned down one by one. Around the 1920s, Bethlehem was discovered by Hasidic Jews from the New York City area, who soon arrived in number to spend the summers in the remaining boarding houses. In fact, that tradition has endured, and it's not uncommon to see bearded men wearing black walking the streets of Bethlehem, or rocking on the porches of Victorian-era homes.

Nearby Littleton, set in a broad valley along the Ammonoosuc River, is the area's commercial hub, but it boasts a surfeit of small-town charm. The town's long main street is still vibrant in an era when many main streets have been abandoned by retailers scrambling for the mall. (That hasn't been a problem here because there *is* no mall.) The street has an eclectic selection of shops—you can buy a wrench, a foreign magazine or literary novel, locally brewed beer, pizza, whole foods, or camping supplies.

These two towns don't offer much in the way of must-see attractions, but offer good lodging, decent restaurants, and pleasant environs, and both are peaceful alternatives for travelers avoiding the tourist bustle to the south.

ESSENTIALS

GETTING THERE Littleton is best reached via I-93; get off at either Exit 41 or 42. Bethlehem is about three miles east of Littleton on Route 302. Get off I-93 at Exit 40 and head east. From the east, follow Route 302 beyond Twin Mountain to Bethlehem.

VISITOR INFORMATION   The **Bethlehem Chamber of Commerce,** P.O. Box 748, Bethlehem, NH 03574 (☎ **603/869-2151**), maintains an information booth in summer on Bethlehem's Main Street near the golf course. The **Littleton Area Chamber of Commerce,** P.O. Box 105, Littleton, NH 03561 (☎ **603/444-6561**), offers information from its storefront office at 141 Main St.

EXPLORING BETHLEHEM

Bethlehem once had 38 resort hotels, but little evidence of that exists today. For a better understanding of the town's rich history, track down "An Illustrated Tour of Bethlehem, Past and Present," available at many shops around town. This unusually informative guide offers a glimpse into the town's past, bringing to life many of the most graceful homes and buildings.

Bethlehem consists of a Main Street, and a handful of side streets. Several antique stores clustered in what passes for downtown are well worth browsing.

Harking back to its more genteel era, Bethlehem still offers two well-maintained 18-hole golf courses amid beautiful North Country scenery. Call for hours and green fees. Both the municipal **Bethlehem Golf Course** (☎ **603/869-5754**) and private **Maplewood Casino and Country Club** (☎ **603/869-3335**) are on Route 302 (Main Street) in Bethlehem.

Just west of Bethlehem on Route 302 is **The Rocks** (☎ **603/444-6228**), a classic, Victorian gentleman's farm that today is the northern headquarters for the Society for the Protection of New Hampshire Forests. Set on 1,200 acres, this gracious estate was built in 1883 by John J. Glessner, an executive with the International Harvester Company. A well-preserved shingled house and an uncommonly handsome barn grace the grounds. Several hiking trails meander through meadows and woodlands on a gentle hillside, where visitors can enjoy open vistas of the wooded mountains across the rolling terrain. The Society operates a Christmas tree farm here, as well as regular nature programs. Admission is free.

WHERE TO STAY

✪ **Adair.** Old Littleton Rd. (just off Exit 40 on Route 93), Bethlehem, NH 03574. ☎ **800/441-2606** or 603/444-2600. Fax 603/444-4823. 8 rms. Summer, foliage season, and winter $125–$175 double; late fall and spring $105–$145 double. Rates include breakfast. AE, MC, V.

Adair just opened in 1992, but has rapidly become one of New England's most esteemed inns. Guests arrive up a long, winding drive flanked by birches and stone walls to arrive at a peaceful, Georgian Revival home that seems far older than its years. Built as a wedding gift for his daughter in 1927 by Washington attorney Frank Hogan (of Hogan & Hartson fame), the inn is set on beautifully landscaped grounds. Inside, the common rooms are open, elegant, and spacious. The guest rooms are impeccably well-furnished with a mix of antiques and reproductions. Innkeepers Patricia and Hardy Banfield have carved a wonderful retreat out of an extraordinary estate. It's the sort of place guests will return to time and again. This is a no-smoking inn.

Dining/Entertainment: If the first-floor sitting room with its fireplace and richly upholstered chairs seems too formal, head downstairs to the Granite Tap Room, a wonderfully informal, granite-lined rumpus room with a VCR and a bar with set-ups (bring your own spirits). For dining, see Tim-Bir Alley, below.

Facilities: A patio overlooks an all-weather tennis court and swimming pool.

🅢 **Hearthside Village.** Rte. 302 (midway between Bethlehem Village and I-93), Bethlehem, NH 03574. ☎ **603/444-1000.** 16 cottages, all showers only. TV. $49.95–$59.95 double ($10 less in off-season). MC, V. Closed mid-Oct to mid-May.

Hearthside Village is a quirky motel court that seems partly conceived by Alfred Hitchcock, partly by Red Grooms. A little bit weird and a little bit charming at the same time, Hearthside claims to be the first motel court built in New Hampshire. The village—a colony of steeply gabled miniature homes—was built by a father and son in two constructive bursts, the first in the 1930s, the second in the late 1940s. The six forties-era cottages are of better quality, with warm knotty-pine interiors. But all cottages are nicely if simply furnished, and most have a fireplaces (Duraflame-style logs only) and handy kitchenettes. Since acquiring the motel in 1990, Rhonda and Steve Huggins have done an outstanding job making it a friendly, fun place that appeals especially to families. There's a pool, an indoor playroom for tots filled with toys, and another recreation room with video games and Ping-Pong for older kids.

Rabbit Hill Inn. Rte. 18, Lower Waterford, VT 05848. ☎ **800/762-8669** or 802/748-5168. Fax 802/748-8342. 20 rms. $179–$269 double. Rates include breakfast and dinner. Discounts available midweek in winter. AE, MC, V. From I-93, take Rte. 18 NW from Exit 44 for approximately 2 miles.

A short hop across the Connecticut River from Littleton is the lost-in-time Vermont village of Lower Waterford with its perfect 1859 church and small library. Amid this cluster of buildings is the stately Rabbit Hill Inn, constructed in 1795. With its prominent gabled roof and imposing columns, the inn easily ranks among the most refined in the Connecticut River Valley. From the porch and many of the guest rooms, the views of the northern White Mountains are unrivaled. The inn's interior is richly furnished with Federal-era antiques. More than half of the rooms have fireplaces, most have air-conditioning, and innkeepers John and Maureen Magee go the extra mile to make this an appealing destination for couples in search of quiet romance. (Honeymoon packages are a specialty.)

Dining/Entertainment: Dinner is included in the rates, and features regional classics along with more creative fare like fresh tomato fettuccine tossed in a jalapeño–sunflower-seed pesto, and braised Vermont pheasant breast with bacon, grapes, and baby artichokes. There's also a pub with a Gaelic flair.

Ⓢ Thayers Inn. Main St., Littleton, NH 03561. ☎ **800/634-8179** or 603/444-6469. 40 rms (3 with shared bath, some with shower only). TV TEL. $42.95–$59.95 double. AE, DC, DISC, MC, V.

Last century President Ulysses S. Grant addressed a streetside crowd from one of the balconies under the imposing eaves of Thayers Inn. You might try that, too, although you might not be as successful at scaring up a crowd. My advice: Just grab a book, have a seat on the balcony, and watch life pass by on Littleton's Main Street. Thayers is a clean, well-run hostelry in an impressive historic building. That's an all-too-rare sight in small towns these days. This solid 1850 inn has a variety of rooms furnished comfortably and eclectically. Notable guests who have stayed here include Bette Davis, Horace Greeley, Nelson Rockefeller, and Richard Nixon. Each room on the four floors is different, and guests are encouraged to poke around and see what's available before deciding on their evening quarters.

WHERE TO DINE

Tim-Bir Alley. In Adair, Old Littleton Rd., Bethlehem. ☎ **603/444-6142.** Reservations recommended. Main courses $13.95–$17.50. No credit cards. Wed–Sun 5:30–9pm. Closed Apr, Nov, and Sun in off-season. REGIONAL/CONTEMPORARY.

Hands down, the best dining in the northern White Mountains is at Tim-Bir Alley, housed in the area's most gracious country inn. Owned by Tim and Biruta Carr, Tim-Bir Alley began in a miniature storefront off a small alley in Littleton. Its reputation for gourmet cuisine outgrew its tiny size, and the pair eventually moved up the hill to Adair, occupying the spacious dining room. The setting is elegant and romantic, and the meals always memorable.

The ingredients are wholesome and basic, but the real art is in the preparation and presentation. Diners might start with a chicken and blue-cheese ravioli in roasted garlic broth, then follow with swordfish cooked with olives and sun-dried tomato, or tournedos of beef with mozzarella and roasted tomato and smoked bacon sauce. Save room for the superb desserts, which range from a pear-walnut tart with maple-caramel sauce to a chocolate-hazelnut pâté.

6 The North Country

I've been traveling to New Hampshire's North Country for more than 25 years, and it's come to serve as a handy touchstone for me. Errol is a town that seems to never change, and that held true even during the boom times of the 1980s. The clean Errol Motel is always there. The Errol Restaurant still serves the best homemade dough-nuts north of Boston. And the land surrounding the town is still possessed of a rug-ged, raw grandeur that hasn't been compromised like many of the former wildlands to the south.

Of course, there's a problem with these lost-in-time areas. It's the nothing-to-see, nothing-to-do syndrome that seems to especially afflict families with young children. You drive for miles and see lots of spruce and pine, an infrequent bog, a glimpse of a shimmering lake, and—if you're lucky—a roadside moose chomping on sedges.

But there *is* plenty to do. White-water kayaking on the Androscoggin River. Ca-noeing on Lake Umbagog. Bicycling along the wide valley floors. And visiting one of the Northeast's grandest, most improbable turn-of-the-century resorts, which hap-pens to keep thriving despite considerable odds against it.

Some recent developments are encouraging for those of us who'd like to see the area remain unchanged. In what may be one of the last bursts of federal largess for a long time to come, the piney shoreline around spectacular Lake Umbagog was pro-tected as a National Wildlife Refuge a few years ago. Part was acquired outright by the federal and state governments (Umbagog straddles the Maine–New Hampshire border), and part was protected through the purchase of development rights from timber companies. The upshot? Umbagog should remain in its more-or-less pristine state for all time.

As for Errol, some shops have closed, some have opened. But the Androscoggin River still flows through. And the police still set up a radar at the bend near the river to catch Canadian speeders heading south toward Old Orchard Beach on Friday, then turn around to catch them heading north on Sundays.

ESSENTIALS

GETTING THERE   Errol is at the junction of Route 26 (accessible from Bethel, Me.) and Route 16 (accessible from Gorham, N.H.).

VISITOR INFORMATION   The **Northern White Mountains Chamber of Commerce,** 164 Main St, Berlin, NH 03570 (☎ **800/992-7480** or 603/752-6060), offers travel information from its offices weekdays between 8:30am and 4:30pm.

OUTDOOR RECREATION

Dixville Notch State Park (☎ **603/788-2155**) offers limited hiking, including a delightful two-mile round-trip hike to Table Rock. Look for the small parking area just east of The Balsams resort (to get there head east from Colebrook on Route 26) on the edge of Lake Gloriette. The loop hike (it connects with a one-half-mile re-turn along Route 25) ascends a scrabbly trail to an open rock with fine views of the resort and the flanking wild hills.

If you're heading to the North Country, be sure to bring your canoe or kayak, since this is a superb area for both white water and flat water.

A great place to learn the fundamentals of white water is at **Saco Bound's Northern Waters** white-water school (☎ **603/482-3848**), located where the Errol Bridge crosses the Androscoggin River. The school offers three- and five-day workshops in the art of getting downstream safely if not dryly. Many of the students camp along the river at the school's campground, although some reside a short walk away at the Errol Motel. Classes involve videos, dry-land training, and frequent forays onto the river—both at the Class I to III rapids at the bridge, and more forgiving rips downstream. The base camp is also a good place for last-minute boat supplies and advice for paddlers exploring the river on their own.

Excellent lake canoeing may be found at **Lake Umbagog,** which sits between Maine and New Hampshire. The lake, which is home to the **Lake Umbagog Wildlife Refuge** (☎ **603/482-3415**), has some 40 miles of shoreline, most of which is wild and remote. Look for osprey and eagles, otter and mink. Some 30 primitive campsites are scattered around the shoreline and on the lake's islands. These are managed by **Umbagog Lake Campground** (☎ **603/482-7795**), and are extremely pricey for backcountry sites ($18 for two). On the other hand, they're well-maintained and you get a lot of wildland for your money. The campground, which is located on Route 26 at the lake's southern tip, also rents canoes.

The area around Errol offers excellent roads for **bicycling**—virtually all routes out of town make for good exploring (although it's mighty hilly heading east). An especially nice trip is south on Route 16 from Errol. The occasional logging truck can be unnerving, but mostly it's an easy and peaceful riverside trip. Consider pedaling as far as what's locally called the Brown Co. Bridge—a simple, wooden logging road bridge that crosses the Androscoggin River. It's a good spot to leap in the river and float through a series of gentle rips before swimming to shore. Some small ledges on the far side of the bridge provide good location for sunning and relaxing.

Biking information and rentals are available in Gorham at **Moriah Sports,** 101 Main St. (☎ **603/466-5050**).

WHERE TO STAY & DINE

✪ **Balsams Grand Resort Hotel.** Dixville Notch, NH 03576. ☎ **800/255-0600** or 603/255-3400 (800/255-0800 in N.H.). Fax 603/255-4221. 200 rms (1 with shower only). TEL. Winter $278–$298 double, including breakfast, dinner, and lift tickets; summer $298–$378 double, including all meals and entertainment; year-round $508–$575 suite. Closed early Apr to late May and mid-Oct to Christmas. AE, DISC, MC, V.

Located on 15,000 private acres in a notch surrounded by 800-foot cliffs, the Balsams is a rare surprise hidden deep in the northern forest. The inn is but one of a handful of great resorts dating back to the 19th century still in operation, and its survival is all the more extraordinary given its remote location. What makes this Victorian grande dame even more exceptional has been its refusal to compromise or bend to the trend of the moment. Bathing suits and jeans are prohibited from the public areas, you'll be ejected from the tennis courts or golf course if you're not neatly attired, and men are required (not requested) to wear jackets at dinner. The resort has also maintained strict adherence to the spirit of the "American plan"—everything but booze is included in the room rate, from green fees to tennis to boats on Lake Gloriette to entertainment in the three lounges in the evening. Even the lift tickets at the resort's downhill ski area are covered.

The Balsams's rigorous Old-World decorum only enriches the mood at this sprawling resort. The rooms are spacious and attractive; the public areas tastefully appointed with resort-style furnishings representing almost every decade between 1866, when the place first opened, and today. Navigating your way through the winding halls is not for the directionally challenged.

Dining/Entertainment: Meals are superb. Especially famous is the sumptuous luncheon buffet, served in summer, and featuring delightful salads, filling entrees like linguine with clam sauce and fried shrimp, and wonderful desserts (when did you last gorge yourself on chocolate eclairs?). There are also three lounges.

Facilities: Two golf courses (one 18-hole, one 9-hole), six tennis courts, a heated outdoor pool, and 45 miles of groomed cross-country ski trails.

ⓢ **Philbrook Farm Inn.** North Rd. (off Rte. 2 between Gorham, N.H., and Bethel, Me.), Shelburne, NH 03581. ☎ **603/466-3831.** 18 rms plus 2 summer cottages (6 rms have shared baths; of the private baths, 1 is tub only, 2 are shower only). $105–$130 double. Rates include breakfast and dinner. No credit cards. Closed Apr and Nov to Dec 26.

The Philbrook Farm Inn is a true New England classic. Set on 1,000 acres between the Mahoosuc Range and the Androscoggin River, this country inn has been owned and operated by the Philbrook family continuously since 1853. The inn has grown haphazardly since the Philbrooks acquired the early farmhouse, with additions in 1861, 1904, and 1934. As a result, the cozy guest rooms on three floors are eclectic—some have a country farmhouse feel, others a more Victorian flavor.

The common areas are spacious and comfortable, with jigsaw puzzles and a century-and-a-half's worth of books lining the shelves. Guests spend their days swimming in the pool, playing croquet, or exploring trails in the nearby hills. Philbrook Farm is a wonderful retreat, well out of the tourist mainstream, and worthy of protection as a local cultural landmark.

Dining/Entertainment: The dining room has a farmhouse-formal feel to it; guests are assigned one table for their stay, and are served by waitresses in crisp, white uniforms. Meals tend toward basic New England fare, with specialities like cod cakes and baked beans with brown bread. Potatoes are served with almost every meal.

Maine 13

by Wayne Curtis

Humorist Dave Barry once wryly suggested that Maine's state motto should be "Cold, but damp."

Cute, but true. There's spring, which tends to last a few blustery, rain-soaked days. There's November, which alternates Arctic winds with gray sheets of rain. And then winter brings a character-building mix of blizzards and ice storms to the fabled coast. (The inland mountains are more or less blessed with uninterrupted snow.)

Ah, but then there's summer. Summer in Maine brings ospreys diving for fish off wooded points; gleaming cumulus clouds building over the steely-blue, rounded peaks of the western mountains; and the haunting whoop of loons echoing off the dense forest walls bordering the lakes. It brings languorous days when the sun rises before most visitors and it seems like noontime at 8am. (There's a tiny but vocal movement afoot to shift Maine to Canada's Atlantic Time Zone, which would move some of the precious daylight from 4 or 5am to the evening, where it might be put to better use.) Maine summers bring a measure of gracious tranquillity, and a placid stay in the right spot can rejuvenate even the most jangled nerves.

The trick comes in finding that right spot. Those who arrive here without a clear plan may find themselves cursing their travel decision. Maine's Route 1 along the coast has its moments, but for the most part it's rather charmless—an amalgam of convenience stores, tourist boutiques, and restaurants catering to bus tours. Acadia National Park can be congested, Mount Katahdin's summit crowded, and some of the more popular lakes become obstacle courses of jet skis.

But Maine's size works to the traveler's advantage. Maine is nearly as large as the other five New England states combined. It has 3,500 miles of coastline, some 3,000 coastal islands, and millions of acres of undeveloped woodland. In fact, more than half of the state exists as "unorganized territories," where no town government exists, and the few inhabitants look to the state for basic services. With all this space, and a little planning, you'll be able to find your piece of Maine.

Wherever your travels take you, be sure to look for the varied layers of history, both natural and human. You'll find the mark of the great glaciers on the scoured mountaintops. You'll find the hand of man in two-century-old mansions on remote coves that bespeak a former affluence when Maine ruled the waves (or at least much of the early trade on those waves). Picking these layers apart is much of the fun in exploring Maine.

1 Enjoying the Great Outdoors

No other northern New England state offers as much diversity in its outdoor recreation as Maine. Bring your mountain bike, hiking boots, sea kayak, canoe, fishing rod, and snowmobile—there'll be plenty for you to do here.

BEACHGOING Swimming at Maine's ocean beaches is for the hearty. The Gulf Stream, which prods warm waters toward the Cape Cod shores to the south, veers toward Iceland south of Maine and leaves the state's 3,500-mile coastline to be washed by the brisk Nova Scotia current, an offshoot of the Arctic Labrador Current. During the "warm" summer months, water temperatures along the south coast can top 60° F during an especially warm spell where the water is shallow, but it's usually cooler than that. The average ocean temperature at Bar Harbor in summer is 54° F.

Maine's beaches are found mostly between Portland and the New Hampshire border. Northeast of Portland there are a handful of fine beaches—including popular **Reid State Park** and **Popham Beach State Park**—but rocky coast defines this territory for the most part. The southern beaches are beautiful, but rarely isolated. Summer homes occupy the low dunes in most areas; mid-rise condos give Old Orchard Beach a "mini-Miami" air. For my money, the best beaches are at **Ogunquit,** which boasts a three-mile-long sandy strand, some of which has a mildly remote character, and **Long Sands Beach** at York, which has a festive, carnival atmosphere right along Route 1A.

Don't overlook the sandy beaches at Maine's wonderful lakes, where the water is tepid by comparison to the frigid Atlantic. A number of state and municipal parks offer access. Especially popular are **Sebago Lake State Park** (☎ 207/693-6613), about 20 miles northwest of Portland, and, for a more rustic experience, **Lily Bay State Park** (☎ 207/695-2700), on Moosehead Lake, eight miles north of Greenville.

BACKPACKING Compared to camping by canoe or sea kayak, backpacking opportunities are relatively limited in Maine. A couple of notable exceptions exist. The 2,000-mile **Appalachian Trail,** which ends (or begins, depending on your direction) at Maine's highest peak, is nothing short of spectacular as it passes through Maine. En route to Mt. Katahdin, it winds through what's known as the "100-Mile Wilderness," a remote, bosky, and boggy stretch where the trail crosses few roads and passes no settlements. It's the quiet habitat of loons and moose, and hikers are but brief transients. Trail guides are available from the **Appalachian Trail Conference,** P.O. Box 807, Harpers Ferry, WV 25425 (☎ 304/535-6331).

Another excellent destination for backcountry exploration is 200,000-acre **Baxter State Park,** 64 Balsam Dr., Millinocket, ME 04462 (☎ 207/723-5140), in the north-central part of the state. The park maintains about 180 miles of backcountry hiking trails. The vast majority of travelers coming to the park are intent on ascending 5,267-foot Mt. Katahdin. But dozens of other peaks are well worth scaling, and just traveling through the deep woods hereabouts is a sublime experience. Reservations are required for backcountry camping, and many of the best spots fill up shortly after the first of the year. Reservations can be made by mail or in person, but not by phone.

Note that there is no backcountry camping at Acadia National Park.

BICYCLING Mount Desert Island and **Acadia National Park** comprise the premier destination for bikers, especially mountain bikers who prefer easy-riding terrain. The 57 miles of well-maintained carriage roads in the national park offer superb cruising through thick forests and to the tops of rocky knolls with ocean views. No cars are permitted on these grass and gravel roads, so you've got them to yourself. Mountain bikes may be rented in Bar Harbor, which has at least three bike shops. The Park Loop Road (toll), while often crowded with slow-moving cars, offers one of the more memorable road biking experiences in the state. The rest of Mount Desert Island is also good for road biking, especially on the quieter western half of the island.

In southern Maine, **Route 103** and **Route 1A** offer pleasant excursions for bikers along the coast. Offshore, bring your bike to the bigger islands for car-free cruising. **Vinalhaven** and **North Haven** in Penobscot Bay, and **Swan's Island** in Blue Hill Bay are all popular destinations for bikers.

CAMPING Car campers in Maine have plenty of choices, from well-developed private campgrounds to primitive backcountry sites. **Baxter State Park** and **Acadia National Park** tend to fill up the fastest, but there's no shortage of other options. Maine has nearly 62,000 acres in state parks (not including 200,000-acre Baxter), a dozen of which offer overnight camping. For more information about the state's parks, contact the **Department of Conservation,** State House Station #22, Augusta, ME 04333 (☎ **207/287-3821**). To make camping reservations at 11 of the state park campgrounds, call between January and August (☎ **800/332-1501** or 207/ 287-3824 in Maine). For reservations at Baxter State Park, see "The North Woods" section of this chapter.

On Maine's western border, the **White Mountain National Forest** offers superb camping at several campgrounds in the mountains of the Evans Notch Ranger District, RR #2, P.O. Box 2270, Bethel, ME 04217 (☎ **207/824-2134**).

Maine also has more than 200 private campgrounds spread throughout the state, many offering full hookups for RVs. For a guide to the private campgrounds, contact the **Maine Campground Owners Association,** 655 Main St., Lewiston, ME 04240 (☎ **207/782-5874**).

CANOEING In the eyes of many, Maine means canoeing. From the thousands of lakes and ponds to the tumbling white water of mountain rivers, Maine offers a big allure for paddlers.

The state's most popular long-distance excursion is the **Allagash Wilderness Waterway** canoe trip, which can be done end-to-end in 7 to 10 days. Some 80 campsites are spaced along the nearly 100-mile route, which includes a 9-mile stretch of Class I–II whitewater. For a map and brochure, contact the Bureau of Parks and Recreation, Maine Department of Conservation, State House Station 22, Augusta, ME 04333. The Allagash is also served by a number of outfitters, who can provide everything from a complete guide service to a simple car shuttle. (See "The North Woods" section of this chapter.)

Other good canoe destinations include the **Saco River,** which ambles out of the White Mountains through western Maine and is noted for its popular sandbars and weekend crowds. There's the upper West Branch of the **Penobscot River,** which winds through moose country and connects to one of Maine's most pristine lakes.

In fact, you can't travel very far in Maine without stumbling upon a great canoe trip. Two excellent sources of information are the *AMC River Guide: Maine* and *Quiet Water Canoe Guide: Maine*, both published by the Appalachian Mountain Club, 5 Joy St., Boston, MA 02108.

FISHING   Maine draws anglers from throughout the Northeast who indulge their grand obsession on Maine's 6,000 lakes and ponds and its countless miles of rivers and streams. Want to find fishing? Just look at a map and head to those big blue areas.

Among the most appealing areas for serious freshwater anglers is the **Grand Lake Stream** region deep in the woods of Washington County, not far from the New Brunswick border and Canada. This area has a strong heritage as a fisherman's settlement, and a number of camps and outfitters cater to the serious angler.

Nearby **Dennys River** and the **St. Croix River** are good destinations for Atlantic salmon; troll the numerous lakes for trout and small-mouth bass. Among the classic fishing lodges in this area are **Weatherby's** (☎ **207/796-5558**) and **Indian Rock Camps** (☎ **800/498-2821** or 207/796-2822).

Nonresident **licenses** are $48 for the season, or $20 for three days. Seven- and fifteen-day licenses are also available. You can purchase licenses at many outdoor shops or general stores. For a booklet of fishing regulations, contact the **Department of Inland Fisheries and Wildlife,** State House Station #41, Augusta, ME 04333 (☎ **207/287-3371**).

HIKING   Maine isn't much of a hiker's state, even though it has 10 peaks over 4,000 feet. The reason is simple. Outside of Baxter State Park and Acadia National Park, Maine has surprisingly little public land. Recreation has historically occurred on the millions of acres of privately owned timber company land, and the emphasis there has been on canoeing, fishing, and hunting, not on recreational hiking.

That's not to say that Maine lacks great places to hike. There are trails, if you know where to look. **Acadia National Park** offers superb and surprisingly quiet hiking, given the huge popularity of the park. Happily for hikers, few visitors venture far from their cars, leaving the trail system relatively unpopulated. In western Maine, 50,000 acres of the **White Mountains** spill over the border from New Hampshire and boast an excellent network of trails. There are a number of pathways in and around Evans Notch that offer opportunities for hikers of all levels. Finally, there's the excellent and generally unheralded **Bigelow Range** near the Sugarloaf/USA ski resort, which offers challenging trails and stunning vistas from high, blustery ridges. The Appalachian Trail traverses the range; a good source of trail information is in the AT guide (see "Backpacking," above).

Two guides to the state's trails are highly recommended. *Fifty Hikes in Southern Maine* by John Gibson is a reliable directory to trails at Evans Notch, Acadia, and the Camden Hills area. *Fifty Hikes in Northern Maine* by Chloe Caputo is the best guide for the Bigelow Range and Baxter State Park. Both are available from **Backcountry Publications,** P.O. Box 175, Woodstock, VT 05091 (☎ **800/245-4151**).

SEA KAYAKING   Sea kayakers nationwide migrate to Maine in the summer for world-class sea-kayaking. The 3,500 miles of rocky coastline and the thousands of offshore islands have created a wondrous sea kayaker's playground. Paddlers can explore protected estuaries far from the surf, or test their skills and determination with excursions across the choppy, open sea to islands far offshore. It's a sport that can be extremely dangerous (the seas can turn on you in a matter of minutes), but can yield plenty of returns for those with the proper equipment and skills.

The nation's first long-distance "water trail" was created here in 1987 when the **Maine Island Trail** was established. This 325-mile waterway winds along the coast from Portland to Machias, and incorporates some 70 state and privately owned islands along the route. Members of the Maine Island Trail Association, a private nonprofit organization, are granted permission to visit and camp on these islands, as long as they follow certain restrictions (for example, don't visit designated islands during seabird nesting season). The association seeks to encourage low-impact, responsible use of these natural treasures. A guidebook, published annually, provides descriptions of all the islands in the network and is free with association membership (note that it's available *only* to members). Membership is $35 per year; contact the **Maine Island Trail Association,** P.O. Box C, Rockland, ME 04841 (☎ **207/ 596-6456** or 207/761-8225).

For novices, Maine has a number of kayak outfitters offering guided excursions ranging from an afternoon to a week. Recommended outfitters include the **Maine Island Kayak Co.,** 70 Luther St., Peaks Island, ME 04108 (☎ **207/766-2373**); **H2Outfitters,** P.O. Box 72, Orr's Island, ME 04066 (☎ **207/833-5257**); and **Maine Sports Outfitters,** P.O. Box 956, Rockport, ME 04856 (☎ **800/244-8799** or 207/236-8797).

SKIING Maine has two major downhill ski resorts along with 10 smaller areas. The two big resorts, **Sugarloaf** and **Sunday River,** came under the same ownership in 1996, but both maintain distinct characters. Sugarloaf is compact and manageable, and offers the highest vertical drop in New England after Vermont's Killington. The resort's base area is self-contained like a campus and is a big hit with families. Sunday River is a younger resort and its base area is still a bit rough around the edges— think of it as more of a brash community college. But it offers diverse skiing terrain and state-of-the-art snowmaking and grooming. I'd go to Sugarloaf if I were expecting heavy natural snowfall; I'd choose Sunday River if the natural snow conditions were marginal or poor.

The medium and small mountains cater primarily to the local market but offer good alternatives for travelers who'd just as soon avoid the flash and crowds of a larger area. Of the mid-sized areas, **Shawnee Peak** and **Saddleback** have small resort complexes at or near their bases, and offer better bargains and fewer crowds; Shawnee Peak is open for night skiing until 10pm six nights each week. **Mt. Abram,** which is near Sunday River, has developed a solid reputation among telemark skiers. For a recorded announcement of current downhill ski conditions statewide, call **207/ 773-7669.**

Cross-country skiers have a glorious mix of terrain to choose from, although groomed cross-country ski areas aren't as extensive in Maine as in neighboring New Hampshire or Vermont. Sunday River, Saddleback, and Sugarloaf all feature cross-country ski areas at or near their downhill complexes. A more remote destination is **The Birches** (☎ **800/825-9453**) on Moosehead Lake with 24 miles of groomed trails. The best place to combine remote backcountry lodging and skiing is **Little Lyford Pond Camps** (☎ via radio phone **207/695-2821**) outside of Greenville— it's accessible in winter only by skiplane or snowmobile.

For further information about cross-country ski areas in Maine, contact the **Maine Nordic Council** (☎ **800/754-9263**).

SNOWMOBILING Snowmobiling is in the midst of a boom in Maine as everyone from mechanics to doctors is discovering the appeal of this sport. Restaurants and lodges that were until recently shuttered through winter are now doing more business in the snowy months than the rest of the year. Communities throughout northern Maine, in particular, are spending tens of thousands of dollars grooming trails nightly for snowmobilers in a bid to attract their attention. Maine's **Interconnected Trail System (ITS)** serves as a superhighway for the North Woods; the woods are also laced with an elaborate network of local trails maintained by local snowmobile clubs. Overall, Maine has 11,000 miles of groomed trails maintained by 260 snowmobile clubs. If you plan your trip right, stops for gas, food, and warming up will be no more than 30 miles apart.

As in the other northern New England states, the farther north you go the better the conditions are likely to be. Of particular note is the new sled trail that follows the perimeter of **Moosehead Lake,** with stops possible at Mt. Kineo and Pittston Farm, both of which offer food and lodging. For more information on the trail or rentals, contact the **Moosehead Region Chamber of Commerce,** P.O. Box 581, Greenville, ME 04441 (☎ 207/695-2702).

WHITE-WATER RAFTING   Maine has three northern rivers that get the adrenaline pumping: the Dead, the Kennebec, and the Penobscot. All three are dam-controlled, which means that good rafting is available throughout the season. The **Dead River** has a limited release schedule; during the average season, it's opened only a half-dozen times for rafting in early summer and fall; smaller releases allow paddling in inflatable kayaks during the summer. The **Kennebec River** offers monstrous waves just below the dam (some say they're comparable to the big water you'll find out West), then tapers off into a gentle afternoon paddle as you float out of a scenic gorge. The West Branch of the **Penobscot River** has a challenging, technical section called the Cribworks at the outset, several serious drops and falls after that, and dramatic views of Mount Katahdin along the route.

For a list of outfitters, contact **Raft Maine,** P.O. Box 3, Bethel, ME 04217 (☎ 800/723-8633 or 207/824-3694).

WINDJAMMING   An ideal way to combine time in the outdoors with relative luxury and an easy-to-digest education in maritime history is aboard a windjammer cruise on the coast. Maine boasts a sizable fleet of vintage sailing ships that offer private cabins, meals, entertainment, and adventure. The ships range in size from 53 to 132 feet, and most are berthed in the region between Bath and Belfast. You choose your adventure: An array of excursions are available, from simple overnights to week-long expeditions sailing among Maine's thousands of scenic islands and coves.

2 The South Coast

There are two good reasons to visit Maine's South Coast: the beaches and the almost tactile sense of history you'll find in the coastal villages.

Thanks to the quirks of geography, almost all of Maine's sandy beaches are located in the 60-mile stretch of coastline between Portland and Kittery. And you're likely to find a sandy spot that appeals to you, whether you prefer dunes and the lulling sound of the surf or the carny atmosphere of a festive beach town. The waves are dependent on the water—during a good Northeast blow they pound the shores and threaten beach houses built decades ago. During the balmy days of midsummer the ocean can be as gentle as a farm pond, with barely audible waves lapping timidly at the shore.

One thing all beaches share in common: They're washed by the frigid waters of the Gulf of Maine. Bouts of swimming tend to be very brief and often accompanied by shrieks and whoops. The beach season is brief and intense, running from July 4th to Labor Day. Before and after, beach towns tend to be rather sleepy.

The South Coast wears its history on its sleeve. More than three centuries ago the early European newcomers first settled here, only to be driven out by hostile Native Americans, who had been pushed to the brink by treaty-breaking British settlers and prodded by the mischievous French. Settlers later reestablished themselves, and by the early 19th century, the southern Maine coast was one of the most prosperous

Southern Maine Coast

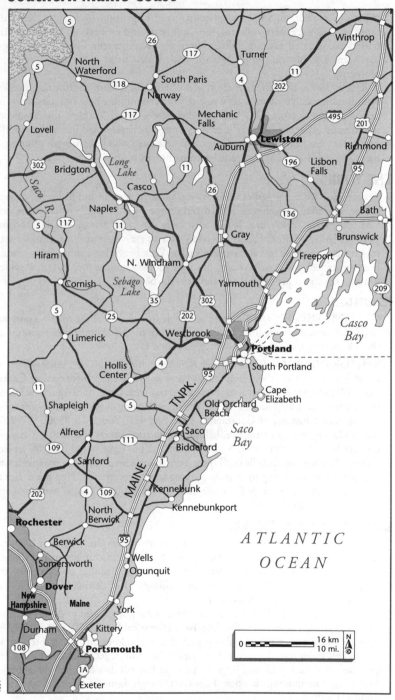

Winthrop

North
Waterford

South Paris

Turner

Norway

Mechanic
Falls

Lewiston

Richmond

Lovell

Auburn

Lisbon
Falls

Bridgton

Long
Lake

Casco

Bath

Naples

Brunswick

Hiram

Gray

Freeport

Cornish

N. Windham

Sebago
Lake

Yarmouth

Casco
Bay

Limerick

Westbrook

Portland

Hollis
Center

South Portland

Shapleigh

Old Orchard
Beach

Cape
Elizabeth

Alfred

Saco

Saco
Bay

Sanford

Biddeford

Kennebunk

North
Berwick

Kennebunkport

Rochester

ATLANTIC
OCEAN

Berwick

Somersworth

Wells

Dover

Ogunquit

New
Hampshire

Maine

York

Durham

Kittery

Portsmouth

Exeter

0   16 km
     10 mi.

N

regions in the nation. Shipbuilders constructed brigantines and sloops, and ship captains plied the eastern seaboard, the Caribbean, and far beyond. Merchants and traders constructed vast warehouses along the rivers to store their goods. Many handsome and historic homes near the coast today attest to the region's former prosperity.

A second wave came in the mid- to late 19th century, when wealthy city dwellers from Boston and New York sought respite from the summer heat and congestion by fleeing to Maine's coast. They built shingled estates (called "cottages") with views of the Atlantic. After the turn of the century, aided by trolleys and buses, the wealthy rusticators were followed by the emerging middle class, who built bungalows near the shore and congregated at oceanside boarding houses to splash in the waves.

THE YORKS

"The Yorks" are comprised of three towns that share a name but little else. In fact, it's rare to find three such well-defined and diverse New England archetypes in such a compact area. York Village is rich with early American history and architecture. York Harbor is redolent of America's late Victorian era, when wealthy urbanites constructed rambling cottages at the ocean's edge. York Beach has a turn-of-the-century beach-town feel, with loud amusements, taffy shops, a modest zoo, and small gabled summer homes set in crowded enclaves near the beach.

ESSENTIALS

GETTING THERE   The Yorks are accessible from Exit 1 of the Maine Turnpike. Route 1A, which departs from Route 1 just south of the turnpike exit, connects all three York towns, and loops north back to Route 1.

VISITOR INFORMATION   Travelers entering the state on I-95 can stock up on travel information for the region and beyond at the **Kittery Information Center** (☎ 207/439-1319), located at a well-marked rest area. Open until 9pm in summer, it's amply stocked with brochures, and the helpful staff can answer many questions.

The **York Chamber of Commerce,** P.O. Box 417, York, ME 03909 (☎ 207/ 363-4422), operates an attractive, helpful information center at 599 Rte. 1, a short distance from the turnpike exit. A trackless trolly (a bus fitted out to look like an old-fashioned trolley) regularly links all three York towns and provides a convenient way to explore without having to scare up parking spots at every stop. Hop the trolley at one of the well-marked stops for a one-hour narrated tour ($3), or disembark along the way and explore by foot.

DISCOVERING LOCAL HISTORY

John Hancock is famed for his oversized signature on the Declaration of Independence. What's not so well known about him is his failure as a businessman. Hancock was the proprietor of Hancock Wharf, a failed enterprise that's only one of the intriguing sites open to the public in **York Village,** a fine destination for those curious about early American history.

First settled in 1624, York Village has several early homes open to the public from mid-June through September. The **Old York Historical Society** (☎ 207/363-4974) operates a community museum comprised of seven buildings spanning three centuries in this quiet riverside town. One ticket ($6 adults, $2.50 children 6 to 16) provides admission to all buildings, or you can buy admission to individual buildings ($2). The museum is open Tuesday through Saturday 10am to 4pm and Sunday 1 to 5pm.

Tickets are available at **Jefferds Tavern,** across from the handsome old burying ground, where changing exhibits document facets of early life. Next door is the

School House, furnished as it might have been in the last century. A 10-minute walk along lightly traveled Lindsay Road will bring you to **Hancock Wharf,** which is next door to the George Marshall Store. Also nearby is the **Elizabeth Perkins House** with its well-preserved Colonial Revival interiors. The newest acquisition is an old bank building, which now houses the society's library and offices. The library is open to historical society members only.

The two don't-miss buildings in the society's collection are the intriguing **Old Gaol,** built in 1719 with its now-musty dungeons for criminals and debtors. The jail is the oldest surviving public building in the United States. Just down the knoll from the jail is the **Emerson-Wilcox House,** built in the mid-1700s. Added on to periodically over the years, it's a virtual catalog of architectural styles and early decorative arts. Docents make the building come alive during a tour.

BEACHES

York Beach actually consists of two beaches—**Long Sands Beach** and **Short Sands Beach**—separated by a rocky headland and a small island capped with scenic Nubble Light. Both offer plenty of room for sunning and Frisbees when the tide is out. When the tide is in, both are a bit cramped. Short Sands fronts the town of York Beach with its candlepin bowling and video arcades. It's the better bet for families who have kids with short attention spans. Long Sands runs along Route 1A, across from a profusion of motels, summer homes, and convenience stores. Parking at both beaches is metered (50¢ per hour).

WHERE TO STAY

For basic accommodations, try York Beach, which has a proliferation of motels and guest cottages facing Long Sands Beach. Even with this abundance, however, it's best to reserve ahead during prime season. And don't expect any real bargains during midsummer, even among the most basic of motels.

If the following inns are booked, try these: **Anchorage Motor Inn** (☎ 207/363-5112), **Sea Latch Motor Inn** (☎ 800/441-2993 or 207/363-4400), or **Sunrise Motel** (☎ 800/242-0752 or 207/363-4542).

Dockside Guest Quarters. Harris Island (P.O. Box 205), York, ME 03909. ☎ **207/363-2868.** Fax 207/363-1977. 21 rms, 2 with shared bath. TV. Mid-June to early Sept $60–$147 double. Rates up to 30% lower in off-season. MC, V. Closed weekdays Nov–May. Drive S on Rte. 103 from Rte. 1A; after bridge, turn left and follow signs.

David and Harriet Lusty established this quiet retreat in 1954, and recent additions (mostly new cottages) haven't taken away any of the friendly, maritime flavor of the place. Situated on an island connected to the mainland by a small bridge, the inn occupies nicely landscaped grounds shady with maples and white pines. Five of the rooms are in the main house, built in 1885, but the bulk of the accommodations are in small, townhouse-style cottages constructed between 1968 and 1974. These are simply furnished, bright, and airy, and all have private decks that overlook the entrance to York Harbor. (Several rooms also offer woodstoves.)

Dining/Entertainment: The inn runs a popular restaurant on the property, serving mounds of fresh seafood and New England classics.

Facilities: The innkeepers provide guests with the use of canoes, rowboats, and a 13-foot Boston Whaler at no additional charge. There's also badminton, croquet, and lounging in the gazebo overlooking the water.

Nevada Motel. Rte. 1A (P.O. Box 885), York Beach, ME 03910. ☎ **207/363-4504.** 21 rms. A/C TV TEL. Mid-June to Labor Day $78 double; off-season $56 double. AE, MC, V. Closed Oct 15–May 15.

This unassuming, classic 1953 beachfront motel is a low, white, two-story affair with turquoise trim offering simple, comfortable rooms, most of which are on the small side. But the sound of surf reaches the rooms through louvered windows (Long Sands Beach is just across Rte. 1A), and there's a spacious deck on the second floor that affords wonderful views across the road to the ocean beyond. The Nevada is popular with a mix of guests, from families to couples, most of whom simply spend their day on the beach.

Stage Neck Inn. Stage Neck (P.O. Box 70), York Harbor, ME 03911. ☎ **800/222-3238** or 207/363-3850. 60 rms. A/C TV TEL. June through Labor Day $135–$205 double; early fall $115–$185 double; winter $85–$130 double; spring $100–$150 double. AE, DISC, MC, V. Head north on 1A from Rte. 1; make second right after York Harbor post office.

A hotel in one form or another has been housing guests on this windswept bluff between the harbor and the open ocean since about 1870. The most current incarnation was constructed in 1972, and it defines modern elegance for the region. The hotel, while indisputably up-to-date, successfully creates a sense of old-fashioned intimacy and avoids the overbearing grandeur to which many modern resorts aspire, often with poor results. Almost every room has a view of the water, and guests enjoy low-key recreational pursuits. And York Harbor Beach is but a few steps away. No smoking.

Dining/Entertainment: The dining room is outstanding, offering dinner entrees ranging from blackened Maine crabcakes to grilled pork médaillons with apple-Dijon-garlic glaze.

Facilities: There are pools indoors and out, a Jacuzzi, and tennis courts overlooking the ocean.

WHERE TO DINE

✪ **Cape Neddick Inn.** 1233 Rte. 1, Cape Neddick. ☎ **207/363-2899.** Reservations recommended. Full dinners $18–$27; light entrees served à la carte $10–$14. AE, MC, V. Summer daily 6–9pm; closed 1 or 2 days weekly during off-season (call ahead). REGIONAL/CONTINENTAL.

This fine inn offers some of the consistently best dining in southern Maine. Located in an elegant structure (largely rebuilt after a recent fire) on a relatively undeveloped stretch of Route 1, the Cape Neddick Inn has a open, handsome dining area that mixes traditional and modern. The old comes in the cozy golden glow of the room. The modern is the artwork, which changes frequently and showcases some of the region's better painters and sculptors.

The highly creative menu also changes frequently to make the most of seasonal products. Depending on the season, the menu might include roasted chicken breast stuffed with shallots, basil, and Boursín cheese and served with an artichoke wine sauce; or a horseradish-and-ginger-encrusted salmon with a soy and sake sauce. Save room for dessert, which tends to be extravagant.

⑤ **Goldenrod Restaurant.** Railroad Rd. and Ocean Ave., York Beach. ☎ **207/363-2621.** Breakfast $2.10–$5.25; lunch and dinner entrees $1.75–$7.50. MC, V. Memorial Day–Labor Day daily 8:30am–10:30pm; closed some weekdays during shoulder seasons. Closed Columbus Day to mid-May. AMERICAN.

This beachtown classic is the place for local color with breakfast or lunch. The Goldenrod has been a summer institution in York Beach since it first opened in 1896. It's easy to find: Look for visitors on the sidewalk gawking at the plate-glass windows, mesmerized by the ancient taffy machines hypnotically churning out taffy in volume, enough to make thousands of dentists very wealthy.

The restaurant, behind the taffy and fudge operation, is low on frills and long on atmosphere. Diners sit on stout oak furniture around a stone fireplace, or at the marble soda fountain. There are dark beams overhead and the sort of linoleum floor you don't see much anymore. Breakfast offerings are the standards: omelets, waffles, griddle cakes, and bakery items. Lunch is fairly predictable, but equally well presented. As for dinner, you'd probably be better served heading to someplace more creative.

OGUNQUIT

Ogunquit has attracted vacationers and artists for more than a century. Ogunquit's fame as an artist's colony dates to 1890, when Charles H. Woodbury arrived and pronounced the place an "artist's paradise." He was followed by artists such as Walt Kuhn, Elihu Vedder, Yasuo Kuniyoshi, and Rudolph Dirks, who was best known for creating the "Katzenjammer Kids" comic strip.

The town bristles with restaurants and inns and can feel overrun with tourists during the peak summer season, especially on weekends. The cure? Head for the expansive beach, which by and large has been protected from development, and is large enough to allow most of the teeming masses to disperse.

ESSENTIALS

GETTING THERE   Ogunquit is located on Route 1 between York and Wells. It's accessible from either Exit 1 or Exit 2 of the Maine Turnpike.

VISITOR INFORMATION   The **Ogunquit Welcome Center,** P.O. Box 2289, Ogunquit, ME 03907 (☎ **207/646-5533** or 207/646-2939), is located on Route 1 south of the village center. It's open daily Memorial Day through Columbus Day, and weekdays during the off-season.

GETTING AROUND   The village of Ogunquit is centered around an awkward four-way intersection that seems fiendishly designed to cause traffic foul-ups in summer. Parking in and around the village is also tight and relatively expensive (expect to pay $5 or $6 per day). As a result, Ogunquit is best reconnoitered on foot, by bike, or on the trackless trolley.

EXPLORING THE TOWN

The village center is good for an hour's browsing among the boutiques (check out the eclectic crafts at **Maya's,** 23 Shore Rd.), or sipping a cappuccino at one of the several coffee emporia.

From the village you can walk the mile to scenic Perkins Cove along **Marginal Way,** a mile-long oceanside pathway once used for herding cattle to pasture. Earlier in this century, the land was bought by a local developer who deeded the right-of-way to the town. The pathway, which is wide and well-maintained, departs across from the Seacastles Resort on Shore Road. It passes tide pools, pocket beaches, and rocky, fissured bluffs, all of which are worth exploring. The scenery can be spectacular (especially after a storm), but Marginal Way can also be spectacularly crowded during fair weather weekends. To elude the crowds, try heading out in the early morning.

Perkins Cove, accessible either from Marginal Way or by driving south on Shore Road and veering left at the "Y" intersection, is a small, well-protected harbor that seems custom-designed for a photo opportunity. As such, it attracts visitors by the busload, carload, and boatload, and can often be congested. A handful of galleries, restaurants, and T-shirt shops catering to the tourist trade occupy a cluster of quaint buildings between the harbor and the sea. An intriguing pedestrian drawbridge is operated by whomever happens to be handy, allowing sailboats to come and go. Perkins Cove is also home to several tour boat operators, who offer trips of various durations throughout the day and at twilight. But if tourist traps give you hives, steer clear of Perkins Cove.

Not far from the cove is **The Ogunquit Museum of Art,** Shore Road (☎ 207/ 646-4909), one of the best small art museums in the country. Set back from the road in a grassy glen overlooking the rocky shore, the museum's spectacular view initially overwhelms the artwork as visitors walk through the door. But stick around a few minutes—the changing exhibits in this architecturally engaging museum of cement block, slate, and glass will get your attention soon enough, since the curators have a track record of staging superb shows and attracting national attention. (Be sure to note the bold, underappreciated work of Henry Strater, the Ogunquit artist who built the museum in 1953.) The museum is open July 1 to September 30 from 10:30am to 5pm Monday through Saturday, and 2 to 5pm on Sunday. Admission is $3 for adults, $2 for seniors.

BEACHES

Ogunquit's main beach is three miles long, and three paid parking lots are located along its length. The most popular access point (with the most expensive parking) is at the foot of Beach Street, which connects to Ogunquit Village. The beach ends at a sandy spit, where the Ogunquit River flows into the sea, and offers changing rooms and a handful of informal restaurants. It's also the most crowded part of the beach. Less crowded, less expensive options are at **Footbridge Beach** (turn on Ocean Avenue off Route 1 north of the village center) and **Moody Beach** (turn on Eldridge Avenue in Wells).

WHERE TO STAY

The Aspinquid. Beach St. (P.O. Box 2408), Ogunquit, ME 03907. ☎ **207/646-7072.** Fax 207/646-1187. 62 rms. A/C MINIBAR TV TEL. June to Labor Day $95–$205 double; shoulder seasons $60–$115 double. AE, MC, V. Closed mid-Oct to mid-Mar.

Built on the site of the old Aspinquid Hotel in 1971, the new Aspinquid is a complex of modern, shingled buildings located an easy stroll across the bridge from Ogunquit's beach. Rooms range from basic motel units to two-room apartments, and all are equipped with most modern amenities. If the beach grows tiresome, on the grounds you'll find a spa, sauna, swimming pool, tennis courts, and a purebred Maine coon cat named Socrates. "If he is an unwanted visitor," notes a letter to the guests, "just shoo him out of your room."

Marginal Way House. Wharf Lane (P.O. Box 697), Ogunquit, ME 03907. ☎ **207/646-8801** or 207/363-6566 in winter. 30 rms, some with showers only. TV. Peak season $75–$150 double; shoulder seasons $40–$130 double. No credit cards. Closed late Oct to mid-Apr.

If you travel for vistas, this is your place. Even if your room lacks a sweeping ocean view (and that's unlikely), you've got the run of the lawn and the guest-house porch, both of which overlook Ogunquit River to the beach and sea beyond. This attractive compound centers around a four-story, mid-19th-century guest house, which is surrounded by four more-or-less modern outbuildings. The whole affair is situated on a large, grassy lot on a quiet cul-de-sac. Indeed, it's hard to believe that you're smack in the middle of Ogunquit, with both the beach and the village just a few minutes' walk away. All rooms have refrigerators ("for the caviar and Champagne," the manager says), and all but two have air-conditioning for those few days when the sea breeze fails. For longer stays, one- and two-bedroom efficiencies are available.

WHERE TO DINE

✪ **Arrows.** Berwick Rd. ☎ **207/361-1100.** Reservations strongly recommended. Main courses $25.95–$29.95. MC, V. May and Columbus Day–Thanksgiving Fri–Sat 6–9:30pm; June and Sept–Columbus Day Wed–Sun 6–9:30pm; July–Aug Tues–Sun 6–9:30pm. Closed Thanks-giving to Apr. Turn uphill at the Key Bank in the village; the restaurant is 1.9 miles on your right. REGIONAL/NEW AMERICAN.

Ask well-heeled Mainers to name the five best restaurants in the state, and it's likely that Arrows will appear on most lists. Since owner/chefs Marc Gaier and Clark Frasier opened Arrows in 1988, they've managed to put Ogunquit on the national culinary map. And they've done so by not only creating an elegant and intimate atmosphere in a pleasant country setting, but by serving up some of the freshest, most innova-tive cooking in New England. The atmosphere is that of a classic European country inn, with oak chairs, white tablecloths, and a smartly uniformed waitstaff. The main dining room has heavy timbers overhead, and lighted views to the lush summer gardens.

The emphasis is on local products—*very* local products. The salad greens are grown in the gardens out back, and much of the rest is grown or raised locally. The food transcends traditional New England, and is concocted with some exotic twists and turns. Frasier lived and traveled widely in Asia, and his Far Eastern experiences often influence the menu, which changes nightly. Typically creative entrees might include grilled yellowfin tuna served with a mélange of golden chanterelles, warm gar-den frisee, walnuts, and a wild mushroom broth; or smoked duck breast with baby bok choy, garlic, jasmine rice fritters, and Szechuan marinated eggplant. The wine list is superb. Arrows is not for the timid of wallet, but makes for a special evening.

Barnacle Billy's & Barnacle Billy's Etc. Perkins Cove. ☎ **207/646-5575.** Reservations not accepted. Lunch $3.65–$11.95; dinner $10.95–$18.95. AE, MC, V. Daily 11am–10pm. Closed Nov to mid-Apr. SEAFOOD.

This pair of side-by-side restaurants under the same ownership are a bit like broth-ers, one of whom became a fisherman, the other an executive. The original Barnacle Billy's, a local landmark since 1961, is a place-your-order-take-a-number-and-wait-on-the-deck-style restaurant with the usual nautical decor and pine furniture inside. Its younger and fancier sibling next door has valet parking, sit-down service, and dem-onstrates better breeding.

In both places, you're largely paying for the same thing: the unobstructed view of Perkins Cove. At the original Barnacle Billy's, that means the food is at the high end of the price range for what you get (on my last visit the iced tea was $1.50 for a glass that was almost all ice). It's best to stick to simple fare, like chowder or boiled lob-ster. The prices are steeper but the value is better next door, where the service seems less weary and more care is taken with the food. Entrees include a variety of broiled, fried, and grilled seafood, along with a selection of poultry and meat.

✪ Hurricane. Oarweed Dr., Perkins Cove. ☎ **207/646-6348.** Reservations recommended. Lunch items $6.95–$12.95; main dinner courses $13.95–$24.95. AE, DC, DISC, MC, V. Mon–Sat 11:30am–4pm, Sun 11:30am–4:30pm; Mon–Thurs 5:30–9:30pm, Fri–Sat 5:30–10:30pm. NEW AMERICAN.

Tucked away amid the T-shirt kitsch of Perkins Cove is one of southern Maine's classiest dining experiences. The plain shingled exterior of the building, set along a curving, narrow lane, doesn't begin to hint at what you'll find on the inside. The narrow dining room is divided into two smallish halves, but soaring windows overlooking the Gulf of Maine make the rooms feel much larger than they actually are. During a storm, you're likely to feel as if you're on the prow of the ship.

Hurricane sneaks in surprises at almost every turn, from the waiters in white shirts and ties (which you don't see that much in Maine beach towns), to the delicate Victorian-style back bar. The cuisine offers pleasant surprises as well, with creative concoctions like an appetizer of deviled Maine lobster cakes served with a tangy fresh salsa. Main courses include a lobster cannelloni with Mascarpone cheese and shiitake mushrooms, and a baked salmon and Brie baklava with a Key Lime béarnaise. Added bonus: Hurricane makes the best martinis in town.

THE KENNEBUNKS

"The Kennebunks" consist of the villages of Kennebunk and Kennebunkport, both situated on the shores of tiny rivers. The region was first settled in the mid-1600s and flourished following the American Revolution when ship captains, ship builders, and successful merchants constructed the imposing, solid homes for which the region is noted. The two villages have decidedly different characters; a visit to these siblings provides contrasting looks at a coastal and an inland town.

While summer is the busy season, winter has its charm: The grand architecture is better seen through leafless trees. When the snow flies, guests find solace curling up in front of a fire at one of the inviting inns.

Kennebunk, an inland town just off the turnpike, is a dignified, small commercial center of white clapboard and brick. **Tom's of Maine,** a maker of natural toothpaste, is headquartered here.

ESSENTIALS

GETTING THERE   Kennebunk is located off Exit 3 of the Maine Turnpike. Kennebunkport is 3¹/₂ miles southeast of Kennebunk on Port Road (Route 35).

VISITOR INFORMATION   The **Kennebunk-Kennebunkport Chamber of Commerce,** P.O. Box 740, Kennebunk, ME 04043 (☎ **207/967-0857**), can answer your questions year-round. It also maintains an information booth (open Memorial Day to Columbus Day) on Route 35 just west of the intersection with Route 9. The **Kennebunkport Information Center** (☎ **207/967-8600**) is off Dock Square (next to Ben & Jerry's) and is open throughout the summer and fall.

EXPLORING KENNEBUNKPORT

Nearby Kennebunkport has name recognition, thanks to President George Bush, whose family has summered here for most of this century. It also has a tweedy, upper-crust feel that you might expect of a town where the former president feels comfortable. This historic village, whose streets were laid out during days of travel by foot and horse, is subject to epic traffic jams around the town center, called **Dock Square.** Your best strategy is to avoid driving near the square; park some distance away, then approach the square by foot.

Ocean Drive from Dock Square to Walkers Point and beyond is lined with opulent summer homes overlooking surf and rocky shore. This stretch is best appreciated by bike or on foot. You'll likely recognize the former president's home at Walkers Point when you arrive. If it's not familiar from the four years it spent in the spotlight, look for the swarming crowds with telephoto lenses.

✪ **The Seashore Trolley Museum.** Log Cabin Rd., Kennebunkport. ☎ **207/967-2800.** Web site http://www.biddeford.com:80/trolley/. $7 adults, $5 seniors, $4 children 6–16. Daily May through mid-Oct; weekends only through mid-Nov. Head north from Kennebunkport on North St.; look for signs.

A short drive north of Kennebunkport on Log Cabin Road is one of the quirkiest and most engaging museums in the state. The Seashore Trolley Museum, a place with an excess of character and an intriguing history, is well worth a visit. This scrapyard masquerading as a museum ("world's oldest and largest museum of its type") was founded in 1939 to preserve a disappearing way of life, and today the collection contains more than 200 trolleys from around the world, including Glasgow, Moscow,

San Francisco, and Rome. Of course, there's also a streetcar named Desire from New Orleans. About 40 of the cars still operate, and the admission charge includes unlimited rides on a two-mile track. The other cars, some of which still contain turn-of-the-century advertising, are on display outdoors and in vast storage sheds.

A good museum inspires awe and educates its visitors on the sly. This one does so deftly, and not until visitors are driving away are they likely to realize how much they learned.

BEACHES

Several local beaches are suitable for an afternoon's relaxation. To the south of the Kennebunk River is **Kennebunk Beach** and **Gooch's Beach;** to the north is **Goose Rocks Beach.** These beaches tend to be less crowded and noisy than the beaches in York and Ogunquit to the south, or Old Orchard Beach to the north. Parking at the beaches requires a permit, which can usually be obtained at the town offices or from your hotel.

WHERE TO STAY

Expensive

Captain Lord. Pleasant St. and Green St. (P.O. Box 800), Kennebunkport, ME 04046. ☎ 207/967-3141. Fax 207/967-3172. Web site www.biddeford.com:80/inntravel/inn0001.html. 16 rms. A/C TEL. $149–$199 double. $60 off during midweek Jan–Apr. Two-night minimum on weekends. Rates include breakfast. DISC, MC, V.

It's simple: This is the best building in Kennebunkport, in the best location, and furnished with the best antiques. The Captain Lord is one of the most architecturally distinguished inns anywhere, housed in a pale-yellow Federal-style home that peers down a shady lawn toward the river. The adjective "stately" is laughably inadequate.

When you enter the downstairs reception area, you'll know immediately that you've transcended the realm of "wannaB&Bs." This is the genuine article, with grandfather clocks and Chippendale highboys—and that's just the front hallway. Off the hall is a comfortable common area with piped-in classical music and a broad brick fireplace. The rooms are furnished with splendid antiques. Some beds are high enough to require a running start to mount. The only complaint I've heard about this place is that it's too nice, too perfect, too friendly. That puts some people on edge. No smoking.

✪ **The Colony.** Ocean Ave. (about a mile from Dock Square; P.O. Box 511), Kennebunkport, ME 04046. ☎ 800/552-2363 or 207/967-3331. Fax 207/967-8738. E-mail colony@cybertours.com. Web site www.cybertours.com/colony/home.html. 135 rms in 4 buildings. TEL. $175–$265 double. Rates include breakfast and dinner. Closed mid-Oct to mid-May. AE, MC, V.

The Colony is one of the handful of oceanside resorts that has preserved intact the classic New England vacation experience. This gleaming white Georgian Revival (built in 1914) lords over the ocean and the mouth of the Kennebunk River. The three-story main inn has 105 rooms, most of which have recently been updated. The rooms are bright and cheery, simply furnished with summer cottage antiques. Rooms in two of the three outbuildings carry over the rustic elegance of the main hotel; the exception is the East House, a 1950s-era motor hotel at the back edge of the property with 20 charmless motel-style rooms.

Guest rooms lack TVs in the main inn, and that's by design. The Boughton family, which has owned the hotel since 1948, encourages guests to leave their rooms in the evening and socialize downstairs in the lobby, on the porch, or at the shuffleboard court, which is lighted for night-time play. During the day, activities include swimming in a heated saltwater pool (or at a small pebble beach across the street), golfing on the putting green overlooking the ocean, or renting bikes and exploring Ocean Avenue.

Dining/Entertainment: The massive, pine-paneled dining room seats up to 400, and guests are assigned one table for throughout their stay. Dinners begin with a relish tray, but quickly progress to a more contemporary era with regional entrees such as rainbow tortellini with lobster marinara sauce, or maple-cured ham with apricot-orange sauce. On Sundays, there's a jazz brunch.

○ White Barn Inn. Beach St. (¹/₄ mile east of junction of Rtes. 9 and 35; P.O. Box 560), Kennebunkport, ME 04046. ☎ **207/967-2321.** Fax 207/967-1100. 24 rms. A/C TEL. $140–$205 double, up to $375 suite. Rates include breakfast. AE, MC, V.

The White Barn Inn pampers its guests like no other in Maine. Upon checking in, guests are shown to one of the inn's parlors and offered sherry or brandy while valets in dark uniforms gather luggage and park the cars. A tour of the inn follows, then guests are left to their own devices. They can avail themselves of the inn's free bikes (including a small fleet of tandems) to head to the beach, or walk across the street and wander the quiet, shady pathways of Saint Anthony's Franciscan Monastery. The innkeepers installed a swimming pool behind the carriage house in 1996.

The inn has a heavily European atmosphere (no surprise: nearly half the staff is here on special visas from Europe), and the emphasis is on service. I'm not aware of any other inn of this size that offers as many unexpected niceties, like robes, fresh flowers in the rooms, bottled water, and turndown service at night. The inn also serves some of the best fare in Maine (see "Where to Dine," below) in the adjoining barn. No smoking.

Moderate

Kennebunkport Inn. Dock Square (P.O. Box 111), Kennebunkport, ME 04046. ☎ **800/248-2621** (out of state) or 207/967-2621. Fax 207/967-3705. 34 rms (some with shower only). A/C TV. Summer $84.50–$189 double; Sept–Oct $79.50–$189 double; off-season $69.50–$179 double. MAP rates available summer and fall. AE, MC, V.

Situated behind a scrim of maple trees a few steps from bustling Dock Square, the Kennebunkport Inn's exterior is busy with an amalgam of dormers, gables, porticos, awnings, and modern additions. Despite all this architectural frenzy, the stately 1899 inn manages the mean feat of both blending in with *and* standing out from its surroundings. Inside, it's impeccably maintained. The rooms are nicely furnished, many with turn-of-the-century antiques. (Some equally well-appointed rooms are located in the adjoining River House, built in the 1930s.)

Downstairs, there's a handsome, clubby lounge and a well-respected dining room, which is open summer and fall. For extended lounging, there's a pool and a relaxing front deck.

WHERE TO DINE

Federal Jack's Restaurant and Brew Pub. Lower Village (south bank of Kennebunk River), Kennebunkport. ☎ **207/967-4322.** Reservations not accepted. Lunch items $5.25–$12.95; main dinner courses $6.25–$21.95. MC, V. Daily 11:30am–4pm; Sun–Thurs 5–9pm, Fri–Sat 5–10pm. PUB FARE.

This light, airy, and modern restaurant is in a new retail complex that sits a bit uneasily amid the scrappy boatyards lining the south bank of the Kennebunk River. From the second-floor perch (look for a seat on the spacious deck in warm weather), you can gaze across the river toward the shops of Dock Square, which is within easy walking distance across the nonworking drawbridge. The menu features basic entrees like hamburgers, barbecue pork ribs, and pizza, but everything is well prepared. Watch for specials like the tasty crab and artichoke bisque.

Don't leave without sampling the Shipyard ales, lagers, and porters brewed downstairs, which are among the best in New England. Shipyard brews a seasonal India Pale Ale in summer that's exceptional. Consider also the ale sampler, which provides tastes of various brews. Nontipplers can enjoy zesty homemade root beer.

✪ **White Barn Inn.** Beach St., Kennebunkport. ☎ **207/967-2321.** Reservations recommended. Fixed-price dinner $56. AE, MC, V. Daily 6–9pm (open later during peak season). Closed Jan. REGIONAL/NEW AMERICAN.

People don't come to the White Barn Inn just for special occasions, like anniversaries or birthdays. They come for *really* special occasions, like anniversaries or birthdays that end in "0" or "5." It's that kind of place (and one that charges that kind of price), but worth saving up for if you're bound and determined to make your stay in Maine unforgettable.

The setting is magical. The restaurant (attached to an equally magical inn; see "Where to Stay," above) is housed in an ancient, rustic barn with a soaring interior that might be compared without embarrassment to a cathedral's nave. (The furnace runs nearly full-time in winter to keep the space comfortable.) There's a copper-topped bar off to one side, rich leather seating in the waiting area, a pianist setting the mood, and an eclectic collection of antiques displayed in the hayloft above. On the tables are floor-length tablecloths, and the chairs feature imported Italian upholstery that recalls early Flemish tapestries.

The menu changes frequently, but depending on the season you might start with a lobster spring roll with daikon, carrots, snowpeas, and cilantro, then graduate to a grilled duckling breast with ginger and sun-dried cherry sauce, or a roast rack of lamb with pecans and homemade barbecue sauce. Anticipate a meal to remember. The White Barn won't disappoint.

Windows on the Water. 12 Chase Hill Rd. (above Lower Village), Kennebunkport. ☎ **800/773-3313** or 207/967-3313. Reservations recommended. Lunch items $6.95–$14.95; main dinner courses $13.95–$23.95. AE, DC, DISC, MC, V. Daily 11:45am–2:30pm; Sun–Thurs 5:30–9pm, Fri 5:30–9:30pm, Sat 5:30–10pm. NEW ENGLAND/INTERNATIONAL.

First off, the name's a bit of a misnomer. It's more like Windows on the Kennebunkport Brewing Co., although some glimpses of the river might be had over the newer buildings, especially from the second-floor dining room. But the compromised views aren't much of a loss, since the interiors of this modern restaurant are tastefully done, with pink tablecloths, oak chairs, and oak accenting. There's also a pleasant garden room with brick flooring and patio furniture, and dining upstairs in a room that's slightly more intimate if somewhat more antiseptic.

The food here is superb. The menu is based on classic New England cuisine, but with cooking techniques and spicing borrowed from around the world. There's seafood fettuccine Milanese, lobster ravioli, and Thai lobster, the latter a delicious concoction served with soy, ginger, coconut milk, and curry. The full dinner menu is available at lunch, along with lighter entrees such as lobster croissants and chicken caesar salad.

3 Portland

Portland is Maine's largest city, and easily one of the most attractive, livable small cities on the East Coast. Actually, Portland has more the feel of a really large town than a small city. Strike up a conversation with a resident, and she's likely to give you an earful about how easy it is to live here. You can buy superb coffee, see great movies, and get delicious pad thai to go (Portland has five Thai restaurants). Yet it's still small enough to walk from one end of town to the other, and postal workers and bank

Greater Portland

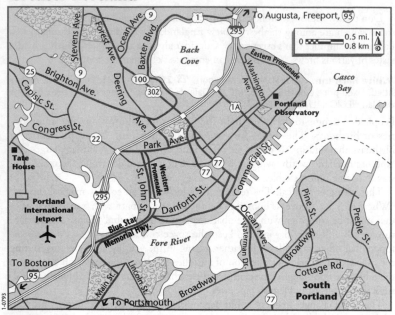

clerks know your name soon after you move here. Despite its outward appearance of being an actual city, Portland has a population of just 65,000 (about half that of Peoria, Il.).

ESSENTIALS

GETTING THERE   Portland is located off the Maine Turnpike (I-95). Coming from the south, downtown is most easily reached by taking Exit 6A off the turnpike, then following I-295 into town. Get off at the Franklin Street exit and follow this eastward until you arrive at the waterfront at the Casco Bay Lines terminal. Turn right on Commercial Street and you'll be at the lower edge of the Old Port. Continue on a few blocks to the visitor's center (see below).

The **Portland International Jetport** is served by regularly scheduled flights on several airlines, including **Business Express** (☎ 800/345-3400), **Continental** (☎ 800/525-0280), **Delta** (☎ 800/221-1212), **USAir** (☎ 800/428-4322), **United** (☎ 800/241-6522), Pine State (☎ 207/879-6111), and **Downeast Express** (☎ 800/983-3247). The small and easily navigated airport is located just across the Fore River from downtown. Metro buses ($1) connect the airport to downtown; cab fare runs about $10.

VISITOR INFORMATION   The **Convention and Visitor's Bureau of Greater Portland,** 305 Commercial St., Portland, ME 04101 (☎ 207/772-4994), stocks a large supply of brochures and is happy to dispense information about local attractions, lodging, and dining. The center is open in summer weekdays 8am to 6pm and weekends 10am to 5pm; hours are shorter during the off-season. Ask for the free *Greater Portland Visitor Guide* with map.

Casco Bay Weekly is a free alternative paper distributed Thursdays at many downtown stores and restaurants. The paper features extensive listings of performers at area clubs and other upcoming events.

ORIENTATION   The city of Portland is divided into two areas: on-peninsula and off-peninsula. (There are also the islands, but more on that below.) Most travelers are destined for the compact peninsula, which is home to the downtown and where most of the city's cultural life and much of its commercial action takes place.

Viewed from the water, Portland's peninsula is shaped like a sway-backed horse, with the Old Port in the low spot near the waterfront, and the peninsula's two main residential neighborhoods (Munjoy Hill and the West End) on the gentle rises overlooking downtown. These two neighborhoods are connected by Congress Street, Portland's main artery of commerce. The western stretch of Congress Street (roughly between Monument Square and State Street) is Portland's emerging Arts District, home to a handsome art museum, three theaters, the campus of the Maine College of Art (located in an old department store), and a growing number of restaurants and boutiques.

PARKING   Parking is notoriously tight in the Old Port area, and the city's parking enforcement is notoriously efficient. Several parking garages are convenient to the Old Port, with parking fees less than $1 per hour.

EXPLORING THE CITY

Any visit to Portland should start with a stroll around the historic **Old Port.** Bounded by Commercial, Congress, Union, and Pearl streets, this several-square-block area near the waterfront contains some of the best commercial architecture in town, a plethora of fine restaurants, a mess of boutiques, and bars thicker than North Woods black flies in June. The narrow streets and intricate brick facades reflect the mid-Victorian era; most of the area was rebuilt following a devastating fire in 1866. Leafy, quaint **Exchange Street** is the heart of the Old Port, with other attractive streets running off and around it.

Children's Museum of Maine. 142 Free St. (next to the Portland Museum of Art). ☎ **207/ 828-1234.** Admission $4 per person (child or adult). Summer Mon–Sat 10am–5pm, Sun noon– 5pm; closed Mon, Tues fall through spring.

The centerpiece exhibit of the Children's Museum is the camera obscura, a room-size "camera" located on the top floor of this regal downtown building. Children gather around a white table in a dark room, where they see magically projected images of city streets and boats plying the harbor. The camera obscura rarely fails to enthrall, and it provides a memorable lesson in how a camera works.

There's plenty more to do here, from running a supermarket checkout counter to sliding down the firehouse pole to piloting the mock space shuttle from a high cockpit. Budget time also for lunch at the cafe, where you can order up a peanut butter and jelly sandwich, a tall glass of milk, and an oatmeal cookie. Make a deal with your kids: They behave during a trip to the art museum next door, and they'll be rewarded with a couple of hours in their own museum.

Maine Historical Society. 489 Congress St. ☎ **207/879-0427.** Gallery and Longfellow house tour $4 adults, $1 children under 12. Gallery only $2 adults, $1 children under 12. Longfellow House and gallery June–Oct Tues–Sun 10am–4pm; gallery only June–Oct Wed–Sat noon–4pm.

Maine Historical Society's "history campus" includes three widely varied buildings in the middle of downtown Portland. The austere brick Wadsworth-Longfellow House dates to 1785 and was built by Gen. Peleg Wadsworth, father of noted poet Henry Wadsworth Longfellow. It's still furnished in an authentic early American style, with many samples from the Longfellow family furniture still on display.

Adjacent to the home is the Maine History Gallery, located in a somewhat garish postmodern building. Changing exhibits explore the rich texture of Maine history. Just behind the Longfellow house is the library of the Maine Historical Society, a popular destination among genealogists. Don't miss the small, peaceful garden hidden in the back next to the library.

⊙ **Portland Head Light & Museum.** Fort Williams Park, 1000 Shore Rd., Cape Elizabeth. ☎ **207/799-2661.** Grounds free; museum admission $2 adults, $1 children 6–18. Park grounds year-round daily sunrise to sunset (until 8:30pm in summer); museum June–Oct daily 10am–4pm; open weekends only in spring and late fall. From Portland, follow State St. across the Fore River to the "T" intersection at Broadway; turn left. At second light turn right on Cottage Rd., which soon becomes Shore Rd.; follow this about 2 miles until you arrive at the park, on your left.

Just a 10-minute drive from downtown Portland, this 1794 lighthouse is one of the most picturesque in the nation. The lighthouse marks the entrance to Portland Harbor, and was occupied continuously from its construction until 1989, when it was automated and the graceful keeper's house (1891) was converted to a small, town-owned museum focusing on the history of navigation. The lighthouse is still active and thus closed to the public, but visitors can wander the park grounds, sit on the rocky headlands, and watch the sailboats and ships come and go. The park has a pebble beach, grassy lawns with ocean vistas, and picnic areas well-suited for informal barbecues.

Portland Museum of Art. 7 Congress Sq. (corner of Congress and High sts.). ☎ **207/775-6148.** Admission $6 adults, $5 students and seniors, $1 children 6–12. Free Fri 5–9pm. Tues–Wed and Sat 10am–5pm, Thurs–Fri 10am–9pm, Sun noon–5pm.

This bold, modern museum was designed by I. M. Pei Associates in 1983, and displays selections from its own fine collections and a parade of touring exhibits. The museum is particularly strong in American artists who had a connection to Maine, including Winslow Homer, Andrew Wyeth, and Edward Hopper, and has fine displays of early American furniture and crafts. The museum shares the Joan Whitney Payson Collection with Colby College (the college gets it one semester every other year). The collection features wonderful European works by Renoir, Degas, and Picasso.

Victoria Mansion. 109 Danforth St. ☎ **207/772-4841.** $4 adults, $2 children under 18. May–Oct Tues–Sat 10am–4pm, Sun 1–5pm; closed Nov–Apr. From the Old Port, head west on Fore St. to Danforth St. near Stonecoast Brewing; bear right and proceed 3 blocks to the mansion.

Widely regarded as one of the most elaborate Victorian brownstone homes in existence, this mansion (also known as the Morse-Libby House) is a remarkable display of high Victorian style. Built between 1859 and 1863 for a Maine businessman who made a fortune in the New Orleans hotel trade, the towering, slightly foreboding home is a prime example of the Italianate style then in vogue. Inside, it appears that not a square inch of wall space was left unmolested by craftsmen or artists (11 artists were hired to paint the murals). The decor is ponderous and somber, but it offers an engaging look at a bygone era.

ON THE WATER

Casco Bay Lines. Commercial and Franklin sts. ☎ **207/774-7871.** Fares vary depending on the run, but are generally $4.50–$13.75 round-trip. Frequent departures 6am–midnight.

Six of the Casco Bay islands have year-round populations and are served by scheduled ferries from downtown Portland. (Most of these are part of the city of Portland; the exception is Long Island, which broke away in a secession bid a few years ago.)

The ferries offer an inexpensive way to view the bustling harbor and get a taste of Maine's islands. Trips range from a 20-minute excursion to Peaks Island (the closest thing to an island suburb with 1,200 year-round residents), to the 5½-hour cruise to Bailey Island and back. All of the islands are well-suited to walking; Peaks Island has a rocky back shore that's easily accessible via the island's paved perimeter road (bring a picnic lunch). Cliff Island is the most remote of the bunch, and has a sedate turn-of-the-century island retreat character.

Eagle Island. Eagle Island Tours, Long Wharf (Commercial St.). ☎ **207/774-6498.** $15 adults, $9 children under 9 (plus state park fee of $1.50 adults, 50¢ children). One departure daily at 10am.

Eagle Island was the summer home of famed Arctic explorer and Portland native Robert E. Peary, who claimed in 1909 to be the first person to reach the North Pole. (His accomplishments have been the subject of exhaustive debate among Arctic scholars, some of whom insist he inflated his claims.) In 1904 Peary built this simple home on a remote, 17-acre island at the edge of Casco Bay; in 1912 he added flourishes in the form of two low stone towers. After his death in 1920 his family kept up the home, then later donated it to the state, which has since managed it as a state park. The home is open to the public, maintained much the way it was when Peary lived here. Island footpaths through the forest allow exploration to the open, seagull-clotted cliffs at the southern tip.

Eagle Tours offers one trip daily from Portland. The four-hour excursion includes a 1½-hour stopover on the island.

MINOR LEAGUE BASEBALL

Portland Sea Dogs. Hadlock Field, P.O. Box 636, Portland, ME 04104. ☎ **800/936-3647** or 207/874-9300. Tickets $4–$6. Season runs Apr–Labor Day.

The Portland Sea Dogs are the Double-A team affiliated with the Florida Marlins, and they play throughout the summer at Hadlock Field, a small stadium near downtown that still retains an old-time feel despite aluminum benches and other improvements. Games here are a great way to spend an afternoon or evening, and are geared toward families, with lots of entertainment between innings and a selection of food that's a couple of notches above basic hot dogs and hamburgers. (Try the tasty french fries and grilled sausages.)

The biggest problem is getting tickets—games tend to sell out a couple of weeks in advance. Pick a date, and call for reservations. If you have general-admission seats, get there at least a half-hour early so you don't end up way down the left field line.

ROAD TRIPS

OLD ORCHARD BEACH   About 12 miles south of Portland is the unrepentantly honky-tonkish beach town of Old Orchard Beach, which offers treats for most of the senses (taste buds excluded). This venerable Victorian-era resort is famed for its amusement park, its pier, and its long, sandy beach, which attracts sun worshippers from all over, especially Quebec. (English-speaking folks quickly feel like a minority here.) Be sure to spend time and money riding some of the stomach-churning rides (if you'd prefer something more relaxing, head for the antique carousel), then walk on the seven-mile-long beach past the mid-rise condos that sprouted in the 1980s like a model train–scale Miami Beach.

The beach is broad and open at low tide; at high tide, space to put your towel down can be hard to come by. In the evenings, teens and young adults dominate the town. For dinner, do as the locals do and buy hot dogs and pizza and cotton candy; save your change for the video arcades.

Old Orchard is just off Route 1 south of Portland. The quickest route is to leave the turnpike at Exit 5, then follow I-195 and the signs to the beach. Be aware that parking is tight, and the traffic can be horrendous during the peak summer months.

SEBAGO LAKE   Maine's second-largest lake is also its most popular. Ringed with summer homes of varying vintages, many dating from the early part of this century, Sebago Lake attracts thousands of vacationers to its cool, deep waters.

You can take a tour of the lake and the ancient canal system between Sebago and Long lakes on the *Songo Queen,* a faux steamship berthed in the town of Naples (☎ 207/693-6861). Or just lie in the sun along the sandy beach at bustling **Sebago Lake State Park** (☎ 207/693-6613) on the lake's north shore (the park is off Route 302; look for signs between Raymond and South Casco). The park has shady picnic areas, a campground, a snack bar, and lifeguards on the beach (entrance fee charged). Even when it's crowded (which is to be expected on summer weekends), it's still always a relaxing place to go. Bring food for barbecuing.

✪ SABBATHDAY LAKE SHAKER COMMUNITY   Route 26 from Portland to Norway is a fast, speedy road through hilly farmland and past new housing developments. At one point the road pinches through a cluster of stately historic buildings that stand proudly beneath towering elms. That's the Sabbathday Lake Shaker Community (☎ 207/926-4597), the last active Shaker community in the nation. The dozen or so Shakers living here today still embrace the traditional Shaker beliefs and maintain a communal, pastoral way of life. The bulk of the community's income comes from the sale of herbs, which have been grown here since 1799.

This community is open to the public daily in summer except on Sundays (when visitors are invited to attend Sunday services). Docents offer tours of the grounds and several buildings, including the graceful 1794 meetinghouse. Exhibits in the buildings showcase the famed furniture lovingly crafted by the Shakers, and include antiques made by Shakers at other U.S. communes. You'll learn a lot about the Shaker ideology with its emphasis on simplicity, industry, and celibacy. After your tour, browse the gift shop for Shaker herbs and teas. Tours last either one hour ($5 adult, $2 children 6–12) or one hour and 45 minutes ($6.50 adult). Open daily except Sunday Memorial Day to Columbus Day from 10am to 4:30pm.

The Shaker village is located about 45 minutes from Portland. Head north on Route 26 (Washington Avenue in Portland). The village is eight miles from Exit 11 (Gray) off the Maine Turnpike.

WHERE TO STAY

Two sizable downtown hotels stand out against the skyline. The **Holiday Inn by the Bay,** 88 Spring St. (☎ 207/775-2311), offers great views of the harbor from about half the rooms, along with the usual chain-hotel creature comforts. The **Radisson Eastland,** 157 High St. (☎ 207/775-5411), is located in Portland's most venerable old hotel, and features two restaurants, a rooftop lounge, and a spacious lobby imbued with an Old-World elegance.

Budget travelers should seek out less expensive accommodations near the Maine Mall in South Portland and off the Maine Turnpike near Westbrook—two areas that are patently charmless, but offer reasonable access to the attractions of downtown, about 10 minutes away. Try **Days Inn** (☎ 207/772-3450) or **Coastline Inn** (☎ 207/772-3838) near the mall, or the **Super 8 Motel** (☎ 207/854-1881) or **Susse Chalet** (☎ 207/774-6101) off turnpike Exit 8 near the Westbrook town line.

The Danforth. 163 Danforth St., Portland, ME 04102. ☎ **800/991-6557** or 207/879-8755. Fax 207/879-8754. 9 rms, some with shower only. A/C TV TEL. $95–$165 double. Rates include breakfast. Rates discounted in the off-season. AE, MC, V.

Downtown Portland

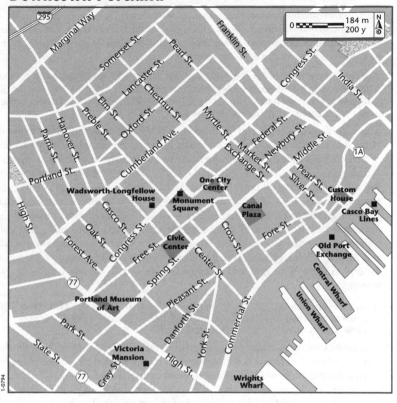

0   184 m
     200 y

295 · Marginal Way
Somerset St.
Pearl St.
Franklin St.
Congress St.
India St.
Lancaster St.
Chestnut St.
Elm St.
Oxford St.
Preble St.
Myrtle St.
Federal St.
Newbury St.
Middle St.
1A
Hanover St.
Paris St.
Cumberland Ave.
Market St.
Exchange St.
Pearl St.
Silver St.
Custom House
Portland St.
Wadsworth-Longfellow House
One City Center
Monument Square
Canal Plaza
Casco Bay Lines
High St.
Casco St.
Congress St.
Free St.
Civic Center
Cross St.
Fore St.
Old Port Exchange
Oak St.
Forest Ave.
Spring St.
Center St.
Central Wharf
77
Portland Museum of Art
Pleasant St.
Union Wharf
Park St.
Danforth St.
Commercial St.
State St.
Victoria Mansion
York St.
Gray St.
High St.
77
Wrights Wharf

1-0794

The Danforth is Portland's newest B&B (it opened in 1994), and brings with it a huge measure of class and elegance. Located in an imposing brick home constructed in 1821, the Danforth is something of a work in progress. It opened with just two guest rooms, but ongoing work has brought the total up to nine, where it will stop. Much of the effort has gone into renovating the building, and as such the guest rooms are still a bit Spartanly furnished. The furnishings should catch up with the opulence of the architecture over time, but even so the inn's extras are exceptional throughout, from the working fireplaces in all rooms but one, to the richly paneled basement billiards room. Innkeeper Barbara Hathaway has done a superb job attending to details, from the direct-line phones in the rooms (equipped with dataports for cyber-travelers) to the smartly uniformed staff to the complimentary guest membership at the city's best health club. The inn is located at the edge of the Spring Street Historic District, and is within walking distance of many downtown attractions.

Inn at Park Spring. 135 Spring St., Portland, ME 04101. ☎ **800/437-8511** or 207/774-1059. 7 rms (2 with shared bath; some with shower only). $60–$115 double. Rates include continental breakfast. AE, DISC, MC, V.

This small in-town B&B is housed in a comfortable, historic brick home dating back to 1835, and is the best located inn for exploring the town on foot. The Portland Museum of Art is just two blocks away, the Old Port about 10 minutes, and great restaurants are all within easy walking distance. Guests can linger or watch television in the front parlor, or chat at the table in the kitchen. The rooms are all corner rooms, and most are bright and sunny. Especially nice is "Spring," with its great morning light and wonderful views of the historic rowhouses on Park Street, and "Gables," one of the shared-bath rooms on the third floor, which has a clean, contemporary design and abundant afternoon sun. Reservations are usually essential here, as the owner lives separately and comes to meet the guests.

○ Pomegranate Inn. 49 Neal St., Portland, ME 04102. ☎ **800/356-0408** or 207/ 772-1006. 8 rms. $95–$165 double. Rates include full breakfast. AE, DISC, MC, V. From the Old Port, take Middle St. (which turns into Spring St.) to Neal St. in the West End (about 1 mile); turn right and proceed to inn. Free on-street parking.

This is Portland's most gracious B&B, and one of the best in northern New England. Housed in a handsome, dove-gray Italianate home in the architecturally distinctive Western Prom neighborhood, the interiors are wondrously decorated with whimsy and elegance—a combination that can be fatally cloying if attempted by someone without impeccably good taste. Look for the bold and exuberant wall paintings by Heidi Gerquest, a local artist, and the wonderfully eclectic antique furniture collected and arranged by owner Isabel Smiles. If you have the chance, peek in some of the unoccupied rooms—they're all quite different with painted floors and faux-marble woodwork. The best room is in the carriage house, which has its own private terrace and fireplace. Breakfasts are invariably creative and tasty. The inn is well situated for exploring the West End, and downtown is about a 15-minute walk away. No smoking.

Portland Regency Hotel. 20 Milk St., Portland, ME 04101. ☎ **800/727-3436** or 207/ 774-4200. Fax 207/775-2150. 95 rms. A/C MINIBAR TV TEL. Summer $149–$229 double; off-season $89–$175 double. AE, CB, DC, DISC, MC, V.

Centrally located on a cobblestone courtyard in the middle of the Old Port, the Regency has the city's premier hotel location. But it's got more than location going for it—it's also one of the most handsome and well-managed hotels in the state. Housed in a historic brick armory, the hotel offers a number of modern guest rooms nicely appointed and furnished with all the standard amenities. The hotel has a well-regarded dining room, an active tavern, and a well-equipped fitness room that doubles as a popular health club among Portlanders. The one complaint I've heard is about the noise: The guest room walls are a bit thin, and on weekends the revelry on the Old Port streets can penetrate even the dense brick exterior walls.

West End Inn. 146 Pine St., Portland, ME 04102. ☎ **800/338-1377** or 207/772-1377. 5 rms (1 with detached bath, 1 with shower only). TV. $89–$169 double. Rates include breakfast. AE, MC, V. Parking on street.

This brick, mansard-roofed Victorian duplex sits in one of Portland's more distinguished residential neighborhoods. And John and Terri Leonard have done a superb job making this urban townhouse into a welcoming retreat. The downstairs parlor features gold-leaf detailing on the ceiling, leather furniture, and Oriental antiques. The five guest rooms on two upstairs floors have canopy beds and are nicely decorated with bold wallpaper and antiques. Look for nice touches like bottles of Poland Spring Water in the rooms, and towels that match the decor in the bathrooms. The inn is well situated for walks in the West End and the Western Prom, two lovely turn-of-the-century neighborhoods with some of Portland's best architecture.

WHERE TO DINE
EXPENSIVE

○ Street & Co. 33 Wharf St. ☎ **207/775-0887.** Reservations recommended. Main courses $11.95–$17.95. AE, MC, V. Sun–Thurs 5:30–9:30pm, Fri–Sat until 10pm. SEAFOOD/ CONTEMPORARY.

This is one of the best seafood restaurants in the state, if not all of New England. A pioneer establishment on now-trendy Wharf Street, Street & Co. specializes in seafood cooked just right. There's no smoke and mirrors—you pass the cramped kitchen on your way in, and some spectators watch the talented chefs practice their art through an alley window. The atmosphere of this intimate spot is a bit like something you might imagine stumbling onto while touring Provence: Low beams, dim lighting, and drying herbs hanging overhead nicely set the mood. Diners are seated at copper-topped tables, designed such that the waiters can deliver steaming skillets right from the stove. Try the lobster diavalo—a spicy mélange of lobster, mussels, and clams in a delectable red sauce. If you're partial to calamari, be sure to order it here. They know how to cook it so it's perfectly tender, something that's becoming a lost art elsewhere. Street & Co. always fills up early, so reservations are strongly recommended. A few tables are reserved for walk-ins each night, though, so if you're in the neighborhood it can't hurt to ask.

✪ **West Side Restaurant.** 58 Pine St. ☎ **207/773-8223.** Reservations recommended. Main courses $11.95–$18.95. MC, V. Tues–Thurs 11:30am–2pm and 5–9pm, Fri 11:30am–2pm and 5–10pm, Sat 9am–1pm and 5–10pm, Sun 9am–2pm and 5–9pm. NEW AMERICAN.

This intimate neighborhood bistro is quiet, elegant, and hugely popular with clued-in Portlanders. It's hard to even read all the way through the enticing menu without body-tackling a waiter and demanding to order immediately. The menu changes every two weeks but often features a good selection of game dishes: There's the Maine venison médaillons with a wild mushroom, tarragon, and red wine sauce; duck breast with cranberries; and a tangy cassoulet with duck, lamb sausage, and pork. Other fine choices include delicate preparations of quail, sweetbreads, veal, salmon, and rabbit. The West Side is off the beaten path, but it's well worth hunting down. In the winter a woodstove makes the place toasty; in summer there's dining on a second-floor deck. Weekend breakfasts and weekday lunches are also first-rate.

MODERATE

ⓢ **Café Uffa!** 190 State St. ☎ **207/775-3380.** Reservations not accepted. Main courses $7.95–$10.95. MC, V. Wed–Sat 5:30–10pm, Sun 9am–2pm. MULTIETHNIC.

If you're looking to stretch your dollar without compromising on quality, this is your place. Launched a couple of years ago by three young friends, Uffa consistently manages to impress Portland's picky eaters with their creative international fare. The specialty is fish grilled to perfect tenderness over a wood-stoked fire, but there's plenty else to choose from. The chefs share a predilection for perfectionism, and even simple side dishes like black beans are cooked with unexpected flair. With its mismatched chairs, last-week's-flea-market decor, and high ceilings, Uffa attracts a young crowd with its aggressively informal styling. Sunday brunches are also superb, but be prepared to wait. There's often a line to get in.

Katahdin. 106 High St. ☎ **207/774-1740.** Reservations not accepted. Main courses $9.95–$14.95. DISC, MC, V. Mon–Thurs 5–10pm, Fri–Sat until 11pm. AMERICAN/REGIONAL.

Katahdin is a noisy, funky place that prides itself on its quirky salt shakers and its eclectic food. Local impoverished artists congregate here and order the nightly blue-plate special, which typically features something basic like meatloaf. Wealthy business folks one table over dine on more delicate fare, like the restaurant's famed crabcakes. Other recommended specialties include the lobster spring roll appetizers, and the entree of grilled sea scallops with a spicy lime vinaigrette. Sometimes the kitchen nods, but for the most part it's good food at good prices. Reservations aren't accepted, but there's a big bar in the dining room where you can enjoy Portland's best martini while waiting for a table.

Uptown Billy's. 1 Forest Ave. ☎ **207/780-0141.** Reservations not accepted. Main courses $6.95–$20.95 (mostly $8–$10). AE, DC, MC, V. Mon–Sat 11:30am–2:30pm and 5–9pm, Fri–Sat until 10pm, Sun 3–8pm. BARBECUE.

Uptown Billy's is the place to go for a plate of pork ribs and a mess o' beans. Billy's started out in an authentic dive across the river in South Portland. Since moving uptown to a slightly larger venue, it's become "bistroized," adding somewhat more dainty dishes like salmon and grilled portobello mushrooms. But it's still best known for the slow-cooked pork spareribs, which require at least a dozen napkins per rack. The meals come with corn bread, buttermilk biscuits, and a choice of side dishes like macaroni and cheese, potatoes, or a zippy coleslaw. Billy's hasn't lost any of its informal charm in the move, and you needn't be embarrassed by the barbecue sauce on your chin. On weekends there's live entertainment, which is typically jazz, blues, or rockabilly.

INEXPENSIVE

Ⓢ **Seng's 2.** 921 Congress St. ☎ **207/879-2577.** No reservations. Main courses $5–$9.95. No credit cards. Daily 11am–10pm. THAI.

Portland's best Thai food is found in a small, somewhat dingy spot in a cheerless part of town near the bus station. Don't come here expecting atmosphere—unless you're a connoisseur of fluorescent lights. Come here expecting a big pile of delicious food at great prices. The spicy pad thai has developed a cult following among knowledgeable Portlanders. Five dollars will buy you a plateful that's nearly big enough for two. The curries are delicious, as are the hot basil leaves with chicken, beef, or tofu. Everything is available to go.

PORTLAND AFTER DARK

Portland is lively in the evenings, especially on summer weekends when the testosterone level in the Old Port seems to rocket into the stratosphere with young men and women prowling the dozens of bars and and spilling over onto the streets. Among the bars favored by locals are **Three-Dollar Dewey's** at the corner of Commercial and Union streets, **Gritty McDuff's Brew Pub** on Fore Street near the foot of Exchange Street, and **BrianBorú,** slightly out of the Old Port on Center Street. All three bars are informal and pubby, with guests sharing long tables with new companions.

Beyond the active Old Port bar scene, a number of clubs offer a good mix of live entertainment throughout the year. Check the free alternative paper, *Casco Bay Weekly,* for performers and showtimes.

4 The Western Lakes & Mountains

Maine's Western Mountains are a treasury of sparkling destinations if your idea of getting away involves heading into the outdoors and away from the crowds. This rugged, brawny region, which stretches northeast from the White Mountains to the Carrabasset Valley, isn't as commercialized as the Maine coast, and the villages aren't as quaint as you'll find in Vermont's Green Mountains. But it has azure lakes, ragged forests of spruce, fir, and lichens, and rolling hills and mountains that take on a distinct blue hue during the summer hiking season.

Cultural amenities are few here, but natural amenities are legion. Hikers have the famed Appalachian Trail, which crosses into Maine in the Mahoosuc Mountains (near where Route 26 enters into New Hampshire), and follows rivers and ridgelines northeast to Bigelow Mountain and beyond. Canoeists and fishermen head to the noted Rangeley Lakes area, a chain of deepwater ponds and lakes that has attracted sportsmen to rustic lodges along their shores for more than a century. And in the winter, skiers can choose among several downhill ski areas, including the two largest ski areas in the state, Sunday River and Sugarloaf.

BETHEL

Until the mid-1980s, Bethel was a sleepy, 19th-century resort town with one of those friendly, family-oriented ski areas that seemed destined for certain extinction. Until a guy named Les Otten came along. This brash, young entrepreneur bought Sunday River Ski Area and proceeded to make it into one of New England's most vibrant and successful ski destinations. (Successful enough that he subsequently snapped up most of the major ski areas in New England, including Killington, Attitash, Sugarbush, Sugarloaf, Mt. Snow, and Waterville Valley.)

With the rise of the ski area, the white-clapboard town of Bethel (located about seven miles from the ski area) has been dragged into the modern era, although it hasn't yet taken on the artificial, packaged flavor of some other New England ski towns. The village (pop. 2,500) is still dominated by a respected prep school, the Gould Academy, and the Bethel Inn, a turn-of-the-century resort that's managed to stay ahead of the tide by adding condos, but without losing its pleasant, timeworn character.

Bethel's stately, historic homes ring the **Bethel Common,** a long, rectangular greensward created in 1807 atop a low, gentle ridge. (It was originally laid out as a street broad enough for the training of the local militia.) The town's historic district encompasses some 27 homes, which represent a wide range of architectural styles popular in the 19th century. The oldest home in the district is the **1813 Moses Mason House,** which is now a fine, small museum housing the collections and offices of the **Bethel Historical Society** (☎ 207/824-2908).

ESSENTIALS

GETTING THERE   Bethel is located at the intersection of Route 26 and Route 2. It's accessible from the Maine Turnpike by heading west on Route 26 from Exit 11. From New Hampshire, drive east on Route 2 from Gorham.

VISITOR INFORMATION   The **Bethel Area Chamber of Commerce,** 30 Cross St., Bethel, ME 04217 (☎ 207/824-2282), has offices near the new movie theater and railroad depot. It's open year-round Monday through Saturday from 9am to 5pm and on Sundays "by chance."

OUTDOOR PURSUITS

Road & Mountain Biking

Hard-core mountain bikers should head to the **Sunday River Mountain Bike Park** (☎ 207/824-3000) at the ski area. Mountain bike trails of every caliber are open to bikers. Experienced trail riders will enjoy taking their bikes by chairlift to the summit, and riding back down on the service roads and bike trails.

Hiking

The **Appalachian Trail** crosses the Mahoosuc Mountains northwest of Bethel. Many of those who've hiked the entire 2,000-mile trail say this stretch is the most demanding on knees and psyches. The trail doesn't forgive; it generally foregoes switchbacks in favor of sheer ascents and descents. It's also hard to find water along the trail during dry weather. Still, it's worth the knee-pounding effort for the views and the unrivaled sense of remoteness.

One stretch of the Appalachian Trail crosses **Old Speck Mountain,** Maine's third highest peak, in Grafton Notch State Park off Route 26. There are no views since the old fire tower closed a few years ago, but an easy-to-moderate hike from Route 26 to an 800-foot cliff called **"The Eyebrow"** provides a good vantage point of the Bear River Valley and the rugged terrain of Grafton Notch. Look for the well-signed parking lot where Route 26 intersects the Appalachian Trail in Grafton Notch State Park. Park your car, then head south on the AT; in 0.1 mile you'll intersect the Eyebrow Trail and its moderate accent to the fine vistas.

The Appalachian Mountain Club's *Maine Mountain Guide* is highly recommended for detailed information about other area hikes.

Alpine Skiing

The East's only **ski train** serves Sunday River from Portland, offering a relaxed way to get to the slopes and back. Launched in 1993 by Sunday River owner Les Otten, this train pulls out of an industrial lot on Portland's outskirts at 6:45am, then follows rivers and historic train routes on its $2^1/4$-hour run to Bethel Station. Skiers are then transferred to a fleet of buses for the final seven-mile shuttle to the slopes, and are usually on the slopes by 9:30 or 10am.

The train cars are spacious if a bit cheerless, and allow sprawling and socializing for up to 283 passengers. Coffee and continental breakfast items are sold on the outbound leg; light meals and beer are available on the return trip. There's an adult-only bar car in the evening.

This isn't just basic transportation—although it's a delight when sloppy snows make driving hazardous. It's a whole experience, and one that's priced right. A weekend trip to sample Portland's restaurants and attractions could easily be packaged with a one- or two-day excursion to Sunday River, combining the best of urban Maine with some of the better skiing in New England.

The train runs on Fridays, Saturdays, and Sundays. When you buy a ski ticket, the train costs $15 round-trip Friday; $20 on weekends. Contact Sunday River (☎ 207/ 824-3000) for more information.

Sunday River Ski Resort. P.O. Box 450, Bethel, ME 04217. ☎ **207/824-3000,** lodging 800/ 543-2754. Vertical drop: 2,340 feet. Lifts: 15 chairlifts (3 high-speed), 1 surface lift. Skiable acreage: 639. Lift tickets: $45 adults weekends, $41 weekdays.

Sunday River has grown by leaps and bounds in recent years, and today competes in the same league as other major New England winter resorts like Mt. Snow and Killington. Unlike ski areas that have developed around a single tall peak, Sunday River has expanded along an undulating ridge that encompasses some seven peaks. Just traversing the resort, stitching runs together with chairlift rides, can take an hour. As a result, you rarely get bored making the same run time and again.

The descents offer something for virtually everyone, from steep bump runs to glade skiing to wide, wonderful intermediate trails. A few years ago, Sunday River was regarded as an intermediate's mountain. That changed dramatically with the expansion to the adjacent peaks and the addition of steep new runs. It's now got the reputation of a mountain with great bumps and sheer descents. Sunday River is also blessed with plenty of water for snowmaking, and makes tons of the stuff using a proprietary snowmaking system.

My chief complaint with Sunday River is that the superb skiing conditions are offset by an uninspiring base area. Everything seems a bit raw and unfinished at the bottom of the mountain. The lodges and condos are architecturally dull, dull, dull, and the less-than-delicate landscaping is the sort created by graceless bulldozers. And spread as widely as it is, there's no real sense of place, as there is at more established resorts like Sugarloaf or Waterville Valley.

Ski Mt. Abram. P.O. Box 120, Locke Mills, ME 04255. ☎ **207/875-5003.** Vertical drop: 1,030 feet. Lifts: 2 chairlifts, 3 T-bars. Skiable acreage: 135. Lift tickets: Adults $28 weekend, $18 midweek; children and teens $16–$22 weekends, $14–$18 midweek.

Mt. Abram is a welcoming intermediate mountain that's perfect for families on the uphill learning curve. It has a friendly, informal atmosphere that's in sharp contrast with nearby Sunday River. You don't have to expend much energy on logistics here planning when to meet up or at what base lodge. You don't have to expend as much cash, either.

WHERE TO STAY

Bethel Inn. On the Common, Bethel, ME 04217. ☎ **800/654-0125** or 207/824-2175. 57 rms (some with showers only). TV TEL. Summer $190–$360 double including breakfast and dinner; winter $150–$260 double including breakfast and dinner. Lodging only in Apr and Nov. Packages available. AE, DC, DISC, MC, V.

The Bethel Inn is a classic, old-fashioned resort built on the common in 1913. You can tell which buildings are part of the inn by their distinctive color—Bethel Inn yellow. The main inn has a quiet, settled air throughout, which seems appropriate since it was built to house patients of Dr. John Gehring, who put Bethel on the map treating nervous disorders through a regimen of healthy country living. (Bethel was once known as "the resting place of Harvard" for all the faculty treated here.) The quaint, homey rooms aren't terribly spacious, but are welcoming and pleasingly furnished with country antiques. The deluxe rooms have separate sitting rooms; modern condominium lodging is also available, but these sorely lack the charm of the inn. While the cost is high, don't be scared off; the inn offers a number of packages that bring down the daily rate if you stay a few days. Call and inquire.

The resort, situated on 200 acres, has a number of welcome amenities, including a fitness center with an outdoor heated pool, a superb golf course, tennis, and the inn's Lake House, picturesquely located amid pines on a small lake a short drive away. In winter, there's cross-country skiing on the inn's 24 miles of trails, and a daily shuttle delivers guests to downhill skiing at Sunday River.

The inn's fine dining room serves notable meals in a classically elegant setting, with specialties like a lobster-filled ravioli appetizer, and venison médaillons and broiled duck breast for main courses. (Angle for a table on the enclosed porch.)

Ⓢ Holidae House. Main St., Bethel, ME 04217. ☎ **207/824-3400.** 7 rms (3 with shower only). TV TEL. Winter $75–$89 double weekends, $45–$58 midweek; summer $60–$70 double. Rates include breakfast. AE, MC, V.

Innkeeper Tom McGinniss has done an extraordinary job making over this century-old village home on Bethel's Main Street. The exterior is unusually handsome, painted in rich but muted colors, and the inside is superbly decorated in a style that nicely straddles high Victorian and low whimsical. Every room is furnished with antiques and Oriental carpets; some have delightful hand-painted ceiling murals and whirlpool tubs. (Number 5 was my favorite, decorated with a surfeit of classically inspired elegance.) The common room is fairly small for an inn of this size, but guests are likely to keep to their rooms most of the time—except perhaps when browsing the antiques shop in the barn out back. (Guests get wholesale prices.) The inn is a five-minute walk from the Bethel Common, and a 10-minute drive to skiing at Sunday River.

L'Auberge Country Inn. Bethel Common (P.O. Box 21), Bethel, ME 04217. ☎ **800/ 760-2774** or 207/824-2774. 7 rms (1 with hall bath). Closed mid-April to mid-May and mid-Oct to Thanksgiving. $60–$100 double, including breakfast ($20 higher weekends and holidays). Two-night minimum on weekends. AE, DISC, MC, V.

L'Auberge was originally built as a barn in the 1890s, but other than a few exposed beams, its lineage isn't immediately evident. Located on a spacious, shady lot down a small lane just off the Bethel Common, the inn has a settled, European air inside. You enter through a high-ceilinged living room with a Steinway, ticking antique hall clock, fireplace, and decanter of sherry. "Kit" the golden retriever may be present to give you a low-key greeting. The rooms are furnished in a comfortable country style, some with stencilling and brass beds. The inn is well-known locally for its dining room, which serves delicately prepared continental fare. Guests choose from three small dining rooms; the best is an intimate space painted "gregarious red" that gives off a gentle, candlelit glow in the evening. (The dining room is open to the public, reservations recommended. Entree prices range from $14 to $24.) In summer, Tuesday nights feature a traditional lobster bake.

WHERE TO DINE

Iron Horse Bar & Grill. Bethel Station (Cross St.), Bethel. ☎ **207/824-0961.** Reservations recommended. Main courses, $9.50–$20. AE, DISC, MC, V. Sun–Thurs 5–9pm (until 10pm Fri–Sat and ski season). AMERICAN.

Housed in two train cars sidetracked at Bethel Station (the new mall/hotel complex at the edge of town), the Iron Horse captures the atmosphere of a long-lost era. Guests enter through a coupling between the two cars. To the right is a lounge car where you might expect to run into John Cheever on his way back to the Westchester suburbs. To the left is the dining car, which has a romantic art deco–ish flair to it, with a striking wall mural in a southwestern motif, white tablecloths, and etched glass partitions. Elegance notwithstanding, diners arrive in jeans in the summer and in ski togs in the winter. (This is Maine, after all.) The entrees are better than you'd find in most trains today, with dishes including Black Angus steak, chicken, seafood, and a selection of game, such as quail and wild boar. Be prepared for less-than-swift service (the waitress told me it's because the kitchen is so narrow), but count on a pleasant evening in unique surroundings.

Moose's Tale. Rte. 2 (at Sunday River Rd.), Bethel. ☎ **207/824-4253.** Reservations not accepted. Main courses $3.95–$13.95 (most $6–$8). MC, V. Daily 11:30am–1am. PUB FARE.

Sunday River Brewing Co. opened this modern brewpub a few years ago on prime real estate at the corner of Route 2 and the Sunday River access road. This is a good choice if your primary objective is to consume superb ales and porters. The brews are excellent; the food (burgers, nachos, chicken wings) doesn't appear to strive for any culinary heights, and certainly doesn't achieve them. The design of the restaurant is a bit idiosyncratic; the best tables are by the stone fireplace in the main dining room, and in a side room near the pool tables. And, of course, there's the bar, which is the optimal place to be after a day skiing the slopes or hiking on the Appalachian Trail. It can get really loud here some nights, especially when local bands are booked.

Mother's. Upper Main St., Bethel. ☎ **207/824-2589.** Reservations accepted for parties of 6 or more. Lunch $4.75–$8; dinner $6.50–$16.50. MC, V. Sun–Fri 11:30am–9:30pm (until 10pm Sat). May be closed briefly in late spring and late fall; call first. AMERICAN.

Appropriate to its name, Mother's is a homey, informal place housed in a pale green Victorian home adorned with gingerbread trim. Inside, diners are ushered to small, darkly paneled rooms, each of which has four or five tables and walls hung with portraits of dour Victorians. (In summer, there's also dining on the front deck.) The meals are basic and well-prepared, and the service is always friendly. For lunch there's hamburgers and crabcake sandwiches; for dinner, try the sea scallops with artichokes, or the pork ribs grilled with a lemon barbecue sauce.

RANGELEY LAKES

Mounted moose heads on the walls, log cabins tucked in the spruce forest, and cool August mornings that demand not one sweater but two come to mind when one speaks of the Rangeley Lakes region. Although Rangeley Lake and its eponymous town are at the heart of the region, it extends much further, consisting of a series of lakes that feed into and flow out of Rangeley. Upstream is Maine's fourth largest lake, Flagstaff, a beautiful, wind-raked body of water created in 1949 when Central Maine Power dammed the Dead River. (Below the dam it's no longer dead; in fact it's now noted for its white-water rafting—see "The North Woods," at the end of this chapter.) From Rangeley Lake, the waters flow into the Cupsuptic Pond, which in turn flow to Mooselookmeguntic Lake, through the Upper and lower Richardson Lakes, down the remote Swift River and to Lake Umbagog, which feeds the head-waters of the Androscoggin River.

The town of Rangeley (pop. 1,063) is the regional center for outdoor activities. It offers a handful of motels and restaurants, a few fishing guides, and a smattering of shops, but little else. Easy-to-visit attractions in the Rangeley area are few, and most regular visitors and residents seem determined to keep it that way. The wise visitor rents a cabin or takes a room at a lodge, then explores the area with the slow pace that seems custom made for the region. Rangeley is Maine's highest town at 1,546 feet, and is usually cool throughout the summer.

ESSENTIALS

GETTING THERE Rangeley is 122 miles north of Portland and 39 miles north-west of Farmington on Route 4. The most scenic approach is on Route 17 from Rumford. Along the way, you'll pass one of the most scenic overlooks in New England, with a sweeping panorama of Mooselookmeguntic Lake and Bemis Mountain.

From New Hampshire, drive 111 miles north on Route 16 from North Conway through Gorham, Berlin, and Errol. Route 16 from Errol to Rangeley is especially remote and scenic.

VISITOR INFORMATION The **Rangeley Lakes Region Chamber of Commerce**, P.O. Box 317, Rangeley, ME 04970 (☎ **800/685-2537** or 207/864-5571), maintains an information booth in town at a small park near the lake that's open year-round Monday through Saturday from 9am to 5pm.

CANOEING

The Rangeley Lakes area is a canoeist's paradise. Azure waters, dense forests, and handsome hills are all part of the allure. Rangeley Lake has a mix of wild forest and old-time camps lining the lakeshore. The southeast coves of Mooselookmeguntic Lake suffered an unfortunate period of haphazard development during the 1980s, but much of the shore, especially along the Phillips Preserve (see "Where to Stay & Dine," below) and the west shore, are still very attractive. Upper Richardson Lake's shore-line is largely owned by the state, and is the most remote and wild of the chain. Primi-tive campsites along the shores of both Upper and Lower Richardson lakes are managed by the **South Arm Campground** (☎ **207/364-5155**), located at the tip of Lower Richardson Lake and accessible via dirt road from the town of Andover.

Canoeists should exercise the usual caution and keep a sharp eye on the weather. Stiff northerly winds can blow through with little warning, making it all but impos-sible to return to where you started. This is especially true on the Upper and Lower

Weird Science

One of the quirkiest destinations in Maine is **Orgonon,** former home of the controversial Viennese psychologist Wilhelm Reich (1897–1957). A tour of his hilltop estate includes a great story about a man with a mission, and an up-close look at an architecturally distinctive stone house. Even if the history of psychology or architecture don't hold any allure for you, take my advice and stop by anyway. It won't be a disappointment.

A brief overview: Wilhelm Reich was an associate of Sigmund Freud during the early days of psychoanalysis. But Reich took Freud's work one step further. He hypothesized that pent-up sexual energy resulted in many neuroses, and believed that a regimen of induced orgasms would result in a psychologically healthy being. This led to his involvement with the sexual politics movement in Europe in the 1930s. His theories forced a break with Freud, and the clouds of World War II forced his departure from Europe.

Once settled in Rangeley, Reich pursued his theories further and developed the science of "orgonomy," which held that units of "orgone" floated freely in the atmosphere, and if captured, could be used to cure patients not only of their neuroses but of illness such as cancer. Reich invented "orgone boxes," which were said to concentrate the orgone from the atmosphere, and patients sat inside to be cured. He also invented a rather large and fearsome-looking orgone gun to capture orgone in the atmosphere, thereby producing rain by altering the atmospheric balance. Reich died in a federal prison in 1957, sentenced for contempt on matters related to the transport of his orgone boxes.

Orgonon, built in 1948 of native fieldstone, has a spectacular view of Dodge Pond and is built in a distinctive American Modern style, which doesn't exactly fit in with the local rustic-lodge motif. Visitors on the one-hour guided tour of the estate can see the orgone boxes and the orgone gun, along with the other intriguing inventions and stark, dramatic canvases created by Reich, who took up painting at age 55.

Orgonon (☎ **207/864-3443**) is located 3.5 miles west of Rangeley on Route 4. Admission is $3 adults, free to children 12 and under; it's open July and August Tuesday through Sunday from 1 to 5pm, and in September on Sunday only.

Richardson lakes, which angle northward—furious winds and frothy whitecaps are not an uncommon summer phenomenon.

HIKING

The **Appalachian Trail** crosses Route 4 about 10 miles south of Rangeley. A strenuous but rewarding hike is along the AT northward to the summit of **Saddleback Mountain,** a 10-mile round-trip that ascends though thick forest and past remote ponds to open, Arctic-like terrain with fine views of the surrounding mountains and lakes. Saddleback actually consists of two peaks over 4,000 feet (hence the name). Be prepared for sudden shifts in weather, and for the high winds that often rake the open ridgeline.

An easier one-mile hike may be found at **Bald Mountain** near the village of Oquossuc, on the northeast shore of Mooselookmeguntic Lake. (Look for the trailhead one mile south of Haines Landing on Bald Mountain Road). The views have grown over in recent years, but you can still catch glimpses of the clear blue waters from above.

ALPINE SKIING

Saddleback Ski Area. P.O. Box 490, Rangeley, ME 04970. ☎ **207/864-5671.** Vertical drop: 1,830 feet. Lifts: 2 double chairs, 3 T-bars. Lift tickets: $32 adult weekend, $19–$27 juniors and students weekend; all tickets $17 midweek.

With only two chairlifts, Saddleback qualifies as a small mountain. But there's the surprise. Because Saddleback has an unexpectedly big-mountain feel. It offers a vertical drop of 1,830 feet, but what makes Saddleback so appealing is its rugged alpine setting (the Appalachian Trail runs across the high, mile-long ridge above the resort) and the old-fashioned trails. Saddleback offered glade skiing and narrow, winding trails well before the bigger ski areas sought to re-create these old-fashioned slopes. The 2.5-mile Lazy River Trail is one of the more scenic beginner's descents in New England.

WHERE TO STAY & DINE

The Rangeley area has a scattering of bed-and-breakfasts, but many travelers destined here plan to spend a week or more either at a sporting camp or a rented waterfront cottage. Among the best-known of the sporting camps is **Grant's Kennebago Camps** (☎ **800/633-4815** or 207/864-3608), situated down a long and dusty logging road on Kennebago Lake—the biggest "fly-fishing only" lake east of the Mississippi. Rates are $100 per person per day, including all meals. **Mooselookmeguntic House** (☎ **207/864-2962**) offers a cluster of cabins on or near the shores of Mooselookmeguntic, along with access to a handsome beach and marina.

For weekly rental of a private cabin, advance planning is essential. A good place to start is the local chamber of commerce's free "Accommodations and Services" pamphlet (☎ **800/685-2537** or 207/864-5364). The chamber can itself book cabins for the week for you.

Rangeley Inn. P.O. Box 398, Rangeley, ME 04907. ☎ **800/666-3687** or 207/864-3341. Fax 207/864-3634. 51 rms (several with shower only). TV (motel only). $69–$119 double. AE, DISC, MC, V.

The architecturally eclectic Rangeley Inn dominates Rangeley's miniature downtown. Parts of this old-fashioned, blue-shingled hotel date back to 1877, but the main wing was built in 1907, with additions in the 1920s and the 1940s. A 15-unit motel annex was built behind the inn on Haley Pond, but those looking for creaky floors and a richer sense of local heritage should request a room in the main, three-floor inn.

The rooms at the inn and motel are each unique—some in the motel have woodstoves, kitchenettes, or whirlpools; in the inn you'll find a handful of rooms with clawfoot tubs perfect for an evening's soaking. The gracious, Old-Worldish dining room serves hearty, filling meals with considerable flair. Ed and Fay Carpenter have run the place since the early 1970s, and have hospitality down to a science. During the heavy tour season (especially fall), bus groups tend to dominate, but the rest of the time it's perfect for couples or families looking for a place to slough off the stress of daily life.

Two Lakeside Campgrounds

While dozens of wilderness campsites, often accessible only by canoe, may be found throughout the region (check with the chamber of commerce for more information), two of the more accessible campgrounds bear mentioning. **Rangeley Lake State Park** (☎ **207/864-3858**) occupies about a mile of shoreline on the south shore of Rangeley Lake. It has 50 attractive campsites with easy access to the waters of Rangeley Lake. Bring a canoe for exploring.

Along a narrow dirt road on the eastern shores of Mooselookmeguntic Lake is the **Stephen Phillips Wildlife Preserve** (☎ **207/864-2003**), a private holding comprised of hundreds of lakeshore acres and several islands. The preserve offers camping on two islands (Toothaker and Students), both of which are accessible by canoe. Lakeside campsites are also available in the scrubby spruce forest that lines the lake; most sites are accessible by walking a few hundred feet from scattered parking areas, providing more of a backcountry experience than you'll find at most drive-in campgrounds. Canoes are available for rent at the office. The fee is $6 per night for two people, and campsite reservations are accepted.

CARRABASSETT VALLEY

The Carrabassett Valley can be summed up in six words: big peaks, wild woods, deep lakes.

The crowning jewel of the region is Sugarloaf Mountain, Maine's second highest peak at 4,237 feet. Distinct from other nearby peaks because of its pyramidal shape, the mountain has been developed for skiing, and offers the highest vertical drop in Maine, the best selection of activities daytime and night, and a wide range of accommodations within easy commuting distance.

Outside of the villages and ski area, it's all rugged hills, tumbling streams, and spectacular natural surroundings. The muscular mountains of the Bigelow Range provide terrain for some of the state's best hiking. And Flagstaff Lake is the place for flatwater canoeing amid majestic surroundings.

ESSENTIALS

GETTING THERE   Kingfield and Sugarloaf are on Route 27. Skiers debate over the best route from the Turnpike. Some exit at Auburn and take Route 4 north to Route 27; others exit in Augusta and take Route 27 straight through. It's a toss-up time-wise, but exiting at Augusta is marginally more scenic.

VISITOR INFORMATION   The **Sugarloaf Area Chamber of Commerce** (☎ **207/235-2100**) offers information year-round from its offices 9.5 miles north of Kingfield on Route 27. The office is open in summer Monday through Saturday 10am to 4pm. In winter, it's open weekdays 8am to 7pm, Saturday 10am to 6pm, and Sunday 11am to 3pm. The chamber will book lodgings in and around Sugarloaf; call **800/843-2732**. For accommodations on the mountain, contact Sugarloaf directly at **800/843-5623**.

ALPINE SKIING

Sugarloaf/USA. R.R. 1, Box 5000, Carrabassett Valley, ME 04947. ☎ **800/843-5623** or 207/237-2000. Web site http://www.sugarloaf.com. Vertical drop: 2,820 feet. Lifts: 13 chairlifts, including 1 gondola and 1 high-speed quad; 1 surface lift. Skiable acreage: 1,400 (snowmaking on 475 acres). Lift tickets: $45 adult weekend; $41 weekday.

Sugarloaf is Maine's big mountain, with the highest vertical drop in New England after Killington in Vermont. And thanks to quirks of geography, it actually feels bigger than it is. From the high snowfields (which account for much of Sugarloaf's huge skiable acreage) or the upper advanced runs like Bubblecuffer or White Nitro, skiers develop a bit of vertigo looking down at the valley floor. Sugarloaf attracts plenty of experts to its hard-core runs, but it's also a superb intermediate mountain, with great cruising runs. A gentle bunny slope extends down through the village; the "green" slopes on the mountain itself are a bit more challenging.

Sugarloaf has more of a destination feel to it than many resorts, since it's nearly three hours from Portland (five from Boston) and gets relatively little day-tripper traffic. Most people who ski Sugarloaf stay at the base complex, a well-run, convivial cluster of hotel rooms, condos, mini-suites, and the like offering 7,500 beds. The accommodations, the mountain, the restaurants, and other area attractions are well-connected by chairlifts and shuttle buses, making for a relaxed visit here even during a fierce blizzard.

CROSS-COUNTRY SKIING

The **Sugarloaf Ski Touring Center** (☎ 207/237-6830) offers 57 miles of groomed trails that weave through the village at the base of the mountain and into the low hills covered with young, scrappy woodlands south of the Carrabassett River. The trails are impeccably groomed for striding and skating, and wonderful views open here and there to Sugarloaf Mountain and the Bigelow Range. The base lodge is simple and attractive, all knotty pine with a cathedral ceiling, and features a cafeteria, towering stone fireplace, and a well-equipped ski shop. Trail fees are $10 daily for adults; $7 to $8 for juniors, seniors, and children. The center is located on Route 27 about one mile south of the Sugarloaf access road. A shuttle bus serves the area in winter.

HIKING

The 12-mile **Bigelow Range** has some of the most dramatic, high-ridge hiking in the state, a close second to Mt. Katahdin. The Bigelow Range consists of a handful of lofty peaks, with Avery Peak (named after Myron Avery, one of the Appalachian Trail's founders) offering perhaps the best views. On exceptionally clear days, hikers can see Mount Washington to the southwest and Mount Katahdin to the northeast.

A strenuous but rewarding hike for fit hikers is the 10.3-mile loop that begins at the **Fire Warden's Trail.** (The trailhead is at the washed-out bridge on Stratton Brook Pond Road, a rugged dirt road that leaves eastward from Route 27 about 2.3 miles north of the Sugarloaf access road.) Follow the Fire Warden's Trail up the extremely steep ridge to the junction with the Appalachian Trail. Head south on the AT, which tops the West Peak and South Horn, two open summits with stellar views. One-quarter mile past Horns Pond, turn south on Horns Pond Trail and descend back to the Fire Warden's Trail to return to your car. Hikers pass two lean-tos along this route (free, first-come, first-served), making this suitable for an overnight hike. Allow about eight hours for the loop; a map and hiking guide are strongly recommended.

Detailed directions for these hikes and many others in the area, may be found in the AMC's *Maine Mountain Guide.*

OTHER OUTDOOR PURSUITS

In summer, Sugarloaf/USA's 18-hole **golf course** (☎ 207/237-2000) attracts golfers by the cartload. It's invariably ranked the number-one golf destination in the state by experienced golfers, who are lured here by the Robert Trent Jones, Jr., course design and dramatic mountain backdrop. Sugarloaf hosts a well-respected golf school during the season.

WHERE TO STAY

For convenience, nothing beats staying right on the mountain in winter. Skiers can pop right out the door and on to the lifts. Sugarloaf is nicely designed to allow skiers access to the village; a long, gentle slope extends from the base of the mountain through the clusters of condos and hotels, allowing skiers to glide home after a long day. A low chairlift takes you up to the base first thing in the morning.

Many of the condos are booked through **Sugarloaf/USA Inn** (☎ 800/843-5623 or 207/237-2000), which handles the reservations of far more than 300 condos and mini-suites. The units are spread throughout the base area, and are of varying vintage and opulence. All guests have access to the Sugarloaf Sports and Fitness Center. Another option at the base village is the **Sugarloaf Mountain Hotel** (☎ **800/527-9879**), a towering structure right at the lifts with more than 100 guest rooms.

The Herbert. Main St. (P.O. Box 67), Kingfield, ME 04947. ☎ **800/843-4372** or 207/265-2000. 40 rms. $80–$140 double; discounts midweek. AE, DC, DISC, MC, V.

The Herbert has the feel of a classic North Woods hostelry—sort of Dodge City meets *Northern Exposure*. Built in downtown Kingfield in 1918, the three-story hotel featured all of the finest accoutrements when it was built—fumed oak paneling and incandescent lights in the lobby (look for the original brass fixtures), a classy dining room, and comfortable rooms. The Herbert's 1982 renovation cost $1 million, and was nicely done—right down to the two stuffed moose heads, the baby grand piano, and the fireplace in the lobby. The rooms are furnished in a fairly simple and basic style, although some feature whirlpool bathtubs (there's also a family whirlpool for rent at $10 per half-hour in the basement). Room furnishings tend toward flea-market antiques, with some newer additions. (This doesn't always translate into charming: I had a cheap imitation brass headboard missing rungs that rattled with every breath I took.) The Herbert is located about 15 miles from the slopes at Sugarloaf/USA.

Three Stanley Avenue. 3 Stanley Ave. (P.O. Box 169), Kingfield, ME 04947. ☎ **207/265-5541.** 6 rms (3 with private bath). Dec–Mar $50–$60 double; Apr–Nov $50–$55 double. All rates include breakfast. Two-night minimum on winter weekends. AE, MC, V.

Three Stanley Avenue is the bed-and-breakfast annex to the better-known restaurant next door, One Stanley Avenue. Set on a shady knoll in a quiet village setting just across the bridge from downtown Kingfield, Three Stanley Avenue has an old-fashioned Victorian boardinghouse feel to it, complete with a garish stained-glass window at the bottom of the stairs. The rooms are comfortably if not luxuriously appointed; three rooms share two baths, the other three have private baths. One of the greatest advantages of this spot is its location, just across a broad lawn from the restaurant, which consistently serves up some of the most creative (and expensive) regional cuisine in the state.

WHERE TO DINE

The Herbert. Main St., Kingfield. ☎ **800/843-4372** or 207/265-2000. Reservations recommended. Main courses, $12.95–$21.95. AE, DC, DISC, MC, V. Daily 5–9pm (until 8pm on Sun). REGIONAL.

This open but intimate dining room off the lobby of The Herbert hotel recalls the days when hotels served the best meals in town. The place has a nice Edwardian gloss to it—right down to the heavy sink for guests to wash their hands. The interior has been prettified somewhat, but not enough to lose its charm for the tourists and locals who flock here for tasty, creative meals. The chef offers some nice interpretations of regional classics, like shiitake mushrooms with venison médaillons, and haddock baked with feta cheese and served with a lemon-garlic dressing. The meals are good, not excellent, but the service is friendly and the experience altogether enjoyable. Come early to enjoy a glass of wine in the lobby before you dine.

✪ **Hug's.** Rte. 27, Carrabassett Valley. ☎ **207/237-2392.** Reservations recommended, especially on weekends. Main courses, $10.95–$16.95. MC, V. Tues–Sun 5–9pm (until 9:30pm on weekends). Closed May–Nov. Located ⁷/₁₀ mile south of the Sugarloaf access road. NORTHERN ITALIAN.

Hug's takes diners well beyond red sauce, offering a broad selection of delicately prepared pastas far finer than one should reasonably expect from a restaurant within the orbit of a ski area. This is a small place, set just off the highway in a fairy tale–like cottage. Inside are two intimate dining rooms; the dominant color is battleship gray, but it's enlivened with lipstick-red tablecloths and intriguing early ski pictures on the walls. Dinners are preceded with a tasty basket of pesto bread (very welcome after a day of hiking or skiing). The dinner selections are outstanding and uncommonly well prepared. The shiitake ravioli with walnut-pesto alfredo is superb, as is the chicken limon. The sole disappointment was the salad, which consisted largely of big, tasteless chunks of iceberg lettuce. (Although another disappointment is that it's closed in summer.) As for the name: No, you won't be greeted with a warm embrace. "Hug" was the original owner's nickname.

5 The Mid-Coast

Veteran Maine travelers contend this part of the coast is fast losing its native charm— it's too commercial, too developed, too much like the rest of the United States. The grousers do have a point, especially regarding Route 1's roadside, but get off the main roads and you'll find pockets where you can catch glimpses of another Maine. Among the sights backroads travelers will stumble upon are quiet inland villages, dramatic coastal scenery, and a rich sense of history, especially maritime history.

FREEPORT & ENVIRONS

If Freeport were a mall (and that's not a far-fetched analogy), L.L. Bean would be the anchor store. It's the business that launched Freeport, elevating its status from just another town off the interstate to one of the two outlet capitals of Maine (the other is Kittery). Freeport still has the form of a classic coastal village (the main "Y" intersection in town was designed such that 100-foot masts could be hauled to the water's edge without making any sharp turns), but it's a village with a twist. Most of the old homes and stores have been converted to upscale shops, and now sell name-brand clothing and housewares. Banana Republic occupies an exceedingly handsome brick Federal-style home; even the McDonald's is in a tasteful, understated Victorian farmhouse—you really have to look for the golden arches.

While a number of more modern buildings have been built to accommodate the outlet boom (there are now more than 100 stores in town), strict planning guidelines have managed to preserve much of the local charm, at least in the village section. Huge parking lots off Main Street are hidden from view, making this one of the more aesthetically pleasant places to shop anywhere in the United States. But even with these vast lots, parking can be hard to find during the peak season, especially on rainy summer days when every cottage-bound tourist between York and Camden decides that a trip to Freeport is a winning idea. Bring a lot of patience, and expect teeming crowds if you come at a busy time.

ESSENTIALS

GETTING THERE   Freeport is on Route 1, but is most commonly reached via I-95 from either Exit 19 or 20.

VISITOR INFORMATION   The **Freeport Merchants Association**, P.O. Box 452, Freeport, ME 04032 (☎ **800/865-1994** or 207/865-1212), publishes a map and directory of retail businesses, restaurants, and overnight accommodations. The free map is available widely around town at stores and restaurants.

The best source of information for the region in general is found at the **Maine State Information Center** (☎ **207/846-0833**) just off I-95 in Yarmouth. This state-run center is stocked with hundreds of brochures and free newspapers, and is staffed with a helpful crew that can provide information on the entire state, but is particularly well-informed about the mid-coast region.

SHOPPING

At last count, Freeport had more than 100 retail shops between Exit 19 at the far lower end of Main Street and Mallett Road, which connects to Exit 20. Shops have recently begun to spread south of Exit 19 toward Yarmouth. If you can't stand missing a single one, get off at Exit 17 and head north on Route 1. Among those with a presence in Freeport are The Gap, Anne Klein, Levi's, Boston Traders, Patagonia, Nike, J. Crew, Timberland, Maidenform, and many others.

L.L. Bean. Main and Bow sts. ☎ **800/341-4341.**

Monster outdoor retailer L.L. Bean traces its roots to the day Leon Leonwood Bean decided that what the world really needed was a good weatherproof hunting shoe. He married a watertight gumshoe bottom with a laced leather upper. Hunters liked it. The store grew. An empire was born.

Today L.L. Bean sells millions of dollars worth of clothing and outdoor goods to customers nationwide through its well-respected catalogs and it continues to draw hundreds of thousands through its door. This modern, multilevel store is the size of a regional mall, but tastefully done with its own indoor trout pond and lots of natural wood. L.L. Bean is open 365 days a year, 24 hours a day (note the lack of locks or latches on the front doors) and it's a popular spot even in the dead of night, especially around summer and holidays. (Stars from rock groups performing in Portland are frequently spotted shopping here after their shows.) Selections include Bean's own trademark clothing, along with home furnishings, books, shoes, and plenty of outdoor gear for camping, fishing, and hunting.

In addition to the main store, L.L. Bean stocks an outlet shop with a relatively small but rapidly changing inventory at discount prices. It's located in a back lot between Main Street and Depot Street—ask at the front desk of the main store for walking directions.

DeLorme's Map Store. Rte. 1 (near Cricket's Restaurant). ☎ **207/865-4171.**

It all started a couple of decades ago with the *Maine Atlas and Gazetteer.* Today, DeLorme produces and sells detailed atlases containing mini-topographic maps for numerous states, as well as award-winning computer CD-ROMs containing detailed road maps for the entire nation. The shop doesn't offer discounts, but the selection of DeLorme products is comprehensive.

Harrington House Museum Store. 45 Main St. ☎ **207/865-0477.**

A shop to benefit the Freeport Historical Society, the Harrington museum store sells a broad array of unique Maine items including antique reproduction furniture, jewelry, and packaged gourmet foods.

J.L. Coombs Shoe Outlet. 15 Bow St. ☎ **207/865-4557.**

A Maine shoemaker since 1830, J.L. Coombs today carries a wide assortment of imported and domestic footwear, including a good selection of those favored by teens and college kids, including Dr. Marten, Ecco, and Mephisto. There's also outerwear by Pendleton and Jackaroos.

Zandhoeven Chocolates. 21 Main St. ☎ **800/897-0677** or **207/865-4405.**

When a pair of Maine friends brought chocolates back from a business trip to Belgium, friends and associates clamored for these rich, delectable sweets and started placing orders for their next trip. A business was born. Their second-floor shop is small but packs a powerful chocolate punch with its array of fresh imported sweets.

WHERE TO STAY

Harraseeket Inn. 162 Main St., Freeport, ME 05032. ☎ **800/342-6423** or 207/865-9377. 54 rms. A/C TV TEL. Summer and fall $155–$235 double; spring and early summer $140–$235 double; winter $105–$215 double. $10 discount midweek. All rates include breakfast buffet. Take Exit 20 off I-95 to Main St. AE, DC, DISC, MC, V.

The Harraseeket Inn is a large, thoroughly modern hotel two blocks north of L. L. Bean. It's to the inn's credit that one could drive down Main Street and not notice it. A late 19th-century home is the soul of the hotel, but most of the rooms are in an architecturally similar 1989 addition that dwarfs the old house. (The new part is of steel and concrete, but not so as you could tell.) Guests can relax in the well-regarded dining room, in the common room with the baby grand player piano, or down in the faux-rustic Broad Arrow Pub with moose head, fireplace, and birchbark canoe. The guest rooms are on the large side and tastefully done, all with quarter-canopy beds and a nice mix of contemporary and antique furniture. About half have fireplaces, and a number have whirlpools. Plans call for construction of another addition with 26 rooms and an indoor pool beginning in December 1996.

EAST ON ROUTE 1
BRUNSWICK & BATH

Brunswick and Bath are two exceptionally handsome historic towns that have a strong commercial past, and today remain vibrant with commercial activity. Many travelers heading on Route 1 up the coast pass through both towns eager to reach the areas with higher billing on the marquee. That's a shame, for both these areas are well worth the detour.

Brunswick was once home to several mills along the Androscoggin River; these have since been converted to offices and the like, but Brunswick's broad Maine Street still bustles with activity. Brunswick is also home to **Bowdoin College,** one of the nation's most respected small colleges. The school was founded in 1794, offered its first classes eight years later, and has since amassed an illustrious roster of prominent alumni, including Nathaniel Hawthorne, Henry Wadsworth Longfellow, Franklin Pierce, and Arctic explorer Robert E. Peary. Bowdoin College has a small museum of Arctic exploration and a fine small art museum. Civil War hero Joshua Chamberlain served as president of the college after the war.

Eight miles to the east, **Bath** is nicely situated on the broad Kennebec River, and is a noted center of shipbuilding. The first U.S.-built ship was constructed downstream at the Popham Bay colony in the early 17th century; in the years since, shipbuilders have constructed more than 5,000 ships. Bath shipbuilding reached its heyday in the late 19th century, but it continues to this day. Bath Iron Works is one of the nation's preeminent boatyards, constructing and repairing ships for the U.S. Navy. The scaled-down military has left Bath shipbuilders in a somewhat tenuous state, but it's still common to see the steely gray ships in the drydock (the best view is from the bridge over the Kennebec), and the towering red-and-white crane moving supplies and parts around the yard.

The **Bath-Brunswick Region Chamber of Commerce,** 59 Pleasant St., Brunswick, ME 04011 (☎ **207/725-8797** or 207/443-9751), offers information and lodging assistance from its offices in downtown Brunswick. The chamber also staffs an information center on Route 1 just west of Bath.

In early August look for posters for the ever-popular **Maine Festival** (☎ 207/ 772-9012), which takes place at Thomas Point Beach between Brunswick and Bath. What started as a sort of counterculture celebration of Maine people and crafts has evolved and grown to a hugely popular mainstream event. Performers from throughout Maine gather at this pretty coveside park (it's a private campground the rest of the summer), and put on shows from noon past dark throughout the first weekend in August. Displays of crafts, artwork, and the products of small Maine businesses are also on display. An admission fee is charged.

You don't have to be a ship aficionado to enjoy the **Maine Maritime Museum and Shipyard,** 243 Washington St. (☎ 207/443-1316). Admission is $7.50 adults, $4.75 children 6 to 17, $21 for a family. Hours are daily from 9:30am to 5pm. But those who do love boats love it here and are hard to drag away. This up-to-date museum on the shores of the Kennebec River (it's just south of Bath Iron Works) features a wide array of displays and exhibits related to the boatbuilders' art. The location is appropriate—it's sited at the former shipyard of Percy and Small, which built some 42 schooners in the late 19th and early 20th century. Indeed, the largest wooden ship ever built in America—the 329-foot *Wyoming*—was constructed on this lot in 1909. If you snoop around in the reeds, you can even find the ways used in launching the ship.

The centerpiece of the museum is the striking brick Maritime History Building. Here, you'll find changing exhibits of maritime art and artifacts. The 10-acre property houses plenty of additional displays, including an intriguing exhibit on lobstering and a complete shipbuilding shop, called the Apprenticeshop. Here, you can watch handsome wooden ships take shape in this year-long program, in which apprentices learn the craft of wooden shipbuilding from the keel up. Kids enjoy the play area (look for pirates from the crow's nest of the play boat). Be sure to wander down to the docks on the river to see what's tied up, or to inquire about cruises on the river (extra charge).

EXPLORING THE HARPSWELL PENINSULA

Extending southwest from Brunswick and Bath is the picturesque Harpswell peninsula. It's actually three peninsulas, like the tines of a pitchfork, if you include the islands of Orrs and Bailey, which are linked to the mainland by bridges. While close to some of Maine's larger towns (Portland is only 45 minutes away), the Harpswell peninsula has a remote, historic feel with sudden vistas across meadows to the blue waters of northern Casco Bay. Toward the southern tips of the peninsulas, the character changes as clusters of colorful Victorian-era summer cottages displace the farmhouses found further inland. Some of these cottages are for rent by the week, but many book up years in advance. Ask local real estate agents if you're interested.

There's no set itinerary for exploring the area. Just drive south until you can't go any farther, then backtrack and strike south again. Among the "attractions" worth looking for are the wonderful ocean and island views from South Harpswell at the tip of the westernmost peninsula (park and wander around for a bit), and the clever **Cobwork Bridge** connecting Bailey and Orrs islands. The humpbacked bridge was built in 1928 of granite blocks stacked in such a way that the strong tides could come and go and not drag the bridge out with it. No cement was used in its construction.

This is a good area for a bowl of chowder or a boiled lobster. One of the best off-the-beaten-track places for chowder is the down-home **Dolphin Marina** (☎ 207/ 833-6000) at Basin Point in South Harpswell. (Look for signs on Route 123 at Ash Point Road near the West Harpswell School.) Find the boatyard, then wander inside, where you'll discover a tiny counter seating six and a handful of pine booths. The fish chowder and lobster stew are reasonably priced and tasty, and the blueberry muffins are delicious.

For lobster, several sprawling establishments specialize in delivering crustaceans fresh from the sea. On the Bailey Island side there's **Cook's Lobster House** (☎ 207/833-6641), which seats 280 diners and has been serving up a choice of shore dinners, most involving lobster, since 1955. Near Harpswell is the **Estes Lobster House** (☎ 207/833-6340), which serves lobster (including an artery-clogging triple lobster plate) amid relaxed, festive surroundings.

The oceanside **Driftwood Inn** (Washington Avenue, Bailey Island, ME 04003; ☎ 207/833-5461, off-season 508/947-1066) dates back to 1910 and is a coastal New England classic. A rustic summer retreat on three acres at the end of a dead-end road, the inn is a compound of three weathered, shingled buildings and a handful of housekeeping cottages on a rocky, oceanside property. The Spartan rooms of time-aged pine have a simple, turn-of-the-century flavor that hasn't been gentrified in the least. Most rooms share baths down the hall, but some have private sinks and toilets. Your primary company will be the constant sound of surf surging in and ebbing out of the fissured rocks. The inn has a small pool and porches with wicker furniture to while away the afternoons, and roadway walks in the area are pleasant, but I'd advise bringing plenty of books and board games. The dining room serves basic fare in a wonderfully austere setting overlooking the sea; meals are extra, although a weekly American plan is available. The Driftwood isn't for those seeking luxury, but it's an ideal location to unwind at the ocean like they used to in the old days. The inn has 18 double rooms, 9 single rooms, and 6 cottages (most rooms share hallways and baths), and rates are $65 to $70 for doubles, $45 to $50 for singles. Weekly rates are $320 per person (including breakfast and dinner), and the cottages go for $425 to $525 per week. Open late May to mid-October; the dining room is open from late June to Labor Day. No credit cards.

BOOTHBAY PENINSULA

Although Boothbay Harbor is 11 miles from Route 1, this small but scenic harbor town exerts an outsized allure on passing tourists, and has become one of the prime destinations of travelers in search of classic coastal Maine. As a result, it's a popular stop for bus tours, and the village has been infiltrated by kitschy shops (T-shirts, stained-glass unicorns) and mediocre restaurants that specialize in fried foods. The harbor is hemmed in somewhat by boxy, bland motels, but there's still an affable charm that manages to rise above the clutter, especially on foggy days when the horns bleat mournfully at the harbor's mouth. And visitors should also find some measure of satisfaction that a nickel will still buy 24 minutes at the town parking meters.

ESSENTIALS

GETTING THERE   Boothbay Harbor is 11 miles south of Route 1 on Route 27. Coming from the west, look for signs shortly after crossing the Sheepscot River at Wiscasset.

VISITOR INFORMATION   There are two visitor information centers in town. A mile before you reach the village is the seasonal **Boothbay Information Center** on your right (open June to October). If you zoom past it or it's closed, don't fret. The year-round **Boothbay Harbor Region Chamber of Commerce,** P.O. Box 356, Boothbay Harbor, ME 04538 (☎ 207/633-2353), is at the intersection of routes 27 and 96.

What to See & Do

Boothbay Harbor is made for walkers. Pedestrians naturally gravitate to the long, narrow footbridge across the harbor, first built in 1901, but it's more of a destination than a link—other than a few restaurants and motels, there's really not much on the other side. The winding, small streets in town also offer plenty of boutiques and shops that cater to the tourist trade and offer decent browsing.

The most enjoyable way to see the Boothbay region is on a boat tour. Nearly two dozen tour boats berth at the harbor or nearby, offering a range of trips from an hour's tour to a full-day excursion to Monhegan Island. You can even observe puffins at their rocky colonies far offshore.

Two of Maine's larger, more modern boat tour firms are based in downtown Boothbay. **Balmy Day Cruises** (☎ 207/633-2284) runs trips to Monhegan Island in the 65-foot *Balmy Days II*, allowing passengers about four hours to explore the island before returning (see "Monhegan Island" section below). The company also offers two-hour dinner cruises with onboard dinners of chicken, lobster roll, and lobster. **Cap'n Fish's Scenic Boat Trips** (☎ 800/636-3244 or 207/633-3244) offers sightseeing trips of one to four hours duration, including puffin and whale watches. The four boats in the fleet each carry between 130 and 150 passengers.

A short excursion to **Ocean Point** is well worthwhile. Follow Route 96 southward from west of Boothbay Harbor, and you'll pass through East Boothbay before striking toward the point. The narrow road runs through piney forests before arriving at the rocky finger; it's one of the few Maine points with a road around its perimeter, allowing wonderful ocean views. Bunches of colorful Victorian-era summer cottages bloom along the roadside like wildflowers.

Where to Stay

Old Resorts

Newagen Seaside Inn. Rte. 27 (P.O. Box 68), Cape Newagen, ME 04552. ☎ **800/654-5242** or 207/633-5242. 26 rms (2 with shower only). $100–$175 double including breakfast. MC, V. Open mid-May to late Sept. Located on south tip of Southport Island; take Rte. 27 from Boothbay Harbor and continue on until the inn sign.

This 1940s-era resort has seen more glamorous days, but it's still a superb small, low-key resort offering stunning ocean views and walks in a fragrant spruce forest. The inn is housed in a low, wide, white-shingled building that's furnished simply with country pine furniture. There's a classically austere dining room with a well-regarded menu, narrow cruise ship–like hallways with pine wainscoting, and a lobby with a fireplace. The rooms are plain and the inn is a bit threadbare in spots, but never mind that. Guests flock here for the 85-acre oceanside grounds filled with decks, gazebos, and walkways that border on the magical. For activities, there's badminton, shuffleboard, horseshoes, tennis, a new freshwater pool surrounded by a great deck for lounging, and an odd saltwater pool at oceanside with a small man-made beach. Rowboats are available free for guests to use. It's hard to overstate the magnificence of the ocean views, which may be the best of any inn in Maine. No smoking.

Spruce Point Inn. Atlantic Ave. (P.O. Box 237), Boothbay Harbor, ME 04538. ☎ **800/553-0289** or 207/633-4152. 65 rms. TV TEL. July–Aug $240–$330 ; June and Sept–Oct $178–$240 double. Rates include breakfast and dinner. AE, MC, V. Open Memorial Day to mid-Oct. Turn right on Union St. in Boothbay Harbor; proceed 2 miles to the inn.

The Spruce Point Inn was originally built as a hunting and fishing lodge in the 1890s, and evolved into a summer resort in 1912. After years of quiet neglect, it benefited in the late 1980s from a long-overdue makeover that thankfully retained much of the rustic charm. The eight guest rooms in the venerable, gabled main lodge are simply furnished and clean, but slightly austere and motel-like. Better are the rooms in the outbuildings flanking the lodge. These have a woodsy, country pine feel, and most have private porches with ocean views. The newer "Ocean Houses," built in 1988 at the back of the property, are contemporary, condominium-like town houses with plenty of amenities but no character whatsoever.

Most guests occupy their time just puttering around the inn's 15-acre oceanfront grounds, or idling in the wicker chairs on the porch overlooking the rocky shore. Slightly more strenuous activities include croquet, shuffleboard, tennis on clay courts, putting on an Astroturf green, swimming at a newly rebuilt oceanside salt-water pool (there's also a heated freshwater pool at the forest's edge), and soaking in the whirlpool. Dinners are memorable events (see below). There's also a free shuttle bus to Boothbay, so guests can dabble in shopping or mild adventure without the hassle of downtown parking.

Inns & B&Bs

Five Gables Inn. Murray Hill Rd. (P.O. Box 335, East Boothbay, ME 04544. ☎ **800/451-5048** or 207/633-4551. 16 rms. $90–$135 double including breakfast buffet. MC, V. Closed Nov–Apr. Drive through East Boothbay on Rte. 96; turn right after crest of hill on Murray Hill Rd.

The 125-year-old Five Gables Inn was painstakingly restored in 1988, and now sits proudly amid a small colony of summer homes on a quiet road above a peaceful cove. It's nicely isolated from the confusion and hubbub of Boothbay Harbor; the activity of choice here is to sit on the deck and enjoy the glimpses of the water through the trees. The rooms are pleasantly appointed, and the common room pleasantly furnished in an upscale country style. The new owners, De and Mike Kennedy from Atlanta, bought the inn in late 1995 and are proving to be as helpful and congenial as their predecessors. This is a no-smoking inn.

Lawnmeer Inn & Restaurant. Rte. 27, Southport, ME 04576. ☎ **800/633-7645** or 207/633-2544. 32 rms. TV. $45–$120 double. MC, V. Closed mid-Oct to mid-May.

The Lawnmeer, situated just a short hop from Boothbay on the northern shore of Southport Island, offers easy access to town and a restful environment. This was originally built as a guest home at the turn of the century, and the main inn has been nicely updated with only a slight loss of charm. More than half of the guest rooms are located in a motel-like annex, which makes up for its lack of character with private balconies offering views of the waterway that separates Southport Island from the mainland. American and continental fare is served in a comfortable, homey dining room with broad windows overlooking the water.

Topside. McKown Hill, Boothbay Harbor, ME 04538. ☎ **207/633-5404.** 28 rms (1 with shower only). July 1–Labor Day $70–$95 double; June and Sept–Oct $50–$85 double. MC, V. Closed mid-Oct to June.

Okay, let's be up-front here. The looming old gray house on the hilltop above the motel-style building may bring to mind the Bates Motel, especially when a full moon is overhead. But get over that. Because Topside offers spectacular ocean views at a good price on its private hilltop compound located right in downtown Boothbay. The inn itself features six comfortable rooms, furnished with a mix of antiques and contemporary furniture. (Some may find the building a bit overly carpeted and wallpapered.) At the edge of the inn's cambered lawn are two outbuildings housing basic motel units, which have paneling and furniture that may recall the era when John Travolta was first popular. Just keep in mind that guests return here year after year not for the dated styling, but for the spectacular ocean views.

WHERE TO DINE

When wandering through town, watch for **"King" Brud and his famous hot-dog cart.** The laconic Brud started selling hot dogs in town in 1943, and he's still at it. If he likes you, he'll give you a free postcard of him and his cart. Dogs are $1. He's usually at the corner of McKown and Commercial streets from 10am till 4pm from June through October.

☉ Boothbay Region Lobstermen's Co-op. Atlantic Ave., Boothbay Harbor. ☎ **207/ 633-4900.** No reservations. Sandwiches $1.25–$8.75; dinners $6.50–$8.95. May–Oct daily 11:30am–8:30pm. By foot: cross footbridge and turn right; follow road for ¹/₃ mile to co-op. No credit cards. SEAFOOD.

"We are not responsible if the seagulls steal your food" reads the sign at the ordering window of this casual, harborside lobster joint. And that sets the tone pretty well. Situated across the harbor from downtown Boothbay, the Lobstermen's Co-op offers no-frills lobster and seafood. You order at a pair of windows, then pick up your meal and carry your tray to either the picnic tables on the dock or inside a garagelike two-story prefab building. Lobsters are priced to market (figure on $8 to $9), with extras like corn-on-the-cob reasonably priced at 85¢. A bank of soda machines provides liquid refreshment for 75¢ a can. This is a fine place for a lobster on a sunny day, but it's uninteresting at best in rain or fog.

Lobsterman's Wharf. Rte. 96, East Boothbay. ☎ **207/633-3443.** Reservations for parties of 6 or more only. Lunch from $4.50; dinner $13.25–$22.95 (mostly $14–$16). AE, MC, V. Closed Nov–Mar. SEAFOOD.

Slightly off the beaten path in East Boothbay, the Lobsterman's Wharf has the comfortable, pubby feel of a popular neighborhood bar, complete with pool table. And that's appropriate, since that's what it is. But it's that rarest of pubs—one that's popular with the locals, but also one that commands the respect of finicky diners and makes travelers feel at home. If the weather's agreeable, sit at a picnic table on the dock, admiring views of a spruce-topped peninsula across the Damariscotta River; you can also grab a table inside amid the festive nautical decor. Entrees include a tasty mixed-seafood grill, a barbecue shrimp and ribs platter, grilled swordfish with béarnaise, and succulent fresh lobster offered four different ways.

❁ Spruce Point Inn. Atlantic Ave, Boothbay Harbor. ☎ **800/553-0289** or 207/633-4152. Reservations recommended. Main courses $14.75–$24.25. AE, MC ,V. Daily 7:30am–9:30am and 6–9pm. Closed mid-Oct to Memorial Day. Turn right on Union St. in Boothbay Harbor; proceed 2 miles to the inn. AMERICAN.

This classic resort dining room is certain to surprise you with its creativity. And what else would you expect from an inn that won a recent statewide cooking contest with a recipe for "lobster succotash"? Diners are seated in an elegant, formal dining room—the tables are lined up with an almost military precision, the maître d' wears a tux, and men are requested to wear jackets at dinner. Guests enjoy wonderful sunset views across the mouth of Boothbay Harbor as they peruse the menu, which offers an inviting mix of seafood and meat dishes. The lobster spring rolls are terrific for starters. Next, you might opt for the two-texture duck (served with a shiitake and ginger gravy), or shrimp amaretto. If you're not feeling overly adventurous, you can take refuge in the more basic choices, like pork tenderloin, grilled chicken breast, or filet mignon.

PEMAQUID PENINSULA

The Pemaquid Peninsula is an irregular, rocky wedge driven deep into the Gulf of Maine. It's much less commercial than the Boothbay Peninsula just across the

Damariscotta River, and more inviting for casual exploring. The inland areas are leafy with hardwood trees, and feature plenty of narrow, twisting backroads perfect for bicycling. Closer to the ocean point, the region takes on a more remote, maritime feel, and small harbors and coves predominate. Rugged and rocky Pemaquid Point, at the extreme southern tip of the peninsula, is one of the most dramatic destinations in Maine when the ocean surf is surging.

The **Damariscotta Region Chamber of Commerce,** P.O. Box 13, Main Street, Damariscotta, ME 04543 (☎ **207/563-8340**), is a good source of local information, and maintains a handy information booth on Route 1 during the summer months.

Shaw's Lobster Pond (on the water, New Harbor; ☎ **207/677-2200**) attracts hordes of tourists, but it's no puzzle to figure out why: It's one of the best-situated lobster pounds, with postcard-perfect views of the working harbor and the boats coming and going through the inlet that connects to the open sea. Customers stand in line to place their order, then wait for their name to be called. While waiting, you can stake out a seat on either the open deck or the indoor dining room (go for the deck), or order up some appetizers from the raw bar. This is one of the few lobster places with a full liquor license. Shaw's does not accept reservations or credit cards. Lobsters are priced according to the market (usually $8 to $11). Open noon until 8pm weekdays, 9pm weekends. Closed mid-October until late May.

MONHEGAN ISLAND

Brawny and remote, Monhegan Island is Maine's premier island destination. Starting in the 1870s and continuing to the present day, noted artists discovered the island and came to stay for a spell. These included Rockwell Kent (the artist most closely associated with the island), George Bellows, Edward Hopper, and Robert Henri. The artists gathered in the kitchen of the lighthouse to chat and drink coffee; it's said that the wife of the lighthouse keeper accumulated a tremendously valuable collection of paintings. Today, Jamie Wyeth, scion of the Wyeth clan, claims the island as his part-time home.

It's not hard to figure why artists have long been attracted to the place: There's a mystical quality to it, from the thin light to the startling contrasts of the dark cliffs and the foamy white surf. There's also a remarkable sense of tranquillity to this place, which can only but help focus one's inner vision.

If you have the time, I'd strongly recommend an overnight on the island. Day trips are popular and affordable, but the island's true character doesn't start to emerge until the last day boat sails away and the quiet, rustic appeal of the island starts to percolate back to the surface.

ESSENTIALS

GETTING THERE   Access to Monhegan Island is via boat from either New Harbor, Boothbay Harbor, or Port Clyde. The hour-and-10-minute trip on the *Laura B.* from Port Clyde is the favored route among longtime island visitors. The trip from this rugged fishing village is very picturesque as it passes the Marshall Point Lighthouse and a series of spruce-clad islands before setting out on the open sea. The *Laura B.* is a doughty work boat (cargo including propane tanks and boxes of food is loaded on first; passengers fill in the available niches on the deck and in the small cabin). You can't bring your car, so pack light and wear sturdy shoes. Reservations are advised: **Monhegan Boat Line,** P.O. Box 238, Port Clyde, ME 04855 (☎ **207/ 372-8848**). Parking is available near the dock for a slight additional charge.

VISITOR INFORMATION   Monhegan Island has no formal visitors center, but it's small and friendly enough that you can make inquiries of just about anyone you meet on the island pathways. The clerks at the boat dock in Port Clyde are also quite helpful. Be sure to pick up the inexpensive map of the island's hiking trail at the boat ticket office or at the various shops around the island.

Because a forest fire could destroy this breezy island in short order, smoking is prohibited outside of the village.

WHAT TO SEE & DO

Hike. Walk.

Those are the chief activities on the island, and it's genuinely surprising how much distance you can cover on this 700-acre island (about 1 1/2 miles long and 1/2-mile wide). The village clusters tightly around the harbor; the rest of the island is mostly wildland, laced with some 17 miles of trails. Much of the island is ringed along its shoreline with high, open bluffs atop fissured cliffs. Pack a picnic lunch and hike the trail around the perimeter, and plan to spend much of the day just sitting and reading, or enjoying the surf rolling in against the cliffs. During one afternoon sitting on a bluff near the island's southern tip, I spotted a half-dozen whale spouts over the course of a half hour, but never did agree with my friend whether it was one whale or several.

The inland trails are appealing in a far different way. The deep, dark **Cathedral Woods** are mossy and fragrant; sunlight only dimly filters through the evergreens to the forest floor. Look for the small "fairy houses" in the woods; these fanciful structures of twigs, bark, and other forest-floor detritus are crafted by island kids and visitors. You're welcome to build your own, provided you don't use live moss.

Bird watching is an exceedingly popular activity in the spring and fall. Monhegan Island is on the Atlantic flyway, and a wide variety of birds stop at the island along their migration routes. Bring your binoculars.

The sole "attraction" on the island is the **Monhegan Museum,** located next to the 1824 lighthouse on a high point above the village. The museum, open from July through September, has an engaging collection of historic artifacts and will provide some context for this rugged island's history. But the real draw is the spectacular view from the grassy slope in front of the lighthouse. The vista sweeps across a marsh (which seems to attract a number of deer at twilight), past one of the island's most historic hotels, past melancholy Manana Island and across the sea beyond. Get here early if you want a good seat for the sunset; it seems most visitors to the island congregate here after dinner to watch the sinking of the sun. (Another popular place is the island's southern tip, where the wreckage of the *D.T. Sheridan,* a coal barge, washed up in 1948.)

One other popular activity is to visit the studios of Monhegan artists, who still gather here in great number. Artists often open their workspaces to visitors during limited hours, and are happy to have people stop by and look at their work, talk with them a bit, and perhaps buy something to bring home. Some of the artwork is predictable seascapes and sunsets, but much of it rises above the banal. Look for the bulletin board along the main pathway in the village for walking directions to the studios and a listing of the days they're open.

WHERE TO STAY & DINE

Monhegan House. Monhegan Island, ME 04852. ☎ **800/599-7983** or 207/594-7983. 32 rms (all with shared bath). $70 double. AE, DISC, MC, V. Closed Columbus Day to Memorial Day.

The handsome Monhegan House has been accommodating guests since 1870, and it has the comfortable, worn patina of a venerable lodging house. The accommodations are austere but comfortable; there are no closets, and everyone uses dormitory-style bathrooms down the hall. The downstairs lobby with fireplace is a welcome spot to sit and take the fog-induced chill out of your bones (even in August it can be cool here). The front deck is a nice place to lounge and keep a close eye on the comings and goings of the village.

Trailing Yew. Monhegan Island, ME 04852. ☎ **207/596-0440.** 37 rms in 4 buildings (1 rm with private bath). $108 double, including breakfast, dinner, taxes, and tips. No credit cards. Closed mid-Oct to mid-May.

At the end of long summer afternoons, guests congregate near the flagpole in front of the main building at this rustic hillside compound. They sit in Adirondack chairs or chat with newfound friends. But mostly they're waiting for the ringing of the bell, which signals them in for dinner, as if at summer camp. Inside, guests sit around long tables, introduce themselves to their neighbors, then pour an iced tea and wait for the delicious, family-style dinner. (You're given a choice, but opt for the fresh fish.)

The Trailing Yew, which has been taking in guests since 1929, is a friendly, informal place, popular with hikers and bird watchers (meals are a great time to swap tales of sightings) who tend to make fast friends here amid the welcome adversity of Monhegan Island. Guest rooms are eclectic and simply furnished in a pleasantly dated summer-home style; only one of the four guest buildings has electricity (although all bathrooms have electricity); guests in rooms without electricity are provided a kerosene lamp and instruction in its use (bring a flashlight just in case).

6 Penobscot Bay

Traveling eastward along the Maine coast, you'll notice around Rockland that you're heading nearly due north. The culprit is Penobscot Bay, a sizable bite out of the Maine coast that forces a northerly detour to cross the head of the bay where the Penobscot River flows in at Bucksport.

You'll find some of Maine's best coastal scenery in this area—spectacular offshore islands, high hills along the water's edge, and heavily weathered rocks pounded by the surf. Although the mouth of Penobscot Bay is occupied by two large islands, its waters can still churn with vigor when the seas are running high.

The west shore of Penobscot Bay gets a heavy stream of tourist traffic, especially along Route 1 and the scenic villages of Rockport and Camden. These are good destinations to get a taste of the Maine coast, especially for those in a hurry to get to Acadia National Park. Services for travelers are easy to find, although during the peak season a small miracle will be required to find a guest room without a reservation.

In contrast, the bay's eastern shore, formed by the Blue Hill Peninsula, Cape Rosier, and Deer Isle, is much more remote, laced with shady back roads and dotted with small inns. By and large it's overlooked by the majority of Maine's tourists, especially those who prefer to avoid narrow roads that suddenly dead-end or inexplicably start to loop back on themselves.

ROCKLAND & ENVIRONS

Few visitors refer to Rockland as "quaint." Located on the southwest edge of Penobscot Bay, Rockland has long been proud of its unadorned, blue-collar waterfront town reputation. Built around the fishing industry, Rockland historically dabbled in tourism on the side. But with the decline of the fisheries and the rise of the tourist economy in Maine, the balance is gradually shifting—Rockland is slowly being colonized by restaurateurs and other small-business folks who are painting it with an unaccustomed gloss.

Penobscot Bay

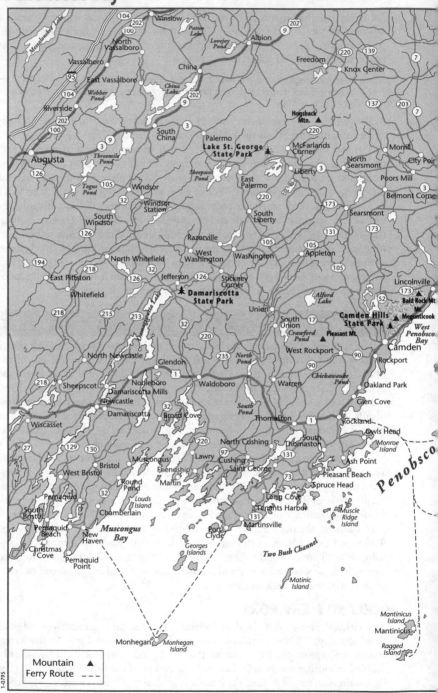

Mountain ▲
Ferry Route − − −

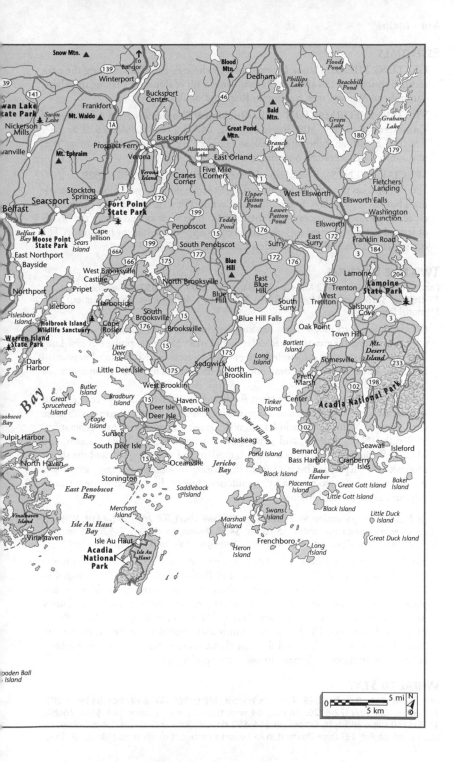

ESSENTIALS

GETTING THERE   Route 1 passes directly through Rockland. During the peak summer season, you can avoid the coastal congestion of Route 1 by taking the Maine Turnpike to Augusta, then heading to Rockland on Route 17.

VISITOR INFORMATION   The **Rockland/Thomaston Area Chamber of Commerce**, P.O. Box 508, Rockland, ME 04841 (☎ **800/562-2529** or 207/ 596-0376), staffs an information desk at Harbor Park. It's open daily 9am to 5pm in summer, open weekdays only the rest of the year.

SPECIAL EVENTS   The **Maine Lobster Festival** (☎ **800/562-2529** or 207/ 596-0376) takes place at Harbor Park the first weekend in August (plus the preceding Thursday and Friday). Entertainers and vendors of all sorts of Maine products— especially the local crustacean—fill the waterfront parking lot and attract thousands of festival-goers who enjoy this pleasant event with a sort of buttery bonhomie. The event includes the Maine Sea Goddess Coronation Pageant.

TWO FINE MUSEUMS

Farnsworth Museum. 352 Main St., Rockland. ☎ **207/596-6457.** $5 adults, $4 seniors, $3 children 8–18. Summer Mon–Sat 10am–5pm, Sun 1–5pm. Closed Mon Columbus Day– Memorial Day.

Rockland, for all its rough edges, has long had historic ties to the arts. Noted sculptor Louise Nevelson grew up in Rockland, and in 1935 cranky philanthropist Lucy Farnsworth bequeathed a fortune large enough to establish Rockland's Farnsworth Museum, which has since become one of the most respected small art museums in New England.

Located in the middle of downtown Rockland, the Farnsworth has a compact but superb collection of paintings and sculptures by renowned American artists with some connection to Maine. This includes not only Louise Nevelson and three generations of Wyeths (N.C., Andrew, and Jamie), but Rockwell Kent, Childe Hassam, and Maurice Prendergast. The display space is modern and well-designed, and the shows professionally prepared. This is a superb destination to while away a rainy afternoon. It's also a good place to reach a fuller understanding of the long, intimate relationship between artists and Maine.

Owls Head Transportation Museum. Rte. 73, Owls Head. ☎ **207/594-4418.** Web site http://www.midcoast.com/~ohtm. $5 adults, $4.50 seniors, $3 children 5–12, $15 families. Apr–Oct daily 10am–5pm; Nov–Mar Mon–Fri 10am–4pm, Sat–Sun 10am–3pm.

You don't have to be a car or plane nut to enjoy a day at the Owl's Head Transportation Museum, located three miles south of Rockland on Route 73. Founded in 1974, the museum has an extraordinary collection of cars, motorcycles, bicycles, and planes, nicely displayed in a tidy, hangarlike building at the edge of the Knox County Airport. Look for the beautiful early Harley Davidson, and the sleek Rolls-Royce Phantom dating from 1929. The museum is also a popular destination for hobbyists and tinkerers, who drive and fly their classic vehicles here for frequent weekend rallies in the summer. Call ahead to ask about special events.

WHERE TO STAY

East Wind Inn. P.O. Box 149, Tenant's Harbor, ME 04860. ☎ **800/241-8439** or 207/ 372-6366. Fax 207/372-6320. 26 rms, 14 with shared bath. Summer $78–$110 double, $125–$150 suites and apts. Off-season $64–$82 double. Rates include continental breakfast. Drive south on Rte. 131 from Thomaston to Tenant's Harbor; turn left at post office. AE, DISC, MC, V.

Windjammer Tours

During the long transition from sail to steam, captains of the fancy new steamships belittled the old-fashioned sailing ships as "windjammers." The term stuck, and through a curious metamorphosis the name evolved into a term of adventure and romance.

Maine is the capital of windjammer cruising in the United States, and two of the most active Maine harbors are Rockland and Camden. Windjammer vacations combine adventure with limited creature comforts—sort of like lodging at a backcountry cabin on the water. Guests typically bunk in small two-person cabins, which usually offer cold running water and a porthole to let in fresh air, but not much else. Cruises last from three days to a week, during which these handsome, creaky vessels poke around the tidy inlets and small coves that ring beautiful Penobscot Bay. It's a superb way to explore Maine's coast the way it's historically been explored—from the outside looking in. The price runs around $100 per day per person, with modest discounts early and late in the season.

Cruises vary from ship to ship, and from week to week, depending on the inclinations of the captains and the vagaries of the mercurial Maine weather. The "standard" cruise often features a stop at one or more of the myriad spruce-studded Maine islands (perhaps with a clambake on shore), hearty breakfasts enjoyed sitting at table belowdecks (or perched cross-legged on the sunny deck), and a palpable sense of maritime history as these handsome ships scud through frothy waters. A windjammer vacation demands you apply all your senses, to smell the tang of the salt air, to hear the rhythmic creaking of the masts in the evening, and to feel the frigid ocean waters as you leap in for a bracing dip.

At least a dozen windjammers offer cruises in the Penobscot Bay region during the summer season (many migrate south to the Caribbean in the winter). The ships vary widely in size and vintage, and guest accommodations range from cramped and rustic to reasonably spacious and well-appointed. Ideally, you'll have a chance to look at a couple of ships to find one that suits you before signing up. If that's not practical, call ahead to the **Maine Windjammer Association** (☎ **800/807-9463**) and request a packet of brochures, which allow decent comparison shopping. If you're angling for a last-minute cruise, stop by the chamber of commerce office at the Rockland waterfront (see "Rockland & Environs," above) and ask if any berths are available.

While all the commercial windjammers are Coast Guard–inspected and each have unique charms, among the notable are the 44-passenger *Victory Chimes* (☎ **800/745-5651** or 207/594-0755), the largest schooner at 132 feet. The smallest in the fleet is the seven-passenger *Summertime* (☎ **800/562-8290**), a 53-foot schooner based in Rockland. The 26-passenger *J&E Riggin* is captained by a native Maine couple, who provide a lively running commentary on Maine history and lore. And the 31-passenger *Angelique* (☎ **800/282-9989** or 207/236-8873), based in Camden, may be the most handsome ship in the fleet, and features two belowdecks hot-water showers.

The East Wind Inn is a gracious anomaly—it manages to attract the corduroyed denizens of the old-money crowd, even though more than half the guest rooms share baths. How do you think old money got that way? Through frugality and thrift, that's how, and the East Wind's shared-bath rates are among the better bargains in the region.

The inn itself, formerly a sail loft, is perfectly situated next to the harbor with water views from all rooms and the long porch. It's a classic seaside inn, with busy wallpaper, simple colonial reproduction furniture, and tidy rooms. (The 10 guest rooms across the way at a former sea captain's house have most of the private baths.) The atmosphere is relaxed almost to the point of ennui, the service very good, and the meals served in an Edwardian-era dining room. The menu includes hearty Yankee fare, usually with an ample selection of fresh-caught seafood.

LimeRock Inn. 96 Limerock St. Rockland, ME 04841. ☎ **800/546-3762** or 207/594-2257. 8 rms (1 with shower only). $100–$160 double, including breakfast. MC, V.

This beautiful Queen Anne–style inn is located on a quiet side street just two blocks from Rockland's Main Street. Originally built for U.S. Rep. Charles Littlefield in 1890, it served as a doctor's residence from 1950 to 1994, after which it was renovated into a gracious inn. The innkeepers—two couples from New Hampshire—have done a stunning job of converting what could be a gloomy manse into one of the region's best choices for overnight accommodation. Excellent attention has been paid to detail throughout, from the choice of country Victorian furniture to the bottles of Poland Spring Water in the rooms. All the guest rooms are welcoming, but among the best is the Island Cottage Room, a bright and airy chamber wonderfully converted from an old shed and featuring a private deck and Jacuzzi. If it's big elegance you're looking for, choose the Grand Manan Room, which has a four-poster bed the size of the Astrodome, a fireplace, and a double Jacuzzi.

WHERE TO DINE

🟢 **Cafe Miranda.** 15 Oak St., Rockland. ☎ **207/594-2034.** Reservations strongly encouraged. Main courses $9.50–$14.50. DISC, MC, V. Tues–Sun 5:30–9:30pm. ECLECTIC/GLOBAL.

The pink flamingo stuck in the flowerbox outside this tiny restaurant and the offbeat notations scrawled on the menu ("Hungry? We have food! Coincidence?!") provide a clue that this isn't your small-town Maine chowderhouse. Further inspection of the menu confirms those suspicions. This tiny restaurant features a huge menu, and it's crammed with cuisines from around the world. Choose from the Szechuan dan dan noodles, poblano chiles stuffed with cheese and cous cous, native mussels steamed in Thai curry, or flank steak wasabi. The one trait all entrees share is a sense of culinary adventure, and for a menu that grazes so far and wide, the chef pulls it off with considerable flair. While the prices aren't cheap compared to basic diner fare available in town, Cafe Miranda offers excellent value for your buck.

CAMDEN

Camden is quintessential coastal Maine. Set at the foot of the wooded Camden Hills around a picturesque harbor that no Hollywood movie set could improve upon, the affluent village of Camden has attracted the gentry of the eastern seaboard for more than 100 years. The quirky mansions of the moneyed set still dominate the shady side streets (many have been converted into bed-and-breakfasts), and Camden is possessed of a grace and sophistication that eludes many other coastal towns.

The best way to enjoy Camden is to park your car as soon as you can—which may mean driving a block or two off Route 1. The village is on a perfect scale to reconnoiter on foot, which allows a leisurely browse of the boutiques and galleries. Don't miss the hidden town park (look behind the library), which was designed by the landscape firm of Frederick Law Olmsted, the nation's most lauded landscape architect. I once stood in this small park at twilight and watched as a schooner maneuvered its way into the harbor, accompanied by the haunting sound of a bagpipe player standing at the bow. In the evening, make your way to **The Waterfront Restaurant** on Bayview Street (☎ 207/236-3747) to secure a seat on the deck overlooking the harbor. Enjoy a snack or cocktail as the evening calm settles over the town.

ESSENTIALS

GETTING THERE   Camden is located on Route 1. Coming from the south, travelers can shave a few minutes off their trip by turning left on Route 90 six miles past Waldoboro, bypassing Rockland. The most traffic-free route from southern Maine is to Augusta via the Maine Turnpike, then via Route 17 to Route 90 to Route 1.

VISITOR INFORMATION   The **Rockport-Camden-Lincolnville Chamber of Commerce,** P.O. Box 919, Camden, ME 04843 (☎ 800/223-5459 or 207/236-4404), dispenses helpful information from its center at the Public Landing in Camden. The chamber is open year-round weekdays from 9am to 5pm and Saturdays 10am to 5pm. In summer, it's also open Sundays noon to 4pm.

OUTDOOR PURSUITS

Camden Hills State Park (☎ 207/236-3109) is nicely situated about a mile north of the village center on Route 1. This 6,500-acre park features an oceanside picnic area, camping at 112 sites, a winding toll road up 800-foot Mt. Battie with spectacular views from the summit, and a variety of well-marked hiking trails.

One easy hike I'd recommend strongly is an ascent to the ledges of **Mount Megunticook,** preferably early in the morning before the crowds have amassed and when the mist still lingers in the valleys. Leave from near the campground and follow the well-maintained trail to these open ledges, which requires only about 30 to 45 minutes' exertion. Spectacular, improbable views of the harbor await, as well as glimpses inland to the gentle valleys. Depending on your stamina and desires, you can continue on the park's trail network to Mount Battie, or into the less-trammeled woodlands on the east side of the Camden Hills.

For a view from the water back to the hills, **Maine Sports Outfitters** (☎ 800/722-0826 or 207/236-8797) offers **sea-kayaking tours** of Camden's scenic harbor. The standard tour lasts four hours, and takes paddlers out to Curtis Island at the outer edge of the harbor. This is an easy, delightful way to get a taste of the area's maritime culture. Longer trips are also available. The outfitter's main shop, located on Route 1 in Rockport, has a good selection of outdoor gear and is worth a stop for outdoor enthusiasts gearing up for local adventures or heading on to Acadia.

WHERE TO STAY

Camden vies with Kennebunkport and Manchester, Vermont, for the title of bed-and-breakfast capital of New England. They're everywhere. Route 1 north of the village center—locally called High Street—is a virtual bed-and-breakfast alley, with many handsome homes converted to lodging. Others are tucked off on side streets. One note: Route 1 is thick with cars and RVs during the summer months, and you may find the steady hum of traffic diminishes the small-town charm of those establishments that flank this otherwise stately, shady road.

Despite the preponderance of B&Bs, the total number of rooms is fairly limited and lodging during peak season is tight. It's best to reserve far in advance. You might also try **Camden Accommodations and Reservations** (☎ 800/236-1920), which offers assistance with everything from booking rooms at resorts to finding cottages for seasonal rental.

Lastly, there's camping at **Camden Hills State Park** (see "Outdoor Pursuits," above).

✪ **Maine Stay.** 22 High St., Camden, ME 04843. ☎ **207/236-9636.** 8 rms (6 with private bath; 4 with shower only). $80–$130 double including breakfast, discounts during the off-season. AE, MC, V.

The Maine Stay is Camden's premiere bed-and-breakfast. Located in a home dating to 1802 but expanded in Greek Revival style in 1840, the Maine Stay is a classic slate-roofed New England homestead set in a shady yard within walking distance of both downtown and Camden Hills State Park. The eight guest rooms on three floors all have ceiling fans and are distinctively furnished with antiques and special decorative touches. My favorite: the new downstairs Carriage House Room, which is away from the buzz of traffic on Route 1 and boasts its own stone patio.

The three downstairs country-style common rooms are perfect for unwinding, and the country kitchen is open to guests at all times—you might even help hand-grind the coffee. Breakfast is served in a country pine dining room, or, when the weather permits, on a deck overlooking the landscaped backyard. Hikers can set out on trails right from the yard into the Camden Hills.

Perhaps the most memorable part of a stay here, however, will be the hospitality of the three hosts—Peter Smith, his wife Donny, and her twin sister, Diana Robson. The trio is genuinely interested in their guests' well-being, and they offer dozens of day-trip suggestions, which are conveniently printed out from the inn's computer for guests to take with them. It's a nice use of a modern technology at an inn that successfully strives to preserve the best of yesterday. No smoking.

✪ **Norumbega.** 61 High St., Camden, ME 04843. ☎ **207/236-4646.** Fax 207/236-0824. 12 rms (three with shower only). TV TEL. July to mid-Oct $195–$450 double; mid-May to June and late Oct, $165–$375 double; Nov to mid-May $135–$295 double. All rates include full breakfast and evening refreshments. AE, MC, V.

You'll have no problem finding Norumbega. Just head north of the village and look for travelers pulled over taking photos of this Victorian-era stone castle overlooking the bay. One of the priciest hostelries in the state, Norumbega is the natural habitat of high-powered businessmen of a certain age. And it's no wonder they're attracted here. The 1886 structure is both wonderfully eccentric and finely built, full of wondrous curves and angles throughout. There's extravagant carved-oak woodwork in the lobby, and a stunning oak and mahogany inlaid floor. The downstairs billiards room is the place to pretend you're a 19th-century railroad baron. (Or an information-age baron—the home was owned for a time by Hodding Carter III.)

The guest rooms have been meticulously restored and furnished with antiques by current owner Murray Keatinge, who bought the place in 1987. Five of the rooms have fireplaces, and the three "garden level rooms" (they're off the downstairs billiards room) have private decks. Two rooms rank among the finest of any inn in the United States—the Library Suite, housed in the original two-story library with interior balcony, and the sprawling Penthouse with its superlative views. The inn is big enough to ensure privacy, but also intimate enough to get to know the other guests—mingling often occurs at breakfast, at the optional evening social hour, and in the afternoon, when the inn puts out its famous fresh-baked cookies.

⑨ **Sunrise Motor Court.** Rte. 1 (HCR 60, Box 545), Lincolnville, ME 04849. ☎ **207/236-3191.** 13 rms (all with shower only). TV. Peak season $49–$59 double; off season $45–$51 double. DISC, MC, V. Closed Columbus Day–Memorial Day.

Situated just far enough beyond the congestion of Camden 4¹/₂ miles north of town to provide a degree of remoteness, the Sunrise Motor Court is a classic 1950s-era establishment with excellent views of the bay—though these views are regrettably across Route 1 and through a latticework of utility lines. Yet, the place boasts a time-worn comfort, like a favorite old sweatshirt. The 13 cabins are arrayed along a grassy hillside at the edge of a wood, and all simply furnished with bed and maybe a few chairs. All boast small decks and outdoor chairs, allowing guests to relax and enjoy the serene view. (Note that two cabins behind the manager's house lack a view.) This is a good bet for budget-conscious travelers who want to experience the Camden area, yet not spend a small fortune doing so.

Whitehall Inn. 52 High St., Camden, ME 04843. ☎ **207/236-3391.** 50 rms, including 10 rms across the street in 2 cottages (5 rms with shared bath). TV TEL. July to late Oct $130–$165 double, including breakfast and dinner ($100–$135 with breakfast only). Discounts in late May and June. AE, MC, V. Closed late Oct–late May.

The Whitehall is a venerable Camden establishment, the sort of place where you half expect to find Cary Grant in a blue blazer tickling the ivories on the 1904 Steinway in the lobby. Set at the edge of town on Route 1 in a structure that dates to 1834, this three-story inn has a striking architectural integrity with its columns, gables, and long roofline. This is the place you think of when you think of the time-worn New England summer inn.

Inside, the antique furnishings—including the handsome Seth Thomas clock, Oriental carpets, and cane-seated rockers on the front porch—are impeccably well cared for. Guest rooms are simple but appealing, and feature rotary dial phones that will provoke nostalgia in older visitors and mild befuddlement among youngest guests. The Whitehall also occupies a minor footnote in the annals of American literature—a young local poet recited her poems here for guests in 1912, stunning the audience with her eloquence. Her name? Edna St. Vincent Millay.

The Whitehall's dining room boasts a slightly faded glory and service that occasionally limps along, but remains a good destination for reliable American fare like veal with sweet vermouth, sage, and prosciutto, or baked haddock stuffed with Maine shrimp. (Entrees $14.75 to $17.50.) And, of course, there's always boiled Maine lobster.

WHERE TO DINE

Peter Ott's. 16 Bayview St. ☎ **207/236-4032.** Reservations not accepted. Main courses $13.95–$22.95 (most $14–$16). MC, V. Daily 5:30–9:30pm during season; closed for a couple of months in winter. AMERICAN.

Peter Ott's has attracted a steady stream of satisfied local customers and repeat-visitor yachtsmen since it opened smack in the middle of Camden in 1974. While it poses as a steakhouse with its simple wooden tables and chairs and its manly meat dishes (like char-broiled Black Angus with mushrooms and onions, and sirloin steak Dijonaise), it's grown beyond that to satisfy more diverse tastes. In fact, the restaurant offers some of the better prepared seafood in town, including a fine pan-blackened seafood sampler and grilled salmon served with a lemon caper sauce. Be sure to leave room for the specialty coffees and its famous deserts, like the lemon-almond crumb tart.

Sea Dog Brewing Co. 43 Mechanic St. ☎ **207/236-6863.** Reservations not accepted. Main courses $2.95–$10.95. AE, DC, DISC, MC, V. Daily 11:30am–3pm and 5–9pm. Located at Knox Mill 1 block west of Elm St. PUB FARE.

The Sea Dog Brewing Co. is one of a handful of brewpubs that have found quick success in Maine, and it makes a decent destination for quick and reliable pub food like nachos or hamburgers. It won't set your taste buds dancing, but it will satisfy basic cravings.

Located in the ground floor of an old woolen mill that's been renovated by MBNA, a national credit-card company, the restaurant has a generic brewpub atmosphere that could be anywhere—maybe the Midwest, maybe a mall. While not original, the place is comfortable with its booths, wooden chairs and tables, a handsome bar, and views through tall windows of the old mill race. And the beers are uniformly excellent, although some suffer from a regrettable cuteness in naming (for example, Old Gollywobbler Brown Ale).

BELFAST TO BUCKSPORT

Hasty travelers more often than not whip around this northerly stretch of Penobscot Bay, scurrying from the tourist enclave of Camden to the tourist enclaves of Bar Harbor and Mount Desert Island. But it's a mistake to hurry through. Because there's some splendid history and architecture to be found here. Most of the businesses, especially off Route 1, cater to the local trade rather than tourists, so you'll find authentic coastal Maine if you but look for it.

This region was once famed for its fine shipbuilding. In the mid-19th century, Belfast and Searsport produced more than their share of ships and captains to pilot them on trading ventures around the globe. In the last century, the now-quiet village of Searsport had 17 active shipyards that turned out some 200 ships. In 1856 alone, 24 ships of more than 1,000 tons were launched from Belfast.

ESSENTIALS

GETTING THERE   Route 1 connects Belfast, Searsport, and Bucksport.

VISITOR INFORMATION   The **Belfast Area Chamber of Commerce,** P.O. Box 58, Belfast, ME 04915 (☎ 207/338-5900), staffs an information booth near the waterfront park that's open in summer. The **Searsport and Stockton Springs Chamber of Commerce,** P.O. Box 139, Searsport, ME 04974 (☎ 207/548-6510), maintains a seasonal information booth on Route 1. Further north, try the **Bucksport Bay Area Chamber of Commerce,** P.O. Box 1880, Bucksport, ME 04416 (☎ 207/469-6818).

EXPLORING THE REGION

Near Belfast's small waterfront park you can take a fun excursion on the scenic **Belfast and Moosehead Lake Railroad** (☎ 800/392-5500 or 207/948-5500). The railroad was chartered in 1867 and financed primarily by the town; in fact, until 1991, the B&ML railroad remained the only railroad in the nation owned by a municipality. The rail line was purchased by entrepreneurs, who have spruced it up considerably. In 1995, the company acquired 11 vintage rail cars from Sweden, including a 1913 steam locomotive, and opened a new station in Unity, near the end of the 33-mile-long line. (The steam train departs from Unity; a diesel train runs from Belfast.)

The 1¹/₂-hour tours offer a wonderful glimpse of inland Maine and its thick forests and rich farmland. (The train also edges along Passagassawakeag River, a name which provokes considerable amusement among all but the most melancholy of children.) The train features a dining car, where beer and wine may be purchased, and entertainment in the form of a holdup by some unsavory desperados known as the Waldo Station Gang. The train tends to be exceptionally popular with children and elderly visitors. An optional tour of northern Penobscot Bay on a handsome riverboat can also be packaged with the train excursions.

The train runs twice daily through from mid-May to the end of October. The fare is $14 for adults, $7 for the first child (ages 3 to 16), and $3.50 for each additional child.

At the northern tip of Penobscot Bay, the Penobscot River squeezes through a dramatic gorge near Verona Island, which Route 1 spans on an attractive suspension bridge. This easily defended pinch in the river was perceived to be of strategic importance in the 1840s, when the solid and imposing **Fort Knox** was constructed. While it was never attacked, the fort was manned during the Civil and Spanish-American Wars, and today is run as a state park (☎ 207/469-7719). It's an impressive edifice to explore, with subterranean chambers that produce wonderful echoes, and graceful granite staircases. Admission is $2 for adults, 50¢ for children under 12, and free for seniors and children under 5.

Penobscot Marine Museum. Church St. at Rte. 1, Searsport. ☎ 207/548-2529. Adults $5, seniors $3.50, children 7–15 $1.50. Mon–Sat 10am–5pm, Sun noon–5pm. Closed mid-Oct to Memorial Day.

The Penobscot Marine Museum is one of the best small museums in New England. Housed in a cluster of eight historic buildings atop a gentle rise in tiny downtown Searsport, the museum does a deft job in educating visitors about the vitality of the local shipbuilding industry, the essential role of international trade to daily life in the 19th century, and the hazards of life at sea. The exhibits are uniformly well organized, and wandering from building to building induces a keen sense of wonderment at the vast enterprise that was Maine's maritime trade.

Among the more intriguing exhibits are a wide selection of dramatic marine paintings (including one stunning rendition of whaling in the Arctic), black-and-white photographs of many of the 286 weathered sea captains who once called Searsport home, photographs of a 1902 voyage to Argentina, and an early home decorated in the style of a sea captain, complete with lacquered furniture and accessories hauled back from trade missions to the Orient. Throughout, the curators have done a fine job both educating and entertaining visitors. It's well worth the price if you're the least interested in Maine's rich culture of the sea.

WHERE TO DINE

Darby's. 105 High St., Belfast. ☎ 207/338-2339. Reservations suggested for after 7pm on weekends. Lunch $3.95–$8.95, dinner $5.75–$13.95. DISC, MC. V. Daily 11am–9pm. AMERICAN/ECLECTIC.

This dark, sometimes smoky restaurant centers around a handsome bar and offers up filling fare that goes the extra culinary mile. Located in a Civil War–era pub with attractive stamped-tin ceilings and a beautiful back bar with Corinthian columns,

Readers Recommend

Young's Lobster Pound. *In the weeks before our trip along the Maine coast, visions of lobster danced in our heads. We expected the happy mollusk to be cheap and plentiful throughout the region; we thought we'd find a down-home lobster pound on every corner. The reality, however, was very different: Lobster was everywhere, but mostly in dinner specials at restaurants that looked pretty much like the ones we had back home. We were surprised at how few and far between the "lobster in the rough" places that we'd envisioned were. But Young's, on Highway 1 just north of Belfast, was exactly the kind of place we were hoping to find: a no-frills joint serving up Maine lobster the way it was meant to be. You enter the hangar-like structure, choose your favorite from the tanks of live lobsters lining the walls (all pulled from the local waters by Young's boats that day), take a seat at one of the picnic tables overlooking the harbor (the view is terrific), and wait for your number to be called. In minutes, you're digging into a paper plate full of steaming lobster, accompanied by perfectly melted butter, vinegar and salt potato chips, and all the handi-wipes you need—all for around $10. It's simply heavenly—and the ideal Maine coast experience.*

—Cheryl Farr, Brooklyn, NY

Darby's is a popular local hangout that boasts a comfortable, neighborhoody feel. Order up a Maine beer while you peruse the menu, which is surprisingly creative. Darby's offers most pub favorites, like burgers and Cajun chicken on a bulkie roll, but also features imports like pad Thai, enchilada verde, and Thai chicken salad. Try the Moroccan lamb or the smoked seafood pasta made with locally smoked fish. And if you like the artwork on the wall, ask about it. It's probably done by a local artist, and it's probably for sale.

Nickerson Tavern. Rte. 1, Searsport. ☎ **207/548-2220.** Reservations recommended, especially on weekends. Main courses $12.50–$18.50. MC, V. Daily 5:30–9:30pm. Closed Mon–Tues off-season; mid-Jan to mid-Mar. REGIONAL/ECLECTIC.

It's easy to miss the Nickerson Tavern, located in a modest 1838 Cape-style home 2.8 miles east of Bucksport's downtown on Route 1. But do yourself a favor and turn around, joining the other gourmands who appreciate this gem set in a rustic part of coastal Maine. After you enter, you're ushered into a small parlor off the entrance. From here, you're seated in either the main dining room, which is decorated in an informal colonial American motif with Indian red paint, early china, and ancient bottles, or one of two smaller, slightly more formal side rooms.

The cuisine draws on regional delicacies, like lobster (of course), chicken, and duckling. The preparation is informed by French style, but dishes are made "without the heaviness and stuffiness of classic presentation," says the chef. You could begin with an appetizer of escargot, baked brie in puff pastry, or Maine mussels steamed in ale with garlic and Dijon mustard. Then select from a delectable array of entrees, including lobster sautéed in butter with a cognac dill cream sauce, raspberry hazelnut chicken, or pork tenderloin served with a sauce of mushrooms, shallots, and capers.

OFF THE BEATEN TRACK: CASTINE, BLUE HILL & DEER ISLE
CASTINE & ENVIRONS

If I had to choose the most elegant village in Maine, I would without hesitation choose Castine. It's not so much the stunningly handsome mid-19th-century homes that fill the side streets, virtually all of which are meticulously maintained. Nor is it the location on a quiet peninsula, 16 miles south of the hubub of tourist-jammed Route 1 via Routes 175 and 166. No, what lends Castine most of its charm are the splendid, towering elm trees, which still overarch many of the village streets. Before Dutch elm disease, much of America once looked like this, and it's easy to slip into a deep nostalgia for this most graceful of trees, even if you're too young to remember America of the elms. Through perseverance and a measure of luck, Castine has managed to keep its elms alive, and it's worth the drive here for this alone.

For American history buffs, Castine offers more than trees. This outpost served as a strategic town in various battles between the British, Dutch, French, and feisty colonials in the centuries after it was settled in 1613. It's been occupied by all of them at some point, and historical personages like Miles Standish and Paul Revere passed through during one epoch or another. (Paul Revere, in one of his less heroic feats, was involved in the ignoble loss of 44 American ships during the Revolution after a failed colonial attack on British-held Castine.) The town has a dignified, aristocratic bearing, and it somehow seems appropriate that Tory-dominated Castine welcomed the British with open arms during the Revolution.

An excellent brief history of Castine by Elizabeth J. Duff is published in brochure form by the Castine Merchant's Association. The brochure, which also includes a walking tour of Castine, is entitled "Welcome to Castine" and is available widely at shops in town and at the state information centers.

One of the town's most intriguing attractions is the **Wilson Museum** (curator's ☎ 207/326-8545; call 5 to 9pm) on Perkins Street, an attractive and quirky anthropological museum constructed in 1921. This small museum contains the collections of John Howard Wilson, a Castine resident and inveterate collector of rifles and other historic artifacts from around the globe. Don't miss the display of summer and winter hearses, or the early American kitchen. The museum is open from the end of May through September. Tuesday through Sunday from 2 to 5pm and admission is free.

The **Castine Inn,** Main Street (P.O. Box 41), Castine, ME 04421 (☎ 207/326-4365, fax 207/326/4570), is a Maine coast rarity—a hotel that was originally built as a hotel (not as a residence), in this case in 1898. This handsome cream-colored village inn, designed in an eclectic Georgian–Federal Revival style, has a fine front porch and attractive gardens. Inside, the lobby takes its cuc from the 1940s, with wingback chairs and loveseats, and a fireplace in the parlor. There's also an intimate, dark lounge decked out in rich green hues, reminiscent of an Irish pub. The elegant dining room has heavy wooden chairs and a wraparound mural by Margaret Parker, one of the inn's owners. The meals served here, incidentally, are the best in town, featuring regional classics like crabmeat cakes, roast venison, fettuccini with mussels, and lobster stew with corn and smoked bacon. Entrees are $12 to $18.

The guest rooms on the two upper floors are attractively if unevenly furnished in early American style—some aren't much of an improvement over standard motel rooms, but others are graciously appointed with antiques. Likewise, some rooms feature glimpses of the harbor, others don't. To avoid disappointment, ask to see your room before you hand over your credit card. The inn has 20 rooms (some with shower only), and rates are $75 to $125 for doubles, including full breakfast. Open mid-May through October. MasterCard and Visa are accepted.

Here's the big activity at the **Pentagöet Inn,** Main Street (P.O. Box 4), Castine, ME 04421 (☎ 800/845-1701 or 207/326-8616): Sit on the wraparound front porch on cane-seated rockers. Watch Castine go by. That's not likely to be overly appealing to those looking for a fast-paced vacation, but it's the perfect salve for those seeking respite from urban life. This quirky yellow and green 1894 structure with its prominent turret is tastefully furnished downstairs with hardwood floors, oval braided rugs, and a woodstove—and somehow it's comforting to see an Encyclopedia Britannica lining the shelves of the sitting room. It's comfortable without being overly elegant, professional without being chilly, personal without being overly intimate.

The rooms on the upper two floors of the main house are furnished nicely and eclectically, with a mix of antiques and old collectibles. The five guest rooms in the adjacent Perkins Street building—a more austere Federal-era house—are furnished simply and feature painted floors. There's no air-conditioning, but all rooms have ceiling fans. No smoking. The inn has 16 rooms (7 with showers only), and rates are $95 to $125 for doubles, including full breakfast. It's open from the end of May through the third week of October. MasterCard and Visa are accepted.

DEER ISLE

Deer Isle is well off the beaten path, but well worth the long detour off Route 1 via Routes 175 and 15 if your tastes run to pastoral countryside with a nautical edge. Loopy, winding roads cross through forest and farmland, and travelers are rewarded with sudden glimpses of the azure ocean and mint-green coves. An occasional settlement crops up now and again.

Deer Isle doesn't cater exclusively to tourists, as many coastal regions do. It's still occupied by fifth-generation fishermen, farmers, longtime rusticators, and artists who prize their seclusion. The village of Deer Isle has a handful of inns and galleries, but its primary focus is to serve locals and summer residents, not transients. The village of Stonington, on the southern tip, is a rough-hewn sea town that's still dominated by fishermen and the occasional quarry worker.

On the island's east side, a trip to the **Haystack Mountain School of Crafts** (☎ 207/348-2306) is a worthy excursion. Just south of the village of Deer Isle, turn east off Route 15 toward Stinson Neck and continue along this scenic road for seven miles. Look for the school's driveway, then head to the visitor's parking area. The campus of this respected summer crafts school is visually stunning.

Stonington basically consists of one street that wraps along the harbor's edge. While a handful of bed-and-breakfasts and galleries have established themselves here, it's still a rough-and-tumble waterfront town with strong links to the sea, and you're likely to observe lots of activity in the harbor as lobstermen and urchin divers come and go. If you hear industrial sounds emanating from just offshore, that's likely to be the quarry on Crotch Island, which has been supplying architectural granite to builders nationwide for more than a century.

Day Trips to Isle au Haut

Rocky and remote Isle au Haut offers the most unique hiking and camping experience in northern New England. This six- by three-mile island, located six miles south of Stonington, was originally named Ile Haut—or High Island—in 1604 by French explorer Samuel de Champlain. The name and its pronunciation evolved—today, it's generally pronounced "aisle-a-ho"—but the island itself has remained steadfastly unchanged over the centuries.

About half of the island is owned by the National Park Service and maintained as an outpost of Acadia National Park (see the next section). A 60-passenger "mailboat" makes a stop in the morning and late afternoon at Duck Harbor, allowing for a solid day of hiking while still returning to Stonington by nightfall. At Duck Harbor the NPS also maintains a cluster of five Adirondack-style lean-tos, which are available for overnight camping. (Advance reservations are essential. Contact **Acadia National Park,** Bar Harbor, ME 04609, or call **207/288-3338.**)

A network of superb hiking trails radiates out from Duck Harbor. Be sure to ascend the island's highest point, 543-foot Duck Harbor Mountain, for exceptional views of the Camden Hills to the west and Mount Desert Island to the east. Nor should you miss the Cliff or Western Head trails, which track along high, rocky bluffs and coastal outcroppings capped with damp, tangled fog forests of spruce. The trails periodically descend down to cobblestone coves, which issue forth with a deep rumble with every incoming wave. A hand-pump near Duck Harbor provides drinking water, but be sure to bring food and refreshments for hiking.

The other half of the island is privately owned, some by fishermen who can trace their island ancestry back three centuries, and some by summer rusticators, whose forebears discovered the bucolic splendor of Isle au Haut in the 1880s. The summer population of the island is about 300, with about 50 die-hards remaining year-round. The mailboat also stops at the small harborside village, which has a few old homes, a handsome church, and tiny schoolhouse, post office, and store. Day-trippers will be better served ferrying straight to Duck Harbor.

The **mail boat** (☎ 207/367-5193) to Isle au Haut leaves from Stonington for the village of Isle au Haut daily at 7 and 11am daily; the *Mink* departs for Duck Harbor daily at 10am. The round-trip boat fare is $18 for adults to either the village or Duck Harbor. Children under 12 are half-price. Reservations are not accepted, but surprisingly few passengers are turned away, even in midsummer. Parking is sometimes a problem, so plan to show up a half-hour before departure.

Sea Kayaking & Camping Along "Merchant's Row"

Peer southward from Stonington and you'll see dozens of spruce-studded islands ringed with a salmon-pink granite between here and the dark, foreboding ridges of Isle au Haut. These islands are collectively called Merchant's Row, and they're invariably ranked by experienced boaters along the coast as the most beautiful in the state. Thanks to these exceptional islands, Stonington is among Maine's most popular destination for sea kayaking. Many of the islands are open to day visitors and overnight camping, and one of the Nature Conservancy islands even hosts a flock of sheep. Experienced kayakers should contact the **Maine Island Trail Association** (☎ 207/761-8225) for more information about paddling here; several of the islands are open only to association members. Aspiring kayakers without experience should sign up for a guided trip. No outfitters are based in Stonington, but several Maine-based outfitters lead multiday camping trips to Merchant's Row and Isle au Haut. Contact **Maine Island Kayak Co.** (☎ 207/766-2373) or **Maine Sports Outfitters** (☎ 207/236-8797).

Where to Stay

Set between an open bay and a millpond, the **Pilgrim's Inn** (Deer Isle, ME 04627; ☎ 207/348-6615) is a historic, handsomely renovated inn in a lovely setting. This four-story, gambrel-roofed structure will especially appeal to those intrigued by early American history. The inn was built in 1793 by Ignatius Haskell, a prosperous sawmill owner. His granddaughter opened the home to boarders, and it's been housing summer guests ever since. The interior is tastefully decorated in a style that's informed by early Americana, but not beholden to historic authenticity. The guest rooms are well-appointed with antiques and painted in muted colonial colors; especially intriguing are the rooms on the top floor with impressive diagonal beams. The inn has 12 rooms and 1 cottage (10 rooms with private bath, 7 with shower only), and rates are $140 to $165 for doubles and $90 to $200 for the cottage, including breakfast and dinner. There is an additional fee of $5 in July and August.

While bikes are available for guest use and just strolling around the village is a pleasure, much inn life revolves around the wonderful dinners, which start with cocktails and hors d'ouevres in the common room at 6pm, followed by one seating at 7pm in the adjacent barn dining room. Only one entree is served at dinner, but it's not likely to disappoint. You might feast on tenderloin of beef with lobster risotto, or a bouillabaisse made of locally caught seafood. Dinner is open to the public by reservation at a fixed price of $29.50. This is a no-smoking inn. Open mid-May through mid-October. MasterCard and Visa are accepted.

BLUE HILL

Blue Hill (pop. 1,900) is fairly easy to find—just look for gently domed, eponymous Blue Hill Mountain, which lords over the northern end of Blue Hill Bay. Set between the mountain and the bay is the quiet historic town of Blue Hill, which clusters along the bay shore and a small stream. There's not much going on in town. This seems to be exactly what attracts summer visitors back time and again—and may explain why there are two excellent bookstores here. Many old-money families still maintain retreats set along the water or in the rolling inland hills. And Blue Hill offers several excellent choices for dining and lodging. It's a good destination for an escape, and will especially appeal to those deft at crafting their own entertainment.

When in the area, be sure to tune into the local community radio station, WERU at 89.9 FM. It started some years back in the chicken coop owned by Peter Yarrow (of Peter, Paul, and Mary fame). The idea was to spread around good music and provocative ideas. It's become slicker and more professional in recent years, but still maintains a pleasantly homespun flavor.

A good way to start your exploration is to ascend the open summit of **Blue Hill Mountain,** from which you'll have superb views of the azure bay and the rocky balds on nearby Mount Desert Island. To reach the trailhead, drive north on Route 172, then turn west (left) on Mountain Road at the Blue Hill Fairgrounds. Drive ⁴/₅ mile and look for the well-marked trail. An ascent of the "mountain" (elevation 940 feet) is about a mile, and requires about 45 minutes. Bring a picnic lunch and enjoy the vistas.

Blue Hill has traditionally attracted more than its fair share of artists, especially, it seems, potters. On Union Street, stop by **Rowantrees Pottery** (☎ 207/374-5535), which has been a Blue Hill institution for more than half a century. The shop was founded by Adelaide Pearson, who said she was inspired to pursue pottery as a career after a conversation with Mahatma Gandhi in India. Rowantrees' pottery is richly hued, and the potters who've succeeded Pearson continue to use glazes made from local resources. **Rackliffe Pottery** (☎ 207/374-2297) was founded by two former Rowantrees potters, and follows a similar local-source philosophy. Visitors are welcome to watch the potters at work. Both shops are open year-round.

Even if you've never been given to swooning over historic homes, you owe yourself a visit to the intriguing **Parson Fisher House** (contact Blue Hill Tea & Tobacco, ☎ 207/374-2161, for information), located on Routes 176 and 15 a half-mile west of the village. Fisher, Blue Hill's first permanent minister, was something of a Renaissance man when he settled here in 1796. Educated at Harvard, Fisher not only delivered sermons in six different languages, including Aramaic, but was a writer, painter, and minor inventor whose energy was evidently boundless. On a tour of his home, which he built in 1814, you can see a clock with wooden works he made, and samples of the books he not only wrote but published and bound himself.

Where to Stay & Dine

The ✪ **Blue Hill Inn,** Union Street (P.O. Box 403), Blue Hill, ME 04614 (☎ 207/374-2844, fax 207/374-2829), has been hosting travelers since 1840, so it should come as no surprise that the place has got hospitality down pat. Situated on one of Blue Hill's busy streets and within walking distance of most everything, this Federal-style inn features an authentic colonial American motif throughout, with the authenticity enhanced by creaky floors, doorjambs slightly out of true, and quirky touches, like a heavy iron safe employed as an end table. Innkeepers Mary and Don Hartley have furnished all the rooms pleasantly with antiques and down comforters.

The one part of the inn that doesn't feel old (and is the least interesting) is the dining room, which is built in a boxy, shedlike addition to the old house. But the superb French-style cooking of chef Andre Strong makes up for the slightly disappointing atmosphere. The limited menu, made chiefly with local, organic ingredients, might start with fiddlehead flan or penne with vodka tomato cream sauce, then follow with rabbit in a mustard wine sauce; lobster with caramelized ginger, shallots, and spinach; or guinea hen with grapes and wild mushrooms. The fixed-price dinner ($30 for five course, $22 for three course) is open to the public, reservations required. This is a no-smoking inn. There are 11 rooms (2 with shower only), and rates are $140 to $190 for a double, including breakfast and dinner. It's closed the first two weeks of December, and from January through March. MasterCard and Visa are accepted.

Coming up the driveway of the ✪ **John Peters Inn,** Route 176 East (P.O. Box 916), Blue Hill, ME 04614 (☎ **207/374-2116**), sends a signal that you're entering into another world, if not another dimension. The narrow dirt road ascends a gentle hill between a row of maples. To the right are glimpses of the bay; to the left is the 1810 home that, with the later architectural embellishments, could be a modest antebellum plantation home.

Inside, it's strictly New England and decorated in antiques with an uncommon elegance and an eye to detail by innkeepers Barbara and Rick Seeger. There's nothing grand here—it's all simple early American style done with exceptionally good taste. The guest rooms, nine of which boast fireplaces and four of which have private phones, all feature loveseats or sofas, and are hard to tear oneself out of. But do try. The inn sits on 25 lovely shorefront acres, and has been lightly landscaped—to do more would be to gild the lily. There's also an unheated outdoor pool that will appeal mostly to those of stout constitution. Breakfast in the simply decorated dining room is a sublime treat, with offerings like freshly squeezed orange juice, poached eggs with asparagus, lobster omelets, and a variety of waffles. This is a no-smoking inn. There are 14 rooms, and rates are $95 to $150 for doubles, including full breakfast. Open May to October. MasterCard and Visa are accepted.

The **Left Bank Bakery and Cafe** (☎ **207/374-2201**) is Maine's preeminent counterculture outpost. Located on Route 172 north of town, the Left Bank serves up good food and good music, although not always accompanied by good service. (On my last visit four workers stood behind the counter chatting amiably while customers waited 15 minutes to place an order.) Tasty fresh-baked products are piled high at the counter in the older front section of the restaurant; a renovated side section down a few steps is open and airy, and hosts regular evening performances by notables like Maria Muldaur, Kenny Rankin, and Mose Alison. Call ahead to find out who's playing.

Firepond, Main Street (☎ **207/374-9970**), located right in the village of Blue Hill, is a drop-dead gorgeous restaurant that happens to serve exceptionally fine food. Ideally sited along a small stream in a former blacksmith's shop, Firepond has old-pine floors and is lavishly decorated with dry and live flowers. The decor flirts with a "Martha Stewart run amok" look, but it pulls back in the nick of time and carries its elegance unusually well. The best seats are downstairs in the covered porch overhanging the stream, but it's hard to go wrong anywhere here for setting a romantic mood. If you're not sure this is the place for you, try this: Stop by the handsome bar with its wrought-iron stools for a drink and an appetizer. The odds are you'll decide that staying for dinner is a good idea.

The meals are adventurous without being overly exotic. When I visited, the chef was in the process of opening a Russian restaurant in New York, and you could see the connection in dishes like "vegetarian caviar," a surprisingly delicate but earthy concoction of cabbage and mushrooms. More traditional regional fare dominates however, with grilled chicken served with a vegetable salsa and amarillo sauce, veal with sun-dried tomatoes, and lobster served on fresh pasta with a cream sauce of Boursín and Romano cheese. Whatever you choose, expect it to be prepared with an exceedingly deft touch. Reservations are recommended, and main courses are between $15.95 and $21.95. American Express, MasterCard, and Visa are accepted. Open daily from 5 to 9:30pm. Closed January to mid-May and Tuesdays in the fall.

Here's some advice: Don't order the boiled lobster at **Jonathan's,** on Main Street (☎ **207/374-5226**). Not that there's anything wrong with it, but you're better off sampling the more innovative cuisine offered here, saving the boiled crustacean for a lobster-pound picnic table. The menu changes frequently, but among the fine dishes apt to be served here are grilled salmon wrapped in grape leaves and served with a feta salad; braised lamb shank simmered in ale and bourbon and served with a maple barbecue sauce; and venison médaillons and wild boar sausage accompanied by portobello and shiitake mushrooms. Appetizers run along the lines of warm salad of smoked mussels and chevre, and grilled sopresatta and shrimp.

Located in the middle of Blue Hill, Jonathan's attracts the local hip crowd as well as the old-money summer denizens. The background music is jazz or light rock, the service brisk and professional, and the wine list is extensive and creative. Guests choose between the barnlike back room with a comfortable knotty-pine feel, or the less elegantly decorated front room facing Main Street, done up in green tablecloths, captain's chairs, and booths of white pine. My vote: Go for the back room— it's bigger, but paradoxically feels more intimate. Reservations are recommended in summer and on weekends year-round. Main courses run from $16.95 to $19.95. MasterCard and Visa are accepted. Open daily 5 to 9:30pm; closed Monday and Tuesday in winter.

7 Mount Desert Island & Acadia National Park

Mount Desert Island is home to spectacular Acadia National Park, and for many visitors the two places are one and the same. It's true, Acadia dominates the economy and defines the spirit of Maine's largest island. And it does feature the most dramatic coastal real estate on the eastern seaboard.

Yet, the national park holdings are only part of the appeal of this popular island, which is connected to the mainland via a short, two-lane causeway. Beyond the parklands are scenic harborside villages and remote backcountry roads, quaint B&Bs and exceptionally fine restaurants, oversized 19th-century summer "cottages" and the unrepentantly ticky-tacky tourist trap of Bar Harbor. Those who arrive on the island expecting untamed wilderness invariably leave disappointed. Those who understand that Acadia National Park is but one chapter (albeit a very long one) in the intriguing story of Mount Desert Island will enjoy their visit more thoroughly.

Mount Desert (pronounced "de-*sert*") is divided into two lobes separated by Somes Sound, the only legitimate fjord in the continental United States. (A fjord is a valley carved by a glacier that is subsequently filled with rising ocean water.) Those with a poetic imagination see Mount Desert shaped as a lobster, with one large claw and one small. Most of the parkland is on the meatier east claw, although large swaths of national park exist on the leaner west claw as well. The eastern side is more developed, with Bar Harbor the center of commerce and entertainment. The western side has a more quiet, settled air, and teems with more wildlife than tourists. The island isn't huge—it's only about 15 miles from the causeway to the island's southernmost tip at Bass Harbor Head—so visitors can take their time adventuring. The best plan is to explore mostly by foot, bicycle, or kayak.

ACADIA NATIONAL PARK

It's not hard to fathom why Acadia is consistently one of the biggest draws in the U.S. national park system. The park's landscape is a rich tapestry of rugged cliffs, restless ocean, and deep, silent woods. Acadia's landscape, like so much of the rest of northern New England, was carved by glaciers some 18,000 years ago. A mile-high ice sheet shaped the land by scouring valleys into their distinctive "U" shapes, rounding many of the once-jagged peaks, and depositing huge boulders about the landscape, such as the famous 10-foot-high "Bubble Rock," which appears to be perched precariously on the side of South Bubble Mountain.

Mount Desert Island/Acadia National Park

The park's more recent roots can be traced back to the 1840s, when noted Hudson River School painter Thomas Cole packed his sketchbooks and casels for a trip to this remote island, then home to a small number of fishermen and boatbuilders. His stunning renditions of the surging surf pounding against coastal granite were later displayed in New York and helped trigger an early tourism boom as urbanites flocked to the island to escape the heat and to "rusticate." By 1872, national magazines were touting Eden (Bar Harbor's name until 1919) as a desirable summer resort. It attracted the attention of wealthy industrialists, and soon became summer home to Carnegies, Rockefellers, Astors, and Vanderbilts, who built massive summer cottages with literally dozens of rooms (one cottage even boasted 28 bathrooms).

By early in this century, the huge popularity and growing development of the island began to concern its most ardent supporters. Boston textile heir and conservationist George Dorr and Harvard president Charles Eliot, aided by the largesse of John D. Rockefeller, Jr., started acquiring large tracts for the public's enjoyment. These parcels were eventually donated to the federal government, and in 1919 the public land was designated Lafayette National Park, the first national park east of the Mississippi. Renamed Acadia in 1929, the park has grown to encompass nearly half the island.

Rockefeller purchased and donated about 11,000 acres—or one-third of the park. He's also responsible for one of the park's most extraordinary features. Around 1905 a row erupted over whether to allow noisy new motorcars on to the island. Resident islanders wanted these new conveniences to boost their mobility; John D. Rockefeller,

Jr., whose fortune was ironically from the oil industry, strenuously objected, preferring the tranquillity of the car-free island. Rockefeller went down to defeat on this issue, and the island was opened to cars in 1913. In response, the multimillionaire set about building an elaborate 57-mile system of carriage roads, featuring a dozen gracefully handcrafted stone bridges. These roads, which are today open only to equestrians, bicyclists, and pedestrians, concentrate most densely around Jordan Pond, but also ascend to some of the most scenic open peaks and wind through sylvan valleys.

ESSENTIALS

GETTING THERE   Acadia National Park is reached from the town of Ellsworth via Route 3. If you're coming from the south, you can avoid the coastal congestion along Route 1 by taking the turnpike to Bangor, picking up I-395 to Route 1A, then continuing south on Route 1A to Ellsworth. While this looks slightly longer on the map, it's by far the quickest route in summer.

Daily flights from Boston to the airport in Trenton, just across the causeway from Mount Desert Island, are offered by **Colgan Air** (☎ **800/272-5488** or 207/ 667-7171).

ENTRY POINTS   The main point of entry to Park Loop Road, the park's most scenic byway, is at the visitor center at **Hulls Cove.** Mount Desert Island consists of an interwoven network of park and town roads, allowing visitors to enter the park at numerous points. A glance at a park map (available at the visitor center) will make these access points self-evident. The entry fee is collected at a toll booth on Park Loop Road one-half mile north of Sand Beach.

VISITOR CENTERS   Acadia maintains two visitor centers. The **Thompson Island Information Center** (☎ **207/288-3411**) on Route 3 is the first you'll pass as you enter Mount Desert Island. This is open May through mid-October and is operated jointly by the park service and the island's chambers of commerce. It's a good stop for lodging and restaurant information; if you're primarily interested in information about the park itself, continue on Route 3 to the National Park Service's **Hulls Cove Visitor Center** (☎ **207/288-5262**), about 7.5 miles beyond Thompson Island. This attractive stone-walled center includes professionally prepared park service displays, such as a large relief map of the island, natural history exhibits, and a short introductory film. You can also request free brochures about hiking trails and the carriage roads, or purchase postcards and more detailed guidebooks. The center is open mid-April through October. In winter, information is available at the park's **headquarters** (☎ **207/288-3338**) on Route 233 between Bar Harbor and Somes Sound.

PARK ACCOMMODATIONS   Unlike many of the other "crown jewel" national parks, Acadia doesn't have its own rustic park lodge. In fact, the park itself offers no overnight accommodations at all, other than two campgrounds (see below). But visitors don't have to go far to find a room. Bar Harbor especially is teeming with motels and inns; the rest of the island has a smattering of hostelries. See "Where to Stay," below.

SEASONS   Visit Acadia in September if you can finagle it. Between Labor Day and the foliage season of early October, the days are often warm and clear, the nights have a crisp northerly tang, and you can avoid the hassles of congestion, crowds, and pesky insects. Not that the park is empty in September. Bus tours seem to proliferate this month, which results in crowds of tourists at the most popular sites. Not to worry: If you walk just a few feet away (literally, in some cases) you can find solitude and an agreeable peacefulness. Hikers and bikers have the trails and carriage roads to themselves.

Summer, of course, is peak season at Acadia. Some of the roads in and around the park can resemble New York's Central Park at rush hour if you arrive at the wrong time. That's no surprise. The weather is perfect for just about any outdoor activity in July and August. Most days are warm (in the 70s or 80s), with afternoons frequently cooler owing to ocean breezes. While sun seems to be the norm, come prepared for rain and fog, which are both frequent visitors to the Maine coast. And once or twice each summer a heat wave will settle into the area, producing temperatures in the 90s, dense haze, and stifling humidity, but this rarely lasts more than two or three days. Soon enough, a brisk north wind will blow in from the Arctic, churning up the waters and forcing visitors into sweaters at night. Sometime around the last two weeks of August, a cold wind will blow through at night and you'll smell the approach of autumn, with winter not far behind it.

AVOIDING THE CROWDS   Late summer and early fall are the best times to miss out on the mobs yet still enjoy the weather. If you do come during midsummer, try to venture out early mornings and early evenings to see the most popular spots, like the Thunder Hole or the summit of Cadillac Mountain. Setting off into the woods is also a good strategy. About four out of five visitors restrict their tours to the loop road and a handful of other major attractions, leaving the Acadia backcountry open for more adventurous spirits. The carriage roads below Jordan Pond are closed to mountain bikes and are a great place for an easy ramble without too much company.

The best guarantee of solitude is to head to the more remote outposts managed by Acadia, especially Isle au Haut and Schoodic Peninsula. These are covered in detail elsewhere in this guide.

REGULATIONS   Guns may not be used in the park; if you have a gun, it must be "cased, broken down, or otherwise packaged against use." Fires and camping are allowed only at designated areas. Pets must be on a leash at all times. Seat belts must be worn in the national park (this is a federal law). Don't remove anything from the park, either man-made or natural; this includes cobblestones from the shore.

FEES   A week-long park pass, which includes unlimited trips on Park Loop Road, costs $5 per car (no extra charge per passenger). Daily passes are not available.

RANGER PROGRAMS   Frequent ranger programs are offered throughout the year. These include talks at campground amphitheaters and tours at various locations around the island. Examples are the Otter Point nature hike, Mr. Rockefeller's bridges walk, Frenchman Bay cruise (rangers provide commentary on commercial trips; make reservations with boat owners), and a discussion of changes in Acadia's landscape. Ask for a schedule of events at the visitor center or either of the two campgrounds.

SEEING THE HIGHLIGHTS

Three or four days are a good minimum for exploring the park. If you're passing through just briefly, try to work in at least three of the four following activities.

DRIVE THE PARK LOOP ROAD   This almost goes without saying, since it's the park's premier attraction. This 20-mile road runs along the island's eastern shore, then loops inland along Jordan Pond and Eagle Lake. The road runs alternately high along the shoulders of brawny coastal mountains, then dips down along the boulder-strewn coastlines. The dark granite is broken by the spires of spruce and fir, and the earthy tones contrast sharply with the frothy white surf and the steely, azure sea. The two-lane road is one-way along the coastal stretches; the right-hand lane serves as a parking area, so it's easy to make frequent stops to admire the vistas.

Ideally, visitors will take at least two trips on the loop road. The first is for the sheer exhilaration and to get a feel for the lay of the land. On the second trip around, plan to stop more frequently, leaving your car behind while you explore the trails and coastline.

Attractions along the coastal loop include the **Robert Abbe Museum of Stone Age Antiquities** (☎ 207/288-3519), a small museum with anthropological artifacts that really isn't worth the $2 admission; scenic **Sand Beach,** which is the only sand beach on the island and offers good swimming during infrequent hot spells and brutally cold swimming the rest of the time; **Thunder Hole** is a shallow oceanside cavern into which the surf surges, compresses, and bursts out with explosive force and a concussive sound (young kids seem to be endlessly mesmerized by this); and **Cadillac Mountain,** at 1,530 feet the highest point on the island and the place first touched by the sun in the United States during certain times of year. The mountain top is accessible by car, but the lot at the summit is often overflowing. You're better off hiking to the top, or scaling a more remote peak.

HIKE A MOUNTAIN This quintessential Acadia experience shouldn't be missed. The park is studded with low "mountains" (they'd be called hills elsewhere) that offer superb views over the island and the open ocean. The trails weren't simply hacked out of the hillside; they were crafted by experienced stonemasons and others with high aesthetic intent. The routes aren't the most direct, or the easiest to build. But they're often the most scenic, taking advantage of fractures in the rocks, picturesque ledges, and sudden vistas. See "Hiking" below for suggested climbs.

BIKE A CARRIAGE ROAD The 57 miles of carriage road built by John D. Rockefeller, Jr., are among the park's most extraordinary hidden treasures. (See introduction above for a brief history.) While built for horse and carriage, these grass-and-gravel roads are ideal for cruising by mountain bike. Park near Jordan Pond and plumb the tree-shrouded roads that lace the area, and take time to admire the stonework on the uncommonly fine bridges. Afterwards, stop for tea and popovers at the Jordan Pond House, which has been an island tradition for over a century, although it's unlikely as much Lycra was in evidence 100 years ago. For bike rentals, see "Mountain Biking," below.

EAT A LOBSTER While you can't feast on boiled lobster served oceanside within Acadia National Park, several lobster pounds offer the opportunity outside the park's borders. The best places are those right on the water, and where there's no pretension or frills. The ingredients for a proper feed at a local lobster pound are a pot of boiling water, a tank of lobsters, some well-worn picnic tables, a good view, and a six-pack of Maine beer. Among the best destinations for lobster are **Beal's Lobster Pier** (☎ 207/244-7178) in Southwest Harbor, which is one of the oldest pounds in the area. **Abel's Lobster Pound** (☎ 207/276-5827) on Route 198 five miles north of Northeast Harbor overlooks the deep blue waters of Somes Sound; eat at picnic tables under the pines or indoors at the restaurant. Abel's is pricier than other lobster pounds, but it's in a spectacular setting. On the mainland just north of the causeway, turn on Route 230 and head four miles to **Oak Point Lobster Pound** (☎ 207/667-8548) for its lobster served up with a sensational view of the island's rocky hills.

Outdoor Pursuits

CANOEING Mount Desert's several ponds offer scenic if limited canoeing, and most have public boat access. Canoe rentals are available at the north end of Long

Pond in Somesville from **National Park Canoe Rentals** (☎ 207/244-5854). Long Pond is the largest of the island ponds, and offers good exploring. Pack a picnic and spend a few hours reconnoitering the pond's three-mile length. Much of the west shore and the southern tip lies within Acadia National Park.

CARRIAGE RIDES   Carriage rides are offered by **Wildwood Stables** (☎ 207/276-3622), a national park concessioner located a half-mile south of Jordan Pond House. The one-hour Day Mountain trip departs three times daily, yields wonderful views, and costs $12 for adults, $7 for children 6 to 12, and $4 for children 2 to 5. Longer tours are also available; reservations are encouraged.

HIKING   Acadia National Park has 120 miles of hiking trails in addition to the 57 miles of carriage roads. The Hulls Cove Visitor Center offers a one-page chart of area hikes; combined with the park map, this is all you'll need since the trails are well-maintained and well-marked. It's not hard to cobble together loop hikes to make your trips more varied. Coordinate your hiking with the weather; if it's damp or foggy, you'll stay drier and warmer strolling the carriage roads. If it's clear and dry, head for the highest peaks with the best views.

Among the most extraordinary trails is the **Dorr Ladder Trail,** which departs from Route 3 near The Tarn just south of the Sieur de Monts entrance to the Loop Road. This trail begins with a Homeric series of stone steps ascending along the base of a vast slab of granite, then passes through crevasses (not for the wide of girth) and up ladders affixed to the unyielding granite. The views east and south are superb.

An easy lowland hike is around **Jordan Pond,** with the northward leg along the pond's east shore on a hiking trail, and the return via carriage road. It's mostly level, with the total loop measuring 3.3 miles. At the north end of Jordan Pond, consider detouring up the prominent, oddly symmetrical mounds called **The Bubbles.** The ascents shouldn't take much more than 20 minutes each; look for signs off the Jordan Pond Shore Trail.

On the western side of the island, an ascent of **Acadia Mountain** and return takes about an hour and a half, but hikers should schedule in some time for lingering while they enjoy the views of Somes Sound and the smaller islands off Mount Desert's southern shores. This 2.5-mile loop hike begins off Route 102 at a trailhead 3 miles south of Somesville. Head eastward through rolling mixed forest, then begin an ascent over ledgy terrain. Be sure to visit both the east and west peaks (the east peak has the better views), and look for hidden balds in the summit forest that afford unexpected vistas.

MOUNTAIN BIKING   Acadia's carriage roads (see introduction, above) offer some of the most scenic, relaxing mountain biking anywhere in the United States. The 57 miles of grassy lanes and gravel road were maintained by John D. Rockefeller, Jr., until his death in 1960. Afterward, they became somewhat shabby and overgrown until a major restoration effort brought them back beginning in 1990. The roads today are superbly restored and maintained. Where the carriage roads cross private land (generally between Seal Harbor and Northeast Harbor), they're closed to mountain bikes. Please respect these restrictions.

A map of the carriage roads is available at the park's visitor center. More detailed guidebooks are sold at area bookstores.

Mountain bike rentals are easily found along Cottage Street in Bar Harbor. Some bike shops include locks and helmets as basic equipment; ask what's included before you rent. Try **Bar Harbor Bicycle Shop** (☎ 207/288-3886) at 141 Cottage St.; **Acadia Outfitters** (☎ 207/288-8118) at 106 Cottage St.; or **Acadia Bike & Canoe** (☎ 207/288-9605) at 48 Cottage St.

SEA KAYAKING   Experienced sea kayakers flock to Acadia to test their paddling skills along the surf at the base of rocky cliffs, to venture out to the offshore islands, and to probe the still, silent waters of Somes Sound. Novice sea kayakers also come to Acadia to try their hand for the first time with guided tours, which are offered by several outfitters. While many new paddlers have found their inaugural experiences gratifying, others complain that the quantity of paddlers taken out on quick tours during peak season make the experience a little too much like a cattle call to truly enjoy. The following outfitters each offer half- and full-day tours: **Acadia Outfitters** (☎ 207/288-8118) at 106 Cottage St.; **Coastal Kayaking Tours** (☎ 207/288-9605) at 48 Cottage St.; and **National Park Sea Kayak Tours** (☎ 207/288-0342) at 137 Cottage St.

CAMPING   The National Park Service maintains two campgrounds within Acadia National Park. Both are extremely popular; during July and August expect both to fill by early to mid-morning. The more popular of the two is **Blackwoods** (☎ 207/288-3274), located on the island's eastern side. Access is from Route 3, five miles south of Bar Harbor. Bikers and pedestrians have easy access to the Loop Road from the campground via a short trail. The campground has no public showers, but an enterprising business offers clean showers for a modest fee at an operation just outside the campground entrance. Camping fees are $15 and limited reservations are accepted through a **commercial reservation service** (☎ 800/365-2267).

   Seawall (☎ 207/244-3600) is on the quieter, western half of the island near the fishing village of Bass Harbor. This is a good base for road biking, and several short coastal hikes are within easy striking distance. The campground is open late May through September on a first-come, first-served basis. No showers. The fee is $13 for those arriving by car, $8 for those coming by foot or bike.

   Private campgrounds handle the overflow. The region from Ellsworth south boasts some 14 private campgrounds, which offer varying amenities. Contact the **Thompson Island Information Center** (☎ 207/288-3411) for details.

BAR HARBOR

After a period of quiet slumber, Bar Harbor has been rejuvenated and rediscovered in recent years as tourists have poured into this area and entrepreneurs have followed them, opening dozens of restaurants, shops, and boutiques. The less charitable regard Bar Harbor as just another tacky tourist mecca—Pigeon Forge, Tennessee, with moosehorns and spruce. And it does share some of those traits—the downtown hosts a proliferation of T-shirt vendors, ice-cream-cone shops, and souvenir places. Crowds spill off the sidewalk and into the street in midsummer, and the traffic and congestion can be truly appalling.

   But Bar Harbor's vibrant history, quirky architecture, and beautiful location along Frenchman Bay allow it to rise above its station in life as mild diversion for tourists. Most of the island's inns, motels, and B&Bs are located here, as are dozens of fine restaurants and fun bars, making it a desirable base of operations. Bar Harbor is also the best destination for the usual supplies and services; there's a decent grocery story and Laundromat, and you can stock up on other necessities of life.

ESSENTIALS

GETTING THERE   Bar Harbor is located on Route 3 about 10 miles southeast of the causeway. It's also accessible by daily bus from Bangor.

VISITOR INFORMATION   The **Bar Harbor Chamber of Commerce,** P.O. Box 158, Bar Harbor, ME 04609 (☎ 207/288-5103), stockpiles a huge amount of

Bar Harbor

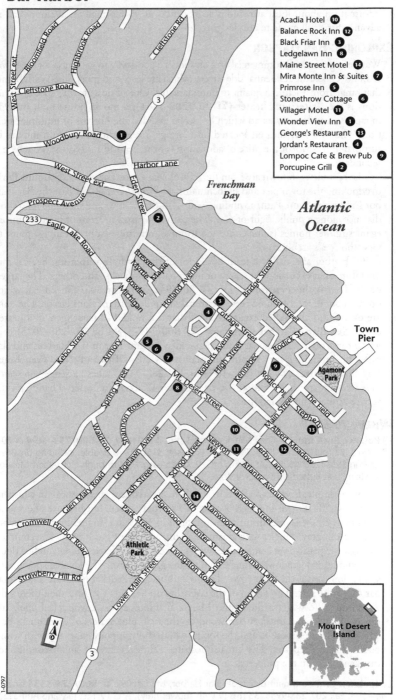

Acadia Hotel **10**
Balance Rock Inn **12**
Black Friar Inn **3**
Ledgelawn Inn **8**
Maine Street Motel **14**
Mira Monte Inn & Suites **7**
Primrose Inn **5**
Stonethrow Cottage **6**
Villager Motel **11**
Wonder View Inn **1**
George's Restaurant **13**
Jordan's Restaurant **4**
Lompoc Cafe & Brew Pub **9**
Porcupine Grill **2**

Frenchman Bay

Atlantic Ocean

Town Pier

Agamont Park

Athletic Park

Mount Desert Island

information about local attractions at its offices at 93 Cottage St. Write or call in advance for a full guide to area lodging.

EXPLORING BAR HARBOR

Wandering the small commercial area on foot is a good way to get a taste of the town. Don't overlook the residential side streets, which are leafy and quiet, lined with homes that range from Victorian quaint to unremarkable. One of downtown's special attractions is the **Criterion Theater** (☎ 207/288-3441), a movie house built in 1932 in a classic art deco style and which has so far avoided the horrors of multiplexification. The 900-seat theater, located on Cottage Street, shows first-run movies in summer and is worth the price of admission for the beautiful interiors; the movie is secondary.

The best views in town are from the foot of Main Street at grassy **Agamont Park,** overlooking the town pier and Frenchman Bay. From here, set off past the Bar Harbor Inn on the Shore Path, a winding, wide trail that follows the shoreline for a short distance along a public right-of-way. The pathway passes in front of many of the elegant summer homes (some converted to inns), offering a superb vantage point to view the area's architecture.

Bar Harbor also makes a terrific base for offshore **whale watching.** Several tour operators offer excursions in search of humpbacks, finbacks, and others. The largest of the fleet is the *Friendship IV* (☎ 800/942-5374 or 207/288-2386), which operates out of the Bluenose Ferry Terminal one mile north of Bar Harbor. The tours are on a fast, twin-hulled excursion boat that can hold 140 passengers in a heated cabin. **Sea Bird Watcher Company** (☎ 800/247-3794 or 207/288-2025) runs whale tours on a 72-foot boat from the Golden Anchor Pier in Bar Harbor, and also offers bird-watching trips to offshore islands to view puffins and terns. **Frenchman Bay Boat Cruises** (☎ 800/508-1499 or 207/288-3322) takes passengers in search of whales aboard the 105-foot, two-deck *Whale Watcher,* and offers a handy pickup service at many hotels and inns.

WHERE TO STAY

✪ **Balance Rock Inn.** 21 Albert Meadow, Bar Harbor, ME 04609. ☎ 800/753-0494 or 207/288-2610. 21 rms. A/C MINIBAR TV TEL. Peak season $150–$350 double, including breakfast; off-season $95–$255 double. AE, DISC, MC, V. Open early May through Oct. Albert Meadow is off Main St. at Butterfield's grocery store.

It's quite simple: If you can afford it, stay here. Everyone seems to speak in whispers, even the staff. It's not so much because it's a snooty place, but because one and all seem in awe of this oceanfront mansion, built in 1903. It's an architecturally elaborate affair of gray shingles with cream, maroon, and forest green trim. The common rooms are expansive yet comfortable, with pilasters and coffered ceilings, arched doorways and leaded windows. There's even a baby grand piano. The favored spot among serious loungers is the front covered patio with its green wicker furniture and a small bar off to the side. The sound of the sea drifts up here gently. And then there's the view, which I'd wager is the best in Maine: You look across a wonderful pool, and down a long lawn framed by hardwoods to the rich, blue waters of Frenchman Bay. The service is impeccable, and the rooms wonderfully appointed, many with whirlpool baths or fireplaces. The inn also features a fitness center in an air-conditioned carriage house on the property.

Ledgelawn Inn. 66 Mount Desert St., Bar Harbor, ME 04609. ☎ 800/274-5334 or 207/288-4596. Fax 207/288-9968. 33 rms (9 with shower only). A/C TV TEL. July and Aug $115–$225 double, including full breakfast; discounts in the off-season. AE, DISC, MC, V. Open late May through late Oct.

The Ledgelawn features a handsome sunporch lounge with a full bar, and when you first set foot inside you half expect to find Bogart flirting with Bacall in a corner. This hulking cream and maroon 1904 "cottage" sits on a village lot amid towering oaks and maples, and has a mid-century elegance to it, although updated with modern amenities; on the property you'll find a pool and hot tub for soaking. Inside, the recently renovated common area around the fireplace has a plush, quiet, upholstered feel. The breakfast room is unexpectedly formal; it feels more like a place for a fancy wedding reception. The guest rooms all vary somewhat as to size and mood, but all are comfortably if not stylishly furnished with antiques and reproductions. Some rooms feature fireplaces that burn Duraflame-style logs.

Mira Monte Inn. 69 Mount Desert St., Bar Harbor, ME 04609. ☎ **800/553-5109** or 207/ 288-4263. Fax 207/288-3115. 12 rms, 3 suites (some with shower only). A/C TV TEL. $115– $150 double, $180 suite. Rates include breakfast. AE, DISC, MC, V. Open May through Oct.

This handsome grayish-green Italianate mansion, built in 1864, is blessed with a profusion of balconies and fireplaces—most guest rooms have one or the other; some have both. The common rooms are furnished in a pleasant country Victorian style, and there's a piano for evening entertainment. The two-acre grounds are handsomely landscaped, and include a cutting garden to keep the house in flowers. There's a nice brick terrace away from the street, which makes a fine a place to enjoy breakfast on warm summer mornings. As for decor, the guest rooms tend to be a bit schizophrenic. Some are dim and almost sepulchral in that heavy Victorian style; others have the bright and airy feel of a country farmhouse. Ask to look first to find a room that fits your tastes. Unless you're traveling with a family, I'd avoid the suites in a separate outbuilding; they're not all that charming, and guests have the vague feel of staying in someone's borrowed apartment.

Mount Desert YWCA. 36 Mount Desert St., Bar Harbor, ME 04609. ☎ **207/288-5008.** 35 rms (all shared bath). $25 single; $85 per week single; $140 per week double. No credit cards.

If you're a woman traveling alone, the undisputed best deal in Bar Harbor is the $25 bed at the YWCA, which is clean and centrally located. It's available only to women, and rooms can be rented by the night or week. If you choose to stay a week or more you'll be assessed a $10 membership fee and a $25 security deposit (refundable). The Y is open year-round, but during summer it fills up rather fast; it's advisable to make reservations early.

Primrose Inn. 73 Mount Desert St., Bar Harbor, ME 04609. ☎ **800/543-7842** or 207/ 288-4031. 10 rms plus 5 efficiencies (1 with shower only). TV TEL. Peak season $90–$145 double, shoulder seasons $85–$140 double; $650–$850 suite per week. Daily rates include breakfast. AE, DISC, MC, V. Open May through late Oct.

This handsome pale-green and maroon Victorian stick-style inn, originally built in 1878, is one of the more noticeable properties on mansion row along Mount Desert Street. Its distinctive architecture has been not only preserved, but improved upon with a major addition in 1987 that added 10 rooms with private baths, and resulted in a number of balconies being added. The inn is comfortable and tinged with elegance inside, although it has a distinctly informal air to it, which encourages guests to mingle and relax in the common room, decorated in a light country Victorian style and complete with piano. The guest rooms are all carpeted, and many feature whirlpools or fireplaces. The suites in the rear are spacious and comfortable, and the efficiencies make sense for families who could benefit from a kitchen (for rent by the week only). Light refreshments are served to all guests in the afternoon.

Pillow Talk

Bar Harbor is the bedroom community for Mount Desert Island, with hundreds of hotel, motel, and inn rooms. Be forewarned that all share one thing in common: They're filled during the busy days of mid-summer. It's essential to book your room as early as possible.

A number of modern hotels and motels cluster along Route 3 just northeast of the village center; this is your best bet if you arrive without reservations.

Be aware that even the most basic of rooms can be frightfully expensive in July and August. There's virtually no motel charging less than $50 during the summer; bed-and-breakfast rates start at about $85.

In the full listings on the adjacent pages there's space enough to review just a handful of the best choices. But these represent only a fraction of the accommodations available. Don't despair if you can't book a room in any of these fine establishments. There are still dozens of other good options, including those listed below.

The Bar Harbor Inn, on Newport Drive (☎ **800/248-3351** or 207/288-3351), is a sprawling complex of 153 rooms in three buildings perfectly situated on the downtown waterfront. Great views abound from Oceanfront and Main Inn; the less expensive Newport building lacks the views but is comfortable and contemporary. Amenities include a pool and dining room overlooking the harbor. The inn is open year-round; rates are $115 to $225 during the peak summer season, and include a continental breakfast.

The Acadia Inn, 98 Eden St. (☎ **800/638-3636** or 207/288-3500), opened in 1996. This modern, stylish three-story hotel features an outdoor pool and Jacuzzi. Peak season rates are $115 to $225, including continental breakfast.

The Golden Anchor, 55 West St. (☎ **800/328-5033** or 207/288-5033), is smack on the waterfront, with some rooms looking across the harbor toward the town pier and others out to Bar Island. (The less expensive rooms have no view at

---

WHERE TO DINE

George's. 7 Stephens Lane. ☎ **207/288-4505.** Reservations recommended. Main courses $20; appetizer, main course, and dessert packages $29. AE, DISC, MC, V. Daily 5:30–10pm; shorter hours after Labor Day. Closed Nov–early May. MEDITERRANEAN-INSPIRED AMERICAN.

You may despair of ever finding George's. Don't. You must persevere. For George's is one of Bar Harbor's classics, offering fine dining in informal surroundings for nearly two decades. (By the way, it's located in the small clapboard cottage behind Main Street's First National Bank.) George's captures the joyous feel of summer nicely in its setting, with four smallish dining rooms (with plenty of open windows) and additional seating on the terrace outside, which is the best place to watch the gentle dusk settle over town. The service is upbeat, and the meals are wonderfully prepared. All entrees sell for one price ($20), and include salad, vegetable, and potato or rice. You won't go wrong with the basic choices, like steamed lobster or roast chicken, but you're better off opting for the more adventurous fare like tangerine scallops or the ever-changing preparations of game or lamb.

Lompoc Cafe and Brewpub. 32 Rodick St. ☎ **207/288-9392.** Reservations not accepted. Sandwiches $3.75–$5.75; dinner $9.95–$13.95. DISC, MC, V. May–Nov daily 11:30am–1am. Closed Dec–April. AMERICAN/ECLECTIC.

The Lompoc Cafe has a well-worn, neighborhood bar feel to it, and it's little wonder that other waiters and waitresses from around Bar Harbor congregate here after hours. The cafe consists of three sections—there's the original bar in the pine-floored

all.) There's a pool and hot tub right at the harbor's edge, and an oceanfront dining room that serves basic fare. Peak season rates range from $110 to $165.

The Park Entrance Oceanfront Motel, Route 3 (☎ **800/288-9703** or 207/288-9703), is nicely situated on 10 handsome waterfront acres close to the park visitor's center. The inn has an attractive private pier and cobblestone beach, and an outdoor swimming pool and Jacuzzi. Summer rates are $129 to $149.

Great views greet guests at the **Atlantic Eyrie Lodge,** on Highbrook Rd. (☎ **800/422-2843** or 207/288-9786), perched on a hillside above Route 3. Peak rates are $125 to $180. Some units have kitchenettes and balconies; all share access to the ocean-view pool.

The oceanside **Holiday Inn SunSpree Resort,** 123 Eden St. (☎ **800/234-6835** or 207/288-9723), has 217 rooms, a children's program, and numerous amenities, including a heated pool, putting green, marina, and restaurant and lounge. Room rates run $149 to $189.

The Colony, Route 3, Hulls Cove (☎ **800/524-1159** or 207/288-3383), consists of a handful of motel rooms and a battery of 55 cottages arrayed around a long green. The Colony is across Route 3 from a cobblestone beach, and a 10-minute drive into Bar Harbor. The rooms are furnished in a simple 1970s style that won't win any awards, but all are comfortable; many have kitchenettes. Summer rates are $50 to $90 for two.

Reputable motels and hotels offering rooms for less than $100 include the conveniently located **Villager Motel,** 207 Main St. (☎ **207/288-3211**), a family-run motel with 63 rooms; the 79-room **Wonder View Inn,** 50 Eden St. (☎ **800/341-1553** or 207/288-3358), with its sweeping bay views; the downtown **Maine Street Motel,** 315 Main St. (☎ **800/333-3188** or 207/288-3188); and the B&B-style **Acadia Hotel,** 20 Mount Desert St. (☎ **207/288-5721**).

dining room, a small, tidy garden just outside (try your hand at bocce ball), and a small, barnlike structure at the garden's edge to handle the overflow. The on-site brewery produces five unique beers, including a locally popular blueberry ale (I don't much care for it), and the smooth Coal Porter, available in sizes up to the 20-ounce "fatty." Whisky drinkers will be busy here: The Lompoc also claims the largest selection of single malts north of Boston. Bar menus are usually predictable but this one has some surprises, with an around-the-world-in-80-minutes-style selection, with tasty entrees like Indonesian chicken, Mediterranean scallops, shrimp étouffé, and Vermont pork tenderloin. Live music is offered some evenings.

Miguel's Mexican Restaurant. 51 Rodick St. ☎ **207/288-5117**. Reservations not accepted. Main courses $6.95–$13.95. MC, V. Tues–Sun 5–9pm. Closed Nov–May. MEXICAN.

Miguel's serves what's possibly the best Mexican food in Maine amid a festive, boisterous atmosphere. It's slightly out of the limelight of downtown Bar Harbor (Rodick Street runs off Cottage Street just west of Main Street), but it's worth making the short trek if you've got a hankering for Mexican. It's not the best place for a quiet dinner—the terra-cotta tiles keep the sound bouncing around—but it is the place for delicious blue-corn crabcakes, shrimp fajitas, or the simple but tasty tacos al carbon. Try the rich, earthy homemade mole sauce, which is available with any dish for an extra 75¢. If you're a drinker with a sweet tooth, the peach daiquiris are dandy.

During warm nights, there's dining on the patio in front, which is a bit quieter and more intimate.

✪ **Porcupine Grill.** 123 Cottage St. ☎ **207/288-3884.** Reservations recommended. Main courses $17.50–$21.95. AE, DC, MC, V. Summer and fall daily 5:30–9:30pm; off-season Fri–Sun only. NEW AMERICAN.

The Porcupine Grill is a pleasant surprise. Housed in a nondescript home on the slightly frayed commercial end of Cottage Street, the grill's interior is beautifully arrayed around a magnificent oak bar, which has the regal presence of a magnificent altar. Guests sit upstairs and down amid a smattering of antiques and enjoy the fresh flowers placed about as they peruse a wonderful menu, which is updated frequently to reflect the seasonal changes in the local bounty. You might begin with the delicate salmon cakes, served with a fresh ginger, chile, and coconut sauce, then move on to filet mignon served with portobello mushrooms and wild-boar bacon, or grilled sea scallops with a peppercorn and sun-dried tomato beurre blanc. The signature Porcupine stew is outstanding—a savory mélange of lobster, scallops, fish, and mussels served in a tomato-caper broth. Desserts are equally superb.

ELSEWHERE ON THE ISLAND

Acadia National Park is the main island attraction, of course, and Bar Harbor has its charm and character. But there's plenty else to explore outside of these areas. Peaceful, charming villages, deep woodlands, and unexpected ocean views are among the jewels that turn up when one peers beyond the usual places.

ESSENTIALS

GETTING AROUND   The east half of the island is best navigated on Route 3, which forms the better part of a loop from Bar Harbor through Seal Harbor and past Northeast Harbor before returning up the eastern shore of Somes Sound. Route 102 and Route 102A provide access to the island's western half.

VISITOR INFORMATION   The best source of information on the island is at the **Thompson Island Information Center** (☎ **207/288-3411**) on Route 3 just south of the causeway connecting Mount Desert Island with the mainland. Another reliable source of local information is **Mount Desert Chamber of Commerce,** P.O. Box 675, Northeast Harbor, ME 04662 (☎ **207/276-5040**).

EXPLORING THE REST OF THE ISLAND

On the tip of the eastern lobe of Mount Desert Island is the staid, prosperous community of **Northeast Harbor,** long one of the favored retreats among the eastern seaboard's upper crust. Those without personal invitations to come as house guests will need to be satisfied with glimpses of the shingled palaces set in the fragrant spruce forests and along the rocky shore. But the village itself is worth investigating. Set around an attractive, narrow harbor, with the glorious Asticou Inn at its head, Northeast Harbor is possessed of a refined sense of elegance that's best appreciated by finding a vantage point, then sitting and admiring.

One of the best, least publicized places for enjoying views of the harbor is from the understatedly spectacular **Asticou Terraces** (☎ **207/276-5130**). Finding the parking lot can be tricky: Head one-half mile south on Route 3 from the junction with Route 198, and look for the small gravel lot on the water side of the road with a sign reading Asticou Terraces. Park here, cross the road on foot, and set off up a magnificent path made of local rock that scales the sheer hillside with expanding views of the harbor and the town. This pathway, with its precise stonework and the occasional bench and gazebo, is one of the Northeast's hidden marvels of landscape architecture. Created by Boston landscape architect Joseph Curtis, who summered here for many years prior to his death in 1928, the pathway seems to blend in almost preternaturally with its spruce-and-fir surroundings, as if it were created by an act of god rather than of man. Curtis donated the property to the public for quiet enjoyment.

Continue on the trail at the top of the hillside and you'll soon arrive at Curtis's cabin (open to the public daily in summer), behind which lies the formal **Thuya Gardens,** which are as manicured as the terraces are natural. These wonderfully maintained gardens, designed by Charles K. Savage, attract flower enthusiasts, students of landscape architecture, and local folks looking for a quiet place to rest. It's well worth the trip. A donation of $2 is requested of visitors to the garden; the terraces are free.

From the harbor visitors can depart on a seaward trip to the beguilingly remote **Cranberry Islands.** You have a couple of options: either travel with a national park guide to Baker Island, the most distant of this small cluster of low islands, and explore the natural terrain. Or hop one of the ferries to either Great or Little Cranberry Island and explore on your own. On Little Cranberry there's a small historical museum run by the National Park Service that's worth seeing. Both islands feature a sense of being well away from it all, but neither offers much in the way of tourist amenities, so travelers should head out prepared for the possibility of shifting weather.

When leaving Northeast Harbor, plan to depart via **Sargent Drive.** This one-way route runs through Acadia National Park along the shore of Somes Sound, affording superb views of this glacially carved inlet.

On the far side of Somes Sound, there's good **hiking** (see "Outdoor Pursuits," above), and the towns of **Southwest Harbor** and **Bass Harbor.** These are both home to fishermen and boatbuilders, and are a far cry from the settlements of the landed gentry at Northeast and Seal harbors across the way.

WHERE TO STAY

Asticou Inn. Rte. 3, Northeast Harbor, ME 04662. ☎ **800/258-3373** or 207/276-3344. 44 rms. TEL. $224–$310 double, including breakfast and dinner. DISC, MC, V. Main inn open early May to mid-Oct; 3-rm B&B cottage open year-round.

The sprawling Asticou Inn, which dates back to 1883, occupies a prime location at the head of Northeast Harbor. Its weathered gray shingles and layered eaves gives it a slightly stern demeanor, but its yellow window shades leaven its appearance with a mild eccentricity. The Asticou is, unfortunately, more elegant on the exterior than on the interior. The furnishings, including the plastic porch furniture, seems to have come from some best-forgotten interregnum between the dapper golden era and the present day. Nonetheless, a wonderful Old World gentility seems to seep from the creaking floorboards and through the thin walls. The rooms are simply furnished in a pleasing summer-home style, as if a more opulent decor was somehow too ostentatious. Jackets are requested on men in the evening; the dinner dance and elaborate buffet on Thursday nights in summer are hallowed island traditions and well worth checking out. Most rooms are located in the main inn, although others are across the road in the cheery Cranberry Lodge. The inn shares its grounds with some unfortunate UFO-like cottages.

Claremont. P.O. Box 137, Southwest Harbor, ME 04679. ☎ **800/244-5036** or 207/244-5036. Fax 207/244-3512. 30 rms (2 with tub only), 12 cottages. TEL. July–Labor Day $115–$145 double, including breakfast; $157–$187 cottage, including breakfast and dinner; off-season from $75 double. No credit cards. Open early June through mid-Oct.

The early prints of the Claremont, built in 1884, show an austere four-story wooden building with one severe gable overlooking Somes Sound from a low, grassy rise. And the place hasn't changed all that much since then. The Claremont offers nothing fancy or elaborate, just simple, clean, classic New England grace. It's wildly appropriate that the state's most high-profile and combative croquet tournament takes place here annually; all those folks in their whites seem right at home. Most of the guest rooms are bright and airy, furnished with antiques and some old furniture that doesn't quite qualify as "antique." The bathrooms are modern. Guests are assessed a premium for a "seaside" room overlooking the water; it's worth it. There's also a series of cottages, available for a three-day minimum. Some of these are set rustically in the piney woods; others offer pleasing views of the sound.

The common areas and dining rooms are pleasantly appointed in an affable country style. There's a library with rockers, a fireplace, and jigsaw puzzles waiting to be assembled. Two other fireplaces in the lobby take the chill out of the morning air. And Lucy and Buster, the inn's dogs—a golden retriever and a Siberian husky—make the place feel like home. Other amenities on the spacious, private grounds include a clay tennis court, rowboats, bicycles (free to guests), and, of course, the impeccably maintained croquet court. Meals are mainly reprises of American classics like grilled salmon, steamed lobster, and ribeye steak served with a mushroom demi-glaze.

Inn at Southwest. Main St. (P.O. Box 593), Southwest Harbor, ME 04679. ☎ **207/ 244-3835.** 9 rms (3 with shower only; 2 with hall bath). Summer and early fall $105–$124 double; off-season $60–$90 double. All rates include full breakfast. MC, V. Open April–Oct.

Jill Lewis and her golden retriever, Bronco, acquired the architecturally quirky Inn at Southwest in early 1995, and both have done a fine job making this mansard-roofed Victorian a hospitable place. There's a decidedly turn-of-the-century air to this elegant home, but it's restrained on the frills. The guest rooms are named after Maine lighthouses, and are furnished with both contemporary and antique furniture. All rooms have ceiling fans and down comforters. Among the most pleasant rooms is Blue Hill Bay on the third floor, with its large bath, sturdy oak bed and bureau, and glimpses of the scenic harbor. Breakfasts are sit-down gourmet, and feature reason-to-get-up specialties like poached pears in wine sauce, eggs Florentine, and crab potato bake.

Le Domaine. Rte. 1 (P.O. Box 496), Hancock, ME 04640. ☎ **800/554-8498** or 207/ 422-3395. Fax 207/422-2316. 7 rms. $200 double ($125 single) including breakfast and dinner. AE, DISC, MC, V.

Although it's a half-hour drive from Mount Desert, Le Domaine has firmly established its reputation as one of the most elegant and delightful destinations in Maine. Set on Route 1 about 10 minutes east of Ellsworth, this inn has the continental flair of an impeccable auberge. While the highway in front can be a bit noisy, the garden and woodland walks out back offer plenty of serenity. The rooms are comfortable and tastefully appointed without being pretentious, but the real draw here is the exquisite dining room. Chef Nicole Purslow carries on the tradition begun by her mother in 1946 by offering superb French country cooking in the handsome candlelit dining room with its pinewood floors and sizable fireplace. The ever-changing sauces make the entrees sing here, and might feature Atlantic salmon with a sorrel and shallot sauce, or rabbit served with a robust prune sauce. Plan to check in by 5:30pm; dinner is served between 6 and 9pm.

WHERE TO DINE

The Burning Tree. Rte. 3, Otter Creek. ☎ **207/288-9331.** Reservations recommended. Main courses $13.75–$19.50. Wed–Mon 5–9pm, daily in Aug. Closed Columbus Day–mid-June. REGIONAL/ORGANIC.

Located on busy Route 3 between Bar Harbor and Northeast Harbor, the Burning Tree is an easy restaurant to speed right by. But that would be a mistake. This low-key restaurant, with its bright, open, and sometimes noisy dining room, serves up the freshest food in the area. Much of the produce and herbs come from its own gardens, with the rest of the ingredients supplied locally wherever possible. Seafood is the specialty here, and it's consistently prepared with equal parts imagination and skill. The menu changes often to reflect local availability. Typical appetizers include chili-orange noodle and scallop salad, and smoked salmon served with a corn and caper relish. Entrees might include Cajun crab and lobster au gratin, grilled swordfish with a watercress-lime sauce, or monkfish baked with clams, artichokes, and olives and served with a saffron orzo. Desserts are equally enticing, especially the ginger-orange cheesecake.

Jordan Pond House. Park Loop Rd., Acadia National Park (near Seal Harbor). ☎ **207/ 276-3316.** Reservations recommended for lunch, tea, and dinner. Lunch $5.50–$12; afternoon tea $5.50–$6.50; dinner $7.50–$14. AE, DISC, MC, V. Late May to late Oct daily 11:30am–8pm (until 9pm July–Aug). Afternoon tea served 2:30–5:30pm. AMERICAN.

The secret to the Jordan Pond House is location, location, location. The restaurant traces its roots back to 1847, when an early farm was established on this picturesque property at the southern tip of a pond looking toward The Bubbles, a pair of sizable glacially sculpted mounds. Tragedy struck in 1979 when the original structure and its birch-bark dining room was leveled by fire. A more modern, two-level dining room was built in its place—it's got less charm, but it still has the location. If the weather's right, ask for a seat on the lawn with its unrivaled views. Afternoon tea is a hallowed Jordan Pond House tradition. Ladies Who Lunch sit next to Lycra-clad mountain bikers, and everyone feasts on the huge, tasty popovers and strawberry jam served with a choice of teas or fresh lemonade. Dinners are reasonably priced, and include classic resort entrees like prime rib, steamed lobster, and baked haddock.

✪ Redfield's. Main St., Northeast Harbor. ☎ **207/276-5283.** Reservations strongly recommended in summer. Main courses $17.95–$19.95. AE, MC, V. June–Oct Mon–Sat 6–9pm; Nov–May Fri–Sat only. CONTEMPORARY.

One of the great surprises of Redfield's is that a restaurant with such a superb sense of service and such a fine mastery over the kitchen can thrive in such a small village. Then again, quietly wealthy Northeast Harbor isn't your typical small village. Located in a storefront in the tiny downtown, this restaurant is decorated with a subtle and restrained elegance. A couple of large sprays of flowers set the tone. Patrons can enjoy a libation at the wonderful marble bar (it was taken from an old soda fountain), then settle in and peruse the short but tempting menu, which draws its inspiration from cuisines around the world. Choices change with some frequency, but might include appetizers of smoked mussels with a sauce of corn, tomato, and serrano chile; or eggplant and roasted red peppers baked with cheddar on a corn tortilla. The delectable entrees are prepared with style and care, and include a salmon filet with ginger-tamari sauce, and venison tenderloin with dried cranberries and blueberries.

8 The North Woods

Think of the much-mimicked perception/reality ads for *Rolling Stone* magazine. Well, there's the perception of Maine's North Woods, and then there's the reality.

The perception is that this is the last outpost of big wilderness in the east, with thousands of acres of unbroken forest, miles of free-running streams, and more azure lakes and rocky mountains than you can shake a canoe paddle at. A look at a road map seems to confirm this, with only a few roads shown here and there amid terrain pocked with lakes. Indeed, Maine accounts for about half of New England, and northern forests with no formal governmental organization—called the "unorganized townships"—comprises about half of Maine. So about one-quarter of New England is undeveloped forestland in northern Maine.

But undeveloped does not mean untouched. The reality is that this forestland is a vast plantation, largely owned and managed by a handful of international paper and timber companies. An extensive network of small timber roads (about 25,000 miles at last count) feed off major arteries and open the region to extensive clear-cutting. This is most visible from the air. In the early 1980s, writer John McPhee noted that much of northern Maine "now looks like an old and badly tanned pelt. The hair is coming out in tufts." That's even more the case now with the acceleration of timber harvesting thanks to technological advances and demands for faster cutting to pay down debts incurred during the buy-and-sell real estate mania of the late 1980s.

While it's not a vast, howling wilderness, the region still has wonderful enclaves where moose and loons predominate, and where it hasn't changed all that much since Thoreau paddled through in the mid-19th century and found it all "moosey and mossy." If you don't arrive expecting utter wilderness, you're less likely to be disappointed.

MOOSEHEAD LAKE REGION

Thirty-two miles long and five miles across at its widest point, Moosehead Lake is Maine's largest lake, and it's a great destination for hikers, boaters, and canoeists. The lake was historically the center of the region's logging activity; paradoxically, that preserved the lake and kept it largely unspoiled by development. Timber companies still own much of the twisting shoreline (although the state has acquired a large amount in recent years), and its 350-mile length is mostly unbroken second- or third-growth forest. The second-home building frenzy of the 1980s had some noticeable impact on the southern reaches of the lake, but the woody shoreline has absorbed most of the boom rather gracefully.

The first thing to know about the lake is that it's not meant to be seen by car. There are some great views from some roads—especially from Route 6/15 as you near Rockwood, and from the high elevations on the way to Lily Bay—but for the most part the roads are away from the shores, and rather uninteresting to drive. To see the lake at its best you should plan to get out on the water by steamship or canoe, or fly above it on a charter float-plane (see below).

Greenville is the "capital" of Moosehead Lake, scenically situated at the southern tip. Most lake services are located here, and you can stock up on groceries and camping supplies. The descent into Greenville on Route 6/15 is getting a bit cluttered with commercial strip development, but the town is still holding on to its remote, woodsy flavor.

ESSENTIALS

GETTING THERE   Greenville is 158 miles from Portland. Take the turnpike to the Newport exit (Exit 39) and head north on Routes 7/11 to Route 23 in Dexter, following that northward to Routes 6/15 near Sangerville. Follow this to Greenville.

VISITOR INFORMATION   The **Moosehead Lake Chamber of Commerce**, P.O. Box 581, Greenville, ME 04441 (☎ **207/695-2702**), maintains an information booth open daily in summer just south of the village on Route 6/15.

OUTDOOR PURSUITS

HIKING   The famed **100-Mile Wilderness** of the Appalachian Trail begins at Monson, south of Greenville, and runs northeast to Abol Bridge near Baxter State

Park. This is a spectacularly remote part of the state, and offers some of the best hiking in Maine. This trip is primarily for independent and experienced backpackers—there are no points along the route to resupply—although day-trips in and out are a possibility.

One especially beautiful stretch of the trail passes by **Gulf Hagas,** sometimes called "Maine's Grand Canyon" (that's a bit grandiose, to my mind). The Pleasant River has carved a canyon as deep as 400 feet through slate in this area; the hiking trail runs along its lip, with side trails extending down to the river, where you can swim in the eddies and cascades. The gulf is accessible as a day hike if you enter the forest via logging roads. Drive north from Milo on Route 11 and follow signs to the Katahdin Iron Works (an intriguing historic site worth exploring), pay your fee at the timber company gate, and ask directions to the gulf. Also nearby is **The Hermitage,** a Nature Conservancy stand of 120-foot white pines that have been spared the woodsman's axe.

Nearer to Greenville, 3,196-foot **Big Squaw Mountain** (home to a ski area called, sensibly enough, Squaw Mountain) offers superb views of Moosehead Lake and the surrounding area from its summit. The hike requires about four hours, and departs about five miles northwest of Greenville on Routes 6/15 (turn west on the gravel paper company road and continue for one mile to the trailhead).

Another inviting hike is **Mount Kineo,** a sheer cliff that rises from the shores of Moosehead. This hike is accessible by water only; near the town of Rockwood look for signs advertising shuttles across the lake to Kineo (folks offering this service seem to change from year to year, so ask around). Once across, you can explore the grounds of the famed old Kineo Mountain House (alas, the grand, 500-guest-room hotel was demolished in 1938), then cut across the golf course and follow the shoreline to the trail that leads to the 1,800-foot summit. The views from the cliffs are dazzling; one hiker I know says he has no problems on any mountain except Kineo, which give him an inexplicable case of vertigo. Be sure to continue on the trail to the old firetower, which you can ascend for a hawk's-eye view of the region.

A number of other hikes are available in the area, but get good guidance as the trails generally aren't as well-marked here as in the White Mountains or Baxter State Park. Ask at the chamber of commerce office, or pick up a copy of *50 Hikes in Northern Maine,* which contains good descriptions of several area hikes. Also, several local hikes are outlined on the Internet at http://www.maineguide.com/mooshead/mooshike.html.

CANOEING

You can follow in Thoreau's footsteps into the Maine woods on a superb canoe excursion down the **West Branch of the Penobscot River.** This 44-mile trip is popularly done in three days. Put in at Roll Dam, north of Moosehead Lake and east of Pittston Farm, and paddle northerly on the smooth waters of the Penobscot. There are several campsites along the river; pick one and spend the night, watching for grazing moose as evening falls. The second day paddle to huge and wild Chesuncook Lake. Near where the river enters the lake is the **Chesuncook Lake House,** a wonderfully remote farmhouse dating from 1864 and open to guests (see "Where to Stay," below). Spend the night here. The final day paddle down Chesuncook Lake with its sweeping views of Mount Katahdin to the east and take out near Ripogenus Dam.

Allagash Canoe Trips, P.O. 713, Greenville 04441 (☎ **207/695-3668**), has been offering guided canoe trips in the North Woods since 1953. A five-day guided camping trip down the West Branch—including all equipment, meals, and transportation—costs $475 for adults, $350 for children.

If you'd prefer to go on your own, shuttling your car from Roll Dam to Ripogenus Dam is easily arranged. **Allagash Wilderness Outfitters** (radio ☎ 207/695-2821) charges $43 to drive your vehicle from one end to the other so it will be awaiting you when you arrive.

WHITE-WATER RAFTING   Big waves and steep drops await rafters on the popular run through Kennebec Gorge at the headwaters of the **Kennebec River,** located southwest of Greenville. Dozens of rafters line up along the boiling stream below the dam, then await the siren that signals the release. Hop in, and you're off, heading off through huge, roiling waves and down precipitous drops with names like Whitewasher and Magic Falls. Most of the excitement is over in the first hour; after that, it's a lazy trip the rest of the way down the river, interrupted only by lunch and the occasional water fight with other rafts. Also nearby is the challenging Dead River, which offers about a half-dozen release dates, mostly during the early summer.

A number of commercial white-water outfits offer trips throughout the summer at a cost of about $75 to $100 per person. **Northern Outdoors,** P.O. Box 100, The Forks, ME 04985 (☎ **800/765-7238**), is the oldest of the bunch, and offers rock-climbing, mountain-biking, and fishing expeditions as well. Rafting companies based in Moosehead Lake region include **Wilderness Expeditions,** P.O. Box 41, Rockwood, ME 04478 (☎ **800/825-9453**); and **Eastern River Expeditions**, Box 1173, Greenville, ME 04441 (☎ **800/634-7238**).

MOOSEHEAD BY STEAMSHIP & FLOAT PLANE   During the lake's golden days of tourism in the late 19th century, visitors could come to the lake by train from New York or Washington, then connect with steamship to the resorts and boarding houses around the lake. A vestige of that era is found at the **Moosehead Marine Museum** (☎ 207/695-2716) in Greenville. A handful of displays in the small building suggest the grandeur of life at Kineo Mountain House, a sprawling Victorian lake resort that once defined elegance. But the real showpiece of the museum is the **S.S. *Katahdin,*** a 115-foot steamship that's been cruising Moosehead's waters since 1914. The two-deck ship (it's now run by diesel rather than steam) offers a variety of sightseeing tours, including a twice-a-week excursion up the lake to the site of the former Kineo Mountain House. Fares vary depending on the length of the trip.

Moosehead from the air is a memorable sight. Stop by **Folsom's Air Service** (☎ 207/695-2821) on the shores of the lake in Greenville just north of the village center on Lily Bay Road. Folsom's has been serving the North Woods since 1946, and has a fleet of five float planes, including a vintage canary-yellow DeHavilland Beaver. A 15-minute tour of the southern reaches of the lake costs $20 per person; longer flights over the region run up to $60. A nice adventure is the canoe-and-fly package. For $85 per person, Folsom's will drop you and a canoe off at Penobscot Farm; paddle up to Lobster Lake, where you'll get picked up and returned to Greenville later that day.

SNOWMOBILING   You'll need more than just good luck finding a room in Greenville some weekends in winter. The town has become a snowmobilers' mecca of sorts, with hundreds of sledders descending on the town during good winter weather before striking out into the remote woods. The new **Moosehead Trail,** which runs around the perimeter of the lake, offers lodging and meals at various stops along the way. For snowmobile rentals, contact the **Kokadjo Trading Post and Camp** (☎ 207/695-3993), which is located about 15 miles north of Greenville, or the **Greenwood Motel** (☎ 207/695-3321).

WHERE TO STAY & DINE

Chesuncook Lake House. P.O. Box 656, Greenville, ME 04441. ☎ **207/745-5330.** 4 rms (all share 2 baths). $170 double, including all meals. No credit cards. Closed Nov–Apr. (2 cottages available in winter.)

The Chesuncook Lake House is a perfect destination for those who like a bit of comfort with their adventure. This 1864 farmhouse, located on the shores of remote Chesuncook Lake, is accessible only via seaplane or 18-mile boat shuttle from Chesuncook Dam. (It can also be reached by canoe; see "Canoeing," above.) It's run with great rustic charm by Bert and Maggie McBurnie, who've been hosting guests here since 1957. (Bert grew up in Chesuncook Village when it was an active logging center; Maggie is from Paris, France.) The rooms are furnished simply and eclectically; there's running water in the shared bathrooms, and gas lamps provide the light in the evening. All meals are included, and Maggie's superb cooking makes good use of produce from her sizable garden. During the day, guests can explore the remnants of Chesuncook Village (Thoreau passed through here in the mid-19th century), canoe over to 3,000-acre Gero Island, or just pass the time on the porch enjoying the views of Mt. Katahdin 35 miles to the east. If you stay three days or longer, the boat shuttle is free; otherwise there's a charge for it.

Greenville Inn. Norris St., Greenville, ME 04441. ☎ **207/695-2206.** 7 rms, 6 cottages (1 rm with hall bath). Summer $105–$165 double; off-season $75–$135 double. All rates include continental breakfast buffet. DISC, MC, V.

This handsome 1895 lumber baron's home sits regally along a hilly side street a short walk from "downtown" Greenville. The interiors are sumptuous, with wonderful cherry and mahogany woodworking and a lovely stained-glass window of a pine tree over the stairwell. There's a handsome small bar, where you can order up a cocktail or Maine beer, then sit in front of the fire or retreat to the front porch to watch the late afternoon sun slip over Squaw Mountain and the lake. Four new cottages were built on the property in 1995, adding to the two others already there. The trim cottages are furnished in a light summer cottage style, and have views of the lake. The dinners served in the elegant dining room are delicious; the popovers are delectable and roughly the size of a football. The restaurant is open to the public, but is usually closed in winter; call first to confirm.

✪ Little Lyford Pond Camps. P.O. Box 1269, Greenville, ME 04441. ☎ **207/695-2821** (radio phone via Folsom's). Fax 207/534-7428. E-mail 73002.2027@compuserve.com. $170 double, including breakfast, lunch, and dinner. Accessible by logging road in summer, by snowmobile or ski-plane in winter. Closed in spring and late fall/early winter. No credit cards.

Kate and Bud Fackelman left Massachusetts for this remote lodge about a decade ago, and they've made this backwoods logging camp one of the most welcoming and comfortable spots in the North Woods. Bud is a renowned veterinary surgeon and maintains a limited practice by flying out from time to time and keeping up with communications through e-mail. Guests stay in small log cabins originally built to house loggers in the 1870s. Each has a small woodstove, propane lantern, cold running water, a private outhouse, and plenty of rustic charm. Guests gather in the more spacious main lodge for meals, to browse the inn's books, and to play board games in the evening. During the day, activities aren't hard to find, from fishing or canoeing at the two ponds down a short trail, or hiking the Appalachian Trail to Gulf Hagas, just two miles away. There's a wood-fired sauna and a solar shower for keeping clean. In winter, the cross-country skiing on the lodging's private network is superb.

BAXTER STATE PARK & ENVIRONS

Baxter State Park is Maine's crown jewel. This 201,000-acre state park in the remote north-central part of the state is unlike more elaborate state parks you might be accustomed to elsewhere—don't look for fancy bathhouses or groomed picnic areas. When you enter Baxter State Park, you enter near-wilderness.

The park was singlehandedly created by former Maine governor and philanthropist Percival Baxter, who used his inheritance and investment profits to buy the property and donate it to the state starting in 1930. Baxter stipulated that it remain "forever wild," and caretakers have done a good job fulfilling his wishes.

You won't find paved roads, RVs, or hook-ups at the eight drive-in campgrounds. (Size restrictions keep the RVs out.) You will find rugged backcountry and beautiful lakes. You'll also find Mount Katahdin, that lone and melancholy granite giant rising above the sparkling lakes and severe boreal forest of northern Maine.

To the north and west of Baxter State Park are several million acres of forestland owned by timber companies and managed primarily for timber production. Twenty-one of the largest timber companies that collectively own much of the land manage recreational access through a consortium called North Maine Woods Inc. If you drive on a logging road far enough, expect to run into a North Maine Woods checkpoint, where you'll be asked to pay a fee for day use or overnight camping on their lands.

One bit of advice: Don't attempt to tour the timberlands by car. Industrial forestland is boring when it's at its best, and downright depressing at its cut-over worst. A better strategy is to select a pond or river for camping or fishing, and spend a couple of days getting to know a small area. Buffer strips have been left around all ponds, streams, and rivers, and it can often feel like you're getting away from it all as you paddle along, even if the forest sometimes has a Hollywood facade feel to it. Be aware that no matter how deep you get into these woods, you may well hear machinery and chainsaws in the distance.

ESSENTIALS

GETTING THERE   Baxter State Park is 86 miles north of Bangor. Take I-95 to Medway (Exit 56), and head west 11 miles on Route 11/157 to the mill town of Millinocket, the last major place for supplies. Head northwest through town and follow signs to Baxter State Park. The less-used entrance is near the park's northeast corner. Take I-95 to the exit for Route 11, drive north through Patten then head west on Route 159 to the park. The speed limit within the park is 20 miles per hour. Motorcycles and ATVs are not allowed within park boundaries.

VISITOR INFORMATION   Baxter State Park offers maps and information from its **headquarters** at 64 Balsam Dr., Millinocket, ME 04462 (☎ **207/723-5140**). For information on canoeing and camping outside of Baxter State Park, contact **North Maine Woods Inc.,** P.O. Box 421, Ashland, ME 04732 (☎ **207/435-6213**). Help finding cottages and outfitters is available through the **Katahdin Area Chamber of Commerce,** 1029 Central St., Millinocket, ME 04462 (☎ **207/723-4443**).

FEES   Baxter State Park visitors with out-of-state license plates are charged a day-use fee of $8 per car. (It's free to Maine residents.) The day-use fee is charged only once per stay for those camping overnight. Camping reservations are by mail or in person only.

The private timberlands managed by North Maine Woods levy a day-use fee of $3.50 per person for Maine residents, $7 per person for nonresidents. Camping fees are additional.

OUTDOOR PURSUITS

HIKING With 180 miles of maintained backcountry trails and 46 peaks (including 18 over 3,000 feet), Baxter State Park is the destination of choice for serious hikers in Maine.

The most serious peak is 5,267-foot **Mount Katahdin**—the northern terminus of the Appalachian Trail. An ascent up this rugged, glacially scoured mountain is a trip you'll not soon forget. Never mind that it's not even a mile high (although a tall cairn on the summit claims to make it so). The raw drama and grandeur of the rocky, windswept summit is equal to anything you'll find in the White Mountains of New Hampshire.

Allow at least eight hours for the round-trip, and be prepared to abandon your plans for another day if the weather takes a turn for the worse while you're en route. The most popular route leaves and returns from **Roaring Brook Campground.** In fact, it's popular enough that it's often closed to day hikers—when the parking lot fills, hikers are shunted to other trails. You ascend first to dramatic **Chimney Pond,** which is set like a jewel in a glacial cirque, then continue to Katahdin's summit via one of two trails. (The **Saddle Trail** is the most forgiving; the **Cathedral Trail** most dramatic.) From here, the descent begins along the aptly named **"Knife's Edge,"** a narrow, rocky spine between Baxter Peak and Pamola Peak. This is not for acrophobes or the squeamish: In places, the trail narrows to two or three feet with a drop of hundreds of feet on either side. It's also not a place to be if high winds or thunderstorms threaten. From here, the trail follows a gentle ridge back down to Roaring Brook.

Katahdin draws the largest crowds, but the park maintains numerous other trails where you'll find more solitude and wildlife. A pleasant day hike is to the summit of **South Turner Mountain,** which offers wonderful views of Mount Katahdin and blueberries for the picking in late summer. The trail also departs from Roaring Brook Campground and requires about three to four hours for a round-trip. To the north, there are several decent hikes out of the **South Branch Pond Campground.** You can purchase a trail map at park headquarters, or consult *Fifty Hikes in Northern Maine.*

CAMPING Baxter State Park has eight campgrounds accessible by car and two backcountry camping areas, but don't count on finding anything open if you show up without reservations. Park headquarters starts taking reservations in January, and dozens of die-hard campers spend a cold night outside headquarters on January 1st to secure the best spots. Many of the most desirable sites sell out well before the snow melts from Katahdin. The park is stubbornly old-fashioned about its reservations, which must be made either in person or by mail, with full payment in advance. No phone reservations are accepted. Don't even mention e-mail. Camping at Baxter State Park costs $6 per person ($12 minimum per tent site), with cabins and bunkhouses available for $17 per person per night.

North Maine Woods Inc. maintains dozens of primitive campsites on private forestland throughout its 2-million-acre holdings. While you may have to drive through massive clear-cuts to reach the campsites, many are located on secluded coves or picturesque points. A map showing logging road access and campsite locations is $3 plus $1 postage from North Maine Woods headquarters (see "Visitor Information," above). Camping fees are $4 per person in addition to the day-use fee outlined above.

WHITE-WATER RAFTING A unique way to view Mount Katahdin is by rafting the West Branch of the Penobscot River. Flowing along the park's southern border, this wild river offers some of the most technically challenging white water in the East. Along the upper stretches it passes through a harrowing gorge that appears to be designed by cubists dabbling in massive blocks of granite. The river widens after this, interspersing sleepy flat water (with views of Katahdin) with several challenging falls and runs through turbulent rapids. At least a dozen rafting companies offer trips on the Penobscot, with prices around $75 to $100 per person, including a lunch along the way. Try **Unicorn Rafting,** P.O. Box T, Brunswick, ME 04011 (☎ **800/ 864-2676**); or **Magic Falls Rafting Co.,** P.O. Box 2820, Winslow, ME 04901 (☎ **800/207-7238** or 207/663-2220).

CANOEING   The state's premiere canoe trip is down the **Allagash River,** which starts just west of Baxter State Park and runs northward for nearly 100 miles to finish at the town of Allagash. The Allagash Wilderness Waterway was the first state-designated wild and scenic river in the country, and was protected in 1970. The river runs through heavily harvested timberlands, but a 500-foot buffer strip of trees protects the forest views along the entire route. The trip begins along a chain of lakes involving light portaging. At Churchill Dam, there's a nice stretch of Class I–II white water for about nine miles, then it's back to lakes and flat-water river paddling. Toward the end, there's a longish portage (about 150 yards) around picturesque Allagash Falls before finishing up above the village of Allagash. (Schedule in enough time for a swim at the base of the falls.) Most paddlers spend between 7 and 10 days making the trip from Telos Dam to Allagash. Eighty campsites are maintained along the route; most have outhouses, fire rings, and picnic tables. The camping fee is $4 per night per person for Maine residents, $5 for nonresidents.

Several outfitters offer Allagash River packages, including canoes, camping equipment, and transportation. **Allagash Wilderness Outfitters,** Box 620, Star Route 76, Greenville, ME 04441 (radio ☎ **207/695-2821**) rents a complete outfit (including canoe, life vests, sleeping bags, tent, saw, axe, shovel, cooking gear, first-aid kit, etc.) for $22 per person per day. Shuttling a car from Telos Dam to Allagash costs $145. **Allagash Canoe Trips** (☎ **207/695-3668**) in Greenville offers guided descents of the river, including all equipment and meals, for $625 adults, $475 children under 18.

SNOWMOBILING   Northern Maine is laced with a magnificent network of snowmobile trails. If the conditions are right, you can even cross over into Canada and take your sled to Quebec. Although a handful of maps and guides outline the network, the trails are still largely a matter of local knowledge. Don't be afraid to ask around. A good place to start is **Shin Pond Village,** R.R.#1, Box 280, Patten, ME 04765 (☎ **207/528-2900**). Six cottages and five guest rooms are available (starting at $40 double for guest rooms and $59 for the cottages), and snowmobile rentals are $100 to $125 per day. Shin Pond is located within one-quarter mile of two ITS trails (the chief snowmobile routes).

Index

WHEREVER YOU TRAVEL, *H*ELP IS NEVER FAR AWAY.

From planning your trip to providing travel assistance along the way, American Express® Travel Service Offices are always there to help.

New England

CONNECTICUT
American Express Travel Service
Stamford
203/359-4244

MAINE
American Express Travel Service
Portland
207/772-8450

MASSACHUSETTS
American Express Travel Service
Boston
617/439-4400

American Express Travel Service
Cambridge
617/868-2600

NEW HAMPSHIRE
Griffin Travel Service (R)
Manchester
603/668-3730

RHODE ISLAND
American Express Travel Service
Cranston
401/943-4545

VERMONT
Milne Travel (R)
Brattleboro
802/254-8844

American-International Travel (R)
Burlington
802/864-9827

Travel

http://www.americanexpress.com/travel

American Express Travel Service Offices are located throughout New England. For the office nearest you, call 1-800-AXP-3429.